KU-114-317

Your personal guide to the content-rich, free online resources for Solomon, *Consumer Behavior,* *Fifth Edition!*

Featuring one-click access to all of the **new** resources created by our award-winning team of educators, myPHLIP provides a **personalized view** of the great new resources available:

NEW **MyPHLIP pages**—Your personal access page unites all your Prentice Hall myPHLIP texts.

NEW **Notes**—Add personal notes to our resources for personal reminders and references.

NEW **Messages**—Instructors can send messages to individual students or to all students linked to your course.

NEW **Student Resources**—Instructors can add premium PHLIP resources for students to view and download (such as our PowerPoints and spreadsheets).

NEW **Syllabus**—New and improved online syllabus tools help instructors add personal syllabi to our site in minutes.

NEW **Business Headlines**—Provide links to articles in today's business news!

NEW **Search**—Search all PHLIP resources for relevant articles and exercises.

NEW **Instructor's Manual**—MyPHLIP Instructor's Manual provides tips and suggestions from our PHLIPfaculty for integrating PHLIP resources into your course.

NEW **Online Learning Solutions**—In Blackboard, WebCT, and Pearson CourseCompass. (Free with New Text Purchase) Standard courses include traditional online course features:
- Online Testing
- Course Managment and Page Tracking
- Gradebook
- Course Information
- Multiple-Section Chat Rooms
- Bulletin Board Conferencing
- Syllabus and Callendar Functions
- E-mail Capability

Combined with the resources you have trusted throughout the years to provide you with the best business resources available:

- **In the News**—New current events articles are added throughout the year. Each article is summarized by our teams of experts, and fully supported by exercises, activities, and instructor materials.

- **Online Study Guide**—Three quizzes are linked to each text chapter and include "hints" for each question. Each quiz is graded immediately upon submission, provides immediate feedback on each given answer, and enables students to e-mail results to the instructor.

- **Research Area**—Your own personal resource library includes tutorials, descriptive links to virtual libraries, and a wealth of search engines and resources.

- **Internet Resources**—provide discipline-specific sites, including preview information that allows you to review site information before you view the site, ensuring you visit the best available business resources found by our learning community.

For the professor

- **Teaching Resources** provide material contributed by professors throughout the world— including teaching tips, techniques, academic papers, and sample syllabi—and **Talk to the Team,** a moderated faculty chat room.

- **Online Faculty Support** includes downloadable supplements, additional cases, articles, links, and suggested answers to Current Events Activities.

- **What's New** gives you one-click access to all newly posted PHLIP resources.

For the student

- **Talk to the Tutor** schedules virtual office hours that allow students to post questions from any supported discipline and receive responses from the dedicated PHLIP/CW faculty team.

- **Writing Resource Center** provides an online writing center that supplies links to online directories, thesauruses, writing tutors, style and grammar guides, and additional tools.

- **Career Center** helps students access career information, view sample résumés, even apply for jobs online.

- **Study Tips** provides an area where students can learn to develop better study skills

www/prenhall.com/solomoncb

CONSUMER BEHAVIOR

The Prentice Hall International Series in Marketing

Philip Kotler, Series Editor

FIFTH EDITION

CONSUMER BEHAVIOR
BUYING, HAVING, AND BEING

Michael R. Solomon
Auburn University

Prentice-Hall International, Inc.

Executive Editor: Whitney Blake
Editor-in-Chief: Jeff Shelstad
Assistant Editor: Anthony Palmiotto
Editorial Assistant: Melissa Pellerano
Media Project Manager: Cindy Harford
Marketing Manager: Shannon Moore
Marketing Assistant: Kathleen Mulligan
Managing Editor (Production): John Roberts
Permissions Coordinator: Suzanne Grappi
Associate Director, Manufacturing: Vincent Scelta
Production Manager: Arnold Vila
Design Manager: Patricia Smythe
Art Director: Kevin Kall
Interior Design: Proof Positive
Cover Design: Kevin Kall
Cover Illustrator: Tom Herzberg
Composition and Full-Service Project Management: Progressive
Printer/Binder: World Color

Credits and acknowledgments borrowed from other sources and reproduced, with permission, in this textbook appear on page 533.

This book may be sold only in those countries to which it is consigned by Prentice-Hall International. It is not to be re-exported and it is not for sale in the U.S.A., Mexico, or Canada.

Copyright © 2002, 1999, 1996, 1994, 1992 by Prentice-Hall, Inc., Upper Saddle River, New Jersey, 07458. All rights reserved. Printed in the United States of America. This publication is protected by Copyright and permission should be obtained from the publisher prior to any prohibited reproduction, storage in a retrieval system, or transmission in any form or by any means, electronic, mechanical, photocopying, recording, or likewise. For information regarding permission(s), write to: Rights and Permissions Department.

10 9 8 7 6 5 4 3 2 1
ISBN 0-13-095008-4

BRIEF CONTENTS

CONTENTS

PREFACE

I love to people-watch, don't you? People shopping, people flirting, people parading. . . . Consumer behavior is the study of people and the products that help to shape their identities. Because I'm a consumer myself, I have a selfish interest in learning more about how this process works—and so do you.

In many courses, students are merely passive observers, learning about topics that affect them indirectly if at all. Not everyone is a plasma physicist, a medieval French scholar, or even an industrial marketer. But we are all consumers. Many of the topics dealt with in this book have both professional and personal relevance to the reader, whether he or she is a student, professor, or marketing practitioner. Nearly everyone can relate to the trials and tribulations associated with last-minute shopping, primping for a big night out, agonizing over an expensive purchase decision, fantasizing about a week in the Caribbean, celebrating a holiday, or commemorating a landmark event, such as a graduation, getting a driver's license, or (dreaming about) winning the lottery.

In this edition I have tried to introduce you to the latest and best thinking by some very bright scientists who develop models and studies of consumer behavior. But, that's not enough. Consumer behavior is an applied science, so we must never lose sight of the role of "horse sense" when we try to apply our findings to life in the real world. That's why you'll find a lot of practical examples to back up these fancy theories. That's also why you'll find a new feature I'm very excited about. It's called "Reality Check," and boy, did I have fun creating it. I was helped by a great panel of college students from around the world. Each was chosen by their professor to represent their universities on the panel, and they did their schools proud. Their comments help to flesh out the material by providing a valuable perspective on ethical and strategic issues discussed in the text. You'll find their take on these questions in every chapter. See whether you agree with them.

Beyond Canned Peas: Buying, Having, and Being

As this book's subtitle suggests, my vision of consumer behavior goes well beyond studying the act of buying—having and being are just as important if not more so. Consumer behavior is more than buying things, such as a can of peas; it also embraces the study of how having (or not having) things affects our lives and how our possessions influence the way we feel about ourselves and about each other—our state of being. I developed the models of consumer behavior that appear at the beginning of text sections to underscore the complex—and often inseparable—interrelationships between the individual consumer and his or her social realities.

In addition to understanding why people buy things, we also try to appreciate how products, services, and consumption activities contribute to the broader social world we experience. Whether shopping, cooking, cleaning, playing basketball, hanging out at the beach, or even looking at ourselves in the mirror, our lives are touched by the marketing system. As if these experiences were not complex enough, the task of understanding the consumer multiplies geometrically when a multicultural perspective is taken. The American experience is important, but it's far from the whole story. This book also considers the many other consumers around the world whose diverse experiences with buying, having, and being are equally vital to understand. In addition to the numerous examples of marketing and consumer practices relating to consumers and companies outside the United States that appear throughout the book, chapters contain boxes called "Multicultural Dimensions" that highlight cultural differences in consumer behavior.

Digital Consumer Behavior: A Virtual Community

As more of us go online everyday, there's no doubt the world is changing—and consumer behavior is evolving faster than you can say World Wide Web. This fifth edition highlights and celebrates the brave new world of digital consumer behavior. Consumers and producers are brought together electronically in ways we have never before experienced. Rapid transmission of information is altering the speed at which new trends develop and the direction in which they travel—especially since the virtual world lets consumers participate in the creation and dissemination of new products.

One of the most exciting aspects of the new digital world is that consumers can interact directly with other people who live around the block or around the world. As a result, the meaning of community is being radically redefined. It's no longer enough to acknowledge that consumers like to talk to each other about products. Now we share opinions and get the buzz about new movies, CDs, cars, clothes—you name it—in electronic communities that may include a housewife in Alabama, a disabled senior citizen in Alaska, or a teen loaded with body piercings in Amsterdam.

We have just begun to explore the ramifications for consumer behavior when a Web surfer can project her own picture onto a Web site to get a virtual makeover or a corporate purchasing agent can solicit bids for a new piece of equipment from vendors around the world in minutes. These new ways of interacting in the marketplace create bountiful opportunities for businesspeople and consumers alike. You will find illustrations of the changing digital world sprinkled liberally throughout this edition. In addition, each chapter features boxes called "Net Profit" that point to specific examples of the Net's potential to improve the way business is conducted.

But, is the digital world always a rosy place? As in the "real world," unfortunately the answer is no. The potential to exploit consumers, whether by invading their privacy, preying on the curiosity of children, or just plain providing false product information, is always there. That's why you'll also find boxes called

"The Tangled Web" that point out some of the abuses of this fascinating new medium. Still, I can't imagine a world without the Web, and I hope you'll enjoy the ways it's changing our field. When it comes to the new virtual world of consumer behavior, you're either on the train or under it.

Consumer Research Is a Big Tent

Like most of the readers of this book, the field of consumer behavior is young, dynamic, and in flux. It is constantly being cross-fertilized by perspectives from many different disciplines—the field is a big tent that invites many diverse views to enter. I have tried to express the field's staggering diversity in these pages. Consumer researchers represent virtually every social science discipline, plus a few from the physical sciences and the arts for good measure. From this melting pot has come a healthy "stew" of research perspectives, viewpoints regarding appropriate research methods, and even deeply held beliefs about what are and what are not appropriate issues for consumer researchers to study in the first place.

The book also emphasizes the importance of understanding consumers in formulating marketing strategy. Many (if not most) of the fundamental concepts in marketing are based on the practitioner's ability to know people. After all, if we don't understand why people behave as they do, how can we identify their needs? If we can't identify their needs, how can we satisfy their needs? If we can't satisfy people's needs, we don't have a marketing concept, so we might as well fold our tents and go home! To illustrate the potential of consumer research to inform marketing strategy, the text contains numerous examples of specific applications of consumer behavior concepts by marketing practitioners as well as examples of windows of opportunity in which such concepts could be used (perhaps by alert strategists after taking this course!). Many of these possibilities are highlighted in special features called "Marketing Opportunities."

The Good, the Bad, and the Ugly

A strategic focus is great, but this book does not assume that everything marketers do is in the best interests of consumers or of their environment. Likewise, as consumers we do many things that are not positive either. People are plagued by addictions, status envy, ethnocentrism, racism, sexism, and many other "isms." Regrettably, there are times when marketing activities—deliberately or not—encourage or exploit these human flaws. This book deals with the totality of consumer behavior, warts and all. Marketing mistakes or ethically suspect activities are also highlighted in special features labeled "Marketing Pitfalls."

On the other hand, marketers have helped to create many wonderful (or at least unusual) things, such as holidays, comic books, techno music, Beanie Babies, and the many stylistic options available to us in the domains of clothing, home design, the arts and cuisine. I have also taken pains to acknowledge the sizable impact of marketing on popular culture. Indeed, the final section of this book reflects very recent work in the field that scrutinizes, criticizes, and sometimes celebrates consumers in their everyday worlds. I hope you will enjoy reading about such wonderful things as much as I enjoyed writing about them.

Ancillary Materials Available

Adopters of the fifth edition will be provided with a useful set of resources, many of which are new to this edition. The improvements to the teaching package include full Web support for professor and students through our My PHLIP Web site (www.prenhall.com/myphlip) and Course Compass, a complete online course management system, a new video library, a set of overhead transparencies featuring advertisements, and a video featuring recent broadcast commercials from around the world. In addition, the following items comprise the support package for *Consumer Behavior*, Fifth Edition.

Instructor's Manual

This manual includes chapter summaries, chapter outline with annotations for video cases and internet exercises, answers to end-of-chapter discussion questions, field projects, and notes for PowerPoint transparencies and ad transparencies.

Test Item File and PH Test Generator

For each chapter, a file of 50 multiple-choice and true/false questions, ranked by difficulty, and a complete test generation system for Windows environments.

PowerPoint Lecture Slides

For each chapter, 25-40 slides which outline the key topics in the chapter, including print ads. A subset of 150 of these slides are available in acetate form as ***transparencies*** to accompany the fifth edition.

Cases in Consumer Behavior by Martha McEnally, Volumes I & II

In two volumes of ten cases each, these case selections vary in length and cover a variety of industries and types of consumer buying situations. Either of both modules can be shrinkwrapped free with the text—ask your sales representative for the appropriate ISBN code for ordering.

Acknowledgments

I am grateful for the many helpful comments on how to improve the fifth edition that were provided by my peer reviewers. Special thanks go to the following people: Cynthia Webster, Mississippi State University; Amy Rummel, Alfred University; and Sylvia D. Clark, St. John's University.

Many other colleagues and friends made significant contributions to this edition. I would like to thank, in particular, the following people who made constructive suggestions or who provided me with a sneak peek at their research materials and manuscripts now in press or under review:

Jennifer Aaker, Stanford University
Mark Alpert, University of Texas
Craig Andrews, Marquette University
Mary Jo Bitner, Arizona State University
Amitava Chattopadhyay, University of British Columbia (Canada)
Susan Fournier, Harvard University
Güliz Ger, Bilkent University (Turkey)
Ron Hill, University of Portland
Charlie Hofacker, Florida State University
Margaret Hogg, University of Manchester (United Kingdom)

Donna Hoffman, Vanderbilt University
Annama Joy, Concordia University (Canada)
Lynn Kahle, University of Oregon
Jerome Kernan, George Mason University
Noreen Klein, Virginia Tech
Robert Kozinets, Northwestern University
Russell Laczniak, Iowa State University
Therese Louie, University of Washington
John Lynch, Duke University
Deborah Roedder John, University of Minnesota
Greg Rose, University of Mississippi
John Sherry, Northwestern University
Itamar Simonson, Stanford University
Robert Veryzyer, Rensselaer Polytechnic Institute
Dan Wardlow, San Francisco State University
Richard Wilk, Indiana University

A special group of professors around the world helped to make the new Reality Check panel a reality. The students they nominated to participate in the panel were delightful to work with, and their numerous thoughtful comments made this innovative experiment a pleasure to carry out. I am indebted to all of them:

Student	University	Sponsoring Professor
Sabrina Aslam	Simon Fraser University, Canada	Judy Zaichkowsky
Giselle Gonzales Aybar	Pontificia Universidad Catolica Madre y Maestra, Dominican Republic	Ray Victor
Dmitri Batsev	University of Alaska Fairbanks	Laura Milner
James Beattie	University of Exeter, England	Andrea Davies
John Dollman IV	West Virginia University	Paula Bone
Jennifer Freet	George Mason University	Laurie Meamber
Pamela Gillen	Dublin City University, Ireland	Darach Turley
Eric Jude Guacena	Virginia Commonwealth University	Deborah Cowles
Michael Hollet	Edith Cowan University, Australia	Ronald Groves
Liv Amber Judd	University of Saskatchewan, Canada	Tammi S. Feltham
Katherine S. Kennedy	James Madison University	C.B. Claiborne
Constanza Montes Larrañaga	Universidad de Chile, Chile	Enrique Manzur Mobarec
I-Cheng Liu (Frank)	Florida State University	Ronald Goldsmith
Liana Mouynes	University of Washington	Therese Louie
Annalise M. Mulholland	Virginia Polytechnic Institute and State University	Noreen Klein
Michelle Purintun	University of Wisconsin-La Crosse	Gwen Achenreiner
Satish Ranchhod	University of Auckland, New Zealand	Brett Martin
Sara Glenn Rast	Southwest Missouri State University	Peggy Gilbert

Concetta Rini	College of William and Mary	Lisa Szykman
Kerri Ruminiski	Idaho State University	Ron LeBlanc
Mai Sasaki	Keio University, Japan	Takeo Kuwahara
Nicole Schragger	Edinburgh University, Scotland	David Marshall
Astrid Spielrein	ASSAS University Paris II, France	Patrick Hetzel
Ho Xiu Rong (Tina)	Nanyang Technological University, Singapore	Roger Marshall
Gregory T. Varveris	DePaul University	Linda F. Alwitt
Fant Walker	University of Mississippi	Greg Rose
Jessica Wells	Utah State University	Cathy Hartman
Jill Wittekind	University of Nevada, Las Vegas	Gillian Naylor
Ayano Yamada	Keio University, Japan	Takeo Kuwahara

Extra special thanks are due to the preparers of the ancillary materials: John R. Brooks Jr. from Houston Baptist University for preparation of the Instructor's Manual and Test Item File, Milton Pressley for preparation of the PowerPoint lecture slides, and Martha McEnally for preparing the selection of cases that accompany the text. These cases are packaged in groups of ten, and are of varying length, and can be packaged free with the fifth edition.

I would also like to thank the good people at Prentice Hall who as always have done yeoman service on this edition. In particular I am indebted to my tenacious editor, Whitney Blake, for helping me to navigate the sometimes treacherous waters of publishing. Thanks also to Bruce Kaplan, Melissa Pellerano, John Roberts, Anthony Palmiotto, Suzanne Grappi, and Richard Allan for their support and great work.

With the support and tolerance of my friends and colleagues, I would never have been able to sustain the illusion that I was still an active researcher while I worked on this edition. I am grateful to my department chair, Carol Warfield, and to Dean June Henton for their continuing support. Special thanks go to two of my courageous doctoral students, Carrie Lego and Natalie Quilty, for their tireless help. Also, I am grateful to my undergraduate students, who have been a prime source of inspiration, examples, and feedback. The satisfaction I have garnered from teaching them about consumer behavior motivated me to write a book I felt they would like to read.

Last but not least, I would like to thank my family and friends for sticking by me during this revision. They know who they are, since their names pop up in chapter vignettes throughout the book. My apologies for "distorting" their characters in the name of poetic license! My gratitude and love go out to my parents, Jackie and Henry, and my in-laws, Marilyn and Phil. My super children, Amanda, Zachary, and Alexandra, always made the sun shine on gray days. Finally, thanks above all to the love of my life—Gail, my wonderful wife, best friend, and occasional research assistant: I still do it all for you.

M.R.S.
Auburn, Alabama
March 2001

ABOUT THE AUTHOR

Michael R. Solomon, Ph.D., is Human Sciences Professor of Consumer Behavior in the Department of Consumer Affairs, College of Human Sciences, at Auburn University. Prior to joining Auburn in 1995, he was Chairman of the Department of Marketing in the School of Business at Rutgers University, New Brunswick, New Jersey. He earned B.A. degrees in Psychology and Sociology magna cum laude at Brandeis University in 1977, and a Ph.D. in Social Psychology at the University of North Carolina at Chapel Hill in 1981. He received the Cutty Sark Men's Fashion Award for his research on the psychological aspects of clothing. In 1996 he was awarded the Fulbright/FLAD Chair in Market Globalization by the U.S. Fulbright Commission and the Government of Portugal.

Prof. Solomon's primary research interests include consumer behavior and lifestyle issues, online research methodologies, the symbolic aspects of products, the psychology of fashion, decoration, and image, and services marketing. He has published numerous articles on these and related topics in academic journals, and he has delivered invited lectures on these subjects in the United Kingdom, Scandinavia, Australia, and Latin America. His research has been funded by the American Academy of Advertising, the American Marketing Association, the U.S. Department of Agriculture, and the U.S. Department of Commerce. He currently sits on the editorial boards of the *Journal of Consumer Behaviour* and the *Journal of Retailing,* and he serves on the Board of Governors of the Academy of Marketing Science. Prof. Solomon was ranked as one of the fifteen most widely cited scholars in the academic behavioral sciences/fashion literature, and as one of the ten most productive researchers in the field of advertising and marketing communications.

In addition to his academic activities, Prof. Solomon is a frequent contributor to mass media. His feature articles have appeared in such magazines as *Psychology Today, Gentleman's Quarterly,* and *Savvy.* He has been quoted in numerous national magazines and newspapers, including *Allure, Elle, Glamour, Mademoiselle, Mirabella, Newsweek, The New York Times, Self, USA Today,* and *The Wall Street Journal.* He has been interviewed numerous times on radio and television, including appearances on *Today, Good Morning America,* CNBC, Channel One, *Inside Edition, Newsweek on the Air,* and National Public Radio. Prof. Solomon serves as an advisor to numerous companies on issues related to consumer behavior, services marketing, retailing, and advertising. He frequently addresses business groups on strategic issues related to consumer behavior. Prof. Solomon currently lives in Auburn, Alabama, with his wife, Gail, their three children, Amanda, Zachary, and Alexandra—and Chloe, their golden retriever.

SECTION

I

THE TRUE COLOR
OF BENETTON.

Your lives and dreams are now available 24 hours a day
For the location of harsh realities nearest you, Call 1-800-000

CONSUMERS IN THE MARKETPLACE

This introductory section provides an overview of the field of consumer behavior. Chapter 1 looks at how the field of marketing is influenced by the actions of consumers and also at how we as consumers are influenced by marketers. It describes the discipline of consumer behavior and some of the different approaches to understanding what makes consumers tick. It also highlights the importance of the study of consumer behavior to such public policy issues as addiction and environmentalism.

◆ ◆ ◆

Section Outline

Chapter 1
An Introduction to Consumer Behavior

ail is killing time before her accounting class by surfing the Web in her room. Between studying for her accounting and marketing exams, she realizes she hasn't looked at any interesting sites in weeks. Enough of the serious stuff, she decides. It's time for some *really* educational surfing.

So, where to go first? Gail figures she'll start at one of the popular women's portals and see what happens. She goes to iVillage.com, where she checks her horoscope (cool! a good day to start a new relationship), scans a few beauty tips, and takes a Great Date quiz (uh-oh, this new guy Bruce she's been seeing may need to be replaced). Similar stuff is going on at Oxygen.com. Then she checks out the new Web site for her sorority at sigmakappa.org, which

invites her to "browse and find out more about how Sigma Kappa is Bringing Sisterhood to Life!" Very nice, but she learned all that at rush. Maybe it's time for something a bit more interesting.

After an hour of surfing some fascinating e-commerce sites—and vowing to return to some of them to reward herself with a present after exams—Gail decides to check out what "real people" are doing on the Web. First she checks in on the clubs she belongs to at collegeclub.com— wow, more than 30 people from her campus are logged on right now! Looks like other students are studying as hard as she is! Then she clicks over to community.com to decide which live webcam she'd like to peek in on

today. The site has tons of them; cameras trained on real guys and women just doing their thing at work or at home. Most of these are pretty boring. There's even a "DissCam" site featuring a balding graduate student who can be observed writing his dissertation! Yawn. Gail checks out the "Campus Views" section where she can select live feeds from many schools ranging from Penn State to Humboldt State. She finally settles on DormCam, a live feed from a room with four residents just doing what students do. For a few minutes, she watches the riveting spectacle of one of the guys brushing his teeth and getting ready to go to class. Hey, it's not exactly an Eminem concert, but it sure beats studying for accounting.

AN INTRODUCTION TO CONSUMER BEHAVIOR

CONSUMER BEHAVIOR: PEOPLE IN THE MARKETPLACE

This book is about people like Gail. It concerns the products and services they buy and use, and the ways these fit into their lives. This introductory chapter describes some important aspects of the field of consumer behavior and some reasons why it's essential to understand how people interact with the marketing system.

For now, though, let's return to one "typical" consumer: Gail, the business major. This brief vignette allows us to highlight some aspects of consumer behavior that will be covered in the rest of the book.

- As a consumer, Gail can be described and compared to other individuals in a number of ways. For some purposes, marketers might find it useful to categorize Gail in terms of her age, gender, income, or occupation. These are some examples of descriptive characteristics of a population, or *demographics*. In other cases, marketers would rather know something about Gail's interests in clothing or music, or the way she spends her leisure time. This sort of information comes under the category of *psychographics*, which refers to aspects of a person's lifestyle and personality. Knowledge of consumer characteristics plays an extremely important role in many marketing applications, such as defining the market for a product or deciding on the appropriate techniques to employ when targeting a certain group of consumers.

- Gail's purchase decisions are heavily influenced by the opinions and behaviors of her sorority sisters. A lot of product information, as well as recommendations to use or avoid particular brands, is transmitted by conversations among real people, rather than by way of television commercials, magazines, billboards, or even bizarre Web sites. The growth of the Web has created thousands of online *consumption communities* where members share views and product recommendations about anything from Barbie dolls to Palm Pilots. The bonds among Gail's group are cemented by the common products they use. There is also pressure on each group member to buy things that will meet with the group's approval. A consumer often pays a price in the form of group rejection or embarrassment when she does not conform to others' conceptions of what is good or bad, "in" or "out."

- As members of a large society, such as the United States, people share certain *cultural values*, or strongly held beliefs about the way the world should be structured. Other values are shared by members of *subcultures*, or smaller groups within the culture, such as Hispanics, teens, Midwesterners, or even "Valley Girls" and "Hell's Angels."

- When examining Web sites, Gail was exposed to many competing "brands." Numerous sites did not capture her attention at all, whereas others were noticed and rejected because they did not fit the "image" with which she identified or to which she aspired. The use of *market segmentation strategies* means targeting a brand only to specific groups of consumers rather than to everybody—even if it means that other consumers who don't belong to this *target market* aren't attracted to that product.

- Brands often have clearly defined images or "personalities" created by product advertising, packaging, branding, and other marketing strategies. The choice of a favorite Web site is very much a lifestyle statement: It says a lot about what a person is interested in, as well as something about the type of person she would like to be. People often choose a product because they like its image, or because they feel its "personality" somehow corresponds to their own. Moreover, a consumer may believe that by buying and using the product or service, its desirable qualities will magically rub off onto him or her.

- When a product, idea, or Web site succeeds in satisfying a consumer's specific needs or desires, it may be rewarded with many years of *brand loyalty*, a bond between product and consumer that is very difficult for competitors to break. Often a change in one's life situation or self-concept is required to weaken this bond.

- Consumers' evaluations of products are affected by their appearance, taste, texture, or smell. A good Web site helps people to feel, taste, and smell with their eyes. We may be swayed by the shape and color of a package, as well as by more subtle factors, such as the symbolism used in a brand name, in an advertisement, or even in the choice of a cover model for a magazine. These judgments are affected by—and often reflect—how a society feels that people should define themselves at that point in time. If asked, Gail might not even be able to say exactly why she considered some Web sites and rejected others. Many product meanings are hidden below the surface of the packaging and advertising, and this book will discuss some of the methods used by marketers and social scientists to discover or apply these meanings.

- As Gail found, our opinions and desires increasingly are shaped by input from around the world, which is becoming a much smaller place due to rapid advancements in communications and transportation systems. In today's global culture, consumers often prize products and services that "transport" them to different places and allow them to experience the diversity of other cultures—even if only to watch others brush their teeth.

What Is Consumer Behavior?

The field of **consumer behavior** covers a lot of ground: It is the study of the processes involved when individuals or groups select, purchase, use, or dispose of products, services, ideas, or experiences to satisfy needs and desires.[2] Consumers take many forms, ranging from an eight-year-old child begging her mother for Pokemon cards to an executive in a large corporation deciding on a multimillion-dollar computer system. The items that are consumed can include anything from canned peas, a massage, democracy, hip-hop music, or hoopster rebel Dennis Rodman. Needs and desires to be satisfied range from hunger and thirst to love, status, or even spiritual fulfillment. Our attachment to everyday products is exemplified by our love affair with colas. The World of Coca-Cola in Las Vegas draws a million visitors a year. Exhibits ask, "What does Coca-Cola mean to you?" and many of the responses tell of strong emotional connections to the brand.[3]

Consumers Are Actors on the Marketplace Stage

The perspective of **role theory** takes the view that much of consumer behavior resembles actions in a play.[4] As in a play, each consumer has lines, props, and costumes necessary to put on a good performance. Because people act out many different roles, they sometimes alter their consumption decisions depending on the particular "play" they are in at the time. The criteria they use to evaluate products and services in one of their roles may be quite different from those used in another role.

Consumer Behavior Is a Process

In its early stages of development, the field was often referred to as *buyer behavior*, reflecting an emphasis on the interaction between consumers and producers at the time of purchase. Most marketers now recognize that consumer behavior is an ongoing process, not merely what happens at the moment a consumer hands over money or a credit card and in turn receives some good or service.

The **exchange**, a transaction in which two or more organizations or people give and receive something of value, is an integral part of marketing.[5] Although exchange remains an important part of consumer behavior, the expanded view emphasizes the entire consumption process, which includes the issues that influence the consumer before, during, and after a purchase. Figure 1.1 illustrates some of the issues that are addressed during each stage of the consumption process.

Consumer Behavior Involves Many Different Actors

A **consumer** is generally thought of as a person who identifies a need or desire, makes a purchase, and then disposes of the product during the three stages in the consumption process. In many cases, however, different people may be involved in this sequence of events. The *purchaser* and *user* of a product might not be the same person, as when a parent picks out clothes for a teenager (and makes selections that can result in "fashion suicide" in the view of the teen). In other cases,

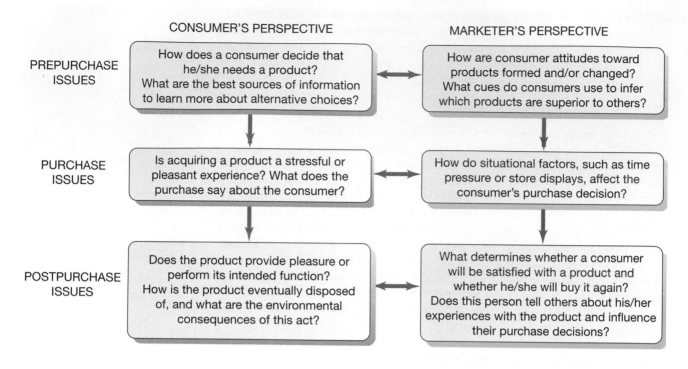

CONSUMER'S PERSPECTIVE   MARKETER'S PERSPECTIVE

PREPURCHASE ISSUES

How does a consumer decide that he/she needs a product? What are the best sources of information to learn more about alternative choices?

How are consumer attitudes toward products formed and/or changed? What cues do consumers use to infer which products are superior to others?

PURCHASE ISSUES

Is acquiring a product a stressful or pleasant experience? What does the purchase say about the consumer?

How do situational factors, such as time pressure or store displays, affect the consumer's purchase decision?

POSTPURCHASE ISSUES

Does the product provide pleasure or perform its intended function? How is the product eventually disposed of, and what are the environmental consequences of this act?

What determines whether a consumer will be satisfied with a product and whether he/she will buy it again? Does this person tell others about his/her experiences with the product and influence their purchase decisions?

Figure 1.1
Some Issues That Arise During Stages in the Consumption Process

another person may act as an *influencer*, providing recommendations for or against certain products without actually buying or using them. For example, a friend's grimace when one tries on a new pair of pants may be more influential than anything a mother or father might do.

Finally, consumers may take the form of organizations or groups. One or several persons may make the decisions involved in purchasing products that will be used by many, as when a purchasing agent orders the company's office supplies. In other organizational situations, purchase decisions may be made by a large group of people—for example, company accountants, designers, engineers, sales personnel, and others—all of whom will have a say in the various stages of the consumption process. As we'll see in Chapter 12, one important type of organization is the family, where different family members play pivotal roles in making decisions regarding products and services used by all.

CONSUMERS' IMPACT ON MARKETING STRATEGY

Surfing cool Web sites is a lot of fun. But, on the more serious side, why should managers, advertisers, and other marketing professionals bother to learn about consumer behavior?

Very simply, understanding consumer behavior is good business. A basic marketing concept holds that firms exist to satisfy consumers' needs. These needs can only be satisfied to the extent that marketers understand the people or organizations that will use the products and services they are trying to sell, and that they do so better than their competitors.

Consumer response is the ultimate test of whether a marketing strategy will succeed. Thus, knowledge about consumers should be incorporated into every facet of a successful marketing plan. Data about consumers helps organizations define the market and identify threats and opportunities to a brand. And, in the wild and wacky world of marketing, nothing is forever: This knowledge also helps to ensure that the product continues to appeal to its core market. The Sony Walkman is a good example of a successful product that needed to update its image. Although Sony revolutionized the mobile music experience and sold almost 300 million Walkmans in the process, recent research found that today's teens see portable cassette players as dinosaurs. The company's advertising agency followed 125 teens to see how they use products in their day-to-day lives. Now the product has been relaunched with a removable "Memory Stick" instead of a cassette player so it can work with MP3 files. The Walkman also needed a fresh message, so Sony's advertising agency decided to use an alien named Plato to appeal to teens. This character was chosen to appeal to today's ethnically diverse marketplace. As the account director explained, "An alien is no one, so an alien is everyone."[6]

Segmenting Consumers

The process of **market segmentation** identifies groups of consumers who are similar to one another in one or more ways, and then devises marketing strategies that appeal to one or more groups. Amazon.com tries to reach multiple segments at the same time, whereas toysrus.com focuses on gifts for kids.[7] Sometimes these market segments are simply the most frequent or loyal users of a brand. For example, in the fast food industry the heavy user accounts for only one of five customers but for about 60 percent of all visits to fast food restaurants. Taco Bell developed the Chalupa, a deep-fried and higher calorie version of its Gordita stuffed taco, to appeal to its heavy users, and Burger King is testing its Great

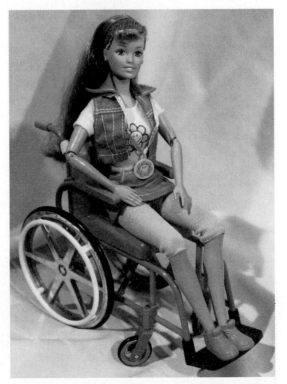

Mattel introduced "Share a Smile Becky," an 11½ inch strawberry blonde in a hot-pink wheelchair, to help break down barriers for kids with disabilities.

MARKETING OPPORTUNITY

DISABLED CONSUMERS ARE STARTING
to be viewed as a profitable marketing
segment rather than as charity cases.
That's not surprising; they comprise
a market of 52 million people with
almost $800 billion in spending power.
This new spirit of "handicapitalism"
is being fueled by the convergence of
three trends: (1) The 1990 Americans
with Disabilities Act created greater
awareness of this population; (2) New
technology such as battery-powered
bicycles and speech-recognition
software is making it easier for these
consumers to interact with others and
with the marketplace (for example,
Nokia makes cell phones that flash or
vibrate for the hard of hearing); and (3)
An aging population ensures continued
growth in the number of disabled people. This new interest in reaching disabled consumers extends to the Web.
Wemedia.com is a Web portal for disabled persons that includes listings for
wheelchair-accessible real estate and
specialized employment services.
DaimlerChrysler and Barnes & Noble
have agreed to sponsor AdapZ.com,
another one-stop Web shop, to encourage the growth of handicapitalism.[9]

American Burger for the same reason. The Checkers burger chain describes its core customer as a single male under age 30 who has a working-class job, loves loud music, doesn't read much, and hangs out with friends.[8] Fries with that?

Aside from heavy usage of a product, there are many dimensions that can be used to slice up a larger market. **Demographics** are statistics that measure observable aspects of a population, such as birthrate, age distribution, and income. The U.S. Census Bureau is a major source of demographic data on families, but many private firms gather additional data on specific population groups as well. The changes and trends revealed in demographic studies are of great interest to marketers, because the data can be used to locate and predict the size of markets for many products, ranging from home mortgages to brooms and can openers. Imagine trying to sell baby food to a single male, or an around-the-world vacation to a couple making $15,000 a year!

In this book, we'll explore many of the important demographic variables that make consumers the same or different from others. We'll also consider other important characteristics that are a bit more subtle, such as differences in consumers' personalities and tastes that can't be objectively measured yet may be tremendously important in influencing product choices. For now, let's summarize a few of the most important demographic dimensions, each of which will be developed in more detail in later chapters.

Finely-tuned segmentation strategies allow marketers to reach only those consumers likely to be interested in buying their products.

Age

Consumers of different age groups obviously have very different needs and wants. Although people who belong to the same age group differ in many other ways, they do tend to share a set of values and common cultural experiences that they carry throughout life.[10] To launch a new shoe called EZ Chuck (a newer version of its classic 1960s Chuck Taylor basketball shoe) that is targeted to teens, Converse is working with teen site bolt.com, where visitors are asked to e-mail the answer to the question: "What does taking it EZ mean to you?" Answers are posted on the site, along with critiques of the new shoe. Converse is hoping to encourage conversation among 12- to 24-year-olds and get this age group into its franchise.[11]

Gender

Many products, from fragrances to footwear, are targeted to either men or women. Differentiating by gender starts at a very early age—even diapers are sold in pink versions for girls and blue for boys. Consumers take these differences seriously: Market research shows that most parents refuse to put male infants in pink diapers![12]

Family Structure

A person's family and marital status is yet another important demographic variable, because this has such a big effect on consumers' spending priorities. Young bachelors and newlyweds are the most likely to exercise; go to bars, concerts, and movies; and consume alcohol. Families with young children are big purchasers of health foods and fruit juices, while single-parent households and those with older children buy more junk food. Home maintenance services are most likely to be used by older couples and bachelors.[17]

NET PROFIT

AS GAIL FOUND, SEGMENTING by gender is alive and well in cyberspace.[13] In France, for example, a group of women started the country's first women's electronic magazine and Web portal called Newsfam.com. These entrepreneurs are hoping to reproduce the success of American sites such as iVillage.com and Women.com.[14] To underscore the idea that men and women differ in their tastes and preferences (the French would say, "Vive la difference!") a Web site for high-tech products called Hifi.com opened a sister site just for women called herhifi.com. It avoids jargon, offers friendly advice, and finds ways to make home entertainment systems relevant to women.[15] Probably a sound strategy, considering that six out of every ten new Internet users are female.[16]

Lange, a ski boot manufacturer, decided to target to women who were looking for a more comfortable boot when the company realized that this segment of the ski boot market is growing quickly. Although the advertising agency debated whether the ad might offend some readers, its managing director noted that it was "done by women, approved by women, and primarily written by women." What do you think?

Social Class and Income

Social class indicates people who are approximately equal in terms of their incomes and social standing in the community. They work in roughly similar occupations, and they tend to have similar tastes in music, clothing, art, and so on. They also tend to socialize with one another, and they share many ideas and values regarding the way one's life should be lived.[18] The distribution of wealth is of great interest to marketers because it determines which groups have the greatest buying power and market potential.

Race and Ethnicity

African Americans, Hispanic Americans, and Asian Americans are the three fastest-growing ethnic groups in the United States. As our society becomes increasingly multicultural, new opportunities develop to deliver specialized products to racial and ethnic groups and to introduce other groups to these offerings.

Sometimes this adaptation is just a matter of putting an existing product into a different context. An African-American product manager at Pillsbury realized that the company had overlooked the importance of baking as a cultural activity for many African-American consumers. At her urging, the company's cornbread twists were packaged with a recipe for corn muffins—in packages delivered to areas with large African-American populations.[19]

Lifestyle

Consumers also have very different lifestyles, even if they share other characteristics such as gender or age. The way we feel about ourselves, the things we value, the things we like to do in our spare time—all of these factors help to determine which products will push our buttons. That's why SoBe Beverages, the fast-growing producer of "New Age drinks," labels its herb concoctions with names like Lizard Fuel that stress attributes such as energy rather than taste. Using an offbeat marketing campaign featuring a "Lizard Love Bus" that shows up at events such as mountain bike races, the company's lifestyle marketing campaign stresses individuality with its tagline: SoBe Yourself.[20]

Geography

Many national marketers tailor their offerings to appeal to consumers who live in different parts of the country. For example, some Southerners are fond of a "good ol' boy" image that leaves others scratching their heads. Although many Northerners regard the name Bubba as a negative term, some businesses in Dixie proudly flaunt the name. Bubba Co. is a Charleston-based firm that licenses products such as Bubba-Q-Sauce. In Florida, restaurants, sports bars, nightclubs, and a limousine firm all proudly bear the name Bubba.[21]

Relationship Marketing: Building Bonds with Consumers

Marketers are carefully defining customer segments and listening to people in their markets as never before. Many of them have realized that a key to success is building relationships between brands and customers that will last a lifetime. Marketers who believe in this philosophy, called **relationship marketing**, interact with customers on a regular basis and give them reasons to maintain a bond with the company over time.

Another revolution in relationship building is being brought to us courtesy of the computer. **Database marketing** involves tracking consumers' buying habits very closely and crafting products and messages tailored precisely to people's wants and needs based on this information. For example, the Ritz-Carlton hotel chain trains associates to enter detailed information into its database so that, if a guest orders decaf coffee from room service, she will also receive decaf on the next visit.[22] Sophisticated companies like American Express, General Motors, and Kraft General Foods are combining and constantly updating information from public records and marketing research surveys—with data volunteered by consumers themselves when they return warranty cards, enter sweepstakes, or purchase from catalogs—to build a complex database that fine-tunes their knowledge of what people are buying and how often.[23]

MARKETING'S IMPACT ON CONSUMERS

For better or for worse, we all live in a world that is significantly influenced by the actions of marketers. We are surrounded by marketing stimuli in the form of advertisements, stores, and products competing for our attention and our dollars. Much of what we learn about the world is filtered by marketers, whether through the affluence depicted in glamorous magazines or the roles played by actors in commercials. Ads show us how we should act with regard to recycling, alcohol consumption, the types of houses and cars we might wish to own—and even how to evaluate others based on the products they buy or don't buy. In many ways we are also "at the mercy" of marketers because we rely on them to sell us products that are safe and perform as promised, to tell us the truth about what they are selling, and to price and distribute these products fairly.

Marketing and Culture

Popular culture, consisting of the music, movies, sports, books, celebrities, and other forms of entertainment consumed by the mass market, is both a product of and an inspiration for marketers. Our lives are also affected in more far-reaching ways, ranging from how we acknowledge cultural events such as marriage, death, or holidays to how we view social issues such as air pollution, gambling, and addictions. Whether it's the Super Bowl, Christmas shopping, presidential elections, newspaper recycling, body piercing, cigarette smoking, in-line skating, or Pokemon cards, marketers play a significant role in our view of the world and how we live in it.

This cultural impact is hard to overlook, although many people do not seem to realize how much their views—their movie and musical heroes, the latest fashions in clothing, food and decorating choices, and even the physical features that they find attractive or ugly in men and women—are influenced by marketers. For example, consider the product icons that companies use to create an identity for their products. Many imaginary creatures and personalities, from the Pillsbury Doughboy to the Jolly Green Giant, at one time or another have been central figures in popular culture. In fact, it is likely that more consumers could recognize such characters than could identify past presidents, business leaders, or artists. Although these figures never really existed, many of us feel as if we "know" them, and they certainly are effective *spokescharacters* for the products they represent. If you don't believe it, visit www.toymuseum.com.

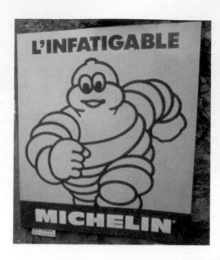

Companies often create product icons to develop an identity for their products. Many made-up creatures and personalities, such as Mr. Clean, Bibendum, the Michelin tire man, and the Pillsbury Doughboy, are widely recognized (and often beloved) figures in popular culture. Bibendum, one of the oldest icons, dates back to the 1890s. He was born at a time when the "machine age" was dawning, so a man constructed of auto parts truly caught the spirit of the times.[24]

The Meaning of Consumption

One of the fundamental premises of the modern field of consumer behavior is that people often buy products not for what they *do*, but for what they *mean*. This principle does not imply that a product's basic function is unimportant, but rather that the roles products play in our lives go well beyond the tasks they perform. The deeper meanings of a product may help it to stand out from other, similar goods and services—all things being equal, a person will choose the brand that has an image (or even a personality!) consistent with the purchaser's underlying needs.

For example, although most people probably couldn't run faster or jump higher if they were wearing Nikes versus Reeboks, many die-hard loyalists swear by their favorite brand. These archrivals are largely marketed in terms of their images—meanings that have been carefully crafted with the help of legions of rock stars, athletes, slickly produced commercials—and many millions of dollars. So, when you buy a Nike "swoosh" you may be doing more than choosing shoes to wear to the mall—you may also be making a lifestyle statement about the type of person you are or wish you were. For a relatively simple item made of leather and laces, that's quite a feat!

Our allegiances to sneakers, musicians, or even soft drinks help us define our place in modern society, and these choices also help each of us to form bonds with others who share similar preferences. This comment by a participant in a focus group captures the curious bonding that can be caused by consumption choices: "I was at a Super Bowl party, and I picked up an obscure drink. Somebody else across the room went 'yo!' because he had the same thing. People feel a connection when you're drinking the same thing."[25]

As we have already seen, a trademark of marketing strategies today is an emphasis on building relationships with customers. The nature of these relationships can vary, and these bonds help us to understand some of the possible meanings products have to us. Here are some of the types of relationships a person might have with a product:

- *Self-concept attachment*—the product helps to establish the user's identity.
- *Nostalgic attachment*—the product serves as a link with a past self.
- *Interdependence*—the product is a part of the user's daily routine.

- *Love*—the product elicits emotional bonds of warmth, passion, or other strong emotion.[26]

One consumer researcher developed a classification scheme in an attempt to explore the different ways that products and experiences can provide meaning to people. This *consumption typology* was derived from a two-year analysis of spectators at Wrigley Field who were attending Chicago Cubs baseball games (of course, studying the hapless Cubbies is bound to produce some unique and frustrating experiences!).[27]

This perspective views consumption as a type of action in which people make use of consumption objects in a variety of ways. Focusing on an event like a ball game also is a useful reminder that when we refer to consumption, we are talking about *intangible* experiences, ideas, and services (the thrill of a home run hit out of the park or the antics of a team mascot) in addition to *tangible objects* (the hot dogs eaten at the ball park). This analysis identified four distinct types of consumption activities:

- *Consuming as experience*—an emotional or aesthetic reaction to consumption objects. This would include reactions such as the pleasure derived from learning how to mark a scorecard or appreciating the athletic ability of a favorite player.
- *Consuming as integration*—learning and manipulating consumption objects to express aspects of the self or society. For example, some fans wear Cubs jerseys to express their solidarity with the team. Attending ball games in person rather than watching them on TV allows the fan to more completely integrate his or her experience with that of the team.
- *Consuming as classification*—the activities that consumers engage in to communicate their association with objects, both to self and to others. For example, spectators might buy souvenirs to demonstrate to others that they are die-hard fans, or the more hard core fans might throw the opposition team's home run ball back onto the field as a gesture of contempt.
- *Consuming as play*—consumers use objects to participate in a mutual experience and merge their identities with that of a group. For example, happy fans might scream in unison and engage in an orgy of "high fives" when one of their team's players hits a home run. This is a different dimension of shared experience than just watching the game at home by oneself.

The Global Consumer

By 2006, the majority of people on Earth will live in urban centers—the number of megacities, defined as urban centers of 10 million or more, is projected to grow to 26 in 2015.[28] One by-product of sophisticated marketing strategies is the movement toward a *global consumer culture*, one in which people around the world are united by their common devotion to brand name consumer goods, movie stars, and celebrities.[29] Some products in particular, such as Levi Strauss, Nike, and McDonald's are associated with a coveted American lifestyle.

Popular culture continues to evolve as the products and styles from different cultures mix and merge in new and interesting ways. For example, although megaperformers from the United States and the United Kingdom dominate the worldwide music industry, there is a movement afoot to include more diverse styles and performers. In Europe local music acts are grabbing larger share and pushing international (i.e., English-speaking acts) down the charts. Revenue from

Spanish-language music has quadrupled in five years. In Asia, new songs are being written to accompany promotions for American movies. For example, in Hong Kong the movie *Lethal Weapon 4* was promoted with a song by a local heavy-metal band called Beyond. Shots from the movie were mixed with clips of band members even though they don't appear in the film and the song is not included in the soundtrack.[30] Madonna doesn't need to lose any sleep just yet, but an explosion of styles from urban rap to North African rai, techno, and world music is lessening the appeal of superstars.[31]

The rise of global marketing means that even smaller companies are looking to expand overseas—and this increases the pressure to understand how customers in other countries are the same or different than in one's own country. In the restaurant industry, for example, Shakey's pizza restaurants are mushrooming in the Philippines, and food from the International House of Pancakes is selling like hot cakes in Tokyo. But menu changes are sometimes called for to please local palates: Schlotzky's in Malaysia offers Smokey Mountain Chicken Crunch with "half-virgin" chicken, and diners in Bob's Big Boy in Thailand snap up Tropical Shrimp, deep fried with "exotic breading."[32] This book will pay special attention to the good and bad aspects of this cultural homogenization. Each chapter features boxes called "Multicultural Dimensions" that spotlight some international aspect of consumer behavior, and this issue will also be explored in depth in Chapter 17.

Virtual Consumption

There's little doubt that the Digital Revolution is one of the most significant influences on consumer behavior right now. Most of us are avid surfers, and it's hard to imagine a time when e-mail, MP3 files, or Palm Pilots weren't an accepted part of daily life. Online retail sales totaled $20 billion in 1999, and Forrester Research predicts that by 2004, 49 million households will be online. U.S. consumers alone will spend $184 billion (7 percent of all retail sales) or nearly $4,000 per household.[33] That's a lot of CDs and sweaters.

Online shopping also lets consumers locate hard-to-find products and creates opportunities for smaller, specialized businesses to thrive. Think about start-up

American products like Levi's jeans are in demand around the world.

Dale color a tu vida con Levi's 517 COLLECTION BOOT CUT

companies like Bigfoot, which sells nothing but enormous shoes up to size 25 EEEE. The company was started by two brothers who each wear size 16 shoes. Their Web site features testimonials, including this one: "I used to have to wear basketball shoes to church. All the other "normal" boys and girls would circle around me, laugh, and point. Thanks to you guys I got a girlfriend, have been accepted in the corporate workplace, and my dog came back!"[34] Satisfying consumers like that is quite a "feat" (sorry!).

Electronic marketing has increased convenience by breaking down many of the barriers caused by time and location. You can shop 24 hours a day without leaving home, you can read today's newspaper without getting drenched picking up a hard copy in a rainstorm, and you don't have to wait for the 6:00 P.M. news to find out what the weather will be like tomorrow—at home or around the globe. And, with the increasing use of handheld devices and wireless communications, you can get that same information—from stock quotes to the weather—even when you're away from your computer.[35]

And, it's not all about businesses selling to consumers (*B2C commerce*). The cyberspace explosion has created a revolution in consumer-to-consumer activity (*C2C commerce*). Just as e-consumers are not limited to local retail outlets in their shopping, they are not limited to their local communities when looking for friends. Picture a small group of local collectors who meet once a month at a local diner to discuss their shared interests over coffee. Now multiply that group by thousands, and include people from all over the world who are united by a shared passion for sports memorabilia, Barbie dolls, Harley-Davidson motorcycles, or refrigerator magnets. Welcome to the new world of *virtual brand communities*. To appreciate the potential marketing power of these brand communities, consider The Hollywood Stock Exchange (hsx.com). This Web site offers a simulated entertainment stock market where traders predict the four-week box office take for each film. Major studios and actors cannot afford to ignore this customer community when making their "real" development and marketing decisions.

The popularity of chat rooms where consumers can go to discuss various topics with like-minded Netizens around the world grows every day. News reports tell us of the sometimes wonderful and sometimes horrific romances that began on the Internet. The Web also provides an easy way for consumers around the world to exchange information about their experiences with products. Amazon.com encourages shoppers to write reviews of books, and you can even rate your professors from A + to F − on virtualratings.com (don't tell your prof about this one; it'll be our secret).

Alas, all is not perfect in the virtual world. E-commerce does have its limitations. Security is one important concern. We hear horror stories of consumers whose credit card numbers and other identity information have been stolen. Some shady companies are making money by prying and then selling personal information to others—one such company promotes itself as "an amazing new tool that allows you to find out EVERYTHING you ever wanted to know about your friends, family, neighbors, employees, and even your boss!"[36] Pretty scary.

Other limitations of e-commerce relate to the actual shopping experience. Although it may be satisfactory to buy a computer or a book on the Internet, buying clothing and other items in which touching the item or trying it on is essential may be less attractive. Even though most companies have very liberal return policies, consumers can still get stuck with large delivery and return shipping charges for items that don't fit or simply aren't the right color.

Some futurists believe that we'll soon reach a point where each of us is wired and online all of the time. We'll each be issued a username and password at birth and a computer device will be implanted in our bodies. That hasn't quite happened yet, but consider the service now offered by a Swiss company called skim.com: Each user is issued a six-digit number that he wears on jackets and backpacks sold by the company. When you see someone on the street or in a club you'd like to get to know better, you go to skim.com, type in the person's number, and send him or her a message. And if you're lucky enough (?) to receive one of these messages, you can decide whether to respond.[37]

Will the Web bring people closer together or drive us each into our own private virtual worlds? In a given week, nearly 70 percent of all 12- to 19-year-olds go online. This is a chance for kids to experiment with new identities as they flirt online.[38] A recent survey found that wired Americans are spending less time with friends and family, less time shopping in stores, and more time working at home after hours. More than one-third of respondents who have access to the Internet reported that they were online at least five hours a week. Also, 60 percent of Internet users said they had reduced their television viewing and one-third said they spent less time reading newspapers.

On the other hand, a study done in 2000 by the Pew Internet and American Life Project reports that more than half of users surveyed feel that e-mail actually strengthens family ties. Users reported far more offline social contact than nonusers.[39] These results argue that people are spending more time than ever with others. It's just that they are forming strong relationships over the Internet instead of in person. But the author of the first survey disagrees. As he observes, "If I go home at 6:30 in the evening and spend the whole night sending e-mail and wake up the next morning, I still haven't talked to my wife or kids or friends. When you spend your time on the Internet, you don't hear a human voice and you never get a hug."[40] So, our new electronic world is both good and bad. Throughout this book, we'll look at some examples of both the pros and cons of virtual consumer behavior in boxes called *Net Profit* and *The Tangled Web*.

Blurred Boundaries: Marketing and Reality

Marketers and consumers coexist in a complicated, two-way relationship. It's often hard to tell where marketing efforts leave off and "the real world" begins. For example, the Internet search site Lycos is the first company to sponsor a team in the Collegiate Professional Basketball League. The league is hoping that Team Lycos will play such opponents as Team Nike, Team America Online, and so on. The league's founder says, "I don't think of us as a basketball league, but as an advertising vehicle built around basketball."[41]

To what degree is the world of popular culture—and even consumers' perceptions of reality—shaped by the efforts of marketers? More than many of us believe, and this influence is increasing dramatically in recent times as companies experiment with new ways to command our attention. On *The X-Files*, Agents Mulder and Scully call each other on Nokia 8860 phones, whereas Regis Philbin on *Who Wants to Be a Millionaire?* calls on "our friends at AT&T" to let contestants phone a friend. Going a step further, the CBS reality-adventure program *Survivor* stranded people on an island and let them compete for products such as a new pair of sneakers or a cold Budweiser—all provided courtesy of the show's sponsors.[42] And how about sleeping with corporations? Holiday Inn Family Suites Resort in Lake Buena Vista, Florida, offers rooms decorated in corporate themes, including the Orange Minute Maid suite and the Edy's Ice Cream suite. A Coca-Cola executive (there is a polar-bear motif in the Coca-Cola suite)

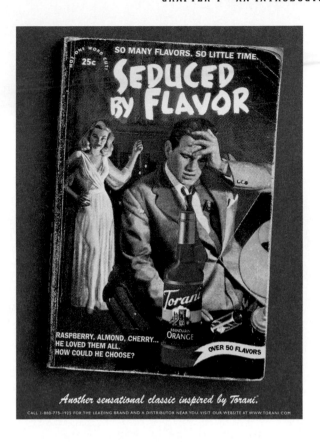

Marketing messages often borrow imagery from other forms of popular culture to connect with an audience. This line of syrups adapts the "look" of a pulp detective novel.

comments that families "feel like they can actually interact with our brands within a room."[43] Now there's a happening vacation for you. . . .

MARKETING ETHICS AND PUBLIC POLICY

In business, conflicts often arise between the goal to succeed in the marketplace and the desire to maximize the well-being of consumers by providing them with safe and effective products and services. Unfortunately, merely giving lip service to the importance of appropriate activities may not be sufficient. For example, an *Advertising Age* study of beer ads on MTV showed that the major brewers often ran commercials in time slots that violated their own voluntary industry guidelines.[44] On the other hand, consumers may expect too much from companies and try to exploit these obligations. Perhaps that explains the woman who sued Celebrity cruise line for more than $2 million in damages because she got hit in the head with a Coco Loco drink that was dropped by a passenger on a deck above her. She claims the line should have known that passengers would try to balance their drinks on the ship's railings![45]

Business Ethics

Business ethics are rules of conduct that guide actions in the marketplace—the standards against which most people in a culture judge what is right and what is wrong, good or bad. These universal values include honesty, trustworthiness,

The potential invasion of consumers' privacy by corporations or governments is a major concern for many, as reflected in this Polish ad.

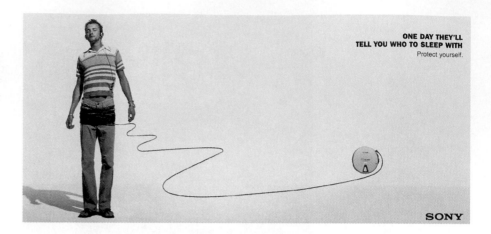

fairness, respect, justice, integrity, concern for others, accountability, and loyalty. Ethical business is good business. A Conference Board survey of U.S. consumers found the most important criterion when forming opinions about corporations is social responsibility in such areas as labor practices, business ethics, and environmental issues.[46] Consumers think better of products made by firms they feel are behaving ethically.[47]

But just what is ethical behavior? Notions of right and wrong differ among people, organizations, and cultures. Some businesses, for example, believe it is all right for salespeople to persuade customers to buy, even if it means giving them false information; other firms feel that anything less than total honesty with customers is terribly wrong. Because each culture has its own set of values, beliefs, and customs, ethical business behaviors are defined quite differently around the world. Giving "gifts" in exchange for getting business from suppliers or customers is common and acceptable in many countries, for example, even though this may be considered bribery or extortion in the United States.

Whether intentionally or not, some marketers do violate their bond of trust with consumers. In some cases, these actions are actually illegal, as when a manufacturer deliberately mislabels the contents of a package. Or a retailer may adopt a "bait-and-switch" selling strategy that lures consumers into the store by offering inexpensive products with the sole intent of getting them to switch to higher-priced goods.

In other cases, marketing practices have detrimental effects on society even though they are not explicitly illegal. Some companies erect billboards for alcohol and tobacco products in low-income neighborhoods; others sponsor commercials depicting groups of people in an unfavorable light to get the attention of a target market. Civil rights groups, for example, charge that the marketing of menthol cigarettes by R. J. Reynolds to African Americans is illegal because menthol cigarettes are less safe than regular brands. A company spokeswoman responds, "This links to the bigger issue that minorities require some special protection. We find that offensive, paternalistic, and condescending."[48] Who is right? Throughout this book, ethical issues related to the practice of marketing are highlighted. Special boxes called "Marketing Pitfalls" feature questionable practices by marketers or the possible adverse effects on consumers of certain marketing strategies.

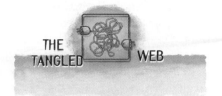

THE TANGLED WEB

TO WHAT EXTENT SHOULD a consumer's personal information be available online? This is one of the most controversial ethical questions today. Scott McNealy, CEO of Sun Microsystems, said in 1999: "You already have zero privacy—get over it." Apparently many consumers don't agree: A study of 10,000 Web users found that 84 percent object to reselling of information about their online activity to other companies. One of the highest profile cases is that of DoubleClick Inc., a company that places "cookies" in your computer to let you receive targeted ads. The trouble began when Double Click bought Abacus Direct, a 90-million-name database, and began compiling profiles linking the two sets of data so clients would know who was receiving what kind of ads.

Double Click's ability to track what you choose to buy and where you choose to surf is just one isolated example, though. Many companies can trace choices you make online and link them to other information about you. For example, when you register online for a product a Globally Unique Identity (GUID) is linked to your name and e-mail address. That means firms like RealJukebox, with 30 million registered users, can relay information to its parent company RealNetworks about the music each user downloads. Comet Systems, which creates customized cursors for companies featuring characters ranging from Pokemon to Energizer bunnies, reports each time a person visits any of the 60,000 Web sites that support its technology.[49] Still other privacy violations are committed by consumers themselves: A site called disgruntledhousewife.com features a column to which women write to describe in excruciating detail the intimate secrets of former lovers. Be careful how you break off a relationship!

How can these thorny ethical issues be solved? One solution is an "infomediary;" an online broker who represents consumers and charges marketers for access to their data. As a Novell executive observed, "Slowly but surely consumers are going to realize that their profile is valuable. For loaning out their identity, they're going to expect something in return."[50] Or, perhaps the solution is to hide your identity: Zero-Knowledge Systems of Montreal sells a software package called Freedom that includes five digital pseudonyms to assign to different identities.

All of these precautions may be irrelevant if regulations now being considered are ever implemented. One now being discussed is an "opt in" proposal that would forbid a Web site from collecting or selling personal data unless the user checked a box letting it do so. These efforts are being resisted by the online commerce lobby, which argues these safeguards would drastically reduce ad revenues.[51]

Needs and Wants: Do Marketers Manipulate Consumers?

One of the most common and stinging criticisms of marketing is that companies convince consumers they "need" many material things and that they will be unhappy and inferior people if they do not have these "necessities." The issue is a complex one, and is certainly worth considering: Do marketers give people what they want, or do they tell people what they *should* want?

Welcome to Consumerspace

Who controls the market—companies or consumers? This question is even more complicated as new ways of buying, having, and being are invented everyday. It seems that the "good old days" of *marketerspace*, a time when companies called the shots and decided what they wanted their customers to know and do, are dead and gone. As we saw with Gail's surfing decisions, many people now feel empowered to choose how, when, or *if* they will interact with corporations as they construct their own *consumerspace*. In turn, companies need to develop and leverage brand equity in bold new ways to attract the loyalty of these consumer "nomads." People still "need" companies—but in new ways and *on their own terms*. As we'll see throughout the book, profound changes in consumer behavior are influencing how people search for product information and evaluate alternative brands. In the brave new world of consumerspace, we have the potential to shape our own marketing destinies.

DESPITE WHAT SOME PEOPLE THINK, ADVERTISING CAN'T MAKE YOU BUY SOMETHING YOU DON'T NEED.

This ad was created by the American Association of Advertising Agencies to counter charges that ads create artificial needs.

FUEL OR FOOL? OIL companies try to convince consumers to buy premium gasolines, even though most don't need higher grades for their cars. As one automotive engineer noted, "Oil company advertising has led people to the conclusion that more expensive fuels will make their cars start easier, get more gas mileage, and last longer. . . . But in most cases this is untrue. . . . Your engine has to be designed to use that extra octane. . . . Otherwise, . . . the extra cost is just lining the pockets of the oil companies."[53] The Federal Trade Commission estimates that 80 to 90 percent of the cars on the road run well on regular, unleaded gasoline. However, nearly one-third of all motorists use midgrade or premium gasoline in their automobiles.[54] Fill 'er up!

Do Marketers Create Artificial Needs?

The marketing system has come under fire from both ends of the political spectrum. On the one hand, some members of the Religious Right believe that marketers contribute to the moral breakdown of society by presenting images of hedonistic pleasure and encouraging the pursuit of secular humanism. On the other hand, some leftists argue that the same deceitful promises of material pleasure function to buy off people who would otherwise be revolutionaries working to change the system.[52] According to this argument, the marketing system creates demand—demand that only its products can satisfy.

A Response: A *need* is a basic biological motive; a *want* represents one way that society has taught us that the need can be satisfied. For example, thirst is biologically based; we are taught to want Coca-Cola to satisfy that thirst rather than, say, goat milk. Thus, the need is already there; marketers simply recommend ways to satisfy it. A basic objective of marketing is to create awareness that needs exist, not to create them.

Are Advertising and Marketing Necessary?

The social critic Vance Packard wrote more than 40 years ago, "Large-scale efforts are being made, often with impressive success, to channel our unthinking habits, our purchasing decisions, and our thought processes by the use of insights gleaned from psychiatry and the social sciences."[55] The economist John Kenneth Galbraith charged that radio and television are important tools to accomplish this manipulation of the masses. Because virtually no literacy is required to use these media, they allow repetitive and compelling communications to reach almost everyone. This criticism may even be more relevant to online communications, where a simple click delivers a world of information to us.

Many feel that marketers arbitrarily link products to desirable social attributes, fostering a materialistic society in which we are measured by what we own. One influential critic even argued that the problem is that we are not materialistic enough—that is, we do not sufficiently value goods for the utilitarian functions they deliver but instead focus on the irrational value of goods for what they symbolize. According to this view, for example, "Beer would be enough for us, without the additional promise that in drinking it we show ourselves to be manly, young at heart, or neighborly. A washing machine would be a useful machine to wash clothes, rather than an indication that we are forward-looking or an object of envy to our neighbors."[56]

A Response: Products are designed to meet existing needs, and advertising only helps to communicate their availability.[57] According to the *economics of information perspective*, advertising is an important source of consumer information.[58] This view emphasizes the economic cost of the time spent searching for products. Accordingly, advertising is a service for which consumers are willing to pay, because the information it provides reduces search time.

Do Marketers Promise Miracles?

Consumers are led to believe through advertising that products have magical properties; products will do special and mysterious things for consumers in a way that will transform their lives. Consumers will be beautiful, have power over others' feelings, be successful, and be relieved of all ills. In this respect, advertising functions as mythology does in primitive societies: It provides simple, anxiety-reducing answers to complex problems.

A Response: Advertisers simply do not know enough about people to manipulate them. Consider that the failure rate for new products ranges from 40 to 80 percent. In testimony before the Federal Trade Commission, one advertising executive observed that although people think that advertisers have an endless source of magical tricks and/or scientific techniques to manipulate people, in reality, the industry is successful when it tries to sell good products and unsuccessful when selling poor ones.[59]

Public Policy and Consumerism

Concern for the welfare of consumers has been an issue since at least the beginning of the twentieth century. Partly as a result of consumers' efforts, many federal agencies have been established to oversee consumer-related activities. These include the Department of Agriculture, the Federal Trade Commission, the Food and Drug Administration, the Securities and Exchange Commission, and the Environmental Protection Agency. After Upton Sinclair's 1906 book *The Jungle* exposed the awful conditions in the Chicago meat-packing industry, Congress was prompted to pass important pieces of legislation—the Pure Food and Drug Act in 1906 and the Federal Meat Inspection Act a year later—to protect consumers. A summary of some important consumer legislation since that time appears in Table 1.1. Other information about consumer-related issues can be found at consumerreports.org and cpsc.gov (The Consumer Product Safety Commission).

Consumerism and Consumer Research

President John F. Kennedy ushered in the modern era of consumerism with his "Declaration of Consumer Rights" in 1962. These include the right to safety, the right to be informed, the right to redress, and the right to choice. The 1960s and 1970s were a time of consumer activism as consumers began to organize to demand better-quality products (and to boycott companies that did not provide them). These movements were prompted by the publication of books such as Rachel Carson's *Silent Spring* in 1962, which attacked the irresponsible use of pesticides, and Ralph Nader's *Unsafe at Any Speed* in 1965, which exposed safety defects in General Motors' Corvair automobile. Many consumers have a vigorous interest in consumer-related issues, ranging from environmental concerns, such as pollution caused by oil spills, toxic waste, and so on, to excessive violence and sex on television or in the lyrics of popular rock and rap songs.

The field of consumer behavior can play an important role in improving our lives as consumers.[60] Many researchers play a role in formulating or evaluating public policies such as ensuring that products are labeled accurately, that people can comprehend important information presented in advertising, or that children are not exploited by program-length toy commercials masquerading as television shows.

Many firms choose to protect or enhance the natural environment as they go about their business activities, a practice known as **green marketing**. The Park Plaza in Boston markets itself as "Boston's Eco-Logical Travel Alternative"; the hotel uses a recycling system that cuts laundry water use by more than half, it installed Thermopane windows to reduce heating costs, and it recycles enough paper to save 300 trees a year.[61] Others have focused their efforts on reducing wasteful packaging, as when Procter & Gamble introduced refillable containers

MULTICULTURAL DIMENSIONS

A PROJECT IN SWEDEN aimed at curbing adolescent drinking illustrates social marketing at work. The Swedish Brewer's Association is investing 10 million Skr (about $7.5 million dollars) in a cooperative effort with the Swedish Non-Violence Project to change teens' attitudes about alcohol consumption.

Consumer researchers working on the project discovered that Swedish adolescents freely admit that they "drink in order to get drunk" and enjoy the feeling of being intoxicated, so persuading them to give up alcohol is a formidable task. However, the teens reported they also are afraid of losing control over their own behavior, especially if there is a risk for them to be exposed to violence. And, while worries about the long-term health effects of drinking don't concern this group (after all, at this age many believe they will live forever), female adolescents reported a fear of becoming less attractive as a result of prolonged alcohol consumption.

Based on these findings, the group commissioned to execute this project decided to stress a more realistic message of "drink if you want to, but within a safe limit. Don't lose control, because if you do, you might get yourself into violent situations." They made up the motto, "Alco-hole in your head" to stress the importance of knowing one's limits. This message is being emphasized along with strong visual images that appear on billboards, in video spots that depict situations involving young drinkers getting out of control, and in school presentations given by young people who will be credible sources for teens.[67]

TABLE 1.1 Sampler of Federal Legislation Intended to Enhance Consumer's Welfare

Year	Act	Purpose
1951	Fur Products Labeling Act	Regulates the branding, advertising, and shipment of fur products.
1953	Flammable Fabrics Act	Prohibits the transportation of flammable fabrics across state lines.
1958	National Traffic and Safety Act	Creates safety standards for cars and tires.
1958	Automobile Information Disclosure Act	Requires automobile manufacturers to post suggested retail prices on new cars.
1966	Fair Packaging and Labeling Act	Regulates packaging and labeling of consumer products. (Manufacturers must provide information about package contents and origin.)
1966	Child Protection Act	Prohibits sale of dangerous toys and other items.
1967	Federal Cigarette Labeling and Advertising Act	Requires cigarette packages to carry a warning label from the Surgeon General.
1968	Truth-in-Lending Act	Requires lenders to divulge the true costs of a credit transaction.
1969	National Environmental Policy Act	Established a national environmental policy and created the Council on Environmental Quality to monitor the effects of products on the environment.
1972	Consumer Product Safety Act	Established the Consumer Product Safety Commission to identify unsafe products, establish safety standards, recall defective products, and ban dangerous products.
1975	Consumer Goods Pricing Act	Bans the use of price maintenance agreements among manufacturers and resellers.
1975	Magnuson-Moss Warranty-Improvement Act	Creates disclosure standards for consumer product warranties and allows the Federal Trade Commission to set policy regarding unfair or deceptive practices.
1990	The Nutrition Labeling and Education Act	Reaffirms the legal basis for the Food and Drug Administration's new rules on food labeling and establishes a timetable for the implementation of those rules. Regulations covering health claims became effective May 8, 1993. Those pertaining to nutrition labeling and nutrient content claims went into effect May 8, 1994.
1998	Internet Tax Freedom Act	Established a three-year moratorium on special taxation of the Internet, including taxation of access fees paid to America Online and other Internet Service Providers. An extension of the moratorium is being considered.

for Downy fabric softener.[62] In other cases, successful marketers are promising donations to charity as purchase incentives or are even donating their own money to good causes.[63] For example, Pierre Omidyar, the creator of eBay who is worth more than $6 billion, is aggressively giving seed money to charities that follow solid business plans. He plans to turn over all but 1 percent of his astounding wealth during the next twenty years.[64]

Social marketing uses marketing techniques normally employed to sell beer or detergent to encourage positive behaviors such as increased literacy and to discourage negative activities such as drunk driving.[65] The Partnership for a Drug Free America, for example, has used more than $3 billion in donated advertising

This cartoon lampoons the widely held belief that marketers manipulate consumers by making us feel inadequate about ourselves. Then they bombard us with products and services we don't really want or need with the promise that we will be better people, more attractive, more successful, and so on if only we will buy them. How valid is this criticism?

to craft messages to young people ("this is your brain on drugs"). As a result, teens are more likely to say that they see or hear antidrug messages and that these have positive effects on them.[66]

THE DARK SIDE OF CONSUMER BEHAVIOR

Despite the best efforts of researchers, government regulators, and concerned industry people, sometimes consumers' worst enemies are themselves. Individuals are often depicted as rational decision makers, calmly doing their best to obtain products and services that will maximize the health and well-being of themselves, their families, and their society. In reality, however, consumers' desires, choices, and actions often result in negative consequences to the individual and/or the society in which he lives.

Some of these actions are relatively harmless, as when a person goes online at www.dogdoo.com to send a bag of dog manure to someone who has made him angry (do not try this at home). Other activities have more onerous consequences than just creating a stink. Some harmful consumer behaviors such as excessive drinking or cigarette smoking stem from social pressures, and the cultural value placed on money encourages activities such as shoplifting or insurance fraud. Exposure to unattainable ideals of beauty and success can create dissatisfaction with the self. Many of these issues will be touched on later in the book, but for now, let's review some dimensions of "the dark side" of consumer behavior.

Addictive Consumption

Consumer addiction is a physiological and/or psychological dependency on products or services. Although most people equate addiction with drugs, virtually any product or service can be seen as relieving some problem or satisfying some need to the point that reliance on it becomes extreme. There is even a Chap Stick Addicts support group with approximately 250 active members![68]

Some psychologists are even raising concerns about "Internet addiction," a condition in which people (particularly college students!) become obsessed by online chat rooms to the point that their "virtual" lives take priority over their real ones.[69] Similar concerns have been raised about addiction to stock trading by so-called "day traders." A message board called "Daytrading and Stock Trading Addiction" (on techstocks.com) notes that unlike a stockbroker, the Internet is always accessible. Telltale signs of addiction: spending 12–14 hours a day at the computer, lying about trading losses, and neglecting one's family.[70] Let's hope these poor souls at least buy low and sell high.

Compulsive Consumption

For some consumers, the expression "born to shop" is taken quite literally. They shop because they are compelled to do so, rather than because shopping is a pleasurable or functional task. **Compulsive consumption** refers to repetitive shopping, often excessive, as an antidote to tension, anxiety, depression, or boredom. "Shopaholics" turn to shopping much the way addicted people turn to drugs or alcohol.[71]

Compulsive consumption is distinctly different from impulse buying, which will be discussed in Chapter 10. The impulse to buy a specific item is temporary, and it centers on a specific product at a particular moment. In contrast, compulsive buying is an enduring behavior that centers on the process of buying, not the purchases themselves. As one woman who spent $20,000 per year on clothing confessed, "I was possessed when I went into a store. I bought clothes that didn't fit, that I didn't like, and that I certainly didn't need."[72]

In some cases, it is fairly safe to say that the consumer, not unlike a drug addict, has little to no control over consumption. Whether alcohol, cigarettes, chocolate, diet colas, or even Chap Stick, the products control the consumer. Even the act of shopping itself is an addicting experience for some consumers. Much negative or destructive consumer behavior can be characterized by three common elements:[73]

1. The behavior is not done by choice.
2. The gratification derived from the behavior is short-lived.
3. The person experiences strong feelings of regret or guilt afterwards.

Gambling is an example of a consumption addiction that touches every segment of consumer society. Whether it takes the form of casino gambling, playing the "slots," betting on sports events with friends or through a bookie, or even buying lottery tickets, excessive gambling can be quite destructive. Taken to extremes, gambling can result in lowered self-esteem, debt, divorce, and neglected children. According to one psychologist, gamblers exhibit a classic addictive cycle: They experience a "high" while in action and depression when they stop gambling, which leads them back to the thrill of the action. Unlike drug addicts, however, money is the substance that hard-core gamblers abuse.[73]

Consumed Consumers

People who are used or exploited, willingly or not, for commercial gain in the marketplace can be thought of as **consumed consumers**. The situations in which consumers *themselves* become commodities can range from traveling road shows that feature dwarfs and midgets to the selling of body parts and babies. Some examples of consumed consumers:

- *Prostitutes*: Expenditures on prostitution in the United States alone are estimated at $20 billion annually. These revenues are equivalent to those in the domestic shoe industry.[75]
- *Organ, blood, and hair donors*: In the United States, more than 11 million people per year sell their blood (not including voluntary donations).[76] A lively market also exists for organs (e.g., kidneys), and some women sell their hair to be made into wigs. Bidding for a human kidney on eBay went to more than $5.7 million before the company ended the auction (it's illegal to sell human organs online—at least so far). The seller wrote, "You can choose either kidney. . . . Of course only one for sale, as I need the other one to live. Serious bids only."[77]
- *Babies for sale*: Several thousand surrogate mothers have been paid to be medically impregnated and carry babies to term for infertile couples.[78] Commercial sperm banks have become big business, and the market is international in scope as many countries rely on imports. The head of one of the largest companies boasts, "We think we can be the McDonald's of sperm." This company markets three grades of sperm including an "extra" grade, which contains twice as many sperm as the average grade. The company can deliver to almost any customer in the world within 72 hours with its special freezing techniques in which the sperm travel in liquid nitrogen tanks.[79]

Illegal Activities

A survey conducted by the McCann-Erickson advertising agency revealed the following tidbits:[80]

- Ninety-one percent of people say they lie regularly. One in three fibs about their weight, one in four about their income, and 21 percent lie about their age. Nine percent even lie about their natural hair color.
- Four out of ten Americans have tried to pad an insurance bill to cover the deductible.
- Nineteen percent say they've snuck into a theater to avoid paying admission.
- More than three out of five people say they've taken credit for making something from scratch when they have done no such thing. According to Pillsbury's CEO, this "behavior is so prevalent that we've named a category after it—speed scratch."

Many consumer behaviors are not only self-destructive or socially damaging, they are illegal as well. Crimes committed by consumers against business have been estimated at more than $40 billion per year.

Consumer Theft

A retail theft is committed every five seconds. **Shrinkage** is the industry term for inventory and cash losses from shoplifting and employee theft. This is a massive problem for businesses that is passed onto consumers in the form of higher prices (about 40 percent of the losses can be attributed to employees rather than shoppers). Shopping malls spend $6 million annually on security, and a family of four

REALITY CHECK

A FASHION PHOTOGRAPHER NAMED

Ron Harris made international news when he set up a Web site, ronsangels.com, that auctions the eggs of fashion models to the highest bidder (minimum bid: $15,000). Harris writes, "Just watch television and you will see that we are only interested in looking at beautiful people. This site simply mirrors our current society, in that beauty usually goes to the highest bidder. . . . Any gift such as beauty, intelligence, or social skills, will help your children in their quest for happiness and success. If you could increase the chance of reproducing beautiful children, and thus giving them an advantage in society, would you?"79

Visit the Web site and see for yourself. Is the buying and selling of humans just another example of consumer behavior at work? Do you agree with Harris that his service is simply a more efficient way to maximize the chance of having happy, successful children? Should this kind of marketing activity be allowed? Would you sell your eggs or sperm on a Web site?

This scenario is reminiscent of Nazi Germany and its obsession in creating a superior race, eugenics experiments and the odious results. Ideally, a child is created out of the loving union of its parents. Beauty is not something that can be created; it comes inherently from a person's soul, their qualities and values, their sense of connection and reason. . . . I wouldn't sell my body parts, and the individuals that would actually consider purchasing eggs-on-line strike me as shallow and not ready to be parents; rather they should purchase a pedigree pet and let it go at that.

Kerri Ruminski,
Idaho State University

While it is common practice for potential parents consider the characteristic of possible donors, he [Harris] has chosen to prey on people's insecurities and concerns regarding their offspring by elevating appearance to be the quintessential trait driving human success. He then tries to use this concern to influence the decision to buy eggs.

Satish Ranchhod,
University of Auckland, New Zealand

We live under capitalism, people are free to do whatever they want. If the person is willing to sell their own eggs for profit, it's their own business. Buying and selling of humans is just another example of consumer behavior at work.

Frank Liu,
Florida State

My first impression was simply just "wow." When I saw the beautiful model's face and body, for a second I thought, "I may want a kid looking exactly like her." The child will be a perfect little boy sitting next to me, and I will be the happiest mother. Mother and the son will be photogenic. . . . Then I thought, "Will the father be in those pictures?" The answer was no. The child would look nothing like his father, and the father will not like the way I am obsessed with beauty. I might be conservative, but I think if this beauty based reproduction becomes popular, the whole definition of family will change.

Mai Sasaki,
Keio University, Japan

For Ron Harris to sell these eggs cannot been seen as any more unethical then what is done at thousands of sperm banks around the world. However, it is poor use of consumer behavior because the demand for such an organization is very low and unprofitable. For many, the birth of their own child is more beautiful then any human on earth and worth more than all the money in the world. I doubt many people will take advantage of this site and soon Ron Harris will be looking for a different marketing ploy.

Jennifer Freet,
George Mason University

This type of activity blatantly announces the emphasis placed on beauty in our society. In this regard, not only is this activity degrading to the parties involved, but it reflects very poorly on our vainglorious society as well. . . . Hawking sperm or eggs online is not only degrading for the couple who end up bidding for them, but it is also degrading for the women and men who have donated and are being selected for their physical attributes rather than their intelligence or social graces. This method of selecting a suitable specimen can be likened to picking a prize stallion or mare at the local animal market.

Sabrina Aslam,
Simon Fraser University, Canada

What's your opinion? Check out the on-line polls at www.prenhall.com/ myphlip. Just follow the little person in the lab coat.

spends about $300 extra per year because of markups to cover shrinkage.[81] Indeed, shoplifting is America's fastest-growing crime. A comprehensive retail study found that shoplifting is a year-round problem that costs U.S. retailers $9 billion dollars annually. The most frequently stolen products are tobacco products, athletic shoes, logo and brand name apparel, designer jeans, and undergarments. The average theft amount per incident is $58.43, up from $20.36 in a 1995 survey.[82]

Adbusters Quarterly is a Canadian magazine devoted to culture jamming. This mock ad skewers Benetton.

The large majority of shoplifting is not done by professional thieves or by people who genuinely need the stolen items.[83] About 2 million Americans are charged with shoplifting each year, but it's estimated that for every arrest, 18 unreported incidents occur.[84] About three-quarters of those caught are middle- or high-income people who shoplift for the thrill of it or as a substitute for affection. Shoplifting is also common among adolescents. Research evidence indicates that teen shoplifting is influenced by factors such as having friends who also shoplift. It is also more likely to occur if the adolescent does not believe that this behavior is morally wrong.[85]

Anticonsumption

Some types of destructive consumer behavior can be thought of as **anticonsumption**, events in which products and services are deliberately defaced or mutilated. In some cases new products are created as parodies of existing ones: Mattel sued MCA Records about a song that labeled Barbie a "blond bimbo girl," and Mattel also took an artist to court for creating a line of dolls including Exorcist Barbie, Tonya Harding Barbie, and Drag Queen Barbie.[86]

Anticonsumption can range from relatively mild acts like spray-painting graffiti on buildings and subways to serious incidences of product tampering or even the release of computer viruses that can bring large corporations to their knees. Anticonsumption can also take the form of political protest in which activists alter or destroy billboards and other advertisements that promote what they feel to be unhealthy or unethical acts. For example, some members of the clergy in areas heavily populated by minorities have organized rallies to protest the proliferation of cigarette and alcohol advertising in their neighborhoods; these protests sometimes include the defacement of billboards promoting alcohol or cigarettes. This practice has been termed **culture jamming**; the term was coined by a San Francisco band called Negativland that released a song called "Dispepsi."

CONSUMER BEHAVIOR AS A FIELD OF STUDY

By now it should be clear that the field of consumer behavior encompasses many things, from the simple purchase of a carton of milk to the selection of a complex networked computer system, from the decision to donate money to a charity to devious plans to rip off a company.

There's an awful lot to understand, and many ways to go about it. Although people have certainly been consumers for a long time, it is only recently that consumption per se has been the object of formal study. In fact, although many business schools now require that marketing majors take a consumer behavior course, most colleges did not even offer such a course until the 1970s.

Interdisciplinary Influences on the Study of Consumer Behavior

Consumer behavior is a very young field, and as it grows, it is being influenced by many different perspectives. Indeed, it is hard to think of a field that is more interdisciplinary. People with training in a very wide range of disciplines—from psychophysiology to literature—can now be found doing consumer research. Consumer researchers are employed by universities, manufacturers, museums, advertising agencies, and governments. Several professional groups, such as the Association for Consumer Research, have been formed since the mid-1970s.

To gain an idea of the diversity of interests of people who do consumer research, consider the list of professional associations that sponsor the field's major journal, the *Journal of Consumer Research*: American Association of Family & Consumer Sciences, the American Statistical Association, the Association for Consumer Research, the Society for Consumer Psychology, the International Communication Association, the American Sociological Association, the Institute of Management Sciences, the American Anthropological Association, the American Marketing Association, the Society for Personality and Social Psychology, the American Association for Public Opinion Research, and the American Economic Association. That's a pretty mixed bag.

So, with all of these researchers from diverse backgrounds interested in consumer behavior, which is the "correct" discipline to look into these issues? You might remember a children's story about the blind men and the elephant. The gist of the story is that each man touched a different part of the animal, and as a result, the descriptions each gave of the elephant were quite different. This analogy applies to consumer research as well. A given consumer phenomenon can be studied in different ways and at different levels depending on the training and interests of the researchers studying it. Table 1.2 illustrates how a "simple" topic like magazine usage can be approached in many different ways.

Figure 1.2 provides a glimpse of some of the disciplines working in the field and the level at which each approaches research issues. These diverse disciplines can be roughly characterized in terms of their focus on micro versus macro consumer behavior topics. The fields closer to the top of the pyramid concentrate

TABLE 1.2	Interdisciplinary Research Issues in Consumer Behavior
Disciplinary Focus	**Magazine Usage Sample Research Issues**
Experimental Psychology: product role in perception, learning, and memory processes	How specific aspects of magazines, such as their design or layout, are recognized and interpreted; which parts of a magazine are most likely to be read
Clinical Psychology: product role in psychological adjustment	How magazines affect readers' body images (e.g., do thin models make the average woman feel overweight?)
Microeconomics/Human Ecology: product role in allocation of individual or family resources	Factors influencing the amount of money spent on magazines in a household
Social Psychology: product role in the behavior of individuals as members of social groups	Ways that ads in a magazine affect readers' attitudes toward the products depicted; how peer pressure influences a person's readership decisions
Sociology: product role in social institutions and group relationships	Pattern by which magazine preferences spread through a social group (e.g., a sorority)
Macroeconomics: product role in consumers' relations with the marketplace	Effects of the price of fashion magazines and expense of items advertised during periods of high unemployment
Semiotics/Literary Criticism: product role in the verbal and visual communication of meaning	Ways in which underlying messages communicated by models and ads in a magazine are interpreted
Demography: product role in the measurable characteristics of a population	Effects of age, income, and marital status of a magazine's readers
History: product role in societal changes over time	Ways in which our culture's depictions of "femininity" in magazines have changed over time
Cultural Anthropology: product role in a society's beliefs and practices	Ways in which fashions and models in a magazine affect readers' definitions of masculine versus feminine behavior (e.g., the role of working women, sexual taboos)

on the individual consumer (micro issues), and those toward the base are more interested in the aggregate activities that occur among larger groups of people, such as consumption patterns shared by members of a culture or subculture (macro issues).

The Issue of Strategic Focus

Many regard the field of consumer behavior as an applied social science. Accordingly, the value of the knowledge generated should be judged in terms of its ability to improve the effectiveness of marketing practice. However some researchers have argued that consumer behavior should not have a strategic focus at all; the field should not be a "handmaiden to business." It should instead focus on the understanding of consumption for its own sake, because the knowledge can be applied by marketers.[87] This rather extreme view is probably not held by most consumer researchers, but it has encouraged many to expand the scope of their work beyond the field's traditional focus on the purchase of consumer goods such as food, appliances, cars, and so on to embrace social problems such as homelessness or preserving the environment. Certainly, it has led to some fiery debates among people working in the field!

Figure 1.2
The Pyramid of Consumer Behavior

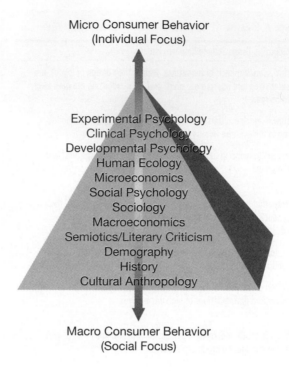

Micro Consumer Behavior
(Individual Focus)

Experimental Psychology
Clinical Psychology
Developmental Psychology
Human Ecology
Microeconomics
Social Psychology
Sociology
Macroeconomics
Semiotics/Literary Criticism
Demography
History
Cultural Anthropology

Macro Consumer Behavior
(Social Focus)

The Issue of Two Perspectives on Consumer Research

One general way to classify consumer research is in terms of the fundamental assumptions the researchers make about what they are studying and how to study it. This set of beliefs is known as a **paradigm**. As in other fields of study, consumer behavior is dominated by a paradigm, but some believe it is in the middle of a *paradigm shift*, which occurs when a competing paradigm challenges the dominant set of assumptions.

The basic set of assumptions underlying the dominant paradigm at this point in time is called **positivism** (or sometimes *modernism*). This perspective has significantly influenced Western art and science since the late sixteenth century. It emphasizes that human reason is supreme, and that there is a single, objective truth that can be discovered by science. Positivism encourages us to stress the function of objects, to celebrate technology, and to regard the world as a rational, ordered place with a clearly defined past, present, and future.

The emerging paradigm of **interpretivism** (or postmodernism) questions these assumptions. Proponents of this perspective argue that there is too much emphasis on science and technology in our society, and that this ordered, rational view of behavior denies the complex social and cultural world in which we live. Others feel that positivism puts too much emphasis on material well-being, and that its logical outlook is dominated by an ideology that stresses the homogenous views of a culture dominated by (dead) white males. Interpretivists instead stress the importance of symbolic, subjective experience, and the idea that meaning is in the mind of the person—that is, we each construct our own meanings based on our unique and shared cultural experiences, so there are no right or wrong answers. In this view, the world in which we live is composed of a pastiche or mixture of images.[88] The value placed on products because they help us to create order in our lives is replaced by an appreciation of consumption as offering a set of

TABLE 1.3	Positivist versus Interpretivist Approaches to Consumer Behavior	
Assumptions	Positivist Approach	Interpretivist Approach
Nature of reality	Objective, tangible Single	Socially constructed Multiple
Goal	Prediction	Understanding
Knowledge generated	Time free Context independent	Time bound Context dependent
View of causality	Existence of real causes	Multiple, simultaneous shaping events
Research relationship	Separation between researcher and subject	Interactive, cooperative with researcher being part of phenomenon under study

SOURCE: Adapted from Laurel A. Hudson and Julie L. Ozanne, "Alternative Ways of Seeking Knowledge in Consumer Research," *Journal of Consumer Research* 14 (March 1988): 508–21. Reprinted with the permission of The University of Chicago Press.

Heard any Volkswagen jokes lately?

An interpretative framework to understanding marketing communications can be illustrated by an analysis of one of the best-known and longest-running (1959–1978) advertising campaigns of all time: The work done by the advertising agency Doyle Dane Bernback for the Volkswagen Beetle. This campaign, widely noted for its self-mocking wit, found many ways to turn the Beetle's homeliness, smallness, and lack of power into positive attributes at a time when most car ads were emphasizing just the opposite. The image created for the humble car was connected to other examples of what scholars of comedy call the "Little Man" pattern. This is a type of comedic character that is related to a clown or a trickster; a social outcast who is able to poke holes in the stuffiness and rigidity of bureaucracy and conformity. Other examples of the "Little Man" character include Hawkeye in the TV sitcom "M.A.S.H.," and the comedians Woody Allen and Charlie Chaplin.

diverse experiences. The major differences between these two perspectives on consumer research are summarized in Table 1.3.

An interpretative framework to understand marketing communications can be illustrated by an analysis of one of the best-known and longest-running (1959–78) advertising campaigns of all time: The work done by the advertising agency Doyle Dane Bernbach for the Volkswagen Beetle. This campaign, widely noted for its self-mocking wit, found many ways to turn the Beetle's homeliness, smallness, and lack of power into positive attributes at a time when most car ads were emphasizing just the opposite. An interpretive analysis of these messages used concepts from literature, psychology, and anthropology to ground the appeal of this approach within a broader cultural context. The image created for the humble car was connected to other examples of what scholars of comedy call the "Little Man" pattern. This is a type of comedic character that is related to a clown or a trickster, a social outcast who is able to poke holes in the stuffiness and rigidity of bureaucracy and conformity. Other examples of the "Little Man" character include Hawkeye in the TV sitcom "M.A.S.H.," the comedian Woody Allen, and Charlie Chaplin. When one looks at the cultural meaning of marketing messages this way, it is perhaps no coincidence that IBM chose the Charlie Chaplin character some years later to help it "soften" its stuffy, intimidating image as it tried to convince consumers that its new personal computer products were user-friendly.

TAKING IT FROM HERE: THE PLAN OF THE BOOK

This book covers many facets of consumer behavior, and many of the research perspectives briefly described in this chapter will be highlighted in later chapters. The plan of the book is simple: It goes from micro to macro. Think of the book as a sort of photograph album of consumer behavior: Each chapter provides a "snapshot" of consumers, but the lens used to take each picture gets successively wider. The book begins with issues related to the individual consumer and expands its focus until it eventually considers the behaviors of large groups of people in their social settings. The topics to be covered correspond to the wheel of consumer behavior presented in Figure 1.3.

Figure 1.3
The Wheel of Consumer Behavior

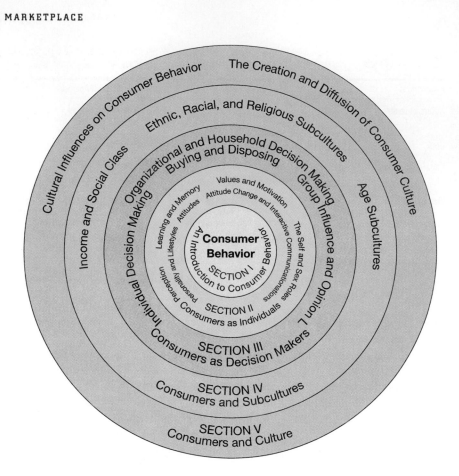

Section II, "Consumers as Individuals," considers the consumer at his or her most micro level. It examines how the individual receives information from his or her immediate environment and how this material is learned, stored in memory, and used to form and modify individual attitudes—both about products and about oneself. Section III, "Consumers as Decision Makers," explores the ways in which consumers use the information they have acquired to make decisions about consumption activities, both as individuals and as group members. Section IV, "Consumers and Subcultures," further expands the focus by considering how the consumer functions as part of a larger social structure. This structure includes the influence of different social groups with which the consumer belongs and/or identifies, including social class, ethnic groups, and age groups. Finally, Section V, "Consumers and Culture," completes the picture as it examines marketing's impact on mass culture. These effects include the relationship of marketing to the expression of cultural values and lifestyles, how products and services are related to rituals and cultural myths, and the interface between marketing efforts and the creation of art, music, and other forms of popular culture that are so much a part of our daily lives.

CHAPTER SUMMARY

- Consumer behavior is the study of the processes involved when individuals or groups select, purchase, use, or dispose of products, services, ideas, or experiences to satisfy needs and desires.

- A consumer may purchase, use, and/or dispose of a product, but these functions may be performed by different people. In addition, consumers may be thought of as role players who need different products to help them play their various parts.
- Market segmentation is an important aspect of consumer behavior. Consumers can be segmented according to many dimensions, including product usage, demographics (the objective aspects of a population, such as age and sex), and psychographics (psychological and lifestyle characteristics). Emerging developments, such as the new emphasis on relationship marketing and the practice of database marketing, mean that marketers are much more attuned to the wants and needs of different consumer groups. This is especially important as people are empowered to construct their own consumerspace—accessing product information where and when they want it and initiating contact with companies on the Internet instead of passively receiving marketing communications.
- The Web is transforming the way consumers interact with companies and with each other. Online commerce allows us to locate obscure products from around the world, and consumption communities provide forums for people to share opinions and product recommendations. The benefits are accompanied by potential problems, including the loss of privacy and the deterioration of traditional social interactions as people log more time online.
- Marketing activities exert an enormous impact on individuals. Consumer behavior is relevant to our understanding of both public policy issues (e.g., ethical marketing practices) and the dynamics of popular culture.
- Although textbooks often paint a picture of the consumer as a rational, informed decision maker, in reality many consumer activities are harmful to individuals or to society. The "dark side" of consumer behavior includes addiction, the use of people as products (consumed consumers), and theft or vandalism (anticonsumption).
- The field of consumer behavior is interdisciplinary; it is composed of researchers from many different fields who share an interest in how people interact with the marketplace. These disciplines can be categorized by the degree to which their focus is micro (the individual consumer) or macro (the consumer as a member of groups or of the larger society).
- There are many perspectives on consumer behavior, but research orientations can roughly be divided into two approaches: The positivist perspective emphasizes the objectivity of science and the consumer as a rational decision maker. The interpretivist perspective, in contrast, stresses the subjective meaning of the consumer's individual experience and the idea that any behavior is subject to multiple interpretations rather than to one single explanation.

KEY TERMS

anticonsumption, p. 27
business ethics, p. 17
compulsive consumption, p. 24
consumed consumers, p. 24
consumer, p. 5
consumer addiction, p. 23
consumer behavior, p. 5

culture jamming, p. 28
database marketing, p. 11
demographics, p. 8
exchange, p. 5
green marketing, p. 21
interpretivism, p. 30
market segmentation, p. 7

paradigm, p. 30
popular culture, p. 11
positivism, p. 30
relationship marketing, p. 10
role theory, p. 5
shrinkage, p. 25
social marketing, p. 22

CONSUMER BEHAVIOR CHALLENGE

1. The chapter states that people play different roles and that their consumption behaviors may differ depending on the particular role they are playing. State whether you agree or disagree with this perspective, giving examples from your personal life. Try to construct a "stage set" for a role you play—specify the props, costumes, and script that you use to play a role (e.g., job interviewee, conscientious student, party animal).

2. Some researchers believe that the field of consumer behavior should be a pure, rather than an applied, science. That is, research issues should be framed in terms of their scientific interest rather than their applicability to immediate marketing problems. Give your views on this issue.

3. Name some products or services that are widely used by your social group. State whether you agree or disagree with the notion that these products help to form group bonds, supporting your argument with examples from your list of products used by the group.

4. Although demographic information on large numbers of consumers is used in many marketing contexts, some people believe that the sale of data on customers' incomes, buying habits, and so on constitutes an invasion of privacy and should be stopped. Is Big Brother watching? Comment on this issue from both a consumer's and a marketer's point of view.

5. List the three stages in the consumption process. Describe the issues that you considered in each of these stages when you made a recent important purchase.

6. State the differences between the positivist and interpretivist approaches to consumer research. For each type of inquiry, give examples of product dimensions that would be more usefully explored using that type of research over the other.

7. What aspects of consumer behavior are likely to be of interest to a financial planner? to a university administrator? to a graphic arts designer? to a social worker in a government agency? to a nursing instructor?

8. Critics of targeted marketing strategies argue that this practice is discriminatory and unfair, especially if such a strategy encourages a group of people to buy a product that may be injurious to them or that they cannot afford. For example, community leaders in largely minority neighborhoods have staged protests against billboards promoting beer or cigarettes in these areas. On the other hand, the Association of National Advertisers argues that banning targeted marketing constitutes censorship, and thus is a violation of the First Amendment. What are your views regarding this issue?

9. Do marketers have the ability to control our desires or the power to create needs? Is this situation changing as the Internet creates new ways to interact with companies? If so, how?

NOTES

1. www.rightgrrl.com/whatwethink.html, accessed June 2, 2000.

2. This definition is similar to the definition of marketing offered by the American Marketing Association: "Marketing is the process of planning and executing the conception, pricing, promotion, and distribution of ideas, goods, and services to create exchanges that satisfy individual and organizational goals" (www.ama.org/about/ama/markdef.asp, accessed May 27, 2000). The focus of study in the consumer behavior discipline is more on the consumer's experience or satisfaction with the product than with

the organizational processes involved in creating or delivering the product. However, these issues obviously are also of great import for many consumer researchers, particularly those with an applied interest. The divergence between academic and applied perspectives will be considered later in this chapter.

3. Jill Rosenfeld, "Experience the Real Thing," *Fast Company.* (January/February 2000): 184.

4. Erving Goffman, *The Presentation of Self in Everyday Life* (Garden City, NY: Doubleday, 1959); George H. Mead, *Mind, Self, and Society* (Chicago: University of Chicago Press, 1934); Michael R. Solomon, "The Role of Products as Social Stimuli: A Symbolic Interactionism Perspective," *Journal of Consumer Research* 10 (December 1983): 319–29.

5. Michael R. Solomon and Elnora W. Stuart, *Marketing: Real People, Real Choices*, 2nd ed. (Upper Saddle River, NJ: Prentice Hall, 2000), pp. 5–6.

6. Quoted in Evan Ramstad, "Walkman's Plan for Reeling in the Ears of Wired Youths," *The Wall Street Journal Interactive Edition* (May 18, 2000).

7. George Anders, "Web Giants Amazon, eToys Bet on Opposing Market Strategies," *The Wall Street Journal Interactive Edition* (November 2, 1999).

8. Jennifer Ordonez, "Cash Cows: Burger Joints Call Them 'Heavy Users'—But Not to Their Faces," *The Wall Street Journal Interactive Edition* (January 12, 2000).

9. Joshua Harris Prager, "People with Disabilities are Next Consumer Niche," *The Wall Street Journal Interactive Edition* (December 15, 1999); Dan Fost, "The Fun Factor: Marketing Recreation to the Disabled," *American Demographics* (February 1998): 54–58; Jeremy Kahn, "Creating an Online Community—and a Market—for the Disabled," *Fortune* (February 7, 2000): 188; J. J. Burnett and P. Pallab, "Assessing the Media Habits and Needs of the Mobility-Disabled Consumer," *Journal of Advertising* 25, no. 3 (1996): 47–59.

10. Natalie Perkins, "Zeroing in on Consumer Values," *Advertising Age* (March 22, 1993): 23.

11. Wayne Friedman, "Converse Pairs with Teen Site Bolt to Kick Off EZ Chuck Athletic Shoe," *Advertising Age* (August 23, 1999): 4.

12. Jennifer Lawrence, "Gender-Specific Works for Diapers—Almost Too Well," *Advertising Age* (February 8, 1993): S10.

13. "Tech Brands Face a Gender Divide," *American Demographics* (February 2000): 16.

14. Amy Barrett, "Site Blends Frivolous, Serious to Draw French Women Online," *The Wall Street Journal Interactive Edition* (April 11, 2000).

15. Erika Check, Walaika Haskins, and Jennifer Tanaka, "Different Appeals," *Newsweek* (March 13, 2000): 15.

16. Casey Greenfield, "Hits & Mrs.," *Yahoo! Internet Life* (March 2000): 132–35.

17. Charles M. Schaninger and William D. Danko, "A Conceptual and Empirical Comparison of Alternative Household Life Cycle Models," *Journal of Consumer Research* 19 (March 1993): 580–94; Robert E. Wilkes, "Household Life-Cycle Stages, Transitions, and Product Expenditures," *Journal of Consumer Research* 22, no. 1 (June 1995): 27–42.

18. Richard P. Coleman, "The Continuing Significance of Social Class to Marketing," *Journal of Consumer Research* 10 (December 1983): 265–80.

19. Linda Keene, "Making a Stale Business Poppin' Fresh," *Sales & Marketing Management* (April 1992): 38–39.

20. Betsy McKay, "SoBe Hopes Edgy Ads Can Induce the Masses to Try Its 'Lizard Fuel,'" *The Wall Street Journal Interactive Edition* (April 28, 2000).

21. Motoko Rich, "Region's Marketers Hop on the Bubba Bandwagon," *The Wall Street Journal Interactive Edition* (May 19, 1999).

22. Alice Z. Cuneo, "Tailor-Made Not Merely 1 of a Kind," *Advertising Age* (November 7, 1994): 22.

23. Robert C. Blattberg and John Deighton, "Interactive Marketing: Exploiting the Age of Addressability," *Sloan Management Review*, 331, no. 1 (Fall 1991): 5–14.

24. Kirk Varnedoe and Adam Gopnik, *High and Low: Modern Art and Popular Culture* (New York: The Museum of Modern Art, 1990).

25. Quoted in "Bringing Meaning to Brands," *American Demographics* (June 1997): 34.

26. Susan Fournier, "Consumers and Their Brands. Developing Relationship Theory in Consumer Research," *Journal of Consumer Research* 24 (March 1998): 343–73.

27. Douglas B. Holt, "How Consumers Consume: A Taxonomy of Consumption Practices," *Journal of Consumer Research*, 22, no. 1 (June 1995): 1–16; personal communication, August 27, 1997.

28. Brad Edmondson, "The Dawn of the Megacity," *Marketing Tools* (March 1999): 64.

29. For a recent discussion of this trend, see Russell W. Belk, "Hyperreality and Globalization: Culture in the Age of Ronald McDonald," *Journal of International Consumer Marketing* 8, no. 3&4 (1995): 23–38.

30. Louise Lee, "No headline," *The Wall Street Journal Interactive Edition* (September 22, 1998).

31. Richard Covington, "Local Bands Leapfrog Global Stars on The Charts," *International Herald Tribune* (1998),

accessed via SS Newslink, February 4, 1998.

32. Robert Frank, "When Small Chains Go Abroad, Culture Clashes Require Ingenuity," *The Wall Street Journal Interactive Edition Edition* (April 12, 2000).

33. Seema Williams, David M. Cooperstein, David E. Weisman, and Thalika Oum, "Post-Web Retail," *The Forrester Report*, Forrester Research, Inc. (September 1999).

34. Susan G. Hauser, "These Guys, Their Big Feet and Her," *The Wall Street Journal Interactive Edition* (January 24, 2000).

35. Some material in this section was adapted from Michael R. Solomon and Elnora W. Stuart, *Welcome to Marketing.Com: The Brave New World of E-Commerce* (Upper Saddle River, NJ: Prentice Hall, 2000).

36. Quoted in Timothy L. O'Brien, "Aided by Internet, Identity Theft Soars," *The New York Times on the Web* (April 3, 2000).

37. Tiffany Lee Brown, "Got Skim?" *Wired* (March 2000): 262.

38. Camille Sweeney, "In a Chat Room You Can Be N E 1," *The New York Times Magazine* [online] (October 17, 1999).

39. Rebecca Fairley Raney, "Study Finds Internet of Social Benefit to Users," *The New York Times on the Web* (May 11, 2000).

40. John Markoff, "Portrait of a Newer, Lonelier Crowd is Captured in an Internet Survey," *The New York Times on the Web* (February 16, 2000).

41. Jonathan B. Weinbach, No headline, *The Wall Street Journal Interactive Edition* (December 7, 1998).

42. Marc Gunther, "Now Starring in Party of Five—Dr. Pepper," *Fortune* (April 17, 2000): 88.

43. Rafer Guzman, "Hotel Offers Kids a Room with a Logo," *The Wall Street Journal Interactive Edition* (October 6, 1999).

44. Chuck Ross and Ira Teinowitz, "Beer Ads Had Wide Underage Reach on MTV," *Advertising Age 4* (January 6, 1997): 36.

45. Frances A. McMorris, "Loaded Coconut Falls Off Deck, Landing Cruise Line in Court," *The Wall Street Journal Interactive Edition* (September 13, 1999).

46. Jennifer Lach, No Headline, *American Demographics* (December 1999): 18.

47. Valerie S. Folkes and Michael A. Kamins, "Effects of Information About Firms' Ethical and Unethical Actions on Consumers' Attitudes," *Journal of Consumer Psychology* 8, no. 3 (1999): 243–59.

48. Quoted in Ira Teinowitz, "Lawsuit: Menthol Smokes Illegally Targeted to Blacks," *Advertising Age* (November 2, 1998): 16.

49. "Firm's Cartoon-Cursor Software Monitors Customers on the Web," *The Wall Street Journal Interactive Edition*

(November 30, 1999); Stuart Elliott, "Internet Company Offers Customized Cursors," *The New York Times on the Web* (November 22, 1999).

50. Quoted in Jennifer Lach, "The New Gatekeepers," *American Demographics* (June 1999): 41–42.

51. Jeffrey Rosen, "The Eroded Self," *The New York Times Magazine* (April 29, 2000).

52. William Leiss, Stephen Kline, and Sut Jhally, *Social Communication in Advertising: Persons, Products, and Images of Well-Being* (Toronto: Methuen, 1986); Jerry Mander, *Four Arguments for the Elimination of Television* (New York: William Morrow, 1977).

53. Matthew L. Wald, "Looking for Savings as Gas Prices Rise," *New York Times* (May 27, 1989): 48.

54. David Ivanovich, "Exxon to Run Commercials Saying Most Cars Don't Need Premium," *Houston Chronicle* (August 15, 1997).

55. Packard (1957); quoted in Leiss et al., *Social Communication*, 11.

56. Raymond Williams, *Problems in Materialism and Culture: Selected Essays* (London: Verso, 1980).

57. Leiss et al., *Social Communication*.

58. George Stigler, "The Economics of Information," *Journal of Political Economy* (1961): 69.

59. Quoted in Leiss et al., *Social Communication*, 11.

60. For consumer research and discussions related to public policy issues, see Paul N. Bloom and Stephen A. Greyser, "The Maturing of Consumerism," *Harvard Business Review* (November–December 1981): 130–39; George S. Day, Assessing the Effect of Information Disclosure Requirements," *Journal of Marketing* (April 1976): 42–52; Dennis E. Garrett, "The Effectiveness of Marketing Policy Boycotts: Environmental Opposition to Marketing," *Journal of Marketing* 51 (January 1987): 44–53; Michael Houston and Michael Rothschild, "Policy-Related Experiments on Information Provision: A Normative Model and Explication," *Journal of Marketing Research* 17 (November 1980): 432–49; Jacob Jacoby, Wayne D. Hoyer, and David A. Sheluga, *Misperception of Televised Communications* (New York: American Association of Advertising Agencies, 1980); Gene R. Laczniak and Patrick E. Murphy, *Marketing Ethics: Guidelines for Managers* (Lexington, MA: Lexington Books, 1985), 117–23; Lynn Phillips and Bobby Calder, "Evaluating Consumer Protection Laws: Promising Methods," *Journal of Consumer Affairs* 14 (Summer 1980): 9–36; Donald P. Robin and Eric Reidenbach, "Social Responsibility, Ethics, and Marketing Strategy: Closing the Gap Between Concept and Application,"

Journal of Marketing 51 (January 1987): 44–58; Howard Schutz and Marianne Casey, "Consumer Perceptions of Advertising As Misleading," *Journal of Consumer Affairs* 15 (Winter 1981): 340–57; Darlene Brannigan Smith and Paul N. Bloom, "Is Consumerism Dead or Alive? Some New Evidence," in Thomas C. Kinnear, ed., *Advances in Consumer Research* 11 (Provo, UT: Association for Consumer Research, 1984), 369–73.

61. L. C. Noechowicz, "America's Hotels Going Green," *Montgomery Advertiser* (September 19, 1996): 4A.

62. "Concerned Consumers Push for Environmentally Friendly Packaging," *Boxboard Containers* (April 1993): 4.

63. Michal Strahilevitz and John G. Myers (1998), "Donations to Charity as Purchase Incentives: How Well They Work May Depend on What You are Trying to Sell," *Journal of Consumer Research* (March 1998), 434–46.

64. Quentin Hardy, "The Radical Philanthropist," *Forbes* (May 1, 2000): 114.

65. Cf. Philip Kotler and Alan R. Andreasen, *Strategic Marketing for Nonprofit Organizations*, 4th ed. (Englewood Cliffs, NJ: Prentice Hall, 1991), Jeff B. Murray and Julie L. Ozanne, "The Critical Imagination: Emancipatory Interests in Consumer Research," *Journal of Consumer Research* 18 (September 1991): 192–244; William D. Wells, "Discovery-Oriented Consumer Research," *Journal of Consumer Research* 19 (March 1993): 489–504.

66. Carol Beardi, "Teen Shift Against Drugs Credited to Paid Media," *Advertising Age* (November 29, 1999): 28.

67. Bertil Swartz, "'Keep Control:' The Swedish Brewers Association Campaign to Foster Responsible Alcohol Consumption Among Adolescents," paper presented at the 1997 ACR Europe Conference, Stockholm, June; Anna Oloffson, Ordpolen Informations AB, Sweden, personal communication, August 1997.

68. Laurie J. Flynn, "Web Site for Chap Stick Addicts," *The New York Times on the Web* (November 1, 1999).

69. "Psychologist Warns of Internet Addiction," *Montgomery Advertiser* (August 18, 1997): 2D.

70. Rebecca Buckman, "These Days, Online Trading Can Become an Addiction," *The Wall Street Journal Interactive Edition* (February 1, 1999).

71. Thomas C. O'Guinn and Ronald J. Faber, "Compulsive Buying: A Phenomenological Explanation," *Journal of Consumer Research* 16 (September 1989): 154.

72. Quoted in Anastasia Toufexis, "365 Shopping Days Till Christmas," *Time* (December 26, 1988): 82; see also Ronald J. Faber and Thomas C. O'Guinn,

"Compulsive Consumption and Credit Abuse," *Journal of Consumer Policy* 11 (1988): 109–21; Mary S. Butler, "Compulsive Buying—It's No Joke," *Consumer's Digest* (September 1986): 55; Derek N. Hassay and Malcolm C. Smith, "Compulsive Buying: An Examination of the Consumption Motive," *Psychology & Marketing* 13 (December 1996): 741–52.

73. Georgia Witkin, "The Shopping Fix," *Health* (May 1988): 73; see also Arch G. Woodside and Randolph J. Trappey III, "Compulsive Consumption of a Consumer Service: An Exploratory Study of Chronic Horse Race Track Gambling Behavior" (working paper #90-MKTG-04, A. B. Freeman School of Business, Tulane University, 1990); Rajan Nataraajan and Brent G. Goff, "Manifestations of Compulsiveness in the Consumer-Marketplace Domain," *Psychology & Marketing* 9 (January 1992): 31–44; Joann Ellison Rodgers, "Addiction: A Whole New View," *Psychology Today* (September/October 1994): 32 (11 pp.).

74. Helen Reynolds, *The Economics of Prostitution* (Springfield, IL: Thomas, 1986).

75. "Precious Drops," *The Economist* (October 14, 1989): 28.

76. Amy Harmon, "Illegal Kidney Auction Pops Up on Ebay's Site," *The New York Times on the Web* (September 3, 1999).

77. Barbara Katz Rothman, "Cheap Labor: Sex, Class, Race and 'Surrogacy'," *Society* 25 (March–April 1988): 21.

78. G. Paschal Zachary, "A Most Unlikely Industry Finds It Can't Resist Globalization's Call," *The Wall Street Journal Interactive Edition* (January 6, 2000).

79. http://www.ronsangels.com/index2.html, accessed 4/3/2000.

80. "Advertisers Face up to the New Morality: Making the Pitch," (Bloomberg), accessed vis SS Newslink (July 8, 1997).

81. "Shoplifting: Bess Myerson's Arrest Highlights a Multibillion-Dollar Problem that Many Stores Won't Talk About," *Life* (August 1988): 32.

82. "New Survey Shows Shoplifting Is A Year-Round Problem," *Business Wire* (April 12, 1998).

83. Catherine A. Cole, "Deterrence and Consumer Fraud," *Journal of Retailing* 65 (Spring 1989): 107–20; Stephen J. Grove, Scott J. Vitell, and David Strutton, "Non-Normative Consumer Behavior and the Techniques of Neutralization," in Terry Childers, et al., eds., *Marketing Theory and Practice*, 1989 AMA Winter Educators' Conference (Chicago: American Marketing Association, 1989); 131–35.

84. Mark Curnutte, "The Scope Of The Shoplifting Problems," *Gannett News Service* (November 29, 1997).

85. Anthony D. Cox, Dena Cox, Ronald D. Anderson, and George P. Moschis, "Social Influences on Adolescent

Shoplifting—Theory, Evidence, and Implications for the Retail Industry," *Journal of Retailing* 69 (Summer 1993) 2: 234–46.

86. Lisa Bannon, "Now, Barbie Favors Legal Suits, Angering Fans and Judges Alike," *The Wall Street Journal Interactive Edition* (January 6, 1998).

87. Morris B. Holbrook, "The Consumer Researcher Visits Radio City: Dancing in the Dark," in Elizabeth C. Hirschman and Morris B. Holbrook, eds., *Advances in Consumer Research* 12 (Provo, UT: Association for Consumer Research, 1985): 28–31.

88. Alladi Venkatesh, "Postmodernism, Poststructuralism and Marketing" (paper presented at the American Marketing Association Winter Theory Conference, San Antonio, February 1992); see also A. Fuat Firat, "Postmodern Culture, Marketing and the Consumer," in Terry Childers, et al., eds., *Marketing Theory and Application* (Chicago: American Marketing Association, 1991); 237–42; A. Fuat Firat and Alladi Venkatesh, "The Making of Postmodern Consumption," in Russell W. Belk and Nikhilesh Dholakia, eds, *Consumption and Marketing: Macro Dimensions* (Boston: PWS-Kent, 1993).

SECTION

II

CONSUMERS AS INDIVIDUALS

In this section, we focus on the internal dynamics of consumers. While "no man is an island," each of us is to some degree a self-contained receptor for information about the outside world. We are constantly confronted with advertising messages, products, other people persuading us to buy something, and even reflections of ourselves that make us happy or sad. Each chapter in this section will consider a different aspect of the individual that is "invisible" to others—but of vital importance to ourselves.

Chapter 2 describes the process of perception, in which information from the outside world about products and other people is absorbed and interpreted. Chapter 3 focuses on the way this information is mentally stored and how it adds to our existing knowledge about the world during the learning process. Chapter 4 discusses our reasons or motivations for absorbing this information and how it is influenced by the values to which we subscribe as members of a particular culture.

Chapter 5 explores how our views about ourselves—particularly our sexuality and our physical appearance—affect what we do, want, and buy. Chapter 6 goes on to consider how people's individual personalities influences these decisions, and how the choices we make in terms of products, leisure activities, and so on help to define our lifestyles.

Chapters 7 and 8 discuss how our attitudes—our evaluations of all these products, messages, and so on—are formed and (sometimes) changed by marketers, and how we as individual consumers engage in our ongoing dialogue with these businesspeople by virtue of our responses to these messages.

◆ ◆ ◆

Section Outline

The European vacation has been wonderful, and this stop in Lisbon is no exception. Still, after two weeks of eating his way through some of the Continent's finest pastry shops and restaurants, Gary's getting a bit of a craving for his family's favorite snack—a good old American box of Oreos and an ice-cold carton of milk. Unbeknownst to his wife, Janeen, he had stashed away some cookies "just in case"—this was the time to break them out.

Now, all he needs is the milk. On an impulse, Gary decides to surprise Janeen with a mid-afternoon treat. He sneaks out of the hotel room while she's napping, and finds the nearest *grosa*. When he heads to the small refrigerated section, though, he's puzzled—no milk here. Undaunted, Gary asks the clerk, *"Leite, por favor?"* The clerk quickly smiles and points to a rack in the middle of the store piled with little white square boxes. No, that can't be right—Gary resolves to work

on his Portuguese. He repeats the question, and again he gets the same answer.

Finally, he investigates and sure enough he sees the boxes, labeled with the brand name Parmalat, contain something called ultra heat treated (UHT) milk. Nasty! Who in the world would drink milk out of a little box that's been sitting on a warm shelf for who knows how long? Gary dejectedly returns to the hotel, his snacktime fantasies crumbling like so many stale cookies. . . .

2

PERCEPTION

INTRODUCTION

Gary would be surprised to learn that many people in the world drink milk out of a box every day. UHT is Grade A pasteurized milk that has been heated until the bacteria causing spoilage are destroyed, and it can last for five to six months without refrigeration if its aseptic container is unopened. Its main manufacturer, the Parmalat Group, is one of the largest dairy companies in the world. Parmalat had $6 billion in sales in 1999.

Shelf-stable milk is particularly popular in Europe, where refrigerator space in homes and stores tends to be more limited than in the United States. Seven out of ten Europeans drink it routinely. The company is trying to crack the American market as well, though analysts are dubious about its prospects. To begin with, milk consumption in the United States is declining steadily as teenagers choose soft drinks instead. Indeed, the Milk Industry Foundation pumped $44 million into an advertising campaign to promote milk drinking ("Got Milk?").

But enticing Americans to drink milk out of a box is even harder. In focus groups, American consumers say they have trouble believing the milk is not spoiled or unsafe. They consider the square, quart-sized boxes more suitable for dry food, and some even feel the name Parmalat sounds too much like baby formulas such as Enfamil or Similac. Parmalat USA is trying to combat this resistance by introducing new containers featuring an image of an old-fashioned milk bottle.

Parmalat is mounting an extensive distribution and marketing campaign in the United States. Parmalat has purchased numerous U.S. dairies and is constructing a new distribution base on the West Coast. The company also invested $30 million in the online grocery store netgrocer.com. In 1999, Parmalat USA sold about $650 million worth of the product, much of it to schools and fast-food chains who appreciate its long shelf life.[1] Still, although Americans may not think twice about drinking a McFlurry from McDonald's made with Parmalat, it's going to be a long, uphill battle to change their perceptions about the proper accompaniment to a bagful of Oreos.

Whether it's the taste of Oreos, the sight of an Obsession perfume ad, or the sound of the music group Offspring, we live in a world overflowing with sensations. Wherever we turn, we are bombarded by a symphony of colors, sounds, and odors. Some of the "notes" in this symphony occur naturally, such as the loud barking of a dog, the shades of the evening sky, or the heady smell of a rose bush. Others come from people: The person sitting next to you in class might sport tinted blonde hair, bright pink pants, and enough nasty perfume to make your eyes water.

Marketers certainly contribute to this commotion. Consumers are never far from advertisements, product packages, radio and television commercials, and billboards, all clamoring for our attention. Sometimes consumers go out of their way to experience "unusual" sensations, whether bungee jumping or playing virtual reality games. On a very popular Peruvian TV show called "Laura en America," contestants show just what people are capable of experiencing (with the right incentive): For $20, two women stripped to their underwear and had buckets of slime covered with toads poured over their bodies. For the same amount, three men raced to gobble down bowls of large tree grubs from the Amazon jungle. For $30, a woman licked the arm pits of a sweaty body builder who had not bathed for two days.[2] You thought college fraternities were out there?

Whether game-show contestants or not, each of us copes with the bombardment of sensations by paying attention to some stimuli and tuning out others. The messages to which we do choose to pay attention often wind up differing from what the sponsors intended, as we each put our "spin" on things by taking away meanings consistent with our own unique experiences, biases, and desires. This chapter focuses on the process of perception, in which sensations are absorbed by the consumer and then are used to interpret the surrounding world.

Sensation refers to the immediate response of our sensory receptors (eyes, ears, nose, mouth, fingers) to basic stimuli such as light, color, sound, odors, and textures. **Perception** is the process by which these sensations are selected, organized, and interpreted. The study of perception, then, focuses on what we add to these raw sensations in order to give them meaning.

Gary's encounter with milk in a box illustrates the perceptual process. He has learned to equate the cold temperature of refrigerated milk with freshness, so he experienced a negative physical reaction when confronted with a product that contradicted his expectations. Gary's evaluation of Parmalat was affected by factors such as the design of the package, the brand name, and even by the section in the grocery store in which the milk was displayed. These expectations are largely affected by a consumer's cultural background. Europeans do not necessarily have the same perceptions of milk, and as a result their reactions to the product are quite different.

Like computers, people undergo stages of information processing in which stimuli are input and stored. Unlike computers, though, we do not passively process whatever information happens to be present. In the first place, only a very small number of the stimuli in our environment are ever noticed. Of these, an even smaller number are attended to. The stimuli that do enter consciousness might not be processed objectively. The meaning of a stimulus is interpreted by

This ad for a luxury car emphasizes the contribution made by all of our senses to the evaluation of a driving experience. In addition to the five channels of sight, sound, touch, smell, and taste, the ad mentions the "sixth sense" of intuition in its treatment of the "power of perception."

the individual, who is influenced by his or her unique biases, needs, and experiences. As shown in Figure 2.1, these three stages of exposure, attention, and interpretation make up the process of perception. Before considering each of these stages, let's step back and consider the sensory systems that provide sensations to us in the first place.

SENSORY SYSTEMS

External stimuli, or sensory inputs, can be received on a number of channels. We may see a billboard, hear a jingle, feel the softness of a cashmere sweater, taste a new flavor of ice cream, or smell a leather jacket. The inputs picked up by our five senses are the raw data that begin the perceptual process. For example, sensory data emanating from the external environment (e.g., hearing a tune on the radio) can generate internal sensory experiences when the song triggers a young man's memory of his first dance and brings to mind the smell of his date's perfume or the feel of her hair on his cheek. These responses are an important part of **hedonic consumption,** the multisensory, fantasy, and emotional aspects of consumers' interactions with products.[3]

Figure 2.1
An Overview of the Perceptual Process

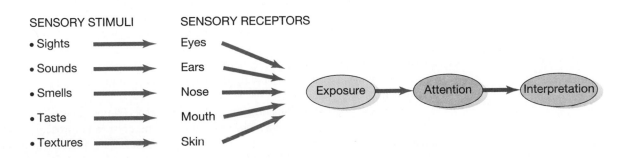

This Finnish ad emphasizes the sensual reasons to visit the city of Helsinki.

The unique sensory quality of a product can play an important role in helping it to stand out from the competition, especially if the brand creates a unique association with the sensation. The Owens-Corning Fiberglass Corporation was the first company to trademark a color when it used a bright pink for its insulation material and adopted the Pink Panther cartoon character as its spokescharacter. Harley-Davidson actually tried to trademark the distinctive sound made by a "hog" revving up.[4]

Vision

Marketers rely heavily on visual elements in advertising, store design, and packaging. Meanings are communicated on the visual channel through a product's color, size, and styling. Colors may even influence our emotions more directly. Evidence suggests that some colors (particularly red) create feelings of arousal and stimulate appetite, and others (such as blue) are more relaxing. Products presented against a backdrop of blue in advertisements are better liked than when a red background is used, and cross-cultural research indicates a consistent preference for blue whether people live in Canada or Hong Kong.[5] American Express chose to name its new card Blue after research showed the color evokes positive feelings about the future. Its advertising agency named blue the color of the new millennium because people associate it with sky and water, "providing a sense of limitlessness and peace."[6]

Some reactions to color come from learned associations. In western countries, black is the color of mourning, whereas in some eastern countries, notably Japan, white plays this role. In addition, the color black is associated with power. Teams in both the National Football League and the National Hockey League

Teeth are very sensitive. They hate violence.

Change from that abrasive dental cream to Phillips. The only dental cream with Phillips Milk of Magnesia.

Phillips
Phillips 2

The whitest and healthiest choice.

This Brazilian toothpaste ad uses vivid perceptual imagery to communicate a product benefit.

who wear black uniforms are among the most aggressive; they consistently rank near the top of their leagues in penalties during the season.[7]

Color plays a dominant role in Web page design; it directs a viewer's eye across the page, ties together design ideas, separates visual areas, organizes contextual relationships, creates mood, and captures attention. Saturated colors such as green, yellow, cyan, and orange are considered the best hues to capture attention, but don't overdo it: Extensive use of these hues can overwhelm people and cause visual fatigue.[8] And, of course, color is a key issue in package design. These choices used to be made casually. For example, the familiar Campbell's Soup can was produced in red and white because a company executive liked the football uniforms at Cornell University! Today, however, color is a serious business, and many companies realize that their color choices can exert a big influence on consumers' assumptions about what is inside the package.

This "package" includes automobiles, where consumers' preferences for exterior hues change with the tides of fashion. That's why DuPont, a leader in the car paint industry, invests heavily in efforts to predict car buyers' tastes in exterior colors one year, three years, and five years down the road. Even car tires are being sold on the basis of color: Michelin came under fire in California for its new "Scorcher" tires that feature yellow, red, or blue treads. A San Francisco supervisor says, "These colored tires may appeal to gangs who will use red and blue skid marks to mark their turf and insult rival gangs." Red and blue are the colors of the Bloods and the Crips, two Southern California gangs.[9] Now, shoppers can log onto the company's B. F. Goodrich brand Web site and order customized tire colors—even if they're not gang members![10]

These decisions help to "color" our expectations of what's inside the package. When introducing a white cheese as a "sister product" to an existing blue "Castello" cheese, a Danish company launched it in a red package under the name of Castello Bianco. The red package was chosen to provide maximum visibility on store shelves. Although taste tests were very positive, sales were disappointing. A subsequent analysis of consumer interpretations showed that the red packaging and the name gave the consumers wrong associations with the product type and its degree of sweetness. Danish consumers had trouble

MULTICULTURAL DIMENSIONS

CULTURAL DIFFERENCES IN COLOR preferences create the need for marketing strategies tailored to different countries. These variations affect products made for kids as well as adults. In Italy, bambini ride in wild yellow and orange strollers. German infants are wheeled about in chartreuse. But in the United States, blue is the only color stroller that sells.[11] And how about their moms? Procter & Gamble (P&G) uses brighter colors in makeup it sells in Latin countries.[12] P&G and other cosmetics companies have found that women in Mexico and South America are willing to pay a premium for bold-colored nail polishes with names such as "Orange Flip." For these women, the natural look is out. As one legal secretary in Mexico City explained, "When you don't wear makeup, men look at you like you are sick or something."[13]

As this Dutch detergent ad illustrates (Flowery orange fades without Dreft), vivid colors are often an attractive product feature.

associating the color red with the white cheese. Also the name Bianco connoted a sweetness that was incompatible with the actual taste of the product. It was relaunched in a white package and given the name "White Castello." Almost immediately sales more than doubled.[14]

Some color combinations come to be so strongly associated with a corporation that they become known as the company's *trade dress*, and the company

This Volkswagen ad pokes fun at the practice of color trend forecasting, which is common in many industries.

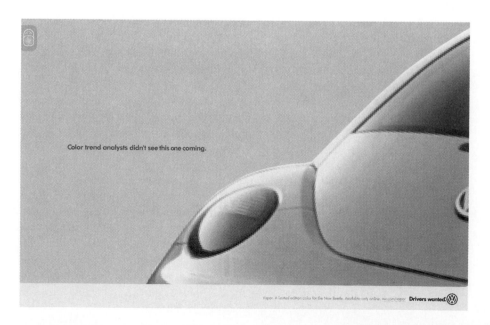

may even be granted exclusive use of these colors. For example, Eastman Kodak has successfully protected its trade dress of yellow, black, and red in court. As a rule, however, trade dress protection is granted only when consumers might be confused about what they are buying because of similar coloration of a competitor's packages.[15]

Smell

Odors can stir emotions or create a calming feeling. They can invoke memories or relieve stress. One study found that consumers who viewed ads for either flowers or chocolate and who also were exposed to flowery or chocolatey odors spent more time processing the product information and were more likely to try different alternatives within each product category.[16]

Some of our responses to scents result from early associations that call up good or bad feelings, and that explains why businesses are exploring connections among smell, memory, and mood.[17] Researchers for Folger's found that for many people the smell of coffee summons up childhood memories of their mothers cooking breakfast, so the aroma reminds them of home. The company turned this insight into a commercial in which a young man in an army uniform arrives home early one morning. He goes to the kitchen, opens a Folger's package, and the aroma wafts upstairs. His mother opens her eyes, smiles, and exclaims, "He's home!"[18]

Fragrance is processed by the limbic system, the most primitive part of the brain and the place where immediate emotions are experienced. One study even found that the scent of fresh cinnamon buns induced sexual arousal in a sample of male students![19] Many new scents are turning up in unexpected places to stimulate these feelings. Procter & Gamble's new Physique shampoo smells like watermelon.[20] Dirt cologne smells like potting soil and is one of 62 "single-note" natural scents produced by Demeter Fragrances. Others include Carrot, Celery, and Cucumber, and single-note fragrances in development include Gasoline and Sweat (charming, right?).[21]

This ad pokes fun at the proliferation of scented ads. Ah, the scent of sweat.

Scented marketing, now a $90 million business, is taking interesting turns. One new wrinkle in the use of scents is fragranced clothes. The textile industry is developing New Age fabrics with "scentual" properties by embedding fragrances in microcapsules that are sewn to clothing. A French lingerie company is selling lingerie that emits scents when touched. Korean men are even buying lavender-scented suits to cover up liquor and cigarette odors.[22] The capsules "pop" when jostled, so the more the man moves the more fragrant he smells—until the capsules wear out, at least.

Sound

Consumers buy millions of dollars' worth of sound recordings each year, advertising jingles maintain brand awareness, and background music creates desired moods.[23] Many aspects of sound affect people's feelings and behaviors. The Muzak Corporation estimates that its recordings are heard by 80 million people every day. This so-called "functional music" is played in stores, shopping malls, and offices to either relax or stimulate consumers. Research shows that workers tend to slow down during midmorning and midafternoon, so Muzak uses a system it calls "stimulus progression" that increases the tempo during those slack times. Muzak has been linked to reductions in absenteeism among factory workers, and even the milk and egg output of cows and chickens is claimed to increase under its influence.[24] Think what it might do for your term papers!

Touch

Although relatively little research has been done on the effects of tactile stimulation on consumer behavior, common observation tells us that this sensory channel is important. Moods are stimulated or relaxed on the basis of sensations reaching the skin, whether from a luxurious massage or the bite of a winter wind. Touch has even been shown to be a factor in sales interactions. In one study diners who were touched by waitpeople gave bigger tips, and food demonstrators in a supermarket who lightly touched customers had better luck in getting shoppers to try a new snack product and to redeem coupons for the brand.[25]

People associate the textures of fabrics and other surfaces with product qualities, and some marketers are exploring how touch can be used in packaging to arouse consumer interest. Some new plastic containers for household beauty items are incorporating "soft touch" resins that provide a soft, friction-like resistance when held. Focus group members who tested one such package for Clairol's new Daily Defense shampoo described the sensations as "almost sexy" and were actually reluctant to let go of the containers![26]

The perceived richness or quality of the material in clothing, bedding, or upholstery is linked to its "feel," whether rough or smooth, flexible or inflexible. A smooth fabric such as silk is equated with luxury; denim is practical and durable. Some of these tactile–quality associations are summarized in Table 2.1. Fabrics that are composed of scarce materials or that require a high degree of processing to achieve their smoothness or fineness tend to be more expensive and thus are seen as being higher-class. Similarly, lighter, more delicate textures are assumed to be feminine. Roughness is often positively valued for men, and smoothness is sought by women.

This Caress ad uses tactile stimulation as a selling point.

Taste

Our taste receptors obviously contribute to our experience of many products, and people form strong preferences for certain flavors. To illustrate, the famous soup cans painted by Andy Warhol sell for a lot of money, but the amount seems to depend on the flavor of the soup can depicted. A painted can of Tomato soup can fetch $10,000, but Black Bean is only worth $4,000. An art gallery owner explains, "People have a strong connection to certain flavors. Maybe it goes back to strong childhood memories."[27]

Specialized companies called "flavor houses" keep busy developing new concoctions to please the changing palates of consumers. For example, consumers' greater appreciation of different ethnic dishes has contributed to increased desires for spicy foods, so the quest for the ultimate pepper sauce is a hot taste trend. More than 50 stores in the United States now specialize in supplying fiery concoctions with names such as Sting and Linger, Hell in a Jar, and Religious Experience (comes in Original, Hot, and Wrath).[28] Some of these sauces are so hot that stores ask customers to sign waivers of legal liability before they will sell them! The "heat" of peppers is measured in units called

TABLE 2.1 Tactile Oppositions in Fabrics

Perception	Male	Female	
High class	Wool	Silk	Fine
Low class	Denim	Cotton	↕
	Heavy ←——→	Light	Coarse

Scovilles. In 1912, Wilbur Scoville asked a five-person panel to see how much sugar water it would take to eliminate the hotness of a pepper. How's this for a hot tip: It takes 1,981 gallons of sweetened water to neutralize a teaspoon of Da' Bomb, which is advertised as the hottest sauce ever made.[29]

At the other extreme of sensation, Japanese beverage companies are catching onto a new fad among younger Japanese consumers who are becoming more health conscious and want to avoid harmful additives: bland, watery drinks. Beverage manufacturers there are working hard to make fruit drinks that you can see through. Coca-Cola introduced a new cold tea with an actor who stares at a bottle and wonders: Is it tea or is it water? Stores are stacked with cartons of "near waters," mineral waters with just a touch of flavor. Sapporo sells a watered-down iced coffee, and Asahi Breweries makes a beer that is as clear as water with a name that sums up this new trend: Beer Water.[30] Not too appealing to Americans, but perhaps good for washing down some hot sauce?

EXPOSURE

Exposure occurs when a stimulus comes within the range of someone's sensory receptors. Consumers concentrate on some stimuli, are unaware of others, and even go out of their way to ignore some messages. An experiment by a Minneapolis bank illustrates consumers' tendencies to miss or ignore information in which they are not interested. After a state law was passed that required banks to explain details about money transfer in electronic banking, the Northwestern National Bank distributed a pamphlet to 120,000 of its customers at considerable cost to provide the required information, which was hardly exciting bedtime reading. In 100 of the mailings, a section in the middle of the pamphlet offered the reader $10 just for finding that paragraph. Not a single person claimed the reward![31] Before we consider what else people may choose not to perceive, let's consider what they are *capable* of perceiving.

Sensory Thresholds

If you have ever blown a dog whistle and watched pets respond to a sound you cannot hear, you won't be surprised to learn that there are some stimuli that people simply are not capable of perceiving. Of course, some people are better able to pick up sensory information than those whose sensory channels may be impaired by disabilities or age. The science that focuses on how the physical environment is integrated into our personal, subjective world is known as **psychophysics.**

The Absolute Threshold
When we define the lowest intensity of a stimulus that can be registered on a sensory channel, we speak of a *threshold* for that receptor. It sounds like a great name for a rock band, but the **absolute threshold** refers to the minimum amount of stimulation that can be detected on a given sensory channel. The sound emitted by a dog whistle is too high to be detected by human ears, so this stimulus is beyond our auditory absolute threshold. The absolute threshold is an important consideration in designing marketing stimuli. A highway billboard might have the most entertaining copy ever written, but this genius is wasted if the print is too small for passing motorists to see it.

The Differential Threshold

The **differential threshold** refers to the ability of a sensory system to detect changes or differences between two stimuli. The mimimum difference that can be detected between two stimuli is known as the **j.n.d.** (just noticeable difference).

The issue of when and if a difference between two stimuli will be noticed by consumers is relevant to many marketing situations. Sometimes a marketer may want to ensure that a change is observed, as when merchandise is offered at a discount. In other situations, the fact that a change has been made may be downplayed, as in the case of price increases or when a product is downsized.

A consumer's ability to detect a difference between two stimuli is relative. A whispered conversation that might be unintelligible on a noisy street can suddenly become public and embarrassingly loud in a quiet library. It is the *relative* difference between the decibel level of the conversation and its surroundings, rather than the absolute loudness of the conversation itself, that determines whether the stimulus will register.

In the nineteenth century, a psychophysicist named Ernst Weber found that the amount of change that is necessary to be noticed is systematically related to the intensity of the original stimulus. The stronger the initial stimulus, the greater a change must be for it to be noticed. This relationship is known as **Weber's Law,** and is expressed in the following equation:

$$K = \frac{\Delta i}{I}$$

where

K = a constant (this varies across the senses)
Δi = the mimimal change in intensity of the stimulus required to produce a j.n.d.
I = the intensity of the stimulus where the change occurs

For example, consider how Weber's Law might work with respect to a product that has had its price decreased for a special sale. A rule-of-thumb used by some retailers is that a markdown should be at least 20 percent for this price cut to make an impact on shoppers. If so, a pair of socks that retails for $10 should be put on sale for $8 (a $2 discount). However, a sports coat selling for $100 would not benefit from a "mere" $2 discount—it would have to be marked down to $80 to achieve the same impact.

Subliminal Perception

Most marketers are concerned with creating messages above consumers' thresholds so they will be noticed. Ironically, a good number of consumers appear to believe that many advertising messages are, in fact, designed to be perceived unconsciously, or *below* the threshold of recognition. Another word for threshold is *limen*, and stimuli that fall below the limen are termed subliminal. **Subliminal perception** occurs when the stimulus is below the level of the consumer's awareness.

Subliminal perception is a topic that has captivated the public for more than 40 years, despite the fact that there is virtually no proof that this process has any effect on consumer behavior.[33] A survey of American consumers found that almost two-thirds believe in the existence of subliminal advertising, and more than one-half are convinced that this technique can get them to buy things they do not really want![34]

MARKETING PITFALLS

THE DISNEY CORPORATION IS one of the most recent victims of concerns about subliminal messages. In 1999 the company recalled 3.4 million copies of its animated video *The Rescuers* because the film included a very brief image of a topless woman (she appeared in two frames of a 110,000-frame film, each for $\frac{1}{30}$ of a second). This picture was embedded as a prank in the master negative way back in 1977, but "the naked truth" surfaced only recently. Disney has been combating rumors of subliminal images in its films for years, and this issue was one of the reasons given for a boycott of the company's products by the Southern Baptist Convention in 1997. In one case, CEO Michael Eisner had to rebut charges on the TV show 60 Minutes that the clergyman in *The Little Mermaid* is shown with an erection. He argued, "Everybody knows it's his knee. It's just people spending too much time looking for things that aren't there."[35] He's probably right in most cases, though whoever pulled off *The Rescuers* prank makes it hard to mount a totally convincing argument.

Campbell's Soup has been gradually modifying its label for the last 125 years. Consumers are rushing to hoard classic Campbell soup cans because in 1999 the company decided to retire the label. The new cans feature photos of actual soup in the bowl but the design retains the distinctive red and white colors and unique script to avert a consumer backlash.[32]

In fact, most examples of subliminal perception that have been "discovered" are not subliminal at all—to the contrary these images are quite visible. Remember, if you can see it or hear it, it is not subliminal, because the stimulus is above the level of conscious awareness! Nonetheless, the continuing controversy about subliminal persuasion has been important in shaping the public's beliefs about advertising and marketers' ability to manipulate consumers against their will.

Subliminal Techniques

Subliminal messages supposedly can be sent on both visual and aural channels. *Embeds* are tiny figures that are inserted into magazine advertising by using high-speed photography or airbrushing. These hidden figures, usually of a sexual nature, supposedly exert strong but unconscious influences on innocent readers. To date, the only real impact of this interest in hidden messages is to sell more copies of "exposés" written by a few authors, and to make some consumers (and students of consumer behavior) look a bit more closely at print ads—perhaps seeing whatever their imaginations lead them to see.

Many consumers also are fascinated by the possible effects of messages hidden on sound recordings. An attempt to capitalize on subliminal auditory perception techniques is found in the growing market for self-help cassettes.

Critics of subliminal persua-
sion often focus on ambigu-
ous shapes in drinks that
supposedly spell out words
like S E X as evidence for
the use of this technique.
This Pepsi ad, while hardly
subliminal, gently borrows
this message format.

These tapes, which typically feature the sound of waves crashing or some other natural sound, supposedly contain subliminal messages to help the listener stop smoking, lose weight, gain confidence, and so on. Despite the rapid growth of this market, there is little evidence that subliminal stimuli transmitted on the auditory channel can bring about desired changes in behavior.[36]

Along with the interest in hidden self-help messages on recordings, some consumers have become concerned about rumors of satanic messages recorded backward on rock music selections. The popular press has devoted much attention to such stories, and state legislatures have considered bills requiring warning labels about these messages. These backward messages do indeed appear on some albums, including Led Zeppelin's classic song "Stairway to Heaven," which contains the lyric "there's still time to change." When played in reverse, this phrase sounds like "so here's to my sweet Satan."

The novelty of such reversals might help to sell records, but the "evil" messages within have no effect.[37] Humans simply don't have a speech perception mechanism operating at an unconscious level that is capable of decoding a reversed signal. On the other hand, subtle acoustic messages such as "I am honest. I won't steal. Stealing is dishonest." are broadcast in more than 1,000 stores in the United States to prevent shoplifting and do appear to have some effect. Unlike subliminal perception, though, these messages are played at a (barely) audible level, using a technique known as threshold messaging.[38] Some evidence indicates, however, that these messages are effective only on individuals who are predisposed to suggestion. For example, someone who might be thinking about taking something on a dare but who feels guilty about it might be deterred, but these soft words will not sway a professional thief.[39]

Does Subliminal Perception Work? Evaluating the Evidence

Some research by clinical psychologists suggests that people can be influenced by subliminal messages under very specific conditions, though it is doubtful that these techniques would be of much use in most marketing contexts. Effective messages must be very specifically tailored to individuals, rather than the mass messages required by advertising.[40] They should also be as close to the liminal threshold as possible. Other discouraging factors include the following issues:

- There are wide individual differences in threshold levels. In order for a message to avoid conscious detection by consumers who have a low threshold, it would have to be so weak that it would not reach those who have a high threshold.
- Advertisers lack control over consumers' distance and position from a screen. In a movie theater, for example, only a small portion of the audience would be in exactly the right seats to be exposed to a subliminal message.
- The viewer must be paying absolute attention to the stimulus. People watching a television program or a movie typically shift their attention periodically and might not even be looking when the stimulus is presented.
- Even if the desired effect is induced, it operates only at a very general level. For example, a message might increase a person's thirst, but not necessarily for a specific drink. Because basic drives are affected, marketers could find that after all the bother and expense of creating a subliminal message, demand for competitors' products increases as well!

Clearly, there are better ways to get our attention—let's see how.

ATTENTION

As you sit in a lecture, you might find your mind wandering (yes, even you!). One minute you are concentrating on the instructor's words, and in the next, you catch yourself daydreaming about the upcoming weekend. Suddenly, you tune back in as you hear your name being spoken. Fortunately, it's a false alarm—the professor has called on another "victim" who has the same first name. But, she's got your attention now. . . .

Attention refers to the extent to which processing activity is devoted to a particular stimulus. As you know from sitting through both interesting and "less interesting" lectures, this allocation can vary depending on both the characteristics of the stimulus (i.e., the lecture itself) and the recipient (i.e., your mental state at the time).

Although we live in an "information society," we can have too much of a good thing. Consumers often are in a state of sensory overload, exposed to far more information than they can or are willing to process. In our society, much of this bombardment comes from commercial sources, and the competition for our attention is increasing steadily. The average adult is exposed to about 3,000 pieces of advertising information every single day.[41] Television networks are jamming a record number of commercials into their shows—an average of 16 minutes and 43 seconds per programming hour.[42] And to make matters worse, this onslaught is growing as we now

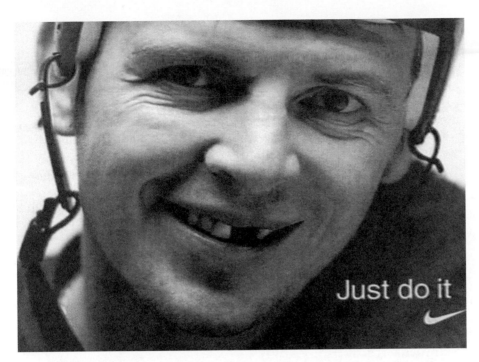

Nike tries to cut through the clutter by spotlighting maimed athletes instead of handsome models.

are bombarded by *banner ads* when we surf the Web as well. These online ads can in fact increase brand awareness after only one exposure, but only if they motivate surfers to click through and see what information is awaiting them.[43]

Because the brain's capacity to process information is limited, consumers are very selective about what they pay attention to. The process of **perceptual selection** means that people attend to only a small portion of the stimuli to which they are exposed. Consumers practice a form of "psychic economy," picking and choosing among stimuli to avoid being overwhelmed. How do they choose? Both personal and stimulus factors help to decide.

Personal Selection Factors

The actions of a Colorado judge illustrate how powerful our own tastes can be in determining what we want to see and hear. He requires young people convicted of violating the city's noise ordinance to listen to music they don't like—including a heavy dose of such "favorites" as Wayne Newton, Dean Martin, and bagpipe recordings.[46] What, no Nine Inch Nails? Experience, which is the result of acquiring and processing stimulation over time, is one factor that determines how much exposure to a particular stimulus a person accepts. Perceptual filters based on our past experiences influence what we decide to process.

Perceptual vigilance is one such factor. Consumers are more likely to be aware of stimuli that relate to their current needs. A consumer who rarely notices car ads will become very much aware of them when she is in the market for a new car. A newspaper ad for a fast-food restaurant that would otherwise go unnoticed becomes significant when one sneaks a glance at the paper in the middle of a five o'clock class.

The flip side of perceptual vigilance is **perceptual defense.** This means that people see what they want to see—and don't see what they don't want to see. If a stimulus is threatening to us in some way, we may not process it—or we distort its meaning so that it's more acceptable. For example, a heavy smoker may

SOME MARKETING ANALYSTS SUGGEST that the Internet has transformed the way business is done—they claim we are now operating in an attention economy. This means that the primary goal is to attract eyeballs, not dollars, to a Web site. The idea is that the amount of information companies can provide to consumers online is infinite—but there's only so much time people can devote to accessing it. So, a goal of interactive media is to buy and sell *attention*, as when a firm is paid to divert the traffic on one Web site to another site.[44] For example, many Web companies including Amazon.com feature affiliate programs that pay people to drive shoppers to merchants via links on their home pages. They get a cut of between 5 and 25 percent of any transaction that results from their lead.[45]

block out images of cancer-scarred lungs because these vivid reminders hit a bit too close to home.

Still another factor is **adaptation,** the degree to which consumers continue to notice a stimulus over time. The process of adaptation occurs when consumers no longer pay attention to a stimulus because it is so familiar. A consumer can become "habituated" and require increasingly stronger "doses" of a stimulus for it to be noticed. A consumer en route to work might read a billboard message when it is first installed, but after a few days, it just becomes part of the passing scenery. Several factors can lead to adaptation:

- *Intensity*: less-intense stimuli (e.g., soft sounds or dim colors) habituate because they have less sensory impact.
- *Duration*: stimuli that require relatively lengthy exposure in order to be processed tend to habituate because they require a long attention span.
- *Discrimination*: simple stimuli tend to habituate because they do not require attention to detail.
- *Exposure*: frequently encountered stimuli tend to habituate as the rate of exposure increases.
- *Relevance*: stimuli that are irrelevant or unimportant will habituate because they fail to attract attention.

Stimulus Selection Factors

In addition to the receiver's mindset, characteristics of the stimulus itself play an important role in determining what gets noticed and what gets ignored. These factors need to be understood by marketers, who can apply them to their messages and packages to boost their chances of cutting through the clutter and commanding attention. This idea even applies to getting animals' attention: A British ad agency did a TV commercial aimed at felines that uses fish and mouse images and sounds to attract catty consumers. In trials, 60 percent of cats showed some form of response to the ad, from twitching their ears to tapping the television screen.[47] That's a better track record than some "people commercials" have shown!

In general, stimuli that differ from others around them are more likely to be noticed (remember Weber's Law). This contrast can be created in several ways:

- *Size*: The size of the stimulus itself in contrast to the competition helps to determine if it will command attention. Readership of a magazine ad increases in proportion to the size of the ad.[48]
- *Color*: As we've seen, color is a powerful way to draw attention to a product or to give it a distinct identity. For example, Black & Decker inaugurated a new line of tools, called Dewalt, targeted to the residential construction industry. The new line was colored yellow instead of black, which made them stand out against other "dull" tools.[50]
- *Position*: Not surprisingly, stimuli that are in places we're more likely to look stand a better chance of being noticed. That's why the competition is so heated among suppliers to have their products displayed in stores at eye level. In magazines, ads that are placed toward the front of the issue, preferably on the right-hand side, also win out in the race for readers' attention. (Hint: The next time you read a magazine, notice which pages you're more likely to spend time looking at.)[51]

A study that tracked consumers' eye movements as they scanned telephone directories also illustrates the importance of a message's position. Consumers scanned listings in alphabetical order, and they noticed 93 percent of quarter-page display ads but only 26 percent of plain

This Australian ad relies upon a stark color contrast to get noticed.

REALITY CHECK *THE SLOGAN FOR THE MOVIE* GODZILLA *was "Size does matter." Should this be the slogan for America as well? Many marketers seem to believe so. The average serving size for a fountain drink has gone from 12 ounces to 20 ounces. An industry consultant explains that the 32-ounce Big Gulp is so popular because "people like something large in their hands. The larger the better." Hardee's Monster Burger, complete with two beef patties and five pieces of bacon, weighs in at 63 grams of fat and more than 900 calories. Clothes have ballooned as well: Kickwear makes women's jeans with 40-inch-diameter legs. The standard for TVs used to be 19 inches; now it's 32 inches. Hulking SUVs have replaced tiny sports cars as the status vehicle of the new millennium. One consumer psychologist theorizes that consuming big things is reassuring: "Large things compensate for our vulnerability," she says. "It gives us insulation, the feeling that we're less likely to die."[49]*

What's up with our fascination with bigness? Is this a uniquely American preference? Do you believe that "bigger is better"? Is this a sound marketing strategy?

 I believe that the importance of size is product-specific. For example, the larger portions of food and drink give consumers the idea of value for money. However, there are products for which their "smallness" is just as important. Men comparing mobile phones are not going to boast about how big theirs is!

Pamela Gillen,
Dublin City University, Ireland

 What exactly are the Americans trying to prove? That their stomachs are in fact bigger than their eyes? I find that eating out in some places in the USA is somewhat an "appetite repressant" namely due to the negative psychological effect that the sight of mountains of food piled sky high can have.

Nicole Schragger,
Edinburgh University, United Kingdom

 It could be said that "bigness" begets "bigness." For example, the increased sizes of cheeseburgers and soft drinks would cause a normal person's size to increase. This would invariably lead to a larger size of clothing as the standard for the average person. It appears to be an endless cycle that has infiltrated every aspect of our lives.

Gregory T. Varveris,
DePaul University

 I think Americans value their possessions and money in a much different way than most other cultures. By this I mean Americans view the items they buy and the money they spend as an extension of themselves. . . . Many Americans are raised with the idea of pursuing their goals by whatever means possible and then enjoying their rewards. As a result, Americans have gained the mindset of "getting more for your money." As a result of this American mindset, many more Americans are overweight and out of shape. . . . We are also becoming a wasteful society producing more than half the world's waste and pollution. These are the negative results of the "bigger is better" attitude and are not likely to go away.

Jennifer Freet,
George Mason University

 I believe this fascination with bigness as a marketing strategy is the way to go for two reasons. First, using such words as "the biggest" or "the best" really does get people's attention. Consumers want to feel as though they are getting more bang for their buck. Second, and most dominating, is the fact that these quotes like "The bigger the better" and "Size does matter" have very strong sexual connotation, which is, as we know a very effective marketing strategy.

Annalise M. Mulholland,
Virginia Polytechnic Institute and State University

 I am not sure that bigness is only noticeable in USA, but compared to Europe, everything there is disproportionate: roads, space, buildings, economy, and number of obese people.

Astrid Spielrein,
ASSAS University Paris II, France

 I believe that bigger is better to a great extent. A lot of this belief has to do with the fact that I grew up in Canada, the second largest land mass where there are very few geographical limitations placed on what one can consume. . . . Additionally, my ethnic heritage is Pakistani and the Pakistanis definitely believe that bigger is better. To them, large houses, cars, and televisions are a sure sign of wealth and prosperity.

Sabrina Aslam,
Simon Fraser University, Canada

 "Size does matter" seems to be America's slogan. When I went to a restaurant in America, I was surprised by the size of a dish. "Am I supposed to eat all this?" was my question. I got used to it, and also gained a lot of weight. Then when I went back to Japan, I could not take the fact that everything was so small. It seemed stingy.

Mai Sasaki,
Keio University, Japan

What's your opinion? Check out the on-line polls at www.prenhall.com/ myphlip. Just follow the little person in the lab coat.

listings. Their eyes were drawn to color ads first, and these were viewed longer than black-and-white ones. In addition, subjects spent 54 percent more time viewing ads for businesses they ended up choosing, which illustrates the influence of attention on subsequent product choice.[52]

- *Novelty*: Stimuli that appear in unexpected ways or places tend to grab our attention. One solution has been to put ads in unconventional places, where there will be less competition for attention. These places include the backs of shopping carts, walls of tunnels, floors of sports stadiums, and yes, even public restrooms.[53] Novelty can also involve crafting brand names that have been associated with some fad or style. For example, the letter z at the end of a brand name is very popular now: We have Beenz online currency, Fritos Racerz, Adaptz.com (a Web site for persons with disabilities), Lugz footwear, Boyz Channel, and Flooz.com. This trend can be traced to the rise of hip hop music: Think of Boyz N the Hood, Heavy D. and the Boyz, Jay-Z, Ghetto Twiinz, Hoodlumz. . . . The letter z now is associated with a hip image or a certain offbeat way of looking at life.[54]

INTERPRETATION

Interpretation refers to the meaning that we assign to sensory stimuli. Just as people differ in terms of the stimuli that they perceive, the eventual assignment of meanings to these stimuli varies as well. Two people can see or hear the same event, but their interpretation of it can be as different as night and day depending on what they had expected the stimulus to be. For example, Vernor's ginger ale did poorly in a taste test against leading ginger ales. When the research team instead introduced it as a new type of soft drink with a tangier taste, it won handily. An executive noted, "People hated it because it didn't meet the preconceived expectations of what a ginger ale should be."[58]

Consumers assign meaning to stimuli based on the **schema,** or set of beliefs, to which the stimulus is assigned. That helps to explain why Gary was so revolted at the thought of warm milk. In a process known as *priming*, certain properties of a stimulus typically will evoke a schema, which leads us to evaluate the stimulus in terms of other stimuli we have encountered that are believed to be similar. Identifying and evoking the correct schema is crucial to many marketing decisions because this determines what criteria will be used to evaluate the product, package, or message. Extra Strength Maalox Whip Antacid flopped even though a spray can is a pretty effective way to deliver the product. But to consumers aerosol whips mean desert toppings, not medication.[59]

Stimulus Organization

One factor that determines how a stimulus will be interpreted is its assumed relationship with other events, sensations, or images. When RJR Nabisco introduced a version of Teddy Grahams (a children's product) for adults, restrained packaging colors were used to reinforce the idea that the new product was for grown-ups. But, sales were disappointing. The box was changed to a bright yellow to convey the idea that this was a fun snack, and buyers' more positive association between a bright primary color and taste led adults to start buying the cookies.[61]

Our brains tend to relate incoming sensations to others already in memory based on some fundamental organizational principles. These principles are based

MARKETING PITFALLS

FAMILIAR PACKAGES AND PRODUCT designs get our attention, but this strategy can backfire when imitators illegally exploit the recognition value of well-known brands. A store named Replicas in Kansas City openly sold fake goods until recently. Brand counterfeiting isn't always that blatant, but the International Anti-Counterfeiting Coalition, an industry group established to combat piracy, estimates that trademark counterfeiting cost U.S. industries $200 billion in lost sales in 1999 alone.[55] A senior FBI official has called brand piracy "the crime of the twenty-first century."[56] Consider that in one year Chinese compact-disk factories produced 3 million legitimate disks and 70 million pirated ones, says the Recording Industry Association of America. An attorney for Microsoft says, "We refer to some countries in Asia as one-disk markets. More than 99 percent of the software is illegitimate copies."[57]

Advertisers know that consumers often will relate an ad to a preexisting schema in order to make sense of it. This Singaporean ad for Toyota evokes a car schema even though the materials used in the picture are chairs and couches one might find inside a house.[60]

on Gestalt psychology, a school of thought that maintains that people derive meaning from the totality of a set of stimuli, rather than from any individual stimulus. The German word **Gestalt** roughly means whole, pattern, or configuration, and this perspective is best summarized by the saying "the whole is greater than the sum of its parts." A piecemeal perspective that analyzes each component of the stimulus separately will be unable to capture the total effect. The Gestalt perspective provides several principles relating to the way stimuli are organized.

The **closure principle** states that people tend to perceive an incomplete picture as complete. That is, we tend to fill in the blanks based on our prior experience. This principle explains why most of us have no trouble reading a neon sign even if several of its letters are burned out. The principle of closure is also at

This Swedish ad relies upon gestalt perceptual principles to insure that the perceiver organizes a lot of separate images into a familiar image.

This Land Rover ad illustrates use of the principle of closure, in which people participate in the ad by mentally filling in the gaps in the sentence.

work when we hear only part of a jingle or theme. Utilization of the principle of closure in marketing strategies encourages audience participation, which increases the chance that people will attend to the message.

The **principle of similarity** tells us that consumers tend to group together objects that share similar physical characteristics. Green Giant relied on this principle when the company redesigned the packaging for its line of frozen vegetables. It created a "sea of green" look to unify all of its different offerings.

The **figure-ground principle** states that one part of a stimulus will dominate (the figure), and other parts recede into the background (the ground). This concept is easy to understand if one thinks literally of a photograph with a clear and sharply focused object (the figure) in the center. The figure is dominant, and the eye goes straight to it. The parts of the configuration that will be perceived as figure or ground can vary depending on the individual consumer as well as other factors. Similarly, in marketing messages that use the figure-ground principle, a stimulus can be made the focal point of the message or merely the context that surrounds the focus.

The Eye of the Beholder: Interpretational Biases

The stimuli we perceive are often ambiguous. It's up to us to determine the meaning based on our past experiences, expectations, and needs. The process of "seeing what you want to see" was demonstrated in a classic experiment in which students at Princeton and Dartmouth viewed a movie of a particularly rough football game between the two schools. Although everyone was exposed to the same stimulus, the degree to which students saw infractions and the blame they assigned for those they did see was quite different depending on which college they attended.[62]

As this experiment demonstrates, consumers tend to project their own desires or assumptions onto products and advertisements. This interpretation process can backfire for marketers, as occurred in these cases:

This billboard for Wrangler jeans makes creative use of the figure-ground principle.

- A Detroit woman mistakenly packed a can of Anheuser-Busch's Bud Ice beer in her grandson's lunch, confusing it with a package of Hawaiian Punch. A Seattle mother thought the brew was a holiday-style can of Pepsi. Her daughter was on the losing end; she got hit with a five-day suspension for bringing beer to school.[63]
- A company called Back to Basics sells a Microbrew line of hair-care products laced with barley, yeast, and hops. They come in names like Honey Wheat Pilsner and Black Cherry Stout, packaged in brown bottles with twist-off caps. Cause for confusion? A company spokesman claims, "People should know enough to put them in the shower, not the fridge."[64]

People often use characteristics of a package to infer its contents. This ad for a fertilizer product reminds us, ". . . they go in your garden, not in your mouth."

Whatever you do, don't get them mixed up.

The bunny on the right is one of 12 Dung Buddies – lovable miniatures made with Zoo Doo fertilizer that dissolves in soil over time. But remember, they go in your garden, not your mouth. **DUNG BUDDY**

The subjective nature of perception is demonstrated by a controversial advertisement developed for Benetton by a French agency. Because a black man and a white man were hand-cuffed together, the ad was the target of many complaints about racism after it appeared in magazines and on billboards around the United States, even though the company has a reputation for promoting racial tolerance. People interpreted it to depict a black man who had been arrested by a white man; their prior assumptions distorted the ad's meaning.[66]

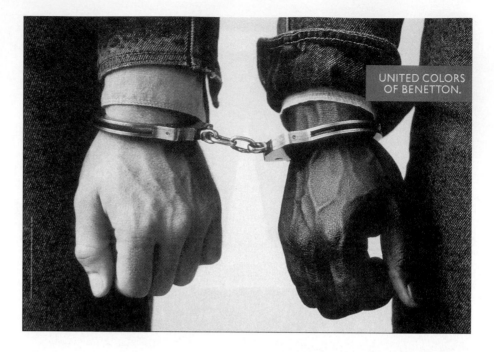

UNITED COLORS OF BENETTON.

- Planters Lifesavers Company introduced a vacuum-packed peanuts package called Planters Fresh Roast. The idea was to capitalize on consumers' growing love affair with fresh roast coffee by emphasizing the freshness of the nuts in the same way. A great idea—until irate supermarket managers began calling to ask who was going to pay to clean the peanut gook out of their stores' coffee-grinding machines.[65]

Semiotics: The Symbols Around Us

When we try to "make sense" of a marketing stimulus, whether a distinctive package, an elaborately staged television commercial, or perhaps a model on the cover of a magazine, we do so by interpreting its meaning in light of associations we have with these images. For this reason, much of the meaning we take away is influenced by what we make of the symbolism we perceive. After all, on the surface many marketing images have virtually no literal connection to actual products. What does a cowboy have to do with a bit of tobacco rolled into a paper tube? How can a celebrity such as ex-basketball star Michael Jordan enhance the image of a soft drink or a fast food restaurant?

For assistance in understanding how consumers interpret the meanings of symbols, some marketers are turning to a field of study known as **semiotics**, which examines the correspondence between signs and symbols and their role in the assignment of meaning.[67] Semiotics is important to the understanding of consumer behavior because consumers use products to express their social identities. Products have learned meanings, and we rely on marketers to help us figure out what those meanings are. As one set of researchers put it, "Advertising serves as a kind of culture/consumption dictionary; its entries are products, and their definitions are cultural meanings."[68]

From a semiotic perspective, every marketing message has three basic components: an object, a sign or symbol, and an interpretant. The **object** is the product that is the focus of the message (e.g., Marlboro cigarettes). The **sign** is the sensory imagery that represents the intended meanings of the object (e.g., the

Figure 2.2
Semiotics

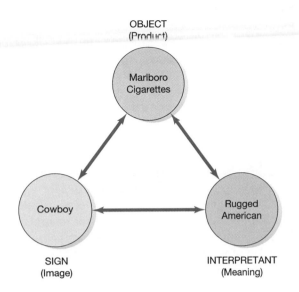

OBJECT
(Product)

Marlboro
Cigarettes

Cowboy

Rugged
American

SIGN
(Image)

INTERPRETANT
(Meaning)

Marlboro cowboy). The **interpretant** is the meaning derived (e.g., rugged, individu-alistic, American). This relationship is diagrammed in Figure 2.2.

According to semiotician Charles Sanders Peirce, signs are related to objects in one of three ways: They can resemble objects, be connected to them, or be conventionally tied to them.[69] An icon is a sign that resembles the product in some way (e.g., Bell Telephone uses an image of a bell to represent itself). An index is a sign that is connected to a product because they share some property (e.g., the pine tree on some of Procter & Gamble's Spic and Span cleanser prod-ucts conveys the shared property of fresh scent). A symbol is a sign that is related to a product through either conventional or agreed-upon associations (e.g., the lion in Dreyfus Fund ads provides the conventional association with fearlessness and strength that is carried over to the company's approach to investments). As we shall see in later chapters, these relationships are often culturally bound; that is, they only make sense to a person who is a member of a particular culture. Marketers who forget that meanings do not automatically transfer from one cul-tural context to another do so at their peril.

One of the hallmarks of modern advertising is that it creates a condition that has been termed **hyperreality.** Hyperreality refers to the becoming real of what is initially simulation of "hype." Advertisers create new relationships between objects and interpretants by inventing new connections between products and benefits, such as equating Marlboro cigarettes with the American frontier spirit.[70]

In a hyperreal environment, over time the true relationship between the sym-bol and reality is no longer possible to discern. The "artificial" associations between product symbols and the real world may take on lives of their own. Consider for example the region of Switzerland that has been renamed "Heidiland" by tourism marketers in honor of the supposed "birthplace" of the imaginary Swiss girl. In the town of Maienfeld, new Heidi attractions are flourish-ing. A Heidi trail leads to a Heidi refreshment stand and then to a man there who poses full time as Heidi's grandfather. Initially officials refused to permit "Welcome to Heidiland" highway signs because Swiss law allows only real place names. The volume of tourists making a pilgrimage to the "home" of this mythi-cal character apparently changed their minds.[71] In our hyperreal world, Heidi lives!

Perceptual Positioning

As we've seen, a product stimulus often is interpreted in light of what we already know about a product category and the characteristics of existing brands. Perceptions of a brand comprise both its functional attributes (e.g., its features, its price, and so on) and its symbolic attributes (its image, and what we think it says about us when we use it). We'll look more closely at issues such as brand image in later chapters, but for now it's important to keep in mind that our evaluation of a product typically is the result of what it means rather than what it does. This meaning—as perceived by consumers—constitutes the product's market position, and it may have more to do with our expectations of product performance as communicated by its color, packaging, or styling than with the product itself.

How does a marketer determine where a product actually stands in the minds of consumers? One technique is to ask them what attributes are important to them, and how they feel competitors rate on these attributes. This information can be used to construct a perceptual map, which is a vivid way to paint a picture of where products or brands are "located" in consumers' minds. GRW Advertising created the perceptual map shown in Figure 2.3 for HMV music stores, a British company. The agency wanted to know more about how its target market, frequent buyers of CDs, perceived the different stores they might patronize. GRW plotted perceptions of such attributes of competitors as selection, price, service, and hipness on an imaginary street map. Based on this research, the firm determined that HMV's strengths were service, selection, and the stores' abilities to cater to local tastes because store managers can order their own stock.

Figure 2.3
HMV Perceptual Map

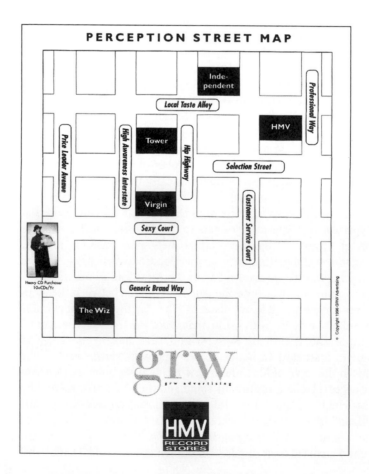

This map was used in the strategic decision to specialize in music products as opposed to competing by offering other items sold by the competition, such as video games, fragrances, and computer CD-ROMs.[72]

A **positioning strategy** is a fundamental part of a company's marketing efforts as it uses elements of the marketing mix (i.e., product design, price, distribution, and marketing communications) to influence the consumer's interpretation of its meaning. For example, although consumers' preferences for the taste of one product over another are important, this functional attribute is only one component of product evaluation. Coca-Cola found this out the hard way when it committed its famous New Coke marketing blunder in the 1980s. New Coke was preferred to Pepsi in blind taste tests (in which the products were not identified) by an average of 55 percent to 45 percent in 17 markets, yet New Coke ran into problems when it replaced the older version. Consumers' impassioned protests and letter-writing campaigns eventually forced the company to bring back "Classic Coke." People do not buy a cola for taste alone; they are buying intangibles such as brand image as well.[73] Coca-Cola's unique position as part of an American, fun-loving lifestyle is based on years of marketing efforts that involve a lot more than taste alone. In 2000 Pepsi revived its Pepsi Challenge; the original promotion was widely believed to have been a driving force behind Coke's disastrous introduction of its sweeter New Coke.[74]

Positioning Dimensions

There are many dimensions that can be used to establish a brand's position in the marketplace. These include:[75]

- *Lifestyle*: Grey Poupon mustard is a "higher class" condiment.
- *Price leadership*: L'Oréal's Noisôme brand face cream is sold in upscale beauty shops, whereas its Plenitude brand is available for one-sixth the

Lexus conveys the sensation of speed in a novel way to position its vehicles.

The new, more powerful GS 430.
A little faster off the line.*

lexus.com

THE PASSIONATE PURSUIT OF PERFECTION. *LEXUS*

price in discount stores—even though both are based on the same chemical formula.[76]

- *Attributes*: Bounty paper towels are "the quicker picker upper."
- *Product class*: The Mazda Miata is a sporty convertible.
- *Competitors*: Northwestern Insurance is "the quiet company."
- *Occasions*: Wrigley's gum is an alternative at times when smoking is not permitted.
- *Users*: Levi's Dockers are targeted primarily to men in their twenties to forties.
- *Quality*: At Ford, "Quality is job 1."

CHAPTER SUMMARY

- Perception is the process by which physical sensations such as sights, sounds, and smells are selected, organized, and interpreted. The eventual interpretation of a stimulus allows it to be assigned meaning. A perceptual map is a widely used marketing tool that evaluates the relative standing of competing brands along relevant dimensions.
- Marketing stimuli have important sensory qualities. We rely on colors, odors, sounds, tastes, and even the "feel" of products when forming evaluations of them.
- Not all sensations successfully make their way through the perceptual process. Many stimuli compete for our attention, and the majority are not noticed or accurately comprehended.
- People have different thresholds of perception. A stimulus must be presented at a certain level of intensity before it can be detected by sensory receptors. In addition, a consumer's ability to detect whether two stimuli are different (the differential threshold) is an important issue in many marketing contexts, such as changing a package design, altering the size of a product, or reducing its price.
- A lot of controversy has been sparked by so-called subliminal persuasion and related techniques, by which people are exposed to visual and aural messages below the threshold. Although evidence that subliminal persuasion is effective is virtually nonexistent, many consumers continue to believe that advertisers use this technique.
- Some of the factors that determine which stimuli (above the threshold level) do get perceived are the amount of exposure to the stimulus, how much attention it generates, and how it is interpreted. In an increasingly crowded stimulus environment, advertising clutter occurs when too many marketing-related messages compete for attention.
- A stimulus that is attended to is not perceived in isolation. It is classified and organized according to principles of perceptual organization. These principles are guided by a gestalt, or overall pattern. Specific grouping principles include closure, similarity, and figure-ground relationships.
- The final step in the process of perception is interpretation. Symbols help us make sense of the world by providing us with an interpretation of a stimulus that is often shared by others. The degree to which the symbolism is consistent with our previous experience affects the meaning we assign to related objects.
- Marketers try to communicate with consumers by creating relationships between their products or services and desired attributes. A semiotic analysis involves the correspondence between stimuli and the meaning of signs. The intended meaning may be literal (e.g., an icon such as a street sign with a

picture of children playing). The meaning may be indexical; it relies on shared characteristics (e.g., the red in a stop sign means danger). Finally, meaning can be conveyed by a symbol, in which an image is given meaning by convention or by agreement of members of a society (e.g., stop signs are octagonal, whereas yield signs are triangular). Marketer-created associations often take on a life of their own as hype is assumed to be real; this condition is known as hyperreality.

KEY TERMS

absolute threshold, p. 50
adaptation, p. 56
attention, p. 54
closure principle, p. 59
differential threshold, p. 51
exposure, p. 50
figure-ground principle, p. 60
gestalt, p. 59
hedonic consumption, p. 43

hyperreality, p. 63
interpretant, p. 63
interpretation, p. 58
j.n.d., p. 51
object, p. 62
perception, p. 42
perceptual defense, p. 55
perceptual selection, p. 55
perceptual vigilance, p. 55

positioning strategy, p. 65
principle of similarity, p. 60
psychophysics, p. 50
schema, p. 58
semiotics, p. 62
sensation, p. 42
sign, p. 62
subliminal perception, p. 51
Weber's Law, p. 51

CONSUMER BEHAVIOR CHALLENGE

1. Many studies have shown that our sensory detection abilities decline as we grow older. Discuss the implications of the absolute threshold for marketers attempting to appeal to the elderly.
2. Interview three to five male and three to five female friends about their perceptions of both men's and women's fragrances. Construct a perceptual map for each set of products. Based on your map of perfumes, do you see any areas that are not adequately served by current offerings? What (if any) gender differences did you obtain regarding both the relevant dimensions used by raters and the placement of specific brands along these dimensions?
3. Assuming that some forms of subliminal persuasion may have the desired effect of influencing consumers, do you think the use of these techniques is ethical? Explain your answer.
4. Assume that you are a consultant for a marketer who wants to design a package for a new premium chocolate bar targeted to an affluent market. What recommendations would you provide in terms of such package elements as color, symbolism, and graphic design? Give the reasons for your suggestions.
5. Do you believe that marketers have the right to use any or all public spaces to deliver product messages? Where would you draw the line in terms of places and products that should be restricted?
6. Using magazines archived in the library, track the packaging of a specific brand over time. Find an example of gradual changes in package design that may have been below the j.n.d.
7. Visit a set of Web sites for one type of product (e.g., personal computers, perfumes, laundry detergents, or athletic shoes) and analyze the colors and other design principles employed. Which sites "work" and which don't? Why?
8. Look through a current magazine and select one ad that captures your attention over the others. Give the reasons.

9. Find ads that utilize the techniques of contrast and novelty. Give your opinion of the effectiveness of each ad and whether the technique is likely to be appropriate for the consumers targeted by the ad.

NOTES

1. Cathy Sivak, "Purposeful Parmalat: Part 1 of 2," *Dairy Field*, 182, no. 9 (September 1999): 1; "North Brunswick, NJ—Based food company signs deal with online grocer," *Home News Tribune* (East Brunswick, NJ) (March 21, 2000).

2. Rick Vecchio, "'Reality TV' Peru Style: Trashy Shows Entertain, Distract During Election Year," *Opelika-Auburn News* (March 15, 2000): 15A.

3. Elizabeth C. Hirschman and Morris B. Holbrook, "Hedonic Consumption: Emerging Concepts, Methods, and Propositions," *Journal of Marketing* 46 (Summer 1982): 92–101.

4. Glenn Collins, "Owens-Corning's Blurred Identity" *New York Times* (August 19, 1994): D4.

5. Amitava Chattopadhyay, Gerald J. Gorn, and Peter R. Darke, "Roses are Red and Violets Are Blue—Everywhere? Cultural Universals and Differences in Color Preference Among Consumers and Marketing Managers," (unpublished manuscript, University of British Columbia, Fall 1999); Joseph Bellizzi and Robert E. Hite, "Environmental Color, Consumer Feelings, and Purchase Likelihood," *Psychology & Marketing* 9 (1992): 347–63; Ayn E. Crowley, "The Two-Dimensional Impact of Color on Shopping," *Marketing Letters*, 1993, Marketing Letters, 4 (January), 59–69; Gerald J. Gorn, Amitava Chattopadhyay, and Tracey Yi, "Effects of Color as an Executional Cue in an Ad: It's in the Shade," (unpublished manuscript, University of British Columbia, 1994).

6. Quoted in Adam Bryant, "Plastic Surgery at AmEx," *Newsweek* (October 4, 1999): 55.

7. Mark G. Frank and Thomas Gilovich, "The Dark Side of Self- and Social Perception: Black Uniforms and Aggression in Professional Sports," *Journal of Personality and Social Psychology* 54, no. 4 (1988): 74–85.

8. Mike Golding and Julie White, *Pantone Color Resource Kit* (New York: Hayden Publishing, 1997); Caroline Lego, *Effective Web Site Design: A Marketing Strategy for Small Liberal Arts Colleges*, Coe College, unpublished honors thesis (1998); T. Long, "Human Factors Principles for the Design of Computer Colour Graphics Display," *British Telecom Technology Journal 2*, no. 3 (1994): 5–14; Morton Walker, *The Power of Color* (Garden City, NY: Avery Publishing Group, 1991).

9. Khanh T. L. Tran, "Plan to Roll Out Colored Tires Brings Politicians' Ire in California," *The Wall Street Journal Interactive Edition* (July 30, 1999).

10. Timothy Aeppel, "Michelin to Let Tire Buyers Order Customized Colors," *The Wall Street Journal Interactive Edition* (May 16, 2000).

11. Barbara Carlton, "Pink, Yellow or Green Just Won't Cut It; American Parents Choose Navy Strollers," *The Wall Street Journal Interactive Edition* (March 25, 1998).

12. Paulette Thomas, "Cosmetics Makers Offer World's Women an All-American Look with Local Twists," *The Wall Street Journal* (May 8, 1995): B1.

13. Dianne Solis, "Cost No Object for Mexico's Makeup Junkies," *The Wall Street Journal* (June 7, 1994): B1.

14. "Ny emballage og nyt navn fordoblede salget," *Markedsforing 12* (1992): 24. Adapted from Michael R. Solomon, Gary Bamossy, and Soren Askegaard, *Consumer Behavior: A European Perspective* (London: Prentice Hall International, 1998).

15. Meg Rosen and Frank Alpert, "Protecting Your Business Image: The Supreme Court Rules on Trade Dress," *Journal of Consumer Marketing* 11, no. 1 (1994): 50–55.

16. Deborah J. Mitchell, Barbara E. Kahn, and Susan C. Knasko, "There's Something in the Air: Effects of Congruent or Incongruent Ambient Odor on Consumer Decision Making," *Journal of Consumer Research* 22 (September 1995): 229–38; for a review of olfactory cues in store environments, see also Eric R. Spangenberg, Ayn E. Crowley, and Pamela W. Henderson, "Improving the Store Environment: Do Olfactory Cues Affect Evaluations and Behaviors?" *Journal of Marketing* 60 (April 1996): 67–80.

17. Pam Scholder Ellen and Paula Fitzgerald Bone, "Does It Matter if It Smells? Olfactory Stimuli as Advertising Executional Cues," *Journal of Advertising* 27, 4 (Winter 1998): 29–40.

18. Jack Hitt, "Does the Smell of Coffee Brewing Remind You of Your Mother?" *New York Times Magazine* (May 7, 2000).

19. Maxine Wilkie, "Scent of a Market," *American Demographics* (August 1995): 40–49.

20. Jack Neff, "Product Scents Hide Absence of True Innovation," *Advertising Age* (February 21, 2000): 22.

21. "That Smells Delightful! Could It Be Creme Brulee Cologne?" *The Wall Street Journal Interactive Edition* (April 8, 1998).

22. Hae Won Choi, "Korean Men Seek Fashion Scents and Lavender Suits Them Just Fine," *The Wall Street Journal Interactive Edition* (February 15, 1999).

23. Gail Tom, "Marketing with Music," *Journal of Consumer Marketing* 7 (Spring 1990): 49–53; J. Vail, "Music as a Marketing Tool," *Advertising Age* (November 4, 1985): 24.

24. Otto Friedrich, "Trapped in a Musical Elevator," *Time* (December 10, 1984): 3.

25. Jacob Hornik, "Tactile Stimulation and Consumer Response," *Journal of Consumer Research* 19 (December 1992): 449–58.

26. "Touch Looms Large as a Sense That Drives Sales," *BrandPackaging* (May/June 1999): 39–40.

27. Paulo Prada, No Headline, *The Wall Street Journal Interactive Edition* (March 15, 1999).

28. Becky Gaylord, "Bland Food Isn't So Bad— It Hurts Just to Think About This Stuff," *The Wall Street Journal* (April 21, 1995): B1.

29. Dan Morse, "From Tabasco to Insane: When You're Hot, It May Not Be Enough," *The Wall Street Journal Interactive Edition* (May 15, 2000).

30. Yumiko Ono, "Flat, Watery Drinks Are All the Rage as Japan Embraces New Taste Sensation," *The Wall Street Journal Interactive Edition* (August 13, 1999).

31. "$10 Sure Thing," *Time* (August 4, 1980): 51.

32. Dana Canedy, "After 102 Years, Campbell Alters Soup Labels," *New York Times on the Web* (August 26, 1999).

33. For a recent study that did find some evidence that unconscious processing of subliminal embeds affected both upbeat and negative feelings in response to ads, see Andrew B. Aylesworth, Ronald C. Goodstein, and Ajay Kalra, "Effect of Archetypal Embeds on Feelings: An Indirect Route to Affecting Attitudes?" *Journal of Advertising* 28, 3 (Fall 1999): 73–81.

34. Michael Lev, "No Hidden Meaning Here: Survey Sees Subliminal Ads," *New York Times* (May 3, 1991): D7.

35. Bruce Orwall, "Disney Recalls 'The Rescuers' Video Containing Images of

Topless Woman," *The Wall Street Journal Interactive Edition* (January 11, 1999).

36. Philip M. Merikle, "Subliminal Auditory Messages: An Evaluation," *Psychology & Marketing* 5, no. 4 (1988): 355–72.

37. Timothy E. Moore, "The Case Against Subliminal Manipulation," *Psychology & Marketing* 5 (Winter 1988): 297–316.

38. Sid C. Dudley, "Subliminal Advertising: What Is the Controversy About?" *Akron Business and Economic Review* 18 (Summer 1987): 6–18; "Subliminal Messages: Subtle Crime Stoppers," *Chain Store Age Executive* 2 (July 1987): 85; "Mind Benders," *Money* (September 1978): 24.

39. Timothy E. Moore, "The Case Against Subliminal Manipulation," *Psychology & Marketing* 5 (Winter 1988): 297–316.

40. Joel Saegert, "Why Marketing Should Quit Giving Subliminal Advertising the Benefit of the Doubt," *Psychology & Marketing* 4 (Summer 1987): 107–20. See also Dennis L. Rosen and Surendra N. Singh, "An Investigation of Subliminal Embed Effect on Multiple Measures of Advertising Effectiveness," *Psychology & Marketing* 9 (March/April 1992): 157–73; for a more recent review see Kathryn T. Theus, "Subliminal Advertising and the Psychology of Processing Unconscious Stimuli: A Review of Research," *Psychology & Marketing* (May/June 1994): 271–90.

41. James B. Twitchell, *Adcult USA: The Triumph of Advertising in American Culture* (New York: Columbia University Press, 1996).

42. Joe Flint, "TV Networks Are 'Cluttering' Shows with a Record Number of Commercials," *The Wall Street Journal Interactive Edition* (March 2, 2000).

43. Gene Koprowsky, "Eyeball to Eyeball," *Critical Mass* (Fall 1999): 32.

44. John Browning and Spencer Reiss, "Encyclopedia of the New Economy, Part I," *Wired* (March 1998), 105.

45. "Raking It In on the Web," *Trend Letter* (March 2, 2000): 6.

46. "Court Orders Bagpipes for Noise Violations," *Montgomery Advertiser* (March 6, 1999): 1A.

47. Lucy Howard, "Trying to Fool a Feline," *Newsweek* (February 8, 1999): 8.

48. Roger Barton, *Advertising Media* (New York: McGraw-Hill, 1964).

49. Quoted in *Atlanta Journal-Constitution*, accessed via SS Newslink May 2, 1998.

50. Suzanne Oliver, "New Personality," *Forbes* (August 15, 1994): 114.

51. Adam Finn, "Print Ad Recognition Readership Scores: An Information Processing Perspective," *Journal of Marketing Research* 25 (May 1988): 168–77.

52. Gerald L. Lohse, "Consumer Eye Movement Patterns on Yellow Pages Advertising," *Journal of Advertising* 26, 1 (Spring 1997): 61–73.

53. Michael R. Solomon and Basil G. Englis (Fall 1994), "Reality Engineering: Blurring the Boundaries Between Marketing and Popular Culture," *Journal of Current Issues and Research in Advertising*, 16, no. 2 (Fall): 1–18; "Toilet Ads," *Marketing* (December 5, 1996): 11; "Rare Media Well Done," *Marketing* (January 16, 1997): 31.

54. Stuart Elliott, "The Popularity of the Letter 'Z'," *New York Times on the Web* (October 26, 1999).

55. Richard Espinoza, "The Battle Against Counterfeit Trademark," *Kansas City Star* (December 24, 1998) (Simon & Schuster College Newslink, January 6, 1999).

56. Quoted in David Stipp, "Farewell, My Logo," *Fortune* (May 27, 1996): 128–40.

57. Quoted in Stipp, "Farewell, My Logo," p. 135.

58. Quoted in Tim Davis, "Taste Tests: Are the Blind Leading the Blind?" *Beverage World*, no.3 (April 1987): 44.

59. Robert M. McMath, "Image Counts," *American Demographics* (May 1998): 64.

60. Michael A. Keating, "A Crowning And Mysterious Achievement," *American Demographics* (March 1995): 13.

61. Anthony Ramirez, "Lessons in the Cracker Market: Nabisco Saved New Graham Snack," *New York Times* (July 5, 1990): D1.

62. Albert H. Hastorf and Hadley Cantril, "They Saw a Game: A Case Study," *Journal of Abnormal and Social Psychology* 49 (1954): 129–34; see also Roberto Friedmann and Mary R. Zimmer, "The Role of Psychological Meaning in Advertising," *Journal of Advertising* 17, no. 1 (1988): 31–40.

63. Gannett News Service, "Grandmother Packs Lunch with 'Punch'," *Montgomery Advertiser* (March 28, 1996): 2A.

64. Quoted in "Brew Ha Ha," *Newsweek* (May 25, 1998): 8.

65. Robert M. McMath, "Chock Full of (Pea)nuts," *American Demographics* (April 1997): 60.

66. Kim Foltz, "Campaign on Harmony Backfires for Benetton," *New York Times* (November 20, 1989): D8.

67. See David Mick, "Consumer Research and Semiotics: Exploring the Morphology of Signs, Symbols, and Significance," *Journal of Consumer Research* 13 (September 1986): 196–213.

68. Teresa J. Domzal and Jerome B. Kernan, "Reading Advertising: The What and How of Product Meaning," *Journal of Consumer Marketing* 9 (Summer 1992): 48–64.

69. Arthur Asa Berger, *Signs in Contemporary Culture: An Introduction to Semiotics* (New York: Longman, 1984); David Mick, "Consumer Research and Semiotics: Exploring the Morphology of Signs, Symbols, and Significance," *Journal of Consumer Research* 13 (September 1986): 196–213; Charles Sanders Peirce, in Charles Hartshorne, Paul Weiss, and Arthur W. Burks, eds., *Collected Papers* (Cambridge, MA: Harvard University Press, 1931–58).

70. Jean Baudrillard, *Simulations* (New York: Semiotext(e), 1983); A. Fuat Firat and Alladi Venkatesh, "The Making of Postmodern Consumption," in Russell Belk and Nikhilesh Dholakia, eds., *Consumption and Marketing: Macro Dimensions* (Boston: PWS-Kent, 1993); A. Fuat Firat, "The Consumer in Postmodernity," in Rebecca H. Holman and Michael R. Solomon, eds., *Advances in Consumer Research* 18 (Provo, UT: Association for Consumer Research, 1991): 70–76.

71. Ernest Beck, "A Minefield in Maienfeld: 'Heidiland' Is Taking Over," *The Wall Street Journal Interactive Edition* (October 2, 1997).

72. Stuart Elliott, "Advertising: A Music Retailer Whistles A New Marketing Tune to Get Heard Above the Cacophony of Competitors," *New York Times* (July 2, 1996): D7; Personal communication, GRW Advertising April 1997).

73. See Tim Davis, "Taste Tests: Are the Blind Leading the Blind?" *Beverage World* 3 (April 1987): 43–44.

74. Betsy McKay, "Pepsi to Revive a Cola-War Barb: The Decades-Old Blind Taste Test," *The Wall Street Journal Interactive Edition* (March 21, 2000).

75. Adapted from Michael R. Solomon and Elnora W. Stuart, *Marketing: Real People, Real Choices*, 2nd ed. (Upper Saddle River, NJ: Prentice Hall, 2000).

76. William Echikson, "Aiming at High and Low Markets," *Fortune* (March 22, 1993): 89.

Ah, Sunday morning! The sun is shining, the birds are singing and Joe is feeling groovy! He puts on his vintage Levi's 501 jeans (circa 1968) and his Woodstock T-shirt (the "real" Woodstock, not that fake abomination they put on back in the 1990s, thank you) and saunters down to the kitchen. Joe smiles in anticipation of his morning plans. First, he's

going to treat himself to a precious bowl of Quisp. Rare boxes of the cereal that was first created in 1965 sell for $10 at his grocery store in Buffalo, but after discovering that he can buy it online at netgrocer.com for $2.99 he's a happy camper. What a beautiful day to "commune" with Quisp, the propeller-headed alien character he's loved over the years. Then, perhaps a little online browsing at hippy.com, where he can check out some famous hippy quotes, visit the hippy chat room, and locate the next festival in the area on the site's Hip Planet Event

Guide. Joe's got a "tune in, turn on, and drop out" vacation in mind as he eagerly awaits the opening of the first HempWorld Resort in Hawaii, where according to the Web site (HempWorldResorts.com/pstindex.html) guests can "sleep, bathe, and clothe in hemp. Have a hemp oil massage, then a hemp dish with hemp beer or hemp wine and hemp ice-cream or hemp cheesecake for dessert." Joe throws a Jefferson Airplane record on the turntable (ah, the sublime joys of vinyl), sits back on his Barcalounger, and lets the memories rush in.

3

LEARNING AND MEMORY

THE LEARNING PROCESS

It's the twenty first century, but Joe's never really left the 1960s. Of course, now he's got the money to surround himself with stuff from that era. He'd better—his vintage Levi's jeans collection alone is worth many thousands of dollars. In fact, the underground market for pre-1970s Levi's 501 and 201 jeans is so strong that Levi Strauss & Co. is manufacturing its own official "vintage line" of denim wear replicas and selling them in selected boutiques for $225.[1]

Joe's a stickler for authenticity, and he is even willing to pay a premium for everyday items like cereal. Again, he's not alone. Until recently Quaker's quirky Quisp corn cereal (say that ten times fast) was on its last legs and sold only 92,000 boxes a year, but everything changed when the manufacturer created a link between Quisp's Web site at Quisp.com and netgrocer.com. Almost overnight, the brand became the number one seller on the site, even beating out favorites such as Cheerios and Frosted Flakes. The Quaker brand manager who saved the cereal explained, "It's the cereal I ate when I was a kid and people around here want to keep it going."[2] Quisp memorabilia has joined the other vintage products that are hot at auction sites where Quisp decoder rings can go for more than $600. The craze for vintage American products is even stronger in Japan, where "previously worn" pairs of Adidas, Nike, and Converse sneakers sell for as much as $1,000.[3]

Many marketers realize that long-standing, learned connections between products and memories are a potent way to build and keep brand loyalty. Some companies are bringing their old trademark characters out of retirement, including the Campbell Soup Kids, the Pillsbury Doughboy, Betty Crocker, and Planters' Mr. Peanut.[4] Several familiar faces returned in major advertising campaigns recently, including the Jolly Green Giant (born in 1925), Charlie the Tuna (who first appeared in 1961), and even Charmin's Mr. Whipple, who was brought out of retirement in 1999.[5] In this chapter, we'll explore how learned associations among feelings, events, and products—and the memories they evoke—are an important aspect of consumer behavior.

Learning is a relatively permanent change in behavior caused by experience. The learner need not have the experience directly; we can also learn by observing events that affect others.[6] We learn even when we are not trying: Consumers recognize many brand names and can hum many product jingles, for example, even for products they themselves do not use. This casual, unintentional acquisition of knowledge is known as *incidental learning*.

Learning is an ongoing process. Our knowledge about the world is being revised constantly as we are exposed to new stimuli and receive ongoing feedback that allows us to modify our behavior when we find ourselves in similar situations at a later time. The concept of learning covers a lot of ground, ranging from a consumer's simple association between a stimulus such as a product logo (e.g., Coca-Cola) and a response (e.g., "refreshing soft drink") to a complex series of cognitive activities (e.g., writing an essay on learning for a consumer behavior exam). Psychologists who study learning have advanced several theories to explain the learning process. These theories range from those focusing on simple stimulus-response connections (behavioral theories) to perspectives that regard consumers as complex problem solvers who learn abstract rules and concepts by observing others (cognitive theories). Understanding these theories is important to marketers as well, because basic learning principles are at the heart of many consumer purchase decisions.

BEHAVIORAL LEARNING THEORIES

Behavioral learning theories assume that learning takes place as the result of responses to external events. Psychologists who subscribe to this viewpoint do not focus on internal thought processes. Instead, they approach the mind as a "black box" and emphasize the observable aspects of behavior, as depicted in Figure 3.1. The observable aspects consist of things that go into the box (the stimuli, or events perceived from the outside world) and things that come out of the box (the responses, or reactions to these stimuli).

This view is represented by two major approaches to learning: classical conditioning and instrumental conditioning. According to this perspective, people's experiences are shaped by the feedback they receive as they go through life. Similarly, consumers respond to brand names, scents, jingles, and other marketing stimuli based on the learned connections they have formed over time. People

Figure 3.1
The Consumer as a "Black Box":
A Behaviorist Perspective on Learning

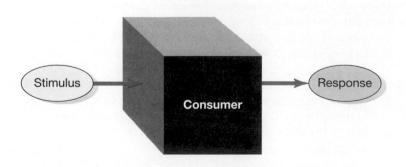

also learn that actions they take result in rewards and punishments, and this feed-back influences the way they will respond in similar situations in the future. Consumers who receive compliments on a product choice will be more likely to buy that brand again, but those who get food poisoning at a new restaurant will not be likely to patronize it in the future.

Classical Conditioning

Classical conditioning occurs when a stimulus that elicits a response is paired with another stimulus that initially does not elicit a response on its own. Over time, this second stimulus causes a similar response because it is associated with the first stimulus. This phenomenon was first demonstrated in dogs by Ivan Pavlov, a Russian physiologist doing research on digestion in animals.

Pavlov induced classically conditioned learning by pairing a neutral stimulus (a bell) with a stimulus known to cause a salivation response in dogs (he squirted dried meat powder into their mouths). The powder was an unconditioned stimulus (UCS) because it was naturally capable of causing the response. Over time, the bell became a conditioned stimulus (CS); it did not initially cause salivation, but the dogs learned to associate the bell with the meat powder and began to salivate at the sound of the bell only. The drooling of these canine consumers because of a sound, now linked to feeding time, was a conditioned response (CR).

This basic form of classical conditioning demonstrated by Pavlov primarily applies to responses controlled by the autonomic (e.g., salivation) and nervous (e.g., eye blink) systems. That is, it focuses on visual and olfactory cues that induce hunger, thirst, sexual arousal, and other basic drives. When these cues are consistently paired with conditioned stimuli such as brand names, consumers may learn to feel hungry, thirsty, or aroused when later exposed to the brand cues.

Classical conditioning can have similar effects for more complex reactions, too. Even a credit card becomes a conditioned cue that triggers greater spending, especially because it is a stimulus present only in situations in which consumers are spending money. People learn they can make larger purchases with credit cards,

THE TANGLED WEB

LEARNING TO LOVE CYBERSEX: About one-third of all visits to Web sites are to sexually-oriented pages. This easy availability of formerly forbidden material has spawned a new disorder: cybersex addiction. According to one physician, "Sex on the Net is like heroin. It grabs them and takes over their lives." For some sex surfers, though, the problem is even worse. Therapists report patients who develop a conditioned response to the computer and become aroused even before turning it on.[7]

Many classic advertising campaigns consist of product slogans that have been repeated so many times that they are etched in consumer's minds. The ad shown here brags about the high awareness of the Chiquita banana jingle ("I'm Chiquita banana, and I'm here to say...").

and they also have been found to leave larger tips than when paying by cash.[8] Small wonder that American Express reminds us, "Don't leave home without it."

Repetition

Conditioning effects are more likely to occur after the (CS) conditioned and unconditioned (UCS) stimuli have been paired a number of times.[9] Repeated exposures increase the strength of stimulus-response associations and prevent the decay of these associations in memory.

Many classic advertising campaigns consist of product slogans that have been repeated so many times that they are etched in consumers' minds. Conditioning will not occur or will take longer if the CS is only occasionally paired with the UCS. One result of this lack of association may be extinction, which occurs when the effects of prior conditioning are reduced and finally disappear. This can occur, for example, when a product is overexposed in the marketplace so that its original allure is lost. The Izod Lacoste polo shirt, with its distinctive crocodile crest, is a good example of this effect—when the once-exclusive crocodile started to appear on baby clothes and many other items, it lost its cachet and was successfully challenged as a symbol of casual elegance by other contenders, such as the Ralph Lauren polo player. Lacoste is trying to resurrect the ailing brand by associating it with celebrities like Matt Lauer and burnishing its image as an upscale garment.[10]

Stimulus Generalization

Stimulus generalization refers to the tendency of stimuli similar to a CS to evoke similar, conditioned responses. For example, Pavlov noticed in subsequent studies that his dogs would sometimes salivate when they heard noises that only resembled a bell, such as keys jangling.

People also react to other, similar stimuli in much the same way they responded to the original stimulus. A drugstore's bottle of private brand mouthwash deliberately packaged to resemble Listerine mouthwash may evoke a similar response among consumers, who assume that this "me-too" product shares other characteristics of the original. Indeed, consumers in one study on shampoo brands tended to rate those with similar packages as similar in quality and performance as well.[11] This "piggybacking" strategy can cut both ways: When the quality of the me-too product turns out to be lower than that of the original brand, consumers may exhibit even more positive feelings toward the original. However, if the quality of the two competitors is perceived to be about equal, consumers may conclude the price premium they are paying for the original is not worth it.[12]

In a recent twist on this principle, some companies are using a strategy called *masked branding* that deliberately hides a product's true origin. For example, giant corporation General Motors distanced itself from its Saturn brand and positioned the carmaker as a small-town business run by ordinary people, and Levi Strauss markets its Red Tab line to appeal to young consumers who don't want to be associated with an "old" brand. Blue Moon beers are positioned as sophisticated and the label lists the manufacturer as the Blue Moon Brewing Co., although in reality the beer is made by Coors, while Miller Brewing Co. created a dummy company called Plank Road Brewery when it launched its Icehouse and Red Dog beers.[13]

Stimulus Discrimination

Stimulus discrimination occurs when a stimulus similar to a CS is not followed by a UCS. When this happens, reactions are weakened and will soon disappear. Part of the learning process involves making a response to some stimuli but not to other, similar stimuli. Manufacturers of well-established brands commonly urge consumers not to buy "cheap imitations" because the results will not be what they expect.

Marketing Applications of Behavioral Learning Principles

Many marketing strategies focus on the establishment of associations between stimuli and responses. Behavioral learning principles apply to many consumer phenomena, ranging from the creation of a distinctive brand image to the perceived linkage between a product and an underlying need.

The transfer of meaning from an unconditioned stimulus to a conditioned stimulus explains why "made-up" brand names like Marlboro, Coca-Cola, or IBM can exert such powerful effects on consumers. The association between the Marlboro Man and the cigarette is so strong that in some cases the company no longer even bothers to include the brand name in its ads. When nonsense syllables (meaningless sets of letters) are paired with such evaluative words as beauty or success, the meaning is transferred to the fake words. This change in the symbolic significance of initially meaningless words shows that even complex meanings can be conditioned by fairly simple associations.[14] This study found that attitudes formed through classical conditioning are enduring.[15] These associations are crucial to many marketing strategies that rely on the creation and perpetuation of **brand equity**, in which a brand has strong positive associations in a consumer's memory and commands a lot of loyalty as a result.[16]

Applications of Repetition

One advertising researcher argued that more than three exposures to a marketing communication are wasted. The first exposure creates awareness of the product, the second demonstrates its relevance to the consumer, and the third serves as a reminder of the product's benefits.[17] However, even this bare bones approach implies that repetition is needed to ensure that the consumer is actually exposed to (and processes) the message at least three times. As we saw in Chapter 2, this exposure is by no means guaranteed because people tend to tune out or distort many marketing communications. Marketers attempting to condition an association must ensure that the consumers they have targeted will be exposed to the stimulus a sufficient number of times in order to make it "stick."

On the other hand, it is possible to have too much of a good thing. Consumers can become so used to hearing or seeing a marketing stimulus that they no longer pay attention to it. This problem, known as *advertising wearout*, can be alleviated by varying the way in which the basic message is presented. For example, the tax preparation firm of H&R Block is famous for its long-standing "Another of the seventeen reasons to use H&R Block" campaign.

Applications of Conditioned Product Associations

Advertisements often pair a product with a positive stimulus to create a desirable association. Various aspects of a marketing message, such as music, humor, or imagery, can affect conditioning. In one study, for example, subjects who viewed a slide of pens paired with either pleasant or unpleasant music were more likely to later select the pen that appeared with pleasant music.[18]

The order in which the conditioned stimulus and the unconditioned stimulus is presented can affect the likelihood that learning will occur. Generally speaking, the conditioned stimulus should be presented prior to the unconditioned stimulus. The technique of backward conditioning, such as playing a jingle (the UCS) and then showing a soft drink (the CS) generally is not effective.[19] Because sequential presentation is desirable for conditioning to occur, classical conditioning is not as effective in static situations, such as in magazine ads, in which (in contrast to TV or radio) the marketer cannot control the order in which the CS and the UCS are perceived.

Just as product associations can be formed, they can be extinguished. Because of the danger of extinction, a classical conditioning strategy may not be as effective for products that are frequently encountered, as there is no guarantee they will be accompanied by the CS. A bottle of Pepsi paired with the refreshing sound of a carbonated beverage being poured over ice may seem like a good application of conditioning. Unfortunately, the product would also be seen in many other contexts in which this sound was absent, reducing the effectiveness of a conditioning strategy.

By the same reasoning, a novel tune should be chosen over a popular one to pair with a product, as the popular song might also be heard in many situations in which the product is not present.[20] Music videos in particular may serve as effective UCSs because they often have an emotional impact on viewers, and this effect may transfer to ads accompanying the video.[21]

Applications of Stimulus Generalization

The process of stimulus generalization is often central to branding and packaging decisions that attempt to capitalize on consumers' positive associations with an existing brand or company name. The marketing value of an admired stimulus is clearly demonstrated at universities with winning sports teams, where loyal fans snap up merchandise from clothing to bathroom accessories emblazoned with the school's name—about $2.5 billion a year of college merchandise. This business did not even exist 20 years ago, when schools were reluctant to commercialize their images. Texas A&M was one of the first schools that even bothered to file for trademark protection, and that was only after someone put the Aggie logo on a line of handguns. Today, it's a different story. All this fuss over sweatshirts, drink coasters, and trash cans emblazoned with school logos is welcomed by many college administrators—universities collectively earn more than $100 million per year in royalties.[22] Strategies based on stimulus generalization include the following:

- *Family branding*: a variety of products capitalize on the reputation of a company name. Companies such as Campbell's, Heinz, and General Electric rely on their positive corporate images to sell different product lines.
- *Product line extensions*: related products are added to an established brand. Dole, which is associated with fruit, introduced refrigerated juices and juice bars, whereas Sun Maid went from raisins to raisin bread. Other extensions include Woolite rug cleaner, Cracker Jack gourmet popping corn, and Ivory shampoo.[23] However, there is a down side: An extension has the potential to weaken the parent brand, as the Carnation Company discovered. The company cancelled plans for "Lady Friskies," a contraceptive dog food, after tests indicated it would reduce sales of regular Friskies.[24]
- *Licensing*: well-known names are "rented" by others. This strategy is increasing in popularity as marketers try to link their products and

services with well-established figures—licensing has become so common-place that even imprisoned cult leader Charles Manson received royalties on T-shirts bearing his likeness.[25] Recent licensing efforts include a new line of home furnishing products called Disney Home, Pokemon Character Body Art (a line of personal care products for kids—we hope), and even Three Stooges Beer. Nyuk![26]

- *Look-alike packaging*: distinctive packaging designs create strong associations with a particular brand. As noted earlier, this linkage often is exploited by makers of generic or private label brands who wish to communicate a quality image by putting their products in very similar packages.[27] Imitating the look of an existing successful brand is common in today's crowded marketplace. One study found that a negative experience with an imitator brand increased evaluations of the original brand. A positive experience with the imitator had the opposite effect of decreasing evaluations of the original brand.[28]

Applications of Stimulus Discrimination

An emphasis on communicating a product's distinctive attributes vis-à-vis its competitors is an important aspect of positioning, where consumers learn to dif-ferentiate a brand from its competitors (see Chapter 2). This is not always an easy task, especially in product categories in which the brand names of many of the alternatives look and sound alike.

Companies with a well-established brand image try to encourage stimulus discrimination by promoting the unique attributes of their brand—hence the constant reminders for American Express Traveler's Checks: "Ask for them by name." On the other hand, a brand name that is used so widely that it is no longer distinctive becomes part of the public domain and can be used by competitors, as has been the case for such products as aspirin, cellophane, the yo-yo, and the escalator.

Instrumental Conditioning

Instrumental conditioning, also known as operant conditioning, occurs as the individual learns to perform behaviors that produce positive outcomes and to avoid those that yield negative outcomes. This learning process is most closely associated with the psychologist B. F. Skinner, who demonstrated the effects of instrumental conditioning by teaching pigeons and other animals to dance, play Ping-Pong, and perform other activities by systematically rewarding them for desired behaviors.[29]

Whereas responses in classical conditioning are involuntary and fairly sim-ple, those in instrumental conditioning are made deliberately to obtain a goal and may be more complex. The desired behavior may be learned over a period of time, as intermediate actions are rewarded in a process called shaping. For example, the owner of a new store may award prizes to shoppers just for coming in, hoping that over time they will continue to drop in and eventually even buy something.

Also, whereas classical conditioning involves the close pairing of two stim-uli, instrumental learning occurs as a result of a reward received following the desired behavior. Learning takes place over a period of time, during which other behaviors are attempted and abandoned because they are not reinforced. A good way to remember the difference is to keep in mind that in instrumental learn-ing, the response is performed because it is instrumental to gaining a reward or

NET PROFIT

MARKETING RESEARCHERS FRE-QUENTLY FACE the problem of con-sumers' reluctance to disclose personal information in surveys. Can online techniques help to overcome this bar-rier? Perhaps, if automated questioning can be made to resemble human inter-actions. One study found that when a computer appears to possess charac-teristics normally associated with human behavior, such as using every-day language and turn taking in con-versations, consumers respond favor-ably and form a relationship with the machine. In other words, they transfer rules they have learned in human inter-action to a man–machine context. The research found that consumers are more likely to divulge personal infor-mation when the computer divulges information first, and the degree of inti-mate disclosure gradually escalates. For example, the computer may dis-close the fact that there are times when it crashes for no apparent reason and then ask the consumer to recipro-cate by disclosing something about the respondent herself. And, those con-sumers who had engaged in self-disclosure and reciprocity with a computer were likely to evaluate products described online more favorably than those that had not engaged in this interaction.[30] So, go give your com-puter a nice big hug.

avoiding a punishment. Consumers over time come to associate with people who reward them and to choose products that make them feel good or satisfy some need.

Instrumental conditioning occurs in one of three ways. When the environment provides **positive reinforcement** in the form of a reward, the response is strengthened and appropriate behavior is learned. For example, a woman who gets compliments after wearing Obsession perfume will learn that using this product has the desired effect, and she will be more likely to keep buying the product. **Negative reinforcement** also strengthens responses so that appropriate behavior is learned. A perfume company might run an ad showing a woman sitting home alone on a Saturday night because she did not use its fragrance. The message to be conveyed is that she could have avoided this negative outcome if only she had used the perfume. In contrast to situations in which we learn to do certain things in order to avoid unpleasantness, **punishment** occurs when a response is followed by unpleasant events (such as being ridiculed by friends for wearing an offensive smelling perfume)—we learn the hard way not to repeat these behaviors.

To help in understanding the differences among these mechanisms, keep in mind that reactions from a person's environment to behavior can be either positive or negative, and that these outcomes or anticipated outcomes can be applied or removed. That is, under conditions of both positive reinforcement and punishment the person receives a reaction after doing something. In contrast, negative reinforcement occurs when a negative outcome is avoided—the removal of something negative is pleasurable and hence is rewarding.

Finally, when a positive outcome is no longer received, extinction is likely to occur, and the learned stimulus–response connection will not be maintained (as when a woman no longer receives compliments on her perfume). Thus positive and negative reinforcement strengthen the future linkage between a response and an outcome because of the pleasant experience. This tie is weakened under conditions of both punishment and extinction because of the unpleasant experience. The relationships among these four conditions are easier to understand by referring to Figure 3.2.

An important factor in operant conditioning is the set of rules by which appropriate reinforcements are given for a behavior. The issue of what is the most effective reinforcement schedule to use is important to marketers, because it relates to the amount of effort and resources they must devote to rewarding consumers to condition desired behaviors. Several schedules are possible:

- *Fixed-interval reinforcement*: After a specified time period has passed, the first response that is made brings the reward. Under such conditions, people tend to respond slowly right after being reinforced, but their responses speed up as the time for the next reinforcement looms. For example, consumers may crowd into a store for the last day of its seasonal sale and not reappear until the next one.
- *Variable-interval reinforcement*: The time that must pass before reinforcement is delivered varies around some average. Because the person does not know exactly when to expect the reinforcement, responses must be performed at a consistent rate. This logic is behind retailers' use of so-called secret shoppers, people who periodically test for service quality by posing as a customer at unannounced times. Because store employees never know exactly when to expect a visit, high quality must be maintained constantly "just in case."
- *Fixed-ratio reinforcement*: Reinforcement occurs only after a fixed number of responses. This schedule motivates people to continue performing

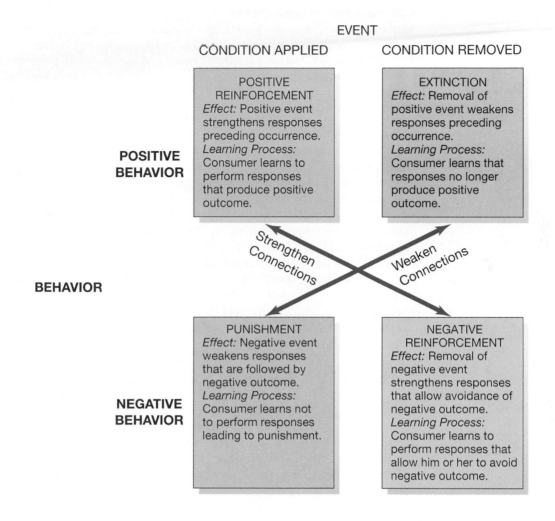

Figure 3.2
Four Types of Learning Outcomes

the same behavior over and over. For example, a consumer might keep buying groceries at the same store in order to earn a prize after collecting 50 books of trading stamps.

• *Variable-ratio reinforcement*: The person is reinforced after a certain number of responses, but he or she does not know how many responses are required. People in such situations tend to respond at very high and steady rates, and this type of behavior is very difficult to extinguish. This reinforcement schedule is responsible for consumers' attraction to slot machines. They learn that if they keep throwing money into the machine, they will eventually win something (if they don't go broke first).

Applications of Instrumental Conditioning Principles

Principles of instrumental conditioning are at work when a consumer is rewarded or punished for a purchase decision. Business people shape behavior by gradually reinforcing consumers for taking appropriate actions. For example, a car dealer might encourage a reluctant buyer to just sit in a floor model, then suggest a test drive, and then try to close the deal.

Reinforcement of Consumption

Marketers have many ways to reinforce consumers, ranging from a simple thank you after a purchase to substantial rebates and follow-up phone calls. For example, a life insurance company obtained a much higher rate of policy renewal among a group of new customers who received a thank you letter after each payment, compared to a control group that did not receive any reinforcement.[31]

Frequency Marketing

A popular technique known as **frequency marketing** reinforces regular purchasers by giving them prizes with values that increase along with the amount purchased. This instrumental learning strategy was pioneered by the airline industry, which introduced "frequent flyer" programs in the early 1980s to reward loyal customers. The practice has spread to other business as well, ranging from video stores to fast-food places. Perhaps the most enthusiastic fan of frequency marketing is David Phillips. He became known as the Pudding Guy because he earned a lifetime of free plane rides after noticing a frequent flyer offer on a chocolate pudding package. Phillips bought enough pudding to win 1.25 million frequent-flier miles from American Airlines. He donated the pudding to local food banks; in exchange for free pudding, workers agreed to peel off the labels as they dished out the stuff. The final tally: 12,150 cups of pudding.[32] Whipped cream with that?

COGNITIVE LEARNING THEORY

In contrast to behavioral theories of learning, **cognitive learning theory** approaches stress the importance of internal mental processes. This perspective views people as problem solvers who actively use information from the world around them to master their environment. Supporters of this view also stress the role of creativity and insight during the learning process.

Is Learning Conscious or Not?

A lot of controversy surrounds the issue of whether or when people are aware of their learning processes. Whereas behavioral learning theorists emphasize the routine, automatic nature of conditioning, proponents of cognitive learning argue that even these simple effects are based on cognitive factors: Expectations are created that a stimulus will be followed by a response (the formation of expectations requires mental activity). According to this school of thought, conditioning occurs because subjects develop conscious hypotheses and then act on them.

On the one hand, there is some evidence for the existence of nonconscious procedural knowledge. People apparently do process at least some information in an automatic, passive way, which is a condition that has been termed mindlessness.[33] When we meet someone new or encounter a new product, for example, we have a tendency to respond to the stimulus in terms of existing categories we have learned, rather than taking the trouble to formulate new ones. Our reactions in these cases are activated by a trigger feature, some stimulus that cues us toward a particular pattern. For example, men in one study rated a car in an ad as superior on a variety of characteristics if a seductive woman (the trigger feature) was present, despite the fact that the men did not believe the woman's presence actually had an influence on their evaluations.[34]

Nonetheless, many modern theorists are beginning to regard some instances of automatic conditioning as cognitive processes, especially where expectations are formed about the linkages between stimuli and responses. Indeed, studies using masking effects, which make it difficult for subjects to learn CS/UCS associations, show substantial reductions in conditioning.[35] An adolescent girl may observe that women on television and in real life seem to be rewarded with compliments and attention when they smell nice and wear alluring clothing. She figures out that the probability of these rewards occurring is greater when she wears perfume, and so she deliberately wears a popular scent to obtain the reward of social acceptance.

Observational Learning

Observational learning occurs when people watch the actions of others and note the reinforcements they receive for their behaviors—learning occurs as a result of vicarious rather than direct experience. This type of learning is a complex process; people store these observations in memory as they accumulate knowledge, perhaps using this information at a later point to guide their own behavior. This process of imitating the behavior of others is called modeling. For example, a woman shopping for a new kind of perfume may remember the reactions her friend received on wearing a certain brand several months earlier, and she will base her behavior on her friend's actions. The modeling process is a powerful form of learning, and people's tendencies to imitate others' behaviors can have negative effects. Of particular concern is the potential of television shows and movies to teach violence to children. Children may be exposed to new methods of aggression by models (e.g., cartoon heroes) in the shows they watch. At some later point, when the child becomes angry, these behaviors will be imitated.

A classic study demonstrates the effect of modeling on children's actions. Kids who watched an adult stomp on, knock down, and otherwise torture a large inflated "Bobo doll" repeated these behaviors when later left alone in a room with the doll; children who did not witness these acts did not.[36] Unfortunately, the relevance of this study to violent TV shows seems quite clear.

Figure 3.3 shows that in order for observational learning in the form of modeling to occur, four conditions must be met:[37]

1. The consumer's attention must be directed to the appropriate model, who for reasons of attractiveness, competence, status, or similarity it is desirable to emulate.
2. The consumer must remember what is said or done by the model.

Figure 3.3
Components of Observational Learning

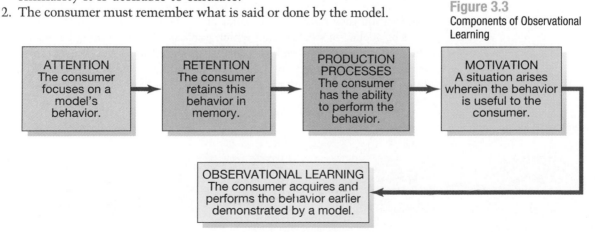

3. The consumer must convert this information into actions.
4. The consumer must be motivated to perform these actions.

Applications of Cognitive Learning Principles

Consumers' ability to learn vicariously by observing how the behavior of others is reinforced makes the lives of marketers much easier. Because people do not have to be directly reinforced for their actions, marketers do not necessarily have to actually reward or punish them for purchase behaviors (think how expensive or even ethically questionable that might be!). Instead, they can show what happens to desirable models who use or do not use their products, knowing that consumers will often be motivated to imitate these actions at a later time. For example, a perfume commercial might depict a woman surrounded by a throng of admirers who are providing her with positive reinforcement for using the product. Needless to say, this learning process is more practical than providing the same attention to each woman who actually buys the perfume!

Consumers' evaluations of models go beyond simple stimulus-response connections. For example, a celebrity's image elicits more than a simple reflexive response of good or bad.[38] It is a complex combination of many attributes. In general, the degree to which a model will be emulated depends on his or her social attractiveness. Attractiveness can be based on several components, including physical appearance, expertise, or similarity to the evaluator.

THE ROLE OF MEMORY IN LEARNING

Memory involves a process of acquiring information and storing it over time so that it will be available when needed. Contemporary approaches to the study of memory employ an information-processing approach. They assume that the mind is in some ways like a computer: Data is input, processed, and output for later use in revised form. In the **encoding** stage, information is entered in a way the system will recognize. In the **storage** stage, this knowledge is integrated with what is already in memory and "warehoused" until needed. During **retrieval,** the person accesses the desired information.[39] The memory process is summarized in Figure 3.4.

Many of our experiences are locked inside our heads, and they may surface years later if prompted by the right cues. Marketers rely on consumers to retain information they have learned about products and services, trusting that it will later be applied in situations in which purchase decisions must be made. During the consumer decision-making process, this internal memory is combined with external memory, which includes all of the product details on packages, in shopping lists, and other marketing stimuli, to permit brand alternatives to be identified and evaluated.[40]

Figure 3.4
The Memory Process

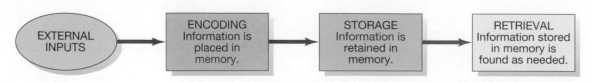

Rocky Road, a classic candy product, uses a brief narrative to remind consumers of its long-lasting value.

Research supports the idea that marketers can distort a consumer's recall of a product experience. What we think we "know" about products can be influenced by advertising messages to which we are exposed after using them. This *post-experience advertising* is more likely to alter actual memories when it is very similar or activates memories about the actual experience. For example, advertising can make a remembered product experience more favorable than it actually was.[41]

Encoding Information for Later Retrieval

The way information is encoded, or mentally programmed, helps to determine how it will be represented in memory. In general, incoming data that are associated with other information already in memory stand a better chance of being retained. For example, brand names that are linked to physical characteristics of a product category (e.g., Coffee Mate creamer or Sani-Flush toilet bowl cleaner) or that are easy to visualize (e.g., Tide detergent or Mercury Cougar cars) tend to be more easily retained in memory than more abstract brand names.[43]

Types of Meaning

A consumer may process a stimulus simply in terms of its sensory meaning, such as its color or shape. When this occurs, the meaning may be activated when the person sees a picture of the stimulus. We may experience a sense of familiarity on seeing an ad for a new snack food we have recently tasted, for example. In many cases, though, meanings are encoded at a more abstract level. Semantic meaning refers to symbolic associations, such as the idea that rich people drink champagne or that fashionable women have navel piercings.

Personal Relevance

Episodic memories are those that relate to events that are personally relevant.[44] As a result, a person's motivation to retain these memories will likely be strong. Couples often have "their song" that reminds them of their first date or wedding. Some especially vivid associations are called *flashbulb memories*. And, recall of the past may have an effect on future behavior. For example, a college fund-raising campaign can get higher donations by evoking pleasant college memories.

One method of conveying product information is through a *narrative* or a story. Much of the social information that an individual acquires is represented in memory this way. Therefore, utilizing this method in product advertising can be an effective marketing technique. Narratives persuade people to construct a mental representation of the information that they are viewing. Pictures aid in this construction and allow for a more developed and detailed mental representation.[45]

NET **PROFIT**

HERE'S A NEW WAY to remember your loved ones. FinalThoughts.com offers a place to store e-mail messages online so they can be sent to family and friends after you die. The creator of the site came up with the idea during a turbulent airplane ride. As the plane shook, he realized he hadn't properly said goodbye to people who mattered to him. The site is set up to encourage advanced planning. Each user chooses a "guardian angel" who will notify the site when the time comes so that the appropriate messages can be sent out. The site also includes resource centers with links to articles on coping with loss and forms that can be used to notify survivors of the deceased's final wishes. Approximately 10,000 customers have signed up; most hope they won't be using the service anytime soon.[42]

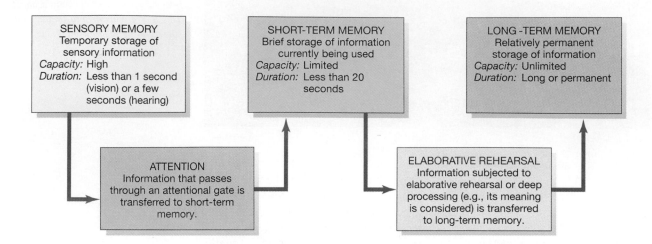

Figure 3.5
Relationships Among Memory Systems

Memory Systems

According to the information-processing perspective, there are three distinct memory systems: sensory memory, short-term memory (STM), and long-term memory (LTM). Each plays a role in processing brand-related information. The interrelationships of these memory systems are summarized in Figure 3.5.

Sensory Memory

Sensory memory permits storage of the information we receive from our senses. This storage is very temporary; it lasts a couple of seconds at most. For example, a person might be walking past a donut shop and get a quick, enticing whiff of something baking inside. Although this sensation would last only for a few seconds, it would be sufficient to allow the person to determine if he or she should investigate further. If the information is retained for further processing, it passes through an attentional gate and is transferred to short-term memory.

Short-Term Memory

Short-term memory (STM) also stores information for a limited period of time, and its capacity is limited. Similar to a computer, this system can be regarded as working memory; it holds the information we are currently processing. Verbal input may be stored acoustically (in terms of how it sounds) or semantically (in terms of what it means).

The information is stored by combining small pieces into larger ones in a process known as chunking. A chunk is a configuration that is familiar to the person and can be manipulated as a unit. For example, a brand name can be a chunk that summarizes a great deal of detailed information about the brand.

Initially, it was believed that STM was capable of processing between five to nine chunks of information at a time, and for this reason phone numbers were designed to have seven digits.[46] It now appears that three to four chunks is the optimal size for efficient retrieval (seven-digit phone numbers can be remembered because the individual digits are chunked, so we may remember a three-digit exchange as one piece of information).[47]

Long-Term Memory

Long-term memory (LTM) is the system that allows us to retain information for a long period of time. In order for information to enter into long-term memory from short-term memory, elaborative rehearsal is required. This process involves thinking about the meaning of a stimulus and relating it to other information already in memory. Marketers sometimes assist in the process by devising catchy slogans or jingles that consumers repeat on their own.

Storing Information in Memory

Relationships among the types of memory are a source of some controversy. The traditional perspective, known as multiple-store, assumes that STM and LTM are separate systems. More recent research has moved away from the distinction between the two types of memory, instead emphasizing the interdependence of the systems. This work argues that depending on the nature of the processing task, different levels of processing occur that activate some aspects of memory rather than others. These approaches are called **activation models of memory**.[48] The more effort it takes to process information (so-called "deep processing"), the more likely it is that information will be placed in long-term memory.

Associative Networks

Activation models propose that an incoming piece of information is stored in an associative network containing many bits of related information organized according to some set of relationships. The consumer has organized systems of concepts relating to brands, manufacturers, and stores.

These storage units, known as **knowledge structures,** can be thought of as complex spider webs filled with pieces of data. This information is placed into nodes, which are connected by associative links within these structures. Pieces of information that are seen as similar in some way are chunked together under some more abstract category. New, incoming information is interpreted to be consistent with the structure already in place.[49]

According to the hierarchical processing model, a message is processed in a bottom-up fashion: Processing begins at a very basic level and is subject to increasingly complex processing operations that require greater cognitive capacity. If processing at one level fails to evoke the next level, processing of the ad is terminated and capacity is allocated to other tasks.[50]

An associative network is developed as links form between nodes. For example, a consumer might have a network for "perfumes." Each node represents a concept related to the category. This node can be an attribute, a specific brand, a celebrity identified with a perfume, or even a related product. A network for perfumes might include concepts like the names Chanel, Obsession, and Charlie, as well as attributes such as sexy and elegant.

When asked to list perfumes, the consumer would recall only those brands contained in the appropriate category. This group constitutes that person's evoked set. The task of a new entrant that wants to position itself as a category member (e.g., a new luxury perfume) is to provide cues that facilitate its placement in the appropriate category. A sample network for perfumes is shown in Figure 3.6.

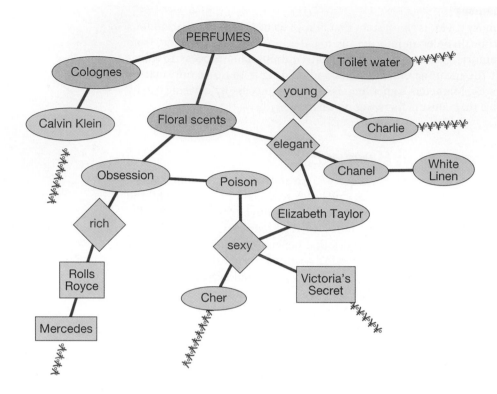

Figure 3.6
An Associative Network for Perfumes

Spreading Activation

A meaning can be activated indirectly; energy spreads across nodes of varying levels of abstraction. As one node is activated, other nodes associated with it also begin to be triggered. Meaning thus spreads across the network, bringing up concepts including competing brands and relevant attributes that are used to form attitudes toward the brand.

This process of spreading activation allows consumers to shift back and forth between levels of meaning. The way a piece of information is stored in memory depends on the type of meaning assigned to it. This meaning type will in turn determine how and when the meaning is activated. For example, the memory trace for an ad could be stored in one or more of the following ways:

- *Brand-specific*: in terms of claims made for the brand
- *Ad-specific*: in terms of the medium or content of the ad itself
- *Brand identification*: in terms of the brand name
- *Product category*: in terms of how the product works or where it should be used
- *Evaluative reactions*: positive or negative emotions, such as "that looks like fun"[51]

Levels of Knowledge

Knowledge is coded at different levels of abstraction and complexity. Meaning concepts are individual nodes (e.g., elegant). These may be combined into a larger unit, called a proposition (also known as a belief). A proposition links two nodes together to form a more complex meaning, which can serve as a single chunk of information. For example, a proposition might be that "Chanel is a perfume for elegant women."

Propositions are in turn integrated to produce a complex unit known as a schema, which as we have already seen is a cognitive framework that is developed through experience. Information that is consistent with an existing schema is encoded more readily.[52] The ability to move up and down among levels of abstraction greatly increases processing flexibility and efficiency. For this reason, young children, who do not yet have well-developed schemas, are not able to make as efficient use of purchase information as are older children.[53]

One type of schema that is relevant to consumer behavior is a script, a sequence of events that is expected by an individual. For example, consumers learn service scripts that guide their behavior in commercial settings. Consumers learn to expect a certain sequence of events, and they may become uncomfortable if the service departs from the script. A service script for a visit to the dentist might include such events as (1) drive to the dentist, (2) read old magazines in the waiting room, (3) hear name called and sit in dentist's chair, (4) dentist puts funny substance on teeth, (5) dentist cleans teeth, and so on. This desire to follow a script helps to explain why such service innovations as automatic bank machines, self-service gas stations, or "scan-your-own" grocery checkouts have met with resistance by some consumers, who have trouble adapting to a new sequence of events.[54]

Retrieving Information for Purchase Decisions

Retrieval is the process whereby information is recovered from long-term memory. As evidenced by the popularity of the TV show *Who Wants to Be a Millionaire?*, people have a vast quantity of information stored in their heads that is not necessarily available on demand. Although most of the information entered in long-term memory does not go away, it may be difficult or impossible to retrieve unless the appropriate cues are present.

Factors Influencing Retrieval

Some differences in retrieval ability are affected by physiological factors. Older adults consistently display inferior recall ability for current items such as prescription drug instructions, though events that happened to them when they were younger may be recalled with great clarity.[55]

Other factors are situational, relating to the environment in which the message is delivered. Not surprisingly, recall is enhanced when the consumer pays more attention to the message in the first place. Some evidence indicates that information about a pioneering brand (the first brand to enter a market) is more easily retrieved from memory than follower brands because the first product's introduction is likely to be distinctive and, for the time being, no competitors divert the consumer's attention.[56] In addition, descriptive brand names are more likely to be recalled than are those that do not provide adequate cues as to what the product is.[57]

The viewing environment of a marketing message also can affect recall. For example, commercials shown during baseball games yield the lowest recall scores among sports programs because the activity is stop-and-go rather than continuous. Unlike football or basketball, the pacing of baseball gives many opportunities for attention to wander even during play. Similarly, General Electric found that its commercials fared better in television shows with continuous activity, such as stories or dramas, compared to variety shows or talk shows that are punctuated by a series of acts.[58] Finally, a large-scale analysis of TV commercials found that

The popular TV game show Who Wants to be a Millionaire *tests consumers' memories of cultural events.*

commercials shown first in a series of ads are recalled better than those shown last.[59]

State-Dependent Retrieval

In a process called *state-dependent retrieval,* people are better able to access information if their internal state is the same at the time of recall as when the information was learned. This phenomenon, called the *mood congruence effect,* underscores the desirability of matching a consumer's mood at the time of purchase when planning exposure to marketing communications. A consumer is more likely to recall an ad, for example, if his or her mood or level of arousal at the time of exposure is similar to that in the purchase environment. By recreating the cues that were present when the information was first presented, recall can be enhanced. For example, Life cereal uses a picture of "Mikey" from its commercial on the cereal box, which facilitates recall of brand claims and favorable brand evaluations.[60]

A few marketing researchers are using *hypnosis* to dredge up past memories of experiences with products.[61] Shell Oil was having trouble finding out why there was a decade-long sales slump at the company. After trying many different research methods, managers decided to try focus groups conducted under hypnosis. People were able to go back in their lives to talk about their first experience in a gas station when they were very young. Shell discovered that current preferences for gasoline were related to these very early memories. As a result, the firm is working on ways to make a positive impression on people at a very early age rather than waiting for them to be old enough to get a driver's license.[62]

Familiarity and Recall

As a general rule, prior familiarity with an item enhances its recall. Indeed, this is one of the basic goals of marketers who are trying to create and maintain awareness of their products. The more experience a consumer has with a product, the better use he or she is able to make of product information.[63]

However, there is a possible fly in the ointment: As noted earlier in the chapter, some evidence indicates that extreme familiarity can result in inferior learning and/or recall. When consumers are highly familiar with a brand or an advertisement, they may attend to fewer attributes because they do not believe that any additional effort will yield a gain in knowledge.[64] For example, when consumers are exposed to a radio replay, in which the audio track from a television ad is replayed on the radio, they do very little critical, evaluative processing and instead mentally replay the video portion of the ad.[65]

Salience and Recall

The salience of a brand refers to its prominence or level of activation in memory. As noted in Chapter 2, stimuli that stand out in contrast to their environment are more likely to command attention, which, in turn, increases the likelihood they will be recalled. Almost any technique that increases the novelty of a stimulus also improves recall (a result known as the *von Restorff Effect*).[66] This effect explains why unusual advertising or distinctive packaging tends to facilitate brand recall.[67]

Introducing a surprise element in an ad can be particularly effective in aiding recall even if it is not relevant to the factual information being presented.[68] In addition, mystery ads, in which the brand is not identified until the end of the ad, are more effective at building associations in memory between the product category and that brand—especially in the case of relatively unknown brands.[69]

Pictorial Versus Verbal Cues:
Is a Picture Worth a Thousand Words?

There is some evidence for the superiority of visual memory over verbal memory, but this advantage is unclear because it is more difficult to measure recall of pictures.[70] However, the available data indicate that information presented in picture form is more likely to be recognized later.[71] Certainly, visual aspects of an ad are more likely to grab a consumer's attention. In fact, eye-movement studies indicate that about 90 percent of viewers look at the dominant picture in an ad before they bother to view the copy.[72]

Although pictorial ads may enhance recall, they do not necessarily improve comprehension. One study found that television news items presented with illustrations (still pictures) as a backdrop result in improved recall for details of the news story, even though understanding of the story's content does not improve.[73]

Factors Influencing Forgetting

Marketers obviously hope that consumers will not forget about their products. However, in a poll of more than 13,000 adults, more than half were unable to remember any specific ad they had seen, heard, or read in the last 30 days.[74] Clearly, forgetting by consumers is a big headache for marketers (not to mention a problem for students when studying for exams!).

Early memory theorists assumed that memories simply fade with the passage of time. In a process of **decay,** the structural changes in the brain produced by learning simply go away. Forgetting also occurs due to interference; as additional information is learned, it displaces the earlier information.

Stimulus-response associations will be forgotten if the consumers subsequently learn new responses to the same or similar stimuli in a process known as *retroactive interference*. Or, prior learning can interfere with new learning, a process termed *proactive interference*. Because pieces of information are stored as nodes in memory that are connected to one another by links, a meaning concept that is connected by a larger number of links is more likely to be retrieved. But, as new responses are learned, a stimulus loses its effectiveness in retrieving the old response.[75]

These interference effects help explain problems in remembering brand information. Consumers tend to organize attribute information by brand.[76] Additional attribute information regarding a brand or similar brands may limit the person's ability to recall old brand information. Recall may also be inhibited if the brand name is composed of frequently used words. These words cue competing associations and result in less retention of brand information.[77]

In one study, brand evaluations deteriorated more rapidly when ads for the brand appeared with messages for 12 other brands in the same category than when the ad was shown with ads for 12 dissimilar products.[78] By increasing the salience of a brand, the recall of other brands can be impaired.[79] On the other hand, calling a competitor by name can result in poorer recall for one's own brand.[80]

Finally, a phenomenon known as the *part-list cueing effect* allows marketers to strategically utilize the interference process. When only a portion of the items in a category are presented to consumers, the omitted items are not as easily recalled. For example, comparative advertising that mentions only a subset of competitors (preferably those that the marketer is not very worried about) may inhibit recall of the unmentioned brands with which the product does not favorably compare.[81]

Products as Memory Markers

Products and ads can themselves serve as powerful retrieval cues. Indeed, the three types of possessions most valued by consumers are furniture, visual art, and photos. The most common explanation for this attachment is the ability of these things to call forth memories of the past.[82] Researchers are just beginning to probe the effects of *autobiographical memories* on buying behavior. These memories appear to be one way that advertisements create emotional responses; ads that succeed in getting us to think about our own past also appear to get us to like these ads more—especially if the linkage between the nostalgia experience and the brand is strong.[83]

Products are particularly important as markers when our sense of past is threatened, as when a consumer's current identity is challenged due to some change in role caused by divorce, moving, graduation, and so on.[84] Our possessions often have mnemonic qualities that serve as a form of external memory by prompting consumers to retrieve episodic memories. For example, family photography allows consumers to create their own retrieval cues, with the 11 billion amateur photos taken annually forming a kind of external memory bank for our culture. A sadder example is the popularity in some neighborhoods of memorial T-shirts for friends and family members who have been murdered. The shirts often feature poems and prayers along with a picture of the dead person. This practice has become so common in gang areas that a common threat has become: "Keep it up—you'll end up on a shirt."[85]

The Marketing Power of Nostalgia

Nostalgia has been described as a bittersweet emotion; the past is viewed with both sadness and longing.[86] As Joe's passion for the 1960s illustrates, references to "the good old days" are increasingly common, as advertisers call up memories of youth—and hope these feelings will translate to what they're selling today. That may help to explain why reunions have become such a booming business; about 22 million Americans attend one every year.[87] A stimulus is at times able to evoke a weakened response even years after it was initially perceived, an effect known as *spontaneous recovery*, and this reestablished connection may explain consumers' powerful nostalgic reactions to songs or pictures they have not been exposed to in quite a long time.

Why are nostalgia appeals so welcomed by consumers? According to one consumer analyst, "We are creating a new culture, and we don't know what's going to happen. So we need some warm fuzzies from our past."[88] Or, this strategy may work because more than half of adults think things were better in the past than they are today, according to research by Roper Starch Worldwide.[89] People are flocking to reissues of old package designs for such products as Necco wafers, Coca-Cola, Sun-Maid raisins, and Cracker Jacks. And they are warming to products that use theme songs from their youth, whether Toyota's "Everyday People" (Sly and the Family Stone), the borrowing of the Partridge Family hit, "I Think I Love You" by Levi Strauss, or even Senokot Laxative's special adaptation of "I Feel Good" by James Brown.[90]

Lifetime TV uses a nostaligia appeal to attract female viewers.[91]

Memory and Aesthetic Preferences

In addition to liking ads and products that remind us of our past, our past experiences also help to determine what we like now. Consumer researchers have created a nostalgia index that measures the critical ages during which our preferences are likely to be formed and endure over time. For example, liking for specific songs appears to be related to how old a person was when that song was popular—on average songs that were popular when he or she was 23.5 years old are the most likely to be favored, whereas preferences for fashion models peak at age 33 and for movie stars at age 26 to 27.[97]

Measuring Memory for Marketing Stimuli

Because marketers pay so much money to place their messages in front of consumers, they are naturally concerned that people will actually remember these messages at a later point. It seems that they have good reason to be concerned. In one study, fewer than 40 percent of television viewers made positive links between commercial messages and the corresponding products, only 65 percent noticed the brand name in a commercial, and only 38 percent recognized a connection to an important point.[98]

Even more sadly, only 7 percent of television viewers can recall the product or company featured in the most recent television commercial they watched. This figure represents less than half the recall rate recorded in 1965 and may be attributed to such factors as the increase of 30- and 15-second commercials, and the practice of airing television commercials in clusters rather than in single-sponsor programs.[99]

MULTICULTURAL DIMENSIONS

CLASSIC AMERICAN TV SHOWS are popular around the world, but few are as admired as *Dallas* is in Romania. In that eastern European country, the show's star J. R. Ewing is revered. Although many U.S. viewers saw J. R. as a greedy, unprincipled villain they "loved to hate," in Romania J. R. has become the symbol of American enterprise and a role model for the new capitalists who are trying to transform the country's economy. So, it's only fitting that J. R. was selected to endorse Lukoil, a brand of Russian motor oil. Advertisements in the Romanian market claim that the oil is "the choice of a true Texan."[92] Try selling that brand of nostalgia to the cowboys back home.

REALITY CHECK *SOME DIE-HARD FANS WERE NOT PLEASED*

when the Rolling Stones sold the tune "Start Me Up" for about $4 million to Microsoft, which wanted the classic song to promote its Windows 95 launch. The Beach Boys sold "Good Vibrations" to Cadbury Schweppes for its Sunkist soft drink, Steppenwolf offered its "Born to be Wild" to plug the Mercury Cougar, and even Bob Dylan sold "The Times They Are A-Changin'" to Coopers & Lybrand (now called PriceWaterhouseCoopers).[95]

Other rock legends have refused to play the commercial game, including Bruce Springsteen, the Grateful Dead, Led Zeppelin, Fleetwood Mac, R.E.M., and U2. According to U2's manager, "Rock 'n' roll is the last vestige of independence. It is undignified to put that creative effort and hard work to the disposal of a soft drink or beer or car."[96] Singer Neil Young is espe- cially adamant about not selling out; in his song "This Note's For You," he croons, "Ain't singing for Pepsi, ain't singing for Coke, I don't sing for nobody, makes me look like a joke."

What's your take on this issue? How do you react when one of your favorite songs turns up in a commercial? Is this use of nostalgia an effective way to market a product? Why or why not?

I personally feel that singers that sell their songs to companies like Microsoft, for commercial purposes are doing nothing wrong. I usually enjoy it when I hear my favorite song on a commercial, unless I hate the product it is helping to promote, and even then it does not make me hate the song.

Sara Rast,
Southwest Missouri State University

Although artists such as U2 and R.E.M. may be adamant in their stance against the evils of the main- stream media, they seem to have no qualms against displaying their music on nationally syndicated television and radio airwaves. These are the same musicians who are the self-proclaimed "purists" of the music industry who feel justified charging astronomical concert and merchandise prices, the same artists

who parade around in their multi-million dollar music videos.

Eric Jude Guacena,
Virginia Commonwealth University

When I hear one of my favorite songs turn up in a commercial I am extremely angry because my perceptions and atti- tudes are altered toward the song and also the artist. I have my own interpre- tation of what a song means to me. However when a song is used for a commercial, my previous thoughts are transposed and in result mean less to me. I will no longer like that certain song nearly as much as before it was used for a commercial.

John Dollman IV,
West Virginia University

I think that successful artists are wise to keep ownership of their production, making advertisers and marketers rely on their own creativity to produce

successful advertising campaigns that result in increased sales. Marketers usually alter lyrics of original pieces, changing artists' original work, losing the art of the creative piece. Commercialization of music is a saddening loss of art and pride for many artists who sell their songs to marketing departments.

Jessica Wells,
Utah State University

When I hear a familiar song on a com- mercial, it helps me think back to a certain happy time in my life. This is an effective way to market a product by using classical conditioning. There is an existing relationship between a good song (the unconditioned stimulus) and the feeling of happiness and pleasure (unconditioned response). When a marketer uses a song to advertise a product, that product then becomes the conditioned response, stim- ulating the same feeling of happiness and pleasure (conditioned response).

Annalise M. Mulholland,
Virginia Tech

When I see a product and recognize that one of my favourite songs is being used to market it, I am more likely to pay attention to the ad . . . . For example, one of my favourite songs is "Fly Away" by Lenny Kravitz. It was recently used to promote the Nissan Pathfinder. Normally I would have switched channels when the commercial came on or gotten up for a snack but since I like the song, I paused and watched the commercial. Because of this, I now associate this song with the Nissan Pathfinder and because I like this song, the Pathfinder has a favourable image in my mind.

Sabrina Aslam,
Simon Fraser University, Canada

What's your opinion? Check out the online polls at www.prenhall.com/ myphlip. Just follow the little person in the lab coat.

Recognition Versus Recall

One indicator of good advertising is, of course, the impression it makes on con- sumers. But how can this impact be defined and measured? Two basic measures of impact are recognition and recall. In the typical recognition test, subjects are shown ads one at a time and asked if they have seen them before. In contrast, free recall tests ask consumers to independently think of what they have seen without being prompted for this information first—obviously this task requires greater effort on the part of respondents.

Fossil's product designs evoke memories of earlier, classic styles.

Under some conditions, these two memory measures tend to yield the same results, especially when the researchers try to keep the viewers' interest in the ads constant.[100] Generally, though, recognition scores tend to be more reliable and do not decay over time the way recall scores do.[101] Recognition scores are almost always better than recall scores because recognition is a simpler process and more retrieval cues are available to the consumer.

Both types of retrieval play important roles in purchase decisions, however. Recall tends to be more important in situations in which consumers do not have product data at their disposal, so they must rely on memory to generate this information.[102] On the other hand, recognition is more likely to be an important factor in a store, where consumers are confronted with thousands of product options and information (i.e., external memory is abundantly available) and the task may simply be to recognize a familiar package. Unfortunately, package recognition and familiarity can have a negative consequence in that warning labels may be ignored, because their message is taken for granted and not really noticed.[103]

The Starch Test

A widely used commercial measure of advertising recall for magazines is called *the Starch Test*, a syndicated service founded in 1932. This service provides scores on a number of aspects of consumers' familiarity with an ad, including such categories as "noted," "associated," and "read most." It also scores the impact of the component parts of an overall ad, giving such information as "seen" for major illustrations and "read some" for a major block of copy.[104] Factors such as the size of the ad, whether it appears toward the front or the back of the magazine, if it is on the right or left page, and the size of illustrations play an important role in affecting the amount of attention given to an ad as determined by Starch scores.

Problems with Memory Measures

Although the measurement of an ad's memorability is important, the ability of existing measures to accurately assess these dimensions has been criticized for several reasons, which we explore now.

Response Biases

Results obtained from a measuring instrument are not necessarily due to what is being measured, but rather to something else about the instrument or the respondent. This form of contamination is called a **response bias.** For example, people tend to give "yes" responses to questions, regardless of what is asked. In addition, consumers often have an eagerness to be "good subjects" by pleasing the experimenter. They will try to give the responses they think he or she is looking for. In some studies, the claimed recognition of bogus ads (ads that have not been seen before) is almost as high as the recognition rate of real ads.[105]

Memory Lapses

People are also prone to unintentionally forget information. Typical problems include omitting (leaving facts out), averaging (the tendency to "normalize" memories by not reporting extreme cases), and telescoping (inaccurate recall of time).[106] These distortions call into question the accuracy of product usage databases that rely on consumers to recall their purchase and consumption of food and household items. In one study, for example, people were asked to describe what portion of various foods—small, medium, or large—they ate in a typical meal. However, different definitions of "medium" were used (e.g., $\frac{3}{4}$ cup versus $1\frac{1}{2}$ cups). Regardless of the measurement used, about the same number of people claimed they typically ate "medium" portions.[107]

Memory for Facts Versus Feelings

Although techniques are being developed to increase the accuracy of memory scores, these improvements do not address the more fundamental issue of whether recall is necessary for advertising to have an effect. In particular, some critics argue that these measures do not adequately tap the impact of "feeling" ads in which the objective is to arouse strong emotions rather than to convey concrete product benefits. Many ad campaigns, including those for Hallmark cards, Chevrolet, and Pepsi, use this approach.[108] An effective strategy relies on a long-term buildup of feeling rather than on a one-shot attempt to convince consumers to buy the product.

Also, it is not clear that recall translates into preference. We may recall the benefits touted in an ad but not believe them. Or, the ad may be memorable because it is so obnoxious and the product becomes one we "love to hate." The bottom line: Although recall is important, especially for creating brand awareness, it is not necessarily sufficient to alter consumer preferences. To accomplish this, more sophisticated attitude-changing strategies are needed. These issues will be discussed in Chapters 7 and 8.

CHAPTER SUMMARY

- Learning is a change in behavior that is caused by experience. Learning can occur through simple associations between a stimulus and a response, or via a complex series of cognitive activities.

- Behavioral learning theories assume that learning occurs as a result of responses to external events. Classical conditioning occurs when a stimulus that naturally elicits a response (an unconditioned stimulus) is paired with another stimulus that does not initially elicit this response. Over time, the second stimulus (the conditioned stimulus) comes to elicit the response even in the absence of the first.
- This response can also extend to other, similar stimuli in a process known as stimulus generalization. This process is the basis for such marketing strategies as licensing and family branding, where a consumer's positive associations with a product are transferred to other contexts.
- Operant or instrumental conditioning occurs as the person learns to perform behaviors that produce positive outcomes and avoid those that result in negative outcomes. Whereas classical conditioning involves the pairing of two stimuli, instrumental learning occurs when reinforcement is delivered following a response to a stimulus. Reinforcement is positive if a reward is delivered following a response. It is negative if a negative outcome is avoided by not performing a response. Punishment occurs when a response is followed by unpleasant events. Extinction of the behavior will occur if reinforcement is no longer received.
- Cognitive learning occurs as the result of mental processes. For example, observational learning takes place when the consumer performs a behavior as a result of seeing someone else performing it and being rewarded for it.
- Memory refers to the storage of learned information. The way information is encoded when it is perceived determines how it will be stored in memory. The memory systems known as sensory memory, short-term memory, and long-term memory each play a role in retaining and processing information from the outside world.
- Information is not stored in isolation; it is incorporated into knowledge structures, in which it is associated with other related data. The location of product information in associative networks, and the level of abstraction at which it is coded, help to determine when and how this information will be activated at a later time. Some factors that influence the likelihood of retrieval include the level of familiarity with an item, its salience (or prominence) in memory, and whether the information was presented in pictorial or written form.
- Products also play a role as memory markers; they are used by consumers to retrieve memories about past experiences (autobiographical memories) and are often valued for their ability to do this. This function also contributes to the use of nostalgia in marketing strategies.
- Memory for product information can be measured through either recognition or recall techniques. Consumers are more likely to recognize an advertisement if it is presented to them than to recall one without being given any cues. However, neither recognition nor recall automatically or reliably translate into product preferences or purchases.

KEY TERMS

activation models of memory, p. 85
behavioral learning theories, p. 72
brand equity, p. 75
classical conditioning, p. 73
cognitive learning theory, p. 80

decay, p. 89
encoding, p. 82
frequency marketing, p. 80
instrumental conditioning, p. 77
knowledge structures, p. 85

learning, p. 72
long-term memory, p. 85
memory, p. 82
negative reinforcement, p. 78
nostalgia, p. 91

CONSUMER BEHAVIOR CHALLENGE

1. Identify three patterns of reinforcement and provide an example of how each is used in a marketing context.
2. Describe the functions of short-term and long-term memory. What is the apparent relationship between the two?
3. Devise a "product jingle memory test." Compile a list of brands that are or have been associated with memorable jingles, such as Chiquita Banana or Alka-Seltzer. Read this list to friends, and see how many jingles are remembered. You may be surprised at the level of recall.
4. Identify some important characteristics for a product with a well-known brand name. Based on these attributes, generate a list of possible brand extension or licensing opportunities, as well as some others that would most likely not be accepted by consumers.
5. Collect some pictures of "classic" products that have high nostalgia value. Show these pictures to consumers, and allow them to free associate. Analyze the types of memories that are evoked, and think about how these associations might be employed in a product's promotional strategy.

NOTES

1. Fred Kaplan, "Levi's Latest Vintage Has Some Folks Panting," *The Boston Globe* [Online] (March 21, 1998).
2. Jonathan Eig, "Nostalgic Fans Use Internet to Save Quirky Quisp from a Cereal Killing," *The Wall Street Journal Interactive Edition* (April 24, 2000).
3. Jennifer Cody, "Here's a New Way to Rationalize Not Cleaning Out Your Closets," *New York Times* (June 14, 1994): B1.
4. Stuart Elliott, "At 75, Mr. Peanut Is Getting Expanded Role at Planters,"*New York Times* (September 23, 1991): D15.
5. Todd Pruzan, "Brand Illusions," *New York Times on the Web* (September 12, 1999).
6. Robert A. Baron, *Psychology: The Essential Science* (Boston: Allyn & Bacon, 1989).
7. Quoted in Jane E. Brody, "Cybersex Gives Birth to a Psychological Disorder," *The New York Times on the Web* (May 16, 2000).
8. Richard A. Feinberg, "Credit Cards as Spending Facilitating Stimuli: A Conditioning Interpretation," *Journal of Consumer Research* 13 (December 1986): 348–56.
9. R. A. Rescorla, "Pavlovian Conditioning: It's Not What You Think It Is," *American*

Psychologist 43 (1988): 151–60; Elnora W. Stuart, Terence A. Shimp, and Randall W. Engle, "Classical Conditioning of Consumer Attitudes: Four Experiments in an Advertising Context," *Journal of Consumer Research* 14 (December 1987): 334–39.
10. Leigh Gallagher, "Endangered Species," *Forbes* (May 31, 1999): 105; "Anemic Crocodile," *Forbes* (August 15, 1994): 116.
11. James Ward, Barbara Loken, Ivan Ross, and Tedi Hasapopoulous, "The Influence of Physical Similarity of Affect and Attribute Perceptions from National Brands to Private Label Brands," in Terence A. Shimp et al., eds, *American Marketing Educators' Conference* (Chicago: American Marketing Association, 1986): 51–56.
12. Judith Lynne Zaichkowsky and Richard Neil Simpson, "The Effect of Experience with a Brand Imitator on the Original Brand," *Marketing Letters* 7, no. 1 (1996): 31–39.
13. Janice S. Griffiths and Mary Zimmer, "Masked Brands and Consumers' Need for Uniqueness," *American Marketing Association* (Summer 1998): 145–53.
14. Chris T. Allen and Thomas J. Madden, "A Closer Look at Classical Conditioning,"

Journal of Consumer Research 12 (December 1985): 301–15; Chester A. Insko and William F. Oakes, "Awareness and the Conditioning of Attitudes," *Journal of Personality and Social Psychology* 4 (November 1966): 487–96; Carolyn K. Staats and Arthur W. Staats, "Meaning Established by Classical Conditioning," *Journal of Experimental Psychology* 54 (July 1957): 74–80.
15. Randi Priluck Grossman and Brian D. Till, "The Persistence of Classically Conditioned Brand Attitudes," *Journal of Advertising* 21, no. 1 (1998): 23–31.
16. Kevin Lane Keller, "Conceptualizing, Measuring, and Managing Customer-Based Brand Equity," *Journal of Marketing* 57 (January 1993): 1–22.
17. Herbert Krugman, "Low Recall and High Recognition of Advertising," *Journal of Advertising Research* (February/March 1986): 79–80.
18. Gerald J. Gorn, "The Effects of Music in Advertising on Choice Behavior: A Classical Conditioning Approach," *Journal of Marketing* 46 (Winter 1982): 94–101.
19. Noreen Klein, Virginia Tech, personal communication (April 2000); Calvin Bierley, Frances K. McSweeney and Renee

Vannieuwkerk, "Classical Conditioning of Preferences for Stimuli," *Journal of Consumer Research* 12 (December 1985): 316–23; James J. Kellaris and Anthony D. Cox, "The Effects of Background Music in Advertising: A Reassessment," *Journal of Consumer Research* 16 (June 1989): 113–18.

20. Frances K. McSweeney and Calvin Bierley, "Recent Developments in Classical Conditioning," *Journal of Consumer Research* 11 (September 1984): 619–31.

21. Basil G. Englis, "The Reinforcement Properties of Music Videos: 'I Want My . . . I Want My . . . I Want My . . . MTV'" (Paper presented at the meetings of the Association for Consumer Research, New Orleans, 1989).

22. Dana Rubin, "You've Seen the Game. Now Buy the Underwear," *New York Times* (September 11, 1994): F5.

23. Peter H. Farquhar, "Brand Equity," *Marketing Insights* (Summer, 1989): 59.

24. Farquhar, "Brand Equity."

25. "Charles Manson Gets Royalties on T-Shirts," *New York Times* (November 25, 1993): A21.

26. Jessica Goldbogen, "A Whole New Mickey Mouse," *HFN* 74, no. 16 (April 17, 2000): 10; "Pokemon Character Body Art," *Product Alert* (April 10, 2000): 30; Andee Joyce, "Two Guys, Two Beers . . . But It's Three Stooges on the Label," *Beverage World* 118 (Mar 31–Apr 30, 1999): 675: 12.

27. "Look-Alikes Mimic Familiar Packages," *New York Times* (August 9, 1986): D1.

28. Judith Lynne Zaichkowsky and Richard Neil Simpson, "The Effect of Experience with a Brand Imitator on the Original Brand," *Marketing Letters* 7, no. 1 (1996): 31–39.

29. For a comprehensive approach to consumer behavior based on operant conditioning principles, see Gordon R. Foxall, "Behavior Analysis and Consumer Psychology," *Journal of Economic Psychology* 15 (March 1994): 5–91.

30. Youngme Moon, "Intimate Exchanges: Using Computers to Elicit Self-Disclosure from Consumers," *Journal of Consumer Research* 26, no. 3 (2000): 323–39.

31. Blaise J. Bergiel and Christine Trosclair, "Instrumental Learning: Its Application to Customer Satisfaction," *Journal of Consumer Marketing* 2 (Fall 1985): 23–28.

32. Jane Costello, "Do Offers of Free Mileage Sell? The Proof Is in Pudding Guy," *The Wall Street Journal Interactive Edition* (January 24, 2000).

33. Ellen J. Langer, *The Psychology of Control* (Beverly Hills, CA: Sage, 1983).

34. Robert B. Cialdini, *Influence: Science and Practice*, 2d ed. (New York: William Morrow, 1984).

35. Chris T. Allen and Thomas J. Madden, "A Closer Look at Classical Conditioning," *Journal of Consumer Research* 12

(December 1985): 301–15; see also Terence A. Shimp, Elnora W. Stuart, and Randall W. Engle, "A Program of Classical Conditioning Experiments Testing Variations in the Conditioned Stimulus and Context," *Journal of Consumer Research* 18 (June 1991): 1–12.

36. Terence A. Shimp, "Neo-Pavlovian Conditioning and Its Implications for Consumer Theory and Research," in Thomas S. Robertson and Harold H. Kassarjian, eds., *Handbook of Consumer Behavior* (Upper Saddle River, NJ: Prentice Hall, 1991).

37. Albert Bandura, *Social Foundations of Thought and Action: A Social Cognitive View* (Upper Saddle River, NJ: Prentice Hall, 1986).

38. Bandura, *Social Foundations of Thought and Action*.

39. R. C. Atkinson and I. M. Shiffrin, "Human Memory: A Proposed System and Its Control Processes," in K. W. Spence and J. T. Spence, eds., *The Psychology of Learning and Motivation: Advances in Research and Theory* 2 (New York: Academic Press, 1968): 89–195.

40. James R. Bettman, "Memory Factors in Consumer Choice: A Review," *Journal of Marketing* (Spring 1979): 37–53; for a study that explores the relative impact of internal versus external memory on brand choice, see Joseph W. Alba, Howard Marmorstein, and Amitava Chattopadhyay, "Transitions in Preference over Time: The Effects of Memory on Message Persuasiveness," *Journal of Marketing Research* 29, no. 4 (1992): 406–16.

41. Kathryn R. Braun, "Postexperience Advertising Effects on Consumer Memory," *Journal of Consumer Research* 25 (March 1999): 319–34.

42. David S. Koeppel, "Tales from the Crypt: Storing e-Mail to be Sent After Your Death," *The New York Times on the Web* (April 13, 2000).

43. Kim Robertson, "Recall and Recognition Effects of Brand Name Imagery," *Psychology & Marketing* 4 (Spring 1987): 3–15.

44. Endel Tulving, "Remembering and Knowing the Past," *American Scientist* 77 (July/August 1989): 361.

45. Rashmi Adaval and Robert S. Wyer Jr. "The Role of Narratives in Consumer Information Processing," *Journal of Consumer Psychology* 7, no. 3 (1998): 207–46.

46. George A. Miller, "The Magical Number Seven, Plus or Minus Two: Some Limits on Our Capacity for Processing Information," *Psychological Review* 63 (1956): 81–97.

47. James N. MacGregor, "Short-Term Memory Capacity: Limitation or Optimization?" *Psychological Review* 94 (1987): 107–8.

48. See Catherine A. Cole and Michael J. Houston, "Encoding and Media Effects on Consumer Learning Deficiencies in the Elderly," *Journal of Marketing Research* 24 (February 1987): 55–64; A. M. Collins and E. F. Loftus, "A Spreading Activation Theory of Semantic Processing," *Psychological Review* 82 (1975): 407–28; Fergus I. M. Craik and Robert S. Lockhart, "Levels of Processing: A Framework for Memory Research," *Journal of Verbal Learning and Verbal Behavior* 11 (1972): 671–84.

49. Walter A. Henry, "The Effect of Information-Processing Ability on Processing Accuracy," *Journal of Consumer Research* 7 (June 1980): 42–48.

50. Anthony G. Greenwald and Clark Leavitt, "Audience Involvement in Advertising: Four Levels," *Journal of Consumer Research* 11 (June 1984): 581–92.

51. Kevin Lane Keller, "Memory Factors in Advertising: The Effect of Advertising Retrieval Cues on Brand Evaluations," *Journal of Consumer Research* 14 (December 1987): 316–33. For a discussion of processing operations that occur during brand choice, see Gabriel Biehal and Dipankar Chakravarti, "Consumers Use of Memory and External Information in Choice: Macro and Micro Perspectives," *Journal of Consumer Research* 12 (March 1986): 382–405.

52. Susan T. Fiske and Shelley E. Taylor, *Social Cognition* (Reading, MA: Addison-Wesley, 1984).

53. Deborah Roedder John and John C. Whitney Jr., "The Development of Consumer Knowledge in Children: A Cognitive Structure Approach," *Journal of Consumer Research* 12 (March 1986): 406–17.

54. Michael R. Solomon, Carol Surprenant, John A. Czepiel, and Evelyn G. Gutman, "A Role Theory Perspective on Dyadic Interactions: The Service Encounter," *Journal of Marketing* 49 (Winter 1985): 99–111.

55. Roger W. Morrell, Denise C. Park, and Leonard W. Poon, "Quality of Instructions on Prescription Drug Labels: Effects on Memory and Comprehension in Young and Old Adults," *The Gerontologist* 29 (1989): 345–54.

56. Frank R. Kardes, Gurumurthy Kalyanaram, Murali Chandrashekaran, and Ronald J. Dornoff, "Brand Retrieval, Consideration Set Composition, Consumer Choice, and the Pioneering Advantage," (unpublished manuscript, The University of Cincinnati, Ohio, 1992).

57. Judith Lynne Zaichkowsky and Padma Vipat, "Inferences from Brand Names" (paper presented at the European meeting of the Association for Consumer Research, Amsterdam, June 1992).

58. Herbert E. Krugman, "Low Recall and High Recognition of Advertising," *Journal of Advertising Research* (February/March 1986): 79–86.

59. Rik G. M. Pieters and Tammo H. A. Bijmolt, "Consumer Memory for Television Advertising: A Field Study of Duration, Serial Position, and Competition Effects," *Journal of Consumer Research* 23 (March 1997): 362–72.

60. Keller, "Memory Factors in Advertising."

61. Michelle Wirth Fellman, "Mesmerizing Method Gets Real Results," *Marketing News* (July 20, 1998): 1.

62. Ruth Shalit, "The Return of the Hidden Persuaders," www.salon.com (September 27, 1999).

63. Eric J. Johnson and J. Edward Russo, "Product Familiarity and Learning New Information," *Journal of Consumer Research* 11 (June 1984): 542–50.

64. Eric J. Johnson and J. Edward Russo, "Product Familiarity and Learning New Information," in Kent Monroe, ed., *Advances in Consumer Research* 8 (Ann Arbor, MI: Association for Consumer Research, 1981): 151–55; John G. Lynch and Thomas K. Srull, "Memory and Attentional Factors in Consumer Choice: Concepts and Research Methods," *Journal of Consumer Research* 9 (June 1982): 18–37.

65. Julie A. Edell and Kevin Lane Keller, "The Information Processing of Coordinated Media Campaigns," *Journal of Marketing Research* 26 (May 1989): 149–64.

66. Lynch and Srull, "Memory and Attentional Factors in Consumer Choice."

67. Joseph W. Alba and Amitava Chattopadhyay, "Salience Effects in Brand Recall," *Journal of Marketing Research* 23 (November 1986): 363–70; Elizabeth C. Hirschman and Michael R. Solomon, "Utilitarian, Aesthetic, and Familiarity Responses to Verbal Versus Visual Advertisements," in Thomas C. Kinnear, ed., *Advances in Consumer Research* 11 (Provo, UT: Association for Consumer Research, 1984): 426–31.

68. Susan E. Heckler and Terry L. Childers, "The Role of Expectancy and Relevancy in Memory for Verbal and Visual Information: What is Incongruency?" *Journal of Consumer Research* 18 (March 1992): 475–92.

69. Russell H. Fazio, Paul M. Herr, and Martha C. Powell, "On the Development and Strength of Category-Brand Associations in Memory: The Case of Mystery Ads," *Journal of Consumer Psychology* 1, no. 1 (1992): 1–13.

70. Hirschman and Solomon, "Utilitarian, Aesthetic, and Familiarity Responses to Verbal Versus Visual Advertisements."

71. Terry Childers and Michael Houston, "Conditions for a Picture-Superiority Effect on Consumer Memory," *Journal of Consumer Research* 11 (September 1984): 643–54; Terry Childers, Susan Heckler, and Michael Houston, "Memory for the Visual and Verbal Components of Print Advertisements," *Psychology & Marketing* 3 (Fall 1986): 147–50.

72. Werner Krober-Riel, "Effects of Emotional Pictorial Elements in Ads Analyzed by Means of Eye Movement Monitoring," in Thomas C. Kinnear, ed., *Advances in Consumer Research* 11 (Provo, UT: Association for Consumer Research, 1984): 591–96.

73. Hans-Bernd Brosius, "Influence of Presentation Features and News Context on Learning from Television News," *Journal of Broadcasting & Electronic Media* 33 (Winter 1989): 1–14.

74. Raymond R. Burke and Thomas K. Srull, "Competitive Interference and Consumer Memory for Advertising," *Journal of Consumer Research* 15 (June 1988): 55–68.

75. Burke and Srull, "Competitive Interference and Consumer Memory for Advertising."

76. Johnson and Russo, "Product Familiarity and Learning New Information."

77. Joan Meyers-Levy, "The Influence of Brand Name's Association Set Size and Word Frequency on Brand Memory," *Journal of Consumer Research* 16 (September 1989): 197–208.

78. Michael H. Baumgardner, Michael R. Leippe, David L. Ronis, and Anthony G. Greenwald, "In Search of Reliable Persuasion Effects: II. Associative Interference and Persistence of Persuasion in a Message-Dense Environment," *Journal of Personality and Social Psychology* 45 (September 1983): 524–37.

79. Alba and Chattopadhyay, "Salience Effects in Brand Recall."

80. Margaret Henderson Blair, Allan R. Kuse, David H. Furse, and David W. Stewart, "Advertising in a New and Competitive Environment: Persuading Consumers to Buy," *Business Horizons* 30 (November/December 1987): 20.

81. Lynch and Srull, "Memory and Attentional Factors in Consumer Choice."

82. Russell W. Belk, "Possessions and the Extended Self," *Journal of Consumer Research* 15 (September 1988): 139–68.

83. Hans Baumgartner, Mita Sujan, and James R. Bettman, "Autobiographical Memories, Affect and Consumer Information Processing," *Journal of Consumer Psychology* 1 (January 1992): 53–82; Mita Sujan, James R. Bettman, and Hans Baumgartner, "Autobiographi-cal Memories and Consumer Judgments" (Working Paper No. 183, Pennsylvania State University, University Park, 1992).

84. Russell W. Belk, "The Role of Possessions in Constructing and Maintaining a Sense of Past," in Marvin E. Goldberg, Gerald Gorn, and Richard W. Pollay, eds., *Advances in Consumer Research* 16, (Provo, UT: Association for Consumer Research, 1989): 669–78.

85. Dan Morse, no headline, *The Wall Street Journal Interactive Edition* (February 4, 1999).

86. Susan L. Holak and William J. Havlena, "Feelings, Fantasies, and Memories: An Examination of the Emotional Components of Nostalgia," *Journal of Business Research* 42 (1998): 217–26.

87. Paula Mergenhagen, "The Reunion Market," *American Demographics* (April 1996): 30–34.

88. Quoted in Keith Naughton and Bill Vlasic, "Nostalgia Boom," *Business Week* (March 23, 1998): 59–64.

89. Diane Crispell, "Which Good Old Days," *American Demographics* (April 1996): 35.

90. Keith Naughton and Bill Vlasic, "Nostalgia Boom," *Business Week* (March 23, 1998): 59–64.

91. Jane L. Levere, "Lingerie Maker Hopes Monroe Image Hasn't Lost Sizzle," *The New York Times News Service* (February 10, 1997).

92. Roger Thurow, "Bucharest is Plastered with J. R. Ewing in an Ad Push by Russian Oil Company," *The Wall Street Journal Interactive Edition* (December 21, 1999).

93. Jean Halliday, "VW Beetle: Liz Vanzura," *Advertising Age* (June 28, 1999): S4.

94. Daniel Howes, "VW Beetle is a Bust in Europe, Where Golf Is Car of Choice" *Detroit News* (April 13, 1999): B1.

95. Thomas F. Jones, "Our Musical Heritage Is Being Raided," *San Francisco Examiner* May 23, 1997.

96. Quoted in Kevin Goldman, "A Few Rockers Refuse to Turn Tunes into Ads," *New York Times* (August 25, 1995): B1.

97. Morris B. Holbrook and Robert M. Schindler, "Some Exploratory Findings on the Development of Musical Tastes," *Journal of Consumer Research* 16 (June 1989): 119–24; Morris B. Holbrook and Robert M. Schindler, "Market Segmentation Based on Age and Attitude Toward the Past: Concepts, Methods, and Findings Concerning Nostalgic Influences on Consumer Tastes," *Journal of Business Research* 37 (September 1996)1: 27–40.

98. "Only 38% of T.V. Audience Links Brands with Ads," *Marketing News* (January 6, 1984): 10.

99. "Terminal Television," *American Demographics* (January 1987): 15.

100. Richard P. Bagozzi and Alvin J. Silk, "Recall, Recognition, and the Measurement of Memory for Print Advertisements," *Marketing Science* 2 (1983): 95–134.

101. Adam Finn, "Print Ad Recognition Readership Scores: An Information Processing Perspective," *Journal of Marketing Research* 25 (May 1988): 168–77.

102. Bettman, "Memory Factors in Consumer Choice."

103. Mark A. Deturck and Gerald M. Goldhaber, "Effectiveness of Product Warning Labels: Effects of Consumers' Information Processing Objectives," *Journal of Consumer Affairs* 23, no. 1 (1989): 111–25.

104. Finn, "Print Ad Recognition Readership Scores."

105. Surendra N. Singh and Gilbert A. Churchill Jr., "Response-Bias-Free Recognition Tests to Measure Advertising Effects," *Journal of Advertising Research* (June/July 1987): 23–36.

106. William A. Cook, "Telescoping and Memory's Other Tricks," *Journal of Advertising Research* 27 (February/March 1987): 5–8.

107. "On a Diet? Don't Trust Your Memory," *Psychology Today* (October 1989): 12.

108. Hubert A. Zielske and Walter A. Henry, "Remembering and Forgetting Television Ads," *Journal of Advertising Research* 20 (April 1980): 7–13; Cara Greenberg, "Future Worth: Before It's Hot, Grab It," *New York Times* (1992): C1; S. K. List, "More Than Fun and Games," *American Demographics* 4 (August 1992): 44.

As Basil scans the menu at the trendy health food restaurant Judy has dragged him to, he reflects on what a man will give up for love. Now that Judy has become a die-hard vegetarian, she's slowly but surely working on him to forsake those juicy steaks and burgers for healthier fare. He can't even hide from tofu and other vegan delights at school;

the dining facility in his dorm just started offering "veggie" alternatives to its usual assortment of greasy "mystery meats" and other delicacies he has come to love.

Judy is totally into it; she claims that eating this way not only cuts out unwanted fat, but is good for the environment. Just

his luck to fall head-over-heels for a "tree-hugger."

As Basil gamely tries to decide between the stuffed artichokes with red pepper vinaigrette and the grilled marinated zucchini, fantasies of a sizzling 24-ounce T-bone dance before his eyes.

4

MOTIVATION AND VALUES

INTRODUCTION

Judy certainly is not alone in believing that eating green is good for the body, the soul, and the planet. It is estimated that seven percent of the general population is vegetarian, and women and younger people are even more likely to adopt a meatless diet. An additional ten to twenty percent of consumers are interested in vegetarian options in addition to their normal fare of dead animals. To reach these veggie lovin' consumers, many companies have developed meat-free products and services. For example, Healthy's Inc., a natural foods company, launched PlanetVeggie.com—"the world's first and only all-vegetarian cyber superstore." It also sidelines as a vegetarian resource offering nutrition and vegetarian lifestyle advice. Some college cafeterias have tried to meet the growing interest in things green by contracting with a branded franchise called Global Vegetarian to provide vegetarian recipes to students.[1]

The forces that drive people to buy and use products are generally straightforward, as when a person chooses what to have for lunch. As hard-core vegans demonstrate, however, even the consumption of basic food products may also be related to wide-ranging beliefs regarding what is appropriate or desirable. In some cases, these emotional responses create a deep commitment to the product. Sometimes people are not even fully aware of the forces that drive them toward some products and away from others. Often these choices are influenced by the person's values—his or her priorities and beliefs about the world.

To understand motivation is to understand why consumers do what they do. Why do some people choose to bungee jump off a bridge or stand in Times Square screaming for Carson Daly to bring them up to the studio on MTV's Total Request Live (TRL) show, whereas others spend their leisure time playing chess or gardening? Whether to quench a thirst, kill boredom, or to attain some deep spiritual experience, we do everything for a reason, even if we can't articulate what that reason is. Marketing students are taught from Day One that the goal of marketing is to satisfy consumers' needs. However, this insight is useless unless we can discover *what* those needs are and *why* they exist. A beer commercial once asked, "Why ask why?" In this chapter, we'll find out.

THE MOTIVATION PROCESS

Motivation refers to the processes that cause people to behave as they do. It occurs when a need is aroused that the consumer wishes to satisfy. Once a need has been activated, a state of tension exists that drives the consumer to attempt to reduce or eliminate the need. This need may be *utilitarian* (i.e., a desire to achieve some functional or practical benefit, as when a person loads up on green vegetables for nutritional reasons) or it may be *hedonic* (i.e., an experiential need, involving emotional responses or fantasies, as when Basil thinks longingly about a juicy steak). The desired end state is the consumer's **goal.** Marketers try to create products and services that will provide the desired benefits and permit the consumer to reduce this tension.

Whether the need is utilitarian or hedonic, a discrepancy exists between the consumer's present state and some ideal state. This gulf creates a state of tension.

This ad for exercise equipment shows men a desired state (as dictated by contemporary Western culture), and suggests a solution (purchase of the equipment) to attain it.

The magnitude of this tension determines the urgency the consumer feels to reduce the tension. This degree of arousal is called a **drive.** A basic need can be satisfied in any number of ways, and the specific path a person chooses is influenced both by his or her unique set of experiences and by the values instilled by the culture in which the person has been raised.

These personal and cultural factors combine to create a **want,** which is one manifestation of a need. For example, hunger is a basic need that must be satisfied by all; the lack of food creates a tension state that can be reduced by the intake of such products as cheeseburgers, double fudge Oreo cookies, raw fish, or bean sprouts. The specific route to drive reduction is culturally and individually determined. Once the goal is attained, tension is reduced and the motivation recedes (for the time being). Motivation can be described in terms of its *strength*, or the pull it exerts on the consumer, and its *direction*, or the particular way the consumer attempts to reduce motivational tension.

MOTIVATIONAL STRENGTH

The degree to which a person is willing to expend energy to reach one goal as opposed to another reflects his or her underlying motivation to attain that goal. Many theories have been advanced to explain why people behave the way they do. Most share the basic idea that people have some finite amount of energy that must be directed toward certain goals.

Biological Versus Learned Needs

Early work on motivation ascribed behavior to instinct, the innate patterns of behavior that are universal in a species. This view is now largely discredited. For one thing, the existence of an instinct is difficult to prove or disprove. The instinct is inferred from the behavior it is supposed to explain (this type of circular explanation is called a *tautology*).[2] It is like saying that a consumer buys products that are status symbols because he or she is motivated to attain status, which is hardly a satisfying explanation.

Drive Theory

Drive theory focuses on biological needs that produce unpleasant states of arousal (e.g., your stomach grumbles during a morning class). We are motivated to reduce the tension caused by this arousal. Tension reduction has been proposed as a basic mechanism governing human behavior.

In a marketing context, tension refers to the unpleasant state that exists if a person's consumption needs are not fulfilled. A person may be grumpy if he hasn't eaten, or he may be dejected or angry if he cannot afford that new car he wants. This state activates goal-oriented behavior, which attempts to reduce or eliminate this unpleasant state and return to a balanced one called **homeostasis.**

Those behaviors that are successful in reducing the drive by satisfying the underlying need are strengthened and tend to be repeated. (This aspect of the learning process was discussed in Chapter 3.) Your motivation to leave class early to grab a snack would be greater if you hadn't eaten in 24 hours than if you had eaten only two hours earlier. If you did sneak out and got indigestion after, say, wolfing down a package of Twinkies, you would be less likely to repeat this behavior the next time you wanted a snack. One's degree of motivation, then, depends on the distance between one's present state and the goal.

Drive theory runs into difficulties when it tries to explain some facets of human behavior that run counter to its predictions. People often do things that increase a drive state rather than decrease it. For example, people may delay gratification. If you know you are going out for a lavish dinner, you might decide to forego a snack earlier in the day even though you are hungry at that time.

Expectancy Theory

Most current explanations of motivation focus on cognitive factors rather than biological ones to understand what drives behavior. **Expectancy theory** suggests that behavior is largely pulled by expectations of achieving desirable outcomes—positive incentives—rather than pushed from within. We choose one product over another because we expect this choice to have more positive consequences for us. Thus the term drive is used here more loosely to refer to both physical and cognitive processes.

MOTIVATIONAL DIRECTION

Motives have direction as well as strength. They are goal oriented in that specific objectives are desired to satisfy a need. Most goals can be reached by a number of routes, and the objective of marketers is to convince consumers that the alternative they offer provides the best chance to attain the goal. For example, a consumer who decides that she needs a pair of jeans to help her reach her goal of being accepted by others can choose among Levi's, Wranglers, Jnco, Calvin Klein, and many other alternatives, each of which promises to deliver certain benefits.

Needs Versus Wants

The specific way a need is satisfied depends on the individual's unique history, learning experiences, and cultural environment. The particular form of consumption used to satisfy a need is termed a want. For example, two classmates may feel their stomachs rumbling during a lunchtime lecture. If neither person has eaten since the night before, the strength of their respective needs (hunger) would be about the same. However, the ways each person goes about satisfying this need might be quite different. The first person may be a vegan like Judy who fantasizes about gulping down a big handful of trail mix, whereas the second person may be a meat hound like Basil who is aroused by the prospect of a greasy cheeseburger and fries.

Types of Needs

People are born with a need for certain elements necessary to maintain life, such as food, water, air, and shelter. These are called *biogenic needs*. People have many other needs, however, that are not innate. *Psychogenic needs* are acquired in the process of becoming a member of a culture. These include the need for status, power, affiliation, and so on. Psychogenic needs reflect the priorities of a culture, and their effect on behavior will vary from environment to environment. For example, an American consumer may be driven to devote a good chunk of his income to products that permit him to display his wealth and status, whereas his Japanese counterpart may work equally hard to ensure that he does not stand out from his group.

Some critics argue that many of our "needs" are actually wants that have been created by marketers who prey on our insecurities. What do you think?

Consumers can also be motivated to satisfy either utilitarian or hedonic needs. The satisfaction of *utilitarian needs* implies that consumers will emphasize the objective, tangible attributes of products, such as miles per gallon in a car; the amount of fat, calories, and protein in a cheeseburger; and the durability of a pair of blue jeans. *Hedonic needs* are subjective and experiential; consumers might rely on a product to meet their needs for excitement, self-confidence, fantasy, and so on. Of course, consumers can be motivated to purchase a product because it provides *both* types of benefits. For example, a mink coat might be bought because of the luxurious image it portrays and because it also happens to keep one warm through the long cold winter.

Motivational Conflicts

A goal has *valence,* which means that it can be positive or negative. A positively valued goal is one toward which consumers direct their behavior; they are motivated to *approach* the goal and will seek out products that will be instrumental in attaining it. However, not all behavior is motivated by the desire to approach a goal. As we saw in the previous chapter's discussion of negative reinforcement, consumers may instead be motivated to avoid a negative outcome. They will structure their purchases or consumption activities to reduce the chances of attaining this end result. For example, many consumers work hard to *avoid* rejection, a negative goal. They will stay away from products that they associate with social disapproval. Products such as deodorants and mouthwash frequently rely on consumers' negative motivation by depicting the onerous social consequences of underarm odor or bad breath.

Because a purchase decision can involve more than one source of motivation, consumers often find themselves in situations in which different motives, both positive and negative, conflict with one another. Because marketers are attempting to satisfy consumers' needs, they can also be helpful by providing possible solutions to these dilemmas. As shown in Figure 4.1, three general types

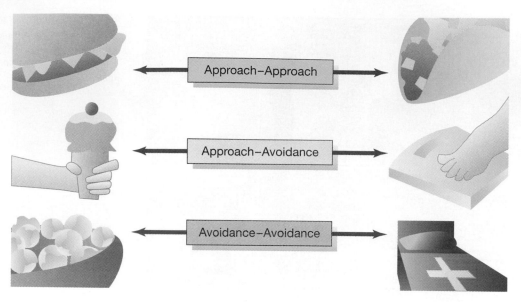

Figure 4.1
Three Types of Motivational Conflicts

of conflicts can occur: approach–approach, approach–avoidance, and avoidance–avoidance.

Approach–Approach Conflict

In an approach–approach conflict, a person must choose between two desirable alternatives. A student might be torn between going home for the holidays or going on a skiing trip with friends. Or, she might have to choose between two CDs.

The **theory of cognitive dissonance** is based on the premise that people have a need for order and consistency in their lives and that a state of tension is created when beliefs or behaviors conflict with one another. The conflict that arises when choosing between two alternatives may be resolved through a process of cognitive dissonance reduction, one in which people are motivated to reduce this inconsistency (or dissonance) and thus eliminate unpleasant tension.[3]

A state of dissonance occurs when there is a psychological inconsistency between two or more beliefs or behaviors. It often occurs when a consumer must make a choice between two products, both of which usually possess both good and bad qualities. By choosing one product and not the other, the person gets the bad qualities of the chosen product and loses out on the good qualities of the unchosen one.

This loss creates an unpleasant, dissonant state that the person is motivated to reduce. People tend to convince themselves, after the fact, that the choice they made was the smart one by finding additional reasons to support the alternative they chose, or perhaps by "discovering" flaws with the option they did not choose. A marketer can resolve an approach–approach conflict by bundling several benefits together. For example, Miller Lite's claim that it is "less filling" and "tastes great" allows the drinker to "have his beer *and* drink it too."

Approach–Avoidance Conflict

Many of the products and services we desire have negative consequences attached to them as well. We may feel guilty or ostentatious when buying a status-laden product such as a fur coat, or we might feel like a glutton when contemplating

The Partnership for a Drug-Free America points out the negative consequences of drug addiction for those who are tempted to start.

a tempting package of Twinkies. When we desire a goal but wish to avoid it at the same time, an approach–avoidance conflict exists.

Some solutions to these conflicts include the proliferation of fake furs, which eliminate guilt about harming animals to make a fashion statement, and the success of diet foods, such as those produced by Weight Watchers, that promise good food without the calories (weight-watchers.com). Many marketers try to overcome guilt by convincing consumers that they are deserving of luxuries (e.g., when the model for L'Oréal cosmetics exclaims, "Because I'm worth it!").

Avoidance–Avoidance Conflict

Sometimes consumers find themselves "caught between a rock and a hard place." They may face a choice with two undesirable alternatives, for instance the option of either throwing more money into an old car or buying a new one. Marketers frequently address this conflict with messages that stress the unforeseen benefits of choosing one option (e.g., by emphasizing special credit plans to ease the pain of car payments).

Classifying Consumer Needs

Much research has been done on classifying human needs. On the one hand, some psychologists have tried to define a universal inventory of needs that could be traced systematically to explain virtually all behavior. One such effort, developed by Henry Murray, delineates a set of 20 psychogenic needs that (sometimes in combination) result in specific behaviors. These needs include such dimensions as *autonomy* (being independent), *defendance* (defending the self against criticism), and even *play* (engaging in pleasurable activities).[4]

Murray's need structure serves as the basis for a number of widely used personality tests such as the Thematic Apperception Technique (TAT) and the Edward's Personal Preference Schedule (EPPS). In the TAT, test subjects are shown four to six ambiguous pictures and asked to write answers to four directing questions about the pictures. These questions are: (1) What is happening?; (2) What has led up to this situation?; (3) What is being thought?; (4) What will happen? Four minutes of writing time is allowed for each story. Each answer is then analyzed for references to certain needs and scored whenever that need is mentioned. The theory behind the test is that people will freely project their own subconscious needs to the ambiguous picture. By getting their responses to the picture, you are really getting at the person's true needs for achievement or affiliation or whatever other need may be dominant. Murray believed that everyone has the same basic set of needs, but that individuals differ in their priority ranking of these needs.[5]

Specific Needs and Buying Behavior

Other motivational approaches have focused on specific needs and their ramifications for behavior. For example, individuals with a high *need for achievement* strongly value personal accomplishment.[6] They place a premium on products and services that signify success because these consumption items provide feedback about the realization of their goals. These consumers are good prospects for products that provide evidence of their achievement. One study of working women found that those who were high in achievement motivation were more likely to choose clothing they considered businesslike and less likely to be interested in apparel that accentuated their femininity.[7] Some other important needs that are relevant to consumer behavior include the following:

- *Need for affiliation* (to be in the company of other people):[8] This need is relevant to products and services that are "consumed" in groups and alleviate loneliness, such as team sports, bars, and shopping malls.
- *Need for power* (to control one's environment):[9] Many products and services allow consumers to feel that they have mastery over their surroundings, ranging from "hopped-up" muscle cars and loud boom boxes (large portable radios) that impose one's musical tastes on others to luxury resorts that promise to respond to the customer's every whim.
- *Need for uniqueness* (to assert one's individual identity):[10] This need is satisfied by products that pledge to accentuate a consumer's distinctive qualities. For example, Cachet perfume claims to be "as individual as you are."

Maslow's Hierarchy of Needs

One influential approach to motivation was proposed by the psychologist Abraham Maslow. Maslow's approach is a general one, originally developed to understand personal growth and the attainment of "peak experiences."[11] Maslow formulated a hierarchy of biogenic and psychogenic needs in which levels of motives are specified. A hierarchical approach implies that the order of development is fixed—that is, a certain level must be attained before the next, higher one is activated. This universal approach to motivation has been embraced by marketers because it (indirectly) specifies certain types of product benefits people might be looking for, depending on the different stages in their development and/or their environmental conditions.

These levels are summarized in Figure 4.2. At each level, different priorities exist in terms of the product benefits a consumer is looking for. Ideally, an individual progresses up the hierarchy until his or her dominant motivation is a focus on

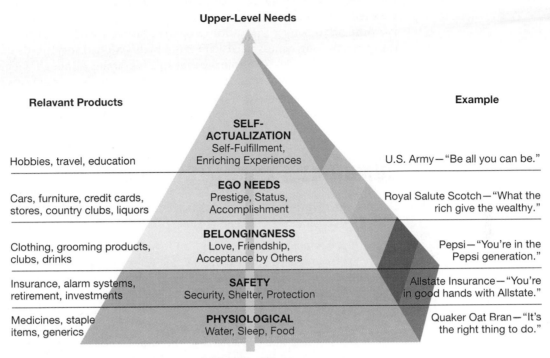

Upper-Level Needs

Relevant Products   **Example**

SELF-ACTUALIZATION
Self-Fulfillment, Enriching Experiences

Hobbies, travel, education   U.S. Army—"Be all you can be."

EGO NEEDS
Prestige, Status, Accomplishment

Cars, furniture, credit cards, stores, country clubs, liquors   Royal Salute Scotch—"What the rich give the wealthy."

BELONGINGNESS
Love, Friendship, Acceptance by Others

Clothing, grooming products, clubs, drinks   Pepsi—"You're in the Pepsi generation."

SAFETY
Security, Shelter, Protection

Insurance, alarm systems, retirement, investments   Allstate Insurance—"You're in good hands with Allstate."

PHYSIOLOGICAL
Water, Sleep, Food

Medicines, staple items, generics   Quaker Oat Bran—"It's the right thing to do."

Lower-Level Needs

Figure 4.2
Levels of Needs in the Maslow Hierarchy

"ultimate" goals, such as justice and beauty. Unfortunately, this state is difficult to achieve (at least on a regular basis); most of us have to be satisfied with occasional glimpses, or *peak experiences.*

The basic lesson of Maslow's hierarchy is that one must first satisfy basic needs before progressing up the ladder (i.e., a starving man is not interested in status symbols, friendship, or self-fulfillment). That implies that consumers value different product attributes depending upon what is currently available to them. For example, consumers in the former Eastern bloc are now bombarded with images of luxury goods, yet may still have trouble obtaining basic necessities. In one study Romanian students named the products they hoped to acquire. Their wish lists included not only the expected items such as sports cars and the latest model televisions, but also staples like water, soap, furniture, and food.[12]

The application of this hierarchy by marketers has been somewhat simplistic, especially as the same product or activity can satisfy a number of different needs. For example, one study found that gardening can satisfy needs at every level of the hierarchy:[13]

- *Physiological:* "I like to work in the soil."
- *Safety:* "I feel safe in the garden."
- *Social:* "I can share my produce with others."
- *Esteem:* "I can create something of beauty."
- *Self-actualization:* "My garden gives me a sense of peace."

Another problem with taking Maslow's hierarchy too literally is that it is culture-bound. The assumptions of the hierarchy may be restricted to Western culture. People in other cultures (or, for that matter, in Western culture itself) may question the order of the levels as specified. A religious person who has taken a vow of celibacy would not necessarily agree that physiological needs must be satisfied before self-fulfillment can occur.

Similarly, many Asian cultures operate on the premise that the welfare of the group (belongingness needs) are more highly valued than needs of the individual (esteem needs). The point is that this hierarchy, although widely applied in marketing, should be valued because it reminds us that consumers may have different need priorities in different consumption situations and at different stages in their lives, not because it exactly specifies a consumer's progression up the ladder of needs.

CONSUMER INVOLVEMENT

Do consumers form strong relationships with products and services? If you don't believe so, consider these recent events:

- A consumer in Brighton, England loves a local restaurant called the All In One so much, he had its name and phone number tattooed on his forehead. The owner remarked, "I'm not going to give him free pizza, because he did it of his own free will. But whenever he comes in, he'll go straight to the front of the queue."[14]
- *Lucky* is a new magazine devoted to shopping for shoes and other fashion accessories. The centerfold of the first issue featured rows of makeup sponges. The editor observes, "It's the same way that you might look at a golf magazine and see a spread of nine irons. *Lucky* is addressing one interest in women's lives, in a really obsessive, specific way."[15]
- After being jilted by his girlfriend, a Tennessee man tried to marry his car. His plan was thwarted, however, after he listed his fiancee's birthplace as Detroit, her father as Henry Ford, and her blood type as 10W40. Under Tennessee law, only a man and a woman can legally wed.[16] So much for that exciting honeymoon at the carwash.

These examples illustrate that people can get pretty attached to products. As we have seen, a consumer's motivation to attain a goal influences his or her desire to expend the effort necessary to attain the products or services believed to be instrumental in satisfying that objective. However, not everyone is motivated to the same extent—one person might be convinced he or she can't live without the latest style or modern convenience, whereas another is not interested in this item at all.

Involvement is defined as "a person's perceived relevance of the object based on their inherent needs, values, and interests."[17] The word *object* is used in the generic sense and refers to a product (or a brand), an advertisement, or a purchase situation. Consumers can find involvement in all these *objects*. Because involvement is a motivational construct, it can be triggered by one or more of the different antecedents, as shown in Figure 4.3. The antecedents are something about the person, something about the object, and something about the situation. On the right hand side of Figure 4.3 are the results or consequences of being involved with the *object*.

Involvement can be viewed as the motivation to process information.[18] To the degree that there is a perceived linkage between a consumer's needs, goals, or values and product knowledge, the consumer will be motivated to pay attention to product information. When relevant knowledge is activated in memory, a motivational state is created that drives behavior (e.g., shopping). As involvement

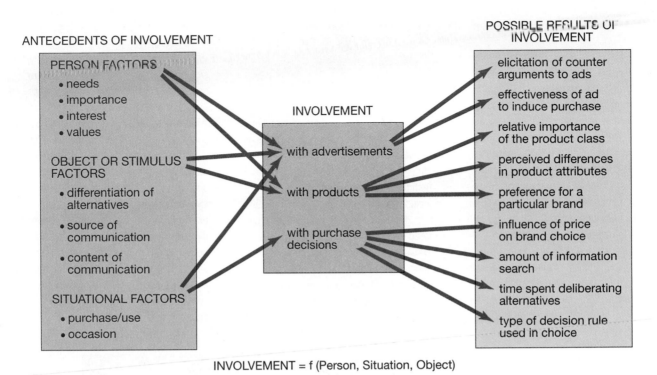

INVOLVEMENT = f (Person, Situation, Object)

The level of involvement may be influenced by one or more of these three factors. Interactions among persons, situation and object factors are likely to occur.

Figure 4.3
Conceptualizing Involvement

with a product increases, the consumer devotes more attention to ads related to the product, exerts more cognitive effort to understand these ads, and focuses attention on the product-related information in them.[19]

Levels of Involvement: From Inertia to Passion

The type of information processing that will occur thus depends on the consumer's level of involvement. It can range from *simple processing,* in which only the basic features of a message are considered, all the way to *elaboration,* in which the incoming information is linked to one's preexisting knowledge system.[20]

A person's degree of involvement can be conceived as a continuum, ranging from absolute lack of interest in a marketing stimulus at one end to obsession at the other (collecting football stars' smelly socks probably falls into that category). Consumption at the low end of involvement is characterized by **inertia,** in which decisions are made out of habit because the consumer lacks the motivation to consider alternatives. At the high end of involvement, we can expect to find the type of passionate intensity reserved for people and objects that carry great meaning for the individual. For example, the passion of some consumers for famous people (those living, such as Michael Jordan, or—supposedly—dead, such as Elvis Presley) demonstrates the high end of the involvement continuum. For the most part, however, a consumer's involvement level with products falls somewhere in the middle, and the marketing strategist must determine the relative level of

MULTICULTURAL DIMENSIONS

PRESUMABLY, A PERSON WHO has had all of his or her needs satisfied lives in "paradise." Conceptualizations of paradise have implications for the marketing and consumption of any products, such as vacation travel, that seek to invoke an ideal state. However, the definition of just what constitutes paradise appears to differ across cultures. To pursue this idea further, the concept of paradise was compared between groups of American and Dutch college students. Informants in both cultures constructed a collage of images to illustrate their overall concept of paradise, and they wrote an essay to accompany and explain this collage. Some similarities were evident in the two societies; both Americans and

Dutch emphasized the personal, experiential aspects of paradise, saying "paradise is different for everyone . . . a feeling . . . a state of being." In addition, individuals in both societies said that paradise must include family, friends, and significant others.

However, the Dutch and Americans differed in important and interesting ways. The Americans consistently emphasized hedonism, materialism, individuality, creativity, and issues of time and space consistent with a society in which time is segmented and viewed almost as a commodity

(more on this in Chapter 10). Conversely, the Dutch respondents showed a concern for social and environmental responsibility, collective societal order and equality, and a balance between work and play as part of paradise. For instance, one Dutch student said that "Respect for animals, flowers, and plants . . . regenerating energy sources, such as wind, water, and sun are all important parts of paradise." Marketers should expect that, because concepts of paradise differ somewhat, different images and behaviors may be evoked when Americans and Dutch are confronted with marketing messages such as "Hawaii is paradise," or "you can experience paradise when you drive this car."[20]

A Dutch respondent's collage emphasizes this person's conception of paradise as a place where there is interpersonal harmony and concern for the environment.

importance to understand how much elaboration of product information will occur.

The Many Faces of Involvement

As previously defined, involvement can take many forms. Involvement can be cognitive, as when a "Webhead" is motivated to learn all she can about the latest specs of a new multimedia PC, or emotional, as when the thought of a new Armani suit gives a clotheshorse goosebumps.[22] Further, the very act of buying the Armani may be very involving for people who are passionately devoted to shopping. To complicate matters further, advertisements, such as those produced for Nike or Adidas, may themselves be involving for some reason (e.g., because they make us laugh, cry, or inspire us to work harder).

It seems that involvement is a fuzzy concept, because it overlaps with other things and means different things to different people. Indeed, the consensus is that there are actually several broad types of involvement related to the product, the message, or the perceiver.[23]

Product Involvement

Product involvement is related to a consumer's level of interest in a particular product. Many sales promotions are designed to increase this type of involvement. In a contest sponsored by Dare perfume, for example, women submitted details of their most intimate trysts by letter or by phone to radio talk shows. The winning stories were edited into a romance novel published by Bantam Books. These books, in turn, were given away as a gift with the purchase of the perfume.[24]

Message–Response Involvement

Message–response involvement (also known as *advertising involvement*), refers to the consumer's interest in processing marketing communications.[25] Television is considered a low-involvement medium because it requires a passive viewer who exerts relatively little control (remote control "zipping" notwithstanding) over content (on the other hand, the young fans of MTV's *TRL Show* certainly seem pretty involved with this experience!). In contrast, print is a high-involvement medium. The reader is actively involved in processing the information and is able to pause and reflect on what he or she has read before moving on.[26] The role of message characteristics in changing attitudes is discussed further in Chapter 8.

Purchase Situation Involvement

Purchase situation involvement refers to differences that may occur when buying the same object for different contexts. Here the person may perceive a great deal of social risk or none at all. What a person thinks when consuming the product for themselves or when others consume the product they buy is not always obvious or intuitive. For example, when you want to impress someone you may try to buy a brand or a product with a certain image that you think reflects good taste. When you have to buy a gift for someone in an obligatory situation, for example, a wedding gift for a cousin you do not really like, you may not care what image the gift portrays. Or you may actually pick something cheap that reflects your desire to distance yourself from that cousin.

MEASURING INVOLVEMENT

The measurement of involvement is important for many marketing applications. For example, research evidence indicates that a viewer who is more involved with a television show will also respond more positively to commercials contained in that show, and that these spots will have a greater chance of influencing his or her purchase intentions.[27] Therefore, many research companies such as Involvement Marketing Inc. measure the level of consumer involvement to make predictions on the success of advertising campaigns. One of the most widely used measures of the state of involvement is the scale shown in Table 4.1. It is the most widely used because it is context free and therefore applicable to products, advertisements, and purchase situations.

| **TABLE 4.1** | A Scale to Measure Involvement |

To Me [Object to be Judged] Is		
1.	important	_:_:_:_:_:_:_	unimportant*
2.	boring	_:_:_:_:_:_:_	interesting
3.	relevant	_:_:_:_:_:_:_	irrelevant*
4.	exciting	_:_:_:_:_:_:_	unexciting*
5.	means nothing	_:_:_:_:_:_:_	means a lot to me
6.	appealing	_:_:_:_:_:_:_	unappealing*
7.	fascinating	_:_:_:_:_:_:_	mundane*
8.	worthless	_:_:_:_:_:_:_	valuable
9.	involving	_:_:_:_:_:_:_	uninvolving*
10.	not needed	_:_:_:_:_:_:_	needed

NOTE: Totaling the 10 items gives a score from a low of 10 to a high of 70.
*Indicates item is reverse scored. For example, a score of 7 for item no. 1 (important/unimportant) would actually be scored as 1.
SOURCE: Judith Lynne Zaichkowsky, "The Personal Involvement Inventory: Reduction, Revision, and Application to Advertising," *Journal of Advertising*, 23 (December 1994)4: 59–70.

Teasing Out the Dimensions of Involvement

A pair of French researchers devised a scale to measure the antecedents of product involvement. Recognizing that consumers can be involved with a product because it is a risky purchase and/or its use reflects on or affects the self, they advocate the development of an *involvement profile* containing five components:[28]

- The personal interest a consumer has in a product category, its personal meaning or importance
- The perceived importance of the potential negative consequences associated with a poor choice of the product (risk importance)
- The probability of making a bad purchase
- The pleasure value of the product category
- The sign value of the product category

These researchers asked a sample of homemakers to rate a set of 14 product categories on each of the those facets of involvement. The results are shown in Table 4.2. These data indicate that no single component captures consumer involvement because this quality can occur for different reasons. For example, the purchase of a durable product such as a vacuum cleaner is seen as risky, because one is stuck with a bad choice for many years. However, the vacuum cleaner does not provide pleasure (hedonic value), nor is it high in sign value (i.e., its use is not related to the person's self-concept). In contrast, chocolate is high in pleasure value but is not seen as risky or closely related to the self. Dresses and bras, on the other hand, appear to be involving for a combination of reasons.

Segmenting by Involvement Levels

A measurement approach of this nature allows consumer researchers to capture the diversity of the involvement construct and also provides the potential to use involvement as a basis for market segmentation. For example, a yogurt manufacturer might find that even though its product is low in sign value for one group of

TABLE 4.2 Involvement Profiles for a Set of French Consumer Products

	Importance of Negative Consequences	Subjective Probability of Mispurchase	Pleasure Value	Sign Value
Dresses	121	112	147	181
Bras	117	115	106	130
Washing machines	118	109	106	111
TV sets	112	100	122	95
Vacuum cleaners	110	112	70	78
Irons	103	95	72	76
Champagne	109	120	125	125
Oil	89	97	65	92
Yogurt	86	83	106	78
Chocolate	80	89	123	75
Shampoo	96	103	90	81
Toothpaste	95	95	94	105
Facial soap	82	90	114	118
Detergents	79	82	56	63

Average product score = 100.
Note the first two antecedents of personal importance and importance of negative consequences are combined in these data.
SOURCE: Gilles Laurent and Jean-Noël Kapferer, "Measuring Consumer Involvement Profiles." *Journal of Marketing Research* 22 (February 1985): 45, Table 3. By permission of American Marketing Association.

consumers, it might be highly related to the self-concept of another market segment, such as health food enthusiasts or avid dieters. The company could adapt its strategy to account for the motivation of different segments to process information about the product.

One study looked at the role of affective versus cognitive and level of involvement (high versus low) in promoting Canadian universities. The researchers found that students who were cognitively high involved conducted an intense search for university information, whereas students who were affectively involved made their university choice based mainly on emotional factors.[29] Note also that involvement with a product class may vary across cultures. Although this sample of French consumers rated champagne high in both sign value and personal value, the ability of champagne to provide pleasure or to be central to self-definition might not transfer to other countries (e.g., Islamic cultures).

Strategies to Increase Involvement

Although consumers differ in their level of involvement with respect to a product message, marketers do not have to just sit back and hope for the best. By being aware of some basic factors that increase or decrease attention, they can take steps to increase the likelihood that product information will get through. A consumer's motivation to process relevant information can be enhanced fairly easily by the marketer who uses one or more of the following techniques:[30]

- Appeal to the consumers' hedonic needs. For example, ads using sensory appeals generate higher levels of attention.[31]
- Use novel stimuli, such as unusual cinematography, sudden silences, or unexpected movements in commercials.
- Use prominent stimuli, such as loud music and fast action, to capture attention in commercials. In print formats, larger ads increase attention. Also, viewers look longer at colored pictures as opposed to black and white.
- Include celebrity endorsers to generate higher interest in commercials. (This strategy will be discussed in Chapter 8.)
- Build a bond with consumers by maintaining an ongoing relationship with them. Learn from the actions of tobacco companies, which have figured out how to keep smokers' loyalties (at least until they die). R. J. Reynolds Co. hosted nearly 3,700 Doral smokers at its factory for Western line dancing lessons, bowling, blackjack, and plenty of free cigarettes. Said one happy attendee, "I'd quit altogether before I'd change brands."[32] Now there's a thought.

A **value** is a belief that some condition is preferable to its opposite. For example, it's safe to assume that most people place a priority on freedom, preferring it to slavery. Others avidly pursue products and services that will make them look young, believing that this is preferable to appearing old. A person's set of values plays a very important role in consumption activities—many products and services are purchased because people believe these products will help to attain a value-related goal.

Two people can believe in the same behaviors (e.g., vegetarianism), but their underlying belief systems may be quite different (e.g., animal activism versus health concerns). The extent to which people share a belief system is a function of individual, social, and cultural forces. Advocates of a belief system often seek out

NET PROFIT

IT'S HUMAN NATURE TO be more involved with a product that's directly relevant to your individual wants and needs. One of the exciting advantages of the Internet is the ability to personalize content so that a Web site offers information or products tailored to individual surfers.[33] According to one study, personalized e-commerce sites boosted new customers by 47 percent in the first year.[34] Consider these different approaches to personalization that build involvement:

- Micromass Communications is developing a site for the American Heart Association that generates pages for visitors based on individual psychological profiles. First-time visitors will respond to an online questionnaire

about their health habits. Then, the site will show users who are at risk of heart disease specifically how to change their lifestyles and reduce cholesterol.[35]

- WhatsHotNow.com is a consumer-driven Internet store offering a selection of sports entertainment and lifestyle merchandise and apparel. The site builds new "stores" each month featuring merchandise requested by its customers. Each time a user visits the site, she sees only the merchandise she's interested in.[36]

- Reflect.com lets consumers custom design cosmetics orders online. The buyer can specify the product formula and shape of the container; the package is labeled with her name. The firm's director of marketing says, "Every product is a gift to yourself, created by you."[37]

- Girls can now customize their own doll at Mattel's My Design Web site, located at www.barbie.com/mydesign. They can specify her skin tone, hair and eye color, and outfits. They can also name the doll, which comes with a personality profile the girls can tailor from choices on the Web site.[38]

others with similar beliefs, so that social networks overlap and as a result believers tend to be exposed to information that supports their beliefs (e.g., "tree-huggers" rarely hang out with loggers).[39]

Core Values

Every culture has a set of values that it imparts to its members.[40] People in one culture might feel that being a unique individual is preferable to subordinating one's identity to the group, whereas another culture may emphasize the virtues of group membership. A study by Wirthlin Worldwide found that the most important values to Asian executives are hard work, respect for learning, and honesty. In contrast, North American businesspeople emphasize the values of personal freedom, self-reliance, and freedom of expression.[41]

And, of course, a culture's values do change over time—not necessarily in positive ways. Right now in Japan young people are working hard to adopt more Western values and behaviors—which explains why the current fashion for young people is bleached blond hair, chalky makeup, and deep tans. But, as the Japanese are being urged by their government to spend more and to be more free in the way they live, more and more teenagers are starting to reject the conservative behavior of the past. The dropout rate among students in junior and senior high school has increased by 20 percent in a two-year period. More than 50 percent of girls have had intercourse by their senior year, a 10 percent increase since the early 1990s.[42]

These differences in values often explain why marketing efforts that are a big hit in one country can flop in another. For example, a hugely successful advertisement in Japan promoted breast cancer awareness by showing an attractive woman in a sundress drawing stares from men on the street as a voice-over says, "If only women paid as much attention to their breasts as men do." The same ad flopped in France because the use of humor to talk about a serious disease offended the French.[43]

In many cases, of course, values are universal. Who does not desire health, wisdom, or world peace? What sets cultures apart is the *relative importance*, or ranking, of these universal values. This set of rankings constitutes a culture's **value system.**[44] For example, one study found that North Americans have more favorable attitudes toward advertising messages that focus on self-reliance, self-improvement, and the achievement of personal goals as opposed to themes stressing family integrity, collective goals, and the feeling of harmony with others. The reverse pattern was found for Korean consumers.[45]

Every culture is characterized by its members' endorsement of a value system. These values may not be equally endorsed by every individual, and in some cases, values may even seem to contradict one another (e.g., Americans appear to value both conformity and individuality, and seek to find some accommodation between the two). Nonetheless, it is usually possible to identify a general set of core *values* that uniquely define a culture. These beliefs are taught to us by *socialization agents,* including parents, friends, and teachers. The process of learning the beliefs and behaviors endorsed by one's own culture is termed **enculturation.** In contrast, the process of learning the value system and behaviors of another culture (often a priority for those who wish to understand consumers and markets in foreign countries) is called **acculturation.**

Core values such as freedom, youthfulness, achievement, materialism, and activity have been claimed to characterize American culture, but even these

TABLE 4.3 Cultural Values Frequently Emphasized in American Advertising: 1900–1980

Overall Value	Themes Included	Proportion of Ads Using Value as Central Theme
Practical	Effectiveness, durability, convenience	44
Family	Nurturance in family, happy home, getting married	17
New	Modernism, improvement	14
Cheap	Economy, bargain, good value	13
Healthy	Fitness, vigor, athleticism	12
Sexy/vain	Good appearance, glamor, eroticism	13
Wisdom	Knowledge, experience	11
Unique	Expense, value, distinctiveness, rarity	10

SOURCE: Adapted from Richard W. Pollay, "The Identification and Distribution of Values Manifest in Print Advertising, 1900–1980." Adapted with the permission of Lexington Books, an imprint of Macmillan, Inc., from *Personal Values and Consumer Psychology* by eds. Robert E. Pitts Jr. and Arch G. Woodside. Copyright © 1984 by Lexington Books.

basic beliefs are subject to change. For example, Americans' emphasis on youth is eroding as the population ages (see Chapter 15). Table 4.3 identifies the dominant values underlying a set of American print ads representing the period from 1900 to 1980. The prevalence of product effectiveness as an underlying advertising theme is obvious.

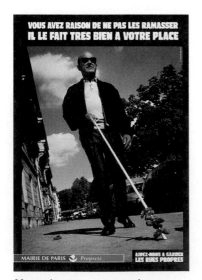

Many advertisements appeal to people's values to perusade them to change or modify their behaviors. This ad sponsored by the City of Paris says to dog owners, "You are quite right not to clean up after your dog. After all, they'll take care of that for you."

Applications of Values to Consumer Behavior

Despite their importance, values have not been as widely applied to direct examinations of consumer behavior as might be expected. One reason is that broad-based concepts such as freedom, security, or inner harmony are more likely to affect general purchasing patterns than to differentiate between brands within a product category. For this reason, some researchers have found it convenient to make distinctions among broad-based *cultural values* such as security or happiness, *consumption-specific values* such as convenient shopping or prompt service, and *product-specific values* such as ease of use or durability.[46] For example, people who value group affiliation and approval place more importance on style and brand name when evaluating the desirability of clothing products.[47]

Because values drive much of consumer behavior (at least in a very general sense), it could be said that virtually all consumer research is ultimately related to the identification and measurement of values. This section will describe some specific attempts by researchers to measure cultural values and apply this knowledge to marketing strategy.

The Rokeach Value Survey

The psychologist Milton Rokeach identified a set of **terminal values,** or desired end states, that apply to many different cultures. The *Rokeach Value Survey*, a scale used to measure these values, also includes a set of **instrumental values,** which are composed of actions needed to achieve these terminal values.[48] These two sets of values appear in Table 4.4.

The List of Values (LOV)

Although some evidence indicates that differences on these global values do translate into product-specific preferences and differences in media usage, the Rokeach Value Survey has not been widely used by marketing researchers.[49] As an alternative, the *List of Values (LOV) Scale* was developed to isolate values with more direct marketing applications. This instrument identifies nine consumer segments based on the values they endorse and relates each value to differences in consumption behaviors. These segments include consumers who place a priority on such values as a sense of belonging, excitement, warm relationships with others, and security. For example, people who endorse the value of sense of belonging are older and more likely to read *Reader's Digest* and *TV Guide*, drink and entertain more, and prefer group activities more than people who do not endorse this value as highly. In contrast, those who endorse the value of excitement are younger and prefer *Rolling Stone* magazine.[50]

TABLE 4.4   Two Types of Values in the Rokeach Value Survey

Instrumental Values	Terminal Values
Ambitious	A comfortable life
Broadminded	An exciting life
Capable	A sense of accomplishment
Cheerful	A world at peace
Clean	A world of beauty
Courageous	Equality
Forgiving	Family security
Helpful	Freedom
Honest	Happiness
Imaginative	Inner harmony
Independent	Mature love
Intellectual	National security
Logical	Pleasure
Loving	Salvation
Obedient	Self-respect
Polite	Social recognition
Responsible	True friendship
Self-controlled	Wisdom

SOURCE: Richard W. Pollay, "Measuring the Cultural Values Manifest in Advertising," *Current Issues and Research in Advertising* (1983): 71–92. Reprinted by permission of University of Michigan Division of Research.

The Means–End Chain Model

Another research approach that incorporates values is termed a *means–end chain model.* This approach assumes that very specific product attributes are linked at levels of increasing abstraction to terminal values. The person has valued end states, and he or she chooses among alternative means to attain these goals. Products are thus valued as the means to an end. Through a technique called **laddering,** consumers' associations between specific attributes and general consequences are uncovered. Consumers are helped to climb up the "ladder" of abstraction that connects functional product attributes with desired end states.[52]

To understand how laddering works, consider the purchase of a diamond ring to symbolize an upcoming marriage. Concrete attributes like size and clarity of the stone are parlayed into abstract and emotional values of love and self-esteem. The diamond industry is very good at keeping an artificially high price on a luxury good through linking the size of the diamond to the size of your paycheck, to the size of your love, and self-worth.

The notion that products are consumed because they are instrumental in attaining more abstract values is central to one application of this technique, called the *Means–End Conceptualization of the Components of Advertising Strategy (MECCAS).* In this approach, researchers first generate a map depicting relationships between functional product or service attributes and terminal values. This information is then used to develop advertising strategy by identifying elements such as the following:[53]

- *Message elements:* the specific attributes or product features to be depicted
- *Consumer benefit:* the positive consequences of using the product or service
- *Executional framework:* the overall style and tone of the advertisement
- *Leverage point*: the way the message will activate the terminal value by linking it with specific product features
- *Driving force:* the end value on which the advertising will focus

This technique was used to develop advertising strategy for Federal Express. The researchers developed a "Hierarchical Value Map" for secretaries, an important group of decision makers in the category of overnight delivery services. As shown in Figure 4.4, concrete attributes of competitive services, such as having a drop box or on-time delivery, were successively related to more abstract benefits, such as "makes me look good" or "saves time." These intermediate levels were then linked, or laddered, to reveal their relationship to the terminal values of peace of mind and self-esteem.

Based on these results, an advertisement was created. Its message elements emphasized Federal Express' satellite communications network. The consumer benefit was the reliability of the service, which made work easier. The executional framework was a humorous one. A secretary is trying to track down an overnight delivery. She and her boss are interrupted and taken to view the Federal Express satellite system. As a result, the secretary sees the benefit of using the company. The leverage point is that using this service allows her to be in control, which in turn provides peace of mind, the driving force (terminal value).

Syndicated Surveys

A number of companies track changes in values through large-scale surveys. The results of these studies are then sold to marketers, who pay a fee to receive regular updates on changes and trends. This approach originated in the mid-1960s,

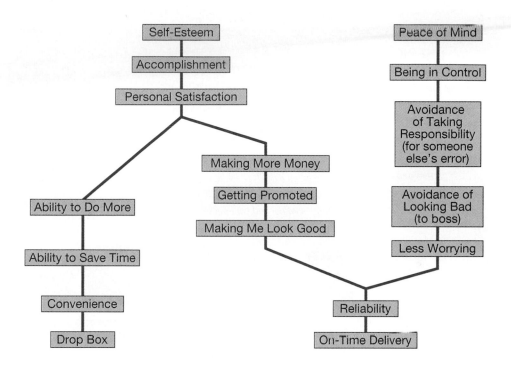

Figure 4.4
Secretaries' Hierarchical Value Map for Overnight Delivery Services

when Playtex was concerned about sagging girdle sales. The company commissioned the market research firm of Yankelovich, Skelly & White to see why sales had dropped. Their research determined that sales had been affected by a shift in values regarding appearance and naturalness. Playtex went on to design lighter, less restrictive garments, while Yankelovich went on to track the impact of these types of changes in a range of industries. Gradually, the firm developed the idea of one big study to track American attitudes. In 1970, the Yankelovich *Monitor*™ was introduced. It is based on two-hour interviews with 4,000 respondents.[54]

For example, the Yankelovich *Monitor* reported a movement among American consumers toward simplification and away from hype as people try to streamline their hectic lives and reduce their concerns about gaining the approval of others through their purchases. Subaru incorporated this finding into its advertising strategy: In one TV spot the voice-over proclaims, "I want a car . . . Don't tell me about wood paneling, about winning the respect of my neighbors. They're my neighbors. They're not my heroes."[55] A successful campaign for Sprite tells us that "Image is nothing. Obey your thirst."

Today, many other syndicated surveys also track changes in values. Some of these are operated by advertising agencies to allow them to stay on top of important cultural trends and help them to shape the messages they craft on behalf of their clients. These services include VALS 2 (more on this in Chapter 6), GlobalScan (operated by the advertising agency Backer Spielvogel Bates), New Wave (the Ogilvy & Mather advertising agency), and the Lifestyles Study conducted by the DDB Needham advertising agency. The Angus Reid Group in Canada surveys changes in values of specific groups or industry segments (for details visit angusreid.com).

REALITY
CHECK

SOME MARKET ANALYSTS SEE A SHIFT in values among young people. They claim that this generation has not had a lot of stability in their lives. They are fed up with superficial relationships and are yearning for a return to tradition. This change is reflected in attitudes toward marriage and family. One survey of 22 to 24-year-old women found that 82 percent thought motherhood was the most important job in the world. Brides *magazine reports a swing toward traditional weddings—80 percent of brides today are tossing their garters and 78 percent are walked down the aisle by Daddy.[51]*

So, what's your take on this? Are young people indeed returning to the values of their parents (or even their grandparents)? How have these changes influenced your perspective on marriage and family?

Market analysts are probably fairly accurate in assessing that younger people want a return to lasting marriages with children. My opinion on marriage is optimistic and I want it to be lasting for my sake and my future children's sake. . . . I believe my feelings on traditional marriages are perhaps more heightened because of my parent's own divorce at a young age. Many of my friends also my age (20–24) that come from divorced families themselves feel strongly about traditional family lifestyles.

Jill Wittekind
University of Nevada, Las Vegas

It's too simplistic to say that young people are returning to or moving away from the values of their parents. We've taken on and modified those values of our parents that are relevant to us and disregarded others. . . . I still view a happy marriage as a major goal in life but like many others my age, I'm willing to wait longer before entering into marriage. We see that in comparison to previous generations there has been a large rise in the number of people living together before marriage as well as the duration of such arrangements. These changes directly reflect the uncertainty young people often feel as we see many relationships failing.

Satish Magan Ranchod
University of Auckland, New Zealand

Despite a recent trend to get married later due to changing life styles and expectations, this surely does not mean that we have lost sight of tradition. I believe that the majority of young people are still quite traditional in terms of wanting to 'tie the knot' in the same way as their parents and grandparents did. Whilst I envisage walking down the aisle by Daddy (any girl's dream) I'm not sure that I would choose to be united before God in the religious sense. That may be the major difference between this generation and previous ones: Whilst getting married is still a popular cultural tradition perhaps the religious aspect has diminished in importance as concrete day-to-day values supersede the abstract.

Nicole Schragger
Edinburgh University, United Kingdom

I would have to say that it is not necessarily a return to traditional beliefs, in as much as it is a quicker rise to maturity and a need for stability. It appears that many "young people" are aging much faster psychologically than those in previous generations. They are being forced to decide what is best for themselves and their loved ones at a younger age than could be said in the past.

Gregory T. Varveris
DePaul University

I don't think that young people are returning to the values of their parents or grandparents. The family's influence on a young person is steadily decreasing as years pass. Due to a constant increase in divorce rates as well as an increase in single parent families, young people are turning to other sources beside family members for advice and information.

John Dollman IV
West Virginia University

Family value is not returning to this generation, but is being seen in a new light. Parents today are using the values their parents taught them with more knowledge and loyalty. The result is a fashionable use of old traditions mixed with new enlightenment.

Jessica Wells
Utah State University

[A] . . . reason for this big swing towards tradition is because a lot of people learned the hard way. In the 60's and 70's there was a big liberal swing when people focused on sex and drugs. And what happened? A lot of addicts with diseases and too many abused children. More people today are realizing that the 60's weren't so groovy after all and that maybe home is really where the heart is.

Annalise M. Mulholland
Virginia Tech

I don't think that young people are returning to the values of their parents. I believe that the swing toward traditional weddings are a trend . . . probably a style that never dies, just like retro music and 60's bellbottoms and stuff.

Tina Ho
Nanyang Technological University, Singapore

What's your opinion? Check out the online polls at www.prenhall.com/myphlip. Just follow the little person in the lab coat.

The 1997 Roper Reports Worldwide Global Consumer Survey reported the views of about 1,000 people in 35 countries. The respondents ranked 56 values by the importance they hold as guiding principles in their lives. The study identified six global values segments, which are summarized in Table 4.5. Some interesting

Reversing a trend of self-denial, this ad illustrates a shift in values toward pleasure and self-indulgence.

differences in core values emerged from this large study. For example, Indonesians rank respecting ancestors as their No. 1 guiding principle. Great Britain leads the world in wanting to protect the family, Brazil has the most fun seekers, the Netherlands is highest in valuing honesty, and Korea is first in valuing health and fitness.[56]

TABLE 4.5 Global Values Segments in the Roper Reports Worldwide Global Consumer Survey

Segment	Profile
Strivers	The largest segment. Emphasis on material and professional goals. One in three people in developing Asia falls into this category.
Devouts	22 percent of adults. Tradition and duty are very important. Most common in developing Asia, Middle East, and Africa.
Altruists	18 percent of adults. Interested in social issues and the welfare of society. More altruists live in Latin America and Russia.
Intimates	15 percent of adults. Value close personal relationships and family. Enjoy cooking and gardening.
Fun Seekers	The youngest group. Found in disproportionate numbers in developed Asia. Like to go to restaurants, bars, and movies.
Creatives	The smallest segment, at 10 percent worldwide. Strong interest in education, knowledge, and technology. More common in Latin America and Western Europe.

SOURCE: Adapted from Tom Miller, "Global Segments from 'Strivers' to Creatives,'" *Marketing News* (July 20, 1998): 11.

Materialism: "He Who Dies with the Most Toys, Wins"

During World War II, members of "cargo cults" in the South Pacific literally worshiped cargo salvaged from crashed aircraft or washed ashore from ships. These people believed that the ships and planes passing near their islands were piloted by their ancestors, and they tried to attract the ships and planes to their villages. They went so far as to construct fake planes from straw in hopes of luring the real ones to their islands.[57]

Although most people don't literally worship material goods in quite this way, things do play a central role in many people's lives. **Materialism** refers to the importance people attach to worldly possessions. Americans inhabit a highly materialistic society in which people often gauge the worth of themselves and others in terms of how much they own (see Chapter 13). The popular bumper sticker, "He Who Dies with the Most Toys, Wins" is a comment on this philosophy. We sometimes take the existence of an abundance of products and services for granted, until we remember how recent this abundance is. For example, in 1950 two of five American homes did not have a telephone, and in 1940 half of all households still did not possess complete indoor plumbing. Today, though, many Americans now energetically seek "the good life," which abounds in material comforts. In fact, one way to think about marketing is, as a system that provides a certain standard of living to consumers. To some extent, then, our lifestyles are influenced by the standard of living we have come to expect and desire.

Materialists are more likely to value possessions for their status and appearance-related meanings, whereas those who do not emphasize this value tend to prize products that connect them to other people or that provide them with pleasure in using them.[58] As a result, products valued by high materialists are more likely to be publicly consumed and to be more expensive. A study that compared specific items valued by both types of people found that products associated with high materialists include jewelry, china, or a vacation home, whereas those

Materialists value visible symbols of success such as expensive watches.

linked to low materialists included a mother's wedding gown, picture albums, a rocking chair from childhood, or a garden.[59]

Although there is still no shortage of materialistic consumers who relish the race to acquire as much as possible before they die, there are signs that a sizable number of Americans are evolving a different value system. The Brain Waves/Market Facts survey reports that about a quarter of the population is displaying a value system characterized by a rejection of tradition and conformity. Significantly, more than half of this group is under the age of 35. They are still interested in achievement, but they are trying to balance life in the fast lane with an emphasis on developing close personal relationships and having fun.

Through observation and in some cases direct experience, these consumers have come to believe that (unlike the "good old days") a diploma does not guarantee a job, getting a job is no guarantee of keeping a job, retirement may not happen, and marriages often fail. This lack of stability has instilled a value of self-reliance and the desire to build personal networks rather than relying on the government or corporations to take care of them, as these institutions did for their parents. Marketing communications like Saab's "Find Your Own Road" and Prudential's "Be Your Own Rock" are designed to appeal to this group.[60]

These changes are not confined to young people. In the past, there was often a sharp divide in values between young and old, but it seems these old categories no longer make sense. As one analyst recently noted, for example, even conservative small towns now often feature "new age" stores and services that are patronized by consumers of all ages. Retailers that used to be considered "bohemian" now are mainstream; grocers such as Fresh Fields sell Mayan Fungus soap and vegetarian dog biscuits to a hodgepodge of consumers. Big corporations such as Apple and The Gap use countercultural figures such as Gandhi and Jack Kerouac in their advertising, and Ben & Jerry's boasts of its unconventional corporate philosophy. It's become hard to separate establishment from anti-establishment as bohemian attitudes of the hippie 1960s have merged with the bourgeois attitudes of the yuppie 1980s to form a new culture that is a synthesis of the two. The people who dominate our culture (this analyst calls them "BoBos, or Bourgeois Bohemians!) now are richer and more worldly than hippies, but more spiritual than yuppies.[61] As we noted earlier, even core values do change over time; stay tuned to see how our always evolving culture continues to put a fresh spin on materialism and other values.

CHAPTER SUMMARY

- Marketers try to satisfy consumer needs, but the reasons any product is purchased can vary widely. The identification of consumer motives is an important step in ensuring that the appropriate needs will be met by a product.
- Traditional approaches to consumer behavior have focused on the abilities of products to satisfy rational needs (utilitarian motives), but hedonic motives (e.g., the need for exploration or for fun) also play a role in many purchase decisions.
- As demonstrated by Maslow's hierarchy of needs, the same product can satisfy different needs, depending on the consumer's state at the time. In addition to his or her objective situation (e.g., have basic physiological needs already been

satisfied?), the consumer's degree of involvement with the product must be considered.

- Consumer motivations are often driven by underlying values. In this context, products take on meaning because they are seen as being instrumental in helping the person to achieve some goal that is linked to a value, such as individuality or freedom. Each culture is characterized by a set of core values to which many of its members adhere.

- *Materialism* refers to the importance people attach to worldly possessions. Although many Americans can be described as being materialists, there are indications of a value shift within a sizable portion of the population.

KEY TERMS

acculturation, p. 117
drive, p. 103
enculturation, p. 117
expectancy theory, p. 104
goal, p. 102
homeostasis, p. 103

inertia, p. 111
instrumental values, p. 118
involvement, p. 110
laddering, p. 120
materialism, p. 124
motivation, p. 102

terminal values, p. 118
theory of cognitive
  dissonance, p. 106
value, p. 116
value system, p. 117
want, p. 103

CONSUMER BEHAVIOR CHALLENGE

1. Describe three types of motivational conflicts, citing an example of each from current marketing campaigns.
2. Devise separate promotional strategies for an article of clothing, each of which stresses one of the levels of Maslow's hierarchy of needs.
3. Collect a sample of ads that appear to appeal to consumers' values. What value is being communicated in each ad, and how is this done? Is this an effective approach to designing a marketing communication?
4. What is your conception of paradise? Construct a collage consisting of images you personally associate with paradise, and compare the results with those of your classmates. Do you detect any common themes?
5. Construct a hypothetical means–end chain model for the purchase of a bouquet of roses. How might a florist use this approach to construct a promotional strategy?
6. Describe how a man's level of involvement with his car would affect how he is influenced by different marketing stimuli. How might you design a strategy for a line of car batteries for a segment of low-involvement consumers, and how would this strategy differ from your attempts to reach a segment of men who are very involved in working on their cars?
7. Interview members of a celebrity fan club. Describe their level of involvement with the "product" and devise some marketing opportunities to reach this group.
8. "High involvement is just a fancy term for expensive." Do you agree?
9. "College students' concerns about the environment and vegetarianism are just a passing fad; a way to look 'cool.'" Do you agree?

NOTES

1. "Study Shows Growing Meatless Market," *Resource: Engineering & Technology for a Sustainable World* 7, no. 3 (March 2000): 15; "What's next.com?" *Direct Marketing* 62, no. 10 (February 2000): 66; Joan Lang, "No Bones About It: Vegetarian Is Hot," *ID: The Voice of Food Service Distribution* 35, no. 7 (July 1999): 70–72; Paul King, "Global Vegetarian Tries to Fill Nonmeat-Eater Niche" *Nation's Restaurant News* 33, no. 2 (October 18, 1999): 20.

2. Robert A. Baron, *Psychology: The Essential Science* (Needham, MA: Allyn & Bacon, 1989).

3. Leon Festinger, *A Theory of Cognitive Dissonance* (Stanford, CA: Stanford University Press, 1957).

4. See Paul T. Costa and Robert R. McCrae, "From Catalog to Classification: Murray's Needs and the Five-Factor Model," *Journal of Personality and Social Psychology* 55, no. 2 (1988): 258–65; Calvin S. Hall and Gardner Lindzey, *Theories of Personality*, 2d ed. (New York: Wiley, 1970); James U. McNeal and Stephen W. McDaniel, "An Analysis of Need-Appeals in Television Advertising," *Journal of the Academy of Marketing Science* 12 (Spring 1984): 176–90.

5. Michael R. Solomon, Judith L. Zaichkowsky, and Rosemary Polegato, *Consumer Behaviour: Buying, Having, and Being—Canadian Edition* (Scarborough, Ontario: Prentice Hall Canada, 1999).

6. See David C. McClelland, *Studies in Motivation* (New York: Appleton-Century-Crofts, 1955).

7. Mary Kay Ericksen and M. Joseph Sirgy, "Achievement Motivation and Clothing Preferences of White-Collar Working Women," in Michael R. Solomon, ed., *The Psychology of Fashion* (Lexington, MA: Lexington Books, 1985): 357–69.

8. See Stanley Schachter, *The Psychology of Affiliation* (Stanford, CA: Stanford University Press, 1959).

9. Eugene M. Fodor and Terry Smith, "The Power Motive as an Influence on Group Decision Making," *Journal of Personality and Social Psychology* 42 (1982): 178–85.

10. C. R. Snyder and Howard L. Fromkin, *Uniqueness: The Human Pursuit of Difference* (New York: Plenum, 1980).

11. Abraham H. Maslow, *Motivation and Personality*, 2d ed. (New York: Harper & Row, 1970).

12. Quoted in Russell W. Belk, "Romanian Consumer Desires and Feelings of Deservingness," in Lavinia Stan, ed., *Romania in Transition* (Hanover, NH: Dartmouth Press, 1997): 191–208, quoted on p. 193.

13. Study conducted in the Horticulture Department at Kansas State University, cited in "Survey Tells Why Gardening's Good," *Vancouver Sun* (April 12, 1997): B12.

14. Quoted in "Forehead Advertisement Pays Off," *Montgomery Advertiser* (May 4, 2000): 7A.

15. Quoted in Alex Kuczynski, "A New Magazine Celebrates the Rites of Shopping," *The New York Times on the Web* (May 8, 2000).

16. "Man Wants to Marry His Car," *Montgomery Advertiser* (March 7, 1999): 11A.

17. Judith Lynne Zaichkowsky, "Measuring the Involvement Construct in Marketing," *Journal of Consumer Research* 12 (December 1985): 341–52.

18. Andrew Mitchell, "Involvement: A Potentially Important Mediator of Consumer Behavior," in William L. Wilkie, ed., *Advances in Consumer Research* 6 (Provo, UT: Association for Consumer Research, 1979): 191–96.

19. Richard L. Celsi and Jerry C. Olson, "The Role of Involvement in Attention and Comprehension Processes," *Journal of Consumer Research* 15 (September 1988): 210–24.

20. Anthony G. Greenwald and Clark Leavitt, "Audience Involvement in Advertising: Four Levels," *Journal of Consumer Research* 11 (June 1984): 581–92.

21. Gary J. Bamossy and Janeen Costa, "Consuming Paradise: A Cultural Construction" (paper presented at the Association for Consumer Research Conference, June 1997, Stockholm); Prof. Janeen Costa, personal communication, August 1997.

22. Judith Lynne Zaichkowsky, "The Emotional Side of Product Involvement," in Paul Anderson and Melanie Wallendorf, eds, *Advances in Consumer Research* 14 (Provo, UT: Association for Consumer Research): 32–35.

23. For a recent discussion of interrelationship between situational and enduring involvement, see Marsha L. Richins, Peter H. Bloch, and Edward F. McQuarrie, "How Enduring and Situational Involvement Combine to Create Involvement Responses," *Journal of Consumer Psychology* 1, no. 2 (1992): 143–53. For more information on the involvement construct see "Special Issue on Involvement" *Psychology and Marketing* 10, no. 4 (July/August 1993).

24. Laurie Freeman, "Fragrance Sniffs out Daring Adventures," *Advertising Age* (November 6, 1989): 47.

25. Rajeev Batra and Michael L. Ray, "Operationalizing Involvement as Depth and Quality of Cognitive Responses," in Alice Tybout and Richard Bagozzi, eds., *Advances in Consumer Research* 10 (Ann Arbor, MI: Association for Consumer Research, 1983): 309–13.

26. Herbert E. Krugman, "The Impact of Television Advertising: Learning Without Involvement," *Public Opinion Quarterly* 29 (Fall 1965): 349–56.

27. Kevin J. Clancy, "CPMs Must Bow to 'Involvement' Measurement," *Advertising Age* (January 20, 1992): 26.

28. Gilles Laurent and Jean-Noël Kapferer, "Measuring Consumer Involvement Profiles," *Journal of Marketing Research* 22 (February 1985): 41–53; this scale was validated on an American sample as well, see William C. Rodgers and Kenneth C. Schneider, "An Empirical Evaluation of the Kapferer–Laurent Consumer Involvement Profile Scale," *Psychology & Marketing* 10, no. 4 (July/August 1993): 333–45. For an English translation of this scale see Jean Noël Kapferer and Gilles Laurent, "Further Evidence on the Consumer Involvement Profile: Five Antecedents of Involvement," *Psychology and Marketing*, 10, no. 4 (July/August 1993: 347–56.

29. Carmen W. Cullen and Scott J. Edgett, "The Role of Involvement in Promoting Management," *Journal of Promotion Management*, 1, no. 2 (1991): 57–71.

30. David W. Stewart and David H. Furse, "Analysis of the Impact of Executional Factors in Advertising Performance," *Journal of Advertising Research* 24, no. 6 (1984): 23–26; Deborah J. MacInnis, Christine Moorman, and Bernard J. Jaworski, "Enhancing and Measuring Consumers' Motivation, Opportunity, and Ability to Process Brand Information from Ads," *Journal of Marketing* 55 (October 1991): 332–53.

31. Morris B. Holbrook and Elizabeth C. Hirschman, "The Experiential Aspects of Consumption: Consumer Fantasies, Feelings, and Fun," *Journal of Consumer Research* 9 (September 1982): 132–40.

32. Gordon Fairclough, "Dancing, Music and Free Smokes in Good Ol' Tobaccoville, N.C.," *The Wall Street Journal Interactive Edition* (October 26, 1999).

33. Natalie T. Quilty, Michael R. Solomon, and Basil G. Englis, "Icons and Avatars: Cyber-Models and Hyper-Mediated Visual Persuasion," paper presented at the Society of Consumer Psychology Conference on Visual Persuasion, Ann Arbor, Michigan, May 2000.

34. Robert D. Hof, "Now It's Your Web," *Business Week* (October 5, 1998): 164.

35. Robert L. Simison, "GM Aims to Become Build-to-Order Firm But Custom Online Sales Are Daunting Task," *The Wall Street Journal Interactive Edition* (February 22, 2000).

36. Stacy Baker, "Wanna Know What's Hot Now . . . ?" *Apparel Industry Magazine* (September 1999): 34–35.

37. Quoted in Jim George and Lisa Joerin, "P&G Brand Dot.Compatible with Internet Marketing," *Brand Packaging* (March/April 2000): 22–24.

38. K. Oanh Ha, "Have It Your Way," *Montgomery Advertiser* (November 9, 1998): 2D.

39. Ajay K. Sirsi, James C. Ward, and Peter H. Reingen, "Microcultural Analysis of Variation in Sharing of Causal Reasoning About Behavior," *Journal of Consumer Research* 22 (March 1996): 345–72.

40. Richard W. Pollay, "Measuring the Cultural Values Manifest in Advertising," *Current Issues and Research in Advertising* 6, no. 1 (1983): 71–92.

41. Paul M. Sherer, "North American and Asian Executives Have Contrasting Values, Study Finds," *The Wall Street Journal* (March 8, 1996): B12B.

42. Howard W. French, "Vocation for Dropouts Is Painting Tokyo Red," *The New York Times on the Web* (March 5, 2000).

43. Sarah Ellison, "Sexy-Ad Reel Shows What Tickles in Tokyo Can Fade Fast in France," *The Wall Street Journal Interactive Edition* (March 31, 2000).

44. Milton Rokeach, *The Nature of Human Values* (New York: Free Press, 1973).

45. Han, Sang-Pil and Sharon Shavitt (1994), "Persuasion and Culture: Advertising Appeals in Individualistic and Collectivistic Societies," *Journal of Experimental Social Psychology* 30, 326–50.

46. Donald E. Vinson, Jerome E. Scott, and Lawrence R. Lamont, "The Role of Personal Values in Marketing and Consumer Behavior," *Journal of Marketing* 41 (April 1977): 44–50.

47. Gregory M. Rose, Aviv Shoham, Lynn R. Kahle, and Rajeev Batra, "Social Values, Conformity, and Dress," *Journal of Applied Social Psychology* 24, no. 17 (1994): 1501–19.

48. Milton Rokeach, *Understanding Human Values* (New York: The Free Press, 1979); see also J. Michael Munson and Edward McQuarrie, "Shortening the Rokeach Value Survey for Use in Consumer Research," in Michael J. Houston, ed., *Advances in Consumer Research* 15 (Provo, UT: Association for Consumer Research, 1988): 381–86.

49. B. W. Becker and P. E. Conner, "Personal Values of the Heavy User of Mass Media," *Journal of Advertising Research* 21 (1981): 37–43; Vinson, Scott, and Lamont, "The Role of Personal Values in Marketing and Consumer Behavior," *Journal of Marketing* 41 (April 1977): 44–50.

50. Sharon E. Beatty, Lynn R. Kahle, Pamela Homer, and Shekhar Misra, "Alternative Measurement Approaches to Consumer Values: The List of Values and the Rokeach Value Survey," *Psychology & Marketing* 2 (1985): 181–200; Lynn R. Kahle and Patricia Kennedy, "Using the List of Values (LOV) to Understand Consumers," *Journal of Consumer Marketing* 2 (Fall 1988): 49–56; Lynn Kahle, Basil Poulos, and Ajay Sukhdial, "Changes in Social Values in the United States During the Past Decade," *Journal of Advertising Research* 28 (February/March 1988): 35–41; see also Wagner A. Kamakura and Jose Alfonso Mazzon, "Value Segmentation: A Model for the Measurement of Values and Value Systems," *Journal of Consumer Research* 18 (September 1991): 28; Jagdish N. Sheth, Bruce I. Newman, and Barbara L. Gross, *Consumption Values and Market Choices: Theory and Applications* (Cincinnati: South-Western Publishing Co., 1991).

51. Helene Stapinski, "Y Not Love?," *American Demographics* (February 1999): 62–68.

52. Thomas J. Reynolds and Jonathan Gutman, "Laddering Theory, Method, Analysis, and Interpretation," *Journal of Advertising Research* 28 (February/March 1988): 11–34; Beth Walker, Richard Celsi, and Jerry Olson, "Exploring the Structural Characteristics of Consumers' Knowledge," in Melanie Wallendorf and Paul Anderson, eds., *Advances in Consumer Research* 14 (Provo, UT: Association for Consumer Research, 1986): 17–21.

53. Thomas J. Reynolds and Alyce Byrd Craddock, "The Application of the MECCAS Model to the Development and Assessment of Advertising Strategy: A Case Study," *Journal of Advertising Research* (April/May 1988): 43–54.

54. "25 Years of Attitude," *Marketing Tools* (November/December 1995): 38–39.

55. William O. Bearden, Richard G. Netemeyer, and Jesse E. Teel, "Measurement of Consumer Susceptibility to Interpersonal Influence," *Journal of Consumer Research* 9, no. 3 (1989): 183–94; Lynn R. Kahle, "Observations: Role-Relaxed Consumers: A Trend of the Nineties," *Journal of Advertising Research* (March/April 1995): 66–71; Lynn R. Kahle and Aviv Shoham, "Observations: Role-Relaxed Consumers: Empirical Evidence," *Journal of Advertising Research* 35, no. 3 (May/June 1995): 59–62.

56. Tom Miller, "Global Segments from 'Strivers' to Creatives," *Marketing News* (July 20, 1998): 11.

57. Russell W. Belk, "Possessions and the Extended Self," *Journal of Consumer Research* 15 (September 1988): 139–68; Melanie Wallendorf and Eric J. Arnould, "'My Favorite Things': A Cross-Cultural Inquiry into Object Attachment, Possessiveness, and Social Linkage," *Journal of Consumer Research* 14 (March 1988): 531–47.

58. Marsha L. Richins, "Special Possessions and the Expression of Material Values," *Journal of Consumer Research* 21 (December, 1994): 522–33.

59. Richins, "Special Possessions and the Expression of Material Values."

60. Paul H. Ray, "The Emerging Culture," *American Demographics* (February 1997): 29.

61. David Brooks, "Why Bobos Rule," *Newsweek* (April 3, 2000): 62–64.

Lisa is trying to concentrate on the report her client is expecting by 5:00. She has always worked hard to maintain this important account for the firm, but today she is distracted thinking about her date last night with Eric. Although things seemed to go okay, why couldn't she shake the feeling that Eric regarded her more as a friend than as a potential romantic partner?

Leafing through *Glamour* and *Cosmopolitan* during her lunch hour, Lisa is struck by all of the articles about ways to become more attractive by dieting, exer-cise, and wearing sexy clothes. Lisa begins to feel depressed as she looks at the svelte models in the many adver-tisements for perfumes, apparel, and makeup. Each woman is more glamorous and beautiful than the next. She could swear that some of them must have had assorted "adjustments"—women just don't look that way in real life. Then again, it's unlikely that Eric could ever be mistaken for hunk model Fabio on the street.

In her down mood, though, Lisa actually entertains the thought that maybe she should look into cosmetic surgery. She even checks out an actual live nose job being perfomed on the Web at onl nesurgery.com. Even though she's never considered herself unattrac-tive, who knows—maybe a new nose or removing that mole on her cheek would make her feel better about herself. On second thought, though, is Eric even worth it?

THE SELF

PERSPECTIVES ON THE SELF

Lisa is not alone in feeling that her physical appearance and possessions affect her "value" as a person. Consumers' insecurities about their appearance are rampant: It has been estimated that 72 percent of men and 85 percent of women are unhappy with at least one aspect of their appearance.[1] Many products, from cars to cologne, are bought because the person is trying to highlight or hide some aspect of the self. In this chapter, we'll focus on how consumers' feelings about themselves shape their consumption practices, particularly as they strive to fulfill their society's expectations about how a male or female should look and act.

Does the Self Exist?

The 1980s were called the "Me Decade" because for many this time was marked by an absorption with the self. More recently, *Self* magazine designated March 7 as Self Day and encourages women to spend a minimum of one hour doing something for themselves.[2]

Although it seems natural to think about each consumer as having a self, this concept is actually a relatively new way of regarding individuals and their relationship to society. The idea that each single human life is unique, rather than a part of a group, only developed in late medieval times (between the eleventh and fifteenth centuries). The notion that the self is an object to be pampered is even more recent. Furthermore, the emphasis on the unique nature of the self is much greater in Western societies.[3] Many Eastern cultures instead stress the importance of a collective self in which the person's identity is derived in large measure from his or her social group.

Both Eastern and Western cultures see the self as divided into an inner, private self and an outer, public self. But where they differ is in terms of which part is seen as the "real you"—the West tends to subscribe to an independent construal of the self, which emphasizes the inherent separateness of each individual. Non-Western cultures, in contrast, tend to focus on an interdependent self in which one's identity is largely defined by the relationships one has with others.[4]

For example, a Confucian perspective stresses the importance of "face"—others' perceptions of the self and maintaining one's desired status in their eyes. One dimension of face is *mien-tzu*—reputation achieved through success and ostentation. Some Asian cultures developed explicit rules about the specific garments and even colors that certain social classes and occupations were allowed to display, and these traditions live on today in Japanese style manuals that provide very detailed instructions for dressing and for addressing a particular individual.[5]

That orientation is a bit at odds with such Western conventions as "Casual Fridays," which encourage employees to express their unique selves (at least within reason). To further illustrate these cross-cultural differences, a recent Roper Starch Worldwide survey compared consumers in thirty countries to see which were the most and least vain. Women living in Venezuela were the chart-toppers; 65 percent said they thought about their appearance all the time.[6] Other high-scoring countries include Russia and Mexico. The lowest scorers lived in the Philippines and Saudi Arabia, where only 28 percent of consumers surveyed agreed with this statement.

Self-Concept

The **self-concept** refers to the beliefs a person holds about his or her own attributes, and how he or she evaluates these qualities. Although one's overall self-concept may be positive, there certainly are parts of the self that are evaluated more positively than others. For example, Lisa feels better about her professional identity than she does about her feminine identity.

Components of the Self-Concept

The self-concept is a very complex structure. It is composed of many attributes, some of which are given greater emphasis when the overall self is being evaluated. Attributes of self-concept can be described along such dimensions as their content (e.g., facial attractiveness versus mental aptitude), positivity or negativity (i.e., self-esteem), intensity, stability over time, and accuracy (i.e., the degree to which one's self-assessment corresponds to reality).[7] As we'll see later in the chapter, consumers' self-assessments can be quite distorted, especially with regard to their physical appearance.

Self-Esteem

Self-esteem refers to the positivity of a person's self-concept. People with low self-esteem expect that they will not perform very well, and they will try to avoid embarrassment, failure, or rejection. In developing a new line of snack cakes, for example, Sara Lee found that consumers low in self-esteem preferred portion-controlled snack items because they felt they lacked self-control.[8] In contrast, people with high self-esteem expect to be successful, will take more risks, and are more willing to be the center of attention.[9] Self-esteem is often related to acceptance by others. As you probably remember from your own experience, high school students who hang out in high-status "crowds" seem to have higher self-esteem than their classmates (even though this may not be deserved!).[10]

Marketing communications can influence a consumer's level of self-esteem. Exposure to ads like the ones Lisa was checking out can trigger a process of *social comparison* in which the person tries to evaluate his or her self by comparing it to the people depicted in these artificial images. This form of comparison appears to be a basic human motive, and many marketers have tapped into this need by supplying idealized images of happy, attractive people who just happen to be using their products.

A study that illustrates the social comparison process showed that female college students tend to compare their physical appearance with models who appear in advertising. Furthermore, study participants who were exposed to beautiful women in advertisements afterwards expressed lowered satisfaction with their own appearance, as compared to other participants who did not view ads with attractive models.[11] Another study demonstrated that young women's perceptions of their own body shapes and sizes can be altered after being exposed to as little as 30 minutes of TV programming.[12]

Self-esteem advertising attempts to change product attitudes by stimulating positive feelings about the self. One strategy is to challenge the consumer's self-esteem and then show a linkage to a product that will provide a remedy. For example, the Marine Corps uses this strategy with its theme "If you have what it takes . . ." Another strategy is outright flattery, as when Virginia Slims cigarettes proclaims, "You've come a long way, baby."

Real and Ideal Selves

Self-esteem is influenced by a process in which the consumer compares his or her actual standing on some attribute to some ideal. A consumer might ask, "Am I as attractive as I would like to be?" "Do I make as much money as I should?" and so on. The **ideal self** is a person's conception of how he or she would like to be, whereas the **actual self** refers to our more realistic appraisal of the qualities we have and don't have.

The ideal self is partly molded by elements of the consumer's culture, such as heroes or people depicted in advertising, who serve as models of achievement or appearance.[13] We might purchase products because they are believed to be instrumental in helping us achieve these goals. Some products are chosen because they are perceived to be consistent with the consumer's actual self, whereas others are used to help in reaching the standard set by the ideal self.

Fantasy: Bridging the Gap Between the Selves

Most people experience a discrepancy between their real and ideal selves, but for some consumers this gap is especially large. These people are especially good targets for marketing communications that employ *fantasy appeals*.[14] A **fantasy** or daydream is a self-induced shift in consciousness, which is sometimes a way of compensating for a lack of external stimulation or of escaping from problems in the real world.[15] Many products and services are successful because they appeal to consumers' fantasies. These marketing strategies allow us to extend our vision of ourselves by placing us in unfamiliar, exciting situations or by permitting us to "try on" interesting or provocative roles. And, with today's technology such as *Cosmopolitan*'s online makeover (virtualmakeover.com) or the virtual preview of sunglass styles superimposed on your scanned photo at rayban.com, consumers can even experiment with different looks before actually taking the plunge in the real world.[16]

Multiple Selves

In a way, each of us really is a number of different people—your mother probably would not recognize the "you" that emerges at a rave at 2:00 A.M. with a group of friends! We have as many selves as we do different social roles. Depending on the situation, we act differently, use different products and services, and even vary in terms of how much we like the "me" that is on display at various times. A person may require a different set of products to play a desired role: She may choose a sedate, understated perfume when she is being her professional self, but splash on something more provocative on Saturday night as she becomes her *femme fatale* self. As we saw in Chapter 1, the dramaturgical perspective on consumer behavior views people as actors who play different roles. We each play many roles, and each has its own script, props, and costumes.[17]

The self can be thought of as having different components, or *role identities*, and only some of these are active at any given time. Some identities (e.g., husband, boss, student) are more central to the self than others, but other identities (e.g., stamp collector, dancer, or advocate for the homeless) may be dominant in specific situations. For example, in a survey done in the United States, the United Kingdom, and some Pacific Rim countries, executives said that different aspects of their personalities come into play depending on whether they are making purchase decisions at home or at work. Not surprisingly, they report being less time conscious, more emotional, and less disciplined in their home roles.[18]

Symbolic Interactionism

If each person potentially has many social selves, how does each develop and how do we decide which self to "activate" at any point in time? The sociological tradition of **symbolic interactionism** stresses that relationships with other people play a large part in forming the self.[19] This perspective maintains that people exist in a symbolic environment, and the meaning attached to any situation or object is determined by the interpretation of these symbols. As members of society, we learn to agree on shared meanings. Thus, we "know" that a red light means stop, the "golden arches" means fast food, and "blondes have more fun."

The meanings of consumers themselves, like other social objects, are defined by social consensus. The consumer interprets his or her own identity, and this assessment is continually evolving as he or she encounters new situations and people. In symbolic interactionist terms, we *negotiate* these meanings over time. Essentially the consumer poses the question, "Who am I in this situation?" The answer to this question is greatly influenced by those around us: "Who do *other people* think I am?" We tend to pattern our behavior on the perceived expectations of others in a form of *self-fulfilling prophecy*. By acting the way we assume others expect us to act, we often wind up confirming these perceptions.

The Looking-Glass Self

This process of imagining the reactions of others toward us is known as "taking the role of the other," or the **looking-glass self.**[20] According to this view, our desire to define ourselves operates as a sort of psychological sonar: We take readings of our own identity by "bouncing" signals off of others and trying to project what impression they have of us. The looking-glass image we receive will differ depending on whose views we are considering.

Like the distorted mirrors in a funhouse, our appraisal of who we are can vary, depending on whose perspective we are taking and how accurately we are able to predict their evaluations of us. A confident career woman such as Lisa may sit

NET PROFIT

TALK ABOUT BEING WIRED. In the fall of 2000, a company called Body Media introduced a line of sensors attached to clothing that monitor a user's vital signs and upload this information to a Web site (bodymedia.com). The "sensewear" includes chest straps, arm bands, and smart rings that monitor heart rate, respiration, and caloric burn rate. Data are mapped onto a personalized Web page. Users can compare their readings to population norms in order to be alerted if a vital sign is abnormal.[27]

morosely at a nightclub, imagining that others see her as an unattractive woman with little sex appeal (whether these perceptions are true or not). A *self-fulfilling prophecy* can operate here because these "signals" can influence Lisa's actual behavior. If she doesn't believe she's attractive, she may choose dowdy clothing that actually does make her less attractive. On the other hand, her confidence in herself in a professional setting may cause her to assume that others hold her "executive self" in even higher regard than they actually do (we've all known people like that!).

Self-Consciousness

There are times when people seem to be painfully aware of themselves. If you have ever walked into a class in the middle of a lecture and noticed that all eyes were on you, you can understand this feeling of *self-consciousness*. In contrast, consumers sometimes behave with shockingly little self-consciousness. For example, people may do things in a stadium, a riot, or at a fraternity party that they would never do if they were highly conscious of their behavior.[21]

Some people seem to be more sensitive in general to the image they communicate to others. On the other hand, we all know people who act as if they're oblivious to the impression they are making! A heightened concern about the nature of one's public "image" also results in more concern about the social appropriateness of products and consumption activities.

Several techniques have been devised to measure this tendency. Consumers who score high on a scale of *public self-consciousness*, for example, are also more interested in clothing and are heavier users of cosmetics.[22] A similar measure is *self-monitoring*. High self-monitors are more attuned to how they present themselves in their social environments, and their product choices are influenced by their estimates of how these items will be perceived by others.[23] Self-monitoring is assessed by consumers' extent of agreement with statements such as "I guess I put on a show to impress or entertain others," or "I would probably make a good actor."[24] High self-monitors are more likely than low self-monitors to evaluate products consumed in public in terms of the impressions they make on others.[25] Similarly, some recent research has looked at aspects of vanity, such as a fixation on physical appearance or on the achievement of personal goals. Perhaps not surprisingly, groups such as college football players and fashion models tend to score higher on this dimension.[26]

CONSUMPTION AND SELF-CONCEPT

By extending the dramaturgical perspective a bit farther, it is easy to see how the consumption of products and services contributes to the definition of the self. For an actor to play a role convincingly, he or she needs the correct props, stage setting, and so on. Consumers learn that different roles are accompanied by constellations of products and activities that help to define these roles.[28] Some "props" are so important to the roles we play that they can be viewed as a part of the extended self, a concept to be discussed shortly.

Products That Shape the Self: You Are What You Consume

Recall that the reflected self helps to shape self-concept, which implies that people see themselves as they imagine others see them. Because what others see includes a person's clothing, jewelry, furniture, car, and so on, it stands to reason

THE TANGLED WEB

A PERSON'S UNIQUE IDENTITY may not be so unique anymore in cyberspace. *Identity theft* is a growing problem—even the former Chairman of the Joint Chiefs of Staff had his identity stolen. This happens when a criminal uses a person's Social Security number and other personal information to secure credit. It is estimated that this crime is committed against 400,000 to 500,000 people a year.[29] Travelers Property Casualty Corporation even offers insurance for people who have their identities stolen. The Federal Trade Commission started a toll-free number for consumers who believe they've been a victim of identity fraud (877-IDTHEFT), and the line receives an average of 400 calls a week.[30]

Consumers often express their self-concepts through their choice of an automobile. These British ads take the process a step farther.

that these products also help to determine the perceived self. A consumer's possessions place him or her into a social role, which helps to answer the question, "Who am I now?"

People use an individual's consumption behaviors to help them make judgments about that person's social identity. In addition to considering a person's clothes, grooming habits, and so on, we make inferences about personality based on a person's choice of leisure activities (e.g., squash versus bowling), food preferences (e.g., tofu and beans versus steak and potatoes), cars, home decorating choices, and so on. People who are shown pictures of someone's living room, for example, are able to make surprisingly accurate guesses about his or her personality.[31] In the same way that a consumer's use of products influences others' perceptions, the same products can help to determine his or her own self-concept and social identity.[32]

A consumer exhibits attachment to an object to the extent that it is used by that person to maintain his or her self-concept.[33] Objects can act as a sort of security blanket by reinforcing our identities, especially in unfamiliar situations. For example, students who decorate their dorm rooms with personal items are less likely to drop out of college. This coping process may protect the self from being diluted in a strange environment.[34]

The use of consumption information to define the self is especially important when an identity is yet to be adequately formed, as occurs when a consumer plays a new or unfamiliar role. **Symbolic self-completion theory** suggests that people who have an incomplete self-definition tend to complete this identity by acquiring and displaying symbols associated with it.[35] Adolescent boys, for example, may use "macho" products such as cars and cigarettes to bolster their developing masculinity; these items act as a "social crutch" during a period of uncertainty about identity.

Loss of Self

The contribution of possessions to self-identity is perhaps most apparent when these treasured objects are lost or stolen. One of the first acts performed by institutions that want to repress individuality and encourage group identity, such as prisons or the military, is to confiscate personal possessions.[36] Victims of burglaries and natural disasters commonly report feelings of alienation, depression, or of being "violated." One consumer's comment after being robbed is typical: "It's the next worse thing to being bereaved; it's like being raped."[37] Burglary victims exhibit a diminished sense of community, lowered feelings of privacy, and less pride in their houses' appearance than do their neighbors.[38]

The dramatic impact of product loss is highlighted by studying postdisaster conditions, in which consumers may have lost literally almost everything but the clothes on their backs following a fire, hurricane, flood, or earthquake. Some people are reluctant to undergo the process of recreating their identity by acquiring new possessions. Interviews with disaster victims reveal that some hesitate to invest the self in new possessions and so become more detached about what they buy. This comment from a woman in her fifties is representative of this attitude: "I had so much love tied up in my things. I can't go through that kind of loss again. What I'm buying now won't be as important to me."[39]

Self/Product Congruence

Because many consumption activities are related to self-definition, it is not surprising to learn that consumers demonstrate consistency between their values (see Chapter 4) and the things they buy.[40] **Self-image congruence models** suggest that products will be chosen when their attributes match some aspect of the self.[41] These models assume a process of cognitive matching between product attributes and the consumer's self-image.[42]

Although results are somewhat mixed, the ideal self appears to be more relevant than the actual self as a comparison standard for highly expressive social products such as perfume. In contrast, the actual self is more relevant for everyday, functional products. These standards are also likely to vary by usage situation.[43] For example, a consumer might want a functional, reliable car to commute to work every day and a flashier model with more "zing" when going out on a date in the evening.

Research tends to support the idea of congruence between product usage and self-image. One of the earliest studies to examine this process found that car owners' ratings of themselves tended to match their perceptions of their cars: Pontiac drivers saw themselves as more active and flashy than did Volkswagen drivers.[44] Congruity also has been found between consumers and their most-preferred brands of beer, soap, toothpaste, and cigarettes relative to their least-preferred brands, as well as between consumers' self-images and their favorite stores.[45] Some specific attributes that have been found to be useful in describing some of the matches between consumers and products include rugged/delicate, excitable/calm, rational/emotional, and formal/informal.[46]

Although these findings make some intuitive sense, we cannot blithely assume that consumers will always buy products whose characteristics match their own. It is not clear that consumers really see aspects of themselves in down-to-earth, functional products that don't have very complex or humanlike images. It is one thing to consider a brand personality for an expressive, image-oriented product such as perfume and quite another to impute human characteristics to a toaster.

Another problem is the old "chicken-and-egg" question: Do people buy products because the products are seen as similar to the self, or do people assume that these products must be similar to themselves because they have bought them? The similarity between a person's self-image and the images of products purchased does tend to increase over the time the product is owned, so this explanation cannot be ruled out.

The Extended Self

As noted earlier, many of the props and settings consumers use to define their social roles in a sense become parts of their selves. Those external objects that we consider a part of us comprise the **extended self.** In some cultures, people literally incorporate objects into the self—they lick new possessions, take the names of conquered enemies (or in some cases eat them), or bury the dead with their possessions.[47]

We don't usually go that far, but some people do cherish possessions as if they were a part of themselves. Many material objects, ranging from personal possessions and pets to national monuments or landmarks, help to form a consumer's identity. Just about everyone can name a valued possession that has a lot of the self "wrapped up" in it, whether it is a beloved photograph, a trophy, an old shirt, a car, or a cat. Indeed, it is often possible to construct a pretty accurate "biography" of someone just by cataloguing the items on display in his or her bedroom or office.

In one study on the extended self, people were given a list of items that ranged from electronic equipment, facial tissues, and television programs to parents, body parts, and favorite clothes. They were asked to rate each in terms of its closeness to the self. Objects were more likely to be considered a part of the extended self if "psychic energy" was invested in the effort to obtain them, or because they were personalized and kept for a long time.[48]

Four levels of the extended self have been described. These range from very personal objects to places and things that allow people to feel as though they are rooted in their larger social environments:[49]

- *Individual level:* Consumers include many of their personal possessions in self-definition. These products can include jewelry, cars, clothing, and so on. The saying "You are what you wear" reflects the belief that one's things are a part of one's identity.
- *Family level:* This part of the extended self includes a consumer's residence and the furnishings in it. The house can be thought of as a symbolic body for the family, and often is a central aspect of identity.
- *Community level:* It is common for consumers to describe themselves in terms of the neighborhood or town from which they come. For farm families or other residents with close ties to a community, this sense of belonging is particularly important.
- *Group level:* Our attachments to certain social groups also can be considered a part of the self—we'll consider some of these consumer subcultures in later chapters. A consumer also may feel that landmarks, monuments, or sports teams are a part of the extended self.

SEX ROLES

Sexual identity is a very important component of a consumer's self-concept. People often conform to their culture's expectations about how those of their gender should act, dress, speak, and so on. Of course, these guidelines change over time, and they can differ radically across societies. It's unclear to what extent gender differences are innate versus culturally shaped—but they're certainly evident in many consumption decisions.

Consider the gender differences market researchers have observed when comparing the food preferences of men versus women. Women eat more fruit; men are more likely to eat meat. As one food writer put it, "Boy food doesn't grow. It is hunted or killed." Men are more likely to eat Frosted Flakes or Corn Pops, but women prefer multigrain cereals. Men are big root beer drinkers; women account for the bulk of sales of bottled water.

The sexes also differ sharply in the quantities of food they eat: When researchers at Hershey's discovered that women eat smaller amounts of candy, the company created a white chocolate confection called Hugs, one of the most successful food introductions of all time. On the other hand, men are more likely to take their food and drink in larger servings. When Lipton advertised its iced tea during the Super Bowl, it told its (predominantly male) viewers, "This ain't no sippin' tea," and encouraged them to chug it down.

Gender Differences in Socialization

A society's assumptions about the proper roles of men and women is communicated in terms of the ideal behaviors that are stressed for each gender (in advertising, among other places). It's likely, for instance, that many women eat smaller quantities because they have been "trained" to be more delicate and dainty.

Gender Goals and Expectations

In many societies, males are controlled by **agentic goals**, which stress self-assertion and mastery. Females, on the other hand, are taught to value **communal goals,** such as affiliation and the fostering of harmonious relations.[51] Each society creates a set of expectations regarding the behaviors appropriate for men and women and finds ways to communicate these priorities. A recent analysis of TV commercials aimed at children in the United States and Australia found that boys continue to be depicted as more knowledgeable, active, aggressive, and instrumental.[52]

This training begins very early; even children's birthday stories reinforce gender roles. One analysis showed that while stereotypical depictions have decreased over time, female characters in children's books are still far more likely to take on nurturant roles such as baking and gift-giving. The adult who prepares the birthday celebration is virtually always the mother—often no adult male is present at all. On the other hand, the male figure in these stories is often cast in the role of a miraculous provider of gifts.[53]

Macho Marketers?

The field of marketing tends to be dominated by male values. Competition rather than cooperation is stressed, and the language of warfare and domination is often used. Strategists often use distinctly masculine concepts: "market penetration" or "competitive thrusts," for example. Academic marketing articles also emphasize agentic rather than communal goals. The most pervasive theme is power and control over others. Other themes include instrumentality (manipulating people for the good

REALITY CHECK

DOES SEX SELL? THERE'S CERTAINLY ENOUGH of it around, whether in print ads, television commercials, or on Web sites. When Victoria's Secret broadcast a provocative fashion show of skimpy lingerie live on the Web (after advertising the show on the Super Bowl), 1.5 million visitors checked out the site before it crashed due to volume. That audience topped the million or so people who viewed videotapes of President Clinton's grand jury testimony. Of course, the retailer was taking a risk because by its own estimate 90 percent of its sales are from women. Some of them did not like this display of skin. One customer said she did not feel comfortable watching the Super Bowl ad with her boyfriend: "It's not that I'm offended by it; it just makes me feel inferior."[50]

Perhaps the appropriate question is not, does sex sell, but should sex sell? What are your feelings about the blatant use of sex to sell products? Do you think this tactic works better when selling to men versus women? Does exposure to unbelievably attractive men and women models only make the rest of us "normal" folks unhappy and insecure? Under what conditions (if any) should sex be used as a marketing strategy?

In 1999, a lingerie store opened on one of Dublin's most famous streets. There was outrage at first as some people suggested that the store lowered the tone of the street with its eye-catching window displays. However, there was a petition handed into Dublin Corporation with thousands of names on it showing support for the outlet. Most of these names were those of women. . . . Whether sex should or should not sell, we have to admit it does. I believe that age and culture affect attitudes towards sexy adverts. Typically, in Ireland at least, it is the older generations that are most shocked by sex appeals. The culture of a country/region is obviously going to affect whether people accept or reject sex in the marketplace.

Pamela Gillen,
Dublin City University, Ireland

There's no question about it that sex does sell! There are limits though. As a young female buying a motorbike (a situation that I have recently been faced with), the last thing I wish to confront are images of fleshy women draped over powerful machines lining the walls of motorbike dealers and motorbike magazines! Is there really any purpose to this label and do these images really enhance the desirability of the bike? I imagine that the male viewpoint would be in direct opposition, but from a female point of view I would go so far as to say that the blatant use of sex in this example is a repellent.

Nicole Schragger,
Edinburgh University, United Kingdom

Exposure to unbelievably attractive men and women models can be effective but can cause some potential customers to become unhappy. A person that is attractive tends to be effective in selling a product. Attractiveness usually symbolizes success. People who are exposed to models strive to imitate their looks and can be persuaded to buy a product. However this can be negative to use supermodels because people might feel that they will not be accepted if they don't look like a model. Sex is an effective and appropriate tool for selling a product if it is done in a tasteful manner.

John Dollman IV,
West Virginia University

Because men are visually stimulated, they are more likely to buy a product when a visual stimulus like semi-dressed women is used in a print or television ad. While sexual tactics are very controversial, they do make a product sell. However, advertisers must be aware that sexual appeals should only be used when the product can portray a sexual advantage to the consumer.

Jessica Wells,
Utah State University

Sex ads have a stronger effect on women than men. You might find this opinion strange but let me explain. Most women feel more insecure and more critical of themselves than do men. Women have more of a need to be attractive to men *and* to other women. Most women feel more of a need to impress and compete against whomever they are with. An example that supports this claim is the comparison of the front page of a woman's magazine versus a man's magazine. In a man's magazine there is usually a picture of a beautiful woman dressed provocatively and that same picture will be on a women's magazine also. The reason marketers do this is because women will feel more insecure when seeing a beautiful woman on the cover and more apt to buy the magazine because they are anxious to find out what they can do to themselves to look so beautiful. On the other hand, a man just wants to see the opposite sex and for the most part could not care less about how they could improve their butt in five days or less!

Annalise M. Mulholland,
Virginia Tech

Sex should sell because it is in one or other way a human necessity, but this topic has to be managed with authenticity, respect, and understanding essential human values.

Giselle Gonzalez Aybar,
Pontificia Universidad Catolica Madre y Maestra, Dominican Republic

The blatant use of sex to sell products seems to be very tacky. There has to be better ideas than that. There are just too many beer advertisements with scantily dressed women running around and you wonder if that has any relevance to the product at all. If women don't come running to you when you don't drink . . . they certainly won't run to you when you do. . . . People should know better than to compare themselves with those models that are paid to look good after tons of makeup, and doing nothing but going to gyms to look good.

Tina Ho,
Nanyang Technological University, Singapore

What's your opinion? Check out the online polls at www.prenhall.com/myphlip. Just follow the little person in the lab coat.

of an organization) and competition.[54] This bias may diminish in coming years, as more marketing researchers begin to stress such factors as emotions and aesthetics in purchase decisions—and as increasing numbers of women major in marketing!

Gender Versus Sexual Identity

Gender role identity is a state of mind as well as body. A person's biological gender (i.e., male or female) does not totally determine whether he or she will exhibit **sex-typed traits**, characteristics that are stereotypically associated with one gender or the other. A consumer's subjective feelings about his or her sexuality are crucial as well.[55]

Unlike maleness and femaleness, masculinity and femininity are *not* biological characteristics. A behavior considered masculine in one culture may not be viewed as such in another. For example, the norm in the United States is that males should be "strong" and repress tender feelings ("real men don't eat quiche"), and male friends avoid touching each other (except in "safe" situations such as on the football field). In some Latin and European cultures, however, it is common for men to hug and kiss one another. Each society determines what "real" men and women should and should not do.

Sex-Typed Products

A popular book was entitled, *Real Men Don't Eat Quiche.* Many products (in addition to quiche) also are *sex-typed.* They take on masculine or feminine attributes, and consumers often associate them with one gender or another.[56] The sex-typing of products is often created or perpetuated by marketers (e.g., Princess telephones, boys' and girls' bicycles, and Luvs color-coded diapers). A new brand of vodka introduced in 2000 called Thor's Hammer illustrates this stereotyping. The booze comes in a short, squat bottle and is described by the company's VP of marketing as being "bold and broad and solid. This is a man's kind of vodka . . . it's not your frosted . . . girly-man vodka." Thor was the Norse god of thunder, and the company claims the name has no connection to the slang phrase "getting hammered," which can happen if you drink too much of the stuff.[57]

This ad for Bijan illustrates how sex-role identities are culturally bound by contrasting the expectations of how women should appear in two different countries.

Androgyny

Masculinity and femininity are not opposite ends of the same spectrum. **Androgyny** refers to the possession of both masculine and feminine traits.[58] Researchers make a distinction between *sex-typed people*, who are stereotypically masculine or feminine, and *androgynous people*, whose mixture of characteristics allows them to function well in a variety of social situations.

Differences in sex-role orientation can influence responses to marketing stimuli, at least under some circumstances.[59] For example, research indicates that females are more likely to undergo more elaborate processing of message content, so they tend to be more sensitive to specific pieces of information when forming a judgment, whereas males are more influenced by overall themes.[60] In addition, women with a relatively strong masculine component in their sex-role identity prefer ad portrayals that include nontraditional women.[61] Some research indicates that sex-typed people are more sensitive to the sex-role depictions of characters in advertising, although women appear to be more sensitive generally to gender-role relationships than men.

In one study, subjects read two versions of a beer advertisement, couched in either masculine or feminine terms. The masculine version contained phrases such as "X beer has the strong aggressive flavor that really asserts itself with good food and good company," and the feminine version made claims such as "Brewed with tender care, X beer is a full-bodied beer that goes down smooth and gentle." People who rated themselves as highly masculine or highly feminine preferred the version that was described in (respectively) very masculine or feminine terms.[62] Sex-typed people in general are more concerned with ensuring that their behavior is consistent with their culture's definition of gender appropriateness.

Women's Sex Roles

In the 1949 movie *Adam's Rib*, Katharine Hepburn played a stylish and competent lawyer. This film was one of the first to show that a woman can have a successful career and still be happily married. The presence of women in positions

Reinforcing gender stereotypes.

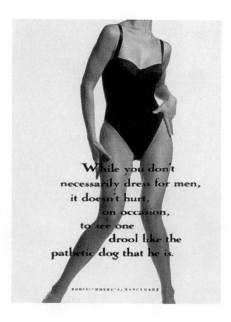

of authority is a fairly recent phenomenon. The evolution of a new managerial class of women has forced marketers to change their traditional assumptions about women as they target this growing market.

Ironically, it seems that in some cases marketers have overcompensated for their former emphasis on women as homemakers. Many attempts to target the vast market of females employed outside the home tend to depict all these women in glamorous, executive positions. This portrayal ignores the facts that the majority of women do not hold such jobs, and that (like men) many work because they have to, rather than for self-fulfillment. This diversity means that not all women should be expected to respond to marketing campaigns that stress professional achievement or the glamour of the working life.

Cheesecake: The Depiction of Women in Advertising

As implied by the ads for Virginia Slims cigarettes—"You've come a long way, baby!"—attitudes about the female sex role have changed remarkably. Still, women continue to be depicted by marketers in stereotypical ways. Consider the popularity of the Singapore Girl in Asia. Encased in her snug sarong, she has been the familiar symbol of Singapore Airlines since 1972—as well as an object of feminist rage. The sarongs are tailored to fit so closely that they have been known to split open during flights. Candidates for the job must be younger than 26, at least 5 ft. 2 inches, slim, and attractive with a good complexion. The rigorous selection process includes a swim suit test in which the women are inspected for scars. A spokesman for the airline said, "We want to present a complete picture of femininity." The airline's slogan: "Singapore Girl, you're a great way to fly."[63]

Ads may also reinforce negative stereotypes. Women are often portrayed as stupid, submissive, temperamental, or as sexual objects who exist solely for the pleasure of men. Although women continue to be depicted in traditional roles, this situation is changing as advertisers scramble to catch up with reality. Women are now as likely as men to be central characters in television commercials. Still, although males are increasingly depicted as spouses and parents, women are still more likely than men to be seen in domestic settings. Also, about 90 percent of all narrators in commercials are male. The deeper male voice is apparently perceived as more authoritative and credible.[64]

Male Sex Roles

The traditional conception of the ideal male as a tough, aggressive, muscular man who enjoys "manly" sports and activities is not dead, but society's definition of the male role is evolving as well. Men in the new millennium are "allowed" to be more compassionate and to have close friendships with other men. In contrast to the depiction of macho men who do not show feelings, some marketers are promoting men's "sensitive" side. An emphasis on male bonding has been the centerpiece of many ad campaigns, especially for beer companies.[65]

Beefcake: The Depiction of Men in Advertising

Men as well as women are often depicted in a negative fashion in advertising. They frequently come across as helpless or bumbling. As one advertising executive put it, "The woman's movement raised consciousness in the ad business as to how women can be depicted. The thought now is, if we can't have women in these old-fashioned traditional roles, at least we can have men being dummies."[68]

MARKETING OPPORTUNITY

AS SEX ROLES FOR males evolve, formerly "feminine products" such as fragrances and hair coloring are being marketed to men. Even nail polish is slowly making its way onto men's bathroom shelves—the Hard Candy line offers its Candy Man collection that includes a metallic gold called Cowboy and a forest green shade named Oedipus. And, responding to pressures felt by many men to look younger, ads aimed at getting men to remove gray hair have tripled during the past decade. Roper Starch Worldwide reports that 36 percent of men have either tried coloring their hair or were open to it. L'Oréal's new Feria line for men's hair includes new hues like Camel (brownish orange) and Cherry Cola. Other vanity products introduced in recent years include Bodyslimmers underwear that sucks in the waist and Super Shaper Briefs that round out the buttocks.[66]

Men in Japan are taking it a step further; it's fashionable for everyone from high school students to professional baseball players to tweeze their eyebrows. Others are putting mud packs on their cheeks and using hairpins, and market researchers are starting to see an interest among men in wearing foundation makeup. These choices illustrate the lengths to which one sex will go to please the other; the men apparently are trying to compete with the large number of boyish, clean cut actors and singers who are now the rage among young Japanese women.[67]

This Australian shoe ad illustrates a common theme in current advertising —the domination of men by women.

Billy, an openly gay doll who is anatomically correct, was created by a London-based firm. He comes with a range of macho outfits including a bell-bottomed sailor and a San Francisco leatherman.

Just as advertisers are often criticized for depicting women as sex objects, the same accusations can be made about how males are portrayed—a practice correspondingly known as "beefcake."[69] An ad campaign for Sansabelt trousers carried the copy, "What women look for in men's pants."

Gay and Lesbian Consumers

The proportion of the population that is gay and lesbian is difficult to determine, and efforts to measure this group have been controversial.[71] However, the respected research company Yankelovich Partners Inc., which has tracked consumer values and attitudes since 1971 in its annual *Monitor*™ survey, now includes a question about sexual identity in its survey. This study was virtually the first to use a sample that reflects the population as a whole instead of polling only smaller or biased groups (such as readers of gay publications) whose responses may not be as representative of all consumers. About 6 percent of respondents identify themselves as gay/homosexual/lesbian. Other data suggest that this proportion is as high as 12 percent in large American cities, where gays and lesbian are more likely to congregate.[72]

These results help to paint a more accurate picture of the potential size and attractiveness of this segment. The gay consumer market spends in the range of $250 to $350 billion a year. A Simmons study of readers of gay publications found that compared to heterosexuals, these consumers are almost 12 times more likely to hold professional jobs, twice as likely to own a vacation home, and eight times more likely to own a notebook computer. Gay consumers also are active Web surfers: The Web site Gay.com attracts one million consumers a month. As many as 65 percent of gay and lesbian internet users go online more than once a day and more than 70 percent make purchases online.[73]

IKEA, a Swedish furniture retailer with stores in several major U.S. markets, broke new ground by running a TV spot featuring a gay couple who purchased a dining room table at the store.[74] Other major companies that now make an effort to market to homosexuals include AT&T, Anheuser-Busch, Apple Computer, Benetton, Levi Strauss, Philip Morris, Seagram, and Sony.[75] And, as civil rights gains are made by gay activists, the social climate is becoming more favorable for firms targeting this market segment.[76] At least in some parts of the country, homosexuality appears to be becoming a bit more mainstream and accepted. Mattel even sold an Earring Magic Ken doll, complete with *faux*-leather vest, lavender mesh shirt, and two-tone hairdo, though the company removed the product from its line following reports that it had become a favorite of gay men.[77]

In addition to gay men, lesbian consumers have recently been in the cultural spotlight. Perhaps the trendiness of "lesbian chic" is due in part to such high-profile cultural figures as tennis star Martina Navratilova, singers k.d. lang and Melissa Etheridge, and actresses Ellen deGeneres and Anne Heche. A readers' survey by a lesbian-oriented publication called *Girlfriends* magazine found that 54 percent hold professional/managerial jobs, 57 percent have partners, and 22 percent have children. But, lesbian women are harder to reach than gay men because they don't tend to concentrate in urban neighborhoods or in bars and don't read as many gay publications. Some marketers have chosen to focus instead on such venues as women's basketball games and women's music festivals.[78] American Express, Stolichnaya vodka, Atlantic Records, and Naya bottled water are among those corporations that run ads in lesbian publications (an ad for American Express Travelers Cheques for Two shows two women's signatures on a check). Acting on research that showed lesbians are four times as likely as the average consumer to own one of their cars, Subaru of America decided to target this market in a big way.

BODY IMAGE

A person's physical appearance is a large part of his or her self-concept. **Body image** refers to a consumer's subjective evaluation of his or her physical self. As was the case with the overall self-concept, this image is not necessarily accurate. A man may think of himself as being more muscular than he really is, or a woman may feel she appears fatter than is the case. It is not uncommon to find marketing strategies that exploit consumers' tendencies to distort their body images by preying on insecurities about appearance, thereby creating a gap between the real and ideal physical self and, consequently, the desire to purchase products and services to narrow that gap. Indeed, the success of the photo chain Glamour Shots, which provides dramatic makeovers to customers (90 percent of them women) and then gives them a pictorial record of their pinup potential, can be traced to the fantasies of everyday people to be supermodels—at least for an hour or two.[79]

A person's feelings about his or her body can be described in terms of **body cathexis.** Cathexis refers to the emotional significance of some object or idea to a person, and some parts of the body are more central to self-concept than are others. One study of young adults' feelings about their bodies found that the respondents were the most satisfied with their hair and eyes and had the least positive feelings about their waists. These feelings also were related to usage of grooming products. Consumers who were more satisfied with their bodies were more frequent users of such "preening" products as hair conditioner, blow dryers, cologne, facial bronzer, tooth polish, and pumice soap.[82]

MARKETING PITFALLS

ARE THE DAYS OF "sensitive men" numbered? A new trend is a return to "old-fashioned" male roles that celebrate leering, boyish behavior—think about the very popular "Man Show" on Comedy Central. An ad for Rheingold beer says, "for the few real men still left," and a character in a Wendy's commercial points out, "This is a burger town, pretty boy."

A new $12 million ad campaign for Brut cologne, targeted to men aged 18–34, exemplifies this new emphasis on being "politically incorrect." The campaign features headlines like "Actually, yes. That outfit does make you look fat." An executive involved with the campaign explains, "These ads reflect the style of how these young guys feel today. It accepts it and speaks in their language that it's good to be Neanderthal again." The campaign was developed after focus groups including men and women of all ages told researchers that crass humor is acceptable now. They were shown a preliminary version, for example, of an ad featuring a man surrounded by buxom women with the tagline, "Brut has been considered an effective treatment for erectile dysfunction." A "disclaimer" says, "Brut antiperspirant should be applied to armpits only." According to the executive, "We showed this to young women in concept form, and they thought it was funny. Certain people might take offense, but overall we were surprised by how both men and women of a wide age range seemed to have a really relaxed attitude about this now." Research findings led to the core insight that drove the campaign: "Inside every man, there's a guy."[70]

This ad for Alize, a cognac drink, is geared toward lesbians.

Ideals of Beauty

A person's satisfaction with the physical image he or she presents to others is affected by how closely that image corresponds to the image valued by his or her culture. In fact, infants as young as two months show a preference for attractive faces.[83] An **ideal of beauty** is a particular model, or *exemplar*, of appearance. Ideals of beauty for both men and women may include physical features (e.g., big breasts or small, bulging muscles or not) as well as clothing styles, cosmetics, hairstyles, skin tone (pale versus tan), and body type (petite, athletic, voluptuous, etc).

Is Beauty Universal?

Recent research indicates that preferences for some physical features over others are "wired in" genetically, and that these reactions tend to be the same among people around the world. Specifically, people appear to favor features associated with good health and youth, attributes linked to reproductive ability and strength. These characteristics include large eyes, high cheekbones, and a narrow jaw. Another cue that apparently is used by people across ethnic and racial groups to signal sexual desirability is whether the person's features are balanced. One study reported that men and women with greater facial symmetry started having sex three to four years earlier than people with asymmetric features!

Men also are more likely to use a woman's body shape as a sexual cue, and it has been theorized that this is because feminine curves provide evidence of reproductive potential. During puberty a typical female gains almost 35 pounds of "reproductive fat" around hips and thighs that supply the approximately 80,000 extra calories needed to support a pregnancy. Most fertile women have waist–hip ratios of 0.6 to 0.8, an hourglass shape that also happens to be the one men rank

Lane Bryant offers lingerie for large women with the slogan "Big girls take back the night."

highest. Even though preferences for overall weight change over time, waist–hip ratios tend to stay in this range. Even the superthin model Twiggy (who pioneered the "waif look" decades before Kate Moss) had a ratio of 0.73.[84] Other positively valued female characteristics include a higher than average forehead, fuller lips, a shorter jaw, and a smaller chin and nose.

Women, on the other hand, favor men with a heavy lower face (an indication of high concentration of androgens that impart strength), those who are slightly above-average height, and males with a prominent brow. One study found these preferences actually fluctuate during the course of a woman's menstrual cycle: Researchers showed women in Japan and Scotland a series of computer-generated photos of male faces that were systematically altered in terms of such dimensions as the size of the jaw and the prominence of the eyebrow ridge.[85] Women in the study preferred the more heavy, masculine features when they were ovulating, but these choices shifted during other parts of their monthly cycles.

Of course, the way these faces are "packaged" still varies enormously, and that's where marketers come in: Advertising and other forms of mass media play a significant role in determining which forms of beauty are considered desirable at any point in time. An ideal of beauty functions as a sort of cultural yardstick. Consumers compare themselves to some standard (often advocated by the fashion media) and are dissatisfied with their appearance to the extent that they don't match up to it.

These cultural ideals often are summed up in a sort of cultural shorthand. We may talk about a "bimbo," a "girl-next-door," or an "ice queen," or we may refer to specific women who have come to embody an ideal, such as Courtney Love, Gwenyth Paltrow, or the late Princess Diana.[86] Similar descriptions for men include "jock," "pretty boy," and "bookworm," or a "Brad Pitt type," a "Wesley Snipes type," and so on.

Ideals of Beauty Over Time

Although beauty may be only skin deep, throughout history women have worked very hard to attain it. They have starved themselves, painfully bound their feet, inserted plates into their lips, spent countless hours under hair dryers, in front of mirrors, and beneath tanning lights, and opted for breast reduction or enlargement operations to alter their appearance and meet their society's expectations of what a beautiful woman should look like.

In retrospect, periods of history tend to be characterized by a specific "look," or ideal of beauty. American history can be described in terms of a succession of dominant ideals. For example, in sharp contrast to today's emphasis on health and vigor, in the early 1800s, it was fashionable to appear delicate to the point of looking ill. The poet Keats described the ideal woman of that time as "a milk white lamb that bleats for man's protection." Other looks have included the voluptuous, lusty woman as epitomized by Lillian Russell, the athletic Gibson Girl of the 1890s, and the small, boyish flapper of the 1920s as exemplified by Clara Bow.[88] One study compared measures of the public's favorite actresses with socioeconomic indicators between 1932 and 1995. When conditions were bad, people preferred actresses with mature features including small eyes, thin cheeks, and a large chin. When the economy was in good shape, however, the public embraced women with babyish features such as large eyes and full cheeks.[89]

In much of the nineteenth century, the desirable waistline for American women was 18 inches, a circumference that required the use of corsets pulled so

MARKETING OPPORTUNITY

A THIRD OF ALL U.S. women wear a size 16 or larger, according to the National Institutes of Health. Throw in size 14s, and that's half of all women, and rising as baby boomers age. Luxury retailers such as Neiman Marcus and Nordstrom's are pushing into this market, which used to be dominated by specialty retailers like Lane Bryant and Forgotten Woman. Wal-Mart successfully extended its Kathie Lee Gifford line into plus sizes, and JC Penney's Web site lets large women "try on" clothes using oversize models.

This oversize business still has room to grow. Big women make up a third to a half of the adult female population, yet large-sizes sales are just 25.4 percent of all women's apparel sales, according to market researcher NPD Group.[80] Lane Bryant has turned its focus from comfortable, baggy styles to the body-hugging fashions popular in smaller sizes. It has carefully groomed a hip image, featuring full-figured celebrity spokesmodels such as former *Playboy* playmate Anna Nicole Smith and Camryn Manheim of *The Practice* TV show. The chain is introducing sexy lingerie with the tagline, "Big girls take back the night." A Lane Bryant executive comments, "If a short-sleeve rib sweater is the hot item this fall it is our challenge to deliver that for our customer, too. But not to do it in a way that makes her look as though she's pushed into a sausage casing."[81]

Cathy reminds us of the large number of products devoted to perfecting the appearance of various body parts.

tight that they routinely caused headaches, fainting spells, and possibly even the uterine and spinal disorders common among women of the time. Although modern women are not quite as "straightlaced," many still endure such indignities as high heels, body waxing, eye-lifts, and liposuction. In addition to the millions spent on cosmetics, clothing, health clubs, and fashion magazines, these practices remind us that—rightly or wrongly—the desire to conform to current standards of beauty is alive and well.

The ideal body type of Western women has changed radically over time, and these changes have resulted in a realignment of *sexual dimorphic markers*—those aspects of the body that distinguish between the sexes. For example, using heights and weights from winners of the Miss America pageant, nutrition experts concluded that many beauty queens are in the undernourished range. In the 1920s, contestants had a body mass index in the range now considered normal—20–25. Since then, an increasing number of winners have had indexes under 18.5, which is the World Health Organization's standard for undernutrition.[90]

Figure 5.1
Waist-Hip Ratios

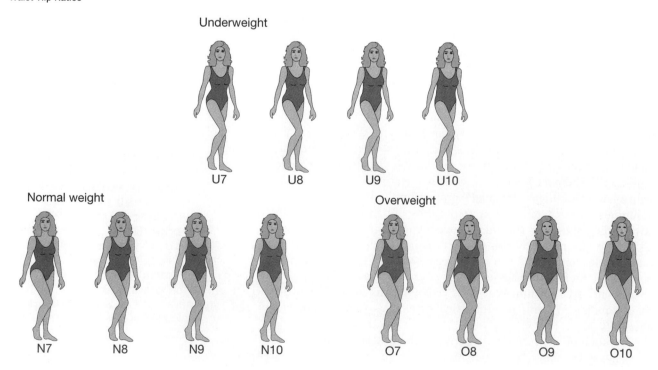

The first part of the 1990s saw the emergence of the controversial "waif" look in which successful models (most notably Kate Moss) were likely to have bodies resembling those of young boys. More recently, the pendulum seems to be shifting back a bit, as the more buxom, "hourglass figure" popular in the 1950s (exemplified by the Marilyn Monroe ideal) has reappeared.[91] One factor leading to this change has been the opposition by feminist groups to the use of overly thin models. Such models, feminists and others charge, encourage starvation diets and eating disorders among women and girls who want to emulate the look. These groups have advocated boycotts against companies such as Coca-Cola and Calvin Klein that have used wafer-thin models in their advertising. Some protesters have even taken to pasting stickers over these ads that read "Feed this woman," or "Give me a cheeseburger."[92]

We can also distinguish among ideals of beauty for men in terms of facial features, musculature, and facial hair—who could confuse Tom Cruise with George Clooney? In fact, one recent national survey that asked both men and women to comment on male aspects of appearance found that the dominant standard of beauty for men is a strongly masculine, muscled body—though women tend to prefer men with less muscle mass than men themselves strive to attain.[93] Advertisers appear to have the males' ideal in mind—a recent study of men appearing in advertisements found that most sport the strong and muscular physique of the male stereotype.[94]

Working on the Body

Because many consumers are motivated to match some ideal of appearance, they often go to great lengths to change aspects of their physical selves. From cosmetics to plastic surgery, tanning salons to diet drinks, a multitude of products and services are directed toward altering or maintaining aspects of the physical self in order to present a desirable appearance. It is difficult to overstate the importance of the physical self-concept (and the desire by consumers to improve their appearance) to many marketing activities.

Fattism

As reflected in the expression "you can never be too thin or too rich," our society has an obsession with weight. Even elementary school children say they would rather be disabled than be obese.[95] The pressure to be slim is continually reinforced both by advertising and by peers. Americans in particular are preoccupied by what they weigh. We are continually bombarded by images of thin, happy people. In a survey of girls aged 12 to 19, 55 percent said they see ads "all the time" that make them want to go on a diet.[96]

How realistic are these appearance standards? Fashion dolls, such as the ubiquitous Barbie, reinforce an unnatural ideal of thinness. The dimensions of these dolls, when extrapolated to average female body sizes, are unnaturally long and thin.[97] If the traditional Barbie doll were a real woman, her dimensions would be 38–18–34! In 1998, Mattel conducted "plastic surgery" on Barbie to give her a less pronounced bust and slimmer hips, but she is still not exactly dumpy.[98] Even newer models feature a body shape that is more athletic and natural, with wider hips and a smaller bust (and for the first time Barbie has a belly button!).[99]

Still, many consumers focus on attaining an unrealistic ideal weight, sometimes by relying on height and weight charts compiled by the insurance industry that show what one *should* weigh. These charts are often outdated because they

NET **PROFIT**

THE NEXT WAVE IN the modeling industry is virtual models—but just like the flesh-and-blood ones they don't come cheap. Elite Models Management was one of the first to move into this new business when it created virtual top model Webbie Tookay to inaugurate its new division, Illusion 2K—Virtual Models and Actresses Management (illusion2k.com). Nodna, a division of the Stockholm-based company Vierte Art, is an agency dedicated to virtual actors (www.nodna.com). The agency offers a variety of "virtualstars" (newly created models and stars), "vuppets" (mascots and animals), and "replicants" (doubles of real people). W Interactive SARL, a French company, also provides Web-based virtual characters in the form of synthetic talking faces that can deliver messages and give product information in a number of different languages. They can be created as cartoon-like people, real people, or famous personalities (www.winteractive.fr).

How do virtual supermodels compare to the real thing? As an Elite executive explains, "Suppose someone hires a regular model to perform in a TV ad. They have to hire a hairdresser, a makeup person, a stylist, a studio, a photographer. Now you can replace all that with a computer crew who will help to develop her movement and animate her." Webbie is loaded with a "personality profile" and she can be engineered to be a voluptuous blonde, a stunning Latina, or an exotic Asian woman.[87] Elle McPherson, look out.

don't take into account today's larger body frames or such factors as muscularity, age, or activity level.[102] Indeed, only 12 percent of blacks and 21 percent of whites (but 43 percent of Hispanics) weigh within the recommended range.[103] American women believe that the "ideal" body size is a 7, an unrealistic goal for most.[104] Even women who are at their best medical weight want on average to be eight pounds lighter.[105]

Body Image Distortions

Many people perceive a strong link between self-esteem and appearance, but some consumers unfortunately exaggerate this connection even more, and sacrifice greatly to attain what they consider to be a desirable body image. Women tend to pick up messages from the media more than men that the quality of their bodies reflects their self-worth, so it is not surprising that most major distortions of body image occur among females. These cultural messages are everywhere—perhaps even in the supermarket if a study conducted by one grocery chain is to be believed. Managers at Tesco, Britain's largest supermarket, were perplexed that its large, 2-pound 2-ounce melons were not selling well, especially when they discovered that sales actually increased when the product was replaced with a smaller, 1-pound 3-ounce version. In research done to explore this curious finding, seven out of 10 women cited unfavorable comparison to their breast size as the reason they avoided the larger fruit. Tesco instructed its produce suppliers to grow smaller melons.[106]

A Swedish firm called Nodna offers its own stable of cybermodels such as Tyra who is shown here.

Men do not tend to differ in ratings of their current figure, their ideal figure, and the figure they think is most attractive to women. In contrast, women rate both the figure they think is most attractive to men and their ideal figure as much thinner than their actual figure.[108] In one survey, two-thirds of college women admitted resorting to unhealthy behavior to control weight. Advertising messages that convey an image of slimness help to reinforce these activities by arousing insecurities about weight.[109]

A distorted body image has been linked to the rise of eating disorders, which are particularly prevalent among young women. People with *anorexia* regard themselves as fat, and virtually starve themselves in the quest for thinness. This condition often results in *bulimia*, which involves two stages. First, binge eating occurs (usually in private), in which more than 5,000 calories may be consumed at one time. The binge is then followed by induced vomiting, abuse of laxatives, fasting, and/or overly strenuous exercise—a "purging" process that reasserts the woman's sense of control.

Most eating disorders are found in white, upper-middle class teenage and college-age young women. Victims often have brothers or fathers who are hypercritical of their weight, and these disorders are also associated with a history of sexual abuse.[110] In addition, binge eating can be encouraged by one's peers. Groups such as athletic teams, cheerleading squads, and sororities may develop positive norms regarding binge eating. In one study of a college sorority, members' popularity within the group increased the more they binged.[111]

Although about 90 percent of teens treated for eating disorders are female, body image disturbances in men may be more widespread than is believed. Increasing cases of *body dysmorphic disorder* (an obsession preoccupied with perceived flaws in appearance) among young males (the average age of onset is 15) are reported by psychiatrists who say that patients' concerns include receding hairlines, facial imperfections, small penises, and inadequate musculature. Symptoms of this disorder include excessive checking of mirrors and attempts to camouflage imagined deformities. Male eating disorders are especially common

Some research indicates that balanced or symmetrical facial features are a cue used by men and women to decide who is attractive. Country singer Lyle Lovett is an example of a man with asymmetrical features. The left picture is the real Lovett; the right is a computerized image that is really two left sides of his face.

among jockeys, boxers, and other athletes who must conform to weight requirements.[112]

As with women, perhaps men are influenced by media images and products encouraging an unrealistic physique. Consider, for example, that if the dimensions of the Original GI Joe action figure were projected onto a real 5'10" man, he would have a 32-inch waist, a 44-inch chest, and 12-inch biceps. Or how about the same exercise for the Batman action figure: If the superhero came to life he would boast a 30-inch waist, 57-inch chest, and 27-inch biceps.[113] Holy steroids, Robin!

Cosmetic Surgery

Consumers are increasingly electing to have cosmetic surgery to change a poor body image or simply to enhance appearance.[114] Virtually any body part is fair game for surgical alteration. For example, bellybutton reconstruction is a popular form of cosmetic surgery in Japan. The navel is an important part of Japanese culture, and mothers often save a baby's umbilical cord in a wooden box. In Japanese, a "bent navel" is a grouch, and a phrase meaning "give me a break" translates as "yeah, and I brew tea in my bellybutton." A popular insult among children is "Your mother has an outie."[115]

Interest in the United States tends to center elsewhere. More than 6 percent of the U.S. adult population has had cosmetic surgery, and the number of procedures rose eightfold from 1990 to 1999.[116] And, going under the knife is not just for women anymore: Men now account for as many as 20 percent of plastic surgery patients, and the number of men having cosmetic surgery rose about 34 percent from 1996 to 1998, with liposuction the most common procedure. Other popular operations for men include the implantation of silicon pectoral muscles (for the chest) and even calf implants to fill out "chicken legs."[117]

As Lisa discovered at the beginning of the chapter, the surgery craze has even spawned several Web sites that feature live Webcasts of real operations, such as onlinesurgery.com. More than 50,000 people tuned in to adoctorinyourhouse.com to watch the singer Carnie Wilson have a gastrointestinal bypass for weight loss.

This 1951 bathing beauty exemplified an ideal of American femininity at that time.

Ironically, the same entrepreneur who owns onlinesurgery.com also owns the highly successful porn site ClubLove.com. He comments on the similarities between the two sites: "They both get inside a world that is forbidden, essentially controversial. They both make you feel a little uneasy and excited. It's like watching the Monica video or news footage from Kosovo."[118]

Breast Augmentation

As the female shoppers at Tesco testified, our culture tends to equate breast size with sex appeal. The impact of breast size on self-concept is demonstrated by consumer research undertaken by an underwear company. While conducting focus groups on bras, an analyst noted that small-chested women typically reacted with hostility when discussing the subject. The participants would unconsciously cover their chests with their arms as they spoke and complained that they were ignored by the fashion industry. To meet this overlooked need, the company introduced a line of A-cup bras called "A-OK" and depicted wearers in a positive light. A new market segment was born.

The modeling industry feeds us images of "perfect" specimens that are used (for better or for worse) as guides for appearance in the "real world".

MULTICULTURAL DIMENSIONS

ALTHOUGH AMERICANS' OBSESSION with thinness is legendary worldwide, the weight-loss obsession is spreading—often with help from American media figures. In traditional Fijian culture, for example, the body ideal for females is, to put it delicately, robust. When a woman started to lose weight, this was cause for concern and a sign of probable illness. Then, a few years ago satellite TV started showing skinny actresses in imported shows such as *Melrose Place* and *Beverly Hills 90210*. Now, the tables have turned and teenaged girls in Fiji are starting to exhibit eating disorders. A study found that teens who watched TV three or more nights per week were 50 percent more likely to feel too fat than were other girls. Participants cited characters such as Heather Locklear as an inspiration for changing their bodies.[100]

Or, consider changes now occurring in the Middle East. As in Fiji, somewhat plumper women have been seen as desirable by Egyptians—and the belly dancing tradition encouraged this. Now, though, weight-loss diets are fashionable. The head of Egyptian television recently announced that overweight female newscasters have three months to shed those extra pounds (10 to 20 pounds in most cases) or they will be fired. Egypt's first lady, Suzanne Mubarak, visits schools to promote thinness, and Egyptian advertising increasingly uses skinny, blond, light-skinned models to sell products to customers who don't look anything like them. An entrepeneur named Samia Allouba is Egypt's answer to Jane Fonda. She sells home-exercise and diet videos, and her twice-weekly exercise program is beamed to millions of potential viewers around the Middle East via satellite. Of course, Fonda never had to face the obstacles Mrs. Allouba does. In deference to Islamic sensibilities, she and female guests exercising on her shows wear only loose-fitting clothes. Though they are doing aerobic exercises, the women aren't allowed to breathe too heavily.[101]

Some women feel that larger breasts will increase their allure and elect to have breast augmentation procedures.[119] Although some of these procedures have generated controversy due to negative side effects, it is unclear whether potential medical problems will deter large numbers of women from choosing surgical options to enhance their (perceived) femininity. And, as Lisa discovered, many companies are promoting nonsurgical alterations by pushing pushup bras that merely create the illusion of a larger cleavage. These products offer "cleavage enhancement" that use a combination of wires and internal pads (called "cookies" in the industry) to create the desired effect.

Body Decoration and Multilation

The body is adorned or altered in some way in every culture. Decorating the self serves a number of purposes.[120]

- *To separate group members from nonmembers:* Chinook Indians of North America pressed the head of a newborn between two boards for a year, permanently altering its shape. In our society, teens go out of their way to adopt distinctive hair and clothing styles that will separate them from adults.
- *To place the individual in the social organization:* Many cultures engage in puberty rites, during which a boy symbolically becomes a man. Young men in Ghana paint their bodies with white stripes to resemble skeletons to symbolize the death of their child status. In Western culture, this rite may involve some form of mild self-mutilation or engaging in dangerous activities.
- *To place the person in a gender category:* The Tchikrin Indians of South America insert a string of beads in a boy's lip to enlarge it. Western women wear lipstick to enhance femininity. At the turn of the century, small lips were fashionable because they represented women's submissive role at that time.[121] Today, big, red lips are provocative and indicate an aggressive

This ad for an online weight-loss site drives home the idea that the media often communicate unrealistic expectations about body shape. One remedy for unrealistic expectations may be MorphOver, an online offering by eFit.com: Users e-mail current photos of themselves, and the photo is altered by nutrition and fitness experts to produce an image of the person at her realistic target weight and size.

This is not normal.
(Despite what you see at the Oscars*.)

sexuality. Some women, including a number of famous actresses and models, receive collagen injections or lip inserts to create large, pouting lips (known in the modeling industry as "liver lips").[122]

- *To enhance sex-role identification:* The modern use of high heels, which podiatrists agree are a prime cause of knee and hip problems, backaches, and fatigue, can be compared with the traditional Oriental practice of footbinding to enhance femininity. As one doctor observed, "When [women] get home, they can't get their high-heeled shoes off fast enough. But every doctor in the world could yell from now until Doomsday, and women would still wear them."[123]
- *To indicate desired social conduct:* The Suya of South America wear ear ornaments to emphasize the importance placed in their culture on listening and obedience. In Western society some gay men may wear an earring

Beverages: Non-Alcoholic

Nunca mais vá à praia de **camis**eta.

DIET PEPSI

Escolha pelo sabor.

You'll never have to go to the beach in a T-shirt again.

Society's emphasis on thinness makes many consumers insecure about their body image. This South American ad promises, "You'll never have to go to the beach in a T-shirt again."

in the left or right ear to signal what role (submissive or dominant) they prefer in a relationship.

- *To indicate high status or rank:* The Hidates Indians of North America wear feather ornaments that indicate how many people they have killed. In our society, some people wear glasses with clear lenses, even though they do not have eye problems, to enhance their perceived status.
- *To provide a sense of security:* Consumers often wear lucky charms, amulets, rabbits' feet, and so on to protect them from the "evil eye." Some modern women wear a "mugger whistle" around their necks for a similar reason.

Tattoos

Tattoos—both temporary and permanent—are a popular form of body adornment (and possibly mutilation). This body art can be used to communicate aspects of the self to onlookers and may serve some of the same functions that other kinds of body painting do in primitive cultures. Tattoos (from the Tahitian *ta-tu*) have deep roots in folk art. Until recently, the images were crude and were primarily either death symbols (e.g., a skull), animals (especially panthers, eagles, and snakes), pinup women, or military designs. More current influences include science fiction themes, Japanese symbolism, and tribal designs.

A tattoo may be viewed as a fairly risk-free way of expressing an adventurous side of the self. Tattoos have a long history of association with people who are social outcasts. For example, the faces and arms of criminals in sixth-century Japan were tattooed as a means to identify them, as were Massachusetts prison inmates in the nineteenth century and concentration camp internees in the twentieth century. These emblems are often used by marginal groups, such as bikers or Japanese *yakuze* (gang members), to express group identity and solidarity.

Body piercing has practically become a mainstream fashion statement.

IT'S NOT NEARLY AS PAINFUL AS PUTTING ON A WEDDING RING.

Body Piercing

Decorating the body with various kinds of metallic inserts also has evolved from a practice associated with some fringe groups to become a popular fashion statement. The initial impetus for the mainstreaming of what had been an underground West Coast fad is credited to Aerosmith's 1993 video "Cryin'" in which Alicia Silverstone gets both a navel ring and a tattoo.[124] Piercings can range from a hoop protruding from a navel to scalp implants, where metal posts are inserted in the skull (do not try this at home!). Publications such as *Piercing Fans International Quarterly* are seeing their circulations soar, and Web sites are attracting numerous followers. This popularity is not pleasing to hard-core piercing fans, who view the practice as a sensual consciousness-raising ritual and are concerned that now people just do it because it's trendy. As one customer waiting for a piercing remarked, "If your piercing doesn't mean anything, then it's just like buying a pair of platform shoes."[125]

CHAPTER SUMMARY

- Consumers' self-concepts are reflections of their attitudes toward themselves. Whether these attitudes are positive or negative, they will help to guide many purchase decisions; products can be used to bolster self-esteem or to "reward" the self.
- Many product choices are dictated by the consumer's perceived similarity between his or her personality and attributes of the product. The symbolic

interactionist perspective on the self implies that each of us actually has many selves, and a different set of products is required as props to play each role. Many things other than the body can also be viewed as part of the self. Valued objects, cars, homes, and even attachments to sports teams or national monuments are used to define the self, when these are incorporated into the extended self.

- A person's sex-role identity is a major component of self-definition. Conceptions about masculinity and femininity, largely shaped by society, guide the acquisition of "sex-typed" products and services.
- Advertising and other media play an important role in socializing consumers to be male and female. Although traditional women's roles have often been perpetuated in advertising depictions, this situation is changing somewhat. The media do not always portray men accurately either.
- A person's conception of his or her body also provides feedback to self-image. A culture communicates certain ideals of beauty, and consumers go to great lengths to attain these. Many consumer activities involve manipulating the body, whether through dieting, cosmetic surgery, piercing, or tattooing.
- Sometimes these activities are carried to an extreme, as people try too hard to live up to cultural ideals. One common manifestation is eating disorders, diseases in which women in particular become obsessed with thinness.
- Body decoration and/or mutilation may serve such functions as separating group members from nonmembers, marking the individual's status or rank within a social organization or within a gender category (e.g., homosexual), or even providing a sense of security or good luck.

KEY TERMS

actual self, p. 133
agentic goals, p. 139
androgyny, p. 142
body cathexis, p. 145
body image, p. 145
communal goals, p. 139

extended self, p. 138
fantasy, p. 133
ideal of beauty, p. 146
ideal self, p. 133
looking-glass self, p. 134

self-concept, p. 132
self-image congruence models, p. 137
sex-typed traits, p. 141
symbolic interactionism, p. 134
symbolic self-completion theory, p. 136

CONSUMER BEHAVIOR CHALLENGE

1. How might the creation of a self-conscious state be related to consumers who are trying on clothing in dressing rooms? Does the act of preening in front of a mirror change the dynamics by which people evaluate their product choices? Why?
2. Is it ethical for marketers to encourage infatuation with the self?
3. List three dimensions by which the self-concept can be described.
4. Compare and contrast the real versus the ideal self. List three products for which each type of self is likely to be used as a reference point when a purchase is considered.
5. Watch a set of ads featuring men and women on television. Try to imagine the characters with reversed roles (i.e., the male parts played by women and vice versa). Can you see any differences in assumptions about sex-typed behavior?

6. To date, the bulk of advertising targeted to gay consumers has been placed in exclusively gay media. If it was your decision to make, would you consider using mainstream media as well to reach gays, who constitute a significant proportion of the general population? Or, remembering that members of some targeted segments have serious objections to this practice, especially when the product (e.g., liquor, cigarettes) may be viewed as harmful in some way, should gays be singled out at all by marketers?

7. Do you agree that marketing strategies tend to have a male-oriented bias? If so, what are some possible consequences for specific marketing activities?

8. Construct a "consumption biography" of a friend or family member. Make a list of and/or photograph his or her most favorite possessions, and see if you or others can describe this person's personality just from the information provided by this catalogue.

9. Some consumer advocates have protested the use of superthin models in advertising, claiming that these women encourage others to starve themselves in order to attain the "waif" look. Other critics respond that the media's power to shape behavior has been overestimated, and that it is insulting to people to assume that they are unable to separate fantasy from reality. What do you think?

10. Interview victims of burglaries, or people who have lost personal property in floods, hurricanes, or other natural disasters. How do they go about reconstructing their possessions, and what effect did the loss appear to have on them?

11. Locate additional examples of self-esteem advertising. Evaluate the probable effectiveness of these appeals—is it true that "Flattery gets you everywhere?"

NOTES

1. Daniel Goleman, "When Ugliness Is Only in Patient's Eye, Body Image Can Reflect Mental Disorder," *New York Times* (October 2, 1991): C13.

2. Ann-Christine P. Diaz, "'Self' Declares Its Own Holiday," *Advertising Age* (January 31, 2000): 20.

3. Harry C. Triandis, "The Self and Social Behavior in Differing Cultural Contexts," *Psychological Review* 96, no. 3 (1989): 506–20; H. Markus and S. Kitayama, "Culture and the Self: Implications for Cognition, Emotion, and Motivation," *Psychological Review* 98 (1991): 224–53.

4. Markus and Kitayama, "Culture and the Self."

5. Nancy Wong and Aaron Ahuvia, "A Cross-Cultural Approach to Materialism and the Self," in Dominique Bouchet, ed., *Cultural Dimensions of International Marketing* (Denmark: Odense University, 1995): 68–89.

6. Lisa M. Keefe, "You're So Vain," *Marketing News* (February 28, 2000): 8.

7. Morris Rosenberg, *Conceiving the Self* (New York: Basic Books, 1979); M. Joseph Sirgy, "Self-Concept in Consumer Behavior: A Critical Review," *Journal of Consumer Research* 9 (December 1982): 287–300.

8. Emily Yoffe, "You Are What You Buy," *Newsweek* (June 4, 1990): 59.

9. Roy F. Baumeister, Dianne M. Tice, and Debra G. Hutton, "Self-Presentational Motivations and Personality Differences in Self-Esteem," *Journal of Personality* 57 (September 1989): 547–75; Ronald J. Faber, "Are Self-Esteem Appeals Appealing?" in Leonard N. Reid, ed., *Proceedings of the 1992 Conference of the American Academy of Advertising* (1992): 230–35.

10. B. Bradford Brown and Mary Jane Lohr, "Peer-Group Affiliation and Adolescent Self-Esteem: An Integration of Ego-Identity and Symbolic-Interaction Theories," *Journal of Personality and Social Psychology* 52, no. 1 (1987): 47–55.

11. Marsha L. Richins, "Social Comparison and the Idealized Images of Advertising," *Journal of Consumer Research* 18 (June 1991): 71–83; Mary C. Martin and Patricia F. Kennedy, "Advertising and Social Comparison: Consequences for Female Preadolescents and Adolescents," *Psychology & Marketing* 10, no. 6 (November/December 1993): 513–30.

12. Philip N. Myers Jr. and Frank A. Biocca, "The Elastic Body Image: The Effect of Television Advertising and Programming on Body Image Distortions in Young Women," *Journal of Communication* 42 (Summer 1992): 108–33.

13. Sigmund Freud, *New Introductory Lectures in Psychoanalysis* (New York: Norton, 1965).

14. Harrison G. Gough, Mario Fioravanti, and Renato Lazzari, "Some Implications of Self Versus Ideal-Self Congruence on the Revised Adjective Check List," *Journal of Personality and Social Psychology* 44, no. 6 (1983): 1214–20.

15. Steven Jay Lynn and Judith W. Rhue, "Daydream Believers," *Psychology Today* (September 1985): 14.

16. Bruce Headlam, "Ultimate Product Placement: Your Face Behind the Ray-Bans," *New York Times* (June 25, 1998): E4.

17. Erving Goffman, *The Presentation of Self in Everyday Life* (Garden City, NY: Doubleday, 1959); Michael R. Solomon, "The Role of Products as Social Stimuli: A Symbolic Interactionism Perspective," *Journal of Consumer Research* 10 (December 1983): 319–29.

18. Julie Skur Hill, "Purchasing Habits Shift for Execs," *Advertising Age* (April 27, 1992): I16.

19. George H. Mead, *Mind, Self and Society* (Chicago: University of Chicago Press, 1934).

20. Charles H. Cooley, *Human Nature and the Social Order* (New York: Scribner's, 1902).

21. J. G. Hull and A. S. Levy, "The Organizational Functions of the Self: An Alternative to the Duval and Wicklund Model of Self-Awareness," *Journal of Personality and Social Psychology* 37 (1979): 756–68; Jay G. Hull, Ronald R. Van Treuren, Susan J. Ashford, Pamela Propsom, and Bruce W. Andrus, "Self-Consciousness and the Processing of Self-Relevant Information," *Journal of Personality and Social Psychology* 54, no. 3 (1988): 452–65.

22. Arnold W. Buss, *Self-Consciousness and Social Anxiety* (San Francisco: Freeman, 1980); Lynn Carol Miller and Cathryn Leigh Cox, "Public Self-Consciousness and Makeup Use," *Personality and Social Psychology Bulletin* 8, no. 4 (1982): 748–51; Michael R. Solomon and John Schopler, "Self-Consciousness and Clothing," *Personality and Social Psychology Bulletin* 8, no. 3 (1982): 508–14.

23. Morris B. Holbrook, Michael R. Solomon, and Stephen Bell, "A Re-Examination of Self-Monitoring and Judgments of Furniture Designs," *Home Economics Research Journal* 19 (September 1990): 6–16; Mark Snyder, "Self-Monitoring Processes," in Leonard Berkowitz, ed., *Advances in Experimental Social Psychology* (New York: Academic Press, 1979): 85–128.

24. Mark Snyder and Steve Gangestad, "On the Nature of Self-Monitoring: Matters of Assessment, Matters of Validity," *Journal of Personality and Social Psychology* 51 (1986): 125–39.

25. Timothy R. Graeff, "Image Congruence Effects on Product Evaluations: The Role of Self-Monitoring and Public/Private Consumption," *Psychology & Marketing* 13, no. 5 (August 1996): 481–99.

26. Richard G. Netemeyer, Scot Burton, and Donald R. Lichtenstein, "Trait Aspects of Vanity: Measurement and Relevance to Consumer Behavior," *Journal of Consumer Research* 21 (March 1995): 612–26.

27. Michael Menduno, "Ready to Wear Health Care," *Wired* (May 2000): 102.

28. Michael R. Solomon and Henry Assael, "The Forest or the Trees? A Gestalt Approach to Symbolic Consumption," in Jean Umiker-Sebeok, ed., *Marketing and Semiotics: New Directions in the Study of Signs for Sale* (Berlin: Mouton de Gruyter, 1987): 189–218.

29. Deborah Lohse, "Travelers Offers Insurance to Borrowers to Cover Expenses of Stolen Identities," *The Wall Street Journal Interactive Edition* (September 29, 1999).

30. Susan J. Wells, "When It's Nobody's Business But Your Own," *The New York Times on the Web* (February 13, 2000).

31. Jack L. Nasar, "Symbolic Meanings of House Styles," *Environment and Behavior* 21 (May 1989): 235–57; E. K. Sadalla, B. Verschure, and J. Burroughs, "Identity Symbolism in Housing," *Environment and Behavior* 19 (1987): 599–87.

32. Michael R. Solomon, "The Role of Products as Social Stimuli: A Symbolic Interactionism Perspective," *Journal of Consumer Research* 10 (December 1983): 319–28; Robert E. Kleine III, Susan Schultz-Kleine, and Jerome B. Kernan, "Mundane Consumption and the Self: A Social-Identity Perspective," *Journal of Consumer Psychology* 2, no. 3 (1993): 209–35; Newell D. Wright, C. B. Claiborne, and M. Joseph Sirgy, "The Effects of Product Symbolism on Consumer Self-Concept," in John F. Sherry Jr. and Brian Sternthal, eds., *Advances in Consumer Research* 19 (Provo, UT: Association for Consumer Research, 1992): 311–18; Susan Fournier, "A Person-Based Relationship Framework for Strategic Brand Management" (doctoral dissertation, University of Florida, 1994).

33. A. Dwayne Ball and Lori H. Tasaki, "The Role and Measurement of Attachment in Consumer Behavior," *Journal of Consumer Psychology* 1, no. 2 (1992): 155–72.

34. William B. Hansen and Irwin Altman, "Decorating Personal Places: A Descriptive Analysis," *Environment and Behavior* 8 (December 1976): 491–504.

35. R. A. Wicklund and P. M. Gollwitzer, *Symbolic Self-Completion* (Hillsdale, NJ: Erlbaum, 1982).

36. Erving Goffman, *Asylums* (New York: Doubleday, 1961).

37. Quoted in Floyd Rudmin, "Property Crime Victimization Impact on Self, on Attachment, and on Territorial Dominance," *CPA Highlights, Victims of Crime Supplement* 9, no. 2 (1987): 4–7.

38. Barbara B. Brown, "House and Block as Territory" (paper presented at the Conference of the Association for Consumer Research, San Francisco, 1982).

39. Quoted in Shay Sayre and David Horne, "I Shop, Therefore I Am: The Role of Possessions for Self Definition," in Shay Sayre and David Horne, eds., *Earth, Wind, and Fire and Water: Perspectives on Natural Disaster* (Pasadena CA: Open Door Publishers, 1996): 353–70.

40. Deborah A. Prentice, "Psychological Correspondence of Possessions, Attitudes, and Values," *Journal of Personality and Social Psychology* 53, no. 6, (1987): 993–1002.

41. Sak Onkvisit and John Shaw, "Self-Concept and Image Congruence: Some Research and Managerial Implications," *Journal of Consumer Marketing* 4 (Winter 1987): 13–24. For a related treatment of congruence between advertising appeals and self-concept, see George M. Zinkhan and Jae W. Hong, "Self-Concept and Advertising Effectiveness: A Conceptual Model of Congruency, Conspicuousness, and Response Mode," in Rebecca H. Holman and Michael R. Solomon, eds., *Advances in Consumer Research* 18 (Provo, UT: Association for Consumer Research, 1991): 348–54.

42. C. B. Claiborne and M. Joseph Sirgy, "Self-Image Congruence as a Model of Consumer Attitude Formation and Behavior: A Conceptual Review and Guide for Further Research" (paper presented at the Academy of Marketing Science Conference, New Orleans, 1990).

43. Jennifer L. Aaker, "The Malleable Self: The Role of Self-Expression in Persuasion," *Journal of Marketing Research* 36 (February 1999): 45–57.

44. Al E. Birdwell, "A Study of Influence of Image Congruence on Consumer Choice," *Journal of Business* 41 (January 1964): 76–88; Edward L. Grubb and Gregg Hupp, "Perception of Self, Generalized Stereotypes, and Brand Selection," *Journal of Marketing Research* 5 (February 1986): 58–63.

45. Ira J. Dolich, "Congruence Relationship Between Self-Image and Product Brands," *Journal of Marketing Research* 6 (February 1969): 80–84; Danny N. Bellenger, Earle Steinberg, and Wilbur W. Stanton, "The Congruence of Store Image and Self Image as It Relates to Store Loyalty," *Journal of Retailing* 52, no. 1 (1976): 17–32; Ronald J. Dornoff and Ronald L. Tatham, "Congruence Between Personal Image and Store Image," *Journal of the Market Research Society* 14, no. 1 (1972): 45–52.

46. Naresh K. Malhotra, "A Scale to Measure Self-Concepts, Person Concepts, and Product Concepts," *Journal of Marketing Research* 18 (November 1981): 456–64.

47. Ernest Beaglehole, *Property: A Study in Social Psychology* (New York: MacMillan, 1932).

48. M. Csikszentmihalyi and Eugene Rochberg-Halton, *The Meaning of Things: Domestic Symbols and the Self* (Cambridge, UK: Cambridge University Press, 1981).

49. Russell W. Belk, "Possessions and the Extended Self," *Journal of Consumer Research* 15 (September 1988): 139–68.

50. Rebecca Quick, no headline, *The Wall Street Journal Interactive Edition* (Feb. 4, 1999).

51. Joan Meyers-Levy, "The Influence of Sex Roles on Judgment," *Journal of Consumer Research* 14 (March 1988): 522–30.

52. Beverly A. Browne, "Gender Stereotypes in Advertising on Children's Television in the 1990s: A Cross-National Analysis," *Journal of Advertising* 27, 1 (Spring 1998): 83–97.

53. Kimberly J. Dodson and Russell W. Belk, "Gender in Children's Birthday Stories," in Janeen Costa, ed., *Gender, Marketing, and Consumer Behavior* (Salt Lake City: Association for Consumer Research, 1996): 96–108.

54. Elizabeth C. Hirschman, "A Feminist Critique of Marketing Theory: Toward Agentic-Communal Balance" (working paper, School of Business, Rutgers University, New Brunswick, NJ, 1990).

55. Eileen Fischer and Stephen J. Arnold, "Sex, Gender Identity, Gender Role Attitudes, and Consumer Behavior," *Psychology & Marketing* 11, no. 2 (March/April 1994): 163–82.

56. Clifford Nass, Youngme Moon, and Nancy Green, "Are Machines Gender Neutral? Gender-Stereotypic Responses to Computers with Voices," *Journal of Applied Social Psychology* 27, no. 10, (1997): 864–76; Kathleen Debevec and Easwar Iyer, "Sex Roles and Consumer Perceptions of Promotions, Products, and Self: What Do We Know and Where Should We Be Headed," in Richard J. Lutz, ed., *Advances in Consumer Research* 13 (Provo, UT: Association for Consumer Research, 1986): 210–14; Joseph A. Bellizzi and Laura Milner, "Gender Positioning of a Traditionally Male-Dominant Product," *Journal of Advertising Research* (June/July 1991): 72–79.

57. Quoted in Hillary Chura, "Barton's New High-End Vodka Exudes a 'Macho Personality,'" *Advertising Age* (May 1, 2000): 8.

58. Sandra L. Bem, "The Measurement of Psychological Androgyny," *Journal of Consulting and Clinical Psychology* 42 (1974): 155–62; Deborah E. S. Frable, "Sex Typing and Gender Ideology: Two Facets of the Individual's Gender Psychology That Go Together," *Journal of Personality and Social Psychology* 56, no. 1 (1989): 95–108.

59. See D. Bruce Carter and Gary D. Levy, "Cognitive Aspects of Early Sex-Role Development: The Influence of Gender Schemas on Preschoolers' Memories and Preferences for Sex-Typed Toys and Activities," *Child Development* 59 (1988): 782–92; Bernd H. Schmitt, France Le Clerc, and Laurette Dube-Rioux, "Sex Typing and Consumer Behavior: A Test of Gender Schema Theory," *Journal of Consumer Research* 15 (June 1988): 122–27.

60. Carol Gilligan, *In a Different Voice: Psychological Theory and Women's Development* (Cambridge, MA: Harvard University Press, 1982); Joan Meyers-Levy and Durairaj Maheswaran, "Exploring Differences in Males' and Females' Processing Strategies," *Journal of Consumer Research* 18 (June 1991): 63–70.

61. Lynn J. Jaffe and Paul D. Berger, "Impact on Purchase Intent of Sex-Role Identity and Product Positioning," *Psychology & Marketing* (Fall 1988): 259–71; Lynn J. Jaffe, "The Unique Predictive Ability of Sex-Role Identity in Explaining Women's Response to Advertising," *Psychology & Marketing* 11, no. 5 (September/October 1994): 467–82.

62. Leila T. Worth, Jeanne Smith, and Diane M. Mackie, "Gender Schematicity and Preference for Gender-Typed Products," *Psychology & Marketing* 9 (January 1992): 17–30.

63. Wayne Arnold, "For the Singapore Girl, It's Her Time to Shine," *New York Times* (December 31, 1999): C4.

64. Daniel J. Brett and Joanne Cantor, "The Portrayal of Men and Women in U.S. Television Commercials: A Recent Content Analysis and Trends Over 15 Years," *Sex Roles* 18 (1988): 595–609.

65. Gordon Sumner, "Tribal Rites of the American Male," *Marketing Insights* (Summer 1989): 13.

66. Jim Carlton, "Hair-Dye Makers, Sensing a Shift, Step Up Campaigns Aimed at Men," *The Wall Street Journal Interactive Edition* (January 17, 2000); Yochi Dreazen, *The Wall Street Journal Interactive Edition* (June 8, 1999); Cyndee Miller, "Cosmetics Makers to Men: Paint Those Nails," *Marketing News* (May 12, 1997): 14.

67. Yumiko Ono, *The Wall Street Journal Interactive Edition* (March 11, 1999).

68. Quoted in Jennifer Foote, "The Ad World's New Bimbos," *Newsweek* (January 25, 1988): 44.

69. Margaret G. Maples, "Beefcake Marketing: The Sexy Sell," *Marketing Communications* (April 1983): 21–25.

70. Quoted in Anthony Vagnoni, "Brut Ad Reeks of Bad-Boy Attitude," *Advertising Age* (October 18, 1999): 24–25.

71. Projections of the incidence of homosexuality in the general population often are influenced by assumptions of the researchers, as well as the methodology they employ (e.g., self-report, behavioral measures, fantasy measures). For a discussion of these factors, see Edward O. Laumann, John H. Gagnon, Robert T. Michael, and Stuart Michaels, *The Social Organization of Homosexuality* (Chicago: University of Chicago Press, 1994).

72. Howard Buford, "Understanding Gay Consumers," *Gay & Lesbian Review*, 7 (Spring 2000): 26–29.

73. Laura Koss-Feder, "Out and About," *Marketing News* (May 25, 1998): 1; Rachel X. Weissman, "Gay Market Power," *American Demographics*, 21, no. 6 (June 1999): 32–33.

74. Kate Fitzgerald, "Ikea Dares to Reveal Gays Buy Tables, Too," *Advertising Age* 3, (March 28, 1994); Cyndee Miller, "Top Marketers Take Bolder Approach in Targeting Gays," *Marketing News* (July 4, 1994): 1; Michael Wilke, "Big Advertisers Join Move to Embrace Gay Market," *Advertising Age* (August 4, 1997): 1.

75. Elliott, "A Sharper View of Gay Consumers"; Kate Fitzgerald, "AT&T Addresses Gay Market," *Advertising Age* (May 16, 1994): 8.

76. Lisa Peñaloza, "We're Here, We're Queer, and We're Going Shopping! A Critical Perspective on the Accommodation of Gays and Lesbians in the U.S. Marketplace," *Journal of Homosexuality*, 31 (Summer 1996): 9–41.

77. Joseph Pereira, "These Particular Buyers of Dolls Don't Say, 'Don't Ask, Don't Tell,'" *The Wall Street Journal* (August 30, 1993): B1.

78. Ronald Alsop, "Lesbians Are Often Left Out When Firms Market to Gays," *The Wall Street Journal Interactive Edition* (October 11, 1999).

79. Stephanie N. Mehta, "Photo Chain Ventures Beyond Big Hair," *The Wall Street Journal* (May 13, 1996): B1.

80. Pollak, Anne Limited, Catherines Miss On Big-Size Boom: Industry Spotlight. *Bloomberg News* [Online] (April 4, 1998).

81. Quoted in Yumiko Ono, "For Once, Fashion Marketers Look to Sell to Heavy Teens," *The Wall Street Journal Interactive Edition* (July 31, 1998).

82. Dennis W. Rook, "Body Cathexis and Market Segmentation," in Michael R. Solomon, ed., *The Psychology of Fashion*, (Lexington, MA: Lexington Books, 1985): 233–41.

83. Carrie Goerne, "Marketing to the Disabled: New Workplace Law Stirs Interest in Largely Untapped Market," *Marketing News* 3 (September 14, 1992): 1; "Retailers Find a Market, and Models, in Disabled," *New York Times* (August 6, 1992): D4.

84. Geoffrey Cowley, "The Biology of Beauty," *Newsweek* (June 3, 1996): 61–66.

85. Corky Siemaszko, "Depends on the Day: Women's Sex Drive a Very Cyclical Thing," *New York Daily News* (June 24, 1999): 3.

86. Englis, Basil G., Michael R. Solomon, and Richard D. Ashmore, "Beauty Before the Eyes of Beholders: The Cultural Encoding

of Beauty Types in Magazine Advertising and Music Television," *Journal of Advertising* 23 (June 1994): 49–64; Michael R. Solomon, Richard Ashmore, and Laura Longo, "The Beauty Match-Up Hypothesis: Congruence Between Types of Beauty and Product Images in Advertising," *Journal of Advertising* 21 (December 1992): 23–34.

87. Quoted in Rachel Emma Silverman, "The Perfect Model: She Won't Age, Gain Weight or Throw Tantrums," *The Wall Street Journal Interactive Edition* (July 16, 1999). See also Victoria Coren "The First Computer-Generated Supermodel Has Arrived . . . and a Chimp That Can Talk," *The Guardian*, (July 27, 1999): 7.

88. Lois W. Banner, *American Beauty* (Chicago: University of Chicago Press, 1980); for a philosophical perspective, see Barry Vacker and Wayne R. Key, "Beauty and the Beholder: The Pursuit of Beauty Through Commodities," *Psychology & Marketing* 10, no. 6 November/December 1993): 471–94.

89. Abraham Tesser and Terry Pettijohn II, reported in "And the Winner Is . . . Wall Street," *Psychology Today* (March/April 1998): 12.

90. "Report Delivers Skinny on Miss America," *Montgomery Advertiser* (March 22, 2000): 5A.

91. Kathleen Boyes, "The New Grip of Girdles Is Lightened by Lycra," *USA Today* (April 25, 1991): 6D.

92. Stuart Elliott, "Ultrathin Models in Coca-Cola and Calvin Klein Campaigns Draw Fire and a Boycott Call," *New York Times* (April 26, 1994): D18; Cyndee Miller, "'Give Them a Cheeseburger'," *Marketing News* (June 6, 1994): 1.

93. Jill Neimark, "The Beefcaking of America," *Psychology Today* (November/December 1994): 32.

94. Richard H. Kolbe and Paul J. Albanese, "Man to Man: A Content Analysis of Sole-Male Images in Male-Audience Magazines," *Journal of Advertising* 25, no. 4 (Winter 1996): 1–20.

95. "Girls at 7 Think Thin, Study Finds," *New York Times* (February 11, 1988): B9.

96. David Goetzl, "Teen Girls Pan Ad Images of Women," *Advertising Age* (September 13, 1999): 32.

97. Elaine L. Pedersen and Nancy L. Markee, "Fashion Dolls: Communicators of Ideals of Beauty and Fashion" (paper presented at the International Conference on

Marketing Meaning, Indianapolis, IN, 1989); Dalma Heyn, "Body Hate," *Ms.* (August 1989): 34; Mary C. Martin and James W. Gentry, "Assessing the Internalization of Physical Attractiveness Norms," *Proceedings of the American Marketing Association Summer Educators' Conference* (Summer 1994): 59–65.

98. Lisa Bannon, "Barbie Is Getting Body Work, and Mattel Says She'll be 'Rad,'" *The Wall Street Journal Interactive Edition* (November 17, 1997).

99. Lisa Bannon, "Will New Clothes, Bellybutton Create 'Turn Around' Barbie," *The Wall Street Journal Interactive Edition* (February 17, 2000).

100. "Fat-Phobia in the Fijis: TV-Thin Is In," *Newsweek (*May 31, 1999): 70.

101. Amy Dockser Marcus, "With an Etiquette of Overeating, It's Not Easy Being Lean in Egypt," *The Wall Street Journal Inter-Active Edition*, (March 4, 1998).

102. "How Much Is Too Fat?" *USA Today* (February 1989): 8.

103. *American Demographics* (May 1987): 56.

104. Deborah Marquardt, "A Thinly Disguised Mcssage," *Ms.* 15 (May 1987): 33.

105. Vincent Bozzi, "The Body In Question," *Psychology Today* 22 (February 1988): 10.

106. "Fruit Cups," *Details* (August 1999): 37.

107. Karen Thomas, "Web Sites Urge Overweight Americans", *USA Today* (January 6, 2000): 10D.

108. Debra A. Zellner, Debra F. Harner, and Robbie I. Adler, "Effects of Eating Abnormalities and Gender on Perceptions of Desirable Body Shape," *Journal of Abnormal Psychology* 98 (February 1989): 93–96.

109. Robin T. Peterson, "Bulimia and Anorexia in an Advertising Context," *Journal of Business Ethics* 6 (1987): 495–504.

110. Jane E. Brody, "Personal Health," *New York Times* (February 22, 1990): B9.

111. Christian S. Crandall, "Social Contagion of Binge Eating," *Journal of Personality and Social Psychology* 55 (1988): 588–98.

112. Judy Folkenberg, "Bulimia: Not For Women Only," *Psychology Today* (March 1984): 10.

113. Stephen S. Hall, "The Bully in the Mirror," *New York Times Magazine*, (downloaded August 22, 1999); Natalie Angier, "Drugs, Sports, Body Image and G.I. Joe," *New York Times* (December 22, 1998): D1.

114. John W. Schouten, "Selves in Transition:

Symbolic Consumption in Personal Rites of Passage and Identity Reconstruction," *Journal of Consumer Research* 17 (March 1991): 412–25.

115. Jane E. Brody, "Notions of Beauty Transcend Culture, New Study Suggests," *New York Times* (March 21, 1994): A14; Norihiko Shirouzu, "Reconstruction Boom in Tokyo: Perfecting Imperfect Belly-buttons," *Wall Street Journal* (October 4, 1995): B1.

116. Nancy Hass, "Nip, Tuck, Click: Plastic Surgery on the Web Is Hip," *The New York Times on the Web*, (September 19, 1999); Celeste McGovern, "Brave New World," *Newsmagazine* (Alberta edition), 26 (February 7, 2000): 50–52.

117. Stephen S. Hall, "The Bully in the Mirror," *New York Times Magazine*, (August 22, 1999); Emily Yoffe, "Valley of the Silicon Dolls," *Newsweek* (November 26, 1990): 72.

118. Quoted in Nancy Hass, "Nip, Tuck, Click: Plastic Surgery on the Web Is Hip," *The New York Times on the Web*, (September 19, 1999).

119. Jerry Adler, "New Bodies For Sale," *Newsweek* (May 27, 1985): 64.

120. Ruth P. Rubinstein, "Color, Circumcision, Tatoos, and Scars," in Michael R. Solomon, ed., *The Psychology of Fashion* (Lexington, MA: Lexington Books, 1985): 243–54; Peter H. Bloch and Marsha L. Richins, "You Look 'Mahvelous': The Pursuit of Beauty and Marketing Concept," *Psychology & Marketing* 9 (January 1992): 3–16. For a visual overview of these processes, visit amnh.org/exhibitions/bodyart/ to view an exhibit mounted by the American Museum of Natural History.

121. Sondra Farganis, "Lip Service: The Evolution of Pouting, Pursing, and Painting Lips Red," *Health* (November 1988): 48–51.

122. Michael Gross, "Those Lips, Those Eyebrows; New Face of 1989 (New Look of Fashion Models)," *New York Times Magazine* (February 13, 1989): 24.

123. Quoted in "High Heels: Ecstasy's Worth the Agony," *New York Post* (December 31, 1981).

124. Accessed via alt.culture on August 22, 1997: pathfinder.com:80/altculture/aentries/p/piercing.html.

125. Quoted in Wendy Bounds, "Body-Piercing Gets Under America's Skin," *The Wall Street Journal* (April 4, 1994): B1.

Jackie and Hank, executives in a high-powered Los Angeles advertising agency, are exchanging ideas about how they are going to spend the big bonus everyone in the firm has been promised for landing the Gauntlet body jewelry account. They can't help but snicker at their friend Margie in accounting, who has been avidly surfing the Net for infor-

mation about a state-of-the-art home theater system she plans to put into her condo. What a couch potato! Hank, who fancies himself a bit of a thrill seeker, plans to blow his bonus on a wild trip to Colorado, where a week of outrageous bungee jumping awaits him (assuming he lives to tell about it, but that uncertainty is half the fun). Jackie replies, "Been there, done that. . . . Believe it or not, I'm staying put right here—heading over to Santa Monica to catch some waves." Seems that she's been bitten by the surfing bug since she started leafing through *Wahine,* a magazine targeted to the growing number of women taking up the sport.

Jackie and Hank are sometimes amazed at how different they are from Margie, who's content to spend her downtime watching sappy old movies or reading books. All three make about the same salary, and Jackie and Margie even went to the same college together. How can their tastes be so different? Oh well, they figure, that's why they make chocolate and vanilla.

6

PERSONALITY AND LIFESTYLES

PERSONALITY

Jackie and Hank are typical of many people who search for new (and even risky) ways to spend their leisure time. This desire has meant big business for the "adventure travel" industry, which specializes in providing white-knuckle experiences. Sports such as bungee jumping, white-water rafting, sky diving, mountain biking, and other physically stimulating activities now account for about one-fifth of the U.S. leisure travel market.[1] And, though once the California beach culture used to relegate women to the status of land-locked "Gidgets" who sat on shore while their boyfriends rode the big one, now it's women who are fueling the sports' resurgence in popularity. Quicksilver Inc., the largest maker of surf apparel, is reaping huge profits with its female surfing gear, which includes a line of boardshorts called Roxy, and at least 20 other companies now offer their own women's lines.[2]

Just what does make Jackie and Hank so different from their more sedate friend Margie? One answer may lie in the concept of **personality,** which refers to a person's unique psychological makeup and how it consistently influences the way a person responds to his or her environment.

In recent years, the nature of the personality construct has been hotly debated. Many studies have found that people do not seem to exhibit stable personalities. In fact, some researchers feel that people do not exhibit consistent behavior across different situations—they argue that this is merely a convenient way to think about other people.

This argument is a bit hard to accept intuitively, possibly because we tend to see others in a limited range of situations, and so most people appear to act consistently. On the other hand, we each know that we are not all that consistent; we may be wild and crazy at times and the model of respectability at others.

Although certainly not all psychologists have abandoned the idea of personality, many now recognize that a person's underlying characteristics are but one part of the puzzle and that situational factors often play a very large role in determining behavior.[3]

Still, some aspects of personality continue to be included in marketing strategies. These dimensions are usually employed in concert with a person's choices of leisure activities, political outlook, aesthetic tastes, and other individual factors to segment consumers in terms of *lifestyles*, a process we'll focus on more fully later in this chapter.

Many approaches to understanding the complex concept of personality can be traced to psychological theorists who began to develop these perspectives in the early part of the twentieth century. These perspectives were qualitative, in the sense that they were largely based on analysts' interpretations of patients' accounts of dreams, traumatic experiences, and encounters with others.

CONSUMER BEHAVIOR ON THE COUCH: FREUDIAN THEORY

Sigmund Freud developed the idea that much of one's adult personality stems from a fundamental conflict between a person's desire to gratify his or her physical needs and the necessity to function as a responsible member of society. This struggle is carried out in the mind among three systems. (Note: These systems do *not* refer to physical parts of the brain.)

Freudian Systems

The **id** is entirely oriented toward immediate gratification—it is the "party animal" of the mind. It operates according to the **pleasure principle;** behavior is guided by the primary desire to maximize pleasure and avoid pain. The id is selfish and illogical. It directs a person's psychic energy toward pleasurable acts without regard for any consequences.

The **superego** is the counterweight to the id. This system is essentially the person's conscience. It internalizes society's rules (especially as communicated by parents) and works to prevent the id from seeking selfish gratification.

Finally, the **ego** is the system that mediates between the id and the superego. It is in a way a referee in the fight between temptation and virtue. The ego tries to balance these opposing forces according to the **reality principle,** whereby it finds ways to gratify the id that will be acceptable to the outside world. These conflicts occur on an unconscious level, so the person is not necessarily aware of the underlying reasons for behavior.

Some of Freud's ideas have also been adapted by consumer researchers. In particular, his work highlights the potential importance of unconscious motives underlying purchases. The implication is that consumers cannot necessarily tell us their true motivation for choosing a product, even if we can devise a sensitive way to ask them directly.

The Freudian perspective also hints at the possibility that the ego relies on the symbolism in products to compromise between the demands of the id and the prohibitions of the superego. The person channels his or her unacceptable desire into acceptable outlets by using products that signify these underlying desires. This is the connection between product symbolism and motivation: The product stands for, or represents, a consumer's true goal, which is socially unacceptable or unattainable. By acquiring the product, the person is able to vicariously experience the forbidden fruit.

Sometimes a Cigar Is Just a Cigar

Most Freudian applications in marketing are related to the sexuality of products. For example, some analysts have speculated that a sports car is a substitute for sexual gratification for many men. Indeed, some men do seem inordinately attached to their cars and may spend many hours lovingly washing and polishing them. An Infiniti ad reinforces the belief that cars symbolically satisfy consumers' sexual needs in addition to their functional ones by describing the J30 model as "what happens when you cross sheet metal and desire."

Others focus on male-oriented symbolism—so-called *phallic symbols*—that appeals to women. Although Freud himself joked that "sometimes a cigar is just a cigar," many popular applications of Freud's ideas revolve around the use of objects that resemble sex organs (e.g., cigars, trees, or swords for male sex organs; tunnels for female sex organs). This focus stems from Freud's analysis of dreams, which he interpreted as communicating repressed desires through symbols.

Motivational Research

The first attempts to apply Freudian ideas to understand the deeper meanings of products and advertisements were made in the 1950s when a perspective known as **motivational research** was developed. This approach was largely based on psychoanalytic (Freudian) interpretations, with a heavy emphasis on unconscious motives. A basic assumption is that socially unacceptable needs are channeled into acceptable outlets. Product use or avoidance is motivated by unconscious forces that are often determined in childhood.

This form of research relies on *in-depth interviews* with individual consumers. Instead of asking many consumers a few general questions about product usage and combining these responses with those of many other consumers in a representative statistical sample, this technique uses relatively few consumers but probes deeply into each person's purchase motivations. An in-depth interview might take several hours and is based on the assumption that the respondent cannot immediately articulate his or her latent, or underlying, motives. These can be derived only after extensive questioning and interpretation on the part of a carefully trained interviewer.

This work was pioneered by Ernest Dichter, a psychoanalyst who was trained in Vienna in the early part of the century. Dichter conducted in-depth interview studies on more than 230 different products, and many of his findings have been incorporated into actual marketing campaigns.[4] For example, Esso (now Exxon) for many years reminded consumers to "Put a Tiger in Your Tank" after Dichter found that people responded well to this powerful animal symbolism containing vaguely sexual undertones. A summary of major consumption motivations identified using this approach appears in Table 6.1.

Motivational research has been attacked for two opposing reasons. Some feel it does not work, whereas others feel it works *too* well. On the one hand, social critics reacted much the same way they had to subliminal perception studies (see Chapter 2). They attacked this school of thought for giving advertisers the power to manipulate consumers.[5] On the other hand, many consumer researchers felt the research lacked sufficient rigor and validity, as interpretations were subjective

TABLE 6.1 Major Motives for Consumption as Identified by Ernest Dichter

Motive	Associated Products
Power-masculinity-virility	Power: Sugary products and large breakfasts (to charge oneself up), bowling, electric trains, hot rods, power tools
	Masculinity-virility: Coffee, red meat, heavy shoes, toy guns, buying fur coats for women, shaving with a razor
Security	Ice cream (to feel like a loved child again), full drawer of neatly ironed shirts, real plaster walls (to feel sheltered), home baking, hospital care
Eroticism	Sweets (to lick), gloves (to be removed by woman as a form of undressing), a man lighting a woman's cigarette (to create a tension-filled moment culminating in pressure, then relaxation)
Moral purity-cleanliness	White bread, cotton fabrics (to connote chastity), harsh household cleaning chemicals (to make housewives feel moral after using), bathing (to be equated with Pontius Pilate, who washed blood from his hands), oatmeal (sacrifice, virtue)
Social acceptance	Companionship: Ice cream (to share fun), coffee
	Love and affection: Toys (to express love for children), sugar and honey (to express terms of affection)
	Acceptance: Soap, beauty products
Individuality	Gourmet foods, foreign cars, cigarette holders, vodka, perfume, fountain pens
Status	Scotch; ulcers, heart attacks, indigestion (to show one has a high-stress, important job!); carpets (to show one does not live on bare earth like peasants)
Femininity	Cakes and cookies, dolls, silk, tea, household curios
Reward	Cigarettes, candy, alcohol, ice cream, cookies
Master over environment	Kitchen appliances, boats, sporting goods, cigarette lighters
Disalienation (a desire to feel connectedness to things)	Home decorating, skiing, morning radio broadcasts (to feel "in touch" with the world)
Magic-mystery	Soups (having healing powers), paints (change the mood of a room), carbonated drinks (magical effervescent property), vodka (romantic history), unwrapping of gifts

SOURCE: Adapted from Jeffrey F. Durgee, "Interpreting Dichter's Interpretations: An Analysis of Consumption Symbolism in *The Handbook of Consumer Motivations*," *Marketing and Semiotics: Selected Papers from the Copenhagen Symposium*, eds., Hanne Hartvig-Larsen, David Glen Mick, and Christian Alstead (Copenhagen, 1991).

and indirect.[6] Because conclusions are based on the analyst's own judgment and are derived from discussions with a small number of people, some researchers are dubious as to the degree to which these results can be generalized to a large market. In addition, because the original motivational researchers were heavily influenced by orthodox Freudian theory, their interpretations usually involved sexual themes. This emphasis tends to overlook other plausible causes for behavior.

Still, motivational research had great appeal to at least some marketers for several reasons, some of which are detailed here.

- Motivational research tends to be less expensive than large-scale, quantitative survey data because interviewing and data-processing costs are relatively minimal.

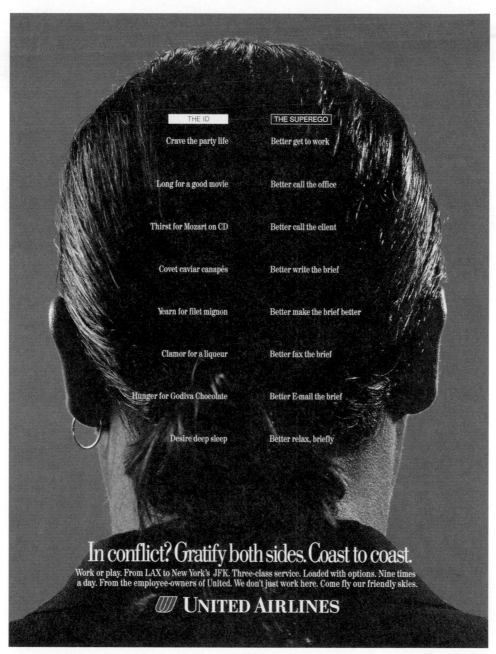

This ad focuses on the conflict between the desire for hedonic gratification (represented by the id) versus the need to engage in rational, task-oriented activities (represented by the superego).

- The knowledge derived from motivational research can possibly help develop marketing communications that appeal to deep-seated needs and thus provide a more powerful hook to reel in consumers. Even if not necessarily valid for all consumers in a target market, these insights can be valuable when used in an exploratory way. For example, the rich imagery that may be associated with a product can be used creatively when developing advertising copy.

- Some of the findings seem intuitively plausible after the fact. For example, motivational studies concluded that coffee is associated with companionship, that people avoid prunes because they remind them of old age, and that men fondly equate the first car they owned as an adolescent with the onset of their sexual freedom.

Other interpretations were hard for some researchers to swallow, such as the observation that to a woman baking a cake symbolizes giving birth, or that men are reluctant to give blood because they feel that their vital fluids are being drained. On the other hand, a pregnant woman is sometimes described as "having a bun in the oven," and Pillsbury claims that "nothing says lovin' like something from the oven." Motivational research for the American Red Cross did find that men (but not women) tend to drastically overestimate the amount of blood that is taken during a donation. The Red Cross counteracted the fear of loss of virility by symbolically equating the act of giving blood with fertilization: "Give the gift of life." Despite its drawbacks, motivational research continues to be employed as a useful diagnostic tool. Its validity is enhanced, however, when used in conjunction with the other research techniques available to the consumer researcher.

Neo-Freudian Theories

Freud's work had a huge influence on subsequent theories of personality. Although Freud opened the door to the realization that explanations for behavior may lurk beneath the surface, many of his colleagues and students felt that an individual's personality was more influenced by how he or she handled relationships with others than by unresolved sexual conflicts. These theorists are often called neo-Freudian (meaning following from or being influenced by Freud).

Karen Horney

One of the most prominent neo-Freudians was a psychoanalyst named Karen Horney. She proposed that people can be described as moving toward others (*compliant*), away from others (*detached*), or against others (*aggressive*).[7] Indeed, one early study found that compliant people are more likely to gravitate toward name-brand products, detached types are more likely to be tea drinkers, and males classified as aggressive prefer brands with a strong masculine orientation (e.g., Old Spice deodorant).[8]

Other well-known neo-Freudians include Alfred Adler, who proposed that many actions are motivated by people's desire to overcome feelings of inferiority relative to others; and Harry Stack Sullivan, who focused on how personality evolves to reduce anxiety in social relationships.[9]

Carl Jung

Carl Jung was also a disciple of Freud's (and was being groomed by Freud to be his successor). However, Jung was unable to accept Freud's emphasis on sexual aspects of personality, and this was a contributing factor in the eventual dissolution of their relationship. Jung went on to develop his own method of psychotherapy, which became known as *analytical psychology*.

Jung believed that people are shaped by the cumulative experiences of past generations. A central part of his perspective was an emphasis on what he called the *collective unconscious*, a storehouse of memories inherited from our ancestral past. For example, Jung would argue that many people are afraid of the dark because their distant ancestors had good reason to exhibit this fear. These shared memories create **archetypes**, or universally shared ideas and behavior patterns.

Archetypes involve themes, such as birth, death, or the devil, that appear frequently in myths, stories, and dreams.

Jung's ideas may seem a bit farfetched, but (at least intuitively) advertising messages often invoke archetypes to link products with underlying meanings. For example, some of the archetypes identified by Jung and his followers include the "old wise man" and the "earth mother."[10] These images appear frequently in marketing messages that use characters such as wizards, revered teachers, or even Mother Nature to convince people of the merits of products.

Trait Theory

One approach to personality is to focus on the quantitative measurement of traits, or identifiable characteristics that define a person. For example, people can be distinguished by the degree to which they are socially outgoing (the trait of *extroversion*)—Margie might be described as an *introvert* (quiet and reserved), whereas her co-worker Jackie is an *extrovert*.

Some specific traits that are relevant to consumer behavior include: *innovativeness* (the degree to which a person likes to try new things); *materialism* (amount of emphasis placed on acquiring and owning products); *self-consciousness* (the degree to which a person deliberately monitors and controls the image of the self that is projected to others), and *need for cognition* (the degree to which a person likes to think about things and by extension expend the necessary effort to process brand information).[11]

Problems with Trait Theory in Consumer Research

Because large numbers of consumers can be categorized according to whether they exhibit various traits, these approaches can, in theory, be used for segmentation purposes. If a car manufacturer, for example, could determine that drivers who fit a given trait profile are more likely to prefer a car with certain features, this match could be used to great advantage. The notion that consumers buy products that are extensions of their personalities makes intuitive sense. As we'll see shortly, this idea is endorsed by many marketing managers, who try to create *brand personalities* that will appeal to different types of consumers.

However, the use of standard personality trait measurements to predict product choices has met with mixed success at best. In general, marketing researchers simply have not been able to predict consumers' behaviors on the basis of measured personality traits. A number of explanations have been offered for these equivocal results.[12]

- Many of the scales are not sufficiently valid or reliable; they do not adequately measure what they are supposed to measure, and their results may not be stable over time.
- Personality tests are often developed for specific populations (e.g., mentally ill people); these tests are then "borrowed" and applied to the general population where their relevance is questionable.
- Often the tests are not administered under the appropriate conditions; they may be given in a classroom or at a kitchen table by people who are not properly trained.
- The researchers often make changes in the instruments to adapt them to their own situations, in the process deleting or adding items and renaming variables. These ad hoc changes dilute the validity of the measures

and also reduce researchers' ability to compare results across consumer samples.

- Many trait scales are intended to measure gross, overall tendencies (e.g., emotional stability or introversion); these results are then used to make predictions about purchases of specific brands.
- In many cases, a number of scales are given with no advance thought about how these measures should be related to consumer behavior. The researchers then use a shotgun approach, following up on anything that happens to look interesting.

Although the use of personality measures by marketing researchers was largely abandoned after many studies failed to yield meaningful results, some researchers have not abandoned the early promise of this line of work. More recent efforts (mainly in Europe) have focused on benefiting from past mistakes. Researchers are using more specific measures of personality traits that they have reason to believe are relevant to economic behavior. They are trying to increase the validity of these measures, primarily by using multiple measures of behavior rather than relying on the common practice of trying to predict purchasing responses from a single item on a personality test. In addition, these researchers have toned down their expectations of what personality traits can tell them about consumers. They now recognize that traits are only part of the solution, and personality data must be incorporated with information about people's social and economic conditions in order to be useful.[13] As a result, some more recent research has had better success at relating personality traits to such consumer behaviors as alcohol consumption among young men or shoppers' willingness to try new, healthier food products.[14]

Brand Personality

In 1886, a momentous event occurred in marketing history—the Quaker Oats man first appeared on boxes of hot cereal. Quakers had a reputation in nineteenth-century America for being shrewd but fair, and peddlers sometimes dressed as Quakers for this reason. When the cereal company decided to "borrow" this imagery for its packaging, this signaled the recognition that purchasers might make the same associations with their product.[15]

These inferences about a product's "personality" are an important part of **brand equity,** which refers to the extent to which a consumer holds strong, favorable, and unique associations with a brand in memory.[16] Building strong brands is good business—if you don't believe it consider that in a study of 760 Fortune 1,000 companies after the stock market took a nosedive in October of 1997, the 20 strongest corporate brands (e.g., Microsoft, GE) actually gained in market value whereas the 20 weakest lost an average of $1 billion each.[17] Name recognition has become so valuable that some companies are completely outsourcing production to focus on nurturing the brand. Nike doesn't own any sneaker factories, and Sara Lee sold off many of its bakeries, meat-processing plant, and textile mills to become a "virtual" corporation. Its CEO commented, "Slaughtering hogs and running knitting machines are businesses of yesterday."[18]

So, how do people think about brands? Advertisers are keenly interested in this question, and several conduct extensive consumer research to help them understand how consumers connect to a brand before they roll out campaigns.

DDB Worldwide does a global study called "Brand Capital" of 14,000 consumers for this purpose; Leo Burnett's "Brand Stock" project involves 28,000 interviews. WPP Group has "BrandZ" and Young & Rubicam has its "Brand Asset Valuator." DDB's worldwide brand planning director observes, "We're not marketing just to isolated individuals. We're marketing to society. How I feel about a brand is directly related and affected by how others feel about that brand." The logic behind this bonding approach is that if a consumer feels a strong connection with a brand, she is less likely to succumb to peer pressure and switch brands.[19]

Some personality dimensions that can be used to compare and contrast the perceived characteristics of brands in various product categories include:[20]

- Old-fashioned, wholesome, traditional
- Surprising, lively, with it
- Serious, intelligent, efficient
- Glamorous, romantic, sexy
- Rugged, outdoorsy, tough, athletic

The following memo was written to help an advertising agency figure out how a client should be portrayed in advertising. Based on this description of the "client," can you guess who he is? "He is creative . . . unpredictable . . . an imp. . . . He not only walks and talks, but has the ability to sing, blush, wink, and work with little devices like pointers. . . . He can also play musical instruments. . . . His walking motion is characterized as a 'swagger.' . . . He is made of dough and has mass."[21] Of course, we all know today that packaging and other physical cues create a "personality" for a product (in this case, the Pillsbury Doughboy!). The marketing activities undertaken on behalf of the product also can influence inferences about its "personality," and some of these actions are shown in Table 6.2.

Indeed, consumers appear to have little trouble assigning personality qualities to all sorts of inanimate products, from personal care products to more mundane, functional ones—even kitchen appliances. In research done by Whirlpool,

TABLE 6.2   Brand Behaviors and Possible Personality Trait Inferences

Brand Action	Trait Inference
Brand is repositioned several times or changes its slogan repeatedly	Flighty, schizophrenic
Brand uses continuing character in its advertising	Familiar, comfortable
Brand charges a high price and uses exclusive distribution	Snobbish, sophisticated
Brand frequently available on deal	Cheap, uncultured
Brand offers many line extensions	Versatile, adaptable
Brand sponsors show on PBS or uses recycled materials	Helpful, supportive
Brand features easy-to-use packaging or speaks at consumer's level in advertising	Warm, approachable
Brand offers seasonal clearance sale	Planful, practical
Brand offers five-year warranty or free customer hot line	Reliable, dependable

SOURCE: Adapted from Susan Fournier, "A Consumer-Brand Relationship Framework for Strategic Brand Management," unpublished doctoral dissertation, University of Florida, 1994, Table 2.2, p. 24.

The Zaltman Metaphor Elicitation Technique (ZMET) is one tool used to assess the strategic aspects of brand personality and is based on the premise that brands are expressed in terms of metaphors; that is, a representation of one thing in terms of another. These associations often are nonverbal, so the ZMET approach is based on a nonverbal representation of brands. Participants collect a minimum of twelve images representing their thoughts and feelings about a topic, and are interviewed in depth about the images and their feelings. Eventually, digital imaging techniques are used to create a collage summarizing these thoughts and feelings, and the person tells a story about the image created. This collage was created by a young woman to express her feelings about Tide detergent. It includes such images as a sunrise to represent freshness and a teddy bear that stands for the soft and comfortable way her laundry feels when she's done. However, the facial expressions also give a clue about her "fondness" for doing laundry![25]

its products were seen as more feminine than were competing brands. They were imagined as a modern, family-oriented woman living in the suburbs—attractive but not flashy. In contrast, the company's KitchenAid brand was envisioned as a modern professional woman who was glamorous, wealthy, and who enjoyed classical music and the theater.[22]

The creation and communication of a distinctive *brand personality* is one of the primary ways marketers can make a product stand out from the competition and inspire years of loyalty to it. This process can be understood in terms of **animism,** the practice found in many cultures whereby inanimate objects are given qualities that make them somehow alive. Animism is in some cases a part of a religion: Sacred objects, animals, or places are believed to have magical qualities or to contain the spirits of ancestors. In our society, objects may be "worshiped" in the sense that they are believed to impart desirable qualities to the owner or they may in a sense become so important to a person that they can be viewed as a "friend."

Two types of animism can be identified to describe the extent to which human qualities are attributed to the product:[23]

Level 1: The object is believed to be possessed by the soul of a being—as is sometimes the case for spokespersons in advertising. This strategy allows the consumer to feel that the spirit of the celebrity is available through the brand. In other cases, a brand may be strongly associated with a loved one, alive or deceased ("My grandmother always served Knott's Berry Farm jam.").

Level 2: Objects are *anthropomorphized,* or given human characteristics. A cartoon character or mythical creation may be treated as if it were a person, and even assumed to have human feelings. Think about familiar spokescharacters such as Charlie the Tuna, the Keebler Elves, or the Michelin Man, or even the frustration some people feel when they come to believe their computer is smarter than they are or may even be "conspiring" to make them crazy! In research for its client Sprint

Business Services, Grey Advertising found that when customers were asked to imagine long-distance carriers as animals, they envisioned AT&T as a lion, MCI as a snake, and Sprint as a puma. Grey used these results to position Sprint as a company that could "help you do more business" rather than taking the more aggressive approach of its competitors.[24]

LIFESTYLES AND PSYCHOGRAPHICS

Jackie, Hank, and Margie strongly resemble one another demographically. They were all raised in middle-class households, have similar educational backgrounds, are about the same age, and work for the same company. However, as their leisure choices show, it would be a big mistake to assume that their consumption choices are similar as well. Each person chooses products, services, and activities that help define a unique *lifestyle*. This section first explores how marketers approach the issue of lifestyle and then how they use information about these consumption choices to tailor products and communications to individual lifestyle segments.

Lifestyle: Who We Are, What We Do

In traditional societies, one's consumption options are largely dictated by class, caste, village, or family. In a modern consumer society, however, people are more free to select the set of products, services, and activities that define themselves and, in turn, create a social identity that is communicated to others. One's choice of goods and services indeed makes a statement about who one is and about the types of people with which one desires to identify—and even those whom we wish to avoid.

Lifestyle refers to a pattern of consumption reflecting a person's choices of how he or she spends time and money. In an economic sense, one's lifestyle represents the way one has elected to allocate income, both in terms of relative allocations to different products and services, and to specific alternatives within these categories.[26] Other somewhat similar distinctions have been made to describe consumers in terms of their broad patterns of consumption, such as those differentiating consumers in terms of those who devote a high proportion of total expenditures to food, advanced technology, or to such information-intensive goods as entertainment and education.[27]

A lifestyle marketing perspective recognizes that people sort themselves into groups on the basis of the things they like to do, how they like to spend their leisure time, and how they choose to spend their disposable income.[28] These choices are reflected, for example, in the growing number of niche magazines that cater to specialized interests. Between 1998 and 1999, *WWF Magazine* (World Wrestling Federation) gained 913,000 readers and *4 Wheel & Off Road* gained 749,000, while mainstream *Reader's Digest* lost more than three million readers and *People* lost more than two million.[29] These finely-tuned choices in turn create opportunities for market segmentation strategies that recognize the potency of a consumer's chosen lifestyle in determining both the types of products purchased and the specific brands most likely to appeal to a designated lifestyle segment.

This ad illustrates the way that products like cars are tightly integrated into consumers' lifestyles, along with leisure activities, travel, music, and so on.

THE TANGLED WEB

THE WEB'S POWER TO unite thousands or even millions of people who share attitudes or consumption preferences is a mixed blessing. Many groups spreading a gospel of hate are using the Internet to reach fellow believers and to recruit new ones. These include neo-Nazi groups, skinheads, and black separatist organizations. As the man who founded the White Aryan Resistance group boasted, "[Now that we are online] our reach is much, much further." And, because the Web is frequented by many relatively affluent, educated people, the targets of these messages are changing as hate groups now can reach those who used to be out of reach. As noted by a spokesman for the Southern Poverty Law Center, a human rights organization that tracks hate groups, "The movement is interested not so much in developing street thugs who beat up people in bars, but college-bound teens who live in middle-class and upper-class homes."[31] Racism is just a click away on the tangled Web.

Lifestyles As Group Identities

Economic approaches are useful in tracking changes in broad societal priorities, but they do not begin to embrace the symbolic nuances that separate lifestyle groups. Lifestyle is more than the allocation of discretionary income. It is a statement about who one is in society and who one is *not*. Group identities, whether of hobbyists, athletes, or drug users, gel around forms of expressive symbolism. The self-definitions of group members are derived from the common symbol system to which the group is dedicated. Such self-definitions have been described by a number of terms, including *lifestyle, taste public, consumer group, symbolic community, and status culture.*[30]

This pattern of consumption often comprises many ingredients that are shared by others in similar social and economic circumstances. Still, each person also provides a unique "twist" to the pattern that allows him or her to inject some individuality into a chosen lifestyle. For example, a "typical" college student (if there is such a thing) may dress much like his or her friends, hang out in the same places, and like the same foods, yet still indulge a passion for marathon running, stamp collecting, or community activism that makes him or her a unique person.

And, lifestyles are not set in stone—unlike the deep-seated values we discussed in Chapter 4—people's tastes and preferences evolve over time, so that consumption patterns that were viewed favorably during one life phase may be laughed at (or sneered at) a few years later. If you don't believe that, simply think back to what you and your friends were wearing five or ten years ago—where *did* you find those clothes?

Because people's attitudes regarding physical fitness, social activism, sex roles for men and women, the importance of home life and family, and so on do change, it is vital for marketers to continually monitor the social landscape to try to anticipate where these changes will lead.

Products Are the Building Blocks of Lifestyles

Consumers often choose products, services, and activities over others because they are associated with a certain lifestyle. For this reason, lifestyle marketing strategies attempt to position a product by fitting it into an existing pattern of consumption. Because a goal of lifestyle marketing is to allow consumers to

The White Aryan Resistance is one of many hate groups with an active presence on the World Wide Web.

Figure 6.1
Linking Products to Lifestyles

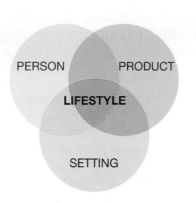

pursue their chosen ways to enjoy their lives and express their social identities, a key aspect of this strategy is to focus on product usage in desirable social settings. The goal of associating a product with a social situation is a long-standing one for advertisers, whether the product is included in a round of golf, a family barbecue, or a night at a glamorous club surrounded by "jet-setters."[32] Thus people, products, and settings are combined to express a certain consumption style, as diagrammed in Figure 6.1

The adoption of a lifestyle marketing perspective implies that we must look at *patterns of behavior* to understand consumers. We can get a clearer picture of

The recreational-vehicle ad shown here demonstrates how a market segment is defined by a particular allocation of time and money to a leisure activity. The ad's claim that the RV dealer has the product that " . . . says you're you!" implies that dedicated RVers derive a significant portion of their self-identities from the activities associated with this lifestyle.

how people use products to define lifestyles by examining how they make choices in a variety of product categories. As one study noted, "all goods carry meaning, but none by itself. . . . The meaning is in the relations between all the goods, just as music is in the relations marked out by the sounds and not in any one note."[33]

Indeed, many products and services do seem to "go together," usually because they tend to be selected by the same types of people. In many cases, products do not seem to "make sense" if unaccompanied by companion products (e.g., fast food and paper plates, or a suit and tie) or are incongruous in the presence of others (e.g., a Chippendale chair in a high-tech office or Lucky Strike cigarettes with a solid gold lighter). Therefore, an important part of lifestyle marketing is to identify the set of products and services that seems to be linked in consumers' minds to a specific lifestyle. And, research evidence suggests that even a relatively unattractive product becomes more appealing when evaluated with other, liked products.[34] Marketers who pursue *co-branding strategies* intuitively understand this: That's why L. L. Bean and Subaru are teaming up for a co-branding deal. According to the VP of marketing at Subaru, "L. L. Bean is a natural partner for Subaru, as both companies provide outdoor enthusiasts with products that enhance their lives."[35]

Product complementarity occurs when the symbolic meanings of different products are related to each other.[36] These sets of products, termed **consumption constellations**, are used by consumers to define, communicate, and perform social roles.[37] For example, the American "yuppie" of the 1980s was defined by such products as a Rolex watch, BMW automobile, Gucci briefcase, a squash racket, fresh pesto, white wine, and brie cheese. Somewhat similar constellations could be found for "Sloane Rangers" in the United Kingdom and "Bon Chic Bon Genres" in France. Although people today take pains to avoid being classified as yuppies, this social role had a major influence on defining cultural values and

Interior designers rely on consumption constellations when choosing items to furnish a room. A decorating style involves integrating products from many different categories—such as appliances, furnishings, knick-knacks, and even artwork—into a unified whole that conveys a certain "look."

consumption priorities in the 1980s.[38] What consumption constellation might characterize you and your friends today?

Psychographics

Consider a marketer who wishes to target a student population. She identifies her ideal consumer as "a twenty-one-year-old senior business major living on a large university campus whose parents make between $30,000 and $60,000 per year." You may know a lot of people who fit this description. Do you think they are all the same? Would they all be likely to share common interests and buy the same products? Probably not, because their lifestyles are likely to differ considerably.

As Jackie's, Hank's, and Margie's choices demonstrated, consumers can share the same demographic characteristics and still be very different people. For this reason, marketers need a way to "breathe life" into demographic data to really identify, understand, and target consumer segments that will share a set of preferences for their products and services. This chapter earlier discussed some of the differences in consumers' personalities that play a role in determining product choices. When personality variables are combined with knowledge of lifestyle preferences, marketers have a powerful lens with which to focus on consumer segments.

This tool is known as **psychographics,** which involves the "use of psychological, sociological, and anthropological factors . . . to determine how the market is segmented by the propensity of groups within the market—and their reasons—to make a particular decision about a product, person, ideology, or otherwise hold an attitude or use a medium."[39] Psychographics can help a marketer fine-tune its offerings to meet the needs of different segments. For example, the Discovery Channel surveyed those who watch at least one-half hour of its programming a week. It found that, in fact, there were eight distinct groups of watchers with different motivations and preferences—psychographic segments that were given descriptive names such as Entertain-Mes, Practicals, Scholars, and Escapists. Based on these results, Discovery was able to tailor its programming to different segments and increase its market share in the competitive cable television industry.[40]

The Roots of Psychographics

Psychographic research was first developed in the 1960s and 1970s to address the shortcomings of two other types of consumer research: *motivational research* and *quantitative survey research*. Motivational research, which involves intensive one-to-one interviews and projective tests, yields a lot of information about a few people. As we've seen though, this information is often idiosyncratic and may not be very reliable. At the other extreme, quantitative survey research, or large-scale demographic surveys, yields only a little information about a lot of people. As some researchers observed, "The marketing manager who wanted to know why people ate the competitor's cornflakes was told '32 percent of the respondents said taste, 21 percent said flavor, 15 percent said texture, 10 percent said price, and 22 percent said don't know or no answer.'"[41]

In many applications, the term psychographics is used interchangeably with lifestyle to denote the separation of consumers into categories based on differences in choices of consumption activities and product usage. There are many psychographic variables that can be used to segment consumers, but they all

NET PROFIT

CHOOSING A LIFESTYLE FOR yourself is complicated enough. Now, the Web lets you "play God" by creating your own family online. By joining The Sims™, you can design and furnish a house and put people in it who look and act as you choose. The Sims™ is a CD-ROM–based game that also features a strong online community— starting at the game's Web site thesims.com you can make up an endless variety of characters, insult your neighbors, fall in love, whatever turns you on. Your "skins" can follow a wide range of career paths (lounge singer, golf caddy, talk show host, maybe even a marketing professor?), and you can "buy" tons of goodies for your virtual family, including hot tubs and giant-screen TV's (and program in nasty stuff like roach infestations to keep Sim life interesting). What's more, you can exchange your simulated world with other players using The Sims Teleportation Device. So what are you waiting for? Get a life.

share the underlying principle of going beyond surface characteristics to understand consumers' motivations for purchasing and using products.

Demographics allow us to describe *who* buys, but psychographics allow us to understand why they do. To illustrate how this approach works, consider a very popular Canadian campaign for Molson Export beer that based its commercials on psychographic findings. Research showed that Molson's target customers tended to be like boys who never grew up, who were uncertain about the future, and who were intimidated by women's new-found freedoms. Accordingly, the ads featured a group of men, "Fred and the boys," whose get-togethers emphasize male companionship, protection against change, and that the beer "keeps on tasting great."[42]

Conducting a Psychographic Analysis

Some early attempts at lifestyle segmentation "borrowed" standard psychological scales (often used to measure pathology or personality disturbances) and tried to relate scores on these tests to product usage. As we saw earlier in the chapter, such efforts were largely disappointing. These tests were never intended to be related to everyday consumption activities and yielded little in the way of explanation for purchase behaviors. The technique is more effective when the variables included are more closely related to actual consumer behaviors. If you want to understand purchases of household cleaning products, you are better off asking people about their attitudes toward household cleanliness than testing for personality disorders!

Psychographic studies can take several different forms:

- *A lifestyle profile* that looks for items that differentiate between users and nonusers of a product
- *A product-specific profile* that identifies a target group and then profiles these consumers on product-relevant dimensions
- *A study that uses personality traits as descriptors,* in which some variable such as concern for the environment is analyzed to see which personality traits are most likely to be related to it
- *A general lifestyle segmentation* in which a large sample of respondents are placed into homogenous groups based on similarities of their overall preferences
- *A product-specific segmentation,* in which questions used in a general approach are tailored to a product category—for example, in a study done specifically for a stomach medicine, the item "I worry too much" might be rephrased as "I get stomach problems if I worry too much." This allows the researcher to more finely discriminate between users of competing brands.[43]

AIOs

Most contemporary psychographic research attempts to group consumers according to some combination of three categories of variables—activities, interests, and opinions—which are known as **AIOs.** Using data from large samples, marketers create profiles of customers who resemble each other in terms of their activities and patterns of product usage.[44] The dimensions used to assess lifestyle are listed in Table 6.3.

To group consumers into common AIO categories, respondents are given a long list of statements and are asked to indicate how much they agree with each one. Lifestyle is thus "boiled down" by discovering how people spend their time,

TABLE 6.3   Lifestyle Dimensions

Activities	Interests	Opinions	Demographics
Work	Family	Themselves	Age
Hobbies	Home	Social issues	Education
Social events	Job	Politics	Income
Vacation	Community	Business	Occupation
Entertainment	Recreation	Economics	Family size
Club membership	Fashion	Education	Dwelling
Community	Food	Products	Geography
Shopping	Media	Future	City size
Sports	Achievements	Culture	Stage in life cycle

SOURCE: William D. Wells and Douglas J. Tigert, "Activities, Interests, and Opinions," *Journal of Advertising Research* 11 (August 1971) 27–35. ©1971 by The Advertising Research Foundation.

what they find interesting and important, and how they view themselves and the world around them, as well as demographic information. By the way, the single most common use of leisure time among Americans overall is—you guessed it— watching television![45]

Typically, the first step in conducting a psychographic analysis is to determine which lifestyle segments are producing the bulk of customers for a particular product. According to a very general rule of thumb frequently used in marketing research, the **80/20 principle,** only 20 percent of a product's users account for 80 percent of the volume of product sold. Researchers attempt to determine who uses the brand and try to isolate heavy, moderate, and light users. They also look for patterns of usage and attitudes toward the product. In many cases, just a few lifestyle segments account for the majority of brand users.[46] Marketers primarily target these heavy users, even though they may constitute a relatively small number of total users.

After the heavy users are identified and understood, the brand's relationship to them is considered. Heavy users may have quite different reasons for using the product; they can be further subdivided in terms of the *benefits* they derive from using the product or service. For instance, marketers at the beginning of the walking shoe craze assumed that purchasers were basically burned-out joggers. Subsequent psychographic research showed that there were actually several different groups of "walkers," ranging from those who walk to get to work to those who walk for fun. This realization resulted in shoes aimed at different segments, from Footjoy Joy-Walkers to Nike Healthwalkers.

Uses of Psychographic Segmentation

Psychographic segmentation can be used in a variety of ways:

- *To define the target market:* This information allows the marketer to go beyond simple demographic or product usage descriptions (e.g., middle-aged men or frequent users).
- *To create a new view of the market:* Sometimes marketers create their strategies with a "typical" customer in mind. This stereotype may not be correct because the actual customer may not match these assumptions. For example, marketers of a facial cream for women were surprised to find

their key market was composed of older, widowed women rather than the younger, more sociable women to whom they were pitching their appeals.

- *To position the product:* Psychographic information can allow the marketer to emphasize features of the product that fit in with a person's lifestyle. Products targeted to people whose lifestyle profiles show a high need to be around other people might focus on the product's ability to help meet this social need.

- *To better communicate product attributes:* Psychographic information can offer very useful input to advertising creatives who must communicate something about the product. The artist or writer obtains a much richer mental image of the target consumer than that obtained through dry statistics, and this insight improves his or her ability to "talk" to that consumer. For example, research conducted for Schlitz beer found that heavy beer drinkers tended to feel that life's pleasures were few and far between. Commercials were developed using the theme that told these drinkers, "You only go around once, so reach for all the gusto you can."[47]

- *To develop overall strategy:* Understanding how a product fits, or does not fit, into consumers' lifestyles allows the marketer to identify new product opportunities, chart media strategies, and create environments most consistent and harmonious with these consumption patterns.

- *To market social and political issues:* Psychographic segmentation can be an important tool in political campaigns and can also be employed to find commonalities among types of consumers who engage in destructive behaviors, such as drug use or excessive gambling. A psychographic study of men aged 18 to 24 who drink and drive highlights the potential for this perspective to help in the eradication of harmful behaviors. Researchers divided this segment into four groups: "good timers," "well adjusted," "nerds," and "problem kids." They found that one group in particular—"good timers"—is more likely to believe that it is fun to be drunk, that the chances of having an accident while driving drunk are low, and that drinking increases one's appeal to the opposite sex. Because the study showed that this group is also the most likely to drink at rock concerts and parties, is most likely to watch MTV, and tends to listen to album-oriented rock radio stations, reaching "good timers" with a prevention campaign was made easier because messages targeted to this segment could be placed where these drinkers are most likely to see and hear them.[48]

Psychographic Segmentation Typologies

Marketers are constantly on the prowl for new insights that will allow them to identify and reach groups of consumers that are united by a common lifestyle. To meet this need, many research companies and advertising agencies have developed their own *segmentation typologies.* Respondents answer a battery of questions that allow the researchers to cluster them into a set of distinct lifestyle groups. The questions usually include a mixture of AIOs, plus other items relating to their perceptions of specific brands, favorite celebrities, media preferences, and so on. These systems are usually sold to companies that want to learn more about their customers and potential customers.

At least at a superficial level, many of these typologies are fairly similar to one another, in that a typical typology breaks up the population into roughly five to eight segments. Each cluster is given a descriptive name, and a profile of the "typical" member is provided to the client. Unfortunately, it is often difficult to compare or evaluate different typologies, as the methods and data used to devise these systems frequently are proprietary; that is, the information is developed and owned by the company, and the company feels that it would not be desirable to release this information to outsiders.

VALS 2

One well-known segmentation system is **The Values and Lifestyles (VALS™) System,** developed at SRI International in California. The original VALS™ system was based on how consumers agreed or disagreed with various social issues such as abortion rights.

After about ten years, SRI discovered that the social issues used to categorize consumers were not as predictive of consumer behavior as they once had been because greater number of people were in agreement with these ideas. SRI searched for a more powerful way to segment consumers, and discovered that certain lifestyle indicators such as "I like a lot of excitement in my life" were better predictors of purchase behavior than the degree to which a person agreed or disagreed with a social value.

The current VALS 2™ system uses a battery of 39 items (35 psychological and four demographic) to divide U.S. adults into groups, each with distinctive characteristics. As shown in Figure 6.2, groups are arranged vertically by their resources (including such factors as income, education, energy levels, and eagerness to buy), and horizontally by self-orientation.

Key to the VALS 2™ system are three self-orientations that comprise the horizontal dimension. Consumers with a Principle orientation make purchase decisions guided by a belief system, and they are not concerned with the views of others. People with a Status orientation make decisions based on the perceived opinions of their peers. Action, or self-oriented individuals, buy products to have an impact on the world around them.

The top VALS 2™ group is termed Actualizers, who are successful consumers with many resources. This group is concerned with social issues and is open to change. As one indication of this group's interest in cutting-edge technology, although only one in ten American adults is an Actualizer, half of all regular Internet users belong to this category.[50]

The next three groups also have sufficient resources but differ in their outlooks on life:[51]

- *Fulfilleds* are satisfied, reflective, and comfortable. They tend to be practical and value functionality.
- *Achievers* are career-oriented and prefer predictability over risk or self-discovery.
- *Experiencers* are impulsive, young, and enjoy offbeat or risky experiences.

The next four groups have fewer resources:

- *Believers* have strong principles and favor proven brands.
- *Strivers* are similar to Achievers, but have fewer resources. They are very concerned about the approval of others.
- *Makers* are action-oriented and tend to focus their energies on self-sufficiency. They will often be found working on their cars, canning their own vegetables, or building their own houses.

MARKETING PITFALLS

WHEN THE R. J. REYNOLDS Company made plans to introduce a new brand of cigarettes, called "Dakota," in several test markets, the tobacco company found out the hard way that a psychographic approach can be controversial. The marketing plan, submitted to the company by an outside consulting firm, specifically targeted the cigarette to 18- to 24-year-old women with a high school education or less who work in entry-level factory or service jobs. This segment is one of the few remaining consumer segments in the United States that exhibits an increase in smoking rates, so from a purely fiscal point of view it clearly has market potential.

The brand was developed to appeal to a lifestyle segment the company called the "Virile Female." This woman has the following psychographic characteristics: Her favorite pastimes are cruising, partying, and going to hot rod shows and tractor pulls with her boyfriend, and her favorite TV shows are *Roseanne* and evening soap operas. Her chief aspirations are to get married in her early twenties and to spend time with her boyfriend, doing whatever he does. More than 100 public health officials signed a resolution asking that Dakota be withdrawn from the market, but R. J. Reynolds claimed that the test brand was simply aimed at current Marlboro smokers. Regardless of the company's intentions, this attempt at lifestyle marketing resulted in a flood of unfavorable publicity as critics charged the company was trying to persuade more young women to take up the habit.[49]

Figure 6.2
VALS 2 Segmentation System

SOURCE: SRI International, Menlo Park, CA

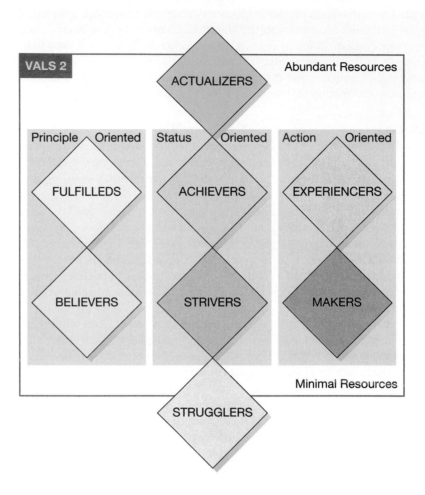

- *Strugglers* are at the bottom of the economic ladder. They are most concerned with meeting the needs of the moment, and have limited ability to acquire anything beyond the basic goods needed for survival.

The VALS 2™ system has been a useful way to understand people like Jackie and Hank. SRI estimates that 12 percent of American adults are thrill seekers, who tend to fall into the system's Experiencer category and who are likely to agree with statements like "I like a lot of excitement in my life" and "I like to try new things." Experiencers like to break the rules, and are strongly attracted to extreme sports such as sky surfing or bungee jumping. Not too surprisingly, fully one-third of consumers aged 18–34 belong in this category, so it has attracted the interest of many marketers who are trying to appeal to younger people (more on this in Chapter 15). For example, VALS 2™ helped Isuzu market its Rodeo sport utility vehicle by focusing on Experiencers, many of whom believe it is fun to break rules in ways that do not endanger others. The car was positioned as a vehicle that lets a driver break the rules. Advertising was created to support this idea by showing kids jumping in mud puddles, running with scissors, and coloring out of the lines.[52] Isuzu sales increased significantly after this campaign. If you want to see what VALS type you would be classified as, go to future.sri.com/VALS/ VALSindex.shtml.

Regional Consumption Differences

If you have traveled to or lived in other parts of the country, you may have experienced the weird feeling of being slightly out of sync with your environment. The people may speak the same language, yet you may have difficulty understanding some things they say. Brands and store names may be confusing; some are familiar and some are not. Some familiar items may masquerade under different names. One person's "hero" is another's "grinder" is another person's "submarine sandwich" is another person's "hoagie."

Citizens of the United States share the same national identity, yet the consumption patterns of different regions have been shaped by unique climates, cultural influences, and resources. Such differences allow us to legitimately talk about "regional personalities" as well as a "national personality." These regional differences often exert a big impact on consumers' lifestyles because many of our preferences in foods, entertainment, and so on are dictated by local customs and the availability of some diversions rather than others: A resident of the Midwest would have to work hard to cultivate a "Florida beach bum" lifestyle, whereas a New Englander might be hard-pressed to find a rodeo show to attend on the weekend.

Food Preferences

Many national marketers regionalize their offerings to appeal to different tastes. Campbell's Soup puts a stronger dose of jalapeño pepper in its nacho cheese soup in the Southwest, and it sells "ranch-style" beans only in Texas.[53]

The Cape Cod Travel Guide *is one of many media vehicles that appeals to regional identification.*

Similarly, some leading brands do significantly better in some parts of the country than others: Kraft Miracle Whip is the nation's overall best-seller in the mayonnaise category, but it only turns in a third-place performance in the Northeast.[54]

Americans even differ in their preferences for "munchies." The average consumer eats 21 pounds of snack foods in a year (hopefully not all at one sitting), but people in the West Central part of the country consume the most (24 pounds per person) whereas those in the Pacific and Southeast regions eat "only" 19 pounds per person. Pretzels are the most popular snack in the mid-Atlantic area, pork rinds are most likely to be eaten in the South, and multigrain chips turn up as a favorite in the West. Not surprisingly, the Hispanic influence in the Southwest has influenced snacking preferences—consumers in that part of the United States eat about 50 percent more tortilla chips than do people elsewhere.[55]

The Arts and Entertainment

The types of entertainment sought by consumers around the country differ markedly as well. Overall, country/western is the most popular form of music (though rock music leads in actual record sales). The blues, R&B, and soul category is rapidly gaining in popularity.[56]

Still, these preferences are by no means uniform across the country. A survey performed for the National Endowment for the Arts showed that jazz and classical music are the most popular in the West and Midwest, and that consumers in the West like museums and the theater more than other Americans.[57]

Geodemography

Geodemography refers to analytical techniques that combine data on consumer expenditures and other socioeconomic factors with geographic information about the areas in which people live in order to identify consumers who share common consumption patterns. This approach is based on the assumption that "birds of a feather flock together;" people who have similar needs and tastes also tend to live near one another, so it should be possible to locate "pockets" of like-minded people who can then be reached more economically by direct mail and other methods. For example, a marketer who wants to reach white, single consumers who are college-educated and tend to be fiscally conservative may find that it is more efficient to mail catalogs to zip codes 20770 (Greenbelt, MD) and 90277 (Redondo Beach, CA) than to adjoining areas in either Maryland or California, where there are fewer consumers who exhibit these characteristics.

A statistical technique called *cluster analysis* allows marketers to identify groups of people who share important characteristics even though they may live in different parts of the country. Geographic information is increasingly being combined with other data to paint an even more complete picture of the American consumer. Several marketing research ventures now employ **single-source data,** in which information about a person's actual purchasing history is combined with geodemographic data, thus allowing marketers to learn even more about the types of marketing strategies that motivate some people—but not others—to respond.

This comprehensive strategy was first implemented in the BehaviorScan project, begun in 1980 by Information Resources, Inc. The system combined

MARKETING OPPORTUNITY

WITH THE AID OF their trusty fax machines and computer modems that allow them to stay online even in remote places, growing numbers of "electronic pioneers" are forging a new lifestyle as they give up life in the big city to work in rural areas. Job growth in nonmetropolitan areas now exceeds that of metros, and counties in vacation or retirement areas or those that have a strong technology infrastructure are leading the way. In fact, farmers and mine workers now make up only 10 percent of the rural population.[58] About 25 million Americans operate a full- or part-time business from home, and another 8.4 million telecommute.[59]

And, whether they live in New York or New Mexico, growing numbers of middle-age and well-educated suburbanites are trying to regain a sense of mastery over their environment by rebuilding their own homes, running their own businesses, managing their own finances, and using their own labor to buy cheaper groceries at warehouse clubs. Aided by technology, they are banking by computer, using specialized software to select mutual funds instead of relying on a broker, and using online travel agents to book vacations. A trend toward "subcontracting" household tasks creates many opportunities for entrepreneurs who see the value of helping these pioneers operate from home.

grocery store UPC scanners, household consumers panels, and responses to different television commercials that were transmitted to selected parts of a market area to track purchases. This type of total approach allows marketers to test the impact of changes in advertising, pricing, shelf placement, and promotions on consumer behavior patterns. Similar systems are now available or under development by other organizations, such as Nielsen and SAMI/ Burke.[60]

Marketers have been successful at adapting sophisticated analytical techniques originally developed for other applications, such as the military and oil and gas exploration. These techniques, which can now employ data at the neighborhood or even household level, are being used in a variety of ways:

- A bank examined its penetration of accounts by customer zip codes.
- A utility company compared demographic data with billing patterns to fine-tune energy conservation campaigns.
- A chain of ice cream stores helped franchisees develop sales promotion programs for local markets by providing them with demographic profiles of actual users and information about the sales potential of untapped customer groups.
- The Western Union Company improved the cost-effectiveness of its network of offices by analyzing the number of Western Union agents needed in an area and determining where new agents would most profitably be located.[61]

One commercial system is ClusterPlus, distributed by Donnelly Marketing. This system assigns each of the country's census block groups into one of 47 clusters. The groupings range in affluence from the "established wealthy" (e.g., Greenwich, Connecticut) to "lowest income black female-headed families" (e.g., the Watts section of Los Angeles). A manufacturer of baking goods used the ClusterPlus system to target consumers who bake from scratch. The top-ranking clusters for this activity were in older, rural, blue-collar areas in the South and Midwest. Commercials for this segment were placed on popular shows such as *Rescue: 911* and *America's Funniest Home Videos,* which are widely watched in these areas.[62]

Another clustering technique is the PRIZM system developed by Claritas, Inc. (PRIZM stands for Potential Rating Index by Zip Market). This system classifies every U.S. zip code into one of 62 categories, ranging from the most affluent "Blue-Blood Estates" to the least well-off "Public Assistance."[63] A resident of Southern California might be classified as "Money & Brains" if he or she lives in Encino (zip code 91316), whereas someone living in Sherman Oaks (zip code 91423) would be a "Young Influential."[64] The system was updated from its original set of 40 clusters to reflect the growing ethnic and economic diversity of the United States; some new clusters include "American Dreams," "Kids & Cul-de-Sacs" and "Young Literati."[65]

Residents of different clusters display marked differences in their consumption of products, from annuities to zip-lock bags. These groupings also are ranked in terms of income, home value, and occupation (i.e., a rough index of social class) on a ZQ (Zip Quality) scale. Table 6.4 provides an idea of how dramatically different the consumption patterns of two clusters can be. This table compares consumption data for "Furs & Station Wagons," the third highest ranking cluster, with "Tobacco Roads," the third lowest.

MULTICULTURAL DIMENSIONS

INCREASINGLY SOPHISTICATED EFFORTS ARE being made to develop lifestyle typologies that transcend national borders. One such approach is Global MOSAIC, developed by a British firm called Experian. This system analyzes consumers in 19 countries including Australia, South Africa, and Peru. Experian boiled down 631 different MOSAIC types to come up with 14 common lifestyles, classifying 800 million people who produce roughly 80 percent of the world's GDP. This allows marketers to identify consumers who share similar tastes around the world. An Experian executive explained, "the yuppie on the upper East side of New York has more in common with a yuppie in Stockholm than a downscale person in Brooklyn." These Yuppies (labeled Education Cosmopolitans in MOSAIC) are the first consumers to accept new products and ideas and are influential in fueling the globalization of lifestyles. Although they are found in every country they are not present in equal proportions. MOSAIC says that they are 10 percent of households in the United States, 7.1 percent in Japan, 5.8 percent in New Zealand, 4.2 percent in Great Britain, and only 3.7 percent in Australia.[68] Figure 6.3 illustrates how an Irish band used this information to identify Americans most likely to want to hear their music.

....

TABLE 6.4 A Comparison of Two PRIZM Clusters			
Furs & Station Wagons (ZQ3)		**Tobacco Roads (ZQ38)**	
New money, parents in 40s and 50s		Racially mixed farm towns in the South	
Newly built subdivisions with tennis courts, swimming pools, gardens		Small downtowns with thrift shops, diners, and laundromats; shanty-type homes without indoor plumbing	
Sample neighborhoods Plano, TX (75075)		**Sample neighborhoods** Belzoni, MI (39038)	
Dunwoody, GA (30338)		Warrenton, NC (27589)	
Needham, MA (02192)		Gates, VA (27937)	
High Usage	**Low Usage**	**High Usage**	**Low Usage**
Country clubs	Motorcycles	Travel by bus	Knitting
Wine by the case	Laxatives	Asthma relief remedies	Live theater
Lawn furniture	Nonfilter cigarettes	Malt liquors	Smoke detectors
Gourmet magazine	Chewing tobacco	*Grit* magazine	*Ms.* magazine
BMW 5 Series	*Hunting* magazine	Pregnancy tests	Ferraris
Rye bread	Chevrolet Chevettes	Pontiac Bonnevilles	Whole-wheat bread
			Mexican foods
Natural cold cereal	Canned stews	Shortening	

NOTE: Usage rates as indexed to average consumption across all 40 clusters.
SOURCE: "A Comparison of Two Prizm Clusters" from *The Clustering of America* by Michael J. Weiss.
Copyright © 1988 by Michael J. Weiss. Reprinted by permission of HarperCollins Publishers, Inc.

The PRIZM system is used to guide media buying and for direct mail targeting. Both *Time* and *Newsweek* have sorted their mailing lists by cluster, sending special editions with ads for luxury products to residents of "Money & Brains" and "Blue-Blood Estates." Colgate–Palmolive sent samples of a new detergent developed for young families to occupants of "Blue-Collar Nursery" cluster, which is largely made up of new families. When Time Inc. Ventures launched *VIBE*, its urban-culture magazine, it needed to convince advertisers that the new outlet was not read solely by inner-city kids. A PRIZM analysis showed that *VIBE* also appealed to "Young Influentials" and even middle-age members of the "Money & Brains" cluster; evidence that led to advertising buys for liquor and electronics marketers.[66]

Although some products may be purchased at an equivalent rate by consumers in two very different clusters, these similarities end when other purchases are taken into account. These differences highlight the importance of going beyond simple product category purchase data and demographics to really understand a market (remember the earlier discussion of product complementarity). For example, high-quality binoculars are bought by people in "Urban Gold Coast," "Money & Brains," and "Blue-Blood Estates" communities, but also by consumers in the "Grain Belt," "New Homesteaders," and "Agri-Business" clusters. The difference is that the former groups use the binoculars to watch birds and other wildlife, but the latter use them to help line up the animals in their gun sights. Furthermore, whereas the bird watchers do a lot of foreign travel, listen to classical music, and host cocktail parties, the bird hunters travel by bus, like country music, and belong to veterans' clubs.

These two bowling centers, both located in a Kansas City suburb, are only six miles apart. However, they are light years apart in terms of the PRIZM clusters they draw upon as their clientele. The architectural firm that designed both centers found that the patrons at Olathe Lanes East came for relaxation and exercise, while those at the West Lanes were hard-core bowlers who came to compete. The customers at East came from three upscale clusters: Young Suburbia, Pools and Patios, and Furs and Station Wagons, and the firm selected an Art Deco motif and used soft lines to create a relaxing, upscale atmosphere. Bowlers at West came from the Blue Collar Nursery, Middle America, Blue Chip Blues, and Shotguns and Pickups clusters. The firm redid the bowling alley, using a Southwest theme with squares and energetic triangles to appeal to these groups.[67]

LIFESTYLE TRENDS: CONSUMER BEHAVIOR IN THE NEW MILLENNIUM

Consumer lifestyles are a moving target. Society's priorities and preferences are constantly evolving, and it is essential for marketers to track these changes and more importantly, try to anticipate them. One "quick and dirty" way to appreciate change is to look at business headings in The Yellow Pages. Within the last few years, these categories have been dropped from many telephone directories: livestock records, mops, and worms. New headings include angels, body piercing, cyber cafes, feng shui, permanent makeup, and aromatherapy.[69]

Of course, many lifestyle changes are rooted in economic and demographic patterns, so understanding these developments usually entails an appreciation of

Figure 6.3
Global Fans of an Irish Rock Band

Source: Michael Weiss, "Parallel Universe," *American Demographics* (October 1999): 58–63.

Global Fans of an Irish Rock Band

When a German-based Irish rock band called the Kelly Family wanted to tour the United States, organizers first classified members of the band's German fan club by Global MOSAIC cluster and found they tended to live in regionally important mid-sized cities. Then marketers ranked U.S. markets with high concentrations of the same clusters and targeted their promotion campaign there.

High
Above Average
Below Average
Low

Top Global MOSAIC Clusters	Top U.S. Media Markets	Top German County Markets
Agrarian Heartlands	Minneapolis	Unteraligau
Career Focused Materialists	Seattle	Bernkastel-Wittlich
Farming Town Communities	Dallas	Hildburghausen
Greys, Blue Sea and Mountain	Nashville	Cloppenburg
Old Wealth	Boston	Donau-Ries

Sources: Global MOSAIC, Experian Micromarketing, Micron Micromarketing-Systeme und Consult GmbH (country size not to scale)

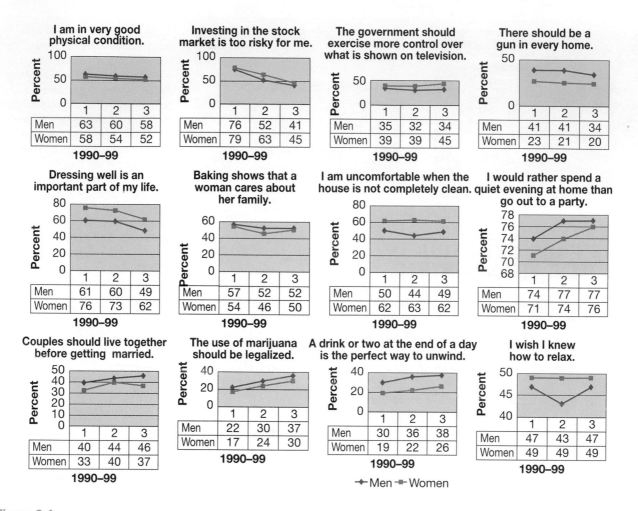

Figure 6.4
Responses to Selected Items in the 1999 DDB Needham Lifestyle Study

factors such as employment rates, educational attainment, and population growth. In the new millennium we see such developments as **affinitization,** in which groups organize around special interests such as immigration policy, the environment, or religious education. In this section, we'll take a look at some of the important lifestyle issues currently shaping consumer behavior.

Trend Forecasting: Peering into the Crystal Ball of Consumer Behavior

If a marketer could see into the future, she would obviously have an enormous advantage when developing products and services that will meet the needs of consumers next year, in five years, or in ten years. No one is able to do that yet, but a number of marketing research firms do try very hard to predict **social trends,** or broad changes in people's attitudes and behaviors. For example, the Lifestyle Monitor, now run by the firm Yankelovich Clancy Shulman, interviews 2,500 American adults annually. Advertising agency Backer Spielvogel Bates' Global Scan program divides markets in 18 countries into psychographic segments and charts changes in attitudes, and advertising agency Ogilvy & Mather scans consumer trends with its New Wave program.[70] Since 1975, the DDB Needham Worldwide advertising agency has been conducting its Lifestyle Study, an ongoing

REALITY CHECK

EXTREME SPORTS. DAY TRADING. CHAT ROOMS. Vegetarianism. Can you predict what will be "hot" in the near future? Identify a lifestyle trend that is just surfacing in your universe. Describe this trend in detail, and justify your prediction. What specific styles and/or products are part of this trend?

Many students on my campus have laptops, beepers and cell phones to be ahead of the game, stay connected and have the perceived advantage. The rest of us look on with curiosity or envy and manage to get by.

Kerri Ruminski
Idaho State University

The ritual of marking the hands with giant X's equates to a lifestyle of being "straight edge." In generic terms, sXe translates to a lifestyle abstaining from alcohol, drugs, and promiscuous sex. The term straight was originated in the early 80's to define a subculture that developed within the confines of the hardcore/punk community. Recently, the trend of sXe is receiving more and more national exposure. It's become quite a reoccurring ritual for musicians to display giant X's on their hands for music videos and national television appearances . . . the premise of sXe was to signify a way of self-discipline and was meant to be reserved for the underground punk rock community. The mainstream music industry has made it their agenda to commercialize straight edge by mass producing anything from t-shirt, stickers, hats, watches, posters, etc. with the sXe insignia. In addition, more and more teenagers are beginning to mimic the artists they watch on television by marking their hands with giant X's as a daily routine.

Eric Jude Guacena
Virginia Commonwealth University

In New Zealand we can see a lifestyle trend emerging in strong movement away from large established brands. . . . This trend among students is most visible through the resurgence of smaller brands and boutique clothing stores which students patronise. These provide a range of choices on how we express our individuality. . . . They can range from high fashion (and often high price) stores such as WORLD to second hand stores carrying a distinctive style of clothes (especially the retro look). However the trend has become much more visible among new brands whose offerings often parody these old establish brands (clothing or otherwise) via the display of a modification of an established brand's logo.

Satish Magan Ranchod
University of Auckland, New Zealand

Wireless Internet will soon be the hottest product to have.

John Dollman IV
West Virginia University

Internet Bars are quickly becoming a hot spot in large cities; a place for busy people to access the World Wide Web, email, chat rooms, and other online access stations while socializing with neighbors. . . . Using rows of personal computer terminals amid a warm, inviting room lined with bars serving drinks and appetizers, Internet Bars provide a place for lounging and studying.

Jessica Wells
Utah State University

Spending a lot of money and buying very expensive items seemed to be the trend of Japan in recent years. . . . But since the start of the recession that seems to have no end, life styles of the Japanese are starting to show much change. Many shows that had things to do with savings were popular and in the beginning of the year 2000 there was a TV series based on a family that had no money. I believe that the products and fashion will start to share the same ideas. Simple in appearance but very fitted to the life styles of the users.

Ayano Yamada
Keio University, Japan

"Natural products," "Low Fat," "No-Fat," "X% less than others," "Dietetic Product" are common in labels of more . . . products. . . . Teenagers (boys and girls) are changing junk food for fruit and natural juice, Coke for Diet Coke . . . What's happening to this generation? Simple: We expect to be healthier than our parents, live more time in better physical and mental conditions. We run away from cancer, tobacco and fat.

Giselle Gonzalez Aybar
Pontificia Universidad Catolica Madre y Maestra, Dominican Republic

Everyone is messaging everybody else with the Short Message System(SMS) on their handphones. Playing games on their Nokia mobiles.

Tina Ho
Nanyang Technological University, Singapore

What's your opinion? Check out the on-line polls at www.prenhall.com/myphlip. Just follow the little person in the lab coat.

study of changes in consumer behavior consisting of a sample of 5,000 Americans' answers to a battery of 1,000 questions. Responses to a few selected items over time are shown in Figure 6.4.

Consumer Trends

Of course, trend forecasting is a bit like reading one's horoscope in the paper. Sometimes forecasts are so general they can't help but come true, and only some proportion of more specific ones actually do. The problem is, we don't

Maidenform, Inc.
"PTA" :30
XMEI-4143

THE MAIDENFORM WOMAN.
YOU NEVER KNOW WHERE SHE'LL TURN UP.

This time I'm making a sensational landing in her Sweet Nothings Demi-Bra. Wide and deep plunge, this feminine front-close bra gives you a high, round, voluptuous look. Definitely executive material in soft, sight-sheer tricot, flexible fill and underwire too.
Sweet Nothings Demi-Bra by Maidenform

The increasing desire among some women to return to domestic activities is reflected in new advertising for Maidenform. In the last decades, the Maidenform woman was depicted (in her underwear!) in professional settings. More recently, she turns up (fully clothed this time) at a PTA meeting. According to an executive who worked on the campaign, "The PTA spot . . . was specifically created to talk to women who are blending motherhood with all the other facets of their lives. . . ."

know until after the fact which ones will. A few trends that have been observed include:

- A decline in concern for the environment. Although Clorox continues to participate in cleanup projects, a spokeswoman confesses, "we do these things despite information that tells us consumers aren't as concerned about litter anymore."[71]
- Emphasis on the value of time-saving products. Oscar Mayer offers pre-cooked bacon, and Papa John's is testing drive-up windows for pizza. Kraft Foods is selling pre-cubed cheese and Sara Lee introduced Ball Park Singles, individually wrapped hot dogs that can be prepared in 20 seconds in a microwave.[72]
- Decreased emphasis on dieting and nutritional foods. Sara Lee's Calzone Creations microwavable sandwiches have 12 grams of saturated fat, 60 percent of an adult's recommended daily intake. Among supermarket shoppers who say they are very concerned about nutrition, just 46 percent say they are worried about fat content, down from 60 percent in 1996.[73]
- Moving toward a more laid-back lifestyle and casual work environment. Inspired by the disheveled look sported by many Silicon Valley startup companies, many firms are instituting a relaxed dress code.

The latest fashion takes this movement to the extreme: Slipper sales have risen 30 percent in the last four years as people are wearing them to work! As one retailer explained, "it is geek chic—the more dressed down you are, the more money you must be making."[74] Note: Do NOT try this on a job interview!

Where to from Here?

Of course, new lifestyle trends constantly are bubbling to the surface. As we'll see in Chapters 15 and 17, many of these set changes in consumer behavior are driven by young consumers who continually are redefining what's hot and what's not. These transformations may come from such growing movements as the new hip hop poets and performance artists who express their alienation from mainstream culture at open-mike nights in poets' cafes. Maybe the gamers who prowl the Internet playing Quake, Obsidian, or Doom will lead the charge, or perhaps "technorganics" who believe in a minimalist lifestyle but who embrace new technologies and spend their time in chat rooms sharing their philosophy of the future will lead the way. Or, the freestylers who value spontaneity and freedom will rule the day (accompanied by the insistent beat of a techno soundtrack) and skateboarding brands such as DC Droors, Menace and Girl, and Chocolate will hit the mainstream. On the other hand, perhaps adherents of "Barrier-Tec" (technology that protects us from pollutants like germs and acid rain) will prevail, and in a few years we will all be sheathed in clothes like those sold by W&LT (Wild and Lethal Trash), a line of street clothing from Europe that features gas masks and other protective gear.[75] Right now, it's anyone's bet: But savvy marketers understand that the only thing they can count on is that lifestyles will continue to change.

CHAPTER SUMMARY

- The concept of *personality* refers to a person's unique psychological makeup and how it consistently influences the way a person responds to his or her environment. Marketing strategies based on personality differences have met with mixed success, partly because of the way these differences in *personality traits* have been measured and applied to consumption contexts. Some approaches have attempted to understand underlying differences in small samples of consumers by employing techniques based on Freudian psychology and variations of this perspective, whereas others have tried to assess these dimensions more objectively in large samples using sophisticated quantitative techniques.

- A consumer's *lifestyle* refers to the ways he or she chooses to spend time and money and how his or her values and tastes are reflected in consumption choices. Lifestyle research is useful to track societal consumption preferences and also to position specific products and services to different segments. Marketers segment by lifestyle differences, often by grouping consumers in terms of their AIOs (activities, interests, and opinions).

- *Psychographic* techniques attempt to classify consumers in terms of psychological, subjective variables in addition to observable characteristics (demographics). A variety of systems, such as VALS, have been developed to identify consumer "types" and to differentiate them in terms of their brand or product preferences, media usage, leisure time activities, and attitudes toward broad issues such as politics and religion.

- Interrelated sets of products and activities are associated with social roles to form *consumption constellations*. People often purchase a product or service because it is associated with a constellation that, in turn, is linked to a lifestyle they find desirable.
- Place of residence often is a significant determinant of lifestyle. Many marketers recognize regional differences in product preferences and develop different versions of their products for different markets. A set of techniques called *geodemography* analyzes consumption patterns using geographical and demographic data, and identifies clusters of consumers who exhibit similar psychographic characteristics.
- Important changes are occurring in consumer priorities and practices in the late 1990s. Some major lifestyle trends include an emphasis on environmentalism, a resurgence of importance placed on value-oriented products and services, a decreased emphasis on nutrition and exercise, renewed interest in devoting more time to families versus careers, and more emphasis on individuality, informal lifestyles and time-saving products and services.

KEY TERMS

80/20 principle, p. 179
affinitization, p. 188
AIOs, p. 178
animism, p. 172
archetypes, p. 168
brand equity, p. 170
consumption constellations, p. 176
ego, p. 164

geodemography, p. 184
id, p. 164
lifestyle, p. 173
motivational research, p. 165
personality, p. 163
pleasure principle, p. 164
product complementarity, p. 176

psychographics, p. 177
reality principle, p. 164
single-source data, p. 184
social trends, p. 188
superego, p. 164
Values and Lifestyles (VALS™)
    System, p. 181

CONSUMER BEHAVIOR CHALLENGE

1. Construct a brand personality inventory for three different brands within a product category. Ask a small number of consumers to rate each brand on about 10 different personality dimensions. What differences can you locate? Do these "personalities" relate to the advertising and packaging strategies used to differentiate these products?
2. In what situations is demographic information likely to be more useful than psychographic data, and vice versa?
3. Alcohol drinkers vary sharply in terms of the number of drinks they may consume, from those who occasionally have one at a cocktail party to regular imbibers. Explain how the 80/20 principle applies to this product category.
4. Compile a set of recent ads that attempt to link consumption of a product with a specific lifestyle. How is this goal usually accomplished?
5. Psychographic analyses can be used to market politicians. Conduct research on the marketing strategies used in a recent, major election. How were voters segmented in terms of values? Can you find evidence that communications strategies were guided by this information?

6. Construct separate advertising executions for a cosmetics product targeted to the Belonger, Achiever, Experiencer, and Maker VALS types. How would the basic appeal differ for each group?

7. Using media targeted to the group, construct a consumption constellation for the social role of college students. What set of products, activities, and interests tend to appear in advertisements depicting "typical" college students? How realistic is this constellation?

8. Geodemographic techniques assume that people who live in the same neighborhood have other things in common as well. Why is this assumption made, and how accurate is it?

9. Single-source data systems give marketers access to a wide range of information about a consumer, just by knowing his or her address. Do you believe this "knowledge power" presents any ethical problems with regard to consumers' privacy? Should access to such information be regulated by the government or other bodies? Should consumers have the right to limit access to these data?

10. Should organizations or individuals be allowed to create web sites that advocate potentially harmful practices? Should hate groups such as The White Aryan Resistance be allowed to recruit members online? Why or why not?

NOTES

1. For an interesting ethnographic account of sky diving as a voluntary high-risk consumption activity, see Richard L. Celsi, Randall L. Rose, and Thomas W. Leigh, "An Exploration of High-Risk Leisure Consumption Through Skydiving," *Journal of Consumer Research* 20 (June 1993): 1–23. See also Jerry Adler, "Been There, Done That," *Newsweek* (July 19, 1993): 43.

2. Ann Marsh, "Surfer Girls," *Forbes* (August 11, 1997): 42.

3. See J. Aronoff and J. P. Wilson, *Personality in the Social Process* (Hillsdale, NJ: Erlbaum, 1985); Walter Mischel, *Personality and Assessment* (New York: Wiley, 1968).

4. Ernest Dichter, *A Strategy of Desire* (Garden City, NY: Doubleday, 1960); Ernest Dichter, *The Handbook of Consumer Motivations* (New York: McGraw-Hill, 1964); Jeffrey J. Durgee, "Interpreting Dichter's Interpretations: An Analysis of Consumption Symbolism" in *The Handbook of Consumer Motivations*, unpublished manuscript (Troy, NY, Rensselaer Polytechnic Institute: 1989); Pierre Martineau, *Motivation in Advertising* (New York: McGraw-Hill, 1957).

5. Vance Packard, *The Hidden Persuaders* (New York: D. McKay, 1957).

6. Harold Kassarjian, "Personality and Consumer Behavior: A Review," *Journal*

of *Marketing Research* 8 (November 1971): 409–18.

7. Karen Horney, *Neurosis and Human Growth* (New York: Norton, 1950).

8. Joel B. Cohen, "An Interpersonal Orientation to the Study of Consumer Behavior," *Journal of Marketing Research* 6 (August 1967): 270–78; Pradeep K. Tyagi, "Validation of the CAD Instrument: A Replication," in Richard P. Bagozzi and Alice M. Tybout, eds., *Advances in Consumer Research* 10 (Ann Arbor, MI: Association for Consumer Research, 1983): 112–14.

9. For a comprehensive review of classic perspectives on personality theory, see Calvin S. Hall and Gardner Lindzey, *Theories of Personality*, 2d ed. (New York: Wiley, 1970).

10. See Carl G. Jung, "The Archetypes and the Collective Unconscious," in H. Read, M. Fordham, and G. Adler, eds., *Collected Works*, vol. 9, part 1 (Princeton: Princeton University Press, 1959).

11. Linda L. Price and Nancy Ridgway, "Development of a Scale to Measure Innovativeness," in Richard P. Bagozzi and Alice M. Tybout, eds., *Advances in Consumer Research* 10 (Ann Arbor, MI: Association for Consumer Research, 1983): 679–84; Russell W. Belk, "Three Scales to Measure Constructs Related to Materialism: Reliability, Validity, and Relationships to Measures of Happiness,"

in Thomas C. Kinnear, ed., *Advances in Consumer Research* 11 (Ann Arbor, MI: Association for Consumer Research, 1984): 291; Mark Snyder, "Self-Monitoring Processes," in Leonard Berkowitz, ed., *Advances in Experimental Social Psychology* (New York: Academic Press, 1979): 85–128; Gordon R. Foxall and Ronald E. Goldsmith, "Personality and Consumer Research: Another Look," *Journal of the Market Research Society* 30, no. 2 (1988): 111–25; Ronald E. Goldsmith and Charles F. Hofacker, "Measuring Consumer Innovativeness," *Journal of the Academy of Marketing Science* 19, no. 3 (1991): 209–21; Curtis P. Haugtvedt, Richard E. Petty, and John T. Cacioppo, "Need for Cognition and Advertising: Understanding the Role of Personality Variables in Consumer Behavior," *Journal of Consumer Psychology* 1 no. 3 (1992): 239–60.

12. Jacob Jacoby, "Personality and Consumer Behavior: How Not to Find Relationships," in *Purdue Papers in Consumer Psychology*, no. 102 (Lafayette, IN: Purdue University, 1969); Harold H. Kassarjian and Mary Jane Sheffet, "Personality and Consumer Behavior: An Update," in Harold H. Kassarjian and Thomas S. Robertson, eds., *Perspectives in Consumer Behavior*, 4th ed. (Glenview, IL: Scott, Foresman, 1991): 291–353; John

Lastovicka and Erich Joachimsthaler, "Improving the Detection of Personality Behavior Relationships in Consumer Research," *Journal of Consumer Research* 14 (March 1988): 583–87; for an approach that ties the notion of personality more directly to marketing issues, see Jennifer L. Aaker, "Dimensions of Brand Personality," *Journal of Marketing Research* 34 (August 1997): 347–57.

13. See Girish N. Punj and David W. Stewart, "An Interaction Framework of Consumer Decision Making," *Journal of Consumer Research* 10 (September 1983): 181–96.

14. J. F. Allsopp, "The Distribution of On-Licence Beer and Cider Consumption and Its Personality Determinants Among Young Men," *European Journal of Marketing* 20, no. 3 (1986): 44–62; Gordon R. Foxall and Ronald E. Goldsmith, "Personality and Consumer Research: Another Look," *Journal of the Market Research Society* 30, no. 2 (April 1988): 111–25.

15. Thomas Hine, "Why We Buy: The Silent Persuasion of Boxes, Bottles, Cans, and Tubes," *Worth* (May 1995): 78–83.

16. Kevin L. Keller, "Conceptualization, Measuring, and Managing Customer-Based Brand Equity," *Journal of Marketing* 57 (January 1993): 1–22.

17. Linda Keslar, "What's in a Name?" *Individual Investor* (April 1999): 101–2.

18. Rebecca Piirto Heath, "The Once and Future King," *Marketing Tools* (March 1998): 38–43.

19. Kathryn Kranhold, "Agencies Beef Up Brand Research to Identify Consumer Preferences," *The Wall Street Journal Interactive Edition* (March 9, 2000).

20. Aaker, "Dimensions of Brand Personality."

21. Quoted in Bradley Johnson, "They All Have Half-Baked Ideas," *Advertising Age* (May 12, 1997): 8.

22. Tim Triplett, "Brand Personality Must Be Managed or It Will Assume a Life of Its Own," *Marketing News* (May 9, 1994): 9.

23. Susan Fournier, "Consumers and Their Brands: Developing Relationship Theory in Consumer Research," *Journal of Consumer Research* 24, no. 4 (March 1998): 343–73.

24. Rebecca Piirto Heath, "The Frontiers of Psychographics," *American Demographics* (July 1996): 38–43.

25. See Gerald Zaltman, Metaphorically Speaking, *Marketing Research* 8, no. 2 (1996): 13–20; Gerald Zaltman, "Rethinking Market Research: Putting People Back In," *Journal of Marketing Research* 34 (November 1997): 424–37; Gerald Zaltman and Robin Higie Coulter, "Seeing the Voice of the Customer: Metaphor-Based Advertising Research," *Journal of Advertising Research*, 35 (1995): 4.

26. Benjamin D. Zablocki and Rosabeth Moss Kanter, "The Differentiation of Life-Styles," *Annual Review of Sociology* (1976): 269–97.

27. Mary Twe Douglas and Baron C. Isherwood, *The World of Goods* (New York: Basic Books, 1979).

28. Zablocki and Kanter, "The Differentiation of Life-Styles."

29. "The Niche's the Thing," *American Demographics* (February 2000): 22.

30. Richard A. Peterson, "Revitalizing the Culture Concept," *Annual Review of Sociology* 5 (1979): 137–66.

31. Quoted in "Hate Group Web Sites on the Rise," *CNN.com*, (February 23, 1999).

32. William Leiss, Stephen Kline, and Sut Jhally, *Social Communication in Advertising* (Toronto: Methuen, 1986).

33. Douglas and Isherwood, *The World of Goods*, quoted on pp. 72–73.

34. Hsee, Christopher K. and France Leclerc, "Will Products Look More Attractive When Presented Separately or Together?" *Journal of Consumer Research* 25 (September 1998): 175–86.

35. Jean Halliday, "L. L. Bean, Subaru Pair for Co-Branding," *Advertising Age* (February 21, 2000): 21.

36. Michael R. Solomon, "The Role of Products as Social Stimuli: A Symbolic Interactionism Perspective," *Journal of Consumer Research* 10 (December 1983): 319–29.

37. Michael R. Solomon and Henry Assael, "The Forest or the Trees? A Gestalt Approach to Symbolic Consumption," in Jean Umiker-Sebeok, ed., *Marketing and Semiotics: New Directions in the Study of Signs for Sale* (Berlin: Mouton de Gruyter, 1988): 189–218; Michael R. Solomon, "Mapping Product Constellations: A Social Categorization Approach to Symbolic Consumption," *Psychology & Marketing* 5, no. 3 (1988): 233–58; see also Stephen C. Cosmas, "Life Styles and Consumption Patterns," *Journal of Consumer Research* 8, no. 4 (March 1982): 453–55.

38. Russell W. Belk, "Yuppies as Arbiters of the Emerging Consumption Style," in Richard J. Lutz, ed., *Advances in Consumer Research* 13 (Provo, UT: Association for Consumer Research, 1986): 514–19.

39. See Lewis Alpert and Ronald Gatty, "Product Positioning by Behavioral Life Styles," *Journal of Marketing* 33 (April 1969): 65–69; Emanuel H. Demby, "Psychographics Revisited: The Birth of a Technique," *Marketing News* (January 2, 1989): 21; William D. Wells, "Backward Segmentation," in Johan Arndt, ed., *Insights into Consumer Behavior* (Boston: Allyn & Bacon, 1968): 85–100.

40. Rebecca Piirto Heath, "Psychographics: 'Q'est-ce que c'est'?" *Marketing Tools* (November/December 1995): 73.

41. William D. Wells and Douglas J. Tigert, "Activities, Interests, and Opinions," *Journal of Advertising Research* 11 (August 1971): 27.

42. Ian Pearson, "Social Studies: Psychographics in Advertising," *Canadian Business* (December 1985): 67.

43. Piirto Heath, "Psychographics: 'Q'est-ce que c'est'?"

44. Alfred S. Boote, "Psychographics: Mind over Matter," *American Demographics* (April 1980): 26–29; William D. Wells, "Psychographics: A Critical Review," *Journal of Marketing Research* 12 (May 1975): 196–213.

45. "At Leisure: Americans' Use of Down Time," *New York Times* (May 9, 1993): E2.

46. Joseph T. Plummer, "The Concept and Application of Life Style Segmentation," *Journal of Marketing* 38 (January 1974): 33–37.

47. Berkeley Rice, "The Selling of Lifestyles," *Psychology Today* (March 1988): 46.

48. John L. Lastovicka, John P. Murry, Erich A. Joachimsthaler, Gurav Bhalla, and Jim Scheurich, "A Lifestyle Typology to Model Young Male Drinking and Driving," *Journal of Consumer Research* 14 (September 1987): 257–63.

49. Anthony Ramirez, "New Cigarettes Raising Issue of Target Market," *New York Times* (February 18, 1990): 28.

50. Rebecca Piirto Heath, "The Frontiers of Psychographics," *American Demographics* (July 1996): 38–43.

51. Martha Farnsworth Riche, "VALS 2," *American Demographics* (July 1989): 25; additional information provided by William D. Guns, Director, Business Intelligence Center, SRI Consulting, Inc., personal communication, May 1997.

52. Rebecca Piirto Heath, "You Can Buy a Thrill: Chasing the Ultimate Rush," *American Demographics* (June 1997): 47–51.

53. Brad Edmonson, "From Dixie to Detroit," *American Demographics* (January 1987): 27.

54. Brad Edmonson, "America's Hot Spots," *American Demographics* (1988): 24–30.

55. Marcia Mogelonsky, "The Geography of Junk Food," *American Demographics* (July 1994): 13–14.

56. Nicholas Zill and John Robinson, "Name That Tune," *American Demographics* (August 1994): 22–27.

57. Edmonson, "From Dixie to Detroit."

58. David Greising, "The Boonies Are Booming," *Business Week* (October 9, 1995): 104.

59. Ronald Henkoff, "Why Every Red-Blooded Consumer Owns a Truck, and

a Five-Pound Jar of Peanut Butter, and a Personal Computer, and a Tool Belt, and a Case of Energy-Saving Light Bulbs, and Why It All Matters on a Nearly Cosmic Scale," *Fortune* (May 29, 1995): 86.

60. Thomas W. Osborn, "Analytic Techniques for Opportunity Marketing," *Marketing Communications* (September 1987): 49–63.

61. Osborn, "Analytic Techniques for Opportunity Marketing."

62. Jonathan Marks, "Clusters Plus Nielsen Equals Efficient Marketing," *American Demographics* (September 1991): 16.

63. Michael J. Weiss, *The Clustering of America* (New York: Harper & Row, 1988).

64. Bob Minzesheimer, "You Are What

You Zip," *Los Angeles* (November 1984): 175.

65. Christina Del Valle, "They Know Where You Live and How You Buy," *Business Week* (February 7, 1994): 89.

66. Del Valle, "They Know Where You Live and How You Buy."

67. Barbara J. Eichhorn, "Selling by Design: Using Lifestyle Analysis to Revamp Retail Space," *American Demographics* (October 1996): 45–48.

68. Quoted in Michael Weiss, "Parallel Universe," *American Demographics* (October 1999): 58–63, p. 62.

69. "Let Your Fingers Do the Trend Forecasting," *Time* (June 1, 1998): 24.

70. Roberta Piirto Heath, "Measuring Minds in the 1990s," *American Demographics* 5 (December 1990): 31.

71. Quoted in Jack Neff, "It's Not Trendy

Being Green," *Advertising Age* (April 10, 2000): 16.

72. Louise Kramer and Judann Pollack, "On the Run," *Advertising Age* (August 24, 1998): 1.

73. Philip Brasher, "Americans Eating More Junk, Worrying Less About Fat and Calories," *Opelika-Auburn* [Alabama] *News* (May 9, 2000): 1A.

74. Quoted in Mark Tatge, "Drop the Dress Shoes and Wear Slippers; See if the Boss Cares," *The Wall Street Journal Interactive Edition* (May 23, 2000).

75. Janine Lopiano-Misdom and Joanne de Luca, *Street Trends* (New York: HarperBusiness, 1997).

t's a lazy Tuesday night, and Jan, Terri, and Nancy are hanging out at Nancy's apartment doing some channel-surfing. Jan clicks to ESPN and the three friends see that there's a women's soccer game on. Jan has been a fan for as long as she can remember—even before the 1999 World Cup that propelled players like Mia Hamm and Brandi Chastain into the media spotlight. She loves the subtle intensity of the game—the traps, the moves, the way players make it look easy to move a ball around a huge field as if it were a small patch of grass. Nancy's a glutton for thrills and chills; she converted to soccer after the emotional cliffhanger of the World Cup final game in which the United States beat China on the team's fifth penalty kick after 120 scoreless minutes. Terri, on the other hand, doesn't know a banana kick from a rainbow kick. Still, you'd have to be living in a cave not to have seen the footage over and over of Brandi Chastain whipping her shirt off to reveal her sports bra when the game was won. Jan even bought one a few weeks later. Still, soccer doesn't really ring her chimes—but as long as she gets to hang out with her girlfriends she doesn't really care if they watch non-contact sports like soccer or contact sports like *The Jerry Springer Show*.

7

ATTITUDES

THE POWER OF ATTITUDES

Jan is just the kind of fan, sponsoring brands like Nike, Gatorade, Adidas, and Bud Light hope will turn women's soccer into an ongoing source of sports fanaticism. Americans' attitudes toward the game have changed dramatically since the women's team lost in the 1996 semifinals in Sweden before a crowd of less than 3,000. The 1999 World Cup was won before an audience of more than 90,000 screaming fans, many of whom were soccer moms who saw the players as important role models for their young daughters. Many traditionally male-dominated sports are now attracting more attention and growing support from women. In 1998 a record 7.5 million women and girls enrolled for soccer teams in the United States. Women now represent just under half of all soccer player registrations.[1]

On the other hand, following Chastain's exuberant show of skin, there is concern about the so-called "Babe Factor" as some critics wonder whether will women's athletics will ever be taken seriously by male fans. Others feel that attitudes toward the game are more complex than that; they argue that sex appeal does not have to be sacrificed for professionalism. The big question is if these positive feelings will endure. The goal of Women's World Cup is to establish a women's professional league during the next few years. This objective parallels the strategy used to launch Major League Soccer in the United States following the 1994 World Cup. Time will tell if this ambitious project will score big or be red-carded and left to dwindle on the sidelines.[2] To score big in professional sports, it's all a question of attitudes.

The term *attitude* is widely used in popular culture. You might be asked, "What is your attitude toward abortion?" A parent might scold, "Young man, I don't like your attitude." Some bars even euphemistically refer to Happy Hour as "an attitude adjustment period." For our purposes, though, an attitude is a lasting, general evaluation of people (including oneself), objects, advertisements, or issues.[3] Anything toward which one has an attitude is called an attitude object (A_o).

An **attitude** is lasting because it tends to endure over time. It is general because it applies to more than a momentary event such as hearing a loud noise, though you might over time develop a negative attitude toward all loud noises. Consumers have attitudes toward a wide range of attitude objects; from very product-specific behaviors (e.g., using Crest toothpaste rather than Colgate) to more general consumption-related behaviors (e.g., how often one should brush one's teeth). Attitudes help to determine whom a person chooses to date, what music he or she listens to, whether he or she will recycle or discard aluminum cans, or whether he or she chooses to become a consumer researcher for a living. This chapter will consider the contents of an attitude, how attitudes are formed, and how they can be measured. It will also review some of the surprisingly complex relationships between attitudes and behavior. In the next chapter, we'll take a closer look at how attitudes can be changed—certainly an issue of prime importance to marketers.

The Functions of Attitudes

The **functional theory of attitudes** was initially developed by psychologist Daniel Katz to explain how attitudes facilitate social behavior.[4] According to this pragmatic approach, attitudes exist *because* they serve some function for the person. That is, they are determined by a person's motives. Consumers who expect that they will need to deal with similar situations at a future time will be more likely to start forming attitudes in anticipation of this event.[5] Two people can each have an attitude toward some object for very different reasons. As a result it can be helpful for a marketer to know *why* an attitude is held before attempting to change it. The following are attitude functions as identified by Katz:

- *Utilitarian function:* The utilitarian function is related to the basic principles of reward and punishment. We develop some attitudes toward

This Norwegian ad addresses young people's smoking attitudes by arousing strong negative feelings. The ad reads (left panel) "Smokers are more sociable than others." (right panel): "While it lasts."

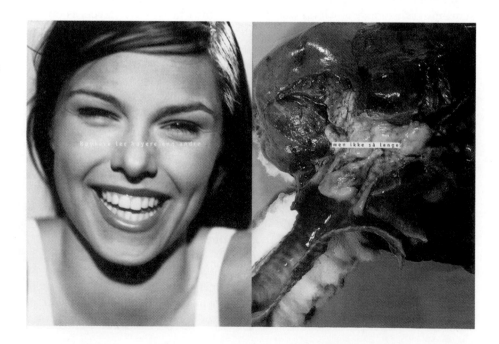

products simply on the basis of whether these products provide pleasure or pain. If a person likes the taste of a cheeseburger, that person will develop a positive attitude toward cheeseburgers. Ads that stress straight-forward product benefits (e.g., you should drink Diet Coke "just for the taste of it") appeal to the utilitarian function.

- *Value-expressive function:* Attitudes that perform a value-expressive function express the consumer's central values or self-concept. A person forms a product attitude not because of its objective benefits, but because of what the product says about him or her as a person (e.g., "What sort of man reads *Playboy*?"). Value-expressive attitudes are highly relevant to lifestyle analyses, which look at how consumers cultivate a cluster of activities, interests, and opinions to express a particular social identity.
- *Ego-defensive function:* Attitudes that are formed to protect the person, either from external threats or internal feelings, perform an ego-defensive function. An early marketing study indicated that housewives in the 1950s resisted the use of instant coffee because it threatened their conception of themselves as capable homemakers.[6] Products that promise to help a man project a "macho" image (e.g., Marlboro cigarettes) may be appealing to his insecurities about his masculinity. Another example is deodorant campaigns that stress the dire, embarrassing consequences of being caught with underarm odor in public.
- *Knowledge function:* Some attitudes are formed as the result of a need for order, structure, or meaning. This need is often present when a person is in an ambiguous situation or is confronted with a new product (e.g., "Bayer wants you to know about pain relievers").

An attitude can serve more than one function, but in many cases a particular one will be dominant. By identifying the dominant function a product serves for consumers—what *benefits* it provides—marketers can emphasize these benefits in their communications and packaging. Ads relevant to the function prompt more favorable thoughts about what is being marketed and can result in a heightened preference for both the ad and the product.

One study determined that for most people coffee serves more of a utilitarian function than a value-expressive function. As a consequence, subjects responded more positively to copy for a (fictitious) coffee that read, "The delicious, hearty flavor and aroma of Sterling Blend coffee comes from a blend of the freshest coffee beans" (utilitarian appeal) than to, "The coffee you drink says something about the type of person you are. It can reveal your rare, discriminating taste" (value-expressive function).[7]

As we saw in the experiences of the three women watching a soccer game, the importance of an attitude object may differ quite a bit for different people. Understanding the attitude's centrality to an individual and to others who share similar characteristics can be useful to marketers who are trying to devise strategies that will appeal to different customer segments. A study of football game attendance illustrates that varying levels of commitment result in different fan "profiles."[8] The study identified three distinct clusters of fans:[9]

- One cluster consisted of the real die-hard fans like Jan who were highly committed to their team and who displayed an enduring love of the game. To reach these fans, the researchers recommend that sports marketers should focus on providing them with greater sports knowledge and relate their attendance to their personal goals and values.

- A second cluster was like Nancy—their attitudes were based on the unique, self-expressive experience provided by the game. They enjoy the stimulation of cheering for a team and the drama of the competition itself. They are more likely to be "brand switchers" who are fair-weather fans, shifting allegiances when the home team no longer provides the thrills they need. This segment can be appealed to by publicizing aspects of the visiting teams, such as advertising the appearance of stars who are likely to give the fans a game they will remember.

- A third cluster was like Terri—they were looking for camaraderie above all. These consumers attend games primarily to take part in small-group activities such as tailgating that accompany the event. Marketers could appeal to this cluster by providing improved peripheral benefits, such as making it easier for groups to meet at the stadium, improving parking, and offering multiple-unit pricing.

The ABC Model of Attitudes

Most researchers agree that an attitude has three components: affect, behavior, and cognition. **Affect** refers to the way a consumer *feels* about an attitude object. **Behavior** involves the person's intentions to *do* something with regard to an attitude object (but, as will be discussed at a later point, an intention does not always result in an actual behavior). **Cognition** refers to the *beliefs* a consumer has about an attitude object. These three components of an attitude can be remembered as the **ABC model of attitudes.**

This model emphasizes the interrelationships among knowing, feeling, and doing. Consumers' attitudes toward a product cannot be determined by simply identifying their beliefs about it. For example, a researcher may find that shoppers "know" a particular camcorder has an 8:1 power zoom lens, autofocus, and a flying erase head, but such findings do not indicate whether they feel these attributes are good, bad, or irrelevant or whether they would actually buy the camcorder.

Hierarchies of Effects

All three components of an attitude are important, but their relative importance will vary depending on a consumer's level of motivation with regard to the attitude object. The differences in athletic interests among the three women in Nancy's apartment illustrate how these elements can be combined in different ways to create an attitude. Attitude researchers have developed the concept of a hierarchy of effects to explain the relative impact of the three components. Each hierarchy specifies that a fixed sequence of steps occurs en route to an attitude. Three different hierarchies are summarized in Figure 7.1.

The Standard Learning Hierarchy. Jan's positive attitude toward women's soccer closely resembles the process by which most attitudes have been assumed to be constructed. A consumer approaches a product decision as a problem-solving process. First, he or she forms beliefs about a product by accumulating knowledge (beliefs) regarding relevant attributes. Next, the consumer evaluates these beliefs and forms a feeling about the product (affect).[10] Over time, Jan assembled information about the sport, began to recognize the players, and learned which teams were superior to others. Finally, based on this evaluation, the consumer engages in a relevant behavior, such as buying the product or supporting a particular team by wearing its jersey. This careful choice process often results in the type of loyalty displayed by Jan; the consumer "bonds" with the product over time and is not easily persuaded to experiment with other brands. The standard learning

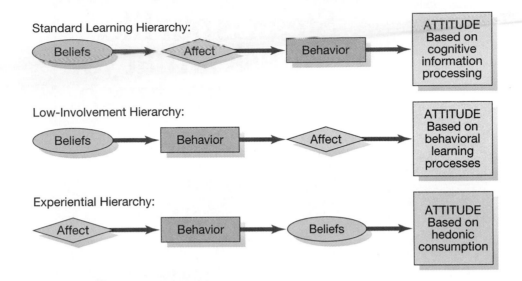

Figure 7.1
Three Hierarchies of Effects

hierarchy assumes that a consumer is highly involved in making a purchase decision.[11] The person is motivated to seek out a lot of information, carefully weigh alternatives, and come to a thoughtful decision.

The Low-Involvement Hierarchy. In contrast to Jan, Nancy's interest in the attitude object (women's soccer) is at best lukewarm. She is not particularly knowledgeable about the sport, and she may have an emotional response to an exciting game but not to a specific team. Nancy is typical of a consumer who forms an attitude via the *low-involvement hierarchy of effects.* In this sequence, the consumer does not initially have a strong preference for one brand over another, but instead acts on the basis of limited knowledge and then forms an evaluation only after the product has been purchased or used.[12] The attitude is likely to come about through behavioral learning in which the consumer's choice is reinforced by good or bad experiences with the product after purchase. Nancy will probably be more likely to tune in to future games if they continue to come down to the wire like the World Cup game.

The possibility that consumers simply don't care enough about many decisions to carefully assemble a set of product beliefs and then evaluate them is important, because it implies that all of the concern about influencing beliefs and carefully communicating information about product attributes may be largely wasted. Consumers aren't necessarily going to pay attention anyway; they are more likely to respond to simple stimulus–response connections when making purchase decisions. For example, a consumer choosing among paper towels might remember that "Bounty is the quicker picker-upper" rather than bothering to systematically compare all of the brands on the shelf.

The notion of low involvement on the part of consumers is a bitter pill for some marketers to swallow. Who wants to admit that what they market is not very important or involving? A brand manager for, say, a brand of bubble gum or cat food may find it hard to believe that consumers don't put that much thought into purchasing her product because she herself spends many of her waking (and perhaps sleeping) hours thinking about it.

For marketers, the ironic silver lining to this low-involvement cloud is that under these conditions, consumers are not motivated to process a lot of complex brand-related information. Instead, they will be swayed by principles of behavioral

This ad for New York's famous Smith & Wollensky restaurant emphasizes that marketers and others associated with a product or service are often more involved with it than are their consumers.

Steak is our life. All we ask is that you make it your lunch.

Smith & Wollensky.
The quintessential New York City steakhouse.
49th St. & 3rd Ave. (212) 753-1530.

Winner of The *Wine Spectator's* 1987 Grand Award.

learning, such as the simple responses caused by conditioned brand names, point-of-purchase displays, and so on. This results in what we might call the *involvement paradox:* The less important the product is to consumers, the more important are many of the marketing stimuli (e.g., packages, jingles) that must be devised to sell it.

The Experiential Hierarchy. Researchers in recent years have begun to stress the significance of emotional response as a central aspect of an attitude. According to the *experiential hierarchy of effects,* consumers act on the basis of their emotional reactions. Terri just enjoys watching the tube with her friends, regardless of what is on. For this reason Coca-Cola is starting to promote Coke in more emotional ways. Consumers told researchers they value attributes like authenticity and optimism as they move toward beverages like water, juices, and flavored teas. To combat this erosion of the cola market, ads for Coke now use phrases like "unique taste sensation" and "sparkle on your tongue." Coke's core proposition now is "Only the unique sensory experience of an ice-cold Coca-Cola brings a magical delight to the real moments of my life."[13]

The experiential perspective highlights the idea that attitudes can be strongly influenced by intangible product attributes, such as package design, and by consumers' reactions toward accompanying stimuli, such as advertising, brand names, and the nature of the setting in which the experience occurs. As discussed in Chapter 4, resulting attitudes will be affected by consumers' hedonic motivations, such as how the product makes them feel or the fun its use will provide. Numerous studies indicate that the mood a person is in when exposed to a marketing message influences how the ad is processed, the likelihood that the information presented will be remembered, and how the person will feel about the advertised item and related products in the future.[14]

One important debate about the experiential hierarchy concerns the independence of cognition and affect. On the one hand, the *cognitive-affective* model

NET PROFIT

THE RECOGNITION THAT EMOTIONAL responses play a key role in product attitudes has sparked renewed interest in developing high-tech approaches to measuring and manipulating emotional responses. Traditionally, these reactions have been measured in terms of physiological arousal, but the problem with this approach is that it is hard to interpret the results because arousal can be either positive or negative.[18] Several companies are marketing more finely-tuned alternatives that track specific responses. IBM is working on a new gadget called the emotion mouse. It tracks the user's skin temperature, heart rate, and even very tiny hand movements, along with the electrical conductivity of the skin, which changes with moisture. The company is a leader in the new field of *affective computing,* where it is hoped that computers will eventually be able to determine the user's current emotional state and actually adjust its interface to reduce frustration, sense when an employee may be burning out, automatically boost computer game action, or base an automatic search for television shows on a user's personal feelings of what is funny. Right now the emotion mouse is about 75 percent successful at determining a user's emotional state. Eventually, these devices are likely to find their way into other objects, such as a car steering wheel that could sense when a driver is getting drowsy or a key chain that will tell a policeman if someone he's stopped seems unusually frightened. And, teachers offering lectures over the Internet may be able to judge the reactions of their faceless students and even replay parts of lectures where students' minds had wandered. Right now an IBM group is working with Microsoft to alter the features of Clippie, the talking paper clip that first appeared in Microsoft Office 97 to offer advice. Many people found the device helpful, but others found it infuriating. The goal is to let the computer sense if you're one of those people who want to strangle the bothersome little paper clip, so Clippie will turn itself off peacefully before you find another way to do it.[19]

argues that an affective judgment is but the last step in a series of cognitive processes. Earlier steps include the sensory registration of stimuli and the retrieval of meaningful information from memory to categorize these stimuli.[15]

On the other hand, the *independence hypothesis* takes the position that affect and cognition involve two separate, partially independent systems; affective responses do not always require prior cognitions.[16] A number one song on the *Billboard* "Top 40" may possess the same attributes as many other songs (e.g., dominant bass guitar, raspy vocals, persistent downbeat), but beliefs about these attributes cannot explain why one song becomes a classic while another sharing the same characteristics winds up in the bargain bin at the local record store. The independence hypothesis does not eliminate the role of cognition in experience. It simply balances this traditional, rational emphasis on calculated decision making by paying more attention to the impact of aesthetic, subjective experience. This type of holistic processing is more likely to occur when the product is perceived as primarily expressive or delivers sensory pleasure rather than utilitarian benefits.[17]

Product Attitudes Don't Tell the Whole Story

Marketers who are concerned with understanding consumers' attitudes have to contend with an even more complex issue: In decision-making situations, people form attitudes toward objects other than the product itself that can influence their ultimate selections. One additional factor to consider is attitudes toward the act of buying in general—as we'll see later in the chapter, sometimes people simply are reluctant, embarrassed, or just plain too lazy to expend the effort to actually obtain a desired product or service.

Attitude Toward the Advertisement

Consumers' reactions to a product are also influenced by their evaluations of its advertising, over and above their feelings about the product itself. Our evaluation of a product can be determined solely by our appraisal of how it's depicted in marketing communications—we don't hesitate to form attitudes toward products we've never even seen in person, much less used.

One special type of attitude object, then, is the marketing message itself. The **attitude toward the advertisement** (A_{ad}) is defined as a predisposition to respond in a favorable or unfavorable manner to a particular advertising stimulus during a particular exposure occasion. Determinants of A_{ad} include attitude toward the advertiser, evaluations of the ad execution itself, the mood evoked by the ad, and the degree to which the ad affects viewers' arousal levels.[20] A viewer's feelings about the context in which an ad appears can also influence brand attitudes. For example, attitudes about an ad and the brand depicted will be influenced if the consumer sees the ad while watching a favorite TV program.[21] The effects demonstrated by A_{ad} emphasize the potential importance of an ad's entertainment value in the purchase process.[22] If consumers are not able to view an ad again, both belief and attitude confidence about that ad rapidly diminishes. This research supports the marketer's effort to pulse or frequently repeat advertisements in the media.[23]

Ads Have Feelings Too

The feelings generated by an ad have the capacity to directly affect brand attitudes. Commercials can evoke a wide range of emotional responses, from disgust to happiness. These feelings can be influenced both by the way the ad is done (i.e., the specific advertising *execution*) and by the consumer's reactions to the advertiser's motives. For example, many advertisers who are trying to craft messages for adolescents and young adults are encountering problems because this age group, having grown up in a "marketing society," tends to be skeptical about attempts to get them to buy things.[24] These reactions can in turn influence memory for advertising content.[25]

At least three emotional dimensions have been identified in commercials: pleasure, arousal, and intimidation.[26] Specific types of feelings that can be generated by an ad include the following:[27]

- *Upbeat feelings:* amused, delighted, playful
- *Warm feelings:* affectionate, contemplative, hopeful
- *Negative feelings:* critical, defiant, offended

FORMING ATTITUDES

We all have lots of attitudes, and we don't usually question how we got them. Certainly, a person isn't born with the conviction that, say, Pepsi is better than Coke, or that alternative music liberates the soul. Where do these attitudes come from?

An attitude can form in several different ways, depending on the particular hierarchy of effects in operation and how the attitude is learned (see Chapter 3). It can occur because of classical conditioning, in which an attitude object such as the Pepsi name is repeatedly paired with a catchy jingle ("You're in the Pepsi Generation"). Or, it can be formed through instrumental conditioning, in which consumption of the attitude object is reinforced (e.g., Pepsi quenches one's thirst). Or the learning of an attitude can be the outcome of a very complex cognitive process. For example, a teenager may come to model the behavior of friends and media figures who drink Pepsi because she believes that this act will allow her to fit in with the desirable images of the Pepsi Generation.

MARKETING PITFALLS

IN A STUDY OF irritating advertising, researchers examined more than 500 prime-time network commercials that had registered negative reactions by consumers. The most irritating commercials were for feminine hygiene products, hemorrhoid medication or laxatives, and women's underwear. The researchers identified the following factors as prime offenders:[28]

- A sensitive product is shown (e.g., hemorrhoid medicine), and its use or package is emphasized.
- The situation is contrived or overdramatized.
- A person is put down in terms of appearance, knowledge, or sophistication.
- An important relationship, such as a marriage, is threatened.
- There is a graphic demonstration of physical discomfort.
- Uncomfortable tension is created by an argument or by an antagonistic character.
- An unattractive or unsympathetic character is portrayed.
- A sexually suggestive scene is included.
- The commercial suffers from poor casting or execution.

Not All Attitudes Are Created Equal

It is thus important to distinguish among types of attitudes, because not all are formed the same way.[29] For example, a highly brand-loyal consumer like Jan, the soccer fan, has an enduring, deeply held positive attitude toward an attitude object, and this involvement will be difficult to weaken. On the other hand, another consumer like Nancy may be a more fickle consumer: She may have a mildly positive attitude toward a product but be quite willing to abandon it when something better comes along. This section will consider the differences between strongly and weakly held attitudes, and briefly review some of the major theoretical perspectives that have been developed to explain how attitudes form and relate to one another in the minds of consumers.

What's your opinion? Check out the on-line polls at www.prenhall.com/ myphlip. Just follow the little person in the lab coat.

REALITY CHECK *MORE THAN 500 UNIVERSITIES HAVE SIGNED up commercial companies to run campus Web sites and e-mail services. These agreements provide Web services to colleges at little or no cost. But, these actions have aroused controversy because the sites are paid for by advertising from major companies. That gives marketers entree to influence the attitudes of thousands of students who are involuntarily exposed to product messages. One professor complained, "We're throwing our freshmen to the wolves. The university has become a shill for the corporate community." But university administrators argue that they could not provide the services by themselves—students expect to be able to fill out financial aid forms and register for classes online. Colleges that do not offer such services may lose their ability to attract students.[30]*

How do you feel about this situation? Do you agree that you're being "thrown to the wolves?" Should companies be able to buy access to your eyeballs from the school you pay to attend?

I don't think it's wrong for companies to be able to advertise to us because all companies do it anyway. It is up to us to be aware and be wise about what we choose to be influenced by.

Liana Mouynes
University of Washington

More power to the universities that are trying to get an edge by having different incentives for students.

Fant Walker
University of Mississippi

A suggestion towards resolving this issue is for each college to display a disclaimer on their webpage informing people of who is paying for the campus website. With this disclaimer, college students are fairly informed of why and where the advertisements are coming from.

Annalise M. Mulholland
Virginia Tech

We are talking about University students here. They have a mind of their own and I don't think that a couple of advertisements would create much effect on them.

Tina Ho
Nanyang Technological University, Singapore

To suggest that online advertising is "throwing students to the wolves" is ridiculous. College students are adults, have been exposed to years of the commercial onslaught and won't be brainwashed by viewing the college home page.

Kerri Ruminiski
Idaho State University

You are not forced to click on the link and visit their website, although some people don't have the maturity to control themselves over credit card applications, but then, sign up booths are all over campus anyway.

Frank Liu
Florida State University

We see advertisements everyday in the pages of our school newspapers, in display cases through out our buildings, and on the tables of our dining halls. We are not oblivious to advertising practice. We are smart, and recognize when an advertisement is trying to persuade us.

Katherine S. Kennedy
James Madison University

Now at my University, we are able to register for classes online. I like this system because we are able to do it at home and at any time we wish to. Not having a website will cause the students to lose interest, therefore, if this is the situation, students might as well accept it.

Mai Sasaki
Keio University, Japan

Levels of Commitment to an Attitude

Consumers vary in their *commitment* to an attitude; the degree of commitment is related to their level of involvement with the attitude object.[31]

- *Compliance:* At the lowest level of involvement, *compliance,* an attitude is formed because it helps in gaining rewards or avoiding punishments from others. This attitude is very superficial; it is likely to change when the person's behavior is no longer monitored by others or when another option becomes available. A person may drink Pepsi because this brand is sold in the cafeteria, and it is too much trouble to go elsewhere for a Coca-Cola.

- *Identification:* A process of identification occurs when attitudes are formed in order to conform with another person or group. Advertising that depicts the social consequences of choosing some products over others is relying on the tendency of consumers to imitate the behavior of desirable models.

- *Internalization:* At a high level of involvement, deep-seated attitudes are internalized and become part of the person's value system. These attitudes are very difficult to change because they are so important to the individual. For example, many consumers had strong attitudes toward Coca-Cola and reacted quite negatively when the company attempted to switch to the New Coke formula. This allegiance to Coke was obviously more than a minor preference for these people; the brand had become intertwined with their social identities, taking on patriotic and nostalgic properties.

The Consistency Principle

Have you ever heard someone say, "Pepsi is my favorite soft drink. It tastes terrible," or "I love my husband. He's the biggest idiot I've ever met"? Probably not too often, because these beliefs or evaluations are not consistent with one another. According to the **principle of cognitive consistency,** consumers value harmony among their thoughts, feelings, and behaviors, and they are motivated to maintain uniformity among these elements. This desire means that, if necessary, consumers will change their thoughts, feelings, or behaviors to make them consistent with their other experiences. The consistency principle is an important reminder that attitudes are not formed in a vacuum. A significant determinant of the way an attitude object will be evaluated is how it fits with other, related attitudes already held by the consumer.

Cognitive Dissonance and Harmony among Attitudes

The **theory of cognitive dissonance** states that when a person is confronted with inconsistencies among attitudes or behaviors, he or she will take some action to resolve this "dissonance," perhaps by changing an attitude or modifying a behavior. The theory has important ramifications for attitudes, because people are often confronted with situations in which there is some conflict between their attitudes and behaviors.[32]

According to the theory, people are motivated to reduce the negative feelings caused by dissonance by somehow making things fit with one another. The theory focuses on situations in which two cognitive elements are inconsistent with one another. A cognitive element can be something a person believes about himself, a behavior he performs, or an observation about his surroundings. For

By describing Cadillac as "my company" the woman in this ad exhibits a high level of attitudinal commitment to her employer.

example, the two *cognitive elements*, "I know smoking cigarettes causes cancer" and "I smoke cigarettes" are *dissonant* with one another. This psychological inconsistency creates a feeling of discomfort that the smoker is motivated to reduce. The magnitude of dissonance depends on both the importance and number of dissonant elements.[33] In other words, the pressure to reduce dissonance is more likely to be observed in high-involvement situations in which the elements are more important to the individual.

Dissonance reduction can occur either by eliminating, adding, or changing elements. For example, the person could stop smoking (eliminating) or remember great aunt Sophie, who smoked until the day she died at age 90 (adding). Alternatively, he might question the research that links cancer and smoking (changing), perhaps by believing industry-sponsored studies that try to refute this connection.

Dissonance theory can help to explain why evaluations of a product tend to increase *after* it has been purchased. The cognitive element "I made a stupid decision" is dissonant with the element "I am not a stupid person" so people tend to find even more reasons to like something after it becomes theirs.

A field study performed at a horse race demonstrated postpurchase dissonance. Bettors evaluated their chosen horse more highly and were more confident of its success *after* they had placed a bet than before. Because the bettor is financially committed to the choice, he or she reduces dissonance by increasing the attractiveness of the chosen alternative relative to the unchosen ones.[34] One implication of this phenomenon is that consumers actively seek support for their purchase decisions, so marketers should supply them with additional reinforcement to build positive brand attitudes.

Self-Perception Theory

Do attitudes necessarily change following behavior because people are motivated to feel good about their decisions? **Self-perception theory** provides an alternative explanation of dissonance effects.[35] It assumes that people use observations of their own behavior to determine what their attitudes are, just as we assume that we know the attitudes of others by watching what they do. The theory states that

This ad for a magazine illustrates that consumers often distort information so that it fits with what they already believe or think they know.

we maintain consistency by inferring that we must have a positive attitude toward an object if we have bought or consumed it (assuming that we freely made this choice). Thus, Jan might say to herself, "I guess I must be into sports pretty big time. I sure choose to watch it a lot."

Self-perception theory is relevant to the *low-involvement hierarchy*, because it involves situations in which behaviors are initially performed in the absence of a strong internal attitude. After the fact, the cognitive and affective components of attitude fall into line. Thus, buying a product out of habit may result in a positive attitude toward it after the fact—why would I buy it if I didn't like it?

Self-perception theory helps to explain the effectiveness of a sales strategy called the **foot-in-the-door technique,** which is based on the observation that a consumer is more likely to comply with a request if he or she has first agreed to comply with a smaller request.[36] The name for this technique comes from the practice of door-to-door selling in which salespeople were taught to plant their foot in a door so the prospect could not slam it on them. A good salesperson knows that he or she is more likely to get an order if the customer can be persuaded to open the door and talk. By agreeing to do so, the customer has established that she or he is willing to listen to the salesperson. Placing an order is consistent with this self-perception. This technique is especially useful for inducing consumers to answer surveys or to donate money to charity. Such factors as the time lag between the first and second request, the similarity between the two requests, and whether the same person makes both requests have been found to influence its effectiveness.[37]

Social Judgment Theory

Social judgment theory also assumes that people assimilate new information about attitude objects in light of what they already know or feel.[38] The initial attitude acts as a frame of reference, and new information is categorized in terms of this existing standard. Just as our decision that a box is heavy depends in part on the weight of other boxes we have lifted, we develop a subjective standard when making judgments about attitude objects.

One important aspect of the theory is the notion that people differ in terms of the information they will find acceptable or unacceptable. They form **latitudes of acceptance and rejection** around an attitude standard. Ideas that fall within a latitude will be favorably received, but those falling outside of this zone will not. Because Jan already had a favorable attitude toward the concept of women playing professional soccer, she is likely to be receptive to ads such as Nike's that promote female athletic participation. If she were opposed to these activities, these messages would probably not be considered.

Messages that fall within the latitude of acceptance tend to be seen as more consistent with one's position than they actually are. This process is called an *assimilation effect*. On the other hand, messages falling in the latitude of rejection tend to be seen as even farther from one's position than they actually are, resulting in a *contrast effect*.[39]

As a person becomes more involved with an attitude object, his or her latitude of acceptance gets smaller. In other words, the consumer accepts fewer ideas that are removed from his or her own position and tends to oppose even mildly divergent positions. This tendency is evident in ads that appeal to discriminating buyers, which claim that knowledgeable people will reject anything but the very best (e.g., "choosy mothers choose Jif peanut butter"). On the other hand, relatively uninvolved consumers will consider a wider range of alternatives. They are less likely to be brand loyal and will be more likely to be brand switchers.[40]

Balance Theory

Balance theory considers relations among elements a person might perceive as belonging together.[41] This perspective involves relations (always from the perceiver's subjective point of view) among three elements, so the resulting attitude structures are called *triads*. Each triad contains: (1) a person and his or her perceptions of; (2) an attitude object and; (3) some other person or object.

These perceptions can be either positive or negative. More importantly, people *alter* these perceptions in order to make relations among them consistent. The theory specifies that people desire relations among elements in a triad to be harmonious, or *balanced*. If they are not, a state of tension will result until somehow perceptions are changed and balance is restored.

Elements can be perceived as going together in one of two ways: They can have either a *unit relation*, in which one element is seen as somehow belonging to or being a part of the other (something like a belief), or a *sentiment relation*, in which the two elements are linked because one has expressed a preference (or dislike) for the other. A dating couple might be seen as having a positive sentiment relation. On getting married, they will have a positive unit relation. The process of divorce is an attempt to sever a unit relation.

To see how balance theory might work, consider the following scenario:

- Alex would like to date Larry, who is in her consumer behavior class. In balance theory terms, Alex has a positive sentiment relation with Larry.
- One day, Larry shows up in class wearing an earring. Larry has a positive unit relation with the earring. It belongs to him and is literally a part of him.
- Alex does not like men who wear earrings. She has a negative sentiment relation with men's earrings.

According to balance theory, Alex faces an unbalanced triad, and she will experience pressure to restore balance by altering some aspect of the triad, as shown in Figure 7.2. She could, for example, decide that she does not like Larry

Figure 7.2
Alternative Routes to Restoring Balance
in a Triad

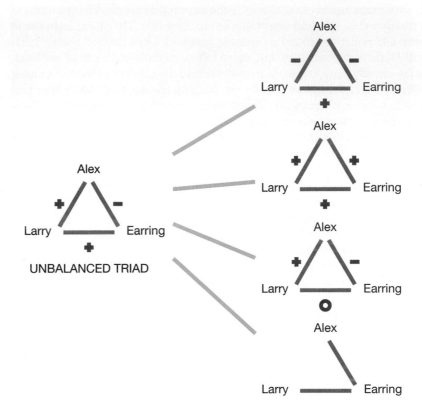

after all. Or, her liking for Larry could prompt a change in her attitude toward earrings. She might even try to negate the unit relation between Larry and the earring by deciding that he must be wearing it as part of a fraternity initiation (thus reducing the free-choice element). Finally, she could choose to "leave the field" by not thinking any more about Larry and his controversial earring.

Note that although the theory does not specify which of these routes will be taken, it does predict that one or more of Alex's perceptions will probably change in order to achieve balance. Although this distortion is most likely an oversimplified representation of most attitude processes, it helps to explain a number of consumer behavior phenomena.

Marketing Applications of Balance Theory

Balance theory reminds us that when perceptions are balanced, attitudes are likely to be stable. On the other hand, when inconsistencies are observed, we are more likely to observe changes in attitudes. Balance theory also helps explain why consumers like to be associated with positively valued objects. Forming a unit relation with a popular product (e.g., buying and wearing fashionable clothing, driving a flashy car) may improve one's chances of being included as a positive sentiment relation in other people's triads.

Finally, balance theory is useful in accounting for the widespread use of celebrities to endorse products. When a triad is not fully formed (e.g., perceptions about a new product or one about which the consumer does not yet have a well-defined attitude), the marketer can create a positive sentiment relation between the consumer and the product by depicting a positive unit relation between the product and a well-known personality. In other cases, behaviors are discouraged when admired people argue against them, as is the goal when athletes appear in antidrug public service advertisements.

This "balancing act" is at the heart of celebrity endorsements, in which marketers hope that the star's popularity will transfer to the product. This strategy will be considered at length in the next chapter. For now, it pays to remember that this creation of a unit relation between product and star can backfire if the public's opinion of the celebrity endorser shifts from positive to negative, as happened when Pepsi pulled an ad featuring Madonna after she was associated with a controversial music video involving religion and sex. The strategy can also cause trouble if the star–product unit relation is questioned, as happened when singer Michael Jackson, who also did promotions for Pepsi, subsequently confessed that he does not drink soda.

ATTITUDE MODELS

A consumer's overall evaluation of a product sometimes accounts for most of his attitude. When market researchers want to assess attitudes, it can be sufficient for them to simply ask a bunch of guys, "How do you feel about Budweiser?" However, as we saw earlier, attitudes can be a lot more complex than that. One problem is that a product or service may be composed of many attributes, or qualities—some of these may be more important than others to particular people. Another problem is that a person's decision to act on his or her attitude is affected by other factors, such as whether it is felt that buying a product would be met with approval by friends or family. As a result *attitude models* have been developed that try to specify the different elements that might work together to influence people's evaluations of attitude objects.

MARKETING OPPORTUNITY

CONSUMERS OFTEN LIKE TO publicize their connections with successful people or organizations (no matter how tenuous the connection) to enhance their own standing. In balance theory terms, they are attempting to create a unit relation with a positively valued attitude object. This tactic has been called "basking in reflected glory."[42]

For example, a series of studies performed at Arizona State University showed how students' desire to identify with a winning image—in this case, ASU's football team—influenced their consumption behaviors. After the team played a game each weekend, observers went around campus and recorded the incidence of school-related items displayed by students (e.g., ASU T-shirts, caps, etc.). The frequency of these behaviors was related to the team's performance. If the team had won, students were more likely to show off their school affiliation (basking in reflected glory) than if the team had lost. This relationship was affected by the magnitude of the win—the bigger the point spread, the more likely were observers to note a sea of ASU insignias the following Monday.

The desire to bask in reflected glory by purchasing products associated with a valued attitude object has created numerous marketing opportunities. College bookstores reap more than $400 million a year by selling items bearing their school's name and logo, and the total market for collegiate licensing amounts to about $750 million annually. The UCLA bookstore alone sells $5 million worth of Bruin items a year. Many schools now license their names (usually for a 6.5 percent royalty) to get a stake in this market (see Chapter 3). Because people tend to identify with successful teams, it is not surprising that the most successful licensing universities also happen to have renowned athletic programs, including Michigan, Ohio State, Florida, Penn State, Texas, Kentucky, Alabama, Florida State, Indiana, and Washington.[43]

College merchandise helps students and fans alike to "bask in reflected glory."

Multiattribute Attitude Models

A simple response does not always tell us everything we need to know about either *why* the consumer feels a certain way toward a product or about what marketers can do to change the consumer's attitude. Beliefs about specific brand attributes can be pivotal for a product. Warner-Lambert discovered this in research it did for its Fresh Burst Listerine mouthwash. A research firm paid 37 families to set up cameras in their bathrooms to watch their daily routines. Users of both Fresh Burst and rival Scope said they used mouthwash to make their breath smell good. But, Scope users swished the liquid and then spit it out, while Listerine users kept the product in their mouths for a long time (one user kept it in until he got in the car and finally spit it out in a sewer a block away!). These findings meant Listerine hadn't shaken its medicine-like image.[44]

Because attitudes can be complex, **multiattribute attitude models** have been extremely popular among marketing researchers. This type of model assumes that a consumer's attitude (evaluation) of an attitude object (A_o) will depend on the beliefs he or she has about several or many attributes of the object. The use of a multiattribute model implies that an attitude toward a product or brand can be predicted by identifying these specific beliefs and combining them to derive a measure of the consumer's overall attitude. We'll describe how these work, using the example of a consumer evaluating a complex attitude object that should be very familiar to you: a college.

Basic multiattribute models specify three elements.[45]

- *Attributes* are characteristics of the A_o. Most models assume that the relevant characteristics can be identified. That is, the researcher can include those attributes that consumers take into consideration when evaluating the A_o. For example, scholarly reputation is an attribute of a college.
- *Beliefs* are cognitions about the specific A_o (usually relative to others like it). A belief measure assesses the extent to which the consumer perceives that a brand possesses a particular attribute. For example, a student might

have a belief that the University of North Carolina has a strong academic standing.

- *Importance weights* reflect the relative priority of an attribute to the consumer. Although an A_o can be considered on a number of attributes, some are likely to be more important than others (i.e., they will be given greater weight). Furthermore, these weights are likely to differ across consumers. In the case of colleges and universities, for example, one student might stress research opportunities, whereas another might assign greater weight to athletic programs.

The Fishbein Model

The most influential multiattribute model is called the *Fishbein model,* named after its primary developer.[46] The model measures three components of attitude:

1. *Salient beliefs* people have about an A_o (i.e., those beliefs about the object that are considered during evaluation)
2. *Object-attribute linkages,* or the probability that a particular object has an important attribute
3. *Evaluation* of each of the important attributes

Note, however, that the model makes some assumptions that may not always be warranted. It assumes that we have been able to adequately specify all of the relevant attributes that, for example, a student will use in evaluating his or her choices about which college to attend. The model also assumes that he or she will go through the process (formally or informally) of identifying a set of relevant attributes, weighing them, and summing them. Although this particular decision is likely to be highly involving, it is still possible that his or her attitude will instead be formed by an overall affective response (a process known as *affect referral*).

By combining these three elements, a consumer's overall attitude toward an object can be computed (we'll see later how this basic equation has been modified to increase its accuracy). The basic formula is

$$A_{ijk} = \Sigma \beta_{ijk} I_{1k}$$

where
i = attribute
j = brand
k = consumer
I = the importance weight given attribute i by consumer k
β = consumer k's belief regarding the extent to which brand j possesses attribute i
A = a particular consumer's (k's) attitude score for brand j

The overall attitude score (A) is obtained by multiplying a consumer's rating of each attribute for all of the brands considered by the importance rating for that attribute.

To see how this basic multiattribute model might work, let's suppose we want to predict which college a high school senior is likely to attend. After months of waiting, Saundra has been accepted to four schools. Because she must now decide among these, we would first like to know which attributes Saundra will consider in forming an attitude toward each school. We can then ask Saundra to assign a rating regarding how well each school performs on each attribute and also determine the relative importance of the attributes to her.

TABLE 7.1 The Basic Multiattribute Model: Saundra's College Decision

Attribute (I)	Importance (I)	Beliefs(B)			
		Smith	Princeton	Rutgers	Northland
Academic reputation	6	8	9	6	3
All women	7	9	3	3	3
Cost	4	2	2	6	9
Proximity to home	3	2	2	6	9
Athletics	1	1	2	5	1
Party atmosphere	2	1	3	7	9
Library facilities	5	7	9	7	2
Attitude score		163	142	153	131

NOTE: These hypothetical ratings are scored from 1 to 10, and higher numbers indicate "better" standing on an attribute. For a negative attribute (e.g. cost), higher scores indicate that the school is believed to have "less" of that attribute (i.e., to be cheaper).

An overall attitude score for each school can then be computed by summing scores on each attribute (after weighing each by its relative importance). These hypothetical ratings are shown in Table 7.1. Based on this analysis, it seems that Saundra has the most favorable attitude toward Smith. She is clearly someone who would like to attend an all-woman's school with a solid academic reputation rather than a school that offers a strong athletic program or a party atmosphere.

Strategic Applications of the Multiattribute Model

Suppose you were the director of marketing for Northland College, another school Saundra was considering. How might you use the data from this analysis to improve your image?

Capitalize on Relative Advantage. If one's brand is viewed as being superior on a particular attribute, consumers like Saundra need to be convinced that this particular attribute is an important one. For example, although Saundra rates Northland's social atmosphere highly, she does not believe this attribute is a valued aspect for a college. As Northland's marketing director, you might emphasize the importance of an active social life, varied experiences, or even the development of future business contacts forged through strong college friendships.

Strengthen Perceived Product/Attribute Linkages. A marketer may discover that consumers do not equate his or her brand with a certain attribute. This problem is commonly addressed by campaigns that stress the product's qualities to consumers (e.g., "new and improved"). Saundra apparently does not think much of Northland's academic quality, athletic programs, or library facilities. You might develop an informational campaign to improve these perceptions (e.g., "little known facts about Northland").

Add a New Attribute. Product marketers frequently try to create a distinctive position from their competitors by adding a product feature. Northland College might try to emphasize some unique aspect, such as a hands-on internship program for business majors that takes advantage of ties to the local community.

Influence Competitors' Ratings. Finally, you might try to decrease the positivity of competitors. This type of action is the rationale for a strategy of comparative advertising. One tactic might be to publish an ad that lists the tuition rates of a number of area schools, as well as their attributes with which Northland can be favorably compared, as the basis for emphasizing the value obtained for the money at Northland.

USING ATTITUDES TO PREDICT BEHAVIOR

Although multiattribute models have been used by consumer researchers for many years, they have been plagued by a major problem: In many cases, knowledge of a person's attitude is *not* a very good predictor of behavior. In a classic demonstration of "do as I say, not as I do," many studies have obtained a very low correlation between a person's reported attitude toward something and his or her actual behavior toward it. Some researchers have been so discouraged that they have questioned whether attitudes are of any use at all in understanding behavior. [47]

This questionable linkage between attitudes and behavior can be a big headache for advertisers: Consumers can love a commercial, yet still not buy the product. For example, one of the most popular TV commercials in recent years featured basketball player Shaquille O'Neal for Pepsi. Although the company spent $67 million on this spot and other similar ones in a single year, sales of Pepsi-Cola fell by close to two percent, even as sales of archrival Coca-Cola increased by eight percent in the same period.[48]

The Extended Fishbein Model

The original Fishbein model, which focused on measuring a consumer's attitude toward a product, has been extended in several ways to improve its predictive ability. The newer version is called the **theory of reasoned action.**[49] This model contains several important additions to the original, and although the model is still not perfect, its ability to predict relevant behavior has been improved.[50] Some of the modifications to this model are considered here.

Intentions Versus Behavior

Like the motivations discussed in Chapter 4, attitudes have both direction and strength. A person may like or dislike an attitude object with varying degrees of confidence or conviction. It is helpful to distinguish between firmly held attitudes and those that are more superficial, especially because an attitude held with greater conviction is more likely to be acted on.[51] One study on environmental issues and marketing activities found, for example, that people who express greater conviction in their feelings regarding environmentally responsible behaviors such as recycling show greater consistency between attitudes and behavioral intentions.[52]

However, as the old expression goes, "the road to hell is paved with good intentions." Many factors might interfere with performance of actual behavior, even if the consumer has sincere intentions. He or she might save up with the intention of buying a stereo system. In the interim, though, any number of things could happen: losing a job, getting mugged on the way to the store, or arriving at the store to find that the desired model is out of stock. It is not surprising, then, that in some instances past purchase behavior has been found to be a better predictor of future behavior than is a consumer's behavioral intention.[53] The theory of reasoned action aims to measure behavioral intentions, recognizing that certain uncontrollable factors inhibit prediction of actual behavior.

Social Pressure

The theory acknowledges the power of other people in influencing behavior. Many of our behaviors are not determined in a vacuum. Much as we may hate to admit it, what we think others would *like* us to do may be more crucial than our own individual preferences. Some research approaches try to assess the extent to which people's "public" attitudes and purchase decisions might be different than what they would do if they were in private. For example, one firm uses a technique it calls "engineered theatre." Researchers go to the actual site where a product is being consumed, such as a bar. They arrange for the wrong product to "mistakenly" be served, and then observe the consumer's "naked response" to the brand and her reaction to consuming the brand in a social context.[54]

In the case of Saundra's college choice, note that she was very positive about going to a predominantly female school. However, if she felt that this choice would be unpopular (perhaps her friends would think she was crazy), she might ignore or downgrade this preference when coming to a decision. A new element, *the subjective norm* (SN), was thus added to include the effects of what we believe other people think we should do. The value of SN is arrived at by including two other factors: (1) the intensity of a *normative belief* (NB) that others believe an action should be taken or not taken, and; (2) the *motivation to comply* (MC) with that belief (i.e., the degree to which the consumer takes others' anticipated reactions into account when evaluating a course of action or a purchase).

Attitude Toward Buying

The model now measures **attitude toward the act of buying** (A_{act}), rather than only the attitude toward the product itself. In other words, it focuses on the perceived consequences of a purchase. Knowing how someone feels about buying or using an object turns out to be more valid than merely knowing the consumer's evaluation of the object itself.[55]

To understand this distinction, consider a problem that might arise when measuring attitudes toward condoms. Although a group of college students might have a positive attitude toward condoms, does this necessarily predict that they will buy and use them? A better prediction would be obtained by asking the students how likely they are to *buy* condoms. A person might have a positive A_o toward condoms, but A_{act} might be negative due to the embarrassment or the hassle involved.

Obstacles to Predicting Behavior in the Theory of Reasoned Action

Despite improvements to the Fishbein model, problems arise when it is misapplied. In many cases, the model is used in ways for which it was not intended, or where certain assumptions about human behavior may not be warranted.[56] Other obstacles to predicting behavior include the following:

- The model was developed to deal with actual behavior (e.g., taking a diet pill), not with the *outcomes* of behavior that are instead assessed in some studies (e.g., losing weight).
- Some outcomes are beyond the consumer's control, such as when the purchase requires the cooperation of other people. For instance, a woman might *want* to get a mortgage, but this intention will be worthless if she cannot find a banker to give her one.
- The basic assumption that behavior is intentional may be invalid in a variety of cases, including impulsive acts, sudden changes in one's situation,

novelty seeking, or even simple repeat buying. One study found that such unexpected events as having guests, changes in the weather, or reading articles about the healthfulness of certain foods exerted a significant effect on actual behaviors.[57]

- Measures of attitude often do not really correspond to the behavior they are supposed to predict, either in terms of the A_o or when the act will occur. One common problem is a difference in the level of *abstraction* employed. For example, knowing a person's attitude toward sports cars may not predict whether he or she will purchase a Mazda Miata. It is very important to match the level of specificity between the attitude and the behavioral intention.

- A similar problem relates to the *time frame* of the attitude measure. In general, the longer the time between the attitude measurement and the behavior it is supposed to assess, the weaker the relationship will be. For example, predictability would improve markedly by asking consumers the likelihood that they would buy a house in the next week as opposed to within the next five years.

- Attitudes formed by direct, personal experience with an A_o are stronger and more predictive of behavior than those formed indirectly, such as through advertising.[58] According to the *attitude accessibility perspective*, behavior is a function of the person's immediate perceptions of the A_o in the context of the situation in which it is encountered. An attitude will guide the evaluation of the object, but *only* if it is activated from memory when the object is observed. These findings underscore the importance of strategies that induce trial (e.g., by widespread product sampling to encourage the consumer to try the product at home, by taste tests, test drives, etc.) as well as those that maximize exposure to marketing communications.

Trying to Consume

Another perspective tries to address some of these problems by instead focusing on consumers' goals and what they believe is required to attain them. The *theory of trying* states that the criterion of behavior in the reasoned action model should be replaced with *trying* to reach a goal.[59] This perspective recognizes that additional factors might intervene between intent and performance—both personal and environmental barriers might prevent the individual from attaining the goal. For example, a person who intends to lose weight may have to deal with numerous issues: He may not believe he is capable of slimming down, he may have a roommate who loves to cook and who leaves tempting goodies lying around the apartment, his friends may be jealous of his attempts to diet and will encourage him to pig out, or he may be genetically predisposed to obesity and cutting down on calories simply will not produce the desired results.

The theory of trying includes several new components that attempt to account for the complex situations in which many factors either help or hurt our changes of turning intentions into actions, as shown in Figure 7.3. These factors include the amount of control the person has over the situation, his or her expectations of success or failure in achieving the goal, social norms related to attaining the goal, and his or her attitude toward the process of trying (i.e., how the action required to attain the goal makes him or her feel, regardless of the outcome). Still other new variables are the frequency and recency of past trying of the behavior—for example, even if a person does not have specific plans to go on a diet in the next month, the frequency with which he or she has tried to do so in

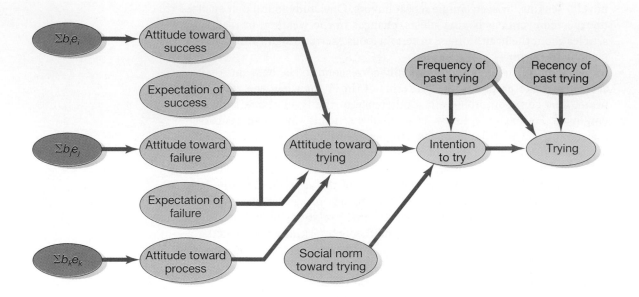

Figure 7.3
Theory of Trying (TT)

the recent past (and the success—however fleeting—he or she may have experienced) would be the best predictor of future attempts to shed some pounds. To predict whether someone would try to lose weight, here are a few sample issues that might be addressed:

- *Past frequency:* How many times in the past year did the person try to lose weight?
- *Recency:* Did he try to lose weight in the last week?
- *Beliefs:* Did he believe he would be healthier if he lost weight?
- *Evaluations of consequences:* Did he believe his girlfriend would be happier if he succeeded in losing weight? Did he believe his friends would make fun of him if he tried but failed to lose weight?
- *The process:* Would the diet make him uncomfortable or depressed?
- *Expectations of success and failure:* Did he believe it likely he would be able to lose weight if he tried?
- *Subjective norms toward trying:* Would the people who are important to him approve of his efforts to lose weight?

Tracking Attitudes over Time

An attitude survey is like a snapshot taken at a single point in time. It may tell us a lot about a brand's position at that moment, but it does not permit many inferences about progress the brand has made over time or any predictions about possible future changes in consumer attitudes. To accomplish that, it is necessary to develop an *attitude-tracking* program. This activity helps to increase the predictability of behavior by allowing researchers to analyze attitude trends during an extended period of time. It is more like a movie than a snapshot. For example, a longitudinal survey conducted by the Food Marketing Institute of consumers' attitudes toward food content during the last decade illustrates how priorities can shift in a fairly short time.[60] Concerns about fat and cholesterol content rose dramatically during this period, and *nutritional issues* such as interest in sugar content decreased.

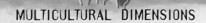

MULTICULTURAL DIMENSIONS

THE THEORY OF REASONED action has primarily been applied in Western settings. Certain assumptions inherent in the model may not necessarily apply to consumers from other cultures. Several cultural roadblocks diminish the universality of the theory of reasoned action.

- The model was developed to predict the performance of any voluntary act. Across cultures, however, many consumer activities, ranging from taking exams and entering military service to receiving an inoculation or even choosing a marriage partner, are not necessarily voluntary.
- The relative impact of subjective norms may vary across cultures. For example, Asian cultures tend to value conformity and "face saving," so it is possible that subjective norms that involve the anticipated reactions of others to the choice will have an even greater impact on behavior for many Asian consumers. Indeed, a recent study conducted among voters in Singapore was able to predict voting for political candidates from their voting intentions, which in turn were influenced by such factors as voters' attitudes toward the candidate, attitudes toward the political party, and subjective norms—which in Singapore included an emphasis on harmonious and close ties among members of the society.[61]
- The model measures behavioral intentions, and thus presupposes that consumers are actively thinking ahead and planning future behaviors. The intention concept assumes that consumers have a linear time sense; they think in terms of past, present, and future. As will be discussed in Chapter 10, this perspective on time is not held by all cultures.
- A consumer who forms an intention is (implicitly) claiming that he or she is in control of his or her actions. Some cultures (e.g., Muslim peoples) tend to be fatalistic and do not necessarily believe in the concept of free will. Indeed, one study comparing students from the United States, Jordan, and Thailand found evidence for cultural differences in assumptions about fatalism and control over the future.[62]

Ongoing Tracking Studies

Attitude tracking involves the administration of an attitude survey at regular intervals. Preferably, the identical methodology is used each time so that results can be reliably compared. Several syndicated services, such as the Gallup Poll or the Yankelovich Monitor, track consumer attitudes over time (see Chapter 6). Results from a tracking study of ecological attitudes among young people in a set of European countries is shown in Figure 7.4.

This activity can be extremely valuable for many strategic decisions. For example, one firm monitored changes in consumer attitudes toward one-stop financial centers. Although a large number of consumers were warm to the idea when it was first introduced, the number of people who liked the concept did not increase over time despite the millions of dollars invested in advertising to promote the centers. This finding indicated some problems with the way the concept was being presented to consumers, and the company decided to "go back to the drawing board," eventually coming up with a new way to communicate the advantages of this service.

Changes to Look For over Time

Some of the dimensions that can be included in attitude tracking include the following:

- *Changes in different age groups:* Attitudes tend to change as people age (a life-cycle effect). In addition, cohort effects occur, whereby members of a particular generation tend to share certain outlooks (e.g., the yuppie). Also, historical effects can be observed as large groups of people are affected

Figure 7.4
Percentage of 16- to 24-Year-Olds Who Agree "We Must Take Radical Action to Cut Down on How We Use Our Cars."

SOURCE: The Henley Centre Frontiers: Planning for Consumer Change in Europe 1996/97.

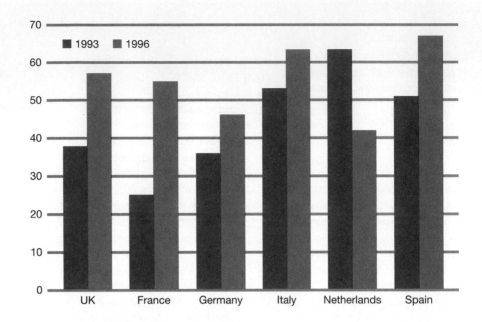

by profound cultural changes (such as the Great Depression or the democratization of Eastern Europe).

- *Scenarios about the future:* Consumers are frequently tracked in terms of their future plans, confidence in the economy, and so on. These measures can provide valuable data about future behavior and yield insights for public policy. For example, Americans tend to overestimate how much they will earn after retirement, which is a potentially dangerous miscalculation.

- *Identification of change agents:* Social phenomena can alter people's attitudes toward basic consumption activities over time, as when consumers' willingness to buy fur changes. Or, consumers' likelihood of desiring a divorce may be affected by such facilitators as changes in the legal system that make this action easier, or by inhibitors, such as the prevalence of AIDS and the value of two paychecks in today's economy.[63]

CHAPTER SUMMARY

- An *attitude* is a predisposition to evaluate an object or product positively or negatively.
- *Social marketing* refers to attempts to change consumers' attitudes and behaviors in ways that are beneficial to the society as a whole.
- Attitudes are made up of three components: *beliefs, affect, and behavioral intentions.*
- Attitude researchers traditionally assumed that attitudes were learned in a fixed sequence, consisting first of the formation of beliefs (*cognitions*) regarding an attitude object, followed by some evaluation of that object (*affect*) and then some action (*behavior*). Depending on the consumer's level of involvement and the circumstances, though, attitudes can result from other hierarchies of effects as well.

- A key to attitude formation is the function the attitude plays for the consumer (e.g., is it utilitarian or ego defensive?).
- One organizing principle of attitude formation is the importance of consistency among attitudinal components—that is, some parts of an attitude may be altered to be in line with others. Such theoretical approaches to attitudes as *cognitive dissonance theory*, *self-perception theory*, and *balance theory* stress the vital role of the need for consistency.
- The complexity of attitudes is underscored by multiattribute attitude models, in which a set of beliefs and evaluations is identified and combined to predict an overall attitude. Factors such as subjective norms and the specificity of attitude scales have been integrated into attitude measures to improve predictability.

KEY TERMS

ABC model of attitudes, p. 200
affect, p. 200
attitude, p. 198
attitude toward the act of
    buying A_{act}, p. 216
attitude toward the advertisement
    (A_{ad}), p. 204
balance theory, p. 209
behavior, p. 200
cognition, p. 200

experiential hierarchy, p. 202
foot-in-the-door technique, p. 208
functional theory of
    attitudes, p. 196
latitudes of acceptance and
    rejection, p. 209
low-involvement hierarchy, p. 201
multiattribute attitude
    models, p. 212

principle of cognitive
    consistency, p. 206
self-perception theory, p. 207
social judgment theory, p. 208
standard learning hierarchy, p. 200
theory of cognitive
    dissonance, p. 206
theory of reasoned action, p. 215

CONSUMER BEHAVIOR CHALLENGE

1. Contrast the hierarchies of effects outlined in the chapter. How will strategic decisions related to the marketing mix be influenced by which hicrarchy is operative among target consumers?
2. List three functions performed by attitudes, giving an example of how each function is employed in a marketing situation.
3. Think of a behavior someone does that is inconsistent with his or her attitudes (e.g., attitudes toward cholesterol, drug use, or even buying things to make him or her stand out or attain status). Ask the person to elaborate on why he or she does the behavior, and try to identify the way the person has resolved dissonant elements.
4. Devise an attitude survey for a set of competing automobiles. Identify areas of competitive advantage or disadvantage for each model you incorporate.
5. Construct a multiattribute model for a set of local restaurants. Based on your findings, suggest how restaurant managers can improve an establishment's image via the strategies described in the chapter.

NOTES

1. Bill Saporito, "Crazy for the Cup: With A 3–0 Start, The U.S. Aims For Another World Soccer Title," *Time* (June 28, 1999): 62–64.

2. Bill Saporito, "Flat-Out Fantastic," *Time* (July 19, 1999): 58; Mark Hyman, "The 'Babe Factor' in Women's Soccer," *Business Week* (July 26, 1999): 118.

3. Robert A. Baron and Donn Byrne, *Social Psychology: Understanding Human Interaction*, 5th ed. (Boston: Allyn & Bacon, 1987).

4. Daniel Katz, "The Functional Approach to the Study of Attitudes," *Public Opinion Quarterly* 24 (Summer 1960): 163–204; Richard J. Lutz, "Changing Brand Attitudes Through Modification of Cognitive Structure," *Journal of Consumer Research* 1 (March 1975): 49–59.

5. Russell H. Fazio, T. M. Lenn, and E. A. Effrein, "Spontaneous Attitude Formation," *Social Cognition* 2 (1984): 214–34.

6. Mason Haire, "Projective Techniques in Marketing Research," *Journal of Marketing* 14 (April 1950): 649–56.

7. Sharon Shavitt, "The Role of Attitude Objects in Attitude Functions," *Journal of Experimental Social Psychology* 26 (1990): 124–48; see also J. S. Johar and M. Joseph Sirgy, "Value-Expressive versus Utilitarian Advertising Appeals: When and Why to Use Which Appeal," *Journal of Advertising* 20 (September 1991): 23–34.

8. For the original work that focused on the issue of levels of attitudinal commitment, see H. C. Kelman, "Compliance, Identification, and Internalization: Three Processes of Attitude Change," *Journal of Conflict Resolution* 2 (1958): 51–60.

9. Lynn R. Kahle, Kenneth M. Kambara, and Gregory M. Rose, "A Functional Model of Fan Attendance Motivations for College Football," *Sports Marketing Quarterly* 5, no. 4 (1996): 51–60.

10. For a study that found evidence of simultaneous causation of beliefs and attitudes, see Gary M. Erickson, Johny K. Johansson, and Paul Chao, "Image Variables in Multi-Attribute Product Evaluations: Country-of-Origin Effects," *Journal of Consumer Research* 11 (September 1984): 694–99.

11. Michael Ray, "Marketing Communications and the Hierarchy-of-Effects," in P. Clarke, ed., *New Models for Mass Communications* (Beverly Hills, CA: Sage, 1973): 147–76.

12. Herbert Krugman, "The Impact of Television Advertising: Learning Without Involvement," *Public Opinion Quarterly* 29 (Fall 1965): 349–56; Robert Lavidge and Gary Steiner, "A Model for Predictive Measurements of Advertising Effectiveness," *Journal of Marketing* 25 (October 1961): 59–62.

13. Stuart Elliott and Constance L. Hays, "Coca-Cola Will Try to Promote Its Top Brand with More Emotion," *The New York Times on the Web* (October 19, 1999).

14. For some recent studies see Andrew B. Aylesworth and Scott B. MacKenzie, "Context Is Key: The Effect of Program-Induced Mood on Thoughts About the Ad," *Journal of Advertising*, 27, no. 2 (Summer 1998): 17; Angela Y. Lee and Brian Sternthal, "The Effects of Positive Mood on Memory," *Journal of Consumer Research* 26 (September 1999): 115–28; Michael J. Barone, Paul W. Miniard and Jean B. Romeo, "The Influence of Positive Mood on Brand Extension Evaluations," *Journal of Consumer Research* 26 (March 2000): 386–401. For a study that compared the effectiveness of emotional appeals across cultures see Jennifer L. Aaker and Patti Williams, "Empathy Versus Pride: The Influence of Emotional Appeals Across Cultures," *Journal of Consumer Research* 25 (December 1998): 241–61.

15. Punam Anand, Morris B. Holbrook, and Debra Stephens, "The Formation of Affective Judgments: The Cognitive–Affective Model Versus the Independence Hypothesis," *Journal of Consumer Research* 15 (December 1988): 386–91; Richard S. Lazarus, "Thoughts on the Relations Between Emotion and Cognition," *American Psychologist* 37, no. 9 (1982): 1019–24.

16. Robert B. Zajonc, "Feeling and Thinking: Preferences Need No Inferences," *American Psychologist* 35, no. 2 (1980): 151–75.

17. Banwari Mittal, "The Role of Affective Choice Mode in the Consumer Purchase of Expressive Products," *Journal of Economic Psychology* 4, no. 9 (1988): 499–524.

18. Patricia Winters Lauro, "Advertisers Want to Know What People Really Think," *The New York Times on the Web* (April 13, 2000).

19. Ian Austen, "Soon: Computers That Know You Hate Them," *The New York Times on the Web* (January 6, 2000).

20. Scot Burton and Donald R. Lichtenstein, "The Effect of Ad Claims and Ad Context on Attitude Toward the Advertisement," *Journal of Advertising* 17, no. 1 (1988): 3–11; Karen A. Machleit and R. Dale Wilson, "Emotional Feelings and Attitude Toward the Advertisement: The Roles of Brand Familiarity and Repetition," *Journal of Advertising* 17, no. 3 (1988): 27–35; Scott B. Mackenzie and Richard J. Lutz, "An Empirical Examination of the Structural Antecedents of Attitude Toward the Ad in an Advertising Pretesting Context," *Journal of Marketing* 53 (April 1989): 48–65; Scott B. Mackenzie, Richard J. Lutz, and George E. Belch, "The Role of Attitude Toward the Ad as a Mediator of Advertising Effectiveness: A Test of Competing Explanations," *Journal of Marketing Research* 23 (May 1986): 130–43; Darrel D. Muehling and Russell N. Laczniak, "Advertising's Immediate and Delayed Influence on Brand Attitudes: Considerations Across Message-Involvement Levels," *Journal of Advertising* 17, no. 4 (1988): 23–34;

Mark A. Pavelchak, Meryl P. Gardner, and V. Carter Broach, "Effect of Ad Pacing and Optimal Level of Arousal on Attitude Toward the Ad," in Rebecca H. Holman and Michael R. Solomon, eds., *Advances in Consumer Research* 18 (Provo, UT: Association for Consumer Research, 1991): 94–99. Some research evidence indicates that a separate attitude is also formed regarding the brand name itself, see George M. Zinkhan and Claude R. Martin Jr., "New Brand Names and Inferential Beliefs: Some Insights on Naming New Products," *Journal of Business Research* 15 (1987): 157–72.

21. John P. Murry Jr., John L. Lastovicka, and Surendra N. Singh, "Feeling and Liking Responses to Television Programs: An Examination of Two Explanations for Media-Context Effects," *Journal of Consumer Research* 18 (March 1992): 441–51.

22. Barbara Stern and Judith Lynne Zaichkowsky, "The Impact of 'Entertaining' Advertising on Consumer Responses," *Australian Marketing Researcher* 14 (August 1991): 68–80.

23. Krishnan, H. Shanker and Robert E. Smith, "The Relative Endurance of Attitudes, Confidence, and Attitude Behavior Consistency: The Role of Information Source and Delay," *Journal of Consumer Psychology* 7, no. 3 (1998): 273–98.

24. For a recent study that examined the impact of skepticism on advertising issues, see David M. Boush, Marian Friestad, and Gregory M. Rose, "Adolescent Skepticism Toward TV Advertising and Knowledge of Advertiser Tactics," *Journal of Consumer Research* 21 (June 1994): 167–75.

25. Basil G. Englis, "Consumer Emotional Reactions to Television Advertising and Their Effects on Message Recall," in S. Agres, J. A. Edell, and T. M. Dubitsky, eds., *Emotion in Advertising: Theoretical and Practical Explorations* (Westport, CT: Quorum Books, 1990): 231–54.

26. Morris B. Holbrook and Rajeev Batra, "Assessing the Role of Emotions as Mediators of Consumer Responses to Advertising," *Journal of Consumer Research* 14 (December 1987): 404–20.

27. Marian Burke and Julie Edell, "Ad Reactions over Time: Capturing Changes in the Real World," *Journal of Consumer Research* 13 (June 1986): 114–18.

28. David A. Aaker and Donald E. Bruzzone, "Causes of Irritation in Advertising," *Journal of Marketing* 49 (Spring 1985): 47–57.

29. Herbert Kelman, "Compliance, Identification, and Internalization: Three Processes of Attitude Change,"

Journal of Conflict Resolution 2 (1958): 51–60.

30. Lisa Guernsey, "Welcome to College. Now Meet Our Sponsor," *The New York Times on the Web* (August 17, 1999).

31. See Sharon E. Beatty and Lynn R. Kahle, "Alternative Hierarchies of the Attitude-Behavior Relationship: The Impact of Brand Commitment and Habit," *Journal of the Academy of Marketing Science* 16 (Summer 1988): 1–10.

32. Leon Festinger, *A Theory of Cognitive Dissonance* (Stanford, CA: Stanford University Press, 1957).

33. Chester A. Insko and John Schopler, *Experimental Social Psychology* (New York: Academic Press, 1972).

34. Robert E. Knox and James A. Inkster, "Postdecision Dissonance at Post Time," *Journal of Personality and Social Psychology* 8, no. 4 (1968): 319–23.

35. Daryl J. Bem, "Self-Perception Theory," in Leonard Berkowitz, ed., *Advances in Experimental Social Psychology* (New York: Academic Press, 1972): 1–62.

36. Jonathan L. Freedman and Scott C. Fraser, "Compliance Without Pressure: The Foot-in-the-Door Technique," *Journal of Personality and Social Psychology* 4 (August 1966): 195–202; for further consideration of possible explanations for this effect, see William DeJong, "An Examination of Self-Perception Mediation of the Foot-in-the-Door Effect," *Journal of Personality and Social Psychology* 37 (December 1979): 221–31; Alice M. Tybout, Brian Sternthal, and Bobby J. Calder, "Information Availability As a Determinant of Multiple-Request Effectiveness," *Journal of Marketing Research* 20 (August 1988): 280–90.

37. David H. Furse, David W. Stewart, and David L. Rados, "Effects of Foot-in-the-Door, Cash Incentives and Follow-ups on Survey Response," *Journal of Marketing Research* 18 (November 1981): 473–78; Carol A. Scott, "The Effects of Trial and Incentives on Repeat Purchase Behavior," *Journal of Marketing Research* 13 (August 1976): 263–69.

38. Muzafer Sherif and Carl I. Hovland, *Social Judgment: Assimilation and Contrast Effects in Communication and Attitude Change* (New Haven, CT: Yale University Press, 1961).

39. See Joan Meyers-Levy and Brian Sternthal, "A Two-Factor Explanation of Assimilation and Contrast Effects," *Journal of Marketing Research* 30 (August 1993): 359–68.

40. Mark B. Traylor, "Product Involvement and Brand Commitment," *Journal of Advertising Research* (December 1981): 51–56.

41. Fritz Heider, *The Psychology of Interpersonal Relations* (New York: Wiley, 1958).

42. R. B. Cialdini, R. J. Borden, A. Thorne, M. R. Walker, S. Freeman, and L. R. Sloan, "Basking in Reflected Glory: Three (Football) Field Studies," *Journal of Personality and Social Psychology* 34 (1976): 366–75.

43. Howard G. Ruben, "College Stores Cash in on School Logos," *Daily News Record* (May 20, 1987): 1.

44. Leslie Kaufman, "Enough Talk," *Newsweek* (August 18, 1997): 48–49.

45. William L. Wilkie, *Consumer Behavior* (New York: Wiley, 1986).

46. M. Fishbein, "An Investigation of the Relationships Between Beliefs About an Object and the Attitude Toward that Object," *Human Relations* 16 (1983): 233–40.

47. Allan Wicker, "Attitudes Versus Actions: The Relationship of Verbal and Overt Behavioral Responses to Attitude Objects," *Journal of Social Issues* 25 (Autumn 1969): 65.

48. Laura Bird, "Loved the Ad. May (or May Not) Buy the Product," *The Wall Street Journal* (April 7, 1994): B1.

49. Icek Ajzen and Martin Fishbein, "Attitude-Behavior Relations: A Theoretical Analysis and Review of Empirical Research," *Psychological Bulletin* 84 (September 1977): 888–918.

50. Morris B. Holbrook and William J. Havlena, "Assessing the Real-to-Artificial Generalizability of Multi-Attribute Attitude Models in Tests of New Product Designs," *Journal of Marketing Research* 25 (February 1988): 25–35; Terence A. Shimp and Alican Kavas, "The Theory of Reasoned Action Applied to Coupon Usage," *Journal of Consumer Research* 11 (December 1984): 795–809.

51. R. P. Abelson, "Conviction," *American Psychologist*, 43 (1988): 267–75; R. E. Petty and J. A. Krosnick, *Attitude Strength: Antecedents and Consequences* (Mahwah, NJ: Erlbaum, 1995); Ida E. Berger and Linda F. Alwitt, "Attitude Conviction: A Self-Reflective Measure of Attitude Strength," *Journal of Social Behavior and Personality* 11, no. 3 (1996): 557–72.

52. Berger and Alwitt, "Attitude Conviction."

53. Richard P. Bagozzi, Hans Baumgartner, and Youjae Yi, "Coupon Usage and the Theory of Reasoned Action," in Rebecca H. Holman and Michael R. Solomon, eds., *Advances in Consumer Research* 18 (Provo, UT: Association for Consumer Research, 1991): 24–27; Edward F. McQuarrie, "An Alternative to Purchase Intentions: The Role of Prior Behavior in Consumer Expenditure on Computers," *Journal of the Market Research*

Society 30 (October 1988): 407–37; Arch G. Woodside and William O. Bearden, "Longitudinal Analysis of Consumer Attitude, Intention, and Behavior Toward Beer Brand Choice," in William D. Perrault Jr., ed., *Advances in Consumer Research* 4 (Ann Arbor, MI: Association for Consumer Research, 1977): 349–56.

54. Andy Greenfield, "The Naked Truth (Studying Consumer Behavior)," *Brandweek* 38, no. 38 (October 13, 1997): 22.

55. Michael J. Ryan and Edward H. Bonfield, "The Fishbein Extended Model and Consumer Behavior," *Journal of Consumer Research* 2 (1975): 118–36.

56. Blair H. Sheppard, Jon Hartwick, and Paul R. Warshaw, "The Theory of Reasoned Action: A Meta-Analysis of Past Research with Recommendations for Modifications and Future Research," *Journal of Consumer Research* 15 (December 1988): 325–43.

57. Joseph A. Cote, James McCullough, and Michael Reilly, "Effects of Unexpected Situations on Behavior-Intention Differences: A Garbology Analysis," *Journal of Consumer Research* 12 (September 1985): 188–94.

58. Russell H. Fazio, Martha C. Powell, and Carol J. Williams, "The Role of Attitude Accessibility in the Attitude-to-Behavior Process," *Journal of Consumer Research* 16 (December 1989): 280–88; Robert E. Smith and William R. Swinyard, "Attitude-Behavior Consistency: The Impact of Product Trial Versus Advertising," *Journal of Marketing Research* 20 (August 1983): 257–67.

59. Richard P. Bagozzi and Paul R. Warshaw, "Trying to Consume," *Journal of Consumer Research* 17, no. 2 (September 1990): 127–40.

60. Barbara Presley Noble, "After Years of Deregulation, a New Push to Inform the Public," *New York Times* (October 27, 1991): F5.

61. Kulwant Singh, Siew Meng Leong, Chin Tiong Tan, and Kwei Cheong Wong, "A Theory of Reasoned Action Perspective of Voting Behavior: Model and Empirical Test," *Psychology & Marketing* 12, no. 1 (January 1995): 37–51.

62. Joseph A. Cote and Patriya S. Tansuhaj, "Culture Bound Assumptions in Behavior Intention Models," in Thom Srull, ed., *Advances in Consumer Research* 16 (Provo, UT: Association for Consumer Research, 1989): 105–9.

63. Matthew Greenwald and John P. Katosh, "How to Track Changes in Attitudes," *American Demographics* (August 1987): 46.

Carrie's sorting through today's mail. Bill, ad, bill, fund-raising letter from a political candidate, an offer for yet another credit card . . . aha! The new edition of *Launch!* Carrie throws down the other junk mail and pops the CD/ROM into her PC. Time to check out the latest music and movies . . . and yes, probably watch some cool commercials also. She's been looking forward to getting her monthly online magazine since she overheard Natalie and Stephanie down at the health club talking about the video interview with Rob Thomas of Matchbox Twenty on this edition.

Carrie fires up the CD/ROM and the interface that looks like a city full of buildings and billboards soon appears. She enters "The Hang" and watches the interview with Thomas.

Then, she clicks on the icon for Toyota and drools through a new commercial for the MR2 Spider. Something to think about. After that, she watches a public service message courtesy of a tobacco company that shows a teenager burning up all of his money to buy cigarettes ("Tobacco is whacko if you're a teen."), and then she previews a few new computer games she might buy for her spaced-out brother Ken. Carrie putters around in a few more locations; she listens to some new music by Gov't Mule, watches a preview of that new Winona Ryder flick (and a Q/A session with the star), and then just for fun she clicks over to the live Launch.com Web site to take a survey and download some more music information. Watching commercials and participating in marketing research projects sure makes a lot more sense when she gets to pick which ones to see and when.

8

ATTITUDE CHANGE AND INTERACTIVE COMMUNICATIONS

CHANGING ATTITUDES THROUGH COMMUNICATION

Consumers are constantly bombarded by messages inducing them to change their attitudes. These persuasion attempts can range from logical arguments to graphic pictures, and from intimidation by peers to exhortations by celebrity spokespeople. And, communications flow both ways—the consumer may seek out information sources in order to learn more about these options. As Carrie's actions show, the choice to access marketing messages on your own terms is changing the way we think about persuasion attempts.

This chapter will review some of the factors that help to determine the effectiveness of marketing communications. Our focus will be on some basic aspects of communication that specifically help to determine how and if attitudes will be created or modified. This objective relates to **persuasion,** which refers to an active attempt to change attitudes. Persuasion is, of course, the central goal of many marketing communications.

Decisions, Decisions: Tactical Communications Options

Suppose a car company wants to create an advertising campaign for a new ragtop targeted to young drivers. As it plans this campaign, it must develop a message that will create desire for the car by potential customers. To craft persuasive messages that might persuade someone to buy this car instead of the many others available, we must answer several questions:

- Who will be shown driving the car in an ad? A NASCAR driver? A career woman? A rock star? The source of a message helps to determine consumers' acceptance of it as well as their desire to try the product.
- How should the message be constructed? Should it emphasize the negative consequences of being left out when others are driving cool cars and you're still tooling around in your old clunker? Should it directly compare the car with others already on the market, or maybe present a fantasy in which a tough-minded female executive meets a dashing stranger while cruising down the highway with the top down?
- What media should be used to transmit the message? Should it be depicted in a print ad? On television? Sold door to door? On a Web site? If a print ad is produced, should it be run in the pages of *Jane? Good Housekeeping? Car and Driver?* Sometimes where something is said can be as important as what is said. Ideally, the attributes of the product should be matched to those of the medium. For example, magazines with high prestige are more effective at communicating messages about overall product image and quality, whereas specialized, expert magazines do a better job at conveying factual information.[1]
- What characteristics of the target market might influence the ad's acceptance? If targeted users are frustrated in their daily lives, they might be more receptive to a fantasy appeal. If they're status-oriented, maybe a commercial should show bystanders swooning with admiration as the car tools by.

The Elements of Communication

Marketers and advertisers have traditionally tried to understand how marketing messages can change consumers' attitudes by thinking in terms of the **communications model,** which specifies that a number of elements are necessary for communication to be achieved. One of these is a source; where the communication originates. Another is the message itself. There are many ways to say something, and the structure of the message has a big effect on how it is perceived. The message must be transmitted via a *medium*, which could be television, radio, magazines, billboards, personal contact, or even a matchbook cover. Toyota placed its message about the Spider in a sophisticated CD/ROM format that it knew would be accessed by young, cutting-edge consumers—just the ones it was trying to reach. The message is then decoded by one or more *receivers* (like Carrie), who interpret it in light of their own experiences. Finally, *feedback* must be received by the source, who uses the reactions of receivers to modify aspects of the message. *Launch* uses the Web to collect such information from its subscribers. The traditional communications process is depicted in Figure 8.1.

An Updated View: Interactive Communications

Although Carrie managed to ignore most of the "junk mail" that arrived at her door, she didn't avoid marketing messages—instead she chose which ones she wanted to see. Although the traditional communications model is not entirely wrong, it also doesn't tell the whole story—especially in today's dynamic world of interactivity, in which consumers have many more choices available to them and greater control over which messages they will choose to process.[2] The traditional model was developed to understand mass communications, in which information

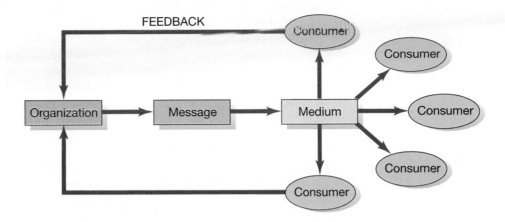

Figure 8.1
The Traditional Communications Model

is transferred from a producer (source) to many consumers (receivers) at one time—typically via print, television, or radio. This perspective essentially views advertising as the process of transferring information to the buyer before a sale. A message is seen as perishable—it is repeated (perhaps frequently) for a fairly short period of time and then it "vanishes" as a new campaign eventually takes its place.

This model was strongly influenced by a group of theorists known as the *Frankfurt School*, which dominated mass communications research for most of this century. In this view, the media exert direct and powerful effects on individuals, and often are used by those in power to brainwash and exploit the population. The receiver is basically a passive being—a "couch potato" who simply is the receptacle for many messages—and who is often duped or persuaded to act based on the information he or she is "fed" by the media.

Uses and Gratifications

Is this an accurate picture of the way we relate to marketing communications? Proponents of **uses and gratifications theory** argue instead that consumers constitute an active, goal-directed audience that draws on mass media as a resource to satisfy needs. Instead of asking what media do *for* or *to* people, they ask what people do *with* the media.[3]

The uses and gratifications approach emphasizes that media compete with other sources to satisfy needs, and that these needs include diversion and entertainment as well as information. This also means that the line between marketing information and entertainment is continuing to blur—especially as companies are being forced to design more attractive retail outlets, catalogs, and Web sites in order to attract consumers. *Launch* accomplishes this by ensuring that the commercial messages it burns into its discs are sufficiently entertaining that its subscribers will *want* to watch them.

This infusion of marketing images into daily life is illustrated by the popularity of the Hello Kitty characters that have popped up on everything from tofu dishes to telephones. This craze originated in Japan and then spread across and into the United States; the Sanrio company earns more than a billion dollars from Hello Kitty products annually. When a Taiwanese bank put Hello Kitty on its checkbooks and credit cards, the lines to get these items were so long many people thought there was a banking crisis.[4] Clearly marketing ideas and products serve as sources of gratification for many—even when others scratch their heads and try to figure out why!

Research with young people in Great Britain finds that they rely on advertising for many gratifications including entertainment (some report that the "adverts" are better than the programs), escapism, play (some report singing along with jingles, others make posters out of magazine ads), and self-affirmation (ads can reinforce their own values or provide role models). It's important to note that this perspective is not arguing that media play a uniformly positive role in our lives, only that recipients are making use of the information in a number of ways. For example, marketing messages have the potential to undermine self-esteem as consumers use the media to establish unrealistic standards for behavior, attitudes, or even their own appearance. A comment by one study participant illustrates this negative impact. She observes that when she's watching TV with her boyfriend, "really, it makes you think 'oh no, what must I be like?' I mean you're sitting with your boyfriend and he's saying 'oh, look at her. What a body!'"[5]

Who's in Charge of the Remote?

Whether for good or bad, though, exciting technological and social developments certainly are forcing us to rethink the picture of the passive consumer, as people increasingly are playing a proactive role in communications. In other words, they are to a greater extent becoming partners—rather than potatoes—in the communications process. Their input is helping to shape the messages they and others like them receive, and furthermore they may seek out these messages rather than sit home and wait to see them on TV or in the paper. This updated approach to interactive communications is illustrated in Figure 8.2.

One of the early signs of this communications revolution was the humble hand-held remote control device. As VCRs began to be commonplace in homes, suddenly consumers had more input into what they wanted to watch—and when. No longer were they at the mercy of the TV networks to decide when to see their favorite shows, and neither did they necessarily have to forsake a show because it conflicted with another's time slot.

Since that time, of course, our ability to control our media environment has mushroomed. Many people have access to video-on-demand or pay-per-view TV. Home-shopping networks encourage us to call in and discuss our passion for cubic zirconium jewelry live on the air. Caller ID devices and answering machines allow us to decide if we will accept a phone call during dinner, and to know the source of the message before picking up the phone. A bit of Web surfing allows us to identify kindred spirits around the globe, to request information about products, and even to provide suggestions to product designers and market researchers.

Figure 8.2
Interactive Communications
Model

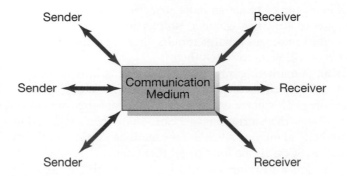

Levels of Interactive Response

A key to understanding the dynamics of interactive marketing communications is to consider exactly what is meant by a response.[6] The early perspective on communications primarily regarded feedback in terms of behavior—did the recipient run out and buy the laundry detergent after being exposed to an ad for it?

However, a variety of other responses are possible as well, including building awareness of the brand, informing us about product features, reminding us to buy a new package when we've run out, and—perhaps most importantly—building a long-term relationship. Therefore a transaction is one type of response, but forward-thinking marketers realize that customers can interact with them in other valuable ways as well. For this reason it is helpful to distinguish between two basic types of feedback.

- *First-order response:* Direct marketing vehicles such as catalogs and television infomercials are interactive—if successful, they result in an order, which is most definitely a response! So, let's think of a product offer that directly yields a transaction as a first-order response. In addition to providing revenue, sales data are a valuable source of feedback that allow marketers to gauge the effectiveness of their communications efforts.
- *Second-order response:* However, a marketing communication does not have to immediately result in a purchase to be an important component of interactive marketing. Messages can prompt useful responses from customers, even though these recipients do not necessarily place an order immediately after being exposed to the communication. Carrie may get around to buying that Spider eventually as a result of being exposed to persuasive messages about it. Customer feedback in response to a marketing message that is not in the form of a transaction is a second-order response.

THE SOURCE

Regardless of whether a message is received by "snail mail" (Net heads' slang for the postal service) or e-mail, common sense tells us that the same words uttered or written by different people can have very different effects. Research on *source effects* has been carried out for more than 40 years. By attributing the same message to different sources and measuring the degree of attitude change that occurs after listeners hear it, it is possible to determine which aspects of a communicator will induce attitude change.[7]

Under most conditions, the source of a message can have a big impact on the likelihood the message will be accepted. The choice of a source to maximize attitude change can tap into several dimensions. The source can be chosen because he or she is an expert, attractive, famous, or even a "typical" consumer who is both likable and trustworthy. Two particularly important source characteristics are *credibility and attractiveness*.[8]

Source Credibility

Source credibility refers to a source's perceived expertise, objectivity, or trustworthiness. This dimension relates to consumers' beliefs that a communicator is competent, and he or she is willing to provide the necessary information to adequately evaluate competing products. A credible source can be particularly persuasive when the consumer has not yet learned much about a product or formed an opinion of it.[9] The decision to pay an expert or a celebrity to tout a product can be a very costly one, but researchers have concluded that on average the investment is worth it simply because the announcement of an endorsement contract is often used by market analysts to evaluate a firm's potential profitability, thereby affecting its expected return. On average, then, the impact of endorsements on stock returns appears to be so positive that it offsets the cost of hiring the spokesperson.[10]

Building Credibility

Credibility can be enhanced if the source's qualifications are perceived as somehow relevant to the product being endorsed. This linkage can overcome other objections people may have to the endorser or the product. Ronald Biggs, whose claim to fame was his 1963 role in "The Great Train Robbery" in the United Kingdom, successfully served as a spokesman in Brazil for a company that makes door locks—a topic about which he is presumably knowledgeable![11] It's important to note that what is credible to one consumer segment may be a turn-off to another. Indeed, rebellious or even deviant celebrities may be attractive to some for just that reason. Basketball player Dennis Rodman, whose outrageous tattoos, fluorescent hair, and tendency to turn up in women's clothing hardly make him a clean-cut sports hero, is swamped with endorsement offers from traditional companies like McDonald's and Comfort Inn. Tommy Hilfiger cultivated a rebellious, street-smart image by using rapper Snoop Doggy Dogg (who was acquitted of murder charges) to help launch his line and Coolio, a former crack addict and thief, as a runway model.[12] Parents may not be thrilled by these message sources—but isn't that the point?

Source Biases

A consumer's beliefs about a product's attributes can be weakened if the source is perceived to be the victim of bias in presenting information.[13] *Knowledge bias* implies that a source's knowledge about a topic is not accurate. *Reporting bias* occurs when a source has the required knowledge, but his or her willingness to convey it accurately is compromised, as when a star tennis player is paid by a racket manufacturer to use its products exclusively. The source's credentials might be appropriate, but the fact that the expert is perceived as a "hired gun" compromises believability. Of course, it's not always clear that a person has been paid to say he loves a product. That's why the Food and Drug Administration blocked Ciba-Geigy Corp. from using Mickey Mantle for an arthritis drug, saying it wasn't clear to consumers he was a paid endorser.[14] And, endorsements can be done subtly—Microsoft was criticized when the software company offered to pay "travel costs" for professors if they present papers at conferences and mention how Microsoft programs helped them in their work.[15]

Source Attractiveness

Source attractiveness refers to the source's perceived social value. This quality can emanate from the person's physical appearance, personality, social status, or his or her similarity to the receiver (we like to listen to people who are like us). A compelling source has great value and endorsement deals are constantly in the works. Even dead sources can be attractive: The great-grandson of the artist Renoir is putting his famous ancestor's name on bottled water, and the Picasso family licensed their name to the French auto maker Citroen.[16] Former boxer George Foreman recently made endorsement history by becoming the first celebrity to sell his name in perpetuity to the company that has sold more than 10 million George Foreman's Lean Mean Fat Reducing Grilling Machines. In exchange for $137.5 million, Foreman agreed never to endorse rival cookware, though he is still free to pitch other products.[17] That's a lot of low-fat hot dogs.

Star Power: Celebrities As Communications Sources

The use of celebrity endorsers is an expensive but common strategy—as golfing sensation Tiger Woods discovered when Nike signed him as its premiere endorser. A celebrity endorsement strategy can pay off handsomely.[18] Indeed, one recent study found that famous faces capture attention and are processed more efficiently by the brain than are "ordinary" faces.[19] Celebrities increase awareness of a firm's advertising and enhance both company image and brand attitudes.[20] A celebrity endorsement strategy can be an effective way to differentiate among similar products; this is especially important when consumers do not perceive many actual differences among competitors, as often occurs when brands are in the mature stage of the product life cycle.

Star power works because celebrities embody *cultural meanings*—they symbolize important categories such as status and social class (a "working-class hero," such as Drew Carey), gender (a "ladies man," such as Leonardo diCaprio), age (the boyish Michael J. Fox), and even personality types (the eccentric Kramer on *Seinfeld*). Ideally, the advertiser decides what meanings the product should convey (that is, how it should be positioned in the marketplace), and then chooses a celebrity who has come to embody a similar meaning. The product's meaning thus moves from the manufacturer to the consumer, using the star as a vehicle.[21]

With all those famous people out there, how does a firm decide who should be the source of its marketing messages? For celebrity campaigns to be effective, the endorser must have a clear and popular image. In addition, the celebrity's image and that of the product he or she endorses should be similar—this is known as the **match-up hypothesis**.[22] Many promotional strategies employing stars fail because the endorser has not been selected very carefully—some marketers just assume that because a person is "famous" he or she will serve as a successful spokesperson. The images of celebrities can be pretested to increase the probability of consumer acceptance. One widely used technique is the so-called *Q rating* (Q stands for quality) developed by a market research company. This rating considers two factors in surveys: consumers' level of familiarity with a name, and the number of respondents who indicate that a person, program, or character is a favorite. Although it yields a rather rough measure, the Q rating acknowledges that mere familiarity with a celebrity's name is not sufficient to gauge popularity, because some widely known people also are widely disliked. The Jenny Craig line of diet foods found this out the hard way when the company had to put the brakes on its controversial ad campaign featuring former Presidential "friend" Monica Lewinsky.

"What Is Beautiful Is Good"

Almost everywhere we turn, beautiful people are trying to persuade us to buy or do something. Our society places a very high premium on physical attractiveness, and we tend to assume that people who are good-looking are smarter, cooler, and happier. Such an assumption is called a *halo effect*, which occurs when persons who rank high on one dimension are assumed to excel on others as well. The

MARKETING PITFALLS

WHAT DOES A COMPANY do when its expensive celebrity endorser "misbehaves?" Pepsi had to abandon its sponsorship of Michael Jackson after the singer was accused of child molestation, and the company had to drop boxer Mike Tyson following allegations of domestic violence. Madonna met a similar fate following the release of her controversial *Like a Prayer* music video. Then, of course, there's O. J. Simpson.

To avoid some of these problems, most endorsement contracts now contain a morality clause that allows the company to release the celebrity if so warranted.[23] Still, some advertisers are looking a lot more favorably at animated spokescharacters such as Bugs Bunny, who tend to stay out of trouble! Even when a firm uses a made-up character to stand for its products, however, the proper image needs to be carefully maintained. The behavior of Quik Bunny Nestle Quik's mascot for more than 50 years is strictly regulated. The actor playing the part is not allowed to talk, and a "Bunny Guidelines Book" lists rules for public appearances including no rolling on the ground that would dirty the costume and no autographs applied to skin or clothing.[24]

REALITY CHECK

MANY, MANY COMPANIES RELY ON CELEBRITY endorsers as communications sources to persuade. Especially when targeting younger people, these spokespeople often are "cool" musicians, athletes, or movie stars. In your opinion, who would be the most effective celebrity endorser today, and why? Who would be the least effective? Why?

Athletes such as Michael Jordan have made a tremendous affect on the lives of young males. Michael Jordan has been married to the same woman for a number of years now and has children by his wife. Michael Jordan's traditional lifestyle promotes stability and respect. Athletes such as Dennis Rodman do not promote good character or a respectable image for young males. Dennis Rodman lacks respect for woman and sex. He presents himself in a manner that fosters womanizing and drug and alcohol use as a cool thing to do.

Jill Wittekind
University of Nevada, Las Vegas

The most recent wave of mobile phone advertising features Zoë Ball as the endorser for the 'One-2-One' telephone network. She is young, good-looking, energetic, down to earth and most importantly radiates a 'happy-go-lucky' attitude. The success of such a marketing campaign lies in her portrayal and in the target market's (in this case young adults) ability to relate to that character or situation. . . . The least effective celebrity endorsers that automatically spring to mind are the Spice Girls (a truly British phenomenon) and whilst they have been pasted on articles from pencil cases to cakes I remain a true

skeptic of their effectiveness . . . if any. . . . To be an effective celebrity endorser one must at least inspire through some unmatched talent, charisma, or admirable quality of which the Spice Girls have none.

Nicole Schragger
Edinburgh University, United Kingdom

The most effective celebrity endorser today is Michael Jordan. This man is amazing not only because of his accomplishments in basketball, but for who he is as a person. He is in the eye of the public all of the time. I can't ever remember a time where he said or did something to offend anybody. He is a well-spoken educated man who has worked extremely hard to achieve his goals. . . . Dennis Rodman is the least effective for many reasons. Rules and regulations are of no concern for Dennis Rodman. He ventures around with the "I don't what I want" attitude. He doesn't symbolize the type of role model that a young person needs to help them through life. Although he is very rich and famous, he has hurt and disappointed many people in doing so. He is not a family man and has been involved with many different women while he tries to raise his daughter.

John Dollman IV
West Virginia University

I would say that Michael Jordan would still be the most effective celebrity to use. . . . I believe that it is very effective to use celebrities that are considered to be aspired to. Michael Jordan definitely falls into this category. I think that the least aspired to celebrity would be someone like Mike Tyson. He is not a good role model, and I don't think companies would want to have him as their spokesman.

Fant Walker
University of Mississippi

Wayne Gretsky, a famous Canadian hockey player, recently retired. He has been perceived as a wholesome hero who made the best of the talents he was born with. However, since his retirement, the products he has endorsed have been vast and quite varied. He has signed endorsement deals with companies such as Goodyear, CIBC, McDonald's, Post, and recently with Anheuser-Busch to promote Budweiser. It seems that every second brand with a spokesperson uses Wayne Gretsky's name or face. In my opinion, he is the least effective spokesperson due to overexposure. Gretzky, it seems, is now just another person paid to promote a product, and therefore I am critical of any opinions he states as an endorser.

Liv Amber Judd
University of Saskatchewan, Canada

What's your opinion? Check out the on-line polls at www.prenhall.com/myphlip. Just follow the little person in the lab coat.

effect can be explained in terms of the consistency principle discussed in Chapter 7, which states that people are more comfortable when all of their judgments about a person go together. This notion has been termed the "what is beautiful is good" stereotype.[25] A physically attractive source tends to facilitate attitude change. His or her degree of attractiveness exerts at least modest effects on consumers' purchase intentions or product evaluation.[26] How does this happen?

One explanation is that physical attractiveness functions as a cue that facilitates or modifies information processing by directing consumers' attention to relevant marketing stimuli. Some evidence indicates that consumers pay more attention to ads that contain attractive models, though not necessarily to the ad copy.[27] In other words, an ad with a beautiful person may stand a better chance of getting noticed but not necessarily read. We may enjoy looking at a beautiful or

To stimulate demand for milk, an industry trade group tapped a huge range of celebrities to show off their milk mustaches.

handsome person, but these positive feelings do not necessarily affect product attitudes or purchase intentions.[28]

Beauty can also function as a source of information. The effectiveness of highly attractive spokespeople in ads appears to be largely limited to those situations in which the advertised product is overtly related to attractiveness or sexuality.[29] The *social adaptation perspective* assumes that information seen to be instrumental in forming an attitude will be more heavily weighted by the perceiver. We filter out irrelevant information to minimize cognitive effort.

Under the right circumstances, an endorser's level of attractiveness constitutes a source of information instrumental to the attitude change process and thus functions as a central, task-relevant cue.[30] An attractive spokesperson, for this reason, is more likely to be an effective source when the product is relevant to attractiveness. For example, attractiveness affects attitudes toward ads about perfume or cologne (where attractiveness is relevant) but not toward coffee ads, where attractiveness is not.

Credibility Versus Attractiveness

How do marketing specialists decide whether to stress credibility or attractiveness when choosing a message source? There should be a match between the needs of the recipient and the potential rewards offered by the source. When this match occurs, the recipient is more motivated to process the message. People who tend to be sensitive about social acceptance and the opinions of others, for example, are more persuaded by an attractive source, whereas those who are more internally oriented are swayed by a credible, expert source.[31]

The choice may also depend on the type of product. A positive source can help to reduce risk and increase message acceptance overall, but particular types of sources are more effective at reducing different kinds of risk. Experts are effective at changing attitudes toward utilitarian products that have high performance risk, such as vacuums (i.e., they may be complex and not work as expected). Celebrities are more effective when they focus on products such as jewelry and furniture that have high *social risk*; the user of such products is aware of their effect on the impression others have of him or her. Finally, "typical" consumers, who are appealing sources because of their similarity to the recipient, tend to be most effective when providing real-life endorsements for everyday products that are low risk, such as cookies.[32]

The Sleeper Effect

Although in general more positive sources tend to increase attitude change, exceptions can occur. Sometimes a source can be obnoxious or disliked and still manage to be effective at getting the product's message across. A case in point is Mr. Whipple, the irritating but well-known television character who scolds toilet paper shoppers, "Please don't squeeze the Charmin!"

In some instances the differences in attitude change between positive sources and less positive sources seem to get erased over time. After a while people appear to "forget" about the negative source and wind up changing their attitudes anyway. This process is known as the **sleeper effect**.[33]

The explanation for the sleeper effect is a subject of debate, as is the more basic question regarding whether and when it really exists. Initially, the dissociative cue hypothesis proposed that over time the message and the source become disassociated in the consumer's mind. The message remains on its own in memory, causing the delayed attitude change.[34]

Another explanation is the *availability-valence hypothesis*, which emphasizes the selectivity of memory owing to limited capacity.[35] If the associations linked to the negative source are less available than those linked to the message information, the residual impact of the message enhances persuasion. Consistent with this view, the sleeper effect has been obtained only when the message was encoded deeply; it had stronger associations in memory than did the source.[36]

THE MESSAGE

A major study of more than 1,000 commercials identified factors that appear to determine whether or not a commercial message will be persuasive. The single most important feature was whether the communications contained a brand-differentiating message. In other words, did the communication stress a unique attribute or benefit of the product? Other good and bad elements are depicted in Table 8.1.[37]

Characteristics of the message itself help to determine its impact on attitudes. These variables include *how* the message is said as well as *what* is said. Some of the issues facing marketers include the following:

- Should the message be conveyed in words or pictures?
- How often should the message be repeated?

TABLE 8.1 Positive and Negative Effects of Elements in Television Commercials	
Positive Effects	**Negative Effects**
Showing convenience of use	Extensive information on components, ingredients, or nutrition
Showing new product or improved features	
Casting background (i.e., people are incidental to message)	Outdoor setting (message gets lost)
	Large number of on-screen characters
Indirect comparison to other products	Graphic displays
Demonstration of the product in use	
Demonstration of tangible results (e.g., bouncy hair)	
An actor playing the role of an ordinary person	
No principal character (i.e., more time is devoted to the product)	

SOURCE: Adapted from David W. Stewart and David H. Furse, "The Effects of Television Advertising Execution on Recall, Comprehension, and Persuasion," *Psychology & Marketing* 2 (Fall 1985): 135–60. Copyright © 1985 by John Wiley & Sons, Inc. Reprinted by permission.

- Should a conclusion be drawn, or should this be left up to the listener?
- Should both sides of an argument be presented?
- Is it effective to explicitly compare one's product to competitors?
- Should a blatant sexual appeal be used?
- Should negative emotions, such as fear, ever be aroused?
- How concrete or vivid should the arguments and imagery be?
- Should the ad be funny?

Sending the Message

The saying "one picture is worth more than ten thousand words" captures the idea that visual stimuli can economically deliver big impact, especially when the communicator wants to influence receivers' emotional responses. For this reason, advertisers often place great emphasis on vivid and creative illustrations or photography.[38]

On the other hand, a picture is not always as effective at communicating factual information. Ads that contain the same information, presented in either visual or verbal form, have been found to elicit different reactions. The verbal version affects ratings on the utilitarian aspects of a product, whereas the visual version affects aesthetic evaluations. Verbal elements are more effective when reinforced by an accompanying picture, especially if the illustration is *framed* (the message in the picture is strongly related to the copy).[39]

Because it requires more effort to process, a verbal message is most appropriate for high-involvement situations, such as in print contexts in which the reader is motivated to really pay attention to the advertising. Because verbal material decays more rapidly in memory, more frequent exposures are needed to obtain the desired effect. Visual images, in contrast, allow the receiver to *chunk* information at the time of encoding (see Chapter 3). Chunking results in a stronger memory trace that aids retrieval over time.[40]

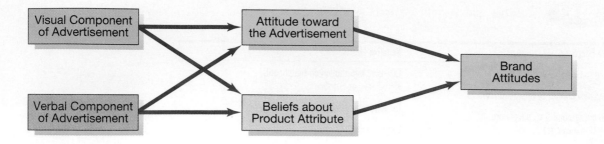

Figure 8.3
Effects of Visual and Verbal
Components of Advertisements
on Brand Attitudes

Visual elements may affect brand attitudes in one of two ways. First, the consumer may form inferences about the brand and change his or her beliefs because of an illustration's imagery. For example, people in a study who saw an ad for a facial tissue accompanied by a photo of a sunset were more likely to believe that the brand came in attractive colors. Second, brand attitudes may be affected more directly; for example, a strong positive or negative reaction elicited by the visual elements will influence the consumer's attitude toward the ad (A_{ad}), which will then affect brand attitudes (A_b). This dual component model of brand attitudes is illustrated in Figure 8.3.[41]

Vividness

Both pictures and words can differ in *vividness*. Powerful descriptions or graphics command attention and are more strongly embedded in memory. The reason may be because they tend to activate mental imagery, whereas abstract stimuli inhibit this process.[42] Of course, this effect can cut both ways: Negative information presented in a vivid manner may result in more negative evaluations at a later time.[43]

The concrete discussion of a product attribute in ad copy also influences the importance of that attribute, because more attention is drawn to it. For example, the copy for a watch that read "According to industry sources, three out of every four watch breakdowns are due to water getting into the case" was more effective than this version: "According to industry sources, many watch breakdowns are due to water getting into the case."[44]

Repetition

Repetition can be a two-edged sword for marketers. As noted in Chapter 3, multiple exposures to a stimulus are usually required for learning (especially conditioning) to occur. Contrary to the saying "familiarity breeds contempt," people tend to like things that are more familiar to them, even if they were not that keen on them initially.[45] This is known as the *mere exposure* phenomenon. Positive effects for advertising repetition are found even in mature product categories—repeating product information has been shown to boost consumers' awareness of the brand, even though nothing new has been said.[46] On the other hand, as we saw in Chapter 2, too much repetition creates *habituation*, whereby the consumer no longer pays attention to the stimulus because of fatigue or boredom. Excessive exposure can cause *advertising wear-out*, which can result in negative reactions to an ad after seeing it too much.[47]

The fine line between familiarity and boredom has been explained by the **two-factor theory,** which proposes that two separate psychological processes are operating when a person is repeatedly exposed to an ad. The positive side of repetition is that it increases familiarity and thus reduces uncertainty about the

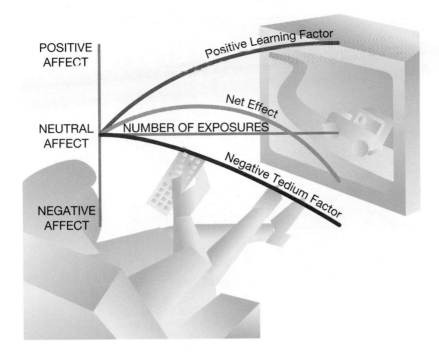

Figure 8.4
Two-Factor Theory and
Advertising Wear-out

product. The negative side is that over time boredom increases with each exposure. At some point the amount of boredom incurred begins to exceed the amount of uncertainty reduced, resulting in wear-out. This pattern is depicted in Figure 8.4. Its effect is especially pronounced when each exposure is of a fairly long duration (such as a 60-second commercial).[48]

The theory implies that advertisers can overcome this problem by limiting the amount of exposure per repetition (such as using 15-second spots). They can also maintain familiarity but alleviate boredom by slightly varying the content of ads over time through campaigns that revolve around a common theme, although each spot may be different. Recipients who are exposed to varied ads about the product absorb more information about product attributes and experience more positive thoughts about the brand than do those exposed to the same information repeatedly. This additional information allows the person to resist attempts to change his or her attitude in the face of a counterattack by a competing brand.[49]

Constructing the Argument

Many marketing messages are similar to debates or trials, in which someone presents arguments and tries to convince the receiver to shift his or her opinion accordingly. The way the argument is presented may be as important as what is said.

One- Versus Two-Sided Arguments

Most messages merely present one or more positive attributes about the product or reasons to buy it. These are known as *supportive arguments*. An alternative is to use a *two-sided message*, in which both positive and negative information is presented. Research has indicated that two-sided ads can be quite effective, yet they are not widely used.[50]

Why would a marketer want to devote advertising space to publicizing a product's negative attributes? Under the right circumstances, the use of *refutational arguments*, in which a negative issue is raised and then dismissed, can be

As this Dutch ad illustrates, the way something is said can be as significant as what is said.

quite effective. This approach can increase source credibility by reducing reporting bias. Also, people who are skeptical about the product may be more receptive to a balanced argument instead of a "whitewash."[51]

This is not to say that the marketer should go overboard in presenting major problems with the product. In the typical refutational strategy, relatively minor attributes are discussed that may present a problem or fall short when compared with competitors. These drawbacks are then refuted by emphasizing positive, important attributes. For example, Avis got a lot of mileage out of claiming to be only the "No. 2" car rental company, whereas an ad for Volkswagen woefully described one of its cars as a "lemon" because there was a scratch on the glove compartment chrome strip.[52] A two-sided strategy appears to be the most effective when the audience is well-educated (and presumably more impressed by a balanced argument).[53] It is also best to use when receivers are not already loyal to the product; "preaching to the choir" about possible drawbacks may raise doubts unnecessarily.

Drawing Conclusions

Should the argument draw conclusions, or should the points merely be presented, permitting the consumer to arrive at his or her own decision? On the one hand, consumers who make their own inferences instead of having them spoon-fed to them will form stronger, more accessible attitudes. On the other, leaving the conclusion ambiguous increases the chance that the desired attitude will not be formed.

The response to this issue depends on the consumers' motivation to process the ad and the complexity of the arguments. If the message is personally relevant, people will pay attention to it and spontaneously form inferences. However, if the arguments are hard to follow or consumers' motivation to follow them is lacking, it is safer for the ad to draw conclusions.[54]

Comparative Advertising

In 1971, the FTC issued guidelines that encouraged advertisers to name competing brands in their ads. This action was taken to improve the information available to consumers in ads, and indeed recent evidence indicates that at least under some conditions this type of presentation does result in more informed decision making.[55] **Comparative advertising** refers to a strategy in which a message compares two or more specifically named or recognizably presented brands and makes a comparison of them in terms of one or more specific attributes.[56] For example, Schering-Plough claimed that "New OcuClear relieves three times longer than Visine," and Bristol-Myers stated that "New Liquid Vanish really does clean tough rust stains below the water line better than Lysol." This strategy can cut both ways, especially if the sponsor depicts the competition in a nasty or negative way. Although some comparative ads result in desired attitude change or positive A_{ad}, they have also been found to be lower in believability and may result in more source derogation (i.e., the consumer may doubt the credibility of a biased presentation).[57] Indeed, in some cultures (such as Asia) comparative advertising is rare because people find such a confrontational approach offensive.

Comparative ads do appear to be effective for new products that are trying to build a clear image by positioning themselves vis a vis dominant brands in the market. They work well at generating attention, awareness, favorable attitudes, and purchase intentions—but ironically consumers may not like the ad itself because of its aggressiveness.[58] But, if the aim is to compare the new brand with the market leader in terms of specific product attributes, merely saying it is as good or better than the leader is not sufficient. For example, the use of the claim "Spring has the same fluoride as Crest" in a study resulted in attitude change for the fictitious product, but the more global statement "Preferred by Europeans in comparison with Crest" did not.[59] And, comparative ads are only credible if they don't reach too far by comparing a brand to a competitor that is obviously superior. Not too surprisingly, for example, a survey of new car buyers found that TV commercials comparing a Nissan Altima to a Mercedes were not effective.[60]

Types of Message Appeals

The *way* something is said can be as significant as *what* is said. A persuasive message can tug at the heartstrings or scare you, make you laugh, make you cry or leave you yearning to learn more. In this section, we'll review the major alternatives available to communicators who wish to *appeal* to a message recipient.

Emotional Versus Rational Appeals

So, which is better: To appeal to the head or to the heart? The answer often depends upon the nature of the product and the type of relationship consumers have with it. This issue was at the core of a fierce debate at Polaroid, a company known for technological innovation rather than "warm and fuzzy" products. Marketers at the photographic products firm argued strenuously that the company

MARKETING PITFALLS

MANY CONSUMERS ARE skeptical about claims made or implied in advertising, and some ads are challenged after being aired, either by the government, by concerned citizens, or by a competitor. About half of those challenged are either modified or taken off the air completely. In some cases, the company makes an attempt to correct the misinformation. One prominent example was a famous Volvo ad that was challenged by the Texas Attorney General's office. In an ad showing a row of cars being crushed by a pickup truck, only the Volvo was unharmed. An investigation revealed that the Volvo used in the ad had been specially reinforced for the shoot. The company later ran ads acknowledging that the dramatization had been faked.

When a marketer makes a specific comparative claim relative to a competing product, he or she must be prepared for the possibility that the rival company will respond with a lawsuit. Many companies have gotten involved in complex lawsuits after using the comparative approach, and the costs of such litigation are high for both parties. As one judge who was involved in a 10-year court battle being fought between two makers of rival analgesics noted, "Small nations have fought for their very survival with less resources." As a result of these and other incidents, marketers are learning to exercise extra care when making product claims, and some are beginning to supply disclaimers to protect themselves against lawsuits.[62]

needed to develop new, "fun" products to recapture younger consumers. Engineers were antagonistic about this idea; they felt a "toy" camera would cheapen Polaroid's reputation. In this case, the marketers prevailed and convinced the engineers to create a small instant camera with a cheap lens to produce fuzzy thumbnail size photos. The I-Zone Instant Pocket camera was born. In a radical move for the company the ad campaign is based on the theme "being a little bit bad is good." One execution features a young man who sticks instant pictures on his nipples and then wiggles his chest. Half of the I-Zone's buyers are 13- to 17-year-old girls, and Polaroid reaped revenues of $270 million for the product in one year. It's now being introduced in new colors like Radical Red, and Polaroid signed teen singer Britney Spears as endorser—as part of the deal during each performance she will use the camera to snap a photo of an adoring fan.[61]

Many companies turned to an emotional strategy after realizing that consumers do not find many differences among brands, especially those in well-established, mature categories. Ads for products ranging from cars (Lincoln Mercury) to cards (Hallmark) focus instead on emotional aspects. Mercury's capitalization on emotional attachments to old rock songs succeeded in lowering the median age of its consumers for some models by 10 years.[63]

The precise effects of rational versus emotional appeals are hard to gauge. Although recall of ad contents tends to be better for "thinking" ads than for "feeling" ads, conventional measures of advertising effectiveness (e.g., day-after recall) may not be adequate to assess cumulative effects of emotional ads. These open-ended measures are oriented toward cognitive responses, and feeling ads may be penalized because the reactions are not as easy to articulate.[64]

Sex Appeals

Echoing the widely-held belief that "sex sells," many marketing communications for everything from perfumes to autos feature heavy doses of erotic suggestions that range from subtle hints to blatant displays of skin. Of course, the prevalence

These ads demonstrate rational versus emotional message appeals. At the time of the initial ad campaign for the new Infiniti automobiles, the ads for rival Lexus (top) emphasized design and engineering, while the ads for Infiniti (bottom) did not even show the car.

of sex appeals varies from country to country (see Chapter 17). Bare flesh is so much a part of French advertising that a minor backlash is brewing as some critics complain the advertising industry is making sex boring![65] Perhaps not surprisingly, female nudity in print ads generates negative feelings and tension among female consumers, whereas men's reactions are more positive.[66] In a case of turnabout being fair play, another study found that males dislike nude males in ads, whereas females responded well to undressed males—but not totally nude ones.[67]

Does sex work? Although the use of sex does appear to draw attention to an ad, its use may actually be counterproductive to the marketer. Ironically, a provocative picture can be too effective; it attracts so much attention that it hinders processing and recall of the ad's contents. Sexual appeals appear to be ineffective when used merely as a "trick" to grab attention. They do, however, appear to work when the product is *itself* related to sex. Overall, though, use of a strong sexual appeal is not very well received.[68]

Humorous Appeals

The use of humor can be tricky, particularly because what is funny to one person may be offensive or incomprehensible to another. Specific cultures may have different senses of humor and use funny material in diverse ways. For example, commercials in the United Kingdom are more likely to use puns and satire than they are in the United States.[70]

Does humor work? Overall, humorous advertisements do get attention. One study found that recognition scores for humorous liquor ads were better than average. However, the verdict is mixed as to whether humor affects recall or product attitudes in a significant way.[71] One function it may play is to provide a source of *distraction*. A funny ad inhibits the consumer from counterarguing (thinking of reasons why he doesn't agree with the message), thereby increasing the likelihood of message acceptance.[72]

Humor is more likely to be effective when the brand is clearly identified and the funny material does not "swamp" the message. This danger is similar to that of beautiful models diverting attention from copy points. Subtle humor is usually better, as is humor that does not make fun of the potential consumer. Finally, humor should be appropriate to the product's image. An undertaker or a bank might want to avoid humor, but other products adapt to it quite well. Sales of Sunsweet pitted prunes improved dramatically based on the claim, "Today the pits, tomorrow the wrinkles."[73]

Fear Appeals

Fear appeals emphasize the negative consequences that can occur unless the consumer changes a behavior or an attitude. Schering-Plough placed ads that read, "A government panel has determined some laxatives may cause cancer." The ads implicated Ex-Lax, a rival brand, even though the Food and Drug Administration hadn't yet made a final determination regarding this issue (Ex-Lax eventually did withdraw the product to reformulate it after the FDA decided to ban its active ingredient).[74] A fear appeal strategy is widely used in marketing communications, though more commonly in social marketing contexts in which organizations are encouraging people to convert to a healthier lifestyle by quitting smoking, using contraception, relying on a designated driver, and so on.

Does fear work? Most research on this topic indicates that these negative appeals are usually most effective when only a moderate threat is used, and when a solution to the problem is presented. Otherwise, consumers will tune out the ad

MULTICULTURAL DIMENSIONS

NIKE IS THE MASTER CRAFTS-
MAN of "in your face" emotional messages about sports that barely acknowledge the shoes they are trying to sell. These appeals have played very well in the United States, but now the company has hit some bumps in the road as it tries to export this attitude overseas. As the company searches for new markets, it is trying to conquer soccer the way it did basketball. An ad in *Soccer America* magazine announced the impending invasion: "Europe, Asia, and Latin America: Barricade your stadiums. Hide your trophies. Invest in some deodorant." This message was not very well received in some soccer quarters, and similarly a successful American TV commercial featuring Satan and his demons playing soccer against Nike endorsers was banned by some European stations on the grounds that it was too scary for children to see and offensive to boot. A British TV ad featuring a French soccer player saying how his spitting at a fan and insulting his coach won him a Nike contract resulted in a scathing editorial against Nike in the sport's international federation newsletter. Nike has a tough task ahead of it: to win over European soccer fans where rival Adidas is king—in a game that traditionally doesn't have the glitz and packaging of basketball. Now a bit chastized, Nike is modifying its "question authority" approach as it tries to win over the sports organizations in countries that don't appreciate its violent messages and antiestablishment themes.[69]

because they can do nothing to solve the problem.[75] This approach also works better when source credibility is high.[76]

When a weak threat is ineffective, this may be because there is insufficient elaboration of the harmful consequences of engaging in the behavior. When a strong threat doesn't work, it may be because *too much* elaboration interferes with the processing of the recommended change in behavior—the receiver is too busy thinking of reasons why the message doesn't apply to him or her to pay attention to the offered solution.[77]

A study that manipulated subjects' degree of anxiety about AIDS, for example, found that condom ads were evaluated most positively when a moderate threat was used. In this context, copy that promoted the use of the condom because "Sex is a risky business" (moderate threat) resulted in more attitude change than either a weaker threat that instead emphasized the product's sensitivity or a strong threat that discussed the certainty of death from AIDS.[78] Similarly, scare tactics have not been as effective as hoped in getting teenagers to decrease their use of alcohol or drugs. Teens simply tune out the message or deny its relevance to them.[79] On the other hand, a study of adolescent responses to social versus physical threat appeals in drug prevention messages found that social threat is a more effective strategy.[80]

Some of the research on fear appeals may be confusing a threat (the literal content of a message, such as saying "engage in safe sex or die") with fear (an emotional response to the message). According to this argument, greater fear does result in greater persuasion—but not all threats are equally effective because different people will respond differently to the same threat. Therefore, the strongest threats are not always the most persuasive because they may not have the desired impact on the perceiver. For example, raising the specter of AIDS is about the strongest threat that can be delivered to sexually active kids—but this tactic is only effective if the kids believe they will get the disease. Because many young people (especially those who live in fairly affluent suburban or rural areas) don't believe that "people like them" will be exposed to the AIDS virus, this strong threat may not actually result in a high level of fear.[81] The bottom line is that more precise measures of actual fear responses are needed before definitive conclusions can be drawn about the impact of fear appeals on consumption decisions.

Humorous ads grab our attention. This one from Budapest says "Very clever. But find another solution. Always lead your dog to a tree. Thank you."

The Message as Art Form: Metaphors Be with You

Marketers may be thought of as storytellers who supply visions of reality similar to those provided by authors, poets, and artists. These communications take the form of stories because the product benefits they describe are intangible and must be given tangible meaning by expressing them in a form that is concrete and visible. Advertising creatives rely (consciously or not) on various literary devices to communicate these meanings. For example, a product or service might be personified by a character such as Mr. Goodwrench, the Jolly Green Giant, or the California Raisins. Many ads take the form of an *allegory*, a story told about an abstract trait or concept that has been personified as a person, animal, or vegetable.

A **metaphor** involves placing two dissimilar objects into a close relationship such that "A is B" whereas a simile compares two objects, "A is like B." This is accomplished because A and B, however seemingly dissimilar, share some quality that is, in turn, highlighted by the metaphor. Metaphors allow the marketer to activate meaningful images and apply them to everyday events. In the stock market, "white knights" battle "hostile raiders" using "poison pills," Tony the Tiger

This Australian toothpaste ad uses a mild fear appeal to promote tooth brushing.

allows us to equate cereal with strength, and the Merrill Lynch bull sends the message that the company is "a breed apart."[82]

Resonance is another type of literary device that is frequently used in advertising. It is a form of presentation that combines a play on words with a relevant picture. Table 8.2 gives some examples of actual ads that rely on the principle of resonance. Whereas metaphor substitutes one meaning for another by connecting two things that are in some way similar, resonance uses an element that has a double meaning, such as a pun in which there is a similarity in the sound of a word but a difference in meaning. For example, an ad for a diet strawberry short-cake dessert might bear the copy "berried treasure" so that qualities associated with buried treasure—being rich, hidden, and associated with adventurous pirates—are conveyed for the brand. Because the text departs from expectations,

TABLE 8.2 Some Examples of Advertising Resonance

Product/Headline	Visual
Embassy Suites: "This Year, We're Unwrapping Suites by the Dozen"	Chocolate kisses with hotel names underneath each
Toyota auto parts: "Our Lifetime Guarantee May Come as a Shock"	Man holding a shock absorber
Bucks filter cigarettes: "Herd of These?"	Cigarette pack with a picture of a stag
Bounce fabric softener: "Is There Something Creeping Up Behind You?"	Woman's dress bunched up on her back due to static
Pepsi: "This Year, Hit the Beach Topless"	Pepsi bottle cap lying on the sand
ASICS athletic shoes: "We Believe Women Should Be Running the Country"	Woman jogging in a rural setting

SOURCE: Adapted from Edward F. McQuarrie and David Glen Mick, "On Resonance: A Critical Pluralistic Inquiry into Advertising Rhetoric," *Journal of Consumer Research* 19 (September 1992): 182, Table 1. Reprinted with permission of The University of Chicago Press.

Many products are personified by make-believe characters.

it creates a state of tension or uncertainty on the part of the viewer until he or she figures out the word play. Once the consumer "gets it," he or she may prefer the ad over a more straightforward message.[83]

Forms of Story Presentation

Just as a story can be told in words or pictures, the way the audience is addressed can also differ. Commercials are structured similarly to other art forms, borrowing conventions from literature and art as they communicate their messages.[84] One important distinction is between a *drama* and *a lecture*.[85] A lecture is like a speech in which the source speaks directly to the audience in an attempt to inform them about a product or persuade them to buy it. Because a lecture clearly implies an attempt at persuasion, the audience will regard it as such. Assuming listeners are motivated to do so, the merits of the message will be weighed, along with the credibility of the source. Cognitive responses, such as counterargumentation, will occur. The appeal will be accepted to the extent that it overcomes objections and is congruent with a person's beliefs.

In contrast, a drama is similar to a play or movie. Whereas an argument holds the viewer at arm's length, a drama draws the viewer into the action. The characters only indirectly address the audience; they interact with each other about a product or service in an imaginary setting. Dramas attempt to be experiential—to involve the audience emotionally. In *transformational advertising*, the consumer associates the experience of product usage with some subjective sensation. Thus, ads for the Infiniti attempted to transform the "driving experience" into a mystical, spiritual event.

THE SOURCE VERSUS THE MESSAGE: SELL THE STEAK OR THE SIZZLE?

Two major components of the communications model, the source and the message, have been reviewed. Which aspect has the most impact on persuading consumers to change their attitudes? Should marketers worry more about *what* is said, or *how* it's said and *who* says it?

The answer is, it depends. Variations in a consumer's level of involvement, as discussed in Chapter 4, result in the activation of very different cognitive processes when a message is received. Research indicates that this level of involvement will determine which aspects of a communication are processed. The situation appears to resemble a traveler who comes to a fork in the road: One or the other path is chosen, and this choice has a big impact on the factors that will make a difference in persuasion attempts.

The Elaboration Likelihood Model

The **elaboration likelihood model (ELM)** assumes that once a consumer receives a message he or she begins to process it.[87] Depending on the personal relevance of this information, the receiver will follow one of two routes to persuasion. Under conditions of high involvement, the consumer takes the central route to persuasion. Under conditions of low involvement, a *peripheral route* is taken instead. This model is diagrammed in Figure 8.5.

The Central Route to Persuasion

When the consumer finds the information in a persuasive message to be relevant or somehow interesting, he or she will carefully attend to the message content. The person is likely to actively think about the arguments presented and generate *cognitive responses* to these arguments. On hearing a radio message warning about drinking while pregnant, an expectant mother might say to herself, "She's right. I really should stop drinking alcohol now that I'm pregnant." Or, she might offer counterarguments, such as "That's a bunch of baloney. My mother had a cocktail every night when she was pregnant with me, and I turned out fine." If a person generates counterarguments in response to a message, it is less likely that he or she will yield to the message, whereas the generation of further supporting arguments by the consumer increases the probability of compliance.[88]

The central route to persuasion is likely to involve the traditional hierarchy of effects, as discussed in Chapter 7. Beliefs are carefully formed and evaluated, and strong attitudes that result will be likely to guide behavior. The implication is that message factors, such as the quality of arguments presented, will be important in determining attitude change. Prior knowledge about a topic results in more thoughts about the message and also increases the number of counterarguments.[89]

The Peripheral Route to Persuasion

In contrast, the peripheral route is taken when the person is not motivated to really think about the arguments presented. Instead, the consumer is likely to use other cues in deciding on the suitability of the message. These cues might include the product's package, the attractiveness of the source, or the context in which the message is presented. Sources of information extraneous to the actual message content are called *peripheral cues* because they surround the actual message.

NET PROFIT

ONE WAY TO INCREASE consumer involvement with marketing messages is to make the viewer part of the story. The newest trend in advertising is "hybrid" campaigns that integrate traditional media with the Web to make the consumer an active participant. Here are some recent hybrid campaigns that hint at the future of interactive communications:

- Tommy Hilfiger's campaign for Tommy jeans featured finalists from an online talent search for unsigned musicians. In addition to voting, consumers were able to download music from the finalists; the winner collected a prize of $810,000 and a recording demo deal.
- Viewers were able to "direct" TV commercials for the Ford Probe. They logged onto focus247.com and picked the cast and plot lines that would be used to create actual spots.
- For its "whatever.com" ads, Nike sent consumers to the Web to pick the endings of three cliffhanger TV spots.[86]

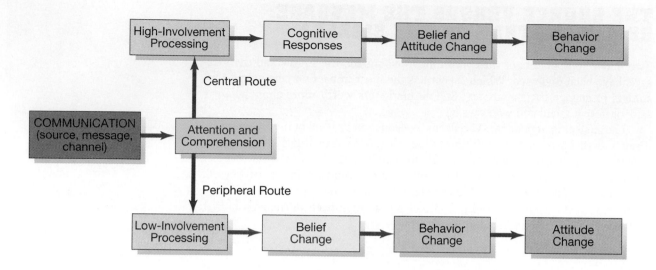

Figure 8.5
The Elaboration Likelihood Model of Persuasion

The peripheral route to persuasion highlights the paradox of low involvement discussed in Chapter 4: When consumers do not care about a product, the stimuli associated with it increase in importance. The implication here is that low-involvement products may be purchased chiefly because the marketer has done a good job in designing a "sexy" package, choosing a popular spokesperson, or perhaps just creating a pleasant shopping environment.

Support for the ELM Model

The ELM model has received a lot of research support.[90] In a typical study, undergraduates were exposed to one of several mock advertisements for Break, a new brand of low-alcohol beer. Using the technique of *thought listing*, they were asked to provide their thoughts about the ads, which were later analyzed by the researchers. Two versions of the ads are shown here.[91] Three independent variables crucial to the ELM model were manipulated.

1. *Message-processing involvement:* Some subjects were motivated to be highly involved with the ads. They were promised a gift of low-alcohol beer for participating in the study and were told that the brand would soon be available in their area. Low-involvement subjects, who were not promised a gift, were told that the brand would be introduced in a distant area.
2. *Argument strength:* One version of the ad used strong, compelling arguments to drink Break (e.g., "Break contains one-half of the amount of alcohol of regular beers and, therefore, has less calories than regular beer."), whereas the other listed only weak arguments (e.g., "Break is just as good as any other regular beer.")
3. *Source characteristics:* Both ads contained a photo of a couple drinking the beer, but their relative social attractiveness was varied by their dress, their posture and nonverbal expressions, and the background information given about their educational achievements and occupations.

Consistent with the ELM model, high-involvement subjects had more thoughts related to the ad messages than did low-involvement subjects, who devoted more cognitive activity to the sources used in the ad. The attitudes of high-involvement subjects were more likely to be swayed by powerful arguments, whereas the attitudes of low-involvement subjects were more likely to be influenced by the ad version using attractive sources. The results of this study, paired with numerous others, indicate that the relative effectiveness of a strong message and a favorable source depends on consumers' level of involvement with the product being advertised.

These results underscore the basic idea that highly involved consumers look for the "steak" (e.g., strong, rational arguments). Those who are less involved are more affected by the "sizzle" (e.g., the colors and images used in packaging or endorsements by famous people). It is important to remember, however, that the same communications variable can be both a central and a peripheral cue, depending on its relation to the attitude object. The physical attractiveness of a model might serve as a peripheral cue in a car commercial, but her beauty might be a central cue for a product such as shampoo, as the product's benefits are directly tied to enhancing attractiveness.[92]

CHAPTER SUMMARY

- Persuasion refers to an attempt to change consumers' attitudes.
- The communications model specifies the elements needed to transmit meaning. These include a source, message, medium, receiver, and feedback.
- The traditional view of communications tends to regard the perceiver as a passive element in the process. Proponents of the uses and gratifications approach instead regard the consumer as an active participant who uses media for a variety of reasons.
- New developments in interactive communications highlight the need to consider the active roles a consumer might play in obtaining product information and building a relationship with a company. A product-related communication that directly yields a transaction is a first-order response. Customer feedback in response to a marketing message that is not in the form of a transaction is a second-order response. This may take the form of a request for more information about a good, service, or organization, or perhaps receipt of a "wish list" from the customer that specifies the types of product information he or she would like to get in the future.
- Two important characteristics that determine the effectiveness of a source are its attractiveness and credibility. Although celebrities often serve this purpose, their credibility is not always as strong as marketers hope.
- Some elements of a message that help to determine its effectiveness are whether it is conveyed in words or pictures, whether an emotional or a rational appeal is employed, the frequency with which it is repeated, whether a conclusion is drawn, whether both sides of the argument are presented, and whether the message includes fear, humor, or sexual references.
- Advertising messages often incorporate elements from art or literature such as dramas, lectures, metaphors, allegories, and resonance.
- The relative influence of the source versus the message depends on the receiver's level of involvement with the communication. The elaboration likelihood model specifies that a less-involved consumer will more likely be swayed by source effects, whereas a more-involved consumer will more likely attend to and process components of the actual message.

KEY TERMS

CONSUMER BEHAVIOR CHALLENGE

1. A government agency wants to encourage the use of designated drivers by people who have been drinking. What advice could you give the organization about constructing persuasive communications? Discuss some factors that might be important, including the structure of the communications, where they should appear, and who should deliver them. Should fear appeals be used, and if so, how?

2. Discuss some conditions in which it would be advisable to use a comparative advertising strategy.

3. Why would a marketer consider saying negative things about his or her product? When is this strategy feasible? Can you find examples of it?

4. A marketer must decide whether to incorporate rational or emotional appeals in its communications strategy. Describe conditions that are more favorable to using one or the other.

5. Collect ads that rely on sex appeal to sell products. How often are benefits of the actual product communicated to the reader?

6. Observe the process of counterargumentation by asking a friend to talk out loud while watching a commercial. Ask him or her to respond to each point in the ad or to write down reactions to the claims made. How much skepticism regarding the claims can you detect?

7. Make a log of all the commercials shown on one network television channel during a two-hour period. Categorize each according to product category, and whether they are presented as drama or argument. Describe the types of messages used (e.g., two-sided arguments), and keep track of the types of spokespeople (e.g., TV actors, famous people, animated characters). What can you conclude about the dominant forms of persuasive tactics currently employed by marketers?

8. Collect examples of ads that rely on the use of metaphors or resonance. Do you feel these ads are effective? If you were working with the products, would you feel more comfortable with ads that use a more straightforward, "hard-sell" approach? Why or why not?

9. Create a list of current celebrities whom you feel typify cultural categories (e.g., clown, mother figure, etc.). What specific brands do you feel each could effectively endorse?

10. The American Medical Association encountered a firestorm of controversy when it agreed to sponsor a line of health care products manufactured by Sunbeam (a decision it later reversed). Should trade or professional organizations, journalists, professors, and others endorse specific products at the expense of other offerings?

NOTES

1. Gert Assmus, "An Empirical Investigation into the Perception of Vehicle Source Effects," *Journal of Advertising* 7 (Winter 1978): 4–10; for a more thorough discussion of the pros and cons of different media, see Stephen Baker, *Systematic Approach to Advertising Creativity* (New York: McGraw-Hill, 1979).

2. Alladi Venkatesh, Ruby Roy Dholakia, and Nikhilesh Dholakia, "New Visions of Information Technology and Post-modernism: Implications for Advertising and Marketing Communications," in Walter Brenner and Lutz Kolbe, eds., *The Information Superhighway and Private Households: Case Studies of Business Impacts* (Heidelberg: Physical-Verlag, 1996): 319–37; Donna L. Hoffman and Thomas P. Novak, "Marketing in Hyper-media Computer-Mediated Environments: Conceptual Foundations," *Journal of Marketing* 60, no. 3 (July 1996): 50–68; for an early theoretical discussion of interactivity in communications para-digms, see R. Aubrey Fisher, *Perspectives on Human Communication* (New York: Macmillan, 1978).

3. First proposed by Elihu Katz, "Mass Communication Research and the Study of Popular Culture: An Editorial Note on a Possible Future for this Journal," *Studies in Public Communication*, 2 (1959): 1–6. For a recent discussion of this approach, see Stephanie O'Donohoe, "Advertising Uses and Gratifications," *European Journal of Marketing* 28, no. 8/9 (1994): 52–75.

4. Annie Huang, "Cartoon Doll Creates Frenzy in Taiwan," *Marketing News* (September 13, 1999): 20.

5. Quoted in O'Donohoe, "Advertising Uses and Gratifications," p. 66.

6. This section is adapted from a discussion in Michael R. Solomon and Elnora W. Stuart, *Marketing: Real People, Real Choices*, 2d ed. (Upper Saddle River, NJ: Prentice Hall, 2000).

7. Carl I. Hovland and W. Weiss, "The Influence of Source Credibility on Com-munication Effectiveness," *Public Opinion Quarterly* 15 (1952): 635–50.

8. Herbert Kelman, "Processes of Opinion Change," *Public Opinion Quarterly* 25 (Spring 1961): 57–78; Susan M. Petroshuis and Kenneth E. Crocker, "An Empirical Analysis of Spokesperson Characteristics on Advertisement and Product Evalua-tions," *Journal of the Academy of Mar-keting Science* 17 (Summer 1989): 217–26.

9. S. Ratneshwar and Shelly Chaiken, "Comprehension's Role in Persuasion: The Case of Its Moderating Effect on the Persuasive Impact of Source Cues," *Journal of Consumer Research* 18 (June 1991): 52–62.

10. Jagdish Agrawal and Wagner A. Kamakura, "The Economic Worth of Celebrity Endorsers: An Event Study Analysis," *Journal of Marketing* 59 (July 1995): 56–62.

11. "Robber Makes It Biggs in Ad," *Advertising Age* (May 29, 1989): 26.

12. Robert LaFranco, "MTV Conquers Madison Avenue," *Forbes* (June 3, 1996): 138.

13. Alice H. Eagly, Andy Wood, and Shelly Chaiken, "Causal Inferences About Com-municators and Their Effect in Opinion Change," *Journal of Personality and Social Psychology* 36, no. 4 (1978): 424–35.

14. Michael Wilke, "FDA Gives OK for Claritin to Use Celebrity Endorser," *Advertising Age* (July 13, 1998): 8.

15. William Dowell, "Microsoft Offers Tips to Agreeable Academics," *Time* (June 1, 1998): 22.

16. Kruti Trivedi, "Great-Grandson of Artist Renoir Uses His Name for Marketing Blitz," *The Wall Street Journal Interactive Edition* (September 2, 1999).

17. Richard Sandomir, "A Pitchman with Punch: George Foreman Sells His Name," *The New York Times on the Web* (January 21, 2000).

18. Judith Graham, "Sponsors Line Up for Rockin' Role," *Advertising Age* (December 11, 1989): 50.

19. Heather Buttle, Jane E. Raymond, and Shai Danziger, "Do Famous Faces Capture Attention," paper presented at *Association for Consumer Research Conference Columbus, Ohio* (October 1999).

20. Michael A. Kamins, "Celebrity and Noncelebrity Advertising in a Two-Sided Context," *Journal of Advertising Research* 29 (June–July 1989): 34; Joseph M. Kamen, A. C. Azhari, and J. R. Kragh, "What a Spokesman Does for a Sponsor," *Journal of Advertising Research* 15, no. 2 (1975): 17–24; Lynn Langmeyer and Mary Walker, "A First Step to Identify the Meaning in Celebrity Endorsers," in Rebecca H. Holman and Michael R. Solomon, eds., *Advances in Consumer Research* 18 (Provo, UT: Association for Consumer Research, 1991): 364–71.

21. Grant McCracken, "Who Is the Celebrity Endorser? Cultural Foundations of the Endorsement Process," *Journal of Consumer Research* 16, no. 3 (December 1989): 310–21.

22. Michael A. Kamins, "An Investigation into the 'Match-Up' Hypothesis in Celebrity Advertising: When Beauty May be Only Skin Deep," *Journal of Advertising* 19, no. 1 (1990): 4–13; Lynn R. Kahle and Pamela M. Homer, "Physical Attractiveness of the Celebrity Endorser: A Social Adaptation Perspective," *Journal of Consumer Research* 11 (March 1985): 954–61.

23. Larry Armstrong, "Still Starstruck," *Business Week* (July 4, 1994): 38; Jeff Giles, "The Risks of Wishing upon a Star," *Newsweek* (September 6, 1993): 38.

24. James Heckman, "Care and Feeding of Mascots," *Marketing News* (March 15, 1999): 1.

25. Karen K. Dion, "What Is Beautiful Is Good," *Journal of Personality and Social Psychology* 24 (December 1972): 285–90.

26. Michael J. Baker and Gilbert A. Churchill Jr., "The Impact of Physically Attractive Models on Advertising Evaluations," *Journal of Marketing Research* 14 (November 1977): 538–55; Marjorie J. Caballero and William M. Pride, "Selected Effects of Salesperson Sex and Attractiveness in Direct Mail Advertisements," *Journal of Marketing* 48 (January 1984): 94–100; W. Benoy Joseph, "The Credibility of Physically Attractive Communicators: A Review," *Journal of Advertising* 11, no. 3 (1982): 15–24; Kahle and Homer, "Physical Attractiveness of the Celebrity Endorser; Judson Mills and Eliot Aronson, "Opinion Change as a Function of Communicator's Attractiveness and Desire to Influence," *Journal of Personality and Social Psychology* 1 (1965): 173–77.

27. Leonard N. Reid and Lawrence C. Soley, "Decorative Models and the Readership of Magazine Ads," *Journal of Advertising Research* 23, no. 2 (1983): 27–32.

28. Marjorie J. Caballero, James R. Lumpkin, and Charles S. Madden, "Using Physical Attractiveness as an Advertising Tool: An Empirical Test of the Attraction Phenomenon," *Journal of Advertising Research* (August/September 1989): 16–22.

29. Baker and Churchill Jr., "The Impact of Physically Attractive Models on Advertising Evaluations"; George E. Belch, Michael A. Belch, and Angelina Villareal, "Effects of Advertising Communications: Review of Research," in *Research in Marketing*, no. 9 (Greenwich, CT: JAI Press, 1987): 59–117; A. E. Courtney and T. W. Whipple, *Sex Stereotyping in Advertising* (Lexington, MA: Lexington Books, 1983).

30. Kahle and Homer, "Physical Attractiveness of the Celebrity Endorser."

31. Kenneth G. DeBono and Richard J. Harnish, "Source Expertise, Source Attractiveness, and the Processing of Persuasive Information: A Functional Approach," *Journal of Personality and Social Psychology* 55, no. 4 (1988): 541–46.

32. Hershey H. Friedman and Linda Friedman, "Endorser Effectiveness by Product Type," *Journal of Advertising Research* 19, no. 5 (1979): 63–71; for a recent study that looked at *non-target market effects*—the effects of

advertising intended for other market segments, see Jennifer L. Aaker, Anne M. Brumbaugh, and Sonya A. Grier, "Non-Target Markets and Viewer Distinctiveness: The Impact of Target Marketing on Advertising Attitudes," *Journal of Consumer Psychology* 9, no. 3 (2000): 127–40.

33. Anthony R. Pratkanis, Anthony G. Greenwald, Michael R. Leippe, and Michael H. Baumgardner, "In Search of Reliable Persuasion Effects: III. The Sleeper Effect Is Dead, Long Live the Sleeper Effect," *Journal of Personality and Social Psychology* 54 (1988): 203–18.

34. Herbert C. Kelman and Carl I. Hovland, "Reinstatement of the Communication in Delayed Measurement of Opinion Change," *Journal of Abnormal Psychology* 48, no. 3 (1953): 327–35.

35. Darlene Hannah and Brian Sternthal, "Detecting and Explaining the Sleeper Effect," *Journal of Consumer Research* 11 (September 1984): 632–42.

36. David Mazursky and Yaacov Schul, "The Effects of Advertisment Encoding on the Failure to Discount Information: Implications For the Sleeper Effect," *Journal of Consumer Research* 15 (June 1988): 24–36.

37. David W. Stewart and David H. Furse, "The Effects of Television Advertising Execution on Recall, Comprehension, and Persuasion," *Psychology & Marketing* 2 (Fall 1985): 135–60.

38. R. C. Grass and W. H. Wallace, "Advertising Communication: Print Vs. TV," *Journal of Advertising Research* 14 (1974): 19–23.

39. Elizabeth C. Hirschman and Michael R. Solomon, "Utilitarian, Aesthetic, and Familiarity Responses to Verbal Versus Visual Advertisements," in Thomas C. Kinnear, ed., *Advances in Consumer Research* 11 (Provo, UT: Association for Consumer Research, 1984): 426–31.

40. Terry L. Childers and Michael J. Houston, "Conditions For a Picture-Superiority Effect on Consumer Memory," *Journal of Consumer Research* 11 (September 1984): 643–54.

41. Andrew A. Mitchell, "The Effect of Verbal and Visual Components of Advertisements on Brand Attitudes and Attitude Toward the Advertisement," *Journal of Consumer Research* 13 (June 1986): 12–24.

42. John R. Rossiter and Larry Percy, "Attitude Change Through Visual Imagery in Advertising," *Journal of Advertising Research* 9, no. 2 (1980): 10–16.

43. Jolita Kiselius and Brian Sternthal, "Examining the Vividness Controversy: An Availability-Valence Interpretation," *Journal of Consumer Research* 12 (March 1986): 418–31.

44. Scott B. Mackenzie, "The Role of Attention in Mediating the Effect of Advertising on Attribute Importance,"

Journal of Consumer Research 13 (September 1986): 174–95.

45. Robert B. Zajonc, "Attitudinal Effects of Mere Exposure," Monograph, *Journal of Personality and Social Psychology* 8 (1968): 1–29.

46. Giles D'Souza and Ram C. Rao, "Can Repeating an Advertisement More Frequently Than the Competition Affect Brand Preference in a Mature Market?" *Journal of Marketing* 59 (April 1995): 32–42.

47. George E. Belch, "The Effects of Television Commercial Repetition on Cognitive Response and Message Acceptance," *Journal of Consumer Research* 9 (June 1982): 56–65; Marian Burke and Julie Edell, "Ad Reactions over Time: Capturing Changes in the Real World," *Journal of Consumer Research* 13 (June 1986): 114–18; Herbert Krugman, "Why Three Exposures May Be Enough," *Journal of Advertising Research* 12 (December 1972): 11–14.

48. Robert F. Bornstein, "Exposure and Affect: Overview and Meta-Analysis of Research, 1968–1987," *Psychological Bulletin* 106, no. 2 (1989): 265–89; Arno Rethans, John Swasy, and Lawrence Marks, "Effects of Television Commercial Repetition, Receiver Knowledge, and Commercial Length: A Test of the Two-Factor Model," *Journal of Marketing Research* 23 (February 1986): 50–61.

49. Curtis P. Haugtvedt, David W. Schumann, Wendy L. Schneier, and Wendy L. Warren, "Advertising Repetition and Variation Strategies: Implications for Understanding Attitude Strength," *Journal of Consumer Research* 21 (June 1994): 176–89.

50. Linda L. Golden and Mark I. Alpert, "Comparative Analysis of the Relative Effectiveness of One- and Two-Sided Communication for Contrasting Products," *Journal of Advertising* 16 (1987): 18–25; Kamins, "Celebrity and Noncelebrity Advertising in a Two-Sided Context"; Robert B. Settle and Linda L. Golden, "Attribution Theory and Advertiser Credibility," *Journal of Marketing Research* 11 (May 1974): 181–85.

51. See Alan G. Sawyer, "The Effects of Repetition of Refutational and Supportive Advertising Appeals," *Journal of Marketing Research* 10 (February 1973): 23–33; George J. Szybillo and Richard Heslin, "Resistance to Persuasion: Inoculation Theory in a Marketing Context," *Journal of Marketing Research* 10 (November 1973): 396–403.

52. Golden and Alpert, "Comparative Analysis of the Relative Effectiveness of One- and Two-Sided Communication for Contrasting Products."

53. Belch et al., "Effects of Advertising Communications."

54. Frank R. Kardes, "Spontaneous Inference Processes in Advertising: The Effects of Conclusion Omission and Involve-

ment on Persuasion," *Journal of Consumer Research* 15 (September 1988): 225–33.

55. Belch et al., "Effects of Advertising Communications"; Cornelia Pechmann and Gabriel Esteban, "Persuasion Processes Associated with Direct Comparative and Noncomparative Advertising and Implications for Advertising Effectiveness," *Journal of Consumer Psychology* 2, no. 4 (1994): 403–32.

56. Cornelia Dröge and Rene Y. Darmon, "Associative Positioning Strategies Through Comparative Advertising: Attribute vs. Overall Similarity Approaches," *Journal of Marketing Research* 24 (1987): 377–89; D. Muehling and N. Kangun, "The Multidimensionality of Comparative Advertising: Implications for the FTC," *Journal of Public Policy and Marketing* (1985): 112–28; Beth A. Walker and Helen H. Anderson, "Reconceptualizing Comparative Advertising: A Framework and Theory of Effects," in Rebecca H. Holman and Michael R. Solomon, eds., *Advances in Consumer Research* 18 (Provo, UT: Association for Consumer Research, 1991): 342–47; William L. Wilkie and Paul W. Farris, "Comparison Advertising: Problems and Potential," *Journal of Marketing* 39 (October 1975): 7–15; R. G. Wyckham, "Implied Superiority Claims," *Journal of Advertising Research* (February/March 1987): 54–63.

57. Stephen A. Goodwin and Michael Etgar, "An Experimental Investigation of Comparative Advertising: Impact of Message Appeal, Information Load, and Utility of Product Class," *Journal of Marketing Research* 17 (May 1980): 187–202; Gerald J. Gorn and Charles B. Weinberg, "The Impact of Comparative Advertising on Perception and Attitude: Some Positive Findings," *Journal of Consumer Research* 11 (September 1984): 719–27; Terence A. Shimp and David C. Dyer, "The Effects of Comparative Advertising Mediated by Market Position of Sponsoring Brand," *Journal of Advertising* 3 (Summer 1978): 13–19; R. Dale Wilson, "An Empirical Evaluation of Comparative Advertising Messages: Subjects' Responses to Perceptual Dimensions," in B. B. Anderson, ed., *Advances in Consumer Research* 3 (Ann Arbor, MI: Association for Consumer Research, 1976): 53–57.

58. Dhruv Grewal, Sukumar Kavanoor, Edward F. Fern, Carolyn Costley, and James Barnes," "Comparative Versus Noncomparative Advertising: A Meta-Analysis," *JM* 61 (October 1997): 1–15.

59. Dröge and Darmon, "Associative Positioning Strategies Through Comparative Advertising: Attribute vs. Overall Similarity Approaches."

60. Jean Halliday, "Survey: Comparative Ads Can Dent Car's Credibility," *Advertising Age* (May 4, 1998): 26.

61. Alec Klein, "The Techies Grumbled, But Polaroid's Pocket Turned into a Huge Hit," *The Wall Street Journal* (May 2, 2000): A1.

62. Dottie Enrico, "Guaranteed! Greatest Advertising Story Ever Told!" *Newsday* (October 16, 1991): 43; Bruce Buchanan and Doron Goldman, "Us vs. Them: The Minefield of Comparative Ads," *Harvard Business Review* 38 (May–June 1989): 50.

63. Edward F. Cone, "Image and Reality," *Forbes* (December 14, 1987): 226.

64. H. Zielske, "Does Day-After Recall Penalize 'Feeling' Ads?" *Journal of Advertising Research* 22 (1982): 19–22.

65. John Lichfield, "French Get Bored with Sex," *The Independent*, London (July 30, 1997).

66. Belch et al., "Effects of Advertising Communications"; Courtney and Whipple, "Sex Stereotyping in Advertising"; Michael S. LaTour, "Female Nudity in Print Advertising: An Analysis of Gender Differences in Arousal and Ad Response," *Psychology & Marketing* 7, no. 1(1990): 65–81; B. G. Yovovich, "Sex in Advertising—The Power and the Perils," *Advertising Age* (May 2, 1983): M4–M5; for an interesting interpretive analysis, cf. Richard Elliott and Mark Ritson, "Practicing Existential Consumption: The Lived Meaning of Sexuality in Advertising," in Frank R. Kardes and Mita Sujan, eds., *Advances in Consumer Behavior* 22 (1995): 740–45.

67. Penny M. Simpson, Steve Horton, and Gene Brown, "Male Nudity in Advertisements: A Modified Replication and Extension of Gender and Product Effects," *Journal of the Academy of Marketing Science* 24, no. 3 (1996): 257–62.

68. Michael S. LaTour and Tony L. Henthorne, "Ethical Judgments of Sexual Appeals in Print Advertising," *Journal of Advertising* 23, no. 3 (September 1994): 81–90.

69. Roger Thurow, "As In-Your-Face Ads Backfire, Nike Finds a New Global Tack," *The Wall Street Journal Interactive Edition* (May 5, 1997).

70. Marc G. Weinberger and Harlan E. Spotts, "Humor in U.S. Versus U.K. TV Commercials: A Comparison," *Journal of Advertising* 18, no. 2 (1989): 39–44.

71. Thomas J. Madden, "Humor in Advertising: An Experimental Analysis" (working paper, no. 83–27, University of Massachusetts, 1984); Thomas J. Madden and Marc G. Weinberger, "The Effects of Humor on Attention in Magazine Advertising," *Journal of Advertising* 11, no. 3 (1982): 8–14; Weinberger and Spotts, "Humor in U.S. Versus U.K. TV Commercials."

72. David Gardner, "The Distraction Hypothesis in Marketing," *Journal of Advertising Research* 10 (1970): 25–30.

73. "Funny Ads Provide Welcome Relief During These Gloom and Doom Days," *Marketing News* (April 17, 1981): 3.

74. "Ex-Lax Taken off Shelves for Now," *Montgomery Advertiser* (August 30, 1997): 1A.

75. Michael L. Ray and William L. Wilkie, "Fear: The Potential of an Appeal Neglected by Marketing," *Journal of Marketing* 34, no. 1 (1970): 54–62.

76. Brian Sternthal and C. Samuel Craig, "Fear Appeals: Revisited and Revised," *Journal of Consumer Research* 1 (December 1974): 22–34.

77. Punam Anand Keller and Lauren Goldberg Block, "Increasing the Effectiveness of Fear Appeals: The Effect of Arousal and Elaboration," *Journal of Consumer Research* 22 (March 1996): 448–59.

78. Ronald Paul Hill, "An Exploration of the Relationship Between AIDS-Related Anxiety and the Evaluation of Condom Advertisements," *Journal of Advertising* 17, no. 4 (1988): 35–42.

79. Randall Rothenberg, "Talking Too Tough on Life's Risks?" *New York Times* (February 16, 1990): D1.

80. Denise D. Schoenbachler and Tommy E. Whittler, "Adolescent Processing of Social and Physical Threat Communications," *Journal of Advertising* 25, no. 4 (Winter 1996): 37–54.

81. "A Drive to Woo Women—and Invigorate Sales," *New York Times* (April 2, 1989).

82. Carrie Goerne, "Gun Companies Target Women: Foes Call It 'Marketing to Fear'," *Marketing News* 2 (August 31, 1992): 1.

83. Edward F. McQuarrie and David Glen Mick, "On Resonance: A Critical Pluralistic Inquiry into Advertising Rhetoric," *Journal of Consumer Research* 19 (September 1992): 180–97.

84. See Linda M. Scott, "The Troupe: Celebrities as Dramatis Personae in Advertisements," in Rebecca H. Holman and Michael R. Solomon, eds., *Advances in Consumer Research* 18 (Provo, UT: Association for Consumer Research, 1991): 355–63; Barbara Stern, "Literary Criticism and Consumer Research: Overview and Illustrative Analysis," *Journal of Consumer Research* 16 (1989): 322–34; Judith Williamson, Decoding Advertisements (Boston: Marion Boyars, 1978).

85. John Deighton, Daniel Romer, and Josh McQueen, "Using Drama to Persuade," *Journal of Consumer Research* 16 (December 1989): 335–43.

86. Michael McCarthy, "Companies are Sold on Interactive Ad Strategy," *USA Today* (March 3, 2000): B1.

87. Richard E. Petty, John T. Cacioppo, and David Schumann, "Central and Peripheral Routes to Advertising Effectiveness: The Moderating Role of Involvement," *Journal of Consumer Research* 10, no. 2 (1983): 135–46.

88. Jerry C. Olson, Daniel R. Toy, and Philip A. Dover, "Do Cognitive Responses Mediate the Effects of Advertising Content on Cognitive Structure?" *Journal of Consumer Research* 9, no. 3 (1982): 245–62.

89. Julie A. Edell and Andrew A. Mitchell, "An Information Processing Approach to Cognitive Responses," in S. C. Jain, ed., *Research Frontiers in Marketing: Dialogues and Directions* (Chicago: American Marketing Association, 1978).

90. See Mary Jo Bitner and Carl Obermiller, "The Elaboration Likelihood Model: Limitations and Extensions in Marketing," in Elizabeth C. Hirschman, and Morris B. Holbrook, eds., *Advances in Consumer Research* 12 (Provo, UT: Association for Consumer Research, 1985): 420–25; Meryl P. Gardner, "Does Attitude Toward the Ad Affect Brand Attitude Under a Brand Evaluation Set?" *Journal of Marketing Research* 22 (1985): 192–98; C. W. Park and S. M. Young, "Consumer Response to Television Commercials: The Impact of Involvement and Background Music on Brand Attitude Formation," *Journal of Marketing Research* 23 (1986): 11–24; Petty, Cacioppo, and Schumann, "Central and Peripheral Routes to Advertising Effectiveness"; for a discussion of how different kinds of involvement interact with the ELM, see Robin A. Higie, Lawrence F. Feick, and Linda L. Price, "The Importance of Peripheral Cues in Attitude Formation for Enduring and Task-Involved Individuals," in Rebecca H. Holman and Michael R. Solomon, eds., *Advances in Consumer Research* 18 (Provo, UT: Association for Consumer Research, 1991): 187–93.

91. J. Craig Andrews and Terence A. Shimp, "Effects of Involvement, Argument Strength, and Source Characteristics on Central and Peripheral Processing in Advertising," *Psychology & Marketing* 7 (Fall 1990): 195–214.

92. Richard E. Petty, John T. Cacioppo, Constantine Sedikides, and Alan J. Strathman, "Affect and Persuasion: A Contemporary Perspective," *American Behavioral Scientist* 31, no. 3 (1988): 355–71.

SECTION

III

i want everything at my party to be yellow
i want yellow balloons, yellow cups, and yellow
icing on my cake because yellow is the prettiest
color ever. except for pink. i want everything at
my party to be pink.

www.iparty.com > birthdays > basics > pink > cups/plates/napkins/favors > order

i want. i click. iparty.com

©1999 Party™ Corp.

CONSUMERS AS DECISION MAKERS

This section explores how we make consumption decisions and discusses the many influences exerted by others during this process. Chapter 9 focuses on the basic sequence of steps we undergo when making a decision. Chapter 10 considers how the particular situation in which we find ourselves affects these decisions and how we go about evaluating the results of our choices. Chapter 11 provides an overview of group processes and discusses the reasons we are motivated to conform to the expectations of others when we choose and display our purchases. Chapter 12 goes on to consider the many instances in which our purchase decisions are made in conjunction with others, especially co-workers or family members.

◆ ◆ ◆

Section Outline

Richard has had it. There's only so much longer he can go on watching TV on his tiny, antiquated black-and-white set. It was bad enough trying to listen to the scratchy music in MTV videos and squinting through *Ally McBeal*. The final straw was when he couldn't tell the Cowboys from the Jaguars during NFL football. When he went next door to watch the second half on Mark's home theater setup, he really realized what he had been missing. Budget or not, it was time to act: A man has to have his priorities.

Where to start looking? The Web, naturally. Richard checks out a few comparison shopping Web sites, including selectsmart.com and deja.com. After narrowing down his options,

he ventures out to scope out a few sets in person. He figures he'll probably get a decent selection (and an affordable price) at one of those huge new warehouse stores. Arriving at Zany Zack's Appliance Emporium, Richard heads straight for the Video Zone in the back—barely noticing the rows of toasters, microwave ovens, and stereos on his way. Within minutes, he's accosted by a smiling salesman in a cheap suit. Even though he could use some help, Richard tells the salesman he's just browsing—he figures these guys don't know what they're talking about, and they're just out to make a sale no matter what.

Richard starts to examine some of the features on the 60-inch color sets. He knew his friend Carol had a set by Prime Wave that she really liked, and his sister Diane had warned him to stay away from the Kamashita. Although Richard finds a Prime Wave model loaded to the max with features such as a sleep timer, on-screen programming menu, cable compatible tuner, and picture-in-picture, he chooses the less-expensive Precision 2000X because it has one feature that really catches his fancy: stereo broadcast reception.

Later that day, Richard is a happy man as he sits in his easy chair, watching Slim Shady do his thing on MTV. If he's going to be a couch potato, he's going in style.

INDIVIDUAL DECISION MAKING

CONSUMERS AS PROBLEM SOLVERS

A consumer purchase is a response to a problem, which in Richard's case is the perceived need for a new TV. His situation is similar to that encountered by consumers virtually every day of their lives. He realizes that he wants to make a purchase, and he goes through a series of steps in order to make it. These steps can be described as: (1) problem recognition, (2) information search, (3) evaluation of alternatives, and (4) product choice. Of course, after the decision is made, the quality of that decision affects the final step in the process, in which learning occurs based on how well the choice worked out. This learning process, of course, influences the likelihood that the same choice will be made the next time the need for a similar decision occurs.

An overview of this decision-making process appears in Figure 9.1. This chapter begins by considering various approaches consumers use when faced with a purchase decision. It then focuses on three of the steps in the decision process: how consumers recognize the problem, or need for a product; their search for information about product choices; and the ways in which they evaluate alternatives to arrive at a decision. Chapter 10 considers influences in the actual purchase situation, as well as the person's satisfaction with the decision.

Because some purchase decisions are more important than others, the amount of effort we put into each one differs. Sometimes the decision-making process is almost automatic; we seem to make snap judgments based on very little information. At other times, coming to a purchase decision begins to resemble a full-time job. A person may literally spend days or weeks thinking about an important purchase such as a new home, even to the point of obsession.

Figure 9.1
Stages in Consumer Decision Making

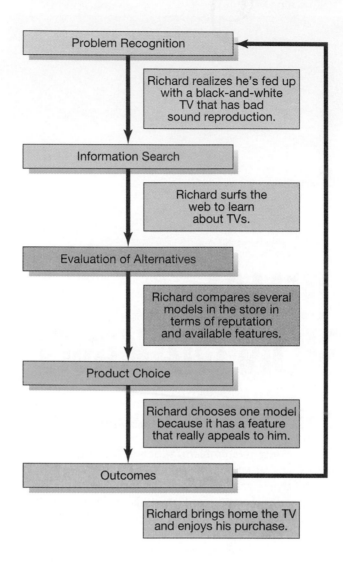

Perspectives on Decision Making

Traditionally, consumer researchers have approached decision makers from a **rational perspective.** In this view, people calmly and carefully integrate as much information as possible with what they already know about a product, painstakingly weigh the pluses and minuses of each alternative, and arrive at a satisfactory decision. This process implies that steps in decision making should be carefully studied by marketing managers to understand how information is obtained, how beliefs are formed, and what product choice criteria are specified by consumers. Products then can be developed that emphasize appropriate attributes, and promotional strategies can be tailored to deliver the types of information most likely to be desired in the most effective formats.[1]

The steps in decision making are followed by consumers for some purchases, but such a process is not an accurate portrayal of many purchase decisions.[2] Consumers simply do not go through this elaborate sequence for every decision. If they did, their entire lives would be spent making such decisions, leaving them very little time to enjoy the things they eventually decide to buy.

This ad by the U.S. Postal Service presents a problem, illustrates the decision-making process and offers a solution.

Researchers are now beginning to realize that decision makers actually possess a repertoire of strategies. A consumer evaluates the effort required to make a particular choice, and then he or she chooses a strategy best suited to the level of effort required. This sequence of events is known as *constructive processing.* Rather than using a big club to kill an ant, consumers tailor their degree of cognitive "effort" to the task at hand.[3]

Some decisions are made under conditions of low involvement, as discussed in Chapter 4. In many of these situations, the consumer's decision is a learned response to environmental cues (see Chapter 3), as when he or she decides to buy something on impulse that is promoted as a "surprise special" in a store. A concentration on these types of decisions can be described as the **behavioral influence perspective.** Under these circumstances, managers must concentrate on assessing the characteristics of the environment, such as the design of a retail outlet or whether a package is enticing, that influence members of a target market.[4]

In other cases, consumers are highly involved in a decision, but still the selections made cannot wholly be explained rationally. For example, the traditional approach is hard pressed to explain a person's choice of art, music, or even a spouse. In these cases, no single quality may be the determining factor. Instead, the **experiential perspective** stresses the *Gestalt,* or totality, of the product or service. Marketers in these areas focus on measuring consumers' affective responses to products or services and develop offerings that elicit appropriate subjective reactions.

Types of Consumer Decisions

One helpful way to characterize the decision-making process is to consider the amount of effort that goes into the decision each time it must be made. Consumer researchers have found it convenient to think in terms of a continuum, which is anchored on one end by habitual decision making and at the other extreme by **extended problem solving.** Many decisions fall somewhere in the middle and are characterized by **limited problem solving.** This continuum is presented in Figure 9.2.

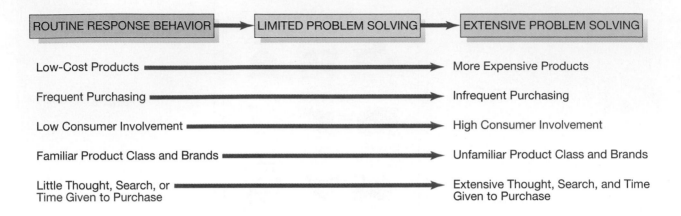

Figure 9.2
A Continuum of Buying
Decision Behavior

Extended Problem Solving

Decisions involving extended problem solving correspond most closely to the traditional decision-making perspective. As indicated in Table 9.1, the extended problem-solving process is usually initiated by a motive that is fairly central to the self-concept (see Chapter 5), and the eventual decision is perceived to carry a fair degree of risk. The consumer tries to collect as much information as possible, both from memory (internal search) and from outside sources (external search). Based on the importance of the decision, each product alternative is carefully evaluated. The evaluation is often made by considering the attributes of one brand at a time and seeing how each brand's attributes shape up to some set of desired characteristics.

Limited Problem Solving

Limited problem solving is usually more straightforward and simple. Buyers are not as motivated to search for information or to evaluate each alternative rigorously. People instead use simple *decision rules* to choose among alternatives. These cognitive shortcuts (more about these later) enable them to fall back on general guidelines, instead of having to start from scratch every time a decision is to be made.

TABLE 9.1   *Characteristics of Limited Versus Extended Problem Solving*

	Limited Problem Solving	Extended Problem Solving
Motivation	Low risk and involvement	High risk and involvement
Information Search	Little search Information processed passively In-store decision likely	Extensive search Information processed actively Multiple sources consulted prior to store visits
Alternative Evaluation	Weakly held beliefs Only most prominent criteria used Alternatives perceived as basically similar Noncompensatory strategy used	Strongly held beliefs Many criteria used Significant differences perceived among alternatives Compensatory strategy used
Purchase	Limited shopping time; may prefer self-service Choice often influenced by store displays	Many outlets shopped if needed Communication with store personnel often desirable

Habitual Decision Making

Both extended and limited problem-solving modes involve some degree of information search and deliberation, though they vary in the degree to which these activities are undertaken. At the other end of the choice continuum, however, are decisions that are made with little to no conscious effort. Many purchase decisions are so routinized that we may not realize we've made them until we look in our shopping carts. Choices characterized by *automaticity* are performed with minimal effort and without conscious control.[5] Although this kind of thoughtless activity may seem dangerous or at best stupid, it is actually quite efficient in many cases. The development of habitual, repetitive behavior allows consumers to minimize the time and energy spent on mundane purchase decisions.

PROBLEM RECOGNITION

Problem recognition occurs whenever the consumer sees a significant difference between his or her current state of affairs and some desired or ideal state. The consumer perceives there is a problem to be solved, which may be small or large, simple or complex. A person who unexpectedly runs out of gas on the highway has a problem, as does the person who becomes dissatisfied with the image of his or her car, even though there is nothing mechanically wrong with it. Although the quality of Richard's TV had not changed, for example, his *standard of comparison* was altered, and he was confronted with a desire he did not have prior to watching his friend's TV.

Figure 9.3 shows that a problem can arise in one of two ways. As in the case of the person running out of gas, the quality of the consumer's *actual state* can move downward (*need recognition*). On the other hand, as in the case of the person who craves a newer, flashier car, the consumer's *ideal state* can move upward (*opportunity recognition*). Either way, a gulf occurs between the actual state and the ideal state.[6] In Richard's case, a problem was perceived as a result of opportunity recognition; his ideal state in terms of television reception quality was altered.

Need recognition can occur in several ways. The quality of the person's actual state can be diminished simply by running out of a product, by buying a product that turns out not to adequately satisfy needs, or by creating new needs

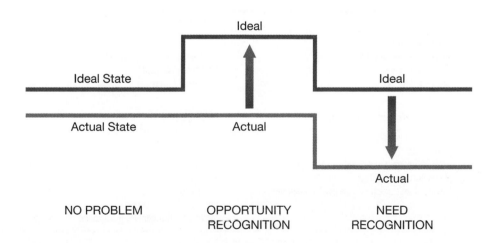

Figure 9.3
Problem Recognition: Shifts in Actual or Ideal States

(e.g., buying a house can set off an avalanche of other choices, because many new things are needed to fill the house). Opportunity recognition often occurs when a consumer is exposed to different or better-quality products. This shift often occurs because the person's circumstances have somehow changed, as when an individual goes to college or gets a new job. As the person's frame of reference shifts, purchases are made to adapt to the new environment.

Although problem recognition can and does occur naturally, this process is often spurred by marketing efforts. In some cases, marketers attempt to create *primary demand*, in which consumers are encouraged to use a product or service regardless of the brand they choose. Such needs are often encouraged in the early stages of a product's life cycle, as, for example, when microwave ovens were first introduced. *Secondary demand*, in which consumers are prompted to prefer a specific brand instead of others, can occur only if primary demand already exists. At this point, marketers must convince consumers that a problem can best be solved by choosing their brand rather than others in a category.

INFORMATION SEARCH

Once a problem has been recognized, consumers need adequate information to resolve it. **Information search** is the process by which the consumer surveys his or her environment for appropriate data to make a reasonable decision. This section will review some of the factors involved in this search.

Types of Information Search

A consumer may explicitly search the marketplace for specific information after a need has been recognized (a process called *prepurchase search*.) On the other hand, many consumers, especially veteran shoppers, enjoy browsing just for the fun of it, or because they like to stay up-to-date on what's happening in the marketplace. They are engaging in *ongoing search*.[7] Some differences between these two search modes are described in Table 9.2.

TABLE 9.2 A Framework for Consumer Information Search	
Prepurchase Search	Ongoing Search
Determinants	
Involvement in the purchase	Involvement with the product
Market environment	Market environment
Situational factors	Situational factors
Motives	
Making better purchase decisions	Building a bank of information for future use
	Experiencing fun and pleasure
Outcomes	
Increased product and market knowledge	Increased product and market knowledge leading to
Better purchase decisions	• future buying efficiencies
Increased satisfaction with the purchase outcome	• personal influence
	Increased impulse buying
	Increased satisfaction from search and other outcomes

SOURCE: Peter H. Bloch, Daniel L. Sherrell, and Nancy M. Ridgway, "Consumer Search: An Extended Framework," *Journal of Consumer Research* 13 (June 1986): 120. Reprinted with permission by The University of Chicago Press.

Internal Versus External Search

Information sources can be roughly broken down into two kinds: internal and external. As a result of prior experience and simply living in a consumer culture, each of us often has some degree of knowledge already in memory about many products. When confronted with a purchase decision, we may engage in *internal search* by scanning our own memory banks to assemble information about different product alternatives (see Chapter 3). Usually, though, even the most market savvy of us needs to supplement this knowledge with external search, by which information is obtained from advertisements, friends, or just plain people-watching.

Deliberate Versus "Accidental" Search

Our existing knowledge of a product may be the result of *directed learning:* on a previous occasion we had already searched for relevant information or experienced some of the alternatives. A parent who bought a birthday cake for one child last month, for example, probably has a good idea of the best kind to buy for another child this month.

Alternatively, we may acquire information in a more passive manner. Even though a product may not be of direct interest to us right now, exposure to advertising, packaging, and sales promotion activities may result in *incidental learning.* Mere exposure over time to conditioned stimuli and observations of others results in the learning of much material that may not be needed for some time after the fact, if ever. For marketers, this result is a benefit of steady, "low-dose" advertising, as product associations are established and maintained until the time they are needed.[8]

In some cases, we may be so expert about a product category (or at least believe we are) that no additional search is undertaken. Frequently, however, our own existing state of knowledge is not satisfactory to make an adequate decision, and we must look elsewhere for more information. The sources we consult for advice vary: They may be impersonal and marketer-dominated sources, such as retailers and catalogs; they may be friends and family members; or they may be unbiased third parties such as *Consumer Reports.*[9]

THE ECONOMICS OF INFORMATION

The traditional decision-making perspective incorporates the *economics-of-information* approach to the search process; it assumes that consumers will gather as much data as needed to make an informed decision. Consumers form expectations of the value of additional information and continue to search to the extent that the rewards of doing so (what economists call the *utility*) exceed the costs. This utilitarian assumption also implies that the most valuable units of information will be collected first. Additional pieces will be absorbed only to the extent that they are seen to augment what is already known.[11] In other words, people will put themselves out to collect as much information as possible, as long as the process of gathering it is not too onerous or time consuming.[12]

Variety seeking can influence a consumer to switch from their favorite product to a less pleasurable item. This can occur even before an individual becomes satiated or tired of their favorite product. Explanations of this phenomenon stems from research that supports the idea that consumers are willing to trade enjoyment for variety and that variety seeking is a choice strategy that occurs as a result of pleasurable memories for a varied sequence.[13]

MARKETING PITFALLS

LABELS PROVIDE VALUABLE information about the proper way to use products, but sometimes they can be . . . less than clear. Here are some examples of "interesting" labels:[10]

- On a Conair Pro Style 1600 hair dryer: WARNING: Do not use in shower. Never use while sleeping.
- Instructions for folding up a portable baby carriage: Step 1: Remove baby.
- A rest stop on a Wisconsin highway: Do not eat urinal cakes.
- On a bag of Fritos: You could be a winner! No purchase necessary. Details inside.
- On some Swanson frozen dinners: Serving suggestion: defrost.
- On Tesco's Tiramisu dessert (printed on bottom of box): Do not turn upside down.
- On Marks & Spencer bread pudding: Product will be hot after heating.
- On packaging for a Rowenta iron: Do not iron clothes on body.
- On Nytol sleeping aid: Warning: May cause drowsiness.

Do Consumers Always Search Rationally?

This assumption of rational search is not always supported. The amount of external search for most products is surprisingly small, even when additional information would most likely benefit the consumer. For example, lower-income shoppers, who have more to lose by making a bad purchase, actually search less prior to buying than do more affluent people.[14]

Like our friend Richard, some consumers typically visit only one or two stores and rarely seek out unbiased information sources prior to making a purchase decision, especially when little time is available to do so.[15] This pattern is especially prevalent for decisions regarding durable goods such as appliances or autos, even when these products represent significant investments. One study of Australian car buyers found that more than a third had made only two or fewer trips to inspect cars prior to buying one.[16]

This tendency to avoid external search is less prevalent when consumers consider the purchase of symbolic items, such as clothing. In those cases, not surprisingly, people tend to do a fair amount of external search, although most of it involves seeking the opinions of peers.[17] Although the stakes may be lower financially, these self-expressive decisions may be seen as having dire social consequences if the wrong choice is made. The level of perceived risk, a concept to be discussed shortly, is high.

In addition, consumers often are observed to engage in *brand switching*, even if their current brand satisfies their needs. For example, researchers for British

This Singaporean beer ad reminds us that not all product decisions are made rationally.

May cause drowsiness, dizzy spells, and vomiting. If affected, carry on. It's normal.

La Guillotine Beer 9·1% Proof. Have a nice coma.

brewer Bass Export who were studying the American beer market discovered a consumer trend toward having a repertoire of two to six favorite brands, rather than sticking to only one. This preference for brand switching led the firm to begin exporting their Tennent's 1885 lager to the United States, positioning the brew as an alternative to young drinkers' usual favorite brands.[18]

Sometimes, it seems that people just plain like to try new things—they are interested in variety seeking, in which the priority is to vary one's product experiences, perhaps as a form of stimulation or to reduce boredom. *Variety seeking* is especially likely to occur when people are in a good mood, or when there is relatively little stimulation elsewhere in their environment.[19] In the case of foods and beverages, variety-seeking can occur due to a phenomenon known as *sensory-specific satiety*. Put simply, this means the pleasantness of a food just eaten drops while the pleasantness of uneaten foods remains unchanged.[20] So even though we have favorites we still like to sample other possibilities. Ironically, consumers actually may switch to less-preferred options for variety's sake even though they enjoy the more familiar option more.[21] On the other hand, when the decision situation is ambiguous or when there is little information about competing brands, consumers tend to opt for the safe choice by selecting familiar brands and maintaining the status quo. Figure 9.4 shows the brand attributes consumers consider most important when choosing among alternatives according to a 1999 survey conducted by *Advertising Age*.

Biases in the Decision-Making Process

Consider the following scenario: You've been given a free ticket to an important football game. At the last minute, though, a sudden snowstorm makes getting to the stadium somewhat dangerous. Would you still go? Now, assume the same game and snowstorm, except this time you paid handsomely for the ticket. Would you head out in the storm in this case?

Analyses of people's responses to this situation and to other similar puzzles illustrates principles of *mental accounting*, in which decisions are influenced by the way a problem is posed (called *framing*), and by whether it is put in terms of gains or losses.[22] In this case, researchers find that people are more likely to risk their personal safety in the storm if they paid for the football ticket. Only the most die-hard fan would fail to recognize that this is an irrational choice, as the risk to the person is the same regardless of whether he or she got a great deal on the ticket. This decision making bias is called the *sunk-cost fallacy*—having paid for something makes us reluctant to waste it.

Another bias is known as *loss aversion*. People place much more emphasis on loss than they do on gain. For example, for most people losing money is more unpleasant than gaining money is pleasant. *Prospect theory*, a descriptive model of choice, finds that utility is a function of gains and losses, and risk differs when the consumer faces options involving gains versus those involving losses.[23]

To illustrate this bias, consider the following choices. For each, would you take the safe bet or choose to gamble?

- Option 1. You're given $30 and then offered a chance to flip a coin: Heads you win $9; tails you lose $9.
- Option 2. You're given a choice of getting $30 outright, or accepting a coin flip that will win you either $39 or $21.

In one study, 70 percent of those given option 1 chose to gamble, compared to just 43 percent of those offered option 2. Yet, the odds are the same for both options! The difference is that people prefer "playing with the house money";

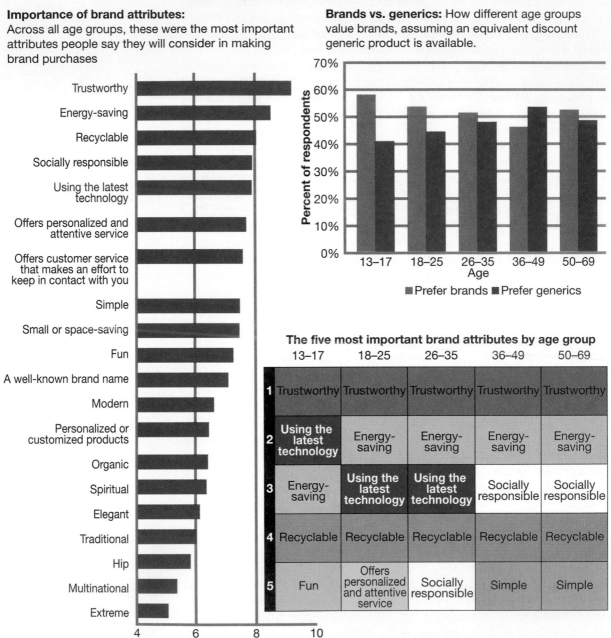

1999 Ad Age/ARC Survey: Brand Attributes

Importance of brand attributes:
Across all age groups, these were the most important attributes people say they will consider in making brand purchases

Brands vs. generics: How different age groups value brands, assuming an equivalent discount generic product is available.

The five most important brand attributes by age group

	13–17	18–25	26–35	36–49	50–69
1	Trustworthy	Trustworthy	Trustworthy	Trustworthy	Trustworthy
2	Using the latest technology	Energy-saving	Energy-saving	Energy-saving	Energy-saving
3	Energy-saving	Using the latest technology	Using the latest technology	Socially responsible	Socially responsible
4	Recyclable	Recyclable	Recyclable	Recyclable	Recyclable
5	Fun	Offers personalized and attentive service	Socially responsible	Simple	Simple

Figure 9.4
Ad Age Poll: Importance of Brand Attributes

they are more willing to take risks when they perceive they're using someone else's resources. So, contrary to a rational decision-making perspective, we value money differently depending on where it comes from. This explains, for example, why someone might choose to blow a big bonus on some frivolous purchase, but they would never consider taking that same amount out of their savings account for this purpose.

Finally, research in mental accounting demonstrates that extraneous characteristics of the choice situation can influence our selections, even though they wouldn't if we were totally rational decision makers. As one example, participants in a survey were provided with one of two versions of this scenario:

> You are lying on the beach on a hot day. All you have to drink is ice water. For the last hour you have been thinking about how much you would enjoy a nice cold bottle of your favorite brand of beer. A companion gets up to go make a phone call and offers to bring back a beer from the only nearby place where beer is sold (either a fancy resort hotel or a small, run-down grocery store, depending on the version you're given). He says that the beer might be expensive and so asks how much you are willing to pay for it. . . . What price do you tell him?

In this survey, the median price given by participants who were in the fancy resort version was $2.65, but those given the grocery store version were only willing to pay $1.50! In both versions the consumption act is the same, the beer is the same, and no "atmosphere" is consumed because the beer is being brought back to the beach.[24] So much for rational decision making!

How Much Search Occurs?

As a general rule, search activity is greater when the purchase is important, when there is a need to learn more about the purchase, and/or when the relevant information is easily obtained and utilized.[25] Consumers differ in the amount of search they tend to undertake, regardless of the product category in question. All things being equal, younger, better-educated people who enjoy the shopping/fact-finding process tend to conduct more information search. Women are more inclined to search than men are, as are those who place greater value on style and the image they present.[26]

The Consumer's Prior Expertise

Should prior product knowledge make it more or less likely that consumers will engage in search? Products experts and novices use very different procedures during decision making. Novices, who know little about a product, should be the most motivated to find out more about it. However, experts are more familiar with the product category, so they should be able to better understand the meaning of any new product information they might acquire.

So, who searches more? The answer is neither: Search tends to be greatest among those consumers who are *moderately knowledgeable* about the product. There is an inverted-U relationship between knowledge and external search effort, as shown in Figure 9.5. People with very limited expertise may not feel they are capable of searching extensively. In fact, they may not even know where to start. Richard, who did not spend a lot of time researching his purchase, is representative of this situation. He visited one store, and he only looked at brands with which he was already familiar. In addition, he focused on only a small number of product features.[27]

The *type* of search undertaken by people with varying levels of expertise differs as well. Because experts have a better sense of what information is relevant to the decision, they tend to engage in *selective search*, which means their efforts are more focused and efficient. In contrast, novices are more likely to rely on the opinions of others and to rely on "nonfunctional" attributes, such as brand name and price, to distinguish among alternatives. They may also process information in a "top-down" rather than a "bottom-up" manner, focusing less on details than on the big picture. For instance, they may be more impressed by the sheer amount

Figure 9.5
The Relationship between Amount
of Information Search and Product
Knowledge

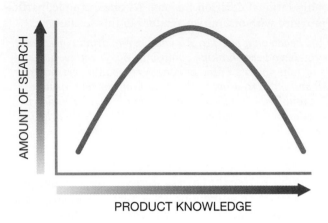

of technical information presented in an ad than by the actual significance of the claims made.[28]

Perceived Risk

As a rule, purchase decisions that involve extensive search also entail some kind of *perceived risk,* or the belief that the product has potentially negative consequences. Perceived risk may be present if the product is expensive or is complex and hard to understand. Alternatively, perceived risk can be a factor when a product choice is visible to others and we run the risk of embarrassment if the wrong choice is made.

Figure 9.6 lists five kinds of risk—including both objective (e.g., physical danger) and subjective factors (e.g., social embarrassment)—as well as the products that tend to be affected by each type. As this figure notes, consumers with greater "risk capital" are less affected by perceived risks associated with the products. For example, a highly self-confident person would be less worried about the social risk inherent in a product, whereas a more vulnerable, insecure consumer might be reluctant to take a chance on a product that might not be accepted by peers.

EVALUATION OF ALTERNATIVES

Much of the effort that goes into a purchase decision occurs at the stage in which a choice must be made from the available alternatives. After all, modern consumer society abounds with choices. In some cases, there may literally be hundreds of different brands (as in cigarettes) or different variations of the same brand (as in shades of lipstick), each screaming for our attention.

Just for fun, ask a friend to name all of the brands of perfume she can think of. The odds are she will reel off three to five names rather quickly, then stop and think awhile before coming up with a few more. It is likely that the first set of brands are those with which she is highly familiar, and she probably wears one or more of these. The list may also contain one or two brands that she does not like and would perhaps like to forget. Note also that there are many, many more brands on the market she did not name at all.

If your friend were to go to the store to buy perfume, it is likely that she would consider buying some or most of the brands she listed initially. She might

MARKETING PITFALLS

TRAVELING BY AIRPLANE IS far safer than other forms of transportation, yet airlines virtually never remind us of the relative safety of air travel for fear of arousing anxieties about flying. Recently, Airbus Industrie broke this taboo by focusing on risk to tout the superiority of its four-engine planes over other models that have only two engines. A print ad showed an Airbus A340 plane flying in ominous skies over dark waters and the caption read, "If you're over the middle of the Pacific, you want to be in the middle of four engines." Needless to say, others in the industry were not pleased by this tactic. An executive of a rival airplane manufacturer wrote, "You exploit the unfounded fears of the traveling public."[29]

Figure 9.6
Five Types of Perceived Risk

	BUYERS MOST SENSITIVE TO RISK	PURCHASES MOST SUBJECT TO RISK
MONETARY RISK	Risk capital consists of money and property. Those with relatively little income and wealth are most vulnerable.	High-ticket items that require substantial expenditures are most subject to this form of risk.
FUNCTIONAL RISK	Risk capital consists of alternative means of performing the function or meeting the need. Practical consumers are most sensitive.	Products or services whose purchase and use requires the buyer's exclusive commitment are most sensitive.
PHYSICAL RISK	Risk capital consists of physical vigor, health, and vitality. Those who are elderly, frail, or in ill health are most vulnerable.	Mechanical or electrical goods (such as vehicles or flammables), drugs and medical treatment, and food and beverages are most sensitive.
SOCIAL RISK	Risk capital consists of self-esteem and self-confidence. Those who are insecure and uncertain are most sensitive.	Socially visible or symbolic goods, such as clothes, jewelry, cars, homes, or sports equipment are most subject to social risk.
PSYCHO-LOGICAL RISK	Risk capital consists of affiliations and status. Those lacking self-respect or attractiveness to peers are most sensitive.	Expensive personal luxuries that may engender guilt; durables; and services whose use demands self-discipline or sacrifice are most sensitive.

also consider a few more possibilities if these were forcefully brought to her attention while at the store—for example, if she is "ambushed" by a representative who is spraying scent samples on shoppers, which is a common occurrence in some department stores.

Identifying Alternatives

How do we decide which criteria are important, and how do we narrow down product alternatives to an acceptable number and eventually choose one instead of others? The answer varies depending on the decision-making process used. A consumer engaged in extended problem solving may carefully evaluate several brands, whereas someone making a habitual decision may not consider any alternatives to their normal brand. Furthermore, some evidence indicates that more extended processing occurs in situations in which negative emotions are aroused due to conflicts among the choices available. This is most likely to occur where difficult tradeoffs are involved, as when a person must choose between the risk involved in undergoing a bypass operation versus the potential improvement in his or her life if the operation is successful.[30]

Minolta features a no-risk guarantee as a way to reduce the perceived risk in buying an office copier.

The alternatives actively considered during a consumer's choice process are his or her evoked set. The **evoked set** comprises those products already in memory (the retrieval set), plus those prominent in the retail environment. For example, recall that Richard did not know much about the technical aspects of television sets, and he had only a few major brands in memory. Of these, two were acceptable possibilities and one was not. The alternatives that the consumer is aware of but would not consider buying are his or her **inert set,** whereas those not entering the game at all comprise the **inept set.** You can easily guess in which set a marketer wants its brand to appear! These categories are depicted in Figure 9.7.

Consumers often include a surprisingly small number of alternatives in their evoked set. One study combined results from several large-scale investigations of consumers' evoked sets and found that the number of products included in these sets is limited, although there are some marked variations by product category

Figure 9.7
Identifying Alternatives: Getting in the Game

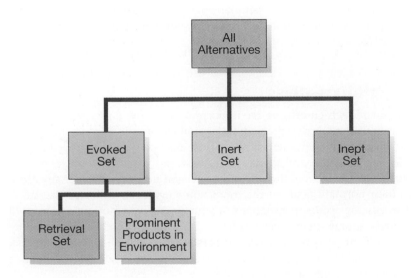

and across countries. For example, the average evoked set size for American beer consumers was fewer than three, whereas Canadian consumers typically considered seven brands. In contrast, whereas auto buyers in Norway studied two alternatives, American consumers on average looked at more than eight models before making a decision.[31]

For obvious reasons, a marketer who finds that her or his brand is not in the evoked set of target market has cause to worry. A product is not likely to be placed in the evoked set after it has previously been considered and rejected. Indeed, a new brand is more likely to be added to the evoked set than is an existing brand that was previously considered but passed over, even after additional positive information has been provided for that brand.[32] For marketers, consumers' unwillingness to give a rejected product a second chance underscores the importance of ensuring that it performs well from the time it is introduced.

Product Categorization

Remember that when consumers process product information, they do not do so in a vacuum. Instead, a product stimulus is evaluated in terms of what people already know about a product or things to which it is similar. A person evaluating a particular 35-mm camera will most likely compare it to other 35-mm cameras rather than to a Polaroid camera, and the consumer would certainly not compare it to a slide projector or VCR. Because the category in which a product is placed determines the other products it will be compared to, *categorization* is a crucial determinant of how a product is evaluated.

The products in a consumer's evoked set are likely to be those that share some similar features. It is important to understand how this knowledge is represented in a consumer's **cognitive structure,** which refers to a set of factual knowledge about products (i.e., beliefs) and the way these beliefs are organized in people's minds.[33] These knowledge structures were discussed in Chapter 4. One reason is that marketers want to ensure that their products are correctly grouped. For example, General Foods brought out a new line of Jell-O flavors, such as Cranberry Orange, that it called Jell-O Gelatin Flavors for Salads. Unfortunately, the company discovered that people would use it only for salad, because the name encouraged them to put the product in their "salad" structure rather than in their "dessert" structure. The product line was dropped.[34]

Levels of Categorization

People group things into categories that occur at different levels of specificity. Typically, a product is represented in a cognitive structure at one of three levels. To understand this idea, consider how someone might respond to these questions about an ice cream cone: What other products share similar characteristics, and which would be considered as alternatives to eating a cone?

These questions may be more complex than they first appear. At one level, a cone is similar to an apple, because both could be eaten as a dessert. At another level, a cone is similar to a piece of pie, because both are eaten for dessert and both are fattening. At still another level, a cone is similar to an ice cream sundae—both are eaten for dessert, are made of ice cream, and are fattening.

It is easy to see that the items a person associates with, say, the category "fattening dessert" influence the choices he or she will make for what to eat after dinner. The middle level, known as a *basic level category*, is typically the most useful in classifying products, because items grouped together tend to have a lot

Figure 9.8
Levels of Abstraction in
Dessert Categories

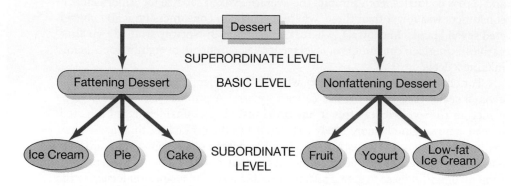

in common with each other but still permit a range of alternatives to be considered. The broader *superordinate category* is more abstract, whereas the more specific *subordinate category* often includes individual brands.[35] These three levels are depicted in Figure 9.8.

Of course, not all items fit equally well into a category. Apple pie is a better example of the subordinate category "pie" than is rhubarb pie, even though both are types of pies. Apple pie is more *prototypical,* and would tend to be considered first, especially by category novices. In contrast, pie experts will tend to have knowledge about both typical and atypical category examples.[36]

Strategic Implications of Product Categorization

Product categorization has many strategic implications. The way a product is grouped with others has very important ramifications for determining both its competitors for adoption and what criteria will be used to make this choice.

Product Positioning. The success of a *positioning strategy* often hinges on the marketer's ability to convince the consumer that his or her product should be considered within a given category. For example, the orange juice industry tried to reposition orange juice as a drink that could be enjoyed all day long ("It's not just for breakfast anymore.") On the other hand, soft drink companies are now attempting the opposite by portraying sodas as suitable for breakfast consumption. They are trying to make their way into consumers' "breakfast drink" category, along with orange juice, grapefruit juice, and coffee. Of course, this strategy can backfire, as Pepsi-Cola discovered when it introduced Pepsi A.M. and positioned it as a coffee substitute. The company did such a good job of categorizing the drink as a morning beverage that customers wouldn't drink it at any other time, and the product failed.[37]

Identifying Competitors. At the abstract, superordinate level, many different product forms compete for membership. The category "entertainment" might comprise both bowling and the ballet, but not many people would consider the substitution of one of these activities for the other. Products and services that on the surface are quite different, however, actually compete with each other at a broad level for consumers' discretionary dollars. Although bowling or ballet may not be a likely trade-off for many people, it is feasible, for example, that a symphony might try to lure away season ticket holders to the ballet by positioning itself as an equivalent member of the category "cultural event."[38]

Consumers are often faced with choices between noncomparable categories, in which a number of attributes exist that cannot be directly related to one

S'alternative.

This ad for Sunkist lemon juice attempts to establish a new category for the product by repositioning it as a salt substitute.

another (the old problem of comparing apples and oranges). The comparison process is easier when consumers can derive an overlapping category that encompasses both items (e.g., entertainment, value, usefulness) and then rate each alternative in terms of that superordinate category.[39]

Exemplar Products. As we saw with the case of apple pie versus rhubarb, if a product is a really good example of a category it is more familiar to consumers and is more easily recognized and recalled.[40] Judgments about category attributes tend to be disproportionately influenced by the characteristics of category exemplars.[41] In a sense, brands that are strongly associated with a category get to "call the shots" by defining the criteria that should be used to evaluate all category members.

Being a bit less than prototypical is not necessarily a bad thing, however. Products that are moderately unusual within their product category may stimulate more information processing and positive evaluations, because they are neither so familiar that they will be taken for granted nor so discrepant that they will be dismissed.[42] A brand that is strongly discrepant (such as Zima, a clear malt beverage) may occupy a unique niche position, whereas those that are moderately discrepant (e.g., local microbrews) remain in a distinct position within the general category.[43]

Locating Products. Product categorization also can affect consumers' expectations regarding the places they can locate a desired product. If products do not clearly fit into categories (e.g., is a rug furniture?), consumers' ability to find them or make sense of them may be diminished. For instance, a frozen dog food that had to be thawed and cooked failed in the market, partly because people could not adapt to the idea of buying dog food in the "frozen foods for people" section of their grocery stores.

PRODUCT CHOICE: SELECTING AMONG ALTERNATIVES

Once the relevant options from a category have been assembled and evaluated, a choice must be made among them.[44] Recall that the decision rules guiding choice can range from very simple and quick strategies to complicated processes requiring much attention and cognitive processing. The choice can be influenced by integrating information from sources such as prior experience with the product or a similar one, information present at the time of purchase, and beliefs about the brands that have been created by advertising.[45]

Evaluative Criteria

When Richard was looking at different television sets, he focused on one or two product features and completely ignored several others. He narrowed down his choices by only considering two specific brand names, and from the Prime Wave and Precision models, he chose one that featured stereo capability.

Evaluative criteria are the dimensions used to judge the merits of competing options. In comparing alternative products, Richard could have chosen from among any number of criteria, ranging from very functional attributes ("does this TV come with remote control?") to experiential ones ("does this TV's sound reproduction make me imagine I'm in a concert hall?").

Another important point is that criteria on which products *differ* from one another carry more weight in the decision process than do those where the alternatives are *similar*. If all brands being considered rate equally well on one attribute (e.g., if all TVs come with remote control), consumers will have to find other reasons to choose one over another. The attributes actually used to differentiate among choices are *determinant attributes.*

Marketers can play a role in educating consumers about which criteria should be used as determinant attributes. For example, consumer research by Church & Dwight indicated that many consumers view the use of natural ingredients as a determinant attribute. The result was promotion of a toothpaste made from baking soda, which the company already manufactured for Church & Dwight's Arm & Hammer brand.[46] And sometimes, the company can even invent a determinant attribute: Pepsi-Cola accomplished this by stamping freshness dates on soda cans. The company spent about $25 million on an advertising and promotional campaign to convince consumers that there's nothing quite as horrible as a stale can of soda—even though it has been estimated that 98 percent of all cans are consumed well before this could be a problem. Six months after introducing the campaign, an independent survey found that 61 percent of respondents felt that freshness dating is an important attribute for a soft drink![47]

The decision about which attributes to use is the result of *procedural learning,* in which a person undergoes a series of cognitive steps before making a choice. These steps include identifying important attributes, remembering whether competing brands differ on those attributes, and so on. In order for a marketer to effectively recommend a new decision criterion, its communication should convey three pieces of information:[48]

1. It should point out that there are significant differences among brands on the attribute.
2. It should supply the consumer with a decision-making rule, such as if (deciding among competing brands), *then* . . . (use the attribute as a criterion).
3. It should convey a rule that can be easily integrated with how the person has made this decision in the past. Otherwise, the recommendation is likely to be ignored because it requires too much mental work.

Cybermediaries

As anyone who's ever typed a phrase like "home theaters" into a search engine knows, the Web delivers enormous amounts of product and retailer information in seconds. In fact, the biggest problem surfers face these days is narrowing down their choices, not beefing them up. In cyberspace, simplification is key. Some people even use Web filters like intermute.com to remove soundtracks, pop-up frames, and other distractions from the sites they find.

With the tremendous number of Web sites available, and the huge number of people surfing the Web each day, how can people organize information and decide where to click? One type of business that is growing to meet this demand is called a **cybermediary.** This is an intermediary that helps to filter and organize online market information so that customers can identify and evaluate alternatives more efficiently.[49] Cybermediaries take different forms.[50]

Directories and *portals* such as Yahoo or fashionmall.com are general services that tie together a large variety of different sites.

Web site evaluators reduce the risk to consumers by reviewing sites and recommending the best ones. For example, Point Communications selects sites that it designates as Top 5 percent of the Web.

Forums, fan clubs, and user groups offer product-related discussions to help customers sift through options (more on these in Chapter 11). Other sites like about.com help to narrow alternatives by actually connecting you with human guides that make recommendations. This approach is especially prevalent in the travel industry, in which several sites now connect surfers to travel experts (often volunteers who just like to share their expertise about travel). These sites include Allexperts.com, BootsnAll.com, and Exp.com.

Financial intermediaries authorize payments from buyer to seller. Payment systems include electronic equivalents to writing checks (Checkfree), paying in cash (Digicash), and sending secure electronic mail authorizing a payment (First Virtual).

Intelligent agents are sophisticated software programs that use *collaborative filtering* technologies to learn from past user behavior in order to recommend new purchases. For example, when you let Amazon.com suggest a new book, it's using an intelligent agent to propose novels based on what you and others like you have bought in the past. This approach was introduced in 1995 (the Stone Age in Web time!) by Firefly to make recommendations for taste-based products such as music, books, and films.[51] Now, a variety of "shopping bots" are available to act as online purchasing shopping agents, including clickthebutton.com, mysimon.com, and dealtime.com. Collaborative filtering is still in its infancy. In the next few years, expect to see many new Web-based methods to simplify the consumer decision-making process. Now if only someone could come up with an easier way to pay for all the great stuff you find courtesy of shopping bots!

Heuristics: Mental Shortcuts

Do we actually perform complex mental calculations every time we make a purchase decision? Get a life! To simplify decisions, consumers often employ decision rules that allow them to use some dimensions as substitutes for others. For example, Richard relied on certain assumptions as substitutes for prolonged information search. In particular, he assumed the selection at Zany Zack's would be more than sufficient, so he did not bother to shop any of Zack's competitors. This assumption served as a shortcut to more extended information processing.[52]

Consumers often simplify choices by using heuristics such as automatically choosing a favorite color or brand.

Especially when limited problem solving occurs prior to making a choice, consumers often fall back on **heuristics,** or mental rules-of-thumb that lead to a speedy decision. These rules range from the very general (e.g., "Higher-priced products are higher-quality products" or "Buy the same brand I bought last time") to the very specific (e.g., "Buy Domino, the brand of sugar my mother always bought").[53]

Sometimes these shortcuts may not be in consumers' best interests. A consumer who personally knows one or two people who have had problems with a particular make of car, for example, might assume he or she would have similar trouble with it and thus overlook the model's overall excellent repair record.[54] The influence of such assumptions may be enhanced if the product has an unusual name, which makes it and the experiences with it more distinctive.[55]

Relying on a Product Signal

One frequently used shortcut is the tendency to infer hidden dimensions of products from observable attributes. The aspect of the product that is visible acts as a *signal* of some underlying quality. Such inferences explain why someone trying to sell a used car takes great pains to be sure the car's exterior is clean and shiny: Potential buyers often judge the vehicle's mechanical condition by its appearance, even though this means they may drive away in a shiny, clean clunker.[56]

When product information is incomplete, judgments are often derived from beliefs about *covariation,* or perceived associations among events that may or may not actually influence one another.[57] For example, a consumer may form an association between product quality and the length of time a manufacturer has been in business. Other signals or attributes believed to coexist with good or bad products include well-known brand names, country of origin, price, and the retail outlets that carry the product.

Unfortunately, consumers tend to be poor estimators of covariation. Their beliefs persist despite evidence to the contrary. In a process similar to the consistency principle discussed in Chapter 7, people tend to see what they are looking for. They will look for product information that confirms their guesses. In one experiment, consumers sampled four sets of products to determine if price and quality were related. Those who believed in this relationship prior to the study elected to sample higher-priced products, thus creating a sort of self-fulfilling prophecy.[58]

Market Beliefs: Is It Better if I Pay More for It?

Consumers often form assumptions about companies, products, and stores. These **market beliefs** then become the shortcuts that guide their decisions—whether or not they are accurate.[59] Recall, for instance, that Richard chose to shop at a large "electronics supermarket" because he *assumed* the selection would be better there than at a specialty store. A large number of market beliefs have been identified. Some of these are listed in Table 9.3. How many do you share?

Do higher prices mean higher quality? The assumption of a *price-quality relationship* is one of the most pervasive market beliefs.[60] Novice consumers may in fact consider price as the only relevant product attribute. Experts also consider this information, although in these cases price tends to be used for its informational value, especially for products (e.g., virgin wool) that are known to have wide quality variations in the marketplace. When this quality level is more standard or strictly regulated (e.g., Harris Tweed sport coats), experts do not weigh price in their decisions. For the most part, this belief is justified; you do tend to

TABLE 9.3	Common Market Beliefs

Brand	All brands are basically the same.
	Generic products are just name brands sold under a different label at a lower price.
	The best brands are the ones that are purchased the most.
	When in doubt, a national brand is always a safe bet.
Store	Speciality stores are great places to familiarize yourself with the best brands; but once you figure out what you want, it's cheaper to buy it at a discount outlet.
	A store's character is reflected in its window displays.
	Salespeople in specialty stores are more knowledgeable than other sales personnel.
	Larger stores offer better prices than small stores.
	Locally owned stores give the best service.
	A store that offers a good value on one of its products probably offers good values on all of its items.
	Credit and return policies are most lenient at large department stores.
	Stores that have just opened usually charge attractive prices.
Prices/Discounts/Sales	Sales are typically run to get rid of slow-moving merchandise.
	Stores that are constantly having sales don't really save you money.
	Within a given store, higher prices generally indicate higher quality.
Advertising and Sales Promotion	"Hard-sell" advertising is associated with low-quality products.
	Items tied to "giveaways" are not a good value (even with the freebee).
	Coupons represent real savings for customers because they are not offered by the store.
	When you buy heavily advertised products, you are paying for the label, not for higher quality.
Product/Packaging	Largest-sized containers are almost always cheaper per unit than smaller sizes.
	New products are more expensive when they're first introduced; prices tend to settle down as time goes by.
	When you are not sure what you need in a product, it's a good idea to invest in the extra features, because you'll probably wish you had them later.
	In general, synthetic goods are lower in quality than goods made of natural materials.
	It's advisable to stay away from products when they are new to the market; it usually takes the manufacturer a little time to work the bugs out.

SOURCE: Adapted from Calvin P. Duncan, "Consumer Market Beliefs: A Review of the Literature and an Agenda for Future Research," in Marvin E. Goldberg, Gerald Gorn, and Richard W. Pollay, eds., *Advances in Consumer Research* 17 (Provo, UT: Association for Consumer Research, 1990): 729–35.

get what you pay for. However, let the buyer beware: The price–quality relationship is not always justified.[61]

Country-of-Origin as a Product Signal

Modern consumers choose among products made in many countries. Americans may buy Brazilian shoes, Japanese cars, clothing imported from Taiwan, or microwave ovens built in South Korea. Consumers' reactions to these imports are mixed. In some cases, people have come to assume that a product made overseas is of better quality (e.g., cameras, cars), whereas in other cases the knowledge that a product has been imported tends to lower perceptions of product quality (e.g., apparel).[62] In general, people tend to rate their own country's products more favorably than do people who live elsewhere, and products from industrialized countries are rated better than are those from developing countries. Roper Starch Worldwide interviewed 30,000 customers in 30 countries regarding their feelings about different cultures around the world.[63] The firm categorized people in terms of their attachment to their own culture versus affinity for other cultures. Among the segments identified were:

- Nationalists (26 percent of the sample): They feel close to their own culture, and their key personal values include duty, respect for ancestors, status, and social stability. These consumers tend to be somewhat older and are likely to be either female homemakers or blue-collar men.

- Internationalists (15 percent of the sample): They feel close to three or more outside cultures. Their key personal values include open-mindedness, learning, creativity, and freedom. They are more likely to be male, well-educated, and upscale.
- Disengaged (7 percent of the sample): These people did not feel great attachment to any culture, including their own. They are bored and disenchanted, and tend to be younger and less educated.

A product's *country-of-origin* in some cases is an important piece of information in the decision-making process.[64] Certain items are strongly associated with specific countries, and products from those countries often attempt to benefit from these linkages. Country-of-origin can function as a *stereotype*—a knowledge structure based on inferences across products. These stereotypes are often biased or inaccurate, but they do play a constructive role in simplifying complex choice situations.[65] Recent evidence indicates that learning of a product's country-of-origin is not necessarily good or bad. Instead, it has the effect of stimulating the consumer's interest in the product to a greater degree. The purchaser thinks more extensively about the product and evaluates it more carefully.[66] The origin of the product thus can act as a product attribute that combines with other attributes to influence evaluations.[67] In addition, the consumer's own expertise with the product category moderates the effects of this attribute. When other information is available, experts tend to ignore country-of-origin information, whereas novices continue to rely on it. However, when other information is unavailable or ambiguous, both experts and novices will rely on this attribute to make a decision.[68]

The tendency to prefer products or people of one's own culture over those from other countries is called **ethnocentrism.** Ethnocentric consumers are likely to feel it is wrong to buy products from other countries, particularly because of the

The growing popularity of faux Irish pubs around the world attests to the power of country stereotypes to influence consumers' preferences. About 800 Irish-themed pubs have been opened in countries including South Africa, Italy, Hong Kong, and Russia. The Irish brewer Guinness PLC encourages the establishment of these outputs, since an Irish pub is mere blarney without Guinness on tap. The company helps owners design the pub and even assists in locating Irish bar staff to dispense its thick brew. As one Guinness executive explained, "We've created a mythology of an Irish ambience."[69] Since Guinness launched its Irish Pub Concept in 1992 it has helped over 1,250 entrepreneurs in 36 countries establish their own Irish pubs. Aspiring Publicans can choose from five pre-set designs: Victorian Dublin, Irish Brewery Pub, Irish Pub Shop, Irish Country Cottage, or Gaelic.

negative effect this may have on the domestic economy. Marketing campaigns stressing the desirability of "buying American" are more likely to appeal to this consumer segment. This trait has been measured on The Consumer Ethnocentrism Scale (CETSCALE) that was devised for this purpose: The scale identifies ethnocentric consumers by their extent of agreement with items such as:

- purchasing foreign-made products is un-American,
- curbs should be put on all imports,
- American consumers who purchase products made in other countries are responsible for putting their fellow Americans out of work.[70]

Choosing Familiar Brand Names: Loyalty or Habit?

Branding is a marketing strategy that often functions as a heuristic. People form preferences for a favorite brand, and then they literally may never change their minds in the course of a lifetime. In a study by the Boston Consulting Group of the market leaders in 30 product categories, it was found that 27 of the brands that were number one in 1930 remain at the top today. These include such perennial favorites as Ivory Soap, Campbell's Soup, and Gold Medal Flour.[73] A major study on brand loyalty commissioned by the WPP Group of advertising agencies surveyed 70,000 consumers in seven world markets and assigned "bonding scores" to brands based on the percentage of respondents who said they had formed an attachment to the brand. In the U.S., Gerber led the pack with a 56 percent score, British Telecom won the day for the United Kingdom, and Lufthansa prevailed in Germany.[74]

A brand commanding fierce loyalty is treasured by marketers, and for good reason. Brands that dominate their markets are as much as 50 percent more profitable than their nearest competitors.[75] Small wonder, then, that companies work very hard to cultivate loyalty. When the Disney Channel failed to appear on Teenage Research Unlimited's survey of the 50 coolest teen brands, the company tried to spice up its image to attract a loyal adolescent following. The channel began to play music videos—even if it meant doctoring some of the lyrics to maintain its clean-cut image. For example, the lyrics to "Genie in a Bottle" by Christina Aguilera were changed from "My body's saying let's go" to "My friends are saying let's go," and "I'm a genie in a bottle, baby, you gotta rub me the right way" became "You gotta treat me the right way."[76] Some efforts to command loyalty are more straightforward, as when Internet Service Providers (ISPs) such as Prodigy and AOL's Compuserve give $400 price cuts on PCs at selected retailers in a deliberate effort to attract a following.[77]

Inertia: The Lazy Customer

Many people tend to buy the same brand just about every time they go to the store. This consistent pattern is often due to **inertia**—a brand is bought out of habit merely because less effort is required. If another product comes along that is for some reason easier to buy (e.g., it is cheaper or the original product is out of stock), the consumer will not hesitate to do so. A competitor who is trying to change a buying pattern based on inertia often can do so rather easily, because little resistance to brand switching will be encountered if the right incentive is offered. When there is little to no underlying commitment to a particular brand, promotional tools such as point-of-purchase displays, extensive couponing, or noticeable price reductions may be sufficient to "unfreeze" a consumer's habitual pattern.

MULTICULTURAL DIMENSIONS

MANY CANADIANS ARE concerned about the dilution of their culture due to the strong U.S. influence, and a backlash is building. According to the Ministry of Canadian Heritage, foreign sources account for 95 percent of movies screened and 83 percent of magazines sold. In a recent poll, 25 percent of the country's citizens identified "life, liberty, and the pursuit of happiness" as a Canadian constitutional slogan rather than an American one.[71] There is a movement afoot to require theaters to offer a fixed share of Canadian movie and to label music as a "Canadian selection" if the music or lyrics are performed by a Canadian or if a live performance was recorded in Canada.

Canadian nationalism was stoked by a recent commercial for Molson Canadian beer called "The Rant" that almost overnight became an unofficial anthem in Canada. A flannel-shirted young Canadian walks onto a stage and calmly begins explaining away Canadian stereotypes: "I'm not a lumberjack or a fur trader. I don't live in an igloo or eat blubber or own a dog sled. . . . My name is Joe and I . . . AM . . . CANADIAN! . . ." The spot debuted during the 2000 Oscar ceremony following a dance routine for the song "Blame Canada" from the "South Park" movie (it's only shown in Canada). The actor in the commecial performs the rant across the country during hockey game intermissions. In six weeks after the ad started airing, the Molson brand gained almost two points in market share.[72]

Brand Loyalty: A "Friend," Tried-and-True

This kind of fickleness will not occur if true **brand loyalty** exists. In contrast to inertia, brand loyalty is a form of repeat purchasing behavior reflecting a conscious decision to continue buying the same brand.[78] For brand loyalty to exist, a pattern of repeat purchase must be accompanied by an underlying positive attitude toward the brand. Brand loyalty may be initiated by customer preference based on objective reasons, but after the brand has been around for a long time and is heavily advertised it can also engender an emotional attachment, either by being incorporated into the consumer's self-image or because it is associated with prior experiences.[79] Purchase decisions based on brand loyalty also become habitual over time, though in these cases the underlying commitment to the product is much firmer.

Compared to an inertia situation in which the consumer passively accepts a brand, a brand-loyal consumer is actively (sometimes passionately) involved with his or her favorite. Because of the emotional bonds that can come about between brand-loyal consumers and products, "true-blue" users react more vehemently when these products are altered, redesigned, or eliminated.[80] For example, when Coca-Cola replaced its tried-and-true formula with New Coke in the 1980s, a firestorm of national call-in campaigns, boycotts, and other protests occurred.

In recent years, marketers have struggled with the problem of *brand parity*, which refers to consumers' beliefs that there are no significant differences among brands. For example, one survey found that more than 70 percent of consumers worldwide believe that all paper towels, soaps, and snack chips are alike.[81] Some analysts even proclaimed that brand names are dead, killed off by private label or generic products that offer the same value for less money.

However, the reports of this death appear to be premature—major brands are making a comeback. This renaissance is attributed to information overload—with too many alternatives (many of them unfamiliar names) to choose from, people are looking for a few clear signals of quality. Following a period in the late 1980s and early 1990s when people had strong doubts about the ability of large companies to produce quality products, more recent surveys indicate consumers slowly are beginning to trust major manufacturers again.[82] Brand names are very much alive in the new millennium.

Decision Rules

Consumers consider sets of product attributes by using different rules, depending on the complexity of the decision and the importance of the decision to them. As we have seen, in some cases these rules are quite simple: People simply rely on a "shortcut" to make a choice. In other cases, though, more effort and thought is put into carefully weighing alternatives before coming to a decision.

One way to differentiate among decision rules is to divide them into those that are *compensatory* versus those that are *noncompensatory*. To aid the discussion of some of these rules, the attributes of TV sets considered by Richard are summarized in Table 9.4. Now, let's see how some of these rules result in different brand choices.

Noncompensatory Decision Rules

Simple decision rules are noncompensatory, meaning that a product with a low standing on one attribute cannot make up for this position by being better on another attribute. In other words, people simply eliminate all options that do not

REALITY CHECK

THINK OF A PRODUCT YOU RECENTLY SHOPPED for online. Describe your search process. How did you become aware you wanted/ needed the product? How did you evaluate alternatives? Did you wind up buying online? Why or why not? What factors would make it more or less likely that you would buy something online versus in a traditional store?

The most recent product I have shopped for on-line is cosmetics. The cosmetics company allows people to customize products to their individual needs. It was easy to get to the web page, but the process consumers had to undergo in order to begin to customize the products was long and I felt it was unnecessary. I did not wind up purchasing any products from the company because I got tired of filling out the questionnaire they required first-time users to fill out.

Sara Rast
Southwest Missouri State University

Recently, I was in dire need for some clothes. Being fully aware that some clothing companies offer special discounts and clearance items via their website, I decided to surf the web and peruse various websites. However, before I purchased anything, I had to analyze the disadvantageous contributing factors that have significant impact on online shopping. I felt a bit skeptical placing my credit card number onto the company's website. In addition, some other disadvantageous factors with online purchasing include size discrepancies, shipping charges, and unknown delivery dates. Once my insecurities of my personal credit confidentiality subsided, I decided to purchase online. Overall, the process was simple and less time consuming than traditional retail shopping. Since then, my preferred method of shopping is online.

Eric Jude Guacena
Virginia Commonwealth University

I am still afraid of buying something online because I can not trust it. In Japan, people do not use credit cards as much as Americans do, I think that is one factor too. When I went to America, I was surprised that people buy Christmas presents from the catalog. I think Americans are more used to shopping online because they are used to shopping from the catalog. . . . Also I am living alone, so I can not stay home when the package arrives. Buying might be simple if you use the web, but receiving is difficult.

Mai Sasaki
Keio University, Japan

Personally, I enjoy seeing what I'm going to buy, checking to see if the products are fresh, if the size and shape are really what I want. I also like to see the new products that are available. Sometimes I walk into the grocery store not knowing what I want to buy or what I want to cook for dinner, but I usually get ideas by walking around and smelling the fresh baked French bread.

Liana Mouynes
University of Washington

I decided to purchase two dozen roses to make corsages for a family event. After searching the local phone book and making several phone calls for pricing, I decided that perhaps an online retailer could provide a lower price. I first used a consumer search engine to look for "fresh flowers." After finding several websites that could offer me wonderful opportunities to have beautiful bouquets delivered anywhere in the world, I decided my search was too vague. I then searched three different search engines for "bulk fresh flowers" and "wholesale fresh flowers." I was able to pinpoint three significant retailers that allowed me to custom order the number of and type of flowers I desired.

I then viewed each of the websites and compared pricing and shipping charges. After finding the least costly retailer, I placed my order. Unfortunately, the website did not provide clear instructions for shipping and phoned me 24 hours later, alerting me that my order could not be shipped immediately. I needed the order to be delivered overnight, so the order was canceled.

I was upset that my order had to be canceled. I had chosen to place my order online for two reasons: to find a less costly alternative to a local retailer and to have my order delivered in a timely manner. I will continue to purchase online from other retailers in the future if instructions for shipping and pricing are clearly defined for me.

Jessica Wells
Utah State University

I know I could buy on the Net everything I need in my daily life (food, leisure, clothes . . .) but I rarely do. I have not integrated Internet as a shopping alternative.

Astrid Spielrein
ASSAS University Paris II, France

I never have bought online. I'm not interested. If I go shopping I want to go out and see. Not to stay seated on a chair, in front of my computer waiting for offers.

Giselle Gonzalez Aybar
Pontificia Universidad Catolica Madre Y maestra, Dominican Republic

meet some basic standards. A consumer such as Richard who uses the decision rule, "Only buy well-known brand names," would not consider a new brand, even if it was equal or superior to existing ones. When people are less familiar with

What's your opinion? Check out the on-line polls at www.prenhall.com/ myphlip. Just follow the little person in the lab coat.

TABLE 9.4   Hypothetical Alternatives for a TV Set

| Attribute | Importance Ranking | Brand Ratings | | |
		Prime Wave	Precision	Kamashita
Size of screen	1	Excellent	Excellent	Excellent
Stereo broadcast capability	2	Poor	Excellent	Good
Brand reputation	3	Excellent	Excellent	Poor
Onscreen programming	4	Excellent	Poor	Poor
Cable-ready capability	5	Good	Good	Good
Sleep timer	6	Excellent	Poor	Good

a product category or are not very motivated to process complex information, they tend to use simple, noncompensatory rules, which are summarized here.[83]

The Lexicographic Rule. When the *lexicographic rule* is used, the brand that is the best on the most important attribute is selected. If two or more brands are seen as being equally good on that attribute, the consumer then compares them on the second most important attribute. This selection process goes on until the tie is broken. In Richard's case, because both the Prime Wave and Precision models were tied on his most important attribute (a 60-inch screen), the Precision was chosen because of its rating on this second most important attribute—its stereo capability.

The Elimination-by-Aspects Rule. Using the *elimination-by-aspects rule*, brands are also evaluated on the most important attribute. In this case, though, specific cutoffs are imposed. For example, if Richard had been more interested in having a sleep timer on his TV (i.e., if it had a higher importance ranking), he might have stipulated that his choice "must have a sleep timer." Because the Prime Wave model had one and the Precision did not, the Prime Wave would have been chosen.

The Conjunctive Rule. Whereas the two former rules involve processing by attribute, the *conjunctive rule* entails processing by brand. As with the elimination-by-aspects procedure, cutoffs are established for each attribute. A brand is chosen if it meets all of the cutoffs, but failure to meet any one cutoff means it will be rejected. If none of the brands meet all of the cutoffs, the choice may be delayed, the decision rule may be changed, or the cutoffs may be modified.

If Richard had stipulated that all attributes had to be rated "good" or better, he would not have been able to choose any of the options. He might then have modified his decision rule, conceding that it was not possible to attain these high standards in the price range he was considering. In this case, perhaps Richard could decide that he could live without on-screen programming, so the Precision model could again be considered.

Compensatory Decision Rules

Unlike noncompensatory decision rules, **compensatory decision rules** give a product a chance to make up for its shortcomings. Consumers who employ these rules tend to be more involved in the purchase and thus are willing to exert the effort to consider the entire picture in a more exacting way. The willingness to let good and bad product qualities balance out can result in quite different choices. For example, if Richard were not concerned about having stereo reception, he might have chosen the Prime Wave model. But because this brand doesn't feature this highly ranked attribute, it doesn't stand a chance when he uses a noncompensatory rule.

Two basic types of compensatory rules have been identified. When using the *simple additive rule,* the consumer merely chooses the alternative that has the largest number of positive attributes. This choice is most likely to occur when his or her ability or motivation to process information is limited. One drawback to this approach for the consumer is that some of these attributes may not be very meaningful or important. An ad containing a long list of product benefits may be persuasive, despite the fact that many of the benefits included are actually standard within the product class and aren't determinant attributes at all.

The more complex version is known as the *weighted additive rule.*[84] When using this rule, the consumer also takes into account the relative importance of positively rated attributes, essentially multiplying brand ratings by importance weights. If this process sounds familiar, it should. The calculation process strongly resembles the multiattribute attitude model described in Chapter 7.

CHAPTER SUMMARY

- Consumers are faced with the need to make decisions about products all of the time. Some of these decisions are very important and entail great effort, whereas others are made on a virtually automatic basis.
- Perspectives on decision making range from a focus on habits that people develop over time to novel situations involving a great deal of risk in which consumers must carefully collect and analyze information prior to making a choice.
- A typical decision process involves several steps. The first is problem recognition, in which the consumer first realizes that some action must be taken. This realization may be prompted in a variety of ways, ranging from the actual malfunction of a current purchase to a desire for new things based on exposure to different circumstances or advertising that provides a glimpse into what is needed to "live the good life."
- Once a problem has been recognized and is seen as sufficiently important to warrant some action, information search begins. This search may range from simply scanning memory to determine what has been done to resolve the problem in the past to extensive fieldwork in which the consumer consults a variety of sources to amass as much information as possible. In many cases, people engage in surprisingly little search. Instead, they rely on various mental shortcuts, such as brand names or price, or they may simply imitate others.
- In the evaluation of alternatives stage, the product alternatives that are considered comprise the individual's evoked set. Members of the evoked set usually share some characteristics; they are categorized similarly. The way products are mentally grouped influences which alternatives will be considered, and some brands are more strongly associated with these categories than are others (i.e., they are more prototypical).
- The World Wide Web has changed the way many consumers search for information. Today, the problem is often weeding out excess detail rather than searching for more. Comparative search sites and intelligent agents help to filter and guide the search process. Cybermediaries such as Web portals may be relied upon to sort through massive amounts of information to simplify the decision making process.
- Research in the field of behavioral economics illustrates that decision making is not always strictly rational. Principles of mental accounting demonstrate that decisions can be influenced by the way a problem is posed (called framing) and whether it is put in terms of gains or losses.

- When the consumer eventually must make a product choice from among alternatives, a number of decision rules may be used. Noncompensatory rules eliminate alternatives that are deficient on any of the criteria the consumer has chosen to use. Compensatory rules, which are more likely to be applied in high-involvement situations, allow the decision maker to consider each alternative's good and bad points more carefully to arrive at the overall best choice.
- Very often, heuristics, or mental rules-of-thumb, are used to simplify decision making. In particular, people develop many market beliefs over time. One of the most common beliefs is that price is positively related to quality. Other heuristics rely on well-known brand names or a product's country of origin as signals of product quality. When a brand is consistently purchased over time, this pattern may be due to true brand loyalty, or simply to inertia because it's the easiest thing to do.

KEY TERMS

behavioral influence
   perspective, p. 257
brand loyalty, p. 278
cognitive structure, p. 269
compensatory decision rules, p. 280
cybermediary, p. 273
ethnocentrism, p. 276

evaluative criteria, p. 272
evoked set, p. 268
experiential perspective, p. 257
extended problem solving, p. 257
heuristics, p. 274
inept set, p. 268
inert set, p. 268

inertia, p. 277
information search, p. 260
limited problem solving, p. 257
market beliefs, p. 274
problem recognition, p. 259
rational perspective, p. 256

CONSUMER BEHAVIOR CHALLENGE

1. If people are not always rational decision makers, is it worth the effort to study how purchasing decisions are made? What techniques might be employed to understand experiential consumption and to translate this knowledge into marketing strategy?
2. List three product attributes that can be used as quality signals and provide an example of each.
3. Why is it difficult to place a product in a consumer's evoked set after it has already been rejected? What strategies might a marketer use in an attempt to accomplish this goal?
4. Define the three levels of product categorization described in the chapter. Diagram these levels for a health club.
5. Discuss two different noncompensatory decision rules and highlight the difference(s) between them. How might the use of one rule versus another result in a different product choice?
6. Choose a friend or parent who grocery shops on a regular basis and keep a log of their purchases of common consumer products during the term. Can you detect any evidence of brand loyalty in any categories based on consistency of purchases? If so, talk to the person about these purchases. Try to determine if his or her choices are based on true brand loyalty or on inertia. What techniques might you use to differentiate between the two?
7. Form a group of three. Pick a product and develop a marketing plan based on each of the three approaches to consumer decision making: rational, experiential, and behavioral influence. What are the major differences in

emphasis among the three perspectives? Which is the most likely type of problem-solving activity for the product you have selected? What characteristics of the product make this so?

8. Locate a person who is about to make a major purchase. Ask that person to make a chronological list of all the information sources consulted prior to making a decision. How would you characterize the types of sources used (i.e., internal versus external, media versus personal, etc.)? Which sources appeared to have the most impact on the person's decision?

9. Perform a survey of country-of-origin stereotypes. Compile a list of five countries and ask people what products they associate with each. What are their evaluations of the products and likely attributes of these different products? The power of a country stereotype can also be demonstrated in another way. Prepare a brief description of a product, including a list of features, and ask people to rate it in terms of quality, likelihood of purchase, and so on. Make several versions of the description, varying only the country from which it comes. Do ratings change as a function of the country-of-origin?

10. Ask a friend to "talk through" the process he or she used to choose one brand rather than others during a recent purchase. Based on this description, can you identify the decision rule that was most likely employed?

11. Push technologies have the potential to make our lives easier by reducing the amount of clutter we need to work through in order to access the information on the Internet that really interests us. On the other hand, perhaps intelligent agents that make recommendations based only on what we and others like us have chosen in the past limit us—they reduce the chance that we will stumble upon something (e.g., a book on a topic we've never heard of, or a music group that's different from the style we usually listen to). Will the proliferation of shopping 'bots make our lives too predictable by only giving us more of the same? Is this a problem?

12. Give one of the scenarios described in the section on biases in decision making to 10 to 20 people. How do the results you obtain compare with those reported in the chapter?

NOTES

1. John C. Mowen, "Beyond Consumer Decision Making," *Journal of Consumer Marketing* 5, no. 1 (1988): 15–25.
2. Richard W. Olshavsky and Donald H. Granbois, "Consumer Decision Making—Fact or Fiction," *Journal of Consumer Research* 6 (September 1989): 93–100.
3. James R. Bettman, "The Decision Maker Who Came in from the Cold" (presidential address), in Leigh McAllister and Michael Rothschild, eds., *Advances in Consumer Research* 20 (Provo, UT: Association for Consumer Research, (1993): 7–11; John W. Payne, James R. Bettman, and Eric J. Johnson, "Behavioral Decision Research: A Constructive Processing Perspective," *Annual Review of Psychology* 4 (1992): 87–131; for an overview of recent developments in individual choice models, see

Robert J. Meyer and Barbara E. Kahn, "Probabilistic Models of Consumer Choice Behavior," in Thomas S. Robertson and Harold H. Kassarjian, eds., *Handbook of Consumer Behavior* (Upper Saddle River, NJ: Prentice Hall, 1991): 85–123.
4. Mowen, "Beyond Consumer Decision Making."
5. Joseph W. Alba and J. Wesley Hutchinson, "Dimensions of Consumer Expertise," *Journal of Consumer Research* 13 (March 1988): 411–54.
6. Gordon C. Bruner III and Richard J. Pomazal, "Problem Recognition: The Crucial First Stage of the Consumer Decision Process," *Journal of Consumer Marketing* 5, no. 1 (1988): 53–63.
7. Peter H. Bloch, Daniel L. Sherrell, and Nancy M. Ridgway, "Consumer Search: An Extended Framework," *Journal of*

Consumer Research 13 (June 1986): 119–26.
8. Girish Punj, "Presearch Decision Making in Consumer Durable Purchases," *Journal of Consumer Marketing* 4 (Winter 1987): 71–82.
9. H. Beales, M. B. Jagis, S. C. Salop, and R. Staelin, "Consumer Search and Public Policy," *Journal of Consumer Research* 8 (June 1981): 11–22.
10. Examples provided by Dr. William Cohen, personal communication, October 1999.
11. Itamar Simonson, Joel Huber, and John Payne, "The Relationship Between Prior Brand Knowledge and Information Acquisition Order," *Journal of Consumer Research* 14 (March 1988): 566–78.
12. John R. Hauser, Glen L. Urban, and Bruce D. Weinberg, "How Consumers Allocate Their Time When Searching for Information," *Journal of Marketing*

Research 30 (November 1993): 452–66; George J. Stigler, "The Economics of Information," *Journal of Political Economy* 69 (June 1961): 213–25; for a set of studies focusing on online search costs see John G. Lynch Jr. and Dan Ariely, "Wine Online: Search Costs and Competition on Price, Quality, and Distribution," unpublished manuscript, Duke University.

13. Ratner, Rebecca K., Barbara E. Kahn, and Daniel Kahneman, "Choosing Less-Preferred Experiences for the Sake of Variety," *Journal of Consumer Research,* 26 (June 1999): 1–15.

14. Cathy J. Cobb and Wayne D. Hoyer, "Direct Observation of Search Behavior," *Psychology & Marketing* 2 (Fall 1985): 161–79.

15. Sharon E. Beatty and Scott M. Smith, "External Search Effort: An Investigation Across Several Product Categories," *Journal of Consumer Research* 14 (June 1987): 83–95; William L. Moore and Donald R. Lehmann, "Individual Differences in Search Behavior for a Nondurable," *Journal of Consumer Research* 7 (December 1980): 296–307.

16. Geoffrey C. Kiel and Roger A. Layton, "Dimensions of Consumer Information Seeking Behavior," *Journal of Marketing Research* 28 (May 1981): 233–39; see also Narasimhan Srinivasan and Brian T. Ratchford, "An Empirical Test of a Model of External Search for Automobiles," *Journal of Consumer Research* 18 (September 1991): 233–42.

17. David F. Midgley, "Patterns of Interpersonal Information Seeking for the Purchase of a Symbolic Product," *Journal of Marketing Research* 20 (February 1983): 74–83.

18. Cyndee Miller, "Scotland to U.S.: 'This Tennent's for You'," *Marketing News* (August 29, 1994): 26.

19. Satya Menon and Barbara E. Kahn, "The Impact of Context on Variety Seeking in Product Choices," *Journal of Consumer Research* 22 (December 1995): 285–95; Barbara E. Kahn and Alice M. Isen, "The Influence of Positive Affect on Variety Seeking Among Safe, Enjoyable Products," *Journal of Consumer Research* 20 (September 1993): 257–70.

20. J. Jeffrey Inman, "The Role of Sensory-Specific Satiety in Consumer Variety Seeking Among Flavors," unpublished manuscript, A. C. Nielsen Center for Marketing Research, University of Wisconsin-Madison, July 1999.

21. Rebecca K. Ratner, Barbara E. Kahn, and Daniel Kahneman, "Choosing Less-Preferred Experiences for the Sake of Variety," *Journal of Consumer Research* 26 (June 1999): 1–15.

22. Gary Belsky, "Why Smart People Make Major Money Mistakes," *Money* (July 1995): 76; Richard Thaler and Eric J. Johnson, "Gambling with the House

Money or Trying to Break Even: The Effects of Prior Outcomes on Risky Choice," *Management Science* 36 (June 1990): 643–60; Richard Thaler, "Mental Accounting and Consumer Choice," *Marketing Science* 4 (Summer 1985): 199–214.

23. Daniel Kahneman and Amos Tversky, "Prospect Theory: An Analysis of Decision Under Risk," *Econometrica* 47 (March 1979): 263–91; Timothy B. Heath, Subimal Chatterjee, and Karen Russo France, "Mental Accounting and Changes in Price: The Frame Dependence of Reference Dependence," *Journal of Consumer Research* 22, no. 1 (June 1995): 90–97.

24. Quoted in Richard Thaler, "Mental Accounting and Consumer Choice," *Marketing Science* 4 (Summer 1985): 199–214, quoted on p. 206.

25. Girish N. Punj and Richard Staelin, "A Model of Consumer Search Behavior for New Automobiles," *Journal of Consumer Research* 9 (March 1983): 366–80.

26. Cobb and Hoyer, "Direct Observation of Search Behavior"; Moore and Lehmann, "Individual Differences in Search Behavior for a Nondurable"; Punj and Staelin, "A Model of Consumer Search Behavior for New Automobiles."

27. James R. Bettman and C. Whan Park, "Effects of Prior Knowledge and Experience and Phase of the Choice Process on Consumer Decision Processes: A Protocol Analysis," *Journal of Consumer Research* 7 (December 1980): 234–48.

28. Alba and Hutchinson, "Dimensions of Consumer Expertise"; Bettman and Park, "Effects of Prior Knowledge and Experience and Phase of the Choice Process on Consumer Decision Processes"; Merrie Brucks, "The Effects of Product Class Knowledge on Information Search Behavior," *Journal of Consumer Research* 12 (June 1985): 1–16; Joel E. Urbany, Peter R. Dickson, and William L. Wilkie, "Buyer Uncertainty and Information Search," *Journal of Consumer Research* 16 (September 1989): 208–15.

29. Daniel Michaels, "Airlines Blast New Ads from Airbus, Say Stoking Safety Fears Doesn't Fly," *The Wall Street Journal Interactive Edition* (November 22, 1999).

30. Mary Frances Luce, James R. Bettman, and John W. Payne, "Choice Processing in Emotionally Difficult Decisions," *Journal of Experimental Psychology: Learning, Memory, and Cognition* 23 (March 1997): 384–405; example provided by Prof. James Bettman, personal communication, December 17, 1997.

31. John R. Hauser and Birger Wernerfelt, "An Evaluation Cost Model of Consideration Sets," *Journal of Consumer Research* 16 (March 1990): 393–408.

32. Robert J. Sutton, "Using Empirical Data to Investigate the Likelihood of Brands Being Admitted or Readmitted into an

Established Evoked Set," *Journal of the Academy of Marketing Science* 15 (Fall 1987): 82.

33. Alba and Hutchison, "Dimensions of Consumer Expertise"; Joel B. Cohen and Kunal Basu, "Alternative Models of Categorization: Toward a Contingent Processing Framework," *Journal of Consumer Research* 13 (March 1987): 455–72.

34. Robert M. McMath, "The Perils of Typecasting," *American Demographics* (February 1997): 60.

35. Eleanor Rosch, "Principles of Categorization," in E. Rosch and B. B. Lloyd, eds., *Recognition and Categorization* (Hillsdale, NJ: Erlbaum, 1978).

36. Michael R. Solomon, "Mapping Product Constellations: A Social Categorization Approach to Symbolic Consumption," *Psychology & Marketing* 5, no. 3 (1988): 233–58.

37. Robert M. McMath, "The Perils of Typecasting," *American Demographics* (February 1997): 60.

38. Elizabeth C. Hirschman and Michael R. Solomon, "Competition and Cooperation Among Culture Production Systems," in Ronald F. Bush and Shelby D. Hunt, eds., *Marketing Theory: Philosophy of Science Perspectives* (Chicago: American Marketing Association, 1982): 269–72.

39. Michael D. Johnson, "The Differential Processing of Product Category and Noncomparable Choice Alternatives," *Journal of Consumer Research* 16 (December 1989): 300–309.

40. Mita Sujan, "Consumer Knowledge: Effects on Evaluation Strategies Mediating Consumer Judgments," *Journal of Consumer Research* 12 (June 1985): 31–46.

41. Rosch, "Principles of Categorization."

42. Joan Meyers-Levy and Alice M. Tybout, "Schema Congruity as a Basis for Product Evaluation," *Journal of Consumer Research* 16 (June 1989): 39–55.

43. Mita Sujan and James R. Bettman, "The Effects of Brand Positioning Strategies on Consumers' Brand and Category Perceptions: Some Insights from Schema Research," *Journal of Marketing Research* 26 (November 1989): 454–67.

44. See William P. Putsis Jr. and Narasimhan Srinivasan, "Buying or Just Browsing? The Duration of Purchase Deliberation," *Journal of Marketing Research* 31 (August 1994): 393–402.

45. Robert E. Smith, "Integrating Information from Advertising and Trial: Processes and Effects on Consumer Response to Product Information," *Journal of Marketing Research* 30 (May 1993): 204–19.

46. Jack Trout, "Marketing in Tough Times," *Boardroom Reports,* no. 2 (October 1992): 8.

47. Stuart Elliott, "Pepsi-Cola to Stamp Dates for Freshness on Soda Cans," *New York Times* (March 31, 1994): D1; Emily

DeNitto, "Pepsi's Gamble Hits Freshness Dating Jackpot," *Advertising Age* (September 19, 1994): 50.

48. Amna Kirmani and Peter Wright, "Procedural Learning, Consumer Decision Making and Marketing Communication," *Marketing Letters* 4, no. 1 (1993): 39–48.

49. Michael Porter, *Competitive Advantage,* (New York: Free Press, 1985).

50. Material in this section adapted from Michael R. Solomon and Elnora W. Stuart, *Welcome to Marketing.com: The Brave New World of E-Commerce,* Englewood Cliffs, NJ: Prentice Hall (2001).

51. Phil Patton, "Buy Here, and We'll Tell You What You Like," *The New York Times on the Web* (September 22, 1999).

52. Robert A. Baron, *Psychology: The Essential Science* (Boston: Allyn & Bacon, 1989); Valerie S. Folkes, "The Availability Heuristic and Perceived Risk," *Journal of Consumer Research* 15 (June 1989): 13–23; Daniel Kahneman and Amos Tversky, "Prospect Theory: An Analysis of Decision Under Risk," *Econometrica* 47 (1979): 263–91.

53. Wayne D. Hoyer, "An Examination of Consumer Decision Making for a Common Repeat Purchase Product," *Journal of Consumer Research* 11 (December 1984): 822–29; Calvin P. Duncan, "Consumer Market Beliefs: A Review of the Literature and an Agenda for Future Research," in Marvin E. Goldberg, Gerald Gorn, and Richard W. Pollay, eds., *Advances in Consumer Research* 17 (Provo, UT: Association for Consumer Research, 1990): 729–35; Frank Alpert, "Consumer Market Beliefs and Their Managerial Implications: An Empirical Examination," *Journal of Consumer Marketing* 10, no. 2 (1993): 56–70.

54. Michael R. Solomon, Sarah Drenan, and Chester A. Insko, "Popular Induction: When Is Consensus Information Informative?" *Journal of Personality* 49, no. 2 (1981): 212–24.

55. Folkes, "The Availability Heuristic and Perceived Risk."

56. Beales et al., "Consumer Search and Public Policy."

57. Gary T. Ford and Ruth Ann Smith, "Inferential Beliefs in Consumer Evaluations: An Assessment of Alternative Processing Strategies," *Journal of Consumer Research* 14 (December 1987): 363–71; Deborah Roedder John, Carol A. Scott, and James R. Bettman, "Sampling Data for Covariation Assessment: The Effects of Prior Beliefs on Search Patterns," *Journal of Consumer Research* 13 (June 1986): 38–47; Gary L. Sullivan and Kenneth J. Berger, "An Investigation of the Determinants of Cue Utilization," *Psychology & Marketing* 4 (Spring 1987): 63–74.

58. John et al., "Sampling Data for Covariation Assessment."

59. Duncan, "Consumer Market Beliefs."

60. Chr. Hjorth-Andersen, "Price as a Risk Indicator," *Journal of Consumer Policy* 10 (1987): 267–81.

61. David M. Gardner, "Is There a Generalized Price-Quality Relationship?" *Journal of Marketing Research* 8 (May 1971): 241–43; Kent B. Monroe, "Buyers' Subjective Perceptions of Price," *Journal of Marketing Research* 10 (1973): 70–80.

62. Durairaj Maheswaran, "Country of Origin as a Stereotype: Effects of Consumer Expertise and Attribute Strength on Product Evaluations," *Journal of Consumer Research* 21 (September 1994): 354–65; Ingrid M. Martin and Sevgin Eroglu, "Measuring a Multi-Dimensional Construct: Country Image," *Journal of Business Research* 28 (1993): 191–210; Richard Ettenson, Janet Wagner, and Gary Gaeth, "Evaluating the Effect of Country of Origin and the 'Made in the U.S.A.' Campaign: A Conjoint Approach," *Journal of Retailing* 64 (Spring 1988): 85–100; C. Min Han and Vern Terpstra, "Country-of-Origin Effects for Uni-National and Bi-National Products," *Journal of International Business* 19 (Summer 1988): 235–55; Michelle A. Morganosky and Michelle M. Lazarde, "Foreign-Made Apparel: Influences on Consumers' Perceptions of Brand and Store Quality," *International Journal of Advertising* 6 (Fall 1987): 339–48.

63. Thomas A. W. Miller, "Cultural Affinity, Personal Values Factors in Marketing," *Advertising Age* (August 16, 1999): H22.

64. See Richard Jackson Harris, Bettina Garner-Earl, Sara J. Sprick, and Collette Carroll, "Effects of Foreign Product Names and Country-of-Origin Attributions on Advertisement Evaluations," *Psychology & Marketing* 11, no. 2 (March/April 1994): 129–45; Terence A. Shimp, Saeed Samiee, and Thomas J. Madden, "Countries and Their Products: A Cognitive Structure Perspective," *Journal of the Academy of Marketing Science* 21, no. 4 (Fall 1993): 323–30.

65. Durairaj Maheswaran, "Country of Origin as a Stereotype: Effects of Consumer Expertise and Attribute Strength on Product Evaluations," *Journal of Consumer Research* 21 (September 1994): 354–65.

66. Sung-Tai Hong and Robert S. Wyer Jr., "Effects of Country-of-Origin and Product-Attribute Information on Product Evaluation: An Information Processing Perspective," *Journal of Consumer Research* 16 (September 1989): 175–87; Marjorie Wall, John Liefeld, and Louise A. Heslop, "Impact of Country-of-Origin Cues on Consumer Judgments in Multi-Cue Situations: A Covariance Analysis," *Journal of the Academy of Marketing Science* 19, no. 2 (1991): 105–13.

67. Wai-Kwan Li and Robert S. Wyer Jr., "The Role of Country of Origin in Product Evaluations: Informational and Standard-of-Comparison Effects," *Journal of Consumer Psychology* 3, no. 2 (1994): 187–212.

68. Maheswaran, "Country of Origin as a Stereotype."

69. Quoted in Howard Banks, "We'll Provide the Shillelaghs," *Forbes* (April 8, 1996): 68, p. 72; see also Brendan I. Koerner, "Spreading the Taste of Ireland," *U.S. News & World Report* (February 24, 1997): 15; for an ethnographic study of the "authenticity" of Irish pubs, see Michael R. Solomon, Caroline K. Lego, Natalie T. Quilty, and Stephanie L. Wright, "A Thirst for the Real Thing in Themed Retail Environments: Consuming Authenticity in Irish Pubs," *Proceedings of the Society for Marketing Advances,* 2000.

70. Items excerpted from Terence A. Shimp and Subhash Sharma, "Consumer Ethnocentrism: Construction and Validation of the CETSCALE," *Journal of Marketing Research* 24 (August 1987): 282.

71. Roger Ricklefs, "Canada Fights to Fend Off American Tastes and Tunes," *The Wall Street Journal Interactive Edition* (September 24, 1998).

72. Adam Bryant, "Message in a Beer Bottle," *Newsweek* (May 29, 2000): 43.

73. Richard W. Stevenson, "The Brands with Billion-Dollar Names," *New York Times* (October 28, 1988): A1.

74. Mereces M. Cardona, "WPP Brand Study Ranks Gerber 1st in U.S. Market," *Advertising Age* (October 5, 1998): 3.

75. Ronald Alsop, "Enduring Brands Hold Their Allure by Sticking Close to Their Roots," *The Wall Street Journal,* centennial ed. (1989): B4.

76. Bruce Orwall, "Some Hip Hopes: Disney Channel Spices Up Its Image for Teenagers," *The Wall Street Journal Interactive Edition* (October 13, 1999).

77. Larry Armstrong, "The Free-PC Game: Lure 'Em In and Lock 'Em Up," *Business Week* (July 19, 1999): 80.

78. Jacob Jacoby and Robert Chestnut, *Brand Loyalty: Measurement and Management* (New York: Wiley, 1978).

79. Anne B. Fisher, "Coke's Brand Loyalty Lesson," *Fortune* (August 5, 1985): 44.

80. Jacoby and Chestnut, *Brand Loyalty.*

81. Ronald Alsop, "Brand Loyalty Is Rarely Blind Loyalty," *The Wall Street Journal* (October 19, 1989): B1.

82. Betsy Morris, "The Brand's the Thing," *Fortune* (March 4, 1996): 72.

83. C. Whan Park, "The Effect of Individual and Situation-Related Factors on Consumer Selection of Judgmental Models," *Journal of Marketing Research* 13 (May 1976): 144–51.

84. Joseph W. Alba and Howard Marmorstein, "The Effects of Frequency Knowledge on Consumer Decision Making," *Journal of Consumer Research* 14 (June 1987): 14–25.

ob is really psyched. The big day has actually arrived: He's going to buy a car! He's had his eye on that silver 1995 Camaro parked in the lot of Russ's Auto-Rama for weeks now. Although the sticker says $2,999, Rob figures he can probably get this baby for a cool $2,000—Russ's looks like just the kind of place where they're hungry to move some cars. Besides, he's already done his homework on the Web. First he found out the wholesale value of similar used Camaros from the Kelley Blue Book (kbb.com), and then he scouted out some cars for sale in his area at autobytel.com. So, Rob figures he's coming in loaded for bear—he's going to show these guys they're not dealing with some rube.

Unlike some of the newer, flashy car showrooms he's been in lately, this place is a real nuts-and-bolts operation—it's so dingy and depressing he can't wait to get out of there and take a shower. Rob dreads the prospect of haggling over the price, but he hopes to convince the salesman to take his offer because he knows the real market value of the car he wants. At the Auto-Rama lot, big signs on all the cars proclaim that today is Russ's Auto-Rama Rip Us Off Day! Things look better than Rob expected—maybe he can get the Camaro for even less than he had planned. He's a bit surprised when a salesperson who introduces herself as Rhoda comes over to him. He had expected to be dealing with a middle-aged man in a loud sport coat (a stereotype he has about used-car

salespeople), but this is more good luck: He figures he won't have to be so tough when dealing with a woman who looks to be about his age.

Rhoda laughs when he offers her $1,800 for the Camaro, pointing out that she can't take such a low bid for such a sweet car to her boss or she'll lose her job. Rhoda's enthusiasm for the car convinces him all the more that he has to have it. When he finally writes a check for $2,700, he's exhausted from all the haggling. What an ordeal! In any case, Rob reminds himself that he at least convinced Rhoda to sell him the car for less than the sticker price—and maybe he can fix it up and sell it for even more in a year or two. That Web surfing really paid off—he's a tougher negotiator than he thought.

10

BUYING AND DISPOSING

INTRODUCTION

Many consumers dread the act of buying a car. In fact, a survey by Yankelovich Partners found that buying a car is the most anxiety provoking and least-satisfying of any retail experience.[1] But, change is in the wind because the car showroom is being transformed. Car shoppers like Rob are logging onto Internet buying services, calling auto brokers who negotiate for them, buying cars at warehouse clubs, and visiting giant auto malls where they can comparison shop.

Rob's experience in buying a car illustrates some of the concepts to be discussed in this chapter. Making a purchase is often not a simple, routine matter of going to a store and quickly picking out something. As illustrated in Figure 10.1, a consumer's choices are affected by many personal factors, such as his or her mood, whether there is time pressure to make the purchase, and the particular situation or context for which the product is needed. In some situations, such as the purchase of a car or a home, the salesperson or realtor plays a pivotal role in the final selection. And today people are using the Web to arm themselves with product and price information before they even enter a dealership or a store, which puts added pressure on retailers to deliver the value they expect.

But the sale doesn't end at the time of purchase. A lot of important consumer activity occurs after a product has been brought home. After using a product, the consumer must decide whether he is satisfied with it. The satisfaction process is especially important to savvy marketers who realize that the key to success is not selling a product one time, but rather forging a relationship with the consumer so that he or she will continue to buy one's products in the future. Finally, just as Rob thought about the resale value of his car, we must also consider how consumers go about disposing of products and how secondary markets (e.g., used-car

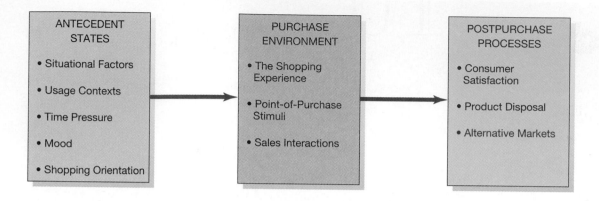

Figure 10.1
Issues Related to Purchase and
Postpurchase Activities

dealers) often play a pivotal role in product acquisition. This chapter considers many issues related to purchase and postpurchase phenomena.

Situational Effects on Consumer Behavior

A *consumption situation* is defined by factors beyond characteristics of the person and of the product that influence the buying and/or using of products and services. Situational effects can be behavioral (e.g., entertaining friends) or perceptual (e.g., being depressed or feeling pressed for time).[2] Common sense tells us that people tailor their purchases to specific occasions, and that the way we feel at a specific point in time affects what we feel like buying or doing. Smart marketers understand these patterns and tailor their efforts to coincide with situations in which people are most prone to buy. For example, book clubs invest

Clothing choices often are heavily influenced by the situation where they need to be worn.

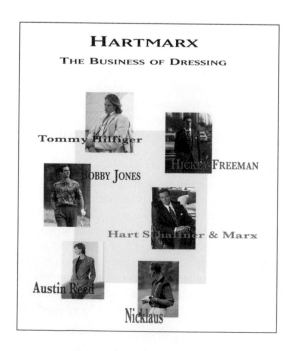

heavily in promotional campaigns in June because many people are looking to stock up on "beach books" to read during the summer.[3]

In addition to the functional relationships between products and usage situation, though, another reason to take environmental circumstances seriously is that the role a person plays at any one time is partly determined by his or her *situational self-image*—he or she basically asks: "Who am I right *now?*" (see Chapter 5).[4] Someone trying to impress his date by playing the role of "man-about-town" may spend more lavishly, ordering champagne instead of beer and buying flowers—purchases he would never consider when he is hanging out with his friends, slurping beer, and playing the role of "one of the boys." Let's see how these dynamics affect the way people think about what they buy.

By systematically identifying important usage situations, market segmentation strategies can position products that will meet the specific needs arising from these situations. Many product categories are amenable to this form of segmentation. For example, consumers' furniture choices are often tailored to specific settings. We prefer different styles for a city apartment, beach house, or an executive suite. Similarly, motorcycles can be distinguished in terms of what riders use them for, including commuting, riding them as dirt bikes, using them on a farm versus highway travel, and so on.[5]

Table 10.1 gives one example of how situations can be used to fine-tune a segmentation strategy. By listing the major contexts in which a product is used (e.g., snow skiing and sunbathing for a suntan lotion) and the different users of the product, a matrix can be constructed that identifies specific product features that

TABLE 10.1 A Person-Situation-Segmentation Matrix for Suntan Lotion

Situation	Young Children		Teenagers		Adult Women		Adult Men		Benefits/Features
	Fair Skin	Dark Skin	Fair Skin	Dark Skin	Fair Skin	Dark Skin	Fair Skin	Dark Skin	
Beach/boat sunbathing	Combined insect repellent				Summer perfume				a. Product serves as windburn protection b. Formula and container can stand heat c. Container floats and is distinctive (not easily lost)
Home-poolside sunbathing					Combined moisterizer				a. Product has large pump dispenser b. Product won't stain wood, concrete, furnishings
Sunlamp bathing					Combined moisturizer and massage oil				a. Product is designed specifically for type of lamp b. Product has an artificial tanning ingredient
Snow skiing					Winter perfume				a. Product provides special protection from special light rays and weather b. Product has antifreeze formula
Person benefit/features	Special protection a. Protection is critical b. Formula is non-poisonous		Special protection a. Product fits in jean pocket b. Product used by opinion leaders		Special protection Female perfume		Special protection Male perfume		

SOURCE: Adapted from Peter R. Dickson, "Person-Situation: Segmentation's Missing Link," *Journal of Marketing* 46 (Fall 1982): 62. By permission of American Marketing Association.

should be emphasized for each situation. For example, during the summer a lotion manufacturer might promote the fact that the bottle floats and is hard to lose, but tout its nonfreezing formula during the winter season.

SOCIAL AND PHYSICAL SURROUNDINGS

A consumer's physical and social environment affects her motives for product usage and how she evaluates products. Important cues include the person's physical surroundings, as well as the amount and type of other consumers also present in that situation. Dimensions of the physical environment, such as decor, smells, and even temperature can significantly influence consumption. One study even found that pumping in certain odors in a Las Vegas casino actually increased the amount of money patrons fed into slot machines![6] We'll take a closer look at some of these factors a bit later in the chapter when considering strategic issues related to store design.

In addition to physical cues, though, groups or social settings significantly affect many of a consumer's purchase decisions. In some cases, the sheer presence or absence of other patrons (*"co-consumers"*) in a setting actually can function as a product attribute, as when an exclusive resort or boutique promises to provide privacy to privileged customers. At other times, the presence of others can have positive value. A sparsely attended ball game or an empty bar can be depressing sights.

The presence of large numbers of people in a consumer environment increases arousal levels, so a consumer's subjective experience of a setting tends to be more intense. This boost, however, can be positive or negative—the experience depends on the consumer's *interpretation* of this arousal. It is important to distinguish between *density* and *crowding* for this reason. The former term refers to the actual number of people occupying a space, while the psychological state of crowding exists only if a negative affective state occurs as a result of this density.[7] For example, 100 students packed into a classroom designed for 75 may result in an unpleasant situation for all concerned, but the same number of people jammed together at a party occupying a room of the same size might just make for a great rave.

In addition, the *type* of consumers who patronize a store or service or who use a product can influence evaluations. We often infer something about a store by examining its customers. For this reason, some restaurants require men to wear a jacket for dinner (and supply a rather tacky one if they don't), and bouncers at some "hot" nightspots handpick people waiting in line based on whether they have the right "look" for the club. To paraphrase the comedian Groucho Marx, "I would never join a club that would have me for a member!"

Temporal Factors

Time is one of consumers' most precious resources. We talk about "making time" or "spending time" and we frequently are reminded that "time is money." Common sense tells us that more careful information search and deliberation occurs when we have the luxury of taking our time. A meticulous shopper who would normally price an item at three different stores before buying might be found sprinting through the mall at 9 P.M. on Christmas Eve, furiously scooping up anything left on the shelves that might serve as a last-minute gift.

Economic Time

Time is an economic variable; it is a resource that must be divided among activities.[8] Consumers try to maximize satisfaction by allocating time to the appropriate combination of tasks. Of course, people's allocation decisions differ; we all know people who seem to play all of the time, and others who are workaholics. An individual's priorities determine his or her *timestyle*.[9]

Many consumers believe they are more pressed for time than ever before, a feeling called **time poverty.** This feeling appears to be due more to perception than to fact. People may just have more options for spending their time and feel pressured by the weight of all of these choices. The average working day at the turn of the twentieth century was 10 hours (six days per week), and women did 27 hours of housework per week, compared to less than five hours weekly now. Of course, in some cases husbands are sharing these burdens more, and in some families maintaining an absolutely spotless home may not be as important as it used to be.[10] Still, about a third of Americans report always feeling rushed—up from 25 percent of the population in 1964.[11] The economic value of time is the basis of a startup company called LassoBucks.com, a Web site that lets people barter time for money. You describe your skill or the service you can offer and when a member of the circle accepts your offer, your account gets credited with the appropriate number of LassoBucks. You then use that currency to buy goods and services from others.[12]

This sense of time poverty has made consumers very responsive to marketing innovations that allow them to save time. With the increase in time poverty, researchers also are noting a rise in *polychronic activity*, or *multi-tasking*, a phenomenon in which consumers do more than one thing at a time.[13] This type of activity is especially prevalent in eating. Consumers often do not allocate a specific time to dining, but instead eat on the run. In a recent poll, 64 percent of respondents said they usually do something else while eating. As one food industry executive commented, "We've moved beyond grazing and into gulping."[14]

Psychological Time

The psychological dimension of time—how it is actually experienced—is an important factor in *queuing theory*, the mathematical study of waiting lines. A consumer's experience of waiting can radically influence his or her perceptions of service quality. Although we assume that something must be pretty good if we have to wait for it, the negative feelings aroused by long waits can quickly turn off customers.[17]

Some products and services are believed to be appropriate for certain times and not for others. One study of fast-food preferences found that consumers were more likely to choose Wendy's rather than other fast-food outlets for an evening meal when they were not rushed than when they were pressed for time.[22] Also, we may be more receptive to advertising messages at certain times (other than a few party animals, who wants to hear a beer commercial at 7 in the morning?). There is some evidence that consumers' arousal levels are lower in the morning than in the evening, which affects their style and quality of information processing.[23]

Marketers have adopted a variety of "tricks" to minimize psychological waiting time. These techniques range from altering customers' perceptions of a line's length to providing distractions that divert attention away from waiting.[24]

- One hotel chain, after receiving excessive complaints about the wait for elevators, installed mirrors near the elevator banks. People's natural tendency to check their appearance reduced complaints, even though the actual waiting time was unchanged.

NET 100 PROFIT

NEW ONLINE BUSINESS CONCEPTS based on improved delivery are popping up all over the Web. Peapod.com brings groceries to customers' doors once a week. Streamline.com will drop off your dry cleaning and get your photos developed.[15] Some manufacturers are trying to automate the process even more. In a British pilot project, the Safeway grocery chain is providing 200 consumers with personal organizers to create shopping lists. By using frequent shopper data, the device can suggest items to replenish based on past purchase patterns. A "smart refrigerator" developed by Frigidaire comes with a bar code scanner so consumers can reorder a fresh bottle of salad dressing, ketchup, or other frequently-used items by scanning the used container across the door. The refrigerator picks up the UPC code and automatically reorders a fresh supply from the grocery store.[16] Now if it can learn to do the dishes.

MULTICULTURAL DIMENSIONS

TO MOST WESTERN CONSUMERS, time is a neatly compartmentalized thing: We wake up in the morning, go to school or work, come home, eat dinner, go out, go to sleep . . . wake up and do it all over again. This perspective is called *linear separable time;* events proceed in an orderly sequence and different times are well-defined: "There's a time and a place for everything." There is a clear sense of past, present, and future. Many activities are performed as the means to some end that will occur later, as when people "save for a rainy day."

This conception of time is not universal. Large cultural differences exist in terms of people's time perspectives.[18] Some cultures run on *procedural time* and ignore the clock completely—people simply decide to do something "when the time is right." Much of the world appears to live on "event time"; for example, in Burundi people might arrange to meet when the cows return from the watering hole, whereas in Madagascar the

response if someone asks how long it takes to get to the market might be, "the time it takes to cook rice."[19]

Alternatively, in *circular* or *cyclic* time, people are governed by natural cycles, such as the regular occurrence of the seasons (a perspective found in many Hispanic cultures). To these consumers, the notion of the future does not make sense, because that time will be much like the present. Because the concept of future value does not exist, these consumers often prefer to buy an inferior product that is available now to waiting for a better one that may be available later. Also, it is hard to convince people who function on circular time to buy insurance or save for a rainy day when they do not think in terms of a linear future.

When groups of college students were asked to draw a picture of time, the resulting

sketches in Figure 10.2 illustrate some of these different temporal perspectives.[20] The drawing at the top left represents procedural time; there is lack of direction from left to right and little sense of past, present, and future. The three drawings in the middle denote cyclical time, with regular cycles designated by markers. The bottom drawing represents linear time, with a segmented time line moving from left to right in a well-defined sequence.

A social scientist compared the pace of life in 31 cities around the world as part of a study on timestyles. He and his assistants timed how long it takes pedestrians to walk 60 feet and postal clerks to sell a stamp.[21] Based on these responses, he claims that the fastest and slowest countries are: Fastest Countries: (1) Switzerland, (2) Ireland, (3) Germany, (4) Japan, (5) Italy Slowest Countries: (31) Mexico, (30) Indonesia, (29) Brazil, (28) El Salvador, (27) Syria

- Airline passengers often complain about waiting to claim their baggage. In one airport, they would walk one minute from the plane to the baggage carousel and then wait seven minutes for their luggage. By changing the layout so that the walk to the carousel took six minutes and bags arrived two minutes after that, complaints were almost entirely eliminated. Continental Airlines plans to install 300 ATM-like machines that allow people to print their own boarding passes and luggage tags. Alaska Airlines allows people to print boarding passes from their home computers to save time.[25]

- Restaurant chains are scrambling to put the fast back into fast food, especially for drive-through lanes, which now account for 65 percent of revenues. In a study that ranked the speed of 25 fast food chains, cars spent an average of 203.6 seconds from the menu board to departure. Wendy's was clocked the fastest at 150.3 seconds. To speed things up and eliminate spills, McDonald's created a salad that comes in a container to fit into car cup holders. Arby's is working on a "high viscosity" version of its special sauce that's less likely to spill. Burger King is testing see-through bags so customers can quickly check their orders before speeding off.[26]

- Grocery stores are trying to reduce the "register rage" experienced by customers who get irritated by long lines and slow clerks. And with good reason: According to a survey, 83 percent of women and 91 percent of men say long lines made them stop going to a particular store. Retailers are testing technologies to reduce or eliminate lines. One approach is called "smart packaging" in which a product has a tag that

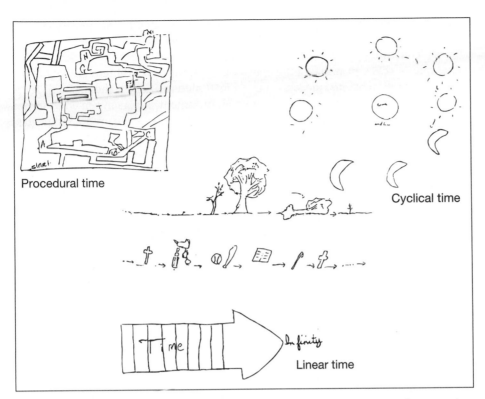

Procedural time

Cyclical time

Linear time

Figure 10.2
Drawings of Time

SOURCE: Esther S. Page-Wood, Carol J. Kaufman, and Paul M. Lane, "The Art of Time," *Proceedings of the Academy of Marketing Science* (1990).

gives off a signal using a radio frequency. A computer at the store's exit picks up the signal, registers the price, and calculates the bill.[27]

Antecedent States: If It Feels Good, Buy It . . .

A person's mood or physiological condition active at the time of purchase can have a big impact on what is bought and can also affect how products are evaluated.[28] One reason is that behavior is directed toward certain goal states,

Recognizing that modern women have many times pressures, Spiegel brings retailing to the office.

as was discussed in Chapter 4. People spend more money in the grocery store if they have not eaten for a while because food is a priority at that time.

A consumer's mood can have a big impact on purchase decisions. For example, stress can impair information-processing and problem-solving abilities.[29] Two dimensions, *pleasure* and *arousal*, determine if a shopper will react positively or negatively to a consumption environment. A person can enjoy or not enjoy a situation, and he or she can feel stimulated or not. As Figure 10.3 indicates, different combinations of pleasure and arousal levels result in a variety of emotional states. For example, an arousing situation can be either distressing or exciting, depending on whether the context is positive or negative (e.g., a street riot versus a street festival). Maintaining an "up" feeling in a pleasant context is one factor behind the success of theme parks such as Disney World, which try to provide consistent doses of carefully calculated stimulation to visitors.[30]

A specific mood is some combination of pleasure and arousal. For example, the state of happiness is high in pleasantness and moderate in arousal, whereas elation is high on both dimensions.[31] A mood state (either positive or negative) biases judgments of products and services in that direction.[32] Put simply, consumers give more positive evaluations when they are in a good mood (this explains the popularity of the business lunch!).

Moods can be affected by store design, the weather, or other factors specific to the consumer. In addition, music and television programming can affect mood, which has important consequences for commercials.[33] When consumers hear happy music or watch happy programs, they have more positive reactions to commercials and products, especially when the marketing appeals are aimed at arousing emotional reactions.[34] When in positive moods, consumers process ads with less elaboration. They pay less attention to specifics of the message and rely more on heuristic processing (see Chapter 9).[35]

SHOPPING: A JOB OR AN ADVENTURE?

Some people shop even though they do not necessarily intend to buy anything at all, whereas others have to be dragged to a mall. Shopping is a way to acquire needed products and services, but social motives for shopping also are important.

Figure 10.3
Dimensions of Emotional States

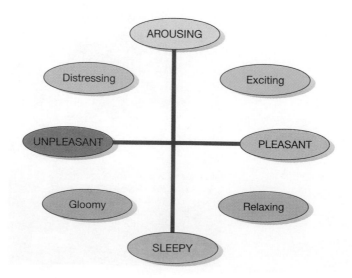

Thus, shopping is an activity that can be performed for either utilitarian (functional or tangible) or hedonic (pleasurable or intangible) reasons.[36]

Reasons for Shopping

The diversity of shopping motives is illustrated by scale items researchers use to assess people's underlying reasons for shopping. One item that measures hedonic value is "During the trip, I felt the excitement of the hunt." When that type of sentiment is compared to a functionally related statement such as "I accomplished just what I wanted to on this shopping trip," the contrast between these two dimensions is clear.[37] Hedonic shopping motives can include the following:[38]

- *Social experiences:* The shopping center or department store has replaced the traditional town square or county fair as a community gathering place. Many people (especially in suburban or rural areas) may have no place else to go to spend their leisure time.
- *Sharing of common interests:* Stores frequently offer specialized goods that allow people with shared interests to communicate.
- *Interpersonal attraction:* Shopping centers are a natural place to congregate. The shopping mall has become a central "hangout" for teenagers. It also represents a controlled, secure environment for the elderly, and many malls now feature "mall walkers' clubs" for early morning workouts.
- *Instant status:* As every salesperson knows, some people savor the experience of being waited on, even though they may not necessarily buy anything. One men's clothing salesman offered this advice: "Remember their size, remember what you sold them last time. Make them feel important! If you can make people feel important, they are going to come back. Everybody likes to feel important!"[39]
- *The thrill of the hunt:* Some people pride themselves on their knowledge of the marketplace. Unlike our car-buying friend Rob, they may relish the process of haggling and bargaining, viewing it almost as a sport.

Which way is it? Do people hate to shop or love it? It depends. Consumers can be segmented in terms of their **shopping orientation,** or general attitudes about shopping. These orientations may vary depending on the particular product categories and store types considered. Rob hates to shop for a car, but he may love to browse in record stores. Industry experts claim that men and women, for example, tend to differ in their shopping styles. Several shopping types have been identified:[40]

- *The economic shopper:* a rational, goal-oriented shopper who is primarily interested in maximizing the value of his or her money.
- *The personalized shopper:* a shopper who tends to form strong attachments to store personnel ("I shop where they know my name").
- *The ethical shopper:* a shopper who likes to help out the underdog and will support locally owned stores rather than big chains.
- *The apathetic shopper:* one who does not like to shop and sees it as a necessary but unpleasant chore.
- *The recreational shopper:* a person who views shopping as a fun, social activity—a preferred way to spend leisure time.

E-Commerce: Clicks Versus Bricks

As more and more Web sites pop up to sell everything from refrigerator magnets to Mack trucks, marketers are hotly debating how this new format will affect how they conduct business.[42] In particular, many are losing sleep wondering whether e-commerce is destined to replace traditional retailing, work in concert with it, or perhaps even fade away to become another fad your kids will laugh about someday. That's unlikely: Online consumer sales totaled $20 billion in 1999, and Forrester Research predicts that by 2004, 49 million households will shop online and spend $184 billion.[43]

For marketers, the growth of online commerce is a sword that cuts both ways: On the one hand, they can reach customers around the world even if they're physically located 100 miles from nowhere. On the other hand, their competition now comes not only from the store across the street, but from thousands of Web sites spanning the globe. A second problem is that offering products directly to consumers has the potential to cut out the middleman—the loyal store-based retailers who carry the firm's products and who sell them at a marked-up price.[44] The "clicks versus bricks" dilemma is raging in the marketing world.

So, can you have your cake and eat it too? Gap thinks so. Its stores and Web site work together to push up sales. Gap's online sales tripled between 1999 and 2000, and are now estimated at $50 to $100 million. That's a lot of jeans and T-shirts bought online, but still a tiny fraction of the company's $9 billion in annual sales. The company was encouraged by a study that found that more than 50 percent of consumers who buy online and in stores spend *more* than when they shopped only at stores. Gap promotes its Web site in its stores by plastering cash registers and window displays with the slogan *surf.shop.ship*. In some high-traffic stores, the chain has even installed "Web lounges" to let shoppers surf gap.com while they're still in the store.[45] One reason retailers such as Gap are pushing e-commerce so heavily is that the Internet can boost sales by luring non-traditional shoppers who don't usually visit their stores. For example, 49 percent of Internet purchases are made by male heads of households, and 68 percent by shoppers older than 40.[46] Those are customers that typically wouldn't "fall into the Gap."

So, what makes e-commerce sites successful? According to a survey by NPD Online, 75 percent of online shoppers surveyed said that good customer service would make them shop at the site again.[47] And many successful e-tailers are learning that using technology to provide extra value for customers is attracting and keeping customers. For example, Eddie Bauer (eddiebauer.com) offers customers a virtual dressing room. The Cover Girl makeup site (covergirl.com) allows women to find colors that match their skin and hair types or to design a total look that's right for their lifestyle. Interactive TV is letting home viewers provide input to the videos played on MTV and to play along with Regis on *Who Wants to be a Millionaire*? Soon MTV viewers will be able to use their remote controls to purchase the CDs that go with the music videos they are seeing.

From the consumer's perspective, electronic marketing has increased convenience by breaking down many of the barriers caused by time and location. You can shop 24 hours a day without leaving home, you can read today's newspaper without getting drenched picking up a hard copy in a rainstorm, and you don't have to wait for the 6:00 P.M. news to find out what the weather will be like tomorrow—at home or around the globe. And, with the increasing use of handheld devices and wireless communications, you can get that same

MULTICULTURAL DIMENSIONS

WHO LOVES TO SHOP the most? In a survey of women around the world, more than 60 percent of women said they enjoy shopping for clothes in every country except Hong Kong, where only 39 percent responded so positively. The "shopping" prize goes to Latin Americans; more than 80 percent of women in countries like Brazil and Colombia agree that clothes shopping is a favorite activity. Other high-scoring countries include France, Italy, and Japan. In comparison, only 61 percent of American women said they like or love to go clothes shopping. Reflecting the casual trend that's swept the country in recent years, the survey indicates that American women are more likely to say that they are not as interested in clothing as they used to be, are more willing to be slightly underdressed at a party rather than slightly overdressed, and they are more willing to wear one comfortable outfit all day long than change clothes to fit each occasion. Almost everywhere in the world, women agreed that store displays are the most important source of information about clothing. Two exceptions are German women, who ranked fashion magazines highest, and Mexican women, who reported that their families are the best place to learn about what to wear.[41]

REALITY CHECK *NEW INTERACTIVE TOOLS ARE BEING INTRODUCED*

that allow surfers on sites such as Landsend.com to view apparel product selections on virtual models in full, 360-degree rotational view. In some cases, the bodies, face, skin coloring, and hairstyles of these models can be modified. In others, the consumer can project his or her own likeness into the space by scanning a photo into a "makeover" program. Boo.com plans to offer three-dimensional pictures that can be rotated for close looks, even down to stitching on a sweater, as well as online mannequins that will incorporate photos of shoppers and mimic voice patterns.[48] *Visit landsend.com or another site that offers a personalized mannequin. Surf around. Try on some clothes.*

Now, tell us about your experience. How helpful was this mannequin? When you shop for clothes online, would you rather see how they look on a body with dimensions the same as yours, or on a different body? What advice can you give Web site designers who are trying to personalize these shopping environments by creating lifelike models to guide you through the site?

The virtual model was more of a novelty and fun to play with than it was useful. It was somewhat useful to see a model of my body type modeling the clothes I was interested in purchasing. However, the virtual model does not replace the accuracy of trying on the clothing personally. Usually, the clothes I purchase from magazines do not look anything like what I expect them to look like. . . . In all honesty, the clothes on airbrushed models on the cover of magazines are what attracted me to purchasing the clothing in the first place. If I had any advice for website designers who create these virtual models, it would be to keep enhancing the graphics and the curves of these models.

Jill Wittekind
University of Nevada, Las Vegas

We often see inaccurate ideals of beauty when browsing through catalogs. If a model looks beautiful in a certain pair of black pants, we are often tempted to buy them, yet hesitate, doubting that a pair of pants could ever look that good on us, let alone even fit us. . . . Having a virtual model that can reproduce a computer image of a woman's exact dimensions is both beneficial not only to the woman herself, but also the company she is considering ordering clothes from. . . . Having this added amenity will likely increase purchases and profit for an on-line catalog, and increase customer satisfaction.

Katherine S. Kennedy
James Madison University

The experience of surfing through these sites is very interesting and original, but at the same time very unreal and idealistic . . . this way of purchasing could never allow the person to touch the fabric's texture, see the details or quality of the clothes, etc. . . . My advice to website designers of this kind of sites is that they must know that people are averse to using unconventional methods for the first time (getting used to technology). . . . If they have virtual mannequins they must be specifically designed according to the consumer's measures (not standard measures, like the mannequins of landsend.com that are really far away from reality).

Constanza Montes Larranga
Universidad de Chile

I tried to build my own model with my body measurements to better assess whether a bathing suit that I like on-line would indeed look good on me. The Web site allowed me to choose the color of my skin, the shape of my face, my hairstyle, and my body measurements to match the model to my own body as closely as possible. It was difficult to come up with all the detailed measurements that were required to build the model, even with a measuring tape at hand. The model did give me a better idea of what the product would look like on me, but I still don't think I would purchase clothing without trying it on first. It was definitely helpful to see the bathing suit on a body that was similar to mine, rather than on someone with completely different measurements. We all know that things don't always look the same on everybody.

Liana Mouynes
University of Washington

Having a virtual model to view apparel is an interesting addition to any on-line store. It is a lot like trying clothes on a Barbie, so it might be popular with women, not men. Most women who shop on-line will probably like the idea of being able to see how the clothes look on a person of their body shape, as not many people are the same shape as models. . . . Although a 3-D model shows how the clothes hang on a body, the model's body is not in motion so you cannot see or feel how the clothes move. At best it will be a fun pastime for Internet explorers, but not for buyers.

Liv Amber Judd
University of Saskatchewan, Canada

I did not find the mannequins particularly helpful in the sites I visited. For example, at Landsend.com, even though I was able to "custom design" my model, she still was not an accurate likeness of me and I had a hard time believing that the clothes I was trying on would really look like that on me. The model I designed using my physical characteristics seemed shorter and stouter than me. Therefore, when I tried on tricky clothing items such as pants and jackets, I seriously doubted that the model was an accurate representation of what the clothing would look like on me. At Boo.com, the model was one of those "perfect" women with "perfect" proportions. . . . I would feel more comfortable trying on clothing with a model that was as close to my physical dimensions as possible.

Sabrina Aslam
Simon Fraser University B.C.

People are not going to buy something like clothes over the Internet unless it is to re-order an item they've previously purchased in a store. People enjoy the attention they get when they walk into a boutique. That sense of belonging is lost over the computer, especially for older women and for those who are techno-phobic. . . . I do not necessarily believe that Internet shopping will be a complete failure but I do not see a bright future for the dot.com companies selling personal items such as jewelry and clothes. Internet shopping will play an important role in re-orders or purchases of such items as books and videos.

Pamela Gillen
Dublin City University

E-commerce sites like bluefly give shoppers the option of shopping without leaving home.

information—from stock quotes to the weather—even when you're away from your computer.

However, all is not perfect in the virtual world. E-commerce does have its limitations. Security is one important concern. We hear horror stories of consumers whose credit cards and other identity information have been stolen. Although an individual's financial liability in most theft cases is limited to $50, the damage to one's credit rating can last for years. Some shady companies are making money by prying and then selling personal information to others—one company promotes itself as "an amazing new tool that allows you to find out EVERYTHING you ever wanted to know about your friends, family, neighbors, employees, and even your boss!"[49] Pretty scary. Almost daily we hear of hackers getting into a business or even a government Web site and causing havoc. Businesses risk the loss of trade secrets and other proprietary information. Many must spend significant amounts to maintain security and conduct regular audits to ensure the integrity of their sites.

Other limitations of e-commerce relate to the actual shopping experience. Although it may be satisfactory to buy a computer or a book on the Internet, buying clothing and other items in which touching the item or trying it on is essential may be less attractive. Even though most companies have very liberal return policies, consumers can still get stuck with large delivery and return shipping charges for items that don't fit or simply aren't the right color. Some of the pros and cons of e-commerce are summarized in Table 10.2. It's clear that traditional shopping isn't quite dead yet—but bricks-and-mortar retailers do need to work harder to give shoppers something they can't get (yet anyway) in the virtual world—a stimulating or pleasant environment in which to browse. Now let's consider how they're doing that.

TABLE 10.2 Pros and Cons of E-Commerce

Benefits of E-Commerce	Limitations of E-Commerce
For the Consumer	**For the Consumer**
Shop 24 hours a day	Lack of security
Less traveling	Fraud
Can receive relevant information in seconds from any location	Can't touch items
More choices of products	Exact colors may not reproduce on computer monitors
More products available to less-developed countries	Expensive to order and then return
Greater price information	Potential breakdown of human relationships
Lower prices so that less affluent can purchase	
Participate in virtual auctions	
Fast delivery	
Electronic communities	
For the Marketer	**For the Marketer**
The world is the marketplace	Lack of security
Decreases costs of doing business	Must maintain site to reap benefits
Very specialized businesses can be successful	Fierce price competition
Real-time pricing	Conflicts with conventional retailers
	Legal issues not resolved

SOURCE: Adapted from Michael R. Solomon and Elnora W. Stuart, *Welcome to Marketing.Com: The Brave New World of E-Commerce* (Upper Saddle River, NJ: Prentice Hall, 2001).

Retailing as Theater

The competition for customers is becoming even more intense as nonstore alternatives from Web sites and print catalogs to TV shopping networks and home shopping parties continue to multiply. With all of these shopping alternatives available, how can a traditional store compete? Shopping malls have tried to gain the loyalty of shoppers by appealing to their social motives as well as providing access to desired goods. The mall is often a focal point in a community. In the United States, 94 percent of adults visit a mall at least once a month. More than half of all retail purchases (excluding autos and gasoline) are made in a mall.[50]

Malls are becoming giant entertainment centers, almost to the point that their traditional retail occupants seem like an afterthought. As one retailing executive put it, "Malls are becoming the new mini-amusement parks."[51] It is now typical to find such features as carousels, miniature golf, and batting cages in a suburban mall. The goal is to provide an experience that will draw people to the mall, and this motivates innovative marketers to blur the line between shopping and theater.[52] Consider these recent developments:

- At the chain of malls run by the Mills Corporation, there is an emphasis on providing interactive experiences. The company is trying to give its 10 malls around the country a single national brand image using the total experience theme. They feature theme restaurants like Rainforest Cafe and virtual reality game centers.[53] The objective to provide "retailtainment" is also evident at Sony's Metreon entertainment center in San Francisco. A bank of movie theaters shows Sony films, and cutting-edge cameras, computers, and video equipment are displayed in shops.[54] Shoppers can play state-of-the-art computer games to their hearts' content on massive floor-to-ceiling screens.

- Vans Inc., a Los Angeles-based sporting goods retailer, opened a 60,000-square foot skate park and off-road bicycle track at the Ontario Mills Mall. As one enthusiastic teenager observed, "All malls should have this. They kick us out of every place else to skate—they might as well make it legal." Bass Pro Shops, a chain of outdoor sports equipment stores, features giant aquariums, waterfalls, trout ponds, archery and rifle ranges, putting greens, and free classes in everything from ice fishing to conservation.[55]

- In the hotel industry, themed rooms have become the rage. California's Madonna Inn features 109 different rooms, such as the Caveman Room, which has natural rock floors and a waterfall. The Swiss Family Robinson Suite at the Anniversary Inn in Salt Lake City lets you sleep in a tree. At the Hotel Monaco in Chicago, you can party like a rock star: For a "mere" $425 at night you stay in a suite that includes a TV that appears to have been thrown through a window as well as a video jukebox and concert photos. In the Blues Brothers suite at the House Of Blues Hotel in Chicago, you can see one of the suits Dan Akroyd wore in the movie *Blues Brothers 2000*.[56]

- The Easy Everything cafe in London is the biggest Internet cafe in the world. An estimated 5,000 people visit everyday, including Europe-crossing backpackers who can check their e-mail. It and other cafes are trying to increase traffic with computer game competitions, training seminars, and wine tastings. Some even feature live feeds from stock exchanges to attract a day-trader clientele.[57]

- Even fast food is blending with entertainment. Burger King unveiled its prototype store design for the twenty-first century. The kitchen is open for viewing so those waiting in line can see flames in the broiler. A virtual fun center features electronic, interactive games for children, including videoconferencing capability, so kids at one Burger King can chat with kids at other Burger Kings.[58]

Store Image

With so many stores competing for customers, how do consumers pick one over another? As with products (see Chapter 6), stores may be thought of as having "personalities." Some stores have very clearly defined images (either good or bad). Others tend to blend into the crowd. They may not have anything distinctive about them and may be overlooked for this reason. This personality, or **store image,** is composed of many different factors. Store features, coupled with such consumer characteristics as shopping orientation, help to predict which shopping outlets people will prefer.[59] Some of the important dimensions of a store's profile are location, merchandise suitability, and the knowledge and congeniality of the sales staff.[60]

These features typically work together to create an overall impression. When shoppers think about stores, they may not say, "Well, that place is fairly good in terms of convenience, the salespeople are acceptable, and services are good." They are more likely to say, "That place gives me the creeps," or "I always enjoy shopping there." Consumers often evaluate stores using a general evaluation, and this overall feeling may have more to do with intangibles such as interior design and the types of people one finds in the store than with aspects such as return policies or credit availability. As a result, some stores are likely to consistently be in consumers' evoked sets (see Chapter 9), whereas others will never be considered.[61]

Atmospherics

Because a store's image is now recognized as a very important aspect of the retailing mix, store designers pay a lot of attention to **atmospherics,** or the "conscious designing of space and its various dimensions to evoke certain effects in buyers."[62] These dimensions include colors, scents, and sounds. For example, stores done in red tend to make people tense, whereas a blue decor imparts a calmer feeling.[63] As was noted in Chapter 2, some preliminary evidence indicates that smells (olfactory cues) also can influence evaluations of a store's environment.[64] A store's atmosphere in turn affects purchasing behavior—one recent study reported that the extent of pleasure reported by shoppers five minutes after entering a store was predictive of the amount of time spent in the store as well as the level of spending there.[65]

Many elements of store design can be cleverly controlled to attract customers and produce desired effects on consumers. Light colors impart a feeling of spaciousness and serenity, and signs in bright colors create excitement. In one subtle but effective application, fashion designer Norma Kamali replaced fluorescent lights with pink ones in department store dressing rooms. The light had the effect of flattering the face and banishing wrinkles, making female customers more willing to try on (and buy) the company's bathing suits.[66] Wal-Mart found that sales were higher in areas of a prototype store lit in natural daylight compared to the more typical artificial light.[67] One study found that brighter in-store lighting influenced people to examine and handle more merchandise.[68]

In addition to visual stimuli, all sorts of cues can influence behaviors.[69] For example, patrons of country-and-western bars drink more when the jukebox music is slower. According to a researcher, "Hard drinkers prefer listening to slower-paced, wailing, lonesome, self-pitying music."[70] Similarly, music can affect eating habits. Another study found that diners who listened to loud, fast music ate more food. In contrast, those who listened to Mozart or Brahms ate less and more slowly. The researchers concluded that diners who choose soothing music at mealtimes can increase weight loss by at least five pounds a month![71]

In-Store Decision Making

Despite all their efforts to "presell" consumers through advertising, marketers increasingly recognize that many purchases are influenced by the store environment. It has been estimated that about two out of every three supermarket purchases are decided in the aisles. The proportion of unplanned purchases is even higher for some product categories. Roughly 85 percent of candy and gum, almost 70 percent of cosmetics, and 75 percent of oral hygiene purchases are unplanned.[72] And, people with lists are just as likely to make spontaneous purchases as those without them.[73]

Spontaneous Shopping

When a shopper is prompted to buy something in the store, one of two different processes may be at work: *Unplanned buying* may occur when a person is unfamiliar with a store's layout or perhaps when under some time pressure; or, a person may be reminded to buy something by seeing it on a store shelf. About one-third of unplanned buying has been attributed to the recognition of new needs while within the store.[76]

In contrast, **impulse buying** occurs when the person experiences a sudden urge that he or she cannot resist. The tendency to buy spontaneously is most

MARKETING OPPORTUNITY

SHOP THE STORE, BUY the soundtrack: Growing recognition of the important role played by a store or restaurant's audio environment has created a new niche, as some companies now are selling musical collections tailored to different activities. These include RCA Victor's "Classical Music for Home Improvements" and Sony Classics' "Cyber Classics," which is billed as music specifically for computer hackers to listen to while programming! In contrast, Sony's "Extreme Classics," packaged for bungee jumpers, claims to be the "loudest and most dangerous music ever written." Whereas a standard hit classical CD might sell 25,000 copies, Polygram's Philips label has sold more than 500,000 units of its "Set Your Life to Music" series including "Mozart in the Morning," and "Baroque at Bathtime." Rising Star Records shipped 10,000 copies of "Classical Erotica" in three months. Both Ralph Lauren and Victoria's Secret are packaging the music played in store outlets, and the bakery chain Au Bon Pain started selling its background music on a CD.[74] Similar spin-offs are in the works by Pottery Barn and Starbucks, which licensed the Blue Note label from Capitol Records for this purpose.[75]

Smart retailers recognize that many purchase decisions are made at the time the shopper is in the store. That's one reason why grocery carts sometimes resemble billboards on wheels.

likely to result in a purchase when the consumers believe acting on impulse is appropriate, such as purchasing a gift for a sick friend or picking up the tab for a meal.[77] To cater to these urges, so-called *impulse items* such as candy and gum are conveniently placed near the checkout. Similarly, many supermarkets have installed wider aisles to encourage browsing, and the widest tend to contain products with the highest profit margins. Low markup items that are purchased regularly tend to be stacked high in narrower aisles to allow shopping carts to speed through.[78] A more recent high-tech tool has been added to encourage impulse buying: A device called the Portable Shopper is a personal scanning gun that allows customers to ring up their own purchases as they shop. The gun was initially developed for Albert Hejin, the Netherlands' largest grocery chain, to move customers through the store more quickly. It's now in use in more than 150 groceries worldwide.[79]

Shoppers can be categorized in terms of how much advance planning they do. *Planners* tend to know what products and specific brands they will buy beforehand.

DRAW-A-PICTURE

1. Think about your image of what kind of person an impulse buyer is. In the space provided below, draw a picture of your image of a typical impulse buyer who is about to make an impulse purchase. Be creative and don't worry about your artistic skills! If you feel that some features of your drawing are unclear, don't hesitate to identify them with a written label.

2. After you have completed your drawing, imagine what is going through your 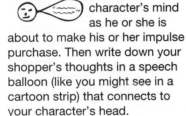 character's mind as he or she is about to make his or her impulse purchase. Then write down your shopper's thoughts in a speech balloon (like you might see in a cartoon strip) that connects to your character's head.

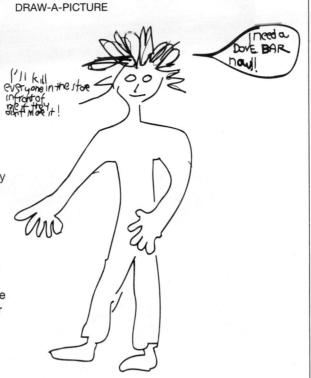

Figure 10.4
One Consumer's Image of an Impulse Buyer

Source: Dennis Rook, "Is Impulse Buying (Yet) a Useful Marketing Concept?" (unpublished manuscript, University of Southern California, Los Angeles, 1990): Fig. 7–A.

Partial planners know they need certain products, but do not decide on specific brands until they are in the store, whereas *impulse purchasers* do no advance planning whatsoever.[80] A consumer who was asked to sketch a typical impulse purchaser, participating in a study on consumers' shopping experiences, drew Figure 10.4.

Point-of-Purchase Stimuli

Impulse purchases increase by 10 percent when appropriate displays are used. Each year, U.S. companies spend more than $13 billion on **point-of-purchase stimuli (POP).** A point-of-purchase stimulus can be an elaborate product display or demonstration, a coupon-dispensing machine, or even someone giving out free samples of a new cookie in the grocery aisle. Some of the more dramatic POP displays have included the following:[81]

- *Timex:* A ticking watch sits in the bottom of a filled aquarium.
- *Kellogg's Corn Flakes:* A button with a picture of Cornelius the Rooster is placed within the reach of children near Corn Flakes. When a child presses the button, he hears the rooster cock-a-doodle-doo.
- *Elizabeth Arden:* The company introduced "Elizabeth," a computer and video makeover system that allows customers to test out their images with different shades of makeup without having to actually apply the products first.
- *Tower Records:* A music sampler allows customers to hear records before buying them and to custom-design their own recordings by mixing and matching singles from assorted artists.
- *Trifari:* This company offered paper punch-out versions of its jewelry so that customers can "try on" the pieces at home.

Music samplers that allow shoppers to check out the latest tunes before buying have become a fixture in many stores. New versions allow listeners to select files, record them on to a CD, and even select the cover and clip art to personalize it.

- *Charmin:* Building on the familiar "Please don't squeeze the Charmin" theme, the company deployed the Charmin Squeeze Squad. Employees hid behind stacks of the toilet tissue and jumped out and blew horns at any "squeezers" they caught in the aisles.
- *The Farnam Company:* As somber music plays in the background, a huge plastic rat draped in a black shroud lay next to a tombstone to promote the company's "Just One Bite" rat poison.

The Salesperson

One of the most important in-store factors is the salesperson.[82] This influence can be understood in terms of **exchange theory,** which stresses that every interaction involves an exchange of value. Each participant gives something to the other and hopes to receive something in return.[83]

What "value" does the customer look for in a sales interaction? There are a variety of resources a salesperson might offer. For example, they might offer expertise about the product to make the shopper's choice easier. Alternatively, the customer may be reassured because the salesperson is a likable person whose tastes are similar and is seen as someone who can be trusted.[84] Rob's car purchase, for example, was strongly influenced by the age and sex of Rhoda, the salesperson with whom he negotiated. In fact, a long stream of research attests to the impact of a salesperson's appearance on sales effectiveness. In sales, as in much of life, attractive people appear to hold the upper hand.[85] In addition, it's not unusual for service personnel and customers to form fairly warm personal relationships; these have been termed *commercial* friendships (think of all those patient bartenders who double as therapists for many people!). Researchers have found that commercial friendships are similar to other friendships in that they can involve affection, intimacy, social support, loyalty, and reciprocal gift-giving. They also work to support marketing objectives such as satisfaction, loyalty, and positive word of mouth.[86]

A buyer/seller situation is like many other dyadic encounters (two-person groups); it is a relationship in which some agreement must be reached about the roles of each participant: A process of *identity negotiation* occurs.[87] For example, if Rhoda immediately establishes herself as an expert (and Rob accepts this position), she is likely to have more influence over him through the course of the relationship. Some of the factors that help to determine a salesperson's role (and relative effectiveness) are their age, appearance, educational level, and motivation to sell.[88]

In addition, more effective salespersons usually know their customers' traits and preferences better than do ineffective salespersons because this knowledge allows them to adapt their approach to meet the needs of the specific customer.[89] The ability to be adaptable is especially vital when customers and salespeople differ in terms of their *interaction styles*.[90] Consumers, for example, vary in the degree of assertiveness they bring to interactions. At one extreme, nonassertive people believe that complaining is not socially acceptable and may be intimidated in sales situations. Assertive people are more likely to stand up for themselves in a firm but nonthreatening way. Aggressives may resort to rudeness and threats if they do not get their way.[91]

POSTPURCHASE SATISFACTION

Consumer satisfaction/dissatisfaction (CS/D) is determined by the overall feelings, or attitude, a person has about a product after it has been purchased. Consumers are engaged in a constant process of evaluating the things they buy as these products are integrated into their daily consumption activities.[94] Despite evidence that customer satisfaction is steadily declining in many industries, good marketers are constantly on the lookout for sources of dissatisfaction so that they can improve.[95] For example, when United Airlines' advertising agency set out to identify specific aspects of air travel that were causing problems, they gave frequent fliers crayons and a map showing different stages in a long-distance trip and asked them to fill in colors using hot hues to symbolize areas causing stress and anger and cool colors for parts of the trip associated with satisfaction and calm feelings. Although jet cabins tended to be filled in with a serene aqua color, lo and behold, ticket counters were colored orange, and terminal waiting areas were fire-red. This research led the airline to focus more on overall operations instead of just in-flight experiences, and the "United Rising" campaign was born.[96]

Perceptions of Product Quality

Just what do consumers look for in products? That's easy: They want quality and value. Especially because of foreign competition, claims of product quality have become strategically crucial to maintaining a competitive advantage.[98] Consumers use a number of cues to infer quality, including brand name, price,

THE TANGLED WEB

WHO SAID THE CUSTOMER is always right? A booming economy has been a mixed blessing for companies because the low level of unemployment makes it tough to find good workers. That's part of the reason why customer satisfaction regarding fast food restaurants, retailers, gas stations, and banks has fallen to its lowest level in 30 years. Managers have to tolerate bad service or find new workers—entire staffs can turn over three times each year. How's this for a bad service experience: A Detroit couple filed a $100 million lawsuit against McDonald's, alleging they were beaten by three McDonald's employees after they tried to return a watery milkshake.

Now employees are venting their hostility toward customers and employers online. At a Web site put up by a disgruntled former employee of a different fast food franchise, we share the pain of this ex-burger flipper: "My memories of adolescence are riddled with the smell of chicken tenders and vanilla shakes. I have seen the creatures that live at the bottom of the dumpster. I have seen the rat by the soda machine. I have seen dead frogs in the fresh salad lettuce. I have seen undercooked meat served to children and I have seen bags of trash piled higher than I stand as they lay less than three feet from the hamburger meat.[92] Super size that order?

A Web site called customerssuck.com gets 1,200 hits a day. Some participants share stupid questions their customers ask, such as "How much is a 99-cent cheeseburger?" whereas others just complain about working conditions and having to be nice to not-so-nice people. The slogan of the site is "the customer is never right."[93]

MARKETING PITFALLS

NOT EXACTLY AN IDEAL test drive: A woman sued a car dealer in Iowa, claiming that a salesperson persuaded her to climb into the trunk of a Chrysler Concorde to check out its spaciousness. He then slammed the trunk shut and bounced the car several times, apparently to the delight of his coworkers. This bizarre act apparently came about because the manager offered a prize of $100 to the salesperson who could get a customer to climb in. At last report, this persuasive salesperson is selling vacuum cleaners door to door.[97]

and even their own estimates of how much money has been put into a new product's advertising campaign.[99] These cues, as well as others such as product warranties and follow-up letters from the company, are often used by consumers to relieve perceived risk and assure themselves that they have made smart purchase decisions.[100]

Although everyone wants quality, it is not clear exactly what it means. Certainly, many manufacturers claim to provide it. The Ford Motor Company emphasizes, *"Quality* is Job 1." Similar claims that have been made at one time or another by car manufacturers include the following:[101]

- *Lincoln-Mercury:* "the highest quality cars of any major American car company"
- *Chrysler:* "quality engineered to be the best"
- *GMC Trucks:* "quality built yet economical"
- *Oldsmobile:* "fulfilling the quality needs of American drivers"
- *Audi:* "quality backed by our outstanding new warranty"

Quality Is What We Expect It to Be

In the book *Zen and the Art of Motorcycle Maintenance,* a cult hero of college students in an earlier generation literally went crazy trying to figure out the meaning of quality.[102] Marketers appear to use the word quality as a catchall term for "good." Because of its wide and imprecise usage, the attribute of "quality" threatens to become a meaningless claim. If everyone has it, what good is it?

To muddy the waters a bit more, satisfaction or dissatisfaction is more than a reaction to the actual performance quality of a product or service. It is influenced by prior expectations regarding the level of quality. According to the *expectancy disconfirmation model,* consumers form beliefs about product performance based on prior experience with the product and/or communications about the product that imply a certain level of quality.[103] When something performs the way we thought it would, we may not think much about it. If, on the other hand, it fails to live up to expectations, negative affect may result. Furthermore, if performance happens to exceed our expectations, we are satisfied and pleased.

This ad for Ford relies on a common claim about quality.

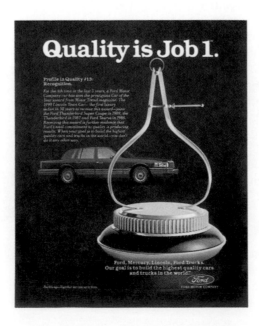

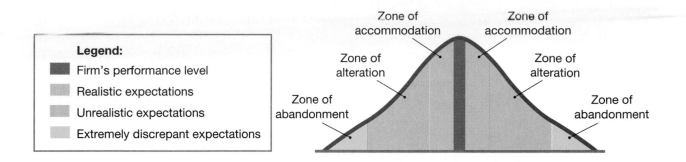

Legend:
- Firm's performance level
- Realistic expectations
- Unrealistic expectations
- Extremely discrepant expectations

Zone of accommodation

Zone of alteration

Zone of abandonment

Figure 10.5
Expectation Zones

To understand this perspective, think about different types of restaurants. People expect to be provided with sparkling clear glassware at fancy restaurants, and they might become upset if they discover a grimy glass. On the other hand, they may not be surprised to find fingerprints on a beer mug at a local greasy spoon; they may even shrug it off because it contributes to the place's "charm." An important lesson for marketers: Don't overpromise if you can't deliver.[104]

This perspective underscores the importance of *managing expectations—* customer dissatisfaction is usually due to expectations exceeding the company's ability to deliver. Figure 10.5 illustrates the alternative strategies a firm can choose in these situations. When confronted with unrealistic expectations about what it can do, the firm can either accommodate these demands by improving the range or quality of products it offers, alter the expectations, or perhaps even choose to abandon the customer if it is not feasible to meet his or her needs.[105] Expectations are altered, for example, when waiters tell patrons in advance that the portion size they have ordered will not be very big, or when new car buyers are warned of strange smells they will experience during the break-in period. A firm also can underpromise, as when Xerox inflates the time it will take for a service rep to visit. When the rep arrives a day earlier, the customer is impressed.

The power of quality claims is most evident when a company's product fails. Here, consumers' expectations are dashed and dissatisfaction results. In these situations, marketers must immediately take steps to reassure customers. When the company confronts the problem truthfully, consumers are often willing to forgive and forget, as was the case for Tylenol (product tampering), Chrysler (disconnecting odometers on executives' cars and reselling them as new), or Perrier (traces of benzene found in the water). When the company appears to be dragging its heels or covering up, on the other hand, consumer resentment will grow, as occurred during Union Carbide's chemical disaster in India and Exxon's massive Alaskan oil spill caused by the tanker *Exxon Valdez.*

Acting on Dissatisfaction

If a person is not happy with a product or service, what can be done? A consumer has three possible courses of action (more than one can be taken):[106]

1. *Voice response:* The consumer can appeal directly to the retailer for redress (e.g., a refund).
2. *Private response:* Express dissatisfaction about the store or product to friends and/or boycott the store. As will be discussed in Chapter 11, negative word-of-mouth (WOM) can be very damaging to a store's reputation.

3. *Third-party response:* The consumer can take legal action against the merchant, register a complaint with the Better Business Bureau, or perhaps write a letter to the newspaper.

In one study, business majors wrote complaint letters to companies. Those who were sent a free sample in response indicated their image of the company significantly improved, but those who received only a letter of apology did not change their evaluations of the company. However, students who got no response reported an even more negative image than before, indicating that some form of response is better than none.[107]

A number of factors influence which route is eventually taken. The consumer may be a generally assertive or meek person. Action is more likely to be taken for expensive products such as household durables, cars, and clothing than for inexpensive products.[108] In addition, consumers who are satisfied with a store are more likely to complain; they take the time to complain because they feel connected to the store. Older people are more likely to complain, and are much more likely to believe the store will actually resolve the problem. Shoppers who get their problems resolved feel even *better* about the store than if nothing went wrong.[109] On the other hand, if the consumer does not believe that the store will respond well to a complaint, the person will be more likely to simply switch than fight.[110] Ironically, marketers should actually *encourage* consumers to complain to them: People are more likely to spread the word about unresolved negative experiences to their friends than they are to boast about positive occurrences.[111]

PRODUCT DISPOSAL

Because people often do form strong attachments to products, the decision to dispose of something may be a painful one. One function performed by possessions is to serve as anchors for our identities: Our past lives on in our things.[112] This attachment is exemplified by the Japanese, who ritually "retire" worn-out sewing needles, chopsticks, and even computer chips by burning them as thanks for good service.[113]

Although some people have more trouble than others in discarding things, even a "pack rat" does not keep everything. Consumers must often dispose of things, either because they have fulfilled their designated functions, or possibly because they no longer fit with consumers' view of themselves. Concern about the environment coupled with a need for convenience has made ease of product disposal a key attribute in categories from razors to diapers.

Disposal Options

When a consumer decides that a product is no longer of use, several choices are available. The person can either (1) keep the item, (2) temporarily dispose of it, or (3) permanently dispose of it. In many cases, a new product is acquired even though the old one still functions. Some reasons for this replacement include a desire for new features, a change in the person's environment (e.g., a refrigerator is the wrong color for a freshly painted kitchen), or a change in the person's role or self-image.[114] Figure 10.6 provides an overview of consumers' disposal options.

The issue of product disposition is doubly vital because of its enormous public policy implications. We live in a throwaway society, which creates problems for the environment and also results in a great deal of unfortunate waste. In a recent survey, 15 percent of adults admit they are pack rats and another 64 percent say

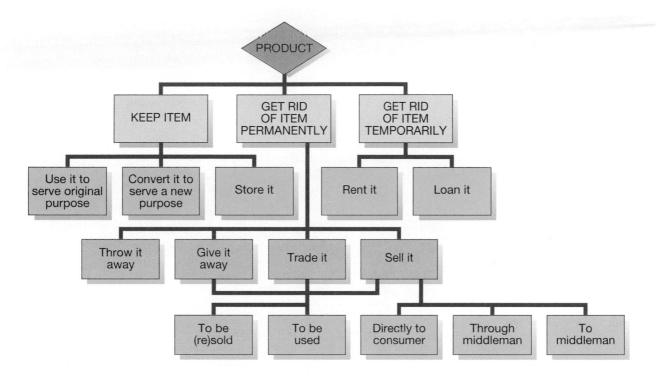

Figure 10.6
Consumers' Disposal Options

Source: Jacob Jacoby, Carol K. Berning, and Thomas F. Dietvorst. "What About Disposition?" *Journal of Marketing* 41 (April 1977):23. By permission of American Marketing Association.

they are selective savers. In contrast, 20 percent say they throw out as much garbage as they can. The consumers most likely to save things are older people and single households.[115]

Training consumers to recycle has become a priority in many countries. Japan recycles about 40 percent of its garbage, and this relatively high rate of compliance is partly due to the social value the Japanese place on recycling: Citizens are encouraged by garbage trucks that periodically rumble through the streets playing classical music or children's songs.[116] Companies continue to search for

This British ad promotes the use of recycled paper.

This Dutch ad says, "And when you've had enough of it, we'll clear it away nicely."

En als u erop uitgekeken bent,
ruimen we hem weer netjes op.

ways to use resources more efficiently, often at the prompting of activist consumer groups. For example, McDonald's restaurants bowed to pressure by eliminating the use of Styrofoam packages, and its outlets in Europe are experimenting with edible breakfast platters made of maize.[117]

A study examined the relevant goals consumers have in recycling. It used a means–end chain analysis of the type described in Chapter 4 to identify how specific instrumental goals are linked to more abstract terminal values. The most important lower-order goals identified were "avoid filling up landfills," "reduce waste," "reuse materials," and "save the environment." These were linked to the terminal values of "promote health/avoid sickness," "achieve life-sustaining ends," and "provide for future generations." Another study reported that the perceived effort involved in recycling was the best predictor of whether people would

Flea markets are an important form of lateral cycling.

go to the trouble—this pragmatic dimension outweighed general attitudes toward recycling and the environment in predicting intention to recycle.[118] By applying such techniques to study recycling and other product disposal behaviors, it will be easier for social marketers to design advertising copy and other messages that tap into the underlying values that will motivate people to increase environmentally responsible behavior.[119]

Lateral Cycling: Junk Versus "Junque"

Interesting consumer processes occur during **lateral cycling,** in which already-purchased objects are sold to others or exchanged for still other things. Many purchases are made secondhand, rather than new. The reuse of other people's things is especially important in our throwaway society because, as one researcher put it, "there is no longer an 'away' to throw things to."[120]

Flea markets, garage sales, classified advertisements, bartering for services, hand-me-downs, and the black market all represent important alternative marketing systems that operate alongside the formal marketplace. For example, the number of used-merchandise retail establishments has grown at about 10 times the rate of other stores.[121] Although traditional marketers have not paid much attention to used-product sellers, factors such as concern about the environment, demands for quality, and cost and fashion consciousness are conspiring to make these "secondary" markets more important.[122]

Interest in antiques, period accessories, and specialty magazines catering to this niche is increasing. Other growth areas include student markets for used computers and textbooks, as well as ski swaps, at which millions of dollars worth of used ski equipment is exchanged. A new generation of secondhand storeowners is developing markets for everything from used office equipment to cast-off kitchen sinks. Many are nonprofit ventures started with government funding. A trade association called the Reuse Development Organization (or *redo*) encourages them. These efforts remind us that recycling is actually the last step in the familiar mantra of the environmental movement: Reduce, reuse, recycle. Only if no use is found for an item should it be shredded and made into something else.[123]

NET PROFIT

FLEA MARKETS ARE ONLINE, and in a big way. People have swapped used items on bulletin boards and newsgroups for years, but now a number of sites have been set up to do this in a more sophisticated fashion. In addition to the tremendously popular auction site ebay.com, other sites such as www.bidfind.com comb the Web to list and sell used goods from Aerosmith memorabilia to zydecos.[124] Sites such as webswap.com and switchouse.com host global swap meets at which people from around the world can buy or sell obscure treasures.[125] Other sites, such as Closeoutnow.com, Liquidation.com, and Retailexchange.com, are springing up to meet the needs of businesses that need to liquidate inventory. Looking for an elegant cashmere coat? Gold cuff links? An equine saddle pad? A home hair cutting kit? All of these items have been left at airline baggage claims, and an online store called unclaimedbaggage.com specializes in the lateral cycling of goodies that people never bothered to claim.[126] Searching for garage sales will never be the same.

CHAPTER SUMMARY

- *The act of purchase* can be affected by many factors. These include the consumer's antecedent state (e.g., his/her mood, time pressure, or disposition toward shopping). Time is an important resource that often determines how much effort and search will go into a decision. Mood can be affected by the degree of pleasure and arousal present in a store environment.
- *The usage context* of a product can be a basis for segmentation; consumers look for different product attributes depending on the use to which they intend to put their purchase. The presence or absence of other people—and the types of people they are—can also affect a consumer's decisions.
- *The shopping experience* is a pivotal part of the purchase decision. In many cases, retailing is like theater—the consumer's evaluation of stores and products may depend on the type of "performance" he or she witnesses. The actors (e.g., salespeople), the setting (the store environment), and props (e.g., store displays) influence this evaluation. A *store image,* like a brand personality,

is determined by a number of factors such as perceived convenience, sophistication, expertise of salespeople, and so on. With increasing competition from nonstore alternatives, the creation of a positive shopping experience has never been more important. Online shopping is growing in importance, and this new way to acquire products has both good (e.g., convenience) and bad (e.g., security) aspects.

- Because many purchase decisions are not made until the time the consumer is actually in the store, *point-of-purchase (POP)* stimuli are very important sales tools. These include product samples, elaborate package displays, place-based media, and in-store promotional materials such as "shelf talkers." POP stimuli are particularly useful in stimulating impulse buying, in which a consumer yields to a sudden urge for a product.
- The consumer's encounter with a salesperson is a complex and important process. The outcome can be affected by such factors as the salesperson's similarity to the customer and his or her perceived credibility.
- *Consumer satisfaction* is determined by the person's overall feeling toward the product after purchase. Many factors influence perceptions of product quality, including price, brand name, and product performance. Satisfaction is often determined by the degree to which a product's performance is consistent with the consumer's prior expectations of how well it will function.
- *Product disposal* is an increasingly important problem. Recycling is one option that will continue to be stressed as consumers' environmental awareness grows. *Lateral cycling* occurs when objects are bought and sold secondhand, fenced, or bartered.

KEY TERMS

atmospherics, p. 301
consumer satisfaction/
   dissatisfaction (CS/D), p. 305
exchange theory, p. 304

impulse buying, p. 301
lateral cycling, p. 311
point-of-purchase stimuli
   (POP), p. 303

shopping orientation, p. 295
store image, p. 300
time poverty, p. 291

CONSUMER BEHAVIOR CHALLENGE

1. Discuss some of the motivations for shopping described in the chapter. How might a retailer adjust his or her strategy to accommodate these motivations?
2. Court cases in recent years have attempted to prohibit special interest groups from distributing literature in shopping malls. Mall management claims that these centers are private property. On the other hand, these groups argue that the mall is the modern-day version of the town square and as such is a public forum. Find some recent court cases involving this free-speech issue, and examine the arguments pro and con. What is the current status of the mall as a public forum? Do you agree with this concept?
3. What are some positive and negative aspects of requiring employees who interact with customers to wear some kind of uniform or of mandating a dress code in the office?
4. Think about exceptionally good and bad salespeople you have encountered in the past. What qualities seem to differentiate them?
5. Discuss the concept of "timestyle." Based on your own experiences, how might consumers be segmented in terms of their timestyles?

6. Compare and contrast different cultures' conceptions of time. What are some implications for marketing strategy within each of these frameworks?

7. The movement away from a "disposable consumer society" toward one that emphasizes creative recycling creates many opportunities for marketers. Can you identify some?

8. Conduct naturalistic observation at a local mall. Sit in a central location and observe the activities of mall employees and patrons. Keep a log of the nonretailing activity you observe (e.g., special performances, exhibits, socializing, etc.). Does this activity enhance or detract from business conducted at the mall? As malls become more like high-tech game rooms, how valid is the criticism that shopping areas are only encouraging more loitering by teenage boys, who don't spend a lot in stores and simply scare away other customers?

9. Select three competing clothing stores in your area and conduct a store image study for them. Ask a group of consumers to rate each store on a set of attributes and plot these ratings on the same graph. Based on your findings, are there any areas of competitive advantage or disadvantage you could bring to the attention of store management?

10. Using Table 10.1 as a model, construct a person/situation segmentation matrix for a brand of perfume.

11. What applications of queuing theory can you find employed among local services? Interview consumers who are waiting in lines to determine how (if at all) this experience affects their satisfaction with the service.

12. The store environment is heating up as more and more companies put their promotional dollars into point-of-purchase efforts. Shoppers are now confronted by videos at the checkout counter, computer monitors attached to their shopping carts, and so on. We're increasingly exposed to ads in nonshopping environments. Recently, a health club in New York was forced to remove TV monitors that showed advertising on the Health Club Media Networks, claiming that they interfered with workouts. Do you feel that these innovations are overly intrusive? At what point might shoppers "rebel" and demand some peace and quiet while shopping? Do you see any market potential in the future for stores that "counter market" by promising a "hands-off" shopping environment?

NOTES

1. Keith Naughton, "Revolution in the Showroom," *Business Week* (February 19, 1996): 70.

2. Pradeep Kakkar and Richard J. Lutz, "Situational Influence on Consumer Behavior: A Review," in Harold H. Kassarjian and Thomas S. Robertson, eds., *Perspectives in Consumer Behavior*, 3d ed., (Glenview, IL: Scott, Foresman, 1981): 204–14.

3. Pradeep Kakkar and Richard J. Lutz, "Situational Influence on Consumer Behavior: A Review," in Harold H. Kassarjian and Thomas S. Robertson, eds., *Perspectives in Consumer Behavior*, 3d ed., (Glenview, IL: Scott, Foresman, 1981): 204–14.

4. Carolyn Turner Schenk and Rebecca H. Holman, "A Sociological Approach to Brand Choice: The Concept of Situational Self-Image," in Jerry C. Olson, ed., *Advances in Consumer Research* 7, (Ann Arbor, MI: Association for Consumer Research, 1980): 610–14.

5. Peter R. Dickson, "Person–Situation: Segmentation's Missing Link," *Journal of Marketing* 46 (Fall 1982): 56–64.

6. Alan R. Hirsch, "Effects of Ambient Odors on Slot-Machine Usage in a Las Vegas Casino," *Psychology & Marketing* 12, no. 7 (October 1995): 585–94.

7. Daniel Stokols, "On the Distinction Between Density and Crowding: Some Implications for Future Research," *Psychological Review* 79 (1972): 275–7.

8. Carol Felker Kaufman, Paul M. Lane, and Jay D. Lindquist, "Exploring More Than 24 Hours a Day: A Preliminary Investigation of Polychronic Time Use," *Journal of Consumer Research* 18 (December 1991): 392–401.

9. Laurence P. Feldman and Jacob Hornik, "The Use of Time: An Integrated Conceptual Model," *Journal of Consumer Research* 7 (March 1981): 407–19; see also Michelle M. Bergadaà, "The Role of Time in the Action of the Consumer," *Journal of Consumer Research* 17 (December 1990): 289–302.

10. Robert J. Samuelson, "Rediscovering the Rat Race," *Newsweek* (May 15, 1989): 57.

11. John P. Robinson, "Time Squeeze," *Advertising Age* (February 1990): 30–33.

12. Gina Imperator, "The Money Value of Time," *Fast Company* (January/February 2000): 40.

13. Lane, Kaufman, and Lindquist, "Exploring More Than 24 Hours a Day."

14. Quoted in Dena Kleiman, "Fast Food? It Just Isn't Fast Enough Anymore,"*New York Times* (December 6, 1989): C12.

15. Jared Sandberg, "NoChores.com," *Newsweek* (August 30, 1999): 30.

16. Jack Neff, "Dawn of the Online Icebox," *Ad Age* (March 15, 1999): 17.

17. See Shirley Taylor, "Waiting for Service: The Relationship Between Delays and Evaluations of Service," *Journal of Marketing* 58 (April 1994): 56–69.

18. Robert J. Graham, "The Role of Perception of Time in Consumer Research," *Journal of Consumer Research* 7 (March 1981): 335–42.

19. Alan Zarembo, "What If There Weren't Any Clocks to Watch?" *Newsweek* (June 30, 1997): 14; based on research reported in Robert Levine, *A Geography of Time: The Temporal Misadventures of a Social Psychologist, or How Every Culture Keeps Time Just a Little Bit Differently* (New York: Basic Books, 1997).

20. Esther S. Page-Wood, Carol J. Kaufman, and Paul M. Lane, "The Art of Time," in *Proceedings of the Academy of Marketing Science* (1990).

21. Zarembo, "What If There Weren't Any Clocks to Watch?"

22. Kenneth E. Miller and James L. Ginter, "An Investigation of Situational Variation in Brand Choice Behavior and Attitude," *Journal of Marketing Research* 16 (February 1979): 111–23.

23. Jacob Hornik, "Diurnal Variation in Consumer Response," *Journal of Consumer Research* 14 (March 1988): 588–91.

24. David H. Maister, "The Psychology of Waiting Lines," in John A. Czepiel, Michael R. Solomon, and Carol F. Surprenant, eds., *The Service Encounter: Managing Employee/Customer Interaction in Service Businesses* (Lexington, MA: Lexington Books, 1985): 113–24.

25. David Leonhardt, "Airlines Using Technology in a Push for Shorter Lines," *The New York Times on the Web* (May 8, 2000).

26. Jennifer Ordonez, "An Efficiency Drive: Fast-Food Lanes, Equipped with Timers, Get Even Faster," *The Wall Street Journal Interactive Edition* (May 18, 2000).

27. Emily Nelson, "Mass-Market Retailers Look to Bring Checkout Lines into the 21st Century," *The Wall Street Journal Interactive Edition* (March 13, 2000).

28. Laurette Dube and Bernd H. Schmitt, "The Processing of Emotional and Cognitive Aspects of Product Usage in Satisfaction Judgments," in Rebecca H. Holman and Michael R. Solomon, eds., *Advances in Consumer Research* 18 (Provo, UT: Association for Consumer Research, 1991): 52–56; Lalita A. Manrai and Meryl P. Gardner, "The Influence of Affect on Attributions for Product Failure," in Rebecca H. Holman and Michael R. Solomon, eds., *Advances in Consumer Research* 18 (Provo, UT: Association for Consumer Research, 1991), 249–54.

29. Kevin G. Celuch and Linda S. Showers, "It's Time to Stress Stress: The Stress–Purchase/Consumption Relationship," in Rebecca H. Holman and Michael R. Solomon, eds., *Advances in Consumer Research* 18 (Provo, UT: Association for Consumer Research, 1991): 284–89; Lawrence R. Lepisto, J. Kathleen Stuenkel, and Linda K. Anglin, "Stress: An Ignored Situational Influence," in Rebecca H. Holman and Michael R. Solomon, eds., *Advances in Consumer Research* 18 (Provo, UT: Association for Consumer Research, 1991): 296–302.

30. See Eben Shapiro, "Need a Little Fantasy? A Bevy of New Companies Can Help," *New York Times* (March 10, 1991): F4.

31. John D. Mayer and Yvonne N. Gaschke, "The Experience and Meta-Experience of Mood," *Journal of Personality and Social Psychology* 55 (July 1988): 102–11.

32. Meryl Paula Gardner, "Mood States and Consumer Behavior: A Critical Review," *Journal of Consumer Research* 12 (December 1985): 281–300; Scott Dawson, Peter H. Bloch, and Nancy M. Ridgway, "Shopping Motives, Emotional States, and Retail Outcomes," *Journal of Retailing* 66 (Winter 1990): 408–27; Patricia A. Knowles, Stephen J. Grove, and W. Jeffrey Burroughs, "An Experimental Examination of Mood States on Retrieval and Evaluation of Advertisement and Brand Information," *Journal of the Academy of Marketing Science* 21 (April 1993): 135–43; Paul W. Miniard, Sunil Bhatla, and Deepak Sirdeskmukh, "Mood as a Determinant of Postconsumption Product Evaluations: Mood Effects and Their Dependency on the Affective Intensity of the Consumption Experience," *Journal of Consumer Psychology* 1, no. 2 (1992): 173–95; Mary T. Curren and Katrin R. Harich, "Consumers' Mood States: The Mitigating Influence of Personal Relevance on Product Evaluations," *Psychology & Marketing* 11, no. 2 (March/April 1994): 91–107; Gerald J. Gorn, Marvin E. Rosenberg, and Kunal Basu, "Mood, Awareness, and Product Evaluation," *Journal of Consumer Psychology* 2, no. 3 (1993): 237–56.

33. Gordon C. Bruner, "Music, Mood, and Marketing," *Journal of Marketing* 54 (October 1990): 94–104; Basil G. Englis, "Music Television and Its Influences on Consumers, Consumer Culture, and the Transmission of Consumption Messages," in Rebecca H. Holman and Michael R. Solomon, eds., *Advances in Consumer Research* 18 (Provo, UT: Association for Consumer Research, 1991): 111–14.

34. Marvin E. Goldberg and Gerald J. Gorn, "Happy and Sad TV Programs: How They Affect Reactions to Commercials," *Journal of Consumer Research* 14 (December 1987): 387–403; Gorn, Goldberg, and Basu, "Mood, Awareness, and Product Evaluation"; Curren and Harich, "Consumers' Mood States."

35. Rajeev Batra and Douglas M. Stayman, "The Role of Mood in Advertising Effectiveness," *Journal of Consumer Research* 17 (September 1990): 203; John P. Murry Jr. and Peter A. Dacin, "Cognitive Moderators of Negative–Emotion Effects: Implications for Understanding Media Context," *Journal of Consumer Research* 22 (March 1996): 439–47; see also Curren and Harich, "Consumers' Mood States"; Gorn, Goldberg, and Basu, "Mood, Awareness, and Product Evaluation."

36. For a scale that was devised to assess these dimensions of the shopping experience, see Barry J. Babin, William R. Darden, and Mitch Griffin, "Work and/or Fun: Measuring Hedonic and Utilitarian Shopping Value," *Journal of Consumer Research* 20 (March 1994): 644–56.

37. Babin, Darden, and Griffin, "Work and/or Fun."

38. Edward M. Tauber, "Why Do People Shop?" *Journal of Marketing* 36 (October 1972): 47–48.

39. Quoted in Robert C. Prus, *Making Sales: Influence as Interpersonal Accomplishment* (Newbury Park, CA: Sage Publications, 1989): 225.

40. Gregory P. Stone, "City Shoppers and Urban Identification: Observations on the Social Psychology of City Life," *American Journal of Sociology* 60 (1954): 36–45; Danny Bellenger and Pradeep K. Korgaonkar, "Profiling the Recreational Shopper," *Journal of Retailing* 56, no. 3 (1980): 77–92.

41. "A Global Perspective . . . on Women and Women's Wear," *Lifestyle Monitor* 14 (Winter 1999/2000): 8–11.

42. Some material in this section was adapted from Michael R. Solomon and Elnora W. Stuart, *Welcome to Marketing.Com: The Brave New World of E-Commerce* (Upper Saddle River, NJ: Prentice Hall, forthcoming).

43. Seema Williams, David M. Cooperstein, David E. Weisman, and Thalika Oum, "Post-Web Retail," *The Forrester Report*, Forrester Research, Inc., September 1999.

44. Rebecca K. Ratner, Barbara E. Kahn, and Daniel Kahneman, "Choosing Less-Preferred Experiences for the Sake of Variety," *Journal of Consumer Research*, 26 (June 1999): 1–15.

45. Louise Lee, "'Clicks and Mortar' at Gap.Com," *Business Week* (October 18, 1999): 150–52.

46. William Rothaker, "E-Commerce Won't Kill Bricks-and-Mortar Retailing," *The Wall Street Journal Interactive Edition* (September 27, 1999).

47. Jennifer Gilbert, "Customer Service Crucial to Online Buyers," *Advertising Age* (September 13, 1999): 52.

48. William Echison, "Designers Climb onto the Virtual Catwalk," *Business Week* (October 11, 1999): 164.

49. Quoted in Timothy L. O'Brien, "Aided by Internet, Identity Theft Soars," *The New York Times on the Web* (April 3, 2000).

50. For a recent study of consumer shopping patterns that views the mall as an ecological habitat, see Peter N. Bloch, Nancy M. Ridgway, and Scott A. Dawson, "The Shopping Mall as Consumer Habitat," *Journal of Retailing* 70, no. 1 (1994): 23–42.

51. Quoted in Jacquelyn Bivins, "Fun and Mall Games," *Stores* (August 1989): 35.

52. Sallie Hook, "All the Retail World's a Stage: Consumers Conditioned to Entertainment in Shopping Environment," *Marketing News* 21 (July 31, 1987): 16.

53. Patricia Winters Lauro, "Developer Promotes Its Malls as Destinations for Fun," *The New York Times on the Web* (October 21, 1999).

54. Alice Z. Cuneo, "'Retailtainment,'" *Advertising Age: The Next Century* (Fall 1999): 68.

55. Janet Ginsburg, "Xtreme Retailing," *Business Week* (December 20, 1999): 120.

56. Kitty Bean Yancey, "To Sleep, Perchance to Theme . . . ," *USA Today* (February 18, 2000): 4D.

57. Stephanie Grunier, "An Entrepreneur Chooses to Court Cafe Society (Cyber Version, Actually)," *The Wall Street Journal Interactive Edition* (September 24, 1999).

58. Richard Gibson, "Burger King Seeks New Sizzle by Implementing Major Changes," *The Wall Street Journal Interactive Edition* (April 14, 1999).

59. Susan Spiggle and Murphy A. Sewall, "A Choice Sets Model of Retail Selection," *Journal of Marketing* 51 (April 1987): 97–111; William R. Darden and Barry J. Babin, "The Role of Emotions in Expanding the Concept of Retail Personality," *Stores* 76, no. 4 (April 1994): RR7–RR8.

60. Most measures of store image are quite similar to other attitude measures, as discussed in Chapter 5. For an excellent bibliography of store image studies, see

Mary R. Zimmer and Linda L. Golden, "Impressions of Retail Stores: A Content Analysis of Consumer Images," *Journal of Retailing* 64 (Fall 1988): 265–93.

61. Spiggle and Sewall, "A Choice Sets Model of Retail Selection."

62. Philip Kotler, "Atmospherics as a Marketing Tool," *Journal of Retailing* (Winter 1973–74): 10–43, 48–64, 50; for a review of some recent research, see J. Duncan Herrington, "An Integrative Path Model of the Effects of Retail Environments on Shopper Behavior," Robert L. King, ed., *Marketing: Toward the Twenty-First Century* (Richmond, VA: Southern Marketing Association, 1991): 58–62; see also Ann E. Schlosser, "Applying the Functional Theory of Attitudes to Understanding the Influence of Store Atmosphere on Store Inferences," *Journal of Consumer Psychology* 7, no. 4 (1998): 345–69.

63. Joseph A. Bellizzi and Robert E. Hite, "Environmental Color, Consumer Feelings, and Purchase Likelihood," *Psychology & Marketing* 9, no. 5 (September/October 1992): 347–63.

64. See Eric R. Spangenberg, Ayn E. Crowley, and Pamela W. Henderson, "Improving the Store Environment: Do Olfactory Cues Affect Evaluations and Behaviors?" *Journal of Marketing* 60 (April 1996): 67–80, for a study that assessed olfaction in a controlled, simulated store environment.

65. Robert J. Donovan, John R. Rossiter, Gilian Marcoolyn, and Andrew Nesdale, "Store Atmosphere and Purchasing Behavior," *Journal of Retailing* 70, no. 3 (1994): 283–94.

66. Deborah Blumenthal, "Scenic Design for In-Store Try-ons," *New York Times* (April 9, 1988).

67. John Pierson, "If Sun Shines in, Workers Work Better, Buyers Buy More," *The Wall Street Journal* (November 20, 1995): B1.

68. Charles S. Areni and David Kim, "The Influence of In-Store Lighting on Consumers' Examination of Merchandise in a Wine Store," *International Journal of Research in Marketing* 11, no. 2 (March 1994): 117–25.

69. Judy I. Alpert and Mark I. Alpert, "Music Influences on Mood and Purchase Intentions," *Psychology & Marketing* 7 (Summer 1990): 109–34.

70. Quoted in "Slow Music Makes Fast Drinkers," *Psychology Today* (March 1989): 18.

71. Brad Edmondson, "Pass the Meat Loaf," *American Demographics* (January 1989): 19.

72. Marianne Meyer, "Attention Shoppers!" *Marketing and Media Decisions* 23 (May 1988): 67.

73. Jennifer Lach, "Meet You in Aisle Three," *American Demographics* (April 1999): 41.

74. Robert La Franco, "Wallpaper Sonatas," *Forbes* (March 25, 1996): 114.

75. Louise Lee, "Background Music Becomes Hoity-Toity," *The Wall Street Journal* (December 22, 1995): B1.

76. Easwar S. Iyer, "Unplanned Purchasing: Knowledge of Shopping Environment and Time Pressure," *Journal of Retailing* 65 (Spring 1989): 40–57; C. Whan Park, Easwar S. Iyer, and Daniel C. Smith, "The Effects of Situational Factors on In-Store Grocery Shopping," *Journal of Consumer Research* 15 (March 1989): 422–33.

77. Dennis W. Rook and Robert J. Fisher, "Normative Influences on Impulsive Buying Behavior," *Journal of Consumer Research* 22 (December 1995): 305–13; Francis Piron, "Defining Impulse Purchasing," in Rebecca H. Holman and Michael R. Solomon, eds., *Advances in Consumer Research* 18 (Provo, UT: Association for Consumer Research, 1991): 509–14; Dennis W. Rook, "The Buying Impulse," *Journal of Consumer Research* 14 (September 1987): 189–99.

78. Michael Wahl, "Eye POPping Persuasion," *Marketing Insights* (June 1989): 130.

79. "Zipping Down the Aisles," *The New York Times Magazine* (April 6, 1997): 30.

80. Cathy J. Cobb and Wayne D. Hoyer, "Planned Versus Impulse Purchase Behavior," *Journal of Retailing* 62 (Winter 1986): 384–409; Easwar S. Iyer and Sucheta S. Ahlawat, "Deviations from a Shopping Plan: When and Why Do Consumers Not Buy as Planned," in Melanie Wallendorf and Paul Anderson, eds., *Advances in Consumer Research* 14 (Provo, UT: Association for Consumer Research, 1987): 246–49.

81. Bernice Kanner, "Trolling in the Aisles," *New York* (January 16, 1989): 12; Michael Janofsky, "Using Crowing Roosters and Ringing Business Cards to Tap a Boom in Point-of-Purchase Displays," *New York Times* (March 21, 1994): D9.

82. See Robert B. Cialdini, *Influence: Science and Practice*, 2d. ed. (Glenview, IL: Scott, Foresman, 1988).

83. Richard P. Bagozzi, "Marketing as Exchange," *Journal of Marketing* 39 (October 1975): 32–39; Peter M. Blau, *Exchange and Power in Social Life* (New York: Wiley, 1964); Marjorie Caballero and Alan J. Resnik, "The Attraction Paradigm in Dyadic Exchange," *Psychology & Marketing* 3, no. 1 (1986): 17–34; George C. Homans, "Social Behavior as Exchange," *American Journal of Sociology* 63 (1958): 597–606; Paul H. Schurr and Julie L. Ozanne, "Influences on Exchange Processes: Buyers' Preconceptions of a Seller's Trustworthiness and Bargaining Toughness," *Journal of Consumer Research* 11 (March 1985): 939–53; Arch G. Woodside and J. W. Davenport, "The Effect of Salesman Similarity and Expertise on Consumer Purchasing Behavior," *Journal of Marketing Research* 8 (1974): 433–36.

84. Paul Busch and David T. Wilson, "An Experimental Analysis of a Salesman's Expert and Referent Bases of Social Power in the Buyer-Seller Dyad," *Journal of Marketing Research* 13 (February 1976): 3–11; John E. Swan, Fred Trawick Jr., David R. Rink, and Jenny J. Roberts, "Measuring Dimensions of Purchaser Trust of Industrial Salespeople," *Journal of Personal Selling and Sales Management* 8 (May 1988): 1.

85. For a study in this area, see Peter H. Reingen and Jerome B. Kernan, "Social Perception and Interpersonal Influence: Some Consequences of the Physical Attractiveness Stereotype in a Personal Selling Setting," *Journal of Consumer Psychology* 2, no. 1 (1993): 25–38.

86. Linda L. Price and Eric J. Arnould, "Commercial Friendships: Service Provider-Client Relationships in Context," *Journal of Marketing* 63 (October 1999): 38–56.

87. Mary Jo Bitner, Bernard H. Booms, and Mary Stansfield Tetreault, "The Service Encounter: Diagnosing Favorable and Unfavorable Incidents," *Journal of Marketing* 54 (January 1990): 7–84; Robert C. Prus, *Making Sales* (Newbury Park, CA: Sage Publications, 1989); Arch G. Woodside and James L. Taylor, "Identity Negotiations in Buyer-Seller Interactions," in Elizabeth C. Hirschman and Morris B. Holbrook, eds., *Advances in Consumer Research* 12 (Provo, UT: Association for Consumer Research, 1985): 443–49.

88. Barry J. Babin, James S. Boles, and William R. Darden, "Salesperson Stereotypes, Consumer Emotions, and Their Impact on Information Processing," *Journal of the Academy of Marketing Science* 23, no. 2 (1995): 94–105; Gilbert A. Churchill Jr., Neil M. Ford, Steven W. Hartley, and Orville C. Walker Jr., "The Determinants of Salesperson Performance: A Meta-Analysis," *Journal of Marketing Research* 22 (May 1985): 103–18.

89. Siew Meng Leong, Paul S. Busch, and Deborah Roedder John, "Knowledge Bases and Salesperson Effectiveness: A Script-Theoretic Analysis," *Journal of Marketing Research* 26 (May 1989): 164; Harish Sujan, Mita Sujan, and James R. Bettman, "Knowledge Structure Differences Between More Effective and Less Effective Salespeople," *Journal of Marketing Research* 25 (February 1988): 81–86; Robert Saxe and Barton Weitz, "The SOCCO Scale: A Measure of the Customer Orientation of Salespeople," *Journal of Marketing Research* 19 (August 1982): 343–51; David M. Szymanski, "Determinants of Selling Effectiveness: The Importance of Declarative Knowledge to the Personal Selling Concept," *Journal of Marketing* 52 (January 1988): 64–77; Barton A. Weitz,

"Effectiveness in Sales Interactions: A Contingency Framework," *Journal of Marketing* 45 (Winter 1981): 85–103.

90. Jagdish M. Sheth, "Buyer-Seller Interaction: A Conceptual Framework," in *Advances in Consumer Research* (Cincinnati, OH: Association for Consumer Research, 1976): 382–86; Kaylene C. Williams and Rosann L. Spiro, "Communication Style in the Salesperson-Customer Dyad," *Journal of Marketing Research* 22 (November 1985): 434–42.

91. Marsha L. Richins, "An Analysis of Consumer Interaction Styles in the Marketplace," *Journal of Consumer Research* 10 (June 1983): 73–82.

92. www.protest.net; accessed June 17, 2000.

93. Keith Naughton, "Tired of Smile-Free Service?" *Newsweek* (March 6, 2000): 44–45.

94. Rama Jayanti and Anita Jackson, "Service Satisfaction: Investigation of Three Models," in Rebecca H. Holman and Michael R. Solomon, eds., *Advances in Consumer Research* 18 (Provo, UT: Association for Consumer Research, 1991): 603–10; David K. Tse, Franco M. Nicosia, and Peter C. Wilton, "Consumer Satisfaction as a Process," *Psychology & Marketing* 7 (Fall 1990): 177–93. For a recent treatment of satisfaction issues from a more interpretive perspective, see Susan Fournier and David Mick, "Rediscovering Satisfaction," *Journal of Marketing* 63 (October 1999): 5–23.

95. Constance L. Hayes, "Service Takes a Holiday," *New York Times*, (December 23, 1998): C1.

96. Leslie Kaufman, "Enough Talk," *Newsweek* (August 18, 1997): 48–49.

97. Calmetta Y. Coleman, "A Car Salesman's Bizarre Prank May End up Backfiring in Court," *The Wall Street Journal* (May 2, 1995): B1.

98. Robert Jacobson and David A. Aaker, "The Strategic Role of Product Quality," *Journal of Marketing* 51 (October 1987): 31–44; for a review of issues regarding the measurement of service quality, see J. Joseph Cronin Jr. and Steven A. Taylor, "Measuring Service Quality: A Reexamination and Extension," *Journal of Marketing* 56 (July 1992): 55–68.

99. Anna Kirmani and Peter Wright, "Money Talks: Perceived Advertising Expense and Expected Product Quality," *Journal of Consumer Research* 16 (December 1989): 344–53; Donald R. Lichtenstein and Scot Burton, "The Relationship Between Perceived and Objective Price-Quality," *Journal of Marketing Research* 26 (November 1989): 429–43; Akshay R. Rao and Kent B. Monroe, "The Effect of Price, Brand Name, and Store Name on Buyers' Perceptions of Product Quality: An Integrative Review," *Journal of Marketing Research* 26 (August 1989): 351–57.

100. Shelby Hunt, "Post-Transactional Communication and Dissonance Reduction," *Journal of Marketing* 34 (January 1970): 46–51; Daniel E. Innis and H. Rao Unnava, "The Usefulness of Product Warranties for Reputable and New Brands," in Rebecca H. Holman and Michael R. Solomon, eds., *Advances in Consumer Research* 18 (Provo, UT: Association for Consumer Research, 1991): 317–22; Terence A. Shimp and William O. Bearden, "Warranty and Other Extrinsic Cue Effects on Consumers' Risk Perceptions," *Journal of Consumer Research* 9 (June 1982): 38–46.

101. Morris B. Holbrook and Kim P. Corfman, "Quality and Value in the Consumption Experience: Phaedrus Rides Again," in Jacob Jacoby and Jerry C. Olson, eds., *Perceived Quality: How Consumers View Stores and Merchandise* (Lexington, MA: Lexington Books, 1985): 31–58.

102. Holbrook and Corfman, "Quality and Value in the Consumption Experience"; Robert M. Pirsig, *Zen and the Art of Motorcycle Maintenance: An Inquiry into Values* (New York: Bantam Books, 1974).

103. Gilbert A. Churchill Jr. and Carol F. Surprenant, "An Investigation into the Determinants of Customer Satisfaction," *Journal of Marketing Research* 19 (November 1983): 491–504; John E. Swan and I. Frederick Trawick, "Disconfirmation of Expectations and Satisfaction with a Retail Service," *Journal of Retailing* 57 (Fall 1981): 49–67; Peter C. Wilton and David K. Tse, "Models of Consumer Satisfaction Formation: An Extension," *Journal of Marketing Research* 25 (May 1988): 204–12; for a discussion of what may occur when customers evaluate a new service for which comparison standards do not yet exist, see Ann L. McGill and Dawn Iacobucci, "The Role of Post-Experience Comparison Standards in the Evaluation of Unfamiliar Services," in John F. Sherry Jr. and Brian Sternthal, eds., *Advances in Consumer Research* 19 (Provo, UT: Association for Consumer Research, 1992): 570–78; William Boulding, Ajay Kalra, Richard Staelin, and Valarie A. Zeithaml, "A Dynamic Process Model of Service Quality: From Expectations to Behavioral Intentions," *Journal of Marketing Research* 30 (February 1993): 7–27.

104. John W. Gamble, "The Expectations Paradox: The More You Offer Customer's, Closer You Are to Failure," *Marketing News* (March 14, 1988): 38.

105. Jagdish N. Sheth and Banwari Mittal, "A Framework for Managing Customer Expectations," *Journal of Market Focused Management* 1 (1996): 137–58.

106. Mary C. Gilly and Betsy D. Gelb, "Post-Purchase Consumer Processes and the Complaining Consumer," *Journal of Consumer Research* 9 (December 1982):

323–28; Diane Halstead and Cornelia Droge, "Consumer Attitudes Toward Complaining and the Prediction of Multiple Complaint Responses," in Rebecca H. Holman and Michael R. Solomon, eds., *Advances in Consumer Research* 18 (Provo, UT: Association for Consumer Research, 1991): 210–16; Jagdip Singh, "Consumer Complaint Intentions and Behavior: Definitional and Taxonomical Issues," *Journal of Marketing* 52 (January 1988): 93–107.

107. Gary L. Clark, Peter F. Kaminski, and David R. Rink, "Consumer Complaints: Advice on How Companies Should Respond Based on an Empirical Study," *Journal of Services Marketing*, 6, no. 1 (Winter 1992): 41–50.

108. Alan Andreasen and Arthur Best, "Consumers Complain—Does Business Respond?" *Harvard Business Review* 55 (July/August 1977): 93–101.

109. Tibbett L. Speer, "They Complain Because They Care," *American Demographics* (May 1996): 13–14.

110. Ingrid Martin, "Expert-Novice Differences in Complaint Scripts," in Rebecca H. Holman and Michael R. Solomon, eds., *Advances in Consumer Research* 18 (Provo, UT: Association for Consumer Research, 1991): 225–31; Marsha L. Richins, "A Multivariate Analysis of Responses to Dissatisfaction," *Journal of the Academy of Marketing Science* 15 (Fall 1987): 24–31.

111. John A. Schibrowsky and Richard S. Lapidus, "Gaining a Competitive Advantage by Analyzing Aggregate Complaints," *Journal of Consumer Marketing* 11, no. 1 (1994): 15–26.

112. Russell W. Belk, "The Role of Possessions in Constructing and Maintaining a Sense of Past," in Marvin E. Goldberg, Gerald Gorn, and Richard W. Pollay, eds., *Advances in Consumer Research* 17 (Provo, UT: Association for Consumer Research, 1989): 669–76.

113. David E. Sanger, "For a Job Well Done, Japanese Enshrine the Chip," *New York Times* (December 11, 1990): A4.

114. Jacob Jacoby, Carol K. Berning, and Thomas F. Dietvorst, "What About Disposition?" *Journal of Marketing* 41 (April 1977): 22–28.

115. Jennifer Lach, "Welcome to the Hoard Fest," *American Demographics* (April 2000): 8–9.

116. Mike Tharp, "Tchaikovsky and Toilet Paper," *U.S. News and World Report* (December 1987): 62; B. Van Voorst, "The Recycling Bottleneck," *Time* (September 14, 1992): 52–54; Richard P. Bagozzi and Pratibha A. Dabholkar, "Consumer Recycling Goals and Their Effect on Decisions to Recycle: A Means-End Chain Analysis," *Psychology & Marketing* 11, no. 4 (July/August 1994): 313–40.

117. "Finally, Something at McDonald's You Can Actually Eat," *Utne Reader* (May/June 1997): 12.

118. Debra J. Dahab, James W. Gentry, and Wanru Su, "New Ways to Reach Non-Recyclers: An Extension of the Model of Reasoned Action to Recycling Behaviors" (paper presented at the meetings of the Association for Consumer Research, 1994).

119. Bagozzi and Dabholkar, "Consumer Recycling Goals and Their Effect on Decisions to Recycle"; see also L. J. Shrum, Tina M. Lowrey, and John A. McCarty, "Recycling as a Marketing Problem: A Framework for Strategy Development," *Psychology & Marketing* 11, no. 4 (July/August 1994): 393–416; Dahab, Gentry, and Su, "New Ways to Reach Non-Recyclers."

120. John F. Sherry Jr., "A Sociocultural Analysis of a Midwestern American Flea Market," *Journal of Consumer Research* 17 (June 1990): 13–30.

121. Diane Crispell, "Collecting Memories," *American Demographics* (November 1988): 38–42.

122. Allan J. Magrath, "If Used Product Sellers Ever Get Organized, Watch Out," *Marketing News* (June 25, 1990): 9; Kevin McCrohan and James D. Smith, "Consumer Participation in the Informal Economy," *Journal of the Academy of Marketing Science* 15 (Winter 1990): 62.

123. "New Kind of Store Getting More Use out of Used Goods," *Montgomery Advertiser* (December 12, 1996): 7A.

124. Yumiko Ono, "The 'Pizza Queen' of Japan Becomes a Web Auctioneer," *The Wall Street Journal Interactive Edition* (March 6, 2000).

125. Catherine Greenman, "Ebay Minus the Cash: Trading Haves for Wants," *The New York Times on the Web* (March 2, 2000).

126. Jessie Hartland, "Lost and Found and Sold," *Travel & Leisure* (February 2000): 102.

Zachary leads a secret life. During the week, he is a straight-laced stock analyst for a major investment firm. The weekend is another story. Come Friday evening, it's off with the Brooks Brothers suit and on with the black leather, as he trades in his BMW for his treasured Harley-Davidson motorcycle. A dedicated member of HOG (Harley Owners Group), Zachary belongs to the faction of Harley riders known as "RUBs" (rich urban bikers). Everyone in his group wears expensive leather vests with Harley insignias and owns customized "Low Riders." Just this week, Zack finally got his new Harley belt buckle when he logged on to The Genuine Harley-Davidson Roadstore at Harley-Davidson.com. As he surfed around the site, he realized the lengths some of his fellow enthusiasts go to make sure others know they are Hog riders. As one of the Harley Web pages observed, "It's one thing to have people buy your products. It's another thing to have them tattoo your name on their bodies." Zack had to restrain himself from buying more Harley stuff; there were jackets, vests, eyewear, belts, buckles, scarves, watches, jewelry, even housewares ("home is the road") for sale. He settled for a set of Harley salt-and-pepper shakers that would be perfect for his buddy Soren's new crib.

Zack has spent a lot of money on his bike and on outfitting himself to be like the rest of the group. But it's worth it. Zachary feels a real sense of brotherhood with his fellow RUBs. The group rides together in two-column formation to bike rallies that sometimes attract up to 300,000 cycle enthusiasts. What a sense of power he feels when they're all cruising together—it's them against the world!

Of course, an added benefit is the business networking he's been able to accomplish during his weekend jaunts with his fellow professionals who also wait for the weekend to "ride on the wild side."[1] Sometimes sharing a secret can pay off in more ways than one.

11

GROUP INFLUENCE AND OPINION LEADERSHIP

REFERENCE GROUPS

Humans are social animals. We all belong to groups, try to please others, and take cues about how to behave by observing the actions of those around us. In fact, our desire to "fit in" or to identify with desirable individuals or groups is the primary motivation for many of our purchases and activities. We will often go to great lengths to please the members of a group whose acceptance we covet.[2]

Zachary's biker group is an important part of his identity, and this membership influences many of his buying decisions. He has spent many thousands of dollars on parts and accessories since acquiring his identity as a RUB. His fellow riders are united by their consumption choices, so total strangers feel an immediate bond with each other when they meet. The publisher of *American Iron*, an industry magazine, observed, "You don't buy a Harley because it's a superior bike, you buy a Harley to be a part of a family."[3]

Zachary doesn't model himself after just *any* biker—only the people with whom he really identifies can exert that kind of influence on him. For example, Zachary's group doesn't have much to do with outlaw clubs, which are primarily composed of blue-collar riders sporting Harley tattoos. The members of his group also have only polite contact with "Ma and Pa" bikers, whose bikes are the epitome of comfort, featuring such niceties as radios, heated handgrips, and floorboards. Essentially, only the RUBs comprise Zachary's *reference group*.

A **reference group** is "an actual or imaginary individual or group conceived of having significant relevance upon an individual's evaluations, aspirations, or behavior."[4] Reference groups influence consumers in three ways. These influences, *informational, utilitarian,* and *value-expressive,* are described in Table 11.1. The chapter focuses on how other people, whether fellow bikers, coworkers, friends, and family, or just casual acquaintances influence our purchase decisions.

TABLE 11.1   Three Forms of Reference Group Influence

Information Influence	• The individual seeks information about various brands from an association of professionals or independent group of experts.
	• The individual seeks information from those who work with the product as a profession.
	• The individual seeks brand-related knowledge and experience (such as how Brand A's performance compares to Brand B's) from those friends, neighbors, relatives, or work associates who have reliable information about the brands.
	• The brand the individual selects is influenced by observing a seal of approval of an independent testing agency (such as *Good Housekeeping*).
	• The individual's observation of what experts do (such as observing the type of car that police drive or the brand of television that repairmen buy) influences his or her choice of a brand.
Utilitarian Influence	• So that he or she satisfies the expectations of fellow work associates, the individual's decision to purchase a particular brand is influenced by their preferences.
	• The individual's decision to purchase a particular brand is influenced by the preferences of people with whom he or she has social interaction.
	• The individual's decision to purchase a particular brand is influenced by the preferences of family members.
	• The desire to satisfy the expectations that others have of him or her has an impact on the individual's brand choice.
Value-Expressive Influence	• The individual feels that the purchase or use of a particular brand will enhance the image others have of him or her.
	• The individual feels that those who purchase or use a particular brand possess the characteristics that he or she would like to have.
	• The individual sometimes feels that it would be nice to be like the type of person that advertisements show using a particular brand.
	• The individual feels that the people who purchase a particular brand are admired or respected by others.
	• The individual feels that the purchase of a particular brand would help show others what he or she is or would like to be (such as an athlete, successful business person, good parent, etc.).

SOURCE: Adapted from G. Whan Park and V. Parker Lessig, "Students and Housewives: Differences in Susceptibility to Reference Group Influence," *Journal of Consumer Research* 4 (September 1977): 102. Reprinted with permission by The University of Chicago Press.

It considers how our preferences are shaped by our group memberships, by our desire to please or be accepted by others, or even by the actions of famous people whom we've never even met. Finally, it explores why some people are more influential than others in affecting consumer's product preferences and how marketers go about finding those people and enlisting their support in the persuasion process.

Types of Reference Groups

Although two or more people are normally required to form a group, the term *reference group* is often used a bit more loosely to describe *any* external influence that provides social cues.[5] The referent may be a cultural figure and have an impact on many people (e.g., Louis Farrakhan) or a person or group whose influence is confined to the consumer's immediate environment (e.g., Zachary's biker club). Reference groups that affect consumption can include parents, fellow motorcycle enthusiasts, the Democratic party, or even the Chicago Bears, the Red Hot Chili Peppers, or Spike Lee.

Obviously, some groups and individuals exert a greater influence than others and affect a broader range of consumption decisions. For example, our parents may play a pivotal role in forming our values toward many important issues, such as attitudes about marriage or where to go to college. This type of influence is **normative influence**—that is, the reference group helps to set and enforce fundamental standards of conduct. In contrast, a Harley-Davidson club might exert **comparative influence,** whereby decisions about specific brands or activities are affected.[6]

Formal Versus Informal Groups

A reference group can take the form of a large, formal organization that has a recognized structure, complete with a charter, regular meeting times, and officers. Or it can be small and informal, such as a group of friends or students living in a dormitory. Marketers tend to be more successful at influencing formal groups because they are more easily identifiable and accessible. However, as a rule it is small, informal groups that exert a more powerful influence on individual consumers. Small, informal groups tend to be more a part of our day-to-day lives and to be more important to us, because they are high in normative influence. Larger, formal groups tend to be more product- or activity-specific and thus are high in comparative influence.

Membership Versus Aspirational Reference Groups

Some reference groups consist of people the consumer actually knows; others are composed of either people the consumer can identify with or admire. Not surprisingly, many marketing efforts that specifically adopt a reference group appeal concentrate on highly visible, widely admired figures (such as well-known athletes or performers).

Because people tend to compare themselves to others who are similar, they are often swayed by knowing how people like them conduct their lives. For this reason, many promotional strategies include "ordinary" people whose consumption activities provide informational social influence. The likelihood that people will become part of a consumer's identificational reference group is affected by several factors, including the following:

- *Propinquity:* As physical distance between people decreases and opportunities for interaction increase, relationships are more likely to form. Physical nearness is called *propinquity.* An early study on friendship patterns in a housing complex showed this factor's strong effects: Residents were much more likely to be friends with the people next door than with those who lived only two doors away. Furthermore, people who lived next to a staircase had more friends than those at the ends of a hall (presumably, they were more likely to "bump into" people using the stairs).[10] Physical structure has a lot to do with whom we get to know and how popular we are.
- *Mere exposure:* We come to like persons or things simply as a result of seeing them more often, which is known as the *mere exposure phenomenon.*[11] Greater frequency of contact, even if unintentional, may help to determine one's set of local referents. The same effect holds when evaluating works of art or even political candidates.[12] One study predicted 83 percent of the winners of political primaries solely by the amount of media exposure given to candidates.[13]

NET PROFIT

MEMBERS OF REFERENCE GROUPS have a huge influence on our tastes and desires, but connecting with like-minded people in the first place can be a challenge in today's hectic world. High-tech entrepreneurs are hard at work to make the matchmaking process easier. Some are developing *affinity portals;* Web sites that provide resources for group members. MyPersonal.com creates affinity portals for college alumni associations, and Ibelong.com has created more than 40 portals for such diverse groups as the AFL-CIO, the National Federation of Republican Women, and the National Association of Underwater Instructors.[7] At each site browsers can find relevant news, chat areas, and shopping opportunities. In return the sponsoring associations get a share of the revenue generated from the site.

How about some *real* matchmaking? Yenta, a software program being developed at MIT, is designed to help individuals find others with common interests. Users communicate with each other anonymously until they decide to meet and exchange identities.[8] Then there are the hundreds of online dating services with such names as singles-dating-online.com and 2hearts.com. Of course, if you're even too shy to meet prospective mates this way you can always try the Lovegety, a $21 device being marketed in Japan. It works this way: Boy sees girl. Boy is too shy to talk to girl. Instead he flicks on his male Lovegety and sends out an infrared signal. If the girl's Lovegety is within five meters of his, it starts to chirp with delight. Depending on her interest, she can send back one of three responses: talk, karaoke, and friend.[9] Wow, nothing like a little romantic karaoke to set the mood.

- *Group cohesiveness: Cohesiveness* refers to the degree that members of a group are attracted to each other and value their group membership. As the value of the group to the individual increases, so too does the likelihood that the group will guide consumption decisions. Smaller groups tend to be more cohesive because in larger groups the contributions of each member are usually less important or noticeable. By the same token, groups often try to restrict membership to a select few, which increases the value of membership to those who are admitted. Exclusivity of membership is a benefit often touted by credit card companies, book clubs, and so on, even though the actual membership base might be fairly large.

The consumer may have no direct contact with reference groups, but they can have powerful influences on his or her tastes and preferences because they provide guidance as to the types of products used by admired people.[14]

Aspirational reference groups comprise idealized figures such as successful business people, athletes, or performers. For example, one study that included business students who aspired to the "executive" role found a strong relationship between products they associated with their *ideal selves* (see Chapter 5) and those they assumed would be owned or used by executives.[15]

Positive Versus Negative Reference Groups

Reference groups may exert *either* a positive or a negative influence on consumption behaviors. In most cases, consumers model their behavior to be consistent with what they think the group expects of them. In some cases, though, consumers may try to distance themselves from other people or groups that function as *avoidance groups.* They may carefully study the dress or mannerisms of a disliked group (e.g., "nerds," "druggies," or "preppies") and scrupulously avoid buying anything that might identify them with that group. For example, rebellious adolescents often resent parental influence and may deliberately do the opposite of what their parents would like as a way of making a statement about their independence. As Romeo and Juliet discovered, nothing makes a dating partner more attractive than a little parental opposition.

Virtual Communities

In ancient times (that is, before the Web was widely accessible), most membership reference groups consisted of people who had face-to-face contact. Now, it's possible to share interests with people whom you've never met—and probably never will. Consider the case of Widespread Panic. The band has never had a

Many products, especially those targeted to young people, are often touted as a way to take the inside track to popularity. This Brazilian ad lets us know about people who don't like a certain shoe.

music video on MTV or cracked the Billboard Top 200. But, it's one of the top 40 touring bands in the United States. How did it get to be so successful? Simple— the group built a virtual community of fans and opened itself up to them. It enlisted listeners to help promote the group in exchange for free tickets and back- stage passes. Then, it went virtual: The band lets fans send messages to its record- ing studio, and hardcore followers can find out vital information such as what band members ate for lunch via regular updates on their Web site.[16]

A **virtual community of consumption** is a collection of people whose online interactions are based upon shared enthusiasm for and knowledge of a specific consumption activity. These anonymous groups grow up around an incredibly diverse set of interests, including everything from Barbie dolls to fine wine.

Virtual communities come in many different forms[17]:

- *Multi-User Dungeons (MUD):* Originally, these were environments in which players of fantasy games met. Now they refer to any computer- generated environment in which people socially interact through the structured format of role and game playing. In a game called EverQuest, on any given night up to 50,000 people can be found roaming around a fantasy land in cyberspace. This is known as a "massively multiplayer game," that combines the stunning graphics of advanced gaming with the social scene of a chat room. Players create a character as a virtual alter ego, which may be a wise elf or a back-stabbing rogue. Some players sell powerful characters on eBay for $1,000 or more. The game is also the cen- ter of an active social scene. Players can travel around in groups of six; in many cases they settle into a regular group and spend two to three hours each night online with the same people. One couple even held a virtual wedding while playing. The bride reported, "We only had one death, a guest who was killed by the guards. It was a lot of fun."[18] Realizing that the average online player logs 17 hours per week, firms such as Sony, Microsoft, and Sega are building their own virtual worlds to get a piece of the action. As one game company executive put it, "This is not a genre of game but a breakthrough new medium. It provides a completely new social, collaborative shared experience. We're basically in the Internet community business."[19]
- *Rooms, rings, and lists:* These include internet relay chat (IRC), otherwise known as *chat rooms. Rings* are organizations of related home pages, and *lists* are groups of people on a single mailing list who share information.
- *Boards:* Online communities organized around interest-specific elec- tronic bulletin boards. Active members read and post messages sorted by date and subject. There are boards devoted to musical groups, movies, wind, cigars, cars, comic strips, even fast food restaurants.

Some communities are created by individuals whose Web pages are hosted on sites such as geocities.com or sixdegrees.com. Others are sponsored by companies who want to give devotees of a product or a lifestyle a congenial place to "meet." There are community sites for specific consumer profiles such as teenage girls (e.g., gurl.com) or college students (collegeclub.com), for themes such as relation- ships (swoon.com), or for people who are fans of a specific product or a TV show. For example, News Digital Media gives Bart Simpson fanatics free Internet access at simpson.com. The site is intended to complement the TV show and to give fans a place to congregate. It also allows the Fox network to gauge viewer reaction to individual episodes of the show.[20]

Virtual communities are still a new phenomenon, but their impact on individuals' product preferences promises to be huge. These loyal consumers essentially are working together to form their tastes, evaluate product quality, and even negotiate for better deals with producers. They place great weight on the judgments of their fellow members. For example, on the official *X-Files* homepage thex-files.com, fans debate the merits of each episode, but also critique and promote the most recent licensed merchandise related to the show. On newsgroup boards such as alt.tv.x-file, they share pricing and quality hints and issue rip-off alerts.

Although consumption communities are largely a grass-roots phenomenon founded by consumers for other consumers, these community members can be reached by marketers—if they are careful not to alienate members by being too aggressive or "commercial." Using newsgroup archives and search engines such as dejanews.com, companies can create a detailed profile of any individual consumer who has posted information. Firms such as Warner Brothers form communities with fans around the world. The company noticed that many fans of Bugs Bunny, Batman, and the Tazmanian Devil were downloading images and sound clips onto their personal Web pages and then selling ad space on those pages. Instead of suing its fans, Warner created an online community called ACME City that builds home pages for registered members. Many corporate-sponsored sites build home pages for new members and ask for nothing in return except personal information on a registration form. They can use this information to fine-tune the online experience by making advertising, contests, and rewards programs more relevant. A community called CyberSites surveys members before exposing them to ads, negotiates group discounts on products sold on the site, and lets members edit their online profile as their tastes change.[21]

In addition, some online startups are profitting by creating Web sites that give people a forum for their opinions about product likes and dislikes. Epinions.com was started by several well-known Silicon Valley venture capitalists. This service both rewards and rates product reviewers in hope of giving them enough incentive to provide useful opinions. Anyone can sign up to give advice on products that fit into the site's 12 categories, and shoppers can rate the reviews on a scale from not useful to very useful. To build credibility and eliminate suspicions that they are merely company shills, advisers can build a page on the site with photos and personal information. Reviewers earn royalties of $1–3 for

Figure 11.1

Virtual Communities

SOURCE: Adapted from Robert V. Kozinets, "E-Tribalized Marketing: The Strategic Implications of Virtual Communities of Consumption," *European Management Journal* 17, 3 (June 1999): 252-264, p. 262.

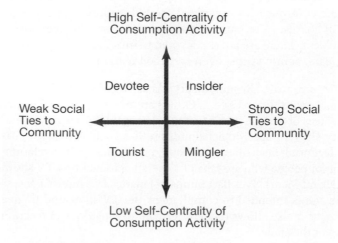

every 10 times their review is read, and their picture can be featured on the front page if their reviews are widely read. According to one of the founders, the site relies on a "Web of trust" in which viewers and advisers tend to be matched up over time with people whose opinions they have come to trust: "It mimics the way word-of-mouth works in the real world." When a recommendation results in a sale, the company earns a referral fee from merchants. Similar sites include Productopia.com and Deja.com.[22]

How do people get drawn into consumption communities? Internet users tend to progress from asocial information gathering ("lurkers" are surfers who like to watch but don't participate) to increasingly affiliative social activities. At first they will merely browse the site, but later they may well be drawn into active participation.

The intensity of identification with a virtual community depends on two factors. The first is that the more central the activity is to a person's self-concept, the more likely he will be to pursue an active membership in a community. The second is that the intensity of the social relationships the person forms with other members of the virtual community helps to determine his extent of involvement. As Figure 11.1 shows, combining these two factors creates four distinct member types:

1. *Tourists* lack strong social ties to the group, and maintain only a passing interest in the activity.
2. *Minglers* maintain strong social ties, but are not very interested in the central consumption activity.
3. *Devotees* express strong interest in the activity, but have few social attachments to the group.
4. *Insiders* exhibit both strong social ties and strong interest in the activity.

Devotees and insiders are the most important targets for marketers who wish to leverage communities for promotional purposes. They are the heavy users of virtual communities. And, by reinforcing usage, the community may upgrade tourists and minglers to insiders and devotees.[23] But marketers have only scratched the surface of this intriguing new virtual world.

When Reference Groups Are Important

Reference group influences are not equally powerful for all types of products and consumption activities. For example, products that are not very complex, that are low in perceived risk, and that can be tried prior to purchase are less susceptible to personal influence.[27] In addition, the specific impact of reference groups may vary. At times it may determine the use of certain products rather than others (e.g., owning or not owning a computer, eating junk food versus health food), whereas at other times it may have specific effects on brand decisions within a product category (e.g., wearing Levi's jeans versus Calvin Klein jeans, or smoking Marlboro cigarettes rather than Virginia Slims).

Two dimensions that influence the degree to which reference groups are important are whether the purchase is to be consumed publicly or privately and whether it is a luxury or a necessity. As a rule, reference group effects are more robust for purchases that are (1) luxuries rather than necessities (e.g., sailboats), because products that are purchased with discretionary income are subject to individual tastes and preferences, whereas necessities do not offer this range of

THE TANGLED WEB

VIRTUAL CONSUMPTION COMMUNITIES HOLD great promise, but there is also great potential for abuse if members can't trust that other visitors are behaving ethically. Many hard-core community members are sensitive to interference from companies and react negatively when they suspect that another member may in fact be a shill of a marketer who wants to influence evaluations of products on the site. One of the reasons for the success of the ebay.com auction site is that buyers rate the quality and trustworthiness of sellers, so a potential bidder can get a pretty good idea of what she's dealing with before participating. In some cases even this system has fallen flat as unscrupulous people find ways to violate the bond of trust.

More generally, e-commerce sites know that consumers give more weight to the opinions of real people, so they are finding ways to let these opinions be included on their Web sites. This trend of posting customer reviews was started by Amazon.com way back in 1995. Now, sellers of computers and other high-priced products post customer reviews.[24] A great idea—but in a highly-publicized lawsuit Amazon was accused of charging publishers to post positive reviews on the site. The company had to offer refunds for all books it recommended and now Amazon tells customers when a publisher has paid for a prominent display on its site.[25] Similarly, some online investment forums have had to hire patrols to keep an eye out for stock promoters who have been hired by companies to create a buzz about their stocks. The Motley Fool site (fool.com), for example, employs 20 full-time "community strollers" who control its message boards on America Online and the Web.[26]

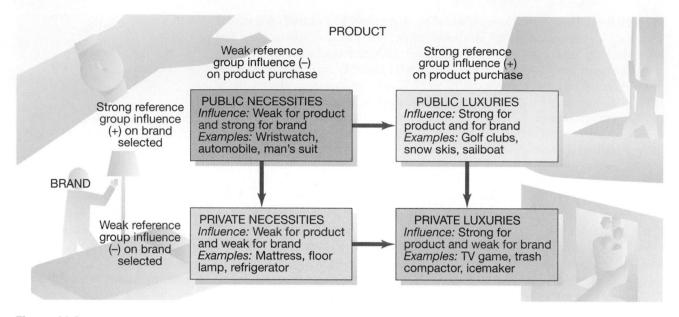

PRODUCT

	Weak reference group influence (–) on product purchase	Strong reference group influence (+) on product purchase
Strong reference group influence (+) on brand selected	**PUBLIC NECESSITIES** *Influence:* Weak for product and strong for brand *Examples:* Wristwatch, automobile, man's suit	**PUBLIC LUXURIES** *Influence:* Strong for product and for brand *Examples:* Golf clubs, snow skis, sailboat
Weak reference group influence (–) on brand selected	**PRIVATE NECESSITIES** *Influence:* Weak for product and weak for brand *Examples:* Mattress, floor lamp, refrigerator	**PRIVATE LUXURIES** *Influence:* Strong for product and weak for brand *Examples:* TV game, trash compactor, icemaker

BRAND

Figure 11.2

Relative Reference Groups Influence on Purchase Intention

choices; and (2) socially conspicuous or visible to others (e.g., living room furniture or clothing), because consumers do not tend to be swayed as much by the opinions of others if their purchases will never be observed by anyone but themselves.[28] The relative effects of reference group influences on some specific product classes are shown in Figure 11.2.

The Power of Reference Groups

Social power refers to "the capacity to alter the actions of others."[29] To the degree that you are able to make someone else do something, whether they do it willingly or not, you have power over that person. The following classification of power bases can help us to distinguish among the reasons a person can exert power over another, the degree to which the influence is allowed voluntarily, and whether this influence will continue to have an effect in the absence of the power source.[30]

- *Referent power:* If a person admires the qualities of a person or a group, he or she will try to imitate those qualities by copying the referent's behaviors (e.g., choice of clothing, cars, leisure activities) as a guide to forming consumption preferences, just as Zack's preferences were affected by his fellow bikers. Prominent people in all walks of life can affect people's consumption behaviors by virtue of product endorsements (e.g., Michael Jordan for Air Nike), distinctive fashion statements (e.g., Madonna's use of lingerie as outerwear), or championing causes (e.g., Jerry Lewis' work for muscular dystrophy). **Referent power** is important to many marketing strategies because consumers voluntarily change behaviors to please or identify with a referent.

- *Information power:* A person can have power simply because he or she knows something others would like to know. Editors of trade publications such as *Women's Wear Daily* often possess power due to their ability to compile and disseminate information that can make or break individual designers or companies. People with **information power** are able to influence consumer opinion by virtue of their (assumed) access to the "truth."

All the clubs you'll never get into in one magazine.

TimeOut New York

The weekly magazine that tells you where to go and what to do.

Exclusive nightclubs have referent power because they determine who is cool enough to be admitted.

- *Legitimate power:* Sometimes people are granted power by virtue of social agreements, such as the power given to policemen and professors. The **legitimate power** conferred by a uniform is recognized in many consumer contexts, including teaching hospitals, in which medical students don white coats to enhance their aura of authority with patients, and banks, in which tellers' uniforms communicate trustworthiness.[31] This form of power may be "borrowed" by marketers to influence consumers. For example, an ad featuring a model wearing a white doctor's coat can add an aura of legitimacy or authority to the presentation of the product ("I'm not a doctor, but I play one on TV").

- *Expert power:* To attract the casual Internet user, U.S. Robotics signed up British physicist Stephen Hawking to endorse its modems. A company executive commented, "We wanted to generate trust. So we found visionaries who use U.S. Robotics technology, and we let them tell the consumer how it makes their lives more productive." Hawking, who has Lou Gehrig's disease and speaks via a synthesizer, says in one TV spot, "My body may be stuck in this chair, but with the Internet my mind can go to the end of the universe."[32] **Expert power** such as that possessed by Hawking is derived from possessing specific knowledge about a content area; it helps to explain the weight many of us assign to reviews of restaurants, books, movies, cars, and so on by critics who specialize in evaluating products on our behalf.[33]

- *Reward power:* When a person or group has the means to provide positive reinforcement (see Chapter 3), that entity will have **reward power** over a consumer to the extent that this reinforcement is valued or desired. The reward may be tangible, as occurs when an employee is given a raise. Or, the reward may be intangible: Social approval or acceptance is often what

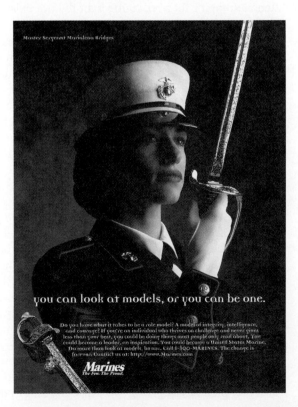

This recruiting ad presents a compelling role model for young women contemplating a career in the armed forces.

is exchanged in return for molding one's behavior to a group or buying the products expected of group members.

- *Coercive power:* A threat is often effective in the short-term, but it does not tend to produce permanent attitudinal or behavioral change. **Coercive power** refers to influencing a person by social or physical intimidation. Fortunately, this type of power is rarely employed in marketing situations, unless you count those annoying calls from telemarketers! However, elements of this power base are evident in fear appeals, intimidation in personal selling, and some campaigns that emphasize the negative consequences that might occur if people do not use a product.

CONFORMITY

The early bohemians who lived in Paris around 1830 made a point of behaving, well, differently from others. One flamboyant figure of the time became famous for walking a lobster on a leash through the gardens of the Royal Palace. His friends drank wine from human skulls, cut their beards in strange shapes, and slept in tents on the floors of their garrets.[34]

Although in every age there certainly are those who "march to their own drummer," most people tend to follow society's expectations regarding how they should act and look (with a little improvisation here and there, of course). **Conformity** refers to a change in beliefs or actions as a reaction to real or imagined group pressure. In order for a society to function, its members develop **norms,** or informal rules that govern behavior. If such a system of agreements did not evolve, social chaos would result. Imagine the confusion if a simple norm such as stopping for a red traffic light did not exist.

Norms change slowly over time, but there is general agreement within a society about which ones should be obeyed, and we adjust our way of thinking to conform to these norms. A powerful example is the change in American society's attitude toward smoking since the 1960s, when this practice was first linked with health concerns such as cancer and emphysema. By the mid-1990s, some communities even outlawed smoking in public places. Although tobacco sales to minors are illegal, most smokers begin puffing before the age of 18. Much of the motivation to begin smoking at an early age is due to peer pressure; the alluring advertising images of smokers as cool, sexy, or mature help to convince many young people that beginning the habit is a path to social acceptance.

Because the power of advertising to influence attitudes is widely recognized, some groups have tried to fight fire with fire by creating antismoking ads that depict smoking as an ugly habit that turns people off. Are these ads effective? One recent study of nonsmoking seventh graders by a pair of consumer researchers examined the kids' perceptions of smokers after being exposed to both cigarette ads and antismoking ads. Results were promising: The researchers found that kids who saw the antismoking ads were more likely to rate smokers lower in terms of both personal appeal and common sense. These findings imply that it is possible to use advertising to debunk myths about the glamour of smoking, especially if used in tandem with other health education efforts.[35]

We conform in many small ways everyday—even though we don't always realize it. Unspoken rules govern many aspects of consumption. In addition to norms regarding appropriate use of clothing and other personal items, we conform to rules that include gift-giving (we expect birthday presents from loved ones and get upset if they do not materialize), sex roles (men often are expected to pick up the check on a first date), and personal hygiene (we are expected to shower regularly to avoid offending others).

Types of Social Influence

Just as the bases for social power can vary, the process of social influence operates in several ways.[36] Sometimes a person is motivated to mimic the behavior of others because this behavior is believed to yield rewards such as social approval or money. At other times, the social influence process occurs simply because the person honestly does not *know* the correct way to respond and is using the behavior of the other person or group as a cue to ensure that he or she is responding correctly.[37] **Normative social influence** occurs when a person conforms to meet the expectations of a person or group.

In contrast, **informational social influence** refers to conformity that occurs because the group's behavior is taken as evidence about reality: If other people respond in a certain way in an ambiguous situation, we may mimic their behavior because this appears to be the correct thing to do.[38]

Conformity is not an automatic process, and many factors contribute to the likelihood that consumers will pattern their behavior after others.[39] Among the factors that affect the likelihood of conformity are the following:

- *Cultural pressures:* Different cultures encourage conformity to a greater or lesser degree. The American slogan "Do your own thing" in the 1960s reflected a movement away from conformity and toward individualism. In contrast, Japanese society is characterized by the dominance of collective well-being and group loyalty over individuals' needs.
- *Fear of deviance:* The individual may have reason to believe that the group will apply *sanctions* to punish behavior that differs from the group's. It is not unusual to observe adolescents shunning a peer who is "different" or a corporation or university passing over a person for promotion because he or she is not a "team player."
- *Commitment:* The more people are dedicated to a group and value membership in it, the more motivated they will be to follow the dictates of the group. Rock groupies and followers of TV evangelists may do anything that is asked of them, and terrorists may be willing to die for the good of their cause. According to the *principle of least interest*, the person or group that is least committed to staying in a relationship has the most power, because that party won't be susceptible to threatened rejection.[40]
- *Group unanimity, size, and expertise:* As groups gain in power, compliance increases. It is often harder to resist the demands of a large number of people than just a few, and this difficulty is compounded when the group members are perceived to know what they are talking about.
- *Susceptibility to interpersonal influence:* This trait refers to an individual's need to identify or enhance his or her image in the opinion of significant others. This enhancement process is often accompanied by the acquisition of products the person believes will impress his or her audience and by the tendency to learn about products by observing how others use them.[41] Consumers who are low on this trait have been called role-relaxed; they tend to be older, affluent, and to have high self-confidence. Based on research identifying role-relaxed consumers, Subaru created a communications strategy to reach

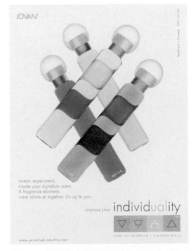

To promote the cause of individuality over conformity, Coty US LLC created Jovan Individuality. Scented tattoos were created for the launch since tattoos have resurfaced as a means of personal expression.

these people. In one commercial, a man is heard saying, "I want a car. . . . Don't tell me about wood paneling, about winning the respect of my neighbors. They're my neighbors. They're not my heroes."

Social Comparison: "How'm I Doing?"

Informational social influence implies that sometimes we look to the behavior of others to provide a yardstick about reality. **Social comparison theory** asserts that this process occurs as a way to increase the stability of one's self-evaluation, especially when physical evidence is unavailable.[42] Social comparison even applies to choices for which there is no objectively correct answer. Stylistic decisions such as tastes in music and art are assumed to be a matter of individual choice, yet people often assume that some choices are "better" or more "correct" than others.[43] If you have ever been responsible for choosing the music to play at a party, you can probably appreciate the social pressure involved in choosing the right "mix."

Although people often like to compare their judgments and actions to those of others, they tend to be selective about precisely whom they will use as benchmarks. Similarity between the consumer and others used for social comparison boosts confidence that the information is accurate and relevant (though we may find it more threatening to be outperformed by someone similar to ourselves).[44] We tend to value the views of obviously dissimilar others only when we are reasonably certain of our own.[45]

In general people tend to choose a *co-oriented peer*, or a person of equivalent standing, when performing social comparison. For example, a study of adult cosmetics users found that women were more likely to seek information about product choices from similar friends to reduce uncertainty and to trust the judgments of similar others.[46] The same effects have been found for evaluations of products as diverse as men's suits and coffee.[47]

Tactical Requests

How do we increase the likelihood that a person will conform to our wishes? The way a request for compliance is phrased or structured can make a difference. One well-known sales tactic is the *foot-in-the-door technique*, in which the consumer is first asked a small request and then is hit up for something bigger.[48] This term is adapted from door-to-door selling. Experienced salespeople know that they are much more likely to make a sale if they first convince a customer to let them in the house to deliver a sales pitch. Once the person has agreed to this small request, it is more difficult to refuse a larger one, because the consumer has legitimized the salesperson's presence by entering into a dialogue. He is no longer a threatening stranger at the door.

Other variations on this strategy include the *low-ball technique*, in which a person is asked for a small favor and is informed after agreeing to it that it will be very costly; or the *door-in-the-face technique*, in which a person is first asked to do something extreme (a request that is usually refused) and then is asked to do something smaller. In each of these cases, people tend to go along with the smaller request, possibly because they feel guilty about denying the larger one.[49]

Group Effects on Individual Behavior

With more people in a group, it becomes less likely any one member will be singled out for attention. People in larger groups or those in situations in which they are likely to be unidentified tend to focus less attention on themselves, so normal restraints on behavior are reduced. You may have observed that people sometimes behave more wildly at costume parties or on Halloween than they do normally. This phenomenon is known as **deindividuation,** a process in which individual identities get submerged within a group.

Social loafing refers to the fact that people do not devote as much to a task when their contribution is part of a larger group effort.[50] Waitresses are painfully aware of social loafing: People who eat in groups tend to tip less per person than when they are eating alone.[51] For this reason, many restaurants automatically tack on a fixed gratuity for groups of six or more.

There is some evidence that decisions made by groups differ from those that would be made by each individual. In many cases, group members show a greater willingness to consider riskier alternatives following group discussion than they would if members made their own decisions with no discussion. This change is known as the *risky shift*.[52]

Several explanations have been advanced to explain this increased riskiness. One possibility is that something similar to social loafing occurs. As more people are involved in a decision, each individual is less accountable for the outcome, so *diffusion of responsibility occurs*.[53] The practice of placing blanks in at least one of the rifles used by a firing squad is one way of diffusing each soldier's responsibility for the death of a prisoner. Another explanation is termed the *value hypothesis*. In this case, riskiness is a culturally valued characteristic, and social pressures operate on individuals to conform to attributes valued by society.[54]

Evidence for the risky shift is mixed. A more general effect appears to be that group discussion tends to increase **decision polarization.** Whichever direction the group members were leaning before discussion began, toward a risky choice or toward a conservative choice, becomes even more extreme in that direction after discussion. Group discussions regarding product purchases tend to create a risky shift for low-risk items, but they yield even more conservative group decisions for high-risk products.[55]

Even shopping behavior changes when people do it in groups. For example, people who shop with at least one other person tend to make more unplanned purchases, buy more, and cover more areas of a store than those who go alone.[57] These effects are due to both normative and informational social influence. Group members may be convinced to buy something to gain the approval of the others, or they may simply be exposed to more products and stores by pooling information with the group. For these reasons, retailers are well-advised to encourage group shopping activities.

Home shopping parties, as epitomized by the Tupperware party, capitalize on group pressures to boost sales.[58] A company representative makes a sales presentation to a group of people who have gathered in the home of a friend or acquaintance. This format is effective because of informational social influence: Participants model the behavior of others who can provide them with information about how to use certain products, especially because the home party is likely to be attended by a relatively homogenous group (e.g., neighborhood homemakers) that serves as a valuable benchmark. Normative social influence also operates because actions are publicly observed. Pressures to conform may be particularly intense and may escalate as more and more group members begin to "cave in" (this process is sometimes termed the bandwagon effect). In addition, deindividuation and/or the risky shift may be activated: As consumers get caught up in the group, they may find themselves willing to try new products they would not normally consider.

MARKETING PITFALLS

A DOWNSIDE TO DEINDIVIDUA-TION can be observed at many college parties, where students are encouraged by their peers to consume almost superhuman volumes of alcohol in group settings. It's been estimated that 4.5 million young people are alcohol-dependent or are problem drinkers. Binge drinking among college students is reaching epidemic proportions. In a two-week period, 42 percent of all college students engage in binge drinking (more than five drinks at a time) versus 33 percent of their noncollege counterparts. One in three students drinks primarily to get drunk, including 35 percent of college women.[56] For most, social pressure to throw inhibitions aside is the culprit.

Resistance To Influence

Many people pride themselves on their independence, unique style, or ability to resist the best efforts of salespeople and advertisers to buy products.[59] Indeed, individuality should be encouraged by the marketing system: Innovation creates change and demand for new products and styles.

Anticonformity Versus Independence

It is important to distinguish between *independence* and *anticonformity*; in anticonformity, defiance of the group is the actual object of behavior.[60] Some people will go out of their way *not* to buy whatever happens to be in at the moment. Indeed, they may spend a lot of time and effort to ensure that they will not be caught "in style." This behavior is a bit of a paradox, because in order to be vigilant about not doing what is expected, one must always be aware of what is expected. In contrast, truly independent people are oblivious to what is expected; they "march to their own drummers."

Reactance

People have a deep-seated need to preserve freedom of choice. When they are threatened with a loss of this freedom, they try to overcome this loss. This negative emotional state is termed **reactance**.[61] For example, efforts to censor books, television shows, or rock music that some people find objectionable may result in an increased desire for these products by the public.[62] Similarly, extremely overbearing promotions that tell consumers they must or should use a product may wind up losing more customers in the long run, even those who were already loyal to the advertised brand! Reactance is more likely to occur when the perceived threat to one's freedom increases and as the threatened behavior's importance to the consumer also increases.

WORD-OF-MOUTH COMMUNICATION

An obscure, 200-year-old breath mint called Altoids is all the rage these days, even though the manufacturer did virtually no advertising for most of the brand's history. How did this happen? The revival began when the mint began to attract a devoted following among smokers and coffee drinkers who hung out in the blossoming Seattle club scene during the 1980s. Until 1993, when manufacturer Callard & Bowers was bought by Kraft, the product was only bought by those "in the know." At that point, the brand's marketing manager persuaded this bigger company to hire advertising agency Leo Burnett to develop a modest promotional effort. The agency decided to publicize the candy by using subway posters sporting retro imagery and other "low-tech" media to avoid making the product seem mainstream—that would turn off the original audience.[63] As the product was shared among young people, its popularity mushroomed. Now, we're in the midst of a breath mint fad: According to Dunhill's director of marketing, "mints have become the latest gentlemanly accessory."[64]

As the Altoids success story illustrates, a lot of product information is conveyed by individuals to other individuals on an informal basis. **Word-of-mouth (WOM)** is product information transmitted by individuals to individuals. Because we get the word from people we know, WOM tends to be more reliable and trustworthy than recommendations we get through more formal marketing channels.

And unlike advertising, WOM often is backed up by social pressure to conform with these recommendations.[65]

If you think carefully about the content of your own conversations in the course of a normal day, you will probably agree that much of what you discuss with friends, family members, or coworkers is product-related: Whether you compliment someone on her dress and ask her where she bought it, recommend a new restaurant to a friend, or complain to your neighbor about the shoddy treatment you got at the bank, you are engaging in WOM. Recall, for example, that many of Zachary's biker purchases were directly initiated by comments and suggestions from his fellow RUBs. Marketers have been aware of the power of WOM for many years, but recently they've been more aggressive about trying to promote and control it instead of sitting back and hoping people will like their products enough to talk about them. In addition to Altoids, recent WOM success stories encompass products as diverse as cars (the VW Beetle), dolls (Beanie Babies), and cult movies (*The Blair Witch Project*).

The Dominance of WOM

As far back as the Stone Age (well, the 1950s, anyway), communications theorists began to challenge the assumption that advertising is the primary determinant of purchases. It is now generally accepted that advertising is more effective at reinforcing existing product preferences than at creating new ones.[66] Studies in both industrial and consumer purchase settings underscore the idea that although information from impersonal sources is important for creating brand awareness, word-of-mouth is relied upon in the later stages of evaluation and adoption.[67] The more positive information consumers get about a product from peers, the more likely they will be to adopt the product.[68]

The influence of others' opinions is at times even more powerful than one's own perceptions. In one study of furniture choices, consumers' estimates of how much their friends would like the furniture was a better predictor of purchase than their own evaluations.[69] In addition, consumers may find their own reasons to push a brand that take the manufacturer by surprise: That's what happened with Mountain Dew, whose popularity among younger consumers can be traced to the "buzz" about the soda's high caffeine content. As an advertising executive explained, "The caffeine thing was not in any of Mountain Dew's television ads. This drink is hot by word-of-mouth."[70] As marketers increasingly recognize the power of WOM to make or break a new product, they are coming up with new ways to get consumers to help them sell. Let's review two successful strategies.

Guerrilla Marketing

Lyor Cohen, a partner in the Def Jam hip hop label, built his business using street marketing tactics. To promote hip hop albums, Def Jam and other labels start building a buzz months before a release, leaking advance copies to deejays who put together "mix tapes" to sell on the street. If the kids seem to like a song, *street teams* then push it to club deejays. As the official release date nears, these groups of fans start slapping up posters around the inner city. They plaster telephone poles, sides of buildings, and car windshields with promotions announcing the release of new albums by artists such as Public Enemy, Jay-Z, DMX, or L. L. Cool J.[71]

These streetwise strategies started in the mid-1970s, when pioneering deejays like Kool DJ Herc and Afrika Bambaataa promoted their parties through graffiti-style flyers. This type of grassroots effort epitomizes **guerrilla marketing**; promotional strategies that use unconventional locations and intensive word-of-mouth campaigns to push products. As Ice Cube observed, "Even though I'm an established artist, I still like to leak my music to a kid on the street and let him duplicate it for his homies before it hits radio."[72]

Today, big companies are buying into guerrilla marketing strategies big time. Coca-Cola did it for a Sprite promotion, and Nike did it to build interest in a new shoe model.[73] When RCA records wanted to create a buzz around teen pop singer Christina Aguilera, they hired a team of young people to swarm the Web and chat about her on popular teen sites such as alloy.com, bolt.com, and gurl.com. They posted information casually, sometimes sounding like fans. Just before one of her albums debuted, RCA also hired a direct marketing company to e-mail electronic postcards filled with song snippets and biographical information to 50,000 Web addresses.[74] Guerrilla marketing delivers: The album quickly went to number one on the charts.

What's your opinion? Check out the online polls at www.prenhall.com/myphlip. Just follow the little person in the lab coat.

REALITY CHECK — *THE STRATEGY OF* VIRAL MARKETING

GETS *customers to sell a product to other customers on behalf of the company. That often means convincing your friends to climb on the bandwagon, and sometimes you get a cut if they wind up buying something.*[77] *Some might argue that means you're selling out your friends (or at least selling to your friends) in exchange for a piece of the action. Others might say you're just sharing the wealth with those you care about. Have you been involved in viral marketing by passing along names of your friends or sending them to a Web site such as* hotmail.com? *If so, what happened? How do you feel about this practice?*

I have been involved with the "surf the net and get paid" type of viral marketing. . . . It could . . . be very annoying to receive unwanted mail from your friends if the person is not interested. From a marketing student's point, I think is a great marketing strategy, but it also could make some people unhappy.

Frank Liu
Florida State University

I had a friend who began working for a website that paid him a lump sum of money if he could get 4,000 users on our campus. He was allowed to hire four marketing representatives, to help him promote the company, sending students from our school to the website. . . . Soon I was throwing flyers in every building of my school. . . . I had to pass along sign up sheets in my classes. . . . My

friend, the leader, kept pressuring us to go back into the same classes, re-forward the e-mails, and keep trying to persuade students to visit the website. Soon, I began to feel like a beggar, hassling my peers to become a user on the site. I didn't understand why we bothered students on our campus, for the benefit of an e-commerce site. . . . It was as though we were doing all the marketing and advertising efforts for them.

Katherine S. Kennedy
James Madison University

I can recall recommending websites services such as hotmail, MSN messenger among others. I've also spread the word about food products, clothing or even car models. I believe that it is most people's nature to recommend a good or service that has proven to be satisfactory and useful for that person. Even though I've never done this for profit, I think I would do it if what I'm "selling" really stands for what

is being promoted. Otherwise, I would consider it almost a non-ethical practice, or at least uncomfortable when it comes to mixing friends and business.

Constanza Montes Larranaga
Universidad de Chile

Honestly, I think it is a huge hassle. I don't think it is a bad idea from the company's standpoint, but I don't know of many people who actually enjoy participating in this process.

Fant Walker
University of Mississippi

The one time I intentionally participated in viral marketing was through physique.com. Their hair care products are ones I particularly like. However, they are pretty expensive. Their website offers a coupon good for one free, full sized product if you send an email to seven friends, recommending the product. After you enter their addresses, your name is inserted in what appears to be a personal message raving about the product's benefits. Were my friends gullible and easily duped people, perhaps I would have felt bad. However, knowing my friends delete most emails before they even read them. I was not concerned.

Concetta Rini
The College of William and Mary

Viral Marketing

Many students are big fans of Hot Mail, a free e-mail service. But, there's no such thing as a free lunch: Hot Mail inserts a small ad on every message sent, making each user a salesperson. The company had five million subscribers in its first year and continues to grow exponentially.[75] **Viral marketing** refers to the strategy of getting customers to sell a product on behalf of the company that creates it. This approach is particularly well-suited to the Web because e-mails circulate so easily. According to a study by Jupiter Communications, only 24 percent of consumers say they learn about new Web sites in magazine or newspaper ads. Instead, they rely on friends and family for new site recommendations, so viral marketing is their main source of information about new sites. The chief executive of Gazooba.com, a company that creates viral marketing promotions, observed that "the return mail address of a friend is a brand that you trust."[76]

Factors Encouraging WOM

WOM is especially powerful when the consumer is relatively unfamiliar with the product category. Such a situation would be expected in the case of new products (e.g., medications to prevent hair loss) or those that are technologically complex (e.g., CD players). As one example, the strongest predictor of a person's intention to buy a residential solar water-heating system was found to be the number of solar-heating users the person knows.[78]

Most WOM campaigns happen spontaneously, as a product begins to develop a regional following, as was the case with Ben & Jerry's ice cream. Occasionally, a "buzz" is intentionally created. Lee jeans did that by creating a "phantom campaign" based on the retro hero Buddy Lee. The company quietly put up posters of Buddy Lee in cities such as New York and Los Angeles and waited for momentum to build before launching TV commercials that were shown during shows like *Dawsons Creek*.[79] Product-related conversations can be motivated by a number of factors:[80]

- A person might be highly involved with a type of product or activity and get pleasure in talking about it. Computer hackers, avid bird watchers, and "fashion plates" seem to share the ability to steer a conversation toward their particular interests.
- A person might be knowledgeable about a product and use conversations as a way to let others know it. Thus, word-of-mouth communication sometimes enhances the ego of the individual who wants to impress others with their expertise.
- A person might initiate such a discussion out of genuine concern for someone else. We are often motivated to ensure that people we care about buy what is good for them, do not waste their money, and so on.
- One way to reduce uncertainty about the wisdom of a purchase is to talk about it. Talking gives the consumer an opportunity to generate more supporting arguments for the purchase and to garner support for this decision from others.

Negative WOM

Word-of-mouth is a two-edged sword that can cut both ways for marketers. Informal discussions among consumers can make or break a product or store. Furthermore, negative word-of-mouth is weighted more heavily by consumers than are positive comments. According to a study by the White House Office of

Consumer Affairs, 90 percent of unhappy customers will not do business with a company again. Each of these people is likely to share their grievance with at least nine other people, and 13 percent of these disgruntled customers will go on to tell more than 30 people of their negative experience.[81] Especially when she is considering a new product or service, the consumer is more likely to pay more attention to negative information than positive information and to relate news of this experience to others.[82] Negative WOM has been shown to reduce the credibility of a firm's advertising and to influence consumers' attitudes toward a product as well as their intention to buy it.[83] And, negative WOM is even easier to spread online. Many dissatisfied customers and disgruntled former employees have been "inspired" to create Web sites just to share their tales of woe with others. For example, a Web site for people to complain about the Dunkin' Donuts chain got to be so popular the company bought it in order to control the bad press it was getting. It grew out of a complaint by the original owner because he could not get skim milk for his coffee.[84] For other protest sites, visit protest.net and prepare to be outraged.

Rumors: Distortion in the Word-of-Mouth Process

In the 1930s, "professional rumormongers" were hired to organize word-of-mouth campaigns to promote clients' products and criticize those of competitors.[85] More recently, Bio Business International, a small Canadian company that markets 100 percent cotton non-chlorine–bleached tampons under the name

Figure 11.3
The Transmission of Misinformation These drawings provide a classic example of the distortions that can occur as information is transmitted from person to person. As each participant reproduced the figure, it gradually changes from an owl to a cat.

Terra Femme, encouraged women to spread a message that tampons made by its American competitors contain dioxin. There is very little evidence to support the claim that these products are dangerous, but as a result of this rumor Procter & Gamble received thousands of complaints about its feminine hygiene products.[86]

A rumor, even if it has no basis in fact, can be a very dangerous thing. As information is transmitted among consumers, it tends to change. The resulting message usually does not at all resemble the original. Social scientists who study rumors have examined the process by which information gets distorted. The British psychologist Frederic Bartlett used the method of *serial reproduction* to examine this phenomenon. As in the game of "Telephone," a subject is asked to reproduce a stimulus, such as a drawing or a story. Another subject is given this reproduction and asked to copy that, and so on. This technique is shown in Figure 11.3. Bartlett found that distortions almost inevitably follow a pattern: They tend to change from ambiguous forms to more conventional ones as subjects try to make them consistent with preexisting schemas. This process, known as *assimilation*, is characterized by *leveling*, in which details are omitted to simplify the structure, or *sharpening*, in which prominent details are accentuated.

OPINION LEADERSHIP

Although consumers get information from personal sources, they do not tend to ask just *anyone* for advice about purchases. If you decide to buy a new stereo, you will most likely seek advice from a friend who knows a lot about sound systems. This friend may own a sophisticated system, or she may subscribe to specialized magazines such as *Stereo Review* and spend free time browsing through electronics stores. On the other hand, you may have another friend who has a reputation for being stylish and who spends his free time reading *Gentlemen's Quarterly* and

THE TANGLED WEB

THERE IS A LONG and "honored" tradition of people inventing fake stories to see who will swallow them—like the one in 1824 in which a man convinced 300 New Yorkers to sign up for a construction project. He claimed all the new building in the lower part of Manhattan (what is now the Wall Street area) was making the island bottom-heavy. As a result it needed to be sawed off and towed out to sea or all of New York City would tip over![87]

The Web is a perfect medium for spreading rumors and hoaxes, and we can only guess how much damage this "project" would cause today if construction crews were recruited via e-mail! Modern day hoaxes abound; many of these are in the form of e-mail chain letters promising instant riches if you pass the message on to ten friends. Your professor will love one variation of this hoax: In a scam called "Win Tenure Fast" academics were told to add their names to a document and then cite it in their own research papers. The idea is that everyone who gets the letter cites the professor's name and with so many citations you're guaranteed to get tenure! If only it were that easy.

Other hoaxes involve major corporations. A popular one promised that if you try Microsoft products you will get a free trip to Disneyland. Nike received several hundred pairs of old sneakers a day after the rumor spread that you would get a free pair of new shoes in exchange for your old, smelly ones (pity the delivery people who had to cart these packages to the company!).[88] Procter & Gamble received more than 10,000 irate calls after a rumor began spreading on newsgroups that its Febreze fabric softener kills dogs. In a pre-emptive strike, the company registered numerous Web site names such as febrezekillspet.com, febrezesucks.com, and ihateprocterandgamble.com to be sure they weren't used by angry consumers.[89] P&G now has a Web site dedicated to fighting rumors: www.pg.com/rumor. Other Web sites, including hoaxkill.com, also are dedicated to tracking hoaxes. The moral: Don't believe everything you click on.

Hoaxkill.com is a website dedicated to tracking hoaxes and debunking product rumors.

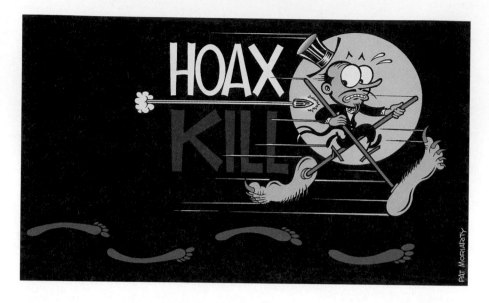

shopping at trendy boutiques. You might not bring up your stereo problem with him, but you may take him with you to shop for a new fall wardrobe.

The Nature of Opinion Leadership

Everyone knows people who are knowledgeable about products and whose advice is taken seriously by others. These individuals are **opinion leaders.** An opinion leader is a person who is frequently able to influence others' attitudes or behaviors.[92] Opinion leaders are extremely valuable information sources for a number of reasons:

1. They are technically competent and thus convincing because they possess expert power.[93]
2. They have prescreened, evaluated, and synthesized product information in an unbiased way, so they possess knowledge power.[94] Unlike commercial endorsers, opinion leaders do not actually represent the interests of one company. Thus, they are more credible because they have no "axe to grind."
3. They tend to be socially active and highly interconnected in their community.[95] They are likely to hold offices in community groups and clubs and to be active outside of the home. As a result, opinion leaders often have legitimate power by virtue of their social standing.
4. They tend to be similar to the consumer in terms of their values and beliefs, so they possess referent power. Note that although opinion leaders are set apart by their interest or expertise in a product category, they are more convincing to the extent that they are *homophilous* rather than *heterophilous. Homophily* refers to the degree that a pair of individuals is similar in terms of education, social status, and beliefs.[96] Effective opinion leaders tend to be slightly higher in terms of status and educational attainment than those they influence but not so high as to be in a different social class.
5. Opinion leaders are often among the first to buy new products, so they absorb much of the risk. This experience reduces uncertainty for others who are not as courageous. Furthermore, whereas company-sponsored

communications tend to focus exclusively on the positive aspects of a product, the hands-on experience of opinion leaders makes them more likely to impart *both* positive and negative information about product performance.

How Influential Is an Opinion Leader?

When marketers and social scientists initially developed the concept of the opinion leader, it was assumed that certain influential people in a community would exert an overall impact on group members' attitudes. Later work, however, began to question the assumption that there is such a thing as a *generalized opinion leader*, somebody whose recommendations are sought for all types of purchases. Very few people are capable of being expert in a number of fields. Sociologists distinguish between those who are *monomorphic*, or expert in a limited field, and those who are *polymorphic*, or expert in several fields.[97] Even opinion leaders who are polymorphic, however, tend to concentrate on one broad domain, such as electronics or fashion.

Research on opinion leadership generally indicates that although opinion leaders do exist for multiple product categories, expertise tends to overlap across similar categories. It is rare to find a generalized opinion leader. An opinion leader for home appliances is likely to serve a similar function for home cleaners but not for cosmetics. In contrast, a fashion opinion leader whose primary influence is on clothing choices may also be consulted for recommendations on cosmetics purchases, but not necessarily on microwave ovens.[98]

Opinion Leaders Versus Other Consumer Types

Early conceptions of the opinion leader role also assumed a static process: The opinion leader absorbs information from the mass media and in turn transmits data to opinion receivers. This view has turned out to be overly simplified; it confuses the functions of several different types of consumers.

Opinion leaders may or may not be purchasers of the products they recommend. As we will see in Chapter 17, early purchasers are known as *innovators*. Opinion leaders who also are early purchasers have been termed *innovative communicators*. One study identified a number of characteristics of college men who were innovative communicators for fashion products. These men were among the first to buy new fashions, and their fashion opinions were incorporated by other students in their own clothing decisions. Other characteristics of the men included the following:[99]

- They were socially active.
- They were appearance-conscious and narcissistic (i.e., they were quite fond of themselves and self-centered).
- They were involved in rock culture.
- They were heavy magazine readers, including *Playboy* and *Sports Illustrated.*
- They were likely to own more clothing, and a broader range of styles, than other students.

Opinion leaders also are likely to be *opinion seekers*. They are generally more involved in a product category and actively search for information. As a result, they are more likely to talk about products with others and to solicit others' opinions as well.[100] Contrary to the static view of opinion leadership, most product-related conversation does not take place in a "lecture" format in which one person does all of the talking. A lot of product-related conversation is prompted

MULTICULTURAL DIMENSIONS

MULTINATIONAL FIRMS ARE ESPECIALLY prone to damage from rumors because they have less control over product quality or local customs. Several marketers in Indonesia, including Nestlé, were hurt by rumors that their foods contain pork, which is prohibited for consumption by the 160 million Muslim consumers in that country. Islamic preachers, or mullahs, responded to these rumors by warning consumers not to buy products that might be tainted with pork fat. Nestlé spent more than $250,000 on an ad campaign to counteract the rumors.[90] In another recent incident in the Middle East, the Egyptian subsidiary of Coca-Cola had to get an edict from Egypt's mufti (top religious authority) ceritfying that the familiar Coca-Cola script logo does not in fact say "No Mohammed, No Mecca" in Arabic after a rumor spread about hidden messages. This problem echoed one experienced a few years earlier by Nike, which recalled 38,000 pairs of shoes because its flaming Air logo resembled the Arabic script for Allah.[91]

Opinion leadership is a big factor in the marketing of athletic shoes. Many styles first become popular in the inner city and then spread by word-of-mouth.

by the situation and occurs in the context of a casual interaction rather than as formal instruction.[101] One study, which found that opinion seeking is especially high for food products, revealed that two-thirds of opinion seekers also view themselves as opinion leaders.[102] This updated view of interpersonal product communication is contrasted with the traditional view in Figure 11.4.

Consumers who are expert in a product category may not actively communicate with others, whereas other consumers may have a more general interest in being involved in product discussions. A consumer category called the **market maven** describes people who are actively involved in transmitting marketplace information of all types. Market mavens are not necessarily interested in certain products and may not necessarily be early purchasers of products; they're just into shopping and staying on top of what's happening in the marketplace. They come closer to the function of a generalized opinion leader because they tend to have a solid overall knowledge of how and where to procure products. The following scale items, to which respondents indicate how much they agree or disagree, have been used to identify market mavens:[103]

1. I like introducing new brands and products to my friends.
2. I like helping people by providing them with information about many kinds of products.
3. People ask me for information about products, places to shop, or sales.

Figure 11.4
Perspectives on the
Communications Process

TRADITIONAL MODEL

```
┌────────────┐      ┌─────────────────┐      ┌────────────┐
│ Mass Media │─────▶│ Opinion Leaders │─────▶│ Recipients │
└────────────┘      └─────────────────┘      └────────────┘
```

UPDATED MODEL

```
                    ┌──────────────┐
                    │ Gatekeepers  │
                    └──────────────┘
          ┌───────────▲    │    ▲───────────┐
          │                ▼                │
┌────────────┐                        ┌────────────┐
│ Mass Media │                        │ Recipients │
└────────────┘                        └────────────┘
          │                                ▲
          └───────────▶┌─────────────────┐─┘
                       │ Opinion Leaders │
                       └─────────────────┘
```

4. If someone asked me where to get the best buy on several types of products, I could tell him or her where to shop.
5. My friends think of me as a good source of information when it comes to new products or sales.
6. Think about a person who has information about a variety of products and likes to share this information with others. This person knows about new products, sales, stores, and so on, but does not necessarily feel he or she is an expert on one particular product. How well would you say this description fits you?

In addition to everyday consumers who are influential in influencing others' purchase decisions, a class of marketing intermediary called the **surrogate consumer** is an active player in many categories. A surrogate consumer is a person who is hired to provide input into purchase decisions. Unlike the opinion leader or market maven, the surrogate is usually compensated for this involvement.

Interior decorators, stockbrokers, professional shoppers, or college consultants can all be thought of as surrogate consumers. Whether or not they actually make the purchase on behalf of the consumer, surrogates' recommendations can be enormously influential. The consumer in essence relinquishes control over several or all decision-making functions, such as information search, evaluation of alternatives, or the actual purchase. For example, a client may commission an interior decorator to redo her house, and a broker may be entrusted to make crucial buy/sell decisions on behalf of investors. The involvement of surrogates in a wide range of purchase decisions tends to be overlooked by many marketers, who may be mistargeting their communications to end consumers instead of to the surrogates who are actually sifting through product information.[104]

Identifying Opinion Leaders

Because opinion leaders are so central to consumer decision making, marketers are quite interested in identifying influential people for a product category. In fact, many ads are intended to reach these influentials rather than the average consumer, especially if the ads contain a lot of technical information. For example, CBS sent a CD-ROM to 10,000 critics, affiliates, advertising agencies, and others it had identified as "influencers" in order to plug the network's prime-time shows.[105]

Unfortunately, because most opinion leaders are everyday consumers and are not formally included in marketing efforts, they are harder to find. A celebrity or an influential industry executive is by definition easy to locate. He or she has national or at least regional visibility or may be listed in published directories. In contrast, opinion leaders tend to operate at the local level and may influence five to 10 consumers rather than an entire market segment. In some cases, companies have been known to identify influentials and involve them directly in their marketing efforts, hoping to create a "ripple effect" as these consumers sing the company's praises to their friends. Many department stores, for example, have fashion panels, usually composed of adolescent girls, who provide input into fashion trends, participate in fashion shows, and so on.

Because of the difficulties involved in identifying specific opinion leaders in a large market, most attempts to do so instead focus on exploratory studies through which the characteristics of representative opinion leaders can be identified and then generalized to the larger market. This knowledge helps marketers target their product-related information to appropriate settings and media. For example, one attempt to identify financial opinion leaders found that these consumers were more likely to be involved in managing their own finances and tended to use a computer to do so. They also were more likely to follow their investments on a daily basis and to read books and watch television shows devoted to financial issues.[106]

The Self-Designating Method

The most commonly used technique to identify opinion leaders is simply to ask individual consumers whether they consider themselves to be opinion leaders. Although respondents who report a greater degree of interest in a product category are more likely to be opinion leaders, the results of surveys intended to identify self-designated opinion leaders must be viewed with some skepticism. Some people have a tendency to inflate their own importance and influence, whereas others who really are influential might not admit to this quality or be conscious of it.[107] Just because we transmit advice about products does not mean other people *take* that advice. For someone to be considered a *bona fide* opinion leader, his or her advice must actually be heard and heeded by opinion seekers. An alternative is to select certain group members (*key informants*) who in turn are asked to identify opinion leaders. The success of this approach hinges on locating those who have accurate knowledge of the group and on minimizing their response biases (e.g., the tendency to inflate one's own influence on the choices of others).

The self-designating method is not as reliable as a more systematic analysis (in which individual claims of influence can be verified by asking others whether the person is really influential), but it does have the advantage of being easy to apply to a large group of potential opinion leaders. In some cases not all members of a community are surveyed. One of the measurement scales developed for self-designation of opinion leaders is shown in Figure 11.5.

Sociometry

A Web-based service call sixdegrees.com is based on the popular play "Six Degrees of Separation." The basic premise is that everyone on the planet indi-

Please rate yourself on the following scales relating to your interactions with friends and neighbors regarding _____.

1. In general, do you talk to your friends and neighbors about _____:

very often				never
5	4	3	2	1

2. When you talk to your friends and neighbors about _____ do you:

give a great deal of information				give very little information
5	4	3	2	1

3. During the past six months, how many people have you told about a new _____?

told a number of people				told no one
5	4	3	2	1

4. Compared with your circle of friends, how likely are you to be asked about new _____?

very likely to be asked				not at all likely to be asked
5	4	3	2	1

5. In discussion of new _____, which of the following happens most?

you tell your friends about _____				your friends tell you about _____
5	4	3	2	1

6. Overall in all of your discussions with friends and neighbors are you:

often used as a source of advice				not used as a source of advice
5	4	3	2	1

Figure 11.5
A Revised and Updated Version of the Opinion Leadership Scale

SOURCE: Adapted from Terry L. Childers, "Assessment of the Psychometric Properties of an Opinion Leadership Scale," *Journal of Marketing Research* 23 (May 1986): 184–88; and Leisa Reinecke Flynn, Ronald E. Goldsmith, and Jacqueline K. Eastman, "The King and Summers Opinion Leadership Scale: Revision and Refinement," *Journal of Business Research* 31 (1994): 55–64.

rectly knows everyone else—or at least knows people who know them. Indeed, it is estimated that the average person has 1,500 acquaintances and that any two people in the United States could be connected by five to six intermediaries.[108] The Web site allows a person to register and provide names and e-mail addresses of other people so that when the user needs to network a connection can be made with others in the database.[109] Its slogan: "You'd be surprised who you know."

This Web site is a digital version of more conventional **sociometric methods,** which trace communication patterns among members of a group. These techniques allow researchers to systematically map out the interactions that take place among group members. By interviewing participants and asking them to whom they go for product information, those who tend to be sources of product-related information can be identified. This method is the most precise, but it is very hard and expensive to implement because it involves very close study of interaction patterns in small groups. For this reason, sociometric techniques are best applied in a closed, self-contained social setting, such as in hospitals, prisons, and army bases, in which members are largely isolated from other social networks.

Many professionals and services marketers depend primarily on word-of-mouth to generate business. In many cases consumers recommend a service provider to a friend or coworker, and in other cases business people will make recommendations to their customers. For example, only 0.2 percent of respondents in one study reported choosing a physician based on advertising. Advice from family and friends was the most widely used criterion.[110]

Sociometric analyses can be used to better understand *referral behavior* and to locate strengths and weaknesses in terms of how one's reputation is communicated through a community.[111] *Network analysis* focuses on communication in social systems, considers the relations among people in a *referral network,* and measures the *tie strength* among them. Tie strength refers to the nature of the bond between people. It can range from strong primary (e.g., one's spouse) to weak secondary (e.g., an acquaintance that one rarely sees). A strong tie relationship may be thought of as a primary reference group; interactions are frequent and important to the individual.

Although strong ties are important, weak ties can perform a *bridging function*. This type of connection allows a consumer access between subgroups. For example, you might have a regular group of friends who serve as a primary reference group (strong ties). If you have an interest in tennis, say, one of these friends might introduce you to a group of people in her dorm who play on the tennis team. As a result, you gain access to their valuable expertise through this bridging function. This referral process demonstrates the strength of weak ties. One study using this method examined similarities in brand choice among members of a college sorority. The researchers found evidence that subgroups, or *cliques*, within the sorority were likely to share preferences for various products. In some cases, even choices of "private" (i.e., socially inconspicuous products) were shared, possibly because of structural variables such as shared bathrooms in the sorority house.[112]

CHAPTER SUMMARY

- Consumers belong to or admire many different groups and are often influenced in their purchase decisions by a desire to be accepted by others.
- Individuals have influence in a group to the extent that they possess social power; types of social power include information power, referent power, legitimate power, expert power, reward power, and coercive power.
- We conform to the desires of others for two basic reasons: (1) People who model their behavior after others because they take others' behavior as evidence of the correct way to act are conforming because of informational social influence, and (2) Those who conform to satisfy the expectations of others or to be accepted by the group are affected by normative social influence.
- Group members often do things they would not do as individuals because their identities become merged with the group; they become deindividuated.
- Individuals or groups whose opinions or behavior are particularly important to consumers are reference groups. Both formal and informal groups influence the individual's purchase decisions, although the impact of reference group influence is affected by such factors as the conspicuousness of the product and the relevance of the reference group for a particular purchase.
- The Web has greatly amplified consumers' abilities to be exposed to numerous reference groups. Virtual consumption communities are composed of people who are united by a common bond—enthusiasm about or knowledge of a specific product or service.
- Opinion leaders who are knowledgeable about a product and whose opinions are highly regarded tend to influence others' choices. Specific opinion leaders are somewhat hard to identify, but marketers who know their general characteristics can try to target them in their media and promotional strategies.
- Other influencers include market mavens, who have a general interest in marketplace activities, and surrogate consumers, who are compensated for their advice about purchases.
- Much of what we know about products comes about through word-of-mouth communication (WOM) rather than formal advertising. Product-related information tends to be exchanged in casual conversations. Guerrilla marketing strategies try to accelerate the WOM process by enlisting consumers to help spread the word.

- Although word-of-mouth often is helpful for making consumers aware of products, it can also hurt companies when damaging product rumors or negative word-of-mouth occurs.
- Emerging marketing strategies try to leverage the potential of the Web to spread information from consumer to consumer extremely quickly. Viral marketing techniques enlist individuals to tout products, services, Web sites, etc. to others on behalf of companies.
- Sociometric methods are used to trace referral patterns. This information can be used to identify opinion leaders and other influential consumers.

KEY TERMS

coercive power, p. 328
comparative influence, p. 321
conformity, p. 328
decision polarization, p. 331
deindividuation, p. 331
expert power, p. 327
guerrilla marketing, p. 334
information power, p. 327
informational social influence, p. 329

legitimate power, p. 327
market maven, p. 340
normative influence, p. 321
normative social influence, p. 329
norms, p. 328
opinion leaders, p. 338
reactance, p. 332
reference group, p. 319
referent power, p. 326

reward power, p. 327
social comparison theory, p. 330
social power, p. 326
sociometric methods, p. 343
surrogate consumer, p. 341
viral marketing, p. 335
virtual community of consumption, p. 323
word of mouth (WOM), p. 332

CONSUMER BEHAVIOR CHALLENGE

1. Compare and contrast the five bases of power described in the text. Which are most likely to be relevant for marketing efforts?
2. Why is referent power an especially potent force for marketing appeals? What factors help to predict whether reference groups will or will not be a powerful influence on a person's purchase decisions?
3. Evaluate the strategic soundness of the concept of guerrilla marketing. For what type of product categories is this strategy most likely to be a success?
4. Discuss some factors that determine the amount of conformity likely to be observed among consumers.
5. Under what conditions are we more likely to engage in social comparison with dissimilar others versus similar others? How might this dimension be used in the design of marketing appeals?
6. Discuss some reasons for the effectiveness of home shopping parties as a selling tool. What other products might be sold this way?
7. Discuss some factors that influence whether membership groups will have a significant influence on a person's behavior.
8. Why is word-of-mouth communication often more persuasive than advertising?
9. Is there such a thing as a generalized opinion leader? What is likely to determine if an opinion leader will be influential with regard to a specific product category?
10. The adoption of a certain brand of shoe or apparel by athletes can be a powerful influence on students and other fans. Should high school and college coaches be paid to determine what brand of athletic equipment their players will wear?

11. The power of unspoken social norms often becomes obvious only when these norms are violated. To witness this result firsthand, try one of the following: stand facing the back wall in an elevator; serve dessert before the main course; offer to pay cash for dinner at a friend's home; wear pajamas to class; or tell someone not to have a nice day.

12. Identify a set of avoidance groups for your peers. Can you identify any consumption decisions that are made with these groups in mind?

13. Identify fashion opinion leaders on your campus. Do they fit the profile discussed in the chapter?

14. Conduct a sociometric analysis within your dormitory or neighborhood. For a product category such as music or cars, ask each individual to identify other individuals with whom they share information. Systematically trace all of these avenues of communication, and identify opinion leaders by locating individuals who are repeatedly named as providing helpful information.

NOTES

1. Details adapted from John W. Schouten and James H. McAlexander, "Market Impact of a Consumption Subculture: The Harley-Davidson Mystique," in Fred van Raaij and Gary Bamossy, eds., *Proceedings of the 1992 European Conference of the Association for Consumer Research* (Amsterdam, 1992); John W. Schouten and James H. McAlexander, "Subcultures of Consumption: An Ethnography of the New Bikers," *Journal of Consumer Research* 22 (June 1995): 43–61. See also Kelly Barron, "Not So Easy Riders." *Forbes* (May 15, 2000).

2. Joel B. Cohen and Ellen Golden, "Informational Social Influence and Product Evaluation," *Journal of Applied Psychology* 56 (February 1972): 54–59; Robert E. Burnkrant and Alain Cousineau, "Informational and Normative Social Influence in Buyer Behavior," *Journal of Consumer Research* 2 (December 1975): 206–15; Peter H. Reingen, "Test of a List Procedure for Inducing Compliance with a Request to Donate Money," *Journal of Applied Psychology* 67 (1982): 110–18.

3. Quoted in Dyan Machan, "Is the Hog Going Soft?" *Forbes* (March 10, 1997): 114–19.

4. C. Whan Park and V. Parker Lessig, "Students and Housewives: Differences in Susceptibility to Reference Group Influence," *Journal of Consumer Research* 4 (September 1977): 102–10.

5. Kenneth J. Gergen and Mary Gergen, *Social Psychology* (New York: Harcourt Brace Jovanovich, 1981).

6. Harold H. Kelley, "Two Functions of Reference Groups," in Harold Proshansky and Bernard Siedenberg, eds., *Basic Studies in Social Psychology* (New York: Holt, Rinehart and Winston, 1965): 210–14.

7. Bob Tedeschi, "A Fresh Spin on 'Affinity Portals' to the Internet," *The New York Times on the Web* (April 17, 2000).

8. Anne Eisenberg, "Find Me a File, Cache Me a Catch," *The New York Times on the Web* (February 10, 2000). For more information see the project Web site: foner.www.media.mit.edu/people/foner/yenta-brief.html.

9. Jon Herskovitz, "Japanese Look for Love," *Advertising Age International* (July 13, 1998): 6.

10. L. Festinger, S. Schachter, and K. Back, *Social Pressures in Informal Groups: A Study of Human Factors in Housing* (New York: Harper, 1950).

11. R. B. Zajonc, H. M. Markus, and W. Wilson, "Exposure Effects and Associative Learning," *Journal of Experimental Social Psychology* 10 (1974): 248–63.

12. D. J. Stang, "Methodological Factors in Mere Exposure Research," *Psychological Bulletin* 81 (1974): 1014–25; R. B. Zajonc, P. Shaver, C. Tavris, and D. Van Kreveid, "Exposure, Satiation and Stimulus Discriminability," *Journal of Personality and Social Psychology* 21 (1972): 270–80.

13. J. E. Grush, K. L. McKeogh, and R. F. Ahlering, "Extrapolating Laboratory Exposure Research to Actual Political Elections," *Journal of Personality and Social Psychology* 36 (1978): 257–70.

14. A. Benton Cocanougher and Grady D. Bruce, "Socially Distant Reference Groups and Consumer Aspirations," *Journal of Marketing Research* 8 (August 1971): 79–81; James E. Stafford, "Effects of Group Influences on Consumer Brand Preferences," *Journal of Marketing Research* 3 (February 1966): 68–75.

15. Cocanougher and Bruce, "Socially Distant Reference Groups and Consumer Aspirations."

16. Greg Jaffe, "No MTV for Widespread Panic, Just Loads of Worshipful Fans," *The Wall Street Journal Interactive Edition* (February 17, 1999).

17. This typology is adapted from material presented in Robert V. Kozinets, "E-Tribalized Marketing: The Strategic Implications of Virtual Communities of Consumption," *European Management Journal* 17, no. 3 (June 1999): 252–64.

18. Tom Weber, "Net's Hottest Game Brings People Closer," *The Wall Street Journal Interactive Edition* (March 20, 2000).

19. Quoted in Marc Gunther, "The Newest Addiction," *Fortune* (August 2, 1999): 122–24.

20. Laurie J. Flynn, "Free Internet Service for Simpsons Fans," *The New York Times on the Web* (January 24, 2000).

21. Neil Gross, "Building Global Communities," *Business Week E.Biz* (March 22, 1999): EB42–EB43.

22. Bob Tedeschi, "Product Reviews from Anyone with an Opinion," *The New York Times on the Web* (October 25, 1999).

23. Robert V. Kozinets, "E-Tribalized Marketing: The Strategic Implications of Virtual Communities of Consumption," *European Management Journal* 17, no. 3 (June 1999): 252–64.

24. Bob Tedeschi, "Online Retailers Find that Customer Reviews Build Loyalty," *The New York Times on the Web* (September 6, 1999).

25. "Bookseller Offers Refunds for Advertised Books," *Opelika-Auburn [Alabama] News* (February 11, 1999): A11.

26. Jason Anders, "When It Comes to Promoters, Boards Say, 'Reader Beware,'" *The Wall Street Journal Interactive Edition* (July 25, 1998).

27. Jeffrey D. Ford and Elwood A. Ellis, "A Re-examination of Group Influence on Member Brand Preference," *Journal of Marketing Research* 17 (February 1980): 125–32; Thomas S. Robertson, *Innovative Behavior and Communication* (New York: Holt, Rinehart and Winston, 1980): Chapter 8.

28. William O. Bearden and Michael J. Etzel, "Reference Group Influence on Product and Brand Purchase Decisions," *Journal of Consumer Research* 9, no. 2 (1982): 183–94.

29. Gergen and Gergen, *Social Psychology:* 312.

30. J.R.P. French Jr. and B. Raven, "The Bases of Social Power," in D. Cartwright, ed., *Studies in Social Power* (Ann Arbor, MI: Institute for Social Research, 1959): 150–67.

31. Michael R. Solomon, "Packaging the Service Provider," *The Service Industries Journal* 5 (March 1985): 64–72.

32. Quoted in Tamar Charry, "Advertising: Hawking, Wozniak Pitch Modems for U.S. Robotics," *The New York Times News Service* (February 5, 1997).

33. Patricia M. West and Susan M. Broniarczyk, "Integrating Multiple Opinions: The Role of Aspiration Level on Consumer Response to Critic Consensus," *Journal of Consumer Research* 25 (June 1998): 38–51.

34. Luc Sante, "Be Different! (Like Everyone Else!)," *The New York Times Magazine* [online], October 17, 1999.

35. Cornelia Pechmann and S. Ratneshwar, "The Effects of Antismoking and Cigarette Advertising on Young Adolescents' Perceptions of Peers Who Smoke," *Journal of Consumer Research* 21, no. 2 (September 1994): 236–51.

36. See Robert B. Cialdini, *Influence: Science and Practice*, 2d ed. (New York: Scott, Foresman, 1988), for an excellent and entertaining treatment of this process.

37. For the seminal work on conformity and social influence, see Solomon E. Asch, "Effects of Group Pressure upon the Modification and Distortion of Judgments," in D. Cartwright and A. Zander, eds., *Group Dynamics* (New York: Harper and Row, 1953); Richard S. Crutchfield, "Conformity and Character," *American Psychologist* 10 (1955): 191–98; Muzafer Sherif, "A Study of Some Social Factors in Perception," *Archives of Psychology* 27 (1935): 187.

38. Burnkrant and Cousineau, "Informational and Normative Social Influence in Buyer Behavior."

39. For a study attempting to measure individual differences in proclivity to confor-mity, see William O. Bearden, Richard G. Netemeyer, and Jesse E. Teel, "Measurement of Consumer Susceptibility to Interpersonal Influence," *Journal of Consumer Research* 15 (March 1989): 473–81.

40. John W. Thibaut and Harold H. Kelley, *The Social Psychology of Groups* (New York: Wiley, 1959); W. W. Waller and R. Hill, *The Family, a Dynamic Interpretation* (New York: Dryden, 1951).

41. William O. Bearden, Richard G. Netemeyer, and Jesse E. Teel, "Measurement of Consumer Susceptibility to Interpersonal Influence," *Journal of Consumer Research* 9, no. 3 (1989): 183–94; Lynn R. Kahle, "Observations: Role-Relaxed Consumers: A Trend of the Nineties," *Journal of Advertising Research* (March/April 1995): 66–71; Lynn R. Kahle and Aviv Shoham, "Observations: Role-Relaxed Consumers: Empirical Evidence," *Journal of Advertising Research* 35, no. 3 (May/June 1995): 59–62.

42. Leon Festinger, "A Theory of Social Comparison Processes," *Human Relations* 7 (May 1954): 117–40.

43. Chester A. Insko, Sarah Drenan, Michael R. Solomon, Richard Smith, and Terry J. Wade, "Conformity as a Function of the Consistency of Positive Self-Evaluation with Being Liked and Being Right," *Journal of Experimental Social Psychology* 19 (1983): 341–58.

44. Abraham Tesser, Murray Millar, and Janet Moore, "Some Affective Consequences of Social Comparison and Reflection Processes: The Pain and Pleasure of Being Close," *Journal of Personality and Social Psychology* 54, no. 1 (1988): 49–61.

45. L. Wheeler, K. G. Shaver, R. A. Jones, G. R. Goethals, J. Cooper, J. E. Robinson, C. L. Gruder, and K. W. Butzine, "Factors Determining the Choice of a Comparison Other," *Journal of Experimental Social Psychology* 5 (1969): 219–32.

46. George P. Moschis, "Social Comparison and Informal Group Influence," *Journal of Marketing Research* 13 (August 1976): 237–44.

47. Burnkrant and Cousineau, "Informational and Normative Social Influence in Buyer Behavior"; M. Venkatesan, "Experimental Study of Consumer Behavior Conformity and Independence," *Journal of Marketing Research* 3 (November 1966): 384–87.

48. J. L. Freedman and S. Fraser, "Compliance Without Pressure: The Foot-in-the-Door Technique," *Journal of Personality and Social Psychology* 4 (1966): 195–202.

49. R. B. Cialdini, J. E. Vincent, S. K. Lewis, J. Catalan, D. Wheeler, and B. L. Darby, "Reciprocal Concessions Procedure for Inducing Compliance: The Door-in-the-Face Effect," *Journal of Personality and Social Psychology* 31 (1975): 200–215.

50. B. Latane, K. Williams, and S. Harkins, "Many Hands Make Light the Work: The Causes and Consequences of Social Loafing," *Journal of Personality and Social Psychology* 37 (1979): 822–32.

51. S. Freeman, M. Walker, R. Borden, and B. Latane, "Diffusion of Responsibility and Restaurant Tipping: Cheaper by the Bunch," *Personality and Social Psychology Bulletin* 1 (1978): 584–87.

52. Nathan Kogan and Michael A. Wallach, "Risky Shift Phenomenon in Small Decision-Making Groups: A Test of the Information Exchange Hypothesis," *Journal of Experimental Social Psychology* 3 (January 1967): 75–84; Nathan Kogan and Michael A. Wallach, *Risk Taking* (New York: Holt, Rinehart and Winston, 1964); Arch G. Woodside and M. Wayne DeLozier, "Effects of Word-of-Mouth Advertising on Consumer Risk Taking," *Journal of Advertising* (Fall 1976): 12–19.

53. Kogan and Wallach, *Risk Taking*.

54. Roger Brown, *Social Psychology* (New York: The Free Press, 1965).

55. David L. Johnson and I. R. Andrews, "Risky Shift Phenomenon Tested with Consumer Product Stimuli," *Journal of Personality and Social Psychology* 20 (1971): 382–85; see also Vithala R. Rao and Joel H. Steckel, "A Polarization Model for Describing Group Preferences," *Journal of Consumer Research* 18 (June 1991): 108–18.

56. J. Craig Andrews and Richard G. Netemeyer, "Alcohol Warning Label Effects: Socialization, Addiction, and Public Policy Issues," in Ronald P. Hill, ed., *Marketing and Consumer Research in the Public Interest* (Thousand Oaks, CA: Sage, 1996): 153–75; "National Study Finds Increase in College Binge Drinking" *Alcoholism & Drug Abuse Weekly* (March 27, 2000): 12–13.

57. Donald H. Granbois, "Improving the Study of Customer In-Store Behavior," *Journal of Marketing* 32 (October 1968): 28–32.

58. Len Strazewski, "Tupperware Locks in New Strategy," *Advertising Age* (February 8, 1988): 30.

59. Gergen and Gergen, *Social Psychology*.

60. L. J. Strickland, S. Messick, and D. N. Jackson, "Conformity, Anticonformity and Independence: Their Dimensionality and Generality," *Journal of Personality and Social Psychology* 16 (1970): 494–507.

61. Jack W. Brehm, *A Theory of Psychological Reactance* (New York: Academic Press, 1966).

62. R. D. Ashmore, V. Ramchandra, and R. Jones, "Censorship as an Attitude Change Induction" (paper presented at meeting of Eastern Psychological Association, New York, 1971); R. A. Wicklund and J. Brehm, *Perspectives on Cognitive Dissonance* (Hillsdale, NJ: Erlbaum, 1976).

63. Pat Wechsler, "A Curiously Strong Campaign," *Business Week* (April 21, 1997): 134.

64. Rachel Beck, "Power-Packing Mints Have Become Fashionable," *Montgomery Advertiser* (June 10, 1998): 1D.

65. Johan Arndt, "Role of Product-Related Conversations in the Diffusion of a New Product," *Journal of Marketing Research* 4 (August 1967): 291–95.

66. Elihu Katz and Paul F. Lazarsfeld, *Personal Influence* (Glencoe, IL: Free Press, 1955).

67. John A. Martilla, "Word-of-Mouth Communication in the Industrial Adoption Process," *Journal of Marketing Research* 8 (March 1971): 173–78; see also Marsha L. Richins, "Negative Word-of-Mouth by Dissatisfied Consumers: A Pilot Study," *Journal of Marketing* 47 (Winter 1983): 68–78.

68. Arndt, "Role of Product-Related Conversations in the Diffusion of a New Product."

69. James H. Myers and Thomas S. Robertson, "Dimensions of Opinion Leadership," *Journal of Marketing Research* 9 (February 1972): 41–46.

70. Quoted in Ellen Neuborne, "Generation Y," *Business Week* (February 15, 1999): 86.

71. Sonia Murray, "Street Marketing Does the Trick," *Advertising Age* (March 20, 2000): S12.

72. Quoted in "Taking to the Streets," *Newsweek* (November 2, 1998): 70–73.

73. Constance L. Hays, "Guerrilla Marketing Is Going Mainstream," *The New York Times on the Web* (October 7, 1999).

74. Wayne Friedman, "Street Marketing Hits the Internet," *Advertising Age* (May 1, 2000): 32; Erin White, "Online Buzz Helps Album Skyrocket to Top of Charts," *The Wall Street Journal Interactive Edition* (October 5, 1999).

75. Jared Sandberg, "The Friendly Virus," *Newsweek* (April 12, 1999): 65–66.

76. Karen J.Bannan, "Marketers Try Infecting the Internet," *The New York Times on the Web* (March 22, 2000).

77. Thomas E. Weber, "Viral Marketing: Web's Newest Ploy May Make You an Unpopular Friend," *The Wall Street Journal Interactive Edition* (September 13, 1999).

78. Dorothy Leonard-Barton, "Experts as Negative Opinion Leaders in the Diffusion of a Technological Innovation," *Journal of Consumer Research* 11 (March 1985): 914–26.

79. Jennifer Lach, "Intelligence Agents," *American Demographics* (March 1999): 52–60.

80. James F. Engel, Robert J. Kegerreis, and Roger D. Blackwell, "Word-of-Mouth Communication by the Innovator," *Journal of Marketing* 33 (July 1969): 15–19.

81. Chip Walker, "Word-of-Mouth," *American Demographics* (July 1995): 38–44.

82. Richard J. Lutz, "Changing Brand Attitudes Through Modification of Cognitive Structure," *Journal of Consumer Research* 1 (March 1975): 49–59; for some suggested remedies to bad publicity, see Mitch Griffin, Barry J. Babin, and Jill S. Attaway, "An Empirical Investigation of the Impact of Negative Public Publicity on Consumer Attitudes and Intentions," in Rebecca H. Holman and Michael R. Solomon, eds., *Advances in Consumer Research* 18 (Provo, UT: Association for Consumer Research, 1991): 334–41; Alice M. Tybout, Bobby J. Calder, and Brian Sternthal, "Using Information Processing Theory to Design Marketing Strategies," *Journal of Marketing Research* 18 (1981): 73–79; see also Russell N. Laczniak, Thomas E. DeCarlo, and Sridhar N. Ramaswami, "Consumers' Responses to Negative Word-of-Mouth Communication: An Attribution Theory Perspective," *Journal of Consumer Psychology*, in press.

83. Robert E. Smith and Christine A. Vogt, "The Effects of Integrating Advertising and Negative Word-of-Mouth Communications on Message Processing and Response," *Journal of Consumer Psychology* 4, no. 2 (1995): 133–51; Paula Fitzgerald Bone, "Word-of-Mouth Effects on Short-Term and Long-Term Product Judgments," *Journal of Business Research* 32 (1995): 213–23.

84. "Dunkin' Donuts Buys Out Critical Web Site," *The New York Times on the Web* (August 27, 1999).

85. Charles W. King and John O. Summers, "Overlap of Opinion Leadership Across Consumer Product Categories," *Journal of Marketing Research* 7 (February 1970): 43–50.

86. Michael Fumento, "Tampon Terrorism," *Forbes* (May 17, 1999): 170.

87. Tina Kelley, "Internet's Chain of Foolery," *New York Times* (July 1, 1999): G1.

88. "Nike Doesn't Want All Those Stinky Shoes," *Montgomery Advertiser* (June 7, 1998): 21.

89. Bradley Johnson, "febrezekillsdogs.com (and Birds, Too)," *Advertising Age* (May 10, 1999): 8.

90. Sid Astbury, "Pork Rumors Vex Indonesia," *Advertising Age* (February 16, 1989): 36.

91. Mae Ghalwash, "Squint Hard, Be Creative in Search for Blasphemy in Coca-Cola Logo," *Opelika-Auburn News* (May 22, 2000): 2A.

92. Everett M. Rogers, *Diffusion of Innovations*, 3d ed. (New York: Free Press, 1983).

93. Leonard-Barton, "Experts as Negative Opinion Leaders in the Diffusion of a Technological Innovation"; Rogers, *Diffusion of Innovations*.

94. Herbert Menzel, "Interpersonal and Unplanned Communications: Indispensable or Obsolete?" in *Biomedical Innovation* (Cambridge, MA: MIT Press, 1981): 155–63.

95. Meera P. Venkatraman, "Opinion Leaders, Adopters, and Communicative Adopters: A Role Analysis," *Psychology & Marketing* 6 (Spring 1989): 51–68.

96. Rogers, *Diffusion of Innovations*.

97. Robert Merton, *Social Theory and Social Structure*, (Glencoe, IL: Free Press, 1957).

98. King and Summers, "Overlap of Opinion Leadership Across Consumer Product Categories"; see also Ronald E. Goldsmith, Jeanne R. Heitmeyer, and Jon B. Freiden, "Social Values and Fashion Leadership," *Clothing and Textiles Research Journal* 10 (Fall 1991): 37–45; J. O. Summers, "Identity of Women's Clothing Fashion Opinion Leaders," *Journal of Marketing Research* 7 (1970): 178–85.

99. Steven A. Baumgarten, "The Innovative Communicator in the Diffusion Process," *Journal of Marketing Research* 12 (February 1975): 12–18.

100. Laura J. Yale and Mary C. Gilly, "Dyadic Perceptions in Personal Source Information Search," *Journal of Business Research* 32 (1995): 225–37.

101. Russell W. Belk, "Occurrence of Word-of-Mouth Buyer Behavior as a Function of Situation and Advertising Stimuli," in Fred C. Allvine, ed., *Combined Proceedings of the American Marketing Association, series*, no. 33, (Chicago: American Marketing Association, 1971): 419–22.

102. Lawrence F. Feick, Linda L. Price, and Robin A. Higie, "People Who Use People: The Other Side of Opinion Leadership," in Richard J. Lutz, ed., *Advances in Consumer Research* 13 (Provo, UT: Association for Consumer Research, 1986): 301–5.

103. For discussion of the market maven construct, see Lawrence F. Feick and Linda L. Price, "The Market Maven," *Managing* (July 1985): 10; scale items adapted from Lawrence F. Feick and Linda L. Price, "The Market Maven: A Diffuser of Marketplace Information," *Journal of Marketing* 51 (January 1987): 83–87.

104. Michael R. Solomon, "The Missing Link: Surrogate Consumers in the Marketing Chain," *Journal of Marketing* 50 (October 1986): 208–18.

105. "CBS Extends Its High-Tech Reach: CD-ROM Goes to 'Influencers'," *PROMO: The International Magazine for Promotion Marketing* (October 1994): 59.

106. Stern and Gould, "The Consumer as Financial Opinion Leader."

107. William R. Darden and Fred D. Reynolds, "Predicting Opinion Leadership for Men's Apparel Fashions," *Journal of Marketing Research* 1 (August 1972): 324–28. A modified version of the opinion leadership scale with improved reliability and validity can be found in Terry L. Childers, "Assessment of the Psychometric Properties of an Opinion Leadership Scale," *Journal of Marketing Research* 23 (May 1986): 184–88.

108. Dan Seligman, "Me and Monica," *Forbes* (March 23, 1998): 76.

109. "Connect," *Newsweek* (May 5, 1997): 11.

110. "Referrals Top Ads as Influence on Patients' Doctor Selections," *Marketing News* (January 30, 1987): 22.

111. Peter H. Reingen and Jerome B. Kernan, "Analysis of Referral Networks in Marketing: Methods and Illustration," *Journal of Marketing Research* 23 (November 1986): 370–78.

112. Peter H. Reingen, Brian L. Foster, Jacqueline Johnson Brown, and Stephen B. Seidman, "Brand Congruence in Interpersonal Relations: A Social Network Analysis," *Journal of Consumer Research* 11 (December 1984): 771–83; see also James C. Ward and Peter H. Reingen, "Sociocognitive Analysis of Group Decision Making Among Consumers," *Journal of Consumer Research* 17 (December 1990): 245–62.

Linda is about as nervous as she can be. Tonight is the first party she and her partner are throwing in their new apartment, and it's really coming down to the wire. Some of her friends and family who were skeptical about Linda's plan to move out of her parents' house and to live with a man will have the chance to say "I told you so" if this debut of her new living arrangement self-destructs.

Life hasn't exactly been a bed of roses since she and Willi moved in together. It's a bit of a mystery—although his desk is tidy and organized at the publishing company where they both work, his personal habits are another story. Willi's really been making an effort to clean up his act, but still Linda's been forced to take on more than her share of cleaning duties—partly out of self-defense because they have to share a bathroom! And, she's learned the

hard way not to trust Willi to do the grocery shopping—he goes to the store with a big list of staples and returns with beer and junk food. You would think that a man who is responsible for buying the firm's multimillion dollar computer network would have a bit more sense when it comes to sticking to a budget and picking out the right household supplies. What's even more frustrating is that although Willi can easily spend a week digging up information about the new big-screen TV they're buying (with her bonus!), she has to virtually drag him by the ear to look at dining room furniture. Then to add insult to injury, he's quick to criticize her choices—especially if they cost too much.

So, how likely is it that while she's at work Willi has been home cleaning up the apartment and mak-

ing some hors d'oeuvres like he promised? Linda did her part by downloading a recipe for crabmeat salad and wasabi caviar from the entertaining section on epicurious .com. She even jotted down some adorable table setting ideas such as napkin holders made out of home-grown bamboo at marthastewart.com. The rest is up to him—at this point she'd be happy if Willi remembers to pick up his underwear from the living room couch. This soiree could turn out to be a real proving ground for their relationship. Linda sighs as she walks into an editors' meeting. She sure has learned a lot about relationships since setting up a new household . . . . living together is going to be a lot bumpier than it's made out to be in romance novels.

12

ORGANIZATIONAL AND HOUSEHOLD DECISION MAKING

INTRODUCTION

Linda's trials and tribulations with Willi illustrate that many consumer decisions are made jointly. The individual decision-making process described in detail in Chapter 9 is, in many cases, overly simplistic because more than one person may be involved in any stage of the problem-solving sequence, from initial problem recognition and information search to evaluation of alternatives and product choice. To further complicate matters, these decisions often involve two or more people who may not have the same level of investment in the outcome, the same tastes and preferences, or the same consumption priorities.

This chapter examines issues related to *collective decision making,* a process in which more than one person is involved in the purchasing process for products or services that may be used by multiple consumers. The first part of the chapter looks at organizational decision making, in which purchases are made on behalf of a larger group. We then move on to focus more specifically on one of the most important organizations to which most of us claim membership—the family unit. We'll consider how members of a family negotiate among themselves and how important changes in modern family structure are affecting this process. The chapter concludes by focusing on how "new employees"—children—learn how to be consumers. First, though, let's focus on decision making that occurs when people leave their families at home and go to work.

ORGANIZATIONAL DECISION MAKING

Many employees of corporations or other organizations make purchase decisions on a daily basis. **Organizational buyers** are people like Willi who purchase goods and services on behalf of companies for use in the process of manufacturing, distribution, or resale. These individuals buy from **business-to-business marketers,** who specialize in meeting the needs of organizations such as corporations, government agencies, hospitals, and retailers. In terms of sheer volume, business-to-business marketing is where the action is: Roughly $2 trillion worth of products and services change hands among organizations, which is actually *more* than is purchased by end consumers.

Organizational buyers have a lot of responsibility. They must decide on the vendors with whom they want to do business and what specific items they require from these suppliers. The items they consider can range in price and significance from paper clips to a multimillion dollar computer system. Obviously, there is a lot at stake in understanding how these important decisions are made.

The organizational buyer's perception of the purchase situation is influenced by a number of factors. These include his *expectations* of the supplier (e.g., product quality, the competence and behavior of the firm's employees, and prior experiences in dealing with that supplier), the *organizational climate* of his own company (i.e., perceptions regarding how the company rewards performance and what it values), and the buyer's *assessment* of his own performance (e.g., whether he believes in taking risks).[1]

Like other consumers, organizational buyers engage in a learning process in which members of the firm share information with one another and develop an "organizational memory" consisting of shared beliefs and assumptions about the proper course of action.[2] Just as a buyer is influenced by "market beliefs" when he goes shopping with the family on the weekend (see Chapter 9), the same person is also an information processor at the office. He (perhaps with fellow employees) attempts to solve problems by searching for information, evaluating alternatives, and making decisions.[3] There are, of course, some important differences between the two situations.

In the Information Age, organizational decision makers must stay on top of clients' complex needs.

Organizational Decision Making Versus Consumer Decision Making

Many factors have been identified to distinguish organizational and industrial purchase decisions from individual consumer decisions. Some of these differences are as follows:[4]

- Purchase decisions made by companies frequently involve many people, including those who do the actual buying, those who directly or indirectly influence this decision, and the employees who will actually use the product or service.
- Organizational and industrial products are often bought according to precise, technical specifications that require a lot of knowledge about the product category.
- Impulse buying is rare (industrial buyers do not suddenly get an "urge to splurge" on lead pipe or silicon chips). Because buyers are professionals, their decisions are based on past experience and a careful weighing of alternatives.
- Decisions often are risky, especially in the sense that a buyer's career may be riding on his demonstration of good judgment.
- The dollar volume of purchases is often substantial, dwarfing most individual consumer grocery bills or mortgage payments. One hundred to 250 organizational customers often account for more than half of a supplier's sales volume, which gives the buyers a lot of influence over the supplier.
- Business-to-business marketing often involves more of an emphasis on personal selling than on advertising or other forms of promotion. Dealing with organizational buyers typically requires more face-to-face contact than is necessary in the case of end consumers.

These important features must be considered when we try to understand the purchasing decisions made by organizations. Still, there are actually more similarities between organizational buyers and ordinary consumers than many people believe. True, organizational purchase decisions do tend to have a higher economic or functional component compared to individual consumer choices, but emotional aspects enter the scene as well. For example, although organizational buyers may appear to the outsider to be models of rationality, their decisions are sometimes guided by brand loyalty, by long-term relationships they have established with particular suppliers, or salespeople, or even by aesthetic concerns.

Intel's development of the hugely successful "Intel Inside" campaign illustrates how important issues such as branding and product image can be in industrial contexts. Competitors had been using Intel's numerical sequencing to label their computer chips since the company had introduced its 286 model. These labels did not, however, guarantee that the rival versions possessed the same architecture as Intel's version, so this created confusion in the marketplace. After trying unsuccessfully to trademark the "386" name, the firm developed the "Intel Inside" logo and persuaded 240 manufacturers to include the new logo in their packaging. In a three-year period, Intel invested more than $500 million in promotional programs and advertising to build recognition of the Intel brand name.[5] This "commodity branding" strategy continues to pay off for the chip maker.

How Do Organizational Buyers Operate?

Like end consumers, organizational buyers are influenced by both internal and external stimuli. Internal stimuli include the buyer's unique psychological characteristics such as willingness to make risky decisions as well as job experience and training. External stimuli include the nature of the organization for which the buyer works as well as the overall economic and technological environment in which the industry is operating. Another set of factors are cultural; vastly different norms for doing business can be found in different countries. For example, Americans tend to be less formal in their interactions than are many of their European or Asian counterparts.

Type of Purchase

The type of item to be purchased influences the organizational buyer's decision-making process. As with consumer purchases, the more complex, novel, or risky the decision, the greater the amount of information search and effort will be devoted to evaluating alternatives. On the other hand, reliance on a fixed set of suppliers for routine purchases is one strategy that greatly reduces the information search and effort in evaluating competing alternatives that would otherwise be required.[6]

Typically, more complex organizational decisions also tend to be made by a group of people (members of a **buying center**) who play different roles in the decision. As we will see later on, this joint involvement is somewhat similar to family decision making, in which more family members are likely to be involved in more important purchases.

The Buyclass Framework

Organizational buying decisions can be divided into three types, which range from the most to the least complex. This classification scheme is called the buyclass theory of purchasing, and it uses three decision-making dimensions to describe the purchasing strategies of an organizational buyer:[7]

1. The level of information that must be gathered prior to making a decision
2. The seriousness with which all possible alternatives must be considered
3. The degree to which the buyer is familiar with the purchase

In practice, these three dimensions relate to how much cognitive effort will be expended in making a purchase decision. Three types of "buyclasses," or strategies based on these dimensions encompass most organizational decision situations.[8] Each type of purchase corresponds to one of the three types of decisions discussed in Chapter 9: habitual decision making, limited problem solving, and extensive problem solving. These strategies are summarized in Table 12.1.

TABLE 12.1 Types of Organizational Buying Decisions

Buying Situation	Extent of Effort	Risk	Buyers Involved
Straight rebuy	Habitual decision making	Low	Automatic reorder
Modified rebuy	Limited problem solving	Low to moderate	One or a few
New task	Extensive problem solving	High	Many

SOURCE: Adapted from Patrick J. Robinson, Charles W. Faris, and Yoram Wind, *Industrial Buying and Creative Marketing* (Boston: Allyn & Bacon, 1967).

A **straight rebuy** is like a habitual decision. It is an automatic choice, as when an inventory level reaches a preestablished reorder point. Most organizations maintain an approved vendor list, and as long as experience with the vendor is satisfactory there is little or no ongoing information search or evaluation.

A **modified rebuy** situation involves limited decision making. It occurs when an organization wants to repurchase a product or service, but with some minor modifications. This decision might involve a limited search for information, most likely by speaking to a few vendors. The decision will probably be made by one or a few people.

A **new task** involves extensive problem solving. Because the decision has not been made before, there is often a serious risk that the product won't perform as it should or that it will be too costly. The organization designates a buying center with assorted specialists to evaluate the purchase, and they typically gather a lot of information before coming to a decision.

Decision Roles

A number of specific roles are played when a collective decision must be made, either by members of a household or by individuals in an organizational buying center.[9] Depending on the decision, some or all of the group members may be involved, and one person may play any number (or even all) of these roles. These roles include:

- *Initiator:* the person who brings up the idea or need.
- *Gatekeeper:* the person who conducts the information search and controls the flow of information available to the group. In organizational contexts the gatekeeper identifies possible vendors and products for the rest of the group to consider.
- *Influencer:* the person who tries to sway the outcome of the decision. Some people may be more motivated than others to get involved, and participants also differ in terms of the amount of power they have to convince others of their choice. In organizations, engineers are often influencers for product information, whereas purchasing agents play a similar role when the group evaluates the vendors that supply these items.
- *Buyer:* the person who actually makes the purchase. The buyer may or may not actually use the product. This person may pay for the item, actually procure it, or both.
- *User:* the person who winds up using the product or service.

B2B E-Commerce

The Web is radically changing the way organizational buyers learn about and select products for their companies. **Business-to-business (B2B) e-commerce** refers to Internet interactions between two or more businesses or organizations. This includes exchanges of information, products, services, or payments. According to Forrester Research, Inc., by 2002 an overwhelming majority (93 percent) of U.S. firms plan to be transacting business on the Web. By 2004, it is projected that total B2B sales will reach $2.7 trillion. Half of those transactions will take place through auctions, bids, and exchanges.[10]

In the simplest form of B2B e-commerce, the Internet provides an online catalog of products and services needed by businesses. Companies like Dell Computer have found their Internet site is important for delivering online technical support, product information, order status information, and customer service to corporate customers. Early on, Dell discovered that it could serve the

THE WEB IS REVOLUTIONIZING the way companies communicate with other firms and even the way they share information with their own people. New cybermiddlemen are popping up to help companies locate each other as they try to source the materials they need to produce their own products. For example, ChemConnect, Inc. of San Francisco matches prospective buyers and sellers of chemical and plastics products at chemconnect.com. FreeMarkets, Inc. of Pittsburgh organizes online auctions for suppliers that bid on contracts for industrial parts.[11] Product designers working for apparel manufacturers like VF Corp. can log into the firm's Intranet and play with product samples and colors in a database as they come up with new clothing ideas. Don't like that color or the way that button looks? A click of a button gives you a new one. In the old days, a new sample would have to be physically produced and evaluated, but now design ideas can be selected and the materials needed to produce them can be located on the desktop.[12] That's business at light speed.

needs of its customers more effectively by tailoring its Internet presence to different customer segments. Dell's Internet site allows shoppers to get recommendations based on their customer segment (home, home office, government, small business, and education). The company saves millions of dollars a year by replacing hard copy manuals with electronic downloads. For its larger customers, Dell provides customer specific, password-protected pages that allow business customers to obtain technical support or to place an order.

THE FAMILY

It is not unusual to read in newspapers and magazines about the death of the family unit. Although it is true that the proportion of people living in a traditional family structure consisting of a married couple with children living at home continues to decline, many other types of families are growing rapidly. Indeed, some experts have argued that as traditional family living arrangements have waned, people are placing even greater emphasis on siblings, close friends, and other relatives in providing companionship and social support.[13] Some people are even joining "intentional families;" these are groups of unrelated people who meet regularly for meals and who spend holidays together.[14]

Defining the Modern Family

The **extended family** was once the most common family unit. It consists of three generations living together and often includes grandparents, aunts, uncles, and cousins. As evidenced by the Cleavers of *Leave It To Beaver* and other TV families of the 1950s, the **nuclear family**—a mother and a father and one or more children (perhaps with a sheepdog thrown in for good measure)—became the model family unit over time. However, many changes have occurred since the days of Beaver Cleaver. Although people may continue to conjure up an image of the typical American family based on old TV shows, demographic data show that this ideal image of the family is no longer a realistic picture.

Just What Is a Household?

When it conducts the national census every 10 years, the U.S. Census Bureau regards any occupied housing unit as a household regardless of the relationships among people living there. A **family household,** as defined by the Census Bureau, contains at least two people who are related by blood or marriage. The Census Bureau and other survey firms compile a massive amount of data on family households, but certain categories are of particular interest to marketers.

There's no doubt that the way we think of family is evolving. Changes in consumers' family structures, such as the upheaval caused by divorce, often represent opportunities for marketers as normal purchasing patterns become unfrozen and people make new choices about products and brands.[15] Significantly more than one million couples divorce in a typical year. In the United States approximately 20 million children under 18 live with just one parent, and in 84 percent of these cases that parent is the mother.[16] Divorces and separations are an accepted part of our culture, and marital breakups are an ever-present theme in books, music, and movies.[17] Reflecting the prevalence of this situation, a few years ago a Canadian entrepreneur created DivorceX, a digital imaging service that removes ex-spouses from family pictures![18]

Folger's Coffee addresses an important need by allowing single people to brew one cup of coffee at a time.

Family Size

Worldwide, surveys show that almost all women want smaller families today. In 1960, the average American household contained 3.3 people, but that number is projected to decline to about 2.5 people by the year 2010.[19]

Family size is dependent on such factors as educational level, the availability of birth control, and religion.[20] The **fertility rate** is determined by the number of births per year per 1,000 women of childbearing age. Marketers keep a close eye on the population's birth rate to gauge how the pattern of births will affect demand for products in the future. The U.S. fertility rate increased dramatically in the late 1950s and early 1960s, when the so-called baby boomers began to reach childrearing age. It declined in the 1970s and began to climb again in the 1980s as baby boomers began to have their own children in a new "baby boomlet."

Nontraditional Family Structures

As noted earlier, the U.S. Census Bureau regards any occupied housing unit as a household, regardless of the relationships among people living there. Thus, one person living alone, three roommates, or two lovers (whether straight or gay) constitute households. Many people share a living arrangement the government calls POSSLQ, which stands for Persons of Opposite Sex Sharing Living Quarters. Like Linda and Willi, this situation is increasingly common: Nearly half of Americans aged 25 to 40 have at some point lived together with a person of the opposite sex.[21] These changes are part of a broader shift toward nonfamily and childless households. By 2010 there is projected to be an increase of 7.4 million childless married-couple households, 6.4 new single-person households, 2.4 million more mixed-family situations, 1.2 million more single parents, 1.1 million more roommate households, and a decrease of 1.5 million married couples with children under 18.[22]

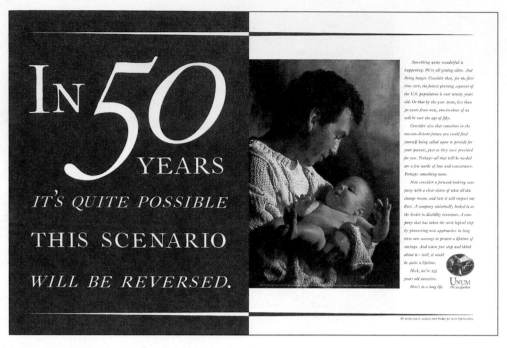

This insurance ad reminds us that people in the "sandwich generation" often must care for their parents in addition to their children.

Who's Living at Home?

Although traditional families are shrinking, ironically in other cases the traditional extended family is very much a reality. Many adults are caring for their own parents as well as for their children. In fact, Americans on average spend 17 years caring for children, but 18 years assisting aged parents.[23] Middle-aged people have been termed "the sandwich generation" because they must attend to those above and below them in age.

In addition to dealing with live-in parents, many adults are surprised to find that their children are living with them longer or are moving back in well after

This ad for Family Circle *magazine humorously emphasizes that some traditional family values persist among young people today.*

their "lease" has expired.[24] As an Argentinian jeans ad asked, "If you are over 20 and still live with your parents, this is wrong. Isn't it high time you started looking for an apartment for them?"

These returnees have been termed **boomerang kids** by demographers. The number of children between 18 and 34 living at home is growing dramatically, and today more than one-fifth of 25-year-old Americans still live with their parents. Young adults who do leave the nest to live by themselves are relatively unlikely to return, whereas those who move in with roommates are more likely to come back. And, young people who move in with a romantic partner are more likely than average to end up back home if the relationship fails![25] If this trend continues, it will affect a variety of markets as boomerang kids spend less on housing and staples and more on discretionary purchases like entertainment.

The Family Life Cycle

A family's needs and expenditures are affected by factors such as the number of people (children and adults) in the family, their ages, and whether one, two, or more adults are employed outside of the home. Two important factors that determine how a couple spends time and money are: (1) whether they have children and; (2) whether the woman works.

Recognizing that family needs and expenditures change over time, marketers apply the **family life cycle (FLC)** concept to segment households. The FLC combines trends in income and family composition with the changes in demands placed upon this income. As we age, our preferences and needs for products and activities tend to change. Households headed by twentysomethings spend less than average on most products and services because their households are small and their incomes are low. Income levels tend to rise (at least until retirement), so that people can afford more over time. Older consumers spend more per capita on luxury items like gourmet foods and upscale home furnishings.[32] In addition, many purchases that must be made at an early age do not have to be repeated very often. For example, we tend to accumulate durable goods such as large appliances and only replace them as necessary.

A life-cycle approach to the study of the family assumes that pivotal events alter role relationships and trigger new stages of life that alter our priorities. These events include couples such as Linda and Willi moving in together, the birth of a first child, the departure of the last child from the house, the death of a spouse, retirement of the principal wage earner, and possibly divorce.[33] Movement through these life stages is indeed accompanied by significant changes in expenditures in leisure, food, durables, and services, even after the figures have been adjusted to reflect changes in income.[34]

This focus on longitudinal changes in priorities is particularly valuable in predicting demand for specific product categories over time. For example, the money spent by a couple with no children on dinners out and vacations will probably be diverted for quite different purchases after the birth of a child. Ironically, although the entertainment industry focuses on winning the hearts and wallets of young consumers, it's the senior citizens who have become America's true party animals. The average household headed by a 65- to 74-year-old spends more on entertainment than does the average household headed by a person under age 25.[35]

A number of models have been proposed to describe family life cycle stages, but their usefulness has been limited because in many cases they have failed to take into account such important social trends as the changing role of women, the acceleration of alternative lifestyles, childless and delayed-child marriages, and single-parent households.

MARKETING OPPORTUNITY

COMPANION ANIMALS ARE OFTEN treated as family members. Many people assume pets share our emotions—perhaps that helps to explain why more than three-quarters of domestic cats and dogs receive presents on holidays and birthdays.[26] Forty-two percent of American households own at least one pet. Americans spend $20 billion a year on their pets (more than they spend on movies and home videos combined).[27] This passion for pets is not confined to the United States: In France, there are twice as many dogs and cats as children.[28] In Britain, pet insurance is a $150 million industry. In pet-crazed Britain, where some restaurants admit animals but not children, more than a million pets are covered by pet insurance. Similarly, about 85 percent of Swedish dogs are covered by health and life insurance.

The inclusion of pets as family members creates many marketing opportunities, ranging from bejeweled leashes to professional dog-walkers.[29] About 20 percent of American kennels now include upscale accommodations for pets.[30] At the Kennel Club in Los Angeles, a pet is pampered in a theme-decorated cottage with a bed, a TV, and a VCR stocked with doggie videos. Pets can also mingle with other dogs for story time and a pupcorn snack. Exercise classes and massage are also available. And what should the well-turned-out pet wear to the kennel? At the Petigree shop operated by Macy's department store, you can buy pink satin party dresses and black dinner jackets for the proper pooch.

Motorola recognizes the new, mobile lifestyles of many modern families. The company positions its paging products to meet the needs of on-the-go parents.

Four variables are necessary to adequately describe these changes: (1) age; (2) marital status; (3) the presence or absence of children in the home; and; (4) the ages of children, if present. In addition, our definition of marital status must be relaxed to include any couple living together who are in a long-term relationship. Thus, although roommates might not be considered "married," a man and woman who have established a household would be, as would two homosexual men who have a similar understanding.

When these changes are considered, this approach allows us to identify a set of categories that include many more types of family situations.[36] These categories,

Choices of living environments provide a useful reflection of changing patterns and preferences in everyday life. The average new single-family home in the United States grew from 1,645 sq. ft. in 1975 to 2,095 sq. ft. in 1995. Americans increasingly prefer homes with privacy, but common living space in the home is growing in popularity. People do more of their living in the kitchen, and formal areas are losing ground. These are being replaced by great rooms that accommodate multiple family activities in one location. When people are asked to design their dream home, common responses include a state-of-the-art kitchen, fireplace, in-ground pool, and Jacuzzi. Women want walk-in closets; men name a game/billiard room, a workshop, or a high-tech entertainment center.[31]

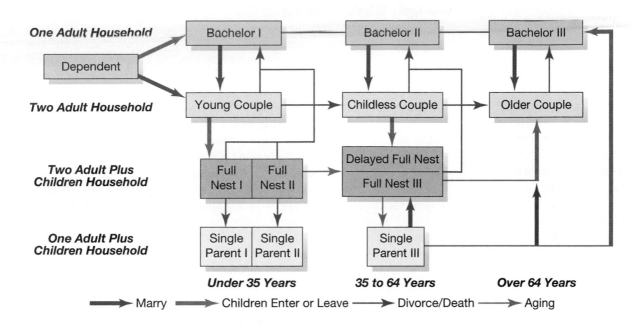

Figure 12.1
Family Life Cycle

SOURCE: Robert E. Wilkes, "Household LIfe-cycle Stages, Transitions, and Product Expenditures," *Journal of Consumer Research* 22 (June 1995): 29. Published by the University of Chicago Press. Used with permission.

shown in Figure 12.1, are derived by dividing consumers into groups in terms of age, whether there is more than one adult present and whether there are children. For example, a distinction is made between the consumption needs of people in the Full Nest I category (in which the youngest child is less than six), the Full Nest II category (in which the youngest child is older than six), the Full Nest III category (in which the youngest child is older than six and the parents are middle-aged), and the Delayed Full Nest (in which the parents are middle-aged but the youngest child is younger than six).

This ad by a furniture manufacturer specifically refers to stages in the family life cycle.

MARKETING OPPORTUNITY

"JOHNNY, BEEP ME WHEN you're done burning that new Phish CD/ROM." Just as corporations differ in terms of their inclination to innovate and adopt new technology, we can also segment families in terms of their desires to be on the cutting-edge. The Yankee Group, a high-tech consulting firm, has studied TAFs—technologically advanced families. These households believe that faster, newer, more-advanced products will facilitate home and work life and make leisure time more fun. TAFs are willing to spend more money today so they don't have to wait to take advantage of technological advances. The Yankee Group estimates that 16.2 percent of American households are TAFs. These families tend to be younger and better-educated, they have more children than the average family, and their median household income is roughly one-third higher. TAFs see themselves as more technologically and financially sophisticated than other consumers. They are usually the first on the block to own the newest digital gadget. Some TAFs admit they are big kids and simply must have the latest shiny toy, but they also believe in the power of technology to help them manage their busy lives. TAFs are more than just an interesting phenomenon to high-tech companies. They also serve as guinea pigs, testing new products and offering clues about what will and won't work for the mass public. IBM uses TAFs to test new products at home before marketing them. As the marketing and sales program director at IBM's Home Networking Solutions observed, "[using TAFs] you can fine-tune the ease of setup, installation, and use of a product that you don't capture in a lab or storyboard."[38]

Life-Cycle Effects on Buying

Consumers classified into these categories show marked differences in consumption patterns. Young bachelors and newlyweds have the most "modern" sex-role attitudes, are the most likely to exercise, to go out to bars, concerts, movies, and restaurants, and to drink alcohol. Although people in their twenties accounts for less than 4 percent of all household spending in the United States, their expenditures are well above average in such categories as apparel, electronics, and gasoline.[37] Families with young children are more likely to consume health foods such as fruit, juice, and yogurt; those made up of single parents and older children buy more junk foods. The dollar value of homes, cars, and other durables is lowest for bachelors and single parents, but increases as people go through the Full Nest and Childless Couple stages. Perhaps reflecting the bounty of wedding gifts, newlyweds are the most likely to own appliances such as toaster ovens and electric coffee grinders. Babysitter and day care usage is, of course, highest among single-parent and Full Nest households, whereas home maintenance services (e.g., lawn mowing) are most likely to be employed by older couples and bachelors. Now, let's review how these different households make all of these decisions in the first place.

THE INTIMATE CORPORATION: FAMILY DECISION MAKING

The decision process within a household unit resembles a business conference. Certain matters are put on the table for discussion, different members may have different priorities and agendas, and there may be power struggles to rival any tale of corporate intrigue. In just about every living situation, whether a conventional family, students sharing a sorority house or apartment, or some other nontraditional arrangement, group members seem to take on different roles just as purchasing agents, engineers, account executives, and others do within a company.

Household Decisions

An understanding of household decision making dynamics is important for marketers. For example, when Chevrolet wanted to win back drivers with its new Venture minivan, the company sent teams of anthropologists to observe families in their natural habitats. Conventional wisdom says that minivan buyers are practical; they care about affordability, lots of features, and plenty of room. But these researchers discovered a different story: The vehicles are seen as part of the family. When consumers were asked to identify the best metaphor for a minivan, many picked a photo of a hang glider because it represents freedom and families on the go. The advertising slogan for the Venture became: "Let's go."[39]

Families make two basic types of decisions.[40] In a **consensual purchase decision,** members agree on the desired purchase, differing only in terms of how it will be achieved. In these circumstances, the family will most likely engage in problem solving and consider alternatives until the means for satisfying the group's goal is found. For example, a household considering adding a dog to the family but concerned about who will take care of it might draw up a chart assigning individuals to specific duties.

Unfortunately, life is not always so easy. In an **accommodative purchase decision,** group members have different preferences or priorities and cannot agree on a purchase that will satisfy the minimum expectations of all involved. It is here

REALITY CHECK   *COLLEGE STUDENTS LIVING AWAY FROM HOME*

can be thought of as having a substitute "family." Whether you live with your parents, with a spouse, or with other students, how are decisions made in your college residence "family?" Do some people take on the role of mother or father or children? Give a specific example of a decision that had to be made and the roles that were played.

Because it is just the three of us, having divorced long ago, my kids and I rely on each other and in many ways, and our traditional parent–child roles blur. Sometimes it's hard to say who is the adult in situations. . . . Mostly, I'm the mom who makes the decisions, demands bathing and eating vegetables; but when my kids ask me how my day was, it's a great role-equalizer.

Kerri Ruminski
Idaho State University

Everything we buy in our house is split 50:50 so one person making all the ultimate decisions is not going to be popular. . . . For example, whoever is in the bathroom when the toilet roll runs out obviously recognises the need that now exists. This can be any unfortunate soul! The next person to go down to the shop is told to buy some more. Now the purchaser does not want to spend money on toilet roll when they could be spending it on food and drink. So, they usually have a quick glance, find the cheapest alternative and throw it into their basket. That is the extent of the search. It is a heuristic—buy the cheapest brand of toilet roll. There is no post-purchase evaluation unless somebody notices that it is of particular poor quality and so next time, the second cheapest toilet roll is bought. Heuristics are very common amongst college residences. They make life easy for everyone. When strangers start out living together these heuristics keep everybody happy and shopping isn't such a daunting task. Examples of heuristics in our apartment are; buy cheese in re-sealable packets, buy large cartons of milk, never buy own brand cereal, etc . . . Straight rebuy is the most common type of decision making process.

Pamela Gillen
Dublin City University, Ireland

When it comes to menial tasks such as grocery shopping, cooking, cleaning, etc, the duties are distributed evenly. A non-verbal rapport exists between my roommate and myself, i.e., we each do our fair share. However, when it comes time for the purchase of luxury items such as television and/or stereo equipment, computer enhancements, etc. being that my roommate has the financial resources to support the decision, the decision is primarily based upon his discretion. However, he does seek some of my input because he's considerate of the space that we share.

Eric Jude Guacena
Virginia Commonwealth University

Household decisions are often made by the core group by reference to common heuristics, and coercive power is used to impress these decisions on other members of the group, even those that were not party to the decision making process. This differs from parental power, which is based on legitimate and reward power.

James Beattie
University of Exeter, United Kingdom

Seeing as my roommate and myself keep our things relatively separate, there is little need for group decision making. The only instance I can think of is at the beginning of the year, deciding who will bring what. . . . However in situations where one has some sort of expertise, we defer our decision making to that person. When it comes to Italian food and restaurants, I am the one most likely to take charge, while my roommate is a fan of Cuban food.

Concetta Rini
The College of William and Mary

What's your opinion? Check out the online polls at www.prenhall.com/ myphlip. Just follow the little person in the lab coat.

that bargaining, coercion, compromise, and the wielding of power are all likely to be used to achieve agreement on what to buy or who gets to use it.

Family decisions often are characterized by an accommodative rather than a consensual decision. For example, about 27 million Americans use computers for work they bring home, and about a third of these people report they must fight other family members for time on the home PC or for access to a phone line. The computer industry is gearing up to sell us multiple computers to solve these problems, but for many of us less-expensive forms of diplomacy are required.[41]

Conflict occurs when there is not complete correspondence in family members' needs and preferences. Although money is the most common source of conflict between marriage partners, TV-viewing choices come in a close second![42] In general, decisions will involve conflict among family members to the extent that they are somehow important or novel or if individuals have strong opinions about good and bad alternatives. The degree to which these factors generate conflict determines the type of decision the family will make.[43] Some specific factors determining the degree of family decision conflict include the following:[44]

- *Interpersonal need* (a person's level of investment in the group): A child in a family situation may care more about what his or her family buys for the house than will a college student who is temporarily living in a dorm.
- *Product involvement and utility* (the degree to which the product in question will be used or will satisfy a need): A family member who is an avid coffee drinker will obviously be more interested in the purchase of a new coffee maker than a similar expenditure for some other item.
- *Responsibility* (for procurement, maintenance, payment, and so on): People are more likely to have disagreements about a decision if it entails long-term consequences and commitments. For example, a family decision about getting a dog may involve conflict regarding who will be responsible for walking it and feeding it.
- *Power* (or the degree to which one family member exerts influence over the others in making decisions): In traditional families, the husband tends to have more power than the wife, who in turn has more than the oldest child, and so on. In family decisions, conflict can arise when one person continually uses the power he or she has within the group to satisfy his or her priorities. For example, if a child believed that his life would end if he did not receive a Nintendo 64 for his birthday, he might be more willing to resort to extreme tactics to influence his parents, perhaps by throwing a tantrum or refusing to participate in family chores.

Sex Roles and Decision-Making Responsibilities

Who "wears the pants" in the family? When one family member chooses a product, this is called an **autonomic decision.** In traditional households, for example, men often have sole responsibility for selecting a car, whereas decorating choices fall to women. **Syncratic decisions,** such as choosing a vacation destination, are made jointly.

According to a study conducted by Roper Starch Worldwide, wives still tend to have the most say when buying groceries, children's toys, clothes, and medicines. Syncratic decisions are common for cars, vacations, homes, appliances, furniture, home electronics, interior design, and long-distance phone services. As the couple's education increases, more decisions are likely to be made together.[45]

Roper sees signs of a shift in marital decision making toward more compromise and turn-taking. For example, the survey firm finds that wives tend to win out in arguments about how the house is kept while husbands get control of the remote control![46] In any case, spouses typically exert significant influence on decision making—even after one of them has died. An Irish study found that many widows claim to sense the continued presence of their dead husbands, and to conduct "conversations" with them about household matters![47] Comments from married women who participated in focus groups conducted for *Redbook* magazine illustrate some of the dynamics of autonomic versus syncratic decision making:

- "We just got our steps done and that was a big project. The contractor would talk (to my husband) and not talk to me. And I said, "Excuse me, I'm here, too."
- "We are looking for a house now, and we're making decisions on which side of town we want it on, what size house do we want, and it's a together decision. That's never how my mother did it."

- "My husband did not want a van, because we have just one child, but I said, "I want a van. And it's not because everyone else has a van. I want comfort." He wanted a convertible. And we got a van."[48]

Identifying the Decision Maker

Figuring out who makes buying decisions is an important issue for marketers so that they know whom to target and whether they need to reach both spouses to influence a choice. For example, when marketing research in the 1950s indicated that women were playing a larger role in household purchasing decisions, lawn mower manufacturers began to emphasize the rotary mower over other power mowers. Rotary mowers, which conceal the cutting blades and engine, were shown in ads featuring young women and smiling grandmothers to downplay fears of injuries.[49]

Researchers have paid special attention to which spouse plays the role of what has been called the **family financial officer (FFO),** the individual who keeps track of the family's bills and decides how any surplus funds will be spent. Among newlyweds, this role tends to be played jointly, and then over time one spouse or the other tends to take over these responsibilities.[51] In traditional families (and especially those with low educational levels), women are primarily responsible for family financial management—the man makes it, and the woman spends it.[52] Each spouse "specializes" in certain activities.[53]

The pattern is different among families in which spouses adhere to more modern sex-role norms. These couples believe that there should be shared participation in family maintenance activities. In these cases, husbands assume more responsibility for laundering, housecleaning, grocery shopping, and so on, in addition to such traditionally "male" tasks as home maintenance and garbage removal.[54]

These responsibilities continue to evolve, especially as women continue to work outside the home and have less time to do the duties traditionally assigned to them. These working mothers often struggle with what one researcher has

Although many men still wear the pants in the family, it's women who buy them. Haggar is redirecting $8 million worth of advertising to target women who shop for and with men. The apparel manufacturer placed menswear ads in about a dozen women's magazines after its research found that women exert tremendous influence over men's clothing choices. In a survey, nearly half of the females polled had purchased men's pants without the man present, and 41 percent said they accompanied the man when he bought pants. Female influence is strongest for decisions involving the matching of colors and the mixing/matching of separates.[50]

Figure 12.2
Leo Mother Types

SOURCE: Cristina Merrill, "Mother's Work Is Never Done," *American Demographics* (September 1999): 30. Reprinted with permission from *American Demographics*.

called the "juggling lifestyle," a frenzied, guilt-ridden compromise between conflicting cultural ideals of motherhood and professionalism.[55] A study by LeoShe, a unit of the Leo Burnett advertising agency that focuses on marketing to women, identified four distinct mother types as shown in Figure 12.2:[56]

- *June Cleaver, the Sequel:* Women who maintain the traditional roles of stay-at-home moms. They are mostly white, highly educated, and upscale.
- *Tug of War:* Women who are forced to work but who aren't happy about it. They tend to be strapped for time, so they buy well-known brand names to make shopping easier.
- *Strong Shoulders:* Women who are in lower income levels but who have a positive view of themselves and their future. More than one-third of the women in this segment are single moms. LeoShe concludes that they are good candidates to try new brands that will help them express themselves.
- *Mothers of Invention:* These women enjoy motherhood and also work out of the home. One reason for their contentment is that their husbands pitch in a lot.

Four factors appear to determine the degree to which decisions will be made jointly or by one or the other spouse.[64]

1. *Sex-role stereotypes:* Couples who believe in traditional sex-role stereotypes tend to make individual decisions for sex-typed products (i.e., those considered to be "masculine" or "feminine").
2. *Spousal resources:* The spouse who contributes more resources to the family has the greater influence.

MULTICULTURAL DIMENSIONS

CULTURAL BACKGROUND PLAYS A big role in determining whether husbands or wives are dominant in the family unit. For example, husbands tend to be more dominant in decision making among couples with a strong Hispanic ethnic identification.[57] Vietnamese-Americans also are more likely to adhere to the traditional model: The man makes the decision for any large purchase, whereas the woman is given a budget to manage the home.[58] In a study comparing marital decision making in the United States versus China, American women reported more "wife decides" situations than did the Chinese.[59] Assumptions about "who's the boss" often are reflected in advertising and marketing strategies. Here are a few examples to illustrate some cross-cultural differences:

- The Coca-Cola Co. developed a campaign to appeal to Latin American women based on an $800,000 research project the company conducted in Brazil. A motherly female kangaroo was found most likely to appeal to women shopping for their families—and who happen to account for 80 percent of Coke's $3.5 billion Brazilian sales. The ads were themed "Mom knows every-

thing," after women in focus groups said they felt the media neglected them even though they were responsible for purchasing all the products in their households.[60]

- A program in India called Butterfly enlists village medicine men to convince local women to take birth control pills. A big obstacle is that women are not accustomed to making these decisions for themselves. The response of one village resident is typical: "I have never taken contraceptives. My husband is my master—he will decide."[61]

- Procter & Gamble produced a commercial for its Ariel laundry detergent in India. A man named Ravi is shown doing the laundry, which is highly unusual in that country. A female voice asks, "Where's the wife?. . . Are you actually going to wash them?. . . man cannot . . . they should not wash clothes . . . [he is] sure to fail."

- Ads showing men doing housework are risky in Asia as well, even though

more Asian women are working outside the home. A South Korean vacuum cleaner ad showed a woman lying on the floor giving herself a facial with slices of cucumber while her husband vacuumed around her. Women there didn't appreciate this ad. As a local ad executive put it, they regarded the ad a challenge to "the leadership of women in the home."[62]

- In contrast, a lot of American advertising sends the message that women should rebel against traditional roles—at least a bit. Research done by Mazda found that its 34- to 42-year-old primary customer did not want to make a complete sacrifice and give up her youthful spirit as she grows older. A commercial for the Mazda 626 shows a mom in her car playing the 1970s rock hit "Rebel, Rebel." As the car stops on a suburban street, the woman gets out dressed in a skirt and high heels with a cake in her hand. The voiceover says, "Do not go gently into that P. T. A. meeting."[63]

---

3. *Experience:* Individual decisions are made more frequently when the couple has gained experience as a decision-making unit.
4. *Socioeconomic status:* Joint decisions are made more by middle-class families than in either higher- or lower-class families.

With many women now working outside of the home, men are participating more in housekeeping activities. In one-fifth of American homes, men do most of the shopping, and nearly one-fifth of men do at least seven loads of laundry a week.[65] Still, as Linda discovered to her chagrin, women continue to do the lion's share of household chores. Ironically, this even appears to be true when the woman's outside income actually exceeds that of her husband's![66] As shown in Table 12.2, a similar situation exists in other western countries such as the United Kingdom. Overall, the degree to which a couple adheres to traditional sex-role norms determines how much their allocation of responsibilities, including consumer decision making, will fall along traditional lines.

Despite recent changes in decision-making responsibilities, women are still primarily responsible for the continuation of the family's **kin-network system:**

TABLE 12.2 Division of Household Tasks in the United Kingdom

Divisions of Household Tasks, 1994	Always the Woman	Usually the Woman	About Equal or Both Together	Usually the Man	Always the Man	All Couples
Washing and ironing	47	32	18	1	1	100
Deciding what to have for dinner	27	32	35	3	1	100
Looking after sick family members	22	26	45	—	—	100
Shopping for groceries	20	21	52	4	1	100
Small repairs around the house	2	3	18	49	25	100

SOURCE: Nicholas Timmins, "New Man Fails to Survive into the Nineties," *The Independent*, January 25, 1996.

They perform the rituals intended to maintain ties among family members, both immediate and extended. This function includes activities such as coordinating visits among relatives, calling and writing family members, sending greeting cards, making social engagements, and so on.[67] This organizing role means that women often make important decisions about the family's leisure activities, and they are more likely to decide with whom the family will socialize.

Heuristics in Joint Decision Making

The **synoptic ideal** calls for the husband and wife to take a common view and act as joint decision makers. According to this ideal, they would very thoughtfully weigh alternatives, assign one another well-defined roles, and calmly make mutually beneficial consumer decisions. The couple would act rationally, analytically, and use as much information as possible to maximize joint utility. In reality, however, spousal decision-making is often characterized by the use of influence or methods that are likely to reduce conflict. A couple "reaches" rather than "makes" a decision. This process has been described as "muddling through."[68]

One common technique for simplifying the decision-making process is the use of *heuristics* (see Chapter 9). Some decision-making patterns frequently observed when a couple makes decisions in buying a new house illustrate the use of heuristics:

- The couple's areas of common preference are based on salient, objective dimensions rather than more subtle, hard-to-define cues. For example, a couple may easily agree on the number of bedrooms they need in the new home, but will have more difficulty achieving a common view of how the home should look.
- The couple agrees on a system of *task specialization* in which each is responsible for certain duties or decision areas and does not interfere on the other's "turf." For many couples, these assignments are likely to be

influenced by their perceived sex roles. For example, the wife may scout out houses in advance that meet their requirements, and the husband determines whether the couple can obtain a mortgage.

- Concessions are based on the intensity of each spouse's preferences. One spouse will yield to the influence of the other in many cases simply because his or her level of preference for a certain attribute is not particularly intense, whereas in other situations he or she will be willing to exert effort to obtain a favorable decision.[69] In cases where intense preferences for different attributes exist, rather than attempt to influence each other, spouses will "trade off" a less-intense preference for a more strongly felt one. For example, a husband who is somewhat indifferent about kitchen design may give in to his wife, but expect that in turn he will be allowed to design his own garage workshop. It is interesting to note that many men apparently want to be very involved in making some decorating decisions and setting budgets—more than women want them to be. According to one survey, 70 percent of male respondents felt the husband should be involved in decorating the den, whereas only 51 percent of wives wanted them to be.[70]

CHILDREN AS DECISION MAKERS: CONSUMERS-IN-TRAINING

Anyone who has had the "delightful" experience of grocery shopping with children in tow knows that kids often have a say (sometimes a loud, whiney one) in what their parents buy.[71] Children make up three distinct markets:[72]

- *Primary market:* Kids spend a lot on their own wants and needs. In 1991 the typical allowance of a 10-year-old was $4.20 a week, and by 1997 this

TABLE 12.3   *Kids' Influence on Household Purchases*

Top 10 Selected Products	Industry Sales (Billions)	Influence Factor (%)	Sales Influence (Billions)
Fruit snacks	0.30	80	0.24
Frozen novelties	1.40	75	1.05
Kids' beauty aids	1.20	70	0.84
Kids' fragrances	0.30	70	0.21
Toys	13.40	70	9.38
Canned pasta	0.57	60	0.34
Kids' clothing	18.40	60	11.04
Video games	3.50	60	2.10
Hot cereals	0.74	50	0.37
Kids' shoes	2.00	50	1.00

SOURCE: "Charting the Children's Market," *Adweek* (February 10, 1992): 42. Reprinted with permission of James J. McNeal, Texas A&M University, College Station, Texas.

FOOD MARKETERS ARE
WORKING hard to capture the hearts
and stomachs of young Web surfers.
Some are designing Web sites to get
attention, such as:

- *nabiscokids.com:* Features an
  Oreo shooting game and a
  Chips Ahoy screen saver.
- *oscar-mayer.com:* Kids learn to
  surf the Web by logging onto
  a World Wide Wiener tutorial.
- *frito-lay.com:* Kids can download wallpaper of Chester
  Cheetah to adorn their computer work space.[78]

But, it's not all about fun stuff.
Marketing researchers say young consumers are reshaping the way America
eats. For many, "homemade" has come
to mean nothing more than "home
heated." They are playing a big role in
the array of ready-made meals, from
pasta to nutrition bars now offered in
supermarkets. Although mothers still
make most grocery decisions, food ads
in magazines aimed at young people
have markedly increased, and food
companies are building "edutainment"
Web pages in addition to game sites.
For example, Ragu's "delizioso" site,
eat.com, promotes its Cheese
Creations! pasta sauce to kids by offering quick, simple recipes, a Go Mama
Go! video game, and a guide to
romance—presumably with tips on
how to gracefully slurp spaghetti
during a dinner date.[79]

weekly stipend had risen to $6.13. And, on average an allowance is only 45 percent of a kid's income. The rest comes from money earned for doing household chores and gifts from relatives. About one-third of this goes to food and beverages with the balance spent on toys, apparel, movies, and games. When marketers at M&M candy figured out who was actually buying a lot of their products, they redesigned vending machines with coin slots lower to the ground to accommodate shorter hands, and sales went up dramatically.

- *Influence market:* **Parental yielding** occurs when a parental decision maker is influenced by a child's request and "surrenders."[73] This is a key driver of product selections because about 90 percent of requests to a parent are by brand name. In recognition of this influence, Mrs. Butterworth's Syrup created a $6 million campaign to target kids directly with humorous ads that show the lengths adults will go to get the syrup bottle to talk to them. An executive who worked on the campaign explained, "We needed to create the nag factor [where kids demand their parents buy the product]."[74]

  The likelihood that yielding will occur partly depends upon the dynamics within a particular family. As we all know, parental styles range from permissive to strict, and they also vary in terms of the amount of responsibility children are given to make decisions.[75] One study documented the strategies kids use to request purchases. Although most children simply asked for things, some other common tactics included saying they had seen it on TV, saying that a sibling or friend has it, or to do chores in return. Other actions were less innocuous; they included directly placing the object in the cart and continuous pleading—often a "persuasive" behavior![76] In addition, the amount of influence children have over consumption is culturally determined. Children who live in individualistic cultures such as the United States have more direct influence, whereas kids in collective cultures like Japan get their way more indirectly.[77] Table 12.3 documents kids' influence in 10 different product categories.

- *Future market:* Kids have a way of growing up to be adults (eventually), and savvy marketers try to lock in brand loyalty at an early age. That explains why Kodak is working so hard to encourage kids to become photographers. Currently, only 20 percent of children aged 5 to 12 own cameras, and they shoot an average of just one roll of film a year. The company produces ads that portray photography as a cool pursuit and as a form of rebellion. Cameras are packaged with an envelope to mail the film directly back so parents can't see the photos.

Consumer Socialization

We've seen that kids are responsible for a lot of marketplace activity, but how do they know what they like and want? Children do not spring from the womb with consumer skills already in memory. **Consumer socialization** is the process "by which young people acquire skills, knowledge, and attitudes relevant to their functioning in the marketplace."[80] Where does this knowledge come from? Friends and teachers certainly participate in this process. For instance, children talk to one another about consumer products, and this tendency increases with age.[81] Especially for young children, though, the two primary socialization sources are the family and the media.

Influence of Parents

Parents' influences in consumer socialization are both direct and indirect. They deliberately try to instill their own values about consumption in their children ("You're going to learn the value of a dollar"). Parents also determine the degree to which their children will be exposed to other information sources, such as television, salespeople, and peers.[83] And, grownups serve as significant models for observational learning (see Chapter 3). Children learn about consumption by watching their parents' behavior and imitating it. This modeling is facilitated by marketers who package adult products in child versions.

Many retailers are trying to attract parents by offering environments where kids and grownups can feel at home. Home Depot conducts weekly workshops for kids. About 30 Starbucks coffee shops nationwide have built kids' play areas to encourage Moms to gather there and drink coffee. Providing a place for kids to jump around while parents relax can pay off: A survey of Burger King customers found that nine of ten parents said they would return to Burger King so their children could play there.[84]

The process of consumer socialization begins with infants, who accompany their parents to stores, where they are initially exposed to marketing stimuli. Within the first two years, children begin to make requests for desired objects. As kids learn to walk, they also begin to make their own selections when they are in stores. By around the age of five, most kids are making purchases with the help of parents and grandparents, and by eight most are making independent purchases and have become full-fledged consumers.[85] The sequence of steps involved in turning kids into consumers is summarized in Figure 12.3.

Three dimensions combine to produce different "segments" of parental styles. Parents characterized by certain styles have been found to socialize their children differently.[86] For example, "authoritarian parents" are hostile, restrictive, and emotionally uninvolved. They do not have warm relationships with their children, they censor the types of media to which their children are exposed, and they tend to have negative views about advertising. "Neglecting parents"

MULTICULTURAL DIMENSIONS

WHO SAYS YOU CAN'T be a kid again? The Japanese are obsessed with "cute" images and products that may strike some Americans as a bit, well, juvenile. All Nippon Airways spent about $1 million in licensing fees and paint to decorate the exterior of three of its 747s with 24-foot-high pocket monsters from Pokemon. Cute characters abound in Japan, including the image of Miffy the bunny on Asahi Bank ATM cards and Hello Kitty charm bags at Shinto shrines. When a Japanese baseball player hits a home run, he is awarded a stuffed animal. Some explain this obsession by noting that the Japanese miss childhood because adulthood in Japan is so demanding and there is such pressure to conform.[82]

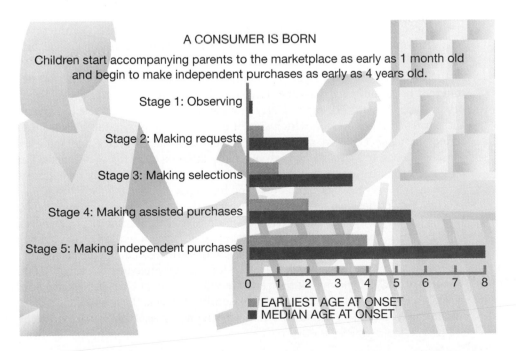

Figure 12.3
Five Stages of Consumer Development by Earliest Age at Onset and Median Age at Onset

MARKETING PITFALLS

ARE MARKETERS ROBBING KIDS of their childhood? Young children have become the target of grownup designers. As a spokesperson for Donna Karan observed, "These seven-year-olds are going on 30. A lot of them have their own sense of style." Maybe so, but perhaps one of the consequences is that they are forced to adopt adult values earlier than they should. One author of a book about kids complains, "We are seeing the deliberate teening of childhood. Parents are giving their kids a lot more choices on what to wear at ever younger ages. The advertisers know this, and they are exploiting the kids' longing to seem sophisticated and grown-up. . . . One of the great things about childhood in the U.S. used to be that kids were protected by the market and allowed to grow their own ideas. Now there is no time to be a kid separate from those pressures. You may have always had kids who are little princesses, but now there are eight-year-old boys that are extremely uptight if they don't get the right Abercrombie & Fitch sweatshirt."[98] Maybe that explains why preteens now account for $200 million of the $3 billion mass-market sales of makeup; a survey of 8- to 12-year-old girls found that two-thirds regularly used cosmetics. Townley Inc. offers fruit-flavored lip gloss for young girls, including the Hello Kitty brand for five-to eight-year-olds. Bath & Body Works sells a line of sparkling cosmetics that includes Coco Crush lipstick and Berry-Go-Round roll-on glitter makeup.[99] So much for the age of innocence.

also do not have warm relationships, but they are more detached from their children and do not exercise much control over what their children do. In contrast, "indulgent parents" communicate more with their children about consumption-related matters and are less restrictive. They believe that children should be allowed to learn about the marketplace without much interference.

Television: "The Electric Babysitter"

It's no secret that kids watch a lot of television. As a result, they are constantly bombarded with messages about consumption, both contained in commercials and in the shows themselves. The media teaches people about a culture's values and myths. The more a child is exposed to television, whether the show is *N.Y.P.D. Blue* or *Sabrina the Teenage Witch*, the more he or she will accept the images depicted there as real.[87] A British TV show called *Teletubbies* targets viewers from three months to two years old. The show has become a national obsession, attracting viewers from more than 20 countries every weekday morning. A Teletubbie record even sold enough copies to make it to the number one spot on the British charts.[88]

In addition to the large volume of programming targeted directly to children, kids are also exposed to idealized images of what it is like to be an adult. Because children over the age of six do about a quarter of their television viewing during prime time, they are affected by programs and commercials targeted to adults. For example, young girls exposed to adult lipstick commercials learn to associate lipstick with beauty.[89]

Sex-Role Socialization

Children pick up on the concept of gender identity (see Chapter 5) at an earlier age than was previously believed—perhaps as young as age one or two. By the age of three, most children categorize driving a truck as masculine and cooking and cleaning as feminine.[90] Even cartoon characters who are portrayed as helpless are more likely to wear frilly or ruffled dresses.[91] Toy companies perpetuate these stereotypes by promoting gender-linked toys with commercials that reinforce sex-role expectations through their casting, emotional tone, and copy.[92]

One function of child's play is to rehearse for adulthood. Children "act out" different roles they might assume later in life and learn about the expectations others have of them. The toy industry provides the props children use to perform these roles.[93] Depending on which side of the debate you're on, these toys either reflect or teach children about what society expects of males and females. Preschool boys and girls do not exhibit many differences in toy preferences, but after the age of five they part company: Girls tend to stick with dolls, whereas boys gravitate toward "action figures" and high-tech diversions.

Industry critics charge that this is because the toy industry is dominated by males, but toy company executives counter that they are simply responding to kids' natural preferences.[94] Indeed, after two decades of working to avoid boy versus girl stereotypes, many companies seem to have decided that differences are inevitable. Toys "R" Us unveiled a new store design after interviewing 10,000 customers, and the chain now has separate sections called Girls World and Boys World. According to the president of Fox Family Channel, "Boys and girls are different, and it's great to celebrate what's special about each."[95] Boys tend to be more interested in battle and competition, whereas girls are more interested in creativity and relationships. This is what experts refer to as "male and female play patterns." Because kids in day care are exposed to other kids earlier on than in the past, these patterns are being observed in younger children then used to be the case.[96]

Recognizing the powerful role toys plays in consumer socialization, doll manufacturers are creating characters they hope will teach little girls about the real world—not the fantasy "bimbo" world that many dolls represent. Recently, a group of California entrepreneurs brought out a line of dolls called Smartees. These characters include Ashley the attorney, Emily the entrepreneur, and Destiny the doctor. A paperback tells each doll's story and includes a sample resume for a person who might have that job in real life.

Not to be outdone, Barbie's recent rebirth as a career woman illustrates how concerns about socialization can be taken to heart by a firm. Although the Barbie doll was introduced as an astronaut in 1964 and as an airline pilot in 1999, there was never much detail about the careers themselves—girls bought the uniform and accessories but they never learned about the professions represented. Now a Working Woman Barbie is on the market as the result of a partnership between Mattel and *Working Woman* magazine. She comes with a miniature computer and cell phone as well as a CD-ROM with information about understanding finances. She is dressed in a grey suit, but the skirt reverses to a red dress to be worn with red platform shoes for her after-work adventures with Ken.[97]

Cognitive Development

The ability of children to make mature, "adult" consumer decisions obviously increases with age (not that grown-ups always make mature decisions). Kids can be segmented by age in terms of their **stage of cognitive development,** or ability to

Lego did research to understand how boys and girls play with its building toys. When executives watched girls play with the toys they noticed they were more likely to build living areas while boys tended to build cars. The company introduced a new version of its product called Paradisa to entice girls to buy more Legos. This set emphasizes the ability to build "socially oriented structures" such as homes, swimming pools, and stables. Sales to girls picked up, though the company still sells most of its sets to boys.

comprehend concepts of increasing complexity. Some evidence indicates that very young children are able to learn consumption-related information surprisingly well.[100]

The foremost proponent of the idea that children pass through distinct stages of cognitive development was the Swiss psychologist Jean Piaget, who believed that each stage is characterized by a certain cognitive structure the child uses to handle information.[101] In one classic demonstration of cognitive development, Piaget poured the contents of a short, squat glass of lemonade into a taller, thinner glass. Five-year-olds, who still believed that the shape of the glass determined its contents, thought this glass held more liquid than the first glass. They are in what Piaget termed a *preoperational stage of development.* In contrast, six-year-olds tended to be unsure, but seven-year-olds knew the amount of lemonade had not changed.

Many developmental specialists no longer believe that children necessarily pass through these fixed stages at the same time. An alternative approach regards children as differing in information-processing capability, or ability to store and retrieve information from memory (see Chapter 3). The following three segments have been identified by this approach:[102]

1. *Limited:* Below the age of six, children do not employ storage and retrieval strategies.
2. *Cued:* Children between the ages of 6 and 12 employ these strategies, but only when prompted.
3. *Strategic:* Children 12 and older spontaneously employ storage and retrieval strategies.

This sequence of development underscores the notion that children do not think in the same way as adults do, and they cannot be expected to use information the same way. It also reminds us that they do not necessarily form the same conclusions as adults do when presented with product information. For example, kids are not as likely to realize that something they see on TV is not "real," and as a result they are more vulnerable to persuasive messages.

Marketing Research and Children

Despite children's buying power, relatively little real data on their preferences or influences on spending patterns is available. Compared to adults, kids are difficult subjects for market researchers. They tend to be undependable reporters of their own behavior, they have poor recall, and they often do not understand abstract questions.[103] This problem is compounded in Europe, where some countries restrict marketers' ability to interview children.

Still, market research can pay off, and many companies, as well as a number of specialized firms, have been successful researching some aspects of this segment.[104] After interviewing elementary school kids, Campbell's Soup discovered that kids like soup but are afraid to admit it because they associate it with "nerds." The company decided to reintroduce the Campbell Kids in its advertising after a prolonged absence, but they are now slimmed down and more athletic to reflect an updated, "un-nerdy" image.[105]

Product Testing

A particularly helpful type of research with children is product testing. Young subjects can provide a valuable perspective on what products will succeed with other kids. These insights are obtained either by watching kids play with toys or

---

THE
TANGLED   WEB

TWO MAJOR DOWNSIDES TO the wealth of information people now can access online is that much of this content is not appropriate for young children, and dotcom companies can collect information from kids that may potentially violate their privacy. We are in the middle of a big debate about the need to block kids from some sites versus the right of free speech that suggests anyone should be able to access whatever they would like. The Children's Advertising Review Unit (CARU) unveiled guidelines for child-oriented Web sites after receiving complaints that kids had trouble distinguishing ads from content. These include clear identification of the sponsor and the right to cancel purchases made online.[111]

The Children's Online Privacy Protection Act took effect in 2000. This legislation requires all Web sites that gather personal information from kids under 13 to have clearly posted privacy policies stating how the data will be used. These sites must gain "verifiable" parental consent before gathering any information. Some people in the industry object to these safeguards; they estimate it will cost a dotcom company $50,000 a year to obtain this verification.[112] How much are we willing to pay to protect our children?

by involving them in focus groups. For example, the Fisher-Price Company maintains a nursery known as the Playlab. Children are chosen from a waiting list of 4,000 to play with new toys while staff members watch from behind a one-way mirror.[106]

Family Fun magazine sponsors an annual Toy of the Year Award to help the toy industry predict which new entries will be a hit or a bust. To do this, 100 children are selected to fill out questionnaires about toys they like and then are shown new toys in focus groups. Finally, the most popular toys are sent to day-care centers, where other kids cast secret ballots.[107] This process works well; in the past the kids have successfully identified hot new toys including the huge hit Tickle Me Elmo.

Message Comprehension

Because children differ in their abilities to process product-related information, many serious ethical issues are raised when advertisers try to appeal directly to them.[108] Kids tend to accept what they see on TV as real, and they do not necessarily understand the persuasive intent of commercials—that they are paid advertisements. Preschool children may not have the ability to make any distinctions between programming and commercials.

Kids' cognitive defenses are not yet sufficiently developed to filter out commercial appeals, so in a sense altering their brand preferences may be likened to "shooting fish in a barrel," as one critic put it.[109] Although some ads include a disclaimer, which is a disclosure intended to clarify a potentially misleading or deceptive statement, the evidence suggests that young children do not adequately understand these either.[110]

Assessing the comprehension of young children is especially hard because preschoolers are not very good at verbal responses. One way around this problem is to show children pictures of kids in different scenarios and ask them to point to the sketch that corresponds to what a commercial is trying to get them to do (see Figure 12.4). The problem with children's processing of commercials has been exacerbated by TV programming that essentially showcases toys (e.g., Jem, G.I. Joe, Transformers). This format has been the target of much criticism because it blurs the line between programming and commercials.[113] Parents' groups object

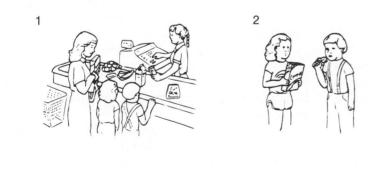

Figure 12.4
The Sketches Used to Measure Children's Perception of the Intent of Commercials

to such shows because, as one mother put it, the "whole show is one big commercial."[114]

CHAPTER SUMMARY

- Many purchasing decisions are made by more than one person. Collective decision making occurs whenever two or more people are involved in evaluating, selecting, or using a product or service.

- Organizational buyers are people who make purchasing decisions on behalf of a company or other group. Although these buyers are influenced by many of the same factors that affect how they make decisions in their personal lives, organizational buying decisions tend to be more rationally based. They are also likely to involve more financial risk, and as they become more complex it is probable that a greater number of people will be involved in making the decision.

- The amount of cognitive effort that goes into organizational decisions is influenced by internal factors, such as the individuals' psychological characteristics, and by external factors, such as the company's willingness to tolerate risk. One of the most important determinants is the type of purchase being considered: The extent of problem solving required depends on whether the product or service to be procured is simply to be reordered (a straight rebuy), ordered with minor modifications (modified rebuy), or if it has never been purchased before or is complex and risky (new task). Online purchasing sites are revolutionizing the way organizational decision makers collect and evaluate product information in business-to-business e-commerce.

- In organizations and in families, several different roles must be played during the decision-making process. These roles include the gatekeeper, influencers, buyers, and users.

- Demographics are statistics that measure a population's characteristics. Some of the most important of these relate to family structure (e.g., the birth rate, the marriage rate, and the divorce rate).

- A household is an occupied housing unit. The number and type of U.S. households is changing in many ways, including delays in getting married and having children, and in the composition of family households, which are increasingly headed by a single parent. New perspectives on the family life cycle, which focuses on how people's needs change as they move through different stages in their lives, are forcing marketers to more seriously consider consumer segments such as homosexuals, divorced persons, and childless couples when they develop targeting strategies.

- Families must be understood in terms of their decision-making dynamics. Spouses in particular have different priorities and exert varying amounts of influence in terms of effort and power. Children are also increasingly influential during a widening range of purchase decisions.

- Children undergo a process of socialization, whereby they learn how to be consumers. Some of this knowledge is instilled by parents and friends, but a lot of it comes from exposure to mass media and advertising. Because children are in some cases so easily persuaded, the ethical aspects of marketing to them are hotly debated among consumers, academics, and marketing practitioners.

KEY TERMS

accommodative purchase
   decision, p. 362
boomerang kids, p. 359
business-to-business (B2B)
   e-commerce, p. 355
business-to-business
   marketers, p. 352
buying center, p. 354
consensual purchase decision, p. 362

consumer socialization, p. 370
extended family, p. 356
family financial officer (FFO), p. 365
family household, p. 356
family life cycle (FLC), p. 359
fertility rate, p. 357
kin-network system, p. 367
modified rebuy, p. 355
new task, p. 355

nuclear family, p. 356
organizational buyers, p. 351
parental yielding, p. 370
stage of cognitive development, p. 373
straight rebuy, p. 355
syncratic decisions, p. 364
synoptic ideal, p. 368

CONSUMER BEHAVIOR CHALLENGE

1. Do you think market research should be performed with children? Give the reasons for your answer.
2. What do you think of the practice of companies and survey firms collecting public data (e.g., from marriage licenses, birth records, or even death announcements) to compile targeted mailing lists? State your opinion from both a consumer's and marketer's perspective.
3. Marketers have been criticized for donating products and services to educational institutions in exchange for free promotion. Is this a fair exchange, in your opinion, or should corporations be prohibited from attempting to influence youngsters in school?
4. For each of the following five product categories—groceries, automobiles, vacations, furniture, and appliances—describe the ways in which you believe a married couple's choices would be affected if they had children.
5. In identifying and targeting newly divorced couples, do you think marketers are exploiting these couples' situations? Are there instances in which you think marketers may actually be helpful to them? Support your answers with examples.
6. Arrange to interview two married couples, one younger and one older. Prepare a response form listing five product categories—groceries, furniture, appliances, vacations, and automobiles—and ask each spouse to indicate, without consulting the other, whether purchases in each category are made by joint or unilateral decisions and to indicate whether the unilateral decisions are made by the husband or the wife. Compare each couples' responses for agreement between husbands and wives relative to who makes the decisions, and compare both couples' overall responses for differences relative to the number of joint versus unilateral decisions. Report your findings and conclusions.
7. Collect ads for three different product categories in which the family is targeted. Find another set of ads for different brands of the same items in which the family is not featured. Prepare a report comparing the probable effectiveness of the two approaches. Which specific categories would most likely benefit from a family emphasis?
8. Observe the interactions between parents and children in the cereal section of a local grocery store. Prepare a report on the number of children who expressed preferences, how they expressed their preferences, and how parents responded, including the number who purchased the child's choice.

9. Watch three hours of children's programming on commercial television stations and evaluate the marketing techniques used in the commercials in terms of the ethical issues raised in the final section of this chapter. Report your findings and conclusions.

10. Select a product category, and using the life-cycle stages given in the chapter, list the variables that will affect a purchase decision for the product by consumers in each stage of the cycle.

11. Consider three important changes in modern family structure. For each, find an example of a marketer who has attempted to be conscious of this change as reflected in product communications, retailing innovations, or other aspects of the marketing mix. If possible, also try to find examples of marketers who have failed to keep up with these developments.

12. Industrial purchase decisions are totally rational. Aesthetic or subjective factors don't—and shouldn't—play a role in this process. Do you agree?

NOTES

1. See J. Joseph Cronin Jr. and Michael H. Morris, "Satisfying Customer Expectations; the Effect on Conflict and Repurchase Intentions in Industrial Marketing Channels," *Journal of the Academy of Marketing Science* 17 (Winter 1989): 41–49; Thomas W. Leigh and Patrick F. McGraw, "Mapping the Procedural Knowledge of Industrial Sales Personnel: A Script-Theoretic Investigation," *Journal of Marketing* 53 (January 1989): 16–34; William J. Qualls and Christopher P. Puto, "Organizational Climate and Decision Framing: An Integrated Approach to Analyzing Industrial Buying," *Journal of Marketing Research* 26 (May 1989): 179–92.

2. James M. Sinkula, "Market Information Processing and Organizational Learning," *Journal of Marketing* 58 (January 1994): 35–45.

3. Allen M. Weiss and Jan B. Heide, "The Nature of Organizational Search in High Technology Markets," *Journal of Marketing Research* 30 (May 1993): 220–33; Jennifer K. Glazing and Paul N. Bloom, "Buying Group Information Source Reliance," *Proceedings of the American Marketing Association Educators' Conference* (Summer 1994): 454.

4. B. Charles Ames and James D. Hlaracek, *Managerial Marketing for Industrial Firms* (New York: Random House Business Division, 1984); Edward F. Fern and James R. Brown, "The Industrial/Consumer Marketing Dichotomy: A Case of Insufficient Justification," *Journal of Marketing* 48 (Spring 1984): 68–77.

5. Kevin Keller, *Strategic Brand Management* (Upper Saddle River, NJ: Prentice Hall 1998); Michael R. Solomon and Elnora W. Stuart, *Marketing: Real People, Real Choices*, 2d ed. (Upper Saddle River, NJ: Prentice Hall, 2000).

6. Daniel H. McQuiston "Novelty, Complexity, and Importance as Causal Determinants of Industrial Buyer Behavior," *Journal of Marketing* 53 (April 1989): 66–79.

7. Patrick J. Robinson, Charles W. Faris, and Yoram Wind, *Industrial Buying and Creative Marketing* (Boston: Allyn & Bacon, 1967).

8. Erin Anderson, Wujin Chu, and Barton Weitz, "Industrial Purchasing: An Empirical Examination of the Buyclass Framework," *Journal of Marketing* 51 (July 1987): 71–86.

9. Fred E. Webster and Yoram Wind, *Organizational Buying Behavior* (Upper Saddle River, NJ: Prentice Hall, 1972).

10. Steven J. Kafka, Bruce D. Temkin, Matthew R. Sanders, Jeremy Sharrard, and Tobias O. Brown, "eMarketplaces Boost B2B Trade," *The Forrester Report*, Forrester Research, Inc., February 2000.

11. Michael Casey, "Power of Internet Changes Supply and Demand Forever," *The Wall Street Journal Interactive Edition* (October 18, 1999).

12. Alison Hardy, "Designing Time and Sampling Money," *Apparel Industry Magazine* (May 2000): 22.

13. Robert Boutilier, "Targeting Families: Marketing to and Through the New Family," *American Demographics Marketing Tools* (Ithaca, NY: 1993): 4–6; W. Bradford Fay, "Families in the 1990s: Universal Values, Uncommon Experiences," *Marketing Research: A Magazine of Management & Applications* 5, no. 1 (Winter 1993): 47.

14. Ellen Graham, "Craving Closer Ties, Strangers Come Together as Family," *The Wall Street Journal* (March 4, 1996): B1.

15. Alan R. Andreasen, "Life Status Changes and Changes in Consumer Preferences and Satisfaction," *Journal of Consumer Research* 11 (December 1984): 784–94; James H. McAlexander, John W. Schouten, and Scott D. Roberts, "Consumer Behavior and Divorce," *Research in Consumer Behavior* 6 (1993): 153–84.

16. Randolph E. Schmid, "Most Americans Still the Marrying Kind, Statistics Show; Trend: The Percentage of Adults Who Are Wed and Living with Their Spouse Is Declining, But Still the Majority," *The Los Angeles Times* (January 17, 1999): 9.

17. "Study Finds Why Marriage Is on the Decline," *Jet* 96 (July 26, 1999): 16–19.

18. Wendy Bounds, "An Easy Way to Get an Ex out of the Picture—and No Lawyer!" *The Wall Street Journal* (June 16, 1994): B1.

19. Diane Crispell, "Family Futures," *American Demographics* (August 1996): 13–14.

20. Karen Hardee-Cleaveland, "Is Eight Enough?" *American Demographics* (June 1989): 60.

21. Brad Edmondson, "Inside the New Household Projections," *The Number News* (July 1996). Available online: www.demographics.com.

22. Brad Edmondson, "Inside the New Household Projections."

23. "Mothers Bearing a Second Burden," *New York Times* (May 14, 1989): 26.

24. Thomas Exter, "Disappearing Act," *American Demographics* (January 1989): 78; see also KerenAmi Johnson and Scott D. Roberts, "Incompletely-Launched and Returning Young Adults: Social Change, Consumption, and Family Environment," in Robert P. Leone and V. Kumar, eds., *Enhancing Knowledge Development in Marketing* (Chicago: American Marketing

Association): 249–54; John Burnett and Denise Smart, "Returning Young Adults: Implications for Marketers," *Psychology & Marketing* 11, no. 3 (May/June 1994): 253–69.

25. Marcia Mogelonsky, "The Rocky Road to Adulthood," *American Demographics* (May 1996): 26.

26. For a review, see Russell W. Belk, "Metaphoric Relationships with Pets," *Society and Animals* 4, no. 2 (1996): 121–46.

27. Diane Crispell, "Pet Projections," *American Demographics* (September 1994): 59; Howard G. Chua-Eoan, "Reigning Cats and Dogs," *Time* (August 16, 1993): 50; Patricia Braus, "Cat Beats Dog, Wins Spot in House," *American Demographics* (September 1993): 24.

28. Quoted in Youssef M. Ibrahim, "French Love for Animals: Too Fervent?" *New York Times* (February 2, 1990): A5.

29. Ian P. Murphy, "A Dog's Life: Products Go Upscale as Owners Pamper Four-Legged Friends," *Marketing News* (August 4, 1997): 1; Woody Hochswender, "The Cat's Meow," *New York Times* (May 16, 1989): B7; Judann Dagnoli, "Toothcare for Terriers," *Advertising Age* (November 20, 1989): 8; "For Fido, Broccoli and Yogurt," *New York Times* (April 16, 1989); William E. Schmidt, "Right, Then: Your Policy Covers Fido for Therapy," *New York Times* (May 15, 1994): 4; Patricia Davis, "New Shampoo for Hoofed Set Has the Mulish Looking Marvelous," *The Wall Street Journal* (August 22, 1995): B1.

30. Anne S. Lewis, "Fancy Fidos Check in at Pet Palazzi," *The Wall Street Journal Interactive Edition* (August 27, 1999).

31. Marcia Mogelonsky, "Reconfiguring the American Dream (House)" *American Demographics* (January 1997): 31–35; Alison M. Torrillo, "Dens Are Men's Territory," *American Demographics* (January 1995): 11.

32. Brad Edmondson, "Do the Math," *American Demographics* (October 1999): 50–56.

33. Mary C. Gilly and Ben M. Enis, "Recycling the Family Life Cycle: A Proposal for Redefinition," in Andrew A. Mitchell, ed., *Advances in Consumer Research* 9 (Ann Arbor, MI: Association for Consumer Research, 1982): 271–76.

34. Charles M. Schaninger and William D. Danko, "A Conceptual and Empirical Comparison of Alternative Household Life Cycle Models," *Journal of Consumer Research* 19 (March 1993): 580–94; Robert E. Wilkes, "Household Life-Cycle Stages, Transitions, and Product Expenditures," *Journal of Consumer Research* 22, no. 1 (June 1995): 27–42.

35. Cheryl Russell, "The New Consumer Paradigm," *American Demographics* (April 1999): 50.

36. These categories are an adapted version of an FLC model proposed by Gilly and Enis (1982). Based on a recent empirical comparison of several competing models, Schaninger and Danko found that this framework outperformed others, especially in terms of its treatment of nonconventional households, though they recommend several improvements to this model as well. See Gilly and Enis, "Recycling the Family Life Cycle"; Schaninger and Danko, "A Conceptual and Empirical Comparison of Alternate Household Life Cycle Markets"; Scott D. Roberts, Patricia K. Voli, and KerenAmi Johnson, "Beyond the Family Life Cycle: An Inventory of Variables for Defining the Family as a Consumption Unit," in Victoria L. Crittenden, ed., *Developments in Marketing Science* 15 (Coral Gables, FL: Academy of Marketing Science, 1992): 71–75.

37. Brad Edmondson, "Do the Math," *American Demographics* (October 1999): 50–56.

38. Quoted in Ristina Ourosa, "Who Are the First Ones out There, Buying the Latest Gadgets? Meet the TAFs," *The Wall Street Journal Interactive Edition* (June 16, 1998).

39. Jennifer Lach, "Intelligence Agents," *American Demographics* (March 1999): 52–60.

40. Harry L. Davis, "Decision Making Within the Household," *Journal of Consumer Research* 2 (March 1972): 241–60; Michael B. Menasco and David J. Curry, "Utility and Choice: An Empirical Study of Wife/Husband Decision Making," *Journal of Consumer Research* 16 (June 1989): 87–97; Conway Lackman and John M. Lanasa, "Family Decision-Making Theory: An Overview and Assessment," *Psychology & Marketing* 10, no. 2 (March/April 1993): 81–94.

41. Neal Templin, "The PC Wars: Who Gets to Use the Family Computer?" *The Wall Street Journal* (October 5, 1995): B1.

42. Shannon Dortch, "Money and Marital Discord," *American Demographics* (October 1994): 11.

43. For research on factors influencing how much influence adolescents exert in family decision making, see Ellen Foxman, Patriya Tansuhaj, and Karin M. Ekstrom, "Family Members' Perceptions of Adolescents' Influence in Family Decision Making," *Journal of Consumer Research* 15, no.4 (March 1989): 482–91; Sharon E. Beatty and Salil Talpade, "Adolescent Influence in Family Decision Making: A Replication with Extension," *Journal of Consumer Research* 21, no. 2 (September 1994): 332–41.

44. Daniel Seymour and Greg Lessne, "Spousal Conflict Arousal: Scale Development," *Journal of Consumer Research* 11 (December 1984): 810–21.

45. Diane Crispell, "Dual-Earner Diversity," *American Demographics* (July 1995): 32–37.

46. "Marriage: The Art of Compromise," *American Demographics* (February 1998): 41.

47. Darach Turley, "Dialogue with the Departed," *European Advances in Consumer Research* 2 (1995): 10–13.

48. "Wives and Money," *American Demographics* (December 1997): 34.

49. Thomas Hine, *Populuxe* (New York: Knopf, 1986).

50. Robert Lohrer, "Haggar Targets Women with $8M Media Campaign," *Daily News Record* (January 8, 1997): 1.

51. Robert Boutilier, "Targeting Families: Marketing to and Through the New Family," *American Demographics Marketing Tools* (Ithaca, NY: 1993).

52. Dennis L. Rosen and Donald H. Granbois, "Determinants of Role Structure in Family Financial Management," *Journal of Consumer Research* 10 (September 1983): 253–58.

53. Robert F. Bales, *Interaction Process Analysis: A Method for the Study of Small Groups* (Reading, MA: Addison-Wesley, 1950); for a cross-gender comparison of food-shopping strategies, see Rosemary Polegato and Judith L. Zaichkowsky, "Family Food Shopping: Strategies Used by Husbands and Wives," *The Journal of Consumer Affairs* 28, no. 2 (1994): 278–99.

54. Alma S. Baron, "Working Parents: Shifting Traditional Roles," *Business* 37 (January/March 1987): 36; William J. Qualls, "Household Decision Behavior: The Impact of Husbands' and Wives' Sex Role Orientation," *Journal of Consumer Research* 14 (September 1987): 264–79; Charles M. Schaninger and W. Christian Buss, "The Relationship of Sex-Role Norms to Household Task Allocation," *Psychology & Marketing* 2 (Summer 1985): 93–104.

55. Craig J. Thompson, "Caring Consumers: Gendered Consumption Meanings and the Juggling Lifestyle," *Journal of Consumer Research* 22 (March 1996): 388–407.

56. Cristina Merrill, "Mother's Work Is Never Done," *American Demographics* (September 1999): 29–32.

57. Cynthia Webster, "Effects of Hispanic Ethnic Identification on Marital Roles in the Purchase Decision Process," *Journal of Consumer Research* 21, no. 2 (September 1994): 319–31; for a recent study that examined the effects of family depictions in advertising among Hispanic consumers, see Gary D. Gregory and James M. Munch, "Cultural Values in International Advertising: An Examination of Familial Norms and Roles in Mexico," *Psychology & Marketing* 14, no. 2 (March 1997): 99–120.

58. John Steere, "How Asian-Americans Make Purchase Decisions," *Marketing News* (March 13, 1995): 9.

59. John B. Ford, Michael S. LaTour, and Tony L. Henthorne, "Perception of Marital Roles in Purchase Decision Processes: A Cross-Cultural Study," *Journal of the Academy of Marketing Science* 23, no. 2 (Spring 1995): 120–31; for a recent study of husband–wife dyad decision making for home purchase decisions, see Chankon Kim and Hanjoon Lee, "A Taxonomy of Couples Based on Influence Strategies: The Case of Home Purchase," *Journal of Business Research* 36, no. 2 (June 1996): 157–68.

60. Claudia Penteado, "Coke Taps Maternal Instinct with New Latin American Ads," *Advertising Age International* (January 1997): 15.

61. Quoted in Miriam Jordan, "India's Medicine Men Market an Array of Contraceptives," *The Wall Street Journal Interactive Edition* (September 21, 1999).

62. Louise Lee, "Ad Agencies in Asia Hit a Nerve, Showing Men Doing Housework," *The Wall Street Journal Interactive Edition* (August 14, 1998).

63. Patricia Winters Lauro, "Sports Geared to Parents Replace Stodgy with Cool," *The New York Times on the Web* (January 3, 2000).

64. Gary L. Sullivan and P. J. O'Connor, "The Family Purchase Decision Process: A Cross-Cultural Review and Framework for Research," *Southwest Journal of Business & Economics* (Fall 1988): 43; Marilyn Lavin, "Husband-Dominant, Wife-Dominant, Joint," *Journal of Consumer Marketing* 10, no. 3 (1993): 33–42.

65. Diane Crispell, "Mr. Mom Goes Mainstream," *American Demographics* (March 1994): 59; Gabrielle Sándor, "Attention Advertisers: Real Men Do Laundry," *American Demographics* (March 1994): 13.

66. Tony Bizjak, "Chore Wars Rage On— Even When Wife Earns the Most," *The Sacramento Bee* (April 1, 1993): A1.

67. Micaela DiLeonardo, "The Female World of Cards and Holidays: Women, Families, and the Work of Kinship," *Signs* 12 (Spring 1942): 440–53.

68. C. Whan Park, "Joint Decisions in Home Purchasing: A Muddling-Through Process," *Journal of Consumer Research* 9 (September 1982): 151–62; see also William J. Qualls and Francoise Jaffe, "Measuring Conflict in Household Decision Behavior: Read My Lips and Read My Mind," in John F. Sherry Jr. and Brian Sternthal, eds., *Advances in Consumer Research* 19 (Provo, UT: Association for Consumer Research, 1992): 522–31.

69. Kim P. Corfman and Donald R. Lehmann, "Models of Cooperative Group Decision-Making and Relative Influence: An Experimental Investigation of Family Purchase Decisions," *Journal of Consumer Research* 14 (June 1987): 1–13.

70. Alison M. Torrillo, "Dens Are Men's Territory," *American Demographics* (January 1995): 11.

71. Charles Atkin, "Observation of Parent-Child Interaction in Supermarket Decision-Making," *Journal of Marketing* 42 (October 1978): 41–45. For more information related to children and consumption, see the government Web site www.child-stats.gov.

72. James U. McNeal, "Tapping the Three Kids' Markets," *American Demographics* (April 1998): 3,737–41.

73. Kay L. Palan and Robert E. Wilkes, "Adolescent-Parent Interaction in Family Decision Making," *Journal of Consumer Research* 24 (September 1997): 159–69.

74. Stephanie Thompson, "Mrs. Butterworth's Changes Her Target," *Advertising Age* (December 20, 1999): 44.

75. Les Carlson, Ann Walsh, Russell N. Laczniak, and Sanford Grossbart, "Family Communication Patterns and Marketplace Motivations, Attitudes, and Behaviors of Children and Mothers," *The Journal of Consumer Affairs* 28, no. 1 (Summer 1994): 25–53; see also Roy L. Moore and George P. Moschis, "The Role of Family Communication in Consumer Learning," *Journal of Communication* 31 (Autumn 1981): 42–51.

76. Leslie Isler, Edward T. Popper, and Scott Ward, "Children's Purchase Requests and Parental Responses: Results from a Diary Study," *Journal of Advertising Research* 27 (October/November 1987): 28–39.

77. Gregory M. Rose, "Consumer Socialization, Parental Style, and Development Timetables in the United States and Japan," *Journal of Marketing* 63, no. 3 (1999): 105–19.

78. David Leonhardt, "Hey Kids, Buy This!" *Business Week* (June 30, 1997): 61.

79. Molly O'Neill, "Teen-Agers Are Reshaping American Eating Habits," *The New York Times on the Web* (March 14, 1998).

80. Scott Ward, "Consumer Socialization," in Harold H. Kassarjian and Thomas S. Robertson, ed., *Perspectives in Consumer Behavior* (Glenview, IL: Scott, Foresman, 1980): 380.

81. Thomas Lipscomb, "Indicators of Materialism in Children's Free Speech: Age and Gender Comparisons," *Journal of Consumer Marketing* (Fall 1988): 41–46.

82. Mary Roach, "Cute Inc.," *Wired* (December 1999): 330–43.

83. George P. Moschis, "The Role of Family Communication in Consumer Socialization of Children and Adolescents," *Journal of Consumer Research* 11 (March 1985): 898–13.

84. Bruce Horovitz, "Targeting the Kindermarket," *USA Today* (March 3, 2000): B1.

85. James U. McNeal and Chyon-Hwa Yeh, "Born to Shop," *American Demographics* (June 1993): 34–39.

86. See Les Carlson, Sanford Grossbart, and J. Kathleen Stuenkel, "The Role of Parental Socialization Types on Differential Family Communication Patterns Regarding Consumption," *Journal of Consumer Psychology* 1, no. 1 (1992): 31–52.

87. See Patricia M. Greenfield, Emily Yut, Mabel Chung, Deborah Land, Holly Kreider, Maurice Pantoja, and Kris Horsley, "The Program-Length Commercial: A Study of the Effects of Television/Toy Tie-Ins on Imaginative Play," *Psychology & Marketing* 7 (Winter 1990): 237–56 for a study on the effects of commercial programming on creative play.

88. Marina Baker, "Teletubbies say 'Eh Oh . . . It's War!'" *The Independent* (March 6, 2000): 7; "A Trojan Horse for Advertisers" *Business Week* (April 3, 2000): 10.

89. Gerald J. Gorn and Renee Florsheim, "The Effects of Commercials for Adult Products on Children," *Journal of Consumer Research* 11 (March 1985): 962–67; for a recent study that assessed the impact of violent commercials on children, see V. Kanti Prasad and Lois J. Smith, "Television Commercials in Violent Programming: An Experimental Evaluation of Their Effects on Children," *Journal of the Academy of Marketing Science* 22, no. 4 (1994): 340–51.

90. Glenn Collins, "New Studies on 'Girl Toys' and 'Boy Toys'," *New York Times* (February 13, 1984): D1.

91. Susan B. Kaiser, "Clothing and the Social Organization of Gender Perception: A Developmental Approach," *Clothing and Textiles Research Journal* 7 (Winter 1989): 46–56.

92. D. W. Rajecki, Jill Ann Dame, Kelly Jo Creek, P. J. Barrickman, Catherine A. Reid, and Drew C. Appleby, "Gender Casting in Television Toy Advertisements: Distributions, Message Content Analysis, and Evaluations," *Journal of Consumer Psychology* 2, no. 3 (1993): 307–27.

93. Lori Schwartz and William Markham, "Sex Stereotyping in Children's Toy Advertisements," *Sex Roles* 12 (January 1985): 157–70.

94. Joseph Pereira, "Oh Boy! In Toyland, You Get More if You're Male," *The Wall Street Journal* (September 23, 1994): B1; Joseph Pereira, "Girls Favorite Playthings: Dolls, Dolls, and Dolls," *The Wall Street Journal* (September 23, 1994): B1.

95. Quoted in Lisa Bannon, "More Kids' Marketers Pitch Number of Single-Sex Products," *The Wall Street Journal Interactive Edition* (February 14, 2000).

96. Lisa Bannon, "More Kids' Marketers Pitch Number of Single-Sex Products," *The Wall Street Journal Interactive Edition* (February 14, 2000).

97. Constance L. Hays, "A Role Model's Clothes: Barbie Goes Professional," *The New York Times on the Web* (April 1, 2000).

98. Kay Hymovitz, quoted in Leslie Kaufman, "New Style Maven: 6 Years Old and Picky," *The New York Times on the Web* (September 7, 1999).

99. Tara Parker-Pope, "Cosmetics Industry Takes Look at the Growing Preteen Market," *The Wall Street Journal Interactive Edition* (December 4, 1998).

100. Laura A. Peracchio, "How Do Young Children Learn to be Consumers? A Script-Processing Approach," *Journal of Consumer Research* 18 (March 1992): 425–40; Laura A. Peracchio, "Young Children's Processing of a Televised Narrative: Is a Picture Really Worth a Thousand Words?" *Journal of Consumer Research* 20, no. 2 (September 1993): 281–93; see also M. Carole Macklin, "The Effects of an Advertising Retrieval Cue on Young Children's Memory and Brand Evaluations," *Psychology & Marketing* 11, no. 3 (May/June 1994): 291–311.

101. Jean Piaget, "The Child and Modern Physics," *Scientific American* 196, no. 3 (1957): 46–51; see also Kenneth D. Bahn, "How and When Do Brand Perceptions and Preferences First Form? A Cognitive Developmental Investigation," *Journal of Consumer Research* 13 (December 1986): 382–93.

102. Deborah L. Roedder, "Age Differences in Children's Responses to Television Advertising: An Information-Processing Approach," *Journal of Consumer Research* 8 (September 1981): 144–53; see also Deborah Roedder John and Ramnath Lakshmi-Ratan, "Age Differences in Children's Choice Behavior: The Impact of Available Alternatives," *Journal of Marketing Research* 29 (May 1992): 216–26; Jennifer Gregan-Paxton and Deborah Roedder John, "Are Young Children Adaptive Decision Makers? A Study of Age Differences in Information Search Behavior," *Journal of Consumer Research* 21, no. 4 (1995): 567–80.

103. Janet Simons, "Youth Marketing: Children's Clothes Follow the Latest Fashion," *Advertising Age* (February 14, 1985): 16.

104. Stipp, "Children as Consumers," see Laura A. Peracchio, "Designing Research to Reveal the Young Child's Emerging Competence," *Psychology & Marketing* 7 (Winter 1990): 257–76, for details regarding the design of research on children.

105. "Kid Power," *Forbes* (March 30, 1987): 9–10.

106. Laura Shapiro, "Where Little Boys Can Play with Nail Polish," *Newsweek* (May 28, 1990): 62.

107. Joseph Pereira, "Pint-Size Judges Make Their Picks for Holiday Favorites This Season," *The Wall Street Journal Interactive Edition* (December 17, 1997); Tom McGee, "Getting Inside Kids' Heads," *American Demographics* (January 1997): 53.

108. Gary Armstrong and Merrie Brucks, "Dealing with Children's Advertising: Public Policy Issues and Alternatives," *Journal of Public Policy and Marketing* 7 (1988): 98–113.

109. Bonnie Reece, "Children and Shopping: Some Public Policy Questions," *Journal of Public Policy and Marketing* (1986): 185–94.

110. Mary Ann Stutts and Garland G. Hunnicutt, "Can Young Children Understand Disclaimers in Television Commercials," *Journal of Advertising* 16 (Winter 1987): 41–46.

111. Ira Teinowitz, "CARU to Unveil Guidelines for Kid-Focused Web Sites," *Advertising Age* (April 21, 1997): 8.

112. Jeri Clausing, "New Privacy Law Forcing Changes to Children's Sites," *The New York Times on the Web* (April 18, 2000).

113. Steve Weinstein, "Fight Heats up Against Kids' TV 'Commershows'," *Marketing News* (October 9, 1989): 2.

114. Alan Bunce, "Are TV Ads Turning Kids into Consumers?" *Christian Science Monitor* (August 11, 1988): 1.

SECTION

IV

CONSUMERS AND SUBCULTURES

The chapters in this section consider some of the social influences that help to determine who we are, with an emphasis on the subcultures that help to determine each of our unique identities. Chapter 13 focuses on factors that define social class, and how membership in a social class exerts a strong pull on what we want to buy with the money we make. Chapter 14 discusses the ways that our ethnic, racial, and religious identifications help to stamp our social identities. Chapter 15 considers how the bonds we share with others who were born at roughly the same time unite us.

◆ ◆ ◆

Section Outline

Finally, the big day has come! Phil is going home with Marilyn to meet her parents. Phil had been doing some contracting work at the securities firm where Marilyn works, and it was love at first sight. Even though Phil had attended the "School of Hard Knocks" on the streets of Brooklyn and Marilyn was fresh out of Princeton, somehow they knew they could work things out despite their vastly different backgrounds. Marilyn's been hinting that the Caldwells have money, but Phil doesn't feel intimidated. After all, he knows plenty of guys from his old neighborhood who have wheeled-and-dealed their way into six figures.

He guesses he can handle one more big shot in a silk suit, flashing a roll of bills and showing off his expensive modern furniture with mirrors and gadgets everywhere you look.

When they arrive at the family estate in Connecticut, Phil looks for a Rolls-Royce parked in the circular driveway, but he sees only a Jeep Cherokee, which must belong to one of the servants. Once inside, Phil is surprised by how simply the house is decorated and by how shabby everything seems. The hall entryway is covered with a faded Oriental rug, and all of the furniture looks really old. In fact, there doesn't seem to be a new stick of furniture anywhere, just a lot of antiques.

Phil is even more surprised when he meets Mr. Caldwell. He had half expected Marilyn's father to be wearing a tuxedo and holding a large glass of cognac like the people he's seen in the movies. In fact, Phil had put on his best shiny Italian suit in anticipation, and he wore his large cubic zirconium pinky ring so this guy would know that he had some money too.

When Marilyn's father emerges from his study wearing an old rumpled cardigan sweater and tennis sneakers, Phil realizes he's definitely not in the old neighborhood anymore.

13

INCOME AND SOCIAL CLASS

CONSUMER SPENDING AND ECONOMIC BEHAVIOR

As Phil's eye-opening experience at the Caldwells' house suggests, there are many ways to spend money, and a wide gulf exists between those who have it and those who don't. Perhaps an equally wide one exists between those who have had it for a long time and those who "made it the hard way—by earning it!" This chapter begins by briefly considering how general economic conditions affect the way consumers allocate their money. Then, reflecting the adage that says "The rich are different," it will explore how people who occupy different positions in society consume in very different ways.

Whether a skilled worker like Phil or a child of privilege like Marilyn, a person's social class has a profound impact on what he does with money and on how consumption choices reflect his "place" in society. As this chapter illustrates, these choices play another purpose as well. The specific products and services we buy are often intended to make sure other people know what our social standing is—or what we would like it to be. Products are frequently bought and displayed as markers of social class; they are valued as *status symbols*. This is especially true in large, modern societies in which behavior and reputation can no longer be counted on to convey one's position in a community.

Income Patterns

Many Americans would probably say that they don't make enough money, but in reality the average American's standard of living continues to improve. These income shifts are linked to two key factors: a shift in women's roles and increases in educational attainment.[1]

Woman's Work

One reason for this increase in income is that there has also been a larger proportion of people of working age participating in the labor force. Mothers with preschool children are the fastest growing segment of working people. Furthermore, many of these jobs are in high-paying occupations such as medicine and architecture, which used to be dominated by men. Although women are still a minority in most professional occupations, their ranks continue to swell. The steady increase in the numbers of working women is a primary cause of the rapid growth of middle- and upper-income families. There are now more than 18 million married couples making more than $50,000 a year—but in almost two-thirds of these families, it is the wife's paycheck that is propelling the couple up the income ladder.[2]

Yes, It Pays to Go to School!

Another factor that determines who gets a bigger piece of the pie is education. Although picking up the tab for college often entails great sacrifice, it still pays off in the long run. College graduates earn about 50 percent more than those who have only gone through high school during the course of their lives. Women without a high school diploma earn only 40 percent as much as women who have a college degree.[3] And, close to half of the increase in consumer spending power during the last decades came from college grads. So, hang in there!

To Spend or Not to Spend, That Is the Question

Consumer demand for goods and services depends both on ability to buy and willingness to buy. Whereas demand for necessities tends to be stable over time, other expenditures can be postponed or eliminated if people don't feel that now is a good time to spend money.[4] For example, a person may decide to "make do" with his current clunker for another year rather than buying a new car right away.

Discretionary Spending

Discretionary income is the money available to a household over and above that required for a comfortable standard of living. American consumers are estimated to wield about $400 billion a year in discretionary spending power. People aged 35 to 55, whose incomes are at a peak, account for about half of this amount. As the population ages and income levels rise, the typical U.S. household is changing the way it spends its money. The most noticeable change is that a much larger share of the budget is spent on shelter and transportation, and less on food and apparel. These shifts are due to factors such as an increase in the prevalence of home ownership (the number of homeowners rose by more than 80 percent in the last three decades) and in the need for working wives to pay commuting costs. On a more cheerful note, households are spending more now on entertainment, reading, and education than in the past. These changes are summarized in Figure 13.1.

Individual Attitudes Toward Money

Many consumers are experiencing doubts about their individual and collective futures, and they are anxious about holding on to what they have. Although half of the respondents in a survey conducted by Roper/Starch Worldwide said they don't believe money can buy happiness, nearly 70 percent still report that if their earnings doubled they would be happier than they are now![5] The Roper/Starch survey found that by far security was the attribute most closely linked to the meaning of money. Other significant associations included comfort, being able to help one's children, freedom, and pleasure. The researchers identified seven distinct types of money personalities that are summarized in Table 13.1.

A consumer's anxieties about money are not necessarily related to how much he or she actually has: Acquiring and managing money is more a state of mind than of wallet. For example, we all know people who are "tightwads" with their money and others whose cash seems to burn a hole in their wallets until they part with it. In recent years being frugal has become a passion for some people, who consider it a point of honor not to pay more than they have to for anything. There is even a publication called *The Tightwad Gazette* that offers its readers advice on buying in bulk, buying used goods, reusing products, and even timing showers to save on water bills.[6]

Money has a variety of complex psychological meanings; it can be equated with success or failure, social acceptability, security, love, or freedom.[7] There are even therapists who specialize in treating money-related disorders, and they report that some people even feel guilty about their success and deliberately make bad investments to reduce this feeling! Some other clinical conditions include *atephobia* (fear of being ruined), *harpaxophiba* (fear of becoming a victim of robbers), *peniaphobia* (fear of poverty), and *aurophobia* (fear of gold).[8]

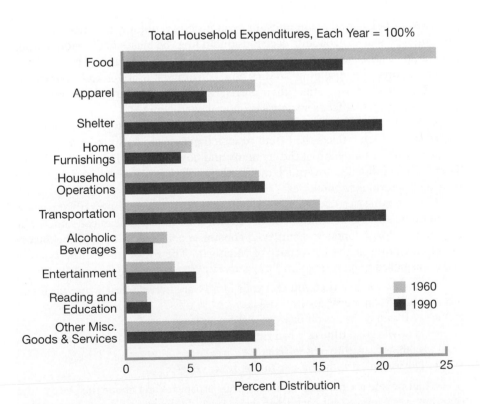

Figure 13.1
The Changing Household Budget

TABLE 13.1 Money Personalities

	Types						
	The Hunter	The Gatherer	The Protector	The Splurger	The Striver	The Nester	The Idealist
Percent of population	13	19	16	14	13	14	10
Mean income	$44,000	$35,000	$36,000	$33,000	$29,000	$31,000	$30,000
Exemplar	Bill Gates (CEO, Microsoft)	Warren Buffet (Nebraska-based Investor)	Paul Newman (actor and entrepreneur)	Elizabeth Taylor (movie star)	Tonya Harding (disgraced figure skater)	Roseanne (comedienne/ actress)	Allen Ginsberg (deceased poet)
Profile	Takes risks to get ahead	Is better safe than sorry	Puts others first	Travels first class or not at all	Is controlled by money	Needs just enough to take care of self	Believe there's more to life than money
Characteristics	Is aggressive and equates money with happiness and achievement; is likely to have unstable personal life	Is a conservative investor with traditional values; tends to be thrifty and tries to minimize borrowing	Believes money is a means of protecting loved ones; tend to be predominantly women; is most likely married	Is self-indulgent; prefers to buy luxury items rather than practical items; is self-centered and not a good planner	Believes money makes the world go round; equates money with power; tends not to be well educated and most likely is divorced	Is not very interested in money; is mostly concerned about meeting immediate needs	Mostly believes that money is the root of all evil; is not very interested in material things

SOURCE: Adapted from Robert Sullivan, "Americans and Their Money" *Worth* (June 1994): 60, based on a survey of approximately 2,000 American consumers conducted by Roper/Starch Worldwide. Reprinted by permission of *Worth* magazine.

Consumer Confidence

The field of **behavioral economics,** or economic psychology, is concerned with the "human" side of economic decisions (including the biases in decision making we examined in Chapter 9). Beginning with the pioneering work of psychologist George Katona, this discipline studies how consumers' motives and their expectations about the future affect their current spending, and how these individual decisions add up to affect a society's economic well-being.[9]

Consumers' beliefs about what the future holds is an indicator of **consumer confidence,** which reflects the extent to which people are optimistic or pessimistic about the future health of the economy and how they will fare down the road. These beliefs influence how much money they will pump into the economy when making discretionary purchases.

Many businesses take forecasts about anticipated spending very seriously, and periodic surveys attempt to "take the pulse" of the American consumer. The Conference Board conducts a survey of consumer confidence, as does the Survey Research Center at the University of Michigan. The following are the types of questions posed to consumers in these surveys:[10]

- Would you say that you and your family are better off or worse off financially than a year ago?
- Will you be better off or worse off a year from now?
- Is now a good time or a bad time for people to buy major household items, such as furniture or a refrigerator?
- Do you plan to buy a car in the next year?

When people are pessimistic about their prospects and about the state of the economy, they tend to cut back their spending and take on less debt. On the other hand, when they are optimistic about the future, they tend to reduce the amount they save, take on more debt, and buy discretionary items. Thus the overall savings rate is influenced by: (1) individual consumers' pessimism or optimism about their personal circumstances such as a sudden increase in personal wealth after buying a high-tech stock; (2) world events such as the severe economic recession that hit Asia a few years ago, and; (3) cultural differences in attitudes toward saving (e.g., the Japanese have a much higher savings rate than do Americans).[11]

SOCIAL CLASS

All societies can be roughly divided into the "haves" and the "have-nots" (though sometimes having is a question of degree). The United States is a place where "all men are created equal," but even so some people seem to be "more equal than others." As Phil's encounter with the Caldwells suggests, a consumer's standing in society—his **social class**—is determined by a complex set of variables, including income, family background, and occupation.

The place one occupies in the social structure is an important determinant not only of *how much* money is spent. This also influences *how* it is spent. Phil was surprised that the Caldwells, who clearly had a lot of money, did not seem to flaunt it. This understated way of living is a hallmark of so-called "old money." People who have had it for a long time don't need to prove they've got it. In contrast, consumers who are relative newcomers to affluence might allocate the same amount of money very differently.

A Universal Pecking Order

In many animal species, a social organization is developed whereby the most assertive or aggressive animals exert control over the others and have the first pick of food, living space, and even mating partners. Chickens, for example, develop a clearly defined *dominance–submission hierarchy*. Within this hierarchy, each hen has a position in which she is submissive to all of the hens above her and dominates all of the ones below her (hence, the origin of the term *pecking order*).[12]

People are not much different. They also develop a pecking order in which they are ranked in terms of their relative standing in society. This standing determines their access to such resources as education, housing, and consumer goods. People try to improve their ranking by moving up in the social order whenever possible. This desire to improve one's lot in life, and often to let others know that one has done so, is at the core of many marketing strategies.

Social Class Affects Access to Resources

Just as marketers try to carve society into groups for segmentation purposes, sociologists have developed ways to describe meaningful divisions of society in terms of people's relative social and economic resources. Some of these divisions involve political power, whereas others revolve around purely economic distinctions. Karl Marx, the nineteenth-century economic theorist, felt that position in a society was determined by one's relationship to the *means of production*. Some people (the haves) control resources, and they use the labor of others to preserve their privileged positions. The have-nots lack control and depend on their own labor for survival, so these people have the most to gain by changing the system. Distinctions among people that entitle some to more than others are perpetuated by those who will benefit by doing so.[13] The German sociologist Max Weber

(1864–1920) showed that the rankings people develop are not one-dimensional. Some involve prestige or "social honor" (he called these *status groups*), some rankings focus on power (or *party*), and some revolve around wealth and property (*class*).[14]

Social Class Affects Taste and Lifestyles

The term social class is now used more generally to describe the overall rank of people in a society. People who are grouped within the same social class are approximately equal in terms of their social standing in the community. They work in roughly similar occupations, and they tend to have similar lifestyles by virtue of their income levels and common tastes. These people tend to socialize with one another and share many ideas and values regarding the way life should be lived.[17]

Social class is as much a state of being as it is of having: As Phil saw, class is also a matter of what one *does* with one's money and how one defines his or her role in society. Although people may not like the idea that some members of society are better off or "different" from others, most consumers do acknowledge the existence of different classes and the effect of class membership on consumption. As one wealthy woman observed when asked to define social class,

> *I would suppose social class means where you went to school and how far. Your intelligence. Where you live. . . . Where you send your children to school. The hobbies you have. Skiing, for example, is higher than the snowmobile. . . . It can't be [just] money, because nobody ever knows that about you for sure.*[18]

Social Stratification

In school, it always seems that some kids get all the breaks. They have access to many resources, such as special privileges, fancy cars, large allowances, or dates with other popular classmates. At work, some people are put on the fast track and are promoted to high-prestige jobs, given higher salaries, and perhaps perks such as a parking space, a large office, or the keys to the executive washroom.

In virtually every context, some people seem to be ranked higher than others. Patterns of social arrangements evolve whereby some members get more resources than others by virtue of their relative standing, power, and/or control in the group.[19] The phenomenon of **social stratification** refers to this creation of artificial divisions in a society: "those processes in a social system by which scarce and valuable resources are distributed unequally to status positions that become more or less permanently ranked in terms of the share of valuable resources each receives."[20]

Achieved Versus Ascribed Status

If you think back to groups you've belonged to, both large and small, you'll probably agree that in many instances some members seem to get more than their fair share of goodies, whereas other individuals are not so lucky. Some of these resources may have gone to people who earned them through hard work or diligent study. This allocation is due to *achieved status*. Other rewards may have been obtained because the person was lucky enough to be born rich or beautiful. Such good fortune reflects *ascribed status*.

Whether rewards go to the "best and the brightest" or to someone who happens to be related to the boss, allocations are rarely equal within a social group.

MARKETING OPPORTUNITY

AS THE OLD SAYING goes, "The rich get richer, and the poor get poorer." Both the top and bottom ends of American income levels are swelling. Since 1980 the wealthiest fifth of the population has increased income by 21 percent, while wages for the bottom 60 percent have stagnated or dipped. America's most powerful brands, from Levi's jeans to Ivory soap, were built on a mass marketing premise, but now that's changing. Stores such as Wal-Mart and Tiffany are reporting big earnings, whereas middle-class outlets such as JCPenney have weak sales. The positioning strategy as chic discount is very successful. Target's bright red bull's eye logo has become a fashion statement for affordable chic.[15] Referred to as "tar-jay" by its many fans, it is a Kmart for yuppies.

This trend has led some companies to try to have their cake and eat it too by developing a two-tiered marketing strategy in which separate plans are crafted for upscale and downscale consumers. For example, Walt Disney's Winnie the Pooh can be purchased as an original line-drawn figure on fine china or on pewter spoons in upscale specialty and department stores, whereas a plump cartoonlike Pooh is available on plastic key chains and polyester bed sheets at Wal-Mart. Gap is remodeling its Banana Republic stores to make them more upscale and simultaneously developing its Old Navy stores for the low end.[16]

Most groups exhibit a structure, or **status hierarchy,** in which some members are somehow better off than others. They may have more authority or power, or they are simply better liked or respected.

Class Structure in the United States

The United States supposedly does not have a rigid, objectively defined class system. Nevertheless, America has tended to maintain a stable class structure in terms of income distribution. Unlike other countries, however, what *does* change are the groups (ethnic, racial, and religious) that have occupied different positions within this structure at different times.[21] The most influential and earliest attempt to describe American class structure was proposed by W. Lloyd Warner in 1941. Warner identified six social classes:[22]

1. Upper Upper
2. Lower Upper
3. Upper Middle
4. Lower Middle
5. Upper Lower
6. Lower Lower

Note that these classifications imply (in ascending order) some judgment of desirability in terms of access to resources such as money, education, and luxury goods. Variations on this system have been proposed over the years, but these six levels summarize fairly well the way social scientists think about class. Figure 13.2 provides one view of the American status structure.

Class Structure Around the World

Every society has some type of hierarchical class structure, which determines people's access to products and services. Of course, the specific "markers" of success depend on what is valued in each culture. For the Chinese, who are just beginning

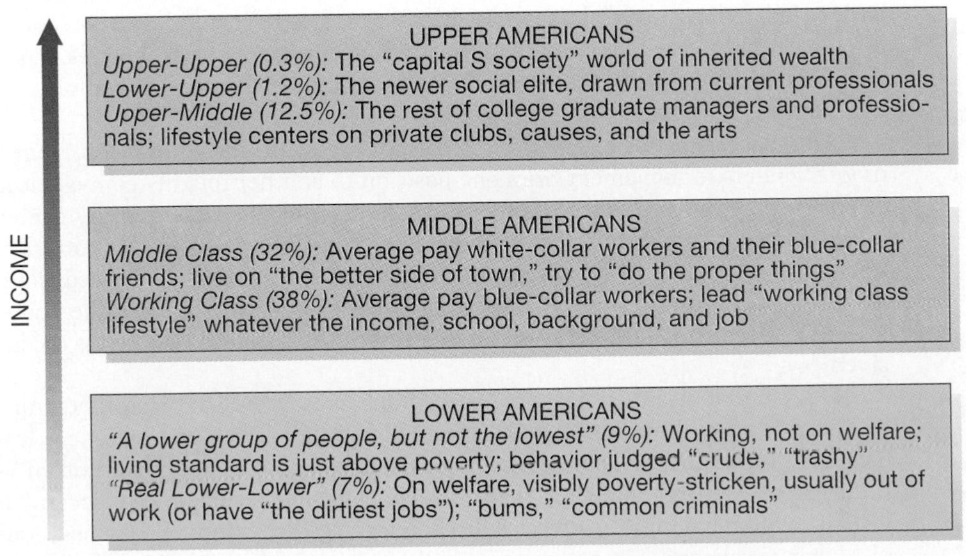

Figure 13.2
A Contemporary View of the American Class Structure

INCOME

UPPER AMERICANS
Upper-Upper (0.3%): The "capital S society" world of inherited wealth
Lower-Upper (1.2%): The newer social elite, drawn from current professionals
Upper-Middle (12.5%): The rest of college graduate managers and professionals; lifestyle centers on private clubs, causes, and the arts

MIDDLE AMERICANS
Middle Class (32%): Average pay white-collar workers and their blue-collar friends; live on "the better side of town," try to "do the proper things"
Working Class (38%): Average pay blue-collar workers; lead "working class lifestyle" whatever the income, school, background, and job

LOWER AMERICANS
"A lower group of people, but not the lowest" (9%): Working, not on welfare; living standard is just above poverty; behavior judged "crude," "trashy"
"Real Lower-Lower" (7%): On welfare, visibly poverty-stricken, usually out of work (or have "the dirtiest jobs"); "bums," "common criminals"

to experience the bounties of capitalism, for example, one marker of success is hiring a bodyguard to protect oneself and one's newly acquired possessions![23]

Japan is a highly status-conscious society in which upscale, designer labels are quite popular, and new forms of status are always being sought. To the Japanese, a traditional rock garden, formerly a vehicle for leisure and tranquillity, has become a sought-after item. Possession of a rock garden implies inherited wealth, because traditionally aristocrats were patrons of the arts. In addition, considerable assets are needed to afford the required land in a country in which real estate is extraordinarily costly. The scarcity of land also helps to explain why the Japanese are fanatic golfers: Because a golf course takes up so much space, membership in a golf club is extremely expensive.[24]

On the other side of the world, there is always Britain: Britain is also an extremely class-conscious country, and at least until recently, consumption patterns were preordained in terms of one's inherited position and family background. Members of the upper class were educated at schools such as Eton and Oxford and spoke like Henry Higgins in *My Fair Lady*. Remnants of this rigid class structure can still be found. "Hooray Henrys" (wealthy young men) play polo at Windsor and hereditary peers still dominate the House of Lords.

The dominance of inherited wealth appears to be fading in Britain's traditionally aristocratic society. According to a survey, 86 of the 200 wealthiest people in England made their money the old-fashioned way: They earned it. Even the sanctity of the Royal Family, which epitomizes the aristocracy, has been diluted through tabloid exposure and the antics of younger family members who have been transformed into celebrities more like rock stars than royalty. As one observer put it, "the royal family has gone down-market . . . to the point that it sometimes resembles soap opera as much as grand opera."[26] In the wake of the return to power of the Labour Party, with Tony Blair as prime minister, and following the harsh criticism of the royal family following Princess Diana's death, there are changes afoot. Whether the changes heralding a "New Britain" will be more substance than form remains to be seen.

Social Mobility

To what degree do people tend to change their social classes? In some societies, such as India, one's social class is very difficult to change, but America is reported to be a country in which "any man (or woman?) can grow up to be president." **Social mobility** refers to the "passage of individuals from one social class to another."[27]

This passage can be upward, downward, or even horizontal. *Horizontal mobility* refers to movement from one position to another roughly equivalent in social status, for instance becoming a nurse instead of an elementary school teacher. *Downward mobility* is, of course, not very desirable, but this pattern is unfortunately quite evident in recent years as farmers and other displaced workers have been forced to go on welfare rolls or have joined the ranks of the homeless. A conservative estimate is that two million Americans are homeless on any given day.[28]

Despite that discouraging trend, demographics in fact decree that there must be *upward mobility* in our society. The middle and upper classes reproduce less (i.e., have fewer children per family) than the lower classes (an effect known as *differential fertility*), and they tend to restrict family size below replacement level (i.e., often having only one child). Therefore, so the reasoning goes, positions of higher status over time must be filled by those of lower status.[29] Overall,

NET PROFIT

MANY HIGH-END MERCHANTS ARE hesitant to sell their wares on the Web. One reason for their reluctance is the importance of exclusivity. If just anyone can buy a luxury item, they fear the snob appeal of the brand name might lose some of its cachet. On the other hand, the average Web user has twice the income of the average American. So, a few high-end retailers are dipping a toe into the waters of e-commerce. Some luxury sites like Bestselections.com and Styleclick.com serve as portals for a number of upscale retailers. Styleclick says that 35 percent of purchases on its site are $500 or more. Luxuryfinder.com is so high-end that it refuses to carry a brand such as Coach leather because those products are too low-end! This site provides services for its well-heeled clientele including a calendar of society events.[25] As the old saying goes, if you have to ask how much it costs you can't afford it.

though, the offspring of blue-collar consumers tend also to be blue-collar, whereas the offspring of white-collar consumers also tend to wind up as white-collars.[30] People tend to improve their positions over time, but these increases are not usually dramatic enough to catapult them from one social class to another.

Components of Social Class

When we think about a person's social class, there are a number of pieces of information we may consider. Two major ones are occupation and income. A third important factor is educational attainment, which is strongly related to income and occupation.

Occupational Prestige

In a system in which (like it or not) a consumer is defined to a great extent by what he or she does for a living, *occupational prestige* is one way to evaluate the "worth" of people. Hierarchies of occupational prestige tend to be quite stable over time, and they also tend to be similar across different societies. Similarities in occupational prestige have been found in countries as diverse as Brazil, Ghana, Guam, Japan, and Turkey.[31]

A typical ranking includes a variety of professional and business occupations at the top (e.g., CEO of a large corporation, physician, and college professor), whereas jobs hovering near the bottom include shoe shiner, ditch digger, and garbage collector. Because a person's occupation tends to be strongly linked to his or her use of leisure time, allocation of family resources, political orientation, and so on, this variable is often considered to be the single best indicator of social class.

Income

The distribution of wealth is of great interest to social scientists and to marketers because it determines which groups have the greatest buying power and market potential. Wealth is by no means distributed evenly across the classes. The top fifth of the population controls about 75 percent of all assets.[32] As we have seen, income per se is not often a very good indicator of social class because the way money is spent is more telling. Still, people need money to obtain the goods and services that they need to express their tastes, so obviously income is still very important. American consumers are getting both wealthier and older, and these changes will continue to influence consumption preferences.

The Relationship Between Income and Social Class

Although consumers tend to equate money with class, the precise relationship between other aspects of social class and income is not clear and has been the subject of debate among social scientists.[33] The two are by no means synonymous, which is why many people with a lot of money try to use it to upgrade their social class.

One problem is that even if a family increases household income by adding wage earners, each additional job is likely to be of lower status. For example, a homemaker who gets a part-time job is not as likely to get one that is of equal or greater status than the primary wage earner's full-time job. In addition, the extra money earned is often not pooled toward the common good of the family. It is instead used by the individual for his or her own personal spending. More money does not then result in increased status or changes in consumption patterns because it tends to be devoted to buying more of the usual rather than upgrading to higher-status products.[34]

The following general conclusions can be made regarding the relative value of social class (i.e., place of residence, occupation, cultural interests, etc.) versus income in predicting consumers choices of products that are bought for functional reasons versus those bought primarily for symbolic reasons (e.g., to convey a desired impression to others).

- Social class appears to be a better predictor of purchases that have symbolic aspects, but low to moderate prices (e.g., cosmetics, liquor).
- Income is a better predictor of major expenditures that do not have status or symbolic aspects (e.g., major appliances).
- Both social class and income data are needed to predict purchases of expensive, symbolic products (e.g., cars, homes).

Measurement of Social Class

Because social class is a complex concept that depends on a number of factors, it is not surprising that it has proven difficult to measure. Early measures included the Index of Status Characteristics developed in the 1940s and the Index of Social Position developed by August Hollingshead in the 1950s.[35] These indices used various combinations of individual characteristics (e.g., income, type of housing) to arrive at a label of class standing. The accuracy of these composites is still a subject of debate among researchers; one recent study claimed that for segmentation purposes, raw education and income measures work as well as composite status measures.[36] One measurement instrument is shown in Figure 13.3.

American consumers generally have little difficulty placing themselves in either the working class (lower middle class) or middle class. Also, the number who reject the idea that such categories exist is rather small.[37] The proportion of consumers identifying themselves as working class tended to rise until about 1960, but it has been declining since then.

Blue-collar workers with relatively high-prestige jobs still tend to view themselves as working class, even though their income levels may be equivalent to many white-collar workers.[38] This fact reinforces the idea that the labels of "working class" or "middle class" are very subjective. Their meanings say at least as much about self-identity as they do about economic well-being.

Problems with Measures of Social Class

Market researchers were among the first to propose that people from different social classes can be distinguished from each other in important ways. Some of these class distinctions still exist, but others have changed.[39] Unfortunately, many of these measures are badly dated and are not as valid today for a variety of reasons.[40]

One reason is that most measures of social class were designed to accommodate the traditional nuclear family, with a male wage earner in the middle of his career and a female full-time homemaker. Such measures have trouble accounting for two-income families, young singles living alone, or households headed by women that are so prevalent in today's society (see Chapter 12).

Another problem with measuring social class is attributable to the increasing anonymity of our society. Earlier studies relied on the *reputational method*, in which extensive interviewing was done within a community to determine the reputations and backgrounds of individuals (see the discussion of sociometry in Chapter 11). This information, coupled with the tracing of interaction patterns

Figure 13.3

Example of a Computerized Index

Interviewer circles code numbers (for the computer) that in his/her judgment best fit the respondent and family. Interviewer asks for detail on occupation, then makes rating. Interviewer often asks the respondent to describe neighborhood in own words. Interviewer asks respondent to specify income—a card is presented to the respondent showing the eight brackets—and records R's response. If interviewer feels this is overstatement or understatement, a "better judgment" estimate should be given, along with an explanation.

	Respondent	Respondent's Spouse
EDUCATION:		
Grammar school (8 yrs or less)	–1 R's Age	–1 Spouse's Age
Some high school (9 to 11 yrs)	–2	–2
Graduated high school (12 yrs)	–3	–3
Some post high school (business, nursing, technical, 1 yr college)	–4	–4
Two, three years of college—possibly Associate of Arts degree	–5	–5
Graduated four-year college (B.A./B.S.)	–7	–7
Master's or five-year professional degree	–8	–8
Ph.D. or six/seven-year professional degree	–9	–9

OCCUPATION PRESTIGE LEVEL OF HOUSEHOLD HEAD: Interviewer's judgement of how head of household rates in occupational status.

(Respondent's description—asks for previous occupation if retired, or if R. is widow, asks husband's: _____)

Chronically unemployed—"day" laborers, unskilled; on welfare	–0
Steadily employed but in marginal semiskilled jobs; custodians, minimum pay factory help, service workers (gas attendants, etc.)	–1
Average-skill assembly-line workers, bus and truck drivers, police and firefighters, route deliverymen, carpenters, brickmasons	–2
Skilled craftsmen (electricians), small contractors, factory foremen, low-pay salesclerks, office workers, postal employees	–3
Owners of very small firms (2–4 employees), technicians, salespeople, office workers, civil servants with average-level salaries	–4
Middle management, teachers, social workers, lesser professionals	–5
Lesser corporate officials, owners of middle-sized businesses (10–20 employees), moderate-success professionals (dentists, engineers, etc.)	–7
Top corporate executives, "big successes" in the professional world (leading doctors and lawyers), "rich" business owners	–9

AREA OF RESIDENCE: Interviewer's impressions of the immediate neighborhood in terms of its reputation in the eyes of the community.

Slum area: people on relief, common laborers	–1
Strictly working class: not slummy but some very poor housing	–2
Predominantly blue-collar with some office workers	–3
Predominantly white-collar with some well-paid blue-collar	–4
Better white-collar area: not many executives, but hardly any blue-collar either	–5
Excellent area: professionals and well-paid managers	–7
"Wealthy" or "society"-type neighborhood	–9

TOTAL SCORE _____

TOTAL FAMILY INCOME PER YEAR:

Under $5,000	–1	$20,000 to $24,999	–5
$5,000 to $9,999	–2	$25,000 to $34,999	–6
$10,000 to $14,999	–3	$35,000 to $49,999	–7
$15,000 to $19,999	–4	$50,000 and over	–8

Estimated Status _____

(Interviewer's estimate: _____ and explanation _____)

R's MARITAL STATUS: Married ____ Divorced/Separated ____ Widowed ____ Single ____ (CODE: ____)

among people, provided a very comprehensive view of social standing within a community. However, this approach is virtually impossible to implement in most communities today. One compromise is to interview individuals to obtain demographic data and to combine these data with the subjective impressions of the interviewer regarding the person's possessions and standard of living.

An example of this approach appears in Figure 13.3. Note that the accuracy of this questionnaire relies largely on the interviewer's judgment, especially regarding the quality of the respondent's neighborhood. These impressions are in danger of being biased by the interviewer's own circumstances, which may affect his or her standard of comparison. Furthermore, the characteristics are described by highly subjective and relative terms: "Slummy" and "excellent" are not objective measures. These potential problems highlight the need for adequate training of interviewers, as well as for some attempt to cross-validate such data, possibly by employing multiple judges to rate the same area.

One problem with assigning any group of people to a social class is that they may not be equal in their standing on all of the relevant dimensions. A person might come from a low-status ethnic group but have a high-status job, whereas another may live in a fancy part of town but did not finish high school. The concept of **status crystallization** was developed to assess the impact of inconsistency on the self and social behavior.[41] The logic behind this idea is that because the rewards from each part of such an "unbalanced" person's life would be variable and unpredictable, stress would result. People who exhibit such inconsistencies tend to be more receptive to social change than are those whose identities are more firmly rooted.

A related problem occurs when a person's social class standing creates expectations that are not met. Some people find themselves in the not-unhappy position of making more money than is expected of those in their social class. This situation is known as an *overprivileged* condition and is usually defined as an income that is at least 25 to 30 percent greater than the median for one's class.[42] In contrast, *underprivileged* consumers, who earn at least 15 percent less than the median, must often allocate a big chunk of their income toward maintaining the impression that they occupy a certain status.

Lottery winners are examples of consumers who become overprivileged virtually overnight. As attractive as winning is to many people, it has its problems. Consumers with a certain standard of living and level of expectations may have trouble adapting to sudden affluence and engage in flamboyant and irresponsible displays of wealth. Ironically, it is not unusual for lottery winners to report feelings of depression in the months after cashing in. They may have trouble adjusting to an unfamiliar world, and they frequently experience pressure from friends, relatives, and businesspeople to "share the wealth." Although you're free to "phone a friend" on *Who Wants to Be a Millionaire?*, the trouble starts after you win and they don't stop phoning *you*.

The traditional assumption is that husbands define a family's social class, whereas wives must live it. Women achieve their social status through their husbands.[43] Indeed, the evidence indicates that physically attractive women tend to "marry up" (*hierogamy*) in social class to a greater extent than attractive men do. Women trade the resource of sexual appeal, which historically has been one of the few assets they were allowed to possess, for the economic resources of men.[44]

The accuracy of this assumption in today's world must be questioned. Many women now contribute equally to the family's well-being, and they work in positions of comparable or even greater status than their spouses. Employed women tend to average both their own and their husband's positions when estimating their own subjective status.[45] Nevertheless, a prospective spouse's social class is often an important "product attribute" when evaluating alternatives in the interpersonal marketplace (as Phil and Marilyn were to find out).

Problems with Social Class Segmentation: A Summary

Social class remains an important way to categorize consumers. Many marketing strategies do target different social classes. However, marketers have failed to use social class information as effectively as they could for the following reasons:

- They have ignored status inconsistency.
- They have ignored intergenerational mobility.
- They have ignored subjective social class (i.e., the class a consumer identifies with rather than the one he or she objectively belongs to).
- They have ignored consumers' aspirations to change their class standing.
- They have ignored the social status of working wives.

HOW SOCIAL CLASS AFFECTS PURCHASE DECISIONS

Different products and stores are perceived by consumers to be appropriate for certain social classes.[46] Working-class consumers tend to evaluate products in more utilitarian terms such as sturdiness or comfort rather than style or fashionability. They are less likely to experiment with new products or styles, such as modern furniture or colored appliances.[47] In contrast, more affluent people living in the suburbs tend to be concerned about appearance and body image, so they are more avid consumers of diet foods and drinks compared to people in more downscale small towns. These differences mean that the cola market, for example, can be segmented by social class.[48]

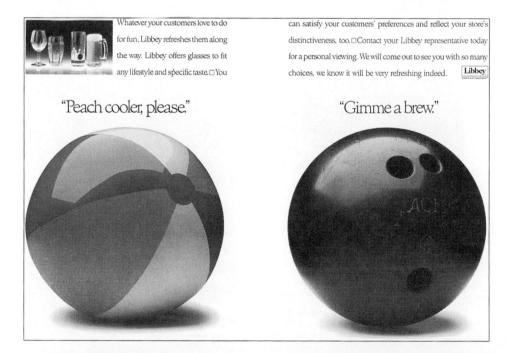

This ad implies that there are social class differences in leisure activities and preferred beverages.

Whatever your customers love to do for fun, Libbey refreshes them along the way. Libbey offers glasses to fit any lifestyle and specific taste. □ You can satisfy your customers' preferences and reflect your store's distinctiveness, too. □ Contact your Libbey representative today for a personal viewing. We will come out to see you with so many choices, we know it will be very refreshing indeed. **Libbey**

"Peach cooler, please."

"Gimme a brew."

Class Differences in Worldview

A major social class difference involves the *worldview* of consumers. The world of the working class (i.e., the lower middle class) is more intimate and constricted. For example, working-class men are likely to name local sports figures as heroes and are less likely to take long vacation trips to out-of-the-way places.[49] Immediate needs, such as a new refrigerator or TV, tend to dictate buying behavior for these consumers, whereas the higher classes tend to focus on more long-term goals, such as saving for college tuition or retirement.[50] Working-class consumers depend heavily on relatives for emotional support and tend to orient themselves in terms of the community rather than the world at large. They are more likely to be conservative and family-oriented. Maintaining the appearance of one's home and property is a priority, regardless of the size of the house.

Although they would like to have more in the way of material goods, working-class people do not necessarily envy those who rank above them in social standing.[51] The maintenance of a high-status lifestyle is sometimes not seen as worth the effort. As one blue-collar consumer commented, "Life is very hectic for those people. There are more breakdowns and alcoholism. It must be very hard to sustain the status, the clothes, and the parties that are expected. I don't think I'd want to take their place."[52]

This person may be right. Although good things appear to go hand in hand with higher status and wealth, the picture is not that clear. The social scientist Émile Durkheim observed that suicide rates are much higher among the wealthy; he wrote in 1897, "The possessors of most comfort suffer most."[53] Durkheim's wisdom may still be accurate today. Many well-off consumers seem to be stressed

This ad for US Magazine *uses a strategy that relies on cultural tastes of consumers in different social classes.*

No killer bees. No monkeys who can drive. No treasure maps found in varicose veins. None of that stuff. US Magazine presents only entertainment news and information; better focused and more comprehensive than People. With 5 million readers per issue and average household incomes above $35,000, our readers aren't just the target, they're the bullseye. **A better class of people.**™

No Manhattan sex slaves.

or unhappy despite or even because of their wealth, a condition sometimes termed *affluenza*.[54] In a *New York Times*/CBS News poll, kids aged 13 to 17 were asked to compare their lives with what their parents experienced growing up. Forty-three percent said they were having a harder time, and upper income teenagers were the most likely to say that their lives were harder and subject to more stress. Apparently, they feel the pressure to get into elite schools and to maintain the family's status.[55]

Taste Cultures, Codes, and Cultural Capital

A **taste culture** differentiates people in terms of their aesthetic and intellectual preferences. This concept helps to illuminate the important yet sometimes subtle distinctions in consumption choices among the social classes.[56] For example, a comprehensive analysis of social class differences using data from 675,000 households suggests that differences in consumption patterns for mass-marketed products have largely disappeared between the upper and upper-middle classes and between the middle and working classes. However, strong differences still

Figure 13.4
Living Room Clusters and Social Class

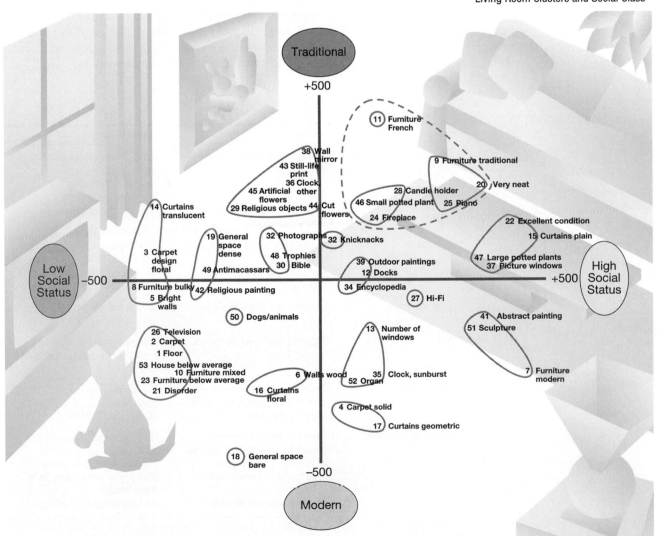

emerge in terms of how consumers spend their discretionary income and leisure time. Upper and upper-middle class people are more likely to visit museums and attend live theater, and middle-class consumers are more likely to go camping and fishing. The upper class are more likely to listen to all-news programs, whereas the middle classes are more likely to tune in country music.[57]

Although analyses based on distinguishing taste cultures have met with criticism due to the implicit value judgments involved, they are valuable because they recognize the existence of groupings based on shared tastes in literature, art, music, leisure activities, and home decoration. In one of the classic studies of social differences in taste, researchers cataloged homeowners' possessions as they were asking them about income and occupation. Clusters of furnishings and decorative items that seemed to appear together with some regularity were identified, and different clusters were found depending on the consumer's social status (see Figure 13.4). For example, religious objects, artificial flowers, and still-life portraits tended to be found together in relatively lower-status living rooms, whereas a cluster containing abstract paintings, sculptures, and modern furniture was more likely to appear in a higher-status home.[58]

Another approach to social class focuses on differences in the types of *codes* (the ways meanings are expressed and interpreted by consumers) used within different social strata. Discovery of these codes is valuable to marketers because this knowledge allows them to communicate to markets using concepts and terms most likely to be understood and appreciated by specific consumers.

TABLE 13.2 Effects of Restricted Versus Elaborated Codes

	Restricted Codes	Elaborated Codes
General characteristics	Emphasize description and contents of objects	Emphasize analysis and interrelationships between objects; i.e., hierarchical organization and instrumental connections
	Have implicit meanings (context dependent)	Have explicit meanings
Language	Use few qualifiers, i.e., few adjectives or adverbs	Have language rich in personal, individual qualifiers
	Use concrete, descriptive, tangible symbolism	Use large vocabulary, complex conceptual hierarchy
Social relationships	Stress attributes of individuals over formal roles	Stress formal role structure, instrumental relationships
Time	Focus on present; have only general notion of future	Focus on instrumental relationship between present activities and future rewards
Physical space	Locate rooms, spaces in context of other rooms and places: e.g., "front room," "corner store"	Identify rooms, spaces in terms of usage; formal ordering of spaces; e.g., "dining room," "financial district"
Implications for marketers	Stress inherent product quality, contents (or trustworthiness, goodness of "real-type"), spokesperson Stress implicit fit of product with total lifestyle Use simple adjectives, descriptors	Stress differences, advantages vis-à-vis other products in terms of some autonomous evaluation criteria Stress product's instrumental ties to distant benefits Use complex adjectives, descriptors

SOURCE: Adapted from Jeffrey F. Durgee, "How Consumer Sub-Cultures Code Reality: A Look at Some Code Types," in Richard J. Lutz, ed., *Advances in Consumer Reasearch* 13 (Provo, UT: Association for Consumer Research, 1986): 332.

The nature of these codes varies among social classes. **Restricted codes** are dominant among the working class, whereas **elaborated codes** tend to be used by the middle and upper classes. Restricted codes focus on the content of objects, not on relationships among objects. Elaborated codes, in contrast, are more complex and depend on a more sophisticated worldview. Some differences between these two general types of codes are provided in Table 13.2. As this table indicates, these code differences extend to the way consumers approach basic concepts such as time, social relationships, and objects.

Marketing appeals constructed with class differences in mind will result in quite different messages. For example, a life insurance ad targeted to a lower-class person might depict in simple, straightforward terms a hard-working family man who feels good immediately after purchasing a policy. A more upscale appeal might depict a more affluent older couple surrounded by photos of their children and grandchildren. It might include extensive copy emphasizing the satisfaction that comes from planning for the future and highlighting the benefits of a whole-life insurance policy.

Clearly, not all taste cultures are created equal. The upper classes have access to resources that enable them to perpetuate their privileged position in society. A French theorist named Pierre Bourdieu has written at length about the process by which people compete for resources, or *capital.* These include *economic capital* (financial resources) and *social capital* (organizational affiliations and networks). The importance of access to social capital is demonstrated by the legions of aspiring professionals who in recent years have taken up golf because so much business is conducted on the greens.

Bourdieu also reminds us of the importance of **cultural capital.** This refers to a set of distinctive and socially rare tastes and practices—knowledge of "refined" behavior that admits a person into the realm of the upper-class.[59] The elites in a society collect a set of skills that enable them to hold positions of power and authority, and they pass these on to their children (think etiquette lessons and debutante balls). These resources gain in value because access to them is restricted. That's part of the reason why people compete so fiercely for admission to elite colleges. Much as we hate to admit it, the rich *are* different.

Targeting the Poor

About 14 percent of Americans live below the poverty line, and this segment has been largely ignored by most marketers. Still, although poor people obviously have less to spend than do rich ones, they have the same basic needs as everyone else. Low-income families purchase staples such as milk, orange juice, and tea at the same rates as average-income families. Minimum wage-level households spend more than average on out-of-pocket health care costs, rent, and food eaten at home.[60] Unfortunately, these resources are harder to obtain due to the reluctance of many businesses to locate in lower-income areas. On average, residents of poor neighborhoods must travel more than two miles to have the same access to supermarkets, large drug stores, and banks as do residents of nonpoor areas.[61] Some businesses have prospered by locating branches in more accessible areas for this large market. For example, Vons Companies, California's largest supermarket operator, is investing $100 million in new stores serving low-income urban areas.[62]

The unemployed do feel alienated in a consumer society because they are unable to obtain many of the items that our culture tells us we "need" to be successful. However, idealized advertising portrayals don't appear to bother low-end consumers who have been interviewed by researchers. Apparently, one way to preserve self-esteem is by placing themselves outside of the culture of consumption and emphasizing the value of a simple way of life with less emphasis on materialism. In some cases, they enjoy the advertising as entertainment without actually yearning for the products; a comment by one 32-year-old British woman is typical, "They're not aimed at me, definitely not. It's fine to look at them, but they're not aimed at me so in the main I just pass over them."[63]

Targeting the Rich

We live in a time in which one can purchase a Pink Splendor Barbie complete with crystal jewelry and a bouffant gown sewn with 24-karat threads.[66] To dress a "living doll," Victoria's Secret offers its Million Dollar Miracle Bra, with more than 100 carats of real diamonds.[67] *Somebody* is buying this stuff.

Many marketers try to target affluent, upscale markets. This practice often makes sense, because these consumers obviously have the resources to expend on costly products (often with higher profit margins). However, it is a mistake to assume that everyone with a high income should be placed into the same market segment. As noted earlier, social class involves more than absolute income. It is also a way of life, and affluent consumers' interests and spending priorities are significantly affected by factors such as where they got their money, how they got it, and how long they have had it.[68]

The number of U.S. millionaires is increasing at roughly 20 times the rate of the population. Many people of diverse backgrounds benefited from the explosive gains of the stock market in the late 1990s, to the point that stereotypes of rich people no longer hold. One study found the typical millionaire is a 57-year-old man who is self-employed, earns a median household income of $131,000, has been married to the same wife for most of his adult life, has children, has never spent more than $399 on a suit or more than $140 for a pair of shoes, and drives a Ford Explorer. Interestingly, many affluent people don't consider themselves to be rich. One tendency noticed by many researchers is that they indulge in luxury goods while pinching pennies on everyday items—buying shoes at Neiman Marcus and deodorant at Wal-Mart, for example.[69]

Old Money

"Old money" families (e.g., the Rockefellers, DuPonts, Fords, etc.) live primarily on inherited funds.[70] One commentator called this group "the class in hiding."[71] Following the Great Depression of the 1930s, monied families became more discreet about exhibiting their wealth, fleeing from mansions such as those found in Manhattan to hideaways in Virginia, Connecticut, and New Jersey.

Merely having wealth is not sufficient to achieve social prominence in these circles. Money must be accompanied by a family history of public service and philanthropy, which is often manifested in tangible markers that enable these donors to achieve a kind of immortality (e.g., Rockefeller University or the Whitney Museum).[72] "Old money" consumers tend to make distinctions among themselves in terms of ancestry and lineage rather than wealth.[73] Old money people (like the Caldwells) are secure in their status. In a sense, they have been trained their whole lives to be rich.

MARKETING PITFALLS

APPROXIMATELY 3.3 MILLION AMERICANS are institutionalized in nursing homes, correctional institutions, and rehabilitation centers. These residents require products that provide escape from boredom, can be traded, and can convey status.[64] Institutionalized consumers are vulnerable in that they face physical constraints on consumption activity, are stigmatized by society, and come disproportionately from lower social classes. They often try to rebuild their identities using goods they obtain from the outside, make themselves, or receive in trades with other inmates or residents. These disadvantaged consumers typically face more limited choices, pay more for comparable goods and services, and have less information on which to make decisions. They often must resort to an underground economy, bartering goods such as cigarettes for sex or drugs.[65]

The Nouveau Riches

Today there are many people—including high-profile billionaires such as Bill Gates, Steve Jobs, and Richard Branson—who can be thought of as "the working wealthy."[74] Others are not quite at that level but are still doing quite well. From 1995 to 1998, the proportion of families with incomes of $50,000 or more rose approximately twenty percent.[75] The Horatio Alger myth, in which a person goes from "rags to riches" through hard work and a bit of luck, is still a powerful force in American society. That's why a commercial showing the actual garage where the two co-founders of Hewlett-Packard first worked strikes a chord in so many.

Although many people do in fact become "self-made millionaires," they often encounter a problem (although not the worst problem one could think of!) after they have become wealthy and change their social status: Consumers who have achieved extreme wealth and have relatively recently become members of upper social classes are known as the *nouveau riches*, a term that is usually used in a derogatory manner to describe newcomers to the world of wealth.

Alas, many nouveau riches are plagued by *status anxiety*. They monitor the cultural environment to ensure that they are doing the "right" thing, wearing the "right" clothes, being seen at the "right" places, using the "right" caterer, and so on.[76] Flamboyant consumption can thus be viewed as a form of symbolic self-completion, whereby the excessive display of symbols thought to denote "class" is used to make up for an internal lack of assurance about the "correct" way to behave.[77]

Advertising directed to this group often plays on these insecurities by empha-sizing the importance of "looking the part." Clever merchandising supplies these consumers with the props necessary to masquerade by playing the role of old money people. For example, ads for *Colonial Homes* magazine feature consumers who "have worked very hard to make it look like they never had to." A housing development near Santa Monica, California epitomizes the demand for ready-made affluent lifestyles. It features completely furnished mansions (complete with linens, dishes, even artwork) and each residence also includes four-car garages, hot tubs, fake boulders doubling as outdoor speaker enclosures, and a built-in computer network. IBM Home Director software controls the lighting and the coffee maker and even phones you anywhere in the world if the tempera-ture gets too high in the wine cellar (don't you just *hate* when that happens?). Buyers choose from one of four different pre-fab lifestyle fantasies: English Country Estate, Tuscan Villa, French Regency, or New York Penthouse.[78] These little gems can be had for as low as $10 million, so don't waste any time putting in your offer!

STATUS SYMBOLS

The "understated" homes described above clearly are meant to showcase their owners' ability to afford them. People have a deep-seated tendency to evaluate themselves, their professional accomplishments and their material well-being relative to others. The popular phrase "keeping up with the Joneses" (in Japan it's "keeping up with the Satos") refers to the comparison between one's standard of living and that of one's neighbors. Many consumers like to feel as if they are special, wealthy, accomplished, even famous. Maybe that explains the success of Tinseltown Studios, a dinner theater in Anaheim, California that lets patrons pretend they are movie stars. Enter the gates, and immediately light bulbs flash

This Jaguar ad uses a blatant appeal to status.

Whether it's a swift horse, a smart hound or an agile car, the English have long known the importance of good breeding.

and autograph seekers close in. Follow the red carpet and watch yourself being interviewed on a giant screen.[79]

However, often it's not enough to have wealth or fame—what matters is that you have more of it than others. A major motivation for the purchase and display of products is not to enjoy them, but rather to let others know that we can afford them. In other words, these products function as **status symbols.** The desire to accumulate these "badges of achievement" is summarized by the popular bumper sticker slogan, "He who dies with the most toys, wins." Status-seeking is a significant source of motivation to procure appropriate products and services that the user hopes will let others know that he or she has "made it."

The quest for status influences both kids and adults, though the symbols we choose to pursue vary as we age. For example, many kids view smoking cigarettes as a status activity because of the numerous movies they've seen that glorify this practice. In one study, ninth graders watched original movie footage with either smoking scenes or control footage with the smoking edited out. Sure enough, when the young viewers saw the actors smoking, this enhanced their perceptions of smokers' social stature and increased their own intent to smoke (the good news: when kids were shown an antismoking advertisement before the film these effects canceled out).[80] Grownups find their own paths to status. Consider the recent trend in men's fashion to weave real gold into clothing. Ties made with 18-karat gold thread are selling for $260. One man spent $9,000 for a black silk tuxedo and a bow tie and cummerbund set flecked with gold thread. Others are buying pinstriped suits from $10 to $20 thousand.[81] Presumably these clothes are dry clean only . . . In any case the moral of the story is that over time the specific products and activities linked to high status will change, but the basic quest for status symbols will always be with us.

Conspicuous Consumption

The motivation to consume for the sake of consuming was first discussed by the social analyst Thorstein Veblen at the turn of the century. Veblen felt that a major role of products was for **invidious distinction**—they are used to inspire envy in others through display of wealth or power.

Veblen coined the term **conspicuous consumption** to refer to people's desire to provide prominent visible evidence of their ability to afford luxury goods. Veblen's work was motivated by the excesses of his time. He wrote in the era of the Robber Barons, where the likes of J. P. Morgan, Henry Clay Frick, and William Vanderbilt were building massive financial empires and flaunting their wealth by throwing lavish parties. Some of these events of excess became legendary, as described in this account:

> There were tales, repeated in the newspapers, of dinners on horseback; of banquets for pet dogs; of hundred-dollar bills folded into guests' dinner napkins; of a hostess who attracted attention by seating a chimpanzee at her table; of centerpieces in which lightly clad living maidens swam in glass tanks, or emerged from huge pies; of parties at which cigars were ceremoniously lighted with flaming banknotes of large denominations.[83]

The Billboard Wife

This flaunting of one's possessions even extended to wives: Veblen criticized the "decorative" role women were often forced to play as they were bestowed with expensive clothes, pretentious homes, and a life of leisure as a way to advertise the wealth of their husbands—a sort of "walking billboard." Fashions such as high-heeled shoes, tight corsets, billowing trains on dresses, and elaborate hairstyles all conspired to ensure that wealthy women could barely move without assistance, much less perform manual labor. Similarly, the Chinese practice of foot-binding prevented women from walking, and they had to be carried from place to place.

The Modern Potlatch

Veblen was inspired by anthropological studies of the Kwakiutl Indians, who lived in the Pacific Northwest. At a ceremony called a *potlatch*, the host showed off his wealth and gave extravagant presents to the guests. The more one gave away, the better one looked to the others. Sometimes, the host would use an even more radical strategy to flaunt his wealth. He would publicly destroy some of his property just to demonstrate how much he had.

This ritual was also used as a social weapon: Because guests were expected to reciprocate, a poorer rival could be humiliated by inviting him to a lavish potlatch. The need to give away as much as the host, even though he could not afford it, would essentially force the hapless guest into bankruptcy. If this practice sounds "primitive," think for a moment about many modern weddings. Parents commonly invest huge sums of money to throw a lavish party and compete with others for the distinction of giving their daughter the "best" or most extravagant wedding, even if they have to save for 20 years to do it.

The Leisure Class

This phenomenon of conspicuous consumption was, for Veblen, most evident among what he termed the *leisure class*, people for whom productive work is taboo. In Marxist terms, such an attitude reflects a desire to link oneself to

MULTICULTURAL DIMENSIONS

IN A LAND WHERE one-child families are the rule, Chinese parents spare few expenses when bringing up baby. They want to show off their pampered child and are eager to surround their "little emperors" with status goods. To meet this need, foreign companies are rushing in, hawking the staples of Western baby care from disposable diapers to Disney crib sheets. These items are expensive luxuries in China, and plenty of families are splurging. Chinese families spend one-third to one-half of their disposable income on their children, according to industry estimates.

The Disney Babies line of T-shirts, rattles, and crib linens—all emblazoned with likenesses of baby Mickey Mouse and other familiar characters—are available in department stores in a dozen or so Chinese cities. These products are true extravagances: A Disney cotton T-shirt, for example, sells for the local equivalent of about $7.25 to $8.45, compared to $1.20 for a Chinese-made shirt. But as a Disney spokesman observed, "New parents are willing to pay the extra. Mickey is portrayed as fun and intelligent in China—characteristics parents want for their children."[82]

REALITY CHECK

STATUS SYMBOLS ARE PRODUCTS THAT ARE valued because they show others how much money or prestige a person has, such as Rolex watches or expensive sports cars. Do you believe that your peer group values status symbols? Why or why not? If yes, what are the products that you think are regarded as status symbols now for consumers your age?

Status symbols of consumers in my age group (20–28) are products such as Tag watches, Prada purses and bags, sports cars such as Mustangs, Saabs, BMWs, and sports utility vehicles. . . . I do believe that my peers value status symbols and think they are better than other people are because they own various material items. . . . I know many people who live beyond their financial means and still own these prestigious items, yet they can barely put food on the table or pay rent.

Jill Wittekind
University of Nevada, Las Vegas

Frequently status symbols . . . reflect a shared preference for lifestyle choices. For example participants in extreme sports such as mountain biking often use their sporting gear as casual clothing, reflecting their choice of activities in their everyday attire. Hence my peer group does still value status symbols, although they are likely to be different for different groups. . . . However some items continue to carry connotations across several groups. The most obvious are our cars. Functionality isn't enough. We need to look cool.

Satish Magan Ranchod
University of Aukland, New Zealand

It appears that every young person is not merely content to appear their own age; they would like to appear older than they actually are. These status symbols allow them a way to achieve that goal. A person in high school would like to appear to be a college student and a college student would like to appear to be in the "real world." Those in college believe that a way that they can appear to be older is by owning possessions that an older person would own. These include a BMW or a Lexus, a house or at the very least, their own apartment. The appearance of independence and stability are sometimes

more important than truly being independent or stable. From a male's opinion, guys tend to want to appear older to attract women. It has been my experience that women prefer older men that are more established or worldlier.

Gregory T. Varveris
DePaul University

In Chile, university students (18–27 years old), usually consume products such as: Cellular telephones: a few years ago, these telephones were a status symbol, but now that it has become a mass product between young people, the status in this product is found on the different and modern models, colors, shapes, uses (internet, MP3).

Fashion clothes . . . Lacoste, Zara, MNG, Polo, Bennetton, Tommy Hilfiger, DKNY, Guess?.

Cars: by the time Chileans turn eighteen, their parents try to buy them the best new car in the market, so they can show their economic status. The most demanded car brands by young people are: Volkswagen Golf, Peugeot 206, Peugeot 306, Rover, Jeep Vitara, Fiat Punto.

Music technology: products such as MP3, mini disks . . .

Digital photograph cameras, with which you can download the photos directly to internet.

Constanza Montes Larranaga
Universidad de Chile

Although many people in my peer group would not admit to this, my peer group is very judgmental of others and their possessions. I think that clothing plays a large part when it comes to judging a person's status. Clothing is one of the first things that people see; therefore, first impressions are sometimes only based on how a person appears to be dressed.

From there, a person's vehicle is the next thing that is looked at. Speaking from experience, I own a minivan because my grandfather gave it to me when he passed away. Every time that someone sees my

minivan, they tease me in some way or the van is given a name such as "The Loaf." . . . To me, a vehicle is one that gets me from point A to point B, but to others it says something about who they are.

Michelle Purintun
University of Wisconsin, LaCrosse

I think that the products related to my peer group are mobile phones (Star Tack), certain types of clothing (such as Zara, Calvin Klein), shoes (Timberland boots, Clarks . . .) and fragrances (CK One, Hugo Boss . . .).

Astrid Spielrein
ASSAS University Paris II, France

The current technological revolution and the expansion of the telecommunications industry provide the ideal breeding ground for status symbols. The mobile communications market is a prime example of this, it is a status symbol to have the latest in mobile technology, the slimmest and lightest mobile phones with WAP (Wireless Application Protocol) technology are very much en vogue. Another strength of this technology is the opportunity for individuality, personalised ring tones, clip on covers and voicemail all service the need to be different. A demonstration of how transitory a status symbol is, is that, after being fashionable amongst teenagers about five years ago, pagers have now all but vanished from the marketplace, as new technology has bypassed them.

James Beattie
University of Exeter, United Kingdom

Cars are always an important status symbol. Expensive, flashy sports cars, or older restored vehicles always turn heads. Other important symbols of status include cell phones, (the smaller the better) designer clothes, such as Tommy Hilfiger, Banana Republic, DKNY, J Crew and Abercrombie and Fitch. More and more, electronic equipment, such as DVD players, CD burners, as well as Palm Pilots and assorted handheld computer devices are signaling status.

Concetta Rini
The College of William and Mary

Ripped jeans (especially the pricey kind that come that way when you buy them) are an example of parody display.

ownership or control of the means of production, rather than to the production itself. Any evidence that one actually has to labor for a living is to be shunned, as suggested by the term the "idle rich."

Like the potlatch ritual, the desire to convince others that one has a surplus of resources creates the need to display evidence of this abundance. Accordingly, priority is given to consumption activities that use up as many resources as possible in nonconstructive pursuits. This *conspicuous waste* in turn shows others that one has the assets to spare. Veblen noted that "we are told of certain Polynesian chiefs, who, under the stress of good form, preferred to starve rather than carry their food to their mouths with their own hands."[84]

Parody Display

As the competition to accumulate status symbols escalates, sometimes the best tactic is to switch gears and go in reverse. One way to do this is to deliberately avoid status symbols—that is, to seek status by mocking it. This sophisticated form of conspicuous consumption has been termed *parody display*.[85] A good example of parody display is the home furnishing style known as High Tech in vogue a few years ago. This motif incorporated the use of industrial equipment (e.g., floors were covered with plates used on the decks of destroyers), and pipes and support beams were deliberately exposed.[86] This decorating strategy is intended to show that one is so witty and "in the know" that status symbols aren't necessary. Hence, the popularity of old, ripped blue jeans, and "utility" vehicles such as Jeeps among the upper classes (like the Caldwells). Thus, "true" status is shown by the adoption of product symbolism that is deliberately not fashionable.

CHAPTER SUMMARY

- The field of behavioral economics considers how consumers decide what to do with their money. In particular, discretionary expenditures are made only when people are able and willing to spend money on items above and beyond their basic needs. Consumer confidence—the state of mind consumers have about their own personal situation, as well as their feelings about their overall economic prospects—helps to determine whether they will purchase goods and services, take on debt, or save their money.

- A consumer's social class refers to his or her standing in society. It is determined by a number of factors, including education, occupation, and income.

- Virtually all groups make distinctions among members in terms of relative superiority, power, and access to valued resources. This social stratification creates a status hierarchy in which some goods are preferred over others and are used to categorize their owners' social class.

- Although income is an important indicator of social class, the relationship is far from perfect. Social class is also determined by factors such as place of residence, cultural interests, and worldview.

- Purchase decisions are sometimes influenced by the desire to "buy up" to a higher social class or to engage in the process of conspicuous consumption, through which one's status is flaunted by the deliberate and nonconstructive use of valuable resources. This spending pattern is a characteristic of the nouveau riches, whose relatively recent acquisition of income, rather than ancestry or breeding, is responsible for their increased social mobility.

- Products often are used as status symbols to communicate real or desired social class. Parody display occurs when consumers seek status by deliberately avoiding fashionable products.

KEY TERMS

behavioral economics, p. 388
conspicuous consumption, p. 405
consumer confidence, p. 388
cultural capital, p. 401
discretionary income, p. 386

elaborated codes, p. 401
invidious distinction, p. 405
restricted codes, p. 401
social class, p. 389
social mobility, p. 392

social stratification, p. 390
status crystallization, p. 396
status hierarchy, p. 391
status symbols, p. 404
taste culture, p. 399

CONSUMER BEHAVIOR CHALLENGE

1. Sears, JCPenney, and, to a lesser degree, Kmart, have made concerted efforts in recent years to upgrade their images and appeal to higher-class consumers. How successful have these efforts been? Do you believe this strategy is wise?

2. What are some of the obstacles to measuring social class in today's society? Discuss some ways to get around these obstacles.

3. What consumption differences might you expect to observe between a family characterized as underprivileged versus one whose income is average for its social class?

4. When is social class likely to be a better predictor of consumer behavior than mere knowledge of a person's income?

5. How do you assign people to social classes, or do you at all? What consumption cues do you use (e.g., clothing, speech, cars, etc.) to determine social standing?

6. Thorstein Veblen argued that women were often used as a vehicle to display their husbands' wealth. Is this argument still valid today?

7. Given present environmental conditions and dwindling resources, what is the future of "conspicuous waste?" Can the desire to impress others with affluence ever be eliminated? If not, can it take on a less dangerous form?

8. Some people argue that status symbols are dead. Do you agree?

9. Using the Status Index presented in Figure 13.3, compute a social class score for people you know, including their parents if possible. Ask several friends (preferably from different places) to compile similar information for people they know. How closely do your answers compare? If you find differences, how can you explain them?

10. Compile a list of occupations and ask a sample of students in a variety of majors (both business and nonbusiness) to rank the prestige of these jobs. Can you detect any differences in these rankings as a function of students' majors?

11. Compile a collection of ads that depict consumers of different social classes. What generalizations can you make about the reality of these ads and about the media in which they appear?

12. The chapter observes that some marketers are finding "greener pastures" by targeting low-income people. How ethical is it to single out consumers who cannot afford to waste their precious resources on discretionary items? Under what circumstances should this segmentation strategy be encouraged or discouraged.

NOTES

1. Data in this section adapted from Fabian Linden, *Consumer Affluence: The Next Wave* (New York: The Conference Board, 1994). For additional information about U.S. income statistics, access Occupational Employment and Wage Estimates at www.bls.gov/oes/oes_data.htm.

2. Sylvia Ann Hewlett, "Feminization of the Workforce," *New Perspectives Quarterly* 98 (July 1, 1998): 66–70.

3. Mary Bowler, "Women's Earnings: An Overview," *Monthly Labor Review* 122 (December 1999): 13–22.

4. Christopher D. Carroll, "How Does Future Income Affect Current Consumption?" *Quarterly Journal of Economics* 109, no. 1 (February 1994): 111–47.

5. Robert Sullivan, "Americans and Their Money," *Worth* (June 1994): 60.

6. For a scale that measures consumer frugality, see John L. Lastovicka, Lance A. Bettencourt, Renee Shaw Hughner, and Ronald J. Kuntze, "Lifestyle of the Tight and Frugal: Theory and Measurement," *Journal of Consumer Research* 26 (June 1999): 85–98.

7. José F. Medina, Joel Saegert, and Alicia Gresham, "Comparison of Mexican-American and Anglo-American Attitudes Toward Money," *The Journal of Consumer Affairs* 30, no. 1 (1996): 124–45.

8. Kirk Johnson, "Sit Down. Breathe Deeply. This Is Really Scary Stuff," *New York Times* (April 16, 1995): F5.

9. Fred van Raaij, "Economic Psychology," *Journal of Economic Psychology* 1 (1981): 1–24.

10. Richard T. Curtin, "Indicators of Consumer Behavior: The University of Michigan Surveys of Consumers," *Public Opinion Quarterly* (1982): 340–52.

11. George Katona, "Consumer Saving Patterns," *Journal of Consumer Research* 1 (June 1974): 1–12.

12. Floyd L. Ruch and Philip G. Zimbardo, *Psychology and Life*, 8th ed. (Glenview, IL: Scott Foresman, 1971).

13. Jonathan H. Turner, *Sociology: Studying the Human System*, 2d ed. (Santa Monica, CA: Goodyear, 1981).

14. Turner, *Sociology*.

15. Keith Naughton, "Hitting the Bull's-Eye," *Newsweek* (October 11, 1999): 64.

16. David Leonhardt, "Two-Tier Marketing," *Business Week* (March 17, 1997): 82.

17. Richard P. Coleman, "The Continuing Significance of Social Class to Marketing," *Journal of Consumer Research* 10 (December 1983): 265–80; Turner, *Sociology*.

18. Quoted by Richard P. Coleman and Lee Rainwater, *Standing in America: New Dimensions of Class* (New York: Basic Books, 1978): 89.

19. Coleman and Rainwater, *Standing in America*.

20. Turner, *Sociology*.

21. James Fallows, "A Talent for Disorder (Class Structure)," *U.S. News & World Report* (February 1, 1988): 83.

22. Coleman, "The Continuing Significance of Social Class to Marketing"; W. Lloyd Warner with Paul S. Lunt, *The Social Life of a Modern Community* (New Haven, CT: Yale University Press, 1941).

23. Nicholas D. Kristof, "Women as Bodyguards: In China, It's All the Rage," *New York Times* (July 1, 1993): A4.

24. James Sterngold, "How Do You Define Status? A New BMW in the Drive. An Old Rock in the Garden," *New York Times* (December 28, 1989): C1.

25. Leslie Kaufman, "Deluxe Dilemma: To Sell Globally or Sell Haughtily?" *The New York Times on the Web* (September 22, 1999).

26. Robin Knight, "Just You Move Over, 'Enry 'Iggins; A New Regard for Profits and Talent Cracks Britain's Old Class System," *U.S. News & World Report* 106 (April 24, 1989): 40.

27. Turner, *Sociology*, p. 260.

28. See Ronald Paul Hill and Mark Stamey, "The Homeless in America: An Examination of Possessions and Consumption Behaviors," *Journal of Consumer Research* 17 (December 1990): 303–21; estimate provided by Dr. Ronald Hill, personal communication, December 1997.

29. Joseph Kahl, *The American Class Structure* (New York: Holt, Rinehart and Winston, 1961).

30. Leonard Beeghley, *Social Stratification in America: A Critical Analysis of Theory and Research* (Santa Monica, CA: Goodyear, 1978).

31. Coleman and Rainwater, *Standing in America*, p. 220.

32. Turner, *Sociology*.

33. See Coleman, "The Continuing Significance of Social Class to Marketing"; Charles M. Schaninger, "Social Class Versus Income Revisited: An Empirical Investigation," *Journal of Marketing Research* 18 (May 1981): 192–208.

34. Coleman, "The Continuing Significance of Social Class to Marketing."

35. August B. Hollingshead and Fredrick C. Redlich, *Social Class and Mental Illness: A Community Study* (New York: Wiley, 1958).

36. John Mager and Lynn R. Kahle, "Is the Whole More Than the Sum of the Parts? Re-evaluating Social Status in Marketing," *Journal of Business Psychology*, 10 (Fall 1995): 3–18.

37. Beeghley, *Social Stratification in America*.

38. R. Vanneman and F. C. Pampel, "The American Perception of Class and Status," *American Sociological Review* 42 (June 1977): 422–37.

39. Donald W. Hendon, Emelda L. Williams, and Douglas E. Huffman, "Social Class System Revisited," *Journal of Business Research* 17 (November 1988): 259.

40. Coleman, "The Continuing Significance of Social Class to Marketing."

41. Gerhard E. Lenski, "Status Crystallization: A Non-Vertical Dimension of Social Status," *American Sociological Review* 19 (August 1954): 405–12.

42. Richard P. Coleman, "The Significance of Social Stratification in Selling," in Martin L. Bell, ed., *Marketing: A Maturing Discipline*, Proceedings of the American Marketing Association 43rd National Conference (Chicago: American Marketing Association, 1960): 171–84.

43. E. Barth and W. Watson, "Questionable Assumptions in the Theory of Social Stratification," *Pacific Sociological Review* 7 (Spring 1964): 10–16.

44. Zick Rubin, "Do American Women Marry Up?" *American Sociological Review* 33 (1968): 750–60.

45. K. U. Ritter and L. L. Hargens, "Occupational Positions and Class Identifications of Married Working Women: A Test of the Asymmetry Hypothesis," *American Journal of Sociology* 80 (January 1975): 934–48.

46. J. Michael Munson and W. Austin Spivey, "Product and Brand-User Stereotypes Among Social Classes: Implications for Advertising Strategy," *Journal of Advertising Research* 21 (August 1981): 37–45.

47. Stuart U. Rich and Subhash C. Jain, "Social Class and Life Cycle as Predictors of Shopping Behavior," *Journal of Marketing Research* 5 (February 1968): 41–49.

48. Thomas W. Osborn, "Analytic Techniques for Opportunity Marketing," *Marketing Communications* (September 1987): 49–63.

49. Coleman, "The Continuing Significance of Social Class to Marketing."

50. Jeffrey F. Durgee, "How Consumer Sub-Cultures Code Reality: A Look at Some Code Types," in Richard J. Lutz, ed., *Advances in Consumer Research* 13 (Provo, UT: Association for Consumer Research, 1986): 332–37.

51. David Halle, *America's Working Man: Work, Home, and Politics Among Blue-Collar Owners* (Chicago: The University of Chicago Press, 1984); David Montgomery, "America's Working Man," *Monthly Review* (1985): 1.

52. Quoted in Coleman and Rainwater, *Standing in America*, p. 139.

53. Quoted in Roger Brown, *Social Psychology* (New York: Free Press, 1965).

54. Kit R. Roane, "Affluenza Strikes Kids," *U.S. News & World Report* (March 20, 2000): 55.

55. Tamar Lewin, "Next to Mom and Dad: It's a Hard Life (or Not)," *The New York Times on the Web* (November 7, 1999).

56. Herbert J. Gans, "Popular Culture in America: Social Problem in a Mass Society or Social Asset in a Pluralist Society?" in Howard S. Becker, ed., *Social Problems: A Modern Approach* (New York: Wiley, 1966).

57. Eugene Sivadas, George Mathew, and David J. Curry, "A Preliminary Examination of the Continuing Significance of Social Class to Marketing: A Geodemographic Replication," *Journal of Consumer Marketing* 41, no. 6 (1997): 463–79.

58. Edward O. Laumann and James S. House, "Living Room Styles and Social Attributes: The Patterning of Material Artifacts in a Modern Urban Community," *Sociology and Social Research* 54 (April 1970): 321–42; see also Stephen S. Bell, Morris B. Holbrook, and Michael R. Solomon, "Combining Esthetic and Social Value to Explain Preferences for Product Styles with the Incorporation of Personality and Ensemble Effects," *Journal of Social Behavior and Personality* 6 (1991): 243–74.

59. Pierre Bourdieu, *Distinction: A Social Critique of the Judgement of Taste* (Cambridge, UK: Cambridge University Press, 1984); see also Douglas B. Holt, "Does Cultural Capital Structure American Consumption?" *Journal of Consumer Research* 1, no. 25 (June 1998): 1–25.

60. Paula Mergenhagen, "What Can Minimum Wage Buy?" *American Demographics* (January 1996): 32–36.

61. Linda F. Alwitt and Thomas D. Donley, "Retail Stores in Poor Urban Neighbor-hoods," *The Journal of Consumer Affairs* 31, no. 1 (1997): 108–27.

62. Susan Chandler, "Data Is Power. Just Ask Fingerhut," *Business Week* (June 3, 1996): 69.

63. Quoted in Richard Elliott, "How Do the Unemployed Maintain Their Identity in a Culture of Consumption?" *European Advances in Consumer Research* 2 (1995): 1–4, p. 3. For a discussion of coping strategies used by impoverished consumers to combat the consequences of limited product availability and restricted income sources see Ronald R. Hill and Debra L. Stephens, "Impoverished Consumer and Consumer Behavior: The Case of the AFDC Mothers," *Journal of Macromarketing*, (Fall 1997): 32–48.

64. Lisa R. Szykman and Ronald Paul Hill, "A Consumer-Behavior Investigation of a Prison Economy," *Research in Consumer Behavior* 6 (1993): 231–60.

65. T. Bettina Cornwell and Terrance G. Gabel, "Out of Sight, Out of Mind: An Exploratory Examination of Institutionalization and Consumption," *Journal of Public Policy & Marketing* 15, no. 2 (Fall 1996): 278–95.

66. Cyndee Miller, "New Line of Barbie Dolls Targets Big, Rich Kids," *Marketing News* (June 17, 1996): 6.

67. Cyndee Miller, "Baubles Are Back," *Marketing News* (April 14, 1997): 1.

68. "Reading the Buyer's Mind," *U.S. News & World Report* (March 16, 1987): 59.

69. Shelly Reese, "The Many Faces of Affluence," *Marketing Tools* (November/December 1997): 44–48.

70. Paul Fussell, *Class: A Guide Through the American Status System* (New York: Summit Books, 1983): 29.

71. Fussell, *Class: A Guide Through the American Status System*, p. 30.

72. Elizabeth C. Hirschman, "Secular Immortality and the American Ideology of Affluence," *Journal of Consumer Research* 17 (June 1990): 31–42.

73. Coleman and Rainwater, *Standing in America*, p. 150.

74. Kerry A. Dolan, "The World's Working Rich," *Forbes* (July 3, 2000): 162.

75. Arthur B. Kennickell, Martha Starr-McCluer, and Brian J. Surette, "Recent Changes in U.S. Family Finances: Results from the 1998 Survey of Consumer Finances," *Federal Reserve Bulletin* (January 2000): 1.

76. Jason DeParle, "Spy Anxiety: The Smart Magazine That Makes Smart People Nervous About Their Standing," *Washingtonian Monthly* (February 1989): 10.

77. For a recent examination of retailing issues related to the need for status, see Jacqueline Kilsheimer Eastman, Leisa Reinecke Flynn, and Ronald E. Goldsmith, "Shopping for Status: The Retail Managerial Implications," *Association of Marketing Theory and Practice* (Spring 1994): 125–30.

78. Jerry Adler and Tara Weingarten, "Mansions Off the Rack," *Newsweek* (February 14, 2000): 60.

79. Debra Goldman, "Paradox of Pleasure," *American Demographics* (May 1999): 50–53.

80. Cornelia Pechmann and Chuan-Fong Shih, "Smoking Scenes in Movies and Antismoking Advertisements Before Movies: Effects on Youth," *Journal of Marketing* 63 (July 1999): 1–13.

81. Susan Carey, "Not All That's Gold Glitters in a $14,000 Pinstriped Suit," *The Wall Street Journal Interactive Edition* (December 13, 1999).

82. Quoted in "Western Companies Compete to Win Business of Chinese Babies," *The Wall Street Journal Interactive Edition* (May 15, 1998).

83. John Brooks, *Showing Off in America* (Boston: Little, Brown, 1981): 13.

84. Thorstein Veblen, *The Theory of the Leisure Class* (1899; reprint, New York: New American Library, 1953): 45.

85. Brooks, *Showing Off in America*.

86. Ibid., p. 31–32.

Maria wakes up early on Saturday morning and braces herself for a long day of errands and chores. As usual, her mother is at work and expects Maria to do the shopping and help prepare dinner for the big family gathering tonight. Of course, her older brother José would never be asked to do the grocery shopping or help out in the kitchen—these are women's jobs.

Family gatherings make a lot of work, and Maria wishes that her mother would use prepared foods once in a while, especially on a Saturday when Maria has an errand or two of her own to do. But no, her mother insists on preparing most of her food from scratch. She rarely uses any convenience products to ensure that the meals she serves are of the highest quality.

Resigned, Maria watches a *telenovela* (soap opera) on Univision while she's getting dressed, and then she heads down to the *carnicería* (small grocery store) to buy a newspaper—there are almost 40 different Spanish newspapers published in her area, and she likes to pick up new ones occasionally. Then Maria buys the grocery items her mother wants; the list is full of well-known brand names that she gets all the time, such as Casera and Goya, so she's able to finish quickly. With any luck, she'll have a few minutes to go to the *mercado* (shopping center) to pick up that new CD by Gloria Trevi that was written up at quepasa.com. She'll listen to it in the kitchen while she chops, peels, and stirs.

Maria smiles to herself: L.A. is a great place to live and what could be better than spending a lively, fun evening with *la familia*.

14

ETHNIC, RACIAL, AND RELIGIOUS SUBCULTURES

SUBCULTURES AND CONSUMER IDENTITY

Yes, Maria lives in Los Angeles, not Mexico City. One in four Californians is Latino. Demographers predict that by 2010 Southern California essentially will be a Latino "subcontinent," culturally distinct from the rest of the United States.[1]

Hispanic Americans have much in common with members of other racial and ethnic groups who live in the United States. They observe the same national holidays, their expenditures are affected by the country's economic health, and they may join together in rooting for Team USA in the Olympics. Nonetheless, American citizenship may provide the raw material for some consumption decisions, but others are profoundly affected by the enormous variations in the social fabric of the United States. The United States truly is a "melting pot" of hundreds of diverse and interesting groups, from Italian and Irish Americans to Mormons and Seventh-Day Adventists. Consider that in some American school systems, including New York City, Chicago, and Los Angeles, more than 100 languages are now spoken![2]

Consumers' lifestyles are affected by group memberships *within* the society-at-large. These groups are known as **subcultures**, whose members share beliefs and common experiences that set them apart from others. Every consumer belongs to many subcultures. These memberships can be based on similarities in age, race or ethnic background, place of residence, or even a strong identification with an activity or art form. Whether "Dead Heads," "Netizens," or skinheads, each group exhibits its own unique set of norms, vocabulary, and product insignias (such as the skulls and roses that signify the Grateful Dead subculture). A recent study of contemporary Mountain Men in the United States illustrates the binding influence of a subculture on its members. Researchers found that

Contemporary Mountain Men share a strong sense of identity and community.

members of this group shared a strong sense of identity, and these ties were reinforced by such items as tipis, buffalo robes, buckskin leggings, and beaded moccasins that created a sense of community among fellow mountain men.[3]

These "communities" can even gel around fictional characters and events. Many devotees of *Star Trek*, for example, immerse themselves in a make-believe world of starships, phasers, and Vulcan neck pinches (sorry to break the news, but no, this show is not real!). Gene Roddenberry, *Star Trek*'s creator, realized early on that people who identify with the show would also value products that identify them as members of this subculture. Sure enough, sales of *Star Trek* merchandise top $1 billion, and approximately three million people attend the more than 3,000 *Star Trek* conventions that are held each year. Some Trekkers have even formed more specialized subcultures within the larger one. One group of fans is devoted to the Klingons, an aggressive warrior race that long battled the Federation. These loyal followers boast their own language (*tlhIngan*, which was created by a linguist for one of the *Star Trek* movies), fan zines, food, and even a summer camp.[4]

ETHNIC AND RACIAL SUBCULTURES

Ethnic and religious identity is a significant component of a consumer's self-concept. An **ethnic subculture** is a self-perpetuating group of consumers who are held together by common cultural or genetic ties, and is identified both by its members and by others as being a distinguishable category.[6]

NET PROFIT

KING FOR A DAY? SURE, the Net allows people to form their own communities—but how about your own nation? Numerous "micronations" exist in cyberspace, some complete with their own monarchs and constitutions. Here's a sampler of these cyber-subcultures:

- www.talossa.com: The King of Talossa lives with his father and sister near the University of Wisconsin—Milwaukee campus. At age 14 (more than 20 years ago), he proclaimed his bedroom a sovereign nation. The name of the country comes from a Finnish word meaning "inside the house." The roughly 60 citizens of Talossa have a body of law, four political parties, an online journal, local holidays, and even a flag. They also have their own lan-

guage and maintain a dictionary with 28,000 entries. The government meets monthly on the Web, and once a year citizens who live near Milwaukee gather in person for TalossaFest. Becoming a citizen is very difficult: You are required to read one online book about the country and purchase at least two of the 16 others for sale on the Web site. Candidates must pass a test on Talossan history, compose an essay titled "What Talossa Means to Me," and be approved by both parliamentary houses. This is for real: Some citizens spend more than 20 hours a week on the Web site, engaging in

political discussions or posting gossip to a bulletin board.[5]

- www.freedonia.org: This micronation is a collective of libertarians based in Boston. Its monarch is a Babson College student who goes by the name of Prince John I. Members have minted their own line of currency, but for now the capital of the country is Prince John's house.
- www.new-utopia.com: This micronation proposes to build a chain of islands in international waters and sells citizenship bonds over the Web for $1,500. The country's founder goes by the name of Prince Lazarus Long. Buyer beware: The Prince does not have the best of diplomatic relations with the Securities Exchange Commission due to these sales.

In some countries, Japan, for instance, ethnicity is almost synonymous with the dominant culture because most citizens claim the same homogenous cultural ties (although even Japan has sizeable minority populations, most notably people of Korean ancestry). In a heterogenous society such as the United States, many different cultures are represented, and consumers may expend great effort to keep their subcultural identification from being submerged into the mainstream of the dominant society.

Marketers cannot ignore the stunning diversity of cultures that are reshaping mainstream society. Ethnic minorities spend more than $600 billion a year on products and services, so firms must devise products and communications strategies tailored to the needs of these subcultures. And this vast market is growing all the time: Immigrants now make up 10 percent of the U.S. population and will account for 13 percent by 2050.[7]

Almost half of all Fortune 1,000 companies have an ethnic marketing program up and running. For example, AT&T sponsors Chinese Dragon Boat Festival races and Cuban folk festivals; it also airs advertisements that are aimed at 30 different cultures, including messages in languages such as Tagalog, spoken by Filipinos, and Twi, a West African dialect. As AT&T's director of multicultural marketing observed, "Marketing today is part anthropology."[8]

Ethnicity and Marketing Strategies

Although some people feel uncomfortable with the notion that people's racial and ethnic differences should be explicitly taken into account when formulating marketing strategies, the reality is that these subcultural memberships are frequently paramount in shaping people's needs and wants. Research indicates, for example, that members of minority groups are more likely to find an advertising

Tex-Mex cusine is popular in Scandinavia. This ad appeared in a Swedish magazine.

spokesperson from their own group to be more trustworthy, and this enhanced credibility in turn translates into more positive brand attitudes.[9] Membership in ethnic subcultures is often predictive of consumer variables such as level and type of media exposure, food and apparel preferences, political behavior, leisure activities, and even willingness to try new products. For example, a diary study of 8,000 respondents that asked people to note how they allocated their time found that African Americans spent the most time on religious activities, Caucasians put in the most hours on housework, and Asian Americans devoted the most time to education.[10]

In addition, the way marketing messages should be structured depends on subcultural differences in how meanings are communicated. Sociologists make a distinction between *high-context cultures* and *low-context cultures*. In a high-context culture, group members tend to be tightly knit, and they are likely to infer meanings that go beyond the spoken word. Symbols and gestures, rather than words, carry much of the weight of the message. Compared to Anglos, many minority cultures are high-context and have strong oral traditions, so perceivers will be more sensitive to nuances in advertisements that go beyond the message copy.[11]

Is Ethnicity a Moving Target?

Although ethnic marketing is in vogue with many firms, the process of actually defining and targeting members of a distinct ethnic group is not always so easy in our "melting pot" society. The popularity of golfer Tiger Woods illuminates the complexity of ethnic identity in the United States. Although Woods has been lauded as an African American role model, in reality he is a model of multiracialism. His mother is Thai, and he also has Caucasian and Indian ancestry. Other popular cultural figures are also multiracial, including actor Keanu Reeves (Hawaiian, Chinese, and Caucasian), singer Mariah Carey (black Venezuelan and white), and Dean Cain of Superman fame (Japanese and Caucasian).[12] Indeed, it is estimated that 70 to 90 percent of people who call themselves African Americans are actually of mixed lineage, and the same is true of many Caucasians.

This trend toward the blurring of ethnic and racial boundaries will only increase over time—the number of married couples of different races or ethnic groups has doubled since 1980. These couples tend to be upscale, well-educated, and young. For example, fully two-thirds of Hispanics with some college education outmarry. Intermarriage rates are highest among people of Asian descent; approximately 12 percent of Asian men and 25 percent of Asian women marry non-Asians.[13] Multicultural households are attractive targets: A study of consumer spending revealed that multicultural households exceeded white households in five categories, including groceries, entertainment, personal care products, clothing, and education. They also outspend whites on more expensive goods, such as cars and homes.[14] Still, portraying mixed couples in advertising is a risky business because there is resentment in some minority communities about people who outmarry. That explains why Philips Electronics decided to focus on a diverse "tribe" of multicultural young people rather than depicting mixed-race couples in its advertising campaign.[15]

Products that are marketed with an ethnic appeal are not necessarily intended for consumption only by the ethnic subculture from which they originate. *De-ethnicitization* refers to the process whereby a product formerly associated with a specific ethnic group is detached from its roots and marketed to other subcultures. This process is illustrated by bagels, a bread product formerly associated with Jewish culture and now mass-marketed. Recent variations include jalapeño bagels, blueberry bagels, and even a green bagel for St. Patrick's Day. A California company even markets tiny bagels as "bagel seeds."[18] Bagels now account for 3 to 6 percent of all American breakfasts, and bagel franchisers such as Bruegger's Corporation and the Einstein/Noah Bagel Corporation are opening hundreds of stores in cities that had never heard of a bagel just a few years ago.[19]

A similar attempt to assimilate ethnic products into mainstream culture is underway by Goya Foods, a major marketer of Hispanic food products. As one company executive noted, "Several food items such as tacos . . . and burritos were once considered the domain of an ethnic group, and now they're mainstream."[20] To underscore this evolution, consider the fact that salsa is now the most popular condiment in the United States, outselling ketchup by $40 million.[21]

The "Big Three" American Subcultures

Three groups that account for much of America's current growth are African Americans, Hispanic Americans, and Asian Americans. The Hispanic population is projected to surpass the black population in the year 2013, at which time there will be 42.1 million Hispanic Americans and 42 million African Americans. The Asian American population, though smaller in absolute numbers, is the fastest-growing racial group. This growth is largely due to immigration; the number of Asian immigrants who arrive in the United States each year is actually greater than the number who are born in the country.[22]

New Ethnic Groups

The dominant American culture has historically exerted pressure on immigrants to divest themselves of their origins and to become absorbed into mainstream society. As President Theodore Roosevelt put it in the early part of the last century, "We welcome the German or the Irishman who becomes an American. We have no use for the German or the Irishman who remains such."[23]

Tiger Woods multiracial background illustrates the complexity of ethnic identity in the United States.

The bulk of American immigrants historically came from Europe, but immigration patterns have shifted dramatically. New immigrants are much more likely to be Asian or Hispanic. As these new waves of immigrants settle in the United States, marketers are attempting to track their consumption patterns and adjust their strategies accordingly. These new arrivals—whether Arabs, Asians, Russians, or people of Caribbean descent—are best marketed to in their native languages. They tend to cluster together geographically, which makes them easy to reach. The local community is the primary source for information and advice, so word of mouth is especially important (see Chapter 11). Figure 14.1 shows how new waves of immigrants are changing the ethnic composition of major American cities.

One striking example is the growing numbers of American consumers who have immigrated from India. This group is relatively affluent and is growing. Many Indian Americans live in urban portions of New York and New Jersey, but the largest number reside in California. The first wave of an immigrant group often consists of relatively well-off people, and that is the case here. In 1990, 30 percent of Indian Americans were employed in professional specialty occupations, compared to 13 percent of the general population. These consumers also own a large number of businesses, partly because family networks allow the businesses to grow—it is common for residents to pool resources and form associations enabling them to buy in bulk and sell at lower prices. This segment places great value on education and financial security, has a very high savings rate, and buys a lot of insurance. A growing number of Indo-American magazines such as *Masala, Onward,* and *Hum* have sprung up to straddle two cultures and appeal to young people.[24]

Ethnic and Racial Stereotypes

A controversial Taco Bell television commercial illustrates how marketers (intentionally or not) use ethnic and racial stereotypes to craft promotional communications. The spot for the restaurant's Wild Burrito featured dark-skinned "natives" with painted faces who danced around in loincloths. Following an uproar in the African American community, the ad was withdrawn.[25]

Many subcultures have powerful stereotypes associated with them. Members of a subgroup are assumed to possess certain traits, even though these assumptions are often erroneous. The same trait can be cast either positively or negatively, depending on the communicator's intentions and biases. For example, the Scottish stereotype in the United States is largely positive, so the supposed frugality of this ethnic group is viewed favorably. Scottish imagery has been used by 3M to denote value (e.g., Scotch tape) and also by a motel chain that offers inexpensive lodging. However, invoking the Scottish "personality" might carry quite different connotations to consumers in Britain or Ireland. One person's "thrifty" is another's "stingy."

Ethnic symbolism has been used in the past by marketers as a shorthand to connote certain product attributes. The images employed were often crude and unflattering. Blacks were depicted as subservient, Mexicans as bandits.[26] As the Civil Rights movement gave more power to minority groups and their rising economic status commanded respect from marketers, these negative stereotypes began to disappear. Frito-Lay responded to protests by the Hispanic community and stopped using the Frito Bandito character in 1971, and Quaker Foods gave Aunt Jemima a makeover in 1989.

MARKETING PITFALLS

AS PEOPLE FROM DIFFERENT racial and ethnic groups intermarry, it is becoming increasingly difficult for the U.S. Census Bureau and other organizations to classify consumers into neat ethnic and racial categories. Federal agencies typically use four broad racial designations—American Indian or Alaskan Native, Asian or Pacific Islander, black, and white. However, many people cannot fit neatly into one of these categories, especially if they come from multiracial families. Other people resent the "mushing together" of many diverse groups under these broad headings. For example, Arab Americans are designated on one part of the census survey as "white, non-European," a category that also includes those of Sudanese, Iranian, and Scandinavian backgrounds. This classification issue has implications for marketers and policy makers because these statistics are used to allocate government funds (and college scholarships!), determine if companies are violating antidiscrimination laws, and allocate marketing budgets for target marketing strategies.[16] The Association for MultiEthnic Americans is one group that fought for changes to the 2000 census, which finally included a multiracial category. The Census Bureau estimates that 1 to 2 percent of Americans will classify themselves as multiracial.[17]

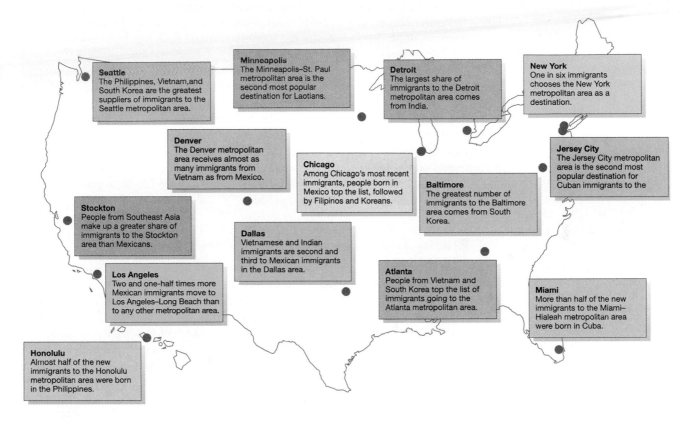

Figure 14.1
America's Newest Markets

The use of subtle (and sometimes not so subtle) ethnic stereotypes in movies illustrates how the media can perpetuate assumptions about ethnic or racial groups. In 1953, the Disney animated feature *Peter Pan* caricatured Native Americans as tomahawk-wielding savages (absurdly led by a blonde, blue-eyed Tiger Lily!), but in the more recent movie *Pocahontas* the company tried to be more sensitive to stereotypes. Still, objections were raised about the historical accuracy of this feature: Disney turned the 12-year-old heroine into a more mature, older character because it was felt that a 12-year-old in love with a 27-year-old man would not be received well by modern audiences.[27] Disney also drew fire from the Arab American community about the movie *Aladdin*, and some controversial lyrics were changed when the movie was released on video.

AFRICAN AMERICANS

African Americans comprise a significant racial subculture and account for 12 percent of the U.S. population. Although black consumers do differ in important ways from whites, the African American market is hardly as homogenous as many marketers seem to believe. Historically, blacks were separated from mainstream society (unfortunately, not by choice). More recently, though, increasing economic success and the many cultural contributions of this group that have been absorbed by mainstream white culture have, in some instances, blurred the lines between American blacks and whites.

Indeed, some commentators have argued that black–white differences are largely illusory. Different consumption behaviors are more likely due to differences in income, the relatively high concentration of African Americans in urban areas, and other dimensions of social class. With some exceptions, the overall spending patterns of blacks and whites are roughly similar. Both blacks and white spend about two-thirds of their incomes on housing, transportation, and food.[29]

Several major magazines, such as *Jet, Ebony, Essence,* and *Black Enterprise,* target this segment exclusively, and with great success. *Jet,* for example, claims to reach more than 90 percent of the black male audience.[30] And a new generation of magazines is springing up to meet the demands of this growing market, including titles such as *The Source, Vibe, Shade,* and *Image.*[31] There are even multicultural romance novels that feature African American heroes and heroines. The basic elements of a romance novel remain, but these books provide numerous references to African American culture, and the heroine is more likely to possess "curly brown locks" than "cascading blond hair."[32]

Black–White Consumption Differences

Nonetheless, there clearly are some differences between blacks and whites in consumption priorities and marketplace behaviors that demand marketers' attention.[33] One reason is the vast market potential of this group: If African Americans comprised a separate nation, their buying power would rank twelfth in Western countries.[34] Because of the growing economic power of this segment, black consumers often represent a fresh opportunity for otherwise saturated markets. Sometimes these differences are subtle but still can be important. When Coffee-Mate discovered that African Americans tend to drink their coffee with sugar and cream much more than Caucasians do, the company mounted a promotional blitz using black media and in return benefited from double-digit increases in sales volume and market share for this segment.[35] Volvo North America created its first advertising campaign targeting African Americans after research showed that car crashes are the leading cause of death among African-American children, who are half as likely to use seat belts as other children.[36]

HISPANIC AMERICANS

The Hispanic subculture is a sleeping giant, a segment that, until recently, was largely ignored by many U.S. marketers. The growth and increasing affluence of this group has now made it impossible to overlook, and Hispanic consumers such as Maria and her family are now diligently courted by major corporations. Marketers especially like the fact that Hispanics tend to be brand-loyal. In one study, about 45 percent reported that they always buy their usual brand, whereas only one in five said they frequently switch brands.[39] Another study found that Hispanics who strongly identify with their ethnic origin are more likely to seek Hispanic vendors, to be loyal to brands used by family and friends, and to be influenced by Hispanic media.[40] This segment is also highly concentrated geographically by country of origin, which makes them relatively easy to reach. More than 50 percent of all Hispanic Americans live in the Los Angeles, New York, Miami, San Antonio, San Francisco, and Chicago metropolitan areas.[41]

Nike made history in 1993 by running the first Spanish-language commercial ever broadcast in prime time on a major American network. The spot, which ran during the All-Star baseball game, featured boys in tattered clothes playing ball in the Dominican Republic, or *La Tierra de Mediocampistas* (the Land of

MARKETING PITFALLS

THE MASS MERCHANDISING OF ethnic products is widespread and growing. Aztec Indian designs appear on sweaters, gym shoes are sold trimmed in kente cloth from an African tribe, and greeting cards bear likenesses of Native American sand paintings. However, many people are concerned about the borrowing—and in some cases, misinterpretation—of distinctive symbolism. Consider, for example, the storm of protest from the international Islamic community over what started as a simple dress design for the House of Chanel. In a fashion show, supermodel Claudia Schiffer wore a strapless evening gown designed by Karl Lagerfeld. The dress included Arabic letters that the designer believed spelled out a love poem. Instead, the message was a verse from the Koran, the Muslim holy book. To add insult to injury, the word "God" happened to appear over the model's right breast. Both the designer and the model received death threats, and the controversy subsided only after the three versions of the dress that had been made (and priced at almost $23,000) were burned.[28] Some industry experts feel that it's acceptable to appropriate symbols from another culture even if the buyer does not know their original meaning. They argue that even in the host society there is often disagreement about these meanings. What do you think?

Shortstops). This title refers to the fact that more than 70 Dominicans have played for major league ball clubs, many of whom started at the shortstop position. This ground-breaking spot also laid bare some of the issues involved in marketing to Hispanics: Many found the commercial condescending (especially the ragged look of the actors), and felt that it promoted the idea that Hispanics don't really want to assimilate into mainstream Anglo culture.[42]

If nothing else, though, this commercial by a large corporation was a wake-up call for many companies. Many are rushing to sign Hispanic celebrities, such as Daisy Fuentes and Rita Moreno, to endorse their products.[43] Others are developing separate Spanish-language campaigns, often with entirely different emphases calculated to appeal to the unique characteristics of this market. For example, the California Milk Processor Board discovered that its hugely successful "Got milk?" campaign was not well received by Hispanics because biting, sarcastic humor is not part of the Hispanic culture. In addition, the notion of milk deprivation is not funny to the Hispanic homemaker because running out of milk means she has failed her family. To make matters worse, "Got milk?" translates as "Are you lactating?", so Spanish-language versions were tailored to Latino moms by saying instead, "And you, have you given them enough milk today?" with tender scenes centered around cooking flan in the family kitchen.[44]

One of the most notable characteristics of the Hispanic market is its youth: The median age of Hispanic Americans is 23.6, compared with the U.S. average of 32. Many of these consumers are "young biculturals" who bounce back and forth between hip-hop and Rock en Espanol, blend Mexican rice with spaghetti sauce, and spread peanut butter and jelly on tortillas.[45] Latino youth are changing mainstream culture. By the year 2020, the U.S. Census Bureau estimates that the number of Hispanic teens will grow by 62 percent compared with 10 percent growth in teens overall. They are looking for spirituality, stronger family ties, and more color in their lives—three hallmarks of Latino culture. Music crossovers are leading the trend, including pop idol Ricky Martin and Big Pun, the first Latino hip-hop artist to go platinum. In fashion, they are popularizing guayabera shirts that were once popular with old Cuban men and baseball shirts with the number 77—the former area code for Puerto Rico.[46] In recognition of this growing market, music retailer Wherehouse Entertainment opened a separate division called Tu Musica (Your Music).[47] Packaged goods companies are also doing more to grab a share of the Hispanic youth market. For example, Frito-Lay discovered that Hispanics are only half as likely to eat salty snacks than the general market, so it looked for a way to appeal to this growing segment. In focus groups, young Hispanics said that Frito-Lay products tasted too mild and they wanted bolder flavors. This research led to the development of new products to capture these consumers, such as Frito's Flamin' Hot Sabrositos.[48]

A second notable characteristic of this market is that family size tends to be large. The average Hispanic household contains 3.5 people, compared to only 2.7 for other U.S. households. These differences obviously affect the overall allocation of income to various product categories. For example, Hispanic households spend 15 to 20 percent more of their disposable income than the national average on groceries.[53] That helps to explain why General Mills developed a breakfast cereal called Buñuelitos specifically for this market. The brand name is an adaptation of *buñuelos,* a traditional Mexican pastry served on holidays.[54]

The importance of the family to Hispanics like Maria cannot be overstated. Preferences to spend time with family influence the structure of many consumption activities. As one illustration, the act of going to the movies has a different

MARKETING PITFALLS

R. J. REYNOLDS TOBACCO IGNITED a lot of controversy when it announced plans to test-market a menthol cigarette, called Uptown, specifically to black consumers in the Philadelphia area. Although the marketing of cigarettes to minorities is not a novel tactic, it was the first time a company explicitly acknowledged the strategy. Many critics attacked the proposal, arguing that the campaign would exploit poor blacks—especially as black people suffer from a higher incidence of tobacco-related diseases than any other group. For its part, Reynolds claimed that its actions were a natural result of shrinking markets and the need to more finely target increasingly small segments. Unlike other ethnic groups that do not seem to display marked cigarette preferences, the tastes of African American consumers are easy to pinpoint. According to Reynolds, 69 percent of black consumers prefer menthol, more than twice the rate of smokers overall. After market research indicated that blacks tend to open cigarette packs from the bottom, the company decided to pack Uptowns with the filters facing down. Following a storm of criticism by both private health groups and government officials (including the Secretary of Health and Human Services), the company announced that it was canceling its test-marketing plans.[37] But the story's not over: In 1999 Philip Morris announced plans to test yet another new menthol cigarette, Marlboro Mild, in order to break into the minority-dominated menthol market now dominated by Lorillard's Newport.[38]

meaning for many Hispanics, who tend to regard this activity as a family outing. One study found that 42 percent of Hispanic moviegoers attend in groups of three or more, as compared with only 28 percent of Anglo consumers.[55]

Behaviors that underscore one's ability to provide well for the family are reinforced in this subculture. Clothing one's children well is regarded in particular as a matter of pride. In contrast, convenience and a product's ability to save time is not terribly important to the Hispanic homemaker. Women like Maria's mother are willing to purchase labor-intensive products if it means that their families will benefit. For this reason, a time-saving appeal short-circuited for Quaker Foods, which found that Hispanic women tend to cook Instant Quaker Oats on the stove as if it were regular oatmeal, refrigerate it, and serve it later as a pudding.[56] Similarly, telephone company promotions that emphasize cheaper rates for calling family members would offend many Hispanic consumers, who would view deterring a phone call home just to save money as an insult![57] This orientation also explains why generic products do not tend to do well in the Hispanic market; these consumers value the quality promised by well-known brand names.

Appealing to Hispanic Subcultures

As with other large subcultural groups, marketers are discovering that the Hispanic market is not homogenous. Subcultural identity is not as much with being Hispanic as it is with the particular country of origin. Mexican Americans, who make up about 62 percent of all Hispanic Americans, are also the fastest-growing subsegment; their population has grown by 40 percent since 1980. Cuban Americans are by far the wealthiest subsegment, but they also are the smallest Hispanic ethnic group.[58] Many Cuban American families with high educational levels fled Fidel Castro's communist regime in the late 1950s and early 1960s, worked hard for many years to establish themselves, and are now firmly entrenched in the Miami political and economic establishment. Because of this affluence, businesses in South Florida now make an effort to target "YUCAs" (young, upwardly mobile Cuban Americans), especially because the majority of Miami residents are Hispanic American![59]

Marketing Blunders

Many initial efforts to market to Hispanic Americans were, to say the least, counterproductive. Companies bumbled in their efforts to translate advertising adequately or to compose copy that could capture desired nuances. These mistakes do not occur so much anymore as marketers are more sophisticated in dealing with this market and tend to involve Hispanics in advertising production to ensure they are getting it right. The following are some translation mishaps that have slipped through in the past:[60]

- The Perdue slogan, "It takes a tough man to make a tender chicken," was translated as "It takes a sexually excited man to make a chick affectionate."
- Budweiser was promoted as the "queen of beers."
- A burrito was called a *burrada*, which means "big mistake."
- Braniff, promoting its comfortable leather seats, used the headline, *Sentado en cuero*, which was interpreted as "Sit naked."
- Coors beer's slogan to "get loose with Coors" appeared in Spanish as "get the runs with Coors."

NET 100 **PROFIT**

PUBLIC POLICY EXPERTS WORRY that ethnic minorities will get left behind as the general population continues to go online in record numbers. In fact, Hispanics are narrowing this "digital divide" by buying computers at a rate much greater than that of the general population. A 2000 survey found that 42 percent of the nation's Hispanic households have a computer, which is a 68 percent increase over 1998. These purchases are occurring even though household income is much less than average—experts feel that the kids are pushing their parents not to be left behind.[49] Several Hispanic Web portals are operating, including Quepasa.com, StarMedia.com, ElSitio.com (country-specific content), and Terra.com.[50] Terra Networks, which operates Terra.com, is a Spanish company that is an Internet powerhouse in Europe—even though less than 10 percent of Spaniards are online now. The company is targeting the 550 million Spanish speakers worldwide, including an estimated 31 million in the United States.[51] Univision, the Spanish-speaking network that controls 91 percent of the U.S. Hispanic television market, is also trying to capture a big Web audience.[52]

Understanding Hispanic Identity

Native language and culture are important components of Hispanic identity and self-esteem (about three quarters of Hispanics still speak Spanish at home), and these consumers are very sympathetic to marketing efforts that acknowledge and emphasize the Hispanic cultural heritage.[61] More than 40 percent of Hispanic consumers say they deliberately attempt to buy products that show an interest in the Hispanic consumer, and this number jumps to more than two-thirds for Cuban Americans.[62] Indeed, although a lot of Hispanic food, music, and athletes are crossing over into the mainstream, many Hispanics are starting to go the other direction. Today many younger Hispanics are searching for their roots and rediscovering the value of ethnic identity.[63]

The behavior profile of the Hispanic consumer includes a need for status and a strong sense of pride. A high value is placed on self-expression and familial devotion. Some campaigns have played to Hispanics' fear of rejection and apprehension about loss of control and embarrassment in social situations. Conventional wisdom recommends creating action-oriented advertising and emphasizing a problem-solving atmosphere. Assertive role models who are cast in nonthreatening situations are effective.[64]

Level of Acculturation

One important way to distinguish among members of a subculture is to consider the extent to which they retain a sense of identification with their country of origin. **Acculturation** refers to the process of movement and adaptation to one country's cultural environment by a person from another country.[65]

This factor is especially important when considering the Hispanic market because the degree to which these consumers are integrated into the American way of life varies widely. For instance, about 38 percent of all Hispanics live in barrios, or predominantly Hispanic neighborhoods, which tend to be somewhat insulated from mainstream society.[66] Table 14.1 describes one attempt to segment Hispanic consumers in terms of degree of acculturation.

The acculturation of Hispanic consumers can be understood in terms of the **progressive learning model.** This perspective assumes that people gradually learn a new culture as they increasingly come in contact with it. Thus, we would expect the consumer behavior of Hispanic Americans to be a mixture of practices taken from their original culture and those of the new or *host culture.*[67] Research has generally obtained results that support this pattern when factors such as shopping orientation, the importance placed on various product attributes, media preference, and brand loyalty are examined.[68] When the intensity of ethnic identification is taken into account, consumers who retain a strong ethnic identification differ from their more assimilated counterparts in the following ways:[69]

- They have a more negative attitude toward business in general (probably caused by frustration due to relatively low income levels).
- They are higher users of Spanish-language media.
- They are more brand-loyal.
- They are more likely to prefer brands with prestige labels.
- They are more likely to buy brands specifically advertised to their ethnic group.

MARKETING PITFALLS

WHEREAS MANY CORPORATIONS ARE just now waking up to the potential of the Hispanic market, others that sell harmful products such as junk food, cigarettes, and alcohol discovered these consumers long ago. Critics point to a high concentration of liquor stores and related advertising in Hispanic neighborhoods. Available evidence indicates that Mexican-born men stand a greater chance of dying of cirrhosis of the liver and that Hispanic men are also more likely to die of lung cancer than are Anglos. The smoking rate of fourth- and fifth-grade Hispanic boys is roughly five times that of Anglo boys.[70] In many cities, community action groups and others have begun programs to reverse these trends, but it's an uphill battle.

TABLE 14.1 Segmenting the Hispanic American Subculture by Degree of Acculturation

Segment	Size	Status	Description	Characteristics
Established adapters	17%	Upwardly mobile	Older, U.S. born; assimilated into U.S. culture	Relatively low identification with Hispanic culture
Young strivers	16%	Increasingly important	Younger, born in U.S.; highly motivated to succeed; adaptable to U.S. culture	Movement to reconnect with Hispanic roots
Hopeful loyalists	40%	Largest but shrinking	Working class; attached to traditional values	Slow to adapt to U.S. culture; Spanish is dominant langauge
Recent seekers	27%	Growing	Newest; very conservative with high aspirations	Strongest identification with Hispanic background; little use of non-Hispanic media

SOURCE: Adapted from a report by Yankelovich Clancy Shulman, described in "A Subculture with Very Different Needs," *Adweek* (May 11, 1992): 44. By permission of Yankelovich Partners , Inc.

Acculturation

A study of Mexican immigrants that used the research technique of *ethnography* probed the acculturation as they adapt to life in the United States.[71] Interviews and observations of recent arrivals in natural settings revealed that immigrants feel a lot of ambivalence about their move. On the one hand, they are happy about the improvements in the quality of their lives due to greater job availability and educational opportunities for their children. On the other hand, they report bittersweet feelings about leaving Mexico. They miss their friends, their holidays, their food, and the comfort that comes from living in familiar surroundings.

The nature of the transition process is affected by many factors, as shown in Figure 14.2. Individual differences, such as whether the person speaks English, influence how rocky the adjustment will be. The person's contact with **acculturation agents**—people and institutions that teach the ways of a culture, are also crucial. Some of these agents are aligned with the *culture of origin* (in this case, Mexico), including family, friends, the church, local businesses, and Spanish-language media that keep the consumer in touch with her country of origin. Other agents are associated with the *culture of immigration* (in this case, America), and help the consumer to learn how to navigate in the new environment. These include public schools, English-language media, and government agencies.

As immigrants adapt to their new surroundings, several processes come into play. *Movement* refers to the factors motivating people to physically uproot themselves from one location and go to another. In this case, people leave Mexico due to the scarcity of jobs and the desire to provide a good education for their children. On arrival, immigrants encounter a need for *translation.* This means attempting to master a set of rules for operating in the new environment, whether learning how to decipher a different currency or figuring out

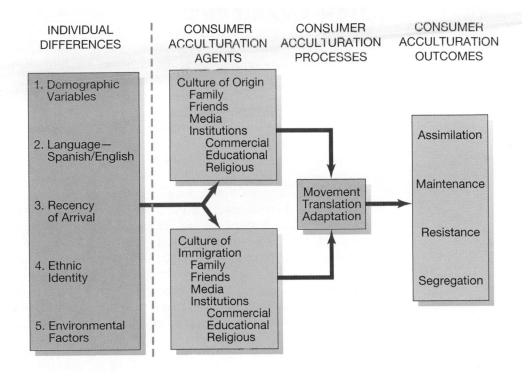

Figure 14.2
A Model of Consumer Acculturation

the social meanings of unfamiliar clothing styles. This cultural learning leads to a process of *adaptation,* by which new consumption patterns are formed. For example, some of the Mexican women interviewed started to wear shorts and pants since settling in the United States, although this practice is frowned upon in Mexico.

During the acculturation process, many immigrants undergo *assimilation,* where they adopt products, habits, and values that are identified with the mainstream culture. At the same time, there is an attempt at *maintenance* of practices associated with the culture of origin. Immigrants stay in touch with people in their country and, like Maria, many continue to eat Spanish foods and read Spanish newspapers. Their continued identification with Mexican culture may cause *resistance,* as they resent the pressure to submerge their Mexican identities and take on new roles. Finally, immigrants (voluntarily or not) tend to exhibit *segregation;* they are likely to live and shop in places that are physically separated from mainstream Anglo consumers.

These processes illustrate that ethnicity is a fluid concept, and the boundaries of a subculture constantly are being recreated. An *ethnic pluralism* perspective argues that ethnic groups differ from the mainstream in varying degrees, and that adaptation to the larger society occurs selectively. Research evidence refutes the idea that assimilation necessarily involves losing identification with the person's original ethnic group. One study found, for example, that many French Canadians show a high level of acculturation, yet still retain a strong ethnic affiliation. The best indicator of ethnic assimilation, these researchers argue, is the extent to which members of an ethnic group have social interactions with members of other groups in comparison to their own.[72]

ASIAN AMERICANS

Although their numbers are still relatively small, Asian Americans are the fastest-growing minority group in the United States. Marketers are just beginning to recognize their potential as a unique market segment, and some are beginning to adapt their products and messages to reach this group. The American advertising industry is spending between $200 million and $300 million to court these consumers.[73] Ford set up a toll-free consumer hotline staffed by operators fluent in three Asian languages, and Sears, Roebuck & Co. holds one-day sales in stores in Asian communities during certain holidays such as the moon festival.[74] WonderBra even launched a special line sized for a slimmer Asian body.[75]

Why all the interest? Asians not only make up the fastest growing population group, but they are generally the most affluent, best educated, and most likely to hold technology jobs of any ethnic subculture. The average household incomes of Asian Americans are more than $2,000 greater than those of Caucasians and $7,000 to $9,000 higher than those of African Americans and Hispanics. These consumers also place a very high priority on education and send a large percentage of their children to college. Of Asian Americans over the age of 25, about a third have completed four or more years of college, twice the graduation rate of whites and more than quadruple that of African Americans and Hispanics.[76]

MARKETING   OPPORTUNITY

REALTORS WHO DO BUSINESS
in areas with a high concentration of Asian American buyers are learning to adapt to some unique cultural traditions. Asians are very sensitive to the design and location of a home, especially as these aspects affect the home's *chi*—an invisible energy current that is believed to bring good or bad luck. Asian home buyers are concerned about whether a prospective house offers a good feng *shui* environment (translated literally as "the wind and the water"). One home developer in San Francisco sold up to 80 percent of its homes to Asian customers after making a few minor design changes, such as reducing the number of "T" intersections in the houses and adding rounded rocks to the garden—harmful *chi* travels in a straight line, whereas gentle *chi* travels on a curved path. It is not unusual for specialists to inspect a home or office to ensure that the *chi* is right before a purchase is transacted.[92]

Segmenting Asian Americans

Asian Americans outspend other ethnic groups in computers, insurance, and international long distance calls.[77] However, earning their business is not always so easy: Asians as a whole do not exhibit much brand loyalty. In one survey of Chinese residents of San Francisco, a third of the respondents could not name the brand of laundry detergent they used.[78] And these consumers also tend to be fairly conservative: Citibank had to drop a New Year's ad targeted to Chinese customers after people complained about the sexual innuendo of corks popping out of champagne bottles![79]

Despite its potential, this group is hard to market to because it actually is composed of subgroups that are culturally diverse and speak many different languages and dialects. The term Asian refers to 20 ethnic groups, with Chinese being the largest and Filipino and Japanese second and third, respectively.[80] Asian Americans still constitute only a small proportion of the population, so mass marketing techniques are often not viable to reach them.[81] Finally, Asian Americans save more of their wages and borrow less, preferring to keep large balances in conservative passbook accounts rather than investing their earnings.

On the other hand, as one Asian American advertising executive noted, "Prosperous Asians tend to be very status-conscious and will spend their money on premium brands, such as BMW and Mercedes-Benz, and the best French cognac and Scotch whiskey."[82] Advertising that features Asian celebrities can be particularly effective. When Reebok used tennis star Michael Chang in one advertisement, shoe sales among Asian Americans soared.[83]

The problems encountered by American marketers when they first tried to reach the Hispanic market also occurred when targeting Asians and Asian Americans. Some attempts to translate advertising messages and concepts into Asian media have backfired. Coca-Cola's slogan, "Coke Adds Life" was translated as "Coke brings your ancestors back from the dead" in Japanese. One company did attempt to run an ad in Chinese to wish the community a Happy New Year, but the characters were upside down.

Other advertisements have overlooked the complex differences among Asian subcultures (e.g., some advertisements targeted to Koreans have used Japanese models), and some have unknowingly been insensitive to cultural practices. Kentucky Fried Chicken, for example, ran into a problem when it described its chicken as "finger-lickin' good" to the Chinese, who don't think licking your fingers is very polite.[84] In another case, a footwear ad depicted Japanese women performing foot binding, a practice done exclusively in China.[85]

Many marketers are discouraged by the lack of media available to reach Asian Americans.[86] Practitioners generally find that advertising in English works best for broadcast ads, whereas print ads are more effective when executed in Asian languages.[87] Filipinos are the only Asians who predominantly speak English among themselves; most Asians prefer media in their own languages.[88] The most frequently spoken languages among Asian Americans are Mandarin Chinese, Korean, Japanese, and Vietnamese.[89] The Bank of America runs commercials in California on Asian language stations, and these efforts have paid off: Asians account for more than 10 percent of the bank's new accounts.[90] And in some cases the large and affluent Asian immigrant population in the United States is creating a new market for Asian products. For example, the Chinese music industry is benefiting from the demand in the Asian American community for the mix of syrupy ballads known as Mandarin Pop. Music idols such as Andy Lau and Jacky Cheung tour the United States, and Chinese record companies are using the Web to build a bigger following overseas. RockaCola.com is one of the largest Chinese music labels in Taiwan and Hong Kong, and another site called YesAsia.com gets 3.2 million hits a month.[91]

RELIGIOUS SUBCULTURES

It seems fair to claim that spirituality is in fashion. For example, the tremendous success of the movie *Titanic* is partly due to its spiritual overtones (yes, Leonardo is good-looking too). Jack is Rose's spiritual guide—he stands for values such as freedom, art, and love—and he gives up his life to save hers. Her immersion in the sea is a kind of baptism, cleansing her of her false self. The popularity of this movie is consistent with the popularity of such books as *The Celestine Prophecy*, movements such as the Promise Keepers, the very high percentage of Americans who believe in angels, and the growth of self-help groups such as Alcoholics Anonymous that proclaim belief in a higher power.[93] American Greetings introduced a Rainbows of Faith line of religious cards, and Hallmark Cards has a similar Morning Light line.[94] When the San Diego Padres baseball team went through a losing streak, a campaign asked fans to "Keep the Faith" and the team resurrected its old mascot, a friar, on its new logo. TV spots introduced the "Gospel of Baseball" and attendance at Padres games has doubled—now there's a miracle![95]

This quest for meaning is influencing mainstream churches as well. They are evolving with the times, and many are adopting an aggressive marketing orientation. In the United States there are approximately 400 *megachurches*, each serving 2,000 or more congregants per week, with a combined annual income of $1.85 billion.[97] Christian bookstores now make less than 40 percent of their sales in books and Bibles, as consumers buy religion-oriented merchandise including apparel (such as a clothing line for born-again Christians called Witness Wear that sells more than $1 million worth of apparel per year), framed art, and

MARKETING   OPPORTUNITY

LESS THAN A THIRD of the six million consumers who buy kosher products are Jewish. Seventh-Day Adventists and Muslims have very similar dietary requirements, and other people simply believe that kosher food is of higher quality. The potential of the kosher market has prompted some of the nation's largest manufacturers to get involved. Wise Potato Chips produces kosher chips, and Eagle Snacks makes kosher snack foods. Of the 330 products made by Pepperidge Farm, 255 are kosher.[102] Manischewitz has launched about 50 new kosher products including fat-free matzo chips, bagel pretzels, and minestrone soup.[103] To attract this broader market, a kosher poultry supplier named Empire ran an ad proclaiming, "Compared to kosher, ordinary chicken doesn't have a chance."[104]

REALITY CHECK

RELIGIOUS SYMBOLISM INCREASINGLY IS BEING USED in advertising, even though some people object to this practice. For example, a French Volkswagen ad for the relaunch of the Golf showed a modern version of the Last Supper with the tag line, "Let us rejoice, my friends, for a new Golf has been born." [96] A group of clergy in France sued the company, and the ad had to be removed from 10,000 billboards. One of the bishops involved in the suit said, "Advertising experts have told us that ads aim for the sacred in order to shock, because using sex does not work any more." Do you agree? Should religion be used to market products? Do you find this strategy effective or offensive? When and where is this appropriate, if at all?

I agree that ads using religious symbols in order to market their product are shocking. I feel that the use of religious symbolism is inappropriate, because religion is sacred and should not be exploited for commercial purposes. I feel that marketing strategies that use religious symbols can be very offensive and should not be used to promote products.

Sara Glenn Rast
Southwest Missouri State University

Growing up in a Catholic family, the beliefs and practices of Catholicism has been engrained into my thought process since the day I was born. Therefore, I feel that it's quite sacrilegious to intertwine religion and advertising. There is no dual meaning behind any type of religion; religion's sole purpose is to provide a means of salvation and worship.

Eric Jude Guacena
Virginia Commonwealth University

I believe that using an advertisement associated with symbolism or religious objects is a very delicate issue, because of the unexpected effects on small religious or ethnic groups. For example, recently in Chile appeared a pharmaceutical shampoo promotion for which was used the image of a guy with dreadlocks just like Bob Marley. The ad showed the phrase "use it brother." Immediately a religious group called "rastafari" reacted saying the advertisement offended directly their lifestyle and beliefs. As a result of this action, the ad was removed and the company incurred great losses.

Constanza Montes Larranaga
Universidad de Chile

I don't really have a problem with religion being used in advertising. If it is not derogatory to God, then I will not be insulted by the advertisements. The ad that was mentioned as an example was not offensive to me but rather creative.

Michelle Purintun
University of Wisconsin-La Crosse

Sacred issues such as religion should not be used as they strike at our core values on an intimate level. The advertisers are therefore penetrating to a very deep personal level with no "right of entry" permit (usually earned through close personal relationship for sacred issues/beliefs). This strategy certainly does shock the audience however it will in the greater majority of cases offend. This offence will be in most cases taken as a personal intrusion into core values and beliefs and will be rejected hence the product will be tagged with the feelings and emotions evoked by the advertisement.

Michael Vernon Hollet
Edith Cowan University, Australia

Whether the marketing campaign is effective or offensive depends upon the ethnic, racial or religious subcultures portrayed. If those portrayed are part of a minority group then the campaign could be widely perceived as distasteful victimisation. The appropriateness of religious marketing campaigns depends upon the market in which they are being deployed. In countries where the predominant religion is losing its cohesiveness and social power, it is more acceptable to make this religion the butt of a joke. However in countries with a more stable religious structure (Italy, Greece) this may be deemed less acceptable. How appropriate an advertising campaign is will unfortunately rarely be measured in terms of how shocking or offensive it is, but more simply in terms of the sales it generates.

James Beattie
University of Exeter, United Kingdom

I do not believe religion should be used to market products, even when that product is religion itself. While many people found the VW ads offensive, I am offended by many of the ads a church in my town posts on its sign. Every week or so the message is changed, but every year around the beginning of May this message appear, "Happy Mother's Day Mom! Thanks for not having an abortion." While the VW ad may have been in poor taste, I believe everyone is capable of taking things a little too far.

Concetta Rini
The College of William and Mary

What's your opinion? Check out the online polls at www.prenhall.com/myphlip. Just follow the little person in the lab coat.

inspirational gifts.[98] In fact, sales of Christian merchandise now exceed $3 billion per year.

Worship is being redesigned to fit into busy lives. For example, the Sausalito Presbyterian Church (SausalitoPresbyterian.com) conducts Saturday night services for people who'd rather watch football or go to the beach on Sunday. As the church's Web site points out, "Following the service, there is plenty of time to go

MULTICULTURAL DIMENSIONS

RELIGIOUS SENSIBILITIES VARY AROUND the world, and big trouble can result if marketers violate taboo subjects in other cultures. Here are some recent examples:

- American restaurants must adapt to local customs in the Middle East, where rules about the mixing of the sexes and the consumption of alcohol are quite strict. Chili's Grill & Bar is known simply as Chili's, and the chain offers a midnight buffet during Ramadan season. McDonald's in Saudi Arabia offers separate dining areas for single men and women and children. Booths must have screens because women can't be seen eating meat.[108]
- An ad for Levi's jeans produced in London shows a young man buying condoms from a pharmacist and hiding them in the small side pocket of his jeans. When he goes to pick up his date, he discovers that her father is the same pharmacist. The commercial was a hit in the United Kingdom, but in a strongly Catholic country like Italy or Spain it was not appreciated.[109]
- A Brazilian ad for Pirelli tires drew heat from religious leaders. The ad shows a soccer superstar with his arms spread and a tire tread on the sole of his foot standing in place of the Christ the Redeemer statue that overlooks Rio de Janeiro.[110]
- An ad in a Danish campaign for the French car manufacturer Renault had to be withdrawn after protests from the Catholic community. The ad described a dialogue during confession between a Catholic priest and a repenting man. The man atones for his sins by praying *Ave Marias* until he confesses to having scratched the paint of the priest's new Renault—then the priest shouts "heathen" and orders the man to pay a substantial penalty to the church.[111]
- Burger King had to modify a commercial it aired on U.S. black radio stations in which a coffeehouse poet reads an ode to a Whopper with bacon. In the original spot the person's name is Rasheed and he uses a common Islamic greeting. A Muslim group called the Council on American–Islamic Relations issued a press release noting that Islam prohibits the consumption of pork products. In the new version the poet was introduced as Willie.[112]

to dinner, the movies, attend a party, or other activities." As a church marketing consultant observes, "Baby boomers think of churches like they think of supermarkets. They want options, choices, and convenience. Imagine if Safeway was open only one hour a week, had only one product, and didn't explain it in English."[99] Clearly, religion is big business.

Ironically, despite this frenzy of faith the number of adults who attend religious services in the United States and other advanced nations is slipping. However, weekly church attendance in the United States still is far higher than in most other developed nations, according to the World Values Survey conducted by Michigan's Institute for Social Research. About 44 percent of Americans attend church once a week (excluding funerals and christenings), compared to 27 percent of Britons, 21 percent of the French, 4 percent of Swedes, and 3 percent of Japanese.[100] More than 90 percent of Americans say they believe in God.

However, recent data comparing reported attendance with actual head counts at services indicate a gap between attitudes and behavior—or, at least, reported behavior. These findings show that about half the respondents who tell pollsters that they go to church services on a regular basis are not telling the truth! Because most people believe that going to church is a socially desirable activity, they are likely to say they do it even when they don't. The growth in religious activity appears to be largely accounted for by women. In a 1999 survey, 86 percent of American women identified with a religious denomination, 75 percent said religion is important in their lives (up from 69 percent in 1996), and 74 percent say they pray every day. Only 36 percent agreed with a Southern Baptist convention statement that "wives should submit graciously to the leadership of their husbands."[101]

The Impact of Religion on Consumption

Religion has not been studied extensively in marketing, possibly because it is seen as a taboo subject.[105] However, the little evidence that has been accumulated indicates that religious affiliation has the potential to be a valuable predictor of consumer behavior.[106] Religious subcultures in particular may exert a significant impact on consumer variables such as personality, attitudes toward sexuality, birthrates and household formation, income, and political attitudes. One early study that examined this issue, for example, found marked differences among Catholic, Protestant, and Jewish college students in preferences for weekend entertainment activities, as well as the criteria used in making these decisions. Price was a relatively more important criterion for Protestants, whereas desire for

Figure 14.3
The Demographics of Religious Subcultures

	Income median annual household income (in thousands)	Employment percent working full time	Education percent college graduates	Property percent owning their own home
Agnostic	$33.3	63.5%	36.3%	59.7%
Assemblies of God	22.2	48.8	13.7	75.1
Baptist	20.6	52.3	10.4	66.6
Brethren	18.5	46.2	11.4	81.4
Buddhist	28.5	59.4	33.4	50.6
Roman Catholic	27.7	54.3	20.0	69.3
"Christian"	20.7	51.8	16.0	63.7
Christian Science	25.8	40.1	33.1	69.0
Churches of Christ	26.6	47.2	14.6	78.1
Congregationalist	30.4	49.7	33.7	80.9
Disciples of Christ	28.8	55.4	39.3	72.3
Eastern Orthodox	31.5	55.1	31.6	72.7
Episcopal	33.0	52.6	39.2	70.6
"Evangelical"	21.9	47.0	21.5	69.7
Hindu	27.8	64.1	47.0	47.1
Holiness	13.7	49.9	5.0	53.7
Jehovah's Witnesses	20.9	44.1	4.7	59.1
Jewish	36.7	50.1	46.7	61.7
Lutheran	25.9	50.0	18.0	76.5
Methodist	25.1	49.6	21.1	75.2
Mormon	25.7	49.9	19.2	74.0
Muslim	24.7	62.5	30.4	43.3
Nazarene	21.6	48.5	12.5	71.2
No religion	27.3	60.5	23.6	60.6
New religious movements	27.5	63.4	40.6	53.4
Pentecostal	19.4	52.8	6.9	60.8
Presbyterian	29.0	48.8	33.8	76.9
"Protestant"	25.7	49.3	22.1	75.4
7th-Day Adventist	22.7	46.0	17.9	54.6
Unitarian	34.8	52.7	49.5	73.2

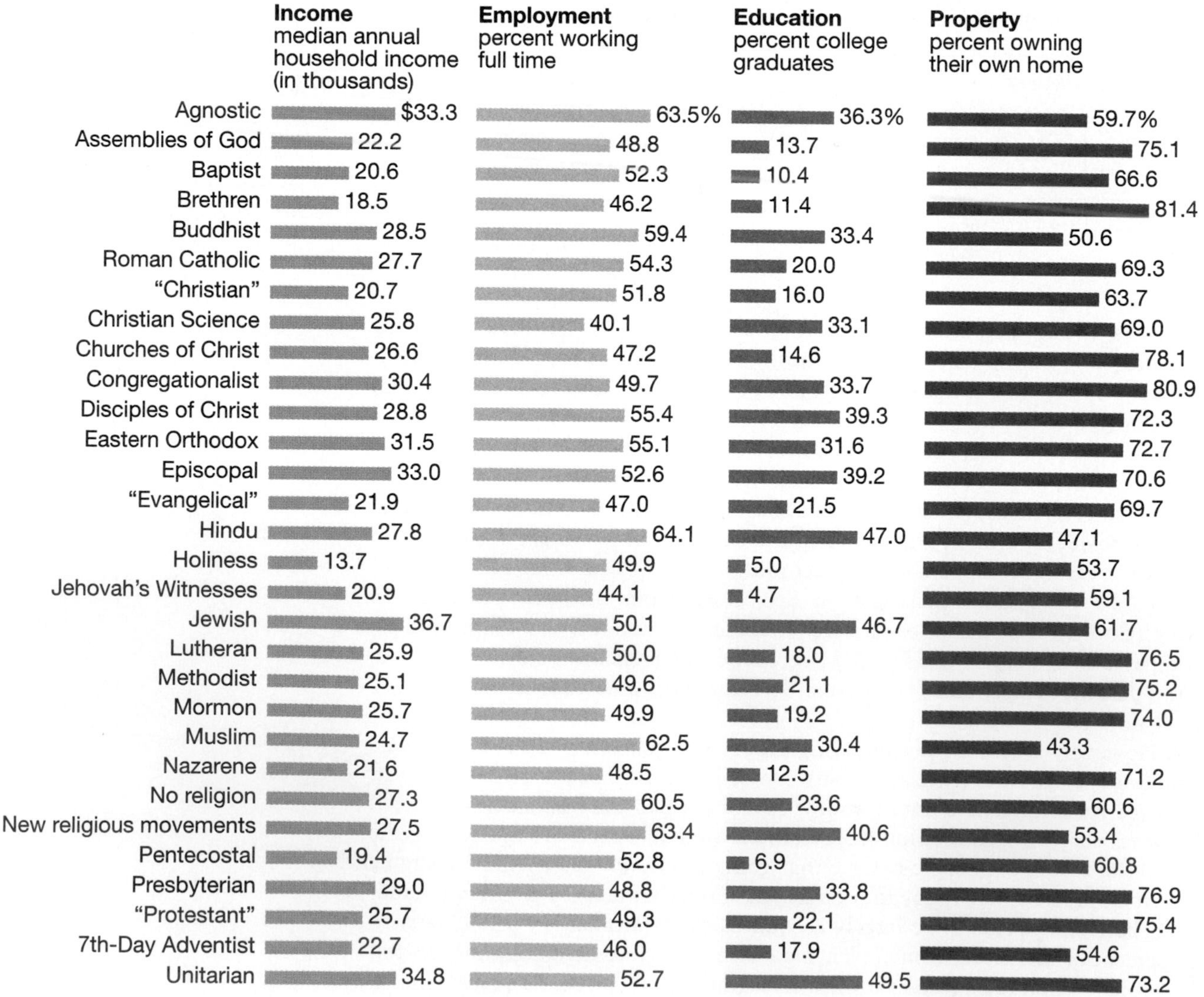

companionship was highest for Jews. Catholics were most likely to designate dancing as a favored activity than were the other two groups, but much less likely to select sex.[107]

What are the dominant religions worldwide? The Barna Research Group (barna.org) estimates that there are 2 billion Christians, 1.2 billion people practising Islam, 900 million are Hindus, 315 million are Buddhists, 15 million are Jews, and a category it terms Primal Indigenous makes up another 190 million. In addition, there are 750,000 practicing Scientologists and 700,000 Rastafarians. Something for everybody.[113]

Among Americans, the majority (57 percent) are Protestant. One-quarter are Catholic. Muslims, Hindus, and Buddhists make up 5 percent of the population, and another 2 percent are Jews. About 12 percent of Americans have no religious preference.[114] A major survey on religious attitudes that included 113,000 respondents sheds some interesting light on the current state of American religions. The study reports that Catholics dominate the New England area, Baptists are pervasive in the South, and Lutherans concentrate in the upper Midwest. Nonbelievers (about 8 percent of American adults) are most likely to be found in the Pacific Northwest and in the Southwestern desert. This survey also highlights the emergence of new religious affiliations. For example, it found that there are more Scientologists than Fundamentalists, and also sizable numbers of followers of wicca (witchcraft) and New Age faiths.[115] Some of the demographic characteristics of many different religious subcultures are summarized in Figure 14.3.

CHAPTER SUMMARY

- Consumers identify with many groups that share common characteristics and identities. These large groups that exist within a society are subcultures, and membership in them often gives marketers a valuable clue about individuals' consumption decisions. A large component of a person's identity is often determined by his or her ethnic origins, racial identity, and religious background. The three largest ethnic and racial subcultures are African Americans, Hispanic Americans, and Asian Americans, but consumers with many diverse backgrounds are beginning to be considered by marketers as well. Indeed, the growing numbers of people who claim multiethnic backgrounds is beginning to blur the traditional distinctions drawn among these subcultures.

- African Americans are a very important market segment. In some respects the market expenditures of these consumers do not differ that much from whites, but blacks are above-average consumers in such categories as personal care products. Hispanic Americans and Asian Americans are other ethnic subcultures that are beginning to be actively courted by marketers. The sizes of both groups are increasing rapidly, and in the coming years one or the other will dominate some major markets. Asian Americans on the whole are extremely well-educated, and the socioeconomic status of Hispanics is increasing as well.

- Key issues for reaching the Hispanic market are consumers' degree of acculturation into mainstream American society and the recognition of important cultural differences among Hispanic subgroups (e.g., Puerto Ricans, Cubans, Mexicans).

- Both Asian Americans and Hispanic Americans tend to be extremely family-oriented and are receptive to advertising that understands their heritage and reinforces traditional family values.

NET **PROFIT**

THE PRACTICE OF RELIGION is being significantly influenced by the Web as numerous spiritually oriented Web sites and portals spring up to meet the needs of spiritual surfers. Indeed, 16 percent of teenagers say that the Internet will substitute for their current church-based religious experience in the next five years.[116] One study estimated that of the 100 million Americans online, 25 percent used the Internet for religious purposes each month, mainly to communicate on e-mail or chat rooms about religious ideas or experiences. Some big religious portals such as Beliefnet.com and SpiritChannel.com hope to attract people from many different religions. According to one participant, "The Internet is an invitation for people who are skeptical. They feel released and can ask the religious questions they want to explore. I've received e-mails at 3 A.M. from people who haven't stepped inside a church in years."[117] Pray for wide bandwidth.

- The quest for spirituality is influencing demand in product categories including books, music, and cinema. Although the impact of religious identification on consumer behavior is not clear, some differences among religious subcultures do emerge. The sensibilities of believers must be considered carefully when marketers use religious symbolism to appeal to members of different denominations.

KEY TERMS

acculturation, p. 423
acculturation agents, p. 424

ethnic subculture, p. 414
progressive learning model, p. 423

subculture, p. 413

CONSUMER BEHAVIOR CHALLENGE

1. R. J. Reynolds' controversial plan to test-market a cigarette to black consumers raises numerous ethical issues about segmenting subcultures. Does a company have the right to exploit a subculture's special characteristics, especially to increase sales of a harmful product such as cigarettes? What about the argument that virtually every business that follows the marketing concept designs a product to meet the needs and tastes of a preselected segment?
2. Describe the progressive learning model and discuss why this phenomenon is important when marketing to subcultures.
3. Born-again Christian groups have been instrumental in organizing boycotts of products advertised on shows they find objectionable, especially those that they feel undermine family values. Do religious groups have a right or a responsibility to dictate the advertising a network should carry?
4. Can you locate any current examples of marketing stimuli that depend on an ethnic stereotype to communicate a message? How effective are these appeals?
5. To understand the power of ethnic stereotypes, conduct your own poll. For a set of ethnic groups, ask people to anonymously provide attributes (including personality traits and products) most likely to characterize each group using the technique of free association. How much agreement do you obtain across respondents? To what extent do the characteristics derive from or reflect negative stereotypes? Compare the associations for an ethnic group between actual members of that group and nonmembers.
6. Locate one or more consumers (perhaps family members) who have immigrated from another country. Interview them about how they adapted to their host culture. In particular, what changes did they make in their consumption practices over time?

NOTES

1. Michael Meyer, "Los Angeles 2010: A Latino Subcontinent," *Newsweek* (November 9, 1992): 32.
2. "The Numbers Game," *Time* (Fall 1993): 17.

3. Russell W. Belk and Janeen Arnold Costa, "The Mountain Man Myth: A Contemporary Consuming Fantasy," *Journal of Consumer Research* 25, no. 3 (1998): 218–40.

4. Erik Davis, "tlhIngan Hol Dajatlh'a' (Do You Speak Klingon?)," *Utne Reader* (March/April 1994): 122–29; additional material provided by personal communication, Prof. Robert V. Kozinets,

Northwestern University, October 1997; and adapted from Philip Kotler, Gary Armstrong, Peggy H. Cunningham, and Robert Warren, *Principles of Marketing*, 3d Canadian ed. (Scarborough, Ontario: Prentice Hall Canada, 1997): 96.

5. Alex Blumberg, "It's Good to Be King," *Wired* (March 2000): 132–49.

6. See Frederik Barth, *Ethnic Groups and Boundaries: The Social Organization of Culture Difference* (London: Allen and Unwin, 1969); Janeen A. Costa and Gary J. Bamossy, "Perspectives on Ethnicity, Nationalism, and Cultural Identity," in J. A. Costa and G. J. Bamossy, eds., *Marketing in a Multicultural World: Ethnicity, Nationalism, and Cultural Identity* (Thousand Oaks, CA: Sage, 1995): 3–26; Michel Laroche, Annamma Joy, Michael Hui, and Chankon Kim, "An Examination of Ethnicity Measures: Convergent Validity and Cross-Cultural Equivalence," Rebecca H. Holman and Michael R. Solomon, eds., *Advances in Consumer Research* 18 (Provo, Utah: Association for Consumer Research, 1991): 150–57; Melanie Wallendorf and Michael Reilly, "Ethnic Migration, Assimilation, and Consumption," *Journal of Consumer Research* 10 (December 1983): 292–302; Milton J. Yinger, "Ethnicity," *Annual Review of Sociology* 11 (1985): 151–80.

7. D'Vera Cohn, "2100 Census Forecast: Minorities Expected to Account for 60% of U.S. Population," *The Washington Post* (January 13, 2000): A5. For interactive demographic graphics, visit www. understandingusa.com.

8. Thomas McCarroll, "It's a Mass Market No More," *Time* (Fall 1993): 80–81.

9. Rohit Deshpandé and Douglas M. Stayman, "A Tale of Two Cities: Distinctiveness Theory and Advertising Effectiveness," *Journal of Marketing Research* 31 (February 1994): 57–64.

10. John Robinson, Bart Landry, and Ronica Rooks, "Time and the Melting Pot," *American Demographics* (June 1998): 18–24.

11. Steve Rabin, "How to Sell Across Cultures," *American Demographics* (March 1994): 56–57.

12. John Leland and Gregory Beals, "In Living Colors," *Newsweek* (May 5, 1997): 58.

13. Linda Mathews, "More Than Identity Rides on a New Racial Category," *New York Times* (July 6, 1996): 1.

14. Tom Maguire, "Ethnics Outspend in Areas," *American Demographics* (December 1998): 12–15.

15. Roberto Suro, "Mixed Doubles," *American Demographics* (November 1999): 57–62.

16. Steven A. Holmes, "Federal Government Is Rethinking Its System of Racial Classification," *New York Times* (July 8, 1994): A18; Mike McNamee, "Should the Census Be Less Black and White?"

Business Week (July 4, 1994): 40; Sándor, "The 'Other' Americans."

17. Christy Fisher, "It's All in the Details," *American Demographics* (April 1998): 45–47.

18. Eils Lotozo, "The Jalapeno Bagel and Other Artifacts," *New York Times* (June 26, 1990): C1.

19. Dana Canedy, "The Shmeering of America," *New York Times* (December 26, 1996): D1.

20. Quoted in Cara S. Trager, "Goya Foods Tests Mainstream Market's Waters," *Advertising Age* (February 9, 1987): S20.

21. Molly O'Neill, "New Mainstream: Hot Dogs, Apple Pie and Salsa," *New York Times* (March 11, 1992): C1.

22. Robert Pear, "New Look at the U.S. in 2050: Bigger, Older and Less White," *New York Times* (December 4, 1992): A1.

23. Quoted in Peter Schrag, *The Decline of the WASP* (New York: Simon and Schuster, 1971): 20.

24. Marcia Mogelonsky, "Asian-Indian Americans," *American Demographics* (August 1995): 32–38.

25. Thomas McCarroll, "It's a Mass Market No More," *Time* (Fall 1993): 80–81.

26. Marty Westerman, "Death of the Frito Bandito," *American Demographics* (March 1989): 28.

27. Betsy Sharkey, "Beyond Tepees and Totem Poles," *New York Times* (June 11, 1995): H1; Paula Schwartz, "It's a Small World . . . and Not Always P.C.," *New York Times* (June 11, 1995): H22.

28. Karyn D. Collins, "Culture Clash," *The Asbury Park Press* (October 16, 1994): D1.

29. William O'Hare, "Blacks and Whites: One Market or Two?" *American Demographics* (March 1987): 44–48.

30. W. Franklyn Joseph, "Blacks' Ambition Enters the Picture," *Advertising Age* (March 14, 1985): 26.

31. Michael E. Ross, "At Newsstands, Black Is Plentiful," *New York Times* (December 26, 1993): F6.

32. Eleena DeLisser, "Romance Books Get Novel Twist and Go Ethnic," *The Wall Street Journal* (September 6, 1994): B1.

33. For studies on racial differences in consumption, see Robert E. Pitts, D. Joel Whalen, Robert O'Keefe, and Vernon Murray, "Black and White Response to Culturally Targeted Television Commercials: A Values-Based Approach," *Psychology & Marketing* 6 (Winter 1989): 311–28; Melvin T. Stith and Ronald E. Goldsmith, "Race, Sex, and Fashion Innovativeness: A Replication," *Psychology & Marketing* 6 (Winter 1989): 249–62.

34. Monroe Anderson, "Advertising's Black Magic Helping Corporate America Tap a Lucrative Market," *Newsweek* (February 10, 1986): 60.

35. Bob Jones, "Black Gold," *Entrepreneur* (July 1994): 62–65.

36. Jean Halliday, "Volvo to Buckle Up African-Americans," *Advertising Age* (February 14, 2000): 28.

37. "Plans for Test Marketing Cigarette Canceled," *The Asbury Park Press* (January 1990): 20; Anthony Ramirez, "A Cigarette Campaign Under Fire," *New York Times* (January 12, 1990): D1; Brad Bennett, "Smoke Signals," *The Asbury Park Press* (July 24, 1994): AA1.

38. Suein L. Hwang, "Philip Morris Tests Menthol Type of Marlboros, Targeting Minorities," *The Wall Street Journal Interactive* (July 26, 1999).

39. Schwartz, "Hispanic Opportunities."

40. Naveen Donthu and Joseph Cherian, "Impact of Strength of Ethnic Identification on Hispanic Shopping Behavior," *Journal of Retailing* 70, no. 4 (1994): 383–93. For another study that compared shopping behavior and ethnicity influences among six ethnic groups, see Joel Herce and Siva Balasubramanian, "Ethnicity and Shopping Behavior," *Journal of Shopping Center Research* 1 (Fall 1994): 65–80.

41. Howard LaFranchi, "Media and Marketers Discover Hispanic Boom," *Christian Science Monitor* (April 20, 1988): 1.

42. Michael Janofsky, "A Commercial by Nike Raises Concerns About Hispanic Stereotypes," *New York Times* (July 13, 1993): D19.

43. Kelly Shermach, "Infomercials for Hispanics," *Marketing News* (March 17, 1997): 1.

44. Rick Wartzman, "When You Translate 'Got Milk' for Latinos, What Do You Get?" *The Wall Street Journal Interactive Edition* (June 3, 1999).

45. Rick Wartzman, "When You Translate 'Got Milk' for Latinos, What Do You Get?" *The Wall Street Journal Interactive Edition* (June 3, 1999).

46. Helene Stapinski, "Generacion Latino," *American Demographics* (July 1999): 62–68.

47. Jeffery D. Zbar, "'Latinization' Catches Retailers' Ears," *Advertising Age* (November 16, 1998): S22.

48. Jennifer Lach, "Intelligence Agents," *American Demographics* (March 1999): 52–60.

49. Katie Hafner, "Hispanics Are Narrowing the Digital Divide," *The New York Times on the Web* (April 6, 2000).

50. Pamela Druckerman, "Loquesea.com Tries to Reach Audience with Edgy Content," *The Wall Street Journal Interactive* (February 9, 2000).

51. David J. Lynch, "Net Company Terra Aims for Hispanic Connection," *USA Today* (January 20, 2000): B1.

52. Ronald Grover, "Univision Peers into Cyberspace," *Business Week* (January 17, 2000): 74.

53. Cheryl Russel, *Racial Ethnic Diversity: Asians, Blacks, Hispanics, Native Americans, &Whites*, 2d ed. May (Ithaca, NY: American Demographics, 1998.

54. Beth Enslow, "General Mills: Baking New Ground," *Forecast* (November/December 1993): 18.

55. "'Cultural Sensitivity' Required When Advertising to Hispanics," *Marketing News* (March 19, 1982): 45.

56. Westerman, "Death of the Frito Bandito."

57. Stacy Vollmers and Ronald E. Goldsmith, "Hispanic-American Consumers and Ethnic Marketing," *Proceedings of the Atlantic Marketing Association* (1993): 46–50.

58. Schwartz, "Rising Status."

59. David J. Wallace, "How to Sell Yucas to YUCAs," *Advertising Age* (February 13, 1989): 5–6; "1994 Survey of Buying Power," *Sales & Marketing Management* (August 30, 1994): A9.

60. Schwartz, "Hispanic Opportunities."

61. "Dispel Myths Before Trying to Penetrate Hispanic Market," *Marketing News* (April 16, 1982): 1.

62. Schwartz, "Hispanic Opportunities."

63. "'Born Again' Hispanics: Choosing What to Be," *The Wall Street Journal Interactive Edition* (November 3, 1999).

64. "'Cultural Sensitivity' Required When Advertising to Hispanics," *Marketing News* (March 19, 1982): 45.

65. See Lisa Peñaloza, "*Atravesando Fronteras*/Border Crossings: A Critical Ethnographic Exploration of the Consumer Acculturation of Mexican Immigrants," *Journal of Consumer Research* 21, no.1 (June 1994): 32–54; Lisa Peñaloza Lisa and Mary C. Gilly, "Marketer Acculturation: The Changer and the Changed," *Journal of Marketing*, 63 (July 1999): 84–104.

66. Sigfredo A. Hernandez and Carol J. Kaufman, "Marketing Research in Hispanic Barrios: A Guide to Survey Research," *Marketing Research* (March 1990): 11–27.

67. Melanie Wallendorf and Michael D. Reilly, "Ethnic Migration, Assimilation, and Consumption," *Journal of Consumer Research* 10 (December 1983): 292–302.

68. Ronald J. Faber, Thomas C. O'Guinn, and John A. McCarty, "Ethnicity, Acculturation and the Importance of Product Attributes," *Psychology & Marketing* 4 (Summer 1987): 121–34; Humberto Valencia, "Developing an Index to Measure Hispanicness," in Elizabeth C. Hirschman and Morris B. Holbrook, eds., *Advances in Consumer Research* 12 (Provo: Association for Consumer Research, 1985): 118–21.

69. Rohit Deshpande, Wayne D. Hoyer, and Naveen Donthu, "The Intensity of Ethnic Affiliation: A Study of the Sociology of Hispanic Consumption," *Journal of Consumer Research* 13 (September 1986): 214–20.

70. Fernando Gonzalez, "Study Finds Alcohol, Cigarette Makers Target Hispanics," *Boston Globe* (November 23, 1989): A11.

71. Peñaloza, "*Atravesando Fronteras*/Border Crossings."

72. Michael Laroche, Chankon Kim, Michael K. Hui, and Annamma Joy, "An Empirical Study of Multidimensional Ethnic Change: The Case of the French Canadians in Quebec," *Journal of Cross-Cultural Psychology* 27, no. 1 (January 1996): 114–31.

73. Greg Johnson and Edgar Sandoval, "Advertisers Court Growing Asian Population: Marketing, Wide Range of Promotions Tied to New Year Typify Corporate Interest in Ethnic Community," *The Los Angeles Times* (February 4, 2000): C1.

74. Alice Z. Cuneo and Jean Halliday Ford, "Penney's Targeting California's Asian Populations," *Advertising Age* (January 4, 1999): 28.

75. Dorinda Elliott, "Objects of Desire," *Newsweek* (February 12, 1996): 41.

76. Richard Kern, "The Asian Market: Too Good to Be True?" *Sales & Marketing Management* (May 1988): 38; Joo Gim Heaney and Ronald E. Goldsmith, "The Asian-American Market Segment: Opportunities and Challenges," *Association of Marketing Theory and Practice* (Spring 1993): 260–65; Betsy Wiesendanger, "Asian-Americans: The Three Biggest Myths," *Sales & Marketing Management* (September 1993): 86.

77. Stuart Elliott, "Marketers Study Nuances to Reach a Valued Audience," *The New York Times on the Web* (March 6, 2000).

78. Wiesendanger, "Asian-Americans."

79. McCarroll, "It's a Mass Market No More."

80. Donald Dougherty, "The Orient Express," *The Marketer* (July/August 1990): 14; Cyndee Miller, "'Hot' Asian-American Market Not Starting Much of a Fire Yet," *Marketing News* (January 21, 1991): 12.

81. Kern, "The Asian Market."

82. Quoted in Dougherty, "The Orient Express," p. 14.

83. Miller, "'Hot' Asian-Market Not Starting Much of a Fire Yet."

84. Marty Westerman, "Fare East: Targeting the Asian-American Market," *Prepared Foods* (January 1989): 48–51.

85. Eleanor Yu, "Asian-American Market Often Misunderstood," *Marketing News* (December 4, 1989): 11.

86. Marianne Paskowski, "Trailblazing in Asian America," *Marketing and Media Decisions* (October 1986): 75–80.

87. Ellen Schultz, "Asians in the States," *Madison Avenue* (October 1985): 78.

88. Dougherty, "The Orient Express."

89. Westerman, "Fare East: Targeting the Asian-American Market."

90. James B. Arndorfer, "A Bank of America Campaign Aims for Asian-Americans," *Advertising Age* (June 9, 1997): 6.

91. Pui-Wing Tam, "Mandarin Pop Is Looking to Penetrate U.S. Markets," *The Wall Street Journal Interactive Edition* (March 31, 2000).

92. Dan Fost, "Asian Homebuyers Seek Wind and Water," *American Demographics* (June 1993): 23–25.

93. Myra Stark, "Titanic Brand Possibilities," *Advertising Age* (March 9, 1998): 36.

94. "Cards Reflect Return to Spiritual Values," *Chain Drug Review*, 21, no. 4 (February 15, 1999).

95. Jennifer Harrison, "Advertising Joins the Journey of the Soul," *American Demographics* (June 1997): 22.

96. Claudia Penteado, "Brazilian Ad Irks Church," *Advertising Age* (March 23, 2000): 11.

97. Tim W. Ferguson, "Spiritual Reality: Mainstream Media Are Awakening to the Avid and Expanding Interest in Religion in the U.S," *Forbes* (January 27, 1997): 70.

98. Tim W. Ferguson and Josephine Lee, "Spiritual Reality," *Forbes* (January 27, 1997): 70; Catherine Dressler, "Holy Socks! This Line Sends a Christian Message," *Marketing News* (February 12, 1996): 5.

99. Richard Cimino and Don Lattin, "Choosing My Religion," *American Demographics* (April 1999).

100. Rebecca Gardyn, "Soul Searchers," *American Demographics* (March 2000): 14; Shelly Reese, "Religious Spirit," *American Demographics* (August 1998).

101. G. Evans Witt, "Women Show Their Spiritual Side," *American Demographics* (April 1999).

102. Delaney, "New Kosher Products, from Tacos to Tofu."

103. Joshua Levine, "You Don't Have to Be Jewish . . ." *Forbes* (April 24, 1995): 154.

104. Yochi Dreazen, "Kosher-Food Marketers Aim More Messages at Non-Jews," *The Wall Street Journal Interactive Edition* (July 30, 1999).

105. For a couple of exceptions see Michael J. Dotson and Eva M. Hyatt, "Religious Symbols as Peripheral Cues in Advertising: A Replication of the Elaboration Likelihood Model," *Journal of Business Research* 48 (2000): 63–68; Elizabeth C. Hirschman, "Religious Affiliation and Consumption Processes: An Initial Paradigm," *Research in Marketing* (Greenwich, CT: JAI Press, 1983): 131–70.

106. See for example Nejet Delener, "The Effects of Religious Factors on Perceived Risk in Durable Goods Purchase Decisions," *Journal of Consumer Marketing* 7 (Summer 1990): 27–38.

107. Hirschman, "Religious Affiliation and Consumption Processes."

108. "Religion Reshapes Realities for U.S. Restaurants in Middle East," *Nation's*

Restaurant News, 32, no. 7 (February 16, 1998).

109. Sarah Ellison, "Sexy-Ad Reel Shows What Tickles in Tokyo Can Fade Fast in France," *The Wall Street Journal Interactive Edition* (March 31, 2000).

110. Claudia Penteado, "Brazilian Ad Irks Church," *Advertising Age* (March 23, 2000): 11.

111. Markedsføring, 10, 1996, p. 22; adapted from Michael R. Solomon, Gary Bamossy, and Soren Askegaard, *Consumer*

Behavior: A European Perspective (London: Prentice Hall International, 1998).

112. "Burger King Will Alter Ad That Has Offended Muslims," *The Wall Street Journal Interactive Edition* (March 15, 2000).

113. "Somebody Say Amen!" *American Demographics* (April 2000): 72.

114. Susan Mitchell, *American Attitudes* 2d ed. (Ithaca, New Strategist Publications, 1998). (Taken from a sample page off the

new strategist publications Web page, www.newstrategist.com).

115. Kenneth L. Woodward, "The Rites of Americans," *Newsweek* (November 29, 1993): 80.

116. "Somebody Say Amen!" *American Demographics* (April 2000): 72.

117. Lori Leibovich, "That Online Religion with Shopping, Too," *The New York Times on the Web* (April 6, 2000).

t's the last week of summer vacation, and Kurt is looking forward to going back to college. It's been a tough summer. He had trouble finding a summer job and seemed to be out of touch with his old friends—and with so much time on his hands just hanging around the house, he and his mother weren't getting along too well. As usual, Kurt is plopped on the couch, aimlessly flipping channels—from *Celebrity Deathmatch* on MTV, to *Bewitched* on Nickelodeon, to a Sony beach volleyball tournament on ESPN, back to MTV. Suddenly, Mrs. Steiner marches in, grabs the remote, and switches the channel to public television. Yet another documentary is on about Woodstock (the original one, way back in 1969). When Kurt protests, "Come on Pam, get a life . . ." his mom snaps back, "Keep your cool. You might actually learn about what it was like to be in college when it really meant something. And what's with the first name stuff? In my day I would never have dreamed of calling my mom or dad by their first name!"

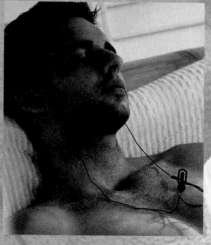

That's when Kurt loses it. He's tired of hearing about the "good old days" of Woodstock, Berkeley, and 20 other places he doesn't care about. Besides, most of his mom's ex-hippie friends now work for the very corporations they used to protest about—who are they to preach to him about doing something meaningful with his life? In disgust, Kurt storms into his room, puts an Outcast CD into his Discman, and pulls the covers up over his head. So much for a constructive use of time. What's the difference, anyway—they'll probably all be dead from the "greenhouse effect" by the time he graduates.

15

AGE SUBCULTURES

AGE AND CONSUMER IDENTITY

The era in which a consumer grows up creates a cultural bond with the millions of others who come of age during the same time period. As we grow older, our needs and preferences change, often in concert with others who are close to our own age. For this reason a consumer's age exerts a significant influence on his identity. All things being equal, we are more likely to have things in common with others of our own age than with those younger or older. As Kurt found out, this identity may become even stronger when the actions and goals of one generation conflict with those of others—an age-old battle.

A marketer needs to communicate with members of an age group in their own language. For example, Sony finally figured out that it had to sponsor events such as beach volleyball to get the attention of young people. When the electronics giant first entered the U.S. car stereo market, it simply hammered on its usual themes of technical prowess and quality. This got nothing but yawns from the 16- to 24-year-olds who make up half of the consumers who buy these products, and Sony ranked a pitiful seventh in the market after 10 years. Finally, the company got the picture—it totally revamped its approach and eventually doubled its car stereo revenues.[1] In this chapter, we'll explore some of the important characteristics of some key age groups and consider how marketing strategies must be modified to appeal to diverse age subcultures.

Age Cohorts: "My Generation"

An **age cohort** consists of people of similar ages who have undergone similar experiences. They share many common memories about cultural heroes (e.g., John Wayne versus Brad Pitt, or Frank Sinatra versus Kurt Cobain), important

Figure 15.1
Household Income by Age

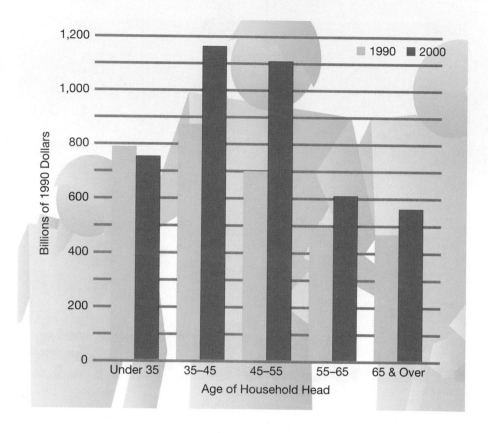

historical events (e.g., the 1976 Bicentennial versus the 2000 Millennium celebration), and so on. Although there is no universally accepted way to divide up people into age cohorts, each of us seems to have a pretty good idea of what we mean when we refer to "my generation."

Marketers often target products and services to a specific age cohort. As shown in Figure 15.1, although middle-aged people make the most money, there's

Members of an age cohort share similar experiences and memories about important historical events like the Millennium.

TABLE 15.1 The Nostalgia Scale

Scale Items

- They don't make 'em like they used to.

- Things used to be better in the good old days.

- Products are getting shoddier and shoddier.

- Technological change will ensure a brighter future (reverse coded).

- History involves a steady improvement in human welfare (reverse coded).

- We are experiencing a decline in the quality of life.

- Steady growth in GNP has brought increased human happiness (reverse coded).

- Modern business constantly builds a better tomorrow (reverse coded).

NOTE: Items are presented on a nine-point scale ranging from strong disagreement (1) to strong agreement (9), and responses are summed.

SOURCE: Morris B. Holbrook and Robert M. Schindler, "Age, Sex, and Attitude toward the Past as Predicters of Consumers' Aesthetic Tastes for Cultural Products," *Journal of Marketing Research* 31 (August 1994): 416. Reprinted by permission of the American Marketing Association.

plenty of market potential attached to other age groups as well. The same offering will probably not appeal to people of different ages, nor will the language and images used to reach them. In some cases separate campaigns are developed to attract consumers of different ages. For example, Norelco found that younger men are far less likely to use electric shavers than are its core customer base of older men. The company launched a two-pronged effort to convince younger men on the one hand to switch from wet shaving to electric, and on the other hand to maintain loyalty among its older following. Ads for Norelco's Speedrazor, aimed at males aged 18 to 35, ran on late-night TV and in *GQ* and *Details.* Messages about the company's triple-head razors, geared to men over 35, ran instead in publications that attract older readers, such as *Time* and *Newsweek.*

Because consumers within an age group confront crucial life changes at roughly the same time, the values and symbolism used to appeal to them can evoke powerful feelings of nostalgia (see Chapter 3). Adults over 30 are particularly susceptible to this phenomenon.[2] However, young people as well as old are influenced by references to their past. In fact, research indicates that some people are more disposed to be nostalgic than others, regardless of age. A scale that has been used to measure the impact of nostalgia on individual consumers appears in Table 15.1.

THE TEEN MARKET: GEN Y LIKE TOTALLY RULES

In 1956, the label "teenage" first entered the general American vocabulary when Frankie Lymon and the Teenagers became the first pop group to identify themselves with this new subculture. Believe it or not, the concept of a teenager is a fairly new idea. Throughout most of history a person simply made the transition from child to adult (often accompanied by some sort of ritual or ceremony, as we'll see in the next chapter). The magazine *Seventeen,* born in 1944, was based on the revelation that young women didn't want to look just like Mom. Following World War II, the teenage conflict between rebellion and conformity

MARKETING OPPORTUNITY

A REUNION IS AN event based on a shared age cohort. People who were not necessarily fond of each other in high school or college come together to celebrate the common experience of having been in school at the same time and place. More than 150,000 reunions are held in the United States each year, attended by 22 million people (the 10-year high school reunion is the most heavily attended). In addition to the boon this nostalgia provides to caterers and professional reunion organizers, some marketers realize that the people who attend reunions represent a valuable customer base. They are self-selected to be fairly successful, because the "failures" tend not to show up. Some companies use reunion-goers to test new products, and travel-related businesses interview attendees about their trips or provide special promotional packages for returning.[3] So, rent that limo, print up some impressive business cards and have a great time.

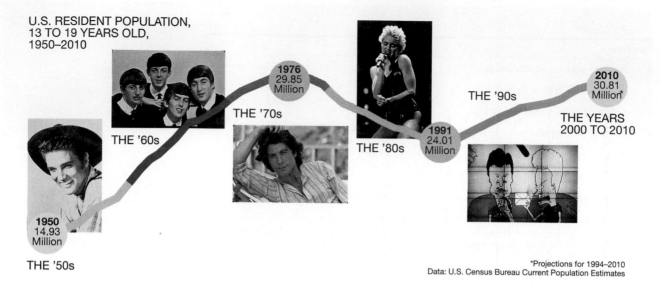

U.S. RESIDENT POPULATION, 13 TO 19 YEARS OLD, 1950–2010

THE '60s

THE '70s

1976
29.85
Million

THE '80s

1991
24.01
Million

THE '90s

2010
30.81
Million*

THE YEARS
2000 TO 2010

1950
14.93
Million

THE '50s

*Projections for 1994–2010
Data: U.S. Census Bureau Current Population Estimates

Figure 15.2

The U.S. Teen Population

began to unfold, pitting Elvis Presley with his slicked hair and suggestive pelvis swivels against the wholesome Pat Boone with his white bucks (see Figure 15.2). Now, this rebellion is often played out for so-called **Generation Y** kids (those born between 1979 and 1994 who are the younger siblings of Generation X, which we'll discuss later) by teen idols such as hip-hop star Eminem or by the confused, sullen teens appearing daily on Ricki Lake and other daytime talk shows.[4]

Teen Values, Conflicts, and Desires

As anyone who has been there knows, the process of puberty and adolescence can be both the best of times and the worst of times. Many exciting changes happen as individuals leave the role of child and prepare to assume the role of adult. These changes create a lot of uncertainty about the self, and the needs to belong and to find one's unique identity as a person becomes extremely important. At this age, choices of activities, friends, and clothes are often crucial to social acceptance. Teens actively search for cues for the "right" way to look and behave from their peers and from advertising. Advertising geared to teens is typically action-oriented and depicts a group of "in" teens using the product.

Teens use products to express their identities, to explore the world and their new-found freedoms in it, and also to rebel against the authority of their parents and other socializing agents. Marketers often do their best to assist in this process. For example, Pepsi capitalized on the surge of teens wearing beepers (presumably to facilitate drug sales) by distributing the devices as part of a sales promotion—participants were beeped weekly with messages from sports and music stars advertising Pepsi and other teen products.[5]

Teenagers in every culture grapple with fundamental developmental issues as they make the transition from childhood to adult. Teenagers throughout history have had to cope with insecurity, parental authority, and peer pressure. According to Teenage Research Unlimited, today the five most important social issues for teens are AIDS, race relations, child abuse, abortion, and the environment. Today's teens often have to cope with additional family responsibilities as well, especially if they live in nontraditional families in which they must take significant responsibility for shopping, cooking, and housework. It's hard work being a teen in the modern world. According to research by the Saatchi & Saatchi advertising agency, there are four themes of conflict common to all teens:

1. *Autonomy versus belonging:* Teens need to acquire independence, so they try to break away from their families. On the other hand, they need to attach themselves to a support structure, such as peers, to avoid being alone. A thriving Internet subculture has developed among many teens to serve this purpose. The Net is the preferred method of communication for many young people because its anonymity makes it easier to talk to people of the opposite sex or of different ethnic and racial groups.[9]

2. *Rebellion versus conformity:* Teens need to rebel against social standards of appearance and behavior, yet they still need to fit in and be accepted by others. Cult products that cultivate a rebellious image are prized for this reason. Hot Topic, a retail chain based in Pomona, California, caters to this need by selling $44 million per year of such "in your face" items as nipple rings, tongue barbells, and purple hair dye.[10]

3. *Idealism versus pragmatism:* Teens tend to view adults as hypocrites, whereas they see themselves as being sincere. They have to struggle to reconcile their view of how the world should be with the realities they perceive around them.

4. *Narcissism versus intimacy:* Teens are often obsessed with their own appearance and needs. On the other hand, they also feel the desire to connect with others on a meaningful level.[11]

Appealing to the Youth Market

Consumers in this age subculture have a number of needs, including experimentation, belonging, independence, responsibility, and approval from others. Product usage is a significant medium through which to express these needs. This age group is growing nearly twice as fast as the general population and is expected to number 30 million by 2005; teens spend an average of $3,000 per year.[13] Much of this money goes toward "feel-good" products: cosmetics, posters, and fast food—with the occasional nose ring thrown in as well. Because they are so interested in many different products and have the resources to obtain them, the teen market is avidly courted by many marketers.

Because modern teens were raised on TV and tend to be more "savvy" than older generations, marketers must tread lightly in attempts to reach them. In particular, the messages must be seen as authentic and not condescending. As one researcher observed, "they have a B.S. alarm that goes off quick and fast. . . . They walk in and usually make up their minds very quickly about whether it's phat or not phat, and whether they want it or don't want it. They know a lot of advertising is based on lies and hype."[18] This wisdom formed the basis for Coca-Cola's introduction of OK soda, a beverage targeted to teens. After a year of field research, the company found that teens responded better to a product that did not overpromise—it was just "OK."[19]

Researching the Youth Market

Research firms are coming up with innovative ways to tap the desires of teens, many of whom don't respond well to traditional survey techniques. Sometimes respondents are given a video camera and are asked to record a "typical" day at school—along with play-by-play commentary to help interpret what's going on.

MULTICULTURAL DIMENSIONS

TEEN REBELLION IS A new phenomenon in Japan, a country known for rigid conformity and constant pressure to succeed. Now more and more teenagers are questioning the rules. The dropout rate among students in junior and senior high school increased by 20 percent in a two-year period. More than 50 percent of girls have had intercourse by their senior year of high school.[6]

Japanese youth are very style-conscious, and currently there are several niches or "tribes," each with very well-defined looks and rules.[7] A popular look for Japanese girls is called the "Gals;" they are easily recognized by their bleached yellow hair, salon-tanned skin, chalk-white lipstick, and seven-inch platform heels. Other groups include the Sports Clique (low-heeled Air Mocs and Gap clothing) and the Back-Harajuku Group (baggy sweatshirts, colorful jeans, sneakers, and long scarves).

To try to win the loyalty of young consumers in Japan, five big companies including Toyota, Matsushita, and Asahi Breweries formed a marketing alliance. They are introducing a range of products, from beer to refrigerators, all with the same brand name of Will (yes, Will). Critics are not sure the plan will work because these companies as of now do not have very modern images, so only time will tell if this ambitious plan Will or won't.[8]

REALITY CHECK

MARKETERS OF ENTRENCHED BRANDS SUCH AS Nike, Pepsi, and Levi Strauss are tearing their hair out over Gen Y consumers. Image-building campaigns (e.g., Michael Jordan endorsing Nike) are not as effective as they once were. Compared to their predecessors, these young consumers seem to be more interested in individuality than in fitting in. For example, Kodak is successfully marketing its "Sticky Film" to young people who use the product to express themselves in original ways. Perhaps this change is partly due to the amount of time young people spend surfing alone on the Web. As a Nike executive put it, "Television drives homogeneity. The Internet drives diversity."[12]

What advice would you give to a marketer who wants to appeal to Gen Y? What are major do's and don'ts? Can you provide some examples of specific marketing attempts targeted to Gen Y that work or don't work?

My marketing advice for marketers such as Nike trying to advertise to Generation Y is to avoid stereotyping in their advertisements. If Nike wants to be diverse in their advertisements they should show other people using Nike shoes or clothes besides athletes. Perhaps Nike should show an advertisement of an average looking college student running to class because he/she is late for class. This would be a nice change to see how different types of people use their Nike shoes.

Jill Wittekind
University of Nevada, Las Vegas

Marketing campaigns that encourage self-expression are likely to be successful depicting characters that young people can relate to. To illustrate this point I will briefly describe a recent advert for Nokia mobile phones that seemed to have won favour amongst youth: A young man seeks to gain the attention of an attractive girl. He does so by asking a friend to keep a close monitor on her lifestyle and movements which the friend communicates to him by phone. Before too long the young man has quit smoking, begun to mimic her movements by following her jogging, buying organic and vegetarian produce and reading poetry all in the aim of impressing and winning her affection. Although this is a very comical and classical depiction of the "boy-chase-girl" scenario it manages to capture the real and common subtleties of teenage-hood which

most of us are able to identify with. I am convinced that being able to identify such a scenario and relating it to a particular product (such as the mobile phone) is the key to marketing success.

Nicole Schragger
Edinburgh University, Scotland

From a marketing perspective, it is important to keep the consumer's attention. Remember they are used to a great deal of sensory information at one time and often lose interest without it. . . . Use real people who are different from one another interacting. And finally, be entertaining because Gen Y consumers do not want to think, just be amused. Look at what is popular to the culture, shows like *The Simpson's, Friends,* and MTV. These are quick paced with a variety of types of people and usually require little cognitive effort. Commercials like the Gap and VW have been good at targeting the Gen Y and incorporating the above.

Jennifer Freet
George Mason University

Gen Y consumers are a smart, and tough group of consumers. Smart and funny, but NOT silly advertising is usually a winning combination. Clever dialogue can also be a key to a successful advertising campaign to Gen Y. For example, the new Molson Canadian "I am Canadian" television advertis-

ing campaign . . . is a fantastic commercial! The commercial begins with a young 20-something man standing on a stage proudly defining the differences between Canadians and the Americans, ". . . it's a toque, not a hat, we don't live in igloos, and the beaver is a proud and noble animal!"

Liv Amber Judd
University of Saskatchewan, Canada

One example of a brand successfully appealing to Generation Y is Gap; they have managed to couple a distinctive brand image with product adaptability. This has been achieved through creating a series of adverts that are enjoyed in their own right and offering a wide range of products, from traditional cut blue jeans to the now fashionable three-quarter-length trousers. This wide range of products allows the Gap brand to be incorporated into many individuals' style, while retaining brand awareness.

James Beattie
University of Exeter, United Kingdom

When marketing to Generation Y, companies should be using the following three concepts: different, interactive, and customized. We are different from everyone else, and you will be different if you use our product. Let's interact and work together to make sure that the product is what you really want. Finally, tell us how can we change the product to meet your unique demand.

Pepsi Cola with their "music points" inside bottle caps should be placed in the marketing Hall of Fame for marketing to Generation Y. Young people buy Pepsi beverages, win points, and put together CD's for themselves with the songs they really like, and they don't have to spend money buying entire albums.

Dmitri Batsev
University of Alaska, Fairbanks

What's your opinion? Check out the online polls at www.prenhall.com/myphlip. Just follow the little person in the lab coat.

Greenfield Consulting Group uses what it calls the "teen-as-creative-director" technique. The firm gives teens camcorders and asks them to complete a two-part creative assignment that will be judged by their peers. A typical task is to create a video collage of the "coolest/hippest/whateverest" things they can find and

NET PROFIT

YOUNG PEOPLE ARE AMONG the most enthusiastic Web surfers. For many, this activity has replaced "old-fashioned fun" such as watching the tube or hanging at the mall. Teens are expected to spend $1.2 billion online, so many firms are working hard to develop Web sites that will capture their interest. Iturf.com, a network of Web sites for teenagers, has the largest traffic numbers among teen-oriented sites. A subsidiary of Delia's (the catalog company that sells youth-oriented fashions), the site logs more than 1.5 million unique visitors per month.[14] Other popular teen sites include Alloy.com and Bolt.com.

According to one market research firm, 62 percent of teenagers log on from home for at least four hours a week. They spend most of their online time doing research, sending and reading e-mail, playing games, or checking out things to buy. And retailers have another reason to be so interested: 10 percent of these kids have a credit card in their own name, and another 9 percent have access to a parent's card (uh-oh!). To counteract parents' concerns about security issues, some start-ups such as Icanbuy, Rocketcash, and Doughnet are creating "digital wallets" that let Mom and Dad set up an account and limit the sites at which money can be spent. What are teens buying? Of teens who make purchases online, 57 percent have bought CDs or cassettes, 38 percent have bought concert or sports tickets, 34 percent bought books and magazines, 32 percent ordered clothing, and 9 percent ordered cell phones or pagers.[15]

Researchers report that teens value privacy when surfing the Web because they view it as a way to express their individuality—that's why it's common for them to have multiple e-mail accounts, each with a different "personality." Major turn-offs: sloppy Web site design, poor navigation, and slow speed.[16] Dotcom companies also need to work on building in some fun and adventure to lure kids away from the mall. As one 13-year-old shopper put it, "The Net kinds of takes away the whole experience—the hunt, the get, and the buy. Web shopping is just too perfect! You type in 'gray cords' and there they are. It's not fun. The fun is in the hunt."[17]

write a song/poem/story that describes what "cool/hip" is all about. After the teens complete their assignments, they present their work to each other at a focus group facility, judge the work collectively, and award prizes of $250 each to the creators of the best video and song/poem/story.

A recent study asked young people in the United States and the Netherlands to write essays about what is "cool" and "uncool" and to create collages representing things that represent being cool to them.[20] The researchers found that being cool has several meanings, though there were a lot of similarities between the two cultures when kids use this term. Some of the common dimensions include having charisma, being in control, and being a bit aloof. And many of the respondents agreed that being cool is a moving target: The harder you try to be cool, the more uncool you are! Some of their actual responses are listed here:

- "Cool means being relaxed, to nonchalantly be the boss of every situation, and to radiate that" (Dutch female).
- "Cool is the perception from others that you've got 'something' which is macho, trendy, hip, etc." (Dutch male).
- "Cool has something stand-offish, and at the same time, attractive." (Dutch male).
- "Being different, but not too different. Doing your own thing, and standing out, without looking desperate while you're doing it" (American male).
- "When you are sitting on a terrace in summer, you see those machos walk by, you know, with their mobile [phones] and their sunglasses. I always think, 'Oh please, come back to earth!' These guys only want to impress. That is just so uncool." (Dutch female).
- "When a person thinks he is cool, he is absolutely uncool" (Dutch female).
- "To be cool we have to make sure we measure up to it. We have to create an identity for ourselves that mirrors what we see in maga-zines, on TV, and with what we hear on our stereos" (American male).

Converse courts the youth market with an edgy message.

In other cases researchers try to interact with young consumers in their own "natural habitats" instead of bringing them into labs or focus group facilities. Firms such as Sputnik and look-look.com use teen informants to report back on the "flavor" that's currently hot on the streets of major urban markets. Other companies send researchers to "live with the natives" and observe how they

Figure 15.3

These are two of the collages created by students in this study. One was created by a Dutch female, and the other by an American male. Can you guess which is which?

really use products in their daily lives. One company sends researchers to spend the night with respondents to observe them up close and personal. During the evening they talk about important stuff such as their skin care routines, but then in the morning the interviewer watches to see what they actually do in the bathroom while primping before school.[21] When the Leo Burnett advertising agency was revamping Heinz ketchup's image to make it cool, the account research team took teens to dinner to see how they actually used ketchup. These meals opened their eyes; new ads focus on teens' need for control by showing ketchup smothering fries "until they can't breathe" and touting new uses for the condiment on pizza, grilled cheese, and potato chips.[22]

Marketers view teens as "consumers-in-training" because brand loyalty often develops during adolescence. A teenager who is committed to a brand may continue to purchase it for many years to come. Such loyalty creates a barrier-to-entry for other brands that were not chosen during these pivotal years. Thus, advertisers sometimes try to "lock in" consumers so that in the future they will buy their brands more or less automatically. As one teen magazine ad director observed, "We . . . always say it's easier to start a habit than stop it."[24]

Teens also exert a big influence on the purchase decisions of their parents (see Chapter 12).[25] Sixty percent of teens, for instance, say they influence the vacation choices of their families.[26] In addition to providing "helpful" advice to parents, teens are increasingly buying products on behalf of the family. The majority of mothers are now employed outside the home and have less time to shop for the family. In fact, seven out of 10 mothers of teens work, and five of those seven are employed full-time.[27]

This fundamental change in family structure has altered the way marketers must conceive of teenage consumers. Although teens are still a good market for discretionary items, in recent years their spending on such "basics" as groceries is even larger than for nonessentials. A market research firm specializing in this segment has gone so far as to label teens *Skippies*—school kids with income and purchasing power.[28] One survey of 16- to 17-year-old girls found that during a three-month period a significant proportion of them purchased staple items such as cereal, frozen meals, cheese, yogurt, and salad dressing.[29] Marketers are beginning to respond to these changes. The number of pages devoted to food advertising in *Seventeen* magazine increased by 31 percent in one year.

Big (Wo)Man on Campus: We're Talking to You!

Advertisers spend approximately $100 million a year on campus to woo college students, who in turn buy about $20 billion worth of products a year. After paying for books, board, and tuition the average student has about $200 per month to spend, so this interest is not surprising. As one marketing executive observed, "This is the time of life where they're willing to try new products. . . . This is the time to get them in your franchise."[33]

Many college students are away from home for the first time, and they must make many buying decisions that used to be made for them by parents, such as the purchase of routine personal care products or of cleaning supplies. Some marketers are attracted by this lack of experience. As one executive put it, "Advertisers look at the college student as someone who can be more easily influenced than someone who has developed brand preferences."[34]

Nevertheless, college students pose a special challenge for marketers, because they are hard to reach via conventional media. Students watch less television than other people, and when they do watch, they are much more likely to do so

MARKETING PITFALLS

CALVIN KLEIN'S STRATEGY OF using adolescent sexuality to sell the company's products dates way back to 1980, when Brooke Shields proclaimed, "Nothing comes between me and my Calvins." Later, ads featuring singer Marky Mark in his underwear sparked a new fashion craze. A few years ago Klein took this approach one very daring step further, when the company unveiled a very controversial advertising campaign featuring young-looking models in situations dripping with sexual innuendo. In one spot, an old man with a gravelly voice says to a scantily clad young boy, "You got a real nice look. How old are you? Are you strong? You think you could rip that shirt off of you? That's a real nice body. You work out? I can tell." The campaign ended when the chairman of Dayton Hudson asked that the stores' names be removed from the ads, and *Seventeen* refused to carry them.[23] By that time, of course, Klein had reaped invaluable volumes of free publicity as teens and adults hotly debated the appropriateness of these images.

PRETEEN GIRLS ARE A major market unto themselves. Marketers use the term **tweens** to describe the 27 million children aged 8–14 who spend $14 billion dollars a year on clothes, CDs, movies, and other "feel good" products. Limited Too sells mostly to 10- and 11-year-old girls and now mails a catalog directly to preteen girls rather than to their parents. Not surprising, because preteen girls buy more than $4.5 billion in clothing a year, Limited Too is developing makeup products targeted to this age segment as well, featuring fragrances such as Sugar Vanilla and Snow Musk.[30]

Tweens are "between" childhood and adolescence and exhibit characteristics of

MARKETING OPPORTUNITY

both age groups. As one tween commented, "When we're alone we get weird and crazy and still act like kids. But in public we act cool, like teenagers." This age group drove the success of movies such as Titanic and boy groups such as 'N Sync—they account for about 9 percent of all CD sales.[31] They like to talk on the phone and in chat rooms, they squeal and shout when the Backstreet Boys take the stage—and they've definitely got marketers' attention.

For example, Kodak made a $75 million, five-year commitment to convince

tween girls to buy its single-use Kodak Max cameras. According to internal research, this segment is 50 percent more likely than boys of the same age to own a camera. When girls are asked to name their most prized possession, 15 percent said photographs, whereas only 4 percent of their male counterparts put photos at the top of their lists. Kodak discovered that a majority of girls keep journals, collect quotes, and maintain online bulletin boards, and the company is betting that this desire to share experiences with friends will turn into a picture-perfect marketing strategy.[32]

after midnight. Students also do not read newspapers as much. AT&T and other large companies have found that the best way to reach students is through their college newspapers; about 90 percent of students read their college paper at least one day a week (usually during a lecture!), which explains why $17 million a year is spent on advertising in college newspapers.[35]

Other strategies to reach students include the widespread distribution of sampler boxes containing a variety of personal care products in student centers and dormitories and the use of posters (termed *wall media*). In addition, a growing number of marketers are capitalizing on the ritual of spring break to reach college students; it is estimated that about 40 percent of students now make the annual trek to points south. Beach promotions used to be dominated by suntan lotion and beer companies, but many others now are well-represented, including Chanel, Hershey, Chevrolet, Procter & Gamble, and Columbia Pictures.[36]

Baby Busters: "Generation X"

The cohort of consumers born between 1960 and 1976 consists of 46 million Americans. This group was labeled **"Generation X"** following the bestselling 1991 novel of that name. They have also been called "slackers" or "baby busters" because of their supposed alienation and laziness, and these stereotypes pervade popular culture in popular movies such as *Clueless* or in the music of groups such as Marilyn Manson.[37]

In the past advertisers fell all over themselves trying to create messages that would not turn off the worldly Generation X cohort. Many of these efforts involved references to old TV shows such as *Gilligan's Island* or vignettes featuring disheveled actors in turned-around baseball caps doing their best to appear blasé. This approach actually turned off a lot of busters because it implies that they have nothing else to do but sit around and watch old television reruns. One of the first commercials of this genre was created for Subaru. It showed a sloppily dressed young man who described the Impreza model as "like punk rock" while denouncing the competition as "boring and corporate." The commercial did not play well with its intended audience, and Subaru eventually switched agencies.

Perhaps one reason appeals to Xers with messages of alienation, cynicism, and despair have not succeeded is that many busters turned out not to be so depressed after all! Generation Xers actually are quite a diverse group—they don't all wear reversed baseball caps and work as burger flippers. Despite the birth of dozens of magazines with names such as *Axcess, Project X*, and *KGB* catering to "riot grrrls" and other angry Xers, the most popular magazine for twentysome-thing women is *Cosmopolitan*. What seems to make this age cohort the angriest is constantly being labeled angry by the media![38] A CNN/Time study found that 60 percent want to be their own boses, and another study revealed that Xers are already responsible for 70 percent of new start-up businesses in the United States. One industry expert observed, "Today's Gen Xer is both values-oriented and value-oriented. This generation is really about settling down." Many people in this segment seem to be determined to have stable families after being latchkey children themselves. Seven out of 10 regularly save some portion of their income, a rate comparable to that of their parents. Xers tend to view the home as an expression of individuality rather than material success. More than half are involved in home improvement and repair projects.[39] They don't sound all that lazy.

The advertising agency Saatchi & Saatchi sent teams of psychologists and cultural anthropologists into the field to study the buster subculture. These researchers identified four key segments:

1. *Cynical Disdainers:* The most pessimistic and skeptical about the world—the stereotypical Xers.

A growing number of marketers are capitalizing on the ritual of Spring Break to reach college students.

2. *Traditional Materialists:* They are upbeat, optimistic about the future, and actively striving for what they continue to view as the American Dream of material prosperity.

3. *Hippies Revisited:* This group tends to espouse the nonmaterialistic values of the 1960s. Their priorities are expressed through music (many continue to be Dead Heads despite the death of Jerry Garcia), retro fashion, and a strong interest in spirituality.

4. *Fifties Machos:* These consumers tend to be young Republicans. They believe in traditional gender roles, are politically conservative, and they are the least accepting of multiculturalism.[40]

BABY BOOMERS

The **baby boomer** age segment (people born between 1946 and 1965) is the source of many fundamental cultural and economic changes. The reason: power in numbers. By 2002, the number of U.S. households headed by people aged 25–44 will decline by 1.7 million, whereas those headed by people aged 45–64 will increase by 5.5 million. By 2008, they will outnumber the younger group by 43 million to 40 million.[41]

Economic Power: He Who Pays the Piper, Calls the Tune

Because of the size and buying power of the boomer group during the last 20 years, marketers pay a lot of attention to this age cohort. Boomers tend to have different emotional and psychological needs than did those who came before them. Domain, a high-fashion furniture chain, found that its core boomer clientele is as concerned about self-improvement as it is about home decoration. The company launched a series of in-store seminars dealing with themes such as women's issues and how to start a business, and found its repeat business doubled since beginning the program.[42]

As teenagers in the 1960s and 1970s, the "Woodstock Generation" created a revolution in style, politics, and consumer attitudes. As they have aged, their collective will has been behind cultural events as diverse as the Free Speech movement and hippies in the 1960s to Reaganomics and yuppies in the 1980s. Now that they are older, they continue to influence popular culture in important ways.

This generation is much more active and physically fit than its predecessors; baby boomers are six percent more likely than the national average to be involved in some type of sporting activity.[45] And boomers are now in their peak earning years. As one commercial for VH1, the music-video network that caters to those who are a bit too old for MTV, pointed out, "The generation that dropped acid to escape reality . . . is the generation that drops antacid to cope with it."

Levi Strauss is a good example of a company that built its core business on the backs (or backsides) of boomers. More recently, though, the apparel maker faced the challenge of keeping aging baby boomers in their franchise as former jeans-wearing hippies got older and lost interest in traditional styles. Levi Strauss answered this challenge by creating a new product category, "New Casuals," that would be more formal than jeans but less casual than dress slacks.

MARKETING OPPORTUNITY

AS THEY AGE, BABY boomers are not interested as they once were in theme parks on steroids. Death-defying roller coasters and headbanger music are a bit less appealing as they prefer to drop their own kids off to frolic in places where they once loved to hang. Park operators are looking at ways to lure boomers back by focusing less on high-tech "scream machines" and more on serene, comfortable surroundings.[43] Disney's Animal Kingdom blends live animals with audio-animatronic creatures, and this portends a movement away from simply collecting ferocious animals and toward collecting entire ecosystems. Other theme park operators are preserving human habitats: At the Port Aventura theme park near Tarragona, Spain, real Cataloniain fishermen drink in fake cantinas—the kind that were destroyed when the old seaport was taken over by developers such as those who built the park in the first place.[44]

This 1962 Pepsi ad highlights the emphasis on youth power that began to shape our culture as baby boomers came of age in the 1960s.

The target audience was men aged 25–49 with higher than average education and income who worked in white collar jobs in major metropolitan areas. The Dockers line was born.[46] Although the Levi's image has suffered among younger consumers who prefer new names such as Diesel and JNCO, the company's role in providing clothes for "Casual Fridays" work environments continues to thrive.

Consumers aged 35 to 44 spend the most on housing, cars, and entertainment. Baby boomers are "feathering their nests;" they account for roughly 40 percent of all the money spent on household furnishings and equipment.[47] In addition, consumers aged 45 to 54 spend the most of any age category on food (30 percent above average), apparel (38 percent above average), and retirement programs (57 percent above average). To appreciate the impact middle-aged consumers have and will have on our economy, consider this: At current spending levels, a 1 percent increase in the population of householders aged 35 to 54 results in an additional $8.9 billion in consumer spending.

In addition to the direct demand for products and services created by this age group, these consumers have also created a new baby boom of their own to keep marketers busy in the future. Because fertility rates have dropped, this new boom is not as big as the one that created the baby boom generation; the new upsurge in the number of children born in comparison can best be described as a **baby boomlet.** Many boomer couples postponed getting married and having children because of the new opportunities and options for women. They began having babies in their late twenties and early thirties, resulting in fewer (but perhaps more pampered) children per family. This new emphasis on children and the family has created opportunities for products such as cars (e.g., the success of the "minivan" concept), services (e.g., the day care industry, as exemplified by the KinderCare chain), and media (e.g., magazines such as *Working Mother* and local magazines for parents that exist in more than 70 American cities).[48]

MARKETING   OPPORTUNITY

AS THE OLDEST MEMBERS of the baby boom generation move into their fifties, businesses are cashing in. Female menopause begins on average at the age of 51, and a new frankness about this life change has led to a boom in self-help books, estrogen supplements, and exercise classes.[49] Men are not immune from life changes, either, as many fall prey to so-called "male menopause." As humorist Dave Barry notes, this is a period when a man wears "enormous pleated pants and designer fragrances, encases his pale porky body in tank tops, and buys a boat shaped like a sexual aid. He then abandons his attractive, intelligent wife to live with a 19-year-old aerobics instructor who once spent an entire summer reading a single magazine article called 'Ten Tips for 'Terrific Toenails.'"

Marketers are eager to provide solutions to "menopausal" men's social anxieties. The Hair Club for Men has about 40,000 members who have received new heads of hair with the help of "hair-replacement engineers." Plastic surgeons also report a sharp rise in the number of men electing to have cosmetic surgery, including nose jobs and liposuction (see Chapter 5). On the other hand, Dave Barry maintains that all these efforts are futile: "Regardless of how many gallons of Oil of Olay you smear on yourself," he warns, "you're going to start aging faster than a day-old bagel on a hot dumpster."[50]

THE GRAY MARKET

The old woman sits alone in her dark apartment while the television blares out a soap opera. Once every couple of days, she slowly and painfully opens her triple-locked door with arthritic hands and ventures out to the corner store to buy essentials such as tea, milk, and cereal, always being sure to pick the least expensive brand. Most of the time she sits in her rocking chair, thinking sadly of her dead husband and the good times she used to have.

Is this the image you have of a typical elderly consumer? Until recently, many marketers did. As a result, they largely neglected the elderly in their feverish pursuit of the baby boomer market. But as our population ages and people are living longer and healthier lives, the game is rapidly changing. A lot of businesses are beginning to replace the old stereotype of the poor recluse. The newer, more accurate image is of an older person who is active, interested in what life has to offer, and is an enthusiastic consumer with the means and willingness to buy many goods and services.

Gray Power: Seniors' Economic Clout

Think about this: By the year 2010, one of every seven Americans will be 65 or older. The U.S. Bureau of Labor Statistics estimates that the mature market will grow by 62 percent between 1987 and 2015, compared to a 19-percent rate of growth for the overall U.S. population.[51] By 2030, 20 percent of the U.S. population will be elderly. And, by 2100 the number of Americans who are at least 100 years old will jump from 65,000 now to more than five million.[52]

None of us may be around to see that, but we can already see the effects of the **gray market** today as consumers aged 55 and older impact the marketplace. Older adults control more than 50 percent of discretionary income and spend more than $60 billion annually in the United States alone.[53] The mature market is the second-fastest growing market segment in the United States, lagging only behind the baby boomers. Such dramatic growth can largely be explained by healthier lifestyles, improved medical diagnoses and treatment, and the resulting increase in life expectancy.

The economic health of older consumers is good and getting better. Some of the important areas that stand to benefit from the surging gray market include exercise facilities, cruises and tourism, cosmetic surgery and skin treatments, and "how-to" books and university courses that offer enhanced learning opportunities. In many product categories seniors spend their money at an even greater rate than other age groups: Householders aged 55 to 64 spend 15 percent more than average per capita. They shell out 56 percent more than the average consumer on women's clothing, and as new grandparents they actually spring for more toys and playground equipment than people aged 25 to 44.[54] In fact, the average grandparent spends an average of about $500 per year on gifts for grandchildren—have you called yours today?[55]

Understanding Seniors

Researchers have identified a set of key values that are relevant to older consumers. For marketing strategies to succeed, they should be related to one or more of these factors:[56]

- *Autonomy:* Mature consumers want to lead active lives and to be self-sufficient. The advertising strategy for Depends, undergarments for incontinent women made by Kimberly-Clark, is centered around actress June Allyson, who plays golf and goes to parties without worrying about her condition.
- *Connectedness:* Mature consumers value the bonds they have with friends and family. Quaker Oats successfully tapped into this value with its ads featuring actor Wilford Brimley, who dispenses grandfatherly advice about eating right to the younger generation.
- *Altruism:* Mature consumers want to give something back to the world. Thrifty Car Rental found in a survey that more than 40 percent of older consumers would select a rental car company if it sponsored a program that gives van discounts to senior citizens' centers. Based on this research, the company launched its highly successful program, "Give a Friend a Lift."

Perceived Age: You're Only as Old as You Feel

Market researchers who work with older consumers often comment that people think of themselves as being 10 to 15 years younger than they actually are. In fact, research confirms the popular wisdom that age is more a state of mind than of body. A person's mental outlook and activity level has a lot more to do with his or her longevity and quality of life than does *chronological age*, the actual number of years lived.

Echoing the saying, "You're only as old as you feel," these ads remind us that a person's perceived age often does not correspond to his or her chronological age.

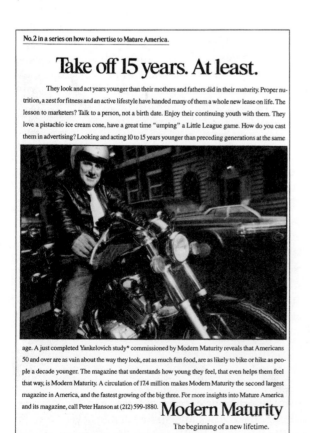

No. 2 in a series on how to advertise to Mature America.

Take off 15 years. At least.

They look and act years younger than their mothers and fathers did in their maturity. Proper nutrition, a zest for fitness and an active lifestyle have handed many of them a whole new lease on life. The lesson to marketers? Talk to a person, not a birth date. Enjoy their continuing youth with them. They love a pistachio ice cream cone, have a great time "umping" a Little League game. How do you cast them in advertising? Looking and acting 10 to 15 years younger than preceding generations at the same age. A just completed Yankelovich study* commissioned by Modern Maturity reveals that Americans 50 and over are as vain about the way they look, eat as much fun food, are as likely to bike or hike as people a decade younger. The magazine that understands how young they feel, that even helps them feel that way, is Modern Maturity. A circulation of 17.4 million makes Modern Maturity the second largest magazine in America, and the fastest growing of the big three. For more insights into Mature America and its magazine, call Peter Hanson at (212) 599-1880. **Modern Maturity**

The beginning of a new lifetime.

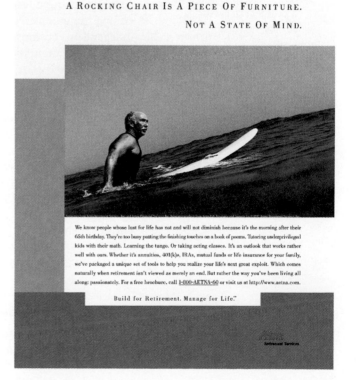

A ROCKING CHAIR IS A PIECE OF FURNITURE.

NOT A STATE OF MIND.

We know people whose lust for life has not and will not diminish because it's the morning after their 65th birthday. They're too busy putting the finishing touches on a book of poems. Tutoring underprivileged kids with their math. Learning the tango. Or taking acting classes. It's an outlook that works rather well with ours. Whether it's annuities, 401(k)s, IRAs, mutual funds or life insurance for your family, we've packaged a unique set of tools to help you realize your life's next great exploit. Which comes naturally when retirement isn't viewed as merely an end. But rather the way you've been living all along: passionately. For a free brochure, call 1-800-AETNA-60 or visit us at http://www.aetna.com.

Build for Retirement. Manage for Life.

THE NET CAN BE a godsend for the elderly, especially those seniors who have difficulty leaving the house to go shopping or who are socially isolated.[59] Senior surfers can reduce unncessary car trips by ordering food to be delivered from companies such as webvan.com, peapod.com, and kozmo.com and arranging for automatic delivery of medications from online pharmacies such as Drugstore.com, PlanetRX.com, or DrugEmporium.com. They can also find new friends online and receive important information and reminders. Some other helpful Web sites include:

- IPing.com—reminders to take medications
- PayMyBills.com—Pay bills online
- Caregiver.org—The Family Caregiver Alliance locates Web pals
- ElderWeb.com—a network of financial and healthcare links
- Seniors-Site.com—message boards for caregivers and seniors

A better yardstick to categorize seniors is **perceived age,** or how old a person feels as opposed to their chronological age. Perceived age can be measured on several dimensions, including "feel-age" (i.e., how old a person feels) and "look-age" (i.e., how old a person looks).[57] The older consumers get, the younger they feel relative to actual age. For this reason, many marketers emphasize product benefits rather than age-appropriateness in marketing campaigns because many consumers will not relate to products targeted to their chronological age.[58]

Segmenting Seniors

The senior subculture is an extremely large market: The number of Americans 65 and older exceeds the entire population of Canada.[60] Because this group is so large, it is helpful to think of the mature market as actually consisting of four subsegments: an "older" group (aged 55–64), an "elderly" group (aged 65–74), an "aged" group (aged 75–84) and finally a "very old" group (85 and up).[61] The elderly market is particularly well-suited for segmentation because older consumers are easy to identify by age and stage in the family life cycle. Most receive Social Security benefits, so they can be located without much effort, and many belong to organizations such as the American Association of Retired Persons (aarp.org), which boasts more than 12 million dues-paying members. AARP's main publication, *Modern Maturity,* has the largest circulation of any American magazine.

In addition to chronological age marketers segment the elderly along such dimensions as the particular years a person came of age (her age cohort), current martial status (e.g., widowed versus married), and a person's health and outlook on life.[62] For example, one ad agency devised a segmentation scheme for American women over the age of 65 using two dimensions: self-sufficiency and perceived opinion leadership.[63] The study discovered many important differences among the groups. For example, the self-sufficient group was found to be more independent, cosmopolitan, and outgoing. Compared to the other seniors, these women were more likely to read a book, attend concerts and sporting events, and dine out.

Several segmentation approaches begin with the premise that a major determinant of elderly marketplace behavior is the way a person deals with being old.[64] **Social aging theories** try to understand how society assigns people to different roles across the life span. For example, when people retire they may reflect society's expectations for someone at this life stage—this is a major transition point when people exit from many relationships.[65] Some people become depressed, withdrawn, and apathetic as they age, some are angry and resist the thought of aging, and others accept the new challenges and opportunities this period of life has to offer. Table 15.2 summarizes some selected findings from one current segmentation approach, **gerontographics,** that divides the mature market into groups based on both level of physical well-being and social conditions such as becoming a grandparent or losing a spouse.

Selling to Seniors

Most older people lead more active, multidimensional lives than we assume. Nearly 60 percent engage in volunteer activities, one in four seniors aged 65 to 72 still works, and more than 14 million are involved in daily care of a grandchild.[66] And, it is crucial to remember that income alone does not express the spending

TABLE 15.2 Gerontographics: Selected Characteristics

Segment	% of 55+ Population	Profile	Marketing Ramifications
Healthy Indulgers	18%	Have experienced the fewest events related to aging, such as retirement or widowhood, and are most likely to behave like younger consumers. Main focus is on enjoying life.	Looking for independent living and are good customers for discretionary services like home cleaning and answering machines.
Healthy Hermits	36%	React to life events like the death of a spouse by becoming withdrawn. Resent that they are expected to behave like old people.	Emphasize conformity. They want to know their appearance is socially acceptable, and tend to be comfortable with well-known brands.
Ailing Outgoers	29%	Maintain positive self-esteem despite adverse life events. They accept limitations but are still determined to get the most out of life.	Have health problems that may require a special diet. Special menus and promotions will bring these people in to restaurants seen as catering to their needs.
Frail Recluses	17%	Have adjusted their lifestyles to accept old age, but have chosen to cope with negative events by becoming spiritually stronger.	Like to stay put in the same house where they raised their families. Good candidates for remodeling, also for emergency-response systems.

SOURCE: Adapted from George P. Moschis, "Life Stages of the Mature Market," *American Demographics* (September 1996): 44–50.

power of this group. Older consumers are finished with many of the financial obligations that siphon off the income of younger consumers. Eighty percent of consumers past age 65 own their own homes, and 80 percent of those homes are owned outright. In addition, child-rearing costs are over. As evidenced by the popularity of the bumper sticker that proudly proclaims "We're Spending Our Children's Inheritance," many seniors now are more inclined to spend money on themselves rather than skimping for the sake of children and grandchildren.

Still, outdated images of mature consumers persist. The editors of *Modern Maturity* reject about a third of the ads submitted to them because they portray older people in a negative light. In one survey, one-third of consumers over age 55 reported that they deliberately did not buy a product because of the way an older person was stereotyped in the product's advertising.[67] To address these negative depictions, marketers can provide more welcoming environments for seniors. Wal-Mart hires older people as greeters to be sure their senior customers feel at home. A California bank named Home Savings of America went even farther by opening branches catering to seniors. The bank supplies coffee and donuts and encourages its older customers to think of the branches as a convenient meeting place and a venue for social interaction.[68]

Product Adaptations

Many consumer products will encounter a more sympathetic reception from seniors if products and the packages they come in are redesigned to be sensitive to physical limitations. Packages are often awkward and difficult to manage, especially for those who are frail or arthritic. Also, many serving sizes are not geared

Jockey Apparel is one of many advertisers that is increasingly featuring attractive older models in its ads.

to smaller families, widows, and other people living alone, and coupons tend to be for family-sized products, rather than for single servings.

Seniors have difficulty with pull-tab cans and push-open milk cartons. Ziploc packages and clear plastic wrap also are difficult to handle. Packages need to be easier to read and should be made lighter and smaller. Finally, designers need to pay attention to contrasting colors. A slight yellowing of the eye's lens as one ages makes it harder to see background colors on packages. Discerning between blues, greens, and violets becomes especially difficult. The closer identifying type colors are to the package's or advertisement's background color, the less visibility and attention they will command.

Carmakers are at the forefront of adapting their products to the needs of the aged. General Motors formed a group called Paragon Team that studies the needs of aging car buyers, and Ford has a similar group of engineers and designers called the Third Age Suit. GM redesigned some Oldsmobile models to include bigger buttons and clearer dashboard displays, and a Cadillac's rearview mirrors automatically dim when hit with headlights. The Lincoln Town Car (the average age of a Lincoln driver is 67) features two sets of radio and air conditioning controls, one on the dashboard and one on the steering wheel, because older drivers have trouble shifting attention from controls to the road. Chrysler engineers are experimenting with collision control systems that sound an alarm when a driver is too close to another car.[69]

Mature Marketing Messages

Older adults respond positively to ads that provide an abundance of information. Unlike other age groups, these consumers usually are not amused, or persuaded, by imagery-oriented advertising. A more successful strategy involves the construction of advertising that depicts the aged as well-integrated, contributing members of society, with emphasis on their expanding their horizons rather than clinging precariously to life. Some basic guidelines for effective advertising to the elderly include the following:[70]

MARKETING PITFALLS

SOME MARKETING EFFORTS

TARGETED to older adults have backfired because they reminded people of their advanced age or depicted their age group in an unflattering way. One of the more infamous blunders was committed by Heinz. A company analyst found that many older people were buying baby food because of the small portions and easy chewing consistency, so Heinz introduced a line of "Senior Foods" made especially for denture wearers. Needless to say, the product failed. Consumers did not want to admit that they required strained foods (even to the supermarket cashier). They preferred to purchase baby foods, which they could pretend they were buying for a grandchild.

- Keep language simple.
- Use clear, bright pictures.
- Use action to attract attention.
- Speak clearly, and keep the word count low.
- Use a single sales message, and emphasize brand extensions to tap consumers' familiarity.
- Avoid extraneous stimuli (i.e., excessive pictures and graphics can detract from the message).

CHAPTER SUMMARY

- People have many things in common with others merely because they are about the same age. Consumers who grew up at the same time share many cultural memories because they belong to a common age cohort, so they may respond well to marketers' nostalgia appeals that remind them of these experiences.
- Four important age cohorts are teens, college students, baby boomers, and older adults. Teenagers are making a transition from childhood to adulthood, and their self-concepts tend to be unstable. They are receptive to products that help them to be accepted and enable them to assert their independence. Because many teens earn money but have few financial obligations, they are a particularly important segment for many nonessential or expressive products, ranging from chewing gum to clothing fashions and music. Due to changes in family structure, many teens also are taking more responsibility for their families' day-to-day shopping and routine purchase decisions. College students are an important but hard-to-reach market. In many cases, they are living alone for the first time, so they are making important decisions about setting up a household. Tweens are an increasingly important market segment; kids aged 8–14 who are making the transition from childhood to adolescence are influential purchasers of clothing, CDs, and other "feel-good" products.
- Baby boomers are the most powerful age segment because of their size and economic clout. As this group ages, its interests have changed and marketing priorities have changed as well. The needs and desires of baby boomers affect demands for housing, child care, automobiles, clothing, and many other products.
- As the population ages, the needs of older consumers will become increasingly influential. Many marketers traditionally ignored seniors because of the stereotype that they are too inactive and spend too little. This stereotype is no longer accurate. Many older adults are healthy, vigorous, and interested in new products and experiences—and they have the income to purchase them. Marketing appeals to this age subculture should focus on consumers' self-concepts and perceived ages, which tend to be more youthful than their chronological ages. Marketers also should emphasize concrete benefits of products because this group tends to be skeptical of vague, image-related promotions.

KEY TERMS

age cohort, p. 437
Baby boomer, p. 448
baby boomlet, p. 449
Generation X, p. 447

Generation Y, p. 440
gerontographics, p. 452
gray market, p. 450

perceived age, p. 452
social aging theories, p. 452
tweens, p. 446

CONSUMER BEHAVIOR CHALLENGE

1. What are some possible marketing opportunities present at reunions? What effects might attending such an event have on consumers' self-esteem, body image, and so on?

2. What are some of the positives and negatives of targeting college students? Identify some specific marketing strategies that you feel have either been successful or unsuccessful at appealing to this segment. What characteristics distinguish the successes from the failures?

3. Why have baby boomers had such an important impact on consumer culture?

4. How has the baby boomlet changed attitudes toward child-rearing practices and created demand for different products and services?

5. "Kids these days seem content to just hang out, surf the Net, and watch mindless TV shows all day." How accurate is this statement?

6. Is it practical to assume that people age 55 and older constitute one large consumer market? What are some approaches to further segmenting this age subculture?

7. What are some important variables to keep in mind when tailoring marketing strategies to older adults?

8. Find good and bad examples of advertising targeted to older consumers. To what degree does advertising stereotype the elderly? What elements of ads or other promotions appear to determine their effectiveness in reaching and persuading this group?

9. If you were a marketing researcher assigned to study what products are "cool," how would you do this? Do you agree with the definitions of "cool" provided by the young people in the chapter?

NOTES

1. Shelly Reese, "The Lost Generation," *Marketing Tools* (April 1997): 50.
2. Bickley Townsend, "Ou Sont les Reiges Díantan? (Where Are the Snows of Yesteryear?)," *American Demographics* (October 1988): 2.
3. Paula Mergenhagen, "The Reunion Market," *American Demographics* (April 1996): 30–34.
4. Stephen Holden, "After the War the Time of the Teen-Ager," *New York Times* (May 7, 1995): E4.
5. Mary Kuntz and Joseph Weber, "The New Hucksterism," *Business Week* (July 1, 1996): 75.
6. Howard W. French, "Vocation for Dropouts Is Painting Tokyo Red," *The New York Times on the Web* (March 5, 2000).
7. Yumiko Ono, "They Say That a Japanese Gal Is an Individualist: Tall, Tan, Blond," *The Wall Street Journal Interactive Edition* (November 19, 1999).
8. Yumiko Ono, "Meet a Beer, a Car, a Refrigerator, and a Fabric Deodorizer, All Named Will," *The Wall Street Journal Interactive Edition* (October 8, 1999).

9. Scott McCartney, "Society's Subcultures Meet by Modem," *The Wall Street Journal* (December 8, 1994): B1.
10. Mary Beth Grover, "Teenage Wasteland," *Forbes* (July 28, 1997): 44–45.
11. Junu Bryan Kim, "For Savvy Teens: Real Life, Real Solutions," (August 23, 1993): S1.
12. Quoted in Ellen Neuborne, "Generation Y," *Business Week* (February 15, 1999): 80, p. 83.
13. Grover, "Teenage Wasteland."
14. Cate T. Corcoran, "Shares of Teen Hub iTurf Surge on Traffic Numbers," *The Wall Street Journal Interactive Edition* (January 24, 2000).
15. Jennifer Gilbert, "New Teen Obsession," *Advertising Age* (February 14, 2000): 38.
16. Melonee McKinney, "A Word from the Y's: E-fficient," *Daily News Record* (January 24, 2000): 30.
17. Julie Connelly, "A Ripe Target for Web Retailers, Teens Keep Heading to the Mall," *The New York Times on the Web* (September 22, 1999).
18. Quoted in Cyndee Miller, "Phat Is Where It's At for Today's Teen Market,"

Marketing News (August 15, 1994): 6; see also Tamara F. Mangleburg and Terry Bristol, "Socialization and Adolescents' Skepticism Toward Advertising," *Journal of Advertising* 27, no. 3 (Fall 1998): 11.
19. Laurie M. Grossman, "Coke Hopes 'OK,' New Drink, Will Be the Toast of Teens," *The Wall Street Journal* (April 21, 1994): B7.
20. Gary J. Bamossy, Michael R. Solomon, Basil G. Englis, and Trinske Antonidies, "You're Not Cool If You Have to Ask: Gender in the Social Construction of Coolness" (paper presented at the Association for Consumer Research Gender Conference, Chicago, June 2000).
21. Jane Bainbridge, Keeping Up With Generation Y," *Marketing* (February 18, 1999): 37–38.
22. Daniel McGinn, "Pour on the Pitch," *Newsweek* (May 31, 1999): 50–51.
23. Margaret Carlson, "Where Calvin Crossed the Line," *Time* (September 11, 1995): 64.
24. Ellen Goodman, "The Selling of Teenage Anxiety," *The Washington Post* (November 24, 1979).

25. Ellen R. Foxman, Patriya S. Tansuhaj, and Karin M. Ekstrom, "Family Members' Perceptions of Adolescents' Influence in Family Decision Making," *Journal of Consumer Research* 15 (March 1989): 482–91.

26. Andrew Malcolm, "Teen-Age Shoppers: Desperately Seeking Spinach," *New York Times* (November 29, 1987): 10.

27. Ibid.

28. John Blades, "Tracking Skippies: TRU Researches Habits of Elusive Groups— Teens," *The Asbury Park Press* (March 2, 1991): C1.

29. Malcolm, "Teen-Age Shoppers."

30. Yumiko Ono, "Limited Too Will Blitz Preteens with Catalogs of Their Very Own," *The Wall Street Journal Interactive Edition* (August 25, 1998).

31. Quoted in Karen Springen, Ana Figueroa, and Nicole Joseph-Goteiner, "The Truth About Tweens," *Newsweek* (October 18, 1999): 62–72.

32. Matthew Grimm, "Snap It, Girlfriend!" *American Demographics* (April 2000): 66–67.

33. Tibbett L. Speer, "College Come-Ons," *American Demographics*, 20 (March 1998): 40–46; quoted in Fannie Weinstein, "Time to Get Them in Your Franchise," *Advertising Age* (February 1, 1988): S6.

34. Quoted in "Advertisers Target College Market," *Marketing News* (October 23, 1987).

35. Beth Bogart, "Word of Mouth Travels Fastest," *Advertising Age* (February 6, 1989): S6; Janice Steinberg, "Media 101," *Advertising Age* (February 6, 1989): S4.

36. Stuart Elliott, "Beyond Beer and Sun Oil: The Beach-Blanket Bazaar," *New York Times* (March 18, 1992): D17.

37. Laura Zinn, "Move Over, Boomers," *Business Week* (December 14, 1992): 7.

38. Scott Donaton, "The Media Wakes Up to Generation X," *Advertising Age* (February 1, 1993): 16; Laura E. Keeton, "New Magazines Aim to Reach (and Rechristen) Generation X," *The Wall Street Journal* (October 17, 1994): B1.

39. Robert Scally, "The Customer Connection: Gen X Grows Up, They're in Their 30s Now," *Discount Store News* 38, no. 20 (October 25, 1999).

40. Faye Rice, "Making Generational Marketing Come of Age," *Fortune* (June 26, 1995): 110–14.

41. Brad Edmondson, "Do the Math," *American Demographics* (October 1999): 50–56.

42. Rice, "Making Generational Marketing Come of Age."

43. Christine Blank, "Parking It for Fun," *American Demographics* (April 1998): 6.

44. T. Trent Gegax, "Booming Amusement Parks: The Theme Is Extreme," *Newsweek* (March 30, 1998): 2.

45. John Fetto, "The Wild Ones," *American Demographics* (February 2000): 72.

46. Kevin Keller, *Strategic Marketing Management* (Upper Saddle River, NJ: Prentice Hall, 1998).

47. Brad Edmondson, "Do the Math," *American Demographics* (October 1999): 50–56.

48. Albert Scardino, "The New Baby Boom Spurs Local Magazines for Parents," *New York Times* (June 26, 1989): D1.

49. Patricia Braus, "Facing Menopause," *American Demographics* (March 1993): 44.

50. Quoted in Blayne Cutler, "Marketing to Menopausal Men," *American Demographics* (March 1993): 49.

51. William Lazer and Eric H. Shaw, "How Older Americans Spend Their Money," *American Demographics* (September 1987): 36; see also Charles D. Schewe and Anne L. Balazs, "Role Transitions in Older Adults: A Marketing Opportunity," *Psychology & Marketing* 9 (March/April 1992): 85–99.

52. D'Vera Cohn, "2100 Census Forecast: Minorities Expected to Account for 60% of U.S. Population," *The Washington Post* (January 13, 2000): A5.

53. Catherine A. Cole and Nadine N. Castellano, "Consumer Behavior," in James E. Binnen, ed., *Encyclopedia of Gerontology*, vol. 1 (San Diego: Academic Press, 1996): 329–39.

54. Cheryl Russell, "The Ungraying of America," *American Demographics* (July 1997): 12.

55. Jeff Brazil, "You Talkin' to Me?" *American Demographics* (December 1998): 55–59.

56. David B. Wolfe, "Targeting the Mature Mind," *American Demographics* (March 1994): 32–36.

57. Benny Barak and Leon G. Schiffman, "Cognitive Age: A Nonchronological Age Variable," in Kent B. Monroe, ed.,

Advances in Consumer Research 8 (Provo, UT: Association for Consumer Research, 1981): 602–6.

58. David B. Wolfe, "An Ageless Market," *American Demographics* (July 1987): 27–55.

59. Dolly Setton, "Cyber Granny," *Forbes* (May 22, 2000): 40.

60. Lenore Skenazy, "These Days, It's Hip to Be Old," *Advertising Age* (February 15, 1988): 8.

61. Lazer and Shaw, "How Older Americans Spend Their Money."

62. L. A. Winokur, "Targeting Consumers," *The Wall Street Journal Interactive Edition* (March 6, 2000).

63. Ellen Day, Brian Davis, Rhonda Dove, and Warren A. French, "Reaching the Senior Citizen Market(s)," *Journal of Advertising Research* (December 1987–January 1988): 23–30.

64. Day et al., "Reaching the Senior Citizen Market(s)"; Warren A. French and Richard Fox, "Segmenting the Senior Citizen Market," *Journal of Consumer Marketing* 2 (1985): 61–74; Jeffrey G. Towle and Claude R. Martin Jr., "The Elderly Consumer: One Segment or Many?" in Beverlee B. Anderson, ed., *Advances in Consumer Research* 3 (Provo, UT: Association for Consumer Research, 1976): 463.

65. Catherine A. Cole and Nadine N. Castellano, "Consumer Behavior," *Encyclopedia of Gerontology*, vol. 1 (1996): 329–39.

66. Rick Adler, "Stereotypes Won't Work with Seniors Anymore," *Advertising Age* (November 11, 1996): 32.

67. Melinda Beck, "Going for the Gold," *Newsweek* (April 23, 1990): 74.

68. Paco Underhill, "Seniors & Stores," *American Demographics* (April 1996): 44–48.

69. Michelle Krebs, "50-Plus and King of the Road," *Advertising Age* (May 1, 2000): S18; Daniel McGinn and Julie Edelson Halpert, "Driving Miss Daisy—and Selling Her the Car," *Newsweek* (February 3, 1997): 14.

70. J. Ward, "Marketers Slow to Catch Age Wave," *Advertising Age* (May 22, 1989): S-1.

FEELING LUCKY?

SECTION

V

LuckySurf.com

CONSUMERS AND CULTURE

The final section of this book looks at consumers as members of a broad cultural system, and reminds us that even everyday, mundane consumption activities often are rooted in deeper meanings. Chapter 16 looks at some of the basic building blocks of culture and the impact that such underlying processes as myths and rituals exert on "modern" consumers. Chapter 17 focuses on the ways that products spread throughout the members of a culture, and across cultures as well. This final chapter considers the process by which some consumer products succeed and others don't, and also examines how successful Western products influence the consumption practices of people around the world.

Section Outline

Whitney is at her wits' end. It's bad enough that she has a deadline looming on that new Christmas promotion for her gift shop. Now, there's trouble on the home front as well: Her son Stephen had to go and flunk his driver's license road exam, and he's just about suicidal because he feels he can't be a "real man" without successfully

obtaining his license. To top things off, now her much-antici-pated vacation to Disney World with her younger stepchildren will have to be postponed because she just can't find the time to get away.

When Whitney meets up with her buddy Shannon at their local Starbucks for their daily "retreat" her mood starts to brighten. Somehow the calm of the cafe rubs off as she savors her grande cappuccino. Shannon consoles her

with her usual assurances, and then she prescribes the ulti-mate remedy to defeat the blues: Go home, take a nice ong bath, and then consume a quart of Starbucks Espresso Swirl ice cream. Yes, that's the ticket. It's amazing how the little things in life can make such a big dif-ference. As she strolls out the door, Whitney makes a mental note to get Shannon a really nice Christmas gift this year. She's earned it.

16

CULTURAL INFLUENCES ON CONSUMER BEHAVIOR

UNDERSTANDING CULTURE

Whitney's daily coffee "fix" is mimicked in various forms around the globe, as people participate in activities that allow them to take a break and affirm their relationships with others. Of course, the products that are consumed in the process can range from black Turkish coffee to Indian tea, or from lager beer to hashish.

Starbucks has experienced phenomenal success by turning the coffee break into a cultural event that, for many, has assumed almost cultlike status. The average Starbucks customer visits 18 times a month, and 10 percent of the clientele stops by twice a day.[1] In 2000 Starbucks announced plans to add 450 U.S. stores to its existing base of more than 2,200 coffeehouses and eventually to add 100 locations in Asia and 50 in Britain to its already 300-plus international stores.[2] And, the chain is innovating to create different kinds of coffee break experiences. It opened an experimental restaurant called Circadia in San Francisco that resurrects the feel of 1960s coffee shops in Greenwich Village. It's decorated with vintage furniture but equipped with high-speed Net connections, credit card swipe machines, and a conference room to accommodate the need of start-up entrepreneurs for meeting places where they can cut power deals.

Culture, a concept crucial to the understanding of consumer behavior, may be thought of as a society's personality. It includes both abstract ideas, such as values and ethics, and material objects and services, such as the automobile, clothing, food, art, and sports, that are produced or valued by a society. Put another way, **culture** is the accumulation of shared meanings, rituals, norms, and traditions among the members of an organization or society.

Consumption choices simply cannot be understood without considering the cultural context in which they are made: Culture is the "lens" through which people view products. Ironically, the effects of culture on consumer behavior are so powerful and far-reaching that their importance is sometimes difficult to grasp. Like a fish immersed in water, we do not always appreciate this power until we encounter a different environment. Suddenly many of the assumptions we had taken for granted about the clothes we wear, the food we eat, the way we address others, and so on no longer seem to apply. The effect of encountering such differences can be so great the term "culture shock" is not an exaggeration.

The importance of these cultural expectations is often only discovered when they are violated. For example, while on tour in New Zealand, the Spice Girls (remember them?) created a stir among New Zealand's indigenous Maoris by performing a war dance only men are supposed to do. A tribal official indignantly stated, "It is not acceptable in our culture, and especially by girlie pop stars from another culture."[3] Sensitivity to cultural issues, whether by rock stars or by brand managers, can only come by understanding these underlying dimensions—that is the goal of this chapter.

A consumer's culture determines the overall priorities that the consumer attaches to different activities and products, and it also mandates the success or failure of specific products and services. A product that provides benefits consistent with those desired by members of a culture at any point in time has a much better chance of attaining acceptance in the marketplace. For example, American culture started to emphasize the concept of a fit, trim body as an ideal of appearance in the mid-1970s. The premium placed on this goal, which stemmed from underlying values such as mobility, wealth, and a focus on the self, greatly contributed to the success of Miller Lite beer at that time. However, when Gablinger introduced a low-cal beer in the 1960s the product failed. This beverage was "ahead of its time" because American consumers were not yet interested in cutting down on calories when drinking brew.

The relationship between consumer behavior and culture is a two-way street. On the one hand, products and services that resonate with the priorities of a culture at any given time have a much better chance of being accepted by consumers. On the other hand, the study of new products and innovations in product design successfully produced by a culture at any point in time provides a window into the dominant cultural ideals of that period. Consider, for example, some American products that reflect underlying cultural processes at the time they were introduced:

- The TV dinner, which hinted at changes in family structure and the onset of a new informality in American home life.
- Cosmetics made of natural materials without animal testing, which reflected consumers' apprehensions about pollution, waste, and animal rights.
- Condoms marketed in pastel carrying cases for female buyers, which signaled changes in attitudes toward sexual responsibility and openness.

Culture is not static. It is continually evolving, synthesizing old ideas with new ones. A cultural system consists of three functional areas:[4]

1. *Ecology:* the way in which a system is adapted to its habitat. This area is shaped by the technology used to obtain and distribute resources (e.g., industrialized societies versus Third World countries). The Japanese, for example, greatly value products that are designed for efficient use of space because of the cramped conditions in that island nation.[5]

2. *Social structure:* the way in which orderly social life is maintained. This includes the domestic and political groups that are dominant within the culture (e.g., the nuclear family versus the extended family; representative government versus dictatorship).

3. *Ideology:* the mental characteristics of a people and the way in which they relate to their environment and social groups. This revolves around the notion that members of a society possess a common **worldview.** They share certain ideas about principles of order and fairness. They also share an ethos, or a set of moral and aesthetic principles. A new theme park in Bombay that caters to India's emerging middle-class called Water Kingdom illustrates how a culture's worldview can be distinctive. Many consumers there are unfamiliar with mixed-sex public activities of this nature, so the park rents swimsuits to women who have never worn one before. No thongs here, though: The suits cover the women from wrists to ankles.[6]

Although every culture is different, four dimensions appear to account for much of this variability:[7]

1. *Power distance:* the way in which interpersonal relationships form when differences in power are perceived. Some cultures emphasize strict, vertical relationships (e.g., Japan), whereas others, such as the United States, stress a greater degree of equality and informality.

2. *Uncertainty avoidance:* the degree to which people feel threatened by ambiguous situations and have beliefs and institutions that help them to avoid this uncertainty (e.g., organized religion).

3. *Masculinity/femininity:* the degree to which sex roles are clearly delineated (see Chapter 5). Traditional societies are more likely to possess very explicit rules about the acceptable behaviors of men and women, such as who is responsible for certain tasks within the family unit.

4. *Individualism:* the extent to which the welfare of the individual versus that of the group is valued (see Chapter 11). Cultures differ in their emphasis on individualism versus collectivism. In **collectivist cultures,** people subordinate their personal goals to those of a stable in-group. In contrast, consumers in **individualist cultures** attach more importance to personal goals, and people are more likely to change memberships when the demands of the group (e.g., workplace, church, etc.) become too costly. Whereas a collectivist society will stress values (see Chapter 4) such as self-discipline and accepting one's position in life, people in individualist cultures emphasize personal enjoyment, excitement, equality, and freedom. Some strongly individualistic cultures include the United States, Australia, Great Britain, Canada, and the Netherlands. Venezuela, Pakistan, Taiwan, Thailand, Turkey, Greece, and Portugal are some examples of strongly collectivist cultures.[8]

Values are very general ideas about good and bad goals. From these flow **norms,** or rules dictating what is right or wrong, acceptable or unacceptable. Some norms, called *enacted norms,* are explicitly decided on, such as the rule that a green traffic light means "go" and a red one means "stop." Many norms, however, are much more subtle. These *crescive norms* are embedded in a culture and are only discovered through interaction with other members of that culture. Crescive norms include the following:[9]

- A **custom** is a norm handed down from the past that controls basic behaviors, such as division of labor in a household or the practice of particular ceremonies.
- A **more** ("mor-ay") is a custom with a strong moral overtone. A more often involves a taboo, or forbidden behavior, such as incest or cannibalism. Violation of a more often meets with strong sanctions from other members of a society.
- **Conventions** are norms regarding the conduct of everyday life. These rules deal with the subtleties of consumer behavior, including the "correct" way to furnish one's house, wear one's clothes, host a dinner party, and so on.

All three types of crescive norms may operate to completely define a culturally appropriate behavior. For example, a more may tell us what kind of food is permissible to eat. Note that mores vary across cultures, so a meal of dog may be taboo in the United States, Hindus shun steak, and Muslims avoid pork products. A custom dictates the appropriate hour at which the meal should be served. Conventions tell us how to eat the meal, including such details as the utensils to be used, table etiquette, and even the appropriate apparel to be worn at dinnertime.

We often take these conventions for granted, assuming that they are the "right" things to do (again, until we travel to a foreign country!). It is good to remember that much of what we know about these norms is learned *vicariously* (see Chapter 3) as we observe the behaviors of actors in television commercials, sitcoms, print ads, and other media.

Cultural differences show up in all kinds of daily activities. For example, when a Big Boy restaurant first opened in Thailand, attracting customers was very difficult. After interviewing hundreds of people the company found out why. Some said the restaurant's "room energy" was bad and that the food was unfamiliar. Others said the Big Boy statue (like the one Dr. Evil rode in the *Austin Powers* movies) made them nervous. One of the restaurant's executives commented, "It suddenly dawned on me that, here I was, trying to get a 3,500-year-old culture to eat 64-year-old food." Now, after the company puts some Thai items on the menu business is picking up.[10] No word yet on the fate of the statue.

MYTHS AND RITUALS

Every culture develops stories and practices that help its members to make sense of the world. When we examine these activities in other cultures, they often seem strange or even unfathomable. Yet, our *own* cultural practices appear quite normal—even though a visitor may find them equally bizarre!

To appreciate how "primitive" belief systems that some may consider bizarre, irrational, or superstitious continue to influence our supposedly "modern" rational society, consider the avid interest of many American consumers in magic. Marketers of health foods, anti-aging cosmetics, exercise programs, and gambling casinos often imply that their offerings have "magical" properties that will ward off sickness, old age, poverty, or just plain bad luck. People by the millions play their "lucky numbers" in the lottery, carry rabbits' feet and other amulets to ward off "the evil eye," and have "lucky" clothing or other products that they believe will bring them good fortune. Sometimes consumers regard "extraordinary" activities such as extreme sports as magical. For example, white-water river rafters report that the rites and rituals they practice on their trips have transformed their lives in profound ways.[11] Software developers even supply "wizards" that help guide the unitiated through their programs!

An interest in the occult tends to be popular when members of a society feel overwhelmed or powerless—magical remedies simplify our lives by giving us "easy" answers. Even a computer is regarded with awe by many consumers as a sort of "electronic magician" with the ability to solve our problems (or in other cases to cause data to magically disappear!).[12] This section will discuss myths and rituals, two aspects of culture common to all societies from the ancients to the modern world.

Myths

A **myth** is a story containing symbolic elements that expresses the shared emotions and ideals of a culture. The story often features some kind of conflict between two opposing forces, and its outcome serves as a moral guide for people. In this way, a myth reduces anxiety because it provides consumers with guidelines about their world. Every society possesses a set of myths that define that culture.

LuckySurf.com, a free lottery site, puts an interesting twist on the common practice of keeping a lucky rabbit's foot.

An understanding of cultural myths is important to marketers, who in some cases (most likely unconsciously) pattern their strategy along a mythic structure. Consider, for example, the way that McDonald's takes on "mythical" qualities.[13] The "golden arches" are a universally recognized symbol, one that is virtually synonymous with American culture. They offer sanctuary to Americans around the world, who know exactly what to expect once they enter. Basic struggles involving good versus evil are played out in the fantasy world created by McDonald's advertising, as when Ronald McDonald confounds the Hamburglar. McDonald's even has a "seminary" (Hamburger University) where inductees go to learn appropriate behavior.

Corporations often have myths and legends as a part of their history, and some make a deliberate effort to be sure newcomers to the organization learn these. Nike designates senior executives as "corporate storytellers" who explain the company's heritage to other employees, including the hourly workers at Nike stores. They tell stories about the founders of Nike, including the coach of the Oregon track team who poured rubber into his family waffle iron to make better shoes for his team—the origin of the Nike waffle sole. The stories emphasize the dedication of runners and coaches involved with the company to reinforce the importance of teamwork. Rookies even visit the track where the coach worked to be sure they grasp the importance of the Nike legends.[14]

The Functions and Structure of Myths

Myths serve four interrelated functions in a culture:[15]

1. *Metaphysical:* They help to explain the origins of existence.
2. *Cosmological:* They emphasize that all components of the universe are part of a single picture.
3. *Sociological:* They maintain social order by authorizing a social code to be followed by members of a culture.
4. *Psychological:* They provide models for personal conduct.

Myths can be analyzed by examining their underlying structures, a technique pioneered by the French anthropologist Claude Lévi-Strauss (no relation to the blue jeans company). Lévi-Strauss noted that many stories involve **binary opposition,** in which two opposing ends of some dimension are represented (e.g., good

This ad for a line of veggie foods borrows the look of wartime propaganda art to imply that eating your broccoli is an heroic act.

versus evil, nature versus technology).[16] Characters, and in some cases, products, are often defined by what they are not rather than what they *are* (e.g., "This is *not* your father's Oldsmobile," "I can't believe it's *not* butter").

Recall from the discussion of Freudian theory in Chapter 6 that the ego functions as a kind of "referee" between the opposing needs of the id and the superego. In a similar fashion, the conflict between mythical opposing forces is sometimes resolved by a *mediating figure* who can link the opposites by sharing characteristics of each. For example, many myths contain animals that have human abilities (e.g., a talking snake) to bridge the gap between humanity and nature, just as cars (technology) are often given animal names (nature) such as Cougar, Cobra, or Mustang.

Myths Abound in Modern Popular Culture

We generally associate myths with the ancient Greeks or Romans, but modern myths are embodied in many aspects of modern popular culture including comic books, movies, holidays, and yes, even commercials. Comic book superheroes demonstrate how myths can be communicated to consumers of all ages in order to teach a lesson about a culture. For example, Marvel Comics' Spiderman character tells stories about balancing the obligations of being a superhero with the need of his alter ego, Peter Parker, to do his homework.[17] Indeed, some of these fictional figures represent a **monomyth,** a myth that is common to many cultures.[18] The most prevalent monomyth involves a hero such as Superman who emerges from the everyday world with supernatural powers and wins a decisive victory over evil forces. He then returns with the power to bestow good things on his fellow men.

Many "blockbuster" movies and hit TV shows draw directly on mythic themes. Although dramatic special effects or attractive stars certainly don't hurt, a number of these movies perhaps also owe their success to their presentation of characters and plot structures, which follow mythic patterns. Three examples of these mythic blockbusters are:[19]

- *Gone with the Wind.* Myths are often set in times of upheaval such as wars. In this story, the North (which represents technology and democracy) is pitted again the South (which represents nature and aristocracy). The movie depicts a romantic era (the antebellum South) in which love and honor were virtues. This era is replaced by the newer forces of materialism and industrialization (i.e., modern consumer culture). The movie depicts a lost era in which man and nature existed in harmony.
- *E.T.: The Extraterrestrial.* E.T. represents a familiar myth involving messianic visitation. The gentle creature from another world visits Earth and performs miracles (e.g., reviving a dying flower). His "disciples" are neighborhood children, who help him combat the forces of modern technology and an unbelieving secular society. The metaphysical function of myth is served by teaching that the humans chosen by God are pure and unselfish.
- *Star Trek:* The television series and movies documenting the adventures of the starship Enterprise are also linked to myths, such as the story of the New England Puritans exploring and conquering a new continent—"the final frontier." Encounters with the Klingons mirror skirmishes with Native Americans. In addition, the quest for paradise was a theme employed in at least 13 out of the original 79 episodes filmed.[20]

The popular Star Trek saga is based on myths, including the quest for paradise.

Commercials can also be analyzed in terms of the underlying mythic themes they represent. For example, commercials for Pepperidge Farm ask consumers to "remember" the good old days (lost paradise) when products were wholesome and natural. The theme of the underdog prevailing over the stronger foe (i.e., David and Goliath) has been used by Chrysler and Avis.[21]

Rituals

A **ritual** is a set of multiple, symbolic behaviors that occur in a fixed sequence and that tend to be repeated periodically.[22] Bizarre tribal ceremonies, perhaps involving animal or human sacrifice, may come to mind when people think of rituals, but in reality many contemporary consumer activities are ritualistic. Just think of Whitney's daily "mental health" trip to Starbucks.

REALITY CHECK *RITUALS CAN PROVIDE US WITH A SENSE OF order and security. In a study of the drinking rituals of college students, the researchers found that drinking imposed order in students' daily lives—from the completion of assignments to what and when to eat. In addition, ritualizing an activity such as drinking provided security and fellowship at a time fraught with confusion and turbulent change.*

Obviously, though, there's a dark side to drinking rituals. Consider the highly publicized death of a Massachusetts Institute of Technology student who died three days after falling into an alcohol-induced coma as the result of a fraternity pledge function.[23] Indeed, although binge drinking is probably the most widely practiced ritual among college students, it also has been described as the most significant health hazard on college campuses today.[24]

What role does drinking play in the social life on your campus? Based on your experience, how does it fit into rituals of college life? Should these practices be changed? If so, how?

Drinking is a major part of the social life at my university. From frat parties to apartment kegs, parties are always going on. Students are frequently finding reasons to drink, to celebrate finishing a test or to ease the stress of a week. When its your birthday, your friends throw you a party, and you and 75 of your close friends party it up. When pledges get initiated, their fraternity throws a party with endless amounts of beer. If a concert comes to town, friends gather and pre-party. . . . Numerous clubs and organizations sponsor non-alcoholic dances and excursions. Theatres showcase plays and films. Just because a student wishes not to drink, does not eliminate him from the party scene. Students are very accepting of non-drinkers. My best friend does not drink, and is still able to be the life of the party, dancing, and smiling with endless energy through the night.

Katherine S. Kennedy
James Madison University

Drinking plays a very important role in the social life here. Students enjoy a few pints after handing in a project, doing a presentation or sitting an exam. It's seen as a type of reward for work done. It is particularly so when students feel under pressure, whether due to personal problems or college issues. . . . Students are proud of their drinking "talents" and "abilities" and often display empty bottles on the windowsill or build a wall of empty cans. Of course it should not be like this but it is practically impossible to change. Going to college is a rite of passage into young adulthood and drinking is one form of expressing this. Students are no longer living at home and have just reached the legal drinking age, which is 18 here in Ireland, so of course major drinking sessions are expected of them by fellow students.

Pamela Gillen
Dublin City University, Ireland

When someone just took a very difficult test and did well on it, they would celebrate by drinking themselves into stupidity. It was a way of rewarding good behavior. When someone took a very difficult test and did not score well on it, they drank in order to forget the bad grade and recover from their failure. When someone was rushing a fraternity, alcohol was always present because someone is more susceptible to outside influences when they are intoxicated. As a celebration for pledging a fraternity, people drank to excess. It was also a mating ritual of sorts. . . . As you can see, alcohol and binge drinking served many goals at the university I attended.

I think that experimentation in all of its forms is a necessary part of college. The classes are an important part of your life (or should be), but it should not be the end all and be all of your existence. Those that confine themselves to their room for all four years and never attempt to experiment with anything new will condemn themselves to a life without any pleasure. As for changing the practices of these college students? I don't think that it's necessarily possible. Several universities have attempted to make their campus dry and I know for a fact that it has not succeeded. Instead of drinking openly (at these campuses) these people drink behind closed and locked doors and the administration looks on with a blind eye. I believe that if anything should be done, a step in the direction of moderation by college students should be done. But then again, who doesn't like to pray to the porcelain god after a long night of drinking?

Gregory T. Varveris
DePaul University

Reality Check continues

Drinking does seem to be linked to ritualistic behavior for many college students. Weekends begin Thursday nights and end on Saturday. For many, drinking has become a ritual by rewarding both achievements and failures. Many students drink after a hard week of exams, to celebrate a new job, or to relax after a stressful paper. It is often a time to build relationships and enjoy the freedom of college life. . . . The importance of having a sober ride, having fun at a party without alcohol, and the effects of peer pressure and drinking should be stressed to students. Drinking helps many students unwind and helps develop relationships with other students. Together, these make the student more successful in college. It may not be right for every student, but is an important aspect of college life that would be difficult to remove.

Jennifer Freet
George Mason University

Drinking seems to be part of Japanese culture which is not only practiced by young college students but also by many of the businessmen of Japan. I think in Japanese culture there are not much times where people speak frankly about each other and about their thoughts. And in such situations alcohol plays an important role.

What is a common ritual in Japan is, when you are served a drink from your elderly, you are not to refuse it. And when the elderly has nothing to drink, the others are to fill up their cup. And in each of these cases, not finishing a drink is considered to be rude. This is practiced heavily among the sports clubs in Japanese colleges. This seems to increase the amounts of drinking, but by drinking, people are allowed to become frank to the elderly, which is not allowed when they are not drunk. This allows these people to have a better relationship to them than without drinks.

Ayano Yamada
Keio University, Japan

Alcohol consumption plays a big role in the lives of many UAF students. Many view Fairbanks, Alaska, as an isolated and boring place to live with not much to do here. Students drink to socialize, make friends, and often times just to get drunk. Not a single event goes without drinking alcohol.

Among the most popular drinking rituals is Case Day . . . The Case Day ritual involves each individual drinking a case of beer in 24 hours (one beer per hour). During that day, most of the students on campus are "hammered." Many students even walk around with marks on their arms to prove, or keep track of, how many drinks they have had so far.

I don't think the drinking rituals at the UAF campus should be changed. They don't hurt anyone. Sooner or later, most young people have this experience anyway. Most of the ones that do realize there are more important things in life than "getting wasted" with friends. As for the ones that don't realize it, oh well, we all make choices in life.

Dmitri Batsev
University of Alaska, Fairbanks

What's your opinion? Check out the online polls at www.prenhall.com/myphlip. Just follow the little person in the lab coat.

Rituals can occur at a variety of levels, as noted in Table 16.1. Some affirm broad cultural or religious values, whereas others occur in small groups or even in isolation. Market researchers discovered, for example, that for many people (like Whitney) the act of late-night ice cream eating has ritualistic elements, often involving a favorite spoon and bowl![25] And, rituals are not always set in stone; they can modified to change with the times. If you don't believe that, check out the wedding cam at discovery.com/cams/wedding/wedding.html. In addition to this innovation, which lets you watch weddings at The Little White Chapel in Las Vegas online, the custom of throwing rice to symbolizes fertility at weddings is evolving as well. In recent years many newlyweds have substituted soap bubbles or jingling bells because of the tendency of birds to eat the rice, which can then expand inside their bodies and cause injury or death. Some enterprising businesses are springing up to work around this problem. The Hole-in-Hand Butterfly Farm in Pennsylvania ships newly hatched butterflies at $100 a dozen. They arrive in dark, cool envelopes that keep them in a resting stage until the package is opened, when they fly out in a crescendo of wagging wings. Another company sells a product called Bio Wedding Rice; this is reconstituted rice that dissolves in water and doesn't harm birds.[26]

TABLE 16.1 Types of Ritual Experience

Primary Behavior Source	Ritual Type	Examples
Cosmology	Religious	Baptism, meditation, mass
Cultural values	Rites of passage Cultural	Graduation, marriage festivals, holidays (Valentine's Day), Super Bowl
Group learning	Civic Group	Parades, elections, trials Fraternity initiation, business negotiations, office luncheons
	Family	Mealtimes, bedtimes, birthdays, Mother's Day, Christmas
Individual aims and emotions	Personal	Grooming, household rituals

SOURCE: Dennis W. Rook "The Ritual Dimension of Consumer Behavior," *Journal of Consumer Research* 12 (December 1985): 251–64. Reprinted with permission of The University of Chicago Press.

Many businesses owe their livelihoods to their ability to supply **ritual artifacts,** or items used in the performance of rituals such as wedding rice, to consumers. Birthday candles, diplomas, specialized foods and beverages (e.g., wedding cakes, ceremonial wine, or even hot dogs at the ball park), trophies and plaques, band uniforms, greeting cards, retirement watches, and now espresso makers are all used in consumer rituals.[27] In addition, consumers often employ a *ritual script,* which identifies the artifacts, the sequence in which they are used, and who uses them. Examples include graduation programs, fraternity manuals, and etiquette books.

Grooming Rituals

Whether brushing one's hair 100 strokes a day or talking to oneself in the mirror, virtually all consumers have private grooming rituals. These are sequences of behaviors that aid in the transition from the private self to the public self or back again. These rituals serve various purposes, ranging from inspiring confidence before confronting the world to cleansing the body of dirt and other impure materials. When consumers talk about their grooming rituals, some of the dominant themes that emerge from these stories reflect the almost mystical qualities attributed to grooming products and behaviors. Many people emphasize a before-and-after phenomenon, whereby the person feels magically transformed after using certain products (similar to the Cinderella myth).[28]

Two sets of binary oppositions expressed in personal rituals are *private/public* and *work/leisure.* Many beauty rituals, for instance, reflect a transformation from a natural state to the social world (as when a woman "puts on her face") or vice versa. In these daily rituals, women reaffirm the value placed by their culture on personal beauty and the quest for eternal youth.[29] This focus is obvious in ads for Oil of Olay Beauty Cleanser, which proclaim "And so your day begins. The Ritual of Oil of Olay." Similarly, the bath is viewed as a sacred, cleansing time, a way to wash away the "sins" of the profane world.[30]

Gift-Giving Rituals

The promotion of appropriate gifts for every conceivable holiday and occasion provides an excellent example of the influence consumer rituals can exert on marketing phenomena. In the **gift-giving ritual,** consumers procure the perfect object, meticulously remove the price tag and carefully wrap it (symbolically changing the item from a commodity to a unique good), and deliver it to the recipient.[31]

Researchers view gift-giving as a form of *economic exchange,* in which the giver transfers an item of value to a recipient, who in turn is somehow obligated to reciprocate. However, gift-giving also can involve *symbolic exchange,* whereby a giver such as Whitney wants to acknowledge her friend Shannon's intangible support and companionship. Some research indicates that gift-giving evolves as a form of social expression. It is more exchange-oriented (instrumental) in the early stages of a relationship, but becomes more altruistic as the relationship develops.[32] One set of researchers identified multiple ways in which giving a gift can affect a relationship. These are listed in Table 16.2.[33]

Every culture prescribes certain occasions and ceremonies for giving gifts, whether for personal or professional reasons. The giving of birthday presents alone is a major undertaking. Each American on average buys about six birthday gifts a year—about one billion gifts in total.[40] Business gifts are an important component in defining professional relationships. Expenditures on business gifts exceed $1.5 billion per year, and great care is taken to ensure that the appropriate gifts are purchased (sometimes with the aid of professional gift consultants). Most executives believe that corporate gift-giving provides both tangible and intangible results including improved employee morale and higher sales.[41]

TABLE 16.2 Effects of Gift-Giving on Social Relationships

Relational Effect	Description	Example
Strengthening	Gift-giving improves the quality of a relationship	An unexpected gift such as one given in a romantic situation
Affirmation	Gift-giving validates the positive quality of a relationship	Usually occurs on ritualized occasions such as birthdays
Negligible Effect	Gift-giving has a minimal effect on perceptions of relationship quality	Informal gift occasions and those in which the gift may be perceived as charity or too good for the current state of the relationship
Negative Confirmation	Gift-giving validates a negative quality of a relationship between the gift giver and receiver	The selection of gift is inappropriate indicating a lack of knowledge of the receiver; alternatively, the gift is viewed as a method of controlling the receiver
Weakening	Gift-giving harms the quality of the relationship between giver and receiver	When there are "strings attached" or the gift is perceived as a bribe, a sign of disrespect, or offensive
Severing	Gift-giving harms the relationship between the giver and receiver to the extent that the relationship is dissolved	When the gift forms part of a larger problem, such as in a threatening relationship; also when a relationship is severed through the receipt of a "parting" gift

SOURCE: Adapted from Julie A. Ruth, Cele C. Otnes, and Frederic F. Brunel, "Gift Receipt and the Reformulation of Interpersonal Relationships," *Journal of Consumer Research* 25 (March 1999): 385–402, Table 1, p. 389.

NET PROFIT

FOR BETTER OR WORSE, the Web is transforming the age-old ritual of buying wedding gifts. Numerous online gift registries take the guesswork out of buying that perfect toaster for the new couple. These sites collect a referral fee from a retailer if a purchase is made.[34] Although registries have been around since the early 1930s, they used to be more subtle—Macy's department store used to publish "Hints on Hinting" to give advice to brides about gently suggesting what to buy.

Competition for the matrimonial market is fierce, so registry sites are scrambling to offer new incentives that will engage the engaged. At theknot.com the couple can even subsidize their honeymoon airfare: They earn a frequent-flier mile for every dollar their guests spend on them. At weddingchannel.com, the lucky couple creates a personal wedding page on which they post directions and pictures, plan toasts and seating arrangements, and tell stories about how they met. Guests pull up updated versions of a gift registry and purchase from retailers directly through the Web site. The Wedding Channel hopes to track its customers (assuming they stay married) and create registries as they celebrate anniversaries and the arrival of babies (uh oh, need another gift!). One of the site's

executives says, "Once I have you, unless you stop me, you are a demographic dream."[35]

The proliferation of these registries is understandable given that this business now takes in $19 billion a year. The average wedding party includes 12 people (including six who get stuck with those awful dresses) plus 150 guests. On average, the bride and groom register for more than 50 products and receive an average of 171 wedding gifts.[36] About half of the couples register at a place they have never shopped before, giving retailers a new customer base. According to the publisher of *Bride's* magazine, "If you can hook this consumer when she is in this life stage, you will fundamentally brand her for life." Wedding registries continue to evolve; some couples have become so brazen that they are requesting specific shares of stock (at Stockgift.com), contributions to fund an around-the-world trip, or even mortgage payments on that new dream house (available on a special registry maintained by the U.S. Department of Housing and Urban Development at hud.gov).

Of course, there are downsides to this new efficiency: Because the wedding couple specifies exactly what they want in advance, the giver doesn't really have to know very much about the recipients. Part of gift-giving is developing or reinforcing a symbolic relationship, but now the process is much more automated. As one etiquette expert disdainfully points out, in the old days (pre-Net) people were supposed to be "zealous with creativity" when selecting a gift. "Now, it's just gimme, gimme, gimme with a dollar amount attached." And in many cases the registry is listed on the invitation itself—a social no-no.[37] Registries also eliminate the likelihood of getting homemade or creative gifts.

In addition, the "surprise factor" goes away, because the recipients can see in advance which gifts they will get by checking what has been purchased on their registry.[38] In fact, you can even "snoop" on what other couples (including celebrities) are getting by accessing their registry information. On the other hand, the Web also offers a solution for that one irritating guest who insists on giving those "unique" psychedelic tie-dyed linens: giftxchange.com is a broker for people who want to unload unwanted gifts in exchange for something they really like.

The gift-giving ritual can be broken down into three distinct stages.[42] During *gestation,* the giver is motivated by an event to procure a gift. This event may be either *structural* (i.e., prescribed by the culture, as when people buy Christmas presents) or *emergent* (i.e., the decision is more personal and idiosyncratic). The second stage is *presentation,* or the process of gift exchange. The recipient responds to the gift (either appropriately or not), and the donor evaluates this response.

In the third stage, known as *reformulation,* the bonds between the giver and receiver are adjusted (either looser or tighter) to reflect the new relationship that emerges after the exchange is complete. Negativity can arise if the recipient feels the gift is inappropriate or of inferior quality. For example, the hapless husband who gives his wife a vacuum cleaner as an anniversary present is asking for trouble, as is the new suitor who gives his girlfriend intimate apparel. The donor may feel the response to the gift was inadequate or insincere or a violation of the **reciprocity norm,** which obliges people to return the gesture of a gift with one of equal value.[43] Both participants may feel resentful for being "forced" to participate in the ritual.[44]

Nivea is well-known for its numerous skin care products. Research conducted for the company as it sought to develop a more consistent brand image for all of its lines in the 1990s confirmed the important, yet intangible, functions played by these items for women as they conduct their private grooming rituals. The company found that consumers associated the Nivea image with scenes depicting moistures, freshness, and relaxation.[39]

In addition to expressing their feelings toward others through consumption, people commonly find (or devise) reasons to give themselves something as well. It is common for consumers to purchase self-gifts as a way to regulate their behavior. This ritual provides a socially acceptable way of rewarding themselves for good deeds, consoling themselves after negative events, or motivating themselves to accomplish some goal.[45] Indeed, retailers report that it is becoming increasingly common for people to treat themselves while they are ostensibly searching for goodies for others. As one shopper admitted recently, "It's one for them, one for me, one for them."[46]

Figure 16-1 is a projective stimulus similar to ones used in research on this phenomenon. Consumers are asked to tell a story based on a picture, and their responses are analyzed to discover the reasons people view as legitimate for rewarding themselves with **self-gifts.** For example, one recurring story that might emerge is that Mary, the woman pictured, had a particularly grueling day at the office and needs a pick-me-up in the form of a new fragrance. This theme could then be incorporated into the promotional campaign for a perfume.

Holiday Rituals

On holidays consumers step back from their everyday lives and perform ritualistic behaviors unique to those times.[50] Holiday occasions are filled with ritual artifacts and scripts and are increasingly cast as a time for giving gifts by enterprising marketers. The Thanksgiving holiday is bursting with rituals for

Figure 16.1

Projective Drawing to Study the Motivations Underlying the Giving of Self-Gifts

Americans; these scripts include serving (in gluttonous portions) foods such as turkey and cranberry sauce that may only be consumed on that day, complaints about how much one has eaten (yet rising to the occasion to somehow find room for dessert), and (for many) a postmeal trip to the couch for the obligatory football game. On Valentine's Day, standards regarding sex and love are relaxed or altered as people express feelings that may be hidden during the rest of the year.

In addition to established holidays, new occasions are invented to capitalize on the need for cards and other ritual artifacts that will then have to be acquired.[51] These cultural events often originate with the greeting card industry, precisely to stimulate demand for more of its products. Some recently invented holidays include Secretaries' Day and Grandparents' Day. In other cases retailers elevate relatively minor holidays to major ones to provide more merchandising opportunities. Most recently the Mexican holiday of Cinco de Mayo has become an excuse for Caucasians to drink a lot of margaritas. True, the day marks a May 5, 1862 victory by a small army over stronger French forces, but it is not Mexican Independence Day. As the president of a Hispanic-American marketing firm notes, "When Mexicans first come to the United States and somebody mentions that they're all excited about some Cinco de Mayo festival, they say, 'What?' It would be like Canadians making a big deal out of the Boston Tea Party. It's a non-event made into a big deal by marketing." On Cinco de Mayo Americans eat 17 million pounds of avocados (guacamole) and sales jump for tequila and other ethnic products as restaurants and bars catch the fever. Tequila maker Jose Cuervo even dropped a "margarita bar" into the water off of Miami to commemorate "Sink-O de Mayo."[52]

Most cultural holidays are based on a myth, and often an historical (e.g., Miles Standish on Thanksgiving) or imaginary (e.g., Cupid on Valentine's Day) character is at the center of the story. These holidays persist because their basic elements appeal to consumers' deep-seated needs.[53] Two of our holidays that are especially rich both in cultural symbolism and in consumption meanings are Christmas and Halloween:

- The Christmas holiday is bursting with myths and rituals, from adventures at the North Pole to those that happen under the mistletoe. The meaning of Christmas has evolved quite dramatically during the last few hundred years. In colonial times, Christmas celebrations resembled carnivals and were most noted for public rowdiness. Most notable was the tradition of "wassailing" in which packs of poor young people would lay siege to the rich, demanding food and drink. By the end of the 1800s, the mobs were so unruly that Protestant America invented a tradition of families having Christmas gatherings around a tree, a practice "borrowed" from early pagan rites.

- In a 1822 poem, Clement Clarke Moore, the wealthy son of New York's Episcopal bishop, invented the modern-day myth of Santa Claus. The Christmas ritual slowly changed to a focus on children.[54] One of the most important holiday rituals still involves Santa Claus, a mythical figure eagerly awaited by children the world over. In opposition to Christ, Santa is a champion of materialism. Perhaps it is no coincidence, then, that he appears in stores and shopping malls—secular temples of consumption. Whatever his origins, the Santa Claus myth serves the purpose of socializing children by teaching them to expect a reward when they are good and that members of society get what they deserve.

- Halloween evolved from a pagan religious observance to a secular event. However, in contrast to Christmas, the rituals of Halloween (e.g., trick-or-treating and costume parties) primarily involve nonfamily members. Halloween is an unusual holiday because its rituals are the opposite of many other cultural occasions. In contrast to Christmas, it celebrates evil instead of good and death rather than birth, and it encourages revelers to extort treats with veiled threats of "tricks" rather than rewarding only the good. Because of these oppositions, Halloween has been described as an *antifestival*, an event in which the symbols associated with other holidays are distorted. For example, the Halloween witch can be viewed as an inverted mother figure. The holiday also parodies the meaning of Easter by stressing the resurrection of ghosts and of Thanksgiving by transforming the wholesome symbolism of the pumpkin pie into the evil jack-o-lantern.[55] Furthermore, Halloween provides a ritualized, and therefore socially sanctioned, context in which people can act out uncharacteristic behaviors and try on new roles: Children can go outside after dark, stay up late, and eat all the candy they like for a night. The otherwise geeky guy who always sits in the back of class comes dressed as Elvis and turns out to be the life of the party.

Halloween observances among adults are booming, changing the character of this holiday. Halloween is now the second most popular party night for adults (after New Year's Eve), and one in four grown-ups wears a costume.[56] The holiday is now becoming trendy in Europe as well, where the French in particular have discovered it as an occasion for festivities, dancing, and the chance to show off new fashions.[57]

The shift in the Halloween ritual has been attributed to adult fears aroused by stories of children receiving tampered candy containing poison or razor blades,

MULTICULTURAL DIMENSIONS

THE IMPORTANCE OF GIFT-GIVING rituals is underscored by Japanese customs, in which the wrapping of a gift is as important (if not more so) than the gift itself. The economic value of a gift is secondary to its symbolic meaning.[47] To the Japanese, gifts are viewed as an important aspect of one's duty to others in one's social group. Giving is a moral imperative (known as *giri*).

Highly ritualized gift giving occurs during the giving of both household/personal gifts and company/professional gifts. Each Japanese has a well-defined set of relatives and friends with which he or she shares reciprocal gift-giving obligations (*kosai*).[48]

Personal gifts are given on social occasions, such as at funerals, to people who are hospitalized, to mark movements from one life stage to another (e.g., weddings, birthdays), and as greetings (e.g., when one meets a visitor). Company gifts are given to commemorate the anniversary of a corporation's founding, the opening of a new building, or when new products are announced.[49] In keeping with the Japanese emphasis on saving face, presents are not opened in front of the giver so that it will not be necessary to hide one's possible disappointment with the present.

which encourage people to plan supervised parties rather than send their children out trick-or-treating.[58] Another factor accounting for the popularity of Halloween among adults is that, unlike other holidays, one does not require a family to celebrate it, which permits single people to participate without feeling lonely or left out.[59]

Rites of Passage

What does a dance for recently divorced people have in common with a fraternity Hell Week? Both are examples of modern **rites of passage,** or special times marked by a change in social status. Every society, both primitive and modern, sets aside times at which such changes occur. Some of these changes may occur as a natural part of consumers' life-cycles (e.g., puberty or death), whereas others are more individual in nature (e.g., getting divorced and reentering the dating market). As Whitney's son discovered when he bombed his driving test, the importance of a rite of passage becomes more obvious when one fails to undergo it at the prescribed time.

Much like the metamorphosis of a caterpillar into a butterfly, consumers' rites of passage consist of three phases.[60] The first stage, *separation*, occurs when the individual is detached from his or her original group or status (e.g., the college

Halloween is evolving from a children's festival to an opportunity for adults to experiment with fantasy roles—and party.

freshman leaves home). *Liminality* is the middle stage, in which the person is literally between statuses (e.g., the new arrival on campus tries to figure out what is happening during orientation week). The last stage, *aggregation*, takes place when the person reenters society after the rite of passage is complete (e.g., the student returns home for Christmas vacation as a college "veteran").

Rites of passage mark many consumer activities, as exemplified by fraternity pledges, recruits at boot camp, or novitiates becoming nuns. A similar transitional state can be observed when people are prepared for certain occupational roles. For example, athletes and fashion models typically undergo a "seasoning" process. They are removed from their normal surroundings (e.g., athletes are taken to training camps, young models are often moved to Paris), indoctrinated into a new subculture, and then returned to the real world in their new roles.

Funeral ceremonies help the living to organize their relationships with the deceased, and action tends to be tightly scripted, down to the costumes (e.g., the ritual black attire, black ribbons for mourners, the body in its best clothes) and specific behaviors (e.g., sending condolence cards or holding a wake). Mourners "pay their last respects," and seating during the ceremony is usually dictated by mourners' closeness to the individual. Even the *cortege* (the funeral motorcade) is accorded special status by other motorists, who recognize its separate, sacred nature by not cutting in as it proceeds to the cemetery.[64]

SACRED AND PROFANE CONSUMPTION

As we saw when considering the structure of myths, many types of consumer activity involve the demarcation, or binary opposition, of categories, such as good versus bad, male versus female—or even regular versus diet. One of the most important of these sets of categories is the distinction between the sacred and the profane. **Sacred consumption** involves objects and events that are "set apart" from normal activities and are treated with some degree of respect or awe. They may or may not be associated with religion, but most religious items and events tend to be regarded as sacred. **Profane consumption** involves consumer objects and events that are ordinary, everyday objects and events that do not share the "specialness" of sacred ones. (Note that profane does not mean vulgar or obscene in this context.)

Domains of Sacred Consumption

Sacred consumption events permeate many aspects of consumers' experiences. We find ways to "set apart" a variety of places, people, and events. In this section, we'll consider some examples of ways that "ordinary" consumption is sometimes not so ordinary after all.

Sacred Places

Sacred places are "set apart" by a society because they have religious or mystical significance (e.g., Bethlehem, Mecca, Stonehenge) or because they commemorate some aspect of a country's heritage (e.g., the Kremlin, the Emperor's Palace in Tokyo, the Statue of Liberty). The sacredness of these places is due to the property of **contamination**—that is, something sacred happened on that spot, so the place itself takes on sacred qualities.

MARKETING PITFALLS

EVEN RITES OF PASSAGE associated with death support an entire industry. At hardiehouse.org/epitaph you can have your epitaph written before you go. There are a number of "virtual cemeteries" where people can remember a loved one in a virtual grave; check out imminentdomain.com.[61] However, death is not all fun and games: Survivors must make fairly expensive purchase decisions, often on short notice and driven by emotional and superstitious concerns. The funeral industry is beginning to be more aggressive in its marketing practices and is even targeting younger consumers who are worried about arranging for their aging parents. (The prepayment of funeral and burial expenses is euphemistically known in the industry as "preneed.") Perhaps because of the emotional tone many of these appeals take, women tend to initiate these purchases.[62] Congress is investigating these sales practices; the average funeral costs more than $5,000 and burial costs can drive the price as high as $7,500. In one case, the Senate heard testimony about an 80-year-old Florida widow who was persuaded months after the death of her husband to purchase more than $125,000 in unneeded goods and services, including a $40,000 casket and a family mausoleum even though she had no family left.[63]

Still other places are created from the profane world and imbued with sacred qualities. Graumann's Chinese Theater in Hollywood, where movie stars leave their footprints in concrete for posterity, is one such place. Even the modern shopping mall can be regarded as a secular "cathedral of consumption," a special place to which community members come to practice shopping rituals. Theme parks are a form of mass-produced fantasy that take on aspects of sacredness. In particular, Disney World and Disneyland (and their outposts in Europe and Japan) are destinations for pilgrimages from consumers around the globe. Disney World displays many characteristics of more traditional sacred places. It is even regarded by some as having healing powers. A trip to the park is the most common "last wish" for terminally ill children.[65]

In many cultures, the home is a particularly sacred place. It represents a crucial distinction between the harsh, external world and consumers' "inner space." Americans spend more than $50 billion a year on interior decorators and home furnishings, and the home is a central part of consumers' identities.[66] "Home is where the heart is." Consumers all over the world go to great lengths to create a special environment that allows them to create the quality of "homeyness." This effect is created by personalizing the home as much as possible, using devices such as door wreaths, mantle arrangements, and a "memory wall" for family photos.[67] Even public places, such as Starbucks cafes, strive for a homelike atmosphere that shelters customers from the harshness of the outside world.

Sacred People

People themselves can be sacred when they are idolized and set apart from the masses. Souvenirs, memorabilia, and even mundane items touched or used by sacred people take on special meanings and acquire value in their own right. Indeed, many businesses thrive on consumers' desire for products associated with famous people. There is a thriving market for celebrity autographs, and objects once owned by celebrities, whether Princess Diana's gowns or John Lennon's guitars, are often sold at auction for astronomical prices.

Sacred Events

Many consumers' activities have also taken on a special status. Public events in particular resemble sacred, religious ceremonies, as exemplified by the recitation of the "Pledge of Allegiance" before a game or the reverential lighting of matches at the end of a rock concert.[68]

For many people, the world of sports is sacred and almost assumes the status of a religion. The roots of modern sports events can be found in ancient religious rites, such as fertility festivals (e.g., the original Olympics).[69] Indeed, it is not uncommon for teams to join in prayer prior to a game. The sports pages are like the scriptures (and we describe ardent fans as reading them "religiously"), the stadium is a house of worship, and the fans are members of the congregation. Devotees engage in group activities, such as tailgate parties and the "Wave." The athletes that fans come to see are godlike; they are reputed to have almost superhuman powers (especially superstars such as Michael Jordan, who is accorded the ability to fly in his Air Nikes).

Athletes are central figures in a common cultural myth, the hero tale. As exemplified by the heroic performance of the U.S. women's soccer team in the 1999 World Cup, often the person must prove herself under strenuous circumstances, and victory is achieved only through sheer force of will. One extremely popular Coke commercial, which featured the football player Mean Joe Greene and an admiring little boy, followed the same plot structure as the fairy tale of

The quest to memorialize Elvis has become an industry—about 20,000 people make a pilgrimage to Graceland each year to "worship" his memory. There is an offical Elvis site: www.elvis-presley.com/, and many other websites devoted to him. Some of the sites are in somewhat poorer taste, such as a Shockwave game called Gimme That Dang Pill, where the object is to flush the Quaaludes down the toilet before Elvis eats them in order to win a virtual fried peanut butter sandwich, (his favorite meal).[70]

The Lion and the Mouse. The injured hero has his confidence restored by the humble mouse/boy, allowing his heroic persona to be rejuvenated. He then shows his gratitude to his benefactor.[71]

Tourism is another example of a sacred, nonordinary experience of extreme importance to marketers. When people travel on vacation, they occupy sacred time and space. The tourist is continually in search of "authentic" experiences that differ from his or her normal world (think of Club Med's motto, "The antidote to civilization").[72] This traveling experience involves binary oppositions between work and leisure and being "at home" versus "away," and often norms regarding appropriate behavior are modified as tourists scramble after illicit or adventurous experiences they would not dream of engaging in at home.

The desire of travelers to capture these sacred experiences in objects forms the bedrock of the souvenir industry, which may be said to be in the business of selling sacred memories. Whether a personalized matchbook from a wedding or New York City salt-and-pepper shakers, souvenirs represent a tangible piece of the consumer's sacred experience.[73] In addition to personal mementos, such as ticket stubs saved from a favorite concert, the following are other types of sacred souvenir icons:[74]

- Local products (e.g., wine from California)
- Pictorial images (e.g., postcards)
- "Piece of the rock" (e.g., seashells, pine cones)
- Symbolic shorthand in the form of literal representations of the site (e.g., a miniature Statue of Liberty)
- Markers (e.g., Hard Rock Cafe T-shirts)

Souvenirs, tacky or otherwise, allow consumers to tangibilize sacred (i.e., out of the ordinary) experiences accumulated as tourists.

From Sacred to Profane, and Back Again

Just to make life interesting, in recent times many consumer activities have moved from one sphere to the other: Some things that were formerly regarded as sacred have moved into the realm of the profane, whereas other, everyday phenomena now are regarded as sacred.[75] Both of these processes are relevant to our understanding of contemporary consumer behavior.

Desacralization

Desacralization occurs when a sacred item or symbol is removed from its special place or is duplicated in mass quantities, becoming profane as a result. For example, souvenir reproductions of sacred monuments such as the Washington Monument or the Eiffel Tower, artworks such as the *Mona Lisa* or Michelangelo's *David*, or adaptations of important symbols such as the American flag by clothing designers, eliminate their special aspects by turning them into unauthentic commodities produced mechanically with relatively little value.[76]

Religion itself has to some extent been desacralized. Religious symbols, such as stylized crosses or New Age crystals, have moved into the mainstream of fashion jewelry.[77] Religious holidays, particularly Christmas, are regarded by many (and criticized by some) as having been transformed into secular, materialistic occasions devoid of their original sacred significance. Even the clergy are increasingly adopting secular marketing techniques. Televangelists rely upon the power of television, a secular medium, to convey their messages. The Catholic Church generated a major controversy after it hired a prominent public relations firm to

Angels are experiencing a renaissance and this ad for a smoke detector uses a guardian angel message to make its point.

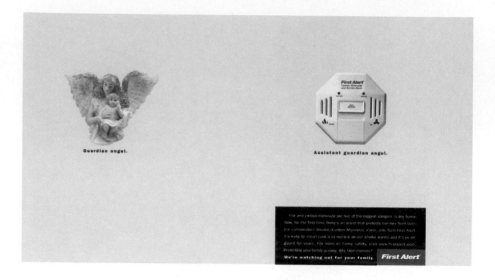

promote its antiabortion campaign.[78] Nonetheless, many religious groups have taken the secular route.

Sacralization

Sacralization occurs when ordinary objects, events, and even people take on sacred meaning to a culture or to specific groups within a culture. For example, events such as the Super Bowl and people such as Elvis Presley have become sacralized to some consumers. Virtually anything can become sacred. Skeptical? Consider that a Web site is thriving by selling unlaundered athletic wear worn by members of the Dallas Cowboys football team. Shoes worn by quarterback Troy Aikman sell for $1,999, and an unwashed practice jersey that retains the sweat of an unknown player goes for $99. Used socks are flying out the door at $19.99 a pair. Says the owner, "Fans who have never been able to touch the Cowboys before now have an opportunity."[79]

Objectification occurs when sacred qualities are attributed to mundane items (like smelly socks). One way that this process can occur is through *contamination*, in which objects associated with sacred events or people become sacred in their own right. This reason explains the desire by many fans for items belonging to, or even touched by, famous people. Even the Smithsonian Institution in Washington, D.C., maintains a display featuring such "sacred items" as the ruby slippers from *The Wizard of Oz*, a phaser from *Star Trek*, and Archie Bunker's chair from the television show *All in the Family*—all reverently protected behind sturdy display glass.

In addition to museum exhibits displaying rare objects, even mundane, inexpensive things may be set apart in *collections*, where they are transformed from profane items to sacred ones. An item is sacralized as soon as it enters a collection, and it takes on special significance to the collector that may be hard to comprehend by the outsider. **Collecting** refers to the systematic acquisition of a particular object or set of objects, and this widespread activity can be distinguished from hoarding, which is merely unsystematic collecting.[80] Collecting typically involves both rational and emotional components; collectors are often obsessed by their objects, but they also carefully organize and exhibit them.[81] Consumers often are ferociously attached to their collections; this passion is exemplified by the comment made in one study by a woman who collects teddy

Objectification occurs when sacred qualities are attributed to mandane items.

bears: "If my house ever burns down, I won't cry over my furniture, I'll cry over the bears."[82]

Some consumer researchers feel that collectors are motivated to acquire their "prizes" in order to gratify a high level of materialism in a socially acceptable manner. By systematically amassing a collection, the collector is allowed to "worship" material objects without feeling guilty or petty. Another perspective is that collecting is actually an aesthetic experience; for many collectors the pleasure emanates from being involved in creating the collection, rather than from passively admiring the items one has scavenged or bought. Whatever the motivation, hard-core collectors often devote a great deal of time and energy to maitaining and expanding their collections, so for many this activity becomes a central component of their extended selves (see Chapter 5).[83]

Name an item, and the odds are that a group of collectors is lusting after it. The contents of collections range from movie posters, rare books, and autographs to *Star Wars* dolls, Elvis memorabilia, old computers, and even junk mail.[84] The 1,200 members of the McDonald's collectors' club trade "prizes" such as sandwich wrappers and Happy Meal trinkets—rare ones such as the 1987 Potato Head Kids Toys sell for $25.[85] And other consumers collect experiences rather than products: Consider the man who has visited more than 10,000 McDonald's restaurants. He keeps a list of unusual menu items and decor, and he defends his

In the 1990s, "Swatch fever" infected many people. The company made more than 500 different models, some of which were special editions designed by artists. Although thousands of people still collect the watches, the frenzy has faded.[87]

hobby this way: "I'm not an oddball or weirdo. I'm a collector of the McDonald's dining experience. So many issues from the last half of this century can be understood, at least partially, from a seat inside a McDonald's. What could be more quintessentially American?" Supersize that?[86]

CHAPTER SUMMARY

- A society's *culture* includes its values, ethics, and the material objects produced by its members. It is the accumulation of shared meanings and traditions among members of a society. A culture can be described in terms of *ecology* (the way people adapt to their habitat), its *social structure*, and its *ideology* (including moral and aesthetic principles).
- *Myths* are stories containing symbolic elements that express the shared ideals of a culture. Many myths involve a *binary opposition*, whereby values are defined in terms of what they are and what they are not (e.g., nature versus technology). Modern myths are transmitted through advertising, movies, and other media.
- A *ritual* is a set of multiple, symbolic behaviors that occur in a fixed sequence and that tend to be repeated periodically. Ritual is related to many consumption activities that occur in popular culture. These include holiday observances, gift-giving, and grooming.
- A *rite of passage* is a special kind of ritual that involves the transition from one role to another. These passages typically entail the need to acquire products and services, called *ritual artifacts*, to facilitate the transition. Modern rites of passage include graduations, fraternity initiations, weddings, debutante balls, and funerals.
- Consumer activities can be divided into *sacred* and *profane* domains. Sacred phenomena are "set apart" from everyday activities or products. People, events, or objects can become sacralized. *Objectification* occurs when sacred qualities are ascribed to products or items owned by sacred people. *Sacralization* occurs when formerly sacred objects or activities become part of the everyday, as when "one-of-a-kind" works of art are reproduced in large quantities. *Desacralization* occurs when objects that previously were considered sacred become commercialized and integrated into popular culture.

KEY TERMS

binary opposition   p. 465
collecting   p. 480
collectivist cultures   p. 463
contamination   p. 476
conventions   p. 464
culture   p. 461
custom   p. 464
desacralization   p. 479

gift-giving ritual   p. 470
individualist cultures   p. 463
monomyth   p. 466
more   p. 464
myth   p. 465
norms   p. 463
profane consumption   p. 476
reciprocity norm   p. 471

rites of passage   p. 475
ritual   p. 467
ritual artifacts   p. 469
sacralization   p. 480
sacred consumption   p. 476
self-gifts   p. 472
worldview   p. 463

CONSUMER BEHAVIOR CHALLENGE

1. Culture can be thought of as a society's personality. If your culture were a person, how would you describe its personality traits?
2. What is the difference between an enacted norm and a crescive norm? Identify the set of crescive norms operating when a man and woman in your culture go out for dinner on a first date. What products and services are affected by these norms?
3. How do the consumer decisions involved in gift-giving differ from other purchase decisions?
4. The chapter argues that not all gift-giving is positive. In what ways can this ritual be unpleasant or negative?
5. What are some of the major motivations for the purchase of self-gifts? Discuss some marketing implications of these.
6. Describe the three stages of the rite of passage associated with graduating from college.
7. Identify the ritualized aspects of football that are employed in advertising.
8. "Christmas has become just another opportunity to exchange gifts and stimulate the economy." Do you agree? Why or why not?

NOTES

1. Bill McDowell, "Starbucks Is Ground Zero in Today's Coffee Culture," *Advertising Age* (December 9, 1996): 1. For a discussion of the act of coffee drinking as ritual, see Susan Fournier and Julie L. Yao, "Reviving Brand Loyalty: A Reconceptualization Within the Framework of Consumer–Brand Relationships" (working paper 96–039, Harvard Business School, 1996).
2. Louise Lee, "Now, Starbucks Uses Its Bean," *Business Week* (February 14, 2000): 92–94; Mark Gimein, "Behind Starbucks' New Venture: Beans, Beatniks, and Booze," *Fortune* (May 15, 2000): 80.
3. "Spice Girls Dance into Culture Clash," *Montgomery Advertiser* (April 29, 1997): 2A.
4. Clifford Geertz, *The Interpretation of Cultures* (New York: Basic Books, 1973); Marvin Harris, *Culture, People and Nature* (New York: Crowell, 1971); John F. Sherry Jr., "The Cultural Perspective in Consumer Research," in Richard J. Lutz, ed., *Advances in Consumer Research* 13 (Provo, UT: Association for Consumer Research, 1985): 573–75.
5. William Lazer, Shoji Murata, and Hiroshi Kosaka, "Japanese Marketing: Towards a Better Understanding," *Journal of Marketing* 49 (Spring 1985): 69–81.
6. Celia W. Dugger, "Modestly, India Goes for a Public Swim," *The New York Times on the Web* (March 5, 2000).
7. Geert Hofstede, *Culture's Consequences* (Beverly Hills, CA: Sage, 1980); see also Laura M. Milner, Dale Fodness, and Mark

W. Speece, "Hofstede's Research on Cross-Cultural Work-Related Values: Implications for Consumer Behavior," in W. Fred van Raaij and Gary J. Bamossy, eds., *European Advances in Consumer Research* (Amsterdam: Association for Consumer Research, 1993): 70–76.
8. Daniel Goleman, "The Group and the Self: New Focus on a Cultural Rift," *New York Times* (December 25, 1990): 37; Harry C. Triandis, "The Self and Social Behavior in Differing Cultural Contexts," *Psychological Review* 96 (July 1989): 506; Harry C. Triandis, Robert Bontempo, Marcelo J. Villareal, Masaaki Asai, and Nydia Lucca, "Individualism and Collectivism: Cross-Cultural Perspectives on Self-Ingroup Relationships," *Journal of Personality and Social Psychology* 54 (February 1988): 323.
9. George J. McCall and J. L. Simmons, *Social Psychology: A Sociological Approach* (New York: The Free Press, 1982).
10. Robert Frank, "When Small Chains Go Abroad, Culture Clashes Require Ingenuity," *The Wall Street Journal Interactive Edition* (April 12, 2000).
11. Eric J. Arnould, Linda L. Price, and Cele Otnes, "Making Consumption Magic: A Study of White-Water River Rafting," *Journal of Contemporary Ethnography* 28, no. 1 (February 1999) 1: 33–68.
12. Molly O'Neill, "As Life Gets More Complex, Magic Casts a Wider Spell," *New York Times* (June 13, 1994): A1.
13. Conrad Phillip Kottak, "Anthropological

Analysis of Mass Enculturation," in Conrad P. Kottak, ed., *Researching American Culture* (Ann Arbor, MI: University of Michigan Press, 1982): 40–74.
14. Eric Ransdell, "The Nike Story? Just Tell It!" *Fast Company* (January–February 2000): 44.
15. Joseph Campbell, *Myths, Dreams, and Religion* (New York: E. P. Dutton, 1970).
16. Claude Lévi-Strauss, *Structural Anthropology* (Harmondsworth: Peregrine, 1977).
17. Jeff Jensen, "Comic Heroes Return to Roots as Marvel Is Cast as Hip Brand," *Advertising Age* (June 8, 1998): 3.
18. Jeffrey S. Lang and Patrick Trimble, "Whatever Happened to the Man of Tomorrow? An Examination of the American Monomyth and the Comic Book Superhero," *Journal of Popular Culture* 22 (Winter 1988): 157.
19. Elizabeth C. Hirschman, "Movies as Myths: An Interpretation of Motion Picture Mythology," in Jean Umiker-Sebeok, ed., *Marketing and Semiotics: New Directions in the Study of Signs for Sale* (Berlin: Mouton de Gruyter, 1987): 335–74.
20. See William Blake Tyrrell, "Star Trek as Myth and Television as Mythmaker," in Jack Nachbar, Deborah Weiser, and John L. Wright, eds., *The Popular Culture Reader* (Bowling Green, OH: Bowling Green University Press, 1978): 79–88.
21. Bernie Whalen, "Semiotics: An Art or Powerful Marketing Research Tool?" *Marketing News* (May 13, 1983): 8.

22. See Dennis W. Rook, "The Ritual Dimension of Consumer Behavior," *Journal of Consumer Research* 12 (December 1985): 251–64; Mary A. Stansfield Tetreault and Robert E. Kleine III, "Ritual, Ritualized Behavior, and Habit: Refinements and Extensions of the Consumption Ritual Construct," in Marvin Goldberg, Gerald Gorn, and Richard W. Pollay, eds., *Advances in Consumer Research* 17 (Provo, UT: Association for Consumer Research, 1990): 31–38.

23. Debbie Treise, Joyce M. Wolburg, and Cele C. Otnes, "Understanding the 'Social Gifts' of Drinking Rituals: An Alternative Framework for PSA Developers," *Journal of Advertising* 28, no. 2 (1999): 17–31.

24. Debbie Treise, Joyce M. Wolburg, and Cele C. Otnes, "Understanding the 'Social Gifts' of Drinking Rituals: An Alternative Framework for PSA Developers," *Journal of Advertising* 28, no. 2 (1999): 17–31.

25. Kim Foltz, "New Species for Study: Consumers in Action," *New York Times* (December 18, 1989): A1.

26. Joyce Cohen, "Here Comes the Bride; Get Ready to Release a Swarm of Live Insects," *The Wall Street Journal* (January 22, 1996): B1. For a study that looked at updated wedding rituals in Turkey, see Tuba Ustuner, Guliz Ger, and Douglas B. Holt, "Consuming Ritual: Reframing the Turkish Henna-Night Ceremony," *Advances in Consumer Research,* Stephen J. Hoch and Robert J. Meyers, eds., (2000): 209–214.

27. For a study that looked specifically at rituals pertaining to birthday parties, see Cele Otnes and Mary Ann McGrath, "Ritual Socialization and the Children's Birthday Party: The Early Emergence of Gender Differences," *Journal of Ritual Studies* 8 (Winter 1994): 73–93.

28. Dennis W. Rook and Sidney J. Levy, "Psychosocial Themes in Consumer Grooming Rituals," in Richard P. Bagozzi and Alice M. Tybout, eds., *Advances in Consumer Research* 10 (Provo, UT: Association for Consumer Research, 1983): 329–33.

29. Diane Barthel, *Putting on Appearances: Gender and Attractiveness* (Philadelphia: Temple University Press, 1988).

30. Quoted in Barthel, *Putting on Appearances: Gender and Advertising.*

31. Russell W. Belk, Melanie Wallendorf, and John F. Sherry Jr., "The Sacred and the Profane in Consumer Behavior: Theodicy on the Odyssey," *Journal of Consumer Research* 16 (June 1989): 1–38.

32. Russell W. Belk and Gregory S. Coon, "Gift Giving as Agapic Love: An Alternative to the Exchange Paradigm Based on Dating Experiences," *Journal of Consumer Research* 20, no. 3 (December 1993): 393–417. See also Cele Otnes, Tina M. Lowrey, and Young Chan Kim, "Gift Selection for Easy and Difficult Recipients: A Social Roles Interpretation," *Journal of Consumer Research* 20 (September 1993): 229–44.

33. Julie A. Ruth, Cele C. Otnes, and Frederic F. Brunel, "Gift Receipt and the Reformulation of Interpersonal Relationships," *Journal of Consumer Research* 25 (March 1999): 385–402.

34. Bob Tedeschi, "Letters to Santa Are No Longer Necessary," *The New York Times on the Web* (November 15, 1999). For an exploration of the role of the bridal salon in the performance of wedding rituals, see Cele Otnes, "Friend of the Bride, and Then Some: The Role of the Bridal Salon in Wedding Planning, in John F. Sherry, ed., *Servicescapes: The Concept of Place in Contemporary Markets* (Lincolnwood, IL: NTC Press, 1998): 229–58.

35. Wendy Bounds, "Here Comes the Bride, Just a Mouse Click Away," *The Wall Street Journal Interactive Edition* (January 14, 1999).

36. Quoted in Cyndee Miller, "Nix the Knick-Knacks; Send Cash," *Marketing News* (May 26, 1997): 1.

37. Quoted in "I Do . . . Take MasterCard," *The Wall Street Journal* (June 23, 2000): W1, p. W1.

38. Deborah Kong, "Web Wish List," *Montgomery Advertiser* (November 8, 1999): 1A.

39. Kevin Keller, *Strategic Marketing Management* (Upper Saddle River, NJ: Prentice Hall 1998).

40. Monica Gonzales, "Before Mourning," *American Demographics* (April 1988): 19.

41. Alf Nucifora, "Tis the Season to Gift One's Best Clients," *Triangle Business Journal* 15, no. 13, (December 3, 1999): 14.

42. John F. Sherry Jr., "Gift Giving in Anthropological Perspective," *Journal of Consumer Research* 10 (September 1983): 157–68.

43. Daniel Goleman, "What's Under the Tree? Clues to a Relationship," *New York Times* (December 19, 1989): C1.

44. John F. Sherry Jr., Mary Ann McGrath, and Sidney J. Levy, "The Dark Side of the Gift," *Journal of Business Research* (1993): 225–44.

45. David Glen Mick and Michelle DeMoss, "Self-Gifts: Phenomenological Insights from Four Contexts," *Journal of Consumer Research* 17 (December 1990): 327; John F. Sherry Jr., Mary Ann McGrath, and Sidney J. Levy, "Monadic Giving: Anatomy of Gifts Given to the Self," in John F. Sherry Jr., ed., *Contemporary Marketing and Consumer Behavior: An Anthropological Sourcebook* (New York: Sage, 1995): 399–432.

46. Quoted in Cynthia Crossen, "Holiday Shoppers' Refrain: 'A Merry Christmas to Me,' " *The Wall Street Journal Interactive Edition* (December 11, 1997).

47. Colin Camerer, "Gifts as Economics Signals and Social Symbols," *American Journal of Sociology* 94 (Supplement 1988): 5, 180–214.

48. Robert T. Green and Dana L. Alden, "Functional Equivalence in Cross-Cultural Consumer Behavior: Gift Giving in Japan and the United States," *Psychology & Marketing* 5 (Summer 1988): 155–68.

49. Hiroshi Tanaka and Miki Iwamura, "Gift Selection Strategy of Japanese Seasonal Gift Purchasers: An Explorative Study" (paper presented at the Association for Consumer Research, Boston, October 1994).

50. See, for example, Russell W. Belk, "Halloween: An Evolving American Consumption Ritual," in Richard Pollay, Jerry Gorn, and Marvin Goldberg, eds., *Advances in Consumer Research* 17 (Provo, UT: Association for Consumer Research, 1990): 508–17; Melanie Wallendorf and Eric J. Arnould, "We Gather Together: The Consumption Rituals of Thanksgiving Day," *Journal of Consumer Research* 18 (June 1991): 13–31.

51. Rick Lyte, "Holidays, Ethnic Themes Provide Built-in F&B Festivals," *Hotel & Motel Management* (December 14, 1987): 56; Megan Rowe, "Holidays and Special Occasions: Restaurants Are Fast Replacing 'Grandma's House' as the Site of Choice for Special Meals," *Restaurant Management* (November 1987): 69; Judith Waldrop, "Funny Valentines," *American Demographics* (February 1989): 7.

52. Quoted in "Cinco de Mayo, a Yawn for Mexicans, Gives Americans a License to Party," *The Wall Street Journal Interactive Edition* (May 5, 2000).

53. Bruno Bettelheim, *The Uses of Enchantment: The Meaning and Importance of Fairy Tales* (New York: Alfred A. Knopf, 1976).

54. Kenneth L. Woodward, "Christmas Wasn't Born Here, Just Invented," *Newsweek* (December 16, 1996): 71.

55. Theodore Caplow, Howard M. Bahr, Bruce A. Chadwick, Reuben Hill, and Margaret M. Williams, *Middletown Families: Fifty Years of Change and Continuity* (Minneapolis, MN: University of Minnesota Press, 1982).

56. Andrea Adelson, "A New Spirit for Sales of Halloween Merchandise," *New York Times* (October 31, 1994): D1.

57. Anne Swardson, "Trick or Treat? In Paris, It's Dress, Dance, Eat," *International Herald Tribune* (October 31, 1996): 2.

58. N. R. Kleinfeld, "The Weird, the Bad and the Scary," *New York Times* (October 15, 1989): 4.

59. Georgia Dullea, "It's the Year's No. 2 Night to Howl," *New York Times* (October 30, 1988): 20.

60. Arnold Van Gennep, *The Rites of Passage,* trans. Maika B. Vizedom and

Shannon L. Caffee (London: Routledge and Kegan Paul, 1960; orig. published 1908); Solomon and Anand, "Ritual Costumes and Status Transition."

61. Rachel Emma Silverman, No Headline, *The Wall Street Journal Interactive Edition* (November 2, 1998).

62. Kelly Shermach, "Pay Now, Die Later: Consumers Urged Not to Delay That Final Decision," *Marketing News* (October 24, 1994): 1.

63. "Aggressive Sales Practices in Funeral Industry Decried," *Montgomery Advertiser* (April 11, 2000): 2A.

64. Walter W. Whitaker III, "The Contemporary American Funeral Ritual," in Ray B. Browne, ed., *Rites and Ceremonies in Popular Culture* (Bowling Green, OH: Bowling Green University Popular Press, 1980): 316–25; for a recent examination of funeral rituals, see Larry D. Compeau and Carolyn Nicholson, "Funerals: Emotional Rituals or Ritualistic Emotions" (paper presented at the Association of Consumer Research, Boston, October 1994).

65. Conrad Phillip Kottak, "Anthropological Analysis of Mass Enculturation," in Conrad P. Kottak, ed., *Researching American Culture* (Ann Arbor, MI: University of Michigan Press, 1982): 40–74.

66. Joan Kron, *Home-Psych: The Social Psychology of Home and Decoration* (New York: Clarkson N. Potter, 1983); Gerry Pratt, "The House as an Expression of Social Worlds," in James S. Duncan, ed., *Housing and Identity: Cross-Cultural Perspectives* (London: Croom Helm, 1981): 135–79; Michael R. Solomon, "The Role of the Surrogate Consumer in Service Delivery," *The Service Industries Journal* 7 (July 1987): 292–307.

67. Grant McCracken, "'Homeyness': A Cultural Account of One Constellation of Goods and Meanings," in Elizabeth C. Hirschman, ed., *Interpretive Consumer Research* (Provo, UT: Association for Consumer Research, 1989): 168–84.

68. Emile Durkheim, *The Elementary Forms of the Religious Life* (New York: Free Press, 1915).

69. Susan Birrell, "Sports as Ritual: Interpretations from Durkheim to Goffman," *Social Forces* 60, no. 2 (1981): 354–76; Daniel Q. Voigt, "American Sporting Rituals," in *Rites and Ceremonies in Popular Culture.*

70. "Elvis Evermore," *Newsweek* (August 11, 1997): 12.

71. Alf Walle, "The Epic Hero," *Marketing Insights* (Spring 1990): 63.

72. Dean MacCannell, *The Tourist: A New Theory of the Leisure Class* (New York: Shocken Books, 1976).

73. Belk et al., "The Sacred and the Profane in Consumer Behavior."

74. Beverly Gordon, "The Souvenir: Messenger of the Extraordinary," *Journal of Popular Culture* 20, no. 3 (1986): 135–46.

75. Belk et al., "The Sacred and the Profane in Consumer Behavior."

76. Belk et al., "The Sacred and the Profane in Consumer Behavior."

77. Deborah Hofmann, "In Jewelry, Choices Sacred and Profane, Ancient and New," *New York Times* (May 7, 1989).

78. "Public Relations Firm to Present Anti-Abortion Effort to Bishops," *New York Times* (August 14, 1990): A12.

79. J. C. Conklin, "Web Site Caters to Cowboy Fans by Selling Sweaty, Used Socks," *The Wall Street Journal Interactive Edition* (April 21, 2000).

80. Dan L. Sherrell, Alvin C. Burns, and Melodie R. Phillips, "Fixed Consumption Behavior: The Case of Enduring Acquisition in a Product Category," in Robert L. King, ed., *Developments in Marketing Science* 14 (1991): 36–40.

81. Belk, "Acquiring, Possessing, and Collecting: Fundamental Processes in Consumer Behavior," cf. 74.

82. Quoted in Ruth Ann Smith, "Collecting as Consumption: A Grounded Theory of Collecting Behavior," (unpublished manuscript, Virginia Polytechnic Institute and State University, 1994): 14.

83. For a discussion of these perspectives, see Smith, "Collecting as Consumption."

84. For an extensive bibliography on collecting, see Russell W. Belk, Melanie Wallendorf, John F. Sherry Jr., and Morris B. Holbrook, "Collecting in a Consumer Culture," in Russell W. Belk, ed., *Highways and Buyways* (Provo, UT: Association for Consumer Research, 1991): 178–215. See also Russell W. Belk, "Acquiring, Possessing, and Collecting: Fundamental Processes in Consumer Behavior," in Ronald F. Bush and Shelby D. Hunt, eds., *Marketing Theory: Philosophy of Science Perspectives* (Chicago: American Marketing Association, 1982): 85–90; Werner Muensterberg, *Collecting: An Unruly Passion* (Princeton, NJ: Princeton University Press, 1994); Melanie Wallendorf and Eric J. Arnould, "'My Favorite Things': A Cross-Cultural Inquiry into Object Attachment, Possessiveness, and Social Linkage," *Journal of Consumer Research* 14 (March 1988): 531–47.

85. Calmetta Y. Coleman, "Just Any Old Thing from McDonald's Can Be a Collectible," *The Wall Street Journal* (March 29, 1995): B1; Ken Bensinger, "Recent Boom in Toy Collecting Leads Retailers to Limit Sales," *The Wall Street Journal Interactive Edition* (September 25, 1998); "PC Lovers Loyal to Classics," *Montgomery Advertiser* (April 2, 2000): 1.

86. Philip Connors, "Like Fine Wine, a 'Collector' Visits McDonald's for Subtle Differences," *The Wall Street Journal Interactive Edition* (August 16, 1999).

87. A Feeding Frenzy for Swatches," *New York Times* (August 29, 1991): C3; Patricia Leigh Brown, "Fueling a Frenzy: Swatch," *New York Times* (May 10, 1992): C1(2); Mary M. Long and Leon G. Schiffman, "Swatch Fever: An Allegory for Understanding the Paradox of Collecting," *Psychology & Marketing* 14, no. 5 (August 1997): 495–509.

s Alexandra is browsing through the racks at her local Abercrombie & Fitch store in Wichita, Kansas, her friend Amanda yells to her, "Alex, check this out! These leopard-skin Capri pants are so tight!" From watching MTV, Alex knows tight means cool, and she agrees. As she takes the pants to the cash register, she's looking

forward to wearing them to school the next day. All of her girlfriends in junior high compete with each other to dress just like the women in Destiny's Child and other hot groups—her friends just won't believe their eyes when they see her tomorrow. Maybe some of the

younger kids in her school might even think she was fresh off the mean streets of New York City! Even though she has never been east of the Mississippi, Alex just knows she would fit right in with all of the Bronx "sistahs" she reads about in her magazines.

17

THE CREATION AND DIFFUSION OF CONSUMER CULTURE

The Creation of Culture

Even though inner-city teens represent only eight percent of all people in that age group and have incomes significantly lower than their white suburban counterparts, their influence on young people's musical and fashion tastes is much greater than these numbers would suggest. Turn on MTV, and it won't be long before a rap video fills the screen. Go to the newsstand, and magazines such as *Vibe* are waiting for you. Numerous Web sites such as vibe.com arc devoted to hip-hop culture, and nightclubs let you peek into what's happening online at sites such as groovetech.com, thewomb.com, raveworld.net, and digitalclubnetwork.com.[1]

In addition to music, "urban" fashion is spreading into the heartland as major retail chains pick up on the craze and try to lure legions of young middle-class shoppers. Macy's and JCPenney carry FUBU ("for us by us"); although this urban clothing company sells a lot of shiny satin baseball jackets, baggy jeans with loops, and fleece tops in the inner city, 40 percent of its sales are to white customers in the suburbs. Even the aristocratic Polo Jeans by Ralph Lauren started its own line to appeal to the hip-hop nation.[2] How does this subculture influence the mass market in so many ways?

Americans always have been fascinated by outsider heroes—whether John Dillinger, Marlon Brando, or Dennis Rodman—who achieve money and fame without being hemmed in by societal constraints. As one executive of a firm that researches urban youth noted, "People resonate with the strong anti-oppression messages of rap, and the alienation of blacks."[3]

Ironically, the only "oppression" Alex has experienced is being grounded by her parents after her mom found a half-smoked cigarette in her room. She lives in a white middle-class area in the Midwest, but she is able to "connect" symbolically with millions of other young consumers by wearing styles that originated far away—even though the original meanings of those styles have little relevance

487

to her. As a privileged member of "white bread" society, her hip-hop clothes have a very different meaning in her suburban world than they would to street kids in New York City or L.A. The fact that she's wearing a style might even be interpreted by these "cutting-edge" types as a sign that this item is no longer in fashion, and it is time to move on to something else.

Big corporations are working hard to capture the next killer fashion being incubated in black urban culture—what is called "flavor" on the streets. For example, Fila, which started as an Italian underwear maker in 1926, initially broke into sportswear by focusing on "lily-white" activities such as skiing and tennis. The company first made a splash by signing Swedish tennis sensation Bjorn Borg as an endorser. Ten years later, the tennis fad faded, but company executives noticed that rap stars such as Heavy D were wearing Fila sweatsuits to symbolize their idealized vision of life in white country clubs. Fila switched gears and went with the flow, and is now the third-leading sneaker marketer, with U.S. revenues of $575 million wholesale.[4]

How did hip-hop music and fashions, which began as forms of expression in the black urban subculture, make it to mainstream America? Here's a brief chronology:

- 1968: Hip-hop is invented in the Bronx by DJ Kool Herc.
- 1973–1978: Urban block parties feature break-dancing and graffiti.
- 1979: A small record company named Sugar Hill becomes the first rap label.
- 1980: Graffiti artists are featured in Manhattan art galleries.
- 1981: Blondie's song "Rapture" hits number one on the charts.
- 1985: Columbia Records buys the Def Jam label.
- 1988: MTV begins *Yo! MTV Raps*, featuring Fab 5 Freddy.
- 1990: Hollywood gets into the act with the hip-hop film *House Party*; Ice-T's rap album is a big hit on college radio stations; amid controversy, white rapper Vanilla Ice hits the big time; NBC launches a new sitcom, *Fresh Prince of Bel Air.*
- 1991: Mattel introduces its Hammer doll (a likeness of the rap star Hammer, formerly known as M. C. Hammer); designer Karl Lagerfeld shows shiny vinyl raincoats and chain belts in his Chanel collection; designer Charlotte Neuville sells gold vinyl suits with matching baseball caps for $800; Isaac Mizrahi features wide-brimmed caps and take-offs on African medallions; Bloomingdale's launches Anne Klein's rap-inspired clothing line by featuring a rap performance in its Manhattan store.
- 1992: Rappers start to abandon this look, turning to low-fitting baggy jeans, sometimes worn backwards; white rapper Marky Mark appears in a national campaign wearing Calvin Klein underwear, exposed above his hip-hugging pants; composer Quincy Jones launches *Vibe* magazine for people who are into hip-hop, and it gains a significant white readership.[5]
- 1993: Hip-hop fashions and slang continue to cross over into mainstream consumer culture. An outdoor ad for Coca-Cola proclaims, "Get Yours 24–7." The company is confident that many viewers in its target market will know that the phrase is urban slang for "always" (24 hours a day, 7 days a week).[6]
- 1994: The late Italian designer Versace pushes oversized overalls favored by urban kids. In one ad, he asks, "Overalls with an oversize look, something like what rappers and homeboys wear. Why not a sophisticated version?"[7]
- 1996: Tommy Hilfiger, a designer who was the darling of the preppie set, turns hip-hop. He gives free wardrobes to rap artists such as Grand Puba

and Chef Raekwon, and in return finds his name mentioned in rap songs—the ultimate endorsement. The September 1996 issue of *Rolling Stone* features the Fugees, with the Hilfiger logo prominently displayed by several band members. In the same year the designer uses rap stars Method Man and Treach of Naughty by Nature as runway models. Hilfiger's new Tommy Girl perfume plays on his name but also is a reference to the New York hip-hop record label Tommy Boy.[8]

- 1997: Coca-Cola features rapper LL Cool J in a commercial that debuts in the middle of the sitcom *In the House*, a TV show starring the singer.[9]
- 1998: In their battle with Dockers for an increased share of the khaki market, Gap launches its first global ad campaign. One of the commercials "Khakis Groove" includes a hip-hop dance performance set to music by Bill Mason.[10]
- 1999: Rapper turned entrepreneur Sean (Puffy) Combs introduces an upscale line of menswear he calls "urban high fashion." New companies FUBU, Mecca, and Enyce attain financial success in the multibillion dollar industry.[11] Lauryn Hill and the Fugees sing at a party sponsored by upscale Italian clothier Emporio Armani and proclaim, "We just wanna thank Armani for giving a few kids from the ghetto some great suits."[12]
- 2000: 360hip-hop.com, a Web-based community dedicated to the hip-hop culture, is launched. In addition to promoting the hip-hop lifestyle, the site allows consumers to purchase clothing and music online while watching video interviews with such artists as Will Smith and Busta Rymes.[13]

It's common for mainstream culture to modify symbols identified with "cutting-edge" subcultures and present these to a larger audience. As this occurs, these cultural products undergo a process of **cooptation** by which their original meanings are transformed by outsiders. In this case, rap music was to a large extent divorced from its original connection with the struggles of young African Americans and is now used as an entertainment format for other fans.[14] One writer sees the white part of the "hip-hop nation" as a series of concentric rings. In the center are those who actually know blacks and understand their culture. The next ring consists of those who have indirect knowledge of this subculture via friends or relatives, but who don't actually rap, spray paint, or break dance. Then, there are those a bit further out who simply play hip-hop between other types of music. Finally come the more suburban "wiggers" who are simply trying to catch on to the next popular craze.[15] The spread of hip-hop fashions and music is just one example of what happens when the meanings created by some members of a culture are interpreted and produced for mass consumption.

This chapter considers how the culture in which we live creates the meaning of everyday products and how these meanings move through a society to consumers. As Figure 17.1 shows, meaning transfer is largely accomplished by such marketing vehicles as the advertising and fashion industries that associate functional products with symbolic qualities. These goods, in turn, impart their meanings to consumers as these products are used by them to create and express their identities.[16] Recall that in Chapter 1 we learned that "one of the fundamental premises of the modern field of consumer behavior is that people often buy products not for what they *do*, but for what they *mean*." This closing chapter brings us full circle as we explore how product symbolism evolves and spreads through our culture.

Figure 17.1
The Movement of Meaning

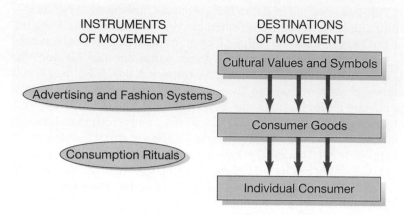

INSTRUMENTS
OF MOVEMENT

DESTINATIONS
OF MOVEMENT

Cultural Values and Symbols

Advertising and Fashion Systems

Consumer Goods

Consumption Rituals

Individual Consumer

Cultural Selection

Nipple rings. Leopard-skin pants. Sushi. High-tech furniture. Postmodern architecture. Chat rooms. Double decaf cappuccino with a hint of cinnamon. We inhabit a world brimming with different styles and possibilities. The food we eat, the cars we drive, the clothes we wear, the places we live and work, the music we listen to—all are influenced by the ebb and flow of popular culture and fashion.

Consumers may at times feel overwhelmed by the sheer number of choices in the marketplace. A person trying to decide on something as routine as a necktie has many hundreds of alternatives to choose from. Despite this seeming abundance, however, the options available to consumers at any point in time actually represent only a small fraction of the total set of possibilities.

The selection of certain alternatives over others—whether automobiles, dresses, computers, recording artists, political candidates, religions, or even scientific methodologies—is the culmination of a complex filtration process resembling a funnel, as depicted in Figure 17.2. Many possibilities initially compete for adoption, and these are steadily winnowed out as they make their way down the path from conception to consumption in a process of **cultural selection.**

Our tastes and product preferences are not formed in a vacuum. Choices are driven by the images presented to us in mass media, our observations of those around us, and even by our desires to live in the fantasy worlds created by marketers. These options are constantly evolving and changing. A clothing style or type of cuisine that is "hot" one year may be "out" the next.

Alex's emulation of hip-hop style illustrates some of the characteristics of fashion and popular culture:

- Styles are often a reflection of deeper societal trends (e.g., politics and social conditions).
- Styles usually originate as an interplay between the deliberate inventions of designers and business people and spontaneous actions by ordinary consumers. Designers, manufacturers, and merchandisers who can anticipate what consumers want will succeed in the marketplace. In the process, they help to fuel the fire by encouraging mass distribution of the item.
- These cultural products can travel widely, often between countries and across continents. Influential people in the media play a large role in deciding which will succeed.

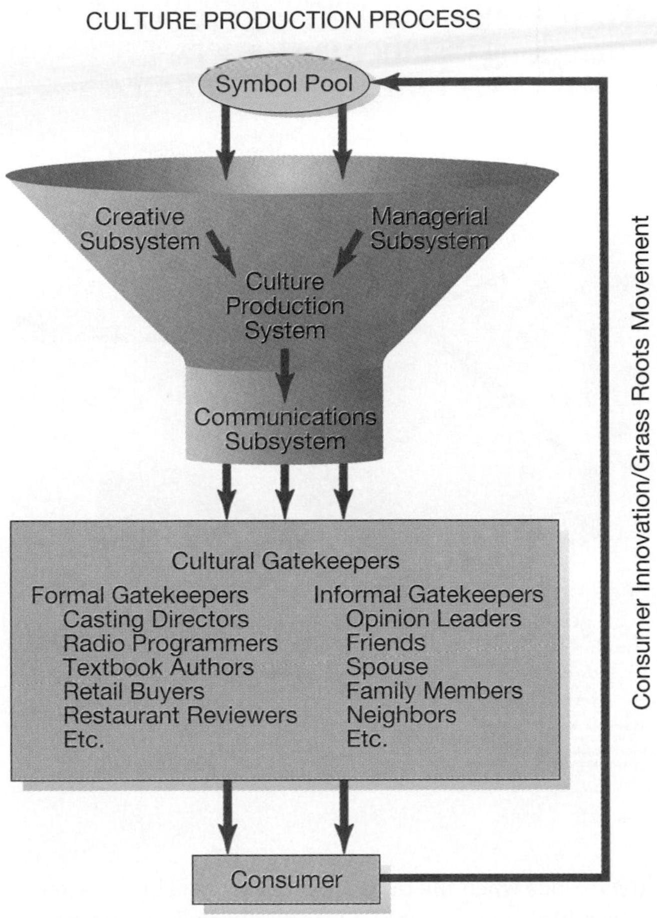

CULTURE PRODUCTION PROCESS

Figure 17.2
The Culture Production Process

Figure 17.2
The Culture Production Process

- A style begins as a risky or unique statement by a relatively small group of people, then spreads as others increasingly become aware of the style and feel confident about trying it.
- Most styles eventually wear out as people continually search for new ways to express themselves and marketers scramble to keep up with these desires.

Culture Production Systems

No single designer, company, or advertising agency is totally responsible for creating popular culture. Every product, whether a hit record, a car, or a new clothing style, requires the input of many different participants. The set of individuals and organizations responsible for creating and marketing a cultural product is a **culture production system (CPS).**[17]

The nature of these systems helps to determine the types of products that eventually emerge from them. Factors such as the number and diversity of competing systems and the amount of innovation versus conformity that is encouraged are important. For example, an analysis of the country/western music industry showed that the hit records it produces tend to be similar to one another

As this AT&T ad demonstrates, many products styles are doomed to become obsolete.

during periods when the industry is dominated by a few large companies, whereas there is more diversity when a greater number of producers are competing within the same market.[18]

The different members of a CPS may not necessarily be aware of or appreciate the roles played by other members, yet many diverse agents work together to create popular culture.[19] Each member does his or her best to anticipate which particular images will be most attractive to a consumer market. Of course, those who are able to consistently forecast consumers' tastes most accurately will be successful over time.

Components of a CPS

A culture production system has three major subsystems: (1) *a creative subsystem* responsible for generating new symbols and products; (2) *a managerial subsystem* responsible for selecting, making tangible, mass producing, and managing the distribution of new symbols and products; and (3) *a communications subsystem* responsible for giving meaning to the new product and providing it with a symbolic set of attributes that are communicated to consumers.

An example of the three components of a culture production system for a record would be: (1) a singer (e.g., rapper Puff Daddy, a creative subsystem); (2) a company (e.g., Bad Boy Records, which manufactures and distributes Puff Daddy's CDs, a managerial subsystem); and (3) the advertising and publicity agencies hired to promote the albums (a communications subsystem). Table 17.1 illustrates some of the many cultural specialists who are required to create a hit CD.

TABLE 17.1 Cultural Specialists in the Music Industry

Specialist	Functions
Songwriter(s)	Compose music and lyrics; must reconcile artistic preferences with estimates of what will succeed in the marketplace
Performer(s)	Interpret music and lyrics; may be formed spontaneously, or may be packaged by an agent to appeal to a predetermined market (e.g., The Monkees, Menudo, and New Kids on the Block)
Teachers and coaches	Develop and refine performers' talents
Agent	Represent performers to record companies
A&R (artist & repertoire) executive	Acquire artists for the record label
Publicists, image consultants, designers, stylists	Create an image for the group that is transmitted to the buying public
Recording technicians, producers	Create a recording to be sold
Marketing executives	Make strategic decisions regarding performer's appearances, ticket pricing, promotional strategies, and so on
Video director	Interpret the song visually to create a music video that will help to promote the record
Music reviewers	Evaluate the merits of a recording for listeners
Disc jockeys, radio program directors	Decide which records will be given airplay and/or placed in the radio stations' regular rotations
Record store owner	Decide which of the many records produced will be stocked and/or promoted heavily in the retail environment

Cultural Gatekeepers

Many judges or "tastemakers" influence the products that are eventually offered to consumers. These **cultural gatekeepers** are responsible for filtering the overflow of information and materials intended for consumers. Gatekeepers include movie, restaurant, and car reviewers; interior designers; disc jockeys; retail buyers; and magazine editors. Collectively, this set of agents is known as the *through-put sector.*[20]

High Culture and Popular Culture

Do Beethoven and Puff Daddy have anything in common? Although both the famous composer and the rap singer are associated with music, many would argue that the similarity stops there. Culture production systems create many kinds of products, but some basic distinctions can be offered regarding their characteristics.

Arts and Crafts

One distinction is between arts and crafts.[21] An **art product** is viewed primarily as an object of aesthetic contemplation without any functional value. A **craft product,** in contrast, is admired because of the beauty with which it performs some function (e.g., a ceramic ashtray or hand-carved fishing lures). A piece of art is original, subtle, and valuable, and typically is associated with the elite of society. A craft tends to follow a formula that permits rapid production. According to this framework, elite culture is produced in a purely aesthetic context and is judged by reference to recognized classics. It is high culture—"serious art."[22]

High Art Versus Low Art

The distinction between high and low culture is not as clear as it may first appear. In addition to the possible class bias that drives such a distinction (i.e., we assume that the rich have culture but the poor do not), high and low culture are blending together in interesting ways. Popular culture reflects the world around us; these phenomena touch rich and poor. In Europe, for example, advertising is widely appreciated as an art form. Some advertising executives are public figures in Great Britain. For more than 10 years, people in France have paid up to $30 to watch an all-night program in a movie theater consisting of nothing but television commercials.[23]

The arts are big business. Americans alone spend more than $2 billion per year to attend arts events.[24] All cultural products that are transmitted by mass media become a part of popular culture.[25] Classical recordings are marketed in much the same way as Top 40 albums, and museums use mass marketing techniques to sell their wares. The Metropolitan Museum of Art has branch gift shops across the United States, some located as boutiques within large department stores.

Marketers often incorporate high art imagery to promote products. They may feature works of art on shopping bags or sponsor artistic events to build public goodwill.[26] When observers from Toyota watched customers in luxury car showrooms, the company found that these consumers tended to view a car as an art

TABLE 17.2 Cultural Formulae in Public Art Forms

Art Form/ Genre	Classic Western	Science Fiction	Hard-Boiled Detective	Family Sitcom
Time	1800s	Future	Present	Anytime
Location	Edge of civilization	Space	City	Suburbs
Protagonist	Cowboy (lone individual)	Astronaut	Detective	Father (figure)
Heroine	Schoolmarm	Spacegal	Damsel in distress	Mother (figure)
Villain	Outlaws, killers	Aliens	Killer	Boss, neighbor
Secondary characters	Townfolk, Indians	Technicians in spacecraft	Cops, underworld	Kids, dogs
Plot	Restore law and order	Repel aliens	Find killer	Solve problem
Theme	Justice	Triumph of humanity	Pursuit and discovery	Chaos and confusion
Costume	Cowboy hat, boots, etc.	High-tech uniforms	Raincoat	Regular clothes
Locomotion	Horse	Spaceship	Beat-up car	Station wagon
Weaponry	Sixgun, rifle	Rayguns	Pistol, fists	Insults

SOURCE: Arthur A. Berger, *Signs in Contemporary Culture: An Introduction to Semiotics* (New York: Longman, 1984): 86. Copyright © 1984. Reissued 1989 by Sheffield Publishing Company, Salem, Wisconsin. Reprinted with permission of the publisher.

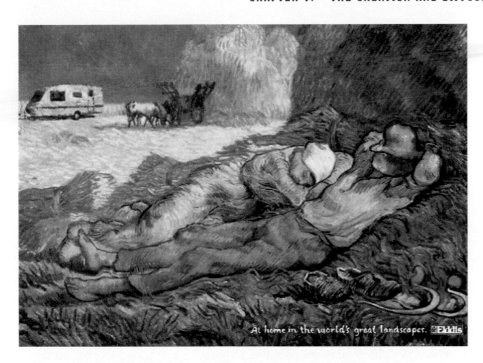

As this British ad illustrates, high art merges with popular culture in interesting ways.

object. This theme was then used in an ad for the Lexus with the caption, "Until now, the only fine arts we supported were sculpture, painting, and music."[27]

Cultural Formulae

Mass culture, in contrast, churns out products specifically for a mass market. These products aim to please the average taste of an undifferentiated audience and are predictable because they follow certain patterns. As illustrated in Table 17.2, many popular art forms, such as detective stories or science fiction, generally follow a **cultural formula,** in which certain roles and props often occur consistently.[28] Romance novels are an extreme case of a cultural formula. Computer programs even allow users to "write" their own romances by systematically varying certain set elements of the story.

Reliance on these formulae also leads to a *recycling* of images, as members of the creative subsystem reach back through time for inspiration. Thus, young people watch retro shows such as *Gilligan's Island* and remakes of *The Brady Bunch*, designers modify styles from Victorian England or colonial Africa, hip-hop DJs sample sound bits from old songs and combine them in new ways, and Gap runs ads featuring now-dead celebrities including Humphrey Bogart, Gene Kelly, and Pablo Picasso dressed in khaki pants. With easy access to VCRs, CD burners, digital cameras, and imaging software, virtually anyone can "remix" the past.[29]

Aesthetic Market Research

Creators of aesthetic products are increasingly adapting conventional marketing methods to fine-tune their mass market offerings. Market research is used, for example, to test audience reactions to movie concepts. Although testing cannot account for such intangibles as acting quality or cinematography, it can determine if the basic themes of the movie strike a responsive chord in the target audience. This type of research is most appropriate for blockbuster movies, which usually follow one of the formulae described earlier. In some cases research is combined with publicity, as when the producers of the Will Smith movie *Men in*

THE TANGLED WEB

A *KNOCKOFF* IS A style that has been deliberately copied and modified, often with the intent to sell to a larger or different market. *Haute couture* clothing styles presented by top designers in Paris and elsewhere are commonly "knocked off" by other designers and sold to the mass market. The Web is making it easier than ever for firms to copy these designs—in some cases so quickly that their pirated styles show up in stores at the same time as the originals. Wildcatters such as First View have set up Web sites to show designers' latest creations, sometimes revealing everything from a new collection. Things have gotten so bad that the House of Chanel requires photographers to sign contracts promising their shots will not be distributed on the Internet.[33] But, isn't imitation the sincerest form of flattery?

Black showed the first 12 minutes of the film to an advance audience and then let them meet the stars to create prerelease buzz.[30]

Even the content of movies is sometimes influenced by consumer research. Typically, free invitations to prescreenings are handed out in malls and movie theaters. Attendees are asked a few questions about the movie, then some are selected to participate in focus groups. Although groups' reactions usually result in only minor editing changes, occasionally more drastic effects result. When initial reaction to the ending of *Fatal Attraction* was negative, Paramount Pictures spent an additional $1.3 million to shoot a new one.[31] Of course, this feedback isn't always accurate—before the megahit *E.T.: The Extra-Terrestrial* was released, consumer research indicated that no one over the age of four would go to see the movie![32] Whoever did that research project needs to phone home.

Reality Engineering

The village of Riverside, Georgia has a colorful history. You can look at the sepia photographs showing the town in the nineteenth century or read excerpts from period novels lauding the settlement's cosmopolitan flair. You'll also discover that the town was used as a Union garrison during the Civil War. There's only one hitch: Riverside didn't exist until 1998. The account of nineteenth-century Riverside is a clever fabrication created to promote a new housing and commercial development. The story "is a figment of our imagination," acknowledges the developer.[34]

Like Riverside, many of the environments in which we find ourselves—whether housing developments, shopping malls, sports stadiums, or theme parks—are largely composed of images and characters spawned by marketing campaigns. **Reality engineering** occurs as elements of popular culture are appropriated

Reality engineering results in the placement of advertising messages almost anywhere.

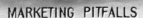

MARKETING PITFALLS

ONE OF THE MOST controversial intersections between marketing and society occurs when companies provide "educational materials" to schools. Many firms including Nike, Hershey, Crayola, Nintendo, and Foot Locker provide free book covers swathed in ads. Almost 40 percent of secondary schools in the United States start the day with a video feed from Channel One, which exposes students to commercials in the classroom in exchange for educational programming. Similarly, an Internet company called ZapMe! gives client schools free computers and Internet connections as well as a network of 11,000 educational sites in exchange for a promise to use the computers at least four hours a day. Commercials run continuously on the lower left-hand quarter of the screen,

and the company has permission to monitor the students' browsing habits, breaking down the data by age, sex, and zip code. In a few cases companies are contracting with schools to run focus groups with their students during the school day in order to get reactions to new product ideas. Coca-Cola signed a ten-year, $8 million exclusive beverage contract with the Colorado Springs, Colorado school system. In some schools third graders practice math by counting Tootsie Rolls, and the kids use reading software sporting the logos of Kmart, Coke, Pepsi, and Cap'n Crunch cereal.

Corporate involvement with schools is hardly new—in the 1920s Ivory Soap spon-

sored soap-carving competitions for students. But, the level of intrusion is sharply increasing, as companies scramble to compensate for the decrease in children's viewership of television on Saturday mornings and weekday afternoons and find themselves competing with videos and computer games for their attention. Many educators argue that these materials are a godsend for resource-poor schools that otherwise could not provide computers and other goodies to their students. On the other hand, a new California law bans the use of textbooks with brand names and company logos. This legislation was prompted by complaints from parents about a middle school math book that uses names like Barbie, Oreos, Nike, and Sony PlayStation in word problems.[37]

by marketers and converted to vehicles for promotional strategies.[35] These elements include sensory and spatial aspects of everyday existence, whether in the form of products appearing in movies, scents pumped into offices and stores, billboards, theme parks, video monitors attached to shopping carts, even faked "documentaries" like *The Blair Witch Project*. This process is accelerating; historical analyses of Broadway plays, best-selling novels and the lyrics of hit songs, for example, clearly show large increases in the use of real brand names over time.[36]

Product Placement

It is quite common to see real brands prominently displayed or to hear them discussed in movies and on television. In many cases, these "plugs" are no accident. **Product placement** refers to the insertion of specific products and the use of brand names in movie and TV scripts. Perhaps the greatest product placement success story was Reese's Pieces; sales jumped by 65 percent after the candy appeared in the film *E.T.*[38]

Some researchers claim that product placement can aid in consumer decision making because the familiarity of these props creates a sense of cultural belonging while generating feelings of emotional security.[39] For better or worse products are popping up everywhere:

- ABC and Nokia entered a $10 million partnership that will include intense exposure of branded mobile phones on the network's shows. ABC gave away Nokia phones in a contest on its daytime soaps and during prime-time hits *Spin City* and *Dharma and Greg*. Also in development are devices that will enable viewers to click on a product being used by a TV character and buy it for themselves. According to an ABC executive, "that world of clicking on a soap star and buying a dress—that's going to happen. That's our future."[40]

MULTICULTURAL DIMENSIONS

PRODUCT PLACEMENT HAS LARGELY been an American phenomenon—until recently. Now, marketers in other countries are discovering the value of placing their brand messages wherever they can. In France, cafes are turning tabletops into billboards for United Airlines, Swatch watches, and other companies. Although some patrons decry the invasion of such commercialism into the "sacred" French practice of lounging at bistros, the owner of a firm that is supplying the ads observes, "We want to make cafes more interesting places for people to visit."[46] *Sacre bleu!*

In China, product placement is emerging as a new way to get noticed. Most commercials on Chinese state-run TV play back-to-back in 10-minute segments, making it difficult for any one 30-second ad to attract attention. So, enterprising marketers are embedding product messages in the shows instead. A soap opera called *Love Talks* features such products as Maybelline lipstick, Motorola mobile phones, and Ponds Vaseline Intensive Care lotion.[47]

- In an action series on the TNN cable network called *18 Wheels of Justice,* the Kenworth truck company spent nearly $1 million and also lent trucks to the show. In exchange, the series features multiple shots of the truck, mentions the company by name in the closing credits, and guarantees a minimum of six minutes of screen time in each episode. Although very few consumers are in the market for 18-wheel trucks, the company hopes that the series will improve the trucking industry's image. To improve the chances of this occurring, the truck is driven by Lucky Vanous, the former Diet Coke hunk model.[41]
- Although IBM sells a lot more computers, Apples are seen in many more TV shows and movies such as *Mission Impossible* and *Independence Day.* Producers like to use the Apple because its image is more hip. But Apple will only let it happen if the brand is identified on screen.[42]
- In the video game Cool Borders, three characters ride past Butterfinger candy bar banners and wear Levi's jeans while attempting to beat opponents' times as recorded on Swatch watches. A Sony PlayStation game called Psybadek outfits its main characters in shoes and clothing from Vans. A Sony executive comments, "We live in a world of brands. We don't live in a world of generics. If a kid is bouncing a basketball in a video game, to us it makes sense that it should be a Spalding basketball."[43]
- Philip Morris paid to place Marlboro cigarettes and signs in *Superman* movies and doled out $350,000 to have Lark cigarettes featured in the James Bond film *License to Kill.* In a lawsuit against the tobacco companies, new evidence was revealed about the Hollywood–Big Tobacco connection. Philip Morris states that "product was supplied" for more than 190 movies between 1978 to 1988.[44]
- The hit CBS show *Survivor* portrayed the adventures of 16 people stranded on a desert island near Borneo for 39 days. They battled for a chance to wear Reeboks, drink Budweiser, and sleep in a Pontiac Aztec sport-utility vehicle.[45]

Traditionally, networks demanded that brand names be "greeked" or changed before they could appear in a show, as when a Nokia cell phone was changed to "Nokio" on *Melrose Place.*[48] Nowadays, though, real products pop up everywhere. Still, to bypass Federal Communications Commission regulations requiring the disclosure of promotional deals, marketers typically don't pay for placements. Instead they pay product placement firms that work with set decorators looking for free props and realism.[49] Warner Bros. is even testing "virtual" product placement. A new technology (the same that lets TV football viewers "see" the first-down line during games) allows a product to be inserted into live or taped video broadcasts.[50] The director of strategic planning at Saatchi & Saatchi New York predicts, "any space you can take in visually, anything you hear in the future will be branded, I believe. It's not going to be the Washington Monument. It's going to be the Washington Post Monument."[51]

Media images, whether of an actor drinking a can of Coke or driving a BMW, appear to significantly influence consumers' perceptions of reality. These depictions affect viewers' notions about what the "real world" is like, including such issues as dating behavior, racial stereotypes, and occupational status.[52] Studies of the **cultivation hypothesis** focus upon the media's ability to distort consumers' perceptions of reality. They show that heavy television viewers tend to overestimate how wealthy people are and the likelihood that they will be victims of a violent crime.[53]

Product placement refers to the insertion of specific products and/or the use of brand names in movies and TV scripts. The popular sitcom Seinfeld *includes blatant references to numerous products, from Junior Mints and Kenny Rogers Fried Chicken to Snapple and Pez.*

The media also exaggerate or distort the frequency of behaviors such as drinking or smoking.[54] A study conducted by the National Partnership for Women and Families illustrates the divergence between life as shown on TV and what occurs in the real world. An analysis of two weeks of prime-time TV shows and movies shown on six broadcast networks revealed several gaps between reality and fantasy. These included a lack of working mothers, fewer parents, and more men then in the U.S. population. Only 13 of 150 episodes showed a character dealing with stress caused by conflicts between the demands of a job versus family. Only 26 of 820 adult TV characters had any caretaking responsibility for an adult relative (one in four U.S. workers does). Fourteen percent of adult TV characters are over 50, compared with 38 percent of the U.S. population. Characters shown taking time off for personal problems encountered no resistance from their bosses. In real life, 34 percent of workers find it difficult to get time off to deal with personal matters.[55] Then again, maybe this kind of escape from reality is why people are watching in the first place.

THE DIFFUSION OF INNOVATIONS

An **innovation** is any product or service that is perceived to be new by consumers. These new products or services occur in both consumer and industrial settings. Innovations may take the form of a clothing style (e.g., skirts for men), a new manufacturing technique (such as the ability to design your own running shoe at customatix.com), or a novel way to deliver a service (such as kozmo.com, which will bring pizzas and videos to you at home).

MARKETING   PITFALLS

REALITY ENGINEERING TOOK A
nasty turn when it was revealed that
the U.S. government used financial
incentives to get television networks
to work antidrug messages into the
scripts of popular TV shows including
*E.R., Chicago Hope, Cosby, The Drew
Carey Show, The Practice,* and *Beverly
Hills 90210.* This effort was initiated
after Congress approved a program to
place antidrug ads on the networks.
The government agreed to give up
some of its ad time (permitting the networks to sell this time at a higher rate
to private companies) as long as the
networks demonstrate their programs
convey antidrug messages. For example, in an episode of WB's *Smart Guy*
series, substance-abusing teenagers
were portrayed as popular characters.
To comply with the government program, the script was changed to make
them losers hiding away in a utility
room taking drugs.[56]

If an innovation is successful (most are not), it spreads through the population. First it is bought or used by only a few people, and then more and more
consumers decide to adopt it, until, in some cases, it seems that almost everyone has bought or tried the innovation. **Diffusion of innovations** refers to the
process whereby a new product, service, or idea spreads through a population.
The rate at which a product diffuses varies. For example, within ten years after
its introduction, cable TV was used by 40 percent of U.S. households, compact
disks by 35 percent, answering machines by 25 percent and color TVs by 20
percent. It took radio 30 years to reach 60 million users and TV 15 years to
reach this number. In contrast, within three years 90 million were surfing the
Web.[57]

Adopting Innovations

A consumer's adoption of an innovation resembles the decision-making sequence
discussed in Chapter 9. The person moves through the stages of awareness, information search, evaluation, trial, and adoption. The relative importance of each
stage may differ depending on how much is already known about a product, as
well as on cultural factors that may affect people's willingness to try new things.[58]
A study of 11 European countries found that consumers in individualistic cultures are more innovative than consumers in collective cultures.[59] However,
even within the same culture, not all people adopt an innovation at the same rate.
Some do so quite rapidly, and others never do at all. Consumers can be placed into
approximate categories based on their likelihood of adopting an innovation. The
categories of adopters, shown in Figure 17.3, can be related to phases of the product life cycle concept used widely by marketing strategists.

As Figure 17.3 shows, roughly one-sixth of the population (innovators and
early adopters) are very quick to adopt new products, and one-sixth of the people
(**laggards**) are very slow. The other two-thirds, so-called **late adopters,** are somewhere in the middle, and these adopters represent the mainstream public. These
consumers are interested in new things, but they do not want them to be *too* new.
In some cases, people deliberately wait to adopt an innovation because they
assume that its technological qualities will be improved or that its price will fall

Figure 17.3
Types of Adopters

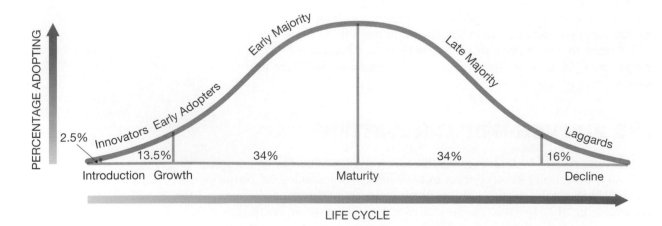

after it has been on the market awhile.[60] Keep in mind that the proportion of consumers falling into each category is an estimate; the actual size of each depends on such factors as the complexity of the product, its cost, and how much risk is associated with trying it.

Even though **innovators** represent only about 2.5 percent of the population, marketers are always interested in identifying them. These are the brave souls who are always on the lookout for novel developments and will be the first to try a new offering. Just as generalized opinion leaders do not appear to exist, innovators tend to be category-specific, as well. A person who is an innovator in one area may even be a laggard in another. A gentleman who prides himself as being on the cutting edge of fashion may have no conception of new developments in recording technology and may still stubbornly cling to his antique phonograph albums even as he searches for the latest *avant-garde* clothing styles in obscure boutiques. Despite this qualification, some generalizations can be offered regarding the profile of innovators.[61] Not surprisingly, for example, they tend to have more favorable attitudes toward taking risks. They also are likely to have higher educational and income levels, and to be socially active.

Early adopters share many of the same characteristics as innovators, but an important difference is their degree of concern for social acceptance, especially with regard to expressive products, such as clothing, cosmetics, and so on. Generally speaking, an early adopter is receptive to new styles because he or she is involved in the product category and also places high value on being in fashion. What appears on the surface to be a fairly high-risk adoption (e.g., wearing a skirt three inches above the knee when most people are wearing them below the knee) is actually not that risky. The style change has already been "field-tested" by innovators, who truly took the fashion risk. Early adopters are likely to be found in "fashion-forward" stores featuring the latest "hot" designers. In contrast, true innovators are more likely to be found in small boutiques featuring as-yet-unknown designers.

MARKETING OPPORTUNITY

INNOVATORS ARE A PRIZE catch for marketers who want a heads-up on how their products will fare in the mass market. Indeed, some innovative companies understand the value of involving their most forward-thinking customers in business decisions before the final product is introduced.[62] For example, more than 650,000 customers tested a beta version of Microsoft Windows 2000. Many were even prepared to pay Microsoft a fee to do this because working with the program would help them understand how it could create value for their own businesses. The value of the research and development investment by customers to Microsoft was estimated at

more than $500 million. Similarly, Cisco gives its customers open access to its resources and systems so that they can solve the problems encountered by other customers.

This approach is more prevalent in high-tech industries, in which many businesses involve lead users in product development. A **lead user** is an involved, experienced customer who is very knowledgeable about the field. Indeed, it is not unusual for high-tech products to be ini-

tially thought of and even prototyped by lead users rather than manufacturers.[63] These customers often experience problems or needs well in advance of others, so their solutions can be applied to other markets. For example, military aircraft must stop before reaching the end of the runway, and the lead user approach resulted in this new technology being applied to antilock braking systems for automobiles. According to one estimate, 70 percent of the innovations in the chemical industry were developed by users rather than manufacturers.[64] The value of this approach for consumer goods is obvious but has yet to be widely applied.

THE
TANGLED   WEB

MP3 (WHICH STANDS FOR
MPEG-1, Layer 3) is a compression
technique that shrinks audio files to
less than a tenth of their original size.
The spread of MP3 is transforming the
way music is produced and sold. A
people's revolution is brewing, and the
music industry is worried, very worried.
The major labels want to encrypt music
so they can sell it online. They formed
the Secure Music Digital Initiative to
create open standards for distributing
music on the Net that controls
copying.[65]

But those efforts aren't stopping
Napster.com and similar sites. Acting
like a music search engine, the software makes it easy to find and copy
music and allows individuals to offer
their own music collections to others.
Napster was created by a 19-year-old
college dropout as a way to get his
roommate to stop complaining about
how hard it was to find the MP3 files
he was looking for on the Internet. Its
use has spread so quickly among college students that the traffic has overloaded university networks. Dozens of
campuses have banned students from
using the service to protect their
networks. The Recording Industry
Association of America filed a lawsuit
to try to shut down the service, and
similar efforts were mounted by some
artists, including Metallica. Napster
argues that it is not liable for music
piracy because it does not keep any of
the music files on its own servers; it
simply allows people to share information. Indeed, the company claims that
the software actually increases sales
by enabling users to sample new
artists.[66] Buying music will never be
the same again.

Behavioral Demands of Innovations

Innovations can be categorized in terms of the degree to which they demand
changes in behavior from adopters. Three major types of innovations have been
identified, though these three categories are not absolutes. They refer, in a relative sense, to the amount of disruption or change they bring to people's lives.

A *continuous innovation* refers to a modification of an existing product, such
as when General Mills introduced a Honey Nut version of Cheerios or Levi's promoted shrink-to-fit jeans. This type of change may be used to set one brand apart
from its competitors. Most product innovations are of this type; that is, they are
evolutionary rather than revolutionary. Small changes are made to position the
product, add line extensions, or merely to alleviate consumer boredom.

Consumers may be lured to the new product, but adoption represents only
minor changes in consumption habits because innovation perhaps adds to the
product's convenience or to the range of choices available. A typewriter company,
for example, many years ago modified the shape of its product to make it more
"user friendly" to secretaries. One simple change was making the tops of the keys
concave, a convention that is carried over on today's computer keyboards. The
reason for the change was that secretaries had complained about the difficulty of
typing with long fingernails on the flat surfaces.

A *dynamically continuous innovation* is a more pronounced change in an
existing product, as represented by self-focusing 35-mm cameras or touch-tone
telephones. These innovations have a modest impact on the way people do things,
requiring some behavioral changes. When introduced, the IBM Selectric typewriter, which uses a typing ball rather than individual keys, permitted secretaries to
instantly change the typeface of manuscripts by replacing one Selectric ball with
another.

A *discontinuous innovation* creates major changes in the way we live. Major
inventions, such as the airplane, the car, the computer, and the television have
radically changed modern lifestyles. The personal computer has, in many cases,
supplanted the typewriter, and it has created the phenomenon of "telecom-
muters" by allowing many consumers to work from their homes. Of course, the
cycle continues, as new continuous innovations (e.g., new versions of software)
are constantly being made for computers; dynamically continuous innovations
such as the "mouse" compete for adoption, and discontinuous innovations such
as wristwatch personal computers loom on the horizon.

Prerequisites for Successful Adoption

Regardless of how much behavioral change is demanded by an innovation, several
factors are desirable for a new product to succeed.[67]

Compatibility. The innovation should be compatible with consumers' lifestyles.
As one illustration, a manufacturer of personal care products tried unsuccessfully
several years ago to introduce a cream hair remover for men as a substitute for
razors and shaving cream. This formulation was similar to that used widely by
women to remove hair from their legs. Although the product was simple and convenient to use, it failed because men were not interested in a product they perceived to be too feminine and thus threatening to their masculine self-concepts.

Trialability. Because an unknown is accompanied by high perceived risk, people
are more likely to adopt an innovation if they can experiment with it prior to
making a commitment. To reduce this risk, companies often choose the expensive strategy of distributing free "trial-size" samples of new products.

Complexity. The product should be low in complexity. A product that is easier to understand and use will be chosen over a competitor. This strategy requires less effort from the consumer, and it also lowers perceived risk. Manufacturers of videocassette recorders, for example, have put a lot of effort into simplifying VCR usage (e.g., on-screen programming) to encourage adoption.

Observability. Innovations that are easily observable are more likely to spread because this quality makes it more likely that other potential adopters will become aware of its existence. The rapid proliferation of fanny packs (pouches worn around the waist in lieu of wallets or purses) was due to their high visibility. It was easy for others to see the convenience offered by this alternative.

Relative Advantage. Most importantly, the product should offer relative advantage over other alternatives. The consumer must believe that its use will provide a benefit other products cannot offer. For example, a product called the Bugchaser is a wristband containing insect repellent. Mothers with young children liked it because it is nontoxic and nonstaining—clear advantages over existing alternatives. In contrast, the Crazy Blue Air Freshener, which was added to windshield wiper fluid and emitted a fragrance when the wipers were turned on, fizzled: People didn't see the need for the product and felt there were simpler ways to freshen their cars if they cared to.

THE FASHION SYSTEM

The **fashion system** consists of all those people and organizations involved in creating symbolic meanings and transferring these meanings to cultural goods. Although people tend to equate fashion with clothing, it is important to keep in mind that fashion processes affect *all* types of cultural phenomena, including music, art, architecture, and even science (i.e., certain research topics and scientists are "hot" at any point in time). Even business practices are subject to the fashion process; they evolve and change depending on which management techniques are "in vogue," such as total quality management or just-in-time inventory control.

Fashion can be thought of as a *code,* or language, that helps us to decipher these meanings.[68] Unlike a language, however, fashion is *context-dependent.* The same item can be interpreted differently by different consumers and in different situations.[69] In semiotic terms (see Chapter 2), the meaning of fashion products often is *undercoded.* There is no one precise meaning, but rather plenty of room for interpretation among perceivers.

At the outset, it may be helpful to distinguish among some confusing terms. **Fashion** is the process of social diffusion by which a new style is adopted by some group(s) of consumers. In contrast, *a fashion* (or style) refers to a particular combination of attributes. And, to be *in fashion* means that this combination is currently positively evaluated by some reference group. Thus, the term *Danish Modern* refers to particular characteristics of furniture design (i.e., a fashion in interior design); it does not necessarily imply that Danish Modern is a fashion that is currently desired by consumers.[70]

Cultural Categories

The meaning that does get imparted to products reflects underlying **cultural categories,** which correspond to the basic ways we characterize the world.[71] Our culture makes distinctions between different times, between leisure and work, and between genders. The fashion system provides us with products that signify these categories. For example, the apparel industry gives us clothing to denote certain times (e.g., evening wear, resort wear), differentiates between leisure clothes and work clothes, and promotes masculine and feminine styles.

These cultural categories affect many different kinds of products. As a result, it is common to find that dominant aspects of a culture at any point in time tend to be reflected in the design and marketing of a wide range of items. This concept is a bit hard to grasp, because on the surface a clothing style, say, has little in common with a piece of furniture or a car. However, an overriding concern with a value such as achievement or environmentalism can determine the types of products likely to be accepted by consumers at any point in time. These underlying themes then surface in a product's design. A few examples of this interdependence will help to demonstrate how a dominant fashion *motif* reverberates across industries.

- Costumes worn by political figures or movie and rock stars can affect the fortunes of the apparel and accessory industries. A movie appearance by actor Clark Gable without a T-shirt (unusual at that time) dealt a severe setback to the men's apparel industry, and Jackie Kennedy's famous "pillbox hat" prompted a rush for hats by women in the 1960s. Other cross-category effects include the craze for ripped sweatshirts instigated by the movie *Flashdance*, a boost for cowboy boots from the movie *Urban Cowboy*, and singer Madonna's legitimation of lingerie as an acceptable outerwear clothing style.
- The Louvre in Paris was remodeled to include a controversial glass pyramid at the entrance designed by the architect I. M. Pei. Shortly thereafter, several designers unveiled pyramid-shaped clothing at Paris fashion shows.[72]
- In the 1950s and 1960s, much of America was preoccupied with

A cultural emphasis on science in the 1950s and 1960s affected product designs, as seen in the design of automobiles with large tail fins (to resemble rockets).

REALITY CHECK *BOOTS WITH SIX-INCH HEELS ARE THE LATEST*

fashion rage among young Japanese women. Several teens have died after tripping over their shoes and fracturing their skulls. However, followers of the style claim they are willing to risk twisted ankles, broken bones, bruised faces, and other dangers associated with the platform shoes. One teenager said, "I've fallen and twisted my ankle many times, but they are so cute that I won't give them up until they go out of fashion."[74]

Many consumers around the world seem to be willing to suffer for the sake of fashion. Others argue that we are merely pawns in the hands of designers, who conspire to force unwieldy fashions down our throats. What do you think? What is and what should be the role of fashion in our society? How important is it for people to be in style? What are the pros and cons of keeping up with the latest fashions? Do you believe that we are at the mercy of designers?

Just last week I went to a dance with a good friend of mine. I bought these awesome black strappy Nine-West sandals, with about a three inch heel. They made my legs look awesome, and I felt pretty confident, ready for a night of fun and partying. He picked me up, and we went to have dinner. My feet began to ache, about 10 minutes into the date. I couldn't walk as fast as Tobey. I almost fell in the gravel parking lot, just trying to keep up with him. Luckily he was a good friend, and took me back to my apartment to get my Reef flip-flops. Walking was much less foreign, and I proceeded to dance the night away. Never again will I sacrifice fun and pleasure for fashion and pain.

Katherine S. Kennedy
James Madison University

Fashion does play an important role for many in society. It is often what bonds groups of people together and makes them the individuals they are. Yet the power of the fashion industry is much more in the hands of the consumers then the designers. What at one time may be very popular, can be unthinkable the next. Take Abercrombie and Fitch, the clothing store, for example. Recently, these clothes were very "in" and now they are viewed as overpriced.

Jennifer Freet
George Mason University

Ultimately people choose their level of involvement in the fashion parade and there is a tendency that young people are strongly influenced by fashions as they have a strong desire through peer group pressure to conform and be "in." Money or price doesn't seem to matter, the label and style are all important.

Michael Vernon Hollet
Edith Cowan University, Australia

I do not think we are in the mercy of the designers because I have never felt that I was forced to be in fashion. But in Japan, like with the six-inch heel boots, when something becomes the trend, that seems like the only thing you can wear to be in fashion. People analyze this by the effect of having to wear uniforms most of their teenage life. I believe fashion is about being able to wear what you want, coordinated with your life style, environment and feeling to look good. . . . I think fashion is one way to entertain yourself.

Ayano Yamada
Keio University, Japan

The move away from homogeneity has forced fashions to extremes. The fact that the high heels Naomi Campbell famously fell over in were at the time mocked as being ridiculous but have now become fashionable represents the degree to which High Street fashion has been forced closer to the catwalk. . . . The fragmentation of consumers . . . has resulted in the diminishment of the size of fashion movements, the world will no longer see the likes of Mods and Rockers, or more recently Punk Rockers, New Romantics and Goths. Fashion movements that straddled continents and united huge numbers of young people have become a thing of the past, they have been replaced by smaller more cohesive groups that take their lead from a more diverse set of cultural gatekeepers.

James Beattie
University of Exeter, United Kingdom

This is a free country, either to spend money or not on the latest fashion by famous designers are up to you. I don't really pay attention to it that much, I usually go for the clothes that look good on me and the ones I can really afford.

Frank Liu
Florida State University

In my opinion, there is no conspiracy involved in introducing new fashion. It is just clever marketing! No one MUST wear six-inch heels. People wear them simply because they want to. I must agree that the fashion nowadays is . . . different and at times even weird. Some groups of people, however, suffer more from trying to keep up with the latest fashion than others. Fashion has always been harder on women than on men. For most men, it is important that the clothes are clean, comfortable, and do not look outdated. Most women, on the other hand, feel more pressure to stay on top of new styles in fashion.

Dmitri Batsev
University of Alaska, Fairbanks

What's your opinion? Check out the online polls at www.prenhall.com/myphlip. Just follow the little person in the lab coat.

science and technology. This concern with "space-age" mastery was fueled by the Russians' launching of the Sputnik satellite, which prompted fears that America was falling behind in the technology race. The theme of technical mastery of nature and of futuristic design became a motif that cropped up in many aspects of American popular culture—from car designs with prominent tailfins to high-tech kitchen styles.

Remember that creative subsystems within a culture production system attempt to anticipate the tastes of the buying public. Despite their unique talents, members of this subsystem are also members of mass culture. Cultural gate-keepers are drawing from a common set of cultural categories, so it's not that surprising that their choices often converge even though they compete against one another to offer the consumer something new or different. The process by which certain symbolic alternatives are chosen over others is termed **collective selection.**[73] As with the creative subsystem, members of the managerial and communications subsystems also seem to develop a common frame of mind. Although products within each category must compete for acceptance in the marketplace, they can usually be characterized by their adherence to a dominant theme or motif—be it "The Western Look," "New Wave," "Danish Modern," or "Nouvelle Cuisine."

Behavioral Science Perspectives on Fashion

Fashion is a very complex process that operates on many levels. At one extreme, it is a societal phenomenon affecting many people simultaneously. At the other, it exerts a very personal effect on individual behavior. A consumer's purchase decisions are often motivated by his or her desire to be in fashion. Fashion products also are aesthetic objects, and their origins are rooted in art and history. For this reason, there are many perspectives on the origin and diffusion of fashion. Although these cannot be described in detail here, some major approaches can be briefly summarized.[75]

Psychological Models of Fashion

Many psychological factors help to explain why people are motivated to be in fashion. These include conformity, variety seeking, personal creativity, and sexual attraction. For example, many consumers seem to have a "need for uniqueness":

Some people argue that consumers are at the mercy of fashion designers. What do you think?

They want to be different, but not too different.[76] For this reason, people often conform to the basic outlines of a fashion, but try to improvise and make a personal statement within these general guidelines.

One of the earliest theories of fashion proposed that "shifting *erogenous zones*" (sexually arousing areas of the body) accounted for fashion changes, and that different zones become the object of interest because they reflect societal trends. J. C. Flugel, a disciple of Freud, proposed in the 1920s that sexually charged areas wax and wane in order to maintain interest, and that clothing styles change to highlight or hide these parts. For example, it was common for Renaissance-era women to drape their abdomens in fabrics in order to give a swollen appearance— successful childbearing was a priority in the disease-ridden fourteenth and fifteenth centuries. Now, some suggest that the current prevalence of the exposed midriff reflects the premium our society places on fitness.[77] It's important to note, by the way, that until very recently the study of fashion focused almost exclusively on its impact on women. Hopefully, this concentration will broaden as scholars and practitioners begin to appreciate that men are affected by many of the same fashion influences.

Economic Models of Fashion

Economists approach fashion in terms of the model of supply and demand. Items that are in limited supply have high value, whereas those readily available are less desirable. Rare items command respect and prestige.

Veblen's notion of conspicuous consumption proposed that the wealthy consume to display their prosperity, for example by wearing expensive (and at times impractical) clothing. As noted in Chapter 13, this approach is somewhat outdated; upscale consumers often engage in *parody display*, by which they deliberately adopt formerly low status or inexpensive products, such as jeeps or jeans. Other factors also influence the demand curve for fashion-related products. These include a *prestige–exclusivity effect*, in which high prices still create high

This ad for Maidenform illustrates that fashions have accentuated different parts of the female anatomy throughout history.

demand, and a *snob effect*, whereby lower prices actually reduce demand ("If it's that cheap, it can't be any good").[78]

Sociological Models of Fashion

The collective selection model discussed previously is an example of a sociological approach to fashion. In addition, much attention has been focused on the relationship between product adoption and class structure.

Trickle-down theory, first proposed in 1904 by Georg Simmel, has been one of the most influential approaches to understanding fashion. It states that there are two conflicting forces that drive fashion change. First, subordinate groups try to adopt the status symbols of the groups above them as they attempt to climb up the ladder of social mobility. Dominant styles thus originate with the upper classes and trickle-down to those below. However, this is where the second force kicks in: Those people in the superordinate groups are constantly looking below them on the ladder to ensure that they are not imitated. They respond to the attempts of lower classes to "impersonate" them by adopting even newer fashions. These two processes create a self-perpetuating cycle of change—the machine that drives fashion.[79]

The trickle-down theory was quite useful for understanding the process of fashion changes when applied to a society with a stable class structure, which permitted the easy identification of lower- versus upper-class consumers. This task is not so easy in modern times. In contemporary Western society, this approach must be modified to account for new developments in mass culture.[80]

- A perspective based on class structure cannot account for the wide range of styles that are simultaneously made available in our society. Modern consumers have a much greater degree of individualized choice than those in the past because of advances in technology and distribution. Just as an adolescent like Alex is almost instantly aware of the latest style trends by watching MTV, elite fashion has been largely replaced by *mass fashion* because media exposure permits many groups to become aware of a style at the same time.

Grassroots innovators typically are people who lack prestige in the dominant culture such as urban youth who are the drivers behind the hip-hop craze.

- Consumers tend to be more influenced by opinion leaders who are similar to them. As a result each social group has its own fashion innovators who determine fashion trends. It is often more accurate to speak of a *trickle-across effect,* whereby fashions diffuse horizontally among members of the same social group.[81]

- Finally, current fashions often originate with the lower classes and *trickle up.* Grassroots innovators typically are people who lack prestige in the dominant culture (e.g., urban youth). Because they are less concerned with maintaining the status quo, they are more free to innovate and take risks.[82]

A "Medical" Model of Fashion

For years and years, the lowly Hush Puppy was a shoe for nerds. Suddenly—almost overnight—the shoe became a chic fashion statement even though the company did nothing to promote this image. Why did this style diffuse through the population so quickly? **Meme theory** has been proposed to explain this process using a medical metaphor. A *meme* is an idea or product that enters the consciousness of people over time—examples include tunes, catch-phrases ("Is that your final answer?"), or styles such as the Hush Puppy. In this view, memes spread among consumers in a geometric progression just as a virus starts off small and steadily infects increasing numbers of people until it becomes an epidemic. Memes "leap" from brain to brain via a process of imitation.

The memes that survive tend to be distinctive and memorable, and the hardiest ones often combine aspects of prior memes. For example, the *Star Wars* movies evoked prior memes relating to Arthurian legend, religion, heroic youth, and 1930s adventure serials. Indeed, George Lucas studied comparative religion and mythology as he prepared his first draft of the *Star Wars* saga, "The Story of Mace Windu."[83]

The meme idea is itself catching on. A Web site called memepool.com is a pool for ideas that attracts 7,000 users a day who post random thoughts that others may adopt.[84] More generally, the diffusion of many products in addition to Hush Puppies seem to follow the same basic path. The product initially is used by a few people, but change happens in a hurry when the process reaches the moment of critical mass—which one author has called the *tipping point.* For example, Sharp introduced the first low-price fax machine in 1984 and sold about 80,000 in that year. There was a slow climb in the number of users for the next three years. Then, suddenly in 1987 enough people had fax machines that it made sense for everyone to have one—Sharp sold a million units that year. Cell phones followed the same trajectory.[85]

Cycles of Fashion Adoption

In the early 1980s, Cabbage Patch dolls were all the rage among American children. Faced with a limited supply of the product, some retailers reported near-riots among adults as they tried desperately to buy the dolls for their children. A Milwaukee disc jockey jokingly announced that people should bring catcher's mitts to a local stadium because 2,000 dolls were going to be dropped from an airplane. Listeners were instructed to hold up their American Express cards so their numbers could be aerially photographed. More than two dozen anxious parents apparently didn't get the joke; they showed up in subzero weather, mitts in hand.[87]

MARKETING PITFALLS

LARGE COMPANIES THAT TRY to stay on top of hot fashion trends face a disturbing paradox: Young consumers are drawn to happening street fashions such as those produced by small entrepreneurs. For example, when Dinah Mohajer was a student at USC, she needed blue nail polish to go with her blue platform shoes, and mixed up her own batch. Her friends loved the idea, and she started Hard Candy with a loan from her parents. Soon Drew Barrymore, Cher, and even Antonio Banderas were wearing Hard Candy colors such as Trailer Trash, Jail Bait, and Fiend.[86]

But as soon as these styles are "discovered" and mass produced, they are no longer cool. In the old days, couture houses and major retailers set the styles, but with the advent of the Web and numerous small 'zines produced by individuals or small companies, the big guys no longer have the final say on what is cool. In fact, established brand names may be distrusted by young consumers. One way around this dilemma is to spin off a separate division and try to distance it from the parent company, as Levi-Strauss did with its Silver Tab boutique label and Miller did with its boutique brewery called Red Dog.

This Jim Beam ad illustrates the cyclical nature of fashion.

Although the Cabbage Patch craze lasted for a couple of seasons, it eventually died out, and consumers moved on to other things, such as Teenage Mutant Ninja Turtles, which grossed more than $600 million in 1989.[88] The Mighty Morphin Power Rangers eventually replaced the Turtles, and they in turn were deposed by Beanie Babies and Giga Pets before the invasion of Pokemon.[89] What will be next?

Fashion Life Cycles

Although the longevity of a particular style can range from a month to a century, fashions tend to flow in a predictable sequence. The fashion life cycle is quite similar to the more familiar product life cycle. An item or idea progresses through basic stages from birth to death, as shown in Figure 17.4.

The diffusion process discussed earlier in the chapter is intimately related to the popularity of fashion-related items. To illustrate how this process works, consider how the **fashion acceptance cycle** works in the popular music business. In the *introduction stage*, a song is listened to by a small number of music innovators. It may be played in clubs or on "cutting-edge" college radio stations, which is exactly how "grunge rock" groups such as Nirvana got their start. During the *acceptance stage*, the song enjoys increased social visibility and acceptance by large segments of the population. A record may get wide airplay on Top 40 stations, steadily rising up the charts "like a bullet."

In the *regression stage*, the song reaches a state of social saturation as it becomes overused, and eventually it sinks into decline and obsolescence as new songs rise to take its place. A hit record may be played once an hour on a Top 40

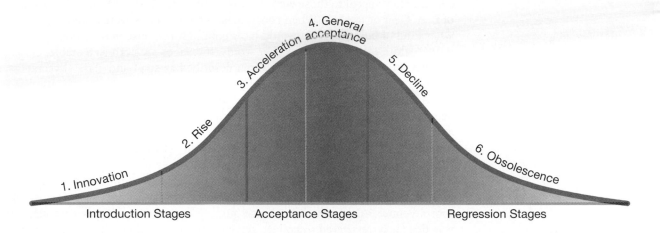

Figure 17.4
A Normal Fashion Cycle

station for several weeks. At some point, though, people tend to get sick of it and focus their attention on newer releases. The former hit record eventually winds up in the discount rack at the local record store.

Figure 17.5 illustrates that fashions are characterized by slow acceptance at the beginning, which (if the fashion is to "make it") rapidly accelerates, peaks, and then tapers off. Different classes of fashion can be identified by considering the relative length of the fashion acceptance cycle. Many fashions exhibit a moderate cycle, taking several years to work their way through the stages of acceptance and decline; others are extremely long-lived or short-lived.

A **classic** is a fashion with an extremely long acceptance cycle. It is in a sense "antifashion" because it guarantees stability and low risk to the purchaser for a long period of time. Keds sneakers, introduced in 1917, have been successful

Figure 17.5
Comparison of the Acceptance Cycles of Fads, Fashions, and Classics

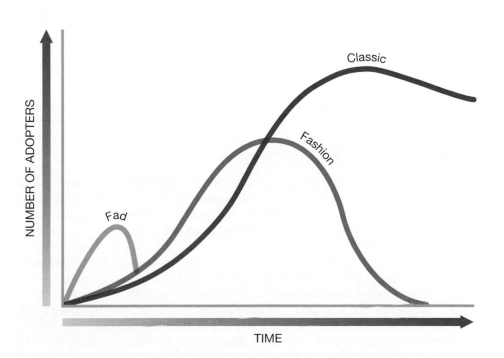

because they appeal to those who are turned off by the high-fashion, trendy appeal of L. A. Gear or Reebok. When consumers in focus groups were asked to imagine what kind of building Keds would be, a common response was a country house with a white picket fence. In other words, the shoes are seen as a stable, classic product. In contrast, Nikes were often described as steel-and-glass skyscrapers, reflecting their more modern image.[90]

A **fad** is a very short-lived fashion. Fads are usually adopted by relatively few people. Adopters may all belong to a common subculture, and the fad "trickles across" members but rarely breaks out of that specific group. Some successful fad products include hula hoops, snap bracelets, and pet rocks—to learn more about these and other "must have" products visit badfads.com.

Streaking was a fad that hit college campuses in the mid-1970s. This term referred to students running naked through classrooms, cafeterias, dorms, and sports venues. Although the practice quickly spread across many campuses, it was primarily restricted to college settings. Streaking highlights several important characteristics of fads.[91]

- The fad is nonutilitarian; it does not perform any meaningful function.
- The fad is often adopted on impulse; people do not undergo stages of rational decision making before joining in.
- The fad diffuses rapidly, gains quick acceptance, and is short lived.

Fad or Trend?

In 1988, a company called Clearly Canadian began testing a clear soft drink, and during the next few years others jumped on board. Colgate-Palmolive spent $6 million developing a clear version of Palmolive dishwashing liquid. By 1992 Colgate was selling clear soap, Coors introduced a clear malt beverage called Zima, and consumers could even choose clear gasoline for their cars. Clear products were so ubiquitous that they were spoofed on *Saturday Night Live* in a fake commercial for Crystal Gravy: "You can see your meat!" It was clear that the beginning of the end was in sight for this fad. The comments of one 25-year-old research participant in a study about clear drinks sums up the problem: "When I first started drinking them, I thought they were interesting. But once it became a fad I thought, 'this isn't cool anymore.'"[92]

The first company to identify a trend and act on it has an advantage, whether the firm is Starbucks (gourmet coffee), Nabisco (Snackwell's low-fat cookies and crackers), or Taco Bell (value pricing). See figure 17.6 which illustrates some fad cycles. Nothing is certain, but some guidelines help to predict if the innovation will endure as a long-term trend or is just a fad, destined to go the way of hula hoops, Pet Rocks, and Wally Wallwalkers:[93]

- Does it fit with basic lifestyle changes? If a new hairstyle is hard to care for, this innovation will not be consistent with women's increasing time demands. On the other hand, the movement to shorter-term vacations is more likely to last because this innovation makes trip planning easier for harried consumers.
- What are the benefits? The switch to poultry and fish from beef came about because these meats are healthier, so a real benefit is evident.
- Can it be personalized? Enduring trends tend to accommodate a desire for individuality, whereas styles such as mohawk haircuts or the grunge look are inflexible and don't allow people to express themselves.
- Is it a trend or a side effect? An increased interest in exercises is part of a basic trend toward health consciousness, although the specific form of

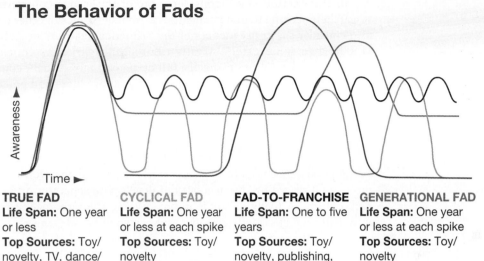

The Behavior of Fads

TRUE FAD
Life Span: One year or less
Top Sources: Toy/novelty, TV, dance/music, fashion
Demographics: All
Example: Pet Rock

CYCLICAL FAD
Life Span: One year or less at each spike
Top Sources: Toy/novelty
Demographics: All
Example: Yo-yos

FAD-TO-FRANCHISE
Life Span: One to five years
Top Sources: Toy/novelty, publishing, movies
Demographics: All
Example: Barbies

GENERATIONAL FAD
Life Span: One year or less at each spike
Top Sources: Toy/novelty
Demographics: Children and nostalgic adults
Example: Trolls

Figure 17.6

exercise that is "in" at any given time will vary (e.g., low-impact aerobics versus in-line skating).

- What other changes have occurred in the market? Sometimes the popularity of products is influenced by *carryover effects.* The miniskirt fad in the 1960s brought about a major change in the hosiery market, as sales of pantyhose and tights grew from 10 percent of this product category to more than 80 percent in two years. Now, sales of these items are declining due to the casual emphasis in dressing.
- Who has adopted the change? If the innovation is not adopted by working mothers, baby boomers, or some other important market segment, it is not likely to become a trend.

TRANSFERRING PRODUCT MEANINGS TO OTHER CULTURES

Innovations know no geographic boundaries; in modern times they travel across oceans and deserts with blinding speed. Just as Marco Polo brought noodles from China and colonial settlers introduced Europeans to the "joys" of tobacco, today multinational firms are constantly working to conquer new markets by convincing legions of foreign consumers to desire what they make.

As if understanding the dynamics of one's culture weren't hard enough, these issues get even more complicated when we take on the daunting task of learning about the practices of other cultures. The consequences of ignoring cultural sensitivities can be costly. This oversight became evident, for example, during the 1994 soccer World Cup. Both McDonald's and Coca-Cola made the mistake of reprinting the Saudi Arabian flag, which includes sacred words from the Koran, on disposable packaging used in promotions. Despite their delight at having a Saudi team in contention for the cup, Muslims around the world protested this borrowing of sacred imagery and both companies had to scramble to correct their gaffe.[94]

In this section, we'll consider some of the issues confronting consumer researchers seeking to understand the cultural dynamics of other countries. We'll also consider the consequences of the "Americanization" of global culture. As U.S. (and to some extent, Western European) marketers continue to export Western popular culture to a globe full of increasingly affluent consumers, many are eagerly waiting to replace their traditional products and practices with the likes of McDonald's, Levi's, and MTV.

Think Globally, Act Locally

As corporations compete in many markets around the world, the debate has intensified regarding the necessity of developing separate marketing plans for each culture. A lively debate is in progress regarding the need to "fit in" to the local culture. Let's briefly consider each viewpoint.

Adopt a Standardized Strategy

Proponents of a standardized marketing strategy argue that many cultures, especially those of industrialized countries, have become so homogenized that the same approach will work throughout the world. By developing one approach for multiple markets, a company can benefit from economies of scale because it does not have to incur the substantial time and expense of developing a separate strategy for each culture.[95] This viewpoint represents an **etic perspective,** which focuses on commonalities across cultures. An etic approach to a culture is objective and analytical; it reflects impressions of a culture as viewed by outsiders.

Adopt a Localized Strategy

On the other hand, many marketers endorse an **emic perspective** stressing variations within a culture. They feel that each culture is unique, with its own value system, conventions, and regulations. This perspective argues that each country has a *national character,* a distinctive set of behavior and personality characteristics.[96] An effective strategy must be tailored to the sensibilities and needs of each specific culture. An emic approach to a culture is subjective and experiential; it attempts to explain a culture as it is experienced by insiders.

Sometimes this strategy involves modifying a product or the way it is positioned to make it acceptable to local tastes. For example, consider the challenge faced by the brewing industry in the Middle East. Alcohol-free beers are growing in popularity, and Saudi market leader Moussey has been doing business there for more than 20 years. Still, selling such a product in a country where alcohol consumption is punishable by flogging can be tricky. These drinks are called malt

Multinational corporations such as McDonald's are aggressively expanding around the world.

beverages instead of beer, and they can only be marketed through special promotions. Stroh's Schlitz No-Alcohol brand is touted vaguely as "The famous American beverage."[97]

In other situations adaptation demands more than wordplay. Consumers in some cultures simply do not like some products that are popular elsewhere. Snapple failed in Japan because consumers there were turned off by the drink's cloudy appearance and the pulp floating in the bottles. Similarly, Frito-Lay stopped selling Ruffles potato chips (too salty) and Cheetos (the Japanese didn't appreciate having their fingers turn orange after eating a handful).[98] Cheetos are made in China, but the local version doesn't contain any cheese, which is not a staple of the Chinese diet. Instead, local flavors are available in varieties like Savory American Cream and Japanese Steak.[99]

Cultural Differences Relevant to Marketers

So, which perspective is correct—the emic or the etic? Perhaps it will be helpful to consider some of the ways cultures vary in terms of their product preferences and norms regarding what types of products are appropriate or desirable.

Given the sizeable variations in tastes within the United States alone, it is hardly surprising that people around the world have developed their own unique preferences. Unlike Americans, for example, Europeans favor dark chocolate over milk chocolate, which they regard as suitable only for children. Sara Lee sells its pound cake with chocolate chips in the United States, raisins in Australia, and coconuts in Hong Kong. Crocodile handbags are popular in Asia and Europe, but not in the United States. Americans' favorite tie colors are red and blue, whereas Japanese men prefer olive, brown, and bronze.[100]

Marketers must be aware of a culture's norms regarding sensitive topics such as taboos and sexuality. Opals signify bad luck to the British, whereas hunting dog or pig emblems are offensive to Muslims. The Japanese are superstitious about the number four. *Shi*, the word for four, is also the word for death. For this reason, Tiffany sells glassware and china in sets of five in Japan.

Does Global Marketing Work?

So, after briefly considering some of the many differences one encounters across cultures, does global marketing work? Perhaps the more appropriate question is, "*When* does it work?"

Although the argument for a homogenous world culture is appealing in principle, in practice it has met with mixed results. One reason for the failure of global marketing is that consumers in different countries have different conventions and customs, so they simply do not use products the same way. Kellogg, for example, discovered that in Brazil big breakfasts are not traditional—cereal is more commonly eaten as a dry snack. In fact, significant cultural differences can even show up within the same country: Advertisers in Canada know that when they target consumers in French-speaking Quebec their messages must be much different from those addressed to their fellow countrymen who live in English-speaking Canada. Ads in Montreal tend to be a lot racier than those in Toronto, reflecting differences in attitudes toward sexuality between consumers with French versus British roots.[102]

Some large corporations, such as Coca-Cola, have been successful in crafting a single, international image. Still, even Coca-Cola must make minor modifications to the way it presents itself in each culture. Although Coke commercials

STRONGLY HELD VALUES CAN make life very difficult for marketers who sell personal-care products. This is the case with tampons; 70 percent of American women use them, but only 100 million out of a potential market of 1.7 billion eligible women around the world do. Resistance to using this product posed a major problem for Tambrands. This company makes only one product, so it needs to sell tampons in as many countries as possible to continue growing. But, Tambrands has trouble selling its feminine hygiene products in some cultures such as Brazil, where many young women fear they will lose their virginity if they use a tampon. A commercial developed for this market included an actress who says in a reassuring voice, "Of course, you're not going to lose your virginity."

MULTICULTURAL DIMENSIONS

Prior to launching a new global advertising campaign for Tampax in 26 countries, the firm's advertising agency conducted research and divided the world into three clusters based on residents' resistance to using tampons. Resistance was so intense in Muslim countries that the agency didn't even try to sell there!

In Cluster One (including the United States, the United Kingdom, and Australia), women felt comfortable with the idea and offered little resistance. A teaser ad was developed to encourage more frequency of use: "Should I sleep with it, or not?"

In Cluster Two (including France, Israel, and South Africa), about 50 percent of women use the product, but some concerns about the loss of virginity remain. To counteract these objections, the marketing strategy focused on obtaining the endorsements of gynecologists within each country.

In Cluster Three (including Brazil, China, and Russia), Tambrands encountered the greatest resistance. To try to make inroads in these countries, the researchers found that the first priority is simply to explain how to use the product without making women feel squeamish—a challenge they still are trying to puzzle out.[101] If they do—and that's a big if—they will have changed the consumer behavior of millions of women and added huge new markets to their customer base in the process.

are largely standardized, local agencies are permitted to edit them to highlight close-ups of local faces.[103] As the world's borders fade due to advances in communications, many companies such as Coca-Cola continue to develop global advertising campaigns. In some cases they are encountering obstacles to acceptance, especially in less-developed countries or in those areas that are only beginning to embrace Western-style materialism as a way of life, such as Eastern Europe.[104]

To maximize the chances of success for these multicultural efforts, marketers must locate consumers in different countries who nonetheless share a common worldview. This is more likely to be the case among people whose frame of reference is relatively more international or cosmopolitan, or who receive much of their information about the world from sources that incorporate a worldwide perspective. Who is likely to fall into this category? Two consumer segments are particularly good candidates: (1) affluent people who are "global citizens" and who are exposed to ideas from around the world through their travels, business contacts, and media experiences; and (2) young people whose tastes in music and fashion are strongly influenced by MTV and other media that broadcast many of the same images to multiple countries. For example, viewers of MTV Europe in Rome or Zurich can check out the same "buzz clips" as their counterparts in London or Luxembourg.[108]

The Diffusion of Consumer Culture

Coca-Cola is the drink of choice among young people in Asian countries, and McDonald's is the favorite restaurant.[109] The National Basketball Association sells $500 million of licensed merchandise every year *outside* of the United States.[110] Walk the streets of Lisbon or Buenos Aires, and you'll be accosted by the sight of Nike hats, Gap T-shirts, and Levi's jeans at every turn. The allure of

MARKETING PITFALLS

THE LANGUAGE BARRIER IS one obvious problem confronting marketers who wish to break into foreign markets. Travelers abroad commonly encounter signs in tortured English such as a note to guests at a Tokyo hotel saying, "You are invited to take advantage of the chambermaid," a notice at a hotel in Acapulco reassuring people that "The manager has personally passed all the water served here," or a dry cleaner in Majorca who urged passing customers to "drop your pants here for best results." And local product names often raise eyebrows to visiting Americans, who may be surprised to stumble on a Japanese coffee creamer called Creap, a Mexican bread named Bimbo, or even a Scandinavian product that unfreezes car locks called Super Piss.[105]

Chapter 14 noted some gaffes made by U.S. marketers when advertising to ethnic groups in their own country. Imagine how these mistakes are compounded outside of the United States! One technique that is used to avoid this problem is *back-translation*, in which a translated ad is retranslated into the original language by a different interpreter to catch errors. Some specific translation obstacles that have been encountered around the world include the following:[106]

- Electrolux vacuum cleaners were marketed in the United States by the Scandinavian manufacturer with the slogan: "Nothing sucks like an Electrolux."
- Colgate introduced a toothpaste in France called Cue, which also happens to be the name of a well-known porn magazine.
- When Parker marketed a ballpoint pen in Mexico, its ads were supposed to say "It won't leak in your pocket and embarrass you." The translation actually said "It won't leak in your pocket and make you pregnant."[107]
- Fresca (a soft drink) is Mexican slang for lesbian.
- Ford had several problems in Spanish markets. The company discovered that a truck model it called Fiera means "ugly old woman" in Spanish. Its Caliente model, sold in Mexico, is slang for a streetwalker. In Brazil, Pinto is a slang term meaning "small male appendage."
- When Rolls-Royce introduced its Silver Mist model in Germany, it found that the word "mist" is translated as excrement. Similarly, Sunbeam's hair curling iron, called the Mist-Stick, translated as manure wand. To add insult to injury, Vicks is German slang for sexual intercourse, so the company had to change its name to Wicks in this market.

consumer culture has spread throughout the world. In a global society, people are quick to borrow from other cultures, especially those they admire. For example, many Koreans are influenced by the cultural scene in Japan, which they view as a very sophisticated country. Japanese rock bands are more popular than Korean bands, and other exports such as comic books, fashion magazines, and game shows are eagerly snapped up. A Korean researcher explains, "Culture is like water. It flows from stronger nations to weaker ones. People tend to idolize countries that are wealthier, freer, and more advanced, and in Asia that country is Japan."[111]

I'd Like to Buy the World a Coke . . .

The West (and especially the United States) is a net exporter of popular culture. Many consumers have learned to equate Western lifestyles in general and the English language in particular with modernization and sophistication. Some Japanese pay the equivalent of one-half million dollars for shrunken versions of U.S. homes. The more avid Americophiles among them have been known to stage cookouts around imported brick barbecues and trade in their Toyotas for expensive imports such as Chevy vans.[112] Teenagers in Tokyo can occasionally be seen cruising the streets with surfboards strapped to the tops of their cars.

Despite the proliferation of American pop culture around the world, there are signs that this invasion is slowing. Japanese consumers, for example, are beginning to exhibit waning interest in foreign products as the health of their country's economy declines. Some of the latest "hot" products in Japan now include green tea and *yukata*, traditional printed cotton robes donned after the evening bath.[113]

Several locally made products are catching on in parts of Eastern Europe due to their lower prices and improved quality. Some Muslims are rejecting Western symbols as they adhere to a green Islam philosophy that includes using natural, traditional products.[114]

Critics in other countries deplore the creeping Americanization of their cultures. The French have been the most outspoken opponents of this influence. They have even tried to ban the use of such "Franglish" terms as *le drugstore, le fast food,* and even *le marketing.*[115] Resistance to the diffusion of American culture is best summarized in the words of one French critic who described the Euro Disney theme park as "a horror made of cardboard, plastic, and appalling colors—a construction of hardened chewing gum and idiotic folklore taken straight out of a comic book written for obese Americans."[116] Fair enough, but after making adjustments to accommodate local expectations (such as serving wine with meals at the park), Euro Disney is thriving—and for better or worse there's a McDonald's on the Champs d'Elysees in Paris.

Emerging Consumer Cultures in Transitional Economies

In the early 1980s the American TV show *Dallas* was broadcast by the Romanian Communist government to point out the decadence of Western capitalism. This strategy backfired, and instead the devious (but rich!) J. R. became a revered icon in parts of Eastern Europe and the Middle East. A popular tourist attraction outside of Bucharest includes a big white log gate that announces (in English) the name, "South Fork Ranch."[117] Western "decadence" appears to be infectious.[118]

More than 60 countries have a gross national product of less than $10 billion, and there are at least 135 transnational companies with revenues greater than that. The dominance of these marketing powerhouses has helped to create a **globalized consumption ethic.** People the world over are increasingly surrounded by tempting images of luxury cars, glam rock stars on MTV, and modern appliances that make life easier. They begin to share the ideal of a material lifestyle and value well-known brands that symbolize prosperity. Shopping evolves from a wearying, task-oriented struggle to locate even basic necessities to a leisure activity. Possessing these coveted items becomes a mechanism to display one's status (see Chapter 13)—often at great personal sacrifice. In Romania, for example, Kent cigarettes are an underground currency, even though the cost of smoking a pack a day of foreign cigarettes would cost the average Romanian his or her entire yearly salary.

After the downfall of communism, Eastern Europeans emerged from a long winter of deprivation into a springtime of abundance. The picture is not all rosy, however, because attaining consumer goods is not easy for many in **transitional economies.** This refers to a country (examples include China, Portugal, and Romania) that is struggling with the difficult adaptation from a controlled, centralized economy to a free-market system. In these situations rapid change is required on social, political, and economic dimensions as the populace suddenly is exposed to global communications and external market pressures.[119]

Some of the consequences of the transition to capitalism include a loss of confidence and pride in the local culture, as well as alienation, frustration, and an increase in stress as leisure time is sacrificed to work ever harder to buy consumer goods. The yearning for the trappings of Western material culture is perhaps most evident in parts of Eastern Europe, where citizens who threw off the shackles of communism now have direct access to coveted consumer goods from the United States and Western Europe—if they can afford them. One analyst observed, "as former subjects of the Soviet empire dream it, the American dream has very little to do with liberty and justice for all and a great deal to do with soap operas and the Sears Catalogue."[120]

As the global consumption ethic spreads, the products wished for in different cultures become homogenized. For example, Christmas is now celebrated among some urbanites in Muslim Turkey, though gift-giving even on birthdays is not customary in many parts of the country. Chinese women demand Western cosmetics costing up to a quarter of their salaries, ignoring domestically produced competitors. As one Chinese executive noted, "Some women even buy a cosmetic just because it has foreign words on the package."[121]

Creolization

Does this homogenization mean that in time consumers who live in Nairobi, New Guinea, or the Netherlands will all be indistinguishable from those in New York or Nashville? Probably not, because the meanings of consumer goods often mutate to be consistent with local customs and values. For example, in Turkey some urban women use ovens to dry clothes and dishwashers to wash muddy spinach. Or, a traditional clothing style such as a *bilum* worn in Papua New Guinea may be combined with Western items such as Mickey Mouse shirts or baseball caps.[122] These processes make it unlikely that global homogenization will overwhelm local cultures, but rather that there will be multiple consumer cultures, each blending global icons such as Nike's pervasive "swoosh" with indigenous products and meanings.

A process called **creolization** occurs when foreign influences are absorbed and integrated with local meanings. Modern Christianity adapted the pagan Christmas tree into its own rituals. In India handicapped beggars sell bottles of Coke from tricycles, and a popular music hybrid called Indipop mixes traditional styles with rock, rap, and reggae.[123] In the United States young Hispanic Americans bounce between hip-hop and Rock en Espanol, blend Mexican rice with spaghetti sauce, and spread peanut butter and jelly on tortillas.[124]

The creolization process sometimes results in bizarre permutations of products and services when they are modified to be compatible with local customs. Consider these creolized adaptations, for example:[125]

- In Peru, Indian boys carry rocks painted to look like transistor radios.
- In highland Papua New Guinea, tribesmen put Chivas Regal wrappers on their drums and wear Pentel pens instead of nosebones.
- Bana tribesmen in the remote highlands of Kako, Ethiopia pay to watch *Pluto the Circus Dog* on a Viewmaster.
- When a Swazi princess marries a Zulu king, she wears a traditional costume of red touraco wing feathers around her forehead and a cape of windowbird feathers and oxtails and the kindis wrapped in a leopard skin. But the ceremony is recorded on a Kodak movie camera while the band plays "The Sound of Music."
- The Japanese use Western words as a shorthand for anything new and exciting, even if they do not understand their meaning. Cars are given names such as Fairlady, Gloria, and Bongo Wagon. Consumers buy *deodoranto* (deodorant) and *appuru pai* (apple pie). Ads urge shoppers to *stoppu rukku* (stop and look), and products are claimed to be *yuniku* (unique).[126] Coca-Cola cans say, "I feel Coke & sound special," and a company called Cream Soda sells products with the slogan, "Too old to die, too young to happy."[127] Other Japanese products with English names include Mouth Pet (breath freshener), Pocari Sweat

Globalization has become an integral part of the marketing strategy of many, if not most, major corporations.

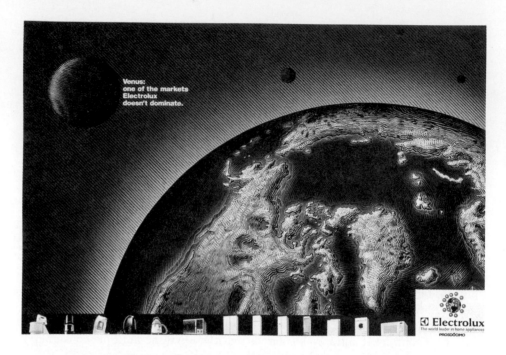

("refreshment water"), Armpit (electric razor), Brown Gross Foam (hair-coloring mousse), Virgin Pink Special (skin cream), Cow Brand (beauty soap), and Mymorning Water (canned water).[128]

CHAPTER SUMMARY

- The styles prevalent in a culture at any point in time often reflect underlying political and social conditions. The set of agents responsible for creating stylistic alternatives is termed a *culture production system (CPS)*. Factors such as the types of people involved in this system and the amount of competition by alternative product forms influence the choices that eventually make their way to the marketplace for consideration by end consumers.

- Culture is often described in terms of high (or elite) forms and low (or popular) forms. Products of popular culture tend to follow a *cultural formula* and contain predictable components. On the other hand, these distinctions are blurring in modern society as imagery from "high art" is increasingly being incorporated into marketing efforts.

- *Reality engineering* occurs as elements of popular culture are appropriated by marketers and converted to vehicles for promotional strategies. These elements include sensory and spatial aspects of everyday existence, whether in the form of products appearing in movies, scents pumped into offices and stores, billboards, theme parks, or video monitors attached to shopping carts.

- *Diffusion of innovations* refers to the process whereby a new product, service, or idea spreads through a population. *Innovators* and *early adopters* are quick to adopt new products, and *laggards* are very slow. A consumer's decision to adopt a new product depends on his or her personal characteristics as well as on characteristics of the innovation itself. Products stand a better chance of being adopted if they demand relatively little change in behavior from users, are easy to understand, and provide a relative advantage compared to existing products.

• The *fashion system* includes everyone involved in the creation and transference of symbolic meanings. Meanings that express common *cultural categories* (e.g., gender distinctions) are conveyed by many different products. New styles tend to be adopted by many people simultaneously in a process known as *collective selection.* According to meme theory, ideas spread through a population in a geometric progression much as a virus infects many people until it reaches epidemic proportions. Other perspectives on motivations for adopting new styles include psychological, economic, and sociological models of fashion.

• Fashions tend to follow cycles that resemble the product life cycle. The two extremes of fashion adoption, *classics* and *fads,* can be distinguished in terms of the length of this cycle.

• Because a consumer's culture exerts such a big influence on his or her lifestyle choices, marketers must learn as much as possible about differences in cultural norms and preferences when marketing in more than one country. One important issue is to the extent to which marketing strategies must be tailored to each culture versus standardized across cultures. Followers of an *etic perspective* believe that the same universal messages will be appreciated by people in many cultures. Believers in an *emic perspective* argue that individual cultures are too unique to permit such standardization; marketers must instead adapt their approaches to be consistent with local values and practices. Attempts at global marketing have met with mixed success; in many cases this approach is more likely to work if the messages appeal to basic values or if the target markets consist of consumers who are more internationally rather than locally oriented.

• The United States is a net exporter of popular culture. Consumers around the world have eagerly adopted American products, especially entertainment vehicles and items that are linked symbolically to a uniquely American lifestyle (e.g., Marlboro cigarettes, Levi's jeans). Despite the continuing "Americanization" of world culture, some consumers are alarmed by this influence, and are instead emphasizing a return to local products and customs. In other cases, they are integrating these products with existing cultural practices in a process known as *creolization.*

KEY TERMS

art product, p. 493
classic, p. 511
collective selection, p. 506
cooptation, p. 489
craft product, p. 493
creolization, p. 519
cultivation hypothesis, p. 498
cultural categories, p. 503
cultural formula, p. 495
cultural gatekeepers, p. 493
cultural selection, p. 490

culture production system (CPS), p. 491
diffusion of innovations, p. 500
early adopters, p. 501
emic perspective, p. 514
etic perspective, p. 514
fad, p. 512
fashion, p. 503
fashion acceptance cycle, p. 510
fashion system, p. 503
globalized consumption ethic, p. 518

innovation, p. 499
innovators, p. 501
laggards, p. 500
late adopters, p. 500
lead user, p. 501
meme theory, p. 509
product placement, p. 497
reality engineering, p. 496
transitional economies, p. 518
trickle-down theory, p. 508

CONSUMER BEHAVIOR CHALLENGE

1. Is it appropriate for large corporations to market small boutique brands and hide the true origins of these products?
2. Some consumers complain that they are "at the mercy" of designers: They are forced to buy whatever styles are in fashion, because nothing else is available. Do you agree that there is such a thing as a "designer conspiracy?"
3. What are the basic differences between a fad, a fashion, and a classic? Provide examples of each.
4. What is the difference between an art and a craft? How would you characterize advertising within this framework?
5. The chapter mentions some instances in which market research findings influenced artistic decisions, as when a movie ending was reshot to accommodate consumers' preferences. Many people would most likely oppose this practice, claiming that books, movies, records, or other artistic endeavors should not be designed to merely conform to what people want to read, see, or hear. What do you think?
6. Due to increased competition and market saturation, marketers in industrialized countries are increasingly trying to develop Third World markets by encouraging people in underdeveloped countries to desire Western products. Asian consumers alone spend $90 billion a year on cigarettes, and U.S. tobacco manufacturers continue to push relentlessly into these markets. Cigarette advertising, often depicting glamorous Western models and settings, is found just about everywhere, on billboards, buses, storefronts, and clothing, and many major sports and cultural events are sponsored by tobacco companies. Some companies even hand out cigarettes and gifts in amusement areas, often to preteens. Should this practice be encouraged, even if the products being marketed may be harmful to consumers' health (e.g., cigarettes) or divert needed money away from the purchase of essentials? If you were a trade or health official in a Third World country, what guidelines, if any, might you suggest to regulate the import of luxury goods from advanced economies?
7. Comment on the growing practices described as reality engineering. Do marketers "own" our culture, and should they?

NOTES

1. Khanh T. L. Tran, "Lifting the Velvet Rope: Night Clubs Draw Virtual Throngs with Webcasts," *The Wall Street Journal Interactive Edition* (August 30, 1999).
2. Quoted in Lauren Goldstein, "Urban Wear Goes Suburban," *Fortune* (December 21, 1998): 169–72, p. 172.
3. Quoted in Spiegler, "Marketing Street Culture: Bringing Hip-Hop Style to the Mainstream,": 30.
4. Joshua Levine, "Badass Sells," *Forbes* (April 21, 1997): 142.
5. Nina Darnton, "Where the Homegirls Are," *Newsweek* (June 17, 1991): 60; "The Idea Chain," *Newsweek* (October 5, 1992): 32.
6. Cyndee Miller, "X Marks the Lucrative Spot, But Some Advertisers Can't Hit

Target," *Marketing News* (August 2, 1993): 1.
7. Ad appeared in *Elle* (September 1994).
8. Spiegler, "Marketing Street Culture: Bringing Hip-Hop Style to the Mainstream"; Levine, "Badass Sells."
9. Jeff Jensen, "Hip, Wholesome Image Makes a Marketing Star of Rap's LL Cool J," *Advertising Age* (August 25, 1997): 1.
10. Alice Z. Cuneo, "Gap's 1st Global Ads Confront Dockers on a Khaki Battlefield," *Advertising Age* (April 20, 1998): 3–5.
11. Jancee Dunn, "How Hip-Hop Style Bum-Rushed the Mall," *Rolling Stone* (March 18, 1999): 54–59.
12. Quoted in Teri Agins, "The Rare Art of 'Gilt by Association': How Armani Got Stars to

Be Billboards," *The Wall Street Journal Interactive Edition* (September 14, 1999).
13. Eryn Brown, "From Rap to Retail: Wiring the Hip-Hop Nation," *Fortune* (April 17, 2000): 530.
14. Elizabeth M. Blair, "Commercialization of the Rap Music Youth Subculture," *Journal of Popular Culture* 27 (Winter 1993): 21–34; Basil G. Englis, Michael R. Solomon, and Anna Olofsson, "Consumption Imagery in Music Television: A Bi-Cultural Perspective," *Journal of Advertising* 22 (December 1993): 21–34.
15. Spiegler, "Marketing Street Culture: Bringing Hip-Hop Style to the Mainstream."

16. Grant McCracken, "Culture and Consumption: A Theoretical Account of the Structure and Movement of the Cultural Meaning of Consumer Goods," *Journal of Consumer Research* 13 (June 1986): 71–84.

17. Richard A. Peterson, "The Production of Culture: A Prolegomenon," in Richard A. Peterson, ed., *The Production of Culture, Sage Contemporary Social Science Issues*, 33 (Beverly Hills, CA: Sage, 1976): 7–22.

18. Richard A. Peterson and D. G. Berger, "Entrepreneurship in Organizations: Evidence from the Popular Music Industry," *Administrative Science Quarterly* 16 (1971): 97–107.

19. Elizabeth C. Hirschman, "Resource Exchange in the Production and Distribution of a Motion Picture," *Empirical Studies of the Arts* 8, no. 1 (1990): 31–51; Michael R. Solomon, "Building Up and Breaking Down: The Impact of Cultural Sorting on Symbolic Consumption," in J. Sheth and E. C. Hirschman, eds., *Research in Consumer Behavior* (Greenwich, CT: JAI Press, 1988), 325–51.

20. See Paul M. Hirsch, "Processing Fads and Fashions: An Organizational Set Analysis of Cultural Industry Systems," *American Journal of Sociology* 77, no. 4 (1972): 639–59; Russell Lynes, *The Tastemakers* (New York: Harper and Brothers, 1954); Michael R. Solomon, "The Missing Link: Surrogate Consumers in the Marketing Chain," *Journal of Marketing* 50 (October 1986): 208–19.

21. Howard S. Becker, "Arts and Crafts," *American Journal of Sociology* 83 (January 1987): 862–89.

22. Herbert J. Gans, "Popular Culture in America: Social Problem in a Mass Society or Social Asset in a Pluralist Society?" in Howard S. Becker, ed., *Social Problems: A Modern Approach* (New York: Wiley, 1966).

23. Peter S. Green, "Moviegoers Devour Ads," *Advertising Age* (June 26, 1989): 36.

24. John P. Robinson, "The Arts in America," *American Demographics* (September 1987): 42.

25. Michael R. Real, *Mass-Mediated Culture* (Upper Saddle River, NJ: Prentice Hall, 1977).

26. Annetta Miller, "Shopping Bags Imitate Art: Seen the Sacks? Now Visit the Museum Exhibit," *Newsweek* (January 23, 1989): 44.

27. Kim Foltz, "New Species for Study: Consumers in Action," *New York Times* (December 18, 1989): A1.

28. Arthur A. Berger, *Signs in Contemporary Culture: An Introduction to Semiotics* (New York: Longman, 1984).

29. Michiko Kakutani, "Art Is Easier the 2d Time Around," *New York Times* (October 30, 1994): E4.

30. Nigel Andrews, "Filming a Blockbuster Is One Thing; Striking Gold Is Another," *Financial Times* (January 20, 1998).

31. Helene Diamond, "Lights, Camera . . . Research!" *Marketing News* (September 11, 1989): 10.

32. Nigel Andrews, "Filming a Blockbuster Is One Thing; Striking Gold Is Another," *Financial Times* (January 20, 1998).

33. Robin Givhan, "Designers Caught in a Tangled Web," *The Washington Post* (April 5, 1997): C1.

34. "A Brand-New Development Creates a Colorful History," *The Wall Street Journal Interactive Edition*, February 18, 1998.

35. Michael R. Solomon and Basil G. Englis, "Reality Engineering: Blurring the Boundaries Between Marketing and Popular Culture," *Journal of Current Issues and Research in Advertising* 16, no. 2 (Fall 1994): 1–17.

36. T. Bettina Cornwell and Bruce Keillor, "Contemporary Literature and the Embedded Consumer Culture: The Case of Updike's Rabbit," in Roger J. Kruez and Mary Sue MacNealy, eds., *Empirical Approaches to Literature and Aesthetics: Advances in Discourse Processes* 52 (Norwood, NJ: Ablex, 1996): 559–72; Monroe Friedman, "The Changing Language of a Consumer Society: Brand Name Usage in Popular American Novels in the Postwar Era," *Journal of Consumer Research* 11 (March 1985): 927–37; Monroe Friedman, "Commercial Influences in the Lyrics of Popular American Music of the Postwar Era," *Journal of Consumer Affairs* 20 (Winter 1986): 193.

37. Peggy J. Farber, "Schools for Sale," *Advertising Age* (October 25, 1999): 22.

38. Benjamin M. Cole, "Products That Want to Be in Pictures," *Los Angeles Herald Examiner* (March 5, 1985): 36; see also Stacy M. Vollmers and Richard W. Mizerski, "A Review and Investigation into the Effectiveness of Product Placements in Films," in Karen Whitehill King, ed., *Proceedings of the 1994 Conference of the American Academy of Advertising*: 97–102; Solomon and Englis, "Reality Engineering: Blurring the Boundaries Between Marketing and Popular Culture."

39. Denise E. DeLorme and Leonard N. Reid, "Moviegoers' Experiences and Interpretations of Brands in Films Revisited," *Journal of Advertising* 28, no. 2 (1999): 71–90.

40. Quoted in Marc Gunther, "Now Starring in *Party of Five*—Dr. Pepper," *Fortune* (April 17, 2000): 88, p. 90.

41. Sally Beatty, "In New TV Series, Big-Rig Maker Decides to Team Up with Hollywood," *The Wall Street Journal Interactive Edition* (October 29, 1999).

42. Jennifer Tanaka and Marc Peyser, "The Apples of Their Eyes," *Newsweek* (November 30, 1998): 58.

43. Benny Evangelista, "Advertisers Get into the Video Game," *San Francisco Chronicle* [online], (January 18, 1999).

44. Nancy Marsden, "Lighting Up the Big Screen," *San Francisco Examiner* [online], (August 4, 1998).

45. Joe Flint, "Sponsors Get a Role in CBS Reality Show," *The Wall Street Journal Interactive Edition* (January 13, 2000).

46. Sarah Ellison, "French Cafes Now Serve Up Logos du Jour with Au Laits," *The Wall Street Journal Interactive Edition* (June 2, 2000).

47. Peter Wonacott, "Chinese TV Is an Eager Medium for (Lots of) Product Placement," *The Wall Street Journal Interactive Edition* (January 26, 2000).

48. Fara Warner, "Why It's Getting Harder to Tell the Shows from the Ads," *The Wall Street Journal* (June 15, 1995): B1.

49. Warner, "Why It's Getting Harder to Tell the Shows from the Ads."

50. Chuck Ross, "Warner Bros. to Test 'Virtual' Ad Concept," *Advertising Age* (March 17, 1999): 1.

51. Quoted in Mary Kuntz and Joseph Weber, "The New Hucksterism," *Business Week* (July 1, 1996): 75, p. 78.

52. George Gerbner, Larry Gross, Nancy Signorielli, and Michael Morgan, "Aging with Television: Images on Television Drama and Conceptions of Social Reality," *Journal of Communication* 30 (1980): 37–47.

53. L. J. Shrum, Robert S. Wyer Jr., and Thomas C. O'Guinn, "The Effects of Television Consumption on Social Perceptions: The Use of Priming Procedures to Investigate Psychological Process," *Journal of Consumer Research* 24 (March 1998): 447–68; Stephen Fox and William Philber, "Television Viewing and the Perception of Affluence," *Sociological Quarterly* 19 (1978): 103–12; W. James Potter, "Three Strategies for Elaborating the Cultivation Hypothesis," *Journalism Quarterly* 65 (Winter 1988): 930–39; Gabriel Weimann, "Images of Life in America: The Impact of American T.V. in Israel," *International Journal of Intercultural Relations* 8 (1984): 185–97.

54. "Movie Smoking Exceeds Real Life," *The Asbury Park Press* (June 20, 1994): A4.

55. Lynn Elber, "TV Offers Fantasy Depiction of Real-Life Family, Work Life, Study Says," *Montgomery Advertiser* (June 11, 1998): B1.

56. David Bauder, "Networks Given Financial Incentive for Anti-Drug Messages," *Opelika-Auburn News* (January 14, 2000): 6A.

57. Robert Hof, "The Click Here Economy," *Business Week* (June 22, 1998): 122–28.

58. Eric J. Arnould, "Toward a Broadened Theory of Preference Formation and the Diffusion of Innovations: Cases from Zinder Province, Niger Republic," *Journal of Consumer Research* 16 (September 1989): 239–67; Susan B. Kaiser, *The Social Psychology of Clothing* (New York: Macmillan, 1985); Thomas S.

Robertson, *Innovative Behavior and Communication* (New York: Holt, Rinehart and Winston, 1971).

59. Jan-Benedict E. M., Steenkamp, Frenkel ter Hofstede, and Michel Wedel, "A Cross-National Investigation into the Individual and National Cultural Antecedents of Consumer Innovativeness," *Journal of Marketing*, 63, no. 7 (1999): 55–69.

60. Susan L. Holak, Donald R. Lehmann, and Fareena Sultan, "The Role of Expectations in the Adoption of Innovative Consumer Durables: Some Preliminary Evidence," *Journal of Retailing* 63 (Fall 1987): 243–59.

61. Hubert Gatignon and Thomas S. Robertson, "A Propositional Inventory for New Diffusion Research," *Journal of Consumer Research* 11 (March 1985): 849–67.

62. C. K. Prahalad and Venkatram Ramaswamy, "Co-Opting Customer Competence," *Harvard Business Review* (Jan/Feb 2000): 79–87.

63. Eric von Hipple, "Users as Innovators," *Technology Review* 80 (January 1978): 3–11.

64. Jakki Mohr, *Marketing of High-Technology Products and Services* (Upper Saddle River, NJ: Prentice Hall, 2001).

65. N'Gai Croal and Andrew Murr, "Rockin' the Boat," *Newsweek* (March 22, 1999): 63–64.

66. Amy Harmon, "Powerful Music Software Has Industry Worried," *The New York Times on the Web* (March 7, 2000).

67. Everett M. Rogers, *Diffusion of Innovations*, 3d ed. (New York: The Free Press, 1983).

68. Umberto Eco, *A Theory of Semiotics* (Bloomington, IN: Indiana University Press, 1979).

69. Fred Davis, "Clothing and Fashion as Communication," in Michael R. Solomon, ed., *The Psychology of Fashion* (Lexington, MA: Lexington Books, 1985): 15–28.

70. Melanie Wallendorf, "The Formation of Aesthetic Criteria Through Social Structures and Social Institutions," in Jerry C. Olson, ed., *Advances in Consumer Research* 7 (Ann Arbor, MI: Association for Consumer Research, 1980): 3–6.

71. Grant McCracken, "Culture and Consumption: A Theoretical Account of the Structure and Movement of the Cultural Meaning of Consumer Goods," *Journal of Consumer Research* 13 (June 1986): 71–84.

72. "The Eternal Triangle," *Art in America* (February 1989): 23.

73. Herbert Blumer, *Symbolic Interactionism: Perspective and Method* (Upper Saddle River, NJ: Prentice Hall, 1969); Howard S. Becker, "Art as Collective Action," *American Sociological Review* 39 (December 1973);

Richard A. Peterson, "Revitalizing the Culture Concept," *Annual Review of Sociology* 5 (1979): 137–66.

74. Calvin Sims, "For Chic's Sake, Japanese Women Parade to the Orthopedist," *The New York Times on the Web* (November 26, 1999).

75. For more details, see Kaiser, *The Social Psychology of Clothing*; George B. Sproles, "Behavioral Science Theories of Fashion," in Michael R. Solomon, ed., *The Psychology of Fashion*, (Lexington, MA: Lexington Books, 1985): 55–70.

76. C. R. Snyder and Howard L. Fromkin, *Uniqueness: The Human Pursuit of Difference* (New York: Plenum Press, 1980).

77. Linda Dyett, "Desperately Seeking Skin," *Psychology Today* (May/June 1996): 14; Alison Lurie, *The Language of Clothes* (New York: Random House, 1981).

78. Harvey Leibenstein, *Beyond Economic Man: A New Foundation for Microeconomics* (Cambridge, MA: Harvard University Press, 1976).

79. Georg Simmel, "Fashion," *International Quarterly* 10 (1904): 130–55.

80. Grant D. McCracken, "The Trickle-Down Theory Rehabilitated," in Michael R. Solomon, ed., *The Psychology of Fashion* (Lexington, MA: Lexington Books, 1985): 39–54.

81. Charles W. King, "Fashion Adoption: A Rebuttal to the 'Trickle-Down' Theory," in Stephen A. Greyser, ed., *Toward Scientific Marketing* (Chicago: American Marketing Association, 1963): 108–25.

82. Alf H. Walle, "Grassroots Innovation," *Marketing Insights* (Summer 1990): 44–51.

83. Robert V. Kozinets, "Fandoms' Menace/Pop Flows: Exploring the Metaphor of Entertainment as Recombinant/Memetic Engineering," *Association for Consumer Research* (October 1999). The new science of memetics, which tries to explain how beliefs gain acceptance and predict their progress, was spurred by Richard Dawkins, who in the 1970s proposed culture as a Darwinian struggle among "memes" or mind viruses—see Geoffrey Cowley, "Viruses of the Mind: How Odd Ideas Survive," *Newsweek* (April 14, 1997): 14.

84. Janet Kornblum, "Everybody into the Mempool for Links to Some Very Odd Sites," *USA Today* (May 4, 2000): 3D.

85. Malcolm Gladwell, *The Tipping Point*, (NY: Little, Brown and Co., 2000).

86. Gregory Beals and Leslie Kaufman, "The Kids Know Cool," *Newsweek* (March 31, 1997): 48–49.

87. "Cabbage-Hatched Plot Sucks in 24 Doll Fans," *New York Daily News* (December 1, 1983).

88. "Turtlemania," *The Economist* (April 21, 1990): 32.

89. John Lippman, "Creating the Craze for Pokemon: Licensing Agent Bet on U.S. Kids," *The Wall Street Journal Interactive Edition* (August 16, 1999).

90. Anthony Ramirez, "The Pedestrian Sneaker Makes a Comeback," *New York Times* (October 14, 1990): F17.

91. B. E. Aguirre, E. L. Quarantelli, and Jorge L. Mendoza, "The Collective Behavior of Fads: The Characteristics, Effects, and Career of Streaking," *American Sociological Review* (August 1989): 569.

92. Quoted in Kathleen Deveny, "Anatomy of a Fad: How Clear Products Were Hot and Then Suddenly Were Not," *The Wall Street Journal* (March 15, 1994): B1.

93. Martin G. Letscher, "How to Tell Fads from Trends," *American Demographics* (December 1994): 38–45.

94. "Packaging Draws Protest," *Marketing News* (July 4, 1994): 1.

95. Theodore Levitt, *The Marketing Imagination* (New York: The Free Press, 1983).

96. Terry Clark, "International Marketing and National Character: A Review and Proposal for an Integrative Theory," *Journal of Marketing* 54 (October 1990): 66–79.

97. Tara Parker-Pope, "Nonalcoholic Beer Hits the Spot in Mideast," *The Wall Street Journal* (December 6, 1995): B1.

98. Norihiko Shirouzu, "Snapple in Japan: How a Splash Dried Up," *The Wall Street Journal* (April 15, 1996): B1.

99. Glenn Collins, "Chinese to Get a Taste of Cheese-Less Cheetos," *New York Times* (September 2, 1994): D4.

100. Julie Skur Hill and Joseph M. Winski, "Goodbye Global Ads: Global Village Is Fantasy Land for Marketers," *Advertising Age* (November 16, 1987): 22.

101. Yumiko Ono, "Tambrands Ads Try to Scale Cultural, Religious Obstacles," *The Wall Street Journal Interactive Edition* (March 17, 1997).

102. Clyde H. Farnsworth, "Yoked in Twin Solitudes: Canada's Two Cultures," *New York Times* (September 18, 1994): E4.

103. Hill and Winski, "Goodbye Global Ads."

104. See, for example, Russell W. Belk and Güliz Ger, "Problems of Marketization in Romania and Turkey," *Research in Consumer Behavior* 7 (JAI Press, 1994): 123–55.

105. Steve Rivkin, "The Name Game Heats Up," *Marketing News* (April 22, 1996): 8.

106. David A. Ricks, "Products That Crashed into the Language Barrier," *Business and Society Review* (Spring 1983): 46–50; "Speaking in Tongues," @ Issue: 3, no. 1 (Spring 1997): 20–23.

107. Shelly Reese, "Culture Shock," *Marketing Tools* (May 1998): 44–49.

108. MTV Europe, personal communication, 1994; see also Teresa J. Domzal and Jerome B. Kernan, "Mirror, Mirror: Some Postmodern Reflections on Global Advertising," *Journal of Advertising* 22, no. 4 (December 1993): 1–20; Douglas P. Holt,

"Consumers' Cultural Differences as Local Systems of Tastes: A Critique of the Personality-Values Approach and an Alternative Framework," *Asia Pacific Advances in Consumer Research* 1 (1994): 1 7.

109. Normandy Madden, "New GenerAsians Survey Gets Personal with Asia-Pacific Kids," *Advertising Age International* (July 13, 1998): 2.

110. "They All Want to Be Like Mike," *Fortune* (July 21, 1997): 51–53.

111. Quoted in Calvin Sims, "Japan Beckons, and East Asia's Youth Fall in Love," *New York Times* (December 5, 1999): 3.

112. Michael Williams and Miho Inada, "Japanese Families Learn to Play House the American Way," *The Wall Street Journal* (January 16, 1995): A1.

113. Jennifer Cody, "Now Marketers in Japan Stress the Local Angle," *The Wall Street Journal* (February 23, 1994): B1.

114. Ger and Belk, "I'd Like to Buy the World a Coke: Consumptionscapes of the 'Less Affluent World.'"

115. Sherry and Camargo, "May Your Life Be Marvelous"; "French Council Eases Language Ban," *New York Times* (July 31, 1994): 12.

116. Quoted in Alan Riding, "Only the French Elite Scorn Mickey's Debut," *New York Times* (1992): A1.

117. Prof. Russell Belk, University of Utah, personal communication, (July 25, 1997).

118. Material in this section adapted from Güliz Ger and Russell W. Belk, "I'd Like to Buy the World a Coke: Consumptionscapes of the 'Less Affluent World,'" *Journal of Consumer Policy* 19, no. 3 (1996): 271–304; Russell W. Belk, "Romanian Consumer Desires and Feelings of Deservingness," in Lavinia Stan, ed., *Romania in Transition* (Hanover, NH: Dartmouth Press, 1997): 191–208; see also Güliz Ger, "Human Development and Humane Consumption: Well Being Beyond the Good Life," *Journal of Public Policy and Marketing* 16 (1997): 110–25.

119. Prof. Güliz Ger, Bilkent University, Turkey, personal communication, (July 25, 1997).

120. Erazim Kohák, "Ashes, Ashes . . . Central Europe After Forty Years," *Daedalus* 121 (Spring 1992): 197–215, p. 209; quoted in Belk, "Romanian Consumer Desires and Feelings of Deservingness."

121. Quoted in Sheryl WuDunn, "Cosmetics from the West Help to Change the Face of China," *New York Times* (May 6, 1990): 16.

122. This example courtesy of Prof. Russell Belk, University of Utah, personal communication, (July 25, 1997).

123. Miriam Jordan, "India Decides to Put Its Own Spin on Popular Rock, Rap and Reggae," *The Wall Street Journal Interactive Edition* (January 5, 2000); Rasul Bailay, "Coca-Cola Recruits Paraplegics for 'Cola War' in India," *The Wall Street Journal Interactive Edition* (June 10, 1997).

124. Rick Wartzman, "When You Translate 'Got Milk' for Latinos, What Do You Get?" *The Wall Street Journal Interactive Edition* (June 3, 1999).

125. Eric J. Arnould and Richard R. Wilk, "Why Do the Natives Wear Adidas: Anthropological Approaches to Consumer Research," *Advances in Consumer Research* 12 (Provo, UT: Association for Consumer Research, 1985): 748–52.

126. John F. Sherry Jr. and Eduardo G. Camargo, "'May Your Life Be Marvelous': English Language Labeling and the Semiotics of Japanese Promotion," *Journal of Consumer Research* 14 (September 1987): 174–88.

127. Bill Bryson, "A Taste for Scrambled English," *New York Times* (July 22, 1990): 10; Rose A. Horowitz, "California Beach Culture Rides Wave of Popularity in Japan," *Journal of Commerce* (August 3, 1989): 17; Elaine Lafferty, "American Casual Seizes Japan: Teenagers Go for N.F.L. Hats, Batman and the California Look," *Time* (November 13, 1989): 106.

128. Lucy Howard and Gregory Cerio, "Goofy Goods," *Newsweek* (August 15, 1994): 8.

GLOSSARY

ABC model of attitudes a multidimensional perspective stating that attitudes are jointly defined by affect, behavior, and cognition

Absolute threshold the minimum amount of stimulation that can be detected on a given sensory channel

Accommodative purchase decision the process using bargaining, coercion, compromise, and the wielding of power to achieve agreement among group members who have different preferences or priorities

Acculturation the process of learning the beliefs and behaviors endorsed by another culture

Acculturation agents friends, family, local businesses, and other reference groups that facilitate the learning of cultural norms

Activation models of memory approaches to memory stressing different levels of processing that occur and activate some aspects of memory rather than others, depending on the nature of the processing task

Actual self a person's realistic appraisal of his or her qualities

Adaptation the process that occurs when a sensation becomes so familiar that it no longer commands attention

Affect the way a consumer feels about an attitude object

Affinitization a recent development in which groups organize around special interests such as immigration policy, the environment, or religious education

Age cohort a group of consumers of approximately the same age who have undergone similar experiences

Agentic goals an emphasis on self-assertion and mastery, often associated with traditional male gender roles

AIOs (activities, interests, and opinions) the psychographic variables used by researchers in grouping consumers

Androgyny the possession of both masculine and feminine traits

Animism cultural practices whereby inanimate objects are given qualities that make them somehow alive

Anticonsumption the actions taken by consumers that involve the deliberate defacement or mutilation of products

Archetype a universally shared idea or behavior pattern, central to Carl Jung's conception of personality; archetypes involve themes—such as birth, death, or the devil—that appear frequently in myths, stories, and dreams

Art product a creation viewed primarily as an object of aesthetic contemplation without any functional value

Atmospherics the use of space and physical features in store design to evoke certain effects in buyers

Attention the assignment of processing activity to selected stimuli

Attitude a lasting, general evaluation of people (including oneself), objects, or issues

Attitude object (A_o) anything toward which one has an attitude

Attitude toward the act of buying (A_{act}) the perceived consequences of a purchase

Attitude toward the advertisement (A_{ad}) a predisposition to respond favorably or unfavorably to a particular advertising stimulus during a particular exposure occasion

Autocratic decisions those purchase decisions that are made almost exclusively by one or the other spouse

Baby boomers a large cohort of people born between the years of 1946 and 1964 who are the source of many important cultural and economic changes

Baby boomlet a modest surge of children born to baby boomers, who have until recently delayed having children and are less likely to have large families in comparison to their parents

Balance theory a theory that considers relations among elements a person might perceive as belonging together, and people's tendency to change relations among elements in order to make them consistent or "balanced"

Behavior a consumer's actions with regard to an attitude object

Behavioral economics the study of the behavioral determinants of economic decisions

Behavioral influence perspective the view that consumer decisions are learned responses to environmental cues

Behavioral learning theories the perspectives on learning that assume that learning takes place as the result of responses to external events

Binary opposition a defining structural characteristic of many myths in which two opposing ends of some dimension are represented (e.g., good versus evil, nature versus technology)

Body cathexis a person's feelings about aspects of his or her body

Body image a consumer's subjective evaluation of his or her physical self

Boomerang kids grown children who return to their parents' home to live

Brand equity a brand that has strong positive associations in a consumer's memory and commands a lot of loyalty as a result

Brand loyalty a pattern of repeat product purchases accompanied by an underlying positive attitude toward the brand

Business ethics rules of conduct that guide actions in the marketplace

Business-to-Business (B2B) e-commerce Internet interactions between two or more businesses or organizations

Business-to-business marketers specialists in meeting the needs of organizations such as corporations, government agencies, hospitals, and retailers

Buying center the part of an organization charged with making purchasing decisions

Classic a fashion with an extremely long acceptance cycle

Classical conditioning the learning that occurs when a stimulus eliciting a response is paired with another stimulus that initially does not elicit a response on its own but will cause a similar response over time because of its association with the first stimulus

Closure principle the gestalt principle that describes a person's tendency to supply missing information in order to perceive a holistic image

Coercive power influencing a person by social or physical intimidation

Cognition the beliefs a consumer has about an attitude object

Cognitive learning theory approaches that stress the importance of internal mental processes. This perspective views people as problem solvers who actively use information from the world around them to master their environment

Cognitive structure the set of factual knowledge, or beliefs about a product, and the way these beliefs are organized

Collecting the systematic acquisition of a particular object or set of objects

Collective selection the process by which certain symbolic alternatives tend to be jointly chosen over others by members of a society

Collectivist cultures cultural orientation that encourages people to subordinate their personal goals to those of a stable in-group; values such as self-discipline and group accomplishment are stressed

Communal goals an emphasis on affiliation and the fostering of harmonious relations, often associated with traditional female gender roles

Communications model a framework specifying that a number of elements are necessary for communication to be achieved, including a source, message, medium, receivers, and feedback

Comparative advertising a strategy in which a message compares two or more specifically named or recognizably presented brands and makes a comparison of them in terms of one or more specific attributes

Comparative influence the process whereby a reference group influences decisions about specific brands or activities

Compensatory decision rules a set of rules that allow information about attributes of competing products to be averaged in some way; poor standing on one attribute can potentially be offset by good standing on another

Compulsive consumption the process of repetitive, often excessive, shopping used to relieve tension, anxiety, depression, or boredom

Conformity a change in beliefs or actions as a reaction to real or imagined group pressure

Consensual purchase decision a decision in which the group agrees on the desired purchase and differs only in terms of how it will be achieved

Conspicuous consumption the purchase and prominent display of luxury goods to provide evidence of a consumer's ability to afford them

Consumed consumers those people who are used or exploited, whether willingly or not, for commercial gain in the marketplace

Consumer a person who identifies a need or desire, makes a purchase, and/or disposes of the product

Consumer addiction a physiological and/or psychological dependency on products or services

Consumer behavior the processes involved when individuals or groups select, purchase, use, or dispose of products, services, ideas, or experiences to satisfy needs and desires

Consumer confidence the state of mind of consumers relative to their optimism or pessimism about economic conditions; people tend to make more discretionary purchases when their confidence in the economy is high

Consumer satisfaction/dissatisfaction (CS/D) the overall attitude a person has about a product after it has been purchased

Consumer socialization the process by which people acquire skills that enable them to function in the marketplace

Consumption constellations a set of products and activities used by consumers to define, communicate, and perform social roles

Contamination when a place or object takes on sacred qualities due to its association with another sacred person or event

Convention norms regarding the conduct of everyday life

Cooptation a cultural process by which the original meanings of a product or other symbol associated with a subculture are modified by members of mainstream culture

Craft product a creation valued because of the beauty with which it performs some function; this type of product tends to follow a formula that permits rapid production, and it is easier to understand than an art product

Creolization foreign influences are absorbed and integrated with local meanings

Cultivation hypothesis a perspective emphasizing media's ability to distort consumers' perceptions of reality

Cultural capital a set of distinctive and socially rare tastes and practices that admits a person into the realm of the upper class

Cultural categories the grouping of ideas and values that reflect the basic ways members of a society characterize the world

Cultural formula a sequence of media events in which certain roles and props tend to occur consistently

Cultural gatekeepers individuals who are responsible for determining the types of messages and symbolism to which members of mass culture are exposed

Cultural selection the process by which some alternatives are selected over others by cultural gatekeepers

Culture the values, ethics, rituals, traditions, material objects, and services produced or valued by the members of a society

Culture jamming the defacement or alteration of advertising materials as a form of political expression

Culture production system (CPS) the set of individuals and organizations responsible for creating and marketing a cultural product

Custom a norm that is derived from a traditional way of doing things

Database marketing tracking consumers' buying habits very closely, and then crafting products and messages tailored precisely to people's wants and needs based on this information

Decay structural changes in the brain produced by learning decrease over time

Decision polarization the process whereby individuals' choices tend to become more extreme (polarized), in either a conservative or risky direction, following group discussion of alternatives

Deindividuation the process whereby individual identities get submerged within a group, reducing inhibitions against socially inappropriate behavior

Demographics the observable measurements of a population's characteristics, such as birthrate, age distribution, and income

Desacralization the process that occurs when a sacred item or symbol is removed from its special place, or is duplicated in mass quantities, and becomes profane as a result

Differential threshold the ability of a sensory system to detect changes or differences among stimuli

Diffusion of innovation the process whereby a new product, service, or idea spreads through a population

Discretionary income the money available to a household over and above that required for necessities

Drive the desire to satisfy a biological need in order to reduce physiological arousal

Early adopters people who are receptive to new products and adopt them relatively soon, though they are motivated more by social acceptance and being in style than by the desire to try risky new things

Ego the system that mediates between the id and the superego

80/20 principle a rule-of-thumb in volume segmentation, which says that about 20 percent of consumers in a product category (the heavy users) account for about 80 percent of sales

Elaborated codes the ways of expressing and interpreting meanings that are more complex and depend on a more sophisticated worldview, which tend to be used by the middle and upper classes

Elaboration likelihood model (ELM) the approach that one of two routes to persuasion (central versus peripheral) will be followed, depending on the personal relevance of a message; the route taken determines the relative importance of message contents versus other characteristics, such as source attractiveness

Emic perspective an approach to studying (or marketing to) cultures that stresses the unique aspects of each culture

Encoding the process in which information from short-term memory enters into long-term memory in a recognizable form

Enculturation the process of learning the beliefs and behaviors endorsed by one's own culture

Ethnic subculture a self-perpetuating group of consumers held together by common cultural ties

Ethnocentrism the belief in the superiority of one's own country's practices and products

Ethos a set of moral, aesthetic, and evaluative principles

Etic perspective an approach to studying (or marketing to) cultures that stresses commonalities across cultures

Evaluative criteria the dimensions used by consumers to compare competing product alternatives

Evoked set those products already in memory plus those prominent in the retail environment that are actively considered during a consumer's choice process

Exchange a transaction in which two or more organizations or people give and receive something of value

Exchange theory the perspective that every interaction involves an exchange of value

Expectancy theory the perspective that behavior is largely "pulled" by expectations of achieving desirable outcomes, or positive incentives, rather than "pushed" from within

Experiential perspective an approach stressing the gestalt or totality of the product or service experience, focusing on consumers' affective responses in the marketplace

Expert power authority derived from possessing a specific knowledge or skill

Exposure an initial stage of perception during which some sensations come within range of consumers' sensory receptors

Extended family traditional family structure in which several generations live together

Extended problem solving an elaborate decision-making process, often initiated by a motive that is fairly central to the self-concept and accompanied by perceived risk; the consumer tries to collect as much information as possible, and carefully weighs product alternatives

Extended self the definition of self created by the external objects with which one surrounds oneself

Extinction the process whereby a learned connection between a stimulus and response is eroded so that the response is no longer reinforced

Fad a very short-lived fashion

Family financial officer (FFO) the individual in the family who is in charge of making financial decisions

Family household a housing unit containing at least two people who are related by blood or marriage

Family life-cycle (FLC) a classification scheme that segments consumers in terms of changes in income and family composition and the changes in demands placed on this income

Fantasy a self-induced shift in consciousness, often focusing on some unattainable or improbable goal; sometimes fantasy is a way of compensating for a lack of external stimulation or for dissatisfaction with the actual self

Fashion the process of social diffusion by which a new style is adopted by some group(s) of consumers

Fashion acceptance cycle the diffusion process of a style through three stages: introduction, acceptance, and regression

Fashion life-cycle the "career" or stages in the life of a fashion as it progresses from introduction to obsolescence

Fashion system those people and organizations involved in creating symbolic meanings and transferring these meanings to cultural goods

Fear appeal an attempt to change attitudes or behavior through the use of threats or by highlighting negative consequences of noncompliance with the request

Fertility rate a rate determined by the number of births per year per 1,000 women of childbearing age

Figure–ground principle the gestalt principle whereby one part of a stimulus configuration dominates a situation while other aspects recede into the background

Foot-in-the-door technique based on the observation that a consumer is more likely to comply with a request if he or she has first agreed to comply with a smaller request

Frequency marketing a marketing technique that reinforces regular purchasers by giving them prizes with values that increase along with the amount purchased

Functional theory of attitudes a pragmatic approach that focuses on how attitudes facilitate social behavior; attitudes exist because they serve some function for the person

Generation X a widely used term to describe "twentysomething" consumers who are (stereotypically) characterized as being confused, alienated, and depressed

Generation Y kids born between 1979 and 1994 (the younger siblings of Gen Xers)

Geodemography techniques that combine consumer demographic information with geographic consumption patterns to permit precise targeting of consumers with specific characteristics

Gerontographics a segmentation approach that divides the mature market into groups based on both level of physical well-being and social conditions such as becoming a grandparent or losing a spouse

Gestalt meaning derived from the totality of a set of stimuli, rather than from any individual stimulus

Gift-giving ritual the events involved in the selection, presentation, acceptance, and interpretation of a gift

Globalized consumption ethic the global sharing of a material lifestyle including the valuing of well-known multinational brands that symbolize prosperity

Goal a consumer's desired end state

Gray market the economic potential created by the increasing numbers of affluent elderly consumers

Green marketing a marketing strategy involving an emphasis on protecting the natural environment

Guerrilla marketing promotional strategies that use unconventional locations and intensive word-of-mouth campaigns

Hedonic consumption the multisensory, fantasy, and emotional aspects of consumers' interactions with products

Heuristics the mental rules-of-thumb that lead to a speedy decision

Hierarchy of effects a fixed sequence of steps that occurs during attitude formation; this sequence varies depending on such factors as the consumer's level of involvement with the attitude object

Homeostasis the state of being in which the body is in physiological balance; goal-oriented behavior attempts to reduce or eliminate an unpleasant motivational state and return to a balanced one

Hyperreality the becoming real of what is initially simulation or "hype"

Id the system oriented toward immediate gratification

Ideal of beauty a model, or exemplar, of appearance valued by a culture

Ideal self a person's conception of how he or she would like to be

Impulse buying a process that occurs when the consumer experiences a sudden urge to purchase an item that he or she cannot resist

Individualist cultures a cultural orientation that encourages people to attach more importance to personal goals than to group goals; values such as personal enjoyment and freedom are stressed

Inert set the product alternatives that the consumer is aware of but would not consider buying during the choice process

Inept set the product alternatives of which the consumer is not aware and, therefore, are not even included in the consumer's choice process

Inertia the process whereby purchase decisions are made out of habit because the consumer lacks the motivation to consider alternatives

Information power power of knowing something others would like to know

Information search the process whereby a consumer searches for appropriate information to make a reasonable decision

Informational social influence the conformity that occurs because the group's behavior is taken as evidence about reality

Innovation a product or style that is perceived as new by consumers

Innovators people who are always on the lookout for novel developments and will be the first to try a new offering

Instrumental conditioning also known as operant conditioning, occurs as the individual learns to perform behaviors that produce positive outcomes and to avoid those that yield negative outcomes

Instrumental values goals endorsed because they are needed to achieve desired end states, or terminal values

Interpretant the meaning derived from a sign or symbol

Interpretation the process whereby meanings are assigned to stimuli

Interpretivism as opposed to the dominant positivist perspective on consumer behavior, instead stresses the importance of symbolic, subjective experience and the idea that meaning is in the mind of the person rather than existing "out there" in the objective world

Invidious distinction the display of wealth or power to inspire envy in others

Involvement the motivation to process product-related information

J.N.D. (just noticeable difference) the minimum difference between two stimuli that can be detected by a perceiver

Kin–network system the rituals intended to maintain ties among family members both immediate and extended

Knowledge structures organized systems of concepts relating to brands, stores, and other concepts

Laddering a technique for uncovering consumers' associations between specific attributes and general consequences

Laggards consumers who are exceptionally slow to adopt innovations

Late adopters the majority of consumers who are moderately receptive to adopting innovations

Latitudes acceptance and rejection formed around an attitude standard; ideas that fall within a latitude will be favorably received, whereas those falling outside this zone will not

Lateral cycling a process in which already-purchased objects are sold to others or exchanged for other items

Learning a relatively permanent change in a behavior caused by experience

Lead user an involved, experienced customer (usually a corporate customer) who is very knowledgeable about the field

Legitimate power the power granted to people by virtue of social agreements

Lifestyle a set of shared values or tastes exhibited by a group of consumers, especially as these are reflected in consumption patterns

Limited problem solving a problem-solving process in which consumers are not motivated to search for information or to rigorously evaluate each alternative; instead they use simple decision rules to arrive at a purchase decision

Long-term memory the system that allows us to retain information for a long period of time

Looking-glass self the process of imagining the reaction of others toward oneself

Low-involvement hierarchy a means of forming attitudes in which consumers are not motivated to process a lot of complex brand-related information

Market beliefs the specific beliefs or decision rules pertaining to marketplace phenomena

Market maven a person who often serves as a source of information about marketplace activities

Market segmentation the process of identifying groups of consumers who are similar to one another in one or more ways, and then devising marketing strategies that appeal to one or more of these groups

Match-up hypothesis a celebrity's image and that of the product he or she endorses should be similar to maximize the credibility and effectiveness of the communication

Materialism the importance consumers attach to worldly possessions

Meme theory a perspective that uses a medical metaphor to explain how an idea or product enters the consciousness of people over time, much like a virus

Memory a process of acquiring information and storing it over time so that it will be available when needed

Metaphor the use of an explicit comparison ("A" is "B") between a product and some other person, place, or thing

Modified rebuy in the context of the buyclass framework, a task that requires a modest amount of information search and evaluation, often focused on identifying the appropriate vendor

Monomyth a myth with basic characteristics that are found in many cultures

More a custom with strong moral overtones

Motivation an internal state that activates goal-oriented behavior

Motivational research a qualitative research approach, based on psychoanalytic (Freudian) interpretations, with a heavy emphasis on unconscious motives for consumption

Multiattribute attitude models those models that assume that a consumer's attitude (evaluation) of an attitude object depends on the beliefs he or she has about several or many attributes of the object; the use of a multiattribute model implies that an attitude toward a product or brand can be predicted by identifying these specific beliefs and combining them to derive a measure of the consumer's overall attitude

Myth a story containing symbolic elements that expresses the shared emotions and ideals of a culture

Negative reinforcement the process whereby the environment weakens responses to

stimuli so that inappropriate behavior is avoided

New task in the context of the buyclass framework, a task that requires a great degree of effort and information search

Normative influence the process in which a reference group helps to set and enforce fundamental standards of conduct

Normative social influence the conformity that occurs when a person alters his or her behavior to meet the expectations of a person or group

Norms the informal rules that govern what is right or wrong

Nostalgia a bittersweet emotion; the past is viewed with sadness and longing; many "classic" products appeal to consumers' memories of their younger days

Nuclear family a contemporary living arrangement composed of a married couple and their children

Object in semiotic terms, the product that is the focus of a message

Observational learning the process in which people learn by watching the actions of others and noting the reinforcements they receive for their behaviors

Opinion leaders those people who are knowledgeable about products and who are frequently able to influence others' attitudes or behaviors with regard to a product category

Organizational buyers people who purchase goods and services on behalf of companies for use in the process of manufacturing, distribution, or resale

Paradigm a widely accepted view or model of phenomena being studied; the perspective that regards people as rational information processors is currently the dominant paradigm, though this approach is now being challenged by a new wave of research that emphasizes the frequently subjective nature of consumer decision making

Parental yielding the process that occurs when a parental decision maker is influenced by a child's product request

Perceived age how old a person feels as compared to his or her true chronological age

Perception the process by which stimuli are selected, organized, and interpreted

Perceptual map a research tool used to understand how a brand is positioned in consumers' minds relative to competitors

Perceptual defense the tendency for consumers to avoid processing stimuli that are threatening to them

Perceptual selection process by which people attend to only a small portion of the stimuli to which they are exposed

Perceptual vigilance the tendency for consumers to be more aware of stimuli that relate to their current needs

Personality a person's unique psychological makeup, which consistently influences the way the person responds to his or her environment

Persuasion an active attempt to change attitudes

Pleasure principle the belief that behavior is guided by the desire to maximize pleasure and avoid pain

Point-of-purchase stimuli (POP) the promotional materials that are deployed in stores or other outlets to influence consumers' decisions at the time products are purchased

Popular culture the music, movies, sports, books, celebrities, and other forms of entertainment consumed by the mass market

Positioning strategy an organization's use of elements in the marketing mix to influence the consumer's interpretation of a product's meaning vis-à-vis competitors

Positive reinforcement the process whereby rewards provided by the environment strengthen responses to stimuli and appropriate behavior is learned

Positivism a research perspective that relies on principles of the "scientific method" and assumes that a single reality exists; events in the world can be objectively measured; and the causes of behavior can be identified, manipulated, and predicted

Principle of cognitive consistency the belief that consumers value harmony among their thoughts, feelings, and behaviors and that they are motivated to maintain uniformity among these elements

Principle of similarity the gestalt principle that describes how consumers tend to group objects that share similar physical characteristics

Problem recognition the process that occurs whenever the consumer sees a significant difference between his or her current state of affairs and some desired or ideal state; this recognition initiates the decision-making process

Product complementarity the view that products in different functional categories have symbolic meanings that are related to one another

Product placement the process of obtaining exposure for a product by arranging for it to be inserted into a movie, television show, or some other medium

Profane consumption the process of consuming objects and events that are ordinary or of the everyday world

Progressive learning model the perspective that people gradually learn a new culture as they increasingly come in contact with it; consumers assimilate into a new culture, mixing practices from their old and new environments to create a hybrid culture

Psychographics the use of psychological, sociological, and anthropological factors to construct market segments

Psychophysics the science that focuses on how the physical environment is integrated into the consumer's subjective experience

Punishment the learning that occurs when a response is followed by unpleasant events

Racial subculture a self-perpetuating group of consumers who are held together by common genetic ties

Rational perspective a view of the consumer as a careful, analytical decision maker who tries to maximize utility in purchase decisions

Reactance a "boomerang effect" that sometimes occurs when consumers are threatened with a loss of freedom of choice; they respond by doing the opposite of the behavior advocated in a persuasive message

Reality engineering the process whereby elements of popular culture are appropriated by marketers and become integrated into marketing strategies

Reality principle principle that the ego seeks ways that will be acceptable to society to gratify the id

Reciprocity norm a culturally learned obligation to return the gesture of a gift with one of equal value

Reference group an actual or imaginary individual or group that has a significant effect on an individual's evaluations, aspirations, or behavior

Referent power the power of prominent people to affect others' consumption behaviors by virtue of product endorsements, distinctive fashion statements, or championing of causes

Relationship marketing the strategic perspective that stresses the long-term, human side of buyer–seller interactions

Resonance a literary device, frequently used in advertising, that uses a play on words (a double meaning) to communicate a product benefit

Response bias a form of contamination in survey research in which some factor, such as the desire to make a good impression on the experimenter, leads respondents to modify their true answers

Restricted codes the ways of expressing and interpreting meanings that focus on the content of objects and tend to be used by the working class

Retrieval the process whereby desired information is recovered from long-term memory

Reward power when a person or group has the means to provide positive reinforcement to a consumer

Rites of passage sacred times marked by a change in social status

Ritual a set of multiple, symbolic behaviors that occur in a fixed sequence and that tend to be repeated periodically

Ritual artifacts items (consumer goods) used in the performance of rituals

Role theory the perspective that much of consumer behavior resembles actions in a play

Sacralization a process that occurs when ordinary objects, events, or people take on sacred meaning to a culture or to specific groups within a culture

Sacred consumption the process of consuming objects and events that are set apart from normal life and treated with some degree of respect or awe

Schema an organized collection of beliefs and feelings represented in a cognitive category

Self-concept the beliefs a person holds about his or her own attributes and how he or she evaluates these qualities

Self-gifts the products or services bought by consumers for their own use as a reward or consolation

Self-image congruence models the approaches based on the prediction that products will be chosen when their attributes match some aspect of the self

Self-perception theory an alternative (to cognitive dissonance) explanation of dissonance effects; it assumes that people use observations of their own behavior to infer their attitudes toward some object

Semiotics a field of study that examines the correspondence between signs and symbols and the meaning or meanings they convey

Sensation the immediate response of sensory receptors (eyes, ears, nose, mouth, fingers) to such basic stimuli as light, color, sound, odors, and textures

Sensory memory the temporary storage of information received from the senses

Sex-typed traits characteristics that are stereotypically associated with one gender or the other

Shopping orientation a consumer's general attitudes and motivations regarding the act of shopping

Short-term memory the mental system that allows us to retain information for a short period of time

Shrinkage the loss of money or inventory from shoplifting and/or employee theft

Sign the sensory imagery that represents the intended meanings of the object

Single-source data a compilation of information that includes different aspects of consumption and demographic data for a common consumer segment

Situational self-image a person's self-concept at a particular point in time, which is influenced by the specific role he or she is playing at that time

Sleeper effect the process whereby differences in attitude change between positive and negative sources seem to diminish over time

Social aging theories a perspective to understand how society assigns people to different roles across the life span

Social class the overall rank of people in a society; people who are grouped within the same social class are approximately equal in terms of their income, occupations, and lifestyles

Social comparison theory the perspective that people compare their outcomes with others' as a way to increase the stability of their own self-evaluation, especially when physical evidence is unavailable

Social judgment theory the perspective that people assimilate new information about attitude objects in light of what they already know or feel; the initial attitude acts as a frame of reference, and new information is categorized in terms of this standard

Social marketing the promotion of causes and ideas (social products), such as energy conservation, charities, and population control

Social mobility the movement of individuals from one social class to another

Social power the capacity of one person to alter the actions or outcome of another

Social stratification the process in a social system by which scarce and valuable resources are distributed unequally to status positions that become more or less permanently ranked in terms of the share of valuable resources each receives

Social trends broad changes in people's attitudes and behaviors

Sociometric methods the techniques for measuring group dynamics that involve tracing communication patterns in and among groups

Source attractiveness the dimensions of a communicator that increase his or her persuasiveness; these include expertise and attractiveness

Source credibility a communications source's perceived expertise, objectivity, or trustworthiness

Stage of cognitive development the ability to comprehend concepts of increasing complexity as a person ages

Standard learning hierarchy means of forming attitudes that assumes that a consumer is highly involved in making a purchase decision. The person is motivated to seek out a lot of information, carefully weigh alternatives, and come to a thoughtful decision

Status crystallization the extent to which different indicators of a person's status (income, ethnicity, occupation) are consistent with one another

Status hierarchy a ranking of social desirability in terms of consumers' access to resources such as money, education, and luxury goods

Status symbols products that are purchased and displayed to signal membership in a desirable social class

Stimulus discrimination the process that occurs when behaviors caused by two stimuli are different, as when consumers learn to differentiate a brand from its competitors

Stimulus generalization the process that occurs when the behavior caused by a reaction to one stimulus occurs in the presence of other, similar stimuli

Storage the process that occurs when knowledge in long-term memory is integrated with what is already in memory and "warehoused" until needed

Store image a store's "personality," composed of such attributes as location, merchandise suitability, and the knowledge and congeniality of the sales staff

Straight rebuy in the context of the buyclass framework, the type of buying decision that is virtually automatic and requires little deliberation

Subculture a group whose members share beliefs and common experiences that set them apart from other members of a culture

Subliminal perception the processing of stimuli presented below the level of the consumer's awareness

Superego the system that internalizes society's rules and that works to prevent the id from seeking selfish gratification

Surrogate consumer a professional who is retained to evaluate and/or make purchases on behalf of a consumer

Symbolic interactionism a sociological approach stressing that relationships with other people play a large part in forming the self; people live in a symbolic environment, and the meaning attached to any situation or object is determined by a person's interpretation of these symbols

Symbolic self-completion theory the perspective that people who have an incomplete self-definition in some context will compensate by acquiring symbols associated with a desired social identity

Syncratic decisions those purchase decisions that are made jointly by both spouses

Synoptic ideal a model of spousal decision making in which the husband and wife take a common view and act as joint decision makers, assigning each other well-defined roles and making mutually beneficial decisions to maximize the couple's joint utility

Taste culture a group of consumers who share aesthetic and intellectual preferences

Terminal values end states desired by members of a culture

Theory of cognitive dissonance theory based on the premise that a state of tension is created when beliefs or behaviors conflict with one another; people are motivated to reduce this inconsistency (or dissonance) and thus eliminate unpleasant tension

Theory of reasoned action an updated version of the Fishbein multiattribute attitude theory that considers factors such as social pressure and A_{act} (the attitude toward the act of buying a product), rather than attitudes toward just the product itself

Time poverty a feeling of having less time available than is required to meet the demands of everyday living

Transitional economies a country that is adapting from a controlled, centralized economy to a free-market system

Trickle-down theory of fashion the perspective that fashions spread as the result of status symbols associated with the upper classes "trickling down" to other social classes as these consumers try to emulate those with greater status

Tweens a marketing term used to describe children aged 8–14

Two-factor theory the perspective that two separate psychological processes are operating when a person is repeatedly exposed to an ad: repetition increases familiarity and thus reduces uncertainty about the product but over time boredom increases with each exposure, and at some point the amount of boredom incurred begins to exceed the amount of uncertainty reduced, resulting in wear-out

Uses and gratifications theory views consumers as an active, goal-directed audience that draws on mass media as a resource to satisfy needs

VALS (Values and Lifestyles) a psychographic segmentation system used to categorize consumers into clusters, or "VALS Types"

Value a belief that some condition is preferable to its opposite

Value system a culture's ranking of the relative importance of values

Viral marketing the strategy of getting customers to sell a product on behalf of the company that creates it

Virtual community of consumption a collection of people whose online interactions are based upon shared enthusiasm for and knowledge of a specific consumption activity

Want the particular form of consumption chosen to satisfy a need

Weber's Law the principle that the stronger the initial stimulus, the greater its change must be for it to be noticed

Word-of-mouth communication (WOM) product information transmitted by individual consumers on an informal basis

Worldview the ideas shared by members of a culture about principles of order and fairness

CREDITS

Chapter 1

1: Adbusters Media Foundation; 2: L.D. Gordon, The Image Bank; 7: Susan Walsh, AP/Wide World Photos; 8: Juno Online Services L.P.; 9: KSV Communicators; 12: The Proctor & Gamble Company, used by permission; Alain Le Bot/Gamma-Liaison, Inc.; Pillsbury Company; 14: Levi Strauss & Co.; 17: Torani Syrup; 18: Leo Burnett Paris; 19: American Association of Advertising Agencies; 23: Copyright © 1994 by Bill Watterston, courtesy of Universal Press Syndicate; 27: Adbusters Media Foundation; 31: Volkswagen of America.

Chapter 2

38: The Proctor & Gamble Company; 40: PhotoDisc, Inc.; 43: © 1993 by Lexus, a division of Toyota Motor Sales, USA, Inc., used by permission; 44: Sek & Grey Advertising Agency; 45: Giovanni Comunicaoes; 46: The Proctor & Gamble Company; 46: Volkswagen of America, Inc.; 47: Everlast Sports, NY; 49: Unilever Home & Personal Care, USA; 52: Campbell Soup Company; 53: PepsiCo, Inc.; 55: Nike Advertising; 56: Howard Schatz, Leo Burnett Connaghan & May; 59: Saatchi & Saatchi; 59: www.vasakronan.se; 60: Land Rover North America; 61: Mike Carroll, VF Corporation; 61: Zoo Doo Compost Company; 62: Oliverio Toscani for Benetton; 64: GRW Advertising; 65: Chris Wimper Photography, Team One Advertising.

Chapter 3

70: Steve Ragland, Stone; 73: Chiquita Brands, Inc.; 83: Miller Group Advertising; 91: Lifetime Network; 93: Fossil, Inc.

Chapter 4

100: German Meneses Photography; 102: Soloflex, Inc.; 105: Universal Press Syndicate; 107: Partnership for a Drug-Free America; 112: Dr. Janeen Costa, University of Utah; 119: Leo Burnett Paris; 123: E&J Gallo; 124: TAG Heuer USA.

111: Fig. 4.3: Judith Lynne Zaichowsky, "Conceptualizing Involvement," *Journal of Advertising* 15, no. 2 (1986). 121: Fig. 4.4: Adapted from Thomas J. Reynolds and Alyce Byrd Craddock, "The Application of the MECCAS Model to the Development and Assessment of Advertising Strategy: A Case Study," *Journal of Advertising Research* (April/May 1988).

Chapter 5

130: Tony Latham, Tony Stone Images; 136: Mini-Equinox Automobile; 141: Bijan, photographer Jim Koch; 142: Goldsmith/Jeffrey and Bodyslimmers; 144: Dunlop Sport; 144: Totem International; 146: Cognac L&L; 146: Lane Bryant; 148: Universal Press Syndicate; 150: Vierte Art; 151: Lisa Rose, Globe Photos, Inc.; 152: The Coca-Cola Company; 152: Universal Press Syndicate; 154: Nutrio.com Inc.; 155: PepsiCo, Inc.; 156: Body Basics.

148: Fig 5.1: *Newsweek* (June 3, 1996): 65. © 1996 Newsweek, Inc. All rights reserved. Reprinted by permission.

Chapter 6

162: Tony Arruza, The Image Works; 167: United Airlines/WHQ AD; 172: Harvard Graduate School of Business Administration; 173: Rick Chou Photography, Saatchi & Saatchi LA; 174: White Aryan Resistance; 175: Jayco, Inc.; 176: reproduced with the permission of the copyright owner, General Electric Company; 183: Ed Hunter, Cape Cod Travel Guide; 187: BJ's Lifecode Merchandising/Design; 190: Maidenform, Inc.

Chapter 7

196: Ariel Skelley, Corbis/Stock Market; 198: Johns Hopkins Center for Communications Programs; 202: Smith & Wollensky Steakhouse; 207: Cadillac; 208: Woman's Day (Hachette Magazines Inc.); 212: Michael Newman, PhotoEdit.

225: Fig. 7.3: Richard P. Bagozzi and Paul R. Warshaw, "Trying to Consume," *Journal of Consumer Research* 17, no. 2 (September 1990).

Chapter 8

224: Andy Sacks, Stone; 233: Bozell Worldwide, Inc.; 238: Hans Brinker Budget Hotel; 240: Lexus, Infiniti, a division of Nissan Motor Corporation, USA; 242: McCann-Erickson, New York; 243: Young & Rubicam, Sydney, The Proctor & Gamble Company; 244: The Proctor & Gamble Company.

228: Fig 8.2: Adapted from Donna L. Hoffman and Thomas P. Novak, "Marketing in Hypermedia Computer-Mediated Environments: Conceptual Foundations," *Journal of Marketing* 60 (July 1996). 236: Fig 8.3: Andrew A. Mitchell, "The Effect of Verbal and Visual Components on Brand Attitudes and Attitude Toward the Advertisement," *Journal of Consumer Research* 13 (June 1986). With permission of the University of Chicago Press. 237: Fig. 8.4: Adapted from Arno J. Rathans, John L. Swasy, and Lawrence Marks, "Effects of Television Commercial Reception," *Journal of Marketing Research* 23 (February 1986). By permission of American Marketing Association. 246: Fig 8.5: John C. Mowen, *Consumer Behavior*, 2d ed. Copyright © 1990 by Macmillan Publishing Company. Reprinted with permission.

Chapter 9

252: iParty.com; 254: Laima Druska/Stock Boston; 257: U.S. Postal Service; 262: La Guillotine Beer; 268: Minolta Corporation; 271: Sunkist Growers, Inc.; 273: iParty.com; 276: Bernard Wolf/Monkmeyer Press.

Chapter 10

286: Michael Newman/PhotoEdit; 288: Hartmarx Clothing; 293: Copyright © 1991, Spiegel, Inc.; 298: Bluefly Inc.; 302: Byron/Monkmeyer Press; 304: Peter Freed; 306: Ford Motor Company; 309: BDH, Manchester, UK; 310: Volkswagen and DDB Needham Worldwide BV Amsterdam; 310: Rudi Von Brie, PhotoEdit.

294: Fig. 10.3: James Russell and Geraldine Pratt, "A Description of the Affective Quality Attributed to Environment," *Journal of Personality and Social Psychology* 38 (August 1980). Copyright © 1980 by the American Psychological Association. 303: Fig. 10.4: Dennis Rook, "Is Impulse Buying (Yet) a Useful Marketing Concept?" manuscript, University of Southern California, Los Angeles, 1990. 307: Fig. 10.5: Adapted from Jagdish N. Sheth and Banwari Mittal, "A Framework for Managing Customer Expectations," *Journal of Market Focused Management* 1 (1996). 309: Fig 10.6: Jacob Jacoby, Carol K. Berning, and Thomas F. Dietvorst. "What About Disposition?" *Journal of Marketing* 41 (April 1977). By permission of American Marketing Association.

Chapter 11

318: Chris Simpson, Stone; 322: Fabiana; 326: Time Out Magazine; 327: United States Marine Corps; 329: Coty U.S. LLC; 338: cartoondepot.net; 340: Carl Schneider, Liaison Agency, Inc.

326: Fig. 11.2: Adapted from William O. Bearden and Michael J. Etzel, "Reference Group Influence on Product and Brand Decisions," *Journal of Consumer Research* (September 1982). Reprinted with permission of the University of Chicago Press. 336: Fig 11.3: Kenneth J. Gergen and Mary Gergen, *Social Psychology* (New York: Harcourt Brace Jovanovich, 1981); adapted from F. C. Bartlett, *Remembering* (Cambridge, UK: Cambridge University Press, 1932).

Chapter 12

350: Nubar Alexanian, Stock Boston; 352: Unisys Corporation; 357: The Proctor & Gamble Company; 358: UNUM; 358: Copyright © 1992 The Family Circle; 360: Motorola Paging Products Group; 360: Chuck Keeler, Tony Stone Images; 361: Ethan Allen Inc.; 365: Haggar; 373: Tom Prettyman, PhotoEdit.

371: Fig 12.3: Adapted from McNeal and Yeh, *American Demographics* (June 1993): 36. Reprinted by permission of American Demographics, Inc. 375: Fig 12.4: M. Carole Macklin,

"Preschoolers' Understanding of the Informational Function of Television Advertising," *Journal of Consumer Research* 14 (September 1994). Reprinted by permission of the University of Chicago Press.

Chapter 13
382: E. Cicinelli/Swanstock, The Image Bank; **384:** Michael Goldman, FPG International LLC; **397:** Libbey Glass Inc.; **398:** *US Magazine* from Advertising Age (Aug. 27, 1989), by Straight Arrow Publishers, Inc.; **404:** Jaguar Cars, Inc.; **407:** Bob Kramer, Stock Boston.

387: Fig 13.1: Fabian Linden, *Consumer Affluence: The Next Wave* (New York: The Conference Board, 1994). **391: Fig 13.2:** Richard P. Coleman, "The Continuing Significance of Social Class to Marketing," *Journal of Consumer Research* 10 (December 1983). Reprinted with permission of the University of Chicago Press. **395: Fig. 13.3:** Richard P. Coleman, "The Continuing Significance of Social Class to Marketing," *Journal of Consumer Research* 10 (December 1983). Reprinted with permission of the University of Chicago Press. **399: Fig. 13.4:** Edward O. Laumann and James S. House, "Living Room Styles and Social Attributes," *Sociology and Social Research* 54 (April 1970).

Chapter 14
412: Michael Newman, PhotoEdit; **414:** Russ Belk; **416:** Nordfalks AB; **417:** Agence France Presse, Corbis.

419: Fig. 14.1: "Newest Markets," *American Demographics* (September 1988). Reprinted with permission. © American Demographics. **425: Fig. 14.2:** Adapted from Lisa Teñaloza, "*Atravesando Fronteras*/Border Crossings," *Journal of Consumer Research* 21, no. 1 (June 1994). Reprinted by permission of the University of Chicago Press. **430: Fig. 14.3:** Blumrich, "The Religious Pecking Order," *Newsweek* (November 29, 1993). Copyright © 1993 by Newsweek, Inc. All rights reserved. Reprinted by permission.

Chapter 15
436: FPG International LLC; **438:** Jim Bourg/Reuters NewMedia Inc., Corbis; **444:** © 1994 by Converse Inc., all rights reserved; **447:** Christopher Brown, Stock Boston; **449:** PepsiCo, Inc.; **451:** Copyright © Mature Americans, the Daniel Yakelovich Group, 1987; **454:** "Jockey for Her," "So Comfortable," and "Jockey" figure are trademarks of and are used with permission of Jockey International, Inc.

438: Fig. 15.1: Fabian Linden, *Consumer Affluence: The Next Wave* (New York: The Conference Board, 1994). **440: Fig. 15.2:** *Business Week* (April 11, 1994). Photos: Brooks Kraft, Sygma; Sunset Boulevard, Sygma; Michael Childers, Sygma; Sunset Boulevard, Sygma; AP/Wide World Photos.

Chapter 16
458: Luckysurf.com; **460:** Michael Newman, PhotoEdit; **465:** Luckysurf.com; **466:** Amazon Advertising; **466:** Corbis, Sygma; **472:** Nivea; **475:** N. Rogers, Monkmeyer Press; **478:** Bozell Worldwide, Inc.; **479:** Deborah Denker, Liaison Agency, Inc.; **480:** First Alert Inc.; **481:** King Features Syndicate; **481:** Swatch Watch USA.

473: Fig. 16.1: Based on David G. Mick, Michele DeMoss, and Ronald J. Faber, "Latent Motivations and Meanings of Self-Gifts: Implications for Retail Management," research report, Center for Retailing Education and Research, University of Florida, 1990.

Chapter 17
486: Rhoda Sidney, Stock Boston; **492:** AT&T International Communications Services; **495:** Robson-Brown Ad Agency; **496:** Publishers Custom Reprints; **499:** Neal Peters Collection; **504:** Archive Photos; **506:** Paradiset DDB; **507:** Copyright © 1994 by Maidenform Inc.; **508:** Sygma; **510:** Jim Beam Brand, Inc.; **514:** King Features Syndicate; **520:** Fabiana.

490: Fig. 17.1: Adapted from Grant McCracken, "Culture and Consumption: A Theoretical Account of the Structure and Movement Of the Cultural Meaning of Consumer Goods," *Journal of Consumer Research* 13 (June 1986). Reprinted with permission of the University of Chicago Press. **491: Fig. 17.2:** Adapted from Michael R. Solomon, "Building Up and Breaking Down: The Impact of Cultural Sorting on Symbolic Consumption," in J. Sheth and E. C. Hirschman, eds., *Research in Consumer Behavior* (Greenwich, CT: JAI Press, 1988). **511: Fig. 17.4:** Susan Kaiser, *The Social Psychology of Clothing* (Macmillan College Publishing, 1985). Copyright © 1985 by Macmillan College Publishing Company, Inc. reprinted with permission. **511: Fig 17.5:** Susan Kaiser, *The Social Psychology of Clothing* (Macmillan College Publishing, 1985). Copyright © 1985 by Macmillan College Publishing Company, Inc. reprinted with permission. **513: Fig. 17.6:** *Wired* (November 1998): 7.

INDEXES

Name Index

Note: Italicized pages locate illustrations; t locates tables.

Product Index

Subject Index

KU-347-230

301
LEGAL
FORMS
Letters & Agreements

LAWPACK

WITHDRAWN

SL10001855950 5

S/o

SOLIHULL MBC LIBRARIES	
CE	
SL10001855950 5	
Askews	
R347.42055	£19.99
	L8520

301 Legal Forms, Letters & Agreements

First edition 1995
Second edition 1996
    Reprinted 1996
Third edition 1997
    Reprinted 1997
Fourth edition 1998
Fifth edition 1999
Sixth edition 2000
Seventh edition 2001
    Reprinted 2002 (twice) and 2003
Eighth edition 2004
    Reprinted 2005
    Reprinted 2006
Ninth edition 2007

Published by

Lawpack Publishing Limited
76-89 Alscot Road
London SE1 3AW

© 2007 Lawpack Publishing

ISBN: 978-1-905261-33-8

This **Lawpack** publication may not be reproduced in whole or in any form without written permission from the publisher, except that individual forms may be photocopied by the purchaser for his or her own use, but not for resale.

Important facts about this Lawpack book

Legal documents need to achieve four things.:

1. They must be clear.

2. They must be complete enough to deal with all forseeable contingencies and to provide an answer to any reasonable question beginning with the words 'what if?'

3. They must contain all provisions which the law requires.

4. They must not contain anything which would bring into play a law that might make them ineffective.

Lawpack publications are designed to help you prepare legal documents by suggesting matters which you may wish to cover and by providing wording which you may be able to adapt in order to make your meaning clear and by alerting you to various relevant legal rules. However, neither this nor any other publication can take the place of a solicitor on important legal matters. There are three reasons for this. Firstly, the law can be complicated and a book like this can only provide a guide to the basics. Secondly, the particular transaction which you are undertaking may throw up complications for which an 'off the peg' form would not be appropriate. Thirdly, no book can suggest to you all of the matters that ought to be covered in your particular transaction.

This Lawpack publication is sold on the understanding that the publisher, authors and retailer are not engaged in rendering legal services. If legal advice or other expert assistance is required, the services of a competent professional should be sought.

The forms included in this Lawpack publication cover many everyday matters, but we cannot cater for all circumstances. If what you want is not included, we advise you to see a solicitor.

This Lawpack publication is designed only for use in England and Wales. It is not suitable for Scotland or Northern Ireland.

The information this book contains has been carefully compiled from reliable sources but its accuracy is not guaranteed as laws and regulations may change or be subject to differing interpretations. The law is stated as at 1st September 2007.

As with any legal matter, common sense should determine whether you need the assistance of a solicitor rather than relying solely on your own efforts, supplemented by the information and forms in this Lawpack book.

We strongly urge you to consult a solicitor whenever substantial amounts of money are involved, or where you do not understand the instructions or are uncertain how to complete and use a form correctly, or if you have any doubts about its adequacy to protect you, or if what you want to do is not precisely covered by the forms provided or if you are planning to use a form many times (e.g. as a standard form in your business).

EXCLUSION OF LIABILITY AND DISCLAIMER

While every effort has been made to ensure that this Lawpack book provides accurate and expert guidance, it is impossible to predict all the circumstances in which it may be used. Accordingly, neither the publisher, authors, the barrister who has approved the contents of this book, retailer nor any other suppliers shall be liable to any person or entity with respect to any loss or damage caused or alleged to be caused by the information contained in or omitted from this Lawpack publication.

For convenience (and for no other reason) 'him', 'he' and 'his' have been used throughout and should be read to include 'her', 'she' and 'her'.

About *301 Legal Forms...*

This book contains legal forms, letters and agreements to safeguard your legal rights and protect you… your family… your property… and your business from everyday legal problems.

With 301 essential legal documents in one book, you now have available a useful guide for simple legal matters where the inconvenience or cost of using a solicitor would not be proportionate to what is at stake.

Lawpack publications are the ideal way to 'get it in writing'. What better way is there to document your important transactions, avoid costly disputes and enforce your legal rights? In a few minutes you can draw up the legal form or agreement you need to sidestep misunderstandings, comply with legal obligations and avoid liability.

Approved by a barrister, *301 Legal Forms Letters & Agreements* has been approved for consumer use.

How to use *301 Legal Forms, Letters & Agreements...*

It is easy to use Lawpack's *301 Legal Forms, Letters and Agreements* by following these simple instructions.

1   To find the appropriate form, read the two tables of contents. The first lists each form alphabetically. The second groups them by subject.

2   You may find several forms for the same general purpose. To choose the form most appropriate for your specific needs, consult the Contents, beginning on page vii, as a guide to the purpose of each form.

3   Cut out and photocopy the form you want and keep the original so it can be used again in the future. Alternatively you can use the form as a template to prepare your own documents. Letter-type documents can be personalised by being reproduced on your own letterhead.

4   Complete each form fully. Make certain all blanks (name, address, dates, amounts) are filled in. You may need to delete or add provisions in some forms to suit your requirements. If this is necessary, make sure each deletion or insertion is initialled by all parties. If there is not enough space on the document to make your insertion, it is best to type out the entire document, including the insertion, on a new sheet of paper.

5   Some forms have footnoted instructions, which should be observed if you are to use the form properly. Some forms refer to other forms in *301 Legal Forms, Letters & Agreements*, other documents or copies of documents which will need to be attached to the form before use.

6   Some forms have 'health warnings' attached which indicate that a solicitor's advice should be sought. While you should not send forms such as these to other parties without first obtaining legal advice, you can nonetheless use the forms as a means of letting your solicitor know, quickly and economically, precisely what it is you want to achieve.

7   The pronoun 'it' within a form can refer to an individual as well as a business entity. The pronoun 'he' can refer to a woman as appropriate.

About Deeds and Agreements

Under English law a contract does not usually have to be written down to be valid and enforceable. An oral contract generally has just as much validity as a written contract. The problem associated with an oral contract is that if there is a dispute over the contract the only evidence of the terms of the contract is the evidence of each party to the contract which will be based on memory.

The reason why important contracts are written down, therefore, is so that a written record exists of what was agreed between the parties, to minimise the possibility of later disputes.

There are a few important exceptions to the rule that a contract does not have to be in writing. For example, a contract for the disposition of interests in land has to be in writing, and has to conform to the particular requirements of the Law of Property (Miscellaneous Provisions) Act 1989. Guarantees (which are a promise by one person to pay the debt of another if the other person defaults) also have requirements as to writing. Detailed requirements as to writing also affect hire purchase, loan and consumer hire agreements that are caught by the Consumer Credit Act 1974.

A contract exists where two or more parties make mutual promises to each other to take some sort of action or to make some payment to each other. An exchange of goods for money is the simplest form of contract. A simple promise by A to B, however, is not a contract if that promise is not given in exchange for an action or promise by B, because B has given no 'consideration' for A's promise. In order to turn A's promise into an enforceable contract B must also make some promise or payment in return (the 'consideration'). A contract like this involving mutual promises can be referred to as both a contract and an agreement, and both terms are used to mean the same thing in *301 Legal Forms, Letters & Agreements*.

It is sometimes the case that a simple promise by one party to another without consideration is all that the parties wish to achieve. Such an agreement can be made enforceable if, but only if, it is made in what is known as a deed. A deed is a written agreement which is given legal enforceability if it contains a description of itself as a deed and if it is executed in a particular way (see below).

You will find many of the agreements in *301 Legal Forms, Letters & Agreements* are set up as deeds to make them enforceable whether there is consideration or not.

Signature of Agreements

The part of an agreement or deed that the parties sign is known as the attestation clause. In agreements, which are not deeds, an individual signs it himself or through a person authorised to sign on his behalf. A company, being an artificial person distinct from its members or directors, cannot physically sign anything. It is, however, deemed to sign an agreement if any person, acting on the company's authority, signs on its behalf. **Important:** normally, in the case of a company contract, the directors, officers and shareholders cannot be sued if a company fails to honour its obligations under a contract. However, if a person signs for a company without including the words 'for and on behalf of X Ltd' he may be sued personally if the company does not perform its obligations.

Signature of Deeds

In deeds, the attestation clauses are different for companies and individuals. On each deed there is space for two individuals to sign, or two companies, or a combination of the two, depending on who is drawing up the deed. Each party should sign the deed and get a witness to sign and provide his or her name and address. The witness to a deed should not be a relative or cohabitant or the other party to the deed.

Use caution and common sense when using *301 Legal Forms, Letters & Agreements* – or any other do-it-yourself legal product. Whilst these forms are generally considered appropriate for self-use, you must nevertheless decide when you should seek professional legal advice instead. You should consult a solicitor if:

• You need a complex or important agreement.

• Your transaction involves substantial amounts of money or expensive property.

• You don't understand how to use a document – or question its adequacy to fully protect you.

Because we cannot be certain that the forms in this book are appropriate to your circumstances – or are being properly used – we cannot assume any liability or responsibility in connection with their use.

Contents

Contents by Category

I. Business

II.   Buying & Selling

III.   Credit & Debt Collection

IV. Employment

V. Loans & Borrowing

VI. Personal & Family

VII. Residential Tenancy

VIII. Transfers & Assignments

IX. Other Legal Forms

Accident Claim Notice   Form OLF01

Date _____

To _____

_____

_____

Dear _____

You are hereby notified of a claim against you for damages arising from the following accident or injury, to which I believe you and/or your agents are liable.

Description of Accident[1] _____

_____

_____

_____

_____

Date _____

Time _____

Location _____

_____

Please ask your insurance company or solicitor to contact me as soon as possible.

Yours sincerely

Signature _____

Name _____

Address _____

_____

Health warning: A form of this nature will usually precede a court case, in which you may need the help of a solicitor. You should only use this form if the loss of property or injury to yourself is minor and you are willing to act for yourself in any court case, if it is not possible to agree a settlement with the defendant or his insurers. If you do not wish to represent yourself you should leave all correspondence, including an initial letter such as this one, to your solicitor.

[1] Enter a description of the accident. For example 'whilst I was [driving] / [sitting as a passenger in] motor car registration number [____] that car was struck by a motor car, registration number [____] driven by [you] / [your agent]. [As a result, I suffered bodily injury.] or 'During the course of my employment with you I fell from a platform and suffered bodily injury'.

Acknowledgement and Acceptance of Order   Form BS01

Date _____

To _____

_____

_____

Dear _____

Re: Your Order No. _____

We acknowledge receipt of your order no. _____

and confirm our acceptance, which, as advised, is subject to our terms and conditions of business.

Yours sincerely

_____

Note: Only use this form if you have already shown your terms and conditions to the customer, or at the least if you have already alerted your customer to the fact that you have a set of standard terms and conditions. Ideally, you should have a copy of the standard terms and conditions, receipted by the customer before he placed the order, or a copy of those terms, signed by the customer as agreed to by him.

Acknowledgement of Alteration of Order   Form BS02

Date _____

To _____

_____

_____

Dear _____

I refer to your order number dated _____

This letter acknowledges that the order is altered and superseded by the following agreed change in terms

_____

_____

_____

All other terms shall remain as stated.

Please indicate your agreement to the alteration by signing below and signing the enclosed copy of this letter which we should be grateful if you would return to us for our file.

Yours sincerely

_____

The above alteration is acknowledged.

_____

Acknowledging a Notification of Maternity Leave   Form E67

Dear _____

Thank you for informing me of your pregnancy and the date that your baby is due. I am writing to you about your maternity leave and pay.

You are eligible for _____.

You have told me that you would like to begin your maternity leave on _____.
If you want to change this date, you must notify me 28 days before the new intended start date or, if that is not reasonably practicable, as soon as you can. Your maternity leave period will end on _____.[1]
If you want to come back to work before this date, **you must notify me eight weeks before your new intended return date or, if that is not reasonably practicable, as soon as you can.** This is a legal requirement, but obviously it helps with planning. If you don't give notice, the Company has the right to postpone your return for eight weeks from the date you informed me that you would like to return early or the end of your maternity leave period if this is earlier.

If you decide that you do not want to return to work, you will be required to give four weeks' written notice in accordance with your contract of employment.

You are eligible for _____.[2]

The Company will pay you for six weeks at 90 per cent of your average weekly earnings, calculated based on a legal formula, which I have calculated as _____. The Company will then pay you the standard rate of statutory maternity pay of _____for the remaining 33 weeks.[3]

During your period of maternity leave, we will make reasonable contact with you to discuss and plan for your return. If you have any questions, please contact me to discuss any aspects of your maternity entitlements.

Yours sincerely

_____

Personnel Manager

---

[1] i.e. 52 weeks after the start of maternity leave.

[2] If the employee is not eligible, state '*not eligible for statutory maternity pay*'.

[3] If the employee is not entitled to statutory maternity pay, replace with '*I have given you form SMP1, which explains why you do not qualify for statutory maternity pay. You may, however, be entitled to maternity allowance. If you take this form to a Benefits Agency, it will discuss your entitlements with you*'.

Affidavit

Form OLF02

I, _____(name)

of _____(address)

_____(occupation)

MAKE OATH and say as follows:_____

_____

_____

_____

_____

_____

_____

_____

_____

_____

_____

_____

_____

Signature

SWORN AT _____(address)

this _____ day of _____ year _____

before me,

_____

(A Solicitor or Commissioner for Oaths)

Affidavit of Power of Attorney   Form OLF03

I _____ ,

of _____ ,

MAKE OATH and say as follows:

1.   The Power of Attorney granted to me by _____ ,

     on _____ , a true copy of which is annexed hereto, is in full force and effect.

2.   At the time of the execution of _____ [1],

     on _____ I had no knowledge of or actual notice of the revocation or

     termination of the Power of Attorney by death or otherwise.

3.   I make this affidavit for the purpose of inducing _____

     to accept the above described instrument as executed by me as attorney knowing that in accepting

     the aforesaid instrument they will rely upon this affidavit.

SWORN AT _____

the _____ day of _____ year ____

Before me

_____

(A Solicitor or Commissioner for Oaths)

Health warning: Unless the Power of Attorney is an Enduring Power of Attorney made in the form prescribed under the Enduring Power of Attorney Act 1985, it will be automatically revoked if the person who gives the power becomes mentally incapacitated. Therefore, if the Power of Attorney is not an Enduring Power of Attorney and if the person giving the power has become of unsound mind, you must not use this form. If the Power of Attorney is an Enduring Power of Attorney it must be registered once the person giving it has become mentally incapacitated, and no further use must be made of it until registration. Note that when it comes into force (1 October 2007) the Mental Capacity Act 2005 will require new Powers of Attorney to be in the form of 'Lasting Powers of Attorney' instead of in the form of Enduring Powers of Attorney, if they are to remain valid after the maker of the power becomes mentally incapacitated. Please check with the Public Guardianship Office that you are using the right form when you next create a Power of Attorney.

[1]   Describe the document that has been executed under the Power of Attorney.

Affidavit of Title to Goods or other Chattels   Form OLF04

I, _____(name)

of _____(address)

_____ (occupation)

MAKE OATH and say as follows:

1.   I certify that I am now in possession of and am the absolute owner of the following property:

    _____

    _____

2.   I also state that its possession has been undisputed and that I know of no fact or reason that may prevent transfer of this property to the buyer.

3.   I also state that no liens, contracts, debts, or lawsuits exist regarding this property, except the following:

    _____

    _____

4.   [I finally state that I have full power to transfer title to this property to the buyer with [full]/[limited] title guarantee.][1]

_____

Signature

SWORN AT _____(address)

this _____day of _____ year _____.

before me,

_____

(A Solicitor or Commissioner for Oaths)

[1] Do not insert this paragraph without the advice of a solicitor or a licensed conveyancer.

Agreement

Form OLF06

THIS AGREEMENT is made the _____ day of _____ year _____

BETWEEN:

(1) _____ of _____ (the 'First Party');and

(2) _____ of _____ (the 'Second Party').

NOW IT IS HEREBY AGREED as follows:

1.   That in consideration of the promises made herein by the Second Party the First Party hereby promises
      and agrees that it shall:_____

      _____

      _____

      _____

      _____

      _____

      _____

2.   That in consideration of the promises made herein by the First Party the Second Party hereby promises
      that it shall: _____

      _____

      _____

      _____

      _____

      _____

      _____

3.   In consideration of the aforementioned promises, the Parties hereto agree that the following terms
      shall have effect: _____

      _____

      _____

      _____

      _____

      _____

      _____

Continued on next page

Agreement (continued)   Form OLF06

4.   This agreement shall be binding upon the parties, their successors and assigns. This is the entire agreement.

5.   [Nothing in this Agreement is intended to confer any benefit on a third party whether under the Contracts (Rights of Third Parties) Act or otherwise].[1]

IN WITNESS OF WHICH the parties have signed this agreement the day and year first above written.

_____

Signed by or on behalf of the first party

_____

Signed by or on behalf of the second party

---

[1] This should be omitted if the parties desire the agreement to benefit a non-party and if they wish that the non-party should be entitled to sue in respect of it.

Agreement for the Sale of Goods   Form BS03

THIS AGREEMENT is made the _____ day of _____ year _____

BETWEEN:

(1) _____ of _____(the 'Buyer'); and

(2) _____ of _____(the 'Seller').

NOW IT IS HEREBY AGREED as follows:

1.   In consideration for the sum of £ _____, receipt of which the Seller hereby acknowledges, the Seller hereby sells and transfers to the Buyer and his/her successors and assigns absolutely, the following goods (the 'Goods'):

       _____

       _____

       _____

[2.   Although this sale is not made in the course of any business of the Seller, it is nonetheless agreed that the statutory terms as to satisfactory quality set out in the Sale of Goods Act Section 14 shall have effect and it is further agreed that the Goods sold under this agreement shall be fit for their purpose, that is to say: _____

       _____

       _____

       _____]¹

IN WITNESS OF WHICH the parties have signed this agreement the day and year first above written

_____   _____

Signed by or on behalf of the Buyer   Signed by or on behalf of the Seller

_____   _____

in the presence of (witness)   in the presence of (witness)

Name _____   Name _____

Address _____   Address _____

_____   _____

Occupation _____   Occupation _____

¹ Insert the purpose for which the buyer has stated that he intends to use the goods. Under statute, in a sale of goods between private individuals that is not made in the course of the seller's business, there is no automatic promise by the seller to the effect that the goods will be of satisfactory quality or fit for any particular purpose, even where the seller knows of the buyer's purpose for the goods. Paragraph two on this form inserts promises as to quality and fitness for purpose. They can be removed if that is what the parties agree. If the sale is made in the course of the seller's business, the sale is automatically made subject to statutory terms as to quality and fitness for purpose, and there is no power to remove these from the agreement except where the buyer has bought them in the course of the buyer's business and either the buyer buys goods of this type frequently or else if the goods are not of a kind which is normally bought for private use.

Under statute, all sales of goods are subject to a promise by the seller that he has title to the goods that he is selling. The only exception is where he makes it clear that he is selling them with such title as he may have. If he does this, he must add a term revealing anything known to him which makes his title open to question. The statutory promises as to title apply, whether or not the seller is selling in the course of a business. It cannot be excluded from the agreement save where the seller is only selling such title as he has.

Agreement for the Sale of a Vehicle　　　　Form BS04

THIS AGREEMENT is made the _____ day of _____ year _____

BETWEEN:

(1) _____ of _____ (the 'Buyer'); and

(2) _____ of _____ (the 'Seller').

NOW it is HEREBY agreed as follows:

1.　In consideration of the sum of £ _____, receipt of which the Seller acknowledges, the Seller sells and transfers to the Buyer the vehicle (the 'Vehicle'):

Make: _____　　　Model: _____

Registration Number: _____　　　Chassis Number: _____

Year of Manufacture: _____　　　Mileage: _____

Colour: _____　　　Extras: _____

2.　The Seller hereby warrants:

　　_____

3.　The Seller warrants that while the Vehicle was in the Seller's possession, the odometer was not altered or disconnected and that to the best of the Seller's knowledge the odometer reading above:

( ) reflects the actual mileage.

( ) reflects the actual mileage in excess of 99,999 miles.

4.　The Buyer agrees to despatch the Vehicle's Registration Document to DVLA as soon as practicable after signature of this Agreement, informing DVLA of the Buyer's ownership of the Vehicle.

[5.　Save as aforesaid the Seller gives no warranty that the vehicle is of satisfactory quality or that it is fit for any particular purpose].

or

[5.　Although his sale is not made in the course of any business of the Seller, it is nonetheless agreed that the statutory terms as to satisfactory quality set out in the Sale of Goods Act Section 14 shall have effect and it is further agreed that the car shall be fit for its purpose, that is to say:

　　_____]

[6.　In part payment of the purchase price, the Buyer has paid to the Seller the sum of £_____. The remainder of the purchase price, being the sum of £_____ shall be paid to the Seller on or before _____]

[7.　The Seller remains the owner of the car until the entire purchase price is paid].

Continued on next page

Agreement for the Sale of a Vehicle (continued)   Form BS04

[8.   The Buyer shall be entitled to remove the car from the Seller's premises when the entire purchase price is paid, at which time ownership of the car, the risk of loss or damage to it, and the responsibility to insure it will pass to the Buyer. For the avoidance of doubt, if the price is paid by cheque, the price will not be deemed to have been paid until the cheque has cleared].

[9.   This is the entire agreement between the parties. Further, the Buyer accepts that he has not relied upon any statement which the Seller may have made].

10.   The applicable law of this Agreement is English law.

The parties hereto have signed this Agreement the day and year first written above.

SIGNED_____

Signed by or on behalf of the Buyer

SIGNED _____

Signed by or behalf of the Seller

Note: This form is not appropriate where a seller is selling the car in the course of a business to a person who is buying as a consumer, because it allows the parties, if tthey agree, to exclude any warranty of satisfactory quality or fitness for purpose. The law does not allow this where goods (including cars) are sold in the course of a business to a person who is buying as a consumer.

The seller must take care to ensure that the car is roadworthy, as otherwise he could be guilty of a criminal offence, even if the car is not sold in the course of a business.

A check through HPI Ltd should be undertaken by the buyer in order to ensure that the car is not subject to an earlier hire purchase agreement. Although the law gives some protection to private purchasers who innocently buy a car that turns out to be subject to a hire purchase agreement, this protection is by no means foolproof.

Agreement to Assume Debt   Form CDC01

THIS AGREEMENT IS MADE the _____ day of _____ year _____

BETWEEN:

(1) _____ of _____(the 'Creditor');

(2) _____ of _____(the 'Debtor'); and

(3) _____ of _____ (the 'Customer').

1.   The Customer acknowledges that the Customer at present owes the Creditor the sum of

     £_____ (the 'Debt') and that the Customer is currently in the possession of certain assets or

     goods which are the property of the Creditor (the 'Goods').

2.   In consideration of the Creditor transferring ownership of the Goods to the Customer, the Debtor

     unconditionally and irrevocably agrees to assume and pay the Debt, as a principal debtor.

3.   The Debt shall be due and payable on the following terms[1]:_____

     _____

     _____

4.   Nothing in this agreement shall constitute a release or discharge of the obligations of the Customer to

     the Creditor for the payment of the Debt, provided that so long as the Debtor shall promptly pay the

     Debt in the manner above described, the Creditor shall forebear in commencing any action against the

     Customer. In the event of any default, the Creditor shall have full rights, jointly and severally, against

     both the Customer and/or the Debtor for any balance then owing.

5.   This agreement shall be binding upon and inure to the benefit of the parties, their successors and assigns.

Continued on next page

Agreement to Assume Debt (continued)   Form CDC01

IN WITNESS OF WHICH the parties have signed this agreement the day and year first above written

_____   _____
Signed by or on behalf of the Creditor   Signed by or on behalf of the Debtor

_____   _____
in the presence of (witness)   in the presence of (witness)

Name _____   Name _____

Address _____   Address _____

_____   _____

Occupation _____   Occupation _____

_____
Signed by or on behalf of the Customer

_____
in the presence of (witness)

Name _____

Address _____

_____

Occupation _____

Health warning: This form should not be used if the original agreement is one which is regulated under the Consumer Credit Act 1974. Broadly speaking the Act, at the time of writing, applies to any loan, hire or hire purchase agreement for £25,000 or less. This is unless one of a limited number of exceptions applies (for example, a non-cash loan, no more than four instalments are to be paid and they are all to be paid within a year, or if a loan is a low cost loan as defined in the Act). If the Act does regulate the original agreement, it will also regulate any variation to the agreement (such as this one). In those circumstances, this form will not comply with the requirements of the Act and the agreement may therefore be unenforceable. Note also that by the time you use this form, the law may have changed so as to bring within the scope of the Act loans of more than £25,000, save for those which are entered into for the borrower's business, where the borrower's business is a firm with more than three partners. However, you may use this form in all circumstances if the debtor and the customer are both limited companies.

[1] No more than four payments should be provided for, and the debt must be stated to be repayable within one year. Otherwise, the Consumer Credit Act 1974 may apply.

Agreement to Compromise Debt

Form CDC02

THIS DEED is made the _____ day of _____ year _____

BETWEEN:

(1) _____ of _____(the 'Customer'); and

(2) _____ of _____(the 'Creditor').

WHEREAS:

(A)   The Customer and the Creditor acknowledge that the Customer is indebted to the Creditor in the sum
       of £ _____ (the 'Debt'), which sum is now due and payable.

(B)   The Creditor agrees to forgo payment of part of the Debt.

[(C)   A dispute has arisen between the Customer and the Creditor which they have agreed to compromise
       on the terms of this Deed.]

NOW THIS DEED WITNESSES as follows:

1.   [In pursuance of the agreement to compromise the said dispute] the parties agree that the Creditor
       shall accept £ _____ (the 'Sum') in full and final settlement of the Debt and in complete
       discharge and satisfaction of all monies due, provided the Sum is punctually paid as follows: _____

       _____

       _____

2.   Should the Customer fail to pay the Sum on the terms set out in paragraph 1 the entire Sum shall fall
       due and the Creditor shall have full rights to prosecute its claim for the full total of the Debt, less any
       payments made.

3.   Upon default, the Customer agrees to pay all reasonable solicitors' fees and costs of collection.

4.   This agreement shall be binding upon and inure to the benefit of the parties, their successors and
       assigns.

Continued on next page

Agreement to Compromise Debt (continued)   Form CDC02

IN WITNESS OF WHICH the parties have executed this deed the day and year first above written

(Individual)   (Company)

_____   Signed for and on behalf of:

Signed by the Customer   _____Ltd

_____   _____

in the presence of (witness)   Director

Name _____

Address _____   _____

_____   Director/Secretary

Occupation _____
                                         Signed for and on behalf of:

                                         _____Ltd

_____

Signed by the creditor   _____

                                         Director

_____

in the presence of (witness)   _____

Name _____   Director/Secretary

Address _____

_____

Occupation _____

Health warning: This form should not be used if the original agreement is one which is regulated under the Consumer Credit Act 1974. Broadly speaking the Act, at the time of writing, applies to any loan, hire or hire purchase agreement for £25,000 or less. This is unless one of a limited number of exceptions applies (for example, a non-cash loan, if no more than four instalments are to be paid and they are all to be paid within a year, or if a loan is a low cost loan). If the Act does regulate the original agreement, it will also regulate any variation to the agreement (such as this one). In those circumstances, this form will not comply with the requirements of the Act and the agreement may therefore be unenforceable. Note also that by the time you use this form, the law may have changed so as to bring within the scope of the Act loans of more than £25,000, save for those which are entered into for the borrower's business, where the borrower's business is a firm with more than three partners. However, you may use this form in all circumstances if the debtor and the Customer are both limited companies.

Unless the agreement takes the form of a Deed, the Customer may not be able to rely upon it, because a promise by a Creditor to accept a lesser sum in full satisfaction of his debt will often fail if there is no consideration. In order to overcome this problem, the parties can either use the form of a Deed (such as appears above) or they can agree that the customer will make an additional promise to the Creditor going beyond a mere promise to pay the reduced sum. Just about anything will do. Paying a peppercorn in addition to the new sum will do. Most commonly, a debt is compromised because a disagreement has arisen as to how much is owing or as to whether anything is owing at all. The compromise of such an agreement will be sufficient consideration. If that is what you are doing, mention in a paragraph under 'whereas' the fact that a disagreement has arisen and that it is being compromised on the terms set out in this document.

Agreement to Extend Debt Payment Form CDC03

THIS DEED is made the _____ day of _____ year _____

BETWEEN:

(1) _____ of _____ (the 'Customer'); and

(2) _____ of _____ (the 'Creditor').

WHEREAS:

(A) The Customer and the Creditor acknowledge that the Customer is indebted to the Creditor in the sum of £ _____ (the 'Debt'), which sum is now due and payable.

(B) The Creditor agrees to extend the term for payment of the Debt.

NOW THIS DEED WITNESSES as follows:

1. The Creditor agrees to the payment of the Debt on extended terms, together with interest on the unpaid balance payable in the following manner: _____

  _____

  _____

2. The Customer agrees to pay the Debt to the Creditor together with interest thereon under the terms set out in paragraph 1.

3. In the event that the Customer shall fail to make any payment on the due date, the Creditor shall have full rights to collect the entire balance then remaining which amount shall be immediately due and payable and the Creditor shall be entitled to interest, both before and after any judgment, at the rate of _____% per annum on the said balance until judgment or sooner payment.

4. In the event of default, the Customer agrees to pay all reasonable solicitors' fees and costs of collection.

5. At the election of the Creditor, the Customer agrees to execute note(s) evidencing the balance then due on terms consistent with this agreement.

6. This agreement shall be binding upon and inure to the benefit of the parties, their successors and assigns.

Continued on next page

Agreement to Extend Debt Payment (continued)　　　Form CDC03

IN WITNESS OF WHICH the parties have executed this deed the day and year first above written

(Individual)　　　　　　　　　　　　　　　　　　(Company)

_____　　Signed for and on behalf of:

Signed by the Customer　　　　　　　　_____Ltd

_____　　_____

in the presence of (witness)　　　　　　Director

Name _____

Address _____

_____　　Director/Secretary

Occupation _____

_____　　Signed for and on behalf of:

Signed by the creditor　　　　　　　　_____Ltd

_____　　_____

in the presence of (witness)　　　　　　Director

Name _____

Address _____

_____　　Director/Secretary

Occupation _____

Health warning: This form should not be used if the original agreement is one which is regulated under the Consumer Credit Act 1974. Broadly speaking the Act, at the time of writing, applies to any loan, hire or hire purchase agreement for £25,000 or less. This is unless one of a limited number of exceptions applies (for example, a non-cash loan, no more than four instalments are to be paid and they are all to be paid within a year, or if a loan is a low cost loan). If the Act does regulate the original agreement, it will also regulate any variation to the agreement (such as this one). In those circumstances, this form will not comply with the requirements of the Act and the agreement may therefore be unenforceable. Note also that by the time you use this form, the law may have changed so as to bring loans of more than £25,000, save for those which are entered into for the borrower's business, within the scope of the Act loans of more than £25,000, save for those which are entered into for the borrower's business, where the borrower's business is a firm with more than three partners. However, you may use this form in all circumstances if the debtor and the Customer are both limited companies.

It is important that the document is signed and witnessed as provided for, because otherwise the promise to give time to pay may not be effective.

Agreement to Extend Performance Date   Form CDC04

THIS DEED is made the _____ day of _____ year _____

BETWEEN:

(1) _____ of _____ (the 'First Party'); and

(2) _____ of _____ (the 'Second Party').

WHEREAS:

(A) The parties entered into an agreement dated _____ year _____ (the 'Agreement') which provides that full performance of the Agreement shall be completed by both parties on or before _____ year _____, (the 'Completion Date').

(B) The parties acknowledge that the Agreement cannot be performed and completed by both parties by the Completion Date and therefore wish to extend the date for mutual performance of the Agreement.

NOW THIS DEED WITNESSES as follows:

1. The parties hereby agree that the date for performance of the Agreement be continued and extended to _____ o'clock on _____day_____month_____year _____, [time being of the essence][1].

2. No other variation of the terms of the Agreement, nor any extension of time for its performance is to be implied. The parties' rights in respect of any breach of the Agreement including, for the avoidance of doubt, any rights to claim damages for delayed completion, are hereby reserved.

3. This agreement shall be binding upon and inure to the benefit of the parties, their successors and assigns.

Continued on next page

Agreement to Extend Performance Date (continued)   Form CDC04

IN WITNESS OF WHICH the parties have executed this deed the day and year first above written

(Individual)

(Company)

_____

Signed for and on behalf of:

Signed by the First Party

_____Ltd

_____

Director

in the presence of (witness)

Name _____

Address _____

Director/Secretary

_____

Occupation _____

Signed for and on behalf of:

_____Ltd

_____

Signed by the Second Party

Director

_____

in the presence of (witness)

Name _____

Address _____

Director/Secretary

_____

Occupation _____

---

[1]   If you include these words it will mean that if one party is late in performing an obligation under the contract, the other party is free to terminate it, even if the delay is entirely trivial.

Agreement to Sell Personal Property (not land)   Form OLF07

THIS AGREEMENT is made the _____ day of _____ year _____

BETWEEN:

(1) _____ of _____ (the 'Buyer'); and

(2) _____ of _____ (the 'Seller').

NOW IT IS HEREBY AGREED as follows:

1.   The Seller agrees to sell, and the Buyer agrees to buy the following property (the 'Property'):

     _____

2.   The Buyer agrees to pay to the Seller and the Seller agrees to accept as total purchase price, inclusive
     of Value Added Tax if any, the sum of £ _____, payable as follows:

     £ _____ deposit herewith paid; and

     £ _____ the balance payable on delivery by cash, or cheque supported by bankers card.

3.   The Seller warrants it has good and legal title to the Property, full authority to sell the Property, and
     that the Property shall be sold free of all liens, charges, encumbrances, liabilities and adverse claims of
     every nature and description whatsoever.

[4.   The Property is sold as seen, and the Seller disclaims any warranty of working order or condition of the
     Property except that it shall be sold in its present condition, reasonable wear and tear excepted.][1]

5.   The parties hereto agree to transfer title on _____ year _____, at the address of the
     Seller.

6.   This agreement shall be binding upon and inure to the benefit of the parties, their successors and assigns.

IN WITNESS OF WHICH the parties have signed this agreement the day and year first above.[1]

_____   _____
Signed by the Buyer   Signed by the Seller

_____   _____
in the presence of (witness)   in the presence of (witness)
Name _____   Name _____
Address _____   Address _____

_____   _____
Occupation _____   Occupation _____

[1] Delete unless either (1) the seller is not selling in the course of a business or (2) the buyer is buying in the course of a business and
    either he buys property of this type frequently or the property is not of a type which is normally acquired for private use.

Alteration to Terms of Employment   Form E68

Date _____ [1]

To _____

_____

_____

This letter is to let you know that the terms and conditions of your contract have been amended as set out below.

If you wish to discuss any of these changes or require any further information, please let me know.

Date changes effective: _____

New wages/salary: _____

New hours of work: _____

New location: _____

Changes to duties and responsibilities: _____

Please acknowledge receipt of this letter and your agreement to the terms set out in it by signing the attached copy of this letter and returning it to _____. You should retain the top copy with your contract of employment.

_____

Signed

for

_____

I, _____, acknowledge that I have received a statement of alteration to the particulars of my employment as required by section 1 of the Employment Rights Act 1996 and agree to the terms set out in that statement.

_____

Signed

_____

Dated

[1] This must be no later than one month after the change to the terms of employment.

Anti-Gazumping Agreement   Form BS05

(AN EXCLUSIVITY CONTRACT BETWEEN THE BUYER & SELLER OF PROPERTY)

THIS AGREEMENT is made the _____ day of _____ year _____

BETWEEN

(1) _____ of _____(the 'Seller');

and

(2) _____ of _____(the 'Buyer').

BACKGROUND

A   The parties have, subject to contract, agreed to a transaction ('the Sale') in which the Seller will sell and
     the Buyer will buy the property described in the First Schedule ('the Property') at the price of
     (£ _____).

B   The solicitors specified in the Second Schedule ('the Seller's Solicitors') will act for the Seller on the
     Sale.

C   The solicitors specified in the Third Schedule ('the Buyer's Solicitors') will act for the Buyer on the Sale.

NOW IT IS HEREBY AGREED as follows:

1. Exclusivity Period

  1.1   The Exclusivity Period shall begin on the exchange of this Agreement and shall end (subject to
        Clause 5.1 below) at 5 pm on the _____ day after the Buyer's Solicitors receive the draft
        contract from the Seller's Solicitors pursuant to Clause 2(b) below or on _____, whichever
        shall be the earlier.

  1.2   If and for as long as the Buyer complies with his obligations under this Agreement, the Seller
        agrees that during the Exclusivity Period neither the Seller nor anyone acting on the Seller's
        behalf will:

        (a)   seek purchasers for the Property;

        (b)   allow any prospective purchaser or mortgagee or any surveyor, valuer or other person
              acting on his or their behalf to enter the Property (other than under clause 4.3 below);

        (c)   provide a draft contract or property information concerning the Property to anyone other
              than the Buyer's Solicitors;

        (d)   negotiate or agree with anyone other than the Buyer or the Buyer's Solicitors any terms for
              the sale of the Property;

        (e)   enter into any commitment, whether or not legally binding, to proceed with any other
              potential purchaser following the expiry of the Exclusivity Period.

2. Seller's instructions to solicitors

  The Seller will immediately:

        (a)   appoint the Seller's Solicitors to act for him on the Sale; and

        (b)   instruct them to send to the Buyer's Solicitors as soon as practicable a draft contract for the Sale
              and such information about the Property as accords with good conveyancing practice and to
              deal promptly and reasonably with any enquiries asked by the Buyer's Solicitors and with any
              amendments to the draft contract proposed by the Buyer's Solicitors.

3. Buyer's instructions to solicitors

  The Buyer will immediately:

        (a)   appoint the Buyer's Solicitors to act for him on the Sale; and

        (b)   instruct them to make all necessary searches and enquiries as soon as practicable and to deal
              promptly and in accordance with good conveyancing practice with the draft contract for the Sale
              and such title and other information about the Property as they receive from the Seller's
              Solicitors and to negotiate with the Seller's Solicitors promptly and reasonably any amendments
              to the draft contract which the Buyer's Solicitors propose.

4. Surveys, mortgages, etc.

  4.1   If the Buyer requires a mortgage loan in connection with the purchase of the Property, the Buyer

Continued on next page

Anti-Gazumping Agreement (continued) — Form BS05

shall within [one week] from the date of this Agreement apply to such building society, bank or other prospective lender ('the Mortgagee') as may reasonably be expected to lend the required amount to the Buyer and the Buyer shall complete such application forms and pay such fees as the Mortgagee shall require in order to process the Buyer's application as quickly as possible.

4.2 If the Buyer or the Mortgagee require the Property to be surveyed and/or valued, the Buyer will use all reasonable endeavours to arrange for the survey and/or valuation inspection to take place within _____ days of the date of this Agreement.

4.3 The Seller will give such access to the Property as is reasonably required by any surveyor or valuer appointed by the Buyer or the Mortgagee for the purpose of surveying and/or valuing the Property.

5. Good faith and withdrawal

5.1 During the Exclusivity Period the Seller and the Buyer will deal with each other in good faith and in particular (but without limiting the above):

(a) if during the Exclusivity Period the Buyer decides not to buy the Property or becomes unable to buy the Property, he will immediately give written notice to that effect to the Seller and the Exclusivity Period will then cease;

(b) if during the Exclusivity Period the Seller decides not to proceed with the Sale or becomes unable to sell the Property, he will immediately give written notice to that effect to the Buyer and the Buyer's obligations under this Agreement will cease but the restrictions imposed on the Seller by Clause 1.2 above shall continue until the expiry of the Exclusivity Period.

(c) The Buyer shall promptly furnish to the Seller any information which the Seller may reasonably require with regard to the Buyer's performance of his obligations under this Agreement and will not assert any claim of legal professional privilege in answer to such a request.

5.2 Nothing in Clause 5.1 above or elsewhere in this Agreement will impose on the Seller any greater duty to disclose matters affecting the Property than are imposed by statute or common law.

5.3 If the Buyer shall fail to comply with his obligations under this Agreement in any material respect or if the Buyer shall indicate to the Buyer that he is unwilling or unable to proceed save upon terms that the purchase price shall be reduced, the Seller shall be entitled to terminate the Exclusivity Period forthwith, and thereafter all obligations of the Seller under this Agreement will cease.

6. Miscellaneous

6.1 This Agreement does not form part of any other contract.

6.2 In this Agreement the expression 'property information' includes title details and any other information about the Property which a prudent prospective buyer or his solicitors would require the seller or his solicitors to provide.

6.3 The headings shall not affect the interpretation of this Agreement.

THE FIRST SCHEDULE	THE SECOND SCHEDULE	THE THIRD SCHEDULE
The Property	The Seller's Solicitors	The Buyer's Solicitors
_____	_____	_____
_____	_____	_____
_____	_____	_____

SIGNED_____   SIGNED_____

by or on behalf of the Seller   by or on behalf of the Buyer

Health warning: It is important to know what this agreement can and what it cannot achieve. It can create an enforceable obligation in the seller, during a defined period, not to take any steps to sell the property to somebody else. The practical effect of such an obligation is that the seller will be more likely than not to keep to his promise that he would sell the property to the buyer on certain terms. Moreover, the various promises that are made about how the negotiations are conducted will, if they are not observed, tend to expose the true intentions of a buyer or seller who is just a time-waster. The Agreement cannot, however, create a legal obligation on the seller to negotiate in any particular way or actually to sell the property. Until everything is agreed there would be merely an 'agreement to agree' which would be too vague to be enforceable.

If you want to impose an obligation on a seller to sell the property to you at a given price and upon given terms, but you are not yet in a position to commit yourself the only way in which you can do it is by getting the seller to agree to grant you an option. For that, however, you will need a solicitor or licensed conveyancer to help you.

Application to be Accepted as a Guarantor   Form LB12

_____ Ltd.

Name of Company for which you wish to be a guarantor _____

Company's Registration No. _____

Company's address _____

_____

Your name _____

Your address _____

_____

How long have you been at this address? _____ years ____ months

(If less than one year, please give previous address _____

_____)

Your date of birth _____

Your home telephone number _____

Your work telephone number _____

Your mobile phone number _____

Your email address _____

Do you

☐ Own your home?

    If yes:

    Current value £ _____

    What percentage of the equity do you own? _____

    Is it mortgaged? If yes, name each mortgagee and state the amount of the mortgage debt.

    _____

☐ Rent your home?

    If yes, please give name and address of landlord?

    _____

☐ Other (please give details) _____

_____

Your bank _____

Address of Branch _____

Account number _____

Continued on next page

Application to be Accepted as a Guarantor (continued)   Form LB12

Employer's name _____

Employer's address _____

_____

Employer's telephone number _____

Employer's email address _____

Your current monthly salary £ _____

Are you self-employed? _____

If yes:

Please give name and address of your accountants:

_____

_____

What profits from that business did you declare as your income on your most recent tax return

£ _____

Date of return _____

If applicable, please state the maximum amount which you are prepared to guarantee:

£ _____

Is there any other matter which you regard as relevant to your application which you would like to tell us

about? _____

_____

I hereby apply for approval to be a guarantor for the above-mentioned company.

I authorise you _____ [1] in connection with this application to make enquires of and

to receive information about me from any bank, accountant, landlord, mortgagee, employer or credit

reference agency which you consider appropriate.

_____

(signed)

_____

(dated)

---

[1] Insert name of company giving credit.

Applicant's Request for an Employment Reference   Form E03

Date   _____

To   _____

_____

_____

Dear   _____

The above named has applied to us for the position of _____ and has given us your name as a referee. We understand that _____ was employed by you from _____ to _____ as a _____. We should be grateful if you would confirm that this is the case and let us know whether, in your opinion, she performed her tasks competently and conscientiously.

We should also be grateful if you would let us know whether you would consider _____ a reliable and responsible employee. Could you also let us know the reasons why she left your employment?

We assure you that any reply you may give will be treated in the strictest confidence.

A stamped addressed envelope is enclosed.

Yours sincerely

_____

Application to Open a Credit Account Form CDC05

with _____ Ltd

Company Name	
Address	Invoice Address (if different)
Tel No.	Fax No.

Name of Buyer		
VAT Registration No. Company Reg. No.	Value of Initial Order £	Requested Credit Limit £
Trade Reference (1)	Trade Reference (2)	Bank Reference

Parent Company (if applicable)

I hereby agree to the terms and conditions of sale accompanying this application.

NAME _____

POSITION _____

SIGNED _____ DATE _____

OFFICE USE ONLY					
	Date	Agency Rating	Credit Limit	Authorised	Date
Application Rec'd		Accounts Rec'd			
Refs Applied For					
Account Opened					

Account No. _____   Credit Limit _____

Health warning: Use this form only where the customer is a limited liability company or where for some other reason the Consumer Credit Act 1974 does not apply.

Assignment of Accounts Receivable with Non-Recourse   Form TA01

THIS AGREEMENT is made the _____ day of _____ year _____

BETWEEN:

(1) _____ of _____ (the 'Assignor'); and

(2) _____ of _____ (the 'Assignee').

NOW IT IS HEREBY AGREED as follows:

1.   In consideration for the payment of the sum of £ _____ (receipt of which the Assignor hereby acknowledges) the Assignor hereby assigns and transfers to the Assignee all rights, title and interest in and to the account(s) receivable described as follows (the 'Accounts'):

     _____

     _____

     _____

2.   The Assignor warrants that the Account(s) are due and the Assignor has not received payment for the same or any part thereof.

3.   The Assignor further warrants that it has full title to the Accounts, full authority to sell and transfer the Accounts and that the Accounts are sold free and clear of all liens, encumbrances and any known claims.

4.   This Agreement shall be binding upon and inure to the benefit of the parties, their successors and assigns.

5.   Upon being required by the Assignee so to do the Assignor shall forthwith instruct each person indebted under the Accounts herein assigned, that payment should be made direct to the Assignee.

IN WITNESS OF WHICH the parties have signed this Agreement the day and year first above written

_____   _____

Signed by or on behalf of the Assignor   Signed by or on behalf of the Assignee

_____   _____

in the presence of (witness)   in the presence of (witness)

Name _____   Name _____

Address _____   Address _____

_____   _____

Occupation _____   Occupation _____

Note: Non-recourse means that the risk of the debtor not paying is on the assignee and that if the parties wish to place the risk on the assignor they should add a term stating 'if the indebtedness due under any Account shall not be paid by _____, the Assignee shall be entitled to require the Assignor to repurchase the Account for the sum that was paid by the Assignee to the Assignor in respect of the same plus interest at _____% per annum from that date.

Assignment of Contract

THIS DEED is made the _____ day of _____ year _____

BETWEEN:

(1) _____ of _____(the 'Assignor');

(2) _____ of _____(the 'Assignee'); and

(3) _____ of _____(the 'Third Party').

WHEREAS:

(A)   The Assignor and the Third Party have entered into an agreement dated_____ _____ year _____ (the 'Agreement').

(B)   With the consent of the Third Party the Assignor wishes to assign all its rights and obligations under the Agreement to the Assignee.

NOW THIS DEED WITNESSES as follows:

1.   The Assignor warrants and represents that the Agreement is in full force and effect and is fully assignable.

2.   In consideration of £_____ paid by the [Assignee to the Assignor], [Assignor to the Assignee] The Assignor hereby assigns its rights under the Agreement to the Assignee and the Assignee hereby assumes and agrees to perform all the remaining and executory obligations of the Assignor under the Agreement and agrees to indemnify and hold the Assignor harmless from any claim or demand resulting from non-performance or defective performance by the Assignee.

[3.   The Assignee shall be entitled to all monies remaining to be paid under the Agreement, which rights are also assigned hereunder.]

4.   The Assignor warrants that the Agreement has not been modified and that the terms contained therein remain in force. [The Assignor further agrees to indemnify the Assignee and hold the Assignee harmless from any claim or demand resulting from non-performance or defective performance by the Assignor prior to the date hereof.]

5.   The Assignor further warrants that it has full right and authority to transfer the Agreement and that the Agreement rights herein transferred are free of lien, encumbrance or adverse claim.

[6.   The Third Party agrees to the assignment of the Agreement upon the terms stated herein, [and agrees further that as regards any future non-performance or defective performance he shall have recourse only against the Assignee] or [but without prejudice to his right of recourse against the Assignor in respect of any non-performance or defective performance, whenever the same may occur.]]

IN WITNESS OF WHICH the parties have executed this deed the day and year first above written

Continued on next page

Assignment of Contract (continued)   Form TA02

(Individual)   (Company)

_____   Signed for and on behalf of _____

Signed by the Assignor   _____Ltd

_____   _____

in the presence of (witness)   Director

Name _____

Address _____   _____

_____   Director/Secretary

Occupation _____

_____   Signed for and on behalf of:_____

Signed by the Assignee   _____Ltd

_____   _____

in the presence of (witness)   Director

Name _____

Address _____   _____

_____   Director/Secretary

Occupation _____

Note: In law, it is possible to assign the benefit of a contract without the consent of the other party to the contract. However, care needs to be taken to ensure that the other party knows about the assignment. It is also possible for one party to delegate performance of the contract to somebody else without such consent, unless personal performance is part of what is expected, say in a contract to paint a portrait.

However, if one party has duties under the contract, it is not possible to assign the legal responsibility to perform those duties without the consent of the other party to the contract. For example, if I contract to deliver a tonne of coal, I can perform that contract by getting somebody else to deliver it, but I remain responsible to ensure that it is delivered and that it is of the correct grade. Therefore, if the contract is not properly performed, I can be sued, although I may have delegated its performance.

The effect of this form is to provide for one person to take over the benefits and the performance of the duties under a contract which arise in the future, and to be indemnified for any breaches of contract which the assignor may have committed before the assignment. Sometimes, a contract is profitable, and a person will pay for the privilege of taking it over. Sometimes, a contract is unprofitable, and a person will pay for the privilege of having someone else take it on. In this form you will find wording in square brackets to cover either possibility. Make sure that you strike out the one which does not apply.

There are also square brackets to cover the question of whether the third party is to continue to have a remedy against the Assignor after the assignment. Again make sure that you strike out the one which does not apply, and that it is altered, if necessary, in such a way as to reflect your intentions.

Assignment of Insurance Policy   Form TA04

THIS DEED is made the _____ day of _____ year _____

BETWEEN:

(1) _____ of _____ (the 'Assignor'); and

(2) _____ of _____ (the 'Assignee').

WHEREAS:

(A)   The Assignor is the holder of a Policy of Insurance number _____ issued by the

_____ Insurance Company (the 'Policy').

(B)   The Assignor wishes to assign the benefit of the Policy to the Assignee.

NOW THIS DEED WITNESSES as follows:

1.   The Assignor warrants that the Policy is in full force and effect and all premiums thereon have been paid in full to date.

2.   The Assignor further warrants that he/she has full authority to transfer the Policy, and shall execute all further documents as may be required by the Insurance Company or broker to effect this Assignment.

3.   The Assignor hereby assigns to the Assignee and the Assignee hereby accepts the assignment of the Policy and all the obligations and benefits attaching thereto.

4.   This assignment shall by binding upon and inure to the benefit of the parties, their successors and assigns.

IN WITNESS OF WHICH the parties have executed this deed the day and year first above written

(Individual)   (Company)

_____   Signed for and on behalf of _____

Signed by the Assignor   _____Ltd

_____

in the presence of (witness)   _____

Name _____   Director

Address _____   _____

_____   Director/Secretary

Occupation _____

_____   Signed for and on behalf of:

Signed by the Assignee   _____Ltd

_____

in the presence of (witness)   _____

Name _____   Director

Address _____   _____

_____   Director/Secretary

Occupation _____

Note: This form is suitable for a case where property is being sold along with the benefit of an insurance policy. It is not suitable where an insurance policy is being assigned as security for a debt owed by the Assignor to the Assignee. **Above all, remember that it is absolutely essential** for the insurance company to be informed about the sale and to agree to the assignment of the property before the sale takes place, as otherwise the policy could be made void. If you only want to assign your entitlement to monies which you are expecting to receive under a claim that has already been made, as opposed to the right to be insured against future mishaps, then you only need to use a form for the assignment of a debt, modified slightly so as to specify the payment the name of the insurance company and the nature of the claim. In that case, too, it is wise to discuss the matter with the insurance company in advance.

Assignment of Money Due   Form TA05

THIS agreement is made the _____ day of _____ year _____

BETWEEN:

(1) _____ of _____ (the 'Assignor'); and

(2) _____ of _____ (the 'Assignee').

WHEREAS:

(A) The Assignor is entitled to the payment of certain monies under a contract dated _____ year _____ ('the Contract') and made between the Assignor and_____ _____ (the 'the Third Party').

(B) The Assignor wishes to assign the benefit of the Contract to the Assignee.

NOW IT IS HEREBY AGREED as follows:

1. In consideration for the sum of £_____, receipt of which the Assignor hereby acknowledges, the Assignor assigns and transfers to the Assignee all monies now due and payable to the Assignor and to become due and payable to the Assignor under the terms of the Contract to the Assignee.

2. The Assignor hereby warrants that there has been no breach of the Contract by any party, and that the Assignor is in full compliance with all the terms and conditions of the Contract, and that he has not assigned or encumbered all or any rights under said contract.

3. The Assignor authorises and directs the Third Party to deliver any and all cheques, drafts, or payments to be issued pursuant to Contract to the Assignee; and further authorises the Assignee to receive such cheques, drafts, or payments from, and to collect any and all funds due or to become due pursuant thereto.

4. The Assignee will at the Assignor's request, immediately serve notice in writing upon the Third Party informing him of the assignment to the Assignee of the Assignor's rights under and in respect of the Contract and requiring him to forward to the Assignee a copy of the notice, signed by the Third Party.

IN WITNESS OF WHICH the parties have signed this agreement the day and year first above written

_____   _____
Signed by or on behalf of the Assignor   Signed by or on behalf of the Assignee

_____   _____
in the presence of (witness)   in the presence of (witness)

Name _____   Name _____

Address _____   Address _____

_____   _____
Occupation _____   Occupation _____

Note: It is essential to inform the Third Party of the assignment as soon as possible, because it is only after notice that the third party will be obliged to pay the Assignee instead of the Assignor. Until the third party is informed, the Assignee will have no remedy against him if he pays the debt to the Assignor, and although the Assignee would have a remedy against the Assignor, that remedy will not necessarily be worth anything against an Assignor who has accepted a payment to which he is no longer entitled.

The assignment is complete as soon as the third party knows of it, no matter who informs him. As a practical matter, however, it is best if the Assignor informs him, because otherwise the third party will be left in doubt as to whether the debt has really been assigned, and he will probably not act upon the assignment without the Assignor's confirmation. If the Assignor refuses to confirm the assignment, the third party will be entitled not to pay until a court decides the matter.

Assignment of Option   Form TA06

THIS AGREEMENT is made the _____ day of _____ year _____

BETWEEN:

(1) _____ of _____(the 'Assignor'); and

(2) _____ of _____(the 'Assignee').

WHEREAS:

(A)   The Assignor has been granted the following option (the 'Option')[1]: _____

_____

_____

_____

(B)   The Assignor wishes to sell the Option to the Assignee.

NOW IT IS HEREBY AGREED as follows:

1.   In consideration for the payment of £ _____, receipt of which the Assignor hereby acknowledges, the Assignor hereby assigns to the Assignee his/her entire interest in the Option and all his/her right thereunder to the Assignee with [Full]/[Limited]/Title Guarantee.

2.   The Assignee, by accepting the transfer of this Option, agrees to exercise the Option, if at all, according to its terms.

3.   This agreement shall be binding upon and inure to the benefit of the parties, their successors and assigns.

IN WITNESS OF WHICH the parties have signed this agreement as a deed the day and year first above written

_____   _____

Signed by or on behalf of the Assignor   Signed by or on behalf of the Assignee

_____   _____

in the presence of (witness)   in the presence of (witness)

Name _____   Name _____

Address _____   Address _____

_____   _____

Occupation _____   Occupation _____

Note: This form is not appropriate for an assignment of an interest in land. For such an assignment use the form TA07.

The words 'Full Title Guarantee' and 'Limited Title Guarantee' incorporate different promises into the assignment. It is best to refer to a solicitor about these. For present purposes these promises relate to the absence of charges and incumbrances. If the Title Guarantee is full, the Assignor promises that the Option is free of any such charges etc except those which he could not reasonably be expected to know about. If the Title Guarantee is Limited, the Assignor promises merely that the Assignor has not charged the Option and that he is not aware of anyone else having done so since the time it was created or last sold. As a rough guide, Limited Title Guarantee is appropriate where the Assignor has inherited the Option, whereas Full Title Guarantee is appropriate where the Assignor has paid for it. If the Option has been created in writing, then set out a full description of all of the documents which have created the Option. Better still, state that the documents are attached to the Option and then attach them.

Note that an Option cannot be assigned if it is personal to the Assignor. The Option should be examined carefully in order to determine whether there is a potential problem here.

[1]   Enter Option details, in particular the price paid for the Option, the items which the Assignor has the right to purchase and the deadline for exercising the Option. An Option is personal if it is intended by the person granting it and the person to whom it is granted that it should be exercisable only by the grantee and not by anyone to whom he might assign the Option.

Assignment of Option to Purchase Land   Form TA07

THIS AGREEMENT is made the _____ day of _____ year _____

BETWEEN:

(1) _____ of _____(the 'Assignor'); and

(2) _____ of _____(the 'Assignee').

WHEREAS:

(A)   The Assignor is the holder of an option granted on _____ to purchase property located at

_____ which expires on _____ year _____ (the

'Option'), a copy of which is annexed.

(B)   The Assignor wishes to sell the Option to the Assignee.

NOW IT IS HEREBY AGREED as follows:

1.   In consideration for the payment of £ _____, receipt of which the Assignee hereby

acknowledges, the Assignor hereby transfers his/her entire interest in the Option and all his/her rights

thereunder with [Full]/[Limited] Title Guarantee to the Assignee absolutely.

2.   The Assignor warrants that the Option is fully assignable.

3.   The Assignee, by accepting the transfer of the Option, agrees to exercise the Option, if at all, according

to its terms.

4.   This agreement shall be binding upon and inure to the benefit of the parties, their successors and assigns.

IN WITNESS OF WHICH the parties have signed this agreement as a Deed the day and year first above written.

_____   _____

Signed by or on behalf or the Assignor   Signed by or on behalf of the Assignee

_____   _____

in the presence of (witness)   in the presence of (witness)

Name _____   Name _____

Address _____   Address _____

_____   _____

Occupation _____   Occupation _____

Note: The words 'Full Title Guarantee' and 'Limited Title Guarantee' incorporate different promises into the Assignment. It is best to refer to a solicitor about these. For present purposes, these promises relate to the absence of charges and incumbrances. If the Title Guarantee is Full, the Assignor promises that the Option is free of any such charges etc except those which he could not reasonably be expected to know about. If the Title Guarantee is Limited, the Assignor promises merely that the Assignor has not charged the Option and that he is not aware of anyone else having done so since the time it was created or last sold. As a rough guide, Limited Title Guarantee is appropriate where the Assignor has inherited the Option, whereas Full Title Guarantee is appropriate where the Assignor has paid for it.

An Option cannot be assigned if it is personal to the Assignor. The Option should be examined carefully in order to determine whether there is a potential problem here.

An Option is the right to enter into a binding contract. Contracts for the sale of land usually involve large sums of money and are often complicated. Make certain that you fully understand the obligations which you are taking on and the rights which you are acquiring under the contract to which the Option refers. If you have any doubts at all, see your solicitor.

It is very important to register a Notice of the Option and of the Assignee's entitlement under this Option at H.M. Land Registry, as otherwise the interest created by this Option will be defeated if the land is sold to somebody else and if the sale is registered.

It is important to remember that the grant or assignment of an Option for the purchase of an interest in land may be subject to Stamp Duty Land Tax and must be declared to the Stamp Duty Land Tax Office by the Grantee or Assignee on a form SDLT1 even if no tax is payable. There are strict time limits which must be observed, otherwise you may be liable for a fine. The helpline for the Office is 0845 6030135. It is especially important to note that an Option to acquire any interest in land must be granted in writing and observe the requirements set out in the Law of Property (Miscellaneous Provisions) Act 1989. See a solicitor to make sure that the Option is valid.

Authorisation to Release Confidential Information   Form OLF08

Date _____

To _____

_____

_____

Dear _____

I hereby authorise and request you to send copies of the following documents which I believe to be in your possession and which contain confidential information concerning me to:

Name _____

Address _____

_____

_____

Documents: _____

_____

_____

_____

_____

[I shall of course reimburse you for any reasonable costs incurred by you in providing the requested information.]

Yours sincerely

Signature _____

Name _____

Address _____

_____

Authorisation to Release Employment Information   Form E04

Date _____

To _____

_____

_____

Dear _____

I hereby authorise and request you to send the information ticked below to:

☐   the following party: _____

☐   any third party _____

The information to be released includes: (tick)

☐   Salary

☐   Position/department/section

☐   Date employment commenced

☐   Part-time/full-time or hours worked

☐   Garnishee orders or wage attachments, if any

☐   Reason for redundancy

☐   Medical/accident/illness reports

☐   Work performance rating

☐   Other:_____

Yours sincerely

Employee Signature _____

Print Name_____

Position or Title _____

Department _____

Authorisation to Release Medical Information   Form OLF09

Date _____

To _____

_____

_____

Dear _____

I hereby authorise and request that you release and deliver to: _____

_____

_____

_____

_____

all my medical records, files, charts, x-rays, laboratory reports, clinical records, and such other information concerning me that is in your possession. I would also request that you do not disclose any information concerning my past or present medical condition to any other person without my express written permission.

Yours sincerely

Signature _____

Printed Name _____

In the presence of

Witness's address _____

_____

Authorisation to Return Goods
Form BS06

Date _____

To _____

_____

_____

Dear _____

This letter is to confirm that we shall accept the return of certain goods we have supplied to you and credit your account. The terms for return are:

1. The value of the goods returned shall not exceed £ _____.

2. We shall deduct _____ % of the invoice value as a handling charge and credit your account with the balance.

3. All return goods shall be in a re-saleable condition and must be goods we either currently stock or can return to our supplier for credit. We reserve the right to refuse the return of goods that do not correspond with this description.

4. You shall be responsible for the costs of shipment and the risk of loss or damage in transit. Goods shall not be accepted for return until we have received, inspected and approved the goods at our place of business.

5. Our agreement to accept returns for credit is expressly conditional upon your agreement to settle any remaining balance due on the following terms: _____

_____

_____

Yours sincerely

_____

Health warning: Do not use this form if your customer has suggested that the goods are defective, or if he has purchased the goods in a consumer sale as to which see the notes to form BS03 above. This is to avoid you committing a breach of the Consumer Transactions (Restrictions on Statements) Order 1976 (as amended).

Board Resolution: Appointment of Auditors   Form C07

THE COMPANIES ACT 1985
PRIVATE COMPANY LIMITED BY SHARES
WRITTEN RESOLUTION OF THE BOARD OF DIRECTORS

Company Number: _____

_____ LIMITED

Pursuant to the Articles of Association of the Company, the undersigned, being all the directors of the company, hereby resolve:

THAT _____

of _____ be the auditors

of the Company with effect from _____ at a fee to be agreed.[1]

Directors' signatures: Date of each signature:

_____   _____

_____   _____

_____   _____

[1] Generally, the directors may appoint only the first auditors of the company who may hold office until the conclusion of the first general meeting at which accounts are presented to the members. The auditors must then be reappointed at this general meeting or, subject to the giving of special notice, an alternative auditor can be appointed by a resolution of the shareholders. The directors may also, however, fill any casual vacancy in the office of auditor – such appointment is only effective until the conclusion of the next general meeting at which accounts are presented to the shareholders. It should be noted that, in the case of private companies only, an elective resolution may be passed which removes the requirement for auditors to be reappointed annually. A copy of such a resolution must be reported to Companies House within 15 days of its being passed.

Many small private companies are exempt from having to appoint auditors.

Details of the exemptions and the requirements as to filing documents can be found on the Companies House website at www.companieshouse.gov.uk.

Board Resolution:
Approval and Registration of Transfer of Shares

THE COMPANIES ACT 1985
PRIVATE COMPANY LIMITED BY SHARES
WRITTEN RESOLUTION OF THE BOARD OF DIRECTORS

Company Number: _____

_____ LIMITED

Pursuant to the Articles of Association of the Company, the undersigned, being all the directors of the Company, hereby resolve:

THAT in accordance with the Company's Articles of Association and subject to its being presented with a duly stamped share transfer form the directors approve the transfer of _____ shares of _____ each from _____

to _____ on _____,

THAT the name of _____be entered in the register of members in respect of the shares transferred to him/her and THAT the Secretary be instructed to prepare a share certificate in respect of the shares transferred and to deliver it to _____

_____.[1]

Directors' signatures: Date of each signature:

_____   _____

_____   _____

_____   _____

---

[1] Check the articles - they may have a restriction on the transfer of shares. Table A places no restrictions on transfers of fully-paid shares. They may also allow the directors to refuse to register a transfer, although again Table A does not allow them to refuse to register the transfer of fully-paid shares. However, it does entitle the directors to require proof that the transferor is entitled to make the transfer (e.g. by requiring registration of the share certificate).

Board Resolution: Form C14
Approval of Directors' Report and Accounts

THE COMPANIES ACT 1985
PRIVATE COMPANY LIMITED BY SHARES
WRITTEN RESOLUTION OF THE BOARD OF DIRECTORS

Company Number: _____

_____ LIMITED

Pursuant to the Articles of Association of the Company, the undersigned, being all the directors of the Company, hereby resolve:

THAT the directors' report and accounts for the year ended _____

have been prepared in accordance with the Companies Act 1985[1] and are hereby approved, and _____

_____

be authorised to sign the report and the balance sheet on behalf of the Company.

Directors' signatures: Date of each signature:

_____   _____

_____   _____

_____   _____

Note: A director or two directors must sign the balance sheet. The directors' report must be signed by either a director or by the company secretary. Where different individuals sign, the resolution should be amended to reflect this. Any copy of the balance sheet and of the report which is laid before the general meeting of the company must state the name of the person who signed it on behalf of the company. Note that there are penalties for late filing of these documents. If yours is a 'small company' you may wish to check whether various possible exemptions for filing directors' reports and for abbreviating the company's accounts apply to your company.

[1] From 1 October 2007 the provisions of the Companies Act 2006 relating to accounts will be in force from which time you should refer to the provisions of the Companies Act 2006. You should check with Companies House to see to what extent any legislative requirements may be altered in the future with regard to the company's accounts and the filing of them.

Board Resolution:
Proposal of Alteration of Articles

Form C32

THE COMPANIES ACT 1985
PRIVATE COMPANY LIMITED BY SHARES
WRITTEN RESOLUTION OF THE BOARD OF DIRECTORS

Company Number: _____

_____ LIMITED

Pursuant to the Articles of Association of the Company the undersigned, being all the directors of the Company, hereby resolve:

THAT an [extraordinary general]/[A] meeting of the Company be convened[1] to authorise the alteration of the Articles as set out below

(1) By deletion of Articles _____

 and _____

 and altering the subsequent numbering accordingly.

(2) By the addition of the new Articles as set out in the attached document to be

 numbered _____

 and _____ .

Directors' signatures: Date of each signature:

_____   _____

_____   _____

_____   _____

[1] At present 21 clear days' notice must be given (i.e. not counting the day when notice is received or when the meeting is held); although in the case of a private company, the holders of 95 per cent of the shares which entitle the holder to attend the meeting may if they agree specify a shorter period of notice.

From 1 October 2007 only 14 days' notice will be required of any meeting of a private company unless it is proposed to pass a resolution requiring special notice, in which case 28 days' notice will be required. Although a 'special resolution' is required to alter the articles, 'special notice' is not required. Therefore, 14 days' notice will suffice for this purpose. Also, the holders of 90 percent of the voting shares will be able to consent to short notice of the meeting except where a resolution requiring special notice is to be considered. A special resolution requires a majority of 75 per cent. The company is required by law to keep copies of all board resolutions and all minutes Af general meetings for 10 years.

Board Resolution to Call [Annual] General Meeting   Form B04

_____ Limited

We, being all the directors of _____Limited

who are entitled to receive notice of a meeting of the directors, RESOLVE that an annual general meeting of

the Company shall be convened on the _____ day of _____ year _____ for the

following purposes: _____

_____

_____

_____

_____

_____

_____

_____

_____

and that the secretary be instructed to give notice of the meeting to all shareholders [and obtain the

consent of all members to the meeting being held on short notice].[1]

Dated this _____ day of _____ year _____

_____

Director's Signature

_____

Director's Signature

_____

Director's Signature

[1] 21 clear days' notice must be given (i.e. not counting the day when notice is received or when the meeting is held). If the meeting is
     to be held on short notice, add the wording in square brackets.

From 1 October 2007 private companies are no longer obliged to hold an annual general meeting. Whenever a meeting is to be held
only 14 days' notice will be required unless it is proposed to pass a resolution requiring special notice, in which case 28 days' notice will
be required. The form is retained because many companies will find it convenient to hold AGMs. Also, the holders of 90 percent of the
voting shares will be able to consent to short notice of the meeting except where a resolution requiring special notice is to be
considered. A special resolution requires a majority of 75 percent. The company is required by law to keep copies of all board
resolutions and all minutes of general meetings for 10 years.

Board Resolution to Call Extraordinary General Meeting

Form B05

_____ Limited

We, being all the directors of _____Limited
who are entitled to receive notice of a meeting of directors, RESOLVE that an extraordinary general meeting
of the company be convened forthwith for the purpose of considering and, if thought fit, passing the
following resolution(s) as (a) special resolution(s) or (an) ordinary resolution(s) as appropriate[1]: _____

_____

_____

_____

_____

_____

_____

[The Company Secretary be instructed to arrange to obtain the consent of the requisite majority of
members to the meeting being held on short notice.]

Dated this _____ day of _____ year _____

_____

Director's Signature

_____

Director's Signature

_____

Director's Signature

[1] 21 clear days' notice must be given (i.e. not counting the day when notice is received or when the meeting is held). If the meeting is
to be held on short notice then add the words in square brackets. The requisite majority is 95 per cent of the shareholders. Certain
types of resolution, for example to remove a director before the end of the term or to remove auditors, require 'special notice' of 28
days. Note that forms for these types of resolution are found elsewhere in this book.

From 1 October 2007 the distinction between annual general meetings and extraordinary general meetings will be abolished in the
case of private companies. For resolutions made after that date use form B04 instead of this form.

Breach of Contract Notice   Form OLF10

Date _____

To _____

_____

_____

Dear _____

We refer to the agreement between us dated _____, which provides that:

_____

_____

_____

PLEASE TAKE NOTE that you are in breach of your obligations under the agreement as follows: _____

_____

_____

_____

We invite you to remedy the breach by immediately taking steps to do the following: _____

_____

_____

_____

If you fail to remedy the breach as requested within 14 days of the date of this letter, such period being provided in clause _____ of the agreement, we shall have no alternative but to commence legal proceedings to claim damages from you as a result of the breach. We will also hold you liable for the costs of those proceedings.

Yours sincerely

Name _____

Address _____

_____

Note: Use this form if , but only if, you do not wish to put an end to the contract altogether. If you think it would be best to refuse to perform any more of your obligations under it, and to refuse to accept any further performance of it by the other party, you could deprive yourself of this option if you use this form. Remember, however that putting an end to a contract because of the other party's breach can be very risky, because if you are not entitled to end the contract, the other party will be able to claim against you for breach. Therefore, if you want to put an end to the contract, it is essential that you to consult a solicitor.

Builder/Decorator Contract   Form OLF11

DATED_____

BETWEEN

(1)   _____ of _____

      _____ (the 'Employer');

      and

(2)   _____ of _____

      _____(the 'Contractor').

NOW IT IS HEREBY AGREED :

1.   The Contractor shall carry out the Works as defined below ('the Works').

2.   The Works shall be[1] _____

      _____

      _____

      _____

      _____

      _____

      _____

      Any plans or specifications that form part of the description of the Works are attached, have been
      signed by both parties and form part of this Contract.

3.   The Works shall be carried out at_____('the Site')
      under the direction of _____(['the Foreman']/
      ['the Architect'] / ['the Surveyor'])*.

4.   The Employer shall pay to the Contractor for the Works £ _____ payable as follows:
      _____.

      or [The Contractor shall every ____ weeks during the course of this Contract submit to [the
      Foreman]/[the Architect]/[the Surveyor]* a claim for payment for the works thus far done and shall
      provide all documents which may be necessary to support the claim whereupon the Employer shall
      pay to the Contractor the amount certified by [the Foreman]/[the Architect]/[the Surveyor]* as being
      the value of the works done during the period to which the certificate relates. [_____ per cent of the
      said sum shall be retained for a period of 6 months following practical completion (as defined below)
      at which time the Employer shall pay the same to the Contractor subject to such deductions in respect
      of unremedied defects, not evident at the time of practical completion, as the Contractor and
      Employer may agree or as may be determined by a court or arbitrator]. For the purposes of this
      Contract 'Practical Completion' shall mean the apparent completion of the works (as amended in
      accordance with Clause 11 hereof)) without the presence of any evident omission or defect.]

Continued on next page

Builder/Decorator Contract (continued) Form OLF11

5. The Contractor shall begin the Works on or before _____ and shall complete the Works on or before _____ (the 'Completion Date') or such later date as may be determined under Clause 12 hereof. If the Works have not been completed by the Completion Date or later as aforesaid the Contractor shall pay or allow to the Employer £_____ for every_____ or part_____ between the Completion Date and the date of actual completion as liquidated damages which sum the parties agree is a reasonable pre-estimate of losses arising from such delay. The Contractor shall not, however, be responsible for delays outside his control and not reasonably foreseeable by him.

6. The_____ shall obtain every licence, permission or authority required for the exercise of the Works and the _____ shall pay all the fees or charges in respect of them.

7. In carrying out the Works, the Contractor shall use all reasonable skill, care and diligence, suitable good quality materials and comply with any higher specifications of materials or workmanship contained in the description of the Works and shall further comply with all applicable building regulations and other statutory provisions and shall at its own expense procure all appropriate certifications that such regulations have been complied with.

8. The Contractor shall take all reasonable precautions to minimise disruption and the risk of any loss or damage at the Site arising out of the execution of the Works. On completion of the Works the Contractor shall leave the Site clean and tidy to the reasonable satisfaction of the Employer and shall make good at his own cost all damage caused by execution of the Works.

9. The Contractor shall promptly make good any defects or faults which appear within six months of the date of actual completion and are due to materials or workmanship not being in accordance with this Contract entirely at his own expense insofar as the cost of such remedy may exceed the sum retained in accordance with Clause 4 hereof.

10. The Contractor shall be responsible for any loss or damage to the Site and any death or personal injury or damage to property arising out of the execution of the Works. The Contractor confirms that he has or will obtain adequate insurance (being not less than £_____) against any liability and will produce evidence of it to the Employer on request. The Works shall be at the Contractor's risk until completion. The [Employer]/[Contractor]*shall obtain and maintain throughout the period prior to Practical Completion, a policy of insurance in the joint names of the Contractor and the Employer against any damage to the Site as may be caused by fire, lightning, aircraft, explosion, earthquake, storm, flood, escape of water or oil, riot, malicious damage, theft or attempted theft (including theft of materials not fixed), falling trees and branches and aerials, subsidence, heave, landslip, collision, and accidental damage to underground services (such cover to include professional fees, demolition and site clearance costs). The nature of the Works and the periods during which the Site is likely to be unoccupied shall be disclosed in the proposal for the policy. Such policy shall require that sums paid

Continued on next page

Builder/Decorator Contract (continued)   Form OLF11

out thereunder shall be paid to the Employer.

11. The Employer shall be entitled to vary, delete or add to the Works. In the case of any such variation or addition the price of the Works shall be increased or decreased by a reasonable amount, taking into account the rates for which work is charged under this Contract.

12. If there shall be any variation of the Works under Clause 11 hereof or if there shall be any delay to the Works by reason of the occurrence of matters, which were not caused by any act or omission of the Contractor, or which the occurrence of which was not reasonably foreseeable by the Contractor, the date for practical completion of the Works shall be extended by such reasonable period as [the Foreman]/[the Architect]/[the Surveyor]* _____ shall determine.

IN WITNESS OF WHICH the parties hereto have signed this Agreement the day and year first above written.

SIGNED   _____

Signed by or on behalf of the Contractor   in the presence of (witness)

Name   _____

Address   _____

_____

Dated   _____   Occupation   _____

SIGNED   _____

Signed by the Employer _____   in the presence of (witness)

Name   _____

Address   _____

_____

Dated   _____   Occupation   _____

Note that this contract should only be used where the contractor has engaged the builder to work on his residence.

¹ It may be desirable to price each item separately.

*Delete as appropriate.

Builders' Work Complaint   Form GS03

Date _____

To _____

_____

_____

Ref Estimate No. _____

Dear _____

You carried out building work at the following address: _____

_____

as per the above estimate finishing on: _____.

I am writing to inform you that the work has proved to be defective in the following manner: _____

_____

_____

_____

[The terms of our Contract] or [The Supply of Goods and Services Act 1982 and the common law]* requires that you should have completed the work with reasonable skill and care using appropriate materials of suitable quality. The defects described above clearly indicate that you have not fulfilled your legal obligations and that you are in breach of contract.

While reserving my rights, I am giving you the opportunity to carry out remedial repairs free of charge. Failing that I will obtain quotations from other builders and will have them carry out the work, claiming any expenses incurred from you as I am entitled to do by law.

I look forward to hearing from you within seven days.

Yours sincerely

Signature _____

Name _____

Address _____

_____

Tel. _____

* Delete as appropriate

Cancellation of an Order to Stop a Cheque   Form OLF12

Date _____

To _____

_____

_____

Dear _____

On _____ ,
we requested you to stop payment on the following cheque that we issued:

Cheque No: _____

Dated: _____

Amount: _____

Payable to: _____

Account No: _____

We have now advised the payee to re-present the cheque for payment, and we should be grateful if you would now honour the cheque on re-presentation.

Yours sincerely

Signature _____

Account _____

Account No. _____

Certificate of Product Conformity   Form BS07

_____ Ltd

To:				Order No:	
				Ref No:	
FAO:				Date:	
Product ID	Qty	Description	Spec no.	Model no	Test reports

This certifies that all of the above goods have been inspected, tested and unless otherwise stated conform in all respects to the order requirements.

Signed _____

Customer Services Manager

Change of Name Deed   Form PF19

THIS DEED (which is intended to be enrolled at the Central Office of the Supreme Court) is made by me [formerly] [now] called _____ ¹ of _____ this_____day of_____20__

WITNESSES AND IT IS HEREBY DECLARED

1   I am a [Commonwealth citizen]/[British citizen]/[British Overseas Territories Citizen]/[British Overseas Citizen [under section _____ of the British Nationality Act 1981]²

2   I absolutely renounce and abandon the use of my former name of _____ and assume adopt and determine to take and use the name of _____ ³

3   I authorise and require all persons at all times to refer to describe and address me as

    _____

4   I declare that I am [single]/[married]/[divorced]/[a widow[er]/[a civil partner]/[[a former civil partner under a civil partnership which has ended by [death][dissolution]]

[5 [I confirm that the forenames which I am renouncing and the use of which I am abandoning in this Deed have not been conferred upon me in a ceremony of baptism] [Although the change of name herein effected involves the change of forenames, which were conferred upon me in a ceremony of baptism, I confirm that I have decided to use my new forenames in place of my former forenames, notwithstanding the decision of. Mr. Justice Vaisey in *re Parrott*]]⁴

SIGNED AS A DEED AND DELIVERED:

By the above-named:

Formerly known as:

In the presence of

Name :_____

Address:_____

Name:_____

Address;_____

Continued on next page

Change of Name Deed (continued)   Form PF19

[I, _____ of _____address hereby certify that I am the [husband]/[wife]/[civil partner] of the above-mentioned _____ ⁵ and that I hereby consent to the Change of Name effected by this Deed from _____ ⁶ to _____ ⁷ and to the enrolment of this Deed in the Central Office of the Supreme Court.

Signed _____

In the presence of:

Name _____

Address _____

Name _____

Address_____] ⁸

Note: As long as you do not use a name for a dishonest purpose, you may use any name that you wish and you do not need to execute any document in order to do so. There is no magic in a Deed Poll. A Deed Poll, however, can provide evidence of your change of name which may be useful if you wish to have dealings in a name other than the one on your birth certificate, and it may be essential for certain official purposes. The most persuasive evidence of change of name is a Deed Poll which has been registered in the Central Office of the High Court in London. In order for such a Deed to be capable of registration, it will need to contain the details in this form. When you apply to register your Deed Poll, you will also need to submit various other documents, as set out in the Enrolment of Deeds (Change of Name) Regulations 1994 (SI 1994/604) as amended by The Enrolment of Deeds (Change of Name) (Amendment) Regulations 2005 (SI 2005/2056). These are available on the government website www.opsi.gov.uk.

You will be very unlikely to need a Deed Poll at all if the only reason why you are changing your name is that you are a woman and are changing your surname to that of your husband. Your marriage certificate will suffice.

If you are married or in a civil partnership, you will need the consent of your spouse or civil partner in order for your Deed Poll to be registered.

If you are registering a change of name for a child you should certainly consult a solicitor.

¹ Insert name you are changing from.

² Omit the reference to the British Nationality Act if you are a Commonwealth Citizen, and are not a British Citizen, British Overseas Territories Citizen or British Overseas Citizen. If you were born before 1st January 1983 and were a Citizen of the United Kingdom and Colonies and had the right to live in the UK as of that date without any restriction of the time you could remain there, insert 'Section 11'. Insert 'Section 1' if you were born on or after 1st January 1983 and were born in the UK and your father or mother was a British citizen or ordinarily resident in the UK without any restriction on the period he or she could remain there. If none of the foregoing applies to you, or if you are uncertain about it, consult a solicitor.

³ Insert new name.

⁴ Omit this clause if you are changing only your surname.

⁵ Insert old name.

⁶ Insert old name.

⁷ Insert new name.

⁸ Delete this section if you are not married or in a civil partnership.

Change in Pay or Grading Following Job Evaluation Form E05

Date _____

To _____

_____

_____

Dear _____

Following our job evaluation review it has been decided to upgrade your job title to _____
_____with effect from
_____

From that date your salary will be increased to £ _____ per _____.

All other terms and conditions of your employment remain unchanged.

We offer our congratulations on your promotion, and hope that you enjoy your new position.

Yours sincerely

_____

Change in Sales Representative Agreement   Form E06

Date _____

To _____

_____

_____

Dear _____

I refer to the sales representative agreement between us dated _____ ,
a copy of which is attached.

This letter acknowledges that the agreement is modified and superseded by the following agreed change in
terms: _____

_____

_____

_____

All other terms shall remain as stated.

Please sign below to indicate your acceptance of the modified terms.

Yours sincerely

_____

_____

Company

I agree to the above modification:

_____

Sales Representative

Note: Changes in the terms of the engagement of a commercial agent should be by true consent and should not be imposed, in case the
agent is able to say that the change amounted to a repudiation of the agency agreement, therefore entitling him to compensation under
the Commercial Agents (Council Directive) Regulations 1993. The principal should therefore be careful to preserve correspondence
evidencing such consent, and should keep a memorandum detailing how the change was for the benefit of both parties.

Change of Address Notice   Form PF01

Date _____

To _____

_____

_____

Dear _____

Please note that as from _____, our address will change from:

_____

_____

_____

to

_____

_____

_____

Our new telephone number will be _____

and fax number _____

Please make note of the above information and direct all future correspondence to us at our new address. Thank you.

Yours sincerely

_____

Child Guardianship Consent Form   Form PF02

I _____ ,

of _____ ,

hereby appoint _____ ,

of _____ , _____ ,

as the legal guardian of my child(ren). The guardian shall have the following powers:_____

_____

_____

_____

_____

_____

_____

_____

_____

_____

_____

Signed this _____ day of _____ , year _____.

_____

_____

Heath warning: You should take legal advice when appointing a guardian for your children and this form will enable you to give instructions to your solicitor more efficiently.

Cohabitation Agreement (for Unmarried Partners)   Form PF03

THIS DEED OF AGREEMENT is made the _____ day of _____ year _____

BETWEEN:

(1) _____ of _____ ('the First Party'); and

(2) _____ of _____ ('the Second Party').

WHEREAS:

(a)   The Parties live together and wish to enter this Agreement to set out their rights and responsibilities towards each other.

(b)   The Parties intend that this Agreement will be legally binding on them.

1.   OWNERSHIP OF THE HOME

The Parties [live]/[are about to live] at the address given above ('the Home') which is a property [about to be] purchased in their joint names/in the sole name of the First/Second Party*.

2.   DIVISION OF PROCEEDS OF SALE OF THE HOME

Where the Home is owned in joint names:

Option 1:   The rights and interests of the Parties in the Home and its net proceeds of sale are set out in a Declaration of Trust dated _____ and are not in any way varied or affected by this Deed.

Option 2:   The Parties agree that they shall hold the beneficial interest in the Home:

as tenants in common in equal shares.

[Before any division of the proceeds is made the parties shall each receive out of the said proceeds the sums which they have respectively contributed out of their own resources (such sums not to bear interest) and if the net proceeds of sale shall be insufficient to enable the parties to recover the entirety of their said contributions they shall each receive such proportion of the same as their respective contributions bear to the totality of the contributions made until the net proceeds shall have been exhausted.]

OR

as to _____ % for the First Party and as to _____ % for the Second Party.

OR

in the proportions in which they contribute to the purchase of the Home whether by contribution to the purchase price, payment of mortgage instalments and mortgage-linked endowment premiums, or by way of improvements which add to the value of the Home (and if the Parties cannot agree the value of any such improvements the value shall be determined by a valuer appointed by the President of the Royal Institution of Chartered Surveyors).

Where the Home is owned in the sole name of one Party:

Option 3:   The Parties agree that they shall hold the beneficial interest in the Home:

as tenants in common in equal shares

[Before any division of the proceeds is made the parties shall each receive out of the said proceeds the sums which they have respectively contributed out of their own resources

(*delete as appropriate)

Continued on next page

Cohabitation Agreement (for Unmarried Partners) (cont) Form PF03

(such sums not to bear interest) and if the net proceeds of sale shall be insufficient to enable the parties to recover the entirety of their said contributions they shall each receive such proportion of the same as their respective contributions bear to the totality of the contributions made until the net proceeds shall have been exhausted].

OR

as to _____ % for the First Party and as to _____ % for the Second Party.

OR

in the proportions in which they contribute to the purchase of the Home whether by contribution to the purchase price, payment of mortgage instalments and mortgage-linked endowment premiums, or by way of improvements which add to the value of the Home (and if the Parties cannot agree the value of any such improvements the value shall be determined by a valuer appointed by the President of the Royal Institution of Chartered Surveyors).

Option 4:   The Parties agree that the First/Second* Party is the sole beneficial owner of the Home and that regardless of contributions to the purchase maintenance or improvement of the Home the other Party is not and will not acquire any beneficial interest in the Home or in its proceeds of sale.

3.   CONTENTS AND PERSONAL BELONGINGS

Any household and personal item shall be owned:

Option 1:   Entirely by the Party who acquired it (whether by inheritance, gift, purchase or otherwise).

Option 2:   By both Parties equally (regardless of when or by whom it was acquired) unless the Parties expressly agree otherwise in writing provided however that any items used exclusively by one of the parties shall belong entirely to that party. Unless the Parties shall agree otherwise within one month of the date of termination of this Agreement all jointly owned items shall be sold and the net proceeds of sale divided equally between them.

4.   BANK OR BUILDING SOCIETY ACCOUNTS

It is agreed that:

Option 1:   The Parties do not intend to open a joint account. Each Party shall maintain separate bank or building society accounts and the money in each account will remain his or her separate property.

Option 2:   The Parties shall maintain a joint bank or building society account ('The Joint Account'). The Parties shall pay into the Joint Account sums sufficient to meet their agreed share of common expenses (referred to in clause 5). The money in the Joint Account shall belong to the Parties in equal shares regardless of the actual sums which either of them may have paid into or withdrawn from the Joint Account. Any money in any bank or building society account maintained separately by either Party shall belong to that Party alone. Any investments purchased with monies in the joint account shall belong to the parties in equal shares.

(*delete as appropriate)

Continued on next page

Cohabitation Agreement (for Unmarried Partners) (cont) Form PF03

5. COMMON EXPENSES

Common household expenditure including mortgage repayments, mortgage-linked endowment premiums, ground rent, service charges, rental payments, buildings and household insurance premiums, council or other local taxes, charges for water rates, gas, electricity, telephone, television licence and rental, food, decoration and repairs shall be:

Option 1:   paid by the First/Second* Party alone.

Option 2:   shared equally by the Parties.

Option 3:   paid as to _____ % by the first Party and as to _____ % by the Second Party.

Unless otherwise agreed in writing, the rights of the parties shall not be affected by any excess or shortfall which may occur in respect of such payments whilst the parties are cohabiting. If they should cease to cohabit and if either party shall pay more than his or her share of the above, he or she shall be entitled to be credited in respect of the excess and the other party shall be debited for the same, but such credit or debit shall not attract interest. Any entitlement to such credit is without prejudice to any entitlement which a party who has left the Home might have for the payment of an occupation rent by the party who remains in residence.

6. VARIATION/TERMINATION

This Agreement shall be varied only by written agreement of the Parties. This Agreement shall terminate by written agreement of the Parties or upon the death or marriage of either one of them or upon the Party's separation for a period exceeding three months following which [the Home] [and any property owned jointly or in common by the parties] shall be valued and either sold and the proceeds divided, either Party being at liberty to buy the Home.

SIGNED AS A DEED

by the said   _____

Name   _____

in the presence of

Signature _____

Name   _____

Address_____

SIGNED AS A DEED

by the said _____

Name _____

in the presence of

Signature _____

Name _____

Address _____

Health Warning: This form should only be used in order to enable you to put down your thoughts so that you can instruct a solicitor or licensed conveyancer more quickly and cheaply. On no account should anyone make a cohabitation agreement without the assistance of a solicitor or licensed conveyancer. This is because any court which is later asked to enforce such an agreement will need to be satisfied that the agreement was not obtained by the misuse of the trust and confidence which one party placed in the other; or (worse still) that the agreement was gained through the use of pressure. Taking independent advice from a solicitor or licensed conveyancer will help to ensure that the agreement is fair, that the often complicated circumstances of the parties are taken properly into account and that it is less open to legal challenge. It will also ensure that various possible complications (e.g. who is to live at the property prior to its being sold and for how long) can be thought through and provided for.

The form of ownership provided for in these forms does not allow for one party's share to be inherited by the other party upon death. **It is essential that you make a Will disposing of your property, especially your interest in the home. Note there is no automatic transfer upon death of your property to a partner to whom you are not married or in a civil partnership with, no matter how long you may have lived together.**

Note: Clauses in square brackets should be deleted as appropriate and both Parties should initial the deletion.

Company Let
(For a Furnished or Unfurnished House or Flat)

Form RT01

The PROPERTY _____

_____

The LANDLORD _____

_____

_____

The TENANT _____LIMITED/PLC

whose Registered Office is at _____

_____

_____

_____(Company Registration No._____)

The TERM _____ months beginning on

_____

⎡ Subject to the right for either party at any time during the Term to end this

Agreement earlier by giving to the other written notice of _____

week(s)/month(s)* ⎤

The RENT £ _____ per week/month* payable in advance on the _____ of each

week/month*

The DEPOSIT £ _____

⎡ The INVENTORY means the list of the Landlord's possessions at the Property which has been signed by

the Landlord and the Tenant   (delete if unfurnished) ⎤

DATED _____   _____

SIGNED _____   _____

_____   _____

(The Landlord)   (Director/Secretary for and on

behalf of The Tenant)

THIS AGREEMENT comprises the particulars detailed above and the terms and conditions printed overleaf
whereby the Property is hereby let by the Landlord and taken by the Tenant for the Term at the Rent.

Terms and Conditions on next page

(*delete as appropriate)

Company Let Terms & Conditions   Form RT01

1. The Tenant will:
   1.1 pay the Rent at the times and in the manner aforesaid without any deduction abatement or set-off whatsoever
   1.2 pay all charges in respect of any electric, gas, water and telephonic or televisual services used at or supplied to the Property and Council Tax or any similar property tax that might be charged in addition to or replacement of it
   1.3 keep the interior of the Property in a good, clean and tenantable state and condition and not damage or injure the Property or any part of it
   1.4 yield up the Property at the end of the Term in the same clean state and condition it was in at the beginning of the Term and if any item listed on the Inventory requires repair, replacing, cleaning or laundering pay for the same (fair wear and tear and damage by fire or similar catastrophes not caused by the Tenant excepted).
   1.5 maintain at the Property and keep in a good and clean condition all of the items listed in the Inventory
   1.6 not make any alteration or addition to the Property nor without the Landlord's prior written consent to do any redecoration or painting of the Property
   1.7 not do or omit to do anything on or at the Property which may be or become a nuisance or annoyance to any other occupiers of the property or owners or occupiers of adjoining or nearby premises or which may in any way prejudice the insurance of the Property or cause an increase in the premium payable therefore
   1.8 not without the Landlord's prior written consent allow or keep any pet or any kind of animal at the Property
   1.9 not use or occupy the Property in any way whatsoever other than as a private residence
   1.10 not assign, sublet, charge or part with or share possession or occupation of the Property or any part thereof provided however that the Tenant may permit the residential occupation of the Property as a whole by the Tenant's officers and employees, so long as the Tenant continues to be responsible for the Rent and all other outgoings and does not make any charge whatsoever in respect of the same to the occupier and no relationship of landlord and tenant is created or allowed to arise between the tenant and the occupier and provided further that the Landlord's prior written consent (not to be unreasonably withheld) is obtained to each such occupier
   1.11 allow the Landlord or anyone with the Landlord's written permission to enter the Property at reasonable times of the day to inspect its condition and state of repair, carry out any necessary repairs and gas inspections, or during the last month of the term, show the Property to prospective new tenants, provided the Landlord has given reasonable prior notice (except in emergency)
   1.12 pay interest at the rate of 4% above the Base Lending Rate for the time being of the Landlord's bankers upon any Rent or other money due from the Tenant under this Agreement which is more than 3 days in arrears in respect of the period from when it became due to the date of payment

2. Subject to the Tenant paying the rent and performing his/her obligations under this Agreement the Tenant may peaceably hold and enjoy the Property during the term without interruption from the Landlord or any person rightfully claiming under or in trust for the Landlord

3. The Landlord will:
   3.1 keep in repair the structure and exterior of the Property (including drains gutters and external pipes)
   3.2 keep in repair and proper working order the installations at the property for the supply of water, gas and electricity and for sanitation (including basins, sinks, baths and sanitary conveniences)
   3.3 keep in repair and proper working order the installations at the Property for space heating and heating water

But the Landlord will not be required to:
   3.4 carry out works for which the Tenant is responsible by virtue of his/her duty to use the Property in a tenant-like manner
   3.5 rebuild or reinstate the Property in the case of destruction or damage by fire or by tempest flood or other inevitable accident

4. In the event of the Rent being unpaid for more than 10 days after it is due (whether demanded

Continued on next page

Company Let Terms & Conditions (continued)   Form RT01

or not) or there being a breach of any other of the Tenant's obligations under this Agreement or the Tenant entering into liquidation or having a receiver or administrative receiver appointed then the Landlord may re-enter the Property and this Agreement shall thereupon determine absolutely but without prejudice to any of the Landlord's other rights and remedies in respect of any outstanding obligations on the part of the Tenant. Note: The Landlord cannot recover possession under this clause without a court order while anyone is living at the property

5. The Deposit

    5.1   The Deposit will be held by the Landlord and will be refunded to the Tenant at the end of the Term (however it ends) at the forwarding address provided to the Landlord but less any reasonable deductions properly made by the Landlord to cover any reasonable costs incurred or losses caused to him by any breaches of the obligations in his Agreement by the Tenant. No interest will be payable to the Tenant in respect of the Deposit money

    5.2   The Deposit shall be re-payable to the Tenant as soon as reasonably practicable, however the Landlord shall not be bound to return the Deposit until after he has had a reasonable opportunity to assess the reasonable cost of any repairs required as a result of any breaches of his obligations by the Tenant or other sums properly due to the Landlord under clause 5.1 However, the Landlord shall not, save in exceptional circumstances, retain the Deposit for more than one month after the end of the tenancy

    5.3   If at any time during the Term the Landlord is obliged to deduct from the Deposit to satisfy the reasonable costs occasioned by any breaches of the obligations of the Tenant the Tenant shall make such additional payments as are necessary to restore the full amount of the Deposit

6. The Landlord hereby notifies the Tenant under Section 48 of the Landlord & Tenant Act 1987 that any notices (including notices in proceedings) should be served upon the Landlord at the address stated with the name of the Landlord overleaf

7. In the event of damage to or destruction of the Property by fire or any other catastrophe not caused by the Tenant the Tenant shall be relieved from payment of the Rent to the extent that the Tenant's use and enjoyment of the Property is thereby prevented and from performance of its obligations as to the state and condition of the Property to the extent of and so long as there prevails such damage or destruction.

8. So long as the reference to a right of early termination in the definition of the 'TERM' overleaf (the 'early termination right') has not been deleted then either party may at any time during the Term terminate this Agreement by giving to the other prior written notice to that effect, the length of such notice to be that stated in the early termination right, and upon the expiry of said notice this Agreement shall end with no further liability of either party save for any antecedent breach

9. Where the context so admits:

    9.1   The 'Landlord' includes the persons for the time being entitled to the reversion expectant upon this Tenancy

    9.2   The 'Tenant' includes any persons deriving title under the Tenant

    9.3   The 'Property' includes all of the Landlord's fixtures and fittings at or upon the Property

    9.4   The 'Term' shall mean the period stated in the particulars overleaf or any shorter or longer period in the event of an earlier termination or an extension or holding over respectively

10. All references to the singular shall include the plural and vice versa and any obligations or liabilities of more than one person shall be joint and several and an obligation on the part of a party shall include an obligation not to allow or permit the breach of that obligation

Concession Note (Seller's - Where Bulk Goods do not Conform to Description or Sample)

Form E05

_____Ltd

To _____Ltd   Concession Note No _____

_____

_____   Customer Order No _____

Please indicate whether or not you accept the concession for material/product non-conformity described below by completing this form and returning it to us as soon as possible. We will only despatch goods upon receipt of your approval. PLEASE NOTE THAT A REFUSAL TO APPROVE DOES NOT AFFECT YOUR STATUTORY RIGHTS.

Product Code   Product Description

Details of [alleged] non-conformity   _____

Description of goods now proposed
 to be supplied   _____

Details of Concession offered   _____

                                      _____

                                      _____

Customer Service Officer

In consideration of the concession, we are prepared to accept goods of the description appearing above in substitution for those originally ordered and in full satisfaction of any claims which we may have in respect of the order.

Name _____   Position _____

Signed _____   Date _____

Confidentiality Agreement   Form E08

THIS AGREEMENT is made the _____ day of _____ year _____

BETWEEN:

(1) _____(the 'Company'); and

(2) _____ (the 'Employee').

WHEREAS:

(A) The Company agrees to give the Employee access to certain confidential information relating to the affairs of the Company solely for purposes of: _____

_____

_____

_____

_____

_____

(B) The Employee agrees to obtain, inspect and use such information only for the purposes described above, and otherwise to hold such information confidential and secret pursuant to the terms of this agreement.

[(C) The Employee and the Company are in discussions with a view to the possible future employment of the Employee by the Company, and in consideration of the Company entering into such discussions and in further consideration of the payment to the Employee by the Company of the sum of one pound, the Employee has agreed to give the undertakings hereinafter contained.]

NOW IT IS HEREBY AGREED as follows:

1.   The Company has or shall furnish to the Employee confidential information ('Information'), described on the attached list, and may further allow suppliers, customers, employees or representatives of the Company to furnish such information to the Employee. Such Information includes but is not limited to the information described on the attached list attached hereto. It also includes any confidential or proprietory information, trade secrets and Information about the Company's customers, suppliers and employees which may be furnished to the Employee.

The Employee agrees to hold all such Information in trust and confidence and agrees that the Information shall be used only for the contemplated purpose, and not for any other.

2.   No copies may be made or retained of the Information without the Company's written consent.

3.   [If the discussions between the Employee and the Company shall conclude without the Employee being employed by the Company or] upon demand by the Company, all Information, including written notes, photographs, or memoranda containing the same shall be promptly returned to the Company. The Employee shall retain no copies or written documentation relating thereto.

4.   This Information shall not be disclosed to any third party, whether or not an employee of the Company, unless the third party agrees to execute and be bound by the terms of this agreement, and disclosure is first approved by the Company in writing.

Continued on next page

Confidentiality Agreement (continued)

Form E08

5. The Employee shall have no obligation with respect to any information known by the Employee, or generally known within the industry prior to date of this agreement, or that shall become common knowledge within the industry thereafter, or which the Employee is entitled to disclose pursuant to the Public Interest Disclosure Act 1998.

6. The Employee acknowledges the Information disclosed herein contains proprietary or trade secrets and in the event of any breach, the Company shall be entitled to apply for injunctive relief and to claim for damages of breach.

7. This agreement shall be binding upon and inure to the benefit of the parties, their successors and assigns.

8. This constitutes the entire agreement between the parties. Any amendments to this agreement shall only be valid if both parties confirm such amendments in writing.

IN WITNESS OF WHICH the parties have signed this agreement the day and year first above written

Signed for and on behalf of the Company by

_____

Director

_____

Director/Secretary

_____

Signed by or on behalf of the Employee

_____

in the presence of (witness)

Name _____

Address _____

_____

Occupation _____

Note: The matters arising in respect of an employee or an independent consultant with regard to confidentiality are often very similar. It is suggested that you examine Form E12 to see if any of the clauses in that form may usefully be added or substituted for those in this form.

Confirmation of Agreement to Pay | Form CDC06

Date _____

To _____

_____

_____

Dear _____

We send you this letter to confirm our agreement, made on _____,
that you will pay your overdue balance of £ _____ according to the following terms:

_____

_____

_____

If this letter does not conform to our agreement, please inform us immediately.

We understand your financial difficulties and, to accommodate you, will accept payments on these extended terms provided each payment is punctually made when due. If any of the payments now agreed to be made by you are not met in full on or before the date specified above (time being of the essence) the entire sums outstanding shall immediately be due and payable.

Whilst this balance remains outstanding we shall supply you on a cash on delivery basis.

We are pleased this matter could be resolved on terms satisfactory to us both, and we look forward to your payments and continued business.

Please indicate your agreement to the above by signing and returning to us a copy of this letter.

Yours sincerely

_____

Note: Do not use this form where the original agreement is regulated by the Consumer Credit Act 1974.

Confirmation of Verbal Order   Form BS09

Date _____

To   _____

      _____

      _____

Dear _____

This letter confirms our verbal order of _____.

A copy of our confirmatory purchase order containing the stated terms is enclosed as order

no.: _____

Please confirm in writing by return that the confirmatory purchase order accurately records our agreement.

Thank you for your cooperation.

Yours sincerely

_____

Conflict of Interest Declaration   Form E09

Employee   _____

Company   _____
           _____

I acknowledge that I have read the Company policy statement concerning conflicts of interest and I hereby declare that neither I, nor any other person to which I may be connected as set out in the Companies Act 2006 section 252 to 254, has any conflict of interest with the Company as would constitute a violation of that Company policy. Furthermore, I declare that during my employment, I shall continue to maintain my affairs in accordance with the requirements of the Company policy and to disclose any conflict of interest which may arise between the Company and any person with whom or with which I may be connected.

_____

Employee's Signature

_____

Date

Consent to Release of Information   Form E11

To _____

From Personnel Office

A request for certain employment information concerning you has been received from: _____

_____

_____

_____

_____

Please tick below those items of information that you permit us to disclose.

☐   Salary

☐   Position

☐   Department

☐   Supervisor

☐   Health records

☐   Dates of employment

☐   Hours worked

☐   Wage attachments

☐   Reason for redundancy

☐   Other:

_____

_____

_____

Employee Signature _____   Date _____

Please return this form to the Personnel Office as soon as possible. Your consent on this occasion will not constitute a consent to release information on future occasions.

Consent to Short Notice of an Annual General Meeting   Form B01

_____ Limited

We, the undersigned, being all members for the time being of the company having the right to attend and vote at the Annual General Meeting of such company convened to be held at _____

_____

_____ on the _____ day of _____ year ____

(the attached notice being the notice convening the meeting), hereby agree:

[a)][1] in accordance with section [369(3) of the Companies Act 1985][2] [307 of the Companies Act 2006] of the

Companies Act 1985 to the holding of such meeting notwithstanding that less than the statutory

period of notice thereof has been given; [and

b)   to accept service of documents in accordance with section 238(1) of the Companies Act 1985

notwithstanding that the documents were sent less than 21 days before the meeting.][3]

Dated this _____ day of _____ year ____.

_____

Member's signature

_____

Member's signature

_____

Member's signature

_____

Member's signature

Note: From 1 October 2007 private companies are no longer obliged to hold an annual general meeting. Whenever a meeting is to be held only 14 days' notice will be required unless it is proposed to pass a resolution requiring special notice, in which case 28 days' notice will be required. The form is retained because many companies will find it convenient to hold AGMs. Also, the holders of 90 percent of the voting shares will be able to consent to short notice of the meeting except where a resolution requiring special notice is to be considered. A special resolution requires a majority of 75 percent. The company is required by law to keep copies of all board resolutions and all minutes of general meetings for 10 years.

[1] Delete from 1 October 2007.

[2] Delete from 1 October 2007.

[3] Delete from 1 October 2007.

Consent to Short Notice of an Extraordinary General Meeting

Form B02

_____ Limited

We, the undersigned, being a majority in number of the members of the company holding not less than [95 per cent] [90 per cent]¹ of the issued share capital having a right to attend and vote at the Extraordinary General Meeting of the said company convened by a Notice of Meeting dated _____ year _____ and to be held on _____ year _____, hereby agree to the holding of such meeting and to the proposing and passing of the special resolutions on the day and at the time and place set out in such Notice, notwithstanding that less than the statutory period of the Notice thereof has been given to us.

Dated this _____ day of _____ year ___.

_____

Member's signature

_____

Member's signature

_____

Member's signature

_____

Member's signature

Note: From 1 October 2007 the distinction between AGMs and EGMs for private companies will be abolished. This form may be retained because companies may find it convenient to hold AGMs and to distinguish between those meetings and other meetings. Also, the holders of 90 percent of the voting shares will be able to consent to short notice of the meeting except where a resolution requiring special notice is to be considered.

¹ Delete '95 per cent' from 1 October 2007.

Consultant Non-Disclosure Agreement   Form E12

THIS AGREEMENT is made the _____ day of _____ year _____

BETWEEN:

(1) _____ of _____ (the 'Client'); and

(2) _____ of _____ (the 'Consultant').

WHEREAS the Client and the Consultant are in negotiations with a view to the Client retaining the Consultant as an outside Consultant and in the course of such negotiations the Client may furnish the Consultant with certain information that is confidential as hereinafter defined AND WHEREAS the Consultant in consideration of the Client taking part in such negotiations and in the further consideration of the payment to the Consultant by the Client of the sum of one pound (receipt of which the Consultant hereby acknowledges) the Consultant has agreed to make the warranties, representations, agreements and to enter into the covenants hereinafter set out.

NOW the Consultant hereby warrants, represents, covenants, and agrees as follows:

1. **Engagement.** The Consultant, prior to and in the course of engagement by the Client, may or will have access to or learn certain information belonging to the Client that is proprietary and confidential (Confidential Information).

2. **Definition of Confidential Information.** Confidential Information as used throughout this agreement means any secret or proprietary information relating directly to the Client's business and that of the Client's affiliated companies and subsidiaries, including, but not limited to, products, customer lists, pricing policies, employment records and policies, operational methods, marketing plans and strategies, product development techniques or plans, business acquisition plans, new personnel acquisition plans, methods of manufacture, technical processes, designs and design projects, inventions and research programs, trade 'know-how,' trade secrets, specific software, algorithms, computer processing systems, object and source codes, user manuals, systems documentation, and other business affairs of the Client and its affiliated companies and subsidiaries.

3. **Non-disclosure.** The Consultant agrees to keep strictly confidential all Confidential Information and will not, without the Client's express written authorisation, signed by one of the Client's authorised officers, use, sell, market, or disclose any Confidential Information to any third person, firm, corporation, or association for any purpose, other than to the Consultants employees and advisors for the purpose of the conduct of negotiations with the Client or the discharge of its duties to the Client. The Consultant further agrees not to make any copies of any documents (whether in written or machine readable form) containing the Confidential Information except upon the Client's written authorisation, signed by one of the Client's authorised officers, namely _____ and will not remove any copy or sample of Confidential Information from the premises of the Client without such authorisation, save for the purpose of communicating the same to its employees or advisors for the purposes aforesaid. The Consultant will not disclose any information or provide any copies of documents as aforesaid to such persons without first having procured the signature of such person to a copy of this agreement and without having delivered the same to the Client. The Consultant shall be liable to the Client for any

Continued on next page

Consultant Non-Disclosure Agreement (cont)   Form E12

loss or damage caused by any use made of the information by any person to whom the Consultant may have disclosed information or provided copies as aforesaid.

4. **Return of Material.** Upon receipt of a written request from the Client, the Consultant will return to the Client all copies of documents and all samples or other items from which confidential information can be acquired that, at the time of the receipt of the notice, are in the Consultant's possession.

5. **Obligations Continue Past Term.** The obligations imposed on the Consultant shall continue with respect to each item of the Confidential Information following the termination of the business relationship between the Consultant and the Client, and such obligations shall not terminate until such item shall cease to be secret and confidential and shall be in the public domain, unless such event shall have occurred as a result of wrongful conduct by the Consultant or the Consultant's advisers agents, servants, officers, or employees or a breach of the covenants set forth in this agreement.

6. **Equitable Relief.** The Consultant acknowledges and agrees that a breach of the provisions of Paragraph 3 or 4 of this Agreement would cause the Client to suffer irreparable damage that could not be adequately remedied by an action at law. Accordingly, the Consultant agrees that the Client shall have the right to seek specific performance of the provisions of Paragraph 3 to enjoin a breach or attempted breach of the provision thereof, such right being in addition to all other rights and remedies that are available to the Client at law, in equity, or otherwise.

7. **Invalidity.** If any provision of this agreement or its application is held to be invalid, illegal, or unenforcable in any respect, the validity, legality, or enforceability of any of the other provisions and applications therein shall not in any way be affected or impaired.

IN WITNESS OF WHICH the parties have signed this agreement the day and year first above written

_____   _____

Signed by or on behalf of the Client   Signed by or on behalf of the Consultant

_____   _____

in the presence of (witness)   in the presence of (witness)

Name _____   Name _____

Address _____   Address _____

_____   _____

Occupation _____   Occupation _____

Note: The matters arising in respect of an independent consultant and of an employee with regard to confidentiality are often very similar. It is suggested that you examine form E08 to see if any of the clauses in that form may usefully be added or substituted for those in this form.

Contract for the Sale of Goods by Delivery   Form BS10

THIS AGREEMENT is made the _____ day of _____ year _____

BETWEEN:

(1) _____(the 'Seller'); and

(2) _____(the 'Buyer').

NOW IT IS HEREBY AGREED as follows:

1. In consideration for the payment of £ _____ (the 'Purchase Price'), on the terms set out below, the Seller agrees to sell and the Buyer agrees to buy the following goods (the 'Goods'):

    _____

    _____

2. The Buyer agrees to pay the Purchase Price and the Seller agrees to accept such payment on the following terms:_____

    _____

    _____

3. The Seller agrees that the Goods will be delivered to the Buyer's place of business by _____ . The shipping costs are estimated at £ _____ and will be paid by the _____.

4. The Buyer will have competent persons available to take delivery of the Goods at such time as the Seller or the Seller's carrier shall indicate that the goods are to be delivered.

5. The risk in the Goods shall pass from the Seller to the Buyer upon delivery.

6. The Seller represents that it has legal title to the Goods and full authority to sell the goods. The Seller also represents that the Goods are sold free and clear of all liens, mortgages, indebtedness, or liabilities.

7. No variation of this Contract will be effective unless it is in writing and is signed by both parties. [Time is of the essence for the purposes of this Contract].[1] This Contract binds and benefits both the Buyer and Seller and any successors. This Contract, including any attachments, is the entire agreement between the Buyer and Seller.

IN WITNESS OF WHICH the parties have signed this agreement the day and year first above written.

_____   _____
Signed by or on behalf of the Seller   Signed by or on behalf of the Buyer

_____   _____
in the presence of (witness)   in the presence of (witness)

Name _____   Name _____

Address _____   Address _____

_____   _____

Occupation _____   Occupation _____

Contractor/Subcontractor Agreement | Form E13

THIS AGREEMENT is made the _____ day of _____ year _____

BETWEEN:

(1) _____.of _____ (the 'Contractor'); and

(2) _____ of _____(the 'Subcontractor').

WHEREAS:

(A)   The Contractor has entered into an agreement ('the Main Contract') dated _____

year _____, with _____ (the 'Company') for the performance of certain

works (the 'Works'),

(B)   The Contractor wishes to subcontract certain portions of the Works to the Subcontractor.

NOW IT IS HEREBY AGREED as follows:

1.   The Subcontractor, as an independent contractor, agrees to furnish all of the labour and materials as

may reasonably be required to complete the following portions of the Works: _____

_____

_____

_____

_____

_____

Any plans or specifications attached hereto shall form part of this Agreement.

2.   The Subcontractor agrees that the following portions of the Works will be completed by the dates

specified:

Work _____   Date _____

_____   _____

_____   _____

_____   _____

_____   _____

_____   _____

_____   _____

_____   _____

Or

[The Subcontractor agrees that it will undertake any part or parts of the works under this Agreement

within [three] working days of being directed by the Contractor to begin the same, and will complete

them promptly so as to enable the Contractor to perform his obligations in respect of the Main

Contract.]

3.   The Subcontractor agrees to perform this work in a workmanlike manner and with proper materials so

as to achieve compliance with the Contractor's obligations under the Main Contract according to

standard practices.

Continued on next page

Contractor/Subcontractor Agreement (continued)   Form E13

The Contractor agrees to pay the Subcontractor £ _____ as payment for the full performance of its obligations hereunder. This sum will be paid to the Subcontractor in instalments upon satisfactory completion of stages of the work as follows:

_____

4. The Contractor and Subcontractor may agree to extra services and work, but any such extras must be set out and agreed to in writing by both the Contractor and the Subcontractor.

5. The Subcontractor agrees to indemnify and hold the Contractor harmless from any claims or liability arising from the Subcontractor's work under this Contract but shall not be liable for losses caused by circumstances beyond the control or reasonably foreseeable by the Subcontractor.

6. No modification of this agreement will be effective unless it is in writing and is signed by both parties. This agreement binds and benefits both parties and any successors. This document, including any attachments is the entire agreement between the parties.

[7. For the purposes of the Contracts (Rights of Third Parties) Act 1999 this agreement does not confer any right of action in respect of it upon any person who is not a party to it.]

8. This Agreement shall not constitute or give rise to a partnership or joint venture.

IN WITNESS OF WHICH the parties have signed this agreement the day and year first above written

_____

Signed by or on behalf of the Contractor

_____

in the presence of (witness)

Name _____

Address _____

_____

Occupation _____

_____

Signed by or on behalf of the Subcontractor

_____

in the presence of (witness)

Name _____

Address _____

_____

Occupation _____

Credit Information   Form CDC07

Date _____

To _____

_____

_____

Dear _____

Re _____

This letter is in reply to your request for credit information on the above account. Accordingly, we submit the following information:

1.   The account was opened with us on _____ year _____

2.   The account's present balance is:

                Under 30 days   £_____

                30-60 days   £_____

                60-90 days   £_____

                Over 90 days   £_____

                Total owed   £_____

3.   The credit limit is:

_____

4.   Other credit information:

_____

_____

_____

We are pleased to be of service to you and trust this information will be held in strict confidence.

Yours sincerely

_____

Please note that this information is given without responsibility on the part of this Company or any of its officers or employees for the accuracy or completeness of such information.

Health warning: Do not provide information without first having obtained permission from the person to whom the data relates.

Credit Information Request · Form CDC08

Date _____

To _____

_____

_____

Dear _____

Thank you for your recent order dated _____

We would be pleased to offer you credit under our standard terms and conditions. In order to enable us to do so, we should be grateful if you would supply us with the following references and information regarding your financial status[1]:

_____

_____

_____

_____

_____

The referees you name will not provide any information about you to us, unless you authorise them to do so. Please therefore include in your reply, letters signed by you on your headed notepaper, addressed to the referees and giving them authority to provide credit information about you to us.

Pending receipt of this information we suggest C.O.D. terms or a deposit of £ _____ to enable us to deliver your order. Upon receipt of your confirmation we shall immediately deliver your order.

Of course, all credit information submitted shall be held in strict confidence.

Yours sincerely

_____

[1] Enter reference/information details which you require.

Credit Reference

Form CDC09

Date _____

To _____

_____

_____

Dear _____

Re _____

In response to your letter dated _____, the above mentioned has been known to us for _____ years. Over that period they have satisfactorily and promptly discharged all their obligations to us.

We have extended them credit and they have never abused our trust nor delayed payment of due accounts. We would, without hesitation, extend credit to them in the amount you have indicated.

We are giving this reference in an endeavour to be helpful to you. We must, however, make it clear that in doing so we accept no responsibility to you for the accuracy or completeness of this information.

Yours sincerely

_____

Note: Do not provide any credit reference unless you are authorised to do so by the person to whom it relates.

Damaged Goods Acceptance With Price Reduction Form BS11

Date _____

To _____

_____

_____

Dear _____

In fulfilment of our order dated _____, we have received goods from you which are defective in the following manner:

_____

_____

_____

_____

By reason of the presence of these defects the goods are not of satisfactory quality. We are therefore entitled to and do reject the goods.

We accordingly request that you collect the goods immediately. Although we will take reasonable care for the safekeeping of the goods for a maximum of 14 days from the date of this letter, the goods are henceforth at your risk.

[Notwithstanding the matters stated above, we would be prepared to retain the goods provided that we are accorded a price reduction of £_____. Please advise us as to whether your propose to accord this reduction or to remove the goods.]

Yours sincerely

_____

Note: Unless the sale is a consumer sale this form should not be used if the defects are minor and easily remediable, as in such circumstances it would be open to the seller to say that the rejection of the goods was improper, in which case the seller might be able both to recover the goods and to sue for the value of the profits lost on the sale.

Debt Acknowledgement   Form CDC10

The undersigned hereby confirms and acknowledges to _____ ('the Creditor')
that the undersigned is indebted to the Creditor in the amount of £ _____ as of the date hereof, which
amount is due and owing and includes all accrued interest and other permitted charges to date. The
undersigned further acknowledges that there are no credits or rights of set off against the balance owing.

Signed this _____ day of _____ year _____.

In the presence of

Witness _____   Debtor_____

Note: From the point of view of the Debtor, there is no point to signing an acknowledgment such as this unless something is given in
return, such as an agreement by the Creditor that the sum stated is all that is owing, or an undertaking by the Creditor to give more
time to pay.

Defect Report Memorandum   Form BS12

_____ **Ltd**

Date:		Report No:		
Product code:		Description:		Batch:

Defect:

Non-conformity details:

Non-conformity cause:

Corrective action to be taken:

Signed _____

Customer Services Officer

Result of corrective action:

Signed _____ Date: _____

Customer Services Officer

Defective Goods Notice   Form BS13

Date   _____

To   _____

_____

_____

Dear   _____

This is to inform you that we have received goods delivered by you as per your invoice or order no. _____, dated _____.

Certain goods as listed on the attached sheet are defective or do not comply with our order for the following reasons:

_____

_____

_____

_____

Accordingly, we wish to return these goods in exchange for a credit note in the amount of £_____. We also intend to return the goods to you at your cost unless you collect them. Please confirm the credit and also issue instructions for the return of the goods.

You are advised by this notice that we reserve our legal rights.

We look forward to your prompt reply.

Yours sincerely

_____

Demand for Delivery   Form BS14

Date _____

To _____

_____

_____

Dear _____

We have made full payment to you in the sum of £ _____ for the delivery of certain goods pursuant to our accepted order dated _____. [Despite the fact that our agreement specified that the goods should be delivered to us by _____ or [Despite the fact that delivery later than _____ was unreasonable in all the circumstances], the goods have still not been delivered. We demand delivery of the goods in accordance with our order.

Unless the goods are received by us on or before _____, which gives you an entirely reasonable period within which to comply with this notice, we shall consider you to be in repudiatory breach of contract and we shall thereupon expect a full refund. We reserve such further rights as we have under the law arising out of any loss or damages sustained.

We would appreciate immediate notification of your intentions in this matter.

Yours sincerely

_____

Note: This notice should only be served if there has been unreasonable delay, or if the contract specifies a date for delivery and that date has passed. Once there has been unreasonable delay or the date for delivery has passed, the notice may be served, but then the time specified for delivery should be a reasonable time in the light of the circumstances prevailing at the time when the notice is served. If a new promise has been made by the seller for delivery by a given date, such a date could be used. Otherwise, it is a matter of what, in common sense, is fair to both parties. Remember that if the notice is served prematurely, or if it specifies an unreasonably early date for compliance, the service of the notice could itself amount to a breach of contract and give rise to a claim against you.

The issues arising in connection with this form are very similar to those arising in connection with form BS16. It is suggested that you examine form BS16 to see if any of the clauses in that form may usefully be added or substituted for those in this form.

Demand for Explanation of Rejection of Goods — Form BS15

Date _____

To _____

_____

_____

Dear _____

Re _____

On _____, we shipped the following goods to you pursuant to your order no.
_____, dated _____:

_____

_____

_____

On _____, we received notice that you had rejected delivery of these goods without satisfactory explanation. We therefore request that you provide us with an adequate explanation for this rejection. Unless we are provided with such explanation within 10 days, we will have no option but to enforce payment for these goods.

Please be advised that we reserve all our rights under the law.

Thank you for your immediate attention to this matter.

Yours sincerely

_____

Demand for Payment (Final) Form CDC11

Date _____

To _____
_____
_____

Dear _____

We have tried on several occasions to secure payment of your overdue account but it remains unpaid. Your account is overdue in the amount of £ _____.

This is your final notice. Unless we receive your cheque for _____pounds (£ _____) within ten (10) days, we shall have to consider referring your account to our solicitors for collection.

Please note that immediate payment is in your own best interests as it will save you further interest and costs, and help preserve your credit rating.

Yours sincerely

_____

Demand to Specify Delivery Dates   Form BS16

Date   _____

To   _____

        _____

        _____

Dear   _____

We request that you confirm and specify delivery arrangements in respect of our order dated _____, and further confirm that you will abide by those arrangements.

Failure to provide this confirmation shall constitute a breach of contract and we shall no longer consider ourselves bound by this contract. Further, we shall hold you responsible for all resultant damages recoverable at law.

Please confirm delivery dates, in writing, no later than _____.

Yours sincerely

_____

Note: This notice should only be served if there has been unreasonable delay in providing details for delivery, or if the contract specifies a date for such details to be provided and if that date has passed. Once there has been unreasonable delay or the date for providing details has passed, the notice may be served, but then the time specified for providing details of delivery should be a reasonable time in the light of the circumstances prevailing at the time when the notice is served. If a new promise has been made by the seller for details to be produced by a given date, such a date could be used. Otherwise, it is a matter of what, in common sense, is fair to both parties. Remember that if the notice is served prematurely, or if it specifies an unreasonably early date for compliance, the service of the notice could itself amount to a breach of contract and give rise to a claim against you.

The issues arising in connection with this form are very similar to those arising in connection with the Demand for Delivery form BS14. It is suggested that you examine that form to see if any of the clauses in that form may usefully by added or substituted for those in this form.

Demand to Guarantor for Payment — Form CDC43

Date _____

To _____

_____

_____

Dear _____

As you are aware, we hold your guarantee dated _____, wherein you guaranteed the debt owed to us by _____

_____

You are advised that this debt is now in default. Accordingly, demand is made upon you as guarantor for full payment on the outstanding debt due us in the amount of £ _____.

In the event payment is not made within _____ (_____) days, we shall be compelled to enforce our rights against you under the guarantee by referring this matter to our solicitors.

Yours sincerely

_____

Note: If the debt has arisen under an agreement which is Regulated under the Consumer Credit Act 1974, the Debtor or Hirer must have been served with an appropriate notice of termination in accordance with that Act and the Consumer Credit (Enforcement Default and Termination Notices) Regulations 1983. It would be advisable to enclose a copy of that notice with this form. If you are not familiar with claims under Regulated agreements, you should consult your solicitor.

Demand to Pay Promissory Note   Form LB02

Date   _____

To   _____

_____

_____

Dear   _____

I refer to a promissory note dated _____ , in the original principal amount of £ _____ and of which I am the holder.

You are in default under the note in that the following payment(s) have not been made:

Payment Date   Amount Due

_____   _____

_____   _____

_____   _____

Accordingly, demand is hereby made for full payment of the entire balance of £ _____ due under the note. In the event payment is not received within _____ days, this note shall be forwarded to our solicitors for collection.

Yours sincerely

_____

Note: If the debt which is the subject of the Promissory Note has arisen under an agreement which is Regulated under the Consumer Credit Act 1974, the Debtor must have been served with an appropriate notice of termination in accordance with that Act and the Consumer Credit (Enforcement Default and Termination Notices) Regulations 1983. It would be advisable to enclose a copy of that notice with this form. If you are not familiar with claims under Regulated agreements, you should consult your solicitor.

Director's Resignation Reserving Rights Against the Company

Form B03

Date _____

To: Board of Directors

_____Limited

_____

_____

Dear Sirs

I resign my office of director of the company with immediate effect and I hereby reserve my right to take all proceedings which may be available to me to recover any fees, expenses, compensation and damages to which I am entitled.

Yours faithfully

_____

Dismissal and Disciplinary Rules and Procedure — Form E14

at _____Limited

1. The Company's aim is to encourage improvement in individual performance and conduct. Employees are required to treat members of the public and other employees equally in accordance with the Equal Opportunities Policy. This procedure sets out the action which will be taken when disciplinary rules are breached.

2. Principles:
   (i)   The list of rules is not to be regarded as an exhaustive list.
   (ii) The procedure is designed to establish the facts quickly and to deal consistently with disciplinary issues. No disciplinary action will be taken until the matter has been fully investigated.
   (iii) At every stage employees will have the opportunity to state their case and be accompanied by a fellow employee of their choice at the hearings.
   (iv) When the Company is contemplating dismissal for disciplinary or non-disciplinary grounds, statutory dispute resolution procedures will be adopted. Where the Company is contemplating taking disciplinary action (other than a warning) statutory dispute resolution procedures will also be adopted.
   (v) Only a Director has the right to suspend or dismiss. An employee may, however, be given a verbal or written warning by their immediate superior.
   (vi) An employee has the right to appeal against any disciplinary decision.

3. The Rules:
   Breaches of the Company's disciplinary rules which can lead to disciplinary action are:
   * failure to observe a reasonable order or instruction;
   * failure to observe a health and safety requirement;
   * inadequate time keeping;
   * absence from work without proper cause (including taking parental leave dishonestly);
   * theft or removal of the Company's property;
   * loss, damage to or misuse of the Company's property through negligence or carelessness;
   * conduct detrimental to the interests of the Company;
   * incapacity for work due to being under the influence of alcohol or illegal drugs;
   * physical assault or gross insubordination;
   * committing an act outside work or being convicted for a criminal offence which is liable adversely to affect the performance of the contract of employment and/or the relationship between the employee and the Company;
   * failure to comply with the Company's Equal Opportunities Policy.

4. The Procedure:
   (a) Oral warning
       If conduct or performance is unsatisfactory, the employee will be given a formal oral warning, which will be recorded. The warning will be disregarded after six months satisfactory service.
   (b) Written warning
       If the offence is serious, if there is no improvement in standards, or if a further offence occurs, a written warning will be given which will include the reason for the warning and a notice that, if there is no improvement after twelve months, a final written warning will be given.
   (c) Final written warning:
       If conduct or performance is still unsatisfactory, or if a further serious offence occurs within the 12-month period, a final warning will be given making it clear that any recurrence of the offence or other serious misconduct within a period of one month will result in dismissal.
   (d) Dismissal
       If there is no satisfactory improvement or if further serious misconduct occurs, the employee will be dismissed.
   (e) Gross misconduct
       If, after investigation, it is confirmed that an employee has committed an offence of the following nature (the list is not exhaustive) the normal consequence will be dismissal:
       theft or damage to the Company's property, incapacity for work due to being under the influence of alcohol or illegal drugs, physical assault and gross insubordination, discrimination or harassment contrary to the Company's Equal Opportunities Policy.
       While the alleged gross misconduct is being investigated the employee may be suspended, during which time he or she will be paid the normal hourly rate. Any decision to dismiss will be taken by the employer only after a full investigation.
   (f) Appeals
       An employee who wishes to appeal against any disciplinary decision must do so
       to:_____ within two working days. The employer will hear the appeal and decide the case as impartially as possible.

Dishonoured Cheque Notice   Form OLF13

Date _____

To _____

_____

_____

Dear _____

Payment of your cheque no. _____ in the sum of £ _____ , dated _____ payable to us has been dishonoured by your bank.

Please therefore ensure sufficient funds are put into your account to enable us to re-present the cheque immediately, or remit your payment in cash to our address by hand.

Yours sincerely

_____

Dismissal Letter for Intoxication on the Job | Form E15

Date _____

To _____

_____

_____

Dear _____

Further to the disciplinary meeting with you on _____. This letter is to inform you that we are terminating your employment with immediate effect from _____. This decision is based on an incident reported to me on _____ by your supervisor, _____ and on your explanation given at the disciplinary meeting. The report recommended your dismissal because of your repeated intoxication during working hours.

As you are aware, the first reported incident of your intoxication on the job was on _____. That report was placed on your personnel file, and you were informed at that time that another incident would result in a disciplinary action or possible dismissal.

This second incident of intoxication adversely affected the operational efficiency and effectiveness of your department and threatened the safety of other employees and this amounts to an act of gross misconduct. Your final pay cheque, including all forms of compensation due to you, can be picked up in the personnel office when you leave. If you wish to appeal against the decision to dismiss you, please notify me within _____ days.

Yours sincerely

_____

Personnel Manager

Before any decision to dismiss is made the statutory dismissal and disciplinary procedure and any contractual procedures may be followed to avoid legal repercussions.

Disputed Account Settlement   Form CDC12

THIS AGREEMENT IS MADE the _____ day of _____ year _____

BETWEEN:

(1) _____ (the 'Creditor'); and

(2) _____ (the 'Debtor').

WHEREAS:

(A)   The Creditor asserts a claim (the 'Claim') against the Debtor in the amount of

    £ _____ arising from the following transaction:

    _____

    _____

    _____

(B)   The Debtor disputes the Claim, and denies the said debt is due.

(C)   The parties have agreed to settle the Claim on the terms hereinafter appearing.

NOW IT IS HEREBY AGREED as follows:

1.   The Debtor agrees to pay the Creditor and the Creditor agrees to accept from the Debtor the sum of

    _____ Pounds (£ _____) in full payment, settlement, satisfaction,

    discharge and release of the Claim.

2.   The Debtor and the Creditor agree that each of them is hereby released from further obligations

    arising out of the transaction and from any liability relating hereto.

IN WITNESS OF WHICH the parties have executed this agreement the day and year first above written

(Individual)   (Company)

_____   Signed for and on behalf of

Signed by the Creditor   _____Ltd

_____   _____

                                                Director

_____   _____

Signed by the Debtor   Director/Secretary

                                                Signed for and on behalf of:

                                                _____Ltd

                                                _____

                                                Director

                                                _____

                                                Director/Secretary

Electricity Bill Query — Form GS06

Date _____

To _____

_____

_____

Ref _____

Dear _____

I have received my bill reference number _____ dated _____ regarding the above account.

I am writing to question the accuracy of the meter reading, as the units of electricity consumed appear to be far above my normal usage for this time of year. I have tested the meter with all electrical appliances in the property turned off and observed the meter still running.

Please therefore arrange for an engineer to test the meter so we can determine its accuracy and settle the matter. Please advise me of any charge for doing this and confirm that costs for meter testing are refundable should the meter indeed prove faulty and that in addition I may be entitled to compensation.

I look forward to hearing from you with a proposed appointment date.

Yours sincerely

_____

Name _____

Address _____

_____

Tel. _____

| Employee Agreement on Confidential Information, Inventions and Patents | Form E16 |

THIS AGREEMENT is made the _____ day of _____ year _____

BETWEEN:

(1) _____(the 'Employee'); and

(2) _____(the 'Company').

NOW IT IS HEREBY AGREED as follows:

In consideration of the employment of the Employee by the Company, the parties agree as follows:

1   The Employee agrees that he will not use any information or material for himself or others, and not take any such material or reproductions thereof from the Company, being apparatus, equipment, drawings, systems, formulae, reports, manuals, invention records, customer lists, computer programmes, or other material embodying trade secrets or confidential technical or business information of the Company or its Affiliates at any time during or after employment by the Company except in the performance of the Employee's duties to the Company.

2.   In this Agreement, the Company's 'Affiliates' shall comprise any subsidiary, holding company or subsidiary of any holding company of which the Company is a subsidiary as well as any person which may be a client, customer or partner of the Company or any other person to who or to which the Company owes any obligation of confidence.

3   The Employee agrees immediately to return all such material and reproductions thereof in his possession to the Company upon request and in any event upon termination of employment.

4.   Except with prior written authorisation by the Company, the Employee agrees not to disclose or publish any trade secret or confidential technical or business information or material of the Company or its Affiliates.

5.   The Employee shall keep a complete and updated record of any and all inventions, patents and improvements, whether patentable or not, which he, solely or jointly, may conceive, make, or first disclose during the period of his employment by the Company and will furnish that record to the Company immediately upon being required to do so.

6.   The Employee confirms that he has no entitlement to any rights relating to any invention which he may make in the course of his employment with the Company save insofar as is provided by the Patents Act 1977 section 39.

7.   The Employee agrees that he will aid the Company or its nominee in the acquisition of any United Kingdom or other Patents which it may wish to acquire in respect of any invention the rights to which belong to the Company or its nominee, by virtue of the same having been made in the course of the employee's employment, and that he will do all lawful acts and execute any documents in relation to such acquisition as may reasonably be requested at any time before and after his employment by the Company, without additional compensation but at the Company's expense.

8.   The Employee agrees that if he accepts employment with any firm or engages in any type of activity on his own behalf or on behalf of any organisation following termination of his employment within the Company, the Employee shall notify the Company in writing within thirty days of the name and

Continued on next page

Employee Agreement on Confidential Information, Inventions and Patents (continued)

address of such organisation and the nature of such activity.

9. The Employee agrees to give the Company timely written notice of any prior employment agreements or patent rights that might conflict with the entitlement of the Company or its Affiliates to benefit from the work undertaken or the inventions made by the Employee.

10. No waiver by either party of any breach by the other party of any provision of this agreement shall be deemed or construed to be a waiver of any succeeding breach of such provision or as a waiver of the provision itself.

11. This agreement shall be binding upon and pass to the benefit of the successors and assigns of the Company and, insofar as the same may be applied thereto, the heirs, legal representatives, and assigns of the Employee.

12. This agreement shall supersede the terms of any prior employment agreement or understanding between the Employee and the Company. This agreement may be modified or amended only in writing signed by an executive officer of the Company and by the Employee.

13. Should any portion of this agreement be held to be invalid, unenforceable or void, such holding shall not have the effect of invalidating the remainder of this agreement or any other part thereof, the parties hereby agreeing that the portion so held to be invalid, unenforceable, or void shall, if possible, be deemed amended or reduced in scope.

14. The Employee acknowledges reading, understanding and receiving a signed copy of this agreement.

IN WITNESS OF WHICH the parties have signed this agreement the day and year first above written

_____

Signed by the Employee

_____

in the presence of (witness)

Name _____

Address _____

_____

Occupation_____

Signed for and on behalf of the Company

_____

Director

_____

Director/Secretary

Employee Disciplinary Report Form E17

Employee _____

Department _____

☐ Written Warning   ☐ Final Warning

1. Statement of the problem: _____

    _____

    _____

2. Prior discussion or warnings on this subject, whether oral or written: _____

    _____

    _____

3. Company policy on this subject: _____

    _____

    _____

4. Summary of corrective action to be taken by the Company and/or Employee: _____

    _____

    _____

5. Consequences of failure to improve performance or correct behaviour: _____

    _____

    _____

6. Employee statement: _____

    _____

    _____

Employee Signature: _____ Date _____

Management Approval: _____ Date _____

Distribution: One copy to Employee, one copy to Supervisor and original to Personnel File.

Employee Dismissal for Lateness   Form E18

Date   _____

To   _____
_____
_____

Dear   _____

Further to our meeting on _____ concerning your timekeeping, I am writing to inform you of my decision.

As discussed, despite receiving verbal and written warnings about your repeated lateness for work, on _____ you arrived late for work. You have been warned that any further lateness may result in the termination of your employment and as you were unable to provide any satisfactory explanation for your lateness, I regret that I have no other option than to give you _____ weeks' notice of the termination of your employment. Your last day of employment will therefore be _____.

If you wish to appeal against your dismissal, please notify me in writing within ___ working days.

Yours sincerely

_____

Before any decision to dismiss is made the statutory dismissal and disciplinary procedure and any contractual procedures may be followed to avoid legal repercussions.

Employee File   Form E19

Employee: _____

Address: _____

Phone: _____ National Insurance No.: _____

DOB: _____ Sex: ☐ M   ☐ F

Marital Status: ☐ Single ☐ Married ☐ Separated ☐ Widowed ☐ Divorced

Name of Spouse: _____No. Dependents _____

In Emergency Notify: _____

Address: _____

_____

_____

Education

Secondary School _____Years: _____

University/College _____Years: _____

Other _____Years: _____

Employment History

Date From /To	Position	Salary _____
_____	_____	£ _____
_____	_____	£ _____
_____	_____	£ _____
_____	_____	£ _____
_____	_____	£ _____
_____	_____	£ _____

Dismissal Information

Date dismissed: _____ Would we re-employ? ☐ Yes ☐ No

Reason for dismissal: _____

_____

_____

_____

_____

_____

Employee Licence
(For a Furnished or Unfurnished House or Flat)

Form RT02

The PROPERTY   _____

_____

The LICENSOR   _____

_____

The LICENSEE   _____

_____

_____

_____

_____

The PERIOD   the period beginning on the date of this Agreement and ending on the date that the Licensee's employment with the Licensor ceases

(delete paragraph if not required)

[Subject to the right of the licensor at any time during the Period to end this Agreement earlier by giving to the licensee written notice

of _____ week(s)/month(s)*]

The LICENCE FEE   £ _____ per week/month* payable in advance on the _____ of each week/month*

The Deposit   £ _____

ete if
urnished)

[The Inventory   means the list of the Licensor's possessions at the Property which has been signed by the Licensor and the Licensee]

DATED   _____

SIGNED   _____   _____

(The Licensor)   (The Licensee)

THIS AGREEMENT comprises the particulars detailed above and the terms and conditions printed overleaf whereby the Property is hereby let by the Licensor and taken by the Licensee for the Period at the Licence Fee.

*delete as appropriate

Terms and Conditions on next page

Employee Licence Terms and Conditions (continued) Form RT02

1. The Licensor requires the Licensee to reside at the Property in order to carry out his employment with the Licensor and on the termination of such employment this Agreement shall immediately terminate.
2. This Licence Agreement is personal to the Licensee
3. The Licensor may deduct the Licence Fee and any other payments due and outstanding from the Licensee under this Agreement from any wages or salary payable by the Licensor to the Licensee
4. The Licensee will pay:
   4.1 the Licence Fee at the times and in the manner set out in this Agreement
   4.2 pay all charges in respect of any electric, gas, water and telephonic or televisual services used at or supplied to the Property and Council Tax or any similar property tax that might be charged in addition to or replacement of it
   4.3 keep the interior of the Property in a good and clean state and condition and not damage or injure the Property or any part of it and if at the end of the Period any item on the Inventory requires repair, replacing, cleaning or laundering the Licensee will pay for the same (reasonable wear and tear and damage by an insured risk excepted)
   4.4 maintain at the Property and keep in a good and clean condition all of the items listed in the Inventory
   4.5 not make any alteration or addition to the Property nor without the Licensor's prior written consent (not to be unreasonably withheld) to do any redecoration or painting of the Property
   4.6 not do or omit to do anything on or at the Property which may be or become a nuisance or annoyance to any other occupiers of the Property or owners or occupiers of adjoining or nearby premises or which may in any way prejudice the insurance of the Property or cause an increase in the premium payable
   4.7 not without the Licensor's prior consent (not to be unreasonably withheld) allow or keep any pet or any kind of animal at the Property
   4.8 pay the Licensor's reasonable legal or other costs and expenses reasonably incurred as a result of any breaches by the Licensee of his obligations under this Agreement
   4.9 not use or occupy the Property in any way whatsoever other than as a private residence
   4.10 not part with or share possession of occupation of the Property or any part thereof provided however that members of the Licensee's immediate family may reside at the Property with the Licensee so long as no relationship of Licensor and Licensee is thereby created or allowed to arise between the Licensee and any family member
   4.11 allow the Licensor or anyone with the Licensor's written permission to enter the Property at reasonable times of the day to inspect its condition and state of repair, carry out any necessary repairs and gas inspections, or during the last month of the term, show the Property to prospective new licensee, provided the Licensor has given 48 hours written notice beforehand (except in emergency)
   4.12 provide the Licensor with a forwarding address when the Licence comes to an end and remove all rubbish and all personal items (including the Licensees own furniture and equipment) from the property before leaving
   4.13 pay interest at the rate of 4% above the Base Lending Rate for the time being of the Licensor's bankers upon any Licence Fee or other money due from the Licensee under this Agreement which is more than 14 days in arrears in respect of the period from when it became due to the date of payment
5. The Deposit
   5.1 will be held by the Licensor and will be refunded to the Licensee at the end of the Term (however it ends) but less any reasonable deductions properly made by the Licensor to cover any reasonable costs incurred by or losses caused to him by any breaches of the Licensee's obligations under this Agreement. No interest will be payable by the Licensor to the Licensee in respect of the Deposit money
   5.2 shall be repaid to the Licensee, at the forwarding address provided to the Licensor, as soon as reasonably practicable. However the Licensor shall not be bound to return the Deposit until he is satisfied that no money is repayable to the Local Authority if the Licensee has been in receipt of Housing Benefit and until after he has had a reasonable opportunity to assess the reasonable cost of any repairs required as a result of any breaches of his obligations by the Licensee or other sums properly due to the Licensor under clause 5.1 above, save that except in exceptional circumstances the Licensor shall not retain the Deposit for more than one month
   5.3 if at any time during the Term the Licensor needs to use any part of the Deposit to cover any reasonable costs incurred as a result of any breaches of his obligations by the Licensee or other sums properly due to the Licensor, the Licensee shall upon demand pay by way of additional rent to the Licensor any additional payments needed to restore the full amount of the Deposit
6. The Licensor will keep in repair
   6.1 the structure and exterior of the Property (including drains gutters and external pipes)
   6.2 the installations at the Property for the supply of water, gas and electricity and for sanitation (including basins, sinks, baths and sanitary conveniences), and
   6.3 the installations at the Property for space heating and heating water
   But the Licensor will not be required to:
   6.4 carry out works for which the licensee is responsible, eg by virtue of clauses 4.3 and 4.4 above
   6.5 reinstate the Property in the case of substantial damage or destruction.
7. In the event of substantial damage to or destruction the Licensee shall be relieved from payment of the Licence Fee to the extent that the Licensee's use and enjoyment of the Property is thereby prevented and from performance of its obligations as to the state and condition of the Property to the extent of and so long as there prevails such damage or destruction (except to the extent that the insurance is prejudiced by any act or default of the Licensee)
8. So long as the reference to a right of early termination in the definition of the 'PERIOD' overleaf (the 'early termination right') has not been deleted then Licensor may at any time during the Period terminate this Agreement by giving to the Licensee prior written notice to that effect, the length of such notice to be that stated in the early termination right, and upon the expiry of the notice period this Agreement shall end with no further liability of either party save for any existing breach, [provided that the Licensee will not be obliged to vacate the premises unless suitable alternative accommodation shall have been offered to him.]
9 Upon the termination of his employment the Licensee shall vacate the Property forthwith. Note that if possession of the Property has not been surrendered and anyone is living at the Property then the Licensor must obtain a court order for possession before reentering the Property. This clause does not affect the Tenant's rights under the Protection from Eviction Act 1977.
10. Where the context so admits:
    10.1 The 'Licensor' includes the persons for the time being entitled to the reversion expectant upon this Licence
    10.2 The 'Property' includes all of the Licensor's fixtures and fittings at or upon the Property
    10.3 The 'Period' shall mean the period stated in the particulars overleaf or any shorter or longer period in the event of an earlier termination or an extension or holding over respectively
11. All references to the singular shall include the plural and vice versa and any obligations or liabilities of more than one person shall be joint and several and an obligation on the part of a party shall include an obligation not to allow or permit the breach of that obligation

Employee Non-Competition and Confidentiality Agreement

Form E20

_____ ('the Employee'), of _____ (address) and employed or about to be employed by _____ ('the Company') hereby makes these convenants to the Company in consideration for the Company:

[hiring the Employee in the position of _____]*

[continuing to employ the Employee with the following change in the nature of the employment]*

(delete as applicable)

Employee's Covenants:

BETWEEN:

(1) _____ (the 'Company'); and

(2) _____ (the 'Employee').

NOW IT IS HEREBY AGREED as follows:

In consideration of the employment or change in the nature of the employment of the Employee by the Company the Employee covenants as follows:

1. The Employee hereby agrees not directly or indirectly to compete with the business of the Company and its successors and assigns during the period of employment and for a period of _____ [months][years] following termination of employment and within a distance of _____ mile(s) of _____ notwithstanding the cause or reason for the termination or redundancy.

2. The phrase 'not compete with the business of' as used herein shall mean that the Employee shall not directly or indirectly own (whether as proprietor or as shareholder), manage, operate, act as consultant to or be employed in a business substantially similar to and in competition with any business of the Company of which the Employee had been engaged, save that this definition shall not extend to the ownership of shares in any public limited company.

3. The Employee further agrees, not for a period of _____ to solicit customers of the Company who have transacted business with the Company during the Employee's employment and that he will not for the like period solicit suppliers or employees of the Company with the intention of inducing them to cease to supply the Company or to leave the Company's employment.

4. The Employee acknowledges that the Company and its affiliates hold certain trade, business, and financial secrets in connection with the business. The Employee covenants not to divulge to any party at any time, directly or indirectly, during the term of employment or any time afterwards, unless directed by the Board of Directors, any confidential information acquired by the Employee about the Company or its affiliates, including, but not limited to, customer lists, trade secrets, documents, financial statements, correspondence, patents, processes, formulas, research, intellectual property, expenses, costs or other confidential information of any kind, or any other data that could be used by third parties to the disadvantage of the Company. This paragraph shall cease to apply to information that is in the public domain other than by way of unauthorised disclosure. This paragraph shall also not apply to disclosures that the Employee is entitled to make under the Public Interest Disclosure Act. The Employee further agrees that, throughout his employment and thereafter, he will not use such secrets, knowledge data or information for his purposes or for those of any third party.

Continued on next page

Employee Non-Competition and Confidentiality Agreement (continued)

5. If the Employee breaches this covenant, the Company shall have the right, in addition to all other rights available hereunder and by law, to prevent the Employee from continuing such breach. The Employee confirms the he/she has had the opportunity to discuss and negotiate this Covenant fully and confirm his/her understanding and acceptance of it. If any part of this Covenant is declared invalid, then the Employee agrees to be bound by a Covenant as near to the original as lawfully possible. This paragraph shall survive the term and termination of employment. The Employee shall further be liable for all costs of enforcement.

6. No waiver of a right by the Company constitutes a waiver of any other right of the Company, and a temporary waiver by the Company does not constitute a permanent waiver or any additional temporary waiver. These Covenants may be modified only in writing and signed by the Employee and the Company. If any portion of these Covenants is declared invalid, these Covenants shall continue in effect as if the invalid portion had never been part hereof.

7. This agreement shall be binding upon and inure to the benefit of the parties, their successors and assigns.

IN WITNESS OF WHICH the parties have signed this agreement the day and year first above written

_____

Signed by the Employee

_____

in the presence of (witness)

Name _____

Address _____

_____

Occupation _____

_____

Signed for and on behalf of the Company

_____

Director

_____

Director/Secretary

Health Warning: Restrictions on competition will not be enforceable unless they are necessary to protect the Employer's customer base and unless it is not practical to do so by a simple prohibition on soliciting or doing work for those customers. If you make the restriction too extensive, the court will not cut it back. Instead the restriction will fail altogether. As a guide, you should ask yourself what are the minimum restrictions which will stop your customers from following the Employee to his new job. Things to think about are: (1) how important is personal contact: for an accountant or a hairdresser; this will be more important than for a typist; (2) how frequently does a customer typically use your service: the more frequent the use, the quicker it is to get the customer to transfer his loyalty from your former employee to his replacement; (3) is your business in a town or in the country: an exclusion from working within a one mile radius may be reasonable in the country, but not in central London. If the restriction is important to you, consult a solicitor to make sure you get it right. Otherwise, think carefully before trying to impose an exclusion area of more than a half-mile radius or a time period of more than six months. Restrictions on disclosing confidential information, as opposed to restrictions on competition, however, need not be so limited.

It is important to ensure that this agreement is signed at the same time or before the time when the employment begins or changes. If you spring it on an Employee who is already working for you in the job which it is intended he should remain in, the court will be more likely to refuse to enforce it, both because there may be doubts as to whether the Employer is giving anything in exchange for the covenant (this is known as 'consideration') and because the Employer's actions may be regarded as oppressive. If the employment has already begun, take a solicitor's advice.

Employee Suspension Notice   Form E22

Date _____

To _____

_____

_____

Dear _____

You have received informal notices that your conduct has been found to be unsatisfactory. On _____ a formal Warning Notice was placed on your permanent employment record. Your unacceptable conduct has continued; in particular you have:

_____

_____

_____

You are herewith suspended from work for a period of _____ commencing _____. Suspension shall be without pay; however, your health and pension benefits shall continue during the suspension providing you return to work immediately following the suspension period.

YOU MAY BE SUBJECT TO DISMISSAL IN THE FUTURE IF YOU CONTINUE TO VIOLATE COMPANY POLICY.

_____

Company Representative

ACKNOWLEDGED

Date _____

_____

Employee

Note: An Employer is only entitled to suspend in this way if the contract allows it to do so, or if its disciplinary policy allows it to do so.

Employee Warning   Form E23

Date _____

To _____

_____

_____

Dear _____

Further to our meeting I write to confirm the outcome of our discussion. In this meeting we discussed your work performance and I informed you that your work performance is unsatisfactory for the following reasons: _____

_____

_____

_____

_____

_____

We discussed the reasons why your performance has fallen below the standard expected and we considered how an improvement might be achieved: _____

_____

_____.

We informed you that we expect immediate correction of the problem, and will monitor your performance for a period of _____ weeks/months to ensure an improvement is achieved.

If there is any question about this notice or if we can help you improve your performance or correct the difficulties, then please discuss this matter with your supervisor at the earliest possible opportunity.

_____

Company Representative

Employer's Request for Reference

Form E25

Date _____

Ref _____

To _____

_____

_____

Dear _____

Re _____

The above-named candidate has applied for a position within our company and has given your name as a previous employer reference. The information requested below will help us evaluate the candidate. We will consider your comments in strict confidence. Please fill in the details below and return this letter in the envelope provided. Thank you for your cooperation.

Yours sincerely

_____

Personnel Department

Please indicate:

Position within your firm: _____

Employed from _____to _____

Salary £ _____

Please rate the applicant on the basis of his/her employment with you (good/ fair/ poor):

Ability _____   Conduct _____   Attitude _____

Efficiency _____   Attendance _____   Punctuality _____

What was the reason for dismissal or redundancy? _____

_____

Would you re-employ him/her? _____. If not, please give reason: _____

_____

_____

Signature and Title

Employment Confirmation Offer Letter — Form E26

Date _____

To _____

_____

_____

Dear _____

Following your interview at this office on_____

I am pleased to offer you the above position with _____ ('the Company') subject to satisfactory references[1] and a medical report.[2] It is the Company's final decision as to whether such references meet with its requirements. You are advised not to resign from your present position until I have confirmed to you that your references have been received and are satisfactory to us. We will endeavour to obtain your references as quickly as possible.

If you accept this offer of employment, your job will be based at _____.

Your employment will commence on _____ and the first four weeks will be treated as a probationary period during which time your employment may be terminated by yourself or by the Company on one week's notice.

Your duties and responsibilities will be as set out in the attached job description and you will be responsible to _____.

Your basic salary at the commencement of your employment will be _____ payable monthly in arrears by bank credit transfer on the last day of each month. Your normal weekly hours will be from _____.

You will be entitled to _____ holiday in every year, in addition to the normal statutory entitlement, of which no more than *two* weeks may be taken consecutively. The holiday year runs from _____.

The Company will be entitled to terminate your appointment by giving you written notice of _____. You are required to give the Company *one week's* notice of your intention to terminate your employment with the Company.

Your other terms of employment will be provided on your first day of employment.[3]

Continued on next page

Employment Confirmation Offer Letter (continued)   Form E26

If you wish to accept this offer of employment, I would be grateful if you could confirm your acceptance by signing and returning one copy of this letter in the stamped addressed envelope enclosed.[4]

I do hope that you will accept this offer. In the meantime, if you wish to discuss any aspect of this offer, please do not hesitate to contact me.

Yours sincerely

_____

Personnel Manager

---

[1] References are usually taken up at this stage, the offer being made subject to satisfactory references. A candidate who receives a job offer subject to satisfactory references should not resign from his current employment until all the conditions have been satisfied. In the public sector, offers are usually made unconditional only after all the conditions are met.

[2] Medical examinations of prospective Employees are not a legal requirement, although Employers are recommended to carry them out now that health and safety in the workplace is so important. A prospective Employee is not obliged to agree to have a medical examination, although if he did refuse it would be reasonable for the prospective Employer not to make an offer.

[3] Alternatively, these may be set out in an enclosed statement of particulars of employment or incorporated into this letter.

[4] Once this offer has been accepted, the parties have entered into a contractual relationship and the Employer will need to issue either a full contract or a statement of particulars of employment.

Employment Contract   Form E27

THIS AGREEMENT IS MADE the _____.[1]

BETWEEN (1) _____ (the 'Employer') and (2)_____ (the 'Employee')

This document sets out the terms and conditions of employment which are required to be given to the Employee under section 1 of the Employment Rights Act 1996 and which apply at the date hereof.

1. Commencement and Job Title

The Employer agrees to employ the Employee from _____ in the capacity of _____. No employment with a previous employer will be counted as part of the Employee's period of continuous employment.[2] The Employee's duties which this job entails are set out in the job description attached to this statement. The job description may, from time to time, be reasonably modified as necessary to meet the needs of the Employer's business.

2. Salary

The Employer shall pay the Employee a salary of £_____ per year payable by credit transfer at monthly intervals on the last day of each month. The Company shall review the Employee's salary at such intervals as it shall, at its sole discretion, decide.

3. Hours of Employment

The Employee's normal hours of employment shall be _____ to _____ on _____ to _____ during which time the Employee may take up to one hour for lunch between the hours of _____ and _____, and the Employee may, from time to time, be required to work such additional hours as is reasonable to meet the requirements of the Employer's business at an overtime rate of £_____ per hour.

4. Holidays

The Employee shall be entitled to _____ days' holiday per calendar year at full pay in addition to the normal public holidays. Holidays must be taken at times convenient to the Employer and sufficient notice of the intention to take holiday must be given to the Employee's supervisor. No more than two weeks' holiday must be taken at any one time unless permission is given by the Employee's supervisor.

The Employee shall be entitled to payment in lieu of holiday accrued due but untaken at the date of termination of his employment. If, at the date of termination, the Employee has taken holiday in excess of his accrued entitlement, a corresponding deduction will be made from his final payment.

5. Sickness

5.1 If the Employee is absent from work on account of sickness or injury, he or someone on his behalf should inform the Employer of the reason for the absence as soon as possible but no later than *12.00pm* on the working day on which absence first occurs.

5.2 *The Company reserves the right to ask the Employee at any stage of absence to produce a medical certificate and/or to undergo a medical examination.*

5.3 The Employee shall be paid normal remuneration during sickness absence for a maximum of _____ in any period of _____ provided that the Employee provides the Employer with a medical certificate in the case of absence of more than _____. Such remuneration will be less the amount of any statutory sick pay or social security sickness benefits to which the Employee may be entitled. Entitlement to payment is subject to notification of absence and production of medical certificates as required above.[3]

Continued on next page

Employment Contract (continued)   Form E27

6. Collective Agreements

There are no collective agreements in force directly relating to the terms of your employment.[4]

7. Pension

The Employee shall be entitled to join the Employer's pension scheme, the details of which are set out in the Employer's booklet/leaflet which is entitled _____ and which is available on request. A contracting-out certificate under the Pension Schemes Act is in force in respect of this employment.[5]

8. Termination

The Employer may terminate this Agreement by giving written notice to the Employee as follows:

    (a)   With not less than one week's notice during the first two years of continuous employment; then

    (b)   With not less than a further one week's notice for each full year of continuous employment after the first two years until the 12th year of continuous employment; and

    (c)   With not less than 12 weeks' notice after 12 years of continuous employment.[6] The Employer may terminate this Agreement without notice or payment in lieu of notice in the case of serious or persistent misconduct such as to cause a major breach of the Employer's disciplinary rules.

The Employee may terminate this Agreement by one week's written notice to the Employer.

After notice of termination has been given by either party, the Employer may in its absolute discretion give the Employee payments in lieu of all or any part of any notice; or, provided the Employee continues to be paid and to enjoy his full contractual benefits under the terms of this Agreement, the Employer may in its absolute discretion for all or part of the notice period exclude the Employee from the premises of the Employer and require that he carries out duties other than those specified in his job description or require that he carries out no duties at all until the termination of his employment.

The normal retirement age for the employment shall be 65.

9. Confidentiality

The Employee is aware that during his employment he may be party to confidential information concerning the Employer and the Employer's business. The Employee shall not, during the term of his employment, disclose or allow the disclosure of any confidential information (except in the proper course of his employment).

After the termination of this Agreement the Employee shall not disclose or use any of the Employer's trade secrets or any other information which is of a sufficiently high degree of confidentiality to amount to a trade secret. The Employer shall be entitled to apply for an injunction to prevent such disclosure or use and to seek any other remedy including without limitation the recovery of damages in the case of such disclosure or use.

The obligation of confidentiality both during and after the termination of this Agreement shall not apply to any information which the Employee is enabled to disclose under the Public Interest Disclosure Act 1998 provided the Employee has first fully complied with the Employer's procedures relating to such external disclosures.

10. Non-Competition

For a period of _____[7] after the termination of this Agreement the Employee shall not solicit or seek business from any customers or clients of the Employer who were customers or clients of the Employer at the time during the _____[8] immediately preceding the termination of this Agreement.

11. Dismissal, Discipline and Grievance

The Employer's Dismissal and Disciplinary Rules and Procedure and the Grievance and Appeal Procedure in connection with these rules are set out in the Employer's *Staff Handbook* which is attached hereto.

Continued on next page

Employment Contract (continued)   Form E27

12. Notices

All communications including notices required to be given under this Agreement shall be in writing and shall be sent either by personal service or by first class post to the parties' respective addresses.

13. Severability

If any provision of this Agreement should be held to be invalid it shall to that extent be severed and the remaining provisions shall continue to have full force and effect.

14. Staff Handbook

Further details of the arrangements affecting your employment are published in the *Staff Handbook* as issued and/or amended from time to time. These are largely of an administrative nature, but, so far as relevant, are to be treated as incorporated in this Agreement.

15. Prior Agreements

This Agreement cancels and is in substitution for all previous letters of engagement, agreements and arrangements (whether oral or in writing) relating to your employment,[9] all of which shall be deemed to have been terminated by mutual consent. This Agreement and the *Staff Handbook*[10] constitute the entire terms and conditions of your employment and any waiver or modification must be in writing and signed by the parties to this Agreement.

16. Governing Law

This Agreement shall be construed in accordance with the laws of England & Wales and shall be subject to the exclusive jurisdiction of the English courts.

Please acknowledge receipt of this statement and your agreement to the terms set out in it by signing the attached copy of this letter and returning it to _____.

IN WITNESS OF WHICH the parties hereto have signed this Agreement the day and year first above written.

SIGNED

_____   _____
Signed by or on behalf of   in the presence of (witness)

Name _____

Address _____

_____

Dated _____   Occupation _____

SIGNED

_____   _____
Signed by the employee   in the presence of (witness)

Name _____

Address _____

_____

Dated _____   Occupation _____

Continued on next page

Employment Contract (continued)   Form E27

---

[1] This must be no later than two months after the employment commences. Any changes must be notified to the Employee within one month of the change. No statement is required to be given to an Employee employed under a contract for less than one month.

[2] If employment with a previous Employer is to be counted as a period of continuous employment, this, and the date it began, must be stated.

[3] If the Employer does not wish to pay normal remuneration during sickness, it should state that the statutory sick pay rules apply.

[4] Where a collective agreement directly affects the terms and conditions of employment, the following should be inserted as clause 6: 'The terms of the collective agreement dated [_____] made between [_____] and [_____] shall be deemed to be included in this Agreement'.

[5] Where no pension scheme exists, this must be stated and where no contracting out certificate is in force, this must also be stated.

[6] These are the minimum periods required by law but they may be increased by agreement.

[7] The Employer may choose the number of months or years that are necessary to protect its business needs, but any more than two years is likely to render this clause unenforceable at law.

[8] This period should be between one and two years if it is to remain enforceable by the Employer.

[9] Where Opt-Out Agreement for Working Time Regulations purposes has already been signed, add the words 'other than an Opt-Out Agreement dated [_____]'.

[10] Where Opt-Out Agreement referred to in footnote 9 is signed, add the words 'and the Opt-Out Agreement dated [_____] '.

Enquiry on Overdue Account   Form CDC13

Date _____

To _____

_____

_____

Dear _____

We have not received payment on your overdue account, and would appreciate it if you could offer your explanation by completing this form. Please tick the applicable reason, fill in the details and return this form to us.

☐   We need copies of unpaid invoices: _____

☐   We have credits outstanding: _____

☐   Payment was sent on _____.

☐   Payment will be sent on _____.

☐   Other: _____

Thank you for your kind attention.

Yours sincerely

_____

Equal Opportunities Policy   Form E28

at _____ Limited

The Company's aim is to ensure that all of its employees and job applicants are treated equally irrespective of disability, race, colour, religion or religious belief, nationality, ethnic origin, age, sex, marital status or sexual orientation. This policy sets out instructions that all employees are required to follow in order to ensure that this is achieved.

Policy

1. There shall be no discrimination or harassment on account of disability, race, colour, religion or religious belief, nationality, ethnic origin, age, sex, marital status or sexual orientation.
2. The Company shall appoint, train, develop and promote on the basis of merit and ability.
3. Employees have personal responsibility for the practical application of the Company's Equal Opportunity Policy, which extends to the treatment of members of the public and employees.
4. Managers and supervisors who are involved in the recruitment, selection, promotion and training of employees have special responsibility for the practical application of the Company's Equal Opportunity Policy.
5. The Grievance Procedure is available to any employee who believes that he or she may have been unfairly discriminated against.
6. Disciplinary action under the Disciplinary Procedure shall be taken against any employee who is found to have committed an act of unlawful discrimination. Discriminatory conduct and harassment shall be regarded as gross misconduct.
7. If there is any doubt about appropriate treatment under the Company's Equal Opportunities Policy, employees should consult the Personnel Manager.

Exercise of Option   Form OLF14

Date _____

To _____

_____

_____

Dear _____

You are hereby notified that I have elected to and hereby exercise and accept the option dated
_____, executed by you in my favour. I agree to all terms, conditions, and provisions of the option.

Yours sincerely

_____

Signed

_____

Name

Address _____

_____

_____

Expenses Record

Form E29

DATE	RECEIPT NUMBER	EXPENSE	TOTAL	VAT	FUEL/ MILEAGE	CAR EXPENSES	SUBSIST/ UK TRAVEL	OVERSEAS TRAVEL	ENTERTAINMENT CLIENT	ENTERTAINMENT STAFF	PHONE	OFFICE SUPPLIES	SUNDRIES
	1												
	2												
	3												
	4												
	5												
	6												
	7												
	8												
	9												
	10												
	11												
	12												
	13												
	14												
	15												
	16												
	17												
	18												
	19												
	20												
	21												
	22												
	23												
	SUB TOTAL		£	£	£	£	£	£	£	£	£	£	£
	TOTAL CLAIMED	£											

EXPENSE CLAIM FORM MONTH CLAIMANT:

SIGNATURE:

APPROVED:

Extension of Option to Purchase Property   Form OLF15

THIS DEED IS MADE the _____ day of _____ year _____

BETWEEN:

(1) _____(the 'Grantor'); and

(2) _____(the 'Holder').

WHEREAS:

(A)   The Grantor, as the owner of property located at _____

_____ (the 'Property') granted an option to buy the Property to

the Holder on _____ (the 'Original Option'), which expires on

_____. A copy of the said Original Option is attached to this agreement.

(B)   The Holder wishes to extend the term of the Option.

NOW IT IS HEREBY AGREED as follows:

1.   In consideration of the payment to the Grantor by the Holder of the sum of

_____Pounds (£_____),

the receipt of which is hereby acknowledged, the Grantor hereby grants to the Holder a further Option

in the same terms as those contained in the Original Option save that the Option herein granted will

expire at _____ on _____ and save as hereinafter appears.

2.   If the Holder exercises the Option before the expiry of the further term herein granted the payment for

the Option and the payment for extension of the expiration of the Option shall be applied towards the

purchase price of the Property and the Holder shall receive a credit on completion equal to the

amount(s) paid for the Option and any extension.

3.   If the Holder fails to exercise the Option before the expiry of the further term herein agreed the

Grantor shall be entitled to retain absolutely all payment made by the Holder to the Grantor for the

Option and the extension granted herein.

IN WITNESS OF WHICH the parties have signed this Deed the day and year first above written

_____   _____

Signed as a Deed by or on behalf of the Grantor   Signed as a Deed by or on behalf of the Holder

_____   _____

in the presence of (witness)   in the presence of (witness)

Name _____   Name _____

Address _____   Address _____

_____   _____

Occupation _____   Occupation _____

Family Tree   Form P113

Name: _____

Father: _____   Mother: _____

Father's   **Mother's**

Father _____   Father _____

Mother _____   Mother _____

Father's Paternal   **Mother's Paternal**

Grandfather: _____   Grandfather _____

Grandmother: _____   Grandmother: _____

Your siblings _____

Your half siblings _____

_____

Father's Siblings   Mother's Siblings _____

_____   _____

_____   _____

Children of each of Father's siblings   Children of each of Mother's siblings

_____   _____

_____   _____

Grandchildren of each of Father's siblings' children   Grandchildren of each of Mother's siblings' children

_____   _____

_____   _____

Father's half siblings   Mother's half siblings

_____   _____

_____   _____

Children of each of Father's half siblings   Children of each of Mother's half siblings

_____   _____

_____   _____

Paternal grandfather's siblings   Paternal grandmother's siblings

_____   _____

_____   _____

Maternal grandfather's siblings   Maternal Grandmother's siblings

_____   _____

_____   _____

Children of each of paternal grandfather's siblings   Children of each of maternal grandfather's siblings

_____   _____

_____   _____

Continued on next page

Family Tree (continued)   Form P113

Children of each of paternal grandmother's siblings

_____

_____

Children of each of the children of
paternal grandfather

_____

_____

Children of each of the children of
paternal grandmother

_____

Paternal grandfather's half siblings

_____

Maternal grandfather's half siblings

_____

Children of each of paternal grandfather's
half siblings

_____

_____

Children of each of paternal grandmother's
half siblings

_____

Children of each of maternal grandmother's siblings

_____

_____

Children of each of the children of
maternal grandfather

_____

_____

Children of each of the children of
maternal grandmother

_____

Paternal grandmother's half siblings

_____

Maternal grandmother;s half siblings

_____

Children of each of maternal grandfather's
 half siblings

_____

_____

Children of each of maternal grandmother's
 half siblings

_____

Final Notice Before Legal Proceedings   Form OLF16

Date   _____

To   _____

            _____

            _____

Dear   _____

We have repeatedly requested payment of your long overdue account in the amount of
£ _____.

Unless we receive payment in full of this amount within seven days of the date of this letter we shall have
no alternative but to refer your account to our solicitors for recovery.

[We also claim statutory interest from [_____] at the rate of [_____] per cent per annum and the
amount of £_____ under the Late Payment of Commercial Debts (Interest) Act 1998.] / [We reserve our
rights to statutory interest under the Late Payment of Commercial Debts (Interest) Act 1998].

Yours sincerely

_____

Note: Do not claim statutory interest under the Late Payment of Commercial Debts (Interest) Act 1998 unless the debt arises in
connection with the supply of goods or services and unless (1) the debtor has entered into the contract in the course of a business and
(2) the contract is not a regulated agreement under the Consumer Credit Act 1974.

Final Warning Before Dismissal   Form E30

Date _____

To _____

_____

_____

Dear _____

Further to our meeting, I write to confirm our discussion. You have already been warned about your conduct within this Company. Incidents that have since come to our notice are: _____

_____

_____

_____

_____

There has not been a satisfactory improvement in your conduct since your last warning. Accordingly, any continued violations of company policy or failure to conduct yourself according to the rules of the company shall result in immediate termination of your employment without further warning.

We remind you that you have the right of appeal against this warning according to the Terms and Conditions of Employment as supplied to you, and if you wish to exercise this right, please notify me in writing within _____ working days.

Please contact the undersigned or your supervisor if you have any questions.

Yours sincerely

_____

Final Warning for Lateness   Form E31

Date   _____

To   _____

_____

_____

Dear   _____

I refer to our meeting on _____. Despite our verbal and written warnings to you about your timekeeping, there has been no improvement and you have given no satisfactory explanation as to why you continue to be late for work.

Your behaviour is unacceptable. We therefore give you this final warning. If you are late again without offering a reasonable excuse, you will be dismissed.

We remind you that you have the right of appeal against this warning according to the Statement of Terms and Conditions of Employment as supplied to you, and if you wish to exercise this right please notify me in writing within ____ working days.

Please contact the undersigned or your superior if you have any questions.

Yours sincerely

_____

First Warning for Lateness
Form E32

Date _____

To _____

_____

_____

Dear _____

I refer to our meeting on _____. You are aware that your hours of work are from
_____ a.m. to _____ p.m. You have repeatedly arrived for work late.

You have been advised of your bad timekeeping and warned of the possible consequences. Despite those
warnings you continue to be late for work and have offered no reasonable excuse.

Consider this a formal letter of warning. You must be at your place of work strictly in accordance with the
terms of your employment and the hours set. If you are late again without reasonable excuse, disciplinary
action will be taken.

This warning is being recorded on your personnel file. You have a right to appeal against this warning, and if
you wish to exercise this right, please notify me in writing within ____ working days.

Yours sincerely

_____

Form of Letter from Testator to Executor   Form PF07

Date _____

To _____

_____

_____

Dear _____

I am writing to confirm that I have named you as an executor of my Will dated

_____ .

- A copy of my Will is enclosed.*
- My signed original Will has been lodged with _____
- I have named _____ as a co-executor.
- My solicitor is _____ at _____ .*

Please confirm to me in writing that you are willing to act as one of my executors.

Yours sincerely

_____

* delete as necessary

Form of Resolution for Submission to Companies House   Form B08

_____ Limited

Company Number _____

The Companies Act 1985

Ordinary/Special/Extraordinary/Elective resolution of

_____ Limited/Public Limited Company

At an extraordinary general meeting of the above named company, duly convened and held at

_____ on the _____ day of _____ year _____ the following

[resolution][1] / [the resolution, a copy of which is attached hereto], was duly passed as an

ordinary/special/extraordinary/elective resolution[2]:

_____

_____

_____

_____

_____

_____

_____

_____

Signature of Chairman

Note: A full list of the resolutions which need to be filed and of directions as to how to do this are available on the website of Companies House at www.companieshouse.gov.uk. From 1 October 2007 the need for annual general meetings will cease in the case of private companies and the types of resolutions which need to be filed will alter.

[1] If the resolution is oral, set out the text of it; if it is written, attach a copy.

[2] Section 380 of the Companies Act 1985 details resolutions that need to be filed at Companies House; special, extraordinary and elective resolutions must be filed but not all ordinary resolutions need to be filed. The resolution must be delivered to Companies House within 15 days of being passed, accompanied by the appropriate fee, if any.

Funeral Wishes   Form PF08

Funeral Wishes
of

_____ (Name)

Funeral (Burial/Cremation) _____

_____

_____

Undertaker _____

_____

_____

Place of Service _____

_____

_____

Type of service _____

_____

_____

Person Officiating _____

_____

_____

Music Selection _____

_____

_____

Reading Selection _____

_____

_____

Flowers _____

_____

_____

Special Instructions _____

_____

_____

Furnished House/Flat Rental Agreement   Form F301

The PROPERTY _____

_____

The LANDLORD _____

of _____

_____

The TENANT _____

_____

The GUARANTOR _____

of _____

The TERM _____ weeks/months* beginning on _____

The RENT £ _____ per week/month* payable in advance on the _____ of each week/month*

The DEPOSIT £_____ which will be registered with one of the Government authorised tenancy deposit schemes ("the Tenancy Deposit Scheme") in accordance with the Tenancy Deposit Scheme Rules.

The INVENTORY means the list of the Landlord's possessions at the Property which has been signed by the Landlord and the Tenant

DATED _____

Signed and executed as a Deed by the following parties

Landlord	**Tenant**	**Guarantor***
_____	_____	_____
_____	_____	_____
Landlord(s)' name(s)	_____	_____
	Tenant(s)' name(s)	Guarantor's name
_____	_____	_____
_____	_____	_____
Landlord(s)' signature(s)	_____	_____
	Tenant(s)' signature(s)	Guarantor's signature

In the presence of:

Witness signature _____	Witness signature _____	Witness signature _____
Full name _____	Full name _____	Full name _____
Address_____	Address_____	Address_____
_____	_____	_____

(*delete as appropriate)

Continued on next page

Furnished House/Flat Rental Agreement (continued)   Form F301

THIS TENANCY AGREEMENT comprises the particulars detailed above and the terms and conditions printed overleaf whereby the Property is hereby let by the Landlord and taken by the Tenant for the Term at the Rent.

IMPORTANT NOTICE TO LANDLORDS:

1 The details of 'The LANDLORD' near the top of this Agreement must include an address for the Landlord in England or Wales as well as his/her name, or all names in the case of joint Landlords.

2 Always remember to give the written Notice Requiring Possession to the Tenant at least two clear months before the end of the Term.

3 Before granting the tenancy agreement, you should check whether your chosen deposit scheme provider requires you to insert any additional terms concerning the deposit into the tenancy agreement or to alter or delete any of the terms appearing in the form below. Details of the websites of the scheme providers are set out in Note 4 for tenants below. Currently only The Tenancy Deposit Scheme has any such requirements.

4. The information in 'Notice to Tenants' below is important to you as well, because it is relevant to whether or not you should use this form and whether you can get the Property back at the end of the term.

IMPORTANT NOTICE TO TENANTS:

1 In general, if you currently occupy Property under a protected or statutory tenancy and you give it up to take a new tenancy of the same or other accommodation owned by the same Landlord, that tenancy cannot be an Assured Shorthold Tenancy and this Agreement is not appropriate.

2 If you currently occupy Property under an Assured Tenancy which is not an Assured Shorthold Tenancy your Landlord is not permitted to grant you an Assured Shorthold Tenancy of that Property or of alternative property and this Agreement is not appropriate.

3 If the total amount of rent exceeds £25,000 per annum, an Assured Shorthold Tenancy cannot be created and this Agreement is not appropriate. Seek legal advice.

4 Further information about the Government-authorised Tenancy Deposit Schemes can be obtained from their websites: The Deposit Protection Service at www.depositprotection.com, Tenancy Deposit Solutions Ltd at www.mydeposits.co.uk and The Tenancy Deposit Scheme at www.tds.gb.com.

Furnished House/Flat Rental Agreement

Terms and Conditions

Form F301

1. This Agreement is intended to create an Assured Shorthold Tenancy as defined in the Housing Act 1988, as amended by the Housing Act 1996, and the provisions for the recovery of possession by the Landlord in that Act apply accordingly. The Tenant understands that the Landlord will be entitled to recover possession of the Property at the end of the Term.

2. **The Tenant's obligations:**
   2.1 To pay the Rent at the times and in the manner set out above.
   2.2 To pay all charges in respect of any electric, gas, water, sewage and telephonic or televisual services used at or supplied to the Property and Council Tax or any property tax that might be charged in addition to or replacement of it during the Term.
   2.3 To keep the items on the Inventory and the interior of the Property in a good and clean state and condition and not damage or injure the Property or the items on the Inventory (fair wear and tear excepted).
   2.4 To yield up the Property and the items on the Inventory at the end of the Term in the same clean state and condition it/they was/were in at the beginning of the Term (but the Tenant will not be responsible for fair wear and tear caused during normal use of the Property and the items on the Inventory.
   2.5 Not to make any alteration or addition to the Property and not without the prior written consent of the Landlord (consent not to be withheld unreasonably) do any redecoration or painting of the Property.
   2.6 Not do anything on or at the Property which:
      (a) may be or become a nuisance or annoyance to any other occupiers of the Property or owners or occupiers of adjoining or nearby premises
      (b) is illegal or immoral
      (c) may in any way affect the validity of the insurance of the Property and the items listed on the Inventory or cause an increase in the premium payable by the Landlord
      (d) will cause any blockages in the drainage system and in the case of breach of this clause the Tenant to be responsible for the reasonable cost of such repair or other works which will be reasonably required.
   2.7 Not without the Landlord's prior consent (consent not to be withheld unreasonably) allow or keep any pet or any kind of animal at the Property.
   2.8 Not use or occupy the Property in any way whatsoever other than as a private residence.
   2.9 Not assign, sublet, charge or part with or share possession or occupation of the Property (but see clause 5.1 below).
   2.10 To allow the Landlord or anyone with the Landlord's written permission to enter the Property at reasonable times of the day to inspect its condition and state of repair, carry out any necessary repairs and gas inspections, and during the last month of the Term, show the Property to prospective new tenants, provided the Landlord has given at least 24 hours' prior written notice (except in emergency).
   2.11 To pay the Landlord's reasonable costs reasonably incurred as a result of any breaches by the Tenant of his obligations under this Agreement, and further to pay the Landlord's reasonable costs of responding to any request for a consent which the Tenant may make of the Landlord under this Agreement.
   2.12 To pay interest at the rate of 4% above the Bank of England base rate from time to time prevailing on any rent or other money lawfully due from the Tenant under this Agreement which remains unpaid for more than 14

days, interest to be paid from the date the payment fell due until payment.
   2.13 To provide the Landlord with a forwarding address when the tenancy comes to an end and to remove all rubbish and all personal items (including the Tenant's own furniture and equipment) from the Property before leaving.

3. **The Landlord's obligations:**
   3.1 The Landlord agrees that the Tenant may live in the Property without unreasonable interruption from the Landlord or any person rightfully claiming under or in trust for the Landlord.
   3.2 To insure the Property and the items listed on the Inventory and use all reasonable efforts to arrange for any damage caused by an insured risk to be remedied as soon as possible and to provide a copy of the insurance policy to the Tenant if requested.
   3.3 The Landlord will where applicable observe his statutory repairing obligations under the Landlord and Tenant Act 1985 Section 11, the Gas Safety (Installation and Use) Regulations 1998, the Electrical equipment (Safety) Regulations 1994. In outline, the Landlord's obligations under the Landlord and Tenant Act 1985 Section 11 are to keep in repair (where provided by the Landlord)
      3.3.1 the structure and exterior of the Property (including drains gutters and external pipes)
      3.3.2 the installations at the Property for the supply of water, sewage, gas and electricity and for sanitation (including basins, sinks, baths and sanitary conveniences)
      3.3.3 the installations at the Property for space heating and heating water
   3.4 But the Landlord will not be required to
      3.4.1 carry out works for which the Tenant is responsible by virtue of his duty to use the Property in a tenant-like manner
      3.4.2 reinstate the Property in the case of damage or destruction if the insurers refuse to pay out the insurance money due to anything the Tenant has done or failed to do
      3.4.3 rebuild or reinstate the Property in the case of destruction or damage of the Property by a risk not covered by the policy of insurance effected by the Landlord.
   3.5 If the property is a flat or maisonette within a larger building then the Landlord will be under similar obligations for the rest of the building but only in so far as any disrepair will affect the Tenant's enjoyment of the Property and in so far as the Landlord is legally entitled to enter the relevant part of the larger building and carry out the required works or repairs.
   3.5 To arrange for the Tenant's Deposit to be protected by an authorised Tenancy Deposit Scheme and provide the Tenant with the required information in accordance with the provisions of the Housing Act 2004 within 14 days of receipt, and to comply with the rules of the Tenancy Deposit Scheme at all times.

4. **Guarantor**
   If there is a Guarantor, he guarantees that the Tenant will keep to his obligations in this agreement. The Guarantor agrees to pay on demand to the Landlord any money lawfully due to the Landlord by the Tenant.

5. **Ending this Agreement**
   5.1 If the tenant stays on after the end of the fixed term, his tenancy will continue but will run from month-to-month or week-to-week by way of a periodic tenancy arising under the Housing Act 1988. This periodic tenancy can be ended by the Tenant giving at least one

Continued on next page

Furnished House/Flat Rental Agreement
Terms and Conditions (continued)

month's written notice to the Landlord, the notice to expire at the end of a rental period. The foregoing does not limit or affect the Landlord's right to end such a periodic tenancy.

5.2 If at any time

5.2.1 any part of the Rent is outstanding for 21 days after becoming due (whether formally demanded or not) and/or

5.2.2 there is any breach, non-observance or non-performance by the Tenant of any covenant and/or other term of this Agreement which has been notified in writing to the Tenant and the Tenant has failed within a reasonable period of time to remedy the breach and/or pay reasonable compensation to the Landlord for the breach and/or

5.2.3 any of the grounds set out as Grounds 2, 8 or Grounds 10-15 (inclusive) (which relate to breach of any obligation by a Tenant) contained in the Housing Act 1988 Schedule 2 apply

the Landlord may recover possession of the Property and this Agreement shall come to an end. The Landlord retains all his other rights in respect of the Tenant's obligations under this Agreement. Note that if possession of the Property has not been surrendered and anyone is living at the Property then the landlord must obtain a court order for possession before re-entering the Property. This clause does not affect the Tenant's rights under the Protection from Eviction Act 1977.

6. The Deposit

6.1 The Deposit will be held in accordance with the Tenancy Deposit Scheme Rules as issued by the relevant Tenancy Deposit Scheme.

6.2. No interest will be payable to the Tenant by the Landlord in respect of the Deposit save as provided by the Rules of the relevant Tenancy Deposit Scheme.

6.3. Subject to any relevant provisions of the rules of the relevant Tenancy Deposit Scheme, the Landlord shall be entitled to claim from the Deposit the reasonable cost of any repairs or damage to the Property or its contents caused by the Tenant (including any damage caused by the Tenant's family and visitors) and for any rent in arrears and for any other financial losses suffered or expenditure incurred by the Landlord as a result of the Tenant's breach of these terms and conditions, provided the sum claimed by the Landlord is reasonably incurred and is reasonable in amount. The Landlord is not entitled to claim in respect of any damage to the Property or its contents which is due to 'fair wear and tear' i.e. which is as a result of the Tenant and his family (if any) living in the property and using it in a reasonable and lawful manner.

7. Other provisions

7.1 The Landlord hereby notifies the Tenant under Section 48 of the Landlord & Tenant Act 1987 that any notices (including notices in proceedings) should be served upon the Landlord at the address stated with the name of the Landlord overleaf.

7.2 The Landlord shall be entitled to have and retain keys for all the doors to the Property but shall not be entitled to use these to enter the Property without the consent of the Tenant (save in an emergency) or as otherwise provided in this Agreement.

7.3 Any notices or other documents (including any court claim forms in legal proceedings) shall be deemed served on the Tenant during the tenancy by either being left at the Property or by being sent to the Tenant at the Property by first-class post. Notices shall be deemed served the day after being left at the property or the day after posting.

7.4 Any person other than the Tenant who pays the rent due hereunder or any part thereof to the Landlord shall be deemed to have made such payment as agent for and on behalf of the Tenant which the Landlord shall be entitled to assume without enquiry.

7.5 Any personal items left behind at the end of the tenancy after the Tenant has vacated (which the Tenant has not removed in accordance with clause 2.13 above) shall be considered abandoned if they have not been removed within 14 days of written notice to the Tenant from the Landlord, or if the Landlord has been unable to trace the Tenant by taking reasonable steps to do so. After this period the Landlord may remove or dispose of the items as he thinks fit. The Tenant shall be liable for the reasonable disposal costs which may be deducted from the proceeds of sale (if any), and the Tenant shall remain liable for any balance. Any net proceeds of the sale to be returned to the Tenant at the forwarding address provided to the Landlord.

7.6 In the event of destruction to the Property or of damage to it which shall make the same or a substantial portion of the same uninhabitable, the Tenant shall be relieved from paying the rent by an amount proportional to the extent to which the Tenant's ability to live in the Property is thereby prevented, save where the destruction or damage has been caused by any act or default by the Tenant or where the Landlord's insurance cover has been adversely affected by any act or omission on the part of the Tenant.

7.7 Where the context so admits:

7.7.1 The 'Landlord' includes the persons from time to time entitled to receive the Rent.

7.7.2 The 'Tenant' includes any persons deriving title under the Tenant.

7.7.3 The 'Property' includes any part or parts of the Property and all of the Landlord's fixtures and fittings at or upon the Property.

7.7.4 All references to the singular shall include the plural and vice versa and any obligations or liabilities of more than one person shall be joint and several (this means that they will each be liable for all sums due under this Agreement, not just liable for a proportionate part) and an obligation on the part of a party shall include an obligation not to allow or permit the breach of that obligation.

7.7.5 All references to 'he', 'him' and 'his' shall be taken to include 'she', 'her' and 'hers'.

Garage Service Bill Complaint   Form GS08

Date _____

To _____

_____

_____

Dear _____

On _____ I brought in my _____ registration number_____ for repairs
which your reception mechanic estimated would cost £_____. However, when I came to pick the car
up on _____ I was dismayed at being presented with a bill for £_____. I had to pay the bill in
order to drive the car away, but did so expressly under protest, saying I would take the matter up in writing.

[Your reception mechanic never indicated to me that the figure which he quoted was provisional or that I
might have to pay a greater sum. I am therefore entitled, as a matter of contract, to hold you to the figure
quoted. I am therefore entitled to the sum of £_____ representing the difference between the figure
quoted and the figure charged.]
[Even if you were to be correct in saying that no set price had been agreed for the work]/[Although we had
not agreed a set price for the work] I am by law only obliged to pay a reasonable price for your services.
Judging by your initial estimate and also by the enclosed copies of estimates I have since obtained from
[other garages]/[the RAC]/[the AA] of £_____ and £_____ for the same work, I am exercising my
rights under law by rejecting your bill as unreasonably high.

I estimate that the work done on my car was worth £_____, taking into consideration your original
estimate and the others I have obtained, but no more. Please therefore send me a cheque for £_____,
representing the amount you overcharged me within 10 days.

I look forward to hearing from you.

Yours sincerely

_____

Name

_____

Address

_____

Tel.

Garage Service Claim   Form GS09

Date _____

To _____

_____

_____

Dear _____

Re Model _____ Reg. No._____

On _____ I brought in the above vehicle for [a full service] / [repairs to _____].
I was subsequently informed that the following needed attention _____
and agreed to have the necessary work carried out. On picking up the car on _____ I paid the
bill for £_____ in full and received a schedule of the parts tested and work carried out.

However, on _____, just _____ days after it was returned to me, the vehicle developed the
following problems _____ which should not have arisen
after [a full service] / [the above repairs]. I had to have the defect remedied at a cost of £_____, as
evidenced by the enclosed receipt.

Under the Supply of Goods and Services Act of 1982, you are responsible for supplying quality goods and
satisfactory service. Your failure to return my car in satisfactory condition constitutes your breach of contract
and you are liable for the expenses I incurred in having the car repaired.

Please send me a cheque for this sum within 10 days. Otherwise, I shall have no alternative but to issue you
a county court claim for recovery of the amount owed to me without further notice.

Yours sincerely

_____
Name

_____
Address

_____
Tel.

General Assignment
Form TA08

THIS AGREEMENT IS MADE the _____ day of _____ year _____

BETWEEN

(1) _____ (the 'Assignor');and

(2) _____ (the 'Assignee').

NOW IT IS HEREBY AGREED as follows:

1. In consideration for the payment of £_____, receipt of which the Assignor hereby acknowledges, the Assignor hereby unconditionally and irrevocably assigns and transfers to the Assignee all right, title and interest in the following: _____

    _____

    _____

2. The Assignor fully warrants that it has full rights and authority to enter into this assignment and that the rights and benefits assigned hereunder are free and clear of any lien, encumbrance, adverse claim or interest by any third party.

3. The Assignor will, at the behest of the Assignee, forthwith give such notice of this Assignment, as the Assignee may require, to any person who is under any obligation which is assigned to the Assignee under this Agreement.

4. This assignment shall be binding upon and inure to the benefit of the parties, and their successors and assigns.

IN WITNESS OF WHICH the parties have signed this agreement as a Deed the day and year first above written

_____   _____
Signed by or on behalf of the Assignee   Signed by or on behalf of the Assignor

_____   _____
in the presence of (witness)   in the presence of (witness)

Name _____   Name _____

Address _____   Address _____

_____   _____

Occupation _____   Occupation _____

Health Warning: It is essential for the Assignee's protection that the person affected by the assignment (e.g. the debtor under an assigned debt) should be given notice of the assignment.

Note: This form is not to be used for assignments by way of security (i.e. where the Assignee is making a loan to the Assignor and where it is intended that the assignor should get back the thing which is assigned once he has paid the debt).

If the assignment is by way of gift (i.e. if no consideration is to be payable in exchange for the assignment) the assignment must be by Deed.

General Power of Attorney   Form PF09
(Pursuant to the Powers of Attorney Act 1971, Section 10)

THIS GENERAL POWER OF ATTORNEY is made

this_____ day of _____ year _____

BY   _____

            OF _____

                    _____

I APPOINT   _____

                    _____

                    _____

[jointly]/[jointly and severally] to be my attorney(s) in accordance with section 10 of the Powers of Attorney Act 1971.

IN WITNESS whereof I have hereunto set my hand the day and year first above written.

SIGNED as a Deed and Delivered by the said

_____   _____

in the presence of:

Witness's Signature   _____

Full name   _____

Address   _____

                       _____

Occupation   _____

Note:

1. If you are giving this power to more than one person, specify 'jointly' which means that they must all act together and cannot act separately; or 'jointly and severally' which means that they can act together, but also separately if they want to.

2. This form may not be valid if you are a trustee and if you wish to use it to delegate your powers as a trustee. If this applies to you, you should take legal advice.

General Proxy   Form B09

_____ LIMITED

I/We _____ of _____, a member/members of the above

company, hereby appoint _____ of _____

_____, as a proxy to vote in my/our name(s) and on my/our behalf at the

annual/extraordinary general meeting of the company to be held at _____

on _____ year_____ and at any adjournment thereof.

_____

Shareholder

_____

Shareholder

_____

Date

Note:

1. This form complies with the requirements of Article 6 of Table A, the provision most commonly applicable to companies. However, you should check the Articles of your company to make sure that this form is compatible with the procedure set out in them.

2. The Companies Act 1985 requires that the notice of the appointment be lodged with the company (or at such address in the UK as may be specified by the notice of the meeting for which the proxy is to be appointed) 48 hours before the meeting is due to begin. When the Companies Act 2006 section 327 comes into force on 1 October 2007, then any day which is not a working day will no longer count towards the 48 hours. Therefore, if a meeting is due to start at 3pm on the Tuesday following a bank holiday Monday, the deadline for giving notice will be 3pm the previous Thursday.

General Release

Form OLF17

THIS DEED IS MADE the _____ day of _____ year _____

BETWEEN

(1) _____ (the 'First Party');and

(2) _____ (the 'Second Party').

NOW IT IS HEREBY AGREED as follows:

1. The First Party forever releases, discharges, acquits and forgives the Second Party from any and all claims, actions, suits, demands, agreements, liabilities, judgment, and proceedings no matter when the same may have arisen and as more particularly related to or arising from:

    _____
    _____
    _____
    _____

2. This release shall be binding upon and inure to the benefit of the parties, their successors and assigns.

IN WITNESS OF WHICH the parties have executed this deed the date and year first above written

(Individual)

_____

Signed by the First Party

_____

in the presence of (witness)

Name _____

Address _____

_____

Occupation _____

_____

Signed by the Second Party

_____

in the presence of (witness)

Name _____

Address _____

_____

Occupation _____

(Company)

Signed for and on behalf of

_____Ltd

_____

Director

_____

Director/Secretary

Signed for and on behalf of

_____Ltd

_____

Director

_____

Director/Secretary

General Subordination Agreement Between Creditors   Form OLF18

THIS DEED IS MADE the _____ day of _____ year _____

BETWEEN

(1) _____ (the 'First Creditor');and

(2) _____ (the 'Second Creditor').

WHEREAS:

(A)   The First Creditor has a claim against _____ (the 'Debtor') for monies owed to the First Creditor by the Debtor.

(B)   The Second Creditor also has a claim against the Debtor for monies owed to the Second Creditor by the Debtor.

(C)   The Parties agree that the Second Creditor's debt be subordinated to that of the First Creditor.

NOW THIS DEED WITNESSES as follows:

1.   The Second Creditor hereby agrees to subordinate its claims for debts now or hereinafter due to the undersigned from the Debtor to any and all debts that may now for a period of _____ years[1] from the making of this Agreement become or hereinafter be due to the First Creditor from the Debtor.

2.   This subordination shall be unlimited as to amount or duration and shall include the subordination of any secured or unsecured obligation.

3.   At any time when the Debtor may be indebted to the First Creditor, the Second Creditor may not receive payment of any debt owed to the Second Creditor, whether such payment be made by the Debtor or by any guarantor of the Debtor's indebtedness, except as follows: _____.

4.   If the Second Creditor shall receive any payment which it is not entitled under this Agreement to receive, or if any indebtedness which the Second Creditor may have to the Debtor should become the subject of any set-off of any indebtedness which the Debtor may have to the Second Creditor, the Second Creditor shall pay to the First Creditor a sum equal to the amount of such payment or set-off, and in the case of any such sums paid to the Second Creditor, the Second Creditor shall hold the same upon trust for the First Creditor.

5.   This subordination agreement shall be binding upon and inure to the benefit of the parties, their successors and assigns.

Continued on next page

General Subordination Agreement
Between Creditors (continued)

Form OLF18

IN WITNESS OF WHICH the parties have executed this Deed the day and year first above written

(Individual)

_____
Signed by the First Creditor

_____

in the presence of (witness)

Name _____

Address _____

_____

Occupation _____

_____
Signed by the Second Creditor

_____

in the presence of (witness)

Name _____

Address _____

_____

Occupation _____

(Company)

Signed for and on behalf of

_____Ltd

_____

Director

_____

Director/Secretary

Signed for and on behalf of

_____Ltd

_____

Director

_____

Director/Secretary

¹ The period should not exceed 80 years.

Grievance Procedure   Form E33

GRIEVANCE PROCEDURE
at _____ Limited

1. The following procedure shall be applied to settle all disputes or grievances concerning an employee or employees of the Company (but excluding those relating to redundancy selection).

2. Principles:

    (i)   It is the intention of both parties that employees should be encouraged to have direct contact with management to resolve their problems.

    (ii)   The procedure for resolution of grievances and avoidance of disputes is available if the parties are unable to agree a solution to a problem.

    (iii) Should a matter be referred to this procedure for resolution, both parties should accept that it should be progressed as speedily as possible, with a joint commitment that every effort will be made to ensure that such a reference takes no longer than seven working days to complete.

    (iv)   Pending resolution of the grievance, the same conditions prior to its notification shall continue to apply, except in those circumstances where such a continuation would have damaging effects upon the Company's business.

    (v)   It is agreed between the parties that where the grievance is of a collective nature, i.e. affecting more than one employee, it shall be referred initially to (ii) of the procedure.

    (vi)   If the employee's immediate supervisor/manager is the subject of the grievance and for this reason the employee does not wish the grievance to be heard by him or her, it shall be referred initially to (ii) of the procedure.

3. The Procedure:

    (i)   Where an employee has a grievance, he shall raise the matter with his or her immediate supervisor/manager. If the grievance concerns the performance of a duty by the Company in relation to an employee, the employee shall have the right to be accompanied by a fellow worker or trade union official if he makes a request to be so accompanied.

    (ii)   If the matter has not been resolved at (i), it shall be referred to a more senior manager or director and the shop steward, full-time trade union officer, or fellow employee, if requested shall be present. A statement summarising the main details of the grievance and the reasons for the failure to agree must be prepared and signed by both parties.

    (iii) In the event of a failure to agree, the parties will consider whether conciliation or arbitration is appropriate. The Company may refer the dispute to the Advisory Conciliation and Arbitration Service, whose findings may, by mutual prior agreement, be binding on both parties.

Guarantee   Form LB03

THIS AGREEMENT IS MADE the _____ day of _____ year _____

BETWEEN

(1) _____ (the 'Guarantor');and

(2) _____ (the 'Creditor').

NOW IT IS HEREBY AGREED as follows:

1.   As an inducement for the Creditor, from time to time to extend credit to _____
     _____ (the 'Customer'),
     it is hereby agreed that the Guarantor does hereby guarantee to the Creditor the prompt, punctual
     and full payment of all monies now or hereinafter due to the Creditor from the Customer.

2.   Until termination, this Guarantee is unlimited as to amount or duration and shall remain in full force
     and effect notwithstanding any extension, compromise, adjustment, forbearance, waiver, release or
     discharge of any party or guarantor, or release in whole or in part of any security granted for the said
     indebtedness or compromise or adjustment thereto, and the Guarantor waives all notices thereto.

3.   The obligations of the Guarantor shall be primary and not secondary and the Creditor shall not be
     required to exhaust its remedies as against the Customer prior to enforcing its rights under this
     Guarantee against the Guarantor.

4.   The Guarantee hereunder shall be unconditional and absolute and the Guarantor waives all rights of
     subrogation and set-off until all sums due under this guarantee are fully paid.

5   In the event payments due under this Guarantee are not paid punctually upon demand, then the
     Guarantor shall pay all reasonable costs and solicitors fees necessary for the collection and
     enforcement of this Guarantee.

6.   This guarantee may be terminated by the Guarantor upon fourteen (14) days written notice of
     termination being delivered to the Creditor. Such termination shall extend only to credit extended by
     the Creditor after the expiry of the said fourteen (14) day period and not to prior extended credit, or
     goods in transit received by the Customer after the expiry of the fourteen day period.

7.   The Guarantor warrants and represents it has full authority to enter into this Guarantee.

8.   This Guarantee shall be binding upon and inure to the benefit of the parties, their successors and
     assigns.

Continued on next page

Guarantee (continued)   Form LB03

9.   This Guarantee is subject to English law and the parties agree to submit to the exclusive jurisdiction of the English courts in connection with any dispute hereunder.

IN WITNESS OF WHICH the parties have signed this agreement the day and year first above written

_____

Signed by or on behalf of the Guarantor

_____

in the presence of (witness)

Name _____

Address _____

_____

Occupation_____

_____

Signed by or on behalf of the Creditor

_____

in the presence of (witness)

Name _____

Address _____

_____

Occupation_____

Health warning: This form should not be used if the original agreement is one which is regulated under the Consumer Credit Act 1974. Broadly speaking the Act, at the time of writing, applies to any loan, hire or hire purchase agreement for £25,000 or less. There are some exceptions. The most important are that (1) an agreement is not regulated if the borrower or hirer is a limited company or (2) the agreement is 'non-commercial', meaning that it is not made in the course of a business or is a mere one-off. There are other exceptions as well, but you should take a solicitor's advice before deciding that any of these apply to you. If the Act does regulate the original agreement, it will also regulate any variation to the agreement (such as this one). In those circumstances, this form will not comply with the requirements of the Act and the agreement may therefore be unenforceable. Note also that by the time you use this form, the law may have changed so as to apply to loans of more than £25,000.

Holiday Letting Agreement
(for a Holiday Let of Furnished Property)

Form RT03

The PROPERTY   _____

_____

The LANDLORD   _____

_____

The TENANT   _____

_____

_____

_____

The TERM   _____ day(s)/week(s)/month(s)* beginning at 12 noon on _____

and expiring at 10 am on _____

The RENT   £ _____ per week/month* payable in advance on the _____ of each week/month*

or

£_____ payable in advance on the date of this Agreement

The DEPOSIT   £ _____

The INVENTORY   means the list of the Landlord's possessions at the Property which has been _____

signed by the Landlord and the Tenant

DATED   _____

SIGNED   _____   _____

_____   _____

(The Landlord)   _____

(The Tenant)

THIS RENTAL AGREEMENT comprises the particulars detailed above and the terms and conditions printed overleaf whereby the Property is hereby let by the Landlord and taken by the Tenant for the Term at the Rent.

(*delete as appropriate)

IMPORTANT NOTICE TO LANDLORDS:

This Form is intended for use only for a Holiday Let. If the circumstances make it clear that the letting is NOT for the purposes of the Tenant's holiday, for example because the Term is so long, the Courts may hold that it is an Assured Shorthold Tenancy (and you will not be able to obtain an order for possession of the Property for at least six months from the beginning of the tenancy).

Terms and Conditions on next page

Holiday Letting Agreement Terms and Conditions — Form RT03

1. The Tenant shall be entitled to occupy the Property for holiday purposes only and this Agreement shall not confer on the Tenant any security of tenure within the terms of the Housing Act 1988 pursuant to which the occupation shall be deemed to be by way of an excluded tenancy

2. The Tenant will:

    2.1 pay the Rent at the times and in the manner aforesaid

    2.2 keep the interior of the Property in a good, clean and tenantable state and condition and not damage or injure the Property or any part of it

    2.3 yield up the Property at the end of the Term in the same clean state and condition it was in at the beginning of the Term reasonable wear and tear and damage by insured risks excepted

    2.4 maintain at the Property and keep in a good and clean condition all of the contents of the Property as listed on the Inventory, if any, and to replace, repair or cleanse any item(s) which become broken or damaged during the Term

    2.5 not make any alteration or addition to the Property nor to do any redecoration or painting of the Property

    2.6 not do or omit to do anything on or at the Property which may be or become a nuisance or annoyance to any other occupiers of the Property or owners or occupiers of adjoining or nearby premises or which may in any way prejudice the insurance of the Property or cause an increase in the premium payable therefor

    2.7 not without the Landlord's prior written consent (consent not to be withheld unreasonably) allow or keep any pet or any kind or animal at the Property. If any pets are permitted they must be kept under strict control at all times and must not be left unattended in the Property. The Tenant will be responsible for all damage and any extra cleaning caused by the pet(s)

    2.8 not use or occupy the Property in any way whatsoever other than as a private holiday residence for a maximum of _____ persons

    2.9 not assign, sublet, charge or part with or share possession of occupation of the Property or any part thereof

    2.10 allow the Landlord or anyone with the Landlord's written permission to enter the Property at reasonable times of the day to inspect its condition and state of repair, and carry out any necessary repairs and gas inspections, provided the Landlord has given reasonable prior notice (except in emergency)

    2.11 pay interest at the rate of 4% above the Base Lending Rate for the time being of the Landlord's bankers upon any Rent or other money due from the Tenant under this Agreement which is more than 3 days in arrears in respect of the period from when it became due to the date of payment

    2.12 provide the Landlord with a forwarding address when the tenancy comes to an end and remove all rubbish and all personal items (including the Tenant's own furniture and equipment) from the Property before leaving

3. Subject to the Tenant paying the rent and performing his/her obligations under this Agreement the Tenant may peaceably hold and enjoy the Property during the term without interruption from the Landlord or any person rightfully claiming under or in trust for the Landlord

4. In the event of the Rent being unpaid for more than 10 days after it is due (whether demanded or not) or there being a breach of any other of the Tenant's obligations under this Agreement then the Landlord may recover possession of the Property and this Rental Agreement shall thereupon end but without prejudice to any of the Landlord's other rights and remedies in respect of any outstanding obligations on the part of the Tenant. This clause does not affect the Tenant's statutory rights and the Landlord will need to obtain a court order while anyone is living at the Property

5. The Deposit

    5.1 The Deposit will be held by the Landlord and will be refunded to the Tenant at the end of the Term (however it ends) at the forwarding address provided to the Landlord but less any reasonable deductions properly made by the Landlord to cover any reasonable costs incurred or losses caused to him by any breaches of the obligations in his Agreement by the Tenant. No interest will be payable to the Tenant in respect of the Deposit money

    5.2 The Deposit shall be payable to the Tenant as soon as reasonably practicable, however the Landlord shall not be bound to return the Deposit until after he has had a reasonable opportunity to assess the reasonable cost of any repairs required as a result of any breaches of his obligations by the Tenant or other sums properly due to the Landlord under clause 6.1 However, the Landlord shall not, save in exceptional circumstances, retain the Deposit for more than one month after the end of the tenancy

    5.3 If at any time during the Term the Landlord is obliged to deduct from the Deposit to satisfy the reasonable costs occasioned by any breaches of the obligations of the Tenant the Tenant shall make such additional payments as are necessary to restore the full amount of the Deposit

6. The Landlord hereby notifies the Tenant under Section 48 of the Landlord & Tenant Act 1987 that any notices (including notices in proceedings) should be served upon the Landlord at the address stated with the name of the Landlord overleaf

7. In the event of damage to or destruction of the Property by any of the risks insured against by the Landlord the Tenant shall be relieved from payment of the Rent to the extent that the Tenant's use and enjoyment of the Property is thereby prevented and from performance of its obligations as to the state and condition of the Property to the extent of and so long as there prevails such damage or destruction (except to the extent that any policy of insurance that the Landlord may have taken out is prejudiced by any act or default of the Tenant)

8. Where the context so admits:

    8.1 The 'Landlord' includes the persons for the time being entitled to the reversion expectant upon this Tenancy

    8.2 The 'Tenant' includes any persons deriving title under the Tenant

    8.3 The 'Property' includes all of the Landlord's fixtures and fittings at or upon the Property

    8.4 The 'Term' shall mean the period stated in the particulars overleaf or any shorter or longer period in the event of an earlier termination or an extension respectively

9. All references to the singular shall include the plural and vice versa and any obligations or liabilities of more than one person shall be joint and several and an obligation on the part of a party shall include an obligation not to allow or permit the breach of that obligation

House Rules   Form RT04

1. The price for the use of the room (with bed and breakfast and evening meal*) is £ _____ per week

    payable in advance on _____

    of each week.

2. The room will be cleaned and sheets changed on _____ of each week.

3. Guests are requested to keep the room tidy and not to bring any food into it.

4. No overnight visitors are permitted. Any visitors must leave the premises at 10 p.m. when the doors

    will be locked.

5. The volume control on any television, radio, audio system or musical instrument must be turned low so

    that they are not audible from outside the room. The owner reserves the right to require these to be

    turned off if they cause annoyance to them or other occupiers.

6. Communal bathroom and kitchen facilities (if any) must be left clean and tidy by guests after use.

7. Guests may use the sitting room.

8. Guests have use of the bedroom assigned to them but they do not have exclusive possession of it. The

    owner reserves the right to require the guest to move to another room at short notice.

9. Guests must not move furniture, pictures or wall hangings without the consent of the owner, nor

    should they install their own furniture, pictures or wall hanging without such consent.

10. Guests returning to the house after 10 p.m. without prior arrangement with the owner are liable to be

    locked out.

* Delete as appropriate

Note: Guests should be asked to sign a copy of these rules.

House/Flat Share Agreement (Non-Resident Owner)   Form F304

The PROPERTY   _____

_____

The DESIGNATED ROOM   _____

The SHARED PARTS   _____

The LANDLORD   _____

                    of_____

_____

The TENANT   _____

The GUARANTOR*   _____

                    of _____

The TERM   _____ weeks/months* beginning on _____

The RENT   £ _____ per week/month* payable in advance on the _____ of each

                    week/month*

The DEPOSIT   £ _____ which will be registered with one of the Government

                    authorised tenancy deposit schemes ('the Tenancy Deposit Scheme') in

                    accordance with the Tenancy Deposit Scheme Rules

The INVENTORY   means the list of the Landlord's possessions at the Property which has been

                    signed by the Landlord and the Tenant

DATED   _____

Signed and executed as a Deed by the following parties

Landlord	**Tenant**	**Guarantor***
_____	_____	_____
Landlord(s)' name(s)	_____	_____
	_____	_____
	Tenant(s)' name(s)	Guarantor's name
_____	_____	_____
Landlord(s)' signature(s)	_____	_____
	_____	_____
	Tenant(s)' signature(s)	Guarantor's signature

In the presence of:

Witness signature _____   Witness signature _____   Witness signature _____

Full name _____   Full name _____   Full name _____

Address_____   Address_____   Address_____

_____   _____   _____

(*delete as appropriate)

Continued on next page

House/Flat Share Agreement (Non-Resident Owner) (cont)   Form F304

THIS TENANCY AGREEMENT comprises the particulars detailed above and the terms and conditions printed overleaf whereby the Designated Room, with the right to share the use of the Shared Parts with such other persons as the Landlord grants or has granted the right to use those Shared Parts, is hereby let by the Landlord and taken by the Tenant for the Term at the Rent.

IMPORTANT NOTICE TO LANDLORDS:

1 The details of 'The LANDLORD' near the top of this Agreement must include an address for the Landlord in England or Wales as well as his/her name, or all names in the case of joint Landlords.

2 Always remember to give the appropriate written Notice to Terminate to the Tenant two clear months before the end of the Term.

3 Before granting the tenancy agreement, you should check whether your chosen deposit scheme provider requires you to insert any additional terms concerning the deposit into the tenancy agreement or to alter or delete any of the terms appearing in the form below. Details of the websites of the scheme providers are set out in Note 4 for tenants below. Currently only The Tenancy Deposit Scheme has any such requirements.

4. The information in 'Notice to Tenants' below is important to you as well, because it is relevant to whether or not you should use this form and whether you can get the Property back at the end of the term.

IMPORTANT NOTICE TO TENANTS:

1 In general, if you currently occupy this Property under a protected or statutory tenancy and you give it up to take a new tenancy of the same or other accommodation owned by the same Landlord, that tenancy cannot be an Assured Shorthold Tenancy and this Agreement is not appropriate.

2 If you currently occupy this Property under an Assured Tenancy which is not an Assured Shorthold Tenancy your Landlord is not permitted to grant you an Assured Shorthold Tenancy of this Property or of alternative property and this Agreement is not appropriate.

3 If the total amount of rent exceeds £25,000 per annum, an Assured Shorthold Tenancy cannot be created and this Agreement is not appropriate. Seek legal advice.

4 Further information about the Government authorised Tenancy Deposit Schemes can be obtained from their websites: The Deposit Protection Service at www.depositprotection.com, Tenancy Deposit Solutions Ltd at www.mydeposits.co.uk and The Tenancy Deposit Scheme at www.tds.gb.com.

Terms and Conditions on next page

House/Flat Share Agreement (Non-Resident Owner) Form F304
Terms and Conditions

1. This Agreement is intended to create an assured shorthold tenancy as defined in the Housing Act 1988, as amended by the Housing Act 1996, and the provisions for the recovery of possession by the Landlord in that Act apply accordingly. The Tenant understands that the Landlord will be entitled to recover possession of the Property at the end of the Term. Under this Agreement, the Tenant will have exclusive occupation of the Designated Room and will share with other occupiers of the Property the use and facilities of the Shared Parts of the Property.

2. The Tenant's obligations:
   2.1 To pay the Rent at the times and in the manner set out above.
   2.2 To make a proportionate contribution to the costs of all charges in respect of any electric, gas, water and telephone or televisual services used at or supplied to the Property and Council Tax or any similar property tax that might be charged in addition to or replacement of it during the Term.
   2.3 To keep the items on the Inventory and the interior of the Designated Room and Shared Parts of the Property in a good and clean state and condition and not damage or injure the Designated Room and Shared Parts of the Property or the items on the Inventory (fair wear and tear excepted).
   2.4 To yield up the Designated Room and Shared Parts of the Property and the items on the Inventory at the end of the Term in the same clean state and condition it/they was/were in at the beginning of the Term (but the Tenant will not be responsible for fair wear and tear caused during normal use of the Property and the items on the Inventory or for any damage to the Shared Parts of the Property and its contents caused by other tenants and/or their visitors).
   2.5 Not make any alteration or addition to the Property and not without the prior written consent of the Landlord (consent not to be withheld unreasonably) do any redecoration or painting of the Property.
   2.6 Not do anything on or at the Property which:
      (a) may be or become a nuisance or annoyance to any other occupiers of the Property or owners or occupiers of adjoining or nearby premises;
      (b) is illegal or immoral;
      (c) may in any way affect the validity of the insurance of the Property and the items listed on the Inventory or cause an increase in the premium payable by the Landlord.
      (d) will cause any blockages in the drainage system and in the case of breach of this clause the Tenant to be responsible for the reasonable cost of such repair or other works which will be reasonably required.
   2.7 Not without the Landlord's prior consent allow or keep any pet or any kind of animal at the Property.
   2.8 Not use or occupy the Property in any way whatsoever other than as a private residence.
   2.9 Not assign, sublet, charge or part with or share possession or occupation of the Property (but see clause 5.1 below).
   2.10 To allow the Landlord or anyone with the Landlord's written permission to enter the Property at reasonable times of the day to inspect its condition and state of repair, carry out any necessary repairs and gas inspections, and during the last month of the Term, show the Property to prospective new tenants, provided the Landlord has given 24 hours' prior written notice (except in emergency).
   2.11 To pay the Landlord's reasonable costs reasonably incurred as a result of any breaches by the Tenant of his obligations under this Agreement, and further to pay the Landlord's reasonable costs of responding to any request for a consent which the Tenant may make of the Landlord under this Agreement.
   2.12 To pay interest at the rate of 4% above the Bank of England base rate from time to time prevailing on any rent or other money lawfully due from the Tenant under this Agreement which remains unpaid for more than 14 days, interest to be paid from the date the payment fell due until payment.
   2.13 To provide the Landlord with a forwarding address when the tenancy comes to an end and to remove all rubbish and all personal items (including the Tenant's own furniture and equipment) from the Designated Room and Shared Parts of the Property before leaving.

3. The Landlord's obligations:
   3.1 The Landlord agrees that the Tenant may live in Designated Room and Shared Parts of the Property without unreasonable interruption from the Landlord or any person rightfully claiming under or in trust for the Landlord.
   3.2 The Landlord will where applicable observe his statutory repairing obligations under the Landlord and Tenant Act 1985 Section 11, the Gas Safety (Installation and Use) Regulations 1998, the Electrical equipment (Safety) Regulations 1994. In outline, the Landlord's obligations under the Landlord and Tenant Act 1985 Section 11 are to keep in repair (where provided by the Landlord)
   3.3.1 the structure and exterior of the Property (including drains gutters and external pipes)
   3.3.2 the installations at the Property for the supply of water, sewage, gas and electricity and for sanitation (including basins, sinks, baths and sanitary conveniences)
   3.3.3 the installations at the Property for space heating and heating water
   3.4 But the Landlord will not be required to
   3.4.1 carry out works for which the Tenant is responsible by virtue of his duty to use the Property in a tenant-like manner
   3.4.2 reinstate the Property in the case of damage or destruction if the insurers refuse to pay out the insurance money due to anything the Tenant has done or failed to do
   3.4.3 rebuild or reinstate the Property in the case of destruction or damage of the Property by a risk not covered by the policy of insurance effected by the Landlord.
   3.4 If the property is a flat or maisonette within a larger building then the Landlord will be under similar obligations for the rest of the building but only in so far as any disrepair will affect the Tenant's enjoyment of the Property and in so far as the Landlord is legally entitled to enter the relevant part of the larger building and carry out the required works or repairs.
   3.5 To arrange for the Tenant's Deposit to be protected by an authorised Tenancy Deposit Scheme in accordance with the provisions of the Housing Act 2004 within 14 days of receipt, and to comply with the rules of the Tenancy Deposit Scheme at all times.

4. Guarantor
   If there is a Guarantor, he guarantees that the Tenant will keep to his obligations in this agreement. The Guarantor agrees to pay on demand to the Landlord any money lawfully due to the Landlord by the Tenant.

5. Ending this Agreement
   5.1 The Tenant cannot normally end this Agreement before the end of the Term. However after the first three months of the Term, if the Tenant can find a suitable alternative tenant, and provided this alternative tenant

Continued on next page

is acceptable to the Landlord (the Landlord's approval not to be unreasonably withheld) the Tenant may give notice to end the tenancy on a date at least one month from the date that such approval is given by the Landlord. On the expiry of such notice and upon (i) payment by the Tenant to the Landlord of the reasonable expenses reasonably incurred by the Landlord in granting the necessary approval and in granting any new tenancy to the alternative tenant, and (ii) the execution by the alternative tenant of a new tenancy agreement in the form of this Agreement for a period of 6 months or for a period not less than the unexpired portion of the term of this Agreement (if that be greater than 6 months), or for such other period as the Landlord shall approve this tenancy shall end.

5.2   If the Tenant stays on after the end of the fixed term, a new tenancy will arise that will run from month to month or week to week (a 'periodic tenancy'). This periodic tenancy can be ended by the Tenant giving at least one month's written notice to the Landlord, the notice to expire at the end of the rental period.

5.2.1   any part of the Rent is outstanding for 21 days after becoming due (whether formally demanded or not) and/or

5.2.2   there is any breach, non-observance or non-performance by the Tenant of any covenant and/or other term of this Agreement which has been notified in writing to the Tenant and the Tenant has failed within a reasonable period of time to remedy the breach and/or pay reasonable compensation to the Landlord for the breach and/or

5.2.3   any of the grounds set out as Grounds 2, 8 or Grounds 10-15 (inclusive) (which relate to breach of any obligation by a Tenant) contained in the Housing Act 1988 Schedule 2 apply

the Landlord may recover possession of the Property and this Agreement shall come to an end. The Landlord retains all his other rights in respect of the Tenant's obligations under this Agreement. Note that if possession of the Property has not been surrendered and anyone is living at the Property then the landlord must obtain a court order for possession before re-entering the Property. This clause does not affect the Tenant's rights under the Protection from Eviction Act 1977.

6.   The Deposit

6.1   The Deposit will be held in accordance with the Tenancy Deposit Scheme Rules as issued by the relevant Tenancy Deposit Scheme.

6.2.   No interest will be payable to the Tenant by the Landlord in respect of the Deposit save as provided by the Rules of the relevant Tenancy Deposit Scheme.

6.3.   Subject to any relevant provisions of the rules of the relevant Tenancy Deposit Scheme, the Landlord shall be entitled to claim from the Deposit the reasonable cost of any repairs or damage to the Property or its contents caused by the Tenant (including any damage caused by the Tenant's family and visitors) any rent in arrears and for any other financial losses suffered or expenditure incurred by the Landlord as a result of the Tenant's breach of these terms and conditions, provided the sum claimed by the Landlord is reasonably incurred and is reasonable in amount. The Landlord is not entitled to claim in respect of any damage to the Property or its contents which is due to 'fair wear and tear' i.e. which is as a result of the Tenant and his family (if any) living in the property and using it in a reasonable and lawful manner.

7.   Other provisions

7.1   The Landlord hereby notifies the Tenant under Section 48 of the Landlord & Tenant Act 1987 that any notices (including notices in proceedings) should be served upon the Landlord at the address stated with the name of the Landlord overleaf.

7.2   The Landlord shall be entitled to have and retain keys for all the doors to the Property but shall not be entitled to use these to enter the Designated Room without the consent of the Tenant (save in an emergency) or as otherwise provided in this Agreement.

7.3   Any notices or other documents shall be deemed served on the Tenant during the tenancy by either being left at the Property or by being sent to the Tenant at the Property by first-class post. If notices or other documents are served on the Tenant by post they shall be deemed served on the day after posting.

7.4   Any person other than the Tenant who pays the rent due hereunder or any part thereof to the Landlord shall be deemed to have made such payment as agent for and on behalf of the Tenant which the Landlord shall be entitled to assume without enquiry.

7.5   Any personal items left behind at the end of the tenancy after the Tenant has vacated (which the Tenant has not removed in accordance with clause 2.13 above) shall be considered abandoned if they have not been removed within 14 days of written notice to the Tenant from the Landlord, or if the Landlord has been unable to trace the Tenant by taking reasonable steps to do so. After this period the Landlord may remove or dispose of the items as he thinks fit. The Tenant shall be liable for the reasonable disposal costs which may be deducted from the proceeds of sale (if any), and the Tenant shall remain liable for any balance. Any net proceeds of the sale to be returned to the Tenant at the forwarding address provided to the Landlord.

7.6   In the event of destruction to the Property or of damage to it which shall make the same or a substantial portion of the same uninhabitable, the Tenant shall be relieved from paying the rent by an amount proportional to the extent to which the Tenant's ability to live in the Property is thereby prevented , save where the destruction or damage has been caused by any act or default by the Tenant or where the Landlord's insurance cover has been adversely affected by any act or omission on the part of the Tenant.

7.7   Where the context so admits:

7.7.1   The 'Landlord' includes the persons from time to time entitled to receive the Rent.

7.7.2   The 'Tenant' includes any persons deriving title under the Tenant.

7.7.3   The 'Designated Room' and 'Shared Parts' includes any part or parts of the Designated Room and Shared Parts and all of the Landlord's fixtures and fittings in the Designated Room and Shared Parts.

7.7.4   All references to the singular shall include the plural and vice versa and any obligations or liabilities of more than one person shall be joint and several (this means that they will each be liable for all sums due under this Agreement, not just liable for a proportionate part) and an obligation on the part of a party shall include an obligation not to allow or permit the breach of that obligation. Note that joint and several liability will only apply to two or more Tenants signing this Agreement together. Tenants will not have joint and several liability with other tenants in the Property who have signed separate agreements with the Landlord.

7.7.5   All references to 'he', 'him' and 'his' shall be taken to include 'she', 'her' and 'hers'.

Household Inventory

Re _____ (the Property)

No.	Living Room
____	Armchair
____	Ashtray
____	Chairs
____	Coffee table
____	Curtains
____	Cushions
____	Framed picture
____	Stereo system
____	Mirror
____	Net curtains
____	Plant
____	Rug
____	Sofa
____	Table
____	Table lamp
____	Telephone
____	Television
____	Vase
____	Video
____	Wall clock
____	

No.	Kitchen/Dining Room
____	Apron
____	Baking tray
____	Bottle opener
____	Bread bin
____	Carving knives
____	Casserole dish
____	Cheese grater
____	Chopping board
____	Coffee pot

____	Corkscrew
____	Cups
____	Dessert spoons
____	Dinner plates
____	Dishwasher
____	Draining board
____	Egg cups
____	Forks
____	Fridge/Freezer
____	Fruit bowl
____	Frying pans
____	Garlic crusher
____	Glasses
____	Kettle
____	Knives
____	Liquidiser
____	Measuring jug
____	Microwave
____	Milk jug
____	Mugs
____	Mug tree
____	Oven & Hob
____	Pie dishes
____	Potato peeler
____	Pudding/Soup dishes
____	Pyrex dish
____	Roasting dish
____	Rolling pin
____	Salt & pepper pots
____	Sauce pans
____	Scales
____	Serving dishes
____	Side plates
____	Sieve
____	Soup spoons
____	Spatula

____	Storage jars
____	Sugar jug
____	Swing bin
____	Table
____	Tablecloth
____	Table mats
____	Teapot
____	Tea spoons
____	Tea towels
____	Tin opener
____	Toaster
____	Tray
____	Washing machine
____	Washing up bowl
____	Wok
____	Wooden spoons

No.	Bedroom One
____	Blankets
____	Bed sheets
____	Chair
____	Chest of drawers
____	Curtains
____	Double bed
____	Dressing table
____	Duvet
____	Duvet cover
____	Framed picture
____	Lamp
____	Mattress cover
____	Net curtains
____	Pillows
____	Pillow cases

Continued on next page

Household Inventory (continued)   Form RT07

____ Side table

____ Single bed

____ Table mirror

____ Wall mirror

____ Wardrobe

____

____

No.	Bedroom Two

____

____ Blankets

____ Bed sheets

____ Chair

____ Chest of drawers

____ Curtains

____ Double bed

____ Dressing table

____ Duvet

____ Duvet cover

____ Framed picture

____ Lamp

____ Mattress cover

____ Net curtains

____ Pillows

____ Pillow cases

____ Side table

____ Single bed

____ Table mirror

____ Wall mirror

____ Wardrobe

____

No.	Bathroom

____ Basket

____ Floor mat

____ Lavatory brush

____ Shower curtain

____ Soap dish

____ Towels

____ Wall mirror

____ Wooden chair

No.	Storage cupboard

____

____ Broom

____ Bucket

____ Clothes horse

____ Dustpan & brush

____ Iron

____ Ironing board

____ Mop

____ Vacuum cleaner

No.	Hall

____ Coat stand

____ Framed picture

____

Signed _____   _____

(Landlord/Owner)   (Tenant/Sharer)

Indemnity Agreement   Form OLF19

THIS AGREEMENT' IS MADE the _____ day of _____ year _____

BETWEEN

(1) _____(the 'First Party');and

(2) _____ (the 'Second Party').

[NOW THIS DEED WITNESSES as follows:]

1. [In consideration of the Second Party [engaging the First Party as a subcontractor to carry out certain of the works which the First Party has undertaken to complete for _____ under a contract dated _____('the Main Contract'). The First Party agrees to indemnify and save harmless the Second Party and its successors and assigns, from any claim, action, liability, loss, damage or suit, arising from the following:

    [any breach, non -performance, act or omission by the First Party its employees or agents by reason of which the Second Party is rendered liable for breach of the Main Contract or in negligence or for breach of any statutory duty to _____ or to any other person or persons, provided that nothing in this Agreement shall make the First Party liable for any negligence or breach of duty on the part of the Second Party its employees or agent.]

2. In the event of any asserted claim as aforesaid, the Second Party shall provide the First Party immediate written notice of the same, and thereafter the First Party shall pay forthwith upon demand by the Second Party, such costs of defending against the Claim as the Second Party may incur and shall at its own expense give all reasonable assistance to the defence against such claim and shall, protect and save harmless the Second Party from the same and from any loss or liability thereunder.

3. The Second Party shall have the right at its sole discretion to defend, pay or settle the claim on its own behalf without notice to the First Party and with full rights of recourse against the the First Party for all fees, costs, expenses and payments made or agreed to be paid to discharge the claim.

4. Upon default, the First Party further agrees to pay all reasonable solicitor's fees incurred in enforcing this Agreement against the First Party.

5. This Agreement shall be unlimited as to amount or (save as aforesaid) duration.

6. This Agreement shall be binding upon and inure to the benefit of the parties, their successors and assigns.

[7. Nothing in this Agreement is intended to confer any benefit on a third party whether under the Contracts (Rights of Third Parties) Act or otherwise].

Continued on next page

Indemnity Agreement (continued)   Form OLF19

IN WITNESS OF WHICH the parties have executed this Deed the day and year first above written

(Individual)

_____

Signed by the First Party

_____

in the presence of (witness)

Name _____

Address _____

Occupation _____

(Company)

Signed for and on behalf of

_____Ltd

_____

Director

_____

Director/Secretary

_____

Signed by the Second Party

_____

in the presence of (witness)

Name _____

Address _____

_____

Occupation _____

Signed for and on behalf of:

_____Ltd

_____

Director

_____

Director/Secretary

Note: This is merely an example of the sort of transaction which could make an indemnity agreement desirable and which could furnish consideration for it.

[1] If there is no consideration for the indemnity, this document should be stated to be a Deed and executed as such.

Independent Contractor Agreement   Form E34

THIS AGREEMENT IS MADE the _____ day of _____ year _____

BETWEEN:

(1 _____ (the 'Owner');and

(2) _____(the 'Contractor').

WHEREAS:

(A)   The owner resides or operates a business at _____ (the 'Site') and
      wishes to have certain services performed at the Site.

(B)   The Contractor agrees to perform such services under the terms and conditions set forth in this
      agreement.

NOW IT IS HEREBY AGREED as follows:

1.   Description of Work: In return for the payment agreed hereunder the Contractor will perform services
      of the following description at the Site: _____

      _____

      _____

      _____

      _____

      _____

      _____

      _____

      _____

2.   Payment: The Owner will pay the Contractor the sum of _____Pounds (£_____)
      for the work performed under this agreement, in accordance with the following schedule: _____

      _____

      _____

      _____

      _____

3.   Relationship of the Parties: This agreement creates an independent contractor-owner relationship. The
      Owner is interested only in the results to be achieved. [The Contractor is free to decide how those
      results will be achieved, and who is to be engaged by him to achieve those results without reference
      to the Contractor, save that _____]¹
      [The Contractor is entitled to carry out the work himself or to engage other persons to carry out in his
      stead as he may in his discretion decide]. The Contractor is solely responsible for the conduct and
      control of the work. The Contractor is not an agent or employee of the Owner for any purpose.
      Employees of the Contractor are not in any contractual relationship with the Owner and are not
      entitled to any benefits that the Owner provides to the Owner's employees. This is not an exclusive

Continued on next page

Independent Contractor Agreement (continued)   Form E34

agreement. Both parties are free to contract with other parties for similar services. [Save for the particular assignments mentioned in the above schedule, the Owner shall not be obliged to provide work for the Contractor, and the Contractor shall not be obliged to do any work or supply any services].

4.   Liability: The Contractor assumes all risk connected with work to be performed, whether in respect of the premises (or access thereto) on which the work is to be carried out or for providing a safe system of work to those engaged in that work. [The Contractor also accepts all responsibility for the provision of tools and equipment used in the performance of this agreement. To the extent that the Owner's tools and equipment are used, the Contractor shall be responsible for ensuring that they are safe to use and appropriate for the work to be done. If the Contractor shall decide that any tools or equipment are unsafe to use or inappropriate for the work, the Contractor shall provide such tools and equipment which in the Contractor's opinion are necessary. Tools and equipment so provided shall belong to and be at the risk of the Contractor. The Contractor will carry for the duration of this agreement public liability insurance [employers' liability insurance] [and] [contract works insurance] in an amount and on terms acceptable to the Owner. The Contractor agrees to indemnify the Owner for any and all liability or loss arising from the performance of this agreement.

5.   Duration: Either party may cancel this agreement with _____ days' written notice to the other party; otherwise, the contract shall remain in force for a term of _____ _____ from the date hereof, [but this term shall not be construed so as to require the Contractor to perform any work or the Owner to provide any work, save as specifically provided for in this Agreement].

IN WITNESS OF WHICH the parties have signed this agreement the day and year first above written

_____   _____
Signed by or on behalf of the Owner   Signed by or on behalf of the Contractor

_____   _____
in the presence of (witness)   in the presence of (witness)

Name _____   Name _____

Address _____   Address _____

_____   _____

Occupation _____   Occupation _____

Note: If you wish to avoid an employer/employee relationship you cannot achieve this by simply calling yourselves independent contractors. A court would look at the reality of the relationship and make an evaluation in all the circumstances. Important factors would be the degree of control which one party has over the way in which the other works, whether the work is to be done by an individual personally, or whether he is free to delegate performance; whether one party is bound to offer, and the other to do, the work and above all the extent to which the contractor is part of the organisation for which he is working (e.g. whether he is brought in to achieve one project or whether he carries out work of a type which always requires someone to be on hand to do it). In this form there are many parts in square brackets. Include all of those which suit your arrangement, as the more you include, the more likely it will be that you will avoid the relationship of employer/employee. Note that it is generally easier to avoid this relationship if you take on temporary staff through an employment agency. You should consult a solicitor if any doubt arises.

¹   Here insert any restrictions as to times of work, qualifications of workers or such other restrictions on the Contractor's freedom to carry out the work in the manner he chooses as may be necessary.

Insurance Claim Notice — Form PF10

Date _____

To _____
_____
_____

Dear _____

You are hereby notified that I have incurred a loss which I believe is covered by my insurance policy number
_____. Details of the loss are as follows:

1. Type of loss or claim: _____
2. Date and time incurred: _____
3. Location: _____
4. Estimated loss: _____

Please forward a claim form to me as soon a possible.

Yours sincerely

Name _____
Address _____
_____
Telephone No. (Work) _____
Telephone No. (Home) _____
Policy Number _____

Note: that you will have to follow this up with a claim on the insurance company's form and that you must submit it within the time limits set out in your policy.

Internal Customer Complaint Memorandum | Form BS19

Please complete and return this memorandum to Customer Services

Date:	Ref:	Complaint taken by:	
Customer:		Telephone/Letter/Fax	
		Contact:	
		Tel:	
		Fax:	
Nature of complaint:		Product code:	
		Supplier:	
		Qty:	
Action required: By whom: Date:			
Action completed:		Signed off:	
		Date:	

Joint Venture Agreement (Non-Partnership)   Form B10

THIS JOINT VENTURE AGREEMENT IS MADE the _____ day of _____ year _____

BETWEEN:

(1) _____ of _____(the 'First Party")
the proprietor of a business known as _____; and

(2) _____ of _____ (the 'Second Party') the proprietor of a
business known as _____

In consideration of the terms, conditions and covenants hereinafter set forth, the parties agree as follows:

1. The Parties hereby agree to co operate for the purposes of enabling their separate businesses to co-operate with one another in the following respects: _____

    _____

2. The term of the this Agreement shall be _____

3. The Parties shall from time to time contribute equally to meeting the expenses arising under this Agreement without reference to the receipts or profitability of either business. For the avoidance of doubt, nothing in this agreement shall confer upon any Party a right to share in the profits of any other Party or Parties.

4. The relationship between the Parties shall be limited to the performance of the terms and conditions of this agreement. Nothing herein shall be construed to create a partnership between the Parties or to authorise any Party to act as a general agent for another, or to permit any Party to bind the other or others except as set forth in this agreement, or to borrow money on behalf of another Party or Parties, or to use the credit of any Party or Parties for any purpose.

5. This agreement may not be assigned without the prior written consent of all of the other Parties hereto.

6. This agreement shall be governed by and interpreted under the law of England and Wales. Any claim arising out of or relating to this agreement, or the breach thereof, shall be settled by arbitration in accordance with the Rules of the Chartered Institute of Arbitrators and judgment upon the award rendered by the arbitrator(s) may be entered in any court having jurisdiction thereof.

7. Any and all notices to be given pursuant to or under this agreement shall be sent to the party to whom the notice is addressed at the address of the Party stated above and to all the other parties thereto.

8. This agreement constitutes the entire agreement between the Joint Venturers pertaining to the subject matter contained in it, and supersedes all prior and contemporaneous agreements, representations, warranties and understandings of the parties. No supplement, variation or amendment of this agreement shall be binding unless executed in writing by all the parties hereto. No waiver of any of the provisions of this agreement shall be deemed, or shall constitute, a waiver of any other provision, whether similar or not similar, nor shall any waiver constitute a continuing waiver. No waiver shall be binding unless in writing signed by the party making the waiver.

Continued on next page

Joint Venture Agreement (Non-partnership) (continued)   Form B10

IN WITNESS OF WHICH the parties have signed this agreement the day and year first above written

_____   _____
Signed by or on behalf of the First Joint Venturer   Signed by or on behalf of the Second Joint Venturer

_____   _____
in the presence of (witness)   in the presence of (witness)

Name _____   Name _____

Address _____   Address _____

_____   _____

Occupation _____   Occupation _____

Health Warning: Business people occasionally attempt to dress up their arrangements as non-partnership agreements when they are in fact partners. They do this because they know that one partner has the ability to undertake obligations on behalf of all of the other partners and because each individual partner is liable for all of the debts of the firm, even if they were run up without his knowledge or consent and even if he was defrauded.

If things go wrong, and if a court has to decide whether you were in a partnership or not, it will not do you any good merely to point to a form which says that you were not partners. Partnership is defined by the Partnership Act 1890 as 'the relation which subsists between persons carrying on a business in common with a view of profit.' If that is what you are doing, then you are partners, with all that that entails. There is no single test for whether you are in fact partners or not. However, if you share only gross receipts, rather than profits, and if you each run your separate businesses without interference of the other, and if you merely co operate with each other in various limited ways, then you are unlikely to be regarded as partners. An example would be if you share shop premises and take turns looking after each others merchandise and serving each others customers. Another example would be if one of you owns land, and you let the other farm it in exchange for your having a share of what he sells the produce for (as opposed to a share of what he earns after deducting his expenses).

Note also that even if you are not partners in fact, you will be treated as if you were partners if you give outsiders the impression that that is what you are. Avoid using stationery which has both your names on it and make it obvious to everyone that you are running separate businesses.

The form above should help you to frame a co operation agreement where you are not partners. Because of the importance of whether you are partners or not, we strongly recommend that you run your draft agreement past your solicitor.

Note that if a partnership is what you want, and if you also to avoid unlimited liability, the law now permits you to have a Limited Liability Partnership. Ask your solicitor about how you can form one.

Landlord's Reference Requirements   Form RT08

EMPLOYMENT				
Work reference – stating	(a) Job Title	☐ Yes		☐ No
	(b) Length of Employment	☐ Yes		☐ No
	(c) Salary	☐ Yes		☐ No
Last three payslips		☐ Yes		☐ No
If self-employed	(a) Copy of last set of accounts	☐ Yes		☐ No
	(b) accountant's letter – stating			
	(i) length of time known to accountant	☐ Yes		☐ No
	(ii) indication of yearly income	☐ Yes		☐ No

BANK/BUILDING SOCIETY		
Last three bank statements	☐ Yes	☐ No
Building society book	☐ Yes	☐ No

OTHER		
Student identification (e.g. student card or letter of acceptance)	☐ Yes	☐ No
Personal reference (e.g. professional friend)	☐ Yes	☐ No
Reference from current landlord stating:		
(a) how long residing at current address;	☐ Yes	☐ No
(b) whether payment of rent and observance of covenants of your letting agreement has been satisfactory. If you have been residing at your current address for less than 6 months, you must also provide a similar reference from your previous landlord.	☐ Yes	☐ No

Letter Accepting Liability   Form BS20

Date _____

To _____

_____

_____

Dear _____

We have now had an opportunity to investigate your complaint fully.

Whilst we do impose the most rigorous quality control on all our products, unfortunately, on rare occasions, human error allows a product to be despatched that does not reach the standards that we have set ourselves. We accept that this is one of those rare occasions.

We are prepared, at your choice, either to replace the product free of charge to you or to refund your purchase money in full. In either case, we would ask you please to return to us the item in question. We will, of course, reimburse you the cost of postage.

Please accept our apologies for the trouble caused you.

Yours sincerely

_____

Note: By sending this letter you are making a statement which is admissible in evidence in a claim brought by the buyer for 'consequential loss' that is, loss which goes beyond the mere loss of the purchase price. This could be, for example, losses of profits which would have been earned from a machine if it had not been faulty, or disappointment caused by a bad holiday experience.

If you think that there is some doubt about your liability, or if you are worried about a claim for consequential loss, you should put the words 'without prejudice' at the top of the letter, and add before the last paragraph the words 'this offer is conditional upon your accepting it in full satisfaction of any claims you may have arising out of the sale of the above mentioned products'.

Letter Accepting Return of Goods   Form BS21

Date _____

To _____

_____

_____

Re: Your order No. _____

Dear _____

We understand that you are rejecting the goods sent to you under the above order because

_____

_____

_____

_____

Whilst we do not accept your claim, we do not wish any customer to be dissatisfied and for that reason we will accept return of the goods.

Yours sincerely

_____

Letter Accompanying Unsolicited Goods   Form BS22

Date   _____

To   _____

_____

_____

Dear   _____

In order to introduce you to our range of products, we enclose a sample together with a leaflet specifying the prices and normal business terms which we offer.

I will telephone you within the next few days, after you have had an opportunity to inspect the samples, to discuss with you any questions you may have. You are, of course, under no obligation to purchase any of the samples. [If you decide not to purchase we will arrange for their return at our expense, and in the meantime they will be at our risk.][1]/[Whatever decision you may make about future purchases, you are welcome to keep these samples with our compliments.][2]

I look forward to speaking to you, and the pleasure of doing business with you.

Yours sincerely

_____

Health Warning: If you send unsolicited goods with a view to their being acquired by the recipient, then if they are to be acquired for the recipient otherwise than for his business, he is entitled to keep them as if you had made a gift.

If you send unsolicited goods with a view to their being acquired by the recipient for the purposes of his business, you are entitled to ask for them back, but the recipient is under no duty to look after the goods before you arrange for their collection.

Whether or not the goods are sent for the purposes of the recipient's business it is usually a criminal offence to demand payment for them. Do not do this under any circumstances without consulting a solicitor first.

[1] Include this if the goods are intended for use in the recipient's business.

[2] Include this if the goods are not intended for use in the recipient's business.

Letter Acknowledging Complaint   Form BS23

Date _____

To _____

_____

_____

Dear _____

I was sorry to hear of your complaint that _____

_____

I am investigating the matter fully and will contact you again as soon as possible.

Please be assured that we will do our very best to rectify any problem we discover, and if the fault is due to any error or omission on our part, we will discuss appropriate compensation with you.

Yours sincerely

_____

Letter Acknowledging Request for Trade Credit   Form CDC14

Date _____

To _____

_____

_____

Dear _____

To enable us to accommodate your request for trade credit, please let us have the name, address and sort code of your bank to whom we may apply for a reference together with your account number. Please also provide two trade references of companies with whom you have done business over the past three years.

Your bank and trade referees will require your permission to communicate with us about you. Please therefore write to them immediately saying that you wish them to provide us with a reference for you and that they have your authority to discuss your credit worthiness with us. It will be helpful if you provide us with a copy.

We should be grateful if you would let us know the extent of the orders that you anticipate placing with us. Our normal payment terms require full payment within _____ days of invoice.

Yours sincerely

_____

Letter Agreeing Appointment of an Estate Agent   Form BS24

Date _____

To _____

_____

_____

Dear _____

Re _____

We hereby instruct you [as sole agents]* to sell the above mentioned property at a price not less than £ _____ and agree to pay your fees and charges as set out in your letter of _____ subject to the terms in this letter. However, we give you no authority to accept any offer (whether or not 'subject to contract') without our prior written consent.

We reserve the right to withdraw these instructions at any time [and without notice]/[on _____ days' notice], and thereafter to appoint another agent [or to move to a non-exclusive basis with you]*. In such circumstances we shall be under no liability to you unless we proceed to an exchange of contracts with a prospective purchaser whom you have introduced to us [or to whom we have been otherwise introduced during the period of your sole agency].*

Yours sincerely

_____

Delete if the agency is not to be an exclusive agency

Letter Agreeing to Trade Terms   Form CDC15

Date _____

To _____

_____

_____

Dear _____

We confirm that we are pleased to extend to you our normal trade terms. We enclose our terms and conditions of trade and draw your attention in particular to the requirement that accounts are due and payable _____ days from the date of invoice. Interest at the rate of _____% per month is payable on overdue accounts.

The maximum credit allowed will be £ _____. These trade terms may be altered or withdrawn by us at our discretion at any time.

Please sign and return one copy of this letter to confirm these terms. Until the signed copy is received, orders will be accepted on a cash on delivery basis.

Yours sincerely

_____

Letter Alleging Passing Off
Form CDC16

Date _____

To _____

_____

_____

Dear _____

We notice that you are advertising or promoting goods/services under the following [name and/or description]. This will or may mislead prospective purchasers that your goods/services are ours.

We have long marketed goods/services under the name and description ' _____

_____.' Your use of the name ' _____

_____' is misleading and likely to cause confusion with our product.

We demand that you cease further use of this name and make clear to those with whom you have previously dealt that you are not connected with our business and that the product that you offer has no connection with ours.

Unless you confirm this to us within the next ten days, we shall have no option but to instruct our solicitors to commence proceedings against you for an injunction and damages.

Yours sincerely

_____

Health Warning: If you have a registered trade mark, do not mention it in this letter without first taking legal advice, as a groundless complaint of trade mark infringement can lead to your being sued under the Trade Marks Act 1994 Section 21.

Letter Confirming Appointment of Independent Consultant

Date _____

To _____

_____

_____

Re _____

Dear _____

We are writing to confirm your engagement as a consultant for_____ (the 'Company')

commencing on _____.

The terms of your engagement will be:

1.　Your engagement shall continue (subject to Paragraph 7) [for a period of _____months from today]/[for the duration of a project consisting of _____]/[until determined by either of us giving to the other not less than _____ months' written notice].[1]

2.　[Your work will include the following:[2]

_____

_____]

[Your work will include such work of the following

description_____ as we may from time to time offer you and as you may undertake to carry out]. [For the avoidance of doubt, we are not under any obligation to offer you work, and you are not under an obligation to accept any work we may offer.]

3.　[You will devote up to _____ hours per week to the performance of your duties].[3] [You shall be free to carry out your work during any hours which are consistent with the proper completion of your work].

4.　Your place of work shall be _____ [You will, however, be free to work elsewhere at your discretion to the extent that this is consistent with the proper completion of your work].

5.　We shall require regular progress reports on projects in which you are involved.

Continued on next page

6.   The manner in which work is carried out will be entirely for you to decide but you must comply with all reasonable requests from the board of the company. You must ensure that your work is carried out in such manner whereby the company is in no way prejudiced.

7.   [In consideration of you carrying out your work we will pay to you a fee of £ _____ per _____ in arrears].[4] [In consideration of your carrying out your work, we will pay to you a fee of £___ per _____]/[such fee as may be agreed in respect of the same]. You will render us _____ invoices in respect of these fees. If you are registered for VAT, you must show VAT separately on the invoices. Our accountants shall have full access to all records supporting these invoices so as to enable them to audit the invoices rendered. [Payment will be made within 30 days of the rendering of your invoice unless within that time we question it].

8.   You will be responsible for all out-of-pocket expenses incurred by you in the performance of your duties.

9.   You will be responsible for all income tax liabilities and National Insurance or similar contributions in respect of your fees and will indemnify us against all claims that may be made against us in respect of income tax or similar contributions relating to your services.

10. [In addition to the right of determination declared in Paragraph 1], we shall be entitled to terminate your engagement forthwith, without any payment, compensation or damages, if you are guilty of any serious misconduct or material or persistent breach of any of the terms and conditions of your engagement, or you wilfully neglect or refuse to carry out your work or to comply with any instructions reasonably given to you by the board, if you are unable to carry out your work properly, if you bring the name of the company into disrepute, if you have a bankruptcy order made against you or compound with or enter into any voluntary arrangement with your creditors, or if you are convicted of any criminal offence. This will not prejudice any other rights or remedies which we may have against you.[5]

11. One matter upon which we are most insistent concerns confidentiality. You will, in providing your services, gain knowledge of our business, our business contacts, our employees and many of our business secrets. It is fundamental that you will not disclose to anyone or use for your own or another's benefit any confidential information that you acquire. This is both during and after your engagement. In particular, you must not solicit, for the benefit of yourself or any other person, business from any customer or employee of the company for a period of two years after you have last done work for the company. Any and all records or papers of any description which are provided to you by the company or which you may bring into being in the course of carrying out your work for the company are the property of the company and must be immediately delivered to the company on the termination of your engagement.

Continued on next page

Letter Confirming Appointment of Independent Consultant (continued)

12. This agreement shall be governed by the laws of England and Wales to the non-exclusive jurisdiction of whose courts both we and you hereby submit.[6]

If you agree to these terms please sign and return one copy of this letter.

We look forward to working with you.

Yours faithfully

_____

Agreed and accepted

_____

Consultant

Note: If you wish to avoid an employer/employee relationship you will not achieve this simply by calling the worker a 'consultant'. A court would look at the reality of the relationship and make an evaluation in all the circumstances. Important factors would be the degree of control which you have over the way in which the other works, whether the work is to be done by an individual personally, or whether he is free to delegate performance; whether you are bound to offer, and the other to do, the work and above all the extent to which the consultant is part of your organisation (e.g. whether he is brought in to achieve one project or whether he carries out work of a type which always requires someone to be on hand to do it). In the form below there are many parts in square brackets. Include all of those which suit your arrangement, as the more you include, the more likely it will be that you will have avoided the relationship of employer/employee. Note that it is generally easier to avoid this relationship if you take on temporary staff through an employment agency. Because of the importance of the distinction between the relationship of employee and that of independent contractor, you would be wise to consult a solicitor if any doubt arises.

[1] You should delete this clause if you can arrange matters so that you are not obliged to offer any work and if the consultant is not obliged to accept it. If you cannot do that, then you might prefer to provide for a fixed period of the engagement or for the engagement to be for the duration of a particular project. One of the matters which a court would look at in deciding whether a relationship of employer/employee exists is whether there is a duty on one party to provide work for the other, and a duty on the other party to do the work. As always, of course, what you write must reflect the reality of your arrangement with the other party, as the courts are very quick to spot a sham.

[2] If possible, provide only for the consultant to do such work as from time to time may be offered and as they may choose to accept.

[3] This clause should be deleted if possible.

[4] If possible, delete this sentence because payment for a period of time can be an indication of employment.

[5] If you have provided that the engagement is for a fixed period, delete the words 'in addition to the right of determination declared in paragraph 1'. If you have provided that there is no obligation on you to provide work or on the consultant to accept it, then delete this paragraph altogether.

[6] Delete the prefix 'non' if you wish to avoid the possibility of litigation in a foreign court.

Letter Confirming Reason for Instant Dismissal   Form E36

Date _____

To _____

_____

_____

Dear _____

Further to the disciplinary hearing held on _____ ,
I write to confirm, formally, your instant dismissal for gross misconduct effective from today for the following reason(s):

_____

_____

_____

_____

_____

_____

You are aware of the code of discipline (a copy of which is enclosed) which makes it quite clear that this type of behaviour will result in immediate dismissal. You have a right to appeal against this decision, and if you wish to exercise this right, please notify me in writing within ____ working days.

Yours sincerely

_____

Letter Denying Liability on Complaint | Form BS25

Date _____

To _____

_____

_____

Dear _____

We have investigated the complaint contained in your letter of dated_____.
I am satisfied that we are not at fault for the following reasons:

_____

_____

_____

_____

[However, if you remain of the opinion that we were at fault, then I am willing to consider the possibility that the matter be referred to mediation in order to reach a compromise in this dispute. If you agree, we can discuss the appointment of an mediator.]

Yours sincerely

_____

Letter Expelling Partner from Continuing Partnership   Form B11

Date _____

Ref _____

To _____

_____

_____

Dear _____

In accordance with clause _____ of our partnership agreement dated _____,
I/we wish to inform you that you are expelled from the partnership. Your rights to any share in the
partnership profits and assets will be dealt with in accordance with the terms of the partnership agreement.

Yours sincerely

_____

Partner's signature

_____

Partner's signature

Health Warning: If the partnership agreement states that a partner can only be expelled for a reason, you must be satisfied that one of the reasons, set out in the agreement as justifying expulsion, actually exists and that you have acted fairly to the expelled partner in coming to your decision. You should specify the reason in this letter. Before any decision to expel is made, the partner who is to be expelled should be informed of the reason why his expulsion is under consideration, and he should be given an opportunity to answer the allegations which are made against him and to say why he should be allowed to continue as a partner.

Where there is no provision in the agreement requiring that a partner be expelled only for cause, it would still be wise not to do it unless there is a reasonable cause, and to specify that cause in the letter of expulsion. This is because partners are obliged to act with good faith towards one another and because it is possible (although controversial) that a good reason for expulsion may have to be given even where the agreement does not expressly call for this.

If the partnership agreement gives a right to expel for reasons having nothing to do with conduct, for example upon the reaching of a particular age, it is usually best to rely upon this right rather than to raise matters of conduct. However, you should only rely upon such a provision it is in practice is applied to everyone.

Above all, remember that expulsions from partnerships often give rise to bitter and expensive disputes. It is usually a good idea to consult a solicitor before you take any action.

Letter from Employee Intending to Resume Work Before End of Ordinary Maternity Leave

Form E37

Date _____

To _____

_____

_____

Dear _____

This is to inform you that I intend to return to work before the end of my maternity leave period and I am giving you at least eight weeks' notice as required by law.

I intend to return to work on _____.

Your sincerely

_____

Letter Inviting Candidate to Attend Interview   Form E68

Date _____

To _____

_____

_____

Dear Miss Porter

Thank you for sending me your application for the post of _____.

I would very much like to discuss this matter further with you and have arranged an interview at

_____ at these offices. I

should be grateful if you would confirm your attendance.

I look forward to meeting you.

Yours sincerely

_____

Personnel Manager

Letter of Claim Addressed to a Carrier   Form BS26

Date _____

To _____

_____

_____

Dear Sirs

Re: _____

We refer to consignment note no._____ concerning _____ collected by you from _____ for delivery to _____.

We have been notified by the recipient that goods to the value of £ _____ were received which were damaged or missing from the consignment.

We wish formally to notify you of this circumstance under the terms of clause _____ of our contract dated _____ .

We have inspected the goods and estimate the replacement cost to be £ _____ and should be grateful if you would arrange for that sum to be forwarded to us within _____ days of the date hereof, failing which we shall be compelled to refer this matter to our solicitors.

Yours faithfully

_____

Letter of Redundancy   Form E38

Date _____

To   _____

      _____

      _____

Dear _____

Further to our meeting on _____ ,
 it is with deep regret that I must advise you that your employment with us will end on _____
_____ , by reason of redundancy. As you are aware, the company has
experienced a serious decline in business.

Our selection criteria has been as follows_____ . Wherever
possible, we have offered employees other employment, but unfortunately we have been unable to find a
suitable alternative position for you. You are entitled to receive a payment based upon the scale laid down
by law and a tax-free cheque for the amount due is enclosed together with a statement reflecting how this
has been calculated. You are also entitled to _____ [weeks']/[months'] notice [which you will be required to
work]/[which you will not be required to work and subsequently we enclose a cheque in lieu of your notice
period].

We hope that you soon find other suitable employment. If you need a reference from us, please submit our
name with the confidence that our reference will be a good one. You have a right to appeal against this
decision and if you wish to exercise this right, please notify me in writing within [_____] days.

Yours sincerely

_____

Letter Offering to Purchase Leasehold Property   Form OLF20

Date _____

To _____

_____

_____

Dear _____

Re _____

Following my inspection of the above-named property, I am prepared to offer the sum of

£ _____ for your existing lease, on the following terms but subject to contract:

1.   Receipt of a satisfactory survey from my surveyors.
2.   Receipt of my solicitor's advice on the terms of the lease, confirming that it contains no provisions
     adverse to my interests and that it is a lease for _____ years from_____ at a ground rent of £
     _____ per annum payable quarterly in advance (reviewable every three years, the next review
     being in _____).
3.   Your giving us vacant possession by _____.

My company's solicitors are Messrs._____ , to whom I have copied this
letter. Please instruct your solicitors to send a draft contract and copy of the lease to my solicitors. I hope we
are able to proceed to a swift exchange of contracts.

Yours sincerely

_____

[For and on behalf of _____Limited]

Letter re. Landlord's Agent's Authority   Form RT09

Date   _____

Ref   _____

To   _____   (name of Tenant(s))

      _____

      _____

Dear Tenant(s)

Re.   _____(the Property)

Please note that _____

_____

_____(name and address of agent(s))

is/are now authorised to deal with the above property on my/our behalf so that you should until further

notice pay the rent and any other payments due under the tenancy to him/her and deal with him/her/them

in respect of any other matters relating to the property.

Notices, including notices in proceedings, can be received [by me at _____] or [on my

behalf by _____ at _____] in respect of your tenancy.[1] This notice is give pursuant to

Section 48 of The Landlord and Tenant Act 1987.

Yours faithfully

_____

(Landlord's signature and printed name and address)

Letter re. Landlord's Agent's Authority   Form RT09

---

[1] The address for receiving notices must be in England or Wales.

Letter re. Bills   Form RT10

Date   _____

Ref   _____

To   _____   (name and address of Authority)

_____

_____

Dear Sir(s)

Re. _____(the Property)

I am/we are the landlord(s) of the above property and write to advise you that with effect from

_____(date of start of tenancy)

the property has been let to _____

_____

_____(name(s) of Tenant(s))

who will therefore be responsible with effect from that date for the [council tax] [electricity charges] [gas charges] [telephone charges] [water rates] in respect of the property.

Yours faithfully

_____

(Landlord's signature and printed name and address)

Letter Refusing Return of Goods   Form BS27

Date _____

To _____

_____

_____

Dear _____

Re: Your Order No. _____

Today your carrier attempted to return the goods identified in the above order.

We refuse to accept the return of the goods because we have given no permission to you either expressly or implicitly to return the goods without good reason. We therefore ask you to remove them immediately as we can accept no liability for them or for any damage that they may suffer whilst left on our premises.

Yours sincerely

_____

Note: Before using this form and acting upon it, make certain that your customer did not have the right in law to return the goods. In particular note that the customer has the right to return the goods if they are not as described, if they are not fit for the stated purpose for which they were bought, if they do not conform to sample, if they are not of satisfactory quality, or if the correct quantity has not been delivered. The rules as to quantity and satisfactory quality are slightly relaxed in the case of commercial (as opposed to consumer) sales, but again you must proceed with caution. Note also that while the law does not impose a particularly high duty of care on you to look after the goods (assuming them to have been wrongly rejected by the customer) you must not be reckless with them either. Do not leave them out in the rain or in a place where they can be easily stolen.

Letter Refusing Trade or Financial References — Form CDC17

Date _____

To _____
_____
_____

Dear _____

Re _____

We regret that we are unable to comply with your request for a reference in respect of the above named company as it is a policy in this company not to give such references.

Please do not take this letter as any indication whatsoever of the commercial or financial standing of the company. We suggest that you ask them for an alternative referee.

Yours sincerely

_____

Letter Refusing Trade Terms   Form CDC18

Date _____

To _____

_____

_____

Dear _____

We have carefully considered your request for trade terms. Unfortunately, we regret that we are not prepared to extend trade terms to you until you first establish a satisfactory pattern of trade with us. We hope you understand our position on the matter.

Yours sincerely

_____

Letter Rejecting Conditions of Order and Reimposing Conditions of Sale

Form BS28

Date _____

To _____

_____

_____

Dear _____

Re: Your Order No. _____

We refer to your order number _____ which is expressed to be on your standard terms and conditions.

Unfortunately, your standard terms and conditions are unacceptable. We can only supply goods on our standard terms and conditions of sale, a copy of which is enclosed.

[We are despatching your ordered goods on our standard terms and conditions in 48 hours. Acceptance of delivery by you will constitute acceptance of our terms. If you are not prepared to accept our terms you must return the goods immediately, although you may do so at our expense] or [If you would care to confirm your acceptance of our terms by return, we will be delighted to fulfill your order by _____. If, however, you feel you are unable to accept our terms, then regretfully we will have to decline your offer].

Yours sincerely

_____

Letter Rejecting Incorrect Goods   Form BS29

Date _____

To _____

_____

_____

Dear _____

Re: Our Order No _____

Today your carrier attempted to deliver goods identified on the numbered order above.

On examination, the goods delivered were found not to correspond with the [sample] or [description] we had received and we therefore refused to accept delivery of the goods. The carrier was instructed to return them to you.

Yours sincerely

_____

Letter Requesting Trade Terms of Payment   Form CDC19

Date _____

To _____

_____

_____

Dear Sirs

We wish to place orders with you for the following:

_____

_____

_____

Please advise us of your normal trade terms of payment.

If you wish to have references we suggest that you refer to our bankers who are:

_____

_____.

You may also like to refer to _____, with whom we have had business relations.

[We have already given our authority to the above to discuss our credit worthiness with you].

Yours faithfully

_____

Letter Sending a Copy of an Agreement Regulated Under the Consumer Credit Act 1974

Form CDC20

Date _____

To _____

_____

_____

Dear _____

Re: Hire Purchase Agreement No. _____

I refer to the above Hire Purchase Agreement which you signed on _____.
As explained to you when you signed the above agreement, you have time to reconsider your decision. If
you wish to do so you may still cancel the agreement by posting to us a written notice of cancellation as
indicated in the document(s) which accompany this letter.

Yours sincerely

_____

Note: To be sent within seven days of signature of the agreement. The Consumer Credit Act has provisions governing the questions of
when copies of an agreement and notices of cancellation rights have to be provided to the customer. The agreements themselves and
notices of rights to cancel have to follow a formula set out in the Consumer Credit Act 1974 and in regulations made under that Act. **It
is essential that you take legal advice** as to what you must provide to your client, and when you must do it. Failure to observe these
requirements may result in your not being able to enforce your agreement.

Letter Taking Up Bank Reference   Form CDC21

Date   _____

To: The Manager _____

_____

_____ Bank plc

Dear Sir

Re _____ Limited

The above-named company, whose address is _____

_____,

has applied to us for trade credit. They tell us that you are their bankers and that their account number is

_____.

The amount involved will be in the order of £ _____ per month. We should be grateful if you would supply us with a statement as to their creditworthiness and let us know whether they can be considered good for the amount involved.

Yours faithfully

_____

Letter Taking Up Trade Reference   Form CDC22

Date _____

To _____

_____

_____

Dear _____

Re _____Limited

The above-named company has applied to us for trade credit. They tell us that they have a credit account with you and have given us your name as a reference. They have suggested that the amount of their trade with us would be in the order of £ _____ per month.

Would you please let us know, in confidence, whether their account with you has been maintained satisfactorily and whether all invoices have been paid on the date they are due.

A stamped and addressed envelope is enclosed for your reply.

Yours sincerely

_____

Letter Terminating Contract and Invoking Retention of Title Clause

Form OLF21

Date _____

To _____

_____

_____

Dear _____

We have received notification that you have been [put into receivership] / [made subject to a winding up order].

Accordingly, pursuant to our Terms and Conditions, we notify you that we consider our contract with you terminated, and that the full price of the goods delivered to you is immediately due and payable.

It is also the case that under our Terms and Conditions, title in the goods, until they have been paid for in full, remains vested in us [and that you hold on trust for us the proceeds of sale of any goods which you have sold without paying for the same].

We therefore require that you forthwith make payment to us in full, and that you undertake that unless and until payment in full is made, you will not dispose of any of our goods without our express permission.

Yours sincerely

_____

Letter to a Solicitor to Collect a Debt   Form CDC23

Date _____

To _____

_____

_____

Dear _____

Re _____

Debt £_____

Please issue proceedings to recover £ _____ from the above named company.

We enclose a copy of our invoice together with our complete file relating to this debt. Please let us know if you require any further information.

No complaint has been received in respect of this debt and all our applications for payment have been ignored. We draw your attention to our last letter in which we gave warning that unless payment was received, proceedings would be commenced without further notice.

We will let you know immediately if any payment is received by us.

Yours sincerely

_____

Letter to Credit Reference Agency for Report   Form CDC24

Date   _____

To   _____

_____

_____

Dear   _____

Re   _____

We request a detailed credit report on the above. They have requested credit terms representing a monthly risk to us of approximately £ _____. We enclose our cheque for £ _____ and would ask you to fax or post your report to us as soon as possible.

[We enclose a copy letter from the above which authorises credit reference agencies to disclose to us information as to their credit-worthiness].

Yours sincerely

_____

Letter to Credit Reference Agency Requesting Personal Data

Form CDC25

Date _____

To _____

_____

_____

Dear _____

Re: Data Protection Act 1998 (the 'Act')

Please let me know if you hold any personal data concerning me on your records. If you do, I should be grateful for a copy of any such data according to my entitlement under the Act. Accordingly, please indicate to me the evidence of my identity which you require in order that you may honour this request. If it is your practice to deal with these requests via a standard form, please furnish me with a copy. If you wish to make a charge for the supply of this information, please let me know the amount of the charge and the statutory provision under which you are entitled to levy the same.

My details and address are as follows _____.

Yours sincerely

_____

Letter to Customer who has Exceeded Credit Limit — Form CDC26

Date _____

To _____

_____

_____

Dear _____

As you know, your credit limit with us is £ _____. Your account today stands in the sum of £ _____, which is in excess of the credit allowed. Until this amount has been paid we regret that we are not prepared to accept any further orders from you on trade terms.

[Interest at the rate of _____ per cent per month is payable on outstanding accounts [under the terms of our conditions of trading] / [under the Late Payment of Commercial Debts (Interest) Act 1998][1] and this interest will be added to your statement.]

Yours sincerely

_____

---

[1] Do not use the wording which refers to the Late Payment of Commercial Debts (Interest) Act 1998 if the sale was to a person purchasing as a consumer.

Letter to Employee Concerning Salary Rise   Form E39

Date _____

To _____

_____

_____

Dear _____

It is with pleasure that I write to let you know of our decision to increase your salary. The increase is
£ _____ per _____ .

This increase is only partly in recognition of the increase in the cost of living since your last rise. It is also made to reward your loyal and conscientious work, and to let you know that your efforts have been recognised. The increase will take effect from the beginning of this month.

Yours sincerely

_____

Letter to Employee, Absent Believed Sick   Form E41

Date _____

To _____

_____

_____

Dear _____

You have not been to work since _____ , and have failed to contact me to let me know why.

Please let me know at once the reason for your absence from work and, if you are unwell, provide me with a certificate from your doctor. Without this certificate, you are not entitled to any sick pay.

In case you do not know about the sickness regulations, employees are only entitled to statutory sick pay when they are absent from work for four or more consecutive days, up to a limit of 28 weeks in a three-year period. After that you must claim state benefit.

Yours sincerely

_____

Letter to Former Employee Who is Using Confidential Information

Date _____

To _____

_____

_____

Dear _____

It has come to our attention that you are informing our customers that you can supply them at prices below our current price list. You are clearly using the information about our customers and prices that you gained whilst working for us, which is in breach of your duty of confidentiality.

Unless you return to us within seven days all customer and price lists relating to our business that you have in your possession and give us your written promise not to make use of your knowledge of our customers and business, our solicitors will be instructed to make an immediate application to the courts for an injunction to prevent you approaching our customers, and they will be instructed also to bring proceedings to claim damages from you.

Yours sincerely

_____

Letter to Receiver or Liquidator Reclaiming Goods   Form BS30

Date _____

To _____

_____

_____

Dear _____

Re: Our Invoice No.   _____

The goods referred to in the above invoice were delivered to _____

_____ which is now in [receivership] or [liquidation]. The goods were sold

on the condition that legal title remains with us until such time as they are paid for in full and that if they

are not paid for in full within _____ days, under such conditions we reserved the right to enter premises

to recover our goods. A copy of the invoice and of our standard conditions is enclosed.

We have not received payment for the goods within the specified period, and therefore we intend to enter

upon their premises on _____ to reclaim our goods. Please may we have your

undertaking by return not to sell, deal with or otherwise dispose of the goods until such time as they have

been paid for in full or collected by us?

Yours sincerely

_____

Letter to Shareholders and Auditors with Resolution to be Passed

Form B13

Date _____

To _____

_____

_____

Dear _____

The company directors propose:

_____

_____

_____

To give effect to this proposal it is necessary for the shareholders to pass a formal resolution to be recorded in the company's minute book. As I understand that all shareholders have been approached and agree to the proposal, I enclose a formal written resolution.

If you confirm that you are in agreement, please sign the form where indicated and return it to me.

An identical form of resolution has been sent to all other shareholders and to the auditors.

[Under the Companies Act 2006 unanimous consent is no longer required to a written resolution. However, it will require a vote of the holders of a [simple majority][1] [75 per cent majority][2] of the voting shares. If consent is not given by the necessary majority before _____ the resolution will be defeated.

In order to indicate your consent to the resolution, you will need to send a signed and witnessed statement to the registered office on or before _____ identifying the resolution in question and stating that you agree to it].

Yours sincerely

_____

Director/Company Secretary

Note: At present the rule is that unanimous consent is needed to approve a resolution that is not passed at a general meeting. However, when Chapter Two Part 13 of the Companies Act 2006 comes into force on 1 October 2007, it will be possible to pass a resolution with the same sorts of majorities which are needed for resolutions that are passed in general meetings. The catch is that new procedures will have to be followed. Therefore copies of the resolutions must be circulated to all members at the same time and the resolution will have to be accompanied by a notice stating that there is a deadline for passing the motion, and that it will be treated as having been defeated if it is not passed by that date. Unless the articles say otherwise, the period will be 28 days from the circulation of the resolution. Another requirement is that the notice should also state what needs to be done by the member to approve the resolution.

Once the new provisions are in force, you will not require unanimous consent for a written resolution, but the letter will need to include the text which appears in square brackets.

Note, this procedure cannot be used to remove an auditor or director before the end of his or her term and is available only to private companies, not to public ones.

[1] For ordinary resolutions.

[2] For special resolutions.

Written Resolution   Form B13

_____LIMITED

COMPANY NUMBER:_____

The following ordinary/extraordinary/special/elective resolution is signed as a written resolution pursuant to [Section 381A of the Companies Act 1985] or [Section Part 13 Chapter Two of the Companies Act 2006][1] [by the holders of all issued shares] or [by the holders of a majority of _____per cent] in the capital of the company conferring a right to vote thereon as if the resolution had been proposed at a general meeting of the company at the date hereof:

_____

_____

_____

_____

_____

_____

_____

Dated this _____ day of _____ year ____

_____

Shareholder's signature

[1] Delete reference to the 1985 Act from 1 October 2007.

Refer to footnote in the letter to shareholders and auditors on the preceding page.

Note that it is a legal requirement to retain copies of all resolutions for 10 years.

Letter to Auditor

Form B13

Date _____

Ref _____

To Messrs. _____ Chartered Accountants

_____

_____

_____

Dear _____

I enclose a copy of a letter sent to all the shareholders and also a copy of the resolution that we wish to pass. As you can see, we are hoping to pass the motion by written resolution rather than by voting at a general meeting.

A copy of the proposed resolution is being sent to you in accordance with the provisions of section 381(B)(i) of the Companies Act 1985.

Yours sincerely

_____

Company Secretary

Note: Until 1 October 2007, failure to send a letter in this form will be a criminal offence. After that date the requirement is abolished for private companies.

Letter to Unsuccessful Candidate   Form E44

Date _____

To _____
_____
_____

Dear _____

I regret to inform you that, after considering your application and meeting to interview you, I am unable to offer you the position you have applied for. Whilst you were adequately qualified for the position, another applicant was more suited to the position.

I am grateful to you for giving your time and wish you every success in the future.

Yours sincerely

_____

Letter Treating Breach of Contract as Repudiation and Claiming Damages

Form BS31

Date _____

To _____

_____

_____

Dear _____

We refer to the contract between us, under which you agreed to perform the following:

_____

_____

_____

You to have failed to perform your obligation under the contract in the following respects:

_____

_____

_____

Despite our previous protests you have not made good your failure.

We have considered the matter fully and conclude that your failure is a repudiation by you of your obligations under the contract. We consider the contract terminated because of your conduct. We are taking advice from our solicitors as to the remedies available to us and you will hear from them shortly.

[As a result of your breaches we have suffered the following losses and been put to the following expense:_____].[1]

[We require you to repay the sum of £_____ which we have paid to you under the contract, the benefit of which he have lost as a result of your breach].[2]

Yours sincerely

_____

Health warning: Unless the contract says specifically that the particular breach you are complaining of entitles you to treat the contract as at an end, it can be very risky to send this letter. Only the most serious breaches of contract will entitle you to do this. If you send this letter when you are not entitled to do so, you could be said to have repudiated the contract and the other side would be able to sue you. That is why we have included the words 'We have referred this matter to our solicitors.' This is something which you should do in all but the clearest cases.

[1] Add this if you are not referring the matter to your solicitor and if it is applicable.

[2] Add this if you are not referring the matter to your solicitor and if it is applicable.

Licence for use of a Car Parking Space   Form OLF22

Date _____

To   _____

_____

_____

Dear   _____

Premises _____

This is to confirm that we are giving you a licence to park _____ motor car(s) in the car parking area adjacent to the above premises (the 'Licence') subject to the following conditions:

(a)   Only _____ motor car(s) may be parked under the Licence and those motor car(s) shall only be parked in the spaces that we indicate. No special place is reserved for you and we can at any time change the area in which you may park. We accept no liability for any loss or damage to the car(s) or their contents.

(b)   You will provide us with the registration number of the car(s) that will be using this permission. [No vehicle may be parked by virtue of this licence, unless notice of that number has been so provided to us.]

(c)   No vehicle may obstruct the access to the parking area and our vehicle that is parked so as to obstruct the parking or movement of any vehicle belonging to us or any other person will be removed immediately. It is a fundamental condition of this Licence that you agree that we may at any time move any car that we consider is in breach of this term and that, unless it is caused negligently, we shall not be liable for any damage caused by our taking this action.

(d)   You will pay us £_____ per _____ for this Licence, the payment to be made in advance. The first payment shall be made today and subsequent payments shall be made on the _____ day of each _____.

(e)   This licence is personal to you.

(f)   This licence is personal to you and may not be assigned.

[(g)   The parking area is kept locked [daily] from _____ to _____during which time you will not have access to it] or [You will be furnished with a key to the parking area. You are not to duplicate this key without our written permission] / [Your access to the parking area shall be [daily] from _____ to _____].

(h)   You will take care not to cause damage to the parking area or to any property thereon. You will not there engage in unlawful activity nor any activity whereby any policy of insurance may be avoided, you will not allow oil to leak from your vehicle(s) and you will not create any untidiness.

Continued on next page

Licence for use of a Car Parking Space (continued)   Form OLF22

(i)   In the event of any breach of this licence, we shall be entitled to terminate it forthwith, and you shall be liable to indemnify us for such breach and any loss or damage thereby caused.

(i)   This Licence may be terminated by either of us giving to the other seven clear days' notice. [Upon termination of this Licence you shall immediately return to us your key and any copy which you may have received or had made].

Yours sincerely

_____

Health Warning: If the arrangement is for the giving of exclusive use of any garage or parking space, as opposed to shared use, then you should consult a solicitor, as otherwise you might create a tenancy with statutory protection under the Landlord and Tenant Act 1954.

Licence to use Copyright Material   Form OLF23

THIS LICENCE IS MADE the _____ day of _____ year _____

BETWEEN:

(1) _____ of _____(the 'Licensor'); and

(2) _____ of _____(the 'Licensee').

NOW IT IS HEREBY AGREED as follows:

1. In consideration of the sum of £ _____, receipt of which the Licensor hereby acknowledges, the Licensor grants to the Licensee a licence to use, reprint and publish the following material (the 'Copyright Material'):

    _____

    _____

2. The Copyright Material shall be used by the Licensee only in the following manner or publication and for the following period:

    _____

    _____

3. The Copyright Material shall be used by the Licensee only in the following territory of the world:

    _____

    _____

4. The Licence confers [exclusive] / [non-exclusive] rights to the Copyright Material in the aforementioned territory during the aforementioned time.

5. The Licensee agrees that the Licensor shall retain the worldwide copyright in the Copyright Material, and the moral rights of the author of the Copyright Material are hereby asserted.

6. [This Licence shall be binding upon and inure to the benefit of the parties, their successors and assigns] / [This Licence is personal to the Licensee and may not be assigned without the express consent of the Licensor].

7. Nothing in this Agreement is intended to confer any benefit on a third party whether under the Contracts (Rights of Third Parties) Act or otherwise.

IN WITNESS OF WHICH the parties have agreed this licence the day and year first above written

_____   _____

Signed by or on behalf of the Licensor   Signed by or on behalf of the Licensee

_____   _____

in the presence of (witness)   in the presence of (witness)

Name _____   Name _____

Address _____   Address _____

Occupation _____   Occupation _____

Note: If payment is to be other than a single lump sum, there should be a clause which says that if payment of any instalment is delayed by more than a period of _____, the Licensor will be at liberty to terminate the Licence by notice. There should also be a clause in those circumstances which provides that interest at the rate of ___ per cent a year will be payable on any licence fees unpaid at the date when they fall due.

Limited Guarantee

Form LB04

THIS DEED IS MADE the _____ day of _____ year _____

BETWEEN:

(1) _____ (the 'Guarantor'); and

(2) _____ (the 'Creditor').

NOW IT IS HEREBY AGREED as follows:

1. As an inducement to the Creditor to extend credit from time to time to _____ (the 'Customer') the Guarantor unconditionally guarantees to the Creditor the prompt and punctual payment of all sums and the discharge of all obligations due to the Creditor from the Customer, whether such indebtedness or obligations shall exist at the date of this agreement or arise hereafter, and whether such indebtedness or obligation be actual or contingent, or whether it be by way of primary liability or under a guarantee and whether the Customer be solely liable or liable jointly or jointly and severally with any other person or persons, provided that the liability of the Guarantor hereunder shall be limited to the amount of £ _____ as a maximum liability and that the Guarantor shall not be liable under this Guarantee for any greater or further amount.

2. The Guarantor agrees to remain fully bound under this Guarantee, notwithstanding any extension, giving of time, forbearance, indulgence or waiver, or release or discharge to the Customer or the substitution or the release or substitution of any surety or collateral or security for the debt. In the event of default, the Creditor may seek payment directly from the Guarantor without need to proceed first against the Customer.

3. The obligations of the Guarantor shall be as a principal debtor and will arise whether or not the Customer is in default of any obligation.

4. The Guarantor shall pay all costs incurred by the Creditor in enforcing the performance of the obligations of the Customer to discharge its indebtedness and other obligations to the Creditor provided that the total of such costs and any indebtedness of the debtor which the Guarantor may pay shall not exceed the aforementioned sum of £_____ . The Guarantor shall further pay all costs incurred by the Creditor in enforcing this Guarantee. For the avoidance of doubt, these costs will be payable, notwithstanding that the total of such costs and other sums due hereunder may exceed the aforementioned limit.

5   This guarantee may be terminated by the Guarantor upon fourteen (14) days written notice of termination being delivered to the Creditor. Such termination shall apply only to credit extended by the Creditor after the expiry of the said fourteen (14) day period and not to prior extended credit, or goods in transit received by the Customer after the expiry of the fourteen day period.

Continued on next page

Limited Guarantee (continued)   Form LB04

[6.   The person signing on behalf of the Guarantor warrants and represents he has full authority to bind the Guarantor to this guarantee.]

7.   Until all debts of the Customer are fully paid, the Guarantor shall not exercise any rights of subrogation or set-off in competition with the Creditor.

8.   This guarantee shall be binding upon and inure to the benefit of the parties, their successors and assigns.

9.   This guarantee is subject to English law and the parties agree to submit to the exclusive jurisdiction of the English courts in connection with any dispute hereunder.

IN WITNESS OF WHICH the parties have signed this deed the day and year first above written.

(Individual)   (Company)

Signed for and on behalf of

_____   _____Ltd

Signed by the Guarantor

_____   _____

in the presence of (witness)   Director

Name _____

Address _____   _____

_____   Director/Secretary

Occupation Solicitor _____

 I hereby certify that I have explained this Guarantee
to the Guarantor and that he/she is entering into it
of his/her own free will

Signed for and on behalf of:

_____   _____Ltd

Signed by the Creditor

_____   _____

in the presence of (witness)   Director

Name _____

Address _____   _____

_____   Director/Secretary

Occupation _____

Health warning: This guarantee should not be used in the case of any indebtedness governed by the Consumer Credit Act 1974. Note also that if there is any personal or family relationship between the parties (even if they are also business partners), you should not accept this guarantee unless the guarantor has seen a solicitor, who has then certified to you that he has advised the guarantor about the guarantee and that the guarantor is willing to enter into it. The name of the solicitor must be given to you by the guarantor, not by the customer.

Limited Proxy
Form B14

_____ LIMITED

FORM OF PROXY FOR USE BY ORDINARY SHAREHOLDERS

FOR THE ANNUAL GENERAL MEETING TO BE HELD ON

_____

I _____ of _____ being a member

of the above-named company, hereby appoint _____

of _____ or, failing him/her, _____

of _____ or failing him/her the duly appointed chairman of

the meeting as my proxy at the annual general meeting of the company to be held on

_____ and at any adjournment thereof and to vote on my behalf as

directed below.

RESOLUTIONS

Please indicate how you wish your proxy to vote by placing an 'X' in the appropriate box. Unless otherwise

indicated the proxy will exercise his discretion as to how he votes and whether he abstains from voting. __

		For	Against
1.	[Insert text of resolution]	☐	☐
2.	[Insert text of resolution]	☐	☐

_____

Dated

_____

Signature

Notes:

(a) This form of proxy, together with the power of attorney or other authority (if any) under which it was signed, or an office or notarially certified copy thereof, must be lodged [at the company's registered office] not later than 48 hours before the meeting.[1]

(b) A proxy need not be a member of the company.

(c) In the case of joint holders the signature of the first-named will be accepted to the exclusion of all others.

(d) In the case of a corporation this form of proxy should be under its common seal or under the hand of an officer or attorney duly authorised.

(e) Any alterations to this form of proxy should be initialled.

(f) The completion of this form of proxy will not preclude the member from attending and voting in person if he/she so wishes.

[(g) Unless the articles provide otherwise, proxies may only vote on a poll] or [members have the right to appoint more than one proxy provided that such proxy is appointed in respect of the rights of different shares or blocks of shares. All proxies have the right to attend, speak or vote at the meeting.][2]

The notes above should be included in the form as sent out to the members.

[1] The Articles of the Company should be checked on this point as some permit proxies to be lodged up until the commencement of the meeting.

[2] After the Companies Act 2006 section 284 comes into effect on 1 October 2007, you must delete in note G above the first passage in square brackets from the form and you must include the second passage in square brackets.

Living Will   Form PF11

PERSONAL DETAILS

Name _____

Address _____

Date of birth _____

Doctor's details _____

National Health Number _____

I, _____, am of sound mind and make this Advance Directive now on my future medical care to my family, my doctors, other medical personnel and anyone else to whom it is relevant, for a time when, for reasons of physical or mental incapacity, I am unable to make my views known.

INSTRUCTIONS

MEDICAL TREATMENT I **DO NOT** WANT:

I REFUSE medical procedures to prolong my life or keep me alive by artificial means if (including but not limited to the intravenous administration of food or fluids where this is not necessary to ensure my comfort) if:

TICK <u>ONE</u> OF THE BOXES ONLY

(1)   I suffer from a severe physical illness or from severe consequences of a physical injury from which in the opinion of _____ independent medical practitioners it is unlikely that I will ever recover or experience any significant improvement where that illness, or the consequences of that injury (a) cause(s) severe and frequent pain or loss of the use of all of my limbs or (b) is terminal;

or

(2)   I have a severe mental incapacity which, in the opinion of _____ independent medical practitioners, has no likelihood of improvement and in addition I have a severe physical illness or suffer from severe consequences of a physical injury from which in the opinion of _____ medical practitioners it is unlikely that I will ever recover or experience any significant improvement where that illness or the consequences of that injury (a) cause(s) severe and frequent pain or loss of the use of all my limbs or (b) is terminal;

or

(3)   I am permanently unconscious and have been so for a period of at least ____ months and in the opinion of ___ independent medical practitioners there is no likelihood that I will ever recover.

or

(4)   I have a severe mental incapacity which, in the opinion of _____ independent medical practitioners, has no likelihood of improvement and which causes me severe emotional distress.

Continued on next page

Living Will (continued) — Form PF11

MEDICAL TREATMENT I **DO** WANT:

I DO wish to receive any medical treatment which will alleviate pain or distressing symptoms or will make me more comfortable. I accept that this may have the effect of shortening my life.

If I am suffering from any of the conditions above and I am pregnant, I wish to RECEIVE medical procedures which will prolong my life or keep me alive by artificial means only until such time as my child has been safely delivered.

HEALTH CARE PROXY

I wish to appoint _____ of _____

as my Health Care Proxy. S/he should be involved in any decisions about my health care options if I am physically or mentally unable to make my views known. I wish to make it clear that s/he is fully aware of my wishes and I request that his/her decisions be respected.

ADDITIONAL DIRECTIONS ON FUTURE HEALTH CARE

_____

_____

_____

_____

_____

_____

The above directions are to apply even if my life is at risk.

SIGNATURES

Signature _____ Date _____

Witness's signature _____ Date _____

I confirm that my views are still as stated above.

	Date	Signature	Witness' signature
1)	_____	_____	_____
2)	_____	_____	_____
3)	_____	_____	_____
4)	_____	_____	_____

Note: This form operates as a refusal of medical treatment which in some circumstances may be legally binding on your doctors. The effect of signing this form could therefore be to shorten your life in circumstances where your doctors could prolong it. Although you can revoke this Living Will at any time, and although you can permit medical treatment at any time even if you have not revoked it, remember that of course you can only do either of these things if you are conscious and able to express yourself at the time.

For the form to be validly executed: (1) you must sign the form or it must be signed by someone by your direction in your presence; and (2) the signature must be made or acknowledged by you in the presence of a witness; and (3) the witness must sign it or acknowledge his signature in your presence.

Loan Agreement | Form LB05

THIS AGREEMENT IS MADE the _____ day of _____ year _____

BETWEEN:

(1) _____(the 'Borrower'); and

(2) _____(the 'Lender').

NOW IT IS HEREBY AGREED as follows:

1. Loan: Subject to and in accordance with this agreement, its terms, conditions and covenants the Lender agrees to lend to the Borrower on _____ (the 'Loan Date') the principal sum of _____ Pounds (£_____) (the 'Loan').

2. Note: The terms of the Loan shall be evidenced by and further particularised in a Note in the form attached hereto and marked 'A' (the 'Note') executed by the Borrower and delivered to the Lender on the Loan Date.

3. Interest: The Loan shall bear interest on the unpaid principal at an annual rate of_____ percent (_____%). In the event of the default in payment interest at the aforesaid interest rate shall additionally accrue on any overdue payment until the same is discharged.

4. Payment: Payment shall be in accordance with the terms contained in the Note. The Note may, at any time and from time to time, be paid or prepaid in whole or in part without premium or penalty, except that any partial prepayment shall be (a) in multiples of £_____, and (b) of a minimum of £_____. All payments shall be applied firstly to the discharge of any interest which may be due by virtue of a default on the part of the Borrower, and secondly to the instalments (if any) due under the Note in the inverse order of their maturity. [Upon the payment of the outstanding principal in full or all of the instalments, if any, the interest on the Loan shall be computed and shall be paid within five (5) days of the receipt of notice from the Lender, in default of which any such unpaid interest will in turn bear interest at the aforementioned rate.][1]

5. Security: The Borrower agrees to secure the repayment of the Loan by executing those security documents attached hereto as Exhibit B (the 'Security Documents') and shall deliver the Security Documents on the Loan Date. From time to time the Lender may demand, and the Borrower shall execute, additional loan documents which in the Lender's view are reasonably necessary to perfect the Lender's security interests.

6. Representations and Warranties: The undersigned signatory on behalf of the Borrower represents and warrants: (i) that the execution, delivery and performance of this agreement, and the Note and Security Documents have been duly authorised by the Borrower; (ii) that the financial statement submitted to the Lender truly and fairly presents the financial condition of the Borrower as of the date of this agreement knowing that the Lender has relied thereon in granting the Loan; (iii) that the Borrower has no contingent obligations not disclosed or reserved against in said financial statement, and at the present time there are no material, unrealised or anticipated losses from any present commitment of the Borrower; (iv) that there will be no material adverse changes in the financial condition of the Borrower at the time of the Loan Date; (v) that the Borrower will advise the Lender of material adverse changes which occur at any time prior to the Loan Date and thereafter to the date of final payment;

Continued on next page

Loan Agreement (continued)   Form LB05

and (vi) that the Borrower has good and valid title to all of the property given as security hereunder. The said Undersigned represents and warrants that such representations and warranties shall be deemed to be continuing representations and warranties during the entire life of this agreement.

7. Default: In addition to the grounds set out in the Loan Note, the Borrower shall be in default: (i) if any payment due hereunder is not made within (___) days of the date due; (ii) in the event of assignment by the Borrower for the benefit of creditors, or the entry of the Borrower into any voluntary arrangement or the passing of a resolution for the winding up of the Borrower otherwise than for the purpose of amalgamation or reconstruction; (iii) upon the filing of any voluntary or involuntary petition for the bankruptcy or liquidation of the Borrower or the appointment of a receiver or administrator of the Borrower; or (iv) if the Borrower has breached any representation or warranty specified in this agreement. In the event of any such default the entire capital sum and interest due hereunder shall on demand fall due forthwith.

8. If the Borrower shall comprise more than one person, the Borrower's obligations herein shall be joint and several.

9. Governing Law: This agreement, the Note(s) and the Security Documents shall be governed by, construed and enforced in accordance with the law of England and Wales to the jurisdiction of which the parties hereto submit.

IN WITNESS OF WHICH the parties have signed this agreement the day and year first above written

(Borrower)   (Lender)

_____   _____
Signed by the Borrower   Signed by the Lender

_____   _____
in the presence of (witness)   in the presence of (witness)
Name _____   Name _____
Address _____   Address _____

_____   _____

Signed for and on behalf of   Signed for and on behalf of:
_____Ltd   _____Ltd

_____   _____
Director   Director

_____   _____
Director/Secretary   Director/Secretary

Note: This form is to be used in conjunction with the Loan Note (Short Form). This form must only be used in connection with agreements which are not regulated under the Consumer Credit Act 1974. Broadly speaking the Act, at the time of writing, applies to any loan, hire or hire purchase agreement for £25,000 or less. There are some exceptions. The most important are that an agreement is not regulated if the borrower or hirer is a limited company. By the time you use this form, however, the law may have changed so as to regulate agreements for more than £25,000. Therefore, you must check the current position.

¹ Include this passage **only** if you are using the Loan Note and it does not provide for instalments to include interest as well as principal.

Loan Note (Long Form)   Form LB06

THIS DEED IS MADE the _____ day of _____ year _____

BETWEEN:

(1) _____ of _____ (the 'Borrower'); and

(2) _____ of _____ (the 'Lender').

NOW THIS DEED WITNESSES as follows:

1.   The Borrower hereby promises to pay to the order of the Lender the sum of _____

     _____ Pounds (£_____), which the Lender has lent to the Borrower

     (receipt of which the Borrower hereby acknowledges) together with interest thereon at the rate of

     _____% per annum on the unpaid balance. The said amount shall be paid in the following manner:

     _____

     _____

     _____

2.   The terms of this Loan shall be governed by the Loan Agreement of the same date made between the
     Lender and the Borrower and attached hereto.

3.   This note shall at the option of any holder thereof be immediately due and payable upon the
     occurrence of any of the following:

     (a)   Failure of the Borrower to make any payment due hereunder within _____ days of its due date.

     (b)   Breach of any condition of any mortgage, loan agreement, or guarantee granted as collateral
           security for this note.

     (c)   Breach of any condition of any loan agreement or mortgage, if any, having a priority over any
           loan agreement or mortgage on security granted, in whole or in part, as collateral security for
           this note.

     (d)   Upon the death, incapacity, dissolution, receivership, insolvency or liquidation of either of the
           parties hereto, or any endorser or guarantor of this note.

4.   In the event that the Borrower shall be in default of any obligation under the Loan Agreement or this
     note then the Borrower will pay all reasonable solicitors fees and costs. All payments hereunder shall
     be made to such address as may from time to time be designated to the Borrower by the Lender.

5.   If the Borrower shall comprise more than one person, the liability of each such person in respect of the
     obligations herein shall be joint and several.

Continued on next page

Loan Note (Long Form) (continued)   Form LB06

IN WITNESS OF WHICH the parties have signed this deed the day and year first above written

(Borrower)   (Lender)

_____   _____
Signed by the Borrower   Signed by the Lender

_____   _____
in the presence of (witness)   in the presence of (witness)

Name _____   Name _____

Address _____   Address _____

_____   _____

Signed for and on behalf of   Signed for and on behalf of:

_____Ltd   _____Ltd

_____   _____
Director   Director

_____   _____
Director/Secretary   Director/Secretary

Note: This form must only be used in connection with agreements which are not regulated under the Consumer Credit Act 1974. Broadly speaking the Act, at the time of writing, applies to any loan, hire or hire purchase agreement for £25,000 or less. There are some exceptions. The most important are that an agreement is not regulated if the borrower or hirer is a limited company. By the time you use this form, however, the law may have changed so as to regulate agreements for more than £25,000. Therefore, you must check the current position.

Loan Note (Short Form) Form LB07

THIS DEED is made the _____ day of _____ year_____

BY:

_____ of _____ (the 'Borrower').

WHEREAS:

The Borrower is indebted to _____(the 'Lender') in the sum of £ _____

NOW THIS DEED WITNESSES as follows:

[This Loan Note is subject to the terms of the Loan Agreement dated _____ which is attached hereto. The two terms of the Loan Agreement dated _____ which is attached hereto. The two documents are to be read as one document, but if there is any conflict between them, the terms of this Loan Note shall prevail.]

1. The Borrower promises to pay to the order of the Lender the sum of _____ _____ Pounds (£ _____), with annual interest of _____ % on any unpaid balance.

2. This note shall be paid in _____ consecutive and equal instalments of £ _____ each with the first payment being made from the date hereof, and the same amount on the same day of each _____ thereafter. The instalments shall be in discharge of [both principal and interest due hereunder] / [principal only, the interest being payable in accordance with the Loan Agreement after the repayment of the principal].

3. This note may be prepaid without penalty.

4. If any instalment shall be unpaid more than _____ days after the same shall fall due, the same shall bear interest at the aforementioned rate until paid. All payments shall be first applied to such default interest and the balance to instalments in the order in which the same fell due.

5. This note shall be due and payable upon demand by any holder hereof should the Borrower default in any payment beyond _____ days of its due date.

Continued on next page

Loan Note (Short Form) (continued)   Form LB07

IN WITNESS OF WHICH the Borrower has executed this deed the day and year first above written

(Borrower)   (Lender)

_____   _____
Signed by the Borrower   Signed by the Lender

_____   _____
in the presence of (witness)   in the presence of (witness)

Name _____   Name _____

Address _____   Address _____

_____   _____

Signed for and on behalf of   Signed for and on behalf of:

_____Ltd   _____Ltd

_____   _____
Director   Director

_____   _____
Director/Secretary   Director/Secretary

Note: This form may be used in conjunction with the Loan Agreement form LB05. This form must only be used in connection with agreements which are not regulated under the Consumer Credit Act 1974. Broadly speaking the Act, at the time of writing, applies to any loan, hire or hire purchase agreement for £25,000 or less. There are some exceptions. The most important are that an agreement is not regulated if the borrower or hirer is a limited company. By the time you use this form, however, the law may have changed so as to regulate agreements for more than £25,000. Therefore, you must check the current position.

If it is intended for the loan to be governed by the Loan Agreement in this book as well as the Loan Note on this page, appropriate deletions will have to be made in order to avoid contradiction. That is because one of the options in the Loan Note permits instalments to pay off both interest and principal, whereas the Loan Agreement calls for the instalments to be of capital only, with the interest to be paid off at the end.

Loan Payment Record

Borrower: _____ Creditor: _____

Terms: _____

Date Due	Date Paid	Amount	Balance	Arrears	Interest Accruing on Arrears	Payments of Interest Accruing on Arrears
_____	_____	£ _____	£ _____	£ _____	£ _____	£ _____
_____	_____	£ _____	£ _____	£ _____	£ _____	£ _____
_____	_____	£ _____	£ _____	£ _____	£ _____	£ _____
_____	_____	£ _____	£ _____	£ _____	£ _____	£ _____
_____	_____	£ _____	£ _____	£ _____	£ _____	£ _____
_____	_____	£ _____	£ _____	£ _____	£ _____	£ _____
_____	_____	£ _____	£ _____	£ _____	£ _____	£ _____
_____	_____	£ _____	£ _____	£ _____	£ _____	£ _____
_____	_____	£ _____	£ _____	£ _____	£ _____	£ _____
_____	_____	£ _____	£ _____	£ _____	£ _____	£ _____
_____	_____	£ _____	£ _____	£ _____	£ _____	£ _____
_____	_____	£ _____	£ _____	£ _____	£ _____	£ _____
_____	_____	£ _____	£ _____	£ _____	£ _____	£ _____
_____	_____	£ _____	£ _____	£ _____	£ _____	£ _____
_____	_____	£ _____	£ _____	£ _____	£ _____	£ _____
_____	_____	£ _____	£ _____	£ _____	£ _____	£ _____
_____	_____	£ _____	£ _____	£ _____	£ _____	£ _____
_____	_____	£ _____	£ _____	£ _____	£ _____	£ _____
_____	_____	£ _____	£ _____	£ _____	£ _____	£ _____
_____	_____	£ _____	£ _____	£ _____	£ _____	£ _____
_____	_____	£ _____	£ _____	£ _____	£ _____	£ _____
_____	_____	£ _____	£ _____	£ _____	£ _____	£ _____
_____	_____	£ _____	£ _____	£ _____	£ _____	£ _____
_____	_____	£ _____	£ _____	£ _____	£ _____	£ _____
_____	_____	£ _____	£ _____	£ _____	£ _____	£ _____
_____	_____	£ _____	£ _____	£ _____	£ _____	£ _____
_____	_____	£ _____	£ _____	£ _____	£ _____	£ _____
_____	_____	£ _____	£ _____	£ _____	£ _____	£ _____
_____	_____	£ _____	£ _____	£ _____	£ _____	£ _____
_____	_____	£ _____	£ _____	£ _____	£ _____	£ _____
_____	_____	£ _____	£ _____	£ _____	£ _____	£ _____
_____	_____	£ _____	£ _____	£ _____	£ _____	£ _____
_____	_____	£ _____	£ _____	£ _____	£ _____	£ _____
_____	_____	£ _____	£ _____	£ _____	£ _____	£ _____
_____	_____	£ _____	£ _____	£ _____	£ _____	£ _____
_____	_____	£ _____	£ _____	£ _____	£ _____	£ _____
_____	_____	£ _____	£ _____	£ _____	£ _____	£ _____

Location of Important Documents and Summary of Personal Information

Location of Important Documents and
Summary of Personal Information

OF

Name _____

Will _____

_____

Birth Certificate _____

_____

Marriage Certificate _____

_____

Divorce Decree _____

_____

Title Deeds _____

_____

Mortgage Documents _____

_____

Life Insurance Policies _____

_____

Pension Details _____

_____

Share Certificates _____

_____

Other Investment Certificates _____

_____

Loan and H.P. Agreements _____

_____

Continued on next page

Location of Important Documents and   Form PF12
Summary of Personal Information (continued)

Bank Account Details   _____

_____

Building Society Passbooks   _____

_____

Donor Cards   _____

_____

Passport   _____

_____

Household Insurance   _____

_____

Driver's Licence   _____

_____

Tenancy Agreement   _____

_____

Car Insurance   _____

_____

Lodger Agreement   Form F303

The PROPERTY   _____

                    _____

The ROOM   means the room at the Property which has been nominated by the Owner and agreed

                    to by the Lodger

The OWNER   _____

                    _____whose address is the Property above

The LODGER   _____

                    _____

The TERM   _____ weeks/months* beginning on _____

EARLY   ⎡ Either party may at any time end this Agreement earlier than the end of the Term ⎤ (*delete as
TERMINATION   ⎣ by giving to the other written notice of _____ week(s)/month(s)*   ⎦ appropriate)

The PAYMENT   £ _____ per week/month* payable in advance on the _____ of each week/month*

The DEPOSIT   £ _____

The INVENTORY   means the list of the Owner's possessions at the Property/Room* which has been

                    signed by the Owner and the Lodger

DATED   _____

SIGNED   _____   _____

                    (The Owner)   (The Lodger)

THIS HOUSE/FLAT SHARE AGREEMENT comprises the particulars detailed above and the terms and
conditions printed overleaf whereby the Room is licensed by the Owner and taken by the Lodger for
occupation during the Term upon making the Payment.

IMPORTANT NOTICE:

1   This form of Agreement is for use in those cases where the Room is part of a house or flat which the Owner occupies as his/her only
    or principal home, so that an Assured Shorthold Tenancy is not created.

2   This form of Agreement does not require either party to give any form of notice to the other at the end of the fixed Term, but if
    either party wishes to end this Agreement early, as referred to in the definition of the TERM near the middle of this Agreement, then
    a Notice to Terminate may be used.

Terms and Conditions on next page

Lodger Agreement (Terms and Conditions)   Form F303

1. This Agreement is personal to the Lodger, is not assignable, and will terminate automatically without any notice if the Lodger ceases to reside at the Property or at any time more than two of the payments are due and unpaid.

2. The Lodger will:

   2.1 only in conjunction with the occupation of the Room be allowed to share with the other occupiers of the Property the use and facilities of the common parts of the Property (including such bathroom, toilet, kitchen and sitting room facilities as may be at the Property);

   2.2 pay the Payment at the times and in the manner aforesaid;

   2.3 keep the interior of the Room in a good and clean state and condition and not damage or injure the Property or any part of it;

   2.4 yield up the Room at the end of the Term in the same clean state and condition it was in at the beginning of the Term;

   2.5 maintain in the Room and keep in a good and clean condition all of the items listed in the Inventory;

   2.6 not make any alteration or addition to the Room nor without the Owner's prior written consent do any redecoration or painting of the Room;

   2.7 not do or omit to do anything on or at the Property which may be or become a nuisance or annoyance to the Owner or any other occupiers of the Property or Sharers or occupiers of adjoining or nearby premises or which may in any way prejudice the insurance of the Property or cause an increase in the premium payable therefor;

   2.8 not without the Owner's prior consent allow or keep any pet or any kind of animal at the Property;

   2.9 not use or occupy the Room in any way whatsoever other than as a private residence;

   2.10 not to let or purport to let or share any rooms at the property or take in any lodger or paying guest or, without the consent of the Owner to permit any person to sleep, or stay at the property;

   2.11 provide the Owner with a forwarding address when the Agreement comes to an end and remove all rubbish and all personal items (including the Lodger's own furniture and equipment) from the Property before leaving;

   2.12 pay interest at the rate of 4% above the Base Lending Rate for the time being of the Owner's bankers upon any payment or other money lawfully due from the Lodger under this Agreement which is more than 14 days in arrears in respect of the period from when it become due down to the date of payment;

   2.13 make a reasonable and proportionate contribution to the cost according to use of all charges in respect of any electric, gas, water and telephonic or televisual services used at or supplied to the Property and Council Tax or any similar tax that might be charged in addition to or replacement of it during the Term.

3. The Deposit

   3.1 The Deposit will be held by the Owner and will be refunded to the Lodger at the end of the Term (however it ends) but less any reasonable deductions properly made by the Owner to cover any reasonable costs incurred by or losses caused to him by any breaches of the Lodger's obligations under this Agreement. No interest will be payable by the Owner to the Lodger in respect of the deposit money.

   3.2 The Deposit shall be repaid to the Lodger, at the forwarding address provided to the Owner, as soon as reasonably practicable. However the Owner shall not be bound to return the Deposit until he is satisfied that no money is repayable to the Local Authority if the Lodger has been in receipt of Housing Benefit and until after he has had a reasonable opportunity to assess the reasonable cost of any repairs required as a result of any breaches of his obligations by the Lodger or other sums properly due to the Owner under clause 3.1 above, save that except in exceptional circumstances the Owner shall not retain the Deposit for more than one month.

   3.3 At any time during the Term the Owner may apply any part of the Deposit to cover any reasonable costs incurred as a result of any breaches of his obligations by the Lodger or other sums properly due to the Owner, in which case the Lodger shall upon demand pay by way of additional Payment to the Owner any additional payments needed to restore the full amount of the Deposit.

4. In the event of destruction to the Property or of damage to it which shall make the same or a substantial portion of the same uninhabitable, the Lodger shall be relieved from making the payment by an amount proportionate to the extent to which the Lodger's ability to live in the Property is thereby prevented, save where the destruction or damage has been caused by any act or default by the Lodger or where the Owner's insurance cover has been adversely affected by any act or omission on the part of the Lodger.

5. To enable the Lodger to comply with clause 4 above, the Owner will upon request provide to the Lodger a copy of his insurance policy (if any) or an extract of the relevant terms.

6. The Lodger shall not have exclusive possession of the Room and the identity of any other occupiers of the Property shall be in the absolute discretion of the Owner.

7. It is hereby agreed that if the parties agree to the Lodger continuing in occupation of the Room after the end of the Term, his occupation shall still be subject to the Terms and Conditions set out in this Agreement, save that it shall be terminable by either party on [one month's] notice. Such notice may expire at any time, whether or not on a date specified for payment on or at the end of a period of this Agreement or otherwise. If such notice expires on a date other than a date specified for payment, the Lodger shall be entitled to a refund of such part of the final payment as is proportionate to the number of days which follows the expiry of the notice or the end of his occupancy, whichever shall be the later, and this will continue unless and until a new agreement is signed or the Lodger vacates the Property.

8. Where the context so admits:

   8.1 the 'Owner' includes the successors in title to the Owner's interest in the Property;

   8.2 the 'Property' includes all of the Owner's fixtures and fittings at or upon the Property and all of the items listed in the Inventory and (for the avoidance of doubt) the Room;

   8.3 the 'Term' shall mean the period stated in the particulars overleaf or any shorter or longer period in the event of an earlier termination or an extension or holding over respectively;

   8.4 All references to the singular shall include the plural and vice versa and any obligations or liabilities of more than one person shall be joint and several and an obligation on the part of a party shall include an obligation not to allow or permit the breach of that obligation.

   8.5 All references to 'he', 'him' and 'his' shall be taken to include 'she', 'her' and 'hers'.

Lodger/Bed and Breakfast Licence   Form RT22
(For a Room in a Furnished House)

The PROPERTY   _____

                       _____

The ROOM   means the room at the Property which has been agreed between the Licensor and Licensee to be taken by the Licensee

The LICENSOR   _____

                       _____whose address is the Property above

The LICENSEE   _____

                       of _____

The PERIOD   _____weeks/months* beginning on _____
(delete
paragraph if
not required)   [Subject to the right for either party at any time during the Period to end this Agreement earlier by giving to the other written notice of _____ week(s)/month(s)*]

The SERVICES   means the services that the Licensor hereby agrees to provide to the Licensor being to [clean the Room and Property] [provide clean sheets] [provide breakfast] [provide dinner]*

The PAYMENT   £ _____ per week/month* payable in advance on the _____ of each week/month*

                       being payment for the Room and Services

The DEPOSIT   £_____

The INVENTORY   means the list of the Licensor's possessions at the Property which has been signed by the Licensor and the Licensee

DATED   _____

SIGNED   _____   _____

                       _____   _____

                       (The Licensor)   (The Licensee)

THIS AGREEMENT comprises the particulars detailed above and the terms and conditions printed overleaf whereby the Room is licensed by the Licensor and taken by the Licensee for occupation during the Period upon making the Payment.

                                                          (* delete as appropriate)

Terms and Conditions on next page

Lodger/Bed and Breakfast Licence Terms and Conditions   Form RT22

1. This Licence is personal to the Licensee, is not assignable, and will terminate automatically without any notice if the Licensee ceases to reside at the Property or if at any time more than two of the payments are due and unpaid

2. The Licensee will:

    2.1   only in conjunction with the occupation of the Room be allowed to share with the other occupiers of the Property the use and facilities of the common parts of the Property (including such bathroom, toilet, kitchen and sitting room facilities as may be at the Property)

    2.2   pay the Payment at the times and in the manner aforesaid

    2.3   [keep the interior of the Room in a good and clean state and condition and]* not damage or injure the Property or any part of it

    2.4   yield up the Room at the end of the Period in the same clean state and condition it was in at the beginning of the Period

    2.5   maintain in the Room and keep in a good [and clean]* condition all of the items listed in the Inventory

    2.6   not make any alteration or addition to the Room nor without the Licensor's prior written consent to do any redecoration or painting of the Room

    2.7   not do or omit to do anything on or at the Property which may be or become a nuisance or annoyance to the Licensor or any other occupiers of the Property or owners or occupiers of adjoining or nearby premises or which may in any way prejudice the insurance of the Property or cause an increase in the premium payable therefor

    2.8   not without the Licensor's prior consent allow or keep any pet or any kind of animal at the Property

    2.9   not use or occupy the Room in any way whatsoever other than as a private residence

    2.10   not to let or purport to let or share any rooms at the property or take in any lodger or paying guest or, without the consent of the Licensor (not to be unreasonably withheld) to permit any person to sleep, or stay at the property

    2.11   provide the Licensor with a forwarding address when the licence agreement comes to an end and remove all rubbish and all personal items (including the Licensee's own furniture and equipment)

    from the property before leaving

    2.12   pay interest at the rate of 4% above the Base Lending Rate for the time being of the Licensor's bankers upon any payment or other money due from the Licensee under this Agreement which is more than 14 days in arrears in respect of the period from when it become due down to the date of payment

    2.13   make a reasonable and proportionate contribution to the cost according to use of all charges in respect of any electric, gas, water and telephonic or televisual services used at or supplied to the Property and Council Tax or any similar tax that might be charged in addition to or replacement of it during the Period

    2.14   to register with the Local Authority as a Council Tax payer in respect of the room or of the house as the Local Authority may decide and to pay such Council Tax as may be assessed. If the Licensee shall pay less than ___ per cent of the Council Tax which is payable in respect of the [room]/[Property] the Licensee will reimburse the Licensor or any occupant who may be obliged to make up the shortfall. If the Licensee is obliged to pay more than the aforementioned portion of the Council Tax, the Licensor shall reimburse him for the excess The term 'Council Tax' shall include any similar tax that might be charged in addition to or replacement of it during the Period

3. The Deposit

    3.1   The Deposit will be held by the Licensor and will be refunded to the Licensee at the end of the Period (however it ends) but less any reasonable deductions properly made by the Licensor to cover any reasonable costs incurred by or losses caused to him by any breaches of the Licensee's obligations under this Licence. No interest will be payable by the Licensor to the Licensee in respect of the deposit money

    3.2   The Deposit shall be repaid to the Licensee, at the forwarding address provided to the Licensor, as soon as reasonably practicable. However the Licensor shall not be bound to return the Deposit until he is satisfied that no money is repayable to the Local Authority if the Licensee has been in receipt of Housing Benefit and until after he has had a reasonable opportunity to assess the

Continued on next page

Lodger/Bed and Breakfast Licence
Terms and Conditions (cont)

Form RT22

reasonable cost of any repairs required as a result of any breaches of his obligations by the Licensee or other sums properly due to the Licensor under clause 3.1 above, save that except in exceptional circumstances the Licensor shall not retain the Deposit for more than one month

3.3 If at any time during the Period the Licensor needs to use any part of the Deposit to cover any reasonable costs incurred as a result of any breaches of his obligations by the Licensee or other sums properly due to the Licensor, the Licensee shall upon demand pay by way of additional Payment to the Licensor any additional payments needed to restore the full amount of the Deposit

4. In the event of damage to or destruction of the Property by fire or other catastrophe not caused by the Licensee shall be relieved from making the Payment to the extent that the Licensee's use and enjoyment of the Property is thereby prevented and from performance of its obligations as to the state and condition of the Property to the extent of and whilst there prevails any such damage or destruction (except to the extent that the insurance is prejudiced by any act or default of the Licensee)

5. So long as the reference to a right of early termination in the definition of 'the PERIOD' overleaf (the 'early termination right) has not been deleted then either party may at an time during the period terminate this Agreement by giving to the other prior written notice to that effect, the length of such notice to be that stated in the early termination right, and upon the

expiry of said notice this Agreement shall end with no further liability for either party save for any existing breach

6. The Licensee shall not have exclusive possession of the Room and the identity of any other occupiers of the Property shall be in the absolute discretion of the Licensor

7. Where the context so admits:
   7.1 the 'Licensor' includes the successors in title to the Licensor's interest in the Property
   7.2 the 'Property' includes all of the Licensor's fixtures and fittings at or upon the Property and all of the items listed in the Inventory and (for the avoidance of doubt) the Room
   7.3 the 'Period' shall mean the period stated in the particulars overleaf or any shorter or longer period in the event of an earlier termination or an extension or holding over respectively

8. All references to the singular shall include the plural and vice versa and any obligations or liabilities of more than one person shall be joint and several and an obligation on the part of a party shall include an obligation not to allow or permit the breach of that obligation

*Delete as appropriate

Note: If you are providing meals (not just a packet of cereal in the morning, for example) or other substantial services such as cleaning and laundry, or if the occupant is sharing the room with someone else and you genuinely have the right to decide who the sharer is, then the arrangement is a licence and can be brought to an end, simply by your serving a written notice giving the minimum term of notice which the licence prescribes. After expiry of the notice, you can bring proceedings for possession. Note that there are only limited cases that you can expel a lodger without bringing court proceedings, and that you must be sure that your case is one of them before you do so. It can be a criminal offence if you get it wrong.

Remember also that the courts are keen to detect sham arrangements and that therefore the provision of meals or the right to determine sharers must reflect reality. If it does not, you may have created a tenancy, and if you have done that you will need to follow certain strict procedures in order to recover possession.

If you have any doubts, therefore, you should consult a solicitor, whether at the time when you are making the arrangement or seeking to bring it to an end.'

If you wish to impose further obligations on the lodger than are contained in this form, we advise you to read the Office of Fair Trading's 'Guidance on unfair terms in tenancy agreements' which is available online.

Lost Credit Card Notice   Form OLF24

Date _____

To _____

_____

_____

Dear _____

This is to confirm that the credit card described below has been lost or stolen. Please put a stop on all credit in respect of the card. I last remember using the card myself on _____ at _____. I shall destroy the card if subsequently found, and I would be grateful if you could issue me with a replacement card.

Yours faithfully

_____

Cardholder

Address _____

_____

_____

_____

Credit Card Number

Magazine Article Commissioning Contract — Form OLF25

THIS AGREEMENT IS MADE the _____ day of _____ year____

BETWEEN:

(1) _____ (the 'Author'); and

(2) _____ (the 'Publisher').

NOW IT IS HEREBY AGREED as follows:

1.   The Author agrees to deliver an original and one copy of the manuscript which is tentatively titled

_____(the 'Work'),

to the Publisher on or before _____.

The Work is described as:

_____

_____

If the Author fails to deliver the Work within _____ days of the Work due date, the Publisher may terminate this contract. The Article shall be submitted by email/on disk and shall be _____ words in length.

2.   Within _____ days of receipt of the Work, the Publisher agrees to notify the Author if the Publisher finds the work unsatisfactory in form or content. The Publisher also agrees to provide the Author with a list of necessary changes unless in the Publisher's reasonable opinion the Work is incapable of remedy. The Author agrees to make the changes within _____ days of receipt of the list. If the Publisher still reasonably rejects the Work as unsatisfactory, the Publisher may terminate this contract. If the Publisher does not reject the Work within ___ days of the receipt of any changes from the Author, the Work will be deemed to have been accepted.

3.   The Author grants the Publisher the exclusive licence to publish the Work for the period of _____ following the initial publication of the Work. Any rights not specifically granted to the Publisher shall remain with the Author. The Author agrees not to exercise any retained rights in such a manner as to adversely affect the value of the rights granted to the Publisher.

4.   The Publisher shall pay to the Author upon acceptance of the Work the amount of £_____.

5.   The style, format, design, layout, and any required editorial changes of the published work shall be in the sole discretion of the Publisher.

6.   The Author warrants that:

(a)   the Work is the sole creation of the Author;

(b)   the Author is the sole owner of the rights granted under this contract;

(c)   the Work does not infringe the copyright of any other work;

(d)   the Work is original and has not been published before;

(e)   the Work is not in the public domain;

(f)   the Work is not obscene, libellous, and does not invade the privacy of any person;

(g)   all statements of fact in the Work are [true and] based upon reasonable research.

The Author will indemnify the Publisher for any breach of these warranties and for any legal costs which the Publisher may incur by reason of the same.

Continued on next page

Magazine Article Commissioning Contract (cont) Form OLF25

7. The Publisher acknowledges that the Author retains worldwide copyright in the Work.

8. The Publisher agrees that, within [six] months from the receipt of a satisfactory manuscript of the Work, the Work will be published at the Publisher's sole expense. [If the Publisher fails to do so, unless prevented by conditions beyond the Publisher's control, the Author may terminate this Contract.] [If the Publisher fails to publish the Work within one year from receipt, the licence shall cease to be exclusive and the Author will be at liberty to publish the Work as he sees fit.] Notwithstanding any prior acceptance by the Publisher of the Work, the Publisher shall be under no obligation to publish the same if the Publisher reasonably believes that any of the warranties contained in Clause 6 hereof are breached. If any of the said warranties are actually breached, the Publisher may reject the Work and terminate the contract, whereupon all sums paid by the Publisher to the Author shall be returned.

9. This contract is the complete agreement between the Author and Publisher. No modification or waiver of any terms will be valid unless in writing and signed by both parties.

10. Nothing in this Agreement is intended to confer any benefit on a third party whether under the Contracts (Rights of Third Parties) Act or otherwise.

IN WITNESS OF WHICH the parties have signed this agreement the day and year first above written

_____

Signed by the Author

_____

in the presence of (witness)

Name _____

Address _____

_____

Occupation _____

_____

Signed for and on behalf of the Publisher

_____

in the presence of (witness)

Name _____

Address _____

_____

Occupation _____

Mailing List Name Removal Request   Form OLF26

Date _____

The Mailing Preference Service (MPS)

DMA House

70 Margaret Street

London

W1W 8SS

Dear Sirs

I regularly receive unsolicited, 'junk' mail from companies advertising their products. I understand that I can ask you to have my name and this household removed from the mailing lists of companies which send out unsolicited mail, and that this service is free of charge.

[I wish to register my address details so it can be removed from mailing lists].*

[I wish to register a previous occupier at my current address, he/she being _____].*

[I wish to register my previous address, this being _____].*

[I wish to register details of _____, who has died]*

[Although other members of the household wish to register, I would like to continue to receive mail]*

Please put this into action with immediate effect.

Yours faithfully.

_____

Name

_____

Address

*Delete as appropriate

Note: The mailing preference service can also be reached by telephone on 0207 291 3310 or www.mpsonline.org.uk.

Mileage Reimbursement Report   Form E45

Employee Name: _____

Driving Licence No. _____Car Reg No. _____

Make/Model of Vehicle _____

Department _____Month _____

Date	Beginning Reading	Ending Reading	Total Mileage	Reason for Travel

Total mileage this month: _____ @ £ _____ Per Mile = £ _____

Approved by _____ Date _____

Title _____

Minutes of Annual General Meeting   Form B15

_____ LIMITED

MINUTES of the annual general meeting of the Company held at

_____ on._____ at _____ a.m./p.m.

PRESENT _____ (in the chair)

_____

IN ATTENDANCE _____

_____

1.   The Chairman announced that consents to the meeting being held at short notice had been received from all of the members of the Company having a right to attend and vote at the meeting.

2   The Chairman declared that a quorum was present.

3.   It was unanimously agreed that the notice convening the meeting should be taken as read.

4.   The Chairman submitted the Company's profit and loss account for the period ended _____ , together with the balance sheet as at that date and it was resolved that the accounts as submitted to the meeting be and are approved.[1]

5.   It was resolved that a final dividend of _____ p per share in respect of the year ended _____ be declared on the ordinary shares of _____ each in the capital of the company, payable on _____ to the holders of ordinary shares registered at the close of business on _____ .

6.   It was resolved that _____ be re-appointed auditors of the Company until the next general meeting at which accounts are laid before the company, at a fee to be agreed with the board of directors.

7.   It was resolved that _____ , the director(s) retiring by rotation, be re-elected a director(s) of the Company.[2]

8.   It was resolved that the appointment of _____ to the board on _____ be confirmed.[3]

9.   The meeting then ended.

_____

Chairman

Note: From 1 October 2007 it will no longer be a statutory requirement for a private company to hold an AGM. This form is, however, retained because many companies will continue to find this a convenient course.

[1] There is no requirement for the accounts to be approved by the shareholders; they need only be laid before them in general meeting.

[2] In a private company, it is possible to vote on the re-election of directors en bloc although best practice is to vote on each individually.

[3] The reappointment of directors appointed during the year should not be confused with the re-election of directors.

Minutes of Directors' Meeting
Changing Objects of Company

Form B16

Minutes of a meeting of the directors held on the _____ day of _____ year __

Present: _____ (Chairman)

                  _____ (Managing Director)

                  _____ (Director)

In attendance: _____(Company Secretary)

1.   On opening the meeting the Chairman declared that a quorum was in attendance.

2.   The board considered the future activities of the Company. Having determined that the objects of the Company were too restrictive and should be altered, it was decided that the memorandum of association of the Company should be altered by deleting subclause (__) of clause ___ of the memorandum of association and substituting therefor: 'To carry on business as a general commercial company.'

3.   It was resolved that an extraordinary general meeting of the Company be held on _____ the ____ day of _____ year ___ at _____ o'clock for the purpose of considering and, if thought fit, passing as a special resolution the following:
'That the memorandum of association of the Company should be altered by deleting subclause (__) of clause ___ of the memorandum of association and substituting therefor:
'To carry on business as a general commercial company.'
Furthermore, the secretary was instructed to give notice to all shareholders of the extraordinary general meeting and to obtain their consent to the meeting being held on short notice.

4.   There being no further business the meeting was closed.

_____

Chairman

Note: All companies formed after the Companies Act 2006 Section 31 comes into force will have unlimited objects, unless these are specifically restricted in the company's Articles.

Minutes of Extraordinary General Meeting — Form B17

_____ LIMITED

MINUTES of an extraordinary general meeting of the Company held at

_____ on _____ at _____ a.m./p.m.

PRESENT _____ (in the chair)

_____

IN ATTENDANCE _____

_____

1. The Chairman [confirmed that notice of the meeting had been given to all the members of the company having a right to attend and vote at the meeting] / [announced that consents to the meeting being held at short notice had been received from all of the members of the Company having a right to attend and vote at the meeting] .

2. The Chairman declared that a quorum was present.

3. It was unanimously agreed that the notice convening the meeting should be taken as read.

4. The Chairman proposed the following resolution as an ordinary/special resolution: _____

    _____

    _____

5. The Chairman put the resolution to the meeting, took the vote on a show of hands[1] and declared the resolution passed as an ordinary/special resolution of the Company.[2]

6. There being no further business the meeting then closed.

_____

Chairman

Note: If it is intended to pass a resolution removing a director or the auditor from office before the expiry of their term of appointment, then special notice (which is 28 days' notice) of the meeting is required.

From 1 October 2007 private companies will no longer be required to hold an AGM; all meetings will therefore be ordinary and none will be extraordinary. This form may continue to be used. Note that the law requiring 28 days' notice of a meeting, where a resolution requiring special notice is to be considered, remains unchanged.

[1] If a poll is validly demanded, the resolution may not be passed or blocked on a show of hands. The circumstances in which a poll may be demanded and the way in which it should be conducted are set out in the articles (in Table A, the relevant provisions are articles 46-52). The fact that a poll has been demanded, by whom and the result of the poll should be recorded in the minutes.

[2] Repeat points 4 and 5 for each resolution.

Minutes of Extraordinary General Meeting Changing Objects of Company

Form B18

Minutes of an extraordinary general meeting of the members of _____ _____

_____ Limited held at _____ at _____

o'clock on _____ the _____day of _____ year _____

Present: _____ (Chairman)

_____ (Managing Director)

_____ (Members)

In attendance: _____ (Company Secretary)

1. The chairman declared that a quorum was present.

2. The notice convening the meeting was read.

3. It was proposed as a special resolution:

   'That the memorandum of association of the Company be altered by deleting subclause (___) of

   clause ___ and substituting therefor the following subclause:

   'To carry on business as a general commercial company.'

   The resolution was carried unanimously.

4. There being no further business the meeting was closed.

_____

Chairman

Note: All companies formed after the Companies Act 2006 Section 31 comes into force will have unlimited objects, unless these are specifically restricted in the company's articles.

From 1 October 2007 it will no longer be a statutory requirement for a private company to hold an AGM. This form is, however, retained because many companies will continue to find this a convenient course. The notice post 1 October 2007 for a resolution to alter the objects of the company is 14 days.

Minutes of First General Meeting of a Private Company   Form B21

_____ LIMITED

Minutes of the general meeting of the Company held at

_____ on _____ at _____ am/pm

PRESENT _____ (in the chair)

_____

IN ATTENDANCE _____

1. The Chairman announced that consents to the meeting being held at short notice[1] had been received from all of the members[2] of the Company having a right to attend and vote at the meeting.

2. The Chairman declared that a quorum was present.

3. The meeting resolved by a vote of _____ to _____ that _____ should be appointed a director of the Company.[3]

4. The meeting resolved by a vote of _____ to _____ that _____ should be appointed a director of the Company.

5. It was agreed by a majority of _____ per cent that the Company's name should be changed from _____ Ltd. to _____ Ltd.

6. It was agreed that the following amendment should be made to the Company's Articles of Association:[4]

7. The meeting then ended.

_____

Chairman

---

[1] Under the Companies Act 1985, 14 days' notice is required for meetings of a private company, except for the annual general meeting, which requires 21 days' notice. A resolution that needs to be passed as a special resolution (e.g. a resolution to alter the articles or to change the name of the company), can only be passed if 21 days' notice has been given. Certain other resolutions require special notice of 28 days, but these resolutions, by the nature of their subject matter, would not arise at a first meeting. Normally, a first meeting would be intended to serve as the AGM, and therefore 21 days' notice will be required. The Companies Act 2006 abolishes, in the case of private companies, the requirements for annual general meetings and for 21 days' notice for special resolutions. When it comes into effect, 14 days' notice will be sufficient.

[2] Under the Companies Act 1985, the holders of 95 per cent of the shares conferring the power to vote may consent to short notice, except in the case of the AGM where unanimity is required. From 1 October 2007, that the holders of 90 per cent of the shares conferring the right to vote or such higher percentage as the articles may specify (not being more than 95 per cent) can consent to short notice.

[3] A simple majority will suffice.

[4] A 75 per cent majority is required.

Mutual Termination of Contract   Form OLF27

THIS DEED IS MADE the _____ day of _____ year _____

BETWEEN:

(1) _____ of _____(the 'First Party'); and

(2) _____ of _____ (the 'Second Party').

WHEREAS:

(A)   The parties entered into a Contract dated _____ (the 'Contract').

(B)   The parties wish mutually to terminate the Contract and all their obligations and rights thereunder.

NOW IT IS HEREBY AGREED as follows:

1.   The parties hereby agree to terminate the Contract.

2.   The parties further agree that the termination shall be without further recourse by either party against the other and this document shall constitute mutual releases of any further obligations under the Contract, to the same extent as if the Contract had not been entered into in the first instance, [provided that the parties shall hereby undertake to perform the act or acts, if any, described below, which obligations, shall remain binding, notwithstanding this agreement to terminate.

_____

_____]

IN WITNESS OF WHICH the parties have signed this agreement as a Deed the day and year first above written

_____   _____

Signed as a Deed by or on behalf of the First Party   Signed as a Deed by or on behalf of the Second Party

_____

in the presence of (witness)   _____

Name _____   in the presence of (witness)

Address _____   Name _____

_____   Address _____

Occupation _____   _____

Occupation _____

Mutual Releases   Form OLF28

THIS DEED IS MADE the _____ day of _____ year _____

BETWEEN:

(1) _____ of _____ (the 'First Party'); and

(2) _____ of _____ (the 'Second Party').

NOW IT IS HEREBY AGREED as follows:

1. The First Party and the Second Party do hereby completely, mutually and reciprocally release,
    discharge, acquit and forgive each other from all claims, contracts, actions, demands, agreements,
    liabilities, and proceedings of every nature and description that either party has or may have against
    the other, arising from the beginning of time to the date of this agreement, including but not limited
    to an incident or claim described as:

    _____

    _____

    _____

2. This release shall be binding upon and inure to the benefit of the parties, their successors and assigns.

IN WITNESS OF WHICH the parties have signed this agreement as a Deed the day and year first above
written

_____   _____

Signed by or on behalf of the First Party   Signed by or on behalf of the Second Party

_____   _____

in the presence of (witness)   in the presence of (witness)

Name _____   Name _____

Address _____   Address _____

_____   _____

Occupation _____   Occupation _____

National Lottery Syndicate Agreement Form OLF29

SYNDICATE NAME: _____

MANAGER	DATE OF APPOINTMENT	SIGNATURE

MEMBER	INDIVIDUAL STAKE (to be paid IN ADVANCE of of each Draw by the agreed deadline)	DATE JOINED SYNDICATE	MANAGER'S SIGNATURE	MEMBER'S SIGNATURE	DATE LEFT SYNDICATE	MANAGER'S SIGNATURE

The Syndicate will participate in Draws on: Wednesdays only*   (*delete as appropriate)

Saturdays only*

Wednesdays and Saturdays*

Agreed deadline for payment of Individual Stakes: Day (each week): _____

Time: _____

(Syndicate Rules on next page)

National Lottery Syndicate Rules

1. Definitions

    'Draw' means a draw of the Camelot National Lottery in which the Syndicate has agreed to participate;

    'Individual Stake' means the stake payable by each Member as set out in this Agreement and received by the Manager in advance of each Draw by the agreed deadline;

    'Manager' means the Manager of the Syndicate, who shall be appointed and may be replaced at any time without notice by a majority of the Members;

    'Members' means all those persons who have joined and not left the Syndicate;

    'Syndicate Stake' means the total of the Members' Individual Stakes in respect of any Draw.

2. Manager's Responsibilities

    2.1 The Manager will:

       (a) establish a procedure for agreeing the combinations of numbers to be entered by the Syndicate for each Draw;

       (b) buy tickets bearing the agreed numbers for the amount of the Syndicate Stake for each Draw. However, if the Syndicate Stake is not sufficient to buy tickets bearing all agreed combinations of numbers in any Draw, the Manager shall have absolute discretion as to which of the agreed combinations to enter;

       (c) keep a current record of each Member's payment, of each payment which he has made on behalf of any Member, of each reimbursement which such Member may have paid and of each ticket purchased;

       (d) collect any prize money and account to the Members for it in proportion to their Individual Stakes, holding it in trust for the Members in the meantime.

    2.2 If any Member fails to pay his Individual Stake to the Manager in advance of any Draw by the agreed deadline, the Manager may (but shall not be obliged to) pay that Individual Stake on the Member's behalf and, if the Manager does so, the Member will reimburse the Manager forthwith upon demand.

    2.3 The Manager shall not be liable to any Member for any loss or damage arising out of any failing of the Manager under this Agreement, provided that the Manager has acted honestly.

3. Members' Responsibilities

    The Members will each pay their Individual Stake to the Manager in advance of each Draw by the agreed deadline.

4. Ceasing to be a Member

    A Member shall be removed from the Group:

    4.1 if the Member wishes to leave; or

    4.2 at the discretion of the Manager, if the Member fails to pay his Individual Stake in accordance with Rule 3 in respect of any 3 weeks (whether consecutive or non-consecutive); or

    4.3 at the discretion of the Manager, if the Member fails to reimburse the Manager in accordance with Rule 2.2.

5. This Agreement

    5.1 It shall be the responsibility of the Manager to update and amend this Agreement in accordance with any amendment which may be passed by a simple majority of the Members. [Rule 4 may be amended only by the vote of 75 per cent of the members.]

    5.2 The list of Members in this Agreement shall be conclusive as to the membership of the Syndicate at any point in time, provided that a person whose application for membership has been accepted by the Manager and who has duly paid an agreed Individual Stake shall not be excluded from a share of prize money under Rule 2.1(c) merely because the Agreement has not been updated to record that person as a Member.

    5.3 If any person is removed from the list of Members, the Manager shall forthwith notify the member of that fact, but the Manager shall incur no liability to such Member for any loss incurred by reason of any such failure to inform the Member of such removal.

    5.3 The appointment or replacement of the Manager shall take effect whether or not this Agreement has been amended to that effect.

    5.4 This Agreement is subject to English law and the parties submit to the exclusive jurisdiction of the English courts in connection with any dispute hereunder.

Nominee Shareholder's Declaration of Trust

Form b

I, _____, of _____,

hereby acknowledge and declare that I hold _____ fully paid ordinary shares in _____

_____ Ltd ('the Share') registered in my name as nominee of and Trustee for

_____ ('the Owner') and I undertake and agree not to transfer, deal with or dispose

of the Share save as the Owner may from time to time direct and further to give full effect to the trust

hereby declared I hereby deposit with the Owner the Certificate for the Share together with a transfer

thereof executed by me in blank and I hereby expressly authorise and empower the Owner at any time to

complete such transfer by inserting therein the name or names of any transferee or transferees and the date

of the transfer and to complete the same in any other necessary particular and I expressly declare that this

authority is irrevocable by me. Furthermore I irrevocably assign to the Owner the right to receive any

dividends which may be declared on the Share together with all profits and other monies which may be

paid or payable to me from time to time upon the Share or in respect thereof, and I further agree and

undertake to exercise my voting power as Holder of the Share in such manner and for such purpose as the

Owner may from time to time direct or determine.

Dated this _____ day of _____ year _____.

_____

Signature

_____

Signature of Witness

Address _____

_____

_____

_____

Occupation

Note. The Nominee's power to make a disposition of the shares on behalf of the registered owner will cease if the owner becomes
mentally incapable. For this reason, an Enduring Power of Attorney (or a Lasting Power of Attorney after the Mental Capacity Act 2005
comes into force) should also be executed.

Notice for Regulated Hire Purchase or Credit Sale Agreements

Form BS32

NOTE: This form is prescribed by the Consumer Credit (Cancellation Notices and Copies of Documents) Regulations 1983 (S.I. 1983 No. 1557) as amended.

YOUR RIGHT TO CANCEL. You have a right to cancel this agreement. You can do this by sending or taking a WRITTEN notice of cancellation to _____ .

You have FIVE days starting with the day after you receive this copy in which to cancel the agreement. You can use the form provided. If you cancel this agreement, any money you have paid, goods given in part-exchange (or their value) and property given as security must be returned to you. You will not have to make any further payment. If you already have goods under the agreement, you should keep them safe (legal action may be taken against you if you do not take proper care of them). You can wait for them to be collected from you and you need not hand them over unless you receive a written request. If you wish, however, you may return the goods yourself.

NOTE: Complete and return this form only if you wish to cancel the agreement

Date _____

To _____

_____

_____

(Name and address of seller)

I/We hereby give notice that I/we wish to cancel agreement number _____ .

_____

Signature

_____

Signature

Note: We repeat our suggestion that if you enter into contracts which are regulated by the Consumer Credit Act 1974 in the course of your business, you should ask your solicitor to review your documents and contractual procedures.

Notice of Acceptance of Goods   Form BS33

Date _____

Ref _____

To _____

_____

_____

Dear _____

Re: Acceptance of Order

Please note that we have received the following goods, with thanks, as per our

order no. _____ dated _____:

_____

_____

_____

The goods are further identified by invoice no. _____ and consignment note/

packing slip no. _____

Please be advised that we have inspected the goods and they have been received in good condition, and in

conformity with our order.

Yours sincerely

_____

Notice of Annual General Meeting   Form B20

_____ LIMITED

Company Number _____

NOTICE IS HEREBY GIVEN that the ANNUAL GENERAL MEETING of the

above-named Company will be held at _____

on _____ at _____ am/pm for the following purposes.

1.   To consider and adopt the company's accounts and reports of the directors and auditors for the period

      _____

      to _____ .

2.   To declare a dividend.

3.   To re-appoint   _____

      as auditors of the Company until the next general meeting at which accounts are laid before the

      company, at a fee to be agreed with the board of directors.

4.   To elect directors in place of those retiring (see the directors report)[1].

5.   To confirm appointments to the board.

Dated

_____

By order of the board

_____

Secretary

Registered office: _____

_____

A member entitled to attend and vote at the meeting convened by this Notice is entitled to appoint a proxy

to attend and vote on a poll[2] in his/her place. A proxy need not be a member of the Company.

[1] 21 days' notice is required - ie 21 days from the date when the member would receive the notice by ordinary post and the date of the
     meeting. Where a resolution requiring special notice is to be passed, 28 days' notice is required.

     After Part 13 Chapter 3 of the Companies Act 2006 comes into force on 1 October 2007, there will no longer be any requirement on a
     private company to hold an annual general meeting. From that date, the notice requirement for meetings will be 14 days, unless a
     resolution requiring special notice is to be passed in which case it will still be 28 days. The Companies Act 2006 will provide, from 1
     October 2007, that the holders of 90 per cent or such higher percentage as the articles may specify (not being more than 95 per cent)
     can consent to short notice.

[2] Unless the Articles provide otherwise, a proxy may only vote on a poll. At meetings of a private limited company, a proxy has the
     same right as a member to speak on a matter. He also has the right to demand a poll or to join in a demand that there be a poll. Once
     section 285 of the Companies Act 2006 comes into force on 1 October 2007, a proxy will be entitled to vote on a show of hands as
     well as on a poll. Once sections 324 and 325 of that Act come into force on 1 October 2007, the passage in square brackets above
     should be replaced by the following, 'A member entitled to attend and vote at the meeting convened by this Notice is entitled to
     appoint a person as his proxy to exercise all or any of his rights to attend and speak as proxy, or more the meeting. A member so
     entitled can appoint more than one proxy provided that each proxy is appointed to exercise the rights attached to a different share
     or shares held by him or (as the case may be) to a different £10, or multiple of £10, of stock held by him.

Notice of Assignment
Form TA09

Date _____

To _____

_____

_____

Dear _____

I attach a copy of an assignment dated _____ by which I assigned my interest in the contract referred to therein to _____ of _____ (the 'Assignee') Please hold all sums of money affected by such assignment, now or hereafter in your possession, that otherwise are payable to me under the terms of our original agreement, for the benefit of the Assignee, in accordance with the provisions of the assignment.

Yours sincerely

_____

Notice of Cancellation of Purchase Order and Demand for Refund

Form BS34

Date _____

To _____

_____

_____

Dear _____

Re: Cancellation of Purchase Order

On _____, as per our order no. _____, a copy of which is enclosed, we ordered the following goods from you:

_____

_____

_____

We paid for these goods by our cheque no. _____, dated _____ in the amount of £ _____.

On _____, we demanded immediate delivery of the goods. To date, the goods have not been delivered to us.

By this notice we therefore cancel this order, because of late delivery, and demand immediate reimbursement. Unless we receive a refund within 10 days of the date of this letter, we will take immediate legal action. Please be advised that we reserve all our legal rights.

Yours sincerely

_____

Note: If you have paid for the goods and have not received them in the time specified by the contract, you can use this form without difficulty. If you have not paid for the goods, however, be very careful before cancelling your order. You do not have the right to cancel an order because of lateness unless: (1) time is expressed in the contract to be 'of the essence' and the deadline has expired; or (2) the time for delivery has passed, you have given reasonable notice that if the goods are not delivered by a specific date the order will be cancelled, and the new date has passed. If you cancel when you do not have a right to do so, the seller could treat you as being in breach. Therefore, do not cancel unless situation (1) or situation (2) applies. Do not send this notice without first obtaining legal advice.

Even if you have paid for the goods and sent this notice, you should be cautious if the goods are subsequently sent to you. Do not send them back without obtaining legal advice unless the contract says that time for delivery is 'of the essence' or unless a substantial further period has elapsed since you sent this notice of cancellation.

Notice of Claim for Indemnity From Joint-Venturer (Non-Partner)

Form OLF30

Date _____

To _____

_____

_____

Dear _____

Re _____

A claim has been made by_____

to the effect that _____.

Under the terms of our joint venture we agreed to share the relevant expenses [equally] [in the proportions of _____]. We are therefore entitled to ask you to indemnify us accordingly.

Please confirm that you accept liability for this matter (if there is any valid claim) and that you will hold us indemnified to the extent of _____ per cent against the claim and the costs of defending it.

I should be pleased to hear from you as a matter of urgency.

Yours sincerely

_____

Note: This form is appropriate if your agreement was a cooperation agreement between two or more separate businesses, rather than a partnership where you are sharing or where you were sharing profits and losses generally. See form B10. If you are seeking an indemnity from a former partner what you really need is for an account to be taken in order to work out who is entitled to what in such a case this form is not appropriate and you should consult the firm's solicitor or accountant.

Notice of Conditional Acceptance of Faulty Goods   Form BS35

Date _____

To _____

_____

_____

Dear _____

Re: Order Number _____

On _____, we received a delivery from you as per our order no. _____,

dated _____. The goods delivered at that time were faulty for the following reason(s):

_____

_____

_____

Although these goods are defective and we are not obliged to accept them, we would be prepared to do so on the condition that you credit our account with you for £ _____.

This credit will make the total amount payable under this order £ _____.

If you do not accept this proposal within 10 days from the date of this letter, we will reject these goods as faulty and they will be returned to you. In the meantime, they are being kept in their original packing in anticipation of their return. Please be advised that we reserve all our legal rights.

Thank you for your immediate attention to this matter.

Yours sincerely

_____

Note: There is a risk that if you use this form, you may be treated as having 'accepted' the goods because it contains what is in reality an attempt to renegotiate the price. Once goods are accepted, they cannot as a rule be rejected. Therefore do not use this form unless you are prepared to risk having to keep the goods and claim damages for the defects. If you wish not to take the risk, you should reject the goods outright. See form BS39 or 40.

Notice of Conditional Acceptance of Non-Conforming Goods

Form BS36

Date _____

Ref _____

To _____

_____

_____

Dear _____

Re: Order Number _____

On _____, we received delivery from you as per our order no. _____,

dated _____. The goods delivered at that time do not conform to the specifications

that were provided with our order for the following reasons:

_____

_____

Although these goods are non-conforming and we are not obliged to accept them, we would be prepared

to accept these goods on the condition that you credit our account with you for £ _____. This credit will

make the total amount payable under this order £ _____.

If you do not accept this proposal within 10 days from the date of this letter, we will reject these goods as

non-conforming and they will be returned to you. In the meantime, they are being kept in their original

packing in anticipation of their return. Please be advised that we reserve all our legal rights.

Thank you for your immediate attention to this matter.

Yours sincerely

_____

Note: There is a risk that if you use this form, you may be treated as having 'accepted' the goods because it contains what is in reality an attempt to renegotiate the price. Once goods are accepted, they cannot as a rule be rejected. Therefore, do not use this form unless you are prepared to risk having to keep the goods and claim damages for the defects. If you do not wish to take the risk, you should reject the goods outright. See form BS39 or 40.

Notice of Default in Payment   Form LB09

Date_____

To   _____

      _____

      _____

Dear _____

You are hereby notified that your payment of _____ pounds

(£_____) due on or before _____, has not been received by us. If payment is

not made by _____, we shall seek the remedies under the agreement between us

dated _____, together with such other remedies as we may have, and this matter

shall be referred to our solicitors.

Yours sincerely

_____

Notice of Demand for Delivery of Goods   Form BS37

Date _____

Ref _____

To _____

_____

_____

Dear _____

Re: Order Number _____

On _____, as per our order no. _____, a copy of which is enclosed, we ordered the following goods from you:

_____

_____

_____

We paid for these goods by cheque no. _____, dated _____ in the amount of £ _____.

To date, the goods have not been delivered to us. We therefore demand the immediate delivery of these goods. Unless the goods are delivered to us within 10 days of the date of this letter, we will cancel this purchase order and demand return of our money. Please be advised that we reserve all our legal rights.

Thank you for your immediate attention to this matter.

Yours sincerely

_____

Note. Specify a longer period than 10 days if you consider it reasonable to do so in the light of your own requirements and the difficulties which the seller may be experiencing. The more reasonable you are, the more likely it is that you will be held to be entitled to cancel your order after the expiry of the period which you specify. If your contract says that time for delivery is 'of the essence', however, you can specify any period that you like, if the date specified for delivery in the order has already passed.

Notice of Dismissal Letter (Capability)   Form E46

Date   _____

To   _____
_____
_____

Dear   _____

I refer to our meeting on _____.

As I explained at the meeting, you have been unable to carry out your duties to the standards required by the Company. Therefore, we have no alternative but to terminate your employment with the Company with effect from _____.

As you are aware, we have provided you with training and assistance to enable you to improve your performance but without success. In addition, we have attempted to find suitable alternative employment within the Company but regret that nothing is available.

You are entitled to be paid in full, including any accrued holiday pay, during your notice period.

I take this opportunity of reminding you that you are entitled to appeal against this decision through the Company's dismissal and disciplinary procedure. If you wish to exercise this right you must let me know within two working days of receipt of this letter.

It is with regret that we have had to take this action. We should like to thank you for your past efforts for the Company and wish you every success for the future.

Yours sincerely

_____

Personnel Manager

Note: Before any decision to dismiss is made the statutory dismissal and disciplinary procedure and any contractual procedures may be followed to avoid legal repercussions.

Notice of Dismissal Letter (Sickness)   Form E47

Date   _____

To   _____

_____

_____

Dear   _____

I refer to our meeting at your home on   _____.

I was very sorry to hear that your condition has not improved and that it is unlikely that you will be able to resume working.

As we discussed, there is little we can do to assist your return to work and our medical adviser has reported that you are not likely to be well enough to return to to your current job for some time, if at all. We have tried to find some alternative suitable work for you but, as you know, all of the work in this Company is fairly heavy work and there is nothing we can offer you.

I regret that I have no alternative other than to give you notice to terminate your employment with the Company with effect from   _____.

You are entitled to full pay for the period of your notice plus accrued holiday pay. I shall arrange for these sums to be paid to you, and for your P45 to be sent to you as soon as possible.

If your health does improve in the future and you are able to resume working, I would be pleased to discuss re-employing you.

Yours sincerely

_____

Personnel Manager

Note: Before any decision to dismiss is made the statutory dismissal and disciplinary procedure and any contractual procedures may be followed to avoid legal repercussions.

This letter is an example of dismissal due to a terminal illness. Such a letter would have to be reworded if the employee was likely to be able to resume work at some future date.

Notice of Disputed Account   Form CDC27

Date _____

Ref _____

To _____
_____
_____

Dear _____

We refer to your invoice/order/statement no. _____, dated _____, in the amount of £_____.

We dispute the balance you claim to be owed for the following reason(s):

☐ Items invoiced for have not been received.

☐ Prices are in excess of the agreed amount. A credit of £ _____ is claimed.

☐ Our payment of £ _____ made on _____, has not been credited.

☐ Goods delivered to us were not ordered and are available for return on delivery instructions.

☐ Goods were defective as per prior letter.

☐ Goods are available for return and credit as per your sales terms.

☐ Other: _____

Please credit our account promptly in the amount of £_____ so it may be satisfactorily cleared.

Yours sincerely

_____

Notice of Extraordinary General Meeting   Form B23

_____ LIMITED

Company Registered Number _____

NOTICE is hereby given that an extraordinary general meeting of the above-named Company will be held at _____ on _____ the _____day of _____ year _____ at _____ o'clock for the purpose of considering and, if thought fit, passing the following ordinary/special/elective/extraordinary resolutions:

_____

_____

_____

_____

_____

[A member entitled to attend and vote at the meeting convened by this Notice is entitled to appoint a proxy to attend and vote on a poll[1] in his/her place. A proxy need not be a member of the Company.]

Dated this _____ day of _____ year _____.

BY ORDER OF THE BOARD

_____

Company Secretary

Registered office:

_____

_____

_____

_____

Note: Any member entitled to attend and vote at the meeting is entitled to appoint a proxy to attend and vote in his place. A proxy need not be a member of the company. Unless the articles provide otherwise, proxies may vote only on a poll. However, proxies may demand a poll or join in a demand for a poll.

The notice of the meeting must generally be given in line with the requirements contained in the articles. Under statute the minimum period of notice is 14 days for an extraordinary general meeting where no special resolution is to be considered, and 21 days where there is a special resolution. Special notice of 28 days is required for meetings considering resolutions under which the auditors or the directors are to be changed before the end of their terms of office. From 1 October 2007, that the holders of 90 per cent of the shares conferring the right to vote or such higher percentage as the articles may specify (not being more than 95 per cent) can consent to short notice. Where special notice is required, there is no power to consent to short notice. Unless the articles provide otherwise, a proxy may only vote on a poll. At meetings of a private limited company, a proxy has the same right as a member to speak on a matter. He also has the right to demand a poll or to join in a demand that there be a poll. Once section 285 of the Companies Act 2006 comes into force, a proxy will be entitled to vote on a show of hands as well as on a poll.

Once sections 324 and 325 of that Act come into force on 1 October 2007, the passage in square brackets above should be replaced by the following, 'A member entitled to attend and vote at the meeting convened by this Notice is entitled to appoint a person as his proxy to exercise all or any of his rights to attend and speak as proxy. A member so entitled can appoint more than one proxy provided that each proxy is appointed to exercise the rights attached to a different share or shares held by him or (as the case may be) to a different £10, or multiple of £10, of stock held by him.

Notice of Extraordinary General Meeting to Change Objects of Company
Form B24

_____ LIMITED

Company Registered Number _____

NOTICE is hereby given that an extraordinary general meeting of the above named Company will be held at _____ on _____ the _____day of _____ year _____ at _____ o'clock for the purpose of considering and, if thought fit, passing the following special resolution:

'That the memorandum of association of the Company be altered by deleting subclause (__) of clause ____ and substituting therefor the following subclause:

(__) _____To carry on business as a general commercial company.'

[A member entitled to attend and vote at the meeting convened by this Notice is entitled to appoint a proxy to attend and vote on a poll[1] in his/her place. A proxy need not be a member of the Company.]

Dated this _____ day of _____ year _____.

BY ORDER OF THE BOARD

_____

Company Secretary

Registered office:

_____

_____

_____

Note: Any member entitled to attend and vote at the meeting is entitled to appoint a proxy to attend and vote in his place. A proxy need not be a member of the company.

[1] Where a change in the objects clause is desired, it is necessary to give the period of notice which the Articles require in the case of meetings which are to consider special resolutions. The minimum period which the Articles can authorise under the Companies Act 1985 is 21 days. This requirement can be waived with the unanimous consent of the shareholders, or with a slightly lesser majority in some cases. Take advice if unanimity is not available. Unless the Articles provide otherwise, a proxy may only vote on a poll. At meetings of a private limited company, a proxy has the same right as a member to speak on a matter. He also has the right to demand a poll or to join in a demand that there be a poll. Once section 285 of the Companies Act 2006 comes into force on 1 October 2007, a proxy will be entitled to vote on a show of hands as well as on a poll.

After 1 October 2007 the period of notice is 14 days for all resolutions except those where special notice is required (which does _not_ include resolutions to change the company's objects). From 1 October 2007, that the holders of 90 per cent of the shares conferring the right to vote or such higher percentage as the articles may specify (not being more than 95 per cent) can consent to short notice.

Once sections 324 and 325 of that Act come into force on 1 October 2007, the passage in square brackets above should be replaced by the following, 'A member entitled to attend and vote at the meeting convened by this Notice is entitled to appoint a person as his proxy to exercise all or any of his rights to attend and speak as proxy. A member so entitled can appoint more than one proxy provided that each proxy is appointed to exercise the rights attached to a different share or shares held by him or (as the case may be) to a different £10, or multiple of £10, of stock held by him.

Notice of Goods Sold on Approval   Form BS38

Date _____

Ref _____

To _____
_____
_____

Dear _____

Re: Goods Sold on Approval

Please be advised that the following goods are being delivered to you on approval:

_____
_____
_____

If these goods do not meet your requirements, you may return all or a part of them at our expense within
_____ days of your receipt of them.

Any goods sold on approval that are not returned to us by that time will be considered accepted by you and
you will be invoiced for them accordingly.

We trust that you will find our goods satisfactory and thank you for your custom.

Yours sincerely

_____

Note. This form should only be used where the customer has actually agreed to take goods on approval. It must on no account be used where the goods are being sent unsolicited. There is a separate form for that. See BS22.

Notice of Intention to Recover Payment in Default   Form CDC28

Date _____

To _____
_____
_____

Dear _____

Re: Agreement Reference: _____

We refer to the default notice which we issued on _____ in connection with the above agreement. We note that you have failed to make payment of the arrears by _____, as requested in the default notice.

In the circumstances, this letter is our formal demand for payment of the outstanding balance, as detailed below:

Outstanding Balance: £ _____
Less Rebate Allowable *:   £ _____
Amount to be paid: £ _____

* This rebate has been calculated on the assumption that payment of the amount demanded reaches us by _____. If it does not, we shall bring proceedings against you for the outstanding balance claimed and, if this results in our obtaining payment before the sum would have become due under the agreement, we shall allow any appropriate rebate or change once we have received the payment in full.

Your sincerely

_____
Signature of Authorised Signatory on
behalf of the Finance Company

Note: This form must not be used to recover monies owing under any agreement which is regulated by the Consumer Credit Act 1974.

Notice of Particulars of Ownership

As required by the Business Names Act 1985[1]

Insert name of business

Proprietor

Insert full name of business proprietor [2]

Address within Great Britain at which documents relating to the
business may be effectively served on the proprietor

Insert full address

Note: This document should be displayed prominently at your principal place of business. Your obligations to disclose your name and address in business correspondence do not end here. You must also disclose the above information on all business letters, written orders for goods or services to be supplied to the business, invoices and receipts issued in the course of the business and written demands for payment of debts arising in the course of the business.

[1] When Part 41 of the Companies Act 2006 comes into force these words should be replaced by Companies Act 2006.

[2] You should insert here the individual, partners, company or limited partnership which owns or own the business.

Notice of Rejection of Non-conforming Goods — Form BS39

Date _____

Ref _____

To _____

_____

_____

Dear _____

Re: Rejection of Non-Conforming Goods

On _____, we received delivery from you as per our order no. _____, dated _____. The goods delivered at that time do not conform to the specifications that were provided with our order for the following reasons:

_____

_____

_____

We paid for these goods by our cheque no. _____, dated _____, in the amount of £ _____. This cheque has been cashed by you.

By this notice, we reject the delivery of these goods and request reimbursement. Unless we receive a refund of our money within 10 days of the date of this letter, we will take immediate legal action for its recovery. Please further advise us as to your wishes for the return of the rejected goods at your expense. Unless we receive instructions within 10 days of this letter, we accept no responsibility for their safe storage. Please be advised that we reserve all our legal rights.

Thank you for your immediate attention to this matter.

Yours sincerely

_____

Note. If you reject the goods, you must still take some care of them before they are returned, because you can be held liable for gross negligence. If substantial time elapses and the goods have not been taken back, you should obtain legal advice.

Notice of Rejection of Goods   Form BS40

Date _____

Ref _____

To _____

_____

_____

Dear _____

Re: Order no. _____

On _____, we received delivery from you as per our order no. _____,

dated _____. We reject these goods for the following reasons:

_____

_____

We paid for these goods by our cheque no. _____, dated _____, in the amount of

£_____.

By this notice, we reject the delivery of these goods and request reimbursement. Unless we receive a refund of our money within 10 days of the date of this letter, we will take immediate legal action for its recovery. Please further advise us as to your wishes for the return of the rejected goods at your expense. Unless we receive instructions for their return within 10 days of this letter, we accept no responsibility for their safe storage. Please be advised that we reserve all our legal rights.

Thank you for your immediate attention to this matter.

Yours sincerely

_____

Note: You should exercise the right of rejection with caution. In non-consumer sales, the buyer may not reject the goods if the breach is so minor that it would be unreasonable for him to reject.

Be careful in stating the reason for rejecting the goods. Although you will be able later to justify a rejection for reasons other than those which you have previously stated, as long as the reasons existed at the time of rejection, the seller may succeed if he shows that the goods could have been remedied if you had brought the reasons to his attention at the time.

If you reject the goods, you must still take some care of them before they are returned, because you can be held liable for gross negligence. If substantial time elapses and the goods have not been taken back, you should obtain legal advice.

Notice of Replacement of Rejected Goods   Form BS41

Date _____

Ref _____

To _____

_____

_____

Dear _____

Re: Order no. _____

On _____, we delivered the following goods to you as per your

order no._____ , dated_____:

_____

_____

_____

On _____, we received notice that you had rejected delivery of these goods.

Please return the rejected goods to us at our expense using the same carrier that delivered the goods.

[In addition, please be advised that we are shipping replacement goods to you at our expense. If replacement of the rejected goods is not satisfactory, please contact us immediately. We apologise for any inconvenience this may have caused you] / [what we propose to do with your consent is to ship replacement goods to you at our expense by _____. If this is acceptable to you, please let us know immediately. Whatever you decide, we apologise for any inconvenience which this may have caused you].[1]

Yours sincerely

_____

---

[1] If there was no specified date for delivery or if you are unable to deliver replacement goods by the specified date, you should delete the wording in the first set of square brackets.

Notice of Result of Grievance Investigation Form E48

Date _____

Ref _____

To _____

_____

_____

Dear _____

I am writing to let you know that your grievance relating to _____

_____has been fully investigated in accordance with the company's

grievance procedures.

Having considered your complaint and having heard all that has been said by you, and on your behalf, and

having taken full account of all that has been said by your trade union representative, it has been decided

_____

_____

_____

You have a right of appeal against this decision and if you wish to exercise this right, please notify me in

writing within [_____] working days.

Yours sincerely

_____

Notice of Return of Goods Sold on Approval Form BS42

Date _____

Ref _____

To _____

_____

_____

Dear _____

Re: Order no. _____

On _____, as per our order no. _____, a copy of which is enclosed, we received the following goods from you on approval:

_____

_____

_____

_____

_____

Please be advised that we have decided to return these goods to you.

Thank you very much for the opportunity to examine the goods.

Yours sincerely

_____

Notice of Trade Term Violations
Form BS43

Date _____

Ref _____

To _____

_____

_____

Dear _____

We routinely review all our accounts. We have found a record of irregular payments on your account, which frequently leaves balances unpaid beyond our credit terms.

Whilst we value your continued custom, we would also appreciate payment within our agreed credit terms. We look forward to your future co-operation in this matter.

Yours sincerely

_____

Notice of Withheld Delivery

Form BS44

Date _____

Ref _____

To _____
_____
_____

Dear _____

Thank you for your order dated _____. It is now ready for delivery.

However, we find that the following invoices remain unpaid beyond our agreed credit terms:

Invoice no.	Amount	Due date
_____	£ _____	_____
_____	£ _____	_____
_____	£ _____	_____
	£ _____	_____

Please send us your cheque promptly in the amount of £ _____ to clear these invoices.

We shall then deliver your order immediately.

Yours sincerely

_____

Note. Only use this Form if: (a) you have not already promised the goods, or (b) if you have promised the goods, you have done so with reference to conditions which entitle you to refuse delivery if the account is in arrears.

Notice of Wrongful Refusal to Accept Delivery   Form BS45

Date _____

Ref _____

To _____

_____

_____

Dear _____

We refer to your order dated _____, a copy of which is enclosed.

We delivered the goods in accordance with the agreed terms but you have refused to accept them. We now consider the purchase contract to have been wrongfully breached by you.

[Accordingly, we shall not attempt further delivery and shall hold you liable for all damages arising from your failure to fulfil your obligations under the order.]

[Accordingly, we shall hold the goods for you to arrange collection and we shall claim the price and cost of storage if payment of the contract price is not received in accordance with your obligations under the agreement.]

Should you wish to rectify the situation by now accepting shipment you must call us immediately and we shall arrange re-shipment at your expense.

Please contact us immediately should you have any questions on this matter.

Yours sincerely

_____

Note. If property in the goods has passed to the buyer who has wrongly rejected them, you will be entitled to claim the price of the goods instead of damages. Damages are likely to consist of compensation for wasted expenditure in a sale that has gone off, and of loss of profits that you would have made on the sale. There may be more argument about this than there would be about a simple claim for the price. By sending this letter, you might lose the right to claim for the price. You may therefore think it worthwhile to ask your solicitor whether: (a) you can succeed in a claim for the price; and (b) a claim for the price is better from your point of view than a claim for damages.

Notice Requiring Possession: Assured Shorthold Tenancy   Form RT21

ENGLAND & WALES
HOUSING ACT 1988
SECTION 21

Assured Shorthold Tenancy: Notice Requiring Possession

TO _____

    of _____

FROM _____

    of _____

I/We* give you notice that, by virtue of Section 21 of the Housing Act 1988, I/we* require possession of the dwelling house known as

_____

after _____

or, if the alternative date mentioned below is different, after the alternative date. The alternative date is the first date after this notice was given to you which is:

- at least two months after service upon you of this notice, and

- (if your tenancy is for a fixed term which has not ended when this notice is given to you) which is a date not earlier than the end of the fixed term, or

- (if your tenancy is a periodic tenancy when this notice is given to you) which is the last day of a period of your tenancy and not earlier than the earliest date on which your tenancy could (apart from the landlord's inability, under s.5(1) of the Housing Act 1988, to terminate an assured tenancy by notice to quit) lawfully be ended by a notice to quit given to you on the same date as this notice.

DATED _____

SIGNED _____
Landlord/Landlord's agent*

_____

_____

Tenant's acknowledgment of service

I/We acknowledge the service of the notice of which the above is a true copy.

Signed_____ (Tenant(s))   Date_____

Note: This notice may be validly served even if this box has not been signed by the tenant. Make a note as to when, how and by whom it was served, so that you can refer to it later if necessary.

Notice to Cancel Delayed Goods   Form BS46

Date   _____

Ref   _____

To   _____

_____

_____

Dear   _____

We refer to our purchase order or contract dated _____,
a copy of which is enclosed.

Under the terms of the order, the goods were to be delivered by _____.
Due to your failure to deliver the goods within the required time, we hereby cancel this order, reserving such
further rights as we may have.

If the above goods are in transit, they shall be refused or returned at your expense.

Yours sincerely

_____

Note: This form should be used with caution. A delay in the delivery of goods does not justify a cancellation of the order unless it was
agreed in the contract that time should be 'of the essence' or unless after the time for delivery has expired, a further and reasonable
period has been given for performance which is expressed to be 'of the essence' and which has elapsed or unless it was apparent from
the facts as known to both parties, that delay would deprive the buyer of much of the benefit of the contract. Speak to a solicitor if you
are in doubt.

Notice to Dissolve a Two-Party Partnership   Form B25

Date _____

Ref _____

To _____

_____

_____

Dear _____

I hereby give you notice to dissolve the partnership between us on _____.
I request that final accounts of the partnership be drawn up to enable its assets to be distributed in
accordance with the partnership agreement.

Yours sincerely

_____

Note: If the partnership provides for a period of notice to be given for dissolution, the period should be given unless an event has
occurred which entitles the partner giving notice to give notice which is effective immediately. This would be when the party to whom
the notice is addressed has acted in such a way that the breach of his duties is so serious as to make it necessary to terminate the
partnership immediately. If no period of notice is provided for, the termination may be effective at once.

Notice to Employee Being Laid Off and Giving Guarantee Payments
Form E49

Date _____

To _____

_____

_____

Dear _____

I refer to our meeting on _____.

As I explained at that meeting, we regret that because of economic pressure we have no option but to lay you off from work.

The period of lay off shall take effect from _____and shall continue until _____. You shall receive guarantee payments of [_____] per day for the first five days of this period.

I very much regret that we have been forced to take this action, but I should like to assure you that we are working hard to ensure that the period of lay off is kept to a minimum.

Yours sincerely

_____

Personnel Managers

The current daily rate is £19.60 but this can be verified by contacting the Department of Work and Pensions or ACAS.

Notice to Employer of Intention to Take Maternity Leave   Form E50

Date _____

To _____

_____

_____

Dear _____

This is to inform you that I am pregnant and wish to take Maternity Leave. I enclose a medical/ maternity certificate dated _____ from Dr _____.

The expected week of childbirth is _____ and I intend to start taking my Maternity Leave on _____.

Please also let me know if I am entitled to receive Statutory Maternity Pay during my Maternity Leave.

Your sincerely

_____

Note: Notification must be given by the beginning of the 14th week before the expected week of childbirth or, if that is not possible, as soon as is reasonably practicable thereafter.

Notice to Stop Goods In Transit   Form BS47

Date _____

Ref _____

To _____ (Carrier)

_____

_____

Dear _____

You currently have goods of ours in transit under consignment note no. _____

for delivery to:

_____

_____

_____

This is to confirm our previous instruction by telephone to stop delivery of these goods and return them to us; we shall pay return freight charges.

[No negotiable bill of lading or document of title has been delivered to our customer (the consignee).]

A copy of our delivery documents for these goods is enclosed for your reference.

Yours sincerely

_____

Copy to [Customer]: _____

Note: The right to stop goods in transit arises if the seller has not been paid and the buyer has become insolvent. If the goods are stopped and it turns out that the buyer is solvent after all, then the buyer can sue the seller for damages. If a bill of lading or other document of title has been delivered to the buyer, that does not itself defeat the seller's right to stop the goods. However, if the buyer, having received a document of title, then sells the goods on, the seller's rights will be ineffective against the onward purchaser. If the right to stop is exercised, the carrier has a lien against the seller over the goods for the cost of carriage.

Notice to Terminate given by owner – House/Flat Share Licence Agreement – Resident Owner

Form RT14

TO
_____

_____

_____

(name(s) of Sharer)

THE OWNER
_____

_____

_____

(name(s) and address of Owner)

REQUIRES POSSESSION

OF THE PROPERTY

KNOWN AS
_____

_____

_____

(address of the Property)

ON THE
_____

(date for Possession)[1]

SIGNED BY
_____

(the Owner or his/her agent)

(if signed by the agent then the Agent's name and address must also be written here)

_____

_____

DATE OF NOTICE
_____

IMPORTANT NOTICE TO OWNERS/SHARERS:

1. This Notice is not suitable for a Protected or Statutory Tenancy under the Rent Act 1977 or for an Assured Tenancy, or for an Assured Shorthold Tenancy. Do not use this form without taking legal advice if the licensee is in occupation because of his employment.

2. A Licensee or Sharer who does not know if he has any right to remain in possession after the Notice to Terminate runs out can obtain advice from a solicitor. Help with all or part of the cost of legal advice and assistance may be available under the Legal Aid Scheme. The Licensee or Sharer should also be able to obtain information from a Citizens Advice Bureau, a Housing Aid Centre or a Rent Officer.

[1] The date specified should not be a date which is earlier than any expiry date previously agreed. If no such date has been agreed, a reasonable amount of time should be specified given to enable the licensee/sharer to expire one week or one month (as the case may be) after the next rent day.

Notice to Terminate given by sharer – House/Flat Share Licence Agreement – Resident Owner

Form RT14

TO
_____
_____
_____

(name(s) and address of Owner)

I/WE
_____
_____
_____

(name(s) of Sharer)

GIVE YOU NOTICE
THAT OUR
AGREEMENT IN
RESPECT OF
_____
_____
_____

(address of the Property)

IS HEREBY
TERMINATED
WITH EFFECT
FROM THE
_____

(date for Possession)

SIGNED BY
_____

(the Sharer)

DATE OF NOTICE
_____

IMPORTANT NOTICE TO OWNERS/SHARERS:

1. This Notice is not suitable for an Assured Shorthold Tenancy.

2. A Sharer who does not know if he has any right to remain in possession after the Notice to Terminate runs out can obtain advice from a solicitor. Help with all or part of the cost of legal advice and assistance may be available under the Legal Aid Scheme. The Sharer should also be able to obtain information from a Citizens Advice Bureau, a Housing Aid Centre or Rent Officer.

Notification of Business Transfer   Form E53

Date _____

Ref _____

To Trade Union Representative/Employee Representative

_____

_____

Dear _____

I am writing to you in accordance with Regulation 10 of the Transfer of Undertakings (Protection of Employment) Regulations 1981 ('the Regulations') to inform you of a proposal to transfer the business of _____.

It is proposed that the transfer of the Company will take place on or about _____. The reason for the transfer is that:

_____

_____

_____.

The proposed transfer will affect the following employees:

_____

_____

_____

By law, the affected employees will, by virtue of the operation of the Regulations, transfer on their existing terms and conditions of employment and with continuity of employment for statutory and contractual purposes. *[State whether there will be any social or economic implications of the transfer – economic would include loss of pension rights.]*

It [is]/[is not] envisaged that the Company or [_____]¹ will be taking [any] measures in connection with the transfer in relation to those employees who will be affected by the transfer.²

Yours sincerely

---

¹ Name of transferee.

² If measures are envisaged state these – if this is the case there is a duty to consult.

Offer of Employment to Avoid Redundancy   Form E54

Date   _____

Ref   _____

To   _____

_____

_____

Dear   _____

After consultation with our employees and representatives of _____
_____ Union, we regret that we must close the _____
_____ section of the company. This will mean redundancy for some employees.

However, I am pleased to advise you that _____ can offer you suitable,
alternative employment as a _____. The salary and terms of
employment will approximate to what you are currently receiving from us.

Please confirm to me whether you accept this employment offer by [_____]. [If you do not accept
this offer your employment will terminate and you will not be entitled to a redundancy payment.] If you
have any questions about this offer please do not hesitate to contact me.

Yours sincerely

_____

Offer to Settle by Arbitration

Form OLF31

Date _____

To _____

_____

_____

Dear _____

I refer to our dispute regarding _____.

I am sorry that we seem to be unable to reconcile our differing points of view. I am sure that neither of us wishes to resort to the courts and I therefore suggest that we refer the dispute between us to arbitration. I propose:

1. The dispute be referred to arbitration.

2. The arbitrator shall be Mr. _____, who is an expert in these matters. If you cannot agree to him, the arbitrator shall be appointed by the President or Vice-President of the Chartered Institute of Arbitrators.

3. [The Chartered Institute of Arbitrators Arbitration Rules]/[The IDRS Rules of Controlled Cost Arbitration] shall apply. [1]

4. The costs of the arbitration shall be left at the discretion of the arbitrator. Any costs payable in advance shall be borne by the parties equally in the first instance, but the arbitrator may alter the incidence of those costs in his award

5. Only one expert witness shall be allowed for each side.

6. The arbitration shall take place at _____ and the dispute shall be decided in accordance with English law.

7. The making of an award by the arbitrator shall be a condition precedent to any right of action by either of us against the other in respect of the matter in dispute.

If you agree to this suggestion, please sign and return the enclosed copy of this letter.

Yours sincerely

_____

[1] The rules are available on the IDRS website at http://www.idrs.ltd.uk/business/adhoc_arbitration.asp.

One-Off Agency Agreement Form OLF05

THIS AGREEMENT is made the _____ day of _____ year _____

BETWEEN:

(1) _____ (the 'Consignor'); and

(2) _____ (the 'Agent').

NOW IT IS HEREBY AGREED that the terms of consignment are the following:

1. The Agent acknowledges receipt of goods from the Consignor as described on the attached schedule (the 'Goods'). The Goods shall remain the property of the Consignor until sold.

2. The Agent, at its own cost and expense, agrees to keep and display the goods only in its place of business and to keep the same in good order and condition, and agrees to return the same on demand in good order and condition to the Consignor.

3. The Agent agrees to use its best efforts to sell the Goods on behalf of the Consignor for the Consignor's account on cash terms and at such prices as shall from time to time be designated by the Consignor.

4. The Agent agrees, upon sale of the Goods, to keep the sale proceeds due to the Consignor separate and apart from its own funds, and to deliver such proceeds, less commission, to the Consignor, together with an account, within _____ days of sale.

5. The Agent agrees to accept as full payment for its obligations hereunder a commission equal to _____% of the gross sales price exclusive of any VAT, [but the Agent shall also be entitled to receive, in addition to his commission, the VAT which is chargeable to him thereon].

6. The Agent agrees to permit the Consignor to enter its premises during business hours to examine and inspect the Goods.

7. The Agent agrees to issue such accounts for public filing as may reasonably be required by Consignor for the purpose of enabling the Consignor to comply with his legal obligations.

8. The Agent will indemnify the Consignor for any liability which the Consignor may incur as a result of any breach by the Agent of this agreement or as a result of any misrepresentation or warranty given in respect of the Goods which misrepresentation or warranty has not been authorised by the Consignor.

9. Save that the Agent may disclose the identity of the Consignor as the seller of the goods, the Agent must not give any undertaking on behalf of the Consignor or purport to pledge his credit or represent himself as having any association with the Consignor or as being in partnership with him.

IN WITNESS OF WHICH the parties have signed the agreement the day and year first above written

Continued on next page

One-Off Agency Agreement (continued)   Form OLF05

_____   _____
Signed for and on behalf of the Consignor   Signed for and on behalf of the Agent

_____   _____
in the presence of (witness)   in the presence of (witness)

Name _____   Name _____

Address _____   Address _____

_____   _____

Occupation _____   Occupation _____

Note: This form is appropriate where there is a one-off arrangement under which a dealer receives a consignment of goods from someone else for the purpose of selling those goods on behalf of the Consignor. It is not appropriate where there is a series of such arrangements and where the parties have in mind that repeat business for the Consignor's goods is to be created. If that is what you have in mind, you should take advice on the effect of the Commercial Agents (Council Directive) Regulations 1993 which confers various rights on commercial agents.

Option to Buy Land   Form BS48

This Deed is made the _____ day of _____ year ____

BETWEEN:

(1) _____ of _____(the 'Buyer'); and

(2) _____ of _____(the 'Seller').

WHEREAS:

The Seller now owns the following land and/or property (the 'Property'):

_____

_____

NOW IT IS HEREBY AGREED as follows:

1. In consideration of the sum of £ _____ , receipt of which is hereby acknowledged by the Seller, the Seller grants to the Buyer an exclusive option to buy the Property for the following price and on the following terms (the 'Option'):

    _____

    _____

    _____

    _____

    _____

    [on the terms set out in the draft contract stapled hereto]

2. The amount received by the Seller from the Buyer referred to in paragraph 1. above will be credited against the purchase price of the Property if the Option is exercised by the Buyer. If the Option is not exercised, the Seller will retain this payment.

3. The option period will be from the date of this Agreement until _____ at which time the Option will expire unless exercised.

4. During this period, the Buyer has the option and exclusive right to buy the Property on the terms set out herein. The Buyer must notify the Seller in writing of the decision to exercise the Option. A notice may be sent by [first class post to the Seller at _____] / [through a document exchange to the Seller at _____] / [by fax _____] / [by email at _____]. A notice sent by these respective means is deemed to have been received as follows: (a) by first class post at 12 noon on the second working day after posting; (b) through a document exchange at 12 noon on the first day after the date on which it would normally be available for collection by the addressee; (c) by fax: at 12:00 noon on the first working day after despatch; (d) by e-mail: at 12:00 noon on the first working day after despatch.

5. No modification of this agreement will be effective unless it is in writing and is signed by both the Buyer and Seller. This agreement binds and benefits both the Buyer and Seller and any successors. Time is of the essence of this agreement. This document, including any attachments, is the entire agreement between the Buyer and Seller.

Continued on next page

Option to Buy Land (continued)   Form BS48

IN WITNESS OF WHICH the parties have signed this Deed the day and year first above written

_____   _____

Signed as a Deed by or on behalf of the Buyer   Signed as a Deed by or on behalf of the Seller

_____   _____

in the presence of (witness)   in the presence of (witness)

Name _____   Name _____

Address _____   Address _____

_____   _____

Occupation _____   Occupation _____

Important note:

The option is not valid unless signed by both parties or unless each signs a copy and the copies are then exchanged.

The greatest care must be taken in setting out the terms on which the property is to be bought and sold if the option is exercised. See paragraph one. Remember, there is more to the purchase of a property than merely agreeing the price. In all but the most straightforward cases, a solicitor should be consulted. If you have decided not to consult a solicitor, make certain that at the very least the terms are clear on what the property is, the identity of the parties who will buy and sell, what the price is, when possession is to be given and whether an absolute or qualified covenant to title is to be given. The Buyer must also register a notice of his interest at the Land Registry in order to prevent the seller from selling the land to a third party, to defeat the Buyer's interest.

Option to Purchase Goods   Form BS49

This Deed is made the _____ day of _____ year ____

BETWEEN:

(1) _____ of _____(the 'Buyer'); and

(2) _____ of _____ (the 'Seller').

NOW IT IS HEREBY AGREED as follows:

1.   In consideration for the sum of £ _____, receipt of which is hereby acknowledged by the Seller, the Seller grants to the Buyer an option to buy the following goods (the 'Goods') on the terms set out herein.

_____

_____

_____

_____

_____

_____

_____

2.   The Buyer has the option and right to buy the Property within the option period for the full price of £ _____.

3.   This option period shall be from the date of this agreement until _____ ____, at which time the option will expire unless exercised.

4.   During the option period the Buyer has the option and exclusive right to buy the Property on the terms set out herein. The Buyer must notify the Seller in writing of the decision to exercise the Option. A notice may be sent by [first class post to the Seller at _____] / [through a document exchange to the Seller at _____] / [by fax _____] / [by email at _____]. A notice sent by these respective means is deemed to have been received as follows: (a) by first class post at 12 noon on the second working day after posting; (b) through a document exchange at 12 noon on the first day after the date on which it would normally be available for collection by the addressee; (c) by fax: at 12:00 noon on the first working day after despatch; (d) by e-mail: at 12:00 noon on the first working day after despatch.

5.   This Deed shall be binding upon and inure to the benefit of the parties, their successors and assigns.

Continued on next page

Option to Purchase Goods (continued)   Form BS49

IN WITNESS OF WHICH the parties have signed this Deed the day and year first above written

_____   _____
Signed as a Deed by or on behalf of the Buyer   Signed as a Deed by or on behalf of the Seller

in the presence of (witness)   in the presence of (witness)

Name _____   Name _____

Address _____   Address _____

_____   _____

Occupation _____   Occupation _____

Note: Great care must be given in drafting the terms on which the goods will be sold if the option is exercised (see clause 1). You must consider all of the matters which you would consider in a contract for the sale of goods, because if the option is exercised that is what you will have.

Order to Stop a Cheque

Date   _____

To   _____

_____

_____

Dear   _____

Please stop the payment of the following cheque:

Name of Payee: _____

Date of Cheque: _____

Cheque No.:   _____

Amount: _____

If this cheque has already been honoured, please advise me of the date of payment.

Thank you for your co-operation.

Yours sincerely

_____

_____

Name of Account

_____

Account No.

Note: You should use this form if you have reason to believe that the cheque has been lost or stolen. If this is not the case and if the payee is in possession of the cheque, you must only stop it if the payment was a gift or if you have been defrauded or if the payee has committed a breach of your agreement which is so serious as to deny you any benefit of the agreement at all. Anything short of the above will entitle the payee to obtain 'summary judgment' against you within a matter of weeks.

Organ Donation   Form PF14

Organ Donation

of

_____(Full name)

In the hope that I may help others, I hereby make this gift, if medically acceptable, to take effect upon my death.

The words and marks below indicate my wishes:

I give: a)   ☐   any needed organs for transplantation or other therapeutic purposes [or anatomical study or medical research].

               b)   ☐   only the following organs _____

                                _____

                                _____

                        [which may be used for purposes of transplantation or other therapeutic purposes only] / [which may be used for transplantation or other therapeutic purposes or for anatomical or medical study].

               c)   ☐   my entire body, for anatomical or medical study, if needed [save to the extent that any organs may be required for transplantation or other therapeutic purposes].

[I request that after the removal from my body of any organs which may be required my body should be [cremated] / [buried] / [in such manner as_____may direct].

Limitations or special wishes:

_____

_____

Signed by the donor and the following two witnesses, in the presence of each other.

_____   _____

Signature of Donor   Witness, who hereby attests the Donor's signature

_____   _____

Date Signed   Address

_____   _____

Date of Birth   Occupation

_____

Address

Note: Written consent is only required in law if a person wishes his body to be used after his death for public display or anatomical examination. Persons in a 'qualifying relationship' (by which is meant spouses, civil partners, children, parents, siblings, half siblings and friends of long standing) can give consent for the use of organs for therapeutic purposes.

Given the need for speed if an organ is to be used for therapeutic purposes, however, a would-be donor should always give a written direction, tell his family and friends that he has done so, and carry a donor card of the type issued by the Department of Health.

Once you have chosen the paragraph that accords with your wishes, delete the other two paragraphs before you print the form. If there are any passages in square brackets that you wish to delete within the paragraph that you have chosen, make sure that you delete these passages as well before printing.

Overdue Account Reminder   Form CDC29

Date _____

Ref _____

To _____

_____

_____

Dear _____

We sent you a statement a recently. Please note that your account is overdue in the amount of £_____.

Please remit payment to us as soon as possible.

Yours sincerely

_____

Partial Delivery Request

Form BS50

Date _____

Ref _____

To _____

_____

_____

Dear _____

Thank you for your order dated _____. The value of the order is approximately £ _____. We regret that we cannot extend to credit to you for the entire amount.

Accordingly, we suggest that we deliver to you a partial delivery on our standard credit terms reducing the quantities ordered by _____ per cent. Upon payment, we shall deliver the balance of the order.

Please let us know immediately whether you are prepared to accept this proposal, as we will be unable to fulfil any part of your order without such acceptance.

We should be happy to consider an application by you to increase your credit limit.

Yours sincerely

_____

Partnership Agreement

This Partnership agreement is made the _____ day of _____ year ___

BETWEEN

(1)_____ of _____

_____(the 'First Partner');

and

(2)_____ of _____

_____ (the 'Second Partner');

hereinafter together called the 'Partners'.

NOW IT IS HEREBY AGREED as follows:

1. THE BUSINESS

    The Partners shall carry on business in Partnership as _____ under the name of

    _____ at _____

    _____ as from _____ year _____.

2. DURATION OF THE PARTNERSHIP

    The Partnership shall continue until terminated under the terms of this Agreement or until the death

    or bankruptcy of either Partner.

3. CAPITAL

    The Capital of the Partnership shall consist of the sum of £_____which belongs to each Partner

    respectively as follows

    _____

    _____

    Unless otherwise agreed, the capital of the Partnership shall belong to the Partners equally and any

    increase in capital shall be made in equal shares.

4. PROFITS AND LOSSES

    The Partners will share all profits and losses (including capital losses)[equally] [in the following

    proportions

    _____

    _____]

    No partner shall make any drawings on account of his share of the profits without the agreement of

    the other partners. If upon the taking of an account for any accounting period any partner shall have

    overdrawn his account, he shall forthwith restore such overdrawings to the account.

5. BANK

    The Partners shall open an account in the name of the Partnership at _____ Bank

    of _____

    and any money belonging to the Partnership shall be paid into the account and the signatures of

    _____ Partners shall be required on all cheques drawn and on all other instruments and instructions

    made in connection with the account.

Continued on next page

Partnership Agreement (continued)   Form B27

6.   ACCOUNTANTS

The accountants to the Partnership shall be _____

of _____

The Partners shall keep such accounting records as the accountants shall recommend, and each partner shall promptly make accurate entries concerning their activities in accordance with any practice which the accountants shall recommend. The accountants shall be instructed to prepare accounts in respect of each accounting period of the Partnership, such period to end on _____ each year, and the Partners shall agree and sign the accounts.

7.   WORKING PRACTICE

Each Partner shall devote his best efforts and his whole time and attention to the business of the Partnership. He shall not act in competition with the Partnership and he shall conduct himself as regards the other Partners in utmost good faith. Each Partner shall be entitled to take____weeks' holiday in each calendar year at such times as the Partners shall agree. All decisions relating to the Partnership shall be made by unanimous agreement between the Partners unless otherwise agreed [No]/[Neither] Partner shall without the consent of the others _____

_____

_____

_____.

8.   INDEMNITY

Each Partner shall indemnify the other Partners or their estates for any loss which may be incurred by them and which may have been caused by any breach on such Partner's part of any of the terms of this agreement.

9.   RETIREMENT

Any Partner may retire from the Partnership by giving to the other partner or partners not less than _____ months' notice in writing, in which case the other Partner or any of the other Partners shall have the right exercisable by counternotice before the expiry of such notice to purchase the share of the outgoing Partner at the net value of such share. If more than one Partner shall serve such Counternotice the share of the outgoing Partner shall be acquired by them equally. If such counternotice is not served before the expiry of the period of notice the Partnership shall be dissolved. If the share is to be acquired as aforesaid, the net value of the same shall be determined by the Partners and in default of agreement shall be decided by the accountants acting as experts not arbitrators. Goodwill shall be valued as the lower of the cost or the net realisable value of the same (as certified by the accountant). No partner may give notice as aforesaid within a period of ____ months of any other Partner having given such notice.

Any group of Partners holding between them more than [2/3rds] of the Capital may at any time and without specifying a reason require the other Partner or Partners to retire from the Partnership on not less than _____ notice. The Partners giving such notice or any of them shall have the right exercisable by a further notice served during the period of notice, to purchase the share or shares of the outgoing Partner or Partners at the net value of such share, whereupon such share shall be acquired equally by the Partners giving such further notice. If such further notice is not served before

Continued on next page

Partnership Agreement (continued)   Form B27

the expiry of the period of notice, the Partnership shall be dissolved. If the share or shares is or are to be acquired as aforesaid, the net value of the same shall be determined as if the Partners on whom the notice has been served had themselves given notice to retire.

10.   DEATH OR INCAPACITY

If any Partner should die, the surviving Partner or any of the surviving Partners as the case may be shall have the right, exercisable by notice within a period of _____ months of the date of the death, to purchase the share of the deceased Partner as if the deceased Partner had given a notice of retirement. If more than one surviving Partner shall serve such notice, the share of the deceased Partner shall be acquired by such surviving Partners equally. If such notice is not served as aforesaid, the Partnership shall be dissolved.

11.   EXPULSION

If any Partner commits a serious breach or consistent breaches of this Agreement or is guilty of any conduct which may have a serious and detrimental effect on the Partnership [the other Partner] or such other Partners as between them have [2/3rds] of the Capital ('the remaining Partners') may by notice in writing expel such Partner from the Partnership, whereupon the remaining Partners shall have the right, exercisable by notice given within ___ month(s) of the notice of expulsion, to buy out the share(s) of the expelled partner(s) by re-payment to him of his share of the capital only. In the absence of such notice, the Partnership shall be dissolved.

12.   RESTRICTIONS

If the firm shall be dissolved, each Partner shall be free to solicit the clients of the firm. If any Partner(s) shall acquire the shares of any other Partner(s), the persons whose shares have been acquired shall not for a period of _____ years[1] approach or solicit any customers of the firm [and shall not be engaged, whether as partner, director or employee in a business of _____ [2] within a radius of one mile[3] of the said address of this firm.

IN WITNESS OF WHICH the parties hereto have signed this Agreement the day and year first above written.

SIGNED   _____DATED _____
             Signed by the First Partner

SIGNED   _____DATED _____
             Signed by the Second Partner

[1] The purpose of a restriction of this sort is to protect the business, rather than to punish an expelled partner. If the restriction is too broad, a court will refuse to enforce it. When deciding how long the restriction should operate, consider what the minimum period of time would be to enable the remaining partners to prevent a customer from following the expelled partner. A hairdresser, for example, often has a personal following which might last longer than that of a newsagent.

[2] Once again, the purpose of this restriction is to protect the business, not to punish the expelled partner. Make certain, therefore, that the activities which he is restricted from pursuing are the same as the activities of the business as actually conducted. For example, a business selling T-shirts should not forbid a former partner from working in a general clothing shop.

[3] Again, restrict only to the extent necessary. The less customers are likely to travel to a business of the type in question, the smaller the excluded area should be. For example, a hairdresser can be excluded from a wider area than can a greengrocer. The exclusion area in a sparsely populated district can be larger than such an area in central London.

Pay Advice

Form E55

_____ Ltd

Name: _____ Date: _____

Works/Dept No.: _____ Tax Code: _____

National Insurance: _____ Tax Week: _____

Payments	Hours	Rate		Total	
		£	p	£	p
Basic	_____				
Overtime	_____				
Bonus, Holiday, Sick Pay	_____				

Gross Payable

Gross wages to date	
£	. p

Deductions	£	p
Company Pension		
Income Tax		
National Insurance		
Standard rate at ____%		
Reduced rate at ____%		
Other deductions		
Total deductions		
Net Payable		

Tax deducted s to date	
£	. p

Keep this record of your earnings

Permission to Use Photograph   Form OLF33

The copyright owner (the 'Grantor') hereby grants to: _____ (the 'Grantee')
non-exclusive worldwide rights to the following photograph(s), copies of which are appended hereto, for
the following purposes:

_____

_____

_____

_____

This licence will expire on _____.
Use for any other purpose will require an additional licence and may require an additional fee.
The Grantor hereby asserts his/her moral rights as author of the photograph(s), and the following credit
should appear against every usage of the photograph(s) in acknowledgement of those rights:

_____

_____

_____

_____

The Grantor hereby warrants that he/she is the owner of the copyright of the said photograph(s), that
he/she has the right to grant this licence to the Grantee and that the publication of this photograph will not
be libellous and that, if it was taken on or after 1st August 1989, it was not taken for private or domestic
purposes.

In return for the grant of this permission, Grantee has paid the Grantor the sum of £_____ [plus VAT
thereon of £_____] receipt of which the Grantor hereby acknowledges.

Permission is granted on _____.

_____

Signature of Grantor

Permission to use Quotation or Personal Statement   Form OLF34

THIS LICENCE IS MADE the _____ day of _____ year_____

BETWEEN:

(1) _____ of _____(the 'Licensor'); and

(2) _____ of _____(the 'Licensee').

NOW IT IS HEREBY AGREED as follows:

1.   In consideration for the sum of £ _____, receipt of which the Licensor hereby acknowledges, the Licensor hereby grants a non-exclusive worldwide licence to the Licensee (the 'Licence') to use, publish or reprint in whole or in part, the following statement, picture, endorsement, quotation or other material ('the Material'):

       _____

       _____

       _____

2.   This Licence shall extend only to [a publication] / [publications] known as _____ _____, but shall extend to all new editions, reprints, excerpts, advertisements, publicity and promotions for publication.

3.   This Licence shall expire on _____, after which date no further use shall be made of the Material without a further licence for which an additional fee will be chargeable. Without such further licence all use of the Material shall cease and all presentations of the Material in electronic or on-line format shall be deleted.

4.   This agreement shall be binding upon and inure to the benefit of the parties, their successors and assigns.

IN WITNESS OF WHICH the parties have signed this licence the day and year first above written

Signed by or on behalf of the Licensor   Signed by or on behalf of the Licensee

_____   _____

in the presence of (witness)   in the presence of (witness)

Name _____   Name _____

Address _____   Address _____

_____   _____

Occupation _____   Occupation _____

Personal Property Rental Agreement Form PF15

THIS AGREEMENT IS MADE the _____ day of _____ year _____

BETWEEN:

(1) _____ of _____ (the 'Owner'); and

(2) _____ of _____ (the 'Hirer').

NOW IT IS HEREBY AGREED as follows:

1. The Owner hereby rents to the Hirer the following personal property (the 'Property'):

    _____

    _____

2. The Hirer shall pay to the Owner the sum of £ _____ as payment for the rental herein, payable as follows:

    _____

    _____

    _____

3. The Hirer shall during the rental term keep and maintain the Property in good condition and repair and shall be responsible for any loss, damage or destruction to the Property notwithstanding how caused and the Hirer agrees to return the Property in its present condition, reasonable wear and tear excepted.

4. The Hirer shall not during the rental period allow others use of the Property nor pawn or pledge the same nor permit the same to stand as security.

5. The Hirer shall during the rental period [keep the Property at _____] / [shall not take the Property] [out of the United Kingdom] / [more than _____ miles from _____].

6. The rental period shall commence on _____, and terminate on _____, at which date the Property shall be promptly returned to the Owner at _____ or at such other location as the Owner shall reasonably specify.

Continued on next page

Personal Property Rental Agreement (continued)   Form PF15

IN WITNESS OF WHICH the parties have signed this agreement the day and year first above written

_____   _____
Signed by or on behalf of the Owner   Signed by or on behalf of the Renter

_____   _____
in the presence of (witness)   in the presence of (witness)

Name _____   Name _____

Address _____   Address _____

_____   _____

Occupation _____   Occupation _____

Health warning: Do not use this form for a consumer hire agreement, within the meaning of the Consumer Credit Act 1974. A hire agreement is a 'consumer hire agreement' unless (1) it is a small agreement (requiring payments of less than £50) or (2) it is non-commercial (i.e not entered into by the owner in the course of a business) or (3) the hirer is a limited company. At present there is a further exclusion of agreements where the hirer is obliged to pay more than £25,000, but this exclusion will no longer apply once the Consumer Credit Act 2006 Section 1 is in force. There will, however, be two new exclusions. The first applies where the hirer is a partnership with more than three partners. The second applies where the goods are for use in the hirer's business and the payments to be made under the agreement exceed £25,000. Because this is a rapidly changing field, please check for recent developments.

Above all, note that if the hire agreement is a 'consumer hire agreement' it will have to be in a special statutory form and these are beyond the scope of this book.

Pools Syndicate Agreement Rules   Form OLF35

For the Football Pools competition run by: _____

and called: _____

SYNDICATE NAME: _____

MANAGER	DATE OF APPOINTMENT	SIGNATURE

MEMBER	INDIVIDUAL STAKE (to be paid IN ADVANCE of of each Match Day by the agreed deadline)	DATE JOINED SYNDICATE	MANAGER'S SIGNATURE	MEMBER'S SIGNATURE	DATE LEFT SYNDICATE	MANAGER'S SIGNATURE

Agreed deadline for payment of Individual Stakes: Time: _____

Day: _____ days before each Match Day

(Syndicate Rules on next page)

Pools Syndicate Agreement Rules (continued)   Form OLF35

1. Definitions
    'Coupon' means an appropriate coupon or coupons for the agreed pools competition;

    'Individual Stake' means the stake payable by each Member as set out in this Agreement and received by the Manager in advance of each Match Day before the agreed deadline;

    'Manager' means the Manager of the Syndicate, who shall be appointed and may be replaced at any time without notice by a majority of the Members;

    'Match Day' means a day or days of scheduled football matches for which a Coupon may be submitted under the agreed pools competition;

    'Members' means all those persons who have joined and not left the Syndicate;

    'Syndicate Stake' means the total of the Members' Individual Stakes in respect of any Match Day.

2. Manager's Responsibilities
    2.1   The Manager will:
        (a)   establish a procedure for agreeing the match selections to be entered by the Syndicate for each Match Day;
        (b)   complete and enter a Coupon bearing the agreed match selections for the amount of the Syndicate Stake for each Match Day. However, if the Syndicate Stake is not sufficient to buy a Coupon bearing all agreed match selections for any Match Day, the Manager shall have absolute discretion as to which of the match selections to enter;
        (c)   keep a current record of each Member's individual stake, of each individual stake which he, the Manager, may make on behalf of any Member, of each reimbursement of each such stake as any Member may make to the Manager and of each Coupon purchased;
        (d)   collect any prize money and account to the Members for it in proportion to their Individual Stakes, holding it in trust for the Members in the meantime.

2.2   If any Member fails to pay his or her Individual Stake to the Manager in advance of any Match Day by the agreed deadline, the Manager may (but shall not be obliged to) pay that Individual Stake on the Member's behalf and, if the Manager does so, the Member will reimburse the Manager forthwith upon demand.

2.3   The Manager shall not be liable to any Member for any loss or damage arising out of any failing of the Manager under this Agreement, provided that the Manager has acted honestly.

3. Member's Responsibilities
    The Members will each pay their Individual Stake to the Manager in advance of each Match Day by the agreed deadline.

4. Ceasing to be a Member
    A Member shall be removed from the Group:

4.1   if the Member wishes to leave; or

4.2   at the discretion of the Manager, if the Member fails to pay his or her Individual Stake in accordance with Rule 3 in respect of any 3 weeks within a calendar year (whether consecutive or non-consecutive); or

4.3   at the discretion of the Manager, if the Member fails to reimburse the Manager in accordance with Rule 2.2.

5. This Agreement

5.1   It shall be the responsibility of the Manager to update and amend this Agreement in accordance with any amendment which the Members may pass. Any such amendment, other than the removal of a Member in accordance with Rule 4, must have been authorised by majority vote of the Members. [Rule 4 may be amended only by the vote of 75 per cent of he Members.]

5.2   The record of Members shall be conclusive as to membership of the Syndicate at any point in time, provided that a person whose application for membership has been accepted by the Manager and who

Continued on next page

Pools Syndicate Agreement Rules (continued) Form OLF35

has duly paid an agreed Individual Stake shall not be excluded from a share of prize money under Rule 2.1(c) merely because the Record has not been updated to record that person as a Member. The Record shall be evidence of each Member's individual Stake and shall only be challenged on the basis of any proven failure by the manager to record a payment which has actually been made. If the Record is successfully challenged the same shall be altered and any prize money shall be paid out in accordance with the Record as altered.

5.3 If any person is removed from the list of Members, the Manager shall forthwith notify the Member of that fact, but the Manager shall incur no liability to such Member for any loss incurred by reason of any failure to inform the Member of such removal. If any Member shall be removed, the Manager shall have the power to reinstate the Member, but the Member shall not be entitled to receive any share of any prize money which may accrue to the syndicate on any Match Day falling between his removal and his reinstatement.

5.4 The appointment or replacement of the Manager shall take effect whether or not this Agreement has been amended to that effect.

T 5.5 This Agreement is subject to English law and the parties submit to the exclusive jurisdiction of the English courts in connection with any dispute hereunder.

Premarital Agreement   Form PF16

THIS AGREEMENT IS MADE the _____ day of _____ year_____

BETWEEN:

(1) _____ of _____ (the 'First Party'); and

(2) _____ of _____ (the 'Second Party').

WHEREAS:

The parties contemplate legal marriage, and it is their mutual desire to enter into this agreement so that they will continue to own and control their own property, and are getting married because of their love for each other but do not desire that their present respective financial interests be changed by their marriage.

NOW IT IS HEREBY AGREED as follows:

1.   All property which belongs to each of the above parties shall be, and shall remain, their personal estate, including all interest, rents, and profits which may accrue from said property, and said property shall remain free of claim by the other.

2.   The parties shall have at all times the full right and authority, in all respects as if the parties had not married, to use, sell, enjoy, manage, give and convey all property as may presently belong to him or her.

3.   In the event of a separation or divorce, the parties shall have no right against each other by way of claims for support, alimony, maintenance, compensation or division of property existing as of this date.

4.   In the event of separation or divorce, marital property acquired after marriage shall nevertheless remain subject to division, either by agreement or judicial determination.

5.   This agreement shall be binding upon and inure to the benefit of the parties, their successors and assigns.

IN WITNESS OF WHICH the parties have signed this agreement the day and year first above written

_____   _____
Signed by or on behalf of the First Party   Signed by or on behalf of the Second Party

_____   _____
in the presence of (witness)   in the presence of (witness)

Name _____   Name _____

Address _____   Address _____

_____   _____
Occupation _____   Occupation _____

Important Note: Premarital agreements are not binding under English law. The distribution of assets is at the discretion of the court. The court may give some weight to an agreement which both parties have made freely and with full knowledge of the meaning of the agreement and of the relevant facts. It can therefore be worthwhile to enter into such an agreement, even though it may not be clear to what extent the court will be influenced by it.

In order for the agreement to have any influence at all, however, both parties should be independently advised by solicitors. An agreement, such as the one above, should merely be used as a draft when seeking such advice. It can assist you to concentrate on the questions that you will have to think about, and may enable you to take up less of your solicitor's time. When going through it you should ask yourselves whether, in the event of a divorce, you ought to provide (contrary to what this form says) that one of you ought to pay maintenance or a lump sum by instalments to the other for a given period (the amount and the time perhaps increasing according to the time which elapses before separation.

Product Defect Notice   Form BS51

Date _____

Ref _____

To _____

_____

_____

Dear _____

Recently I purchased a product manufactured, distributed or sold by you and described as:

_____

This is to inform you that the product is defective; details as follows:

1.   Date of purchase _____

2.   Nature of defect _____

_____

3.   Injuries or damage _____

4.   Item purchased from _____

This information is provided to give you the earliest possible notice of the claim. Please inform me as to what course of action you intend to take to repair or replace the product and make good any damage.

Yours sincerely

_____

Name

_____

Address

_____

Tel

Note: If you are provided with defective goods, you must make a choice as to whether to reject them and ask for your money back, or accept them and claim money to make up the loss caused by the defect. By sending a Note in the terms in this form you may be regarded as having elected to give up your claim to have your money back. If you think it appropriate to reject the goods, other forms in this book can be used.

Promissory Note   Form CDC30

Principal Amount £ _____ Date _____

I, the undersigned, hereby promise to pay on demand to the order of _____
_____ the sum of _____pounds (£ _____) together with
interest thereon from the date hereof until paid at the rate of ___% per annum.

_____
Signed

_____
Name

_____
Witness

Important Note: Do not use this form for a consumer credit agreement, within the meaning of the Consumer Credit Act 1974. An agreement is a consumer credit agreement unless (1) it is a small agreement (requiring payments of less than £50) or (2) it is non-commercial (i.e. not entered into by the owner in the course of a business) or (3) the borrower is a limited company. At present there is a further exclusion of agreements where the loan is for less than £25,000, but this exclusion will no longer apply once the Consumer Credit Act 2006 Section 1 is in force. There will, however, be two new exclusions. The first applies where the borrower is a partnership with more than three partners. The second applies where the loan is for the purposes of the borrower's business and the loan exceeds £25,000. Because this is a rapidly changing field, please check for recent developments.

Above all, note that if the loan agreement is a consumer credit agreement it will have to be in a special statutory form and these are beyond the scope of this book.

Promissory Note for Repayment by Instalments   Form LB10

1.   I hereby promise to pay to _____ or to his order for value received the sum of _____

     _____Pounds (£ _____), with interest thereon at the rate of _____ % per annum on

     the unpaid balance in the following manner:

     £_____ on _____ date_____

     £_____ on _____ date_____

     £_____ on _____ date_____

     If I should default on any of the above payments, the entire unpaid balance of principal and interest

     shall be paid on demand.

_____   _____

Signed by or on behalf of the Borrower   Signed by or on behalf of the Guarantor

_____   _____

in the presence of (witness)   in the presence of (witness)

Name _____   Name _____

Address _____   Address _____

_____   _____

Occupation _____   Occupation _____

Important Note: It is essential that the dates for payment are specified. Do not say 'by' a given date, or 'on or before' the date. Use 'on.'

Do not use this form for a consumer credit agreement, within the meaning of the Consumer Credit Act 1974. An agreement is a consumer credit agreement unless (1) it is a small agreement (requiring payments of less than £50) or (2) it is non-commercial (i.e. not entered into by the owner in the course of a business) or (3) the borrower is a limited company. At present there is a further exclusion of agreements where the loan is for less than £25,000, but this exclusion will no longer apply once the Consumer Credit Act 2006 Section 1 is in force. There will, however, be two new exclusions. The first applies where the borrower is a partnership with more than three partners. The second applies where the loan is for the purposes of the borrower's business and the loan exceeds £25,000. Because this is a rapidly changing field, please check for recent developments. Above all, note that if the loan agreement is a consumer credit agreement it will have to be in a special statutory form and these are beyond the scope of this book.

Guarantee to Support a Promissory Note   Form LB13

If you_____will discount the promissory note dated _____ of _____, I will in consideration of your so doing, in the event of the said promissory note being dishonoured, pay you the balance owing (including interest) of such dishonoured note.

_____

Signed

_____

Name of Guarantor

_____

Witness,

Solicitor of _____who certifies as follows:

The above named _____has instructed me to advise him/her as to the meaning and effect of this guarantee. I have explained its meaning and effect to him/her and have further explained that the reason why I have been asked to witness this document is to enable you to enforce the guarantee contained therein against him/her should you wish to do so. I am satisfied that he/she understands the obligations contained in the guarantee and that he/she is entering into the same of his/her own free will.

Important note: Do not use this form for a consumer credit agreement, within the meaning of the Consumer Credit Act 1974. An agreement is a consumer credit agreement unless (1) it is a small agreement (requiring payments of less than £50) or (2) it is non-commercial (i.e not entered into by the owner in the course of a business) or (3) the borrower is a limited company. At present there is a further exclusion of agreements where the loan is for less than £25,000, but this exclusion will no longer apply once the Consumer Credit Act 2006 Section 1 is in force. There will, however, be two new exclusions. The first applies where the borrower is a partnership with more than three partners. The second applies where the loan is for the purposes of a borrower's business and the loan exceeds £25,000. Because this is a rapidly changing field, please check for recent developments. Above all, note that if the loan agreement is a consumer credit agreement it will have to be in a special statutory form and these are beyond the scope of this book. If the guarantor is a friend or relative of the borrower, you should insist that the guarantor get independent legal advice, as otherwise it may be very difficult to enforce the guarantee.

Property Inventory

Property Inventory   Form PF17

Property Inventory

OF

_____(NAME)

ITEM	ESTIMATED VALUE	LOCATION

Purchase Order   Form BS52

_____ Ltd

Address: _____

Contact Details: _____

Order to:		Order date:	
		Order no.:	
Deliver to:		Our ref no.:	
		Account no.:	
Delivery date:			

Product no	Description	Quantity	Unit price	Net
			Total Goods	
			Total VAT	
			Total £	

Please quote our order number on all correspondence.

Issued subject to our Conditions of Purchase a copy of which is enclosed.

Signed_____

For & on behalf of _____Limited

[_____] Limited registered in England Reg. No _____

Quotation

Form BS53

_____ Ltd

Address: _____

Contact Details: _____

To: _____ Date: _____

_____ Contact: _____

We have pleasure in providing our quotation as follows:

Your Ref.	Spec No.	Description	Quantity	Unit cost £
			VAT	
			Total	

Delivery time from order:
Payment terms:
Samples available:
SUBJECT TO OUR CONDITIONS OF SALE ENCLOSED

[_____] Limited registered in England Reg. No _____

Receipt Appropriated to a Particular Debt　　　Form BS54

Date _____

Ref _____

To _____

_____

_____

The undersigned hereby acknowledges receipt of the sum of £ _____

paid by _____. It is appropriated to the following debt:

_____

_____

_____

_____

The remaining unpaid balance of this debt is now £ _____.

Signed this _____ day of _____ year _____.

_____

Receipt for Company Property   Form E56

Employee: _____

Identification No: _____

Department/Section: _____

I hereby acknowledge receipt of the company property listed below. I agree to keep the property in good condition and to return it when I leave the company, or earlier on request. I agree to report immediately any loss or damage to the property. In addition, I agree to use the property only for work-related purposes.

1.　Item _____　Received From _____ Date_____

　　Serial No _____　Returned To _____ Date_____

2.　Item _____　Received From _____ Date_____

　　Serial No _____　Returned To _____ Date_____

3.　Item _____　Received From _____ Date_____

　　Serial No _____　Returned To _____ Date_____

4.　Item _____　Received From _____ Date_____

　　Serial No _____　Returned To _____ Date_____

5.　Item _____　Received From _____ Date_____

　　Serial No _____　Returned To _____ Date_____

6.　Item _____　Received From _____ Date_____

　　Serial No _____　Returned To _____ Date_____

_____

Employee

_____

Date

Receipt in Full   Form BS55

Date _____

Ref _____

To _____

_____

_____

The undersigned acknowledges receipt of the sum of £ _____ in full payment of all demands.

_____

Signed

[For and on behalf of _____ Ltd]

Receipt Credited to a Particular Account Form CDC31

Date _____

Ref _____

To _____
_____
_____

The undersigned acknowledges receipt of the sum of £ _____ paid by _____
_____.This payment will be applied and credited to the following account:
_____
_____
_____
_____

This leaves a balance on that account outstanding of £_____ as at the date hereof.

_____

Signed

[For and on behalf of _____ Ltd]

Receipt for non-cash consideration upon Allotment of Shares   Form B28

of

_____Limited

On this date, _____ has purchased _____ shares of common stock

in this company, represented by share certificate number _____. The shareholder has

transferred to the company the following assets, with an agreed fair value of £ _____, in consideration

for the receipt of the shares:

_____

_____

_____

Payment in full has been received for these shares and the share certificate representing the shares has

been issued by the company to the shareholder. Record of this transaction has been recorded in the share

transfer book of this company.

_____

Date

_____

Secretary of the company

_____

Shareholder

Important note: For as long as the Companies Act 1985 section 88 (2) (b) remains in force the company is required to provide Companies House with a copy of any contract under which a shareholder is to acquire shares from a company in exchange for consideration other than cash. If there is no written contract, details of any oral contract must be supplied. The details must include as a minimum, the name of the shareholder, the name of the company, a description of the property which forms the consideration and the agreed price of the property.

This requirement will be abolished when the relevant provision of the 2006 Companies Act comes into force.

Remember that there is a legal requirement to file a 'Return of Allotment' in statutory form whenever shares are allotted. You should consult Companies House immediately after the allotment to obtain the appropriate form. Remember also that it is not permitted to issue shares at a discount. The value attached to the non-cash consideration paid for the shares must therefore be a genuine estimate of its worth.

Redundancy with Ex Gratia Payment   Form E57

Date   _____

To   _____

_____

_____

Dear   _____

Further to our meeting on _____, I write to confirm that with regret you will be made redundant with effect from _____ , due to:

_____

_____

At the meeting we discussed the reasons for reaching this decision and the method in which you had been selected. We have made every effort to find alternative employment for you but I regret that there are no suitable positions available at present.

The redundancy benefits that you are entitled to are:

1.   Statutory redundancy pay   £ _____

2.   Pay in lieu of notice (if less than the full notice is given)   £ _____

3.   Other _____   £ _____

4.   TOTAL   £ _____

In addition, in recognition of your years of good service to the company, you will be paid an ex gratia sum of £ _____ . We will be writing to you separately about your pension entitlement.

Thank you for your past efforts on behalf of the company and I hope that you will soon find other suitable employment. You may submit our name as a reference in the confidence that the reference will be favourable.

If you wish to discuss any aspect of this letter, please do not hesitate to contact me.

Yours sincerely

_____

Note: Before any decision to dismiss is made the statutory dismissal and disciplinary procedure and any contractual procedures must be followed to avoid legal repercussions.

Reference Letter on Employee   Form E58

Private and Confidential

Date _____

Ref _____

To _____

_____

_____

Dear _____

Re _____

In reply to your request for a reference for the above job application, I report to you as follows:

_____

_____

_____

I confirm that the individual was employed by this firm between the dates of

_____ and _____ in the capacity of

_____. My additional comments are as follows:

_____

_____

_____

This reference is given to be of help to you and in fairness to your proposed employee. It is given on the basis that we accept no legal liability and that you must rely upon your own judgment whether or not to proceed with your proposed employment of this individual. We trust you shall hold this reference in strict confidence.

Yours sincerely

_____

Rejected Goods Notice   Form BS56

Date _____

Ref _____

To _____

_____

_____

Dear _____

Please note that on _____, we received goods from you under our order or contract

dated _____.

We hereby notify you of our intent to reject and return the goods for the reason(s) indicated below:

☐   Goods were not delivered within the time specified.

☐   Goods were defective or damaged as described overleaf.

☐   Goods did not conform to sample, advertisement, specifications, or price, as stated overleaf.

☐   An order acknowledgment has not been received, and we therefore ordered these goods from other

      sources.

☐   Goods represent only a partial shipment.

Please credit our account or issue a refund if prepaid, and provide instructions for the return of these goods

at your expense. Return of these goods however shall not be a waiver of any legal claim we may have.

Yours sincerely

_____

Note: A buyer should be careful not to reject goods unless he is confident that he has the right to reject them. If he rejects them when he is not entitled to do so, he will himself be in breach of contract and liable to be sued. Note also that, except in sales to consumers, the buyer does not have the right to reject the goods for defects if the defects are so minor as to make rejection unreasonable.

Reminder of Unpaid Account   Form CDC32

Date _____

Ref _____

To _____

_____

_____

Dear _____

Re: Date   Invoice No.   Invoice Amount

_____   _____   £ _____

Our records indicate that the above account remains outstanding. We would be grateful for an early remittance.

If you have paid the amount within the past seven days, please ignore this letter.

Yours sincerely

_____

Remittance Advice

Form CDC33

Date _____

Ref _____

To _____

_____

_____

Dear _____

We enclose our cheque no._____ in the amount of £ _____. This cheque is only to be credited to the following charges/invoices/orders:

Invoice	Amount
_____	£_____
_____	£_____
_____	£_____
_____	£_____
_____	£_____

Please note that this payment shall only be applied to the items listed and shall not be applied, in whole or in part, to any other, charge, order or invoice that may be outstanding.

Yours sincerely

_____

Rent Review Memorandum   Form RT16

The PROPERTY   _____

Name(s) of   _____
LANDLORD(S)   _____

Name(s) of   _____
TENANT(S)   _____

DATE OF TENANCY   _____

RENT REVIEW DATE   _____

NEW RENT   _____

The Landlord(s) and the Tenant(s) hereby record their agreement that with effect from the rent review date stated above (and subject to any provisions in the tenancy for any further review in the future) the rent payable under the tenancy shall be the figure stated as the new rent above.

SIGNED   _____   _____

                _____   _____

                     (The Landlord(s))   (The Tenant(s))

Note: Do not use this form for a tenancy protected under the Rent Act 1977. It may, however, be used for Business Tenancies or for assured and assured shorthold tenancies (as to which see Housing Act 1988 Section 13 (5)).

Rent Statement

Form RT17

Property _____

Name of Landlord/Owner _____

Address of Landlord/Owner _____

_____

Name of Tenant/Sharer _____

_____

Date Due	Amount Due	Date of Payment	Amount Paid	Cumulative Arrears	Signature of Landlord/Owner

IMPORTANT NOTICE:

This Rent Statement, or a Rent Book, must be supplied to the Tenant/Sharer if the rent/payment is paid weekly.

continued on next page

Rent Statement (continued)   Form RT17

> **IMPORTANT - PLEASE READ THIS:**
>
> **If the rent for the premises you occupy as your residence is payable weekly, the landlord must provide you with a Rent Book or similar document. If you have an Assured Tenancy, including an Assured Shorthold Tenancy (see paragraph 7 below), or a protected or statutory tenancy, the rent book or similar document must contain the notices and information which are appropriate to your type of tenancy properly filled in.**

1. Address of premises _____

2. Name and address of Landlord[1] _____

    _____

    _____

3. Name and address of agent (if any)[1] _____

    _____

    _____

4. The rent payable[1] including/excluding council tax[2] is
    £ _____ per week.

5. Details of accommodation (if any) which the occupier
    has the right to share with other persons _____

    _____

    _____

    _____

6. The other terms and conditions of the tenancy are _

    _____

    _____

    _____

    _____

    _____

    _____

7. If you have an Assured Tenancy or an Assured
    Agricultural Occupancy you have certain rights under
    the Housing Act 1988. These include the right not to be
    evicted from your home unless your Landlord gets a
    possession order from the courts. Unless the property is
    let under an Assured *Shorthold* Tenancy, the courts can
    only grant an order on a limited number of grounds.
    Further details regarding Assured Tenancies are set out
    in the Department for Communities and Local
    Government and the Welsh Assembly Government
    booklet 'Assured and Assured Shorthold Tenancies - a

Guide for Tenants' no. 97HC228C in the series of the
housing booklets. These booklets are available from the
rent officers, council offices and housing aid centres,
some of which also give advice.

8. You may be entitled to get help to pay your rent
    through the housing benefit scheme. Apply to your
    local council for details.

9. It is a criminal offence for your Landlord to evict you
    without an order from the court or to harass you or
    interfere with your possessions or use of facilities in
    order to force you to leave.

10. If you are in any doubt about your legal rights or obli-
    gations, particularly if your Landlord has asked you to
    leave, you should go to a Citizens Advice Bureau, hous-
    ing aid centre, law centre or solicitor. Help with all or
    part of the cost of legal advice from a solicitor may be
    available under the Legal Aid Scheme (now the
    Community Legal Service).

THE HOUSING ACT 1985

*Summary of Part X of the Housing Act 1985, to be inserted in a
Rent Book or similar document.*

1. An occupier who causes or permits his dwelling to be
    overcrowded is liable to prosecution for an offence
    under the Housing Act 1985, and, if convicted, to a fine
    of up to level 2 of the standard scale, and a further fine
    of up to one-tenth of that level in respect of every day
    on which the offence continues after conviction. Any
    part of a house which is occupied by a separate house-
    hold is a 'dwelling'.

2. A dwelling is overcrowded if the number of persons
    sleeping in it is more than the 'permitted number', or is
    such that two or more of those persons, being ten
    years old or over, of opposite sexes (not being persons
    living together as husband and wife), must sleep in the
    same room.

3. The 'permitted number' for the dwelling to which this
    Rent Statement relates is _____ persons. In count-
    ing the number of persons each child under ten
    counts as half a person, and a child of less than a year
    is not counted at all.

4. The name and address of the Local Health Officer is:

    _____

    _____

    Tel:_____

5. The name and address of the landlord or other person
    responsible for repairs is:

    _____

    _____

    Tel:_____

[1] These entries must be kept up-to-date.

[2] Cross out if council tax is not payable to the landlord.

Note: use this form for an assured or assured shorthold tenancy. Do not use it for a protected or statutory tenancy governed by the
Rent Act 1977, where a different form is prescribed. If in doubt, you should consult a solicitor.

Rejection of Claim for Credit Note   Form CDC34

Date _____

Ref _____

To _____

_____

_____

Dear _____

We have investigated your claim that we should credit your account for the following ticked reason(s) which you have given:

☐   Prices are above the agreed amount.

☐   Non-credited payments in the amount of £_____.

☐   Goods invoiced for have not been received.

☐   Goods were not ordered.

☐   Goods were defective or wrongly delivered.

☐   Goods are available for return.

☐   Other:_____.

We regret we must reject your claim for a credit for the following reason:

_____

_____

_____

We now request payment in the amount of £ _____ without further delay. Please contact us if you have any further questions.

Yours sincerely

_____

Request for Advance Payment   Form CDC35

Date _____

Ref _____

To _____
_____
_____

Dear _____

Upon reviewing your past credit record with us, we are compelled to say that we cannot continue to offer credit terms to you. Consequently, future orders can only be delivered with payment in advance.

We regret any inconvenience this may cause, but remind you that this arrangement will allow you to take advantage of the discounts we offer for early payment.

We hope this will be only a temporary arrangement, and that in the near future we can again extend credit terms to you.

Yours sincerely

_____

Request for Bank Credit Reference   Form CDC36

Date   _____

Ref   _____

To   _____

_____

_____

Dear   _____

Re   _____

The above account holder has requested the we obtain a banking reference from you. In order that we may evaluate trade terms for this account. He has requested that we [grant him credit in the amount of £_____] / [that we permit him to run up a bill of £_____ on terms of payment within 30 days of invoicing.] We would appreciate the following information:

1. How long has the account holder had an account with you?
2. What has the average balance on the account been during the last quarter?
3. Is the account holder permitted to overdraw? If yes, what is his permitted overdraft?
4. Does the account holder have any term loans?
5. If the account holder has any term loans, please advise:
   - i) present balance on loans;
   - ii) terms of repayment;
   - iii) is repayment satisfactory;
6. Has the borrower exceeded his overdraft limit within the last 6 months? If yes, please provide details.
7. Is the level of credit which the borrower has requested from us in line with what you would regard as normal, bearing in mind the nature and size of his business?
8. Is the overall banking relationship satisfactory?

Any additional comments or information you provide would be greatly appreciated and, of course, we would equally appreciate any future information involving a change in the account holder's financial situation or their banking relationship with you.

All information will be held in the strictest confidence.

Yours sincerely

_____

I hereby consent to the Bank furnishing to _____ the information requested above.

Signed

_____ Account holder

Request for Credit Reference   Form CDC37

Date   _____

Ref   _____

To   _____

        _____

        _____

Dear   _____

Re   _____

The above named has recently applied to us for credit terms and has cited you as a credit reference. He has requested that we [grant him credit in the amount of £_____] / [that we permit him to run up a bill of £_____ on terms of payment within 30 days of invoicing].

We would be grateful if you could provide us with the following information:

i)   Credit limit.

ii)   Terms.

iii)   How long the credit account has been open.

iv)   Present amount owed.

v)   Payment history.

vi)   Is the level of credit which the borrower has requested from us in line with what you would regard as normal, bearing in mind the nature and size of his business?

vii)   Have you found his dealings with you to be satisfactory?

Any other information you believe to be helpful is welcome. All information will be held in the strictest confidence. We accept your reference without liability on your part.

A pre-paid envelope is enclosed for your convenience. Thank you for your help.

Yours sincerely

_____

I hereby consent to the bank furnishing to _____ the information requested above.

Signed

_____ Applicant for credit

Request for Guarantee   Form CDC38

Date _____

To _____

_____

_____

Dear _____

We often find that we do not have sufficient credit information to allow us to offer trade credit to newly established businesses applying for credit.

We should be happy to offer you our normal trade credit terms if you provide us with the personal guarantee of the directors of your company and we find their credit satisfactory. Accordingly, we enclose our standard guarantee and guarantor's credit application.

Thank you for your interest in our firm and we sincerely hope you will accept our suggestion in order that we may both enjoy a mutually beneficial business relationship.

Yours sincerely

_____

Request for Information on Disputed Charge   Form CDC39

Date _____

Ref _____

To _____

_____

_____

Dear _____

We refer to your letter dated _____ disputing your account balance.
To help us resolve this matter, we ask you to provide us with the following:

☐   Copies of statements dated _____, annotated by you to show disputed amounts.

☐   Copies of any bills containing disputed items, with those items indicated and reasons given.

☐   List of all payments made since _____ with dates of payments and cheque numbers or other details of payment.

☐   Copies of returned goods authorisations.

☐   Credit notes outstanding.

☐   List of goods claimed as not received.

☐   List of goods claimed to be damaged.

☐   List of goods claimed to be non-conforming.

☐   Other:_____.

Upon receipt of the above information, we shall consider your claim at the earliest opportunity and attempt to resolve the issue.

Thank you for your prompt attention to this matter.

Yours sincerely

_____

Request for Quotation   Form BS57

Date   _____

Ref   _____

To   _____

        _____

        _____

Dear Sirs

Re: Request for Quotation

We are interested in purchasing the following goods:

_____

_____

_____

Please provide us with a firm quotation for these goods. Please also provide us with your discount structure for volume purchases and the following information:

i)   Standard terms for payment.

ii)   Availability of an open credit account with your firm. If available, please provide us with the appropriate credit application form.

iii) Delivery costs for orders.

iv)   VAT applicability.

v)   Delivery time for orders from the date of your receipt of a purchase order to our receipt of the goods.

vi)   Length of the validity of the quotation.

Yours faithfully

_____

Request for Replacement Share Certificate   Form B29

To: The Secretary

_____ Limited (the 'Company').

_____

_____

I, _____ do hereby request that the Company (or its registrars) issue to me a duplicate certificate no _____ for _____ shares in the capital of the Company, and I solemnly and sincerely declare that I am the registered holder of those shares and that I believe the original certificate to have been mislaid, destroyed or lost. In consideration of the Company so doing, I hereby indemnify the Company against all claims and demands, monies, losses, damages, costs and expense which may be brought against or be paid, incurred or sustained by the Company by reason or in consequence of the issuing to me of the duplicate certificate, or otherwise howsoever in relation thereto. I further undertake and agree, if the original certificate shall hereafter be found, forthwith to deliver up the same or cause the same to be delivered up to the Company, its registrars or their successors and assigns without cost, fee or reward.

[I make this solemn declaration conscientiously believing the same to be true, and by virtue of the provisions of the Statutory Declarations Act 1835][1]

Dated this _____ day of _____ year ____

_____

Member's signature

Before me

_____

a solicitor/commissioner for oaths

_____

Note: Depending on the size of the shareholding and the possible future value of the same, some companies may also require a bank or insurance company to be party to the indemnity.

[1] If the company wishes to require the request to have the force of a statutory declaration, the wording in square brackets should be added and the signature should be witnessed by a solicitor or commissioner for oaths.

Resignation   Form E59

Date   _____

Ref   _____

To   _____

_____

_____

Dear   _____

This is to inform you that I hereby tender my resignation from the Company with effect from

_____.

Please acknowledge receipt and acceptance of this resignation by signing below and returning to me a copy of this letter.

Yours sincerely

Name   _____

Address   _____

_____

_____

The foregoing resignation is hereby accepted and is effective as of this _____ day of _____

_____ year _____.

Name   _____

Company   _____

Note: Resignation without giving the required contractual or statutory minimum notice may have legal consequences.

Resignation of Director Relinquishing All Claims   Form B30

Date _____

To: Board of Directors

_____ Limited

Dear Sirs

I hereby resign my office of director of the company with immediate effect and confirm that I have no outstanding claims whatsoever against the company.

Yours faithfully

_____

Note: If the Director is receiving a payment or other consideration for loss of office, there are requirements for the members to be informed and for their approval to be obtained and these must be observed, even if the resignation takes this form.

Response to Employee's Complaint   Form E60

Date _____

Ref _____

To _____
_____
_____

Dear _____

We acknowledge receipt of your letter dated _____ regarding your complaint about:

_____
_____
_____
_____

As you are aware, the company follows a standard complaints procedure in these circumstances. I should be grateful if you would complete the attached form and return it to the Personnel Manager as quickly as possible so that we may follow that procedure. An investigation will then be made into the matter.

Yours sincerely

_____

Restaurant Food Poisoning Claim   Form GS27

Date _____

To _____

_____

_____

Ref _____

Dear _____

On _____my party of _____ came to have _____ at your restaurant.
Shortly afterwards _____ members of the group came down with food poisoning. The effects on the
members of my immediate family were as follows:

Name	Time of first onset of symptoms	Description of Symptoms	Duration of symptoms, time off school or work

My GP has concluded that our illnesses were directly caused by the consumption of food served at your
restaurant. As I am sure you are aware, your conduct in selling food which is damaging to health renders you
civilly liable for breach of contract and negligence, as well as criminally liable under the Food Safety Act
1990 Section 8. I therefore hold you responsible to compensate each of us for the suffering we have
endured, time off work and other expenses. The figure I have arrived at as reasonable compensation for
each of us is £_____ being made up as follows:

Name	Amount

I look forward to receiving your payment.

Yours sincerely

_____

Name _____

Address _____

Tel. _____

Note: If the symptoms are severe or if all of the members of your party have not yet fully recovered, or if the financial loss is substantial,
you should consult a solicitor before sending this letter. You should also consider reporting the matter to the health department of the
local authority where the restaurant is located in order to ensure that the evidence is recorded and that repetitions are prevented.

Restaurant Food Quality Complaint   Form BS58

Date _____

To _____
_____
_____

Ref _____

Dear _____

We came for _____ at your restaurant on _____. I was disappointed to find that upon tasting the _____ that had been ordered it was not satisfactory for the following reason: _____.

I expressed my disappointment immediately and requested that the price of the dish be deducted from the bill. But upon receiving the bill for £_____ I discovered nothing had been done to adjust for the uneaten dish. I was given no alternative but to pay the bill in full, which I did under protest, making it clear that I would seek proper compensation from your establishment at a later date.

[You will be aware that the Food Safety Act 1990 makes it a criminal offence to supply food which is not of the 'nature, substance or quality demanded'. As the dish you served [was contaminated]/[did not contain the ingredients which it was described as containing][1] you are liable for a breach of that Act.]

Furthermore, because the purpose of a meal in a restaurant is to obtain enjoyment and because the quality of the dish referred to above was such that no reasonable person could have been expected to consume it, I am entitled to compensation on behalf of myself and the members of the party who accompanied me]/ [to receive compensation for the annoyance and disappointment which you have caused, in addition to a refund for the dish itself.

I shall expect to receive a cheque for £_____ within 10 days. Otherwise, I shall have no alternative but to issue you a county court claim for recovery of the amount owed to me without further notice.

Yours sincerely

_____

Name _____
Address _____
Tel. _____

[1] Do not include the words in square brackets unless the food was uncooked to an extent which was dangerous or unless it was contaminated or did not contain the ingredients which it was said to contain. If there has been such an offence, you should also consider informing the local authority where the restaurant is located. On the other hand, merely serving badly-prepared food is not a criminal offence in itself, although it can give rise to civil liability for breach of contract, as the following letter states.

Restaurant Lost Reservation Claim   Form GS28

Date _____

To _____
_____
_____

Ref _____

Dear _____

On _____ I called your restaurant and made a reservation for _____ at _____ [am] / [pm] for ___ people on_____. [In order to secure the booking I was requested to supply, and did supply, my credit card details.]

Upon our prompt arrival at your restaurant I was told that no booking existed in my name. I was forced to improvise other arrangements which caused me considerable embarrassment and disappointment.

Your failure to keep the reservation I had made constitutes your breach of contract and I am entitled to compensation from you as a result. Considering the travel expenses incurred in getting to your restaurant and the inconvenience suffered I consider £_____ to be a reasonable sum.

Failure to pay me compensation within 10 days shall result in a claim being issued against you in your local small claims court for recovery of the money.

Yours sincerely

_____

Name _____
Address _____
Tel. _____

Revocation of Power of Attorney   Form PF18

THIS DEED OF REVOCATION is made on the _____ day of _____, year_____

by me _____ of _____

WITNESSES as follows:

1.   I revoke the instrument dated _____, year____ (the 'Instrument') in which I appointed
_____ of _____
to be my attorney for the purpose of the [Power of Attorney Act 1971 (Section 10)] / [the Enduring
Powers of Attorney Act 1985 (Section 2)] / [the Mental Capacity Act 2005 (Section 9)].

2.   I declare that all power and authority conferred by the Instrument is now revoked and withdrawn by me.

3.   I verify everything done by my attorney under the Instrument.

4.   This deed of resolution is a deed and has been executed by me as a deed.

IN WITNESS OF WHICH the said _____ has executed this deed the day
and year first above written.

_____

Signature

_____

Signed by Witness

Name _____

Address _____

_____

_____

Occupation_____

Important Note:

Although you can always claim against an agent who misuses his powers under a power of attorney, you can only make a claim based solely on the agent using the power of attorney after revocation, if you have informed him of the revocation.

If your agent has been dealing with people on your behalf, and if they know that he has been acting under a power of attorney, those other people will be entitled to hold you to anything done on your behalf by the agent, until they know about the revocation. Therefore, once you have revoked the power of attorney you must be sure to inform anyone with whom your agent has been dealing on your behalf that the power has been revoked. You must also demand that the agent return the power of attorney to you. If he does not do so, you must immediately see a solicitor in order to get an order compelling him to return it and to forbid him from acting upon it.

Sale Agreement of Moveable Property Subject to Debt   Form BS59

THIS AGREEMENT is made the _____ day of _____ year_____

BETWEEN:

(1)_____(the 'Buyer'); and

(2) _____ (the 'Seller').

NOW IT IS HEREBY AGREED as follows:

1.   In consideration of the sum of £ _____, receipt of which the Seller hereby acknowledges, the Seller hereby transfers and sells the following property to the Buyer (the 'Property'):

_____

_____

_____

2.   The Seller warrants that he/she owns the Property and that he/she has the authority to sell the Property to the Buyer. The Seller also states that the Property is sold subject to the following debt, but that it is otherwise free from encumbrances:

_____

_____

_____

3.   The Buyer and the Seller agree that in respect of the debt they shall apply to the creditor for the substitution of the Buyer in place of the Seller and that they shall execute any instrument which may be necessary to achieve such substitution. Until such substitution is achieved, the Buyer warrants that he/she will pay all instalments due under the debt and that he/she will indemnify and hold the Seller harmless from any claim arising from any failure by the Buyer to pay off this debt.

4.   The Seller also warrants that the Property is in good working condition and otherwise of satisfactory quality as of this date.

IN WITNESS OF WHICH the parties have signed this agreement the day and year first above written

_____   _____

Signed by or on behalf of the Buyer   Signed by or on behalf of the Seller

_____   _____

in the presence of (witness)   in the presence of (witness)

Name _____   Name _____

Address _____   Address _____

_____   _____

Occupation _____   Occupation _____

Note: This agreement should be used for moveable property and not for land or buildings. Because of the legal complexities involved, you should consult a solicitor in relation to land or buildings. You should also be careful not to use this agreement for property which is subject to a hire-purchase agreement, because a sale of such property without the hire purchase company's prior consent will usually entitle the hire purchase company to bring moveable agreement to an end and repossess the property. Before parting with money, the Buyer should ask the creditor to confirm the amount of the debt and the permission which has been given for the property to be sold subject to the debt.

Sales Representative Agreement   Form E61

THIS AGREEMENT is made the _____ day of _____ year____

BETWEEN:

(1) _____ of _____ (the 'Principal'); and

(2) _____ of _____ (the 'Representative').

PARTICULARS

This appointment commences on the _____ day of _____ year____ [for a period of ____ years]

Sales Territory:_____ [in which the Representative shall have the exclusive right to represent the Principal in respect of the Products below-mentioned.]

Products/Services: _____

Commission Rates:

(a)   (subject to (c) below), _____ per cent of the price charged to the customer on all prepaid sales, net of freight, insurance and duties;

(b)   (subject to (c) below), _____ per cent of the price charged to the customer on all credit sales, net of freight, insurance and duties;

(c)   a commission percentage to be negotiated between the Principal and the Representative in advance of sale on all orders on which the Principal allows a quantity discount or other trade concession.

Run Off Period: _____ months from the termination of this Agreement.

[Target: A gross turnover of sale of £_____ a month]

NOW IT IS HEREBY AGREED as follows:

1.   The Representative hereby agrees:

    1.1   To act in good faith towards the Principal.

    1.2   To represent and sell the Principal's Products/Services in the Sales Territory.

    1.3   To represent and state accurately the Principal's policies and terms of trading to all potential and present customers and to make or give no other representations or warranties other than those contained in any standard terms of trading of the Principal.

    1.4   To notify promptly to the Principal all contacts and orders within the Sales Territory, and all enquiries and leads from outside the Sales Territory, to the Principal.

    1.5   Not to solicit orders outside the Sales Territory.

    1.6   To inform the Principal or the Principal's sales manager of any problems concerning customers of the Principal within the Sales Territory.

    1.7   During the period of this Agreement to inform the Principal or the Principal's sales manager if the Representative is representing, or plans to represent, any other trader within the Sales

Continued on next page

Sales Representative Agreement (continued)   Form E61

Territory. In no event shall the Representative be involved directly or indirectly with a competing company or product line within the Sales Territory.

1.8   During the period of this Agreement in no event shall the Representative directly or indirectly sell or solicit orders on behalf of any person other than the Principal in respect of any product which competes with those of the Principal's Products that are the subject of this Agreement.

1.9   For a period of [2 years] after the termination of this Agreement, in no event shall the Representative directly or indirectly sell or solicit orders within the Sales Territory for any product which competes with those of the Principal's Products that are the subject of this Agreement.

1.10   To achieve the Target.

1.11   To provide the Principal upon request with sales reports detailing sales progress within the Sales Territory.

1.12   To return promptly at its expense all materials and samples provided by the Principal to the Representative after the termination of this Agreement.

1.13   Not to pledge the credit of the Principal.

1.14   To indemnify the Principal against any and all loss suffered by the Principal resulting from any breach of this Agreement by the Representative.

2.   The Principal agrees:.

2.1   Not later than the last day of the month following the quarter in which the Principal receives payment in respect of a sale made [as a result of or mainly attributable to the actions or efforts of the Representative] [to any customer within the Territory][1], to provide the Representative with a statement of commission due, and to pay commission to the Representative at the appropriate Commission Rate for that sale. The Principal shall, upon request, allow the Representative any records which the Representative may reasonably require in order to enable him/her to check the accuracy of the statement of commission.

2.2   All sales concluded after the termination of the Agreement but prior to the end of the Run-Off Period which are a result of, or attributable to, the actions or efforts of the Representative during the period of this Agreement shall attract commission at the appropriate Commission Rate and shall be apportioned, as the Principal shall consider to be reasonable, between the Representative and any person who may be appointed to the Sales Territory in replacement of the Representative

2.3.   To provide the Representative with reasonable quantities of business cards, brochures, catalogues, and product samples required for sales purposes.

2.4.   To provide to the Representative details of any enquiries or leads which it may receive from outside the Sales Territory in respect of those of its products which are subject to this Agreement.

Continued on next page

Sales Representative Agreement (continued) Form E61

3.   It is further agreed that:

   3.1   Should refunds be made to any customer of the Principal, a proportion of the commission already paid to the Representative on that transaction, commensurate with the sums refunded, shall be deducted from future commissions to be paid to the Representative by the Principal provided that the refund to the customer shall not have been made necessary through the fault of the Principal.

   3.2   Either Party may terminate this Agreement by giving written notice to the other Party. If the Agreement has run for one year or less when notice is served, one month's notice must be given. If it has run for between one and two years, two months' notice must be given. Otherwise, three months' notice must be given unless one Party has committed a material breach of the terms of this Agreement in which case the other can terminate without notice.

   3.3   Upon termination of the Agreement the Representative shall have the right to be indemnified as provided in the Commercial Agents (Council Directive) Regulations 1993, but the Representative shall have no right to compensation under those Regulations[2].

   3.4   This constitutes the entire Agreement between the Parties. Any amendments to this Agreement shall only be valid if both parties confirm such amendments in writing.

   3.5   This Agreement shall be binding upon the Parties and their successors and assigns.

   3.6   The Parties are not partners or joint venturers, nor is the Representative an employee of the Principal, nor is the Representative able to act as the agent of the Principal except as authorised by this Agreement. Further, the Representative shall not enter into any contract with any customer on the Principal's behalf [without the Principal's prior authority].

   3.7   This Agreement is governed by and shall be construed in accordance with English law.

IN WITNESS OF WHICH the Parties have signed this Agreement the day and year above written

_____   _____

Signed by the Representative   Signed for and on behalf of the Principal

---

[1]   Choose this if the Representative has the exclusive right to represent the Principal within the Territory.

[2]   The Regulations permit the parties to choose between the Representative having the right to an 'indemnity' or to 'compensation' on termination of the Agreement. If neither is specified, the Representative is entitled to compensation. The two remedies can lead to different results. You should take advice from a solicitor as to which is the more appropriate in your case.

Samples and Documents Receipt   Form E62

_____ Ltd

I, _____, employed in the position

of _____, confirm that I have received from the

company the following samples:

No. Rec'd	Serial No.	Description	Value Each	Total Value
_____	_____	_____	_____	_____
_____	_____	_____	_____	_____
_____	_____	_____	_____	_____
_____	_____	_____	_____	_____
_____	_____	_____	_____	_____

In addition I confirm that I have received the following documents:

_____

_____

_____

_____

_____

_____

I accept responsibility to safeguard these materials, to prevent the disclosure of confidential material
otherwise than as may be necessary in discharge of my duties as an employee and to return these (except
those authorised for and delivered to customers) to the company on demand and, in any event, upon
termination of employment

_____

Employee

_____

Date

Second Notice of Overdue Account   Form CDC40

Date _____

Ref _____

To _____

_____

_____

Dear _____

Payment of your account is now unacceptably overdue. Your account balance currently stands as follows.

PAST DUE DATE

Over 30 days	£_____
Over 60 days	£_____
Over 90 days	£_____
Total	£_____

May we please now have your immediate payment without further delay.

[Under the terms of our conditions of trading, interest is payable at the rate of _____ per cent per annum][1]

[Under the Late Payment of Commercial Debts (Interest) Act 1998 statutory interest is payable.][1]

Yours sincerely

_____

[1] Add this in non-consumer credit sales.

Second Warning For Lateness

Form E63

Date _____

To _____
_____
_____

Dear _____

Further to our meeting, I write to confirm the outcome of our discussion about your bad time-keeping, for which you have already been warned on _____.

Despite these verbal and written warnings, you continue to be late for work, in breach of your employment terms. Your hours of work are stated in the Statement of Terms and Conditions of Employment previously given to you. A further copy of the terms and conditions is enclosed.

Since you have ignored the previous warnings, I have no alternative but to issue this second formal warning. If you fail to improve your time-keeping, we may have no option but to consider your dismissal.

This second written warning is being recorded on your personnel file. If you wish to exercise your right of appeal against this warning, please notify me in writing within _____ working days.

Yours sincerely

_____

Security Agreement   Form LB11

THIS DEED IS MADE the _____ day of _____ year _____

BETWEEN:

(1) _____ of _____ (the 'Debtor'); and

(2) _____ of _____ (the 'Secured Party').

WHEREAS:

(A)   The Debtor is indebted to the Secured Party in the Sum of £ _____ (the 'Debt').

(B)   The Secured Party wishes to obtain from the Debtor security for the Debt.

NOW THIS DEED WITNESSES as follows:

1.   The Debtor hereby undertakes to repay all indebtedness and to discharge all obligations which it may owe to the Secured Party whether now or hereafter. WIthout prejudice to the generality of the foregoing, these indebtednesses and obligations include the following:

_____

_____

2.   The Debtor grants to Secured Party of and its successors and assigns a fixed charge over the following property (the 'Security'), which shall include all after-acquired property of a like nature and description and proceeds of sale thereof:

_____

_____

[3.   The Debtor hereby acknowledges to the Secured Party that the Security shall be kept at the Debtor's above address and not moved or relocated without written consent.]/[The Debtor shall not move the Security from the Debtor's above address without informing the Secured Party in advance.

4.   The Debtor warrants that the Debtor owns the Security and that it is free from any other lien, charge, encumbrance or other adverse interest and the Debtor has full power to grant this charge.

5.   The Debtor will keep the Security in good repair, and take all reasonable care to protect it from damage, and will not act in any way so as to prejudice or invalidate any warranty or insurance policy in respect of the Security. The Debtor further will preserve all documents of title and all maintenance records, and will provide copies of the same to the Secured Party forthwith upon demand.

6.   The Debtor will not assign or charge the Security. Should any lien attach to the Security, the Debtor will forthwith procure the discharge of the same. The Debtor will pay any charges or licence fees which may be imposed by any statutory body in respect of the Security.

7.   If the Security should become subject to any incumbrance, the Debtor shall forthwith inform the Secured Party of the same.

8.   The Debtor agrees to execute such assignments, assents or other documents as may reasonably be required by the Secured Party to perfect this Charge.

9.   Upon default in payment or performance of any obligation for which this security interest is granted, or upon breach of any term of this security agreement, or upon the presentation of a petition for the winding up of the Debtor, or upon the appointment of a Receiver or Administrator in respect of the

Continued on next page

Security Agreement (continued)   Form LB11

Debtor or if the Secured Party's surveyor shall decide that there has been any material decrease in the value of the Security then in any such instance the Secured Party may declare all obligations immediately due and payable.

10. Upon the occurrence of any of the events in clause 8 hereof, the Secured Party's rights to enforce this Agreement under section 101 of the Law of Property Act 1925 shall become exercisable. The restrictions upon the exercise of that power contained in section 103 of the said Act shall not apply.

11 The Debtor agrees to to insure the Security against fire, theft, flood, storms, malicious damage and any other risks that the Secured Party, and upon request by the Secured Party forthwith to provide copies of all policies and receipts for premiums. The Secured Party shall be named the beneficiary of any insurance policy taken out for such purpose.

12. Upon default the Debtor shall indemnify the Secured Party for all solicitors' and other fees and costs incurred in the enforcement of this Agreement.

13. Nothing in this Agreement is intended to confer any benefit on a third party whether under the Contracts (Rights of Third Parties) Act or otherwise.

IN WITNESS WHEREOF the parties have signed this deed the day and year first above written.

_____   _____

Signed by or on behalf of the Debtor   Signed by or on behalf of the Secured Party

_____   _____

in the presence of (witness)   in the presence of (witness)

Name _____   Name _____

Address _____   Address _____

_____   _____

Occupation _____   Occupation _____

Important:

Use this form only if the Debtor is a company, rather than an individual. If the Debtor is an individual, a security over 'personal chattels' by which is meant most physical objects not attached to land, will be void unless (1) it is in the form prescribed by the Schedule to the Bills of Sale (1878) Amendment Act 1882; (2) it secures only the types of obligation permitted by the Bills of Exchange Acts; (3) it contains nothing which is inconsistent with the statutory form; (4) it is executed exactly as the Acts prescribe; and (5) it is registered within seven days by the Registry at the High Court having responsibility for bills of sale. In addition, you will have to comply with the formalities prescribed by the Consumer Credit Act 1974. In other words, do not attempt to take security from individuals without obtaining professional advice.

Make certain to register this Agreement at Companies House under Sections 395 – 396 of the Companies Act 1985, as otherwise the Agreement will be void against a liquidator of the Company.

This form is not appropriate for use in respect of the debtor's stock in trade or other items which the debtor is to be free to dispose of and replace from time to time. A security to cover such items must be in the form of a floating charge which is not including in this book.

Settlement Statement   Form CDC41

NOTE: This statement complies with the Consumer Credit (Settlement Information) Regulations 1983 (S.I. 1983 No. 1564).

To _____

_____

_____

_____

(Name and address of customer)

From: _____

_____

_____

_____

(Name and address of creditor)

This statement is given in respect of an agreement dated _____ which was made

between you and _____ in respect of the hire purchase

(credit sale) of _____ _____ and

has the reference number _____.

Settlement date _____ calculated in accordance with regulation 3 of the Consumer Credit (Settlement Information) Regulations 1983.

Amount required to settle the agreement early without any rebate due: £ _____

[Note: Include one of the three alternatives below as appropriate; NB: if the customer is entitled to a rebate, the rebate must be the higher of (a) the customer's entitlement under the agreement, (b) the customer's entitlement under section 95 of the Consumer Credit Act 1974]* *Delete this note before sending*

The customer is not entitled to any rebate for settlement of the outstanding amount before the settlement date.

Rebate calculation made in regard to the Consumer Credit (Rebate on Early Settlement) Regulations 1983.

Rebate made in accordance with the agreement.

[Include the following if a rebate is due]

Amount due under agreement	£ _____
Less: rebate	_____
Amount required to settle:	£ _____

(General information about the operation of the Consumer Credit Act and Regulations made under it is made available by the Office of Fair Trading, www.oft.gov.uk, and advice may be obtained by contacting the local Trading Standards Department or nearest Citizens' Advice Bureau).

Note: Although we have included this form we repeat our suggestion that if you engage in transactions which are regulated by the Consumer Credit Act 1974 in the course of your business you should ask your solicitor to review your contractual forms and procedures.

Share Certificate

Certificate No. _____

Number of Shares _____

_____ LIMITED

This is to Certify that _____

of _____

is/are the Registered holder(s) of _____ [ordinary][1] _____ shares of £ _____ each [_fully] _____ paid[2]

in the above-named Company, subject to the Memorandum and Articles of Association of the Company.

Delete one of the following two sentences.

This document is hereby executed by the company.

The Common Seal of the Company was hereto affixed in the presence of:

_____ Directors

_____ Secretary _____ year _____

[1] If the shares are not ordinary shares, substitute 'preference' or such other class of share as may be.

[2] In the unlikely event that the shares are not fully paid up, state the amount by which they have been paid up and record the share numbers, as well as the certificate number.

Share Subscription/Application   Form B33

I/We offer to acquire _____ ordinary shares of_____

_____ (company) at the offer price of £_____ per share.

I/We attach a cheque or bankers draft for the amount of £_____.

I/We agree to take such shares subject to the Memorandum and Articles of Association of the Company and to be registered on the register of members.

Applicant's name   _____

Applicant's full address   _____

_____

_____

Applicant's signature   _____

Additional joint applicants:

Second Applicant's name   _____

Address   _____

_____

_____

Signature   _____

Third Applicant's name   _____

Address   _____

_____

_____

Signature   _____

Solicitor's Charges: Detailed Account Request   Form GS33

Date   _____

To   _____

_____

_____

Ref   _____

Dear   _____

I am in receipt of your bill dated _____ for the work on _____ but am unclear about the fees I have been charged.

To clarify the matter, please send me a detailed, itemised breakdown of the account of charges for the services you have performed, as I am legally entitled to under Section 64 of the Solicitors Act 1974. If you intend to charge me for this please let me know before proceeding.

I look forward to hearing from you shortly.

Yours sincerely

_____

Name   _____

Address   _____

_____

Tel.   _____

Note: If the client is dissatisfied with the detailed bill, a solicitor's bill can be assessed by the court under the Solicitors Act 1974 Section 70. However, there are time limits for making an application. In particular, the court is entitled to impose conditions on the client or refuse to entertain the application altogether if the challenge is made more than one month after the bill has been delivered to the client. The court also has no power to consider the application except in certain special circumstances, if the client has paid the bill (sometimes even if he has paid under protest) and if more than a year has elapsed since the bill was paid. Note also that the client can be made to pay the costs of a court application, just as in any other litigation. You should therefore seek advice before embarking on this course of action.

You should also consider the alternative, set out in the next form, for requiring your solicitor to obtain a remuneration certificate (although it is only available for non-contentious work, such as conveyancing).

Solicitor's Charges: Remuneration Certificate Request   Form GS32

Date   _____

To   _____

_____

_____

Ref   _____

Dear   _____

I am in receipt of your letter dated _____ detailing the charges for the services you have provided up to _____.

I feel these charges are unreasonably high and should be grateful if you would apply for a Remuneration Certificate from the Law Society on my behalf. As I am sure you are aware I am entitled to such a Certificate stating what should be a reasonable and fair charge for the work you have done.

Please confirm your acceptance of the above.

Yours sincerely

_____

Name   _____

Address   _____

_____

Tel.   _____

Note: The procedure for obtaining a remuneration certificate is free of charge, but applies only if (a) the bill is for £50,000 or less; (b) it has not yet been paid; (c) no more than a month has elapsed from the solicitor informing the client of the right to obtain a certificate; and (d) the Court has not ordered the bill to be assessed. The procedure is as follows: the client requests that the solicitor obtain a certificate, the solicitor obtains a form from the Law Society's Consumer Complaints Service, the solicitor forwards the form to the client and the client fills it in and returns it to the solicitor who will in turn send it along with his file to the Remuneration Department of the Law Society. More information is available on the website of the Law Society at www.lawsociety.org.uk.

Special Notice for the Removal of Auditors   Form B35

Date _____

Ref _____

To The Directors

_____ Limited

_____

_____

Dear Sirs

I hereby give notice pursuant to sections [379 and 391A of the Companies Act 1985]/[312, 510 and 511 of the Companies Act 2006][1] I hereby give special notice of my intention to propose the following ordinary resolution at a General Meeting of the company, to be held not earlier than 28 days from the date of this notice.

Ordinary Resolution

'That _____ be and are hereby removed from office as auditors of the company and that _____ be appointed as auditors of the company in their place to hold office until the conclusion of the next General Meeting at which accounts are laid before the company at a remuneration to be fixed by the directors.'[2]

Dated this _____ day of _____ year___.

Yours faithfully

_____

Note: Virtually the same provisions apply if there is a resolution not to reappoint an auditor whose term has expired. This notice must be given by a member and left at the company's registered office at least 28 days before the general meeting. On receipt of this notice the company must send a copy to the auditors. The company must give notice of this resolution to the members when it gives them notice of the meeting (or, if that is not practicable, either by advertisement in a newspaper having an appropriate circulation or in any other mode allowed by the articles, not less than 21 days before the meeting). The Companies Act give the auditor the right to make representations in writing and to the meeting at which the resolution to remove him is to be considered, as well as to have those representations circulated. 'Note that the Companies Acts give the auditor the right to make representations in writing and to the meeting at which the resolution to remove him is to be considered, as well as to have those representations circulated.'

[1] Delete according to whether or not the cited sections of the Companies Act 2006 are in force when you come to use this form. You may consult Companies House as to whether the sections are in force.

[2] Notice of the removal of an auditor must be given to Companies House on Form 391, to be submitted within 14 days of the resolution being passed.

Special Notice for the Removal of a Director   Form B34

_____ LIMITED

The Directors

_____

In accordance with sections [379 and 303(2) of the Companies Act 1985]/[312 and 168 of the Companies Act 2006], I hereby give special notice of my intention to move the following ordinary resolution at a general meeting of the company, to be held not earlier than 28 days from the date of this notice.

ORDINARY RESOLUTION

That _____ be and is hereby removed from office as a director of the company.

Dated

_____

_____

_____

Note: Use the references to the 2006 Act after 1 October 2007. The removal of a director or the appointment of a replacement must be notified to Companies House within 14 days.

Note also that the Companies Acts give the director the right to make representations in writing to the meeting at which the resolution to remove him is to be considered, as well as to have those representations circulated. You may consult Companies House about this.

This notice must be given by a member and left at the company's registered office at least 28 days before the general meeting. On receipt of this notice the company must send a copy to the director concerned. The company must give notice of this resolution to the members when it gives them notice of the meeting (or, if that is not practicable, either by advertisement in a newspaper having an appropriate circulation or in any other mode allowed by the articles, not less than 21days before the meeting). If the directors are not willing to call a meeting they can be compelled to do so under Section 368 of the Companies Act 1985 or 304 of the Companies Act 2006.

Standard Board Minutes   Form B36

_____ LIMITED

MINUTES of a Meeting of the Board of Directors held at _____

_____ on _____ at _____ a.m./p.m.

PRESENT:

_____(in the chair)

_____

_____

_____

_____

IN ATTENDANCE:

_____

_____

_____

_____

The Chairman confirmed that notice of the meeting had been given to all the directors of the Company and that a quorum of the board of directors was present at the meeting.

_____ declared his/their interest(s) in the following proposed transactions of the Company which were to be discussed at the meeting in accordance with Section [317 Companies Act 1985] / [177 of the Companies Act 2006]:

_____.

IT WAS RESOLVED THAT

_____

_____

_____

_____

There being no further business the meeting then ended.

Chairman: _____

Note: Sections 117 of the 2006 Act is in force from 1 October 2007. The company is required by law to keep copies of all board resolutions for 10 years.

Standard Contractual Terms for Sale of Services Online   Form BS63
where the customer is a business – services and
price negotiated individually

SALE AGREEMENT
_____ [Limited][1]

Address[2] _____

Contact Details[3] _____

Publicly accessible register (if applicable)[4] _____

Relevant supervisory authority (if applicable)[5] _____

Professional body of which a member (if applicable)[6] _____

VAT Registration Number _____

Terms and Conditions

1.   **Parties**: This Agreement is made between _____ Ltd. of _____ ('the Company'), of the one part and the person who is named in the Acceptance Form ('the Customer') of the other part.

2.   **Agreement of Price and Formation of Contract:** The Company will submit a quote for acceptance by the Customer. Acceptance by the Customer shall be by way of e-mail ('the Acceptance Form') in such manner as may be prescribed on this internet site from time to time. [No contract will arise between the Customer and the Company, and the Company shall therefore not be under any obligation to undertake any work, until the Company shall have received payment of the price agreed for the work.]

3.   **Choice of Law and Jurisdiction**: This contract will be governed by the laws of England. Any disputes of whatever nature arising out of or connected with this contract shall be subject to the exclusive jurisdiction of the English Courts.

4.   **The Company's Services:** The Company will

_____.[7] In particular

_____

_____

   4.1   The Company will _____[8]

   4.2   The Company will not _____[9]

5.   If any work undertaken by the Company shall contain any error or omission caused by the Company, the Company shall correct the same or at its discretion refund to the Customer the sums which the Customer shall have paid in respect of the work in question. In all such cases of such error or omission, whether or not the same be caused by the Company's negligence, the Customer's remedies shall be limited to the correction of the work or to a refund as aforesaid. The Company will not be liable for any consequential loss including but not limited to loss of reputation or business or profits.

6.   The Company reserves the right at any time to refuse to do any work which in the Company's opinion:

     •   is unlawful, whether in the United Kingdom or elsewhere;

     •   would involve the publication of offensive or obscene material;

Continued on next page

Standard Contractual Terms for Sale of Services Online   Form BS63
where the customer is a business – services and
price negotiated individually (continued)

- would involve the publication of material which is defamatory;
- would involve a breach of copyright to publish.

If during the course of any work, the Company shall decide to refuse to continue with the same for any of the above reasons, the Company will refund the sums paid by the Customer in respect of the same, less such proportion thereof as in the Company's opinion is appropriate to remunerate the Company for the work undertaken, but (whether or not the Company's refusal to continue the work was justified) the Customer's remedies shall be limited to such refund and the Customer shall not be entitled to damages or other remedy for any consequential loss which it may sustain whether by way of loss or reputation, or loss of business or profits or otherwise.

7. The time taken for performance of the Company's work will be specified in the Company's quote. Unless otherwise stated in the quote, the period will run from the receipt of payment. If the period expires without the work having been completed, the Customer may give to the Company notice by e-mail that the Customer will refuse to accept the work if the same shall not be substantially completed before the expiry of _____ working days. The Customer will be entitled to a refund of all sums paid in respect of the work in question upon the expiry of such notice if the work shall not by then have been substantially completed. The right to serve a notice as aforesaid will affect only the work mentioned in the quote in question. Work done or to be done in pursuance of other quotes will remain unaffected, as will the Company's entitlement to payment therefor. The Customer will not be entitled to any remedy other than a refund in respect of delayed performance or failure to perform, and the Customer shall not be entitled to any remedy for consequential loss, whether for loss of reputation or business or profits or otherwise.

8. The Customer will co-operate with the Company so as to facilitate the Company's performance of its work and will when requested provide such clarifications and instructions as the Company may reasonably require. If the Customer shall fail to provide clarification or instructions requested by the Company, any period for performance referred to in Clause 7 will cease to run until such instructions or clarifications are provided.

9. **Security:** The Company will presume, unless the Company receives an e-mail from the Customer to contrary effect, that information submitted by the Customer is not confidential and that there is no requirement for the encryption of communications between the Customer and the Company in respect of it. If the Customer instructs the Company that any communications are to be encrypted or treated as confidential, the Company will do its best to comply and will arrange encryption with the Customer at no extra charge.

10. **Copyright:** The copyright in the material produced for the Customer shall belong to the Customer, provided however, that the Company shall be entitled to retain a copy of such material for the purposes of enabling it to provide further services to the Customer and also, without the payment of royalties, for the purpose of using the same as precedents to enable it to prepare work for other Customers.

11. **Indemnity:** The Customer warrants that material supplied to the Company does not contain any

Continued on next page

Standard Contractual Terms for Sale of Services Online   Form BS63
where the customer is a business, services and
price negotiated individually (continued)

material which is defamatory, that its publication will not infringe the laws of the United Kingdom or of any country in which the Customer intends to publish or make use of the same and that its publication will not constitute a breach of the rights of any third party. The Customer will indemnify the Company for any claim or loss suffered by the Company arising out of any breach of this warranty.

12. **Privacy**

    12.1   The Company will not disclose any information about the Customer without the Customer's express permission to anyone other than a person whom the Company believes to be authorised by the Customer to receive such information, save where the Company, in its opinion, is obliged to do so by legal process or obligation.

    12.2.   The Customer's remedy for any breach of confidentiality or security by the Company, whether occasioned by the Company's negligence or not, shall be limited to a refund of the monies paid for the work in respect of which the information, the subject of the breach, was supplied. The Customer shall not be entitled to damages or other remedy for any consequential loss which it may sustain whether by way of loss or reputation, or loss of business or profits or otherwise.

13. **Statutory rights**

All restrictions of liability hereinbefore contained shall take effect to the full extent of the laws of England, but they shall not be construed so as to limit the Customer's statutory rights.

Note: This form must on no account be used for the sale of services to consumers (persons who are buying the service otherwise than for the purposes of their business), because the restrictions on liability which this form contains would be likely to infringe the requirements of the Unfair Terms in Consumer Contracts Regulations and the Distance Selling Regulations. Note also that any contract for the sale of services online (whether or not to consumers) will engage the E-Commerce Regulations and will therefore have to contain the information about the company which appears at the beginning of the form.

[1]   Business name.

[2]   Geographic address, not web address.

[3]   Include email address.

[4]   Any publicly accessible register (e.g. companies register) on which you appear (include registration number)

[5]   Authority to which you are subject.

[6]   With which professional body are you registered, what professional rules govern you and where can they be accessed.

[7]   Here provide brief description of the services to be provided.

[8]   Here insert a description of what the company will do.

[9]   Here insert a description of what the company will not do, and what it will rely upon the customer to do.

Summary of Employment Terms   Form E64

Date _____

To _____

_____

_____

Dear _____

We are pleased that you have accepted a position with our company, and should like to take this opportunity to summarise your initial terms and conditions of employment.

1.   Commencement date of employment _____

2.   Position/title _____

3.   Starting salary: _____

4.   Weeks holiday per year: _____

5.   Eligible for holiday starting: _____

6.   Health insurance: _____

_____

7.   Pension/profit-sharing: _____

_____

8.   Other benefits: _____

_____

9.   Other terms/conditions: _____

_____

If this is not in accordance with your understanding, please let me know immediately. We look forward to you joining us.

Yours sincerely

_____

Supplier Questionnaire   Form BS60

_____ Ltd

We are introducing a supplier rating system to meet the requirements of BS5750/ISO9000. We should be grateful if you would complete this questionnaire and return it to us.

Company name _____   Tel _____

Reg. Number_____   Fax _____

Address_____

_____

Post Code_____

Products/Services Provided_____

1) Is your firm registered as a firm of assessed capability
    to BS5750/ISO9000?   Yes ☐   No ☐

2) Does your firm hold any other nationally or internationally
    recognised approvals?   Yes ☐   No ☐

3) Has your firm been approved by an accredited assessing body?   Yes ☐   No ☐
    Please give your certificate number and expiry date _____
    If you answered Yes to question 1) and 3) please move to question 7).

4) Does your firm intend to apply for registration to BS5750/ISO9000?   Yes ☐   No ☐
    If Yes please state when you expect this _____

5) Does your firm have a quality or procedures manual?   Yes ☐   No ☐

6) Does your firm have a documented system to control the following?
    a) recording of changes to customers orders/contracts   Yes ☐   No ☐
    b) receipt and checking of purchased products/services   Yes ☐   No ☐
    c) identification of products during manufacture, storage & delivery   Yes ☐   No ☐
    d) calibration and maintenance of measuring and testing equipment   Yes ☐   No ☐
    e) inspection of products at each stage of manufacturing process   Yes ☐   No ☐
    f) identification, segregation and disposal of
        non-conforming products   Yes ☐   No ☐
    g) investigating and taking action against the cause of
        non-conforming products   Yes ☐   No ☐
    h) personnel training   Yes ☐   No ☐

Continued on next page

Supplier Questionnaire (continued)   Form BS60

7)   Does your firm implement internal quality audits?   Yes ☐   No ☐

8)   Does your firm provide Certificates of Conformity
     for your products?   Yes ☐   No ☐

9)   Does your firm have a Quality Control Officer or nominated
     quality representative?   Yes ☐   No ☐

     Name _____   Position _____

10) Would your firm object to a representative of our company
     visiting you and reviewing your quality system?   Yes ☐   No ☐

11) Additional supplier comments: _____

     _____

     _____

     _____

Questionnaire completed by

Name _____   Signature _____

Position _____   Date _____

Telecoms Bill Dispute   Form GS35

Date _____

To _____

_____

_____

Ref _____

Dear _____

I received your bill dated _____ for £_____the above account.

I am questioning the accuracy of the bill as it appears improbably high and not in line with my usage during the period in question. Please review and adjust the bill or, if necessary, test the line metering and security so we can determine its accuracy and settle the matter. In particular:

_____ [1]

I look forward to hearing from you within 14 days with the appropriate adjustment or the result of a technical investigation. Otherwise, I may refer this matter to the Office of Communications.

Yours sincerely

_____

Name _____

Address _____

_____

Tel. _____

Note: you can reach the Office of Communications at www.ofcom.org.uk.

[1] Supply details, for example, 'the usage shown is twice as great as my usage in any of the previous three months' or 'calls to Lithuania are recorded, and I know no one in that country', or as the case may be.

Tenant's Bank Standing Order Mandate   Form RT20

TO   _____ (Tenant's bank
                      _____ name & address)

PLEASE PAY   _____ (Landlord's bank
                      _____ name & address)
                      _____ ☐☐ ☐☐ ☐☐ (& sort code)

TO THE   _____ (Landlord's account
CREDIT OF   _____ name & account
                                                           number)

THE SUM OF   _____ (Amount in figures
                      _____ & words)

COMMENCING   _____ (Date of first payment)

AND THEREAFTER
EVERY   _____ (Due date & frequency
                                                           e.g. '13th monthly')
UNTIL   _____ (Date of last payment, you
                                                           may write 'until further
                                                           notice')

QUOTING THE   _____ (The address of the
REFERENCE   _____ Property being let)

ACCOUNT NAME   _____ (Tenant's name)
TO BE DEBITED

ACCOUNT No.   _____ (Tenant's A/C No.)
TO BE DEBITED

SIGNED   _____ DATED _____

                      _____
                      (Tenant(s))

Trading Standards Officer Complaint   Form GS37

Date _____

To The Trading Standards Officer

_____ Local Authority

Dear Sir

I am writing to ask that you investigate _____ which I believe is acting in breach of trading standards for the reason briefly described below:

- Product safety: _____
- Consumer Credit: _____
- Counterfeiting: _____
- Misleading Prices or Promotions: _____
- Weights and Measures: _____
- Vehicle Safety: _____
- Overloaded Vehicles: _____
- False Descriptions: _____
- Under Age Sales: _____
- Estate Agents: _____

I am enclosing any documentary evidence I have to support this accusation. Please let me know if I can be of further help in your investigation. I look forward to hearing from you in due course.

Yours faithfully

_____

Name _____

Address _____

_____

Tel. _____

Unfurnished House/Flat Rental Agreement   Form F302

The PROPERTY   _____

_____

The LANDLORD   _____

of _____

_____

The TENANT   _____

_____

The GUARANTOR   _____

of _____

The TERM   _____ weeks/months* beginning on _____

The RENT   £ _____ per week/month* payable in advance on the _____ of each week/month*

The DEPOSIT   £ _____ which will be registered with one of the Government authorised tenancy

deposit schemes ("the Tenancy Deposit Scheme") in accordance with the Tenancy

Deposit Scheme Rules.

DATED   _____

Signed and executed as a Deed by the following parties

Landlord	**Tenant**	**Guarantor***
_____	_____	_____
_____	_____	_____
Landlord(s)' name(s)	_____	_____
	Tenant(s)' name(s)	Guarantor's name
_____	_____	_____
_____	_____	_____
Landlord(s)' signature(s)	_____	_____
	Tenant(s)' signature(s)	Guarantor's signature

In the presence of:

Witness signature _____   Witness signature _____   Witness signature _____

Full name _____   Full name _____   Full name _____

Address_____   Address_____   Address_____

_____   _____   _____

(*delete as appropriate)

Continued on next page

Unfurnished House/Flat Rental Agreement (continued)   Form F302

THIS TENANCY AGREEMENT comprises the particulars detailed above and the terms and conditions printed overleaf whereby the Property is hereby let by the Landlord and taken by the Tenant for the Term at the Rent.

IMPORTANT NOTICE TO LANDLORDS:

1   The details of 'The LANDLORD' near the top of this Agreement must include an address for the Landlord in England or Wales as well as his/her name, or all names in the case of joint Landlords.

2   Always remember to give the written Notice Requiring Possession to the Tenant at least two clear months before the end of the Term if you want the tenant to vacate.

3   Before granting the tenancy agreement, you should check whether your chosen deposit scheme provider requires you to insert any additional terms concerning the deposit into the tenancy agreement or to alter or delete any of the terms appearing in the form below. Details of the websites of the scheme providers are set out in Note 4 for tenants below. Currently only The Tenancy Deposit Scheme has any such requirements.

IMPORTANT NOTICE TO TENANTS:

1   In general, if you currently occupy Property under a protected or statutory tenancy and you give it up to take a new tenancy of the same or other accommodation owned by the same Landlord, that tenancy cannot be an Assured Shorthold Tenancy and this Agreement is not appropriate.

2   If you currently occupy Property under an Assured Tenancy which is not an Assured Shorthold Tenancy your Landlord is not permitted to grant you an Assured Shorthold Tenancy of that Property or of alternative property and this Agreement is not appropriate.

3   If the total amount of rent exceeds £25,000 per annum, an Assured Shorthold Tenancy cannot be created and this Agreement is not appropriate. Seek legal advice.

4   Further information about the Government authorised Tenancy Deposit Schemes can be obtained from their websites: The Deposit Protection Service at www.depositprotection.com, Tenancy Deposit Solutions Ltd at www.mydeposits.co.uk and The Tenancy Deposit Scheme at www.tds.gb.com.

Unfurnished House/Flat Rental Agreement

Terms and Conditions (continued)

Form F302

1. This Agreement is intended to create an Assured Shorthold Tenancy as defined in the Housing Act 1988, as amended by the Housing Act 1996, and the provisions for the recovery of possession by the Landlord in that Act apply accordingly. The Tenant understands that the Landlord will be entitled to recover possession of the Property at the end of the Term.

2. **The Tenant's obligations:**
   2.1 To pay the Rent at the times and in the manner set out above.
   2.2 To pay all charges in respect of any electric, gas, water, sewage and telephonic or televisual services used at or supplied to the Property and Council Tax or any property tax that might be charged in addition to or replacement of it during the Term.
   2.3 To keep the interior of the Property in a good and clean state and condition and not damage or injure the Property (fair wear and tear excepted).
   2.4 To yield up the Property at the end of the Term in the same clean state and condition it was in at the beginning of the Term (but the Tenant will not be responsible for fair wear and tear caused during normal use of the Property and the items listed on the Inventory (if any).
   2.5 Not to make any alteration or addition to the Property and not without the prior written consent of the Landlord (consent not to be withheld unreasonably) do any redecoration or painting of the Property.
   2.6 Not do anything on or at the Property which:
       (a) may be or become a nuisance or annoyance to any other occupiers of the Property or owners or occupiers of adjoining or nearby premises
       (b) is illegal or immoral
       (c) may in any way affect the validity of the insurance of the Property and the items listed on the Inventory (if any) or cause an increase in the premium payable by the Landlord
       (d) will cause any blockages in the drainage system and in the case of breach of this clause the Tenant to be responsible for the reasonable cost of such repair or other works which will be reasonably required.
   2.7 Not without the Landlord's prior consent (consent not to be withheld unreasonably) allow or keep any pet or any kind of animal at the Property.
   2.8 Not use or occupy the Property in any way whatsoever other than as a private residence.
   2.9 Not assign, sublet, charge or part with or share possession or occupation of the Property (but see clause 5.1 below).
   2.10 To allow the Landlord or anyone with the Landlord's written permission to enter the Property at reasonable times of the day to inspect its condition and state of repair, carry out any necessary repairs and gas inspections, and during the last month of the Term, show the Property to prospective new tenants, provided the Landlord has given at least 24 hours' prior written notice (except in emergency).
   2.11 To pay the Landlord's reasonable costs reasonably incurred as a result of any breaches by the Tenant of his obligations under this Agreement, and further to pay the Landlord's reasonable costs of responding to any request for a consent which the Tenant may make of the Landlord under this Agreement.
   2.12 To pay interest at the rate of 4% above the Bank of England base rate from time to time prevailing on any rent or other money lawfully due from the Tenant under this Agreement which remains unpaid for more than 14 days, interest to be paid from the date the payment fell due until payment.
   2.13 To provide the Landlord with a forwarding address

when the tenancy comes to an end and to remove all rubbish and all personal items (including the Tenant's own furniture and equipment) from the Property before leaving.

3. **The Landlord's obligations:**
   3.1 The Landlord agrees that the Tenant may live in the Property without unreasonable interruption from the Landlord or any person rightfully claiming under or in trust for the Landlord.
   3.2 To insure the Property and items listed on the Inventory (if any) and use all reasonable efforts to arrange for any damage caused by an insured risk to be remedied as soon as possible and to provide a copy of the insurance policy to the Tenant if requested.
   3.3 The Landlord will where applicable observe his statutory repairing obligations under the Landlord and Tenant Act 1985 Section 11, the Gas Safety (Installation and Use) Regulations 1998, the Electrical equipment (Safety) Regulations 1994. In outline, the Landlord's obligations under the Landlord and Tenant Act 1985 Section 11 are to keep in repair (where provided by the Landlord)
   3.3.1 the structure and exterior of the Property (including drains gutters and external pipes)
   3.3.2 the installations at the Property for the supply of water, sewage, gas and electricity and for sanitation (including basins, sinks, baths and sanitary conveniences)
   3.3.3 the installations at the Property for space heating and heating water
   3.4 But the Landlord will not be required to
   3.4.1 carry out works for which the Tenant is responsible by virtue of his duty to use the Property in a tenant-like manner
   3.4.2 reinstate the Property in the case of damage or destruction if the insurers refuse to pay out the insurance money due to anything the Tenant has done or failed to do
   3.4.3 rebuild or reinstate the Property in the case of destruction or damage of the Property by a risk not covered by the policy of insurance effected by the Landlord.
   3.4 If the property is a flat or maisonette within a larger building then the Landlord will be under similar obligations for the rest of the building but only in so far as any disrepair will affect the Tenant's and in so far as the Landlord is legally entitled to enter the relevant part of the larger building and carry out the required works or repairs.
   3.4 To arrange for the Tenant's Deposit to be protected by an authorised Tenancy Deposit Scheme in accordance with the provisions of the Housing Act 2004 within 14 days of receipt, and to comply with the rules of the Tenancy Deposit Scheme at all times.

4. **Guarantor**
   If there is a Guarantor, he guarantees that the Tenant will keep to his obligations in this Agreement. The Guarantor agrees to pay on demand to the Landlord any money lawfully due to the Landlord by the Tenant.

5. **Ending this Agreement**
   5.1 The Tenant cannot normally end this Agreement before the end of the Term. However after the first three months of the Term, if the Tenant can find a suitable alternative tenant, and provided this alternative tenant is acceptable to the Landlord (the Landlord's approval not to be unreasonably withheld) the Tenant may give notice to end the tenancy on a date at least one month from the date that such approval is given by the Landlord. On the expiry of such notice and upon (i) payment by the Tenant to the Landlord of the reasonable expenses reasonably incurred by the Landlord in granti-

Continued on next page

ng the necessary approval and in granting any new tenancy to the alternative tenant, and (ii) the execution by the alternative tenant of a new tenancy agreement in the form of this Agreement for a period of 6 months or for a period not less than the unexpired portion of the term of this Agreement (if that be greater than 6 months), or for such other period as the Landlord shall approve this tenancy shall end

5.2   If the Tenant stays on after the end of the fixed term, a new tenancy will arise that will run from month to month or week to week (a 'periodic tenancy'). This periodic tenancy can be ended by the Tenant giving at least one month's written notice to the Landlord, the notice to expire at the end of the rental period.

5.3   If at any time

    5.3.1   any part of the Rent is outstanding for 21 days after becoming due (whether formally demanded or not) and/or

    5.3.2   there is any breach, non-observance or non-performance by the Tenant of any covenant and/or other term of this Agreement which has been notified in writing to the Tenant and the Tenant has failed within a reasonable period of time to remedy the breach and/or pay reasonable compensation to the Landlord for the breach and/or

    5.3.3   any of the grounds set out as Grounds 2, 8 or Grounds 10-15 (inclusive) (which relate to breach of any obligation by a Tenant) contained in the Housing Act 1988 Schedule 2 apply

the Landlord may recover possession of the Property and this Agreement shall come to an end. The Landlord retains all his other rights in respect of the Tenant's obligations under this Agreement. Note that if possession of the Property has not been surrendered and anyone is living at the Property then the landlord must obtain a court order for possession before re-entering the Property. This clause does not affect the Tenant's rights under the Protection from Eviction Act 1977.

6.   The Deposit

6.1   The Deposit will be held in accordance with the Tenancy Deposit Scheme Rules as issued by the relevant Tenancy Deposit Scheme.

6.2.   No interest will be payable to the Tenant by the Landlord in respect of the Deposit save as provided by the Rules of the relevant Tenancy Deposit Scheme.

6.3.   Subject to any relevant provisions of the Rules of the relevant Tenancy Deposit Scheme, the Landlord shall be entitled to claim from the Deposit the reasonable cost of any repairs or damage to the Property or its contents caused by the Tenant (including any damage caused by the Tenant's family and visitors) any rent in arrears and for any other financial losses suffered or expenditure incurred by the Landlord as a result of the Tenant's breach of these terms and conditions, provided the sum claimed by the Landlord is reasonably incurred and is reasonable in amount. The Landlord is not entitled to claim in respect of any damage to the Property or its contents which is due to 'fair wear and tear' i.e. which is as a result of the Tenant and his family (if any) living in the property and using it in a reasonable and lawful manner.

7.   Other provisions

7.1   The Landlord hereby notifies the Tenant under Section 48 of the Landlord & Tenant Act 1987 that any notices (including notices in proceedings) should be served upon the Landlord at the address stated with the name of the Landlord overleaf.

7.2   The Landlord shall be entitled to have and retain keys for all the doors to the Property but shall not be entitled to use these to enter the Property without the consent of the Tenant (save in an emergency) or as otherwise provided in this Agreement.

7.3   Any notices or other documents (including any court claim forms in legal proceedings) shall be deemed served on the Tenant during the tenancy by either being left at the Property or by being sent to the Tenant at the Property by first-class post. Notices shall be deemed served the day after being left at the property or the day after posting.

7.4   Any person other than the Tenant who pays the rent due hereunder or any part thereof to the Landlord shall be deemed to have made such payment as agent for and on behalf of the Tenant which the Landlord shall be entitled to assume without enquiry.

7.5   Any personal items left behind at the end of the tenancy after the Tenant has vacated (which the Tenant has not removed in accordance with clause 2.13 above) shall be considered abandoned if they have not been removed within 14 days of written notice to the Tenant from the Landlord, or if the Landlord has been unable to trace the Tenant by taking reasonable steps to do so. After this period the Landlord may remove or dispose of the items as he thinks fit. The Tenant shall be liable for the reasonable disposal costs which may be deducted from the proceeds of sale (if any), and the Tenant shall remain liable for any balance. Any net proceeds of the sale to be returned to the Tenant at the forwarding address provided to the Landlord.

7.6   In the event of destruction to the Property or of damage to it which shall make the same or a substantial portion of the same uninhabitable, the Tenant shall be relieved from paying the rent by an amount proportional to the extent to which the Tenant's ability to live in the Property is thereby prevented, save where the destruction or damage has been caused by any act or default by the Tenant or where the Landlord's insurance cover has been adversely affected by any act or omission on the part of the Tenant.

7.7   Where the context so admits:

    7.7.1   The 'Landlord' includes the persons from time to time entitled to receive the Rent.

    7.7.2   The 'Tenant' includes any persons deriving title under the Tenant.

    7.7.3   The 'Property' includes any part or parts of the Property and all of the Landlord's fixtures and fittings at or upon the Property.

    7.7.4   All references to the singular shall include the plural and vice versa and any obligations or liabilities of more than one person shall be joint and several (this means that they will each be liable for all sums due under this Agreement, not just liable for a proportionate part) and an obligation on the part of a party shall include an obligation not to allow or permit the breach of that obligation.

    7.7.5   All references to 'he', 'him' and 'his' shall be taken to include 'she', 'her' and 'hers'.

Unsolicited Idea Acknowledgement   Form B37

Date _____

Ref _____

To _____

_____

_____

Dear _____

We appreciate your interest in submitting material for our consideration. Because of complications which may arise if we examine such material before any agreement has been reached about the terms on which we conduct such examination, however, it is our practice to return the material without reading or examining it in any way, and to invite the sender, if he or she wishes, to resubmit the material under the cover of a letter (which must be signed by the sender and witnessed by a person not related to the sender) in the following terms:

'Dear _____,

I would be grateful if you would consider our idea or proposal, the details of which are set out in the material herewith.

In consideration of your reviewing the material, which I have submitted to you unsolicited, I agree to the following terms:

1.   Samples, or written or other material (hereinafter 'material') will be returned only if a stamped addressed envelope is enclosed or carriage is prepaid.

2.   You are not responsible for damage or loss to samples or other submitted material no matter how such loss or damage may occur and whether or not such loss or damage has resulted from your negligence.

3.   You are not obliged to keep confidential any of the material. Without prejudice to the foregoing, you are expressly authorised to copy, lend or reveal the contents of the material to any person or body to whom you may in your absolute discretion consider it desirable to reveal, lend or copy the same for the purpose of facilitating the eventual exploitation of the material. For the avoidance of doubt, you will not in any way be liable for any use which such third party may make of the material without your authority.

Continued on next page

Unsolicited Idea Acknowledgement (continued)   Form B37

4. You will not be obliged to pay me any consideration or compensation in respect of the material unless you and I enter into a separate agreement in respect of the same, provided that this exclusion shall not apply if (a) you use the material or a substantial part thereof, (b) the material includes information which is not in the public domain, and (c) the material which is not in the public domain contributes significantly to the value of the material. If the proviso shall apply, I shall be entitled to compensation, but such compensation shall be no greater than that which a willing seller of the material might be deemed to receive from a willing buyer, and in particular no aggravated or exemplary damages shall be payable.

5   I warrant that I am the owner of all intellectual or other property rights which may subsist in relation to the material, and that I have full power to grant to you exclusive rights in respect of the same. I warrant further that I am not aware of any possible claim which any other person might make in respect of any ownership or entitlement to exploit such property in the material.

6. For the avoidance of doubt, I confirm that I shall have no claim for any compensation or consideration in respect of any part of the material if such material or information included therein has been submitted to you by any other person.

7. If any provision of this agreement shall be held to be invalid, such invalidity shall not affect any other provision of this agreement.

Yours sincerely

_____

Signature

Witness name, address and occupation

_____

_____

_____

Witness signature

Variation of Contract   Form OLF36

THIS DEED is made the_____ day of _____ year _____

BETWEEN

(1) _____ of _____ (the 'First Party');and

(2) _____ of _____ (the 'Second Party').

WHEREAS:

(A)   The two parties above have entered into an agreement dated_____ (the 'Agreement')

(B)   The two parties above now wish to vary the terms of the Agreement.

NOW THIS DEED WITNESSES as follows:

1.   The two parties agree that the following additions and amendments to the Agreement shall apply

_____

_____

2.   All other terms and conditions of the Agreement shall remain in full force and effect.

IN WITNESS OF WHICH the parties have executed this deed the day and year first above written

(Individual)   (Company)

                                                Signed for and on behalf of

_____   _____ Ltd

Signed by the First Party

                                                _____

in the presence of (witness)   Director

Name _____   _____

Address _____   Director/Secretary

_____

Occupation _____

                                                Signed for and on behalf of:

_____   _____Ltd

Signed by the Second Party

                                                _____

in the presence of (witness)   Director

Name _____   _____

Address _____   Director/Secretary

_____

Occupation _____

Variation of Employment Agreement — Form E65

Date _____

Ref _____

To _____
_____
_____

Dear _____

This letter is to inform you that the terms or conditions of your contract have been amended as set out below. Please acknowledge receipt of this letter and your agreement to the terms set out in it by signing the attached copy and returning it to me. You should retain the top copy with your contract of employment.

Please contact me should you wish to discuss any of the changes or require any further information.

Date changes effective: _____

Details of changes are as follows: _____
_____
_____

Yours sincerely

_____

For the Company

I,_____, acknowledge that I have received a statement of alteration to the particulars of my employment, as required by the Employment Rights Act 1996 Section 1, and agree to the terms set out in that agreement.

_____

Signed

_____

Dated

Waiver of Liability and Assumption of Risk   Form OLF37

I, the undersigned, _____ (the 'Customer'), voluntarily make and grant this Waiver of Liability and Assumption of Risk in favour of _____ _____ (the 'Seller') as partial consideration (in addition to monies paid to the Seller) for the opportunity to use the facilities, equipment, materials and/or other assets of the Seller; and/or to receive assistance, training, guidance and/or instruction from the personnel of the Seller; and/or to engage in the activities, events, sports, festivities and/or gatherings sponsored by the Seller; I hereby waive and release any and all claims whether in contract or tort, for any loss or damage that may arise from my aforementioned use or receipt, save for death or personal injury which may be occasioned by your negligence.

I understand and recognise that there are certain risks, dangers and perils connected with such use and/or receipt, which I hereby acknowledge to have been fully explained to me and which I fully understand, and which I nevertheless accept as being acceptable to me. I further agree to use my best judgment in undertaking these activities, and to adhere strictly to all safety instructions and recommendations, which may be communicated to me whether oral or written. I hereby certify that I am a competent adult assuming these risks of my own free will, being under no compulsion or duress.

The facilities, equipment materials and other assets referred to above include, but are not limited to, the following: _____

_____

The assistance, training, guidance and instruction referred to above include but are not limited to the following _____

_____

I warrant that I have the following experience and agree that the Seller may have reliance upon this warranty in permitting me to use the facilities materials equipment and other assets and in furnishing me the guidance, training and instruction above-mentioned: _____

_____

I warrant that the risks about which I have been advised include but are not limited to _____

_____

I warrant that I do not have any medical condition which enhances any of the risks above referred to.

_____

Customer's signature

Name _____

Address _____

_____

Date _____

Age _____

Warranty Increasing Statutory Rights Form BS61

1.   This warranty is given in addition to your statutory rights and does not affect your statutory rights in any way.

2.   We warrant that, in the event that any fault or defect is discovered with the goods within one year of the date of sale, we will, unless the fault or defect has been caused by a misuse of the goods by the purchaser or by the goods being used for a purpose for which they have not been designed, either repair or, at our option, replace the goods free of charge to the purchaser.

Note: These terms can be added, where desired, to any contract for the sale of goods. They can also be displayed in a shop. The wording about statutory rights are intended to make clear that the promises made are for the purpose of adding to statutory protection rather than attempting to restrict it (which is often unlawful). This wording is therefore necessary and should on no account be omitted.

Water Supply Interruption: OFWAT Investigation Request

Form GS39

Date _____

To OFWAT Customer Service Committee

_____

_____

Ref _____

Dear Sirs

This letter is in reference to my complaint with _____ which has still not yet been resolved.

Please refer to the enclosed correspondence relating to this case. I understand I am entitled to [£20 for failure to keep an appointment]/[£20 for failure to respond to a complaint]/[£20 for failure to respond to an account enquiry within 10 working days]/[£20 for failure to tell me in writing at least 48 hours before a planned interruption of water supply][1]/[£20 for failure to restore interrupted supply within the time stated plus £10 for each 24-hour period the supply remains unrestored]/[£20 plus a further £10 for each 24 hour period of unplanned interruption beyond 12 hours (or 48 hours in the case of a 'strategic' water main][2]/[a refund of sewerage charges by reason of flooding from sewers]/[£25 for low pressure lasting more than an hour on two occasions within 28 days]. In addition, the water company is responsible for the damages that occurred as a result of the shut-off.

I should be grateful if you would please look into my claim. It is my understanding that during your investigation my services will not be further interrupted.

Please keep me informed on the status of my case.

Yours faithfully

_____

Name _____

Address _____

_____

Tel. _____

Note: If you have a complaint, you should first take it up with your supplier. If your supplier has not handled your complaint satisfactorily, you should contact the Consumer Council for Water, which can be reached at www.ccwater.org.uk or on 0845 039 2837 or 0121 345 1000. You will be given details for the regional office which you should contact.

[1] £50 in the case of a non-household customer.

[2] In the case of non-household customers £50 for failure to restore on time and £25 for each 24-hour period.

Withheld Delivery Notice   Form BS62

Date _____

Ref _____

To _____
_____
_____

Dear _____

Reference is made to your order no._____ dated _____.

We are withholding delivery of the goods for the reason(s) ticked:

☐   Overdue balance of £_____ must first be paid.

☐   Required payment of £_____ has not been made.

☐   You previously cancelled the order.

☐   You have not provided us with delivery instructions.

☐   Certain goods are back ordered and delivery will be made in a single lot.

☐   Other:_____

Please respond to this notice so we may fulfil your order without further delay or inconvenience.

Yours sincerely

_____

Note: make certain if you are deliberately withholding delivery that you are not placing yourself in breach of contract.

Working Time Regulations Opt Out Agreement   Form E66

WORKING TIME REGULATIONS 1998 OPT-OUT

1. DEFINITIONS

1.1 In this Agreement the following definitions apply:

'Employee' means _____

'the Employer' means _____

'Working Week' means an average of 48 hours each week over a 17-week period

1.2 Unless the context requires otherwise, references to the singular include the plural and references to the masculine include the feminine and vice versa.

1.3 The headings contained in these Terms are for convenience only and do not affect their interpretation.

2. RESTRICTIONS

2.1 The Working Time Regulations 1998 provide that an Employee shall not work in excess of the Working Week unless he agrees in writing that this limit should not apply.

3. CONSENT

3.1 The Employee hereby agrees that the Working Week limit shall not apply to his contract of employment with the Employer.

4. WITHDRAWAL OF CONSENT

4.1 The Employee may end this Agreement by giving the Employer three months' notice in writing.

4.2 For the avoidance of doubt, any notice bringing this Agreement to an end shall not be construed as termination by the Employee of his contract of employment with the Employer.

4.3 Upon the expiry of the notice period set out in clause 4.1, the Working Week limit shall apply with immediate effect.

5. THE LAW

5.1 These Terms are governed by the law of England & Wales and are subject to the exclusive jurisdiction of the courts of England & Wales.[1]

_____

Signed by the Employee

_____

Date